OXFORD
GNVQ

Advanced
BUSINESS

DAN MOYNIHAN & BRIAN TITLEY

Oxford University Press 1995

Oxford University Press, Walton St, Oxford, OX2 6DP

Oxford New York
Athens Auckland Bangkok Bombay
Calcutta Cape Town Dar es Salaam Delhi
Florence Hong Kong Istanbul Karachi
Kuala Lumpur Madras Madrid Melbourne
Mexico City Nairobi Paris Singapore
Taipei Tokyo Toronto

and associated companies in
Berlin Ibadan

Oxford is a trademark of Oxford University Press

© Oxford University Press 1995

First published 1995

A CIP catalogue record for this book is available from the British Library

All rights reserved. No part of this publication may be reproduced, stored in a retrieval system, or transmitted, in any form or by any means, without the prior permission in writing of Oxford University Press. Within the UK, exceptions are allowed in respect of any fair dealing of the purpose of research or private study, or criticism or review, as permitted under the Copyright, Designs and Patents Act, 1988, or in the case of reprographic reproduction in accordance with the terms of licences issued by the Copyright Licensing Agency. Enquiries concerning reproduction outside those terms and in other countries should be sent to the Rights Department, Oxford University Press, at the address above.

ISBN 0 19 833538 5
     0 19 833549 0 (net edition)

Produced and Illustrated by Gecko Ltd, Bicester, Oxon

Printed in Great Britain

The publishers would like to thank the following for permission to reproduce photographs:

Ace Photo Agency: 140 right, 172 bottom, 195 top, 260 middle, 270, 374 top left, 375, 398 top right, 414; Barnaby's Picture Library: 75 bottom middle, 103, 114, 154 middle, 221, 280 top left & right, 398 top left, 415 bottom; Biffa Waste Services: 94; John Birdsall Photography: 495 top left; John Bright & Bros Ltd: 398 middle; British Health & Safety Executive: 134 top right; British Petroleum: 109 top; British School of Motoring: 110 bottom; British Telecom: 59 bottom, 156 top left, 156 bottom left, 165 top, 374 bottom left; Philip Davies: 406 middle; Ford Motor Company Ltd: 145, 201; Format Partners Photo Library: 332 top; Peter Gimbere: 27 top; Greater London Record Office: 300 top left: Chris Honeywell: 172 middle, 177, 181, 184 left, 211; I.B.M. 176 bottom, 178; I.C.I: 384; K9: 140 top; Tony Mays: 300 top right; Archie Miles: 406 bottom middle; National Coal Board: 430; National Motor Museum: 201 left; Nissan: 449; Network: 153; Alan Owens: 405 bottom right; Oxford University Press/ Chris Honeywell 105, 300 bottom right; /Norman McBeath 140 middle left, /Terry Austin Smith 467, /J R Tabberner 105; Alan C Parker/Greenways: 66; Pontin's: 411; Press Association: 33, 71, 77, 195 bottom, 297, 616 top, 680 bottom right, 681 left; Sanyo: 20 middle right, 32 middle, 154 bottom, 156 bottom middle; Martin Sookias: 18, 54, 58 top, 59 top & middle, 93, 109 middle, 110 top, 115, 135, 156 bottom right, 163, 165 top & bottom, 175, 176 top, 179, 184 right, 193 top &bottom left, 197 top, 202, 203, 204, 206, 217, 223, 245, 248 middle, 259, 264, 265, 266, 286, 324, 367 right, 382 bottom left, 416, 483, 495 middle left & bottom right, 496, 507, 508, 593, 616 middle & bottom, 643, 670, 680 top; Sporting Pictures: 246; Tony Stone Images: 127, 154 top, 180 top, 197 middle, 283, 311, 334 bottom right; Telegraph Colour Library: 22 middle and bottom, 61, 75 top middle & bottom, 159 right, 160 top, 180 bottom, 269, 280 bottom, 315, 334 left, 367 left, 374 bottom right, 381, 406 top, 495 bottom left; Tesco plc: 300 bottom left; Thames Valley Police: 104; Toshiba: 494; Tropix: 625; Unipart Group of Companies: 139, 193; Van den Bergh Foods Ltd: 198, 647; Voluntary Service Overseas: 673; Volvo Car UK Ltd: 380; Zefa: 334 top right, 398 bottom

All other photographs courtesy of Oxford University Press

Special thanks to ABTA; British Wool Marketing Board; British Gas plc; British Standards Institute; DHL Worldwide Express; Investors In People; 3i (Investors in Industry); Lacroix Watches; Penguin Books; Rolls Royce plc; TNT.

Contents

Introduction   1
About the Advanced GNVQ course in Business   2
Presenting Data   7
Analysing Data   14
What is Business?   19

Unit 1
Business in the Economy   25
1 The Effects of Demand and Supply on Business   26
2 The Operation of Markets   50
3 The Effects of Government Policy on Markets   70

Unit 2
Business Organizations and Systems   99
4 Business Organizations   100
5 Administrative Systems   131
6 Communications Systems   152
7 Information Processing   171

Unit 3
Marketing   191
8 The Principles and Functions of Marketing   192
9 Market Research   210
10 Marketing Communications   233
11 Customer Service and Sales Methods   258

Unit 4
Human Resources   277
12 Managing Human Resources   278
13 Job Roles and Change at Work   308
14 Job Applications and Interviews   331

Unit 5
Production and Employment in the Economy   361
15 Production   362
16 Investigating Employment   389
17 The Competitiveness of UK Industry   420

Unit 6
Financial Transactions, Costing and Pricing   455
18 Added Value and the Money Cycle   456
19 Financial Transactions and Supporting Documents   470
20 Business Costs   493
21 Pricing Decisions and Strategies   506

Unit 7
Financial Forecasting and Monitoring   527
22 Business Finance   528
23 Cashflow Forecasting   550
24 Profit and Loss Statements and Balance Sheets   567
25 Monitoring Business Performance   591

Unit 8
Business Planning   613
26 The Business Plan – Preparing and Collecting Data   614
27 How to Prepare and Produce a Business Plan   639
28 Planning for Employment or Self-employment   663

Index   695

Preface

This book aims to provide everything that you need in order to pass the mandatory Advanced GNVQ Business units offered by BTEC, City and Guilds and the RSA examinations boards. The book has been carefully written to match closely the 1995 GNVQ Business specifications.

The book can be used as a course text to support either a course with a high proportion of teacher/lecturer contact time or one with less contact time and more supported self-study. Students will find a large number of portfolio activities designed to generate evidence for the GNVQ Portfolio as well as numerous test questions to help prepare students for the end of unit tests. All of the activities and questions have been tried and tested by experienced GNVQ teachers and students!

As well as helping students to pass their Advanced GNVQ with a good grade, the book has been designed to provide a thorough insight into the dynamic and exciting world of business by using a wide range of case studies and real world examples. Each chapter is packed with up to date articles and statistics in order to assist students in carrying out research and in producing coursework using up-to-date research and case studies.

The authors would like to thank the staff at NCVQ without whose consistent and prompt help in providing information this book would not have been possible. Thanks also to Jane, Sarah, Thomas and Julie for their patience and support

Don Moynihan

Brian Titley

Introduction for Students

Introduction

- About the Advanced GNVQ Course in Business
- Presenting Data
- Analysing Data
- What is Business?

About the Advanced GNVQ Course in Business

The Advanced GNVQ in Business is designed to provide you with a broad-based business education. In addition to acquiring a thorough knowledge and understanding of the world of business, you will also achieve a range of core skills which are essential for success in the world of business and enterprise.

This combination of practical business knowledge and core skills will provide a foundation from which you should be able to progress either to further and higher education or into employment and further training.

Evidence requirements

The Advanced GNVQ in Business is a very different qualification to any other course that you may have taken so far. The emphasis in GNVQ is on you, the candidate, doing things to demonstrate your achievement. In order to pass, you must provide evidence of your achievement in the form of a wide variety of different kinds of coursework against the Advanced Business specifications.

The provision of evidence by you, the candidate, is essential. This means that you must carefully plan your work in order to ensure that you build a portfolio of evidence which matches the syllabus specifications. The content and activities in this book are designed to provide you with everything that you need in order to do this.

Course structure: Business and Core Skills Unit

In traditional Advanced Level qualifications your overall grade will usually depend entirely on a final examination. The GNVQ structure is very different. In order to do well in GNVQ, you will need to solve problems, undertake research, work with others, and show a great deal of resourcefulness and initiative throughout your course. This has the advantage that your success in the GNVQ course does not depend on one final exam, but it does require you to work steadily throughout.

To pass the Advanced GNVQ in Business it is necessary to achieve passes in:

- 12 business units
- 3 core skill units

Eight of the twelve business units are mandatory; the remaining four may be picked from a list of optional units provided by your 'awarding body'. Seven of the eight mandatory units also require that unit tests are passed.

Course structure: Unit elements

Each GNVQ unit is divided into a series of **elements**. Each element defines a particular area of knowledge and skill in which you need to demonstrate your competence. The elements are divided into:

- **Performance criteria**: these are the kinds of things that you must demonstrate that you can do

- **Range**: this indicates the broad areas of knowledge and skill which you will be expected to master. These need to be reflected in the coursework you produce to match the performance criteria.

- **Evidence indicators**: these provide some suggestions as to the kinds of activities that you could undertake in order to demonstrate your achievement for the element. This book provides a full range of Portfolio Activities to meet the evidence indicator requirements.

- **Amplification and guidance**: this consists of further explanation designed to clarify the meaning and requirements of the element. It is well worth reading through it in order to see what is required.

It is very important that you read the GNVQ unit and element specifications of your awarding body and that you keep referring back to these as you work through the course. By doing this you will be able to ensure that the work you produce closely matches the Advanced GNVQ Business specifications. Ask your tutor for a copy of these.

Course structure: Core skills

The purpose behind the Advanced GNVQ in Business is to ensure that you not only possess the knowledge required to be successful in business, but also the skills and confidence to apply this knowledge to real problems.

The Advanced GNVQ will not only test what you know, it will also test whether you can apply it. For example, you may know the main components of a marketing strategy for a particular product, but can you evaluate just how good that strategy is? And can you design and plan a marketing strategy of your own? Similarly, you may be able to describe how Information Technology could be used in a business, but can you recommend a specific communications system for a particular firm - and justify your decision? These are the practical skills which the Advanced GNVQ in Business aims to develop.

In order to apply your knowledge, you need to master a number of core skills:

- *Communication*

    3.1 Take part in discussions

    3.2 Produce written materials

    3.3 Use images

    3.4 Read and respond to written materials

- *Application of number*
  - 3.1 Collect and record data
  - 3.2 Tackle problems
  - 3.3 Interpret and present data
- *Information Technology*
  - 3.1 Prepare information
  - 3.2 Process information
  - 3.3 Present information
  - 3.4 Evaluate the use of information

Gathering evidence

You will need to make use of both planned and unplanned evidence of core skills achievement.

In gathering your evidence you should carefully study the core skills specifications produced by NCVQ for students (ask your tutor for a copy). These explain what you need to do. By looking at the specifications in advance you will find that there are opportunities for you to structure your work in particular ways in order to generate evidence against the core skills.

For example, if you are undertaking a market research survey, you may, after looking at the core skills, decide to present graphs of your results and to calculate the mean and range of the data and draw conclusions from this - this will count as evidence towards *Application of number* 3.3. If you fail to look at the skills specifications, you may miss the opportunity to gather the evidence. If you do not plan to do this, you may find that you end up with large gaps in your core skills achievement which cannot be filled.

When you are building your portfolio you may generate unexpected evidence against core skills. For example, during your research you may have spoken with different people, some of whom you did not know, and you may have had to question them in order to check your understanding of what they were saying. This kind of activity will provide evidence towards Communications 3.1. You should record what you have done and present the evidence of unplanned core skills achievement to your GNVQ assessor. Again, you are only likely to be able to do this if you are familiar with the core skills specifications and are actively looking out for evidence opportunities.

Managing your portfolio of evidence

It is your responsibility to provide your GNVQ course assessor with evidence that you have met the performance criteria in the element specifications and core skills. To do this you will need to build up a portfolio of coursework.

The quality and coverage of your portfolio will determine your final grade, so it is very important to maintain a well-ordered and up-to-date portfolio. The portfolio should include evidence not just against the advanced business elements, but also against the core skills.

INTRODUCTION

The evidence requirements of the eight mandatory business units vary widely and you should not expect to produce all of your evidence in the form of written coursework or reports. Some evidence will be in the form of records of your contribution to the work of a group of students, or evidence from your work placement supervisor. Some may be presented in the form of graphs and tabulated data, or video and audio recordings you have produced.

Remember that you need to produce evidence of your course achievements and build this into a portfolio to be assessed at the end of the course. If you lose your work, you lose your evidence and you may have to do the work all over again. You must store your work securely and safely. Keep back-up copies of work produced on a computer on disk. Clearly label your disks and files and never leave your work in an unlocked desk or cabinet. If you have difficulty in finding secure storage space in your school or college, you should consider keeping a personal copy of your main pieces of work at home.

Grading

In your portfolio, it is important to build up evidence of your ability to undertake independent research and gather data and information on your own. Evidence of your research and study skills, together with the quality of your coursework, will help to determine your overall grade.

To obtain a pass, you must successfully complete all the required mandatory, optional, and core skill units in the Advanced GNVQ.

The ways in which you plan, carry out, monitor and review your coursework are very important in determining the grade you will achieve at the end of your course.

Some tips on carrying out research

In GNVQ Business it is particularly important that you investigate and identify your own sources of information and other resources to supplement those supplied by your school or college or in a textbook.

To help gather data and information on real-life business activities, you will find it helpful to:

- Regularly read through the business pages in a good newspaper and build up your own file of cuttings on business topics (these are likely to be very useful for future coursework assignments)
- Take note of the business and economic news on television and radio
- Read *The Economist* magazine (particularly the weekly business summary) as well as monthly Treasury briefings and bank reviews. All these should be available in either your local or school/college library.
- Obtain copies of the annual accounts of Public Limited Companies, particular those which are currently in the news or which interest you. These are usually provided free of charge.
- Ask to be included on the mailing lists for reports from your local Training and Enterprise Council (TEC), Enterprise Agency, Chamber of Commerce and Council Economic Development Unit

- Use publications such as *Social Trends* and *Economic Trends* for statistical information

In producing coursework it is essential that you list all of your sources of information, including sources for statistics, tables and charts, the people you interviewed, telephone calls made, etc. Keep your notes and working documents to show your tutor, in order to provide him/her with proof of the sources that you used.

About this book

This book has been written specially for the new mandatory Advanced GNVQ Business units launched in September 1995. The book is designed to contain everything that you need in order to achieve a good pass in Advanced GNVQ Business. It covers the requirements of the eight mandatory GNVQ units and can therefore be used by candidates taking the Advanced GNVQ in Business with BTEC, RSA, and The City & Guilds.

The text is designed as a comprehensive resource, providing explanations, up-to date business examples, activities, coursework suggestions, and much more:

- **Underpinning knowledge and understanding requirements** of all of the mandatory units in GNVQ Advanced Business needed for success in the course are covered in the text. An overview of the knowledge requirements, or key ideas, is given at the beginning of each chapter. This overview is derived from published NCVQ unit and element specifications.

- **Portfolio Activities,** or coursework tasks, provide everything you need to build a complete portfolio of evidence for assessment. Each Portfolio Activity indicates clearly published GNVQ range statements and the main core skills covered by the activity.

- **Assessment Assignments** at the end of each chapter are specially designed to help you produce evidence to demonstrate your achievement of the performance criteria and range statements in each GNVQ element within the eight mandatory units.

- **Test Questions** at the end of each chapter give you the opportunity to test your understanding of each element and prepare for the mandatory end-of-unit tests.

- **Practice in** *Application of number* **core skills** in presenting and analysing data will be useful to you in a number of Portfolio Activities and Assessment Assignments

- **Lists of useful publications** provide information and data relevant to your studies

- **Lists of useful contacts** in the business world give details of organizations who may be able to provide you with further information

We very much hope that you will learn from and enjoy this book and wish you every success with your Advanced GNVQ qualification.

Dan Moynihan

Brian Titley

INTRODUCTION

Presenting Data

The presentation of numerical data which you collect yourself or find in this book will often form an important part of preparing work to include in your portfolio. The use of tabulation and graphical methods can demonstrate core skills in numeracy and Information Technology if computer software packages are used. However, methods of presenting data are not examined in the final tests.

Rules of data presentation

When presenting data, the following rules should be observed:

1. Tables and graphs should have clear, understandable titles that reflect their content
2. The dependent variable in a graph, for example, sales, output, employment, costs, is normally plotted against the vertical or y axis
3. The independent variable, for example, years, quarters, months, is normally plotted against the horizontal or x axis
4. Each axis should be labelled with the name of the variable and units of measurement
5. Keep the scale of axes simple. As far as possible, draw axes with intervals of 1, 10, 100, or 1,000, etc.
6. Provide a key. Use colours or shading where possible to distinguish between different components
7. Give the source of your data

The main methods of data presentation are considered below.

Tables

Tables are one of the easiest ways to present data, especially if data on a large number of different variables needs to be shown at the same time, or where numbers are required to perform calculations. Tables are also useful for presenting information expressed in words. For example, Table A below presents data on the names, country of origin, industrial sectors, and turnover of the top five European companies in 1992.

▼ Table A: Europe's top 5 companies; by turnover, 1992

Company name	Country	Sector of origin	Sales turnover £ billion
Royal Dutch/Shell Group	Great Britain/ Netherlands	Oil, Gas & Nuclear Fuels	55.03
British Petroleum plc	Great Britain	Oil, Gas and Nuclear Fuels	43.31
Volkswagen AG	Germany	Transport - Manufacture and distribution	34.84
Daimler-Benz AG	Germany	Transport - Manufacture and distribution	33.51
IRI- Istituto per la Riconstruzione Industriale	Italy	Contracting, Construction	31.64

The Times 1000 1994

Advanced Business

Some people argue that graphs are a much better method of displaying numerical information in a readily identifiable way. However, this is not the case if a graph is poorly or inaccurately drawn.

Pie charts

Pie charts are a popular method of presentation. In a pie chart the total amount of data collected is represented by a circle or 'pie'. The circle is then divided into slices, the angle of each slice being proportional to a component within the total.

Consider Table B. If we are to present this information in a pie chart, the 360 degrees in a circle will have to be divided between the trip purposes which make up the total number of bicycle trips in London in 1991.

To calculate the angle of each slice in the pie, a business would need to use the following formula:

$$\frac{\text{Value of the individual component} \times 360°}{\text{Total}}$$

The size of the slice representing work trips per day is therefore calculated as;

$$\frac{112,000 \times 360°}{328,000} = 34°$$

Using the same formula for the other bicycle trip purposes we can derive the pie chart in Figure 1.

Bigger pie charts can show bigger totals. One twice as large as Figure 1 would represent double the number of daily bicycle trips in London.

Bar charts

These are one of the most common methods of graphical presentation. The height of each bar is drawn to be proportional to the value it represents. For example, the data on household size in Table C below is presented in the bar chart in Figure 2.

Bar charts are usually presented vertically, but can also be displayed horizontally. They can present absolute numbers or percentages.

▼ Table B: Purpose of bicycle trips, London 1991

Purpose of trip	Number of trips per day	%
Work	112,000	34
Employer's business	34,000	11
Shopping	47,000	14
Education	43,000	13
Other	93,000	28
Total	328,000	100

Travel in London - London Area Transport Survey 1991 (London Research Centre and Department of Transport, 1994)

▼ Figure 1: Pie chart of purpose of bicycle trips in London, 1991

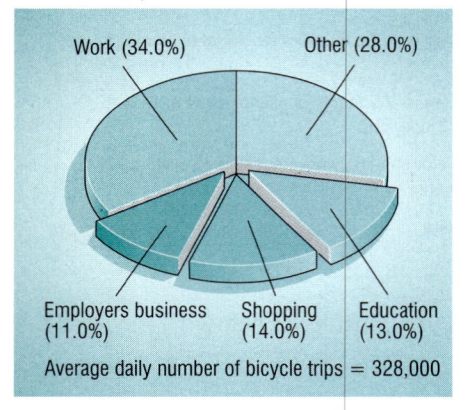

Work (34.0%)　Other (28.0%)
Employers business (11.0%)　Shopping (14.0%)　Education (13.0%)
Average daily number of bicycle trips = 328,000

▼ Table C: Households by size, Great Britain 1991

Size	Number of households (millions)
1 person	5.9
2 people	7.5
3 people	3.5
4 people	3.5
5 people	1.1
6 or more people	0.4
Total	21.9

Social Trends 1994

▼ Figure 2: Bar chart of households by size, GB 1991

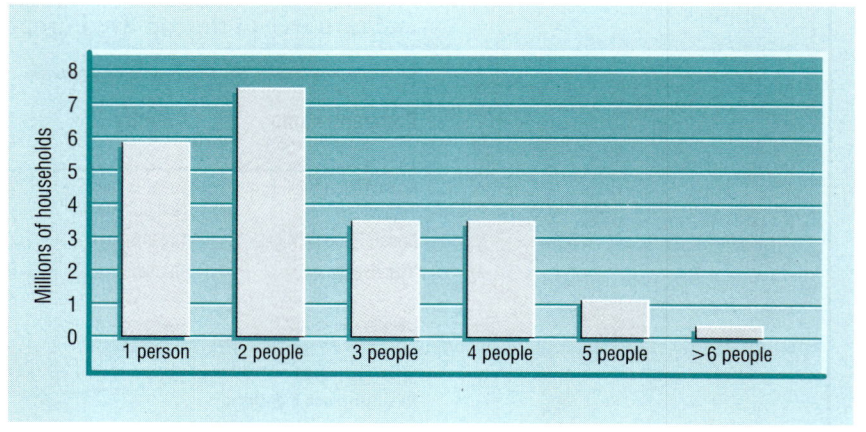

INTRODUCTION

Stacked bar charts
More information can be presented in bar charts by dividing each bar into several component parts. For example, the data in Table D and figure 3 display the average daily flow of motor vehicles per year by type of road.

▼ Figure 3: Stacked bar chart of average daily traffic flow by road type

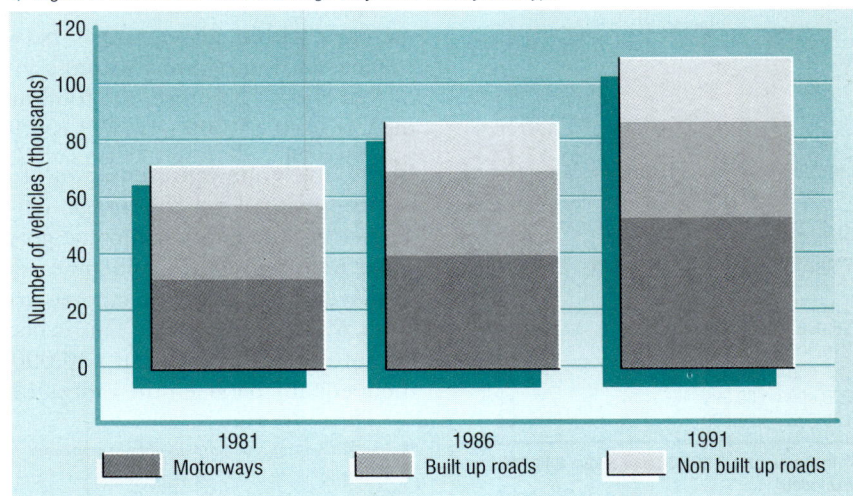

▼ Table D: Average vehicle flow per day; by road type

Great Britain	Number of vehicles (000's)		
Road class	1981	1986	1991
Motorway	30.6	38.3	52.9
Built-up roads	25.9	29.3	33.2
Non-built-up roads	13.5	17.0	22.0
Total	70.0	84.6	108.1

Social Trends 1994

Alternatively, the bars for each road class might be side by side in a **parallel bar chart** as in Figure 4(a). This allows easy comparison of the relative importance of each road class to total road travel. We might also convert the figures for each class in each year to percentages to examine the relative importance of each road class more clearly. Each bar in Figure 4(b) is now the same length, representing the total flow of 100%. The graph shows more clearly the increasing importance of motorways in total road travel over the other roads between 1981 and 1991.

▼ Figure 4: Alternative presentations of traffic flow statistics by road class
4a

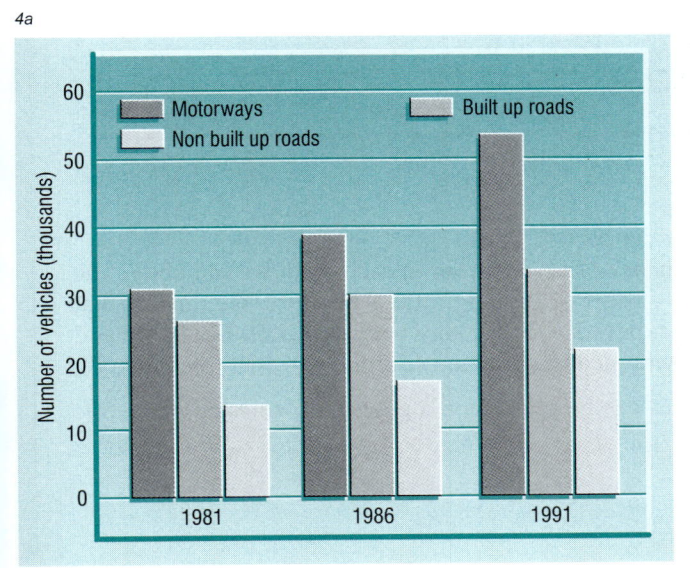

▼ Figure 4: Alternative presentations of traffic flow statistics by road class
4b

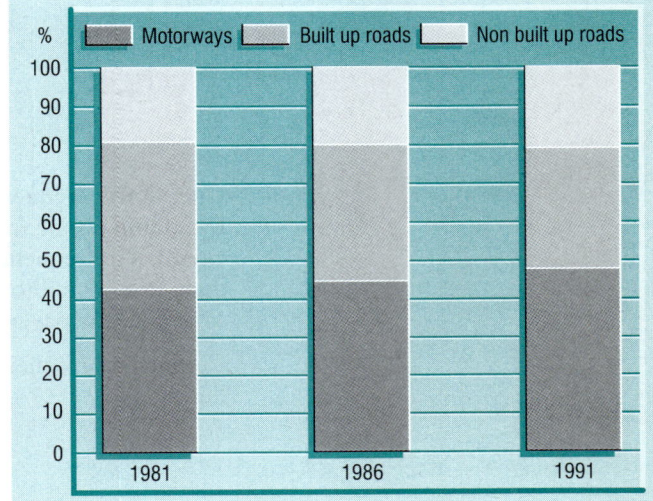

9

Advanced Business

Histograms

Histograms are similar in construction to bar charts except that it is the area of each bar that is proportional to the quantity being illustrated, and not just the height of each bar.

Histograms tend to be used when observations are sorted into convenient groups, known as **classes**. Table E shows the number of taxpayers with incomes within given ranges between £5,000 and £39,999. The total number of observations within a given class is known as the frequency (f) of that class. Therefore, the total number of taxpayers or frequency in the income class £5,000 - £9,999 is 7.9 million.

In the histogram representation of data in Table E, the width of each bar is proportional to the range of values in each class (see Figure 5). Therefore, the bars for income groups 4 and 5 are twice the width of the three bars representing incomes of £19,999 and below. The frequency displayed by the bar for income group 4 is not 3.2 as shown in the table but 1.6 (3.2 ÷ 2 = 1.6). This is because in the table 3.2 million taxpayers fall into the income group £20,000-£29,999 whereas the histogram splits them equally between the ranges £20,000-£24,999 and £25,000-£29,999.

▼ Table E: Number of taxpayers; by gross annual income, UK 1992

Income range*	Class number	Number of taxpayers (millions)
£5,000 – £9,999	1	7.9
£10,000 – £14,999	2	6.1
£15,000 – £19,999	3	3.9
£20,000 – £29,999	4	3.2
£30,000 – £39,999	5	1.0

* Incomes below £5,000 and above £40,000 are excluded

Social Trends 1994

▼ *Figure 5 Histogram of the number of taxpayers; by gross annuals income, UK 1992*

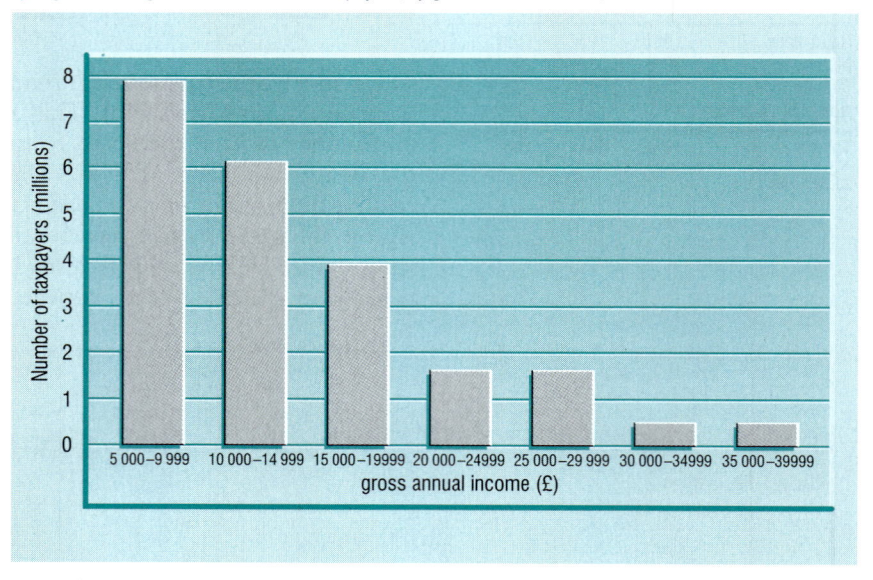

Cumulative frequency curves

By adding up the frequency of observations in each class, we can obtain the **cumulative frequency** - a sort of running total. Therefore, we can say that there are 7.9 million taxpayers with incomes between £5,000 - £9,999 and 15 million taxpayers with incomes between £5,000 - £14,999 (see Table F).

Cumulative frequencies can be plotted on a graph known as an **ogive** (see Figure 6).

INTRODUCTION

▼ Table F: Number of taxpayers; by gross annual income, UK 1992

Income range*	Number of taxpayers (millions)	Cumulative frequency
£5,000 – £9,999	7.9	7.1
£10,000 – £14,999	6.1	15.0 (7.1 + 6.1)
£15,000 – £19,999	3.9	18.9 (15.0 + 3.9)
£20,000 – £29,999	3.2	22.1 (18.9 + 3.2)
£30,000 – £39,999	1.0	23.1 (22.1 + 1.0)
All ranges	23.1	

* Incomes below £5,000 and above £40,000 are excluded

Social Trends 1994

▼ Figure 6: Ogive of UK taxpayers by gross annual income, 1992

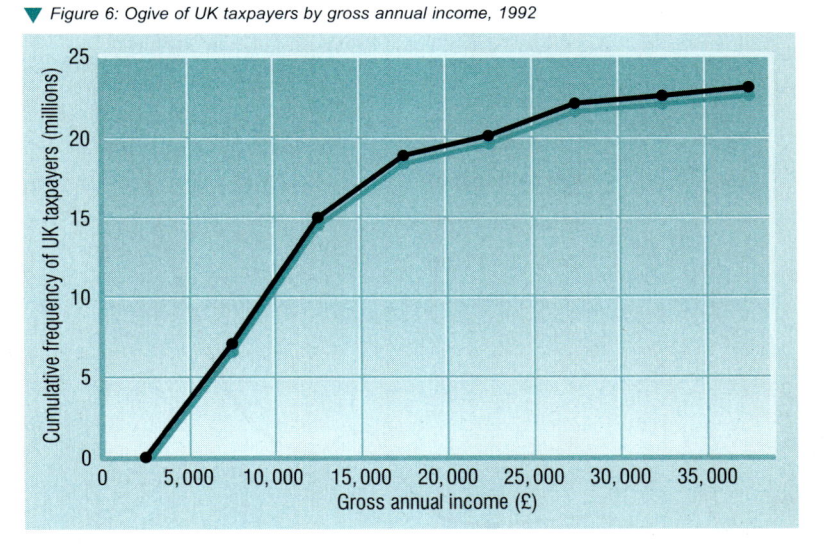

Scatter plots

These are plots of observation values relating one variable to another - for example, firm size by size of profit. To be meaningful, the two variables should be related in some way. The values of one variable are represented along the vertical (y) axis and the value of the other variable along the horizontal (x) axis.

▼ Figure 7: Scatter plot of profits in 1992 against profits in 1991 in the top 25 European companies, 1992

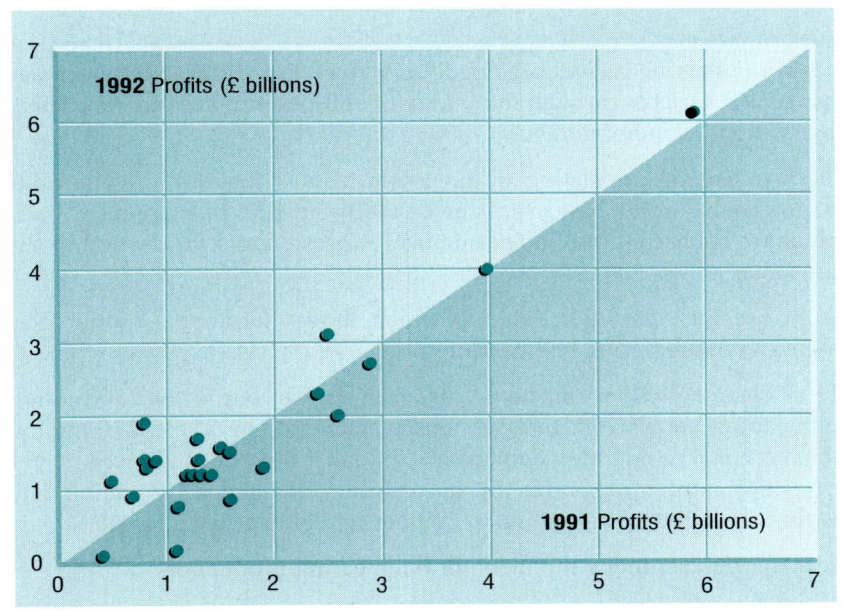

As an example, in the scatter plot in Figure 7, profits in 1992 have been plotted against profits in 1991 for the top 25 European companies, ranked by sales turnover. If the size of profits in each company were the same in each year, all the points would lie along a 45° line drawn through the origin of the axes. Points above the 45° indicate that the profits of that company increased in 1992, while points below the line show profits had fallen.

Line graphs

A mass of points scattered in a graph is not particularly revealing. If it is meaningful to do so, the scatter of points can be joined up in sequence to derive a line graph. These can be used to reveal the relationship between two variables.

For example, Figure 8 shows average radio and TV audiences by time of day. Firms involved in the mass-marketing of their products through TV advertising will be particularly interested in the peaked profile in TV audiences.

▼ Figure 8: Radio and television audiences throughout the day, 1992

1 Persons aged 4 or over.
2 Average audience, Quarter 4, 1992.

Source: Broadcasters' Audience Research Board; Radio Joint Audience Research; AGB Limited; RSL Limited.

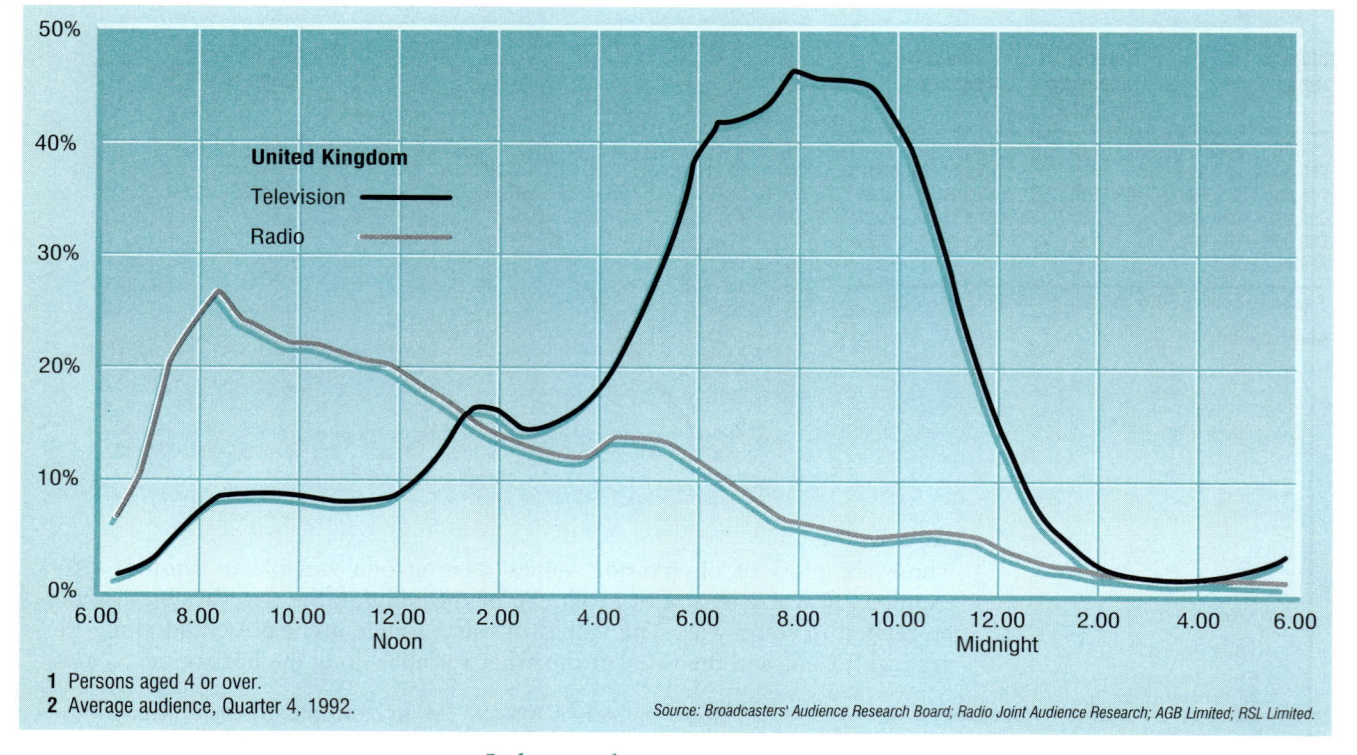

Index numbers

Index numbers or **indices** are simply a way of expressing the percentage change in a variable through time. Many published sources of data present observations as index numbers.

The first stage in calculating an index is to choose a base year. The value of the variable in the base year is given the value 100. In subsequent years values are converted into index numbers expressed as a proportion of the base value.

As an example, consider Table G which shows the annual output of a business manufacturing ball bearings.

Let us choose 1990 as our base year, such that an output of 250 million ball bearings equals 100. In 1991, output increased by 8% to 270 million which is equal to an index number of 108 (i.e. 1.08 x 100). Between 1991 and 1992 output expanded by a further 3.7% and 280 million ball bearings is equivalent to an index number of 112 (i.e. 1.037 x 108).

▼ Table G: Calculating index numbers - an example

Year	Output of ball bearings (millions)	% annual change in output	Index numbers (1990=100)
1990	250	–	100
1991	270	8.00%	108.0
1992	280	3.70%	112.0
1993	265	5.35%	106.0
1994	274	3.39%	109.6

How to calculate index numbers for ball bearing production:

Year 1990: output in base year = 100

Year 1991: $\dfrac{\text{output in 1991} \times 100}{\text{output in base year}} = 108.0$

Year 1992: $\dfrac{\text{output in 1992} \times 108.0}{\text{output in 1991}} = 112.0$

INTRODUCTION

Any data series collected over time can be represented as an index number series. One of the best known indices is the Retail Price Index (RPI), which is used to measure price inflation in the UK (see Unit 1). For example, we could infer from an RPI of 110 that retail prices had, on average, increased by 10% since the base year.

The main advantages of using indices to display movements in variables through time, such as volumes, prices, incomes, expenditures, is that trends can be easily identified and comparisons made between different indices, regardless of the values of the original data they represent.

The activity below will help you get used to looking at tables of numerical data and drawing graphs. You can include the finished activity in your portfolio of work.

Portfolio Activity

Skills: Interpret and present data, Process information

1. Suggest four types of information that can be found from the table above.
2. Choose appropriate data from the table to present in the form of a pie chart, bar chart, and line graph (use a computer to help you if possible).
3. What are the advantages and disadvantages of the graphical forms of presentation you have used over the tabulation?
4. What type of business organization might find the data useful, and why?
5. How might people who own, or might want to own, a house benefit from knowing about the data and what it shows?

▼ *Indicators of investment in dwellings and interest rates, 1990-1993*

Year/Qtr		Orders received by contractors for new houses (GB) (£ million, 1990 prices)	Housing completions (GB)		Average price of new dwellings [1]: mortgages approved £	Selected retail banks: base rates [2] %
			Private enterprise (thousands)	Local authorities new towns and government departments (thousands)		
1990	Q1	1,597	40.8	4.6	79,196	15.00
	Q2	1,427	39.0	4.3	79,051	15.00
	Q3	1,299	39.3	4.2	79,355	15.00
	Q4	1,215	39.9	3.4	79,154	14.00
1991	Q1	1,280	35.2	3.1	76,414	12.50
	Q2	1,387	38.9	3.0	76,640	11.50
	Q3	1,409	38.6	2.3	76,412	10.50
	Q4	1,363	39.0	1.9	76,056	10.50
1992	Q1	1,372	36.5	1.8	74,442	10.50
	Q2	1,326	35.2	1.1	73,349	10.00
	Q3	1,414	25.9	1.0	71,969	9.00
	Q4	1,288	32.4	0.7	72,383	7.00
1993	Q1	1,545	34.4	0.4	74,022	6.00
	Q2	1,633	34.3	0.8	75,360	6.00
	Q3	1,646	33.9	0.6	75,012	6.00
	Q4	1,740	34.9	0.5	74,868	5.50

1. Average prices of dwellings on which building societies have approved mortgages during the period.
2. Interest rate at end of period.

Economic Trends March 1994

Analysing Data

Your research will often result in the gathering of a large amount of data on many different variables, such as sales volumes, output, wage levels, employment, prices, and many more. Each item of data is called an observation. As well as collecting similar information, firms will also collect a huge amount of data using market research to find out the buying habits and tastes of their customers and potential customers (see Unit 3).

Sets of data are often uninformative because of their sheer quantity. If a vast amount of data is to be of use, it must be organized into an easy-to-read format, such as a graph or table. There are also a variety of statistical techniques that can be used to describe and analyse complete samples of data. Together these might help a firm to establish:

- Average sales each day, or the average age of their consumers
- The most likely outcome - for example, the level of stock most often reordered by retailers
- The range of prices which consumers might be willing to pay for a product.
- Trends - for example, the growth in output over the last ten years
- Future outcomes - for example, sales volumes next year, or advertising expenditures on a seasonal basis

When data is presented using statistical methods it is called **quantitative data**. Quantitative data refers to quantities sold per period of time, numbers of shoppers per week or month, etc., and can be presented in numerical or graphical format. The examination of numerical data is known as **quantitative analysis**. *Application of number* core skills will, amongst other things, require you to demonstrate the use and understanding of techniques of quantitative analysis. However, the statistical methods that are explained below are not examined in the final tests.

INTRODUCTION

Measures of central tendency, or averages

When a large amount of data has been collected, it is very useful to work out a central value or **average** which can be used to make sense of the whole dataset. Because averages give a single central value, they are sometimes known as **measures of central tendency**. They are also known as **summary statistics** because they are able to summarize features of a distribution of data in a single value.

Three main kinds of average may be calculated, known as the **mean, median** and the **mode**. Each measure has a number of advantages and disadvantages for the purpose of market research analysis.

The arithmetic mean

The **mean** is the measure most people think of as an average value. It can be calculated very simply by adding together the values of individual sample observations (denoted by $x_1, x_2, x_3 \ldots x_n$) and dividing the total by the number of observations (denoted by n). The formula for calculating the mean ($\bar{x}$) is given by:

$$\bar{x} = \Sigma \frac{(x_1 + x_2 + x_3 + \ldots + x_n)}{n} = \frac{\text{Sum of observations}}{\text{number of observations}}$$

(The sign Σ denotes the sum of all the individual observations).
Consider the following example. A survey of 50 people in a particular town has revealed the following data showing the number of visits each person has made to the cinema in the last year.

▼ Table H: Observed cinema visits per year - an example

13	5	50	13	26	7	50	0	13	50
10	7	13	13	13	0	50	7	50	5
5	50	0	26	5	5	13	5	0	7
5	13	7	50	50	13	10	10	0	10
10	4	10	13	26	50	5	13	5	26

A cinema chain attempting to decide whether or not to set up in the town needs to interpret the data. It is clearly very difficult to get a picture of likely cinema attendances just by looking at the observations in Table H. It would be more useful to work out an average attendance figure and use this as an estimate of attendance in the town as a whole.

The mean of the sample data in Table H is calculated as:

$\bar{x} = 841 \div 50 = 16.82$

That is, average attendance is likely to be around 17 visits per person per year. This is a very high figure and suggests either that the sample may be biased and not representative of all the people in the town, or alternatively that the company should set up there as quickly as possible!

The arithmetic mean is very useful, but can be affected by extreme values. For example, if one person in the sample worked as a film critic, the number of films he or she would see in a year could be well over 1,000. This would make the average figure for the sample equal to 35.9 (i.e. 1841 ÷ 51) and this would give a distorted impression of the number of times each individual could be expected to visit the cinema each year.

The median

The **median** is the middle number in a set of observations. The value of the median does not depend upon the size of any other numbers but simply on which number is in the middle of the group of numbers. Therefore extremely large or small 'freak' values have no effect on it.

For example, the median of 15, 20, 25, 30, 35 is 25. The median of 11, 12, 13, 14, 15, 16 is 13.5. In the first example there was an odd number of observations. Where the number is odd, the median or middle observation can be found using the formula:

$(n+1) \div 2$ = Median for odd number of observations.

In the second example there was an even number of observations. In this case, the median was found by taking the average of the two middle numbers.

When there are a large number of observations, rather than count whether there is an odd or even number, it is easier to use the formula $n \div 2$ to select the middle value.

In a frequency table the median value is worked out by calculating the total or cumulative frequency and dividing by 2. Frequency (f) denotes the number of times each observation occurs.

▼ Table I: Cumulative frequency of cinema visits

No. of visits to cinema (X_n)	Frequency (f)	Cumulative frequency
0	5	5
4	1	6 (5+1)
5	9	15 (6+9)
7	5	20 (15+5)
10	6	26 (20+6)
13	11	37 (26+11)
26	4	41 (37+4)
50	9	50 (41+9)

The median of the above data can be calculated from the cumulative frequency in Table I as the 50th ÷ 2 observation, or 25th observation, which was from an individual who visited the cinema 10 times in one year.

The main problem with using the median to describe a dataset is that it ignores all observations in a sample except the middle value. The median reveals little about the range of observations.

The mode

The **mode** is the observation value which is most common or which occurs most often in a distribution - i.e., the value with the maximum frequency. Therefore, in the survey of 50 cinemagoers, the modal value is 13 visits per year, which was observed from 11 survey respondents (see Table I).

The mode does, however, suffer from the disadvantage that it ignores all values other than the one which occurs the most. Sometimes the most frequently occurring value in a sample is not necessarily representative of the total population. For example, if a cigarette firm were considering launching packets containing 30 cigarettes aimed at heavy smokers, it would need to know how many people smoked over 20 cigarettes per day. Market research may show that the mode of the sample may be one or two cigarettes per day. This measure is unhelpful because the firm is interested in the consumption of heavy smokers who will not be represented in the mode, but whose consumption will be reflected in the mean of the whole sample.

The range

While it is useful to know the central value, or average, of a set of market research information, it can also be very useful to know how the data is spread around the central value. That is, are individual observations widely dispersed or within a narrow range around the average?

Where observation values vary widely, the average value will not be particularly representative of the sample. For example, if a survey revealed that consumers were on average willing to pay £10 for a given product, yet over 50% of those interviewed had said they were willing to pay anything up to £5 either side of the average, a firm could not be confident that setting a price equal to £10 would maximize sales. If, however, the majority would be willing to pay between £9.50 and £10.50, then the price of £10 would be more representative of consumers' willingness to pay.

▼ *Table J: Sweet consumption, packets per month per child under 14 years*

2,	2,	3,	5,	7,	10,	2,	15,	20,	21,	22,	30,	35,	35,	38

The **range** is a simple measure of spread calculated by subtracting the difference between the highest and lowest values in a distribution. Consider the following example of a sample of 16 observations of sweet consumption in packets per month for children aged under 14.

The range of the sample distribution in Table J is calculated as 38 - 2 · 36 packets of sweets per month.

This set of market research data has a mean of 17 packets of sweets with a range, or spread, of values of 36. If, however, the last number was 80 due to a young sweet addict, the range would be 78. Clearly then, the value of the range is distorted by extreme values, and in this case, the measure would not be representative of the majority of observations.

Now try the following activity using a computer spreadsheet. Many software packages have functions which allow you calculate the mean, median, mode, and/or range of a series of highlighted numbers simply by inputting a simple command or using a single keystroke.

Advanced Business

Portfolio Activity

Skills: Interpret and present data

Handywells is a medium-sized high street DIY store. Having in the past sold nails and screws by weight, they are now thinking of introducing pre-packed bags.

In an attempt to find out the amount of nails customers prefer to buy, staff at Handywells were asked to collect information on nail purchases during a typical trading week. Because types of nails and their weights vary so much, it was decided to record only the most popular sizes and types. These were wood nails between 1" and 2".

Each time an amount of nails was weighed, the sales staff wrote down the weight and then converted this figure into the number of nails bought.

If possible, input the data below into a spreadsheet to undertake the following tasks

1. Calculate the mean number of nails purchased per person.
2. Sort the data into ascending order and find the median number of nails purchased.
3. What is the modal number of nails bought per customer?
4. What is the range in the above data? Comment on the usefulness of the range as a measure of the accuracy of the research data above.
5. Compare the mean, median and mode. Which of these three measures would you say is the most representative average for the distribution, and why?
6. Advise Handywells how to make use of their research data and the summary statistics you calculated in questions 1 - 5 in preparing pre-packed bags of nails.

20	20	60	40
25	25	120	25
5	30	45	30
35	40	30	25
560	20	95	40
45	45	30	45
5	30	24	30
20	22	45	18
30	5	75	18
230	15	25	12
15	25	175	25
55	125	8	30
30	18	30	5

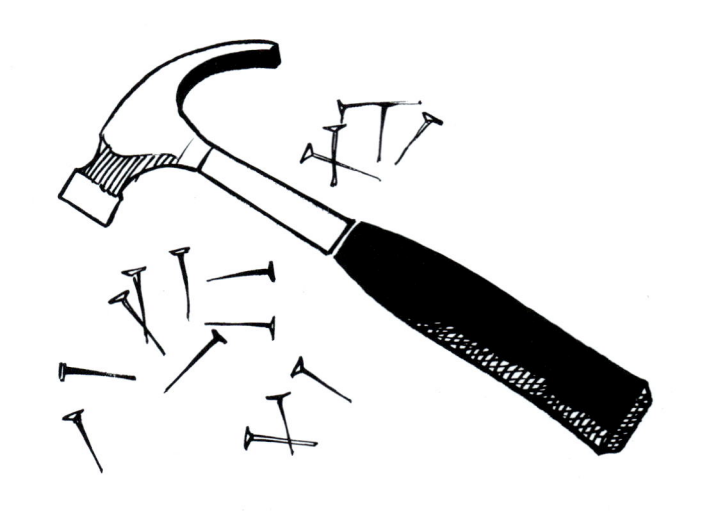

Purchase of nails recorded at Handy Wells

Further reading
Hall, D, Jones, R, Raffo, C: *Business Studies* (Causeway Press Ltd, 1993), Units 13, 14 and 15

INTRODUCTION

What is Business?

Needs and wants

Everyone needs a minimum of food, drink, and clothing or shelter to protect them from climatic extremes. This contrasts to the diversity of limitless human wants in a modern industrial society. People want cars, video recorders, designer clothes, pop concerts, foreign holidays, for the pleasure they give not, because they are necessary to maintain life and ensure survival.

Today, most people earn money to buy the things they need and want by working in a particular occupation, such as nursing, accountancy, bricklaying, or company management. Very few people attempt to satisfy their own needs and wants by their own direct work. That is, in a modern society, most people rely on others to satisfy their **needs** and **wants**.

Simply defined, **business** refers to the cooperation and organization between people, their materials, buildings, and machines, for the purpose of productive activity to satisfy human needs and wants. Everywhere you look today, you will see business activity: people shopping in the high street, factories, transport, the provision of parks and refuse collection by local councils, government taxation and expenditures on hospitals and defence, even pollution. The study of business is therefore the study of productive activity, how it is organized, how it creates wealth, and how that wealth is distributed.

What is a business organization?

A business organization can be defined as a group of people who cooperate with each other for the purpose of productive activity. A number of features are common to all business organizations:

- **A name**: for example, Sony, Tescos, Unilever
- **A mission statement**: to define the overall purpose of the organization - for example 'to serve our customers'
- **Objectives**: business goals such as optimizing profits, sales revenues, market share
- **People**: business owners, managers, and a workforce with a variety of skills and knowledge
- **An organizational structure**: the chain of command which shows who is in charge, who makes decisions, and who carries them out
- **Rules and regulations**: some set by managers, others dictated by government - for example, concerning health and safety
- **A culture**: a set of common values held by people within the organization - for example, 'to work together to achieve a high standard of product or service quality'
- **Records**: for example, of outputs, revenues, staffing levels, absenteeism, by which to judge performance, and for accounting purposes
- **Rewards and incentives**: to motivate employees and ensure they complete set tasks
- **Specialist functions**: e.g. product design, personnel, marketing, accounting, distribution, etc.

Advanced Business

▼ *International specialization*

▲ *Swiss watches*

▼ *Scotch whisky*

What is specialization?

Specialization is a major feature of modern business. It refers to the production of a limited range of goods and services by an individual, firm, region, or even a whole country. For example, despite the output of a wide range of products, Japan is probably best known for its electronic products. Swiss watches, Italian olive oil, Cuban cigars, French wine, and Scotch whisky are all examples of international specialization.

Firms also specialize in particular goods or services. For example, Ford specializes in making cars, MacDonalds specializes in fast foods, Esso specializes in drilling and refining oil. Specialization also takes place within a business organization. Most large organizations have different departments that specialize in activities such as personnel, finance, marketing, and design.

▲ *Japanese videos*

Why is trade necessary?

Specialization was the first step towards a wealthier society. People who were able to produce more clothes, pots, food than they themselves needed or wanted were able to exchange their surplus for other surplus items made by other people or communities. Thus, specialization implies a need to trade.

The earliest form of trade involved swapping goods directly and was known as **barter**. However, this was an inefficient form of exchange because it required a **double coincidence of wants**. That is, in order for trade to take place, a person with, say, a pound of apples who wanted to exchange them for some corn, would need to find a person who had surplus corn which they were willing to trade for apples. If the person with corn wanted pears or something else instead, no trade could take place.

ILL NEVER GET THAT IN MY WALLET!...

Placing a value on a good or service was also difficult. For example, how many apples could be exchanged for a cow, how many cows for a cart, and therefore, how many apples to a cart? Apples and other perishable goods would also rot before too long and so could not be saved to trade at a later date. Because of these problems many people still had to rely on being self-sufficient.

▼ Money is a universally accepted medium of exchange

The role of money

Nowadays, trade is easy. You can walk into any shop and make an exchange. Today, **money** is a universally accepted **medium of exchange** for goods and services. Money overcomes the disadvantages of barter:

- It provides a common measure of the value of all goods and services, i.e. all goods and services can be priced in terms of currency units
- It allows people to save and buy goods and services at a later date
- It allows people and business organizations to buy on credit and defer payment for goods and services received

Without money, trade would be difficult and specialization stifled. Money encourages specialization by making trade easier. People are able to specialize in particular tasks and be paid with money for their services. People will accept the money because they know that suppliers of food, clothing, shelter, and all other goods and services will accept their money in exchange.

International trade has allowed people all over the world to enjoy a wider range of products and share in technological advances made in different countries.

In the UK today, money includes bank notes and coins, and bank and building society accounts (both current and deposit accounts). Cheques and credit cards are not money but simply a way of transferring money between people and organizations.

How does business create wealth?

Business creates wealth by using natural, man-made, and human resources to make goods and services which people need and want. When goods and services are produced, **resources** are used up - woods, metals, clean air, nutrients in the soil, people's labour, and machines. Businesses will pay the owners of resources for their use. For example, people will supply their labour for wages; landowners will supply land for rent; suppliers of materials and equipment will also be paid to supply them. Business activity, therefore, generates incomes which people can use to buy goods and services. If a business is able to sell its goods and services for more than the cost of the resources it used to produce them, it will make a **profit** - the difference between sales revenues and costs.

Why does business involve choice

The resources used for productive activity are scarce compared to limitless human needs and wants. That is, there are just not enough resources to satisfy everyone's needs and wants. Scarcity of productive inputs implies the need for choice. Businesses must decide how to make the best use of

Natural resources

Labour

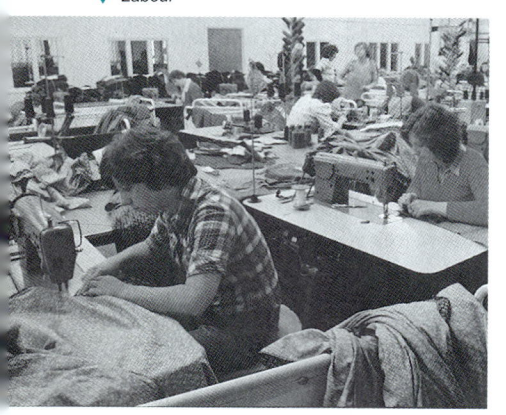

Capital

limited resources. Decisions must therefore be taken on three fundamental questions:

- **What to produce?** For example, should resources be used to satisfy wants for food and housing, or should more resources be devoted to the production of computers and tanks?
- **How to produce?** Where should production take place? What machines and tools are required? How many workers? What skills do they need?
- **For whom to produce?** Should the old and the infirm get more goods and services? Should more go to those people willing and able to pay the most? Or should everyone get an equal share regardless of their needs? The answer to these questions will depend on peoples' opinions or value judgements.

What are resources?

The scarce resources available to a business are called **factors of production**. Factors of production can be grouped under three headings:

- **Natural resources** - usually called raw materials, include: water from rivers and seas; minerals such as coal and oil; chemicals and gases from the air and deep within the earth's crust; plants and animals.
- **Labour** describes **human resources**. People provide the physical and mental effort necessary to make goods and services.
- **Capital** describes all those **man-made resources** used to produce other goods and services. To make the task of production easier, man has invented many tools: pens to write with, computers to calculate, screwdrivers, spanners, shovels, drills. On a much larger scale, turbines drive engines, tractors plough soil, roads and railways enable goods to be transported across land, ships and airplanes provide a means of carriage overseas.

Buildings such as factories, offices and shops are further examples of capital goods which help productive activity.

What is an economy?

Choosing how scarce resources should be used is called the problem of **resource allocation**. An **economy** is any system which attempts to solve the problem of resource allocation and decide what, how, and for whom to produce. Within any economic system three main groups of decision-makers can be identified. These are:

- Government
- Private individuals
- Business organizations (including those which seek to make a profit and those, such as charities, which are 'not for profit')

In a market economy such as the UK, most decisions on what, how, and for whom to produce are made by business organizations owned and controlled by private individuals in the **private sector** of the economy. However, some goods and services will also be provided by the government. In **planned economies** such as China and North Korea, the government takes most of the decisions on how to allocate scarce resources. Government authorities and enterprises, owned and controlled by central and local government, form the **public sector** of an economy.

An economy can be of any size and involve any number of people. For example, there is a **local economy** in every village, town, or city. A **national economy** refers to an entire country, such as the United Kingdom. In turn, the United Kingdom is part of the European economy. Indeed, every country in the world can be considered an economy as long as it is involved in productive activity, however small. All the countries in the world together combine to form the **world economy**.

Who are consumers and producers?

A **consumer** is a person who uses goods and services to satisfy their wants and needs. **Consumption**, therefore, involves the using up of goods and services to satisfy wants. When we watch television we are consuming electricity, the television set, and the services of a television company. When we attend college, we are consuming the services of teachers and lecturers. We consume the books we read, the food we eat, the cars we drive, the beds we sleep on, the banks we use.

Business involves the organization of scarce resources into productive enterprises known as **firms**. The people and enterprises who make goods and services are known as **producers**.

Goods and services are produced to satisfy consumer's wants and needs. **Production**, therefore, is any activity which is designed to satisfy wants. A successful business is, therefore, one that has correctly identified its consumers. A firm that uses resources to produce a commodity which nobody wants will soon go out of business.

Where does production take place?

In business it is necessary to distinguish between the different places in which production is organized.

- A **plant** or **factory** will be located at one particular site. Some plants may occupy a large area of land and house many workers and machines, such as a car plant or steel factory. Other plants may be very small, perhaps a small shed where a carpenter carries out his trade.

- A **firm** refers to a business organization, which can own and control any number of plants. For example, as well as offices, Ford UK controls some 13 different plants in the UK where car parts are produced.

- An **industry** consists of a group of firms all producing similar products or services. For example, the car industry consists of all those firms producing cars. Some industries can be dominated by one firm because its scale of production is large compared to competing firms.

Some useful background reading:

Moynihan, D, and Titley, B: *Economics - A Complete Course* (Oxford University Press, 1993) Chapters 1, 2, and 15

Business in the Economy

unit one

unit 1

chapter 1   The Effects of Demand and Supply on Business (Element 1.1)
chapter 2   The Operation of Markets (Elements 1.2)
chapter 3   The Effects of Government Policy on Markets (Elements 1.3)

Advanced Business

chapter 1
The Effects of Demand and Supply on Business

This chapter investigates the impact of changes in the market conditions of demand and supply on business organizations

Key ideas

Business involves the organization of scarce resources into productive activity to satisfy consumer wants.

Every decision on what to produce has an **opportunity cost** measured as the benefit of the alternative goods or services foregone.

A **market** for a particular good or service consists of all those consumers willing and able to buy it and all those producers willing and able to supply it.

Demand refers to the want or willingness of consumers to buy goods and services. To create an effective demand, consumers must have enough income to pay for goods and services.

A business enterprise must attempt to estimate the potential **effective demand** for their product in order to plan production.

A **market demand curve** for a product is a graphical representation of the relationship between consumer demand and possible product prices

In general, as the price of a product rises, consumer demand will tend to contract.

Price elasticity of demand measures the responsiveness of quantity demanded to a change in the price of a good or service. If demand is **price elastic**, sales revenues will tend to fall as product price is increased. If demand is **price inelastic**, revenues will tend to rise as price rises.

Demand for a product will depend on the level of consumer incomes, the price and availability of rival and complementary products, tastes and fashions, and other factors such as the weather.

Supply refers to the willingness and ability of producers to produce goods and services. In a mixed economy such as the UK, goods and services are produced and supplied to consumers by both private sector and public sector organizations.

A **market supply curve** for a product is a graphical representation of the relationship between producer supply and possible product prices.

In general, the higher the price, the more producers will wish to supply of their products. This is because they will expect to earn more profit as a surplus of revenue over production costs.

The supply of a product will depend on the cost of production, business expectations of sales and profits, technological change, and other factors such as the weather.

Prices at which goods and services are traded are affected by changes in their market demand and supply. A rise in market demand or a fall in the market supply of a product will tend to increase the **market price**. A fall in market demand or an increase in supply will tend to reduce market price.

Section **1.1**

Markets

The satisfaction of consumer wants

Productive resources

Business involves the organization and management of productive resources to produce goods and services to satisfy consumers' wants and needs. Productive resources are:

- **Human resources** - labour
- **Natural resources** - including wood, metal ores, soil, oil, meat, air, and water
- **Man-made resources** - buildings, machines, vehicles, roads, tools, and other equipment

When goods and services are produced, resources are used up - wood, clean air, nutrients in the soil, people's labour, and machines. However, the resources used for productive activity are scarce compared to limitless human needs and wants for food, shelter, clothes, cars, video recorders, holidays, and so on. There are just not enough resources to satisfy everyone's needs and wants. Business organizations must, therefore, decide what goods and services to produce with their limited resources.

Opportunity cost

Every society, no matter what its size, faces a choice, because resources are scarce compared to wants. The real cost of choosing one thing and not another is known as **opportunity cost**. This is the benefit foregone from not choosing the next best alternative. For example, if you choose to buy a compact disc you are making a choice to go without other items you could have bought. Similarly, in business, if an organization chooses to use its resources to produce electric kettles, it must go without the profits it might have earned from producing electric toasters instead.

Individuals, business organizations, even whole nations are continually faced with choice. The real cost of a government decision to build more schools will be the alternatives, such as hospitals or even reduced taxes, foregone. The business that decides to use resources to make clothes reduces the total amount of resources available to make other items.

What is a market?

The goods and services produced by business organizations are sold in markets. A **market** is defined as consisting of all those consumers willing and able to buy goods and services and all those producers willing and able to supply them. For example, the market for televisions will consist of the producers of televisions and the people who buy them. Similarly, there will be a market for cars, hairdressing, video recorders, window cleaning, and all other goods and services. These are called **consumer goods markets**.

▼ *Opportunity cost: resources are scarce and have alternative uses*

Open land

OR

Housing

Business organizations will also operate in many other markets, for example:

- **Capital goods markets** - where items such as machinery and vehicles are bought and sold by business organizations
- **Commodity markets** - where raw materials such as oil, copper and wheat are bought and sold
- **The labour market** - where people are hired for their services
- **The money market** - where people and financial institution borrow and lend money
- **The foreign exchange market** - where people and firms buy and sell foreign currencies if they need to trade overseas
- **The property market** - where people and firms buy and sell houses, offices and factories

A market for a good or service can be of any size and can cover any area. It can involve any number of consumers and producers anywhere in the world willing to exchange a good or service. The market for a local newspaper in Kingston-Upon-Thames is likely to be confined to the immediate area surrounding this town, but the market for newspapers such as the *Daily Mirror* or *The Times* is national. Products like oil, sugar, video recorders, and insurance are sold all over the world. These goods and services have international or world markets.

The interaction of consumer demand and producer supply in a market will determine the price at which a product is sold and the quantity sold. Changes in **market conditions** - that is, changes in the level and strength of consumer demand and/or producer supply - can, therefore, influence how individual businesses use their resources. How markets work is explored in this chapter.

Key words

Resources - the inputs to the production of goods and services

Opportunity cost - the cost of choice measured as the benefit of the next best alternative foregone

Market - any setting in which trade occurs between consumers willing and able to buy a product and producers who are willing and able to supply it

Market conditions - the level and strength of consumer demand and producer supply in a market

Section 1.2

Market demand

What is demand?

Demand refers to the want or willingness of consumers to buy the goods and services produced by business organizations. In order to be an **effective demand**, their wants must be backed up by an ability to pay for goods and services. A business enterprise must attempt to estimate the potential effective demand for their product in order to plan production. To do this, firms can use market research (see 9.1).

Firms can measure the quantity demanded of a good or service at a number of possible prices that may be charged for the product, and over a certain period of time - for example, the number of apples bought per day, videos per week, cars per month or even yearly. This information can be plotted on a graph to derive a **market demand curve**.

In general, all firms observe the following relationship between the price they charge for a good or service and consumer demand:

- As product price falls, the quantity demanded of that product expands
- As product price rises, the quantity demanded of that product contracts (see figure 1.1).

Portfolio Activity 1.1

Range: Demand
Skills: Interpret and present data

Plotting a demand curve

1. The table below lists possible prices for a 1lb bar of milk chocolate. Collect information from at least 20 people at your school or college on the number of chocolate bars they might buy each month at each possible price. Add up the number they would buy at each price and use this data to plot a line graph in the space provided below. Enter price (P) on the vertical (y) axis and quantity demanded (Qd) per month on the horizontal (x) axis. Label the plotted curve D1D1.

(Alternatively enter the data into a computer spreadsheet package to plot an xy graph. Remember to specify the column of prices as your y axis variable).

2. What does the demand curve look like? Describe the relationship between the price of chocolate bars and quantity demanded.

▼ *Resources are scarce and have alternative uses[Chocolate table]*

1LB BAR OF CHOCOLATE

Possible price	Quantity demanded
20p	—
40p	—
60p	—
80p	—
£1.00	—
£1.20	—
£1.40	—
£1.60	—
£1.80	—
£2.00	—

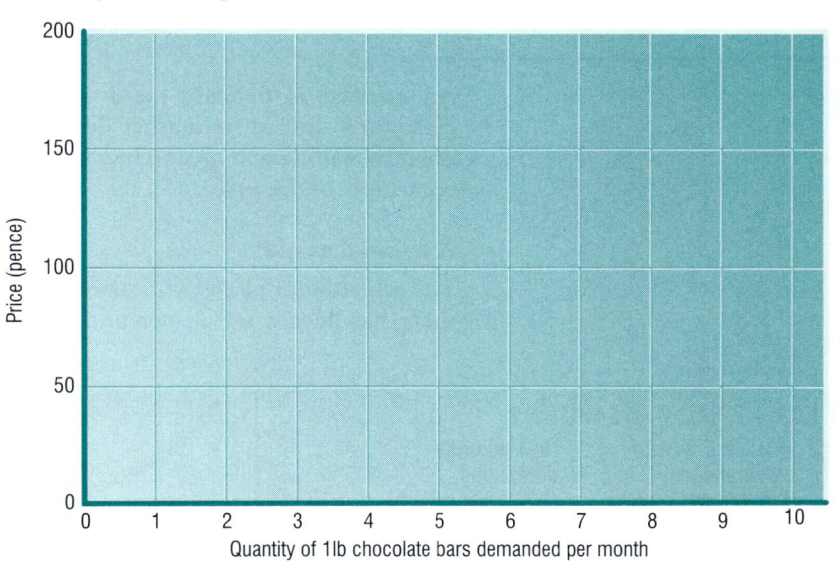

Advanced Business

▼ Figure 1.1: A typical market demand curve

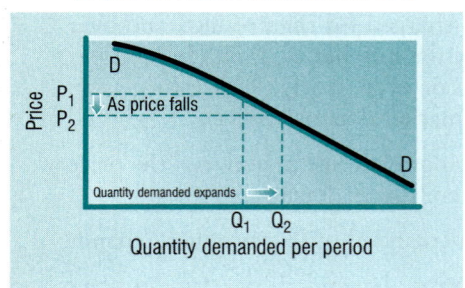

What makes a demand curve shift?

A change in product price causes quantity demanded to expand or contract along a given demand curve. However, over time, consumer demand for a product will be influenced by a number of factors other than price. These will cause the demand curve to shift.

Business organizations sometimes have little control over the conditions that cause consumer demand for their product to increase or decrease. For example, try to think what effect a general rise in household income might have on the demand for goods and services.

An increase in demand

Consider Figure 1.2 below. A firm has estimated the quantity demanded ($Qd1$) each week of its blank video cassettes for a schedule of different prices (P). After one year, the firm estimates market demand again ($Qd2$) and discovers that consumers now demand more video cassettes at each price than before.

The plotted demand curve D1D1 represents the original demand schedule ($Qd1$), while D2D2 represents the increased level of demand ($Qd2$).

▼ Figure 1.2: An increase in demand

MARKET FOR 3 HOUR VIDEO CASSETTES

Possible price (£)	Original quantity demanded (000's per week) (Qd1)	New quantity demanded (000's per week) (Qd2)
12	50	70
10	60	80
8	80	100
6	110	130
4	150	170
2	200	220

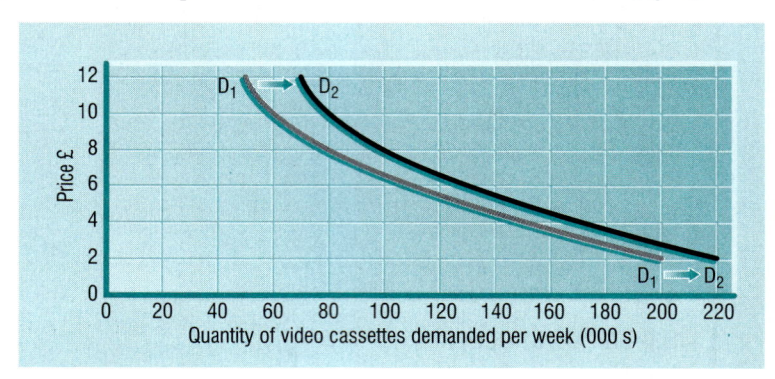

An increase in demand for a good or service can be represented by a rightward shift in its market demand curve. This shows that consumers are now willing and able to buy more of that product than they did before, regardless of the price.

A fall in demand

The schedule of prices and quantity demanded in Figure 1.3 below shows there has been a fall in demand for packets of peanuts at every possible

▼ Figure 1.3: A fall in demand

MARKET FOR 1lB BAG OF PEANUTS

Possible price (£)	Original quantity demanded (000's per month) (Qd1)	New quantity demanded (000's per month) (Qd3)
1.00	400	100
0.80	500	200
0.60	700	400
0.40	1000	700
0.20	1400	1100

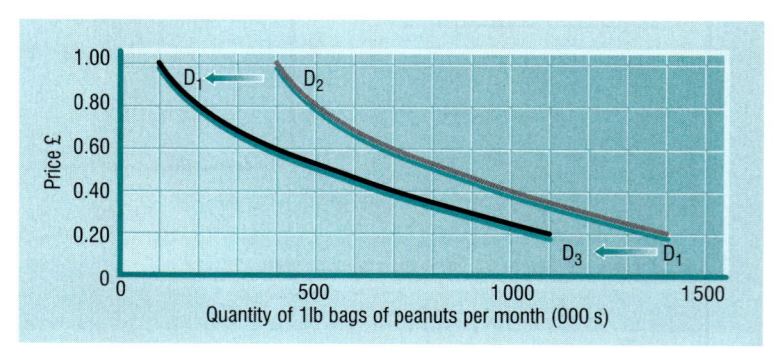

UNIT ONE

CHAPTER 1

price. The fall in demand is represented by a shift in the market demand curve inwards from the right, from D1D1 to D3D3.

A fall in demand for a good or service can be represented by an inward shift of the market demand curve. It shows consumers as only willing and able to buy less than they did before, regardless of price.

Portfolio Activity 1.2

Range: Demand, Effects on business decisions
Skills: Read and respond to written material

Look at the news articles below and, for each one:

1. Identify the things that have changed that might affect the demand for the particular good or service in question, or consumer demand for all products.

2. State whether quantity demanded will tend to rise, fall or remain unchanged as a result of the change you have identified.

3. Draw diagrams to show the likely market demand curves before and after each change.

Most economists still want interest-rate cuts. They believe that, without them, the recovery will slow because of the tax increases scheduled for April. From April National Insurance contributions will go up, VAT will be levied on fuel, and the married couples' allowance and tax relief on mortgage interest payments will come down. Together, these increases, the biggest overall tax rise since the Second World War, will knock 3% off most workers' disposable incomes, according to Steven Bell, chief economist at Morgan Grenfell, a merchant bank. Since pay settlements are barely keeping pace with inflation, this means that most workers will see their real disposable income fall in 1994. That could threaten consumer spending, and those favouring interest-rate cuts want them to counter this.

The Economist 15.1.94

POPULATION CHANGE
United Kingdom

	Population at start of period
Census enumerated	
1901-1911	38,237
1911-1921	42,082
1921-1931	44,027
1931-1951	46,038
Mid-year estimates	
1951-1961	50,290
1961-1971	52,807
1971-1981	55,928
1981-1991	56,352
Mid-year projections	
1991-2001	57,561
2001-2011	59,174
2011-2021	60,033

Social Trends 1994

The Birchfield, on the promenade at Weston-super-Mare on the Bristol Channel, is a 35-bedroomed Victorian hotel which "by a fluke" has been full this week, its owner Mr David Wright said.

On present bookings he expects it to be very quiet in a couple of weeks' time.

The poor weather "has had a dampening effect on people deciding on impulse to go away for the weekend. People are tending to book much later – if the weather is good they may well book a UK holiday, if it is poor they may well go into their travel agents and jet off to somewhere sunny," he said.

Financial Times 16.8.93

Fare rise drives more into cars

MOTORISTS are becoming more pollution conscious as the increasing cost of public transport drives more people to buy their own cars. Between 1981 and 1993, rail, bus and coach fares increased by over 130 per cent while motoring costs rose by just over 80 per cent.

The Times 27.1.94

In general, if the demand for a product tends to rise as incomes rise, the product is said to be a **normal good**. If demand falls as incomes rise, the product is said to be an **inferior good**. For example, as incomes rise, people may prefer to travel by taxi rather than bus.

Disposable income refers to the amount of income people have left to spend or save after paying tax on their income. Clearly, any change in the level of personal tax allowances, income tax or National Insurance contributions is likely to result in a change in the quantity of goods and services demanded.

Figure 1.4: Possible relationships between demand and income

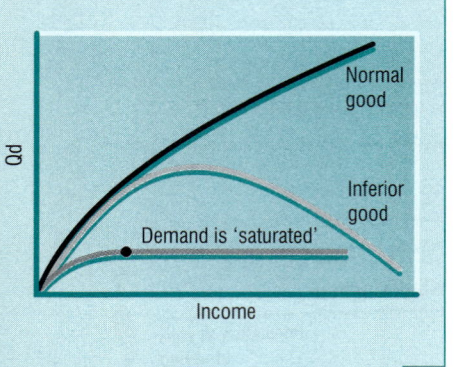

The following factors are likely to cause a shift in the market demand curve for a good or service:

1. Changes in income
Because effective demand is the willingness to buy a product backed by an ability to pay, it is clear that, as incomes rise, consumers will be able to buy more. However, the precise nature of the relationship between income and demand will depend on the type of product considered and the level of consumers' income. For example, a rise in income is unlikely to make most consumers want to buy more salt or newspapers each day or week, but it might allow them to travel less by bus and take the taxi more often, or even to buy a bigger car (see figure 1.4).

2. The prices and availability of other goods and services
Some of the goods and services we buy need other things, or accessories, to go with them. For example, cars need petrol, compact discs need a disc player, bread is consumed with butter or margarine. These **complementary goods** are said to be in **joint demand**.

If the price of new cars falls, consumer demand for them may expand and in turn generate increased demand for petrol. A rise in the price of compact disc players may lead to a fall in the demand for compact discs.

On the other hand, some goods and services are **substitutes**. A product is a substitute when its purchase can replace the want for another good or service. For example, margarine is considered a close substitute for butter. A rise in the price of one may therefore result in a rise in demand for the alternative. Different makes of car are also close substitutes - a fall in the price of Nissan Micras may cause a rise in the demand for Ford Fiestas.

A business organization will find it useful to gather information on changes in the prices and quality of competing and complementary products from rival producers, because any changes in competitors' products can affect demand and, therefore, sales revenue and profit for their own products.

3. Changes in tastes, habits and fashion
The demand for goods and services can change dramatically because of the changing tastes of consumers and fashion. Carefully planned advertising campaigns based on market research information on consumers can also help to create wants and shift demand curves for the advertised products out to the right.

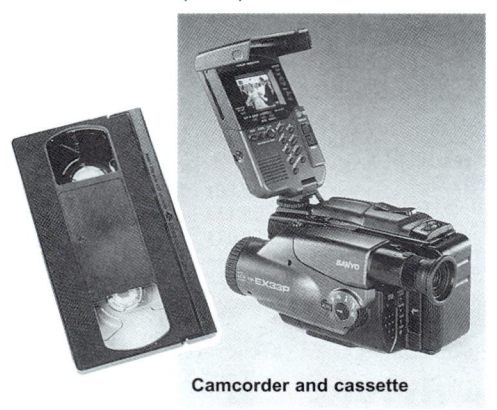

▼ *Complements*

Camcorder and cassette

▼ *Substitutes*

Buses and taxis

Fashion: here today and gone tomorrow...

1960s

Grunge

4. Population change

An increase in population will tend to increase the demand for all goods and services. Population growth in the UK is now negligible. Birth and death rates have fallen and this has resulted in a rise in the average age of the population. The growing number of middle-aged and elderly people has resulted in a changing pattern of demand.

5. Other factors

There are a great many other factors that can affect demand. The weather is one example. A hot summer can boost sales of cold drinks and ices. A cold winter will increase the demand for fuel for heating. Higher interest rates can increase the demand for savings schemes but reduce the amount of money people want to borrow, including mortgages for house purchases.

Changes in laws may also affect demand for some products. For example, it is now illegal to ride a motorbike without a crash helmet.

Key words

Demand - the willingness of consumers to buy goods and services at given prices

Effective demand - demand backed by an ability to pay

Market demand curve - a graphical representation of the relationship between demand for a product and price in a market

Normal good - a good for which demand increases as peoples' incomes rise

Inferior goods - a good for which demand falls as incomes increase

Disposable income - income available to spend on goods and services after income taxes have been deducted

Complementary goods - goods or services which are in joint demand

Substitutes - goods or services which are similar and which compete for consumer demand

---

Section **1.3**

Market supply

The motives for production

Profit or public service?

In a mixed economy such as the UK, goods and services are produced and supplied to consumers by both private sector organizations, owned and controlled by private individuals, and public sector organizations owned and controlled by government bodies and agencies (see 4.3). Some public sector enterprises produce goods and services for sale to consumers, such as a rail journey or a postage stamp. However, many are provided for free at the point of use, such as the National Health Service (NHS), and are instead paid for from tax revenues and government borrowing.

The motive for organizing resources to provide the NHS and a number of other public services, is to provide a service to consumers regardless of their ability to pay. The government also provides a number of goods and services which are of benefit to the nation but which the private sector is unwilling to provide, for example, street lighting, sea defences, and environmental protection. Some publicly provided goods and services are also felt to be too dangerous to be controlled by private organizations, such as nuclear power stations, the armed forces, and law and order.

However, for most private-sector organizations the motive for production is **profit**. Business owners who have invested their money in a business enterprise will wish to earn at least as much from their investment as they could have earned if they had placed their money in a risk-free interest-earning bank account. Profit is the reward for taking a risk and investing money in a business. Business organizations will hope to use their limited resources in the most efficient way to minimize costs and maximize profits.

We can measure the **profit margin** on each unit of output as the difference between the price received from the sale of that unit and the amount it cost to produce. In general, a firm will have an incentive to keep raising output to supply a market as long as the product price exceeds cost. However, the ability of a firm to expand output will depend on the availability of productive resources - raw materials, labour, plant and machinery - and its ability to finance the expansion (see 22.5).

What is supply?

Supply refers to the willingness and ability of producers to make goods and services to satisfy consumers wants and needs.

The **market supply** of a given product represents the sum of the individual supplies of all the producers competing to supply that product to consumers. We can plot information on the amount of a product firms wish to supply to a market on a **market supply curve**. In general, the higher the price, the more of a product a firm will wish to supply because they will expect to earn more profit.

Portfolio Activity 1.3

Range: Supply
Skills: Interpret and present data

1. The following table presents information on the quantity of bean bags that all bean bag producers are willing and able to supply at different prices.

Plot this information as a line graph in an xy graph space with price on the vertical (y) axis and quantity supplied on the horizontal (x) axis. Join up the points and label the resulting curve the **market supply curve** (S1S1).

Alternatively enter the data into a computer spreadsheet to plot the curve.

Possible price per bean bag (£)	Quantity supplied per month
35	18,000
30	16,000
25	13,000
20	10,000
15	6,000
10	1,500

2. What does the market supply curve look like? Describe the relationship between product price and quantity supplied.

3. Use the market supply curve S1S1 to determine how many bean bags would be supplied at a price of
   - £12
   - £28

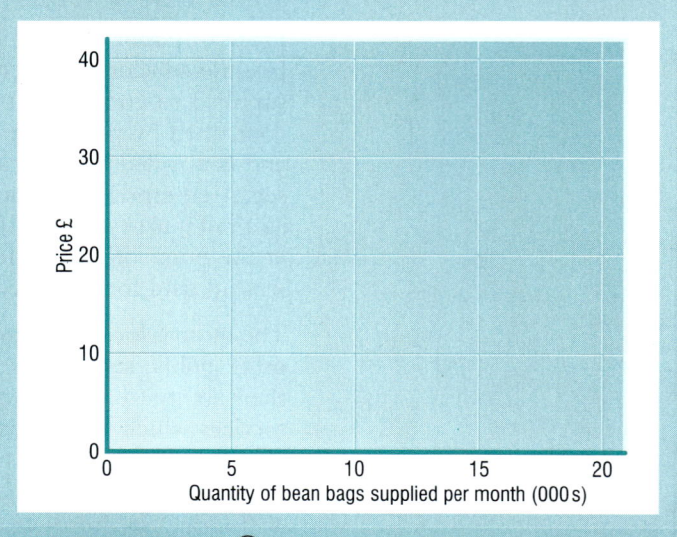

▼ Figure 1.5: A typical market supply curve

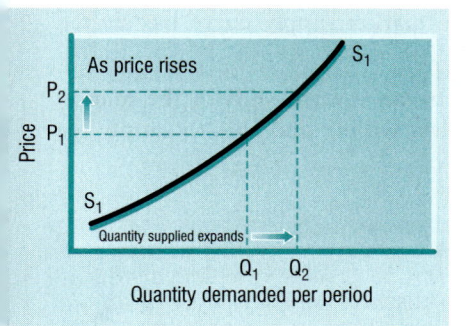

In general, we can observe the following relationships between the quantity supplied of a product and product price (see figure 1.5):

- As product price rises, the quantity supplied of that product expands
- As product price falls, the quantity supplied of that product contracts

Falling prices will generally be expected to reduce firms' sales revenues and consequently reduce their profit margins over and above production costs.

What causes a supply curve to shift?

A change in the price of a product will normally cause the quantity supplied to expand or contract along a given supply curve. However, changes in factors other than the price of the product can cause the whole supply curve to move.

An increase in supply

The schedule of prices (P) and quantity supplied (Qs) in Figure 1.6 shows that there has been an increase in the supply of disposable razors at all possible prices. The plotted market supply curve S1S1 represents the original supply schedule (Qs1), while S2S2 represents the increased level of supply (Qs2).

▼ Figure 1.6: An increase in supply

Price of Razor (pence)	Original monthly supply (Qs1)	New monthly supply (Qs2)
50	12 000	15 000
40	11 000	14 000
30	9 000	12 000
20	6 000	9 000
10	2 000	5 000

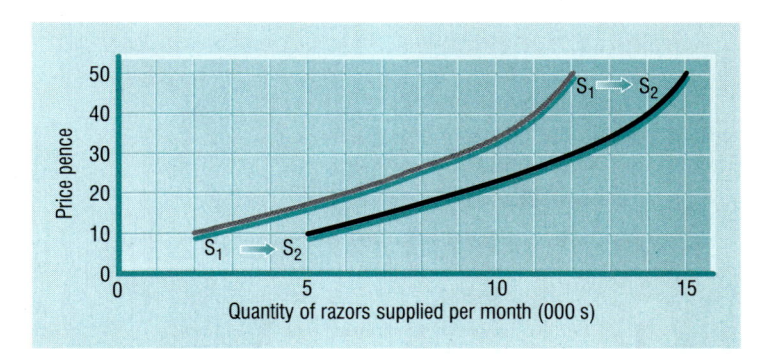

An increase in the supply of a good or service can be represented by a rightward shift in the market supply curve. It shows producers as willing and able to supply more of the product, regardless of price.

A fall in supply

The schedule of prices and quantity supplied in Figure 1.7 below shows

▼ Figure 1.7: A fall in supply

Price of 1lb Potatoes (pence)	Original daily supply (Qs1)	New daily supply (Qs2)
100	60 000	40 000
80	50 000	30 000
60	40 000	20 000
40	30 000	10 000
20	20 000	0

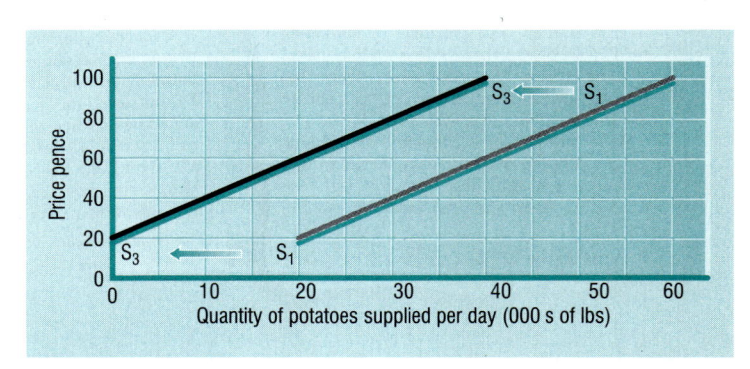

Advanced Business

that there has been a fall in the market supply of potatoes at every possible price from Qs1 to Qs3. The market supply curve has shifted inwards to the left from S1S1 to S3S3.

A fall in supply can be represented by an inward shift in the market supply curve. It shows producers as less willing and able to supply the product, whatever the price.

Portfolio Activity 1.4

Range: Supply, Effects on business decisions
Skills: Read and respond to written material

1. Look at the news articles below and, for each one:

- Identify the changing factor(s) and the potential impact on the supply of the goods or services in question, or generally.
- State whether quantity supplied will tend to rise, fall, or remain unchanged as a result of the changing factor.
- Draw diagrams to show the likely market supply curves before and after each change.

2. Choose a product and investigate the following aspects of supply:

- Who are the suppliers of your product?
- What are the characteristics of the product suppliers (i.e. firm size, location, market share, turnover, profit, ownership, etc.)?
- How do the suppliers compete with each other?
- Evaluate the supply of the product to consumers in terms of price, range, quality, availability, image.

Write a short report based on your findings.

What use could you make of this information if you were considering starting a business to supply the same product?

LIKE MANY RUSSIANS, Mr Igor Prokopov can become emotional at times. And he gets noticeably cross when anyone suggests that the Commonwealth of Independent States is entirely responsible for bringing the western aluminium industry to its knees.

There has been an unprecedented surge in CIS aluminium exports, which European producers say has depressed the price to a point where their industry is on the verge of collapse.

Japan once was a big aluminium producer, he recalls, but now makes virtually none. The Japanese were forced out in the early 1980s because their costs were too high, particularly their energy costs. Nobody blamed the CIS producers for that, so why blame them now?

His spirited defence cuts little ice with the European Commission, which last week imposed restrictions on CIS aluminium imports, insisting that only 60,000 tonnes may be imported between now and the end of November – about half of what might otherwise have been expected.

Financial Times 16.8.93

KEEPING an eye on the shrinking cost of various technologies is also important, say toy manufacturers. Computer chips, for instance, were once formidably expensive, but have now become so cheap that they can be widely used in children's products.

Hasbro has capitalized on low-cost, high-memory chips to produce Talking Barney, a stuffed green dinosaur which says 500 different phrases at random. "Before, six or seven sayings were considered a lot," says Sharon Hartley, vice president of marketing for Playskool, the Hasbro division that makes Talking Barney. "But additional memory has become so cheap now that we've been able to use it in a number of toys."

With the cost of technology diminishing rapidly, toy manufacturers say their products will soon use technologies once thought too expensive even for the adult consumer market.

Financial Times 21.12.93

The Malaysian government has tightened its newly decreed trade restrictions against the UK by outlining a range of projects in which British companies will not be allowed to participate.

British companies calculate that hundreds of millions of pounds' worth of work will be lost in Malaysia and jobs in Britain might be under threat.

Financial Times 28.2.94

Manufacturers see hopes rise

A CONFEDERATION OF BRITISH INDUSTRY survey yesterday painted a more optimistic picture of business trends than last week's report from the British Chambers of Commerce.

An encouraging sign in the CBI survey is that orders and output are increasing faster than forecast in the last report in October. Furthermore, the balance of companies intending to increase spending on plant and machinery over the coming year was positive for the first time since July 1989. More companies have cut domestic prices than raised them over the last four months.

CBI/Financial Times 25.1.94

Factors in market supply

The following factors are likely to cause shifts in the market supply curves of goods and services:

1. Changes in the price of other goods

Price changes act as the signals to private-sector firms to move their resources to and from the production of different goods and services (see 1.4). If the prices of pre-recorded audio cassettes are falling, the potential profit margin between sales revenues and costs will be squeezed and some producers may be attracted to the CD industry in search of higher profits. This will result in an increased supply of compact discs. The supply curve for CDs will shift out to the right as in Figure 1.6.

2. Business optimism and expectations

Fears of an economic downturn may cause some firms to move resources into the production of goods and services they feel will be less affected by falling consumer incomes and demand (see 3.2). For example, high-cost luxury items such as cars and video recorders often fare badly during economic recessions. Conversely, expectations of an economic recovery may result in a re-allocation of scarce resources into new markets, thereby shifting their supply curves out towards the right.

3. Technological advance

Technical progress can mean improvements in the performance of machines, employees, production methods, management control, product quality, etc. This allows more to be produced, often at a lower cost, regardless of the price at which the product is sold. For example, advances in deep-water mining technology and rig design have helped a number of countries to drill for oil in deep oceans once thought too costly to exploit.

4. Global factors

The supply of goods and services can be affected by a variety of factors that cannot be controlled by producers, for example, sudden climatic change, trade sanctions, wars, natural disasters, and political factors. Following the Gulf War in 1990, international restrictions prevented Iraq from selling the oil it produced on the world market. This had the effect of moving the market supply curve of oil in to the left as in Figure 1.7.

5. Business objectives

A firm might seek to increase market share by forcing competitors out of business. This may lead to a fall in market supply.

6. The costs of production

By far the largest determinant of supply is the cost of production, i.e. payments made for raw materials, power supplies, labour, buildings, and machinery.

A fall in the costs of production due, for example, to new technology, will mean that more of a product can be offered at the same price. The profit margin between unit price and unit cost will have increased. The market supply curve will therefore move out to the right. A rise in the cost of production, for example, due to workers winning generous wage rises, or a shortage of raw materials, will have the opposite effect. Market supply will tend to fall at each price.

A firm may actively seek to expand consumer demand for its product in the short run by cutting prices. This will reduce the profit margin between the revenue and cost of each item sold. A firm that expands sales will clearly need to raise output in the short run to meet demand. This may initially incur higher costs – paying labour to work overtime, buying in more materials, or more equipment. However, this assumes a firm will be able to finance expansion. Some may be constrained in the amount of money they can raise from retained profits, bank loans or the sale of shares (see 22.2).

By expanding sales and output an organisation will hope that in the future (the long run) it will be able to reduce the average cost of producing each unit of output, for example, each car, each pair of shoes, or each compact disc. Lower average costs increases potential profit margins between revenues and costs.

Large scale, or mass, production can reduce the cost per unit of output because there are economies of scale (see 20.2). This is because certain costs incurred by a firm are spread over a larger output. Cost such as rents, rates, lighting and heating, telephone usage and more, are called fixed costs because they have to be paid whatever the size of output produced. For example, consider a firm making cakes. On top of the cost of ingredients and wages, it incurs fixed costs of £1000 each month regardless of how many cakes it produces. If it makes 1000 cakes per month then the average fixed cost per cake is £1 (ie £1000/1000). However, doubling output to 2000 cakes per month reduces fixed costs per cake to 50 pence and so on.

Large scale production can bring also costs savings in the form of discounts for buying materials in bulk; lower interest rates on loans from banks who are happier to lend to well established large businesses; or even technical economies because the large firm can afford to employ new faster machines and production processes.

Key words

Profit - an excess of revenues over costs

Profit margin - the difference between the price received from the sale of a unit of output and the cost of producing it

Supply - the willingness of producers to provide goods and services for sale at given prices

Profit margin - the difference between the price received from the sale of a unit of output and how much it cost to produce

Market supply curve - a graphical representation of the relationship between supply and price in a market

Section 1.4 The determination of market prices

The articles opposite suggest that product prices are affected by changes in their market demand and supply. Rising prices are likely to be the result of either a rise in market demand or a fall in the market supply of a product.

The Pope and the Price of Fish

For over 1,000 years the Roman Catholic Church required believers to abstain from consuming meat on Fridays and instead eat fish. However, a liberalization of the regulation of the church abolished this requirement in December 1966.

Frederick W. Bell studied the impact of this liberalization on the price of fish in New England, USA (with a population approximately 45% catholic). The study compared fish prices over a ten-year period before the catholic church abolished the rule with a nine-month period just after. But first he had to correct for the influence of a number of other changing factors on the price of fish: fish imports, prices of close substitutes (poultry and meat); cold storage holdings, and changes in personal incomes, etc. Having corrected for these influences on price, the effect of the liberalization on fish prices can be seen in the following table:

Prices of fish (monthly data 1957-67)

Species	% change in average price due to liberalization
Sea scallops	-17%
Cod	-10%
Haddock	-21%
Whiting	-20%

Bell, FW: 'The Pope and the Price of Fish' in American Economic Review, Vol. 58

The results showed that, for any given quantity of fish, the prices received for fish were lower after the effect of liberalization on demand.

Adapted from Hirshleifer, J: Price Theory and Applications (Prentice Hall International)

▲ Some examples of how demand and supply determine price

Rice price rise

BANX

European consumers will soon be paying more for rice because of poor harvests.
Financial Times 20.1.94

Opec ministers trade frowns for smiles as oil prices rally

Fresh optimism that short-term oil prices are on their way up was clearly reflected in the smiles and jaunty steps of oil ministers at last week's meeting in Vienna of the Organization of Petroleum Exporting Countries.

The Centre for Global Energy Studies in London believes "prices could rise steeply towards the end of the year if Opec continues to restrain output" in the face of sharply rising demand. It recently warned that sudden price rises were possible because stocks held by oil companies are likely to fall sharply by the fourth quarter.
Financial Times 20.6.94

Falling prices, on the other hand, are the likely result of either a fall in consumer demand for the product, or an increase in supply. The interaction of consumer demand and producer supply will ultimately determine the price at which a good or service is traded.

The **market price** of a product can be found at the point at which the market demand and supply curves intersect. At this price, the amount consumers are willing and able to buy is exactly equal to the amount producers are willing to supply. (In **Portfolio Activity 1.5** on page 40 the market price is determined at 40 pence per chocolate bar. At this price producers will supply 200,000 chocolate bars each week - just enough to satisfy consumer demand).

Advanced Business

Portfolio Activity 1.5

Range: Effects on bussiness decisions; Analyse in terms of market price and volume
Skills: Interpret and present data

Consider the following market demand and supply schedules for 500-gram milk chocolate bars.

1. On the graph, plot and label the market demand and supply curves for chocolate bars.

2. From the table, identify the price at which quantity demanded is equal to quantity supplied. This is known as the **market price**. Label the market price P on your graph.

3. At the market price, producers are willing and able to supply as many chocolate bars as consumers are willing and able to buy. That is, there is an equal quantity traded between producers and consumers. Identify the amount equilibrium quantity traded in your table and label it Q on your graph.

4. When quantity demanded exceeds quantity supplied there is an **excess demand** in the market. Similarly if quantity supplied outstrips quantity demanded, there is an **excess supply**.

Figure 1.8: The determination of a market price for chocolate bars

Possible price of chocolate bar (pence)	Quantity demanded per week (Qd)	Quantity supplied per week (Qs)
70	100,000	420,000
60	120,000	330,000
50	150,000	260,000
40	200,000	200,000
30	250,000	120,000
20	320,000	60,000
10	400,000	30,000

Using your graph, state whether there is an excess demand or supply at the following prices:
A 70 pence
B 50 pence
C 35 pence
D 40 pence

5. How do you think firms will alter the price of their chocolate bars if:
A there is excess demand
B there is excess demand
C there is no excess demand or supply?

Figure 1.8 The determination of market price and quantity traded

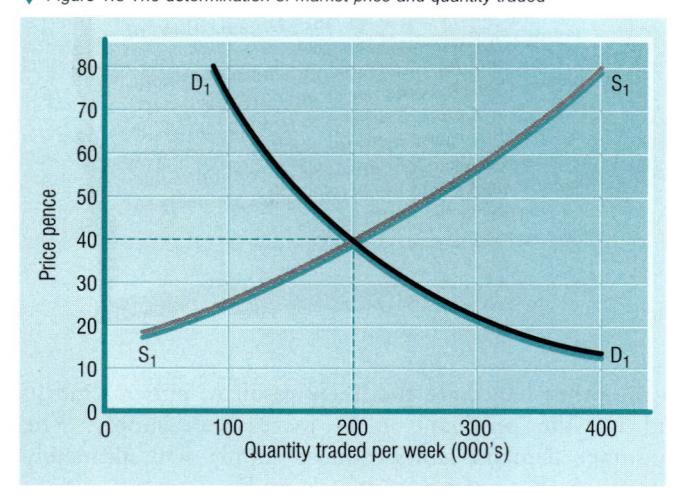

If firms set their prices above the market price - for example, at 80 pence - there will be an **excess supply**. Firms will be producing more chocolate bars than consumers are willing to buy. If consumers are to be persuaded to buy up the excess supply, price will have to fall.

If firms set their prices below the market price, for example at 40 pence, there will be an **excess demand**. There will be pressure on price to rise to 'clear the market'. As the price rises, firms are willing to expand output, while at the same time a rising price causes demand to contract.

The same reasoning applies to any good or service. Only at the market price will consumers' decisions to buy a product match producers' decisions to supply it. There will be no need for price to change unless there is a change in market conditions, i.e. a shift in the market demand or supply curves.

Changes in market price

Four basic movements in the market price for a given product are conceivable if we consider all the possible changes in demand and supply. These are shown in the diagrams below.

▼ An increase in demand results in more being traded at a higher market price as the quantity supplied expands

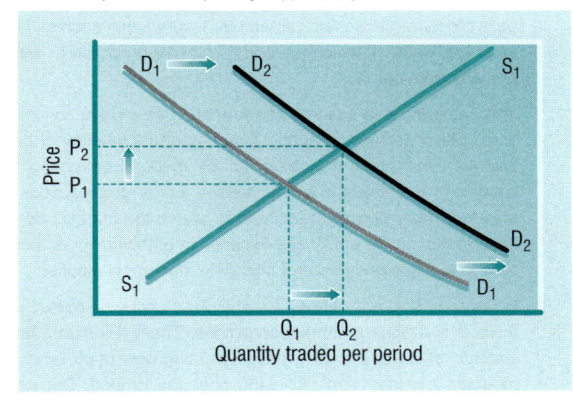

▼ A fall in demand results in less being traded at a lower market price as the quantity supplied contracts

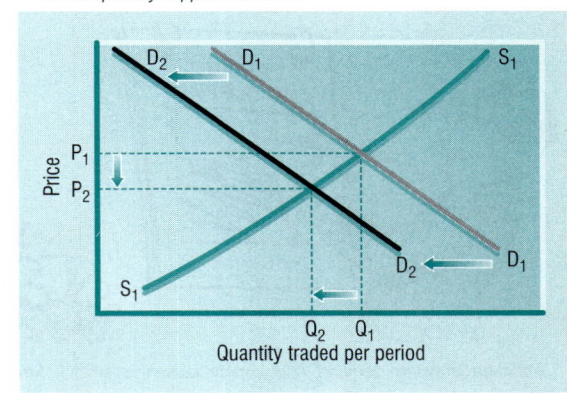

▼ An increase in supply results in more being traded at a lower market price as quantity demanded expands

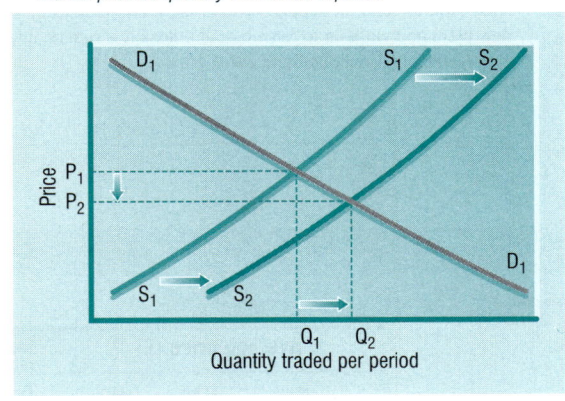

▼ A fall in supply results in less being traded at a higher market price as quantity demanded contracts

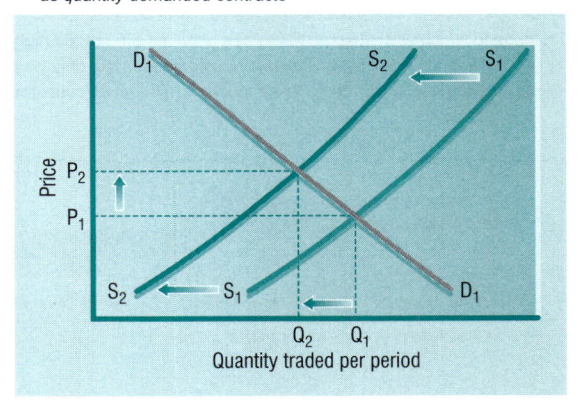

The price mechanism

Changes in demand and supply cause changes in the prices and quantity traded of different products. In most economies, changing prices are a signal to producers to increase or decrease the production of different products. For example, a rise in consumer demand for pork will push up the market price and increase the potential for producers to earn higher profits from the sale of the meat. As a result, a number of food producers may be tempted to use more land, labour and capital to breed and keep more pigs. This leaves fewer resources to be used to make products whose prices are lower or falling. The same is true of most products. In this way, consumers get what they want. This is known as the **price mechanism**.

Advanced Business

Demand and supply analysis in business

It is important for businesses to be able to analyse the effects of a change in market conditions on price and quantity traded, because of the effect it can have on their revenues, profits, and the allocation of scarce resources. However, the world is always changing, and many shifts in both market demand and supply can occur at any given time. It is difficult to predict the effect on price and quantity traded unless the precise size of the changes in demand and supply are known.

Although drawing demand and supply curves is useful, firms are unlikely to have perfect knowledge of their market demand and supply curves. As a result, they will tend to choose prices for their products which fulfil certain business objectives, for example, pricing to achieve a desired mark-up over cost for profit, or pricing low to increase market share or to force competitors out of business (see 21.3). However, they need to be aware of the forces of demand and supply. As we have discovered, if firms set prices low, there is likely to be excess consumer demand which will cause prices to rise. If prices are set too high, sales will suffer and firms may be left with unsold goods. The only way to sell off surplus stocks will be to lower prices to suit what consumers are willing to pay.

The best any business will be able to do is to examine changes in market conditions as they occur and consider the likely direction of movement in market price and quantity traded. For example, information on the business expansion plans of rival firms could suggest an increasing market supply in the future and downward pressure on prices and profits, thus forcing firms with high costs out of the market. On the demand side, rising interest rates may signal a possible fall in consumer demand for luxury items such as hi-fi, videos and cars, many of which are bought on hire purchase or with the help of loans from banks.

The gathering and analysis of information on market conditions which could affect demand or supply is an important function of business. A business that does not examine or respond to changing market conditions is unlikely to be successful. Large organizations are often able to employ specialist analysts to 'watch the market'. Smaller firms have to rely on the ability and experience of their owners, managers or staff to analyse and interpret changing market conditions.

However, firms are unlikely to alter their prices or output every time there is a change in market conditions. There are high administrative costs involved in changing prices, printing new price lists, relabelling products and communicating the changes to staff. Consumers also tend to dislike rapid price changes. It is hard for them to plan their expenditure if prices are continually going up or down.

Similarly, firms are unlikely to cut production levels, lay off workers and shut down plant every time demand falls. A fall in demand might only be temporary. Only if the slump in demand becomes protracted will firms tend to contract supply. In contrast, a firm is unlikely to invest in new plant and workers to raise output unless it is reasonably sure that high levels of product demand will continue.

Portfolio Activity 1.6

Range: Effects on business decisions
Skills: Interpret and present data

You work as a market analyst for a major construction firm. The UK construction market has been depressed for a number of years and the company directors have asked you to produce a market commentary to help clarify past, present and possible future trends in the housing market.

You have collected the following information relevant to your analysis. (Collect additional and more up-to-date information as necessary.)

▼ Average house prices

	Number of mortgages
1971	4,506
1976	5,322
1981	6,336
1986	8,138
1987	8,283
1988	8,564
1989	9,125
1990	9,415
1991	9,815
1992	9,922
1993	9,998

	Average price (£)			Mix-adjusted dwellings Price index (1990=100)
	New dwellings	Other dwellings	All dwellings	
1982	28,205	23,083	23,644	37.7
1983	30,817	25,901	26,471	42.1
1984	33,080	28,557	29,106	46.1
1985	36,103	30,476	31,103	50.2
1986	43,562	35,464	36,276	57.0
1987	49,692	39,336	40,391	66.7
1988	61,873	47,961	49,355	83.8
1989	73,544	52,568	54,846	101.3
1990	75,037	57,760	59,785	100.0
1991	73,507	60,986	62,455	98.6
1992	73,190	59,226	60,821	94.9
1993	73,315	61,423	62,709	94.3

Department of the Environment

Your commentary should include discussion of the following:

- Trends in house prices and new construction
- How the observed changes in house prices are related to changes in the supply of new housing and demand. For example, do recent changes indicate excess supply?
- What affects the demand for new mortgages and therefore the demand for housing?
- What affects the supply of new housing? For example, what has happened to the price of building materials?)

Keep your text short and to the point. The commentary should include graphs of relevant statistical data developed using computer graphics.

Useful additional information sources will include:

- Newspapers
- Specialist magazines aimed at house buyers
- Building societies
- Annual reports of major house builders (e.g. Wimpey, Barratt Homes)

Key words

Market price - the price established in a market for a good or service at the point at which market demand is exactly equal to market supply

Excess demand - when market demand exceeds market supply, usually because price is too low

Excess supply - when market demand is outstripped by market supply, because price is too high

Price mechanism - the influence of changes in market demand and supply, and hence market price, on business decisions to allocate scarce resources to the production of different goods and services

Section 1.5 Elasticity of demand

What is price elasticity of demand?

Producers need to know by how much demand for their products will change, given a change in market price. For example, consider a local bus company that has recently raised its flat rate fare from 70 pence to 90 pence. It discovers that fare revenues collected during peak travel times have increased, but off-peak bus patronage and revenues have fallen. The company concludes that it was unwise to raise off-peak fares. The company made this mistake because it had no knowledge of the price (or fare) elasticity of demand.

Price elasticity of demand measures the responsiveness of quantity demanded to a change in the price of a good or service. Consider two cases:

Figure 1.9 represents the market demand curve for off-peak bus trips. It is relatively flat, showing that a small rise in price causes a much larger fall in demand. Here, demand can be said to be relatively **price elastic**. Quantity demanded stretches or changes a lot given relatively small changes in price.

Figure 1.10 could represent the market demand curve of bus passengers who travel during the morning and evening peak, for example, to and from work. It is relatively steep. Even a quite large increase in fares would have only a marginal effect on

▼ Figure 1.9

Advanced Business

▼ Figure 1.10

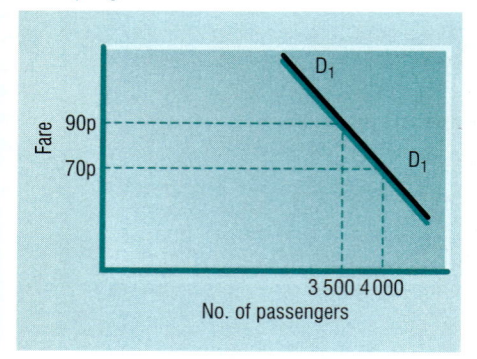

demand. In this case, demand is said to be **price inelastic**. Quantity demanded contracts or expands very little given small changes in price.

Price elasticity of demand and sales revenues

We can calculate the effect on bus company revenues from the increase in fares from Figures 1.9 and 1.10 as follows:

Fare = 70 pence			Fare = 90 pence		
No. of passengers per weekday		Revenue £	No. of passengers per weekday		Revenue £
Peak	4,000	£2,250	Peak	3,500	£3,150
Off-peak	3,000	£2,100	Off-peak	1,000	£900
Total	7,000	£4,350	Total	4,500	£4,050

Because demand is price inelastic during the peak, raising the flat rate fare has increased revenue. There is only a relatively small reduction in the number of passengers, from 4,000 per weekday to 3,500. However, a significant fall in demand during off-peak hours has caused revenue to fall from £2,100 to just £900. If the bus company wants to encourage increased bus use and raise revenues during the off-peak, it will do best to reduce the off-peak fare, because demand here is price elastic. For example, at an off-peak fare of 50 pence, bus patronage rises to 5,000 passengers and revenues would increase to £2,500 per weekday.

Knowledge of how responsive demand is to price changes will allow a firm to forecast the effect on their revenues of a change in the price of their product. For example, a firm attempting to maximize revenue may actually reduce its product prices if demand for them is highly price elastic. Firms may be able to estimate the price elasticity of demand for their products by looking at past data on price changes and sales revenues, or by using market research to find out how much consumers of a product would buy at different prices.

Measuring price elasticity of demand

The price elasticity of demand for a good or service can be measured in two ways:

- By comparing the percentage change in quantity demanded to the percentage change in price that caused it
- By observing what happens to sales revenues following a change in price

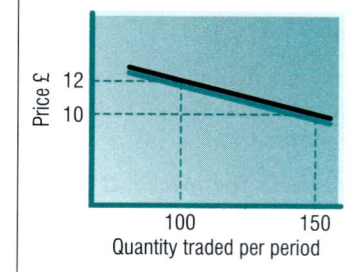

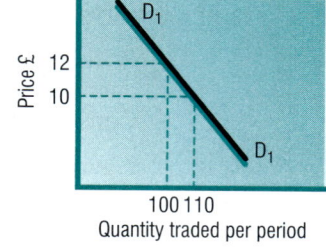

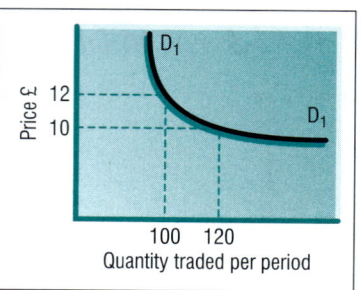

▼ Figure 1.11: Three cases of price elasticity of demand

Demand for a product is **price elastic** when:
- The market demand curve is relatively flat
- The % change in demand is more than the % change in price
- A rise in price reduces revenue
- A reduction in price increases revenue

Demand for a product is **price inelastic** when:
- The market demand curve is relatively steep
- The % change in demand is less than the % change in price
- A rise in price raises revenue
- A reduction in price reduces revenues

Demand for a product is of **unitary elasticity** when:
- The % change in demand is exactly equal to the % change in price
- Revenue remains the same whether the price has been increased or reduced

Portfolio Activity 1.7

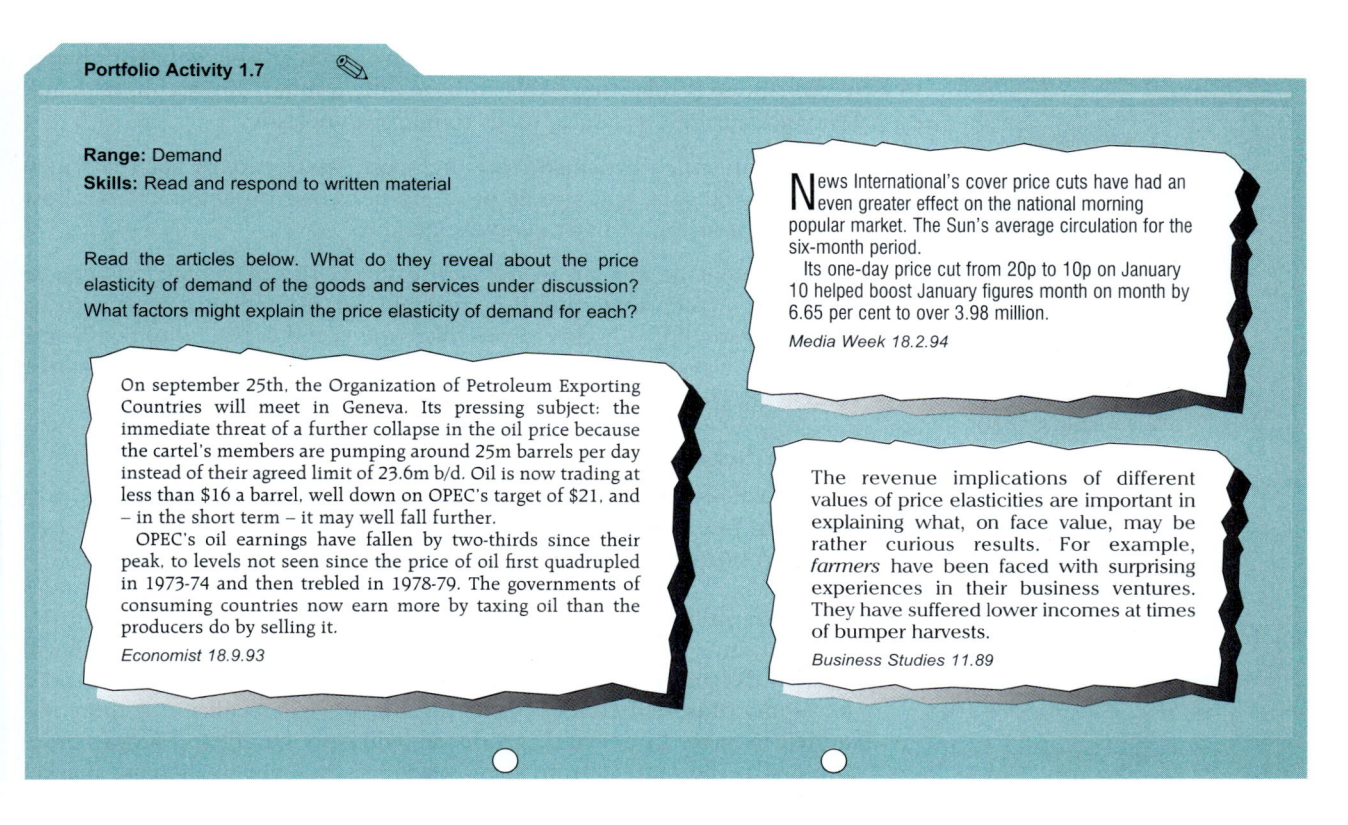

Range: Demand
Skills: Read and respond to written material

Read the articles below. What do they reveal about the price elasticity of demand of the goods and services under discussion? What factors might explain the price elasticity of demand for each?

> On september 25th, the Organization of Petroleum Exporting Countries will meet in Geneva. Its pressing subject: the immediate threat of a further collapse in the oil price because the cartel's members are pumping around 25m barrels per day instead of their agreed limit of 23.6m b/d. Oil is now trading at less than $16 a barrel, well down on OPEC's target of $21, and – in the short term – it may well fall further.
>
> OPEC's oil earnings have fallen by two-thirds since their peak, to levels not seen since the price of oil first quadrupled in 1973-74 and then trebled in 1978-79. The governments of consuming countries now earn more by taxing oil than the producers do by selling it.
>
> *Economist 18.9.93*

> News International's cover price cuts have had an even greater effect on the national morning popular market. The Sun's average circulation for the six-month period.
>
> Its one-day price cut from 20p to 10p on January 10 helped boost January figures month on month by 6.65 per cent to over 3.98 million.
>
> *Media Week 18.2.94*

> The revenue implications of different values of price elasticities are important in explaining what, on face value, may be rather curious results. For example, *farmers* have been faced with surprising experiences in their business ventures. They have suffered lower incomes at times of bumper harvests.
>
> *Business Studies 11.89*

Factors which affect price elasticity of demand

1. If the product is a necessity
Basic foodstuffs are necessary for human survival. The demand for products such as bread and flour tends to be relatively price inelastic.

2. How many substitutes a product has
When consumers are able to choose between a large number of substitutes for a particular product, demand for any one of them is likely to be price elastic.

Demand will tend to be price inelastic where there are few substitutes. For example, medicines, petrol, and some foodstuffs, such as milk, have few close alternatives.

Much advertising is aimed at promoting a brand image that suggests the advertised product has few close substitutes, for example, 'Coke, the real thing' (see 8.3).

3. How long a consumer takes to search for alternative products
If the price of a good or service rises, consumers will attempt to search for cheaper substitutes. The longer they have, the more likely they are to find one. Demand for any product is therefore likely to become more elastic in the long run.

4. The proportion of income spent on a product
Goods and services, like matches, salt, car washes, and newspapers, tend to be price inelastic because they are relatively inexpensive and account

▼ Figure 1.12: Price elasticity of supply and time
Supply is fixed regardless of price at any moment in time

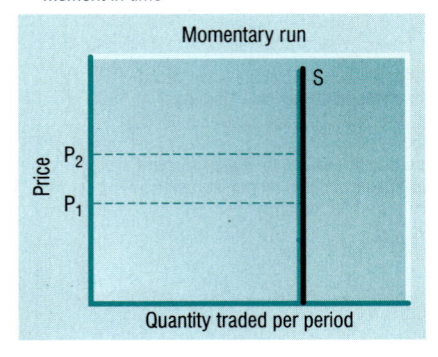

Momentary run

▼ Supply is price inelastic in the short run

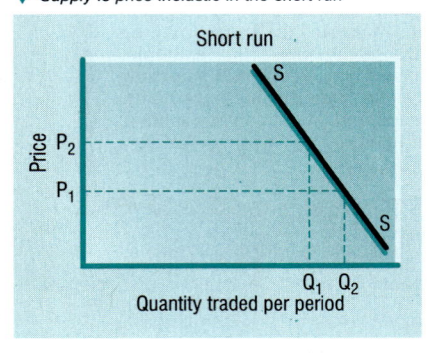

Short run

▼ Supply is price elastic in the long run

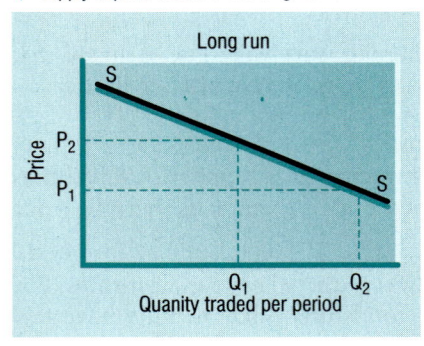

Long run

for only a small proportion of the average consumer's budget. Any change in their price is therefore likely to have only a minor impact on demand. Demand for these products tends to be price inelastic.

On the other hand, demand for high-cost, luxury items such as video recorders and cars, tends to be price elastic. Their purchase will swallow a large proportion of most people's income.

If the percentage change in demand exceeds the percentage change in consumer income that caused it, demand for that product is said to be **income elastic**. Most luxury goods, like videos and cars tend to be income elastic. However, if the percentage change in demand is less than the percentage change in income demand is said to be **income inelastic**.

Price elasticity of supply

Price elasticity of supply measures the responsiveness of supply to a change in price. Supply is said to be **elastic** if a change in price causes a larger proportionate change in quantity supplied of a given product.

What determines price elasticity of supply?

Time: At any given moment in time, the market supply of a product will be fixed. No more can be supplied whatever the product price. Consider the supply of potted conifer plants for sale at garden centres. If there is a sudden increase in demand, producers will only be able to supply more conifers to the market from their stocks. If they are to increase market supply significantly, producers will need to buy more pots, plant more seeds, and wait for the conifers to grow. Similarly, car manufacturers could not meet a significant increase in demand until they have had time to hire more labour, buy in more materials, and even expand into new premises. In general, supply is more price elastic in the long run (see Figure 1.12).

Availability of resources: The ability of firms to expand production will depend on some existing resources being unemployed. Failing that, an increase in the supply of natural, man-made, or human resources will be required: for example, an increasing population of working age, the discovery of more oil and mineral deposits, new production methods that can produce more using fewer resources.

Key words

Price elasticity of demand - the responsiveness of consumer demand to a change in the price of a product

Price elasticity - when demand changes proportionately more than a change in price

Price inelasticity - when demand changes proportionately less than a change in price

Unitary elasticity - when the change in demand is in equal proportion to a change in price

---

Further reading

Moynihan, D, and Titley, B, *Economics - A Complete Course* (Oxford University Press, 1993) Chapter 8

Test questions

The following underpinning knowledge will be examined:

1. Demand for goods and services
2. Supply of goods and services
3. Analyse demand and supply interaction
4. Effects on business decisions of changes in demand and supply
5. Future changes in demand and supply and how these might affect business decisions
6. Report research findings about demand and supply interaction for a particular product.

1 There is an increase in the demand for oranges. This could be explained by:

A An increase in imports of oranges
B A fall in the price of apples
C A successful advertising campaign for oranges
D Poor weather reducing the supply of oranges

2 Which of the following would cause a movement along the market demand curve for gloves?

A A rise in consumer income
B A fall in the price of gloves
C Severe weather conditions
D A change in consumer tastes in knitwear

3 In order for a consumer's demand for a new car to be effective, that consumer must have:

A A want for the car
B A need for a car
C An available supply of cars
D An ability to pay for the car

4 The market demand for bread is very price inelastic. This could be explained by the fact that bread:

A Is a basic necessity
B Has many competing products
C Accounts for a large proportion of household expenditure
D Is poorly advertised

5 The following table shows consumer demand for a given product at different prices:

Price	Market demand
£10	14,000
£11	10,000

The price elasticity of demand for the product can be said to be:

A Of unitary elasticity
B Inelastic
C Elastic
D Of zero elasticity

6 The graph shows two demand curves for compact disc players in a local hi-fi shop:

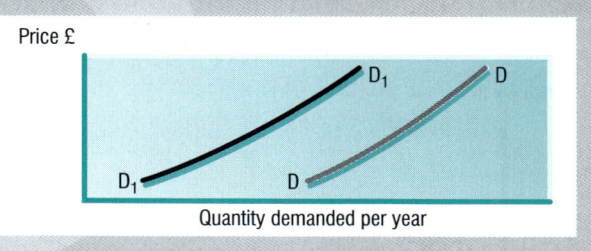

Which factor will have caused the movement from DD to D1D1?

A A fall in the price of vinyl LPs
B An increase in the rate of income tax
C A fall in the price of compact discs
D A fall in the supply of laser components for disc players

7 Mercury has cut charges for phone calls made during off-peak periods. Revenues have increased as a result. It concludes that off-peak demand for phone calls is:

A Price inelastic
B Price elastic
C Unrelated to price
D Of unitary elasticity

8 The graph below shows a change in the market supply of microwave ovens.

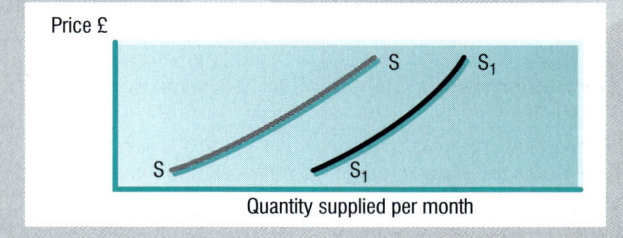

The shift in the supply curve from SS to S1S1 may have been caused by:

A A rise in the price of gas ovens
B A fall in production costs
C An increase in demand for microwave ovens
D A rise in the market price of microwaves

Advanced Business

9 The ability of a producer to supply a good at a given price will be affected by:

A A change in consumer income

B A change in the amount of imported goods

C A change in production technology

D A change in the price of the good

Questions 10-12 are based on the following diagram depicting demand and supply in the market for potatoes:

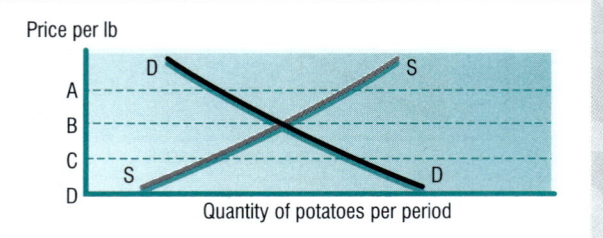

At what price will there be:

10 A stable market price?

11 An excess supply?

12 An excess demand?

13 Which of the following is unlikely to be an important factor in the product pricing decision of a company:

A The prices of close substitutes

B Total production costs

C Consumer willingness to pay

D Shifts in the market supply curve

14 You work for a new company that is about to launch a new mobile phone network to compete with British Telecom and Mercury. In preparation you will need to provide answers to the following questions;

i What factors are likely to affect the demand for mobile phones?

ii What is the likely relationship between consumer demand for mobile phone services and the price per minute of each call. Show this relationship on an appropriate diagram.

iii What impact will your organization have on the supply of mobile phone services? Draw an appropriate diagram to illustrate the impact on supply.

iv What will determine the market price for mobile phone services and how many calls are made? Draw a diagram to illustrate how market price and quantity traded are determined.

v What will happen to market price if there is a fall in demand for mobile phone services? Show this on a diagram.

vi What is price elasticity of demand?

vii Explain how knowledge of the price elasticity of demand for calls made during peak periods and off-peak periods can help the firm decide an appropriate call charging structure.

15 'Potato prices rocket after crop failure'

i Consider the headline above and explain, using appropriate diagrams, why the price of potatoes increased.

ii What is 'effective demand'? Why is it important to firms selling to make a profit?

iii What will be the likely impact on the market price for potatoes if there is a corresponding rise in demand for them?

16 Explain, using diagrams, what will be the likely impact on the market price of butter and the quantity sold of each of the following events:

i Income tax is raised by 2%

ii The price of milk used to make butter rises

iii The price of margarine increases

iv A successful advertising campaign declaring 'butter is best'

v The cost of equipment used to make butter falls

17 'The demand for butter tends to be fairly price inelastic.' Explain this statement and assess the likely impact on butter producers' revenues of a rise in its price.

(assessment assignment)

UNIT ONE

CHAPTER 1

Assessment assignment

Range: Demand
Supply
Effects on business decisions
Analyse in terms of market price and volume and supply

Skills: **Communication**
Prepare written material
Use illustrations and images
Understand and respond to written material
Application of number
Represent and tackle problems
Information Technology
Enter and save information

Understanding the market

You represent a large Korean firm called Proteus. Your firm manufactures cars, hi-fi, and computer equipment. Recently senior management at Proteus have become concerned about the establishment of the Single Market among European Community member states. Although barriers to trade will be removed between EC members, goods from outside the EC will be subject to tariffs. In the last twelve months the price of Proteus cars in Europe has risen by around 15% because of the heavy taxes that must be paid to import the goods. A recent survey of showroom prices has shown that Proteus cars are now dearer than Japanese cars made in plants located inside Europe.

Proteus wants to investigate locating factories within the EC to produce cars, TVs, audio, and computer equipment. If Proteus sets up in the EC, it will be in full competition with other producers such as Ford, Nissan, Sony, Panasonic, Sega, and Nintendo, to name but a few of the foreign-owned companies already operating in Europe.

Proteus are aware that the price of its products will be a key factor in its success. As a first step, Proteus intends to begin the production of computer games and games consoles in the UK. If they are able to break into the market, they will then begin to open other factories across Europe to produce their entire range of goods.

Proteus management have little knowledge of the market for computer games products in the UK and have asked you to report. If possible, your document should be written using a word processor and include computer-generated graphs and diagrams where appropriate.

Tasks

1. What are the main influences on the demand for computer games in the UK?

2. Draw a demand curve for computer games and explain some of the factors that might cause the curve to shift, giving examples relevant to the computer games industry.

3. Sega, Nintendo, and 3DO games and consoles are quite expensive. Proteus could enter the market in the same price range or lower. Management would, therefore, like to know how sales revenues are likely to respond to a higher or lower price. This requires knowledge of the elasticity of demand for computer products. Explain the meaning of elasticity of demand and its relevance to business decision-making.

4. What are the main influences on the elasticity of demand for a product? List these and consider how they apply to the case of computer games and consoles.

5. Investigate the supply of computer games and consoles in the UK.
   - Who are the main producers?
   - What prices do they charge?
   - How much competition will Proteus face in the market?
   - How have prices changed recently and why?

6. What will be the likely impact on the market supply and price of computer games following the entrance of Proteus into the UK market? Draw a market supply curve for computer games in the UK before and after this event.

7. What other factors may affect the market supply of computer games and consoles? Give examples, where possible, with relevance to the computer games industry.

8. Discuss why the management of Proteus need to be aware of influences on the market demand and supply of computer games in the UK when deciding what price to charge for their products.

Alternative

Analyse the market demand and supply of a product of a local business with which you are familiar. Complete the same tasks above. (Change any references to Proteus to the name of your chosen business, and references to computer games to the good or service they produce.)

chapter 2

Advanced Business

chapter 2
The Operation of Markets

This chapter examines the nature and degree of competition in markets, and how the production of goods and services to supply a market can result in external costs and benefits

Key ideas

Market structure refers to the amount of competition among rival firms supplying a market. Competition to supply a market is restricted in some way in most markets for goods and services.

Competition between firms can be on product **price** or through **non-price competition**, such as product image and quality, after-sales care, and promotions.

Advertising can be used to influence consumer demand for a product.

Firms will compete with each other for **customers, sales, market share**, and **product superiority**.

In highly competitive markets firms must accept the prevailing market price at which to sell their products. Firms are **price takers** because no one organization is able to influence the market price.

Firms engaged in **monopolistic competition** will attempt to build consumer loyalty to their product by differentiating it from those of rival producers, usually by creating a **brand image**.

An **oligopoly** consists of a number of large firms that dominate the supply of a particular good or service to a market.

A firm is a **pure monopoly** if it is the sole supplier of a good or service wanted by consumers. By UK law a firm, or group of firms acting together, is a **legal monopoly** if it supplies over 25% of a market.

Monopolies, and oligopolies working together, can create **barriers to entry** to stop new firms seeking to sell a competing product in the markets they dominate.

By restricting the supply of a product to a market, a monopoly is able to influence the market price. A monopoly can act as a **price maker**.

The production of goods and services can result in **external costs**, such as pollution and noise.

The **social cost** to society of a business activity is equal to the **private costs** of that activity - for example, the costs of materials and labour - plus any external costs.

UNIT ONE

Section 2.1 **Competition**

Why do firms compete?

The goods and services produced by business organizations to satisfy consumer wants are sold in markets. In Chapter 1 a **market** was defined as any setting in which exchange takes place between consumers willing and able to buy goods and services and producers willing and able to supply them.

The level and strength of consumer demand and producer supply in a market are known as **market conditions** (see 1.1). The article below illustrates how changing market conditions has affected the allocation of resources in the computer industry.

Few companies have been so admired as International Business Machines (IBM). For nearly three decades IBM seemed to do everything right. It towered over one of the world's greatest industries, computers.

Yet now IBM is an object of pity, its fabulous prosperity washed away by years of losses. For years IBM stubbornly attempted to ignore the trend away from big mainframe computers to desktop personal computers. Instead of adapting, it tried to protect its base: the computing dinosaurs accounted for 42% of IBM's revenues.

At a time when other computer companies, including Sun Microsystems and Compaq, have been reporting hefty profit increases and rolling out innovative products, IBM last week was announcing its most traumatic cutbacks to date. It plans to shed more unprofitable and ill-fitting assets and slash its workforce by some 25,000 employees.

IBM is now seeking to gain strength in the personal computer market. However, competition is increasingly fierce. During the past ten years thousands of companies, many of them start-ups, have entered the market. The industry used to be dominated by proprietary technical standards (usually IBM's) which obliged most big customers to buy all their computer equipment from one supplier (usually IBM). However, technological advance has changed all that. Customers no longer need, or want, to depend on a single supplier and can afford to shop around.

Adapted from The Economist 16.1.93

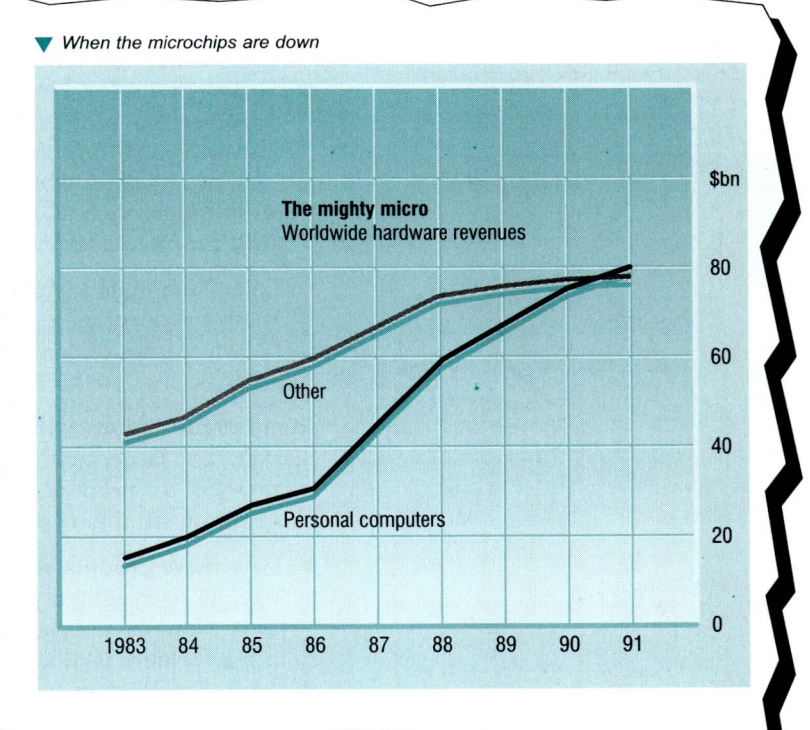

▼ When the microchips are down

The mighty micro
Worldwide hardware revenues

Falling demand for large mainframe computers has resulted in losses at IBM while firms making personal computers (PCs) have seen their sales and profits rise. As a result, IBM is cutting the amount of labour it uses and selling off some capital goods, such as machinery and factory buildings. At the same time a growing number of firms have been attracted to the computer market because of the potential to earn large profits from organizing resources to produce and sell PCs. However, increasing competition to supply PCs has forced their price down as rival suppliers attempt to expand their share of total consumer demand.

51

▼ *Figure 2.1: A fall in demand for mainframe computers*

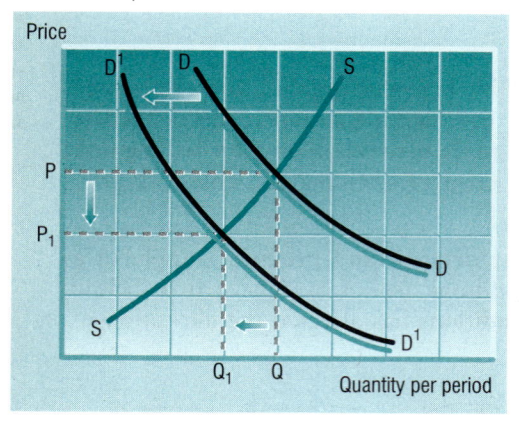

▼ *Figure 2.2: A rise in the supply of personal computers*

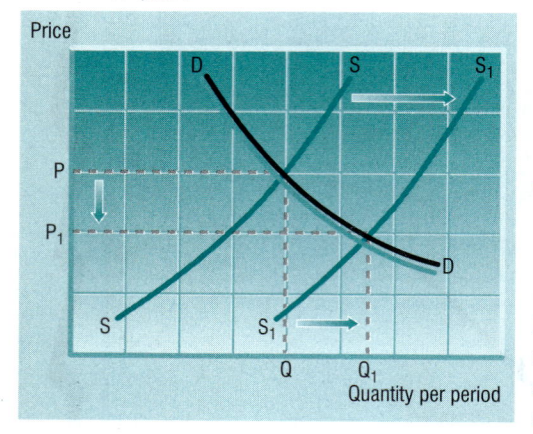

We can represent these changes in market conditions in two diagrams. Figure 2.1 shows the fall in market demand for mainframe computers, resulting in a fall in their price and the profits their producers can expect to earn.

However, the market for personal computers is expanding. Consumer demand is rising and a growing number of firms attracted by the potential for profit are competing to supply the market. **Competition** tends to force market prices down but expand the quantity traded (Figure 2.2). Sales revenues can be expected to grow if demand for the product is **price elastic** (see 1.5).

Firms will compete to supply a market to achieve a number of objectives. These are:

- **To increase their customer base.** Firms will compete with each other on price, product quality and through promotional strategies to increase the number of customers buying their products.

- **To increase sales.** Not only will firms seek to increase the number of customers buying their products but they will also hope that existing customers will buy more. Cutting prices can increase sales revenues from products for which demand is price elastic. Advertising and other promotions, such as free gifts, can help to expand sales without the need for price cuts.

- **To expand market share.** The market share of a firm can be calculated as its proportion of total sales. For example, Sony accounted for 12.3% of sales of recorded music in a world market worth $30 billion in 1994.

Many organizations will aim to increase their share of total sales in a market. The larger an organization's market share, and the more widely established its product, the better able it will be to withstand new competition from new products and firms.

- **To achieve product superiority.** This has two meanings. On one hand it refers to making a product that is clearly better than rival products for reasons of prestige and/or profit. A superior product will help a firm to achieve its objectives of generating sales and expanding market share. But product superiority also means that the product dominates a market by outselling all others - which is not necessarily because it is the best product on the market.

A firm that is able to dominate the supply of a product to market is able to have some influence over the determination of the market price. It is also well placed to fight off competition from smaller rivals.

- **To enhance image.** Firms will also compete on image. Customer perception of an organization will be reflected in sales. A poor image will reduce sales; a good image will help to expand sales and market share.

In response to the growing awareness of environmental issues among consumers in the 1990s, many organizations are trying to present themselves as caring and environmentally friendly. For example, the

Portfolio Activity 2.1

Range: Compare competition
Skills: Read and respond to written material

1. What problems does Cadbury's face in trying to increase sales of its drinks in the USA?
2. Who are Cadbury's main competitors in the USA? What advantages do they have over Cadbury's?
3. Explain what is meant by 'market share'? What is the market share of Cadbury's compared to its main US rivals?
4. What motives does Cadbury's have in trying to buy up the Dr Pepper/Seven-Up companies?
5. How are conditions in the soft drinks market changing? What effect is this likely to have on drink producers?

▼ *Tough competition in soft drinks market*

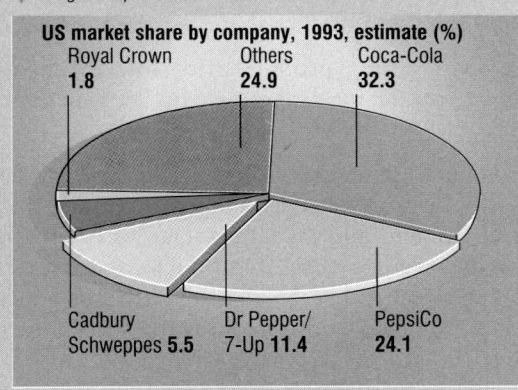

US market share by company, 1993, estimate (%)
- Royal Crown 1.8
- Others 24.9
- Coca-Cola 32.3
- Cadbury Schweppes 5.5
- Dr Pepper/7-Up 11.4
- PepsiCo 24.1

Cadbury's Health in Dr Pepper's Hands

One statistic above all explains best why Cadbury Scweppes, the UK confectionery and soft drinks maker, has to buy Dr Pepper/Seven-Up Companies, the third-largest US soft drinks maker.

Even with famous international brands such as Schweppes and Canada Dry and US ones including A&W and Mott's, Cadbury has to use some 1,000 independent bottlers to cobble together a mere 5.5 per cent of the US soft drinks market.

In contrast, Coca-Cola and PepsiCo use only some 120 bottling companies each, either independents or ones they own directly, to achieve market shares respectively of 32.3 per cent and 24.1 per cent.

Worse, Cadbury's lack of distribution and brand clout in the US jeopardises its global strategy. Unless it achieves critical mass in the US, accounting for one-third of the global soft drinks market, it can never achieve its ambition of becoming the world's largest supplier of non-cola drinks.

Dr Pepper, which claims to be the oldest US soft drinks maker, is the only acquisition Cadbury could make to solve the strategic problem. Dr Pepper may be only the fourth largest US soft drinks brand and Seven-Up the eighth, but they dwarf anything in Cadbury's portfolio. Dr Pepper, for example, sells almost six times the volume of Canada Dry, Cadbury's largest US brand.

Moreover, Dr Pepper was the fastest growing US non-cola drink last year and the Dallas-based company is the largest player in the US non-cola market with a share of more than 40 percent.

With consumers tiring of colas and seeking greater variety in their soft drinks, Coke, Pepsi and other players such as Quaker Oats, through its recent Snapple purchase, are pushing harder than ever into non-cola drinks - putting pressure on the relations of Dr Pepper and Cadbury with their bottlers.

Financial Times 24.1.95

Market share

Market share is a useful indicator of business performance. Market shares are usually calculated from the total value of sales revenue in a particular goods market. For example, in 1993/94 total retail sales of food products in the UK amounted to £57.5 billion. Of this, £8.74 billion was spent in supermarkets owned and controlled by Sainsburys plc. The supermarket chain can therefore be defined as having a 15.2% share of the retail market for food in the UK, compared to a 14.4% share for rivals Tesco. Recently, giant discount stores have been attracted to the lucrative retail food market in the UK. Companies such as Aldi, Netto, and Costco, from Germany, Denmark, and the USA respectively, have located stores in the UK and increased competition in this market. This has created a price war as rivals have cut their prices in an effort to expand, or least maintain, their individual market shares.

▼ *Figure 2.3 UK food retail market shares (year to Spring 1994)*

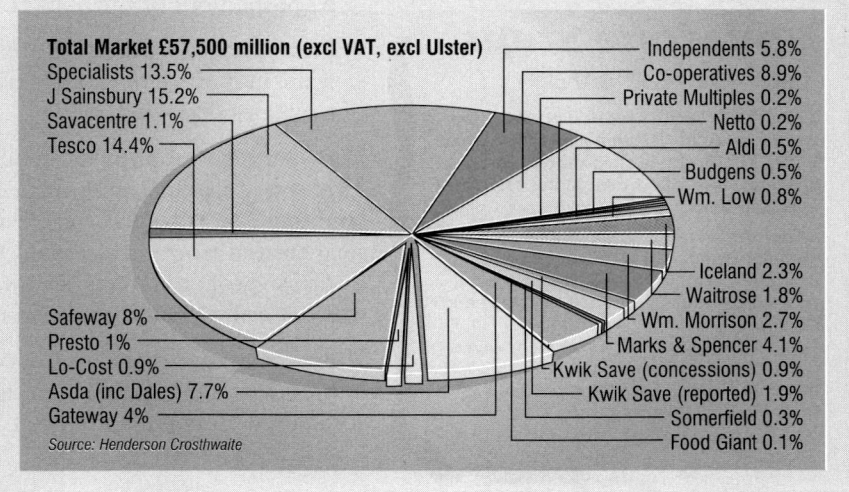

Total Market £57,500 million (excl VAT, excl Ulster)

- Specialists 13.5%
- J Sainsbury 15.2%
- Savacentre 1.1%
- Tesco 14.4%
- Safeway 8%
- Presto 1%
- Lo-Cost 0.9%
- Asda (inc Dales) 7.7%
- Gateway 4%
- Independents 5.8%
- Co-operatives 8.9%
- Private Multiples 0.2%
- Netto 0.2%
- Aldi 0.5%
- Budgens 0.5%
- Wm. Low 0.8%
- Iceland 2.3%
- Waitrose 1.8%
- Wm. Morrison 2.7%
- Marks & Spencer 4.1%
- Kwik Save (concessions) 0.9%
- Kwik Save (reported) 1.9%
- Somerfield 0.3%
- Food Giant 0.1%

Source: Henderson Crosthwaite

Price competition

Non-price competition

Vodafone steps up price war

THE DEVELOPING mobile phone price war was further fuelled yesterday when VODAFONE, the largest mobile phone operator, published new lower tariffs for new and existing services.

The tariffs are partly a response to the imminent launch of an advanced digital service by Mercury One-2-One, a joint venture between Cable and Wireless and US West.

One-2-One is testing its service, which will be launched within the M25 area later this summer at a peak rate tariff of less than 20p a minute.

Financial Times, 1994

Body Shop prides itself on not testing products on animals, while the Co-operative Bank will only invest money in 'green' companies that have a good environmental record.

Types of competition

We can distinguish between competition between organizations on price, and competition on aspects other than price.

Price competition

Cutting price can expand consumer demand. Hence, competition between firms on price is often vigorous.

Ultimately the ability of a firm to undercut rivals to increase sales will be constrained by market conditions and production costs. Cutting prices to expand sales will reduce the margin between revenues and costs. If a firm is to be in a strong position to compete on prices, it must try to reduce its costs by increasing the productivity of its resources.

There are a number of short-term pricing strategies an organization might use in an attempt to expand sales and market share:

- **Penetration pricing** involves setting product price low to encourage sales. This is especially important for a new or existing firm trying to establish a new product.

- **Expansion pricing** is similar to penetration pricing. Product prices are set low to encourage consumers to buy. As demand increases, the firm can raise output to meet demand and take advantage of economies of scale which will lower the average cost of producing each unit (see 20.2). Lower average costs can either be passed onto consumers as lower prices, or, if prices are held steady, the lower costs will increase the firm's profit margins.

- **Destruction pricing** is a more drastic version of penetration pricing, usually practised by larger firms when threatened by new competition from smaller organizations. The objective is to destroy the sales of competitors by setting price very low - even below costs - and sustaining a loss for a short period of time. Smaller firms, unable to take a loss, will be pushed out of the market.

- **Price war.** In markets where the supply side is very competitive, price wars may develop among rival firms employing the various pricing strategies discussed above.

Price wars are not popular among firms even though they frequently occur. This is because engaging in price war is a very high-risk strategy. Gains tend to be shortlived as rival firms continually slash prices in an attempt to steal custom from each other. Only the consumer benefits in the long run, as firms' profits margins are drastically reduced by successive price cuts without a sustained increase in demand for their products.

However, where there is little competition in a market, for example for a new and unique product, a firm may be able to exploit consumers' willingness to pay by pricing at 'what the market can bear'.

- **Market skimming.** Also known as **price creaming**, this involves charging a high price for a new product to yield a high initial profit from consumers who are willing to pay extra because the product is new and unique. As competitors enter the market, prices are reduced to expand the market.

Market skimming is a practice often observed in markets for new consumer technology such as audio and video products, mobile phones, and personal computers. For example, some of the first recordable CD-ROM drives for computers released on to the UK market by organizations such as Phillips and Yamaha in the early 1990s were priced at around £20,000. In 1994 recordable CD-ROM drive prices started at around £1,500 and are set to fall further.

Non-price competition

When consumers buy a product they are looking not just for low price but also for value for money in terms of the quality of the good or service, its size or shape, colour, smell, or taste. Consumers also look for after-sales care in case anything should go wrong and they might want to exchange their product. Firms can compete on all these facets of a product and service to offer consumers what they want.

Promotion is also very important if consumers are to be tempted to buy one product rather than another. Free gifts, money-off coupons, attractive in-store displays, publicity in magazines - these are all methods that can be used to persuade consumers to buy (see 10.2). Advertising, through media such as television or newspapers, is one of the main ways firms compete for sales. Advertising can be used to present features of a product in an attractive way and to persuade people that a product is better than its rivals. By creating an image for a product in the mind of the consumer, advertising can manipulate consumer wants. Organizations are willing to spend many millions of pounds on advertising because, if used effectively, it can create a want among consumers for a new or existing product. By creating a want and increasing the demand for their product a firm will generate sales and may be able to charge a higher price.

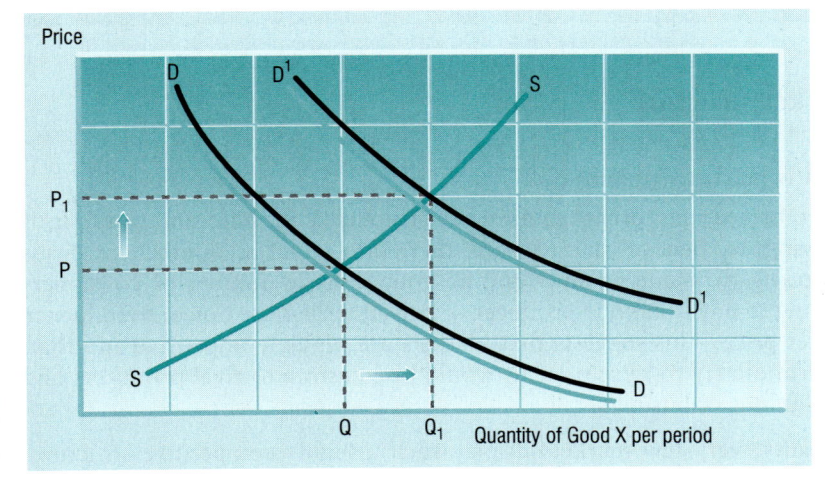

▼ Figure 2.4: Advertising can create wants and increase demand

Competition: good or bad for the consumer?

Both price and non-price competition are good for consumers because they can reduce prices and increase the quality and availability of different product. However, advertising and excessive packaging is sometimes considered wasteful. Prices will reflect the cost of these activities and will, therefore, tend to be higher than they might otherwise be (see "Farewell to green dream")

Farewell to green dream

FANCY unnecessary packaging can double the cost of some goods we buy in the shops.

It is estimated that for every £75 spent on groceries, £10 goes on packaging which ends up in the bin.

A recent survey by Friends of the Earth reveals that loose apples can cost half as much as those pre-wrapped in plastic and polythene.

The same goes for carrots, while green beans, pears and tomatoes can cost a third more.

The majority of overpackaged goods surveyed were between one and ten per cent more expensive, but a significant number were between 10 and 30 per cent more.

Even the little labels that apple growers stick on their fruit cost us an extra 2p in the pound. We eat 840,000 tonnes of apples a year - which means £10m of labels.

Supermarkets insist that the labels help staff and customers to identify different types of apple. But research shows 87 per cent of consumers do not want them.

Daily Mirror 2.8.94

Portfolio activity 2.2

Range: Compare competition, Analyse in terms of competitive pricing and non-pricing strategies

Skills: Produce written material, Collect and record data

Choose an organization you are familiar with, that sells a good or service. Gather information and write a short report on how they compete with their rival organizations. Try to find out:

- Why do they compete?
- What is their market share?
- Who are their main competitors?
- How do their prices compare?
- What forms of non-price competition do they use?
- How effective have their price- and non-price-competitive strategies been?

Key words

Market share - the proportion of total sales revenue in a particular market accounted for by a firm or group of firms

Price competition - competition to sell product by undercutting rivals on price

Non-price competition - competition between firms on aspects of product other than price, for example, quality, packaging, free gifts, advertising

---

Section 2.2 Market structure

What is market structure?

Different markets are organized or structured in different ways. It is tempting to believe that, where there are a large number of firms producing the same product and an equally large number of consumers wanting to buy it, no one producer or consumer has the power to influence market price. This suggests that markets are highly competitive and that, if a firm did try to raise price, it would lose custom to rival producers and soon go out of business.

In reality, very few markets display such a highly competitive structure. Perhaps the world agricultural market is the closest example of near 'perfect competition'. Because there are so many producers of wheat, barley, and other arable crops of such similar quality worldwide, individual producers are forced to sell their produce at prevailing market prices. That is, in competitive markets there are numerous consumers and producers such that no one alone can influence market price - they are all **price takers**.

Competition in a market affects an individual firm's ability to influence the market price for their products. In general, the more competition a business faces from firms making similar products, the less scope it will have to influence price. The focus of an analysis of market structure is therefore on the degree of competition in individual markets.

In general, markets are grouped into four broad categories:

Type of market structure	Number of producers	Can producers influence market price?	Do firms compete on aspects of product other than price?	Can existing producers prevent new firms entering market?
'Perfect competition'	Many	No. All firms are price takers	No - products of individual producers are exactly the same	No
Monopolistic competition	Many	A little	Yes - producers try to differentiate their product using brand image	No
Oligopoly	Few	Yes, by agreeing to fix prices and/or outputs	Yes - fierce competition on product image	Yes
Monopoly	One	Yes. A monopoly can be a price maker	No - no competition, so not necessary	Very much - almost impossible for new firms to enter market

Portfolio Activity 2.3

Range: Types of market
Skills: Produce written material, Collect and record data

Table 2.1 provides data on the share of total output of the five largest producers in a number of UK industries between 1979 and 1987. For example, it shows that 96% of the total UK output of coke ovens was supplied by just five manufacturing firms in 1987.

1. Do the figures suggest UK manufacturing has become more or less competitive? Use data from Table 2.1 to support your argument.
2. What do the figures suggest about the market structure and degree of competition in the different industries?
3. What other information would you require to make a proper assessment of the degree of competition between producers in individual markets? For example, what about competition from foreign firms? Do market prices suggest there is a lack of price competition in these markets? Are the top five firms in each industry necessarily the same five each year? Investigate possible sources of data to provide answers to these and other questions.

▼ Table 2.1: Industry concentration in U.K. manufacturing; % share of total output of 5 largest firms (after accounting for imports).

Industry	1979	1984	1987
Coke ovens	94	56	96
Cement/lime/plaster	85	84	83
Asbestos goods	85	76	88
Glass containers	78	75	80
Fertilisers	75	76	71
Explosives	78	73	68
Adhesive film/cloth/foil	73	58	61
Soap/detergents	76	74	71
Ordnance/ammunition	80	76	56
Insulated wires/cables	81	64	50
Batteries	80	51	48
Elect. equip. for vehicles	72	60	63
Telegraph/telephone equip.	77	69	57
Locomotives/parts	85	81	75
Margarine	87	83	87
Biscuits/crispbread	81	79	75
Ice cream	69	57	50
Tobacco	98	98	97
Wall coverings	74	66	57
Personal hygiene paper prods.	71	61	59

Department of Trade and Industry

Advanced Business

> 4. Investigate the market structure of, and degree of competition in, the following business sectors in the UK:
> - High street banking
> - Petrol stations
> - Domestic passenger flights
> - Electricity supply
> - Fast food retailers
> - A product of your choice

▼ *Some oligopolistic markets*

High street banking

Petrol supplies

Paints

Types of market structure

Monopolistic competition

In reality, most markets display some restriction on competition. Individual producers will often attempt to modify their own products to distinguish them from their rivals. This is called **product differentiation** and is a feature of 'monopolistic competition'. It can be achieved by branding - making differences in the design and packaging of products - as well as the creation of different trade names and product images through advertising. In this way an organization can create and maintain consumer demand for their product. Building consumer loyalty to a product reduces the effectiveness of price cuts and advertising as ways to lure customers away from rival firms.

Oligopolistic competition

Today, most markets can be described as 'oligopolistic'. An **oligopoly** exists if a small number of large firms dominate the supply of a particular good or service to a market.

Price leadership is a feature of many oligopolistic markets. In order to avoid price wars, the firms that dominate the market will tend to price their products in line with each other. In extreme cases they may even collude to 'fix' prices. Sometimes however agreements to fix prices or play 'follow my leader' break down, and price wars can develop among rival firms.

Cartels are formal agreements between firms to regulate prices and/or output, thereby effectively creating a monopoly. The best known cartel is OPEC (Organization of Petroleum Exporting Countries) which attempts to restrict the world supply of crude oil in order to hold up its market price. **Collusion** to fix prices at artificially high levels is illegal in the UK under the terms of the 1956 Restrictive Trade Practices Act (see 3.4).

Because of the relative price stability in oligopolistic markets, they tend to be characterized by aggressive non-price competition for consumers and market share. For example, the growth of shops on petrol station forecourts and the giving of tokens towards free gifts are attempts at non-price competition by a handful of large petrol companies. Similarly,

▼ *Some virtual monopolies*

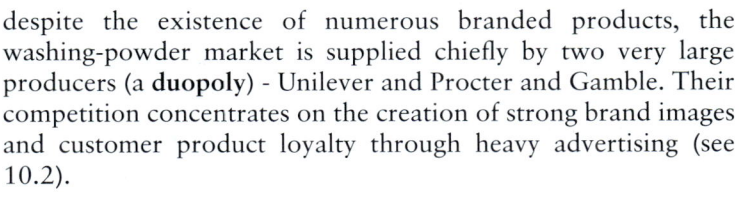

British Gas

Blockbuster Video

BT

despite the existence of numerous branded products, the washing-powder market is supplied chiefly by two very large producers (a **duopoly**) - Unilever and Procter and Gamble. Their competition concentrates on the creation of strong brand images and customer product loyalty through heavy advertising (see 10.2).

Monopoly

A firm is a **pure monopoly** if it is the sole supplier of a good or service wanted by consumers. For example, until 1998 British Gas plc will supply 100% of households connected to the national gas supply grid in the UK. However, as defined by UK law, a legal monopoly is any firm, or group of firms acting together, supplying 25% or more of a market.

A monopoly faces little or no competition and is therefore able to keep profit levels high by setting a high price for its product. Monopolies are often described as **price makers** because they can restrict the supply to a market to force up the market price. However, in order to do this, the monopoly must prevent new firms from entering the market. Any increase in supply from new firms will force prices and profits down.

We can demonstrate the impact of a monopoly on market supply and price in figure 2.5.

Barriers to entry used by monopolies (and oligopolies) to prevent the entry of new firms into their markets can occur naturally, or can be deliberately created by the dominant firms to force new and smaller competitors out of business.

▼ *Figure 2.5: The impact of a monopoly restriction on market supply to force up price*

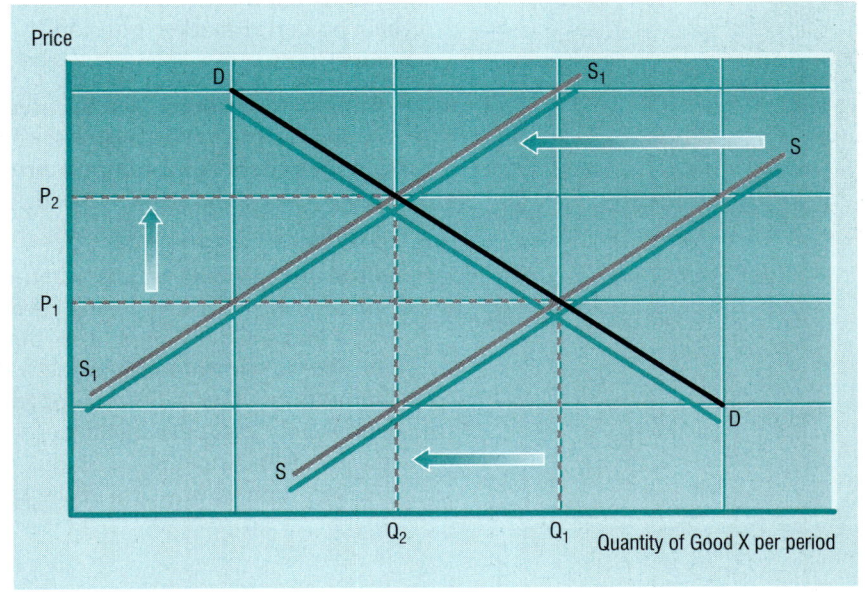

Natural barriers to entry

New firms may be unable to compete with a monopoly because of the advantages a large firm has simply because of its size.

- **Economies of scale.** By increasing in size, a firm may be able to reduce the average cost of producing each unit of output below the costs of smaller organizations (see 20.2). If one firm is able to produce the entire market supply at a lower average cost per unit than a number of smaller firms put together, then it is known as a **natural monopoly**. The gas, electricity and water supply systems are natural monopolies. This is because it does not make economic sense to have more than one set of gas or water pipes or electricity cables supplying each house, office of factory.

- **Capital size.** The supply of a product may involve the input of such a vast amount of capital equipment that new competing firms find it difficult to raise necessary finance to buy or hire their own. For example, consider the amount of capital that would be required to produce electricity to supply the national grid; the Sizewell B nuclear power station will cost an estimated £2.5 billion to build.

- **Historical reasons.** A business may have a monopoly because it was first to enter the market for a product and has built up an established customer base. For example, Lloyds of London dominates the world insurance market primarily because of its established expertise dating back to the 18th century.

- **Legal considerations.** The development of new production methods and products can be expensive but can be encouraged by granting innovative producers **patents** or copyright, so as to to prevent other firms copying their ideas and thereby reducing their potential profits. Also, some monopolies are government-owned, for example, the Post Office.

Artificial barriers to entry

While some monopolies occur naturally, others may achieve and retain their powerful market position by creating their own artificial barriers to competition.

- **Supply restrictions** can be used to prevent new firms obtaining the supplies of materials necessary for production. If suppliers rely heavily on the orders of a monopoly firm, a threat by the firm to obtain supplies from elsewhere is likely to be very effective in deterring them from supplying rival organizations.

- **Predatory pricing** occurs when the dominant firm in a market cuts its prices - at the risk of losing revenue in the short run - in order to force new and smaller competitors out of business. New firms are unlikely to be able to withstand trading at a loss for as long as the larger, established monopoly. Once new competitors have been forced to close, the monopoly can once again raise prices. It was alleged that many of the large airline operators in the UK used this method to force Laker Airways out of business in the early 1980s.

- **Exclusive dealing** involves a monopoly preventing retailers from stocking the products of competing firms. This method of restricting competition is particularly effective if the product supplied by the dominant firm is very popular and the retailer would lose too much trade if they did not sell it. Raleigh, the famous bicycle manufacturer, was found to be using this barrier to competition when they refused to supply large multi-product discount stores with their cycles in 1981.

- **Full line forcing** occurs when large firms refuse to supply retailers unless they stock and sell their full range of products.

Because monopolies and oligopolies have the ability to restrict competition, the UK government has passed a number of laws which can regulate their activities and in extreme cases prevent their formation (see 3.4).

Portfolio Activity 2.4

Range: Types of market, Compare competition, Analyse in terms of price making

Skills: Read and respond to written material, Collect and record data

1. What is an artificial barrier to entry? Explain why it might be against the public interest.
2. What evidence is there from the two articles that artificial barriers are used to restrict entry into the retail perfume and ice cream markets?
3. Draw an appropriate diagram to show the effect on market price of the decision by perfume houses to restrict their supply to authorized retailers only.
4. Gather your own evidence on the existence of artificial barriers to entry in the retail perfume and ice cream markets. Which manufacturers' products are available in different types of outlet? How do prices compare? What forms of non-price competition are practised?

Ask the owners or managers of the retail outlets about their product ranges and any special arrangements they have with their suppliers.

Icy Relations in Europe

Mars, the US confectionery company, has brought actions in Brussels and other European capitals challenging the ice cream distribution arrangements of Unilever, the Anglo-Dutch consumer products manufacturer which is the world's largest ice cream manufacturer.

Mars is challenging Unilever's policy of 'cabinet exclusivity' which involves supplying freezer cabinets to retailers free of charge on condition that they are not used to carry competitors' products.

The US manufacturer claims that 'cabinet exclusivity' unfairly inhibits entry into the ice cream market and penalizes smaller producers'.

Adapted from the Financial Times 16.11.93

Whiff of Controversy Hangs in the Air

Quite a few eyebrows have been raised in response to last week's decision by the UK competition authorities on the complaint by Superdrug, the discount drug store retailer, that perfume manufacturers such as Yves Saint Laurent and Givenchy were refusing to supply it in order to maintain high prices and make monopoly profits.

Many observers find it hard to reconcile the Monopolies and Mergers Commission's two central findings that a 'complex monopoly' existed under which leading perfume houses acted as a group refusing to supply retailers they had not authorized themselves, and recommended resale prices to those they did; yet that these practices 'did not operate in the public interest.'

The perfume houses argue that their products can be satisfactorily sold only in a suitable atmosphere or ambience, where the up-market image of the fragrances is not spoilt by association with more mundane and less expensive goods.

They have further claimed that products that come into contact with the skin require specialist point-of-sale advice and that, while not technically complex, perfume requires a level of special selling expertise.

However, Superdrug and the Consumers' Association have argued that the perfume houses' main purpose in setting up selective distribution systems is to prevent supplies of their perfumes reaching discount retailers such as Superdrug and Tesco. This the CA alleges is an anti-competitive practice.

Size isn't everything!

It would be wrong to think that all large firms exploit their consumers. Many, because of their size, are able to spend a large amount of money on product improvements and more efficient production processes. Cost savings may be passed onto consumers as lower prices. Monopolies and oligopolies may also face competition from products in other markets and from foreign competition. For example, British Gas faces competition from coal and water as a source of energy to produce electricity. Households also have the choice between electricity, solid fuels, or gas to provide heating.

Key words

Market structure - characteristics of a market which determine the behaviour of firms supplying it

Price taker - a firm that has no power to influence market supply or demand and must, therefore, accept the prevailing market price at which to sell its products

Monopolistic competition - a market structure in which a large number of firms compete to supply broadly similar products

Product differentiation - the creation of differences in consumer perceptions of very similar products through brand imaging

Branding - the creation of a brand image for a product through distinctive packaging and advertising

Oligopoly - a market structure with a small number of dominant firms

Cartel - a formal arrangement between firms to agree prices and/or outputs

Collusion - collaboration between firms to 'fix' prices

Duopoly - when two firms dominate market supply

Pure monopoly - a firm that controls the entire supply of a particular good or service to a market

Legal monopoly - as defined by law, a firm, or group of firms acting together, which supplies over 25% of a market

Barriers to entry - constraints used by existing producers in a market to hinder competition from new firms

Natural monopoly - a firm that controls the entire market supply of a product because production at this scale is the most efficient

Price maker - a firm that is able to influence the market price of a product

---

Section 2.3 Social costs and benefits

The benefits and costs of productive activity

The production of electricity allows us to satisfy our needs and wants for light and warmth, televisions, video recorders, and microwave ovens among many other devices. It also satisfies the wants of other producers for power to drive machinery enabling them to supply other goods and services to various product markets.

However, the article opposite suggests that the production of electricity has helped to cause acid rain, radioactive waste, damage to car paintwork, and may even have created health problems. Acid rain has been blamed for killing fish and damaging forests and crops. These are costs additional to the payment of wages, purchase of nuclear fuels, oil and coal, rent and rates paid by electricity generating companies. The costs of environmental damage are borne by other people and organizations.

DAMAGING IMAGE

Electricity is the fuel that environmentalists love to hate. Whether it is produced by coal, oil, orimulsion or nuclear, each causes great offence to somebody and different parts of the green lobby are out to restrict its use.

It is not so surprising, because the electricity industry makes a bigger contribution to environmental damage than any other.

The statistics to support this are mindboggling. The Council for the Protection of Rural Wales gave evidence at a recent parliamentary enquiry to show that the production of electricity in the United Kingdom is responsible for the following:

- 73 per cent of sulphur dioxide emissions, causing acid rain
- 38 per cent of carbon emissions
- 35 per cent of nitrogen dioxides, both worsening global warming
- 90 per cent of the country's radioactive waste

Health fears that overhead cables may contribute to such illnesses as leukaemia, continue to grow.

IN NORTH Yorkshire there is a row over the threat to run overhead power cables in the beautiful Vale of York. On the South Coast, PowerGen's burning of orimulsion has been blamed for damaging car paintwork.

Evening Standard 5.12.94

The costs of growth: economic bads

Economic growth refers to an increase in the total volume of goods and services produced in an economy. Economic growth, therefore, suggests that people are better off because they have more goods and services to enjoy. More people are also likely to be employed and earning incomes. However, there are also costs of growth wider than those faced by industry in buying or hiring the necessary resources to produce more goods and services.

A growth in the total supply of goods and services in an economy can have the following costs and benefits:

The benefits of growth	The costs of growth
1. There are more goods and services for people to enjoy.	1. Growth may only be achieved by producing more capital goods, such as machinery, at the expense of consumer goods
2. Higher levels of output may be achieved by using less labour input so people may enjoy more leisure time.	2. Growth may use up scarce resources more quickly. Natural resources such as oil, coal, and other mineral deposits are finite and cannot be replenished. Space is limited. Using land to build more factories and offices leaves less for parks and woodland.
3. More resources are employed by organizations to produce goods and services.	3. Waste can increase, for example, as a result of unnecessary packaging.
4. Firms may invest more money in new premises, machinery and staff training, providing further jobs and incomes.	4. Technical progress may replace workers with machines. People may remain unemployed for long periods of time, often on limited incomes.
5. Increases in income generate more tax revenue for the government which can be used to produce more roads, schools, hospitals, and other goods and services that can increase the standard of living in a country	5. Increased production may increase pollution and health problems

Economic goods and bads

Producing goods and services to satisfy consumer wants can involve the production of **economic bads** such as pollution and destruction of the

Economic bads

environment. The drive to increase output may also result in less compassionate production methods, for example, battery farming and testing on animals.

When making production decisions, private firms will normally only consider their **private costs**, such as wages, electricity bills, rents and materials, and their **private benefits** or revenues. They will be concerned with the amount of profit they can expect from the activity but will tend to ignore the **external costs** of production. These are costs borne by people and firms not directly involved in the activity that causes them.

Profit = private benefits − private costs

Externalities

An externality arises when the decisions of one person or firm, or group of people or firms, affects others. Negative externalities result in external costs.

Rivers and seas polluted by industrial waste can kill stocks of fish and reduce the output and revenue of the fishing industry. Atmospheric pollution causes acid rain which can damage crops and forests. Buildings may need to be cleaned more often. People can suffer respiratory problems which can result in higher medical bills, paid from higher taxes or medical insurance premiums. These are all examples of **negative externalities**.

However, some productive activity may result in **positive externalities** which give **external benefits**. For example, a large firm may train workers in particular skills which can benefit other firms who employ them at some future date. Firms may also contribute to charities or sponsor sports events which provide wider benefits beyond that of improving the image of the firm.

Social costs and benefits

The total cost to society, or **social cost**, of an organization's decision to produce a particular good or service includes both the private costs of the organization and any external costs. This must be compared to the **social benefit** of that decision before we can judge whether or not it is in the general interest.

Portfolio Activity 2.5

Range: Evaluate social costs and benefits
Skills: Prepare written material, Gather and process data

Collect evidence from newspapers of external costs and benefits resulting from business decisions to produce goods and services.

Compile your newspaper cuttings in a file and for each clipping write a brief note on the external cost(s) and/or benefit(s) it highlights. (Present a balanced view. Do not focus exclusively on external costs, such as pollution and waste. Consider also the benefits to the wider community of having more goods and services, employment opportunities, and incomes).

Social cost = private costs + external costs

The social benefit of a decision to supply a market will be equal to the private benefits of business organizations plus any external benefits. Society will benefit from the production of goods and services through the satisfaction of consumer wants. This is reflected by their willingness to pay firms for products. Sales revenues are the private benefits of firms, while external benefits may include the training they provide, and job creation.

Social benefits = private benefits + external benefits

If the social cost of producing a particular good or service exceeds its social benefit, this suggests that using resources to produce that product is 'uneconomic' from society's point of view - even if the producing firms make a profit. That is, society would be better off if resources were used to produce something else.

If social costs exceed social benefits, the decision to produce a good or service makes society worse off even if the producers make a profit.

Firms will continue to produce a particular good or service if their sales revenues exceed their costs, i.e. they make a profit. However, their production may generate significant external costs thereby making everyone else worse off - i.e. the social cost exceeds the social benefit of production. This suggests the price of the product may be too low because it does not reflect the external costs of production. If prices were higher, less of the product would be consumed, so less would need to be produced and therefore external costs such as pollution could be lower. For example, in 1994 the government announced it was to raise taxes on petrol each year by at least 5% above inflation in an attempt to curb car use and the release of harmful exhaust emissions (see 3.4).

Only if the social benefit of a decision to supply a particular good or service exceeds the social costs of doing so will society be better off as a result.

If social costs are less than social benefits, the decision to produce a good or service will make society better off.

External costs and business decision-making

As consumers have become more aware of issues such as pollution, animal testing, global warming, cruelty in farming, and the protection of the environment, businesses have begun to take more account of external costs in their decision-making. Environmentally-friendly products and labelling, increased waste management, recycling, and cruelty-free products are just some examples of the way firms have reacted to consumer pressure. At first, production costs may be increased as firms change their existing production processes, switch to other suppliers, and/or develop new products. That is, many firms have been forced by changing consumer demand to **internalize** some the external costs of their decisions.

The government may also force firms and consumers to internalize many of the external costs they cause. For example, laws have been passed in the UK to prevent firms polluting the environment. The Clean Air Act and the Environmental Protection Act set limits on the quantities of certain gases firms can release into the atmosphere, and firms that exceed these limits may be heavily fined. Taxes on petrol and smoking are an attempt to reduce the consumption of products which pollute and which may cause health problems among the public at large (see 3.3).

Advanced Business

Portfolio Activity 2.6

Range: Evaluate social costs and benefits
Skills: Read and respond to written material

The article reveals that the waste disposal industry is opposed to the introduction of a tax on landfill rubbish dumping by firms.

1. What are the private costs of firms engaged in waste disposal?
2. 'Waste is an external cost of productive activity to satisfy consumer wants.' Explain this statement.
3. What is the purpose of the landfill tax?
4. How, and why, does the article suggest that business may try to avoid the landfill tax without reducing the amount of waste they produce?

Waste tax hailed as ecological milestone

Britain is to get its first tax on rubbish dumping.

The landfill tax announced by Mr Clarke is intended to deal with Britain's growing waste mountain. It will raise "several hundred million" pounds and come into effect in 1996.

Charles Secrett, director of Friends of the Earth, described the announcement, and its recognition that tax can play a role in environmental protection, as "a very big advance in the cause of sustainable development."

The waste-disposal industry, however, described the proposed tax as futile. An industry source said the levy could add 50 per cent to the cost of disposing of solid waste, an increase that would be borne by local authorities and the consumer.

Miguel Pestana, government affairs manager for Waste Management International, one of the largest operators of landfill sites in Britain, said: "We do not think it will have the positive environmental effects that have been projected."

"The results could be the reverse. The tax could well stimulate the use of substandard landfill disposal options."

There is concern within the industry that waste-disposal authorities may try to cut costs by seeking out cheaper sites and 'cowboy' operators.

Britain produces about 140 million tonnes of waste a year. Raising several hundred million pounds annually would, therefore, mean a landfill tax of £2-£5 a tonne.

Mr Clarke said consultation proposals on the tax would be published shortly. Its aim, according to the Treasury, is to encourage business and consumers to produce less waste and recover more from it.

The Independent 30.11.94

Key words

Economic bads - unwelcome by-products of productive activities designed to satisfy consumer wants

Private cost - the cost of an activity to those private individuals or firms undertaking it

Private benefit - the benefit of an activity to those private individuals or firms undertaking it

Negative externalities - the detrimental effects of decisions by one person or firm, or group of people or firms, on others

External costs - costs borne by people and firms not directly involved in the activity that caused them

Social cost - the cost of an activity to society as a whole, including business

Social benefit - the benefit of an activity to society as a whole, including business

Further reading

Moynihan, D, and Titley, B: Economics - A Complete Course (Oxford University Press, 1993), Chapters 9 and 10

Test questions

The following underpinning knowledge will be tested:
1. Types of markets
2. Compare competition within markets
3. Explain the behaviour of business in different markets
4. Evaluate the social costs and benefits of market operations

1 A firm that supplies 100% of a market is known as:
- A An oligopoly
- B A sole trader
- C A monopoly
- D A duopoly

2 Which of the following is NOT a feature of an oligopolistic market:
- A A small number of firms supply the market
- B Heavy advertising of products
- C strong product brand images
- D price wars

3 Which of the following is an external cost caused by a decision to produce goods and services?
- A The cost of employing a contractor to clean the outside of a building due to airborne pollutants
- B The cost of hiring labour
- C The cost of employing a contractor to maintain the computer network in a firm
- D A fall in the profits of grain producers due to a poor harvest

4 The most likely explanation for the decision by a business owner to turn his sweetshop into a video film rental shop instead is:
- A Consumer demand for video film rental is falling
- B Consumer demand for confectionery is rising
- C Consumer demand for video film rental is rising
- D Consumer demand for all goods and services is falling

Questions 5-7 share the following answer options:
- A Market skimming
- B Destruction pricing
- C Penetration pricing
- D Non-price competition

Which of the above describe the following competitive practices?

5 A firm entering a market for the first time and setting price low to build sales

6 A firm that invests heavily in advertising to launch an entirely new product

7 A firm that launches a new product protected by a patent initially at a high price.

8 Increasing competition in a market is likely to:
- A Raise market price and the quantity sold
- B Lower market price and the quantity sold
- C Raise market price and lower the quantity sold
- D Lower market price and raise the quantity sold

9 Firms will compete to achieve all the following objectives except:
- A Increased market share
- B Higher sales revenues
- C Product superiority
- D Lower market prices

10 The UK government is currently adding a fourth lane to the M25 motorway ring around London at an estimated cost of around £3 billion. The government has argued that the expansion will reduce congestion and help reduce transport costs. Protestors argue that it will simply fill up with more traffic.

i   List two examples of private costs incurred in building the fourth lane on the M25.

ii Suggest and explain two external costs that use of the M25 may cause.

iii Suggest and explain a potential external benefit resulting from a fourth lane.

11

i   Suggest two reasons why firms compete to supply a market with a good or service.

ii What is the difference between price competition and non-price competition? Explain your answer using examples.

iii What is a 'monopoly'?

iv Explain what is meant by 'destruction pricing'. What is it designed to achieve?

v   Other than price, suggest two ways in which a monopoly can restrict new competition to supply a product.

vi Draw a diagram to show the effect of a monopoly restricting the market supply of a product on its market price and quantity traded.

assessment assignment ☞

UNIT ONE

CHAPTER 2

Assessment assignment

Range: Types of Markets
Compare competition
Analyse in terms of competitive pricing and non-pricing strategies
Evaluate social costs and benefits

Skills: Communication
Produce written material
Use images
Application of number
Collect and record data
Information Technology
Prepare information
Present information

The death of vinyl?

The graph below illustrates the changing pattern of consumer demand in the market for recorded music. Consumers are now buying less vinyl records while sales of compact discs are rising.

Trade deliveries of LPs, cassettes, compact discs and singles

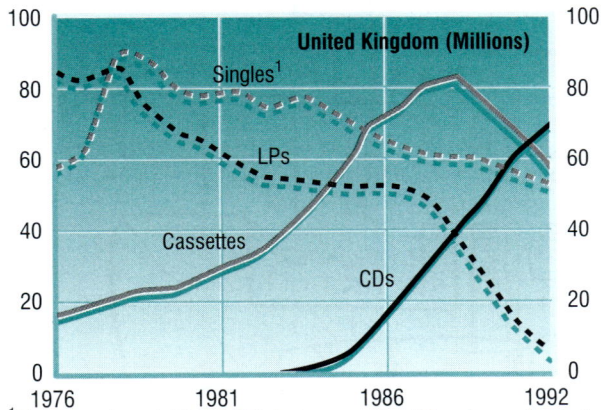

United Kingdom (Millions)

Singles[1], LPs, Cassettes, CDs

1976 — 1981 — 1986 — 1992

[1]The figures include 7" and 12" singles as well as CD and cassette singles

Source: British Phonographic Industry

CD FIRMS CLEARED OF PRICE PLOT RIP-OFF

RECORD companies were controversially cleared of overcharging for compact discs yesterday.

They had been accused of keeping prices artificially high – CDs cost about £1 to make, almost exactly the same as tape cassettes. But they sell in Britain for between £12.99 and £15.99, much more than a cassette and almost double what is charged in the United States.

However, the Monopolies and Mergers Commission ruled that although there is a monopoly by five companies – EMI, PolyGram, Warner, Sony, and BMG – it does not operate against the public interest.

Instead, pricing policies are justified because of strong competition within the industry, according to the watchdog body. The major firms, accounting for about 70 per cent of the UK market, 'competed vigorously among themselves' and also with the independent sector, it added.

Daily Mail 24.6.94

chapter 3

Tasks

Investigate the record industry and produce a short report of your findings to explain:

1. The motives of the organizations that supply records and CDs

2. How, and why, changes in consumer wants have affected the use of resources and production in the record industry

3. The factors that may have caused consumer wants for records and CDs to change. Use appropriate diagrams to illustrate the changes in market conditions you have discussed and their likely impact on market price and quantity traded.

4. How record companies and record shops compete

5. The degree of price and non-price competition in the record industry. Do your findings support the ruling made by the Monopolies and Mergers Commission that record companies have not acted against the public interest?

6. The external costs and benefits of producing records and CDs. (Hint: consider the resources required to produce records and CDs. For example, oil is a raw material for vinyl records and plastic; electricity can be produced by burning oil, gas or coal)

7. Compare your findings on competition and business behaviour in the recorded music market with another product market where there is evidence of a higher or lower degree of business competition. For example, the gas supply industry is a good example of a near-total monopoly, while the markets for agricultural produce and raw materials tend to be highly competitive.

In order to demonstrate Information Technology core skills, your report must be produced with a computer using a word processor or desktop publishing package.

Helpful sources of information include:

- Your local record shop
- Major record companies
- Music Week magazine

Advanced Business

chapter 3
The Effects of Government Policy on Markets

This chapter examines why and how the UK and European Union governments intervene in markets for goods and services

Key ideas

Governments will often intervene in product markets if they feel the market has failed to establish a satisfactory price or quantity traded.

Government intervention will aim to **regulate or increase competition**, **counteract anti-competitive business activities**, **protect consumers** from unfair and dishonest trading, and **safeguard environmental and social interests**.

The government is able to influence market demand and supply by using **fiscal** and **monetary policy instruments**, **competition policy**, **regulation** and **legislation**, **public ownership** and **privatization**.

The use of **taxation** and **public expenditure** to influence the level of aggregate demand in the economy is known as **fiscal policy**. A fiscal boost involves cutting taxes and/or raising public expenditure in an attempt to generate business and employment opportunities.

Monetary policy involves using **interest rates** to control the demand for borrowed funds and to influence the **foreign exchange rate**. Raising interest rates will increase business costs and tend to reduce growth opportunities.

Value Added Tax (VAT) and **customs and excise duties** may be used selectively to raise the price of goods and services to discourage their consumption.

Subsidies may be used selectively to reduce business costs and protect infant industries. **Regional assistance** is available from both the UK and European Union (EU) governments to assist firms and job creation in areas of industrial decline.

Competition policy concerns measures to control **monopolies**, **mergers**, and **restrictive trade practices**, such as price fixing rings.

Nationalization refers to the transfer of a whole industry from private to public ownership. Many former nationalized industries have now been sold back to the private sector. **Privatization** also involves joint ventures between the public and private sectors, deregulation to allow greater competition in supply, and contracting out activities to private organizations to undertake.

Section **3.1**

Government intervention in markets

Market failure

What is wrong with the Market?

In Chapter 1 we learnt how the allocation of resources to different markets is determined by the individual decisions of producers and consumers. Producers will increase their output of goods and services in response to effective consumer demand. A rise in demand forces up market price, providing firms with a profit incentive to extend supply. In this way, freely working markets:

- Respond quickly to consumer wants
- Produce a wide variety of goods and services to meet diverse consumer wants
- Encourage the use of new and more efficient methods of production in order to maximize profits for business owners.

However, the market system may not always produce an outcome that is beneficial to all. For example:

- Resources will be employed only if it is profitable to do so
- Large and powerful monopolies may develop
- The market may fail to provide certain goods and services such as street lighting, law and order, and defence if private firms find it difficult to charge a price for these to individual consumers based on the amount they have consumed.
- The free market may encourage the consumption of harmful goods. For example, producers may be willing to supply dangerous drugs to consumers who are willing and able to pay for them if there are no legal constraints to prevent them doing so.
- Private firms and consumers may ignore the damaging social and environmental effects of their production and consumption decisions
- The system allocates more goods and services to those consumers with the most money. The needs of the poor can often be ignored.

In many countries, therefore, governments intervene in markets in an attempt to correct some of the ways in which it fails to produce a satisfactory outcome, either in terms of the market price of the product or the quantity traded.

▼ *Market failure?*

▼ *Market failure?*

Advanced Business

Portfolio Activity 3.1

Range: Reasons for government intervention, Ways

Skills: Read and respond to written material; Collect and record data

The articles below describe intervention by the UK government in a number of product markets.

INCREASES in fuel duty and energy efficiency grants for pensioners mean that Britain has now set out in full how it will meet its commitment, signed in Rio Janeiro, to freeze emissions of gases which cause global warming by the year 2000

An increase in fuel duty by five per cent a year for the rest of the decade, instead of three per cent announced in Mr Lamont's Budget in March, completes a list of measures estimated to save 10 million tons of carbon dioxide a year. Fuel will rise by 3p a litre immediately.

Daily Telegraph 1.1.93

CUTS PROMISED IN ELECTRICITY PRICES

Savings totalling £2.5bn for electricity users in England and Wales over the next five years will be promised today by the industry's regulator as he unveils price controls that are likely to disappoint consumer groups but please investors.

Prof Stephen Littlechild, director-general of the regulatory body Offer, says his proposals imply reductions of £12-£16 in average household electricity bills in the year from next April. This is equivalent to at least 4 per cent.

Financial Times 11.8.94

Cheers – cough up

The price of a pack of 20 cigarettes rose 11p last night as Mr Clarke continued government policy of trying to cut the number of smokers by increasing tobacco duty above the rate of inflation.

Daily Telegraph 1.12.93

Hill farmers are main aid losers

HILL farmers fared worst from the Government's new spending plans for agriculture — losing £25 million from their cattle and sheep subsidies in a package of measures announced alongside the Budget.

These cuts, which help to offset an overall increase in spending on the farming industry next year under the increasingly expensive Common Agricultural Policy, will leave the Government open to the criticism that it has targeted the poorest group of farmers in the country.

Daily Telegraph 1.1.93

---

1. What impact will each of the measures described above have on the price of the products in question?

2. Explain each of the measures used by the government to influence price.

3. For each product suggest why the government has attempted to influence prices.

4. Consider the price elasticity of demand for cigarettes and petrol. Suggest whether or not the action taken by the government will have the desired effect on consumption. What will be the effect on tax revenues? Explain your answers.

5. Gather information from newspapers and other sources on various measures taken by government to influence prices in different markets. In each case record why the action was taken and the mechanism used to influence price, and explain whether or not you consider the action will be successful.

Why do governments intervene in markets?

The governments of the UK and the European Union (EU) have a great deal of power to intervene in product markets. The reasons why successive governments have used this power are:

1. To regulate prices set by private firms with a significant command over the market supply of a product who may use this power to restrict supply and force up market price

2. To increase or regulate the amount of competition for supply in markets dominated by a one or a handful of large firms

3. To counteract anti-competitive activities, such as price fixing rings

4. To protect consumers from misleading marketing and unscrupulous trading practices

5. To encourage the consumption of a product by keeping prices low, or discourage consumption by keeping prices high. For example, the price of petrol is kept high to conserve a valuable natural resource, but also to discourage car use to reduce harmful exhaust emissions.

6. To raise the incomes of some producers in order to encourage them to continue to supply their product. For example, farmers' incomes have often been protected because if they go out of business a valuable domestic source of food supply is lost.

7. To stabilize prices in markets susceptible to dramatic changes in the conditions of supply and therefore price. For example, unforeseen weather conditions can cause large variations in agricultural harvests. Resulting price changes can discourage both consumption and production.

8. To protect environmental and social interests, such as public health and moral concerns, such as the exploitation of child labour.

9. To protect employment

How do governments intervene in markets?

The UK government can use a number of measures to intervene in markets to influence price and the quantity traded, either directly or indirectly by influencing consumer demand or producer supply.

- **Macro-economic policy.** This refers to measures that attempt to influence the performance of the entire economy in terms of the rate of general price inflation, unemployment, growth in total output, and the balance of overseas trade. The overall level of taxation, public expenditure, and interest rates are policy variables which can be used to effect changes in all markets (see 3.2).

- **Micro-economic policy.** This refers to policies that are directed at individual product markets. For example, specific taxes like those on cigarettes, and subsidies to areas of high unemployment (see 3.3).

- **Legislation and regulation.** Governments can pass laws which regulate business activities. There are a variety of laws to restrict anti-competitive behaviour and regulate the environmental impact of business operations (see 3.4).

The government has also set up a number of 'watchdogs' which set standards of service and regulate price increases in certain industries. For example, the Office of Water Services (OFFWAT) regulates the privatized water supply companies.

- **Public ownership and privatization.** In the past, one way to regulate industries that had significant market power or to protect jobs in firms that were in danger of closing was to take them into public ownership. That is, the government would take over the ownership and control of these organizations. However, since 1979 the Conservative government administrations in the UK have returned many public sector activities to the private sector under a programme of privatization (see 3.5).

The following sections consider these measures in more detail.

Section 3.2 Macro-economic policy

Government policies to control the economy

What is macro-economics?

Macro-economics is the study of how an economy works as a whole, including the overall level of income and prices, total employment and unemployment, the base rate of interest, total savings and investment, the rate of growth in total output, the balance of overseas trade, and the currency exchange rate.

Government macro-economic objectives

Like most governments in the developed world, the UK government has four main macro-economic objectives. These are:

- To achieve low and stable inflation in the general level of prices (see 17.2)
- To reduce unemployment
- To encourage economic growth, i.e. growth in total output
- To secure a favourable balance of payments (i.e. between inflows from inward investment and payments for UK exports, and outflows from UK investment overseas and payments of imports)

It is assumed that if the government can meet these objectives it will create an economic climate which is favourable to business. For example, it is argued that high inflation destroys business confidence and jobs. Business will find it difficult to plan ahead if the costs of their materials and equipment are rising quickly.

When prices rise quickly, consumers cannot afford to buy so many goods and services and so demand falls. People may also save more to protect the value of their savings which are worth less as inflation rises. In addition, if the UK rate of price inflation is higher than other countries, UK goods become less competitively priced and overseas demand for our exports will fall.

As firms experience a fall in demand, they cut back production and shed resources, including labour. Unemployment will therefore tend to rise.

Controlling aggregate demand

Central to the success of macro-economic policy is the control of the level of **aggregate demand** in the economy.

Aggregate demand refers to the demand of all consumers of UK goods and services in the very widest sense. That is, consumption of goods and services by the public, investment in new plant and machinery by firms, expenditure on goods and services by the government, and spending on UK exports by other countries.

Rising aggregate demand is normally characteristic of **economic recovery** and **boom** (see 17.1). Most business organizations experience rising sales and order books. To fulfil orders and meet demand, firms may create employment opportunities and invest in expanding their capacity to produce. However, if firms are unable to keep pace with rising demand, stocks will fall and firms will tend to increase their prices. During an economic boom when total demand outstrips the supply of all goods and services, prices will tend to rise rapidly. Rising prices will eventually choke off demand and, if incomes fail to keep pace with prices, demand will start to fall.

Falling aggregate demand is characteristic of **economic recession** or **slump**. Trading conditions become difficult as demand for goods and services falls and firms experience rising stocks and falling orders. Prices are likely to fall as supply exceeds demand – or at least rise less fast. If recession continues firms will cut back production. Investment in new research and development and machinery will also suffer as long-term plans are cut back. Unemployment tends to rise and growth in the productive capacity of the economy will falter.

The government is able to influence the level of aggregate demand for goods and services and, therefore, business trading conditions and employment opportunities, by using a number of **policy instruments**. These are:

- The general level of taxation
- The general level of public sector expenditure
- The base rate of interest

These policy instruments are used because:

- the amount consumers have to spend on goods and services depends on their level of personal **disposable income** i.e. income after the deduction of tax
- as the interest rate rises, firms tend to reduce their investment in new capital goods, such as machinery
- total public expenditure accounts for around 39% of aggregate demand in the UK

▼ *Aggregate demand*

▲ *Consumer spending*

▲ *Investment*

▲ *Public Expenditure*

▲ *Exports*

- as interest rates fall, the value of the pound in terms of foreign currencies tends to fall, reducing the price of UK goods and services sold abroad.

Fiscal policy

Using taxation and public expenditure to influence the level of aggregate demand in the economy is known as **fiscal policy** (see also 17.2).

- During times of economic recession when trading conditions tend to be poor and unemployment relatively high, the government may give the economy a **fiscal boost** by cutting taxes and/or increasing public expenditure. Increasing capital expenditure, for example, on the construction of new roads and hospitals, will create employment opportunities for firms and people in the construction industry. As the number of people employed increases, the level of expenditure on goods and services will tend to rise.

- During times of high inflation when high demand may be forcing up prices, the government may increase taxes and/or reduce public spending. The same actions will not only affect the demand for UK goods but will also reduce the demand for goods and services imported from abroad if the balance of overseas trade is unfavourable.

There are two main types of tax the UK government can charge:

- **Direct taxes** (collected by the Inland Revenue) are levied directly on the incomes of people and firms, and include income tax, corporation tax, capital gains tax and inheritance tax (see table 3.1). Raising income tax will reduce people's disposable incomes and reduce the level of aggregate demand in the economy. Conversely, cutting corporation tax on business profits will raise the amount firms are able to re-invest in new plant and machinery or pay in dividends to shareholders.

- **Indirect taxes** (collected by the Customs and Excise Department) are levied on goods and services, and therefore only have an indirect effect on incomes via spending. The main indirect tax in the UK is Value Added Tax (VAT). Indirect taxes also include customs duties on the price of some imported goods and excise duties on such items as cigarettes, alcohol, and petrol. Licences for motor vehicles and televisions are also forms of indirect tax.

Raising indirect taxes will at first add to price inflation in the economy because they are added either as a percentage, or as a lump sum, to the price of goods and services. However, as prices rise, people will find they are unable to buy as much with their incomes and so demand for many goods and services will fall. Cutting indirect taxes will have the opposite effect.

▼ Table 3.1 : General Government Receipts, 1994-95

	£ BILLION	
	1993–94	1994–95
Inland Revenue		
Income tax	58·4	64·2
Corporation tax	14·9	20·1
Petroleum revenue tax	0·4	0·7
Capital gains tax	0·7	0·8
Inheritance tax	1·3	1·4
Stamp duties	1·7	1·8
Total Inland Revenue	**77·5**	**89·1**
Customs and Excise		
Value added tax	38·9	43·3
Fuel duties	12·5	14·2
Tobacco duties	6·5	6·8
Spirits duties	1·7	1·7
Wine duties	1·1	1·1
Beer and cider duties	2·4	2·6
Betting and gaming duties	1·1	1·2
Customs duties	2·0	2·0
Agricultural levies	0·2	0·2
Air passenger duty	0·0	0·1
Insurance premium tax	0·0	0·2
Total Customs and Excise	**66·3**	**73·2**
Vehicle excise duties	3·6	3·8
Oil royalties	0·6	0·5
Business rates	12·6	12·3
Other taxes and royalties	5·8	5·9
Total taxes and royalty receipts	**166·4**	**184·9**
Social security contributions	38·7	42·5
Council tax	8·6	8·8
Interest and dividends	5·1	4·2
Gross trading surpluses and rent	5·1	5·2
Other receipts	6·9	6·9
General government receipts	**230·8**	**252·5**
North Sea revenues	1·2	1·6

UNIT ONE

CHAPTER 3

Indirect taxes can also be used selectively to influence the demand and supply of individual goods and services as part of micro-economic policy in the UK (see 3.3).

Employees' National Insurance Contributions (NICs) are not strictly a tax although they are levied as a percentage of earned income in much the same way as income tax. Thus, by raising or lowering NICs the government can affect the level of disposable income and, therefore, consumer demand for goods and services.

What is the Budget?

Each year (usually in late November) the Chancellor of the Exchequer presents the government plans for public spending and revenues for the next 12 months to Parliament. This is known as the **budget**.

The government uses the budget to announce new taxes, abolish old taxes, or revise tax rates. For example, in 1993 the government announced it was to raise the excise duty on petrol by 5% each year over and above the rate of inflation to the year 2,000 in an attempt to curb the use of cars and petrol to reduce harmful vehicle emissions. Increases or cuts in spending on different activities, for example, defence, transport, the heath service, are also announced in the budget.

In the December 1994 budget the UK government announced plans to spend £305 billion during 1995/96 and envisaged raising £207 billion from taxes. A **budget deficit** means that the government plans to spend more than it expects to raise from tax revenues.

A fiscal boost to the economy involves increasing the budget deficit by spending more or cutting taxes. If the government reduces its budget deficit over last year, then it is planning a **fiscal contraction** in an attempt to reduce aggregate demand to reduce price inflation.

Most years, the government has to borrow money to finance the shortfall between expenditure plans and total government revenues, including taxes, interest and dividends on loans and public sector shareholdings, and profits from public sector trading activities, such as the Post Office. The difference between spending plans and revenues each year is what the government must borrow, known as the **Public Sector Borrowing Requiremen**t (PSBR). In 1994/95 the PSBR was £34.5 billion.

Between 1987/88 and 1990/91 government revenues exceeded expenditures and so the government was able to repay some of the **national debt** – the total amount of borrowing by the public sector (some £334 billion in 1994) – and, therefore, reduce yearly interest charges. When this happens the amount repaid is known as the **Public Sector Debt Repayment** (PSDR).

▼ *Figure 3.1: The Public Sector Borrowing Requirement (£ billion)*

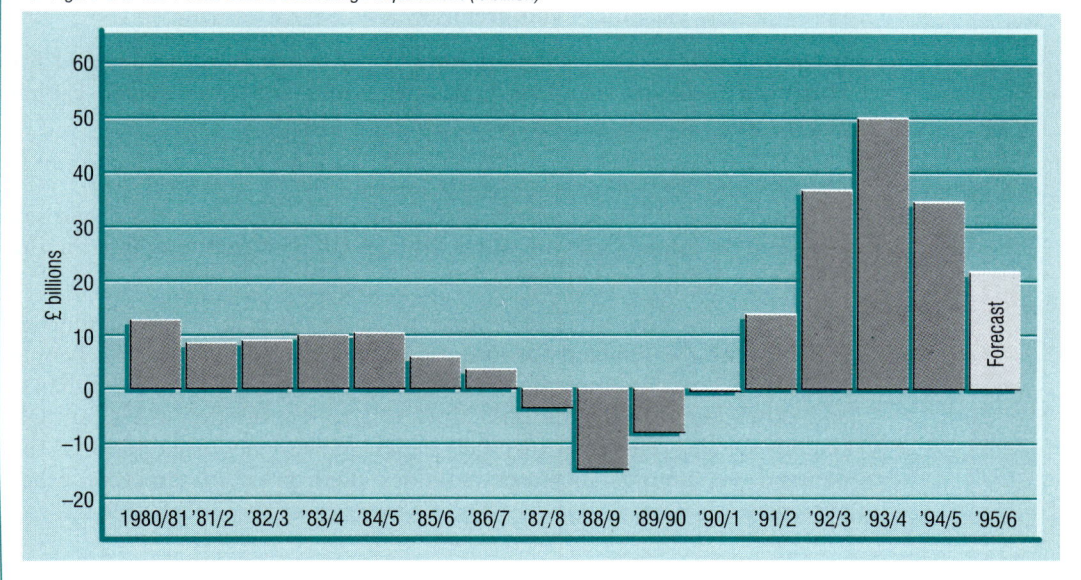

77

Advanced Business

Portfolio Activity 3.2

Range: Ways, Government policies, Evaluate
Skills: Take part in discussions, Collect and record data

Working in groups:

1. Gather information on the most recent budget from newspapers such as the *Financial Times* and *The Independent*, business magazines, bank reports, and budget statements available from the Treasury.

2. Examine the information carefully and identify the key budget changes and how they might affect business activity either directly or indirectly through their impact on the macro-economy.

3. Working on your own, pick a number of key changes to analyse the effects in some detail and produce a word-processed report summary.

4. The report should also record the reaction of business owners and managers you are in contact with. Arrange to phone or visit them when they have some spare time and ask them how they feel the budget changes will affect their business. How do their reactions compare with your own thoughts?

5. Discuss your findings within the group. To what extent do you feel the government should intervene in business and economic activity?

Monetary policy

The main instrument of monetary policy is the interest rate charged on short-term loans from the Bank of England to the monetary sector; banks, finance houses, etc. (see 22.2). The Bank of England is the central bank in the economy and operator of government monetary policy. By raising the interest rate, the government is able to influence the level of aggregate demand as banks and other lenders will usually follow by raising their own **base rates** of interest on loans to consumers and firms.

'Tightening' monetary policy involves raising the rate of interest to make borrowing money more expensive (see figure 3.2). As a result, demand for goods and services will tend to fall. Firms will also tend to borrow less to invest in new machinery and premises.

It follows that reducing interest rates tends to increase the demand for borrowed funds to spend on consumer goods and services and capital goods to expand the productive capacity of firms.

Monetary policy and overseas trade

Interest rates in the UK can also affect the price of goods we buy and sell overseas by influencing the value of the UK currency sterling on the foreign exchange market (see 17.2).

An increase in interest rates relative to those offered in other countries will increase the demand for interest-bearing deposits in the UK. People overseas will wish to increase the amount of money they keep in UK banks and other financial institutions. However, to do this they must buy UK pounds sterling with their own currencies. As with any other good, as the demand for pounds increases, so does their price in terms of other currencies.

▼ Figure 3.2 : UK Interest Rates*, 1984 – 1994

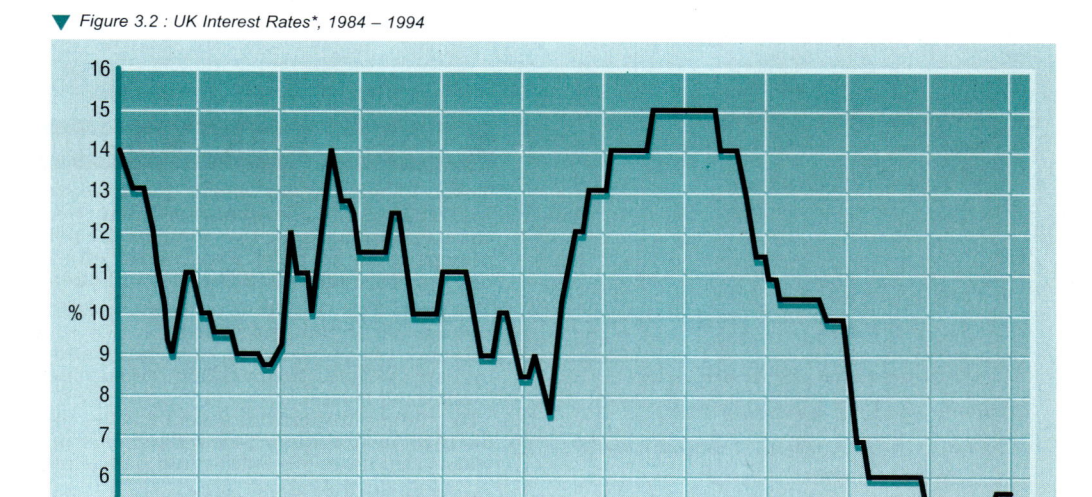

*Selected retail banks base rates
CSO Economic Trends

As the value of the pound rises, exports of UK goods and services sold overseas become more expensive and demand for them is likely to fall. However, the price of imports the UK buys from overseas will also fall, thereby reducing inflation. The level of UK imports of raw materials for use in UK industry is significant. Falling import prices can reduce production costs which can be passed on to UK consumers in lower prices.

When there is downward pressure on the pound, imports will tend to become more expensive. In a bid to reduce the inflationary impact of a fall in the value of the pound, interest rates will often be raised.

It follows that reducing interest rates can help reduce the value of the UK pound and the prices of UK exports overseas. This may create an increase in the demand for our exports and result in export-led growth in the UK economy.

Advanced Business

Portfolio Activity 3.3

Range: Ways, Government policies, Evaluate
Skills: Read and respond to written material, Collect and record data

1. What impact is the fall in the value of sterling likely to have on:
   A Business costs
   B Inflation
   C The price of UK exports sold overseas

2. Why are interest rates likely to rise?

3. What will be the effects of a rise in interest rates on consumers and business?

4. Look at Figure 3.2. What does it indicate about the operation and possible objectives of monetary policy over time?

5. Update Figure 3.2 with movements in interest rates since 1994 using data from *CSO Economic Trends*. What is the government's current policy on interest rates in the UK? Gather evidence from articles in the financial and business press. Make a prediction on what is likely to happen to interest rates over the next year and give reasons for your forecast.

Sterling takes a pounding

Turmoil reigned on world foreign exchange markets yesterday as the pound plunged to its lowest level against the German mark for two years. If the pound continues to plunge it could have a dramatic effect on mortgages, house prices, loans and the cost of holidays abroad.

The most likely outcome of the crisis is a lower pound and a sharp rise in interest rates.

Each 1 per cent rise in bank rates adds £500 million to industry's costs. Business failures may increase, leading to further job losses.

By making imports more expensive, the lower pound is likely to fuel inflation. This will increase pressure for higher wages and more job cuts would be the result.

Value of £1 against the German mark (Dm)

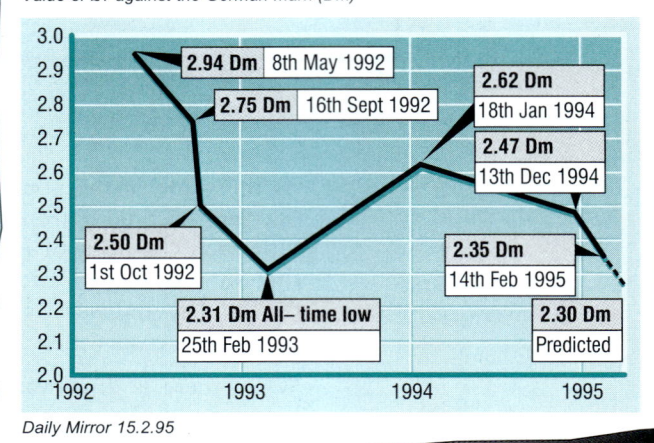

- 2.94 Dm 8th May 1992
- 2.75 Dm 16th Sept 1992
- 2.50 Dm 1st Oct 1992
- 2.31 Dm All-time low 25th Feb 1993
- 2.62 Dm 18th Jan 1994
- 2.47 Dm 13th Dec 1994
- 2.35 Dm 14th Feb 1995
- 2.30 Dm Predicted

Daily Mirror 15.2.95

Incomes and prices policy

Controls on incomes and prices have from time to time been used to control inflation in the UK. Since the end of the Second World War there have been eleven distinct episodes of government restraint on wage and price rises, either in the form of specified upper limits or a complete freeze on increases over given periods of time.

Workers and firms have been hostile to controls placed on their ability to raise wages and prices. History has shown that the controls have no lasting effect. Every time controls have been lifted, workers and firms simply pushed for even higher wages and prices to make up for what they thought they had lost in income and profits during the period of government restraint.

More recently the government has restricted the use of controls on wages to the public sector in order to reduce pressure on public sector spending. In 1993/94 a ceiling of 1.5% was imposed on the wage rises of civil servants, teachers and other public sector workers. The government argued that if pay rises were to exceed this upper limit they could only be financed by a reduction in the number of public sector workers.

> **Key words**
>
> **Macro-economic policy** – government actions designed to influence the whole economy
>
> **Aggregate demand** – the total amount of demand for goods and services in an economy by consumers, firms and governments at home and overseas
>
> **Economic recession** – a period of falling aggregate demand, rising unemployment, and falling output
>
> **Economic recovery** – a period of rising aggregate demand, output and prices, and falling unemployment
>
> **Disposable income** – income left to spend or save after taxes on income and National Insurance Contributions have been deducted
>
> **Policy instruments** – levers which can be used by government to influence macro-economic variables such as price inflation and unemployment
>
> **Fiscal policy** – using taxation and public expenditure to influence the level of aggregate demand
>
> **Fiscal boost** – lowering taxes and/or raising public spending to raise aggregate demand and generate business and employment opportunities
>
> **Direct taxes** – taxes levied on incomes, such as corporation tax on company profits
>
> **Indirect taxes** – taxes raised from expenditure, such as VAT
>
> **The Budget** – the government's annual plans for levels of taxation and public expenditure
>
> **Budget deficit** – when the government plans to spend more than it expects to raise from taxes in a given year
>
> **Public Sector Borrowing Requirement** (PSBR) – the amount the government must borrow in a year to cover a shortfall of government revenues below public expenditure
>
> **National Debt** – the total amount of outstanding government borrowing
>
> **Monetary policy** – the use of interest rates to influence the level of aggregate demand in the economy and the foreign exchange rate
>
> **Foreign exchange rate** – the value of one currency in terms of another, for example £1 = US$1.5

Section 3.3 Micro-economic policy

What is micro-economics?

The study of **micro-economics** focuses on how individual markets work and not how the whole economy works. Thus, it considers how prices are determined by the forces of demand and supply in particular markets.

Micro-economic policy instruments

Unlike macro-economic policy instruments, which are intended to affect the overall level of income, prices, and employment in the economy, micro-economic policy instruments are targeted at particular markets in an attempt to influence the market price and quantity traded.

A number of policy instruments are available;

- Setting price ceilings and floors
- The selective use of indirect taxes
- The selective use of tariffs and quotas on imports
- The selective use of public expenditure

Price floors and ceilings

Governments can impose a fixed price in a given market (see figures 3.3 and 3.4). For example, during the Second World War the prices of many goods in short supply were kept artificially low in the UK. If the prices of goods, such as eggs and meat, had been allowed to find their free market

▼ Figure 3.3: A maximum price

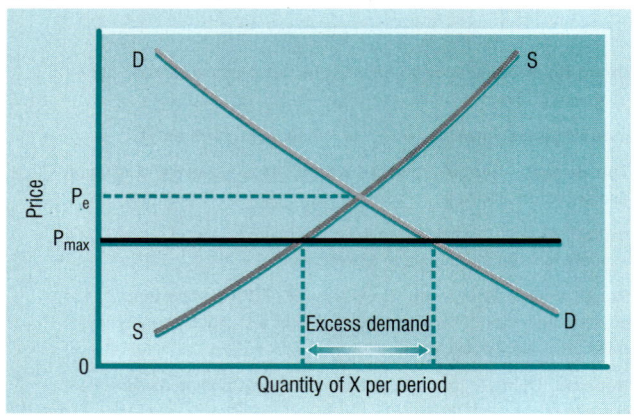

Price ceilings
If a maximum price (**Pmax**) is fixed below the free market price (**Pe**) it will result in an excess of demand. 'Black markets' supplying goods at higher prices to those who can afford to pay may develop.

▼ Figure 3.4: A minimum price

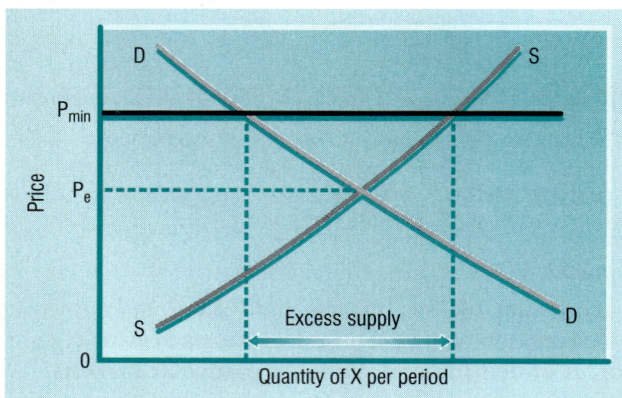

Price floors
A minimum price floor (**Pmin**) imposed above the free market price (**Pe**) will cause an excess of supply over demand.

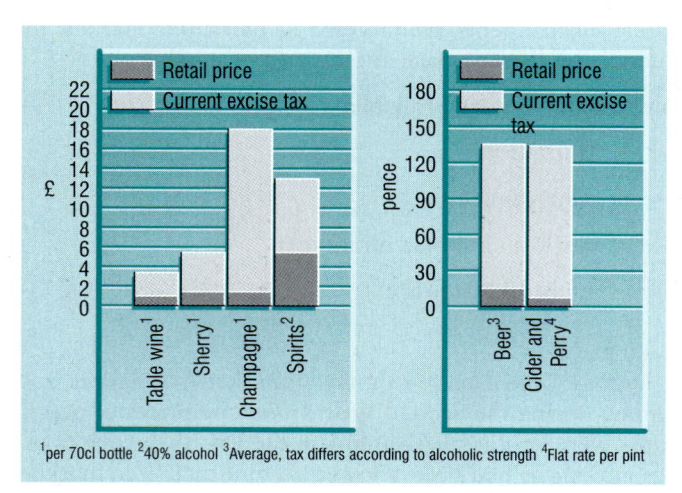

▲ Excise duties on alcohol 1994/95
[1] per 70cl bottle [2] 40% alcohol [3] Average, tax differs according to alcoholic strength [4] Flat rate per pint

price, the shortage of supply would have pushed their price beyond the reach of most people. At various other times, UK governments have imposed ceilings on rents in the rented accommodation market and minimum wage levels in labour markets. These controls have not always been successful.

Price floors in agricultural markets: Price floors have often been used in agricultural markets to protect farm incomes. Cheap imported food and advances in technology mean that most consumers in developed countries can buy their food at a lower cost from foreign producers than from domestic farmers. This has, in part, led to falling wages and employment in agriculture in developed countries during the last fifty years.

However, the use of price floors in agricultural markets has often encouraged over-production and surplus produce must be withdrawn from the market if prices are to be kept high.

Over-production?

The EU Common Agricultural Policy (CAP) aims to guarantee incomes and employment for farmers in Europe by purchasing their surplus produce or even by paying them to leave fields idle using European taxpayers' money. This policy has created vast stockpiles of butter, olive oil, wine, and beef held in EU stores that cannot be sold in the food market without causing food prices, farm incomes, and employment to fall. In this way, EU consumers are subsidizing farmers across Europe. CAP subsidies have the effect of keeping wages and employment higher than would otherwise be the case in a free agricultural labour market.

Indirect taxes

Indirect taxes, namely VAT and customs and excise duties, can be used to influence the price and quantity traded of selected goods and services. **Value Added Tax (VAT)** is an **ad valorem tax**. This means the tax is levied as a percentage of the price of a commodity. VAT, currently set at 17.5% in the UK, is levied on most goods and services.

Apart from raising revenue, indirect taxes are often used to discourage over-consumption of tobacco, alcohol, and petroleum products. For example, the UK government has committed itself to increase the real duty on cigarettes, over and above the effect of inflation, by at least 3% each year.

A tax additional to the price of a product can be regarded as a cost and will therefore shift the supply curve upwards by the amount of the tax.

▼ Figure 3.5: The effect of VAT on supply

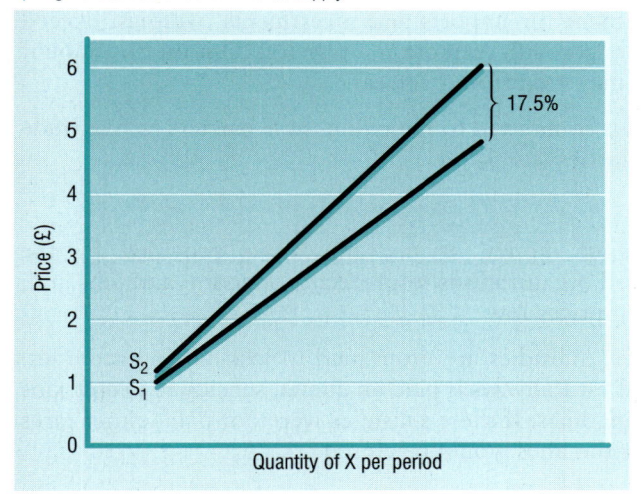

▼ Figure 3.6: The effect of a 50p excise duty on supply

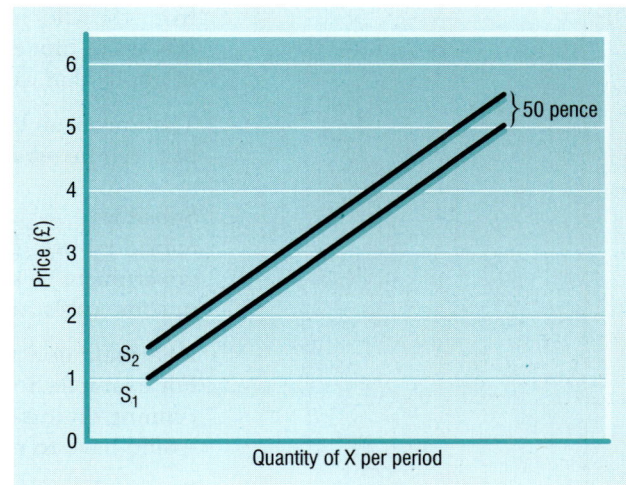

Sharing the burden of tax between consumers and producers

Imposing a tax on a product does not necessarily mean that the price of that product will be raised by the full amount of the tax.

This is because producers might reduce their own prices so that the after-tax price does not discourage consumers from buying their products. Clearly, in this way the tax is a cost to producers because it will reduce their sales revenues and profits.

Portfolio Activity 3.4

Range: Government policies, Evaluate
Skills: Read and respond to written material

1. The article suggests that the price of one litre of juice will rise by the full 17.5% VAT from £1.95 to £2.30. Explain why some producers may be willing to raise prices by less than the full amount of the tax.

2. Explain why the imposition of VAT is predicted to threaten the jobs of 2,000 workers?

3. Investigate indirect taxes on goods and services. What products are exempt from VAT, and why? To what products are customs and excise duties applied, and why? What changes were made to these taxes in the last budget and why? What are the effects of these taxes on consumers and business?

New VAT squeeze on juices

A TAX on healthy fresh fruit drinks is to be imposed next month.

The new VAT squeeze caused uproar last night as the Government rushed it through the Commons in 90 minutes.

A litre of orange juice will go up from £1.95 to £2.30 in supermarkets.

Industry sources grimly predicted a fall in sales, threatening 2,000 jobs – most in South Wales and Northamptonshire.

Labour slated the $17\frac{1}{2}$ per cent tax as "wicked".

But the Treasury claims it is fair to treat fresh fruit juices the same as other drinks.

Tory MP Sir Teddy Taylor called the move "a disgrace".

He said: "This means that VAT has been introduced on to a fresh food without Parliament having had the opportunity to debate it."

Daily Mirror 4.11.93

Tariffs and quotas

Tariffs are taxes placed on the price of selected goods and services imported from overseas in order to discourage their consumption and hence reduce a balance of payments deficit (i.e. when outflows of money from the UK, in payment for imports and investments overseas, exceed inflows of money from abroad). A **quota** is a physical limit on the amount of goods that can be imported from overseas.

The European Union is committed to removing these barriers to free trade between member countries (see 17.3).

Subsidies

Subsidies are grants of money or tax allowances provided by the government to selected organizations to protect production and jobs and, in some cases, to keep prices low.

Loss-making activities: Subsidies are often paid to loss-making activities. For example, South West Railways is paid an annual subsidy to keep trains running on loss-making lines. If these subsidies were not paid, either fares would have to rise or the lines would be closed.

Protection of infant industries: new firms and industries often find it difficult to start up and compete with well established, larger foreign competitors. It is sometimes thought that these industries should be protected from competition from cheap foreign imports. The UK and EU governments may subsidize infant firms to lower their costs of production in the hope that they will eventually grow strong enough to be able to compete. The European video cassette industry is an example. The problem with this kind of policy is that protected industries never learn how to compete with stronger rivals and soon grow dependent on the protection offered. Because they never learn to compete with the best they rarely succeed. There are very few European video firms.

Regional policy: The government provides aid to business organizations in those parts of the UK designated as **development areas** in an attempt to regenerate employment, incomes, and demand in areas of industrial decline. Grants for new capital and plant are available to firms that are able to demonstrate that their productive activities help to create new jobs, or safeguard existing ones (see 22.4). The availability of regional grants may influence the location decisions of new firms.

The EU is also able to offer **structural funds** to contribute towards the cost of actions to deal with structural economic disparities within the EU. Basic rules set out in European Council regulations agreed in July 1993 specified six objectives on which funds are to be spent:

Types of area	Objective
1	Assisting areas lagging behind, e.g. N Ireland, Merseyside
2	Assisting areas of industrial decline
3	Combatting long-term unemployment
4	Helping workers to adapt to industrial change
5a	Assisting the adjustment of agricultural structures
5b	Rural development

The EU has earmarked £120 billion to be spent on these six areas between 1994 and 1999. Just over half will be spent in the four poorest member states: Spain, Portugal, Greece and Ireland. The UK's allocation will total some £9.5 billion – around £3.6 billion of which will be spent on objectives 1, 2 and 5b.

Environmental protection: Subsidies might also be used to encourage more environmentally friendly activities, for example, by subsidizing the construction of recycling facilities and plants. The government is to fund the construction of 1,000 miles of cycle lanes in and around London to encourage people to use bicycles instead of cars in order to reduce transport emissions.

Key words

Price ceiling – a maximum price imposed in a market above which market price will not be allowed to rise

Price floor – a minimum price imposed in a market below which market price will not be allowed to fall

CAP – EU Common Agricultural Policy to stabilize farm incomes in member countries

VAT – Value Added Tax levied on most goods and services

Ad valorem tax – a tax levied as a percentage of the market price of a good or service, such as VAT

Subsidies – grants of money paid to certain firms to cover their production costs in part.

Regional policy – UK and EU measures to promote business and employment opportunities in areas of industrial decline and high unemployment

---

Section 3.4 Legislation and regulation

A number of laws exist in the UK to protect consumers from unfair and anti-competitive trading and to safeguard the environment from abuse by business.

Competition policy

Underpinning government **competition policy** is a view that anti-competitive and restrictive behaviour by dominant firms in markets is against consumers' interests. Legislation and government action to increase the degree of competition in markets has, therefore, aimed to control monopolies and mergers.

Any firm, or group of firms acting together, with a market share of 25% or over is considered to be a monopoly under UK law. **Merger activity** refers to all forms of amalgamation between firms. Amalgamation occurs when two or more firms join together to form a larger enterprise. There are two main ways business amalgamation can take place: takeover or merger.

Takeovers

A takeover occurs when one company buys control of another through the **acquisition** of shares in the ownership of that company.

Takeovers can be **hostile** or **friendly**. A hostile takeover occurs when managers and shareholders in a company resist another firm's bid for ownership. This will normally require the predator company to raise additional funds to purchase ownership. A friendly takeover occurs when one firm invites or allows another to take control. This may be because the firm cannot raise the necessary finance to expand or is struggling to survive in a competitive market.

Mergers

A merger occurs when two or more firms agree to join together to form a new enterprise with a new legal identity. This is usually done by shareholders of the merging companies exchanging their existing shares for new shares in the new organization. The name of the newly created enterprise will normally reflect the names of the merging companies. For example, the merger in 1993 of AKZO and Nobel Industries, two leading European speciality chemicals groups, created the world's largest paints group, AKZO-Nobel.

Reasons for merger activity

The main reason for amalgamation between two or more organizations is to expand market share and increase market power. For example, in 1989 Thomson joined with Horizon to give the combined group a 39% share of the UK package holiday market, compared to the 14% share of their nearest rival.

Other reasons for mergers may include:

- **To enter a new market.** For example, in 1994 Virgin Retail and the Wheelock Pacific trading company, formed a joint venture to open Virgin Megastores in Hong Kong, China, and Taiwan.
- **To defend market position.** A predator may launch a hostile takeover bid for a competing firm, or two firms may agree to merge to warn off competition or counter the threat of a hostile takeover by a rival.
- To secure the supply chain by merging with a supplier
- To enjoy economies of large scale production (see 20.2)
- **For the purpose of asset stripping.** An **asset stripper** will aim to buy up another company at a market value which is less than the value of its total assets (see 22.1). It will then close down any loss-making operations and sell off the more lucrative parts of the acquired firm at a profit.

Competition Laws

The Monopolies and Trade Practices Act 1948 established a Monopolies Commission to investigate dominant firms to see if they acted in the public interest, and recommend further action if they were found to be abusing their market power. The **Monopolies and Mergers Act 1965** extended the powers of the Commission to investigate mergers and takeovers and created the Monopolies and Mergers Commission (MMC).

The **Fair Trading Act 1973** established the **Office of Fair Trading (OFT)** with responsibility for the administration of all policy relating to competition and consumer protection. The OFT is further responsible for monitoring merger activity and referring cases to the MMC for investigation.

The **Restrictive Trade Practices Act 1956** established the **Restrictive Practices Court** with which all firms engaged in restrictive practices have to register. The court then decides whether or not they are acceptable. Examples of restrictive practices include: price-fixing agreements between firms, a dominant supplier insisting that retailers stock all their entire product range or insisting they do not offer the products of rival firms.

The Monopolies and Mergers Commission

The purpose of the **Monopolies and Mergers Commission (MMC)** is to investigate and reach a judgement on whether a particular monopoly or proposed merger is in the public interest. The **1980 Competition Act** extended the powers of the MMC to investigate public sector enterprises and anti-competitive practices.

A merger or takeover falls within the scope of UK legislation if it results in a combined market share exceeding 25%, or if the gross value of combined assets is over £30 million. The MMC is able to recommend to the government the break-up of monopolies or a ban on particular merger and takeover proposals if they are thought to form monopolies which are likely to act against the public interest. For example, in 1991 the merger between Tate and Lyle and British Sugar was stopped by the MMC because the combined enterprise would have gained a 92% share of the UK sugar market.

In recent years there has been an increase in the number of mergers and takeovers in the UK referred by the Office of Fair Trading to the MMC for investigation (see table 3.2). However, in most years the MMC will complete only about 20 investigations, less than 10% of all mergers in any one year. Very few amalgamations are found to be against the public interest, leading some people to argue that the MMC is ineffectual.

Mergers and takeovers which have a 'European dimension', namely those with a combined turnover of more than ECU 5 billion (around £3.7 million in 1994) can be investigated, and if necessary blocked, by the Competition-Directorate of the European Commission.

▼ Table 3.2: Mergers/Takeovers Qualifying under the Fair Trading Act

	Number[1]	Number referred to MMC Gross	Net[2]	Number found against public interest by MMC
1980	182	3	3	0
1981	164	5	4	1
1982	190	8	7	4
1983	192	10	8	2
1984	259	9	7	4
1985	192	6	6	0
1986	313	14	10	1
1987	321	8	6	3
1988	306	10	8	3
1989	281	14	12	1
1990	261	20	17	2

1. 25% market share rule and £30 million asset size criteria
2. Some mergers/takeovers were 'dropped' after referral

Office of Fair Trading

Advanced Business

Portfolio Activity 3.5

Range: Reasons for government intervention, Ways, Evaluate
Skills: Produce written material, Collect and record data, Present information

1. What is a merger? What were the motives behind the merger between Allied Lyons and Carlsberg?

2. Why was the merger intially thought to be against the public interest by the MMC?

3. How might the conditions set by the MMC for the merger to go ahead inject more competition into the beer and lager market?

4. Research and produce a factsheet for business on competition policy in the UK, using desktop publishing software. This should include a description of the role of competition policy, practices that are outlawed, and the responsibilities of the OFT, the MMC, and the Restrictive Practices Court. Recent examples of OFT and MMC investigations from newspaper articles can be included to illustrate points made in your factsheet (see also the Chapter 1 Assignment and Portfolio Activity 2.4).

Monopolies opposition to Allied–Carlsberg link-up

ALLIED-Lyons and the Danish brewer Carlsberg are being forced to re-negotiate plans to merge their British brewing operations after the Monopolies & Mergers Commission decided that the deal would operate against the public interest.

Despite the commission's opposition to the £510m Carlsberg–Tetley merger, primarily on the grounds that it would increase concentration in the lager market, it attracted three conditions which would allow it to proceed.

Allied and Carlsberg, which would together have 21pc of lager production behind Courage's 22pc and Bass' 24pc, said they were confident of finding a "mutually acceptable way forward."

Daily Telegraph 29.7.92

A deal could be finalised in two months. The conditions which the brewers must now thrast out with Sir Brian Carsberg, the director-general of fair trading are:

- that they undertake not to increase the price of beer supplied to Carlsberg's existing regional brewer or independent wholesaler customers for three years.
- that they cut the length of a supply agreement between the merged companies and Allied's pubs from seven to five years.
- that Allied tennants be free, after two years, to buy up to half of their annual lager requirements from other suppliers.

The European Commission, which also investigated the deal, has reached much the same conclusion.

It said the five biggest brewers already account for almost 80pc of beer production and after the merger would brew almost 90pc of lager.

Weighing up the merger, which brings together three of the top selling brands, the Monopolies Commission said it would have both positive and detrimental effects on competition.

The merged company, it said, would be a more effective brewer with a better balanced portfolio of brands able to compete more vigorously against its bigger rivals. But it said removing Carlsberg as an independent supplier to pubs would lessen competition and adversely affect regional brewers and independent wholesalers, particularly in supplying lager to the free trade.

Consumer protection

Consumer protection is about helping consumers get a fair deal when they buy goods and services. Many years ago there was very little consumer protection. The basis of the law relating to the sale and advertising of products was known as *caveat emptor* – 'let the buyer beware'. Consumers had to make purchases at their own risk.

However, a vast array of goods and services are available to consumers today, many imported from overseas. Consumers cannot be expected to have the detailed technical knowledge to evaluate all the different products available. More than ever before, they must rely on business organizations for information and advice on what to buy.

A number of organizations exist to advise consumers and protect their interests from large powerful producers who may be tempted to misinform or be economical with the truth. For example, the Consumers Association publishes the *Which?* magazine series which carry expert product evaluations. TV programmes, such as *Watchdog* perform a similar role and publicize consumer complaints.

A large number of laws exist relating to safety, price, advertising messages, choice, and quality of goods and services (see 11.3). For example, the Food Safety Act 1990 states that all food must be prepared and sold in hygienic conditions, and all pre-packed foods must display a list of contents.

The emphasis in law has changed from *caveat emptor* to *caveat vendor* – 'let the seller beware!'

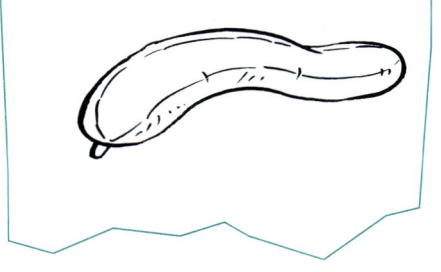

Regulation (and deregulation)

A vast array of rules and regulations apply to business activities in the UK, from the conditions in licenses for public houses and taxis, to shop opening hours and health, safety and environmental standards. An increasing number of regulations from the EU are also affecting UK business, from issues such as the treatment of cider as wine for taxation purposes to the appropriate name for soya milk.

However, the **1994 Deregulation and Contracting Out Act** aims to streamline and remove around 450 statutory regulations on business. Some of the regulations are clearly out of date and need to be replaced, whereas others are thought to be too restrictive and reduce the competitiveness of UK firms. Areas covered in the act include restrictions on shop opening hours, children in pubs, building society lending, and rules applying to mergers. The legislation will also allow the contracting out of public sector services to private firms, which was formerly illegal.

How bendy is your one?

In 1988 the European Commission created four cucumber classifications, setting standards for each class – including the amount of curve per 10cm. Top class cucumbers had to be practically straight. Other cucumbers—the ones with kinks in – were quite legitimate but unclassified.

▼ Deregulation

Legal oddities in line for abolition

One of the strongest arguments for the government's drive against red tape is the sheer oddity of some of the regulations being abolished.

For example, methylated spirits cannot be sold between 10pm on Saturday and 8am on Monday. Meths drinking, the Department of Trade and Industry says, is a thing of the past, so legislation enacted 105 years ago can be repealed.

Scottish hairdressers are not allowed to open on Sunday, English haircuts on the Sabbath are apparently legal.

Shops need a specific licence for selling kettle de-scaler. It is classed as a poison.

Financial Times 20.1.94

A taste of the 450 measures to be swept away:

- A change in the basis of Health and Safety legislation. At present, outdated legislation cannot be removed unless it is replaced
- Changes in the definition of a newspaper proprietor under competition law. The present requirement to investigate newspaper mergers catches some deals not involving newspapers at all
- Companies which have ceased trading will be allowed to apply to be struck off the register, thus being relieved of their Companies Act obligations
- Shops and supermarkets in Scotland will be allowed to sell alcohol on Sunday between 12.30pm and 10pm. This is now prohibited, though pubs are allowed to sell alcohol all day
- The act requiring employment agencies to be licensed is to be repealed.
- Goods vehicles and public service vehicles must now have their licences renewed every five years. This is to be replaced by a system of continuous licensing
- Local authorities will no longer be responsible for the supervision of slaughterhouses
- Duplication in rules for the design and construction of buildings will be eliminated
- Paperwork on the transfer of waste will be simplified
- Several new areas of public service will be subjected to market testing. These include the administration of civil service pension schemes, the enforcement of milk hygiene and the invalid vehicle scheme

However, while the government is aiming to remove some regulations on industry, it is introducing other measures that are intended to influence market outcomes. For example, planning guidance issued to local authorities in 1994 encourages them to take planning decisions that limit the scale of out-of-town developments, particularly large retail outlets, and reduce the use of private cars in favour of increased public transport use. The government is keen to prevent the spread of out-of-town superstores which can be reached only by car, despite the demand for them from the retailers themselves and from shoppers. The guidance strongly recommends placing new shopping, leisure and housing developments close together and near to existing public transport links to limit the need for journey making.

Environmental protection

Laws have been passed which make it illegal to pollute the environment. The **Clean Air Act** and **Environmental Protection Act** set limits on the type and amount of pollutants firms can discharge into the atmosphere, rivers, and seas. A new environment bill under consideration by Parliament in early 1995 proposes to merge the UK's three main environment regulators – the National Rivers Authority, Her Majesty's Inspectorate of Pollution, and the Waste Regulation Authorities. The new Environment Agency for England and Wales and the Scottish Environment Protection Agency will be largely responsible for the control of industrial pollution and waste, and for the regulation of the water environment.

Many firms are now voluntarily developing their own codes of practice regarding the environment due to pressure in the market from consumers. An increasing number of firms are producing environmental performance reports along with their end-of-year profit and loss statements and balance sheets (see 24.1). The Confederation of British Industry (CBI) has also issued guidelines stressing that 'firms should establish policies to secure openness in safety, health and environmental information and should make adequate arrangements for their application in practice'.

Key words

Competition policy – government actions that aim to increase the degree of competition in markets

Merger activity – amalgamations between two or more firms, usually with the intention to increase market share

Takeover – when one firm buys a controlling interest in another firm

Merger – when two or more firms agree to combine their operations

Asset stripping – buying up another firm at a low price with the intention of selling off its assets at a higher price

Office of Fair Trading (OFT) – government body responsible for the administration of all policy relating to competition and consumer protection in the UK.

Monopolies and Mergers Commission (MMC) – government body that investigates legal monopolies, merger activity, and anti-competitive practices by firms. If they are found not to be in the public interest, the MMC can recommend appropriate action.

Deregulation – the removal of statutory restrictions on competition

Section 3.5 **Public ownership and privatization**

Public Ownership

Following the end of the Second World War a number of industries were nationalized in the UK, including coal, steel, and the railways. Nationalization refers to the transfer of a whole industry from private to public ownership by the passing of an act of parliament forcing the private owners of firms to sell their shares to the government. Nationalized industries are defined as those public corporations which trade directly with consumers.

Why were industries nationalized?

UK governments have in the past taken into public ownership entire industries, such as railways, coal, and shipbuilding, for the following reasons:

- **To promote economies of scale:** As firms grow in size they may be able to lower the average cost of producing each unit of output. Economies of scale refer to cost savings associated with large-scale production (see 20.2). Some industries need to be very large, even to the extent that they become a monopoly supplier, in order to take full advantage of the cost savings large-scale production can bring.

- **To control natural monopolies and avoid wasteful duplication:** Imagine five different private firms competing to supply gas to your home. Five sets of pipes would be required where only one is necessary. In this case competition between firms would be wasteful.

  A firm is a **natural monopoly** if the most efficient size of that firm is one that supplies the whole market. Examples of natural monopolies include the supply of gas and water through pipelines, and electricity through the National Grid. In a natural monopoly resources can be combined in the most productive and cost-effective way. State ownership enabled these industries to develop to their most efficient size. However, in private hands such large firms may abuse their market power to push up prices to consumers.

- **For safety:** Some industries, such as nuclear energy, were thought to be too dangerous to be controlled by private entrepreneurs.

- **To protect employment:** Some firms were nationalized because they faced closure as private sector loss-making organizations. For example, in 1975 the government rescued British Leyland to protect the jobs of car workers.

- **To maintain public services:** Private sector firms will not continue to provide goods and services if they make a loss. Under public ownership, loss-making services, such as rail lines and postal services in remote areas, or supplies of gas or electricity to households that consume very little, can be subsidized using tax revenues.

Nationalized industries 1982

- British Coal
- National Girobank
- Electricity (England and Wales)
- British Airways
- N of Scotland Hydro Electric
- British Airports Authority
- S of Scotland Electricity
- British Rail
- British Gas
- British Waterways
- British Steel
- National Bus Company
- British Telecom
- Scottish Transport Group
- Post Office
- British Shipbuilders
- London Transport
- Civil Aviation Authority

Privatization

The Economist 21.8.93

British Gas plc Offer for Sale
by
N M Rothschild & Sons Limited
on behalf of
The Secretary of State for Energy

Under the Offer for Sale in the United Kingdom and separate offerings in the United States, Canada, Japan and Europe

4,025,500,000 Ordinary Shares of 25p each are being offered

at 135p per share

of which 50p is payable now,

45p is payable on 9th June, 1987 and

40p is payable on 19th April, 1988

Since 1979 public ownership of entire industries has been reduced significantly as many nationalized enterprises and other public sector activities have been returned to the private sector. **Privatization** involves private firms taking over public sector activities. It can take many forms:

- **The sale of public sector assets:** Here, shares in government-owned nationalized industries are sold to the general public and private sector firms. The first most significant sale was in 1984 when shares in British Telecom were sold (see figure 3.7).

Privatization also includes the sale of major assets owned by the government. For example, in 1982 the government sold 51% of shares in Britoil, a part of the British National Oil Corporation (BNOC).

The government has also sold shares it held in private sector companies, such as British Petroleum, ICI, and Cable and Wireless.

THE PRIVATIZATION PROGRAMME
SALES TO DATE

1979–80	British Petroleum ICI. Suez Finance Company and other miscellaneous	1981–82	British Sugar Cable and Wireless Amersham International National Freight Miscellaneous plus Crown Agent and Forestry Commission land and property sales	1984–85	Enterprise Oil British Gas onshore oil Sealink ferries Jaguar cars British Telecom	1988–89	British Steel Trustee Savings Bank British Leyland
1980–81	Ferranti Fairey North Sea Oil: Licenses British Aerospace Miscellaneous and small NEB			1985–86	British Airports Royal Ordnance factories	1989–90	Regional Water Authorities
						1990–91	Electricity Area Boards
		1982–83	Britoil Associated British Ports Sales of oil licenses, oil stockpiles and miscellaneous	1986–87	British Gas	1991–92	Electricity Generation
				1987–88	British Airways British Airports Authority Rolls Royce Leyland Bus and Truck	FUTURE SALES	British Rail franchises British Coal Executive Agencies Nuclear electric Scottish nuclear fuels
		1983–84	BR Hotels Cable and Wireless				

▲ *Figure 3.7: The privatization programme*

Nationalized industries 1994

British Coal
Railtrack (rail network & stations)
Post office
Nuclear electric
Scottish nuclear
British shipbuilders
Civil Aviation Authority
London Transport
National Girobank
Scottish Water
British Rail (passenger services)

▼ *Local services are now operated by private firms*

By 1994 about two-thirds of the nationalized industry sector of the early 1980s and more than 920,000 jobs had been transferred to the private sector.

- **Joint ventures with the private sector:** In other cases, privatization can take the form of joint ventures between public sector concerns and private firms, for example the Crossrail project to build a rail link between major rail terminals in east and west London.

- **Contracting out:** Many local authorities now invite private sector firms to compete for jobs such as refuse collection, parking enforcement, school catering, and road-sweeping. This is known as **tendering**. Contracts are awarded on the basis of a private firm providing a low-price, quality service. Also, private firms can now build and operate prisons on behalf of the government. Former police duties, such as prisoner escort services, are also under contract to private firms, such as Group4.

- **Franchising:** In 1994 the government split British Rail up to form Railtrack, a new body responsible for track and signalling infrastructure, and a number of separate train operating organizations responsible for providing passenger services over given areas of network. It is the intention of the government to offer these as **franchises** to different private sector organizations who will compete to win a franchise (see 4.2). They will have to pay Railtrack charges for track access, lease trains from public leasing companies, and pay others for using depots and stations.

  Purchase of a franchise to run a rail service for an agreed period of time will be subject to certain conditions concerning minimum service levels, quality standards, and other requirements such as through ticketing. Franchise operators will be accountable to the new Rail Regulator who will licence all train operators, and to the Health and Safety Executive.

- **Deregulation:** Deregulation does not involve a transfer of ownership between the public and private sector. It refers to the removal of state controls limiting competition in markets (see 3.4). An example is the provision of bus services, which are now free to be provided by private operators in most major UK cities.

In 1993 the government announced that all controls on the gas supply market that currently preserve the British Gas monopoly in the UK would end in April 1998. New gas suppliers will then be able to sell gas to any industrial customer and to new domestic customers.

▼ *A deregulated bus service*

Advanced Business

Portfolio Activity 3.6

Range: Ways, Evaluate
Skills: Produce written material, Collect and record data

Find out about local refuse collection. Has your local council contracted out refuse collection to a private firm or is it still operated by the public sector?

Imagine that the council has employed you as a consultant to consider: A Whether the privatization of refuse collection services has been successful and if private sector involvement should continue, OR B If the service is still a public sector activity, what would be the likely impacts of privatization on the council and local residents.

1. Write a report of your findings. You will need to make a list of the criteria on which you can judge the past and present performance of the local refuse collection service, for example, operating costs, service frequency, workforce levels, customer satisfaction, the cost to local taxpayers, etc. You will need to gather information on your selected performance criteria from the local council and people who live in your area. Also, consider the business objectives of the local council and private contractors who undertake refuse collection services. Do their objectives conflict or complement each other?

2. After you have completed your report, make a short presentation of your findings to your class. Develop charts, posters, or overhead slides as appropriate to illustrate your presentation. Use a computer to help you if available. (If possible, invite a local council official to listen to your presentations and to discuss the findings of your class).

TORIES WANT TO SELL OFF STONEHENGE

THE TORIES want to sell Stonehenge, it was revealed last night.

Treasury ministers, determined to cut public spending, are pressing for the privatization of historic sites– also including Edinburgh Castle and Dover Castle–to raise cash.

Daily Mirror 6.8.94

The arguments for privatization

- **To stop government abuse of monopoly power:** Because consumer demand for commodities such as gas and electricity tends to be price inelastic, it has been argued that governments have in the past simply raised prices to fund increases in public expenditure.

- **To increase efficiency:** It has been argued that public sector activities were inefficient and provided poor services because they faced no competition and did not have to return a profit. Privatization would allow these enterprises to operate for profit. Competition and profit provide the incentive to greater efficiency to reduce costs, lower prices and improve quality.

- **To raise government revenue:** Between 1979 and 1993 sales of nationalized industries raised a total of £50 billion. The sale of British Gas shares raised over £6 billion alone.

- **To give ownership to the people:** People have been encouraged to buy shares in the ownership of privatized industries. As shareholders, they have the right to vote on how these companies should be run and can earn dividends on their shares when these companies make profits.

The arguments against privatization

- **Competition breaks up economies of scale:** If the most efficient size of a firm is one that supplies the whole market for a particular product, then breaking that firm up into a number of smaller competing firms will be inefficient and raise costs and prices.

- **The public interest is no longer protected:** Services that make a loss will be closed by private sector firms aiming for profit. The privatization of the rail network has raised fears that rail services to remote areas and off-peak services which do not earn a profit will be closed.

- **It does not return ownership to the people:** Instead, most shares in the ownership of privatized industries are held by large financial institutions such as banks and insurance companies' funds (see Figure 22.5). Many have also been snapped up by non-UK companies.

- **Private monopolies exploit consumers:** Those opposed to the sale of nationalized industries argue that privatization has created private sector monopolies able to restrict output to force up prices.

However, competition is slowly being introduced into industries without sacrificing their natural monopoly element. For example, Mercury has the right to use British Telecom phonelines, and regional electricity companies will be able to compete to supply households and firms in each others' regions through the national grid after 1998.

The regulation of privatized industries

Because privatization created some private sector monopolies, UK governments have also set up specialist agencies to regulate the activities of these industries:

- **OFTEL** (Office of Telecommunications) set up in 1984 to regulate British Telecom plc
- **OFGAS** (Office of Gas Supplies) created in 1986 to regulate British Gas plc
- **OFWAT** (Office of Water Services) set up in 1989 following the creation of the private regional water companies.
- **OFFER** (Office of Electricity Regulation) created in 1991 to regulate the 12 regional electricity companies
- **ORR** (Office of the Rail Regulator) set up in 1994 to monitor the newly franchised rail services.

Each of the regulators has different powers, but their main functions are to ensure safety requirements, introduce competition where possible, and operate a system of price controls.

Annual price rises are capped by the regulators, the idea being that caps would encourage efficiency as companies would be only be able to earn higher profits if they increased the size of their markets and/or cut their costs. The price caps are usually set with reference to the annual percentage rate of price inflation as measured by the Retail Prices Index (RPI). For example, in 1994 OFGAS allowed British Gas to raise prices for household consumers by only RPI – 4%. As the RPI was below 4% in 1994, British Gas had to cut gas prices.

Portfolio Activity 3.7

Range: Reasons for government intervention, Ways, Evaluate

Skills: Produce written material, Collect and record data, Present information

Investigate a privatized organization such as British Gas or one of the regional electricity supply companies.

1. Produce a list of criteria on which you may judge the performance of the privatized organisation over time from the point of view of its consumers and business owners. Gather evidence on the performance of the organization on each criteria.

2. Produce a word-processed report on:
   - The reasons for the privatization
   - How the industry was privatized
   - How ownership has changed
   - The performance of the industry since privatization (and if possible, before privatization)

   Useful sources of information will be annual reports of your chosen company and business magazine and newspaper articles (including archive material on CD-ROM).

Key words

Nationalization – transferring the ownership of private sector firms in an industry to the public sector

Nationalized industries – public sector enterprises which trade directly with consumers

Privatization – the sale of public sector assets to private individuals and firms

Further reading:

Moynihan, D, and Titley, B: *Economics – A Complete Course* (Oxford University Press 1993) Chapters 10, 16, and 20

Test questions:

The following underpinning knowledge will be tested;
1. The reasons for government intervention in markets
2. The ways in which governments can influence markets
3. Evaluate the effects of government policy on markets

Questions 1–3 share the following answer options:
- A Raise income tax
- B Raise selected excise duties
- C Raise public expenditure
- D Cut interest rates

Which of the above policies would you advise the government to use in an attempt to:

1 Increase employment opportunities?

2 Reduce the consumption of cigarettes?

3 Increase consumer borrowing?

4 Corporation tax rates on company profits have been reduced in recent years. Fiscal policy is being used in this case to:
- A Encourage firms to lower their product prices
- B Enable firms to pass on higher dividends to shareholders
- C Encourage firms to invest in new plant and machinery
- D Encourage firms to pay higher wages

Question 5–7 share the following answer options:
- A To reduce unemployment
- B To reduce pollution
- C To increase competition
- D To protect domestic food supplies

Which of the above objectives do the following organisations or policies seek to achieve?

5 EU Common Agricultural Policy

6 Monopolies and Mergers Commission

7 The Environment Agency

8 Which of the following is unlikely to be a reason for the privatization of public sector activities?
- A To increase business management and efficiency
- B To give consumers more choice
- C To break up economies of scale
- D To raise government revenue

Questions 9–11 share the following answer options:
- A Income tax
- B Corporation tax
- C VAT
- D Tariffs

Which of the above taxes could be increased to:

9 Reduce disposable income?

10 Reduce investment by business?

11 Reduce the demand for imported goods?

12 Which of the following is **not** an argument in favour of imposing restrictions on imports?
- A To reduce domestic unemployment
- B To protect domestic firms from foreign competition
- C To increase consumer choice
- D To protect an infant industry

Questions 13–15 share the following answer options:
- A Competition policy
- B Regional Policy
- C Fiscal Policy
- D Monetary policy

Which of the above policies

13 Uses interest rates to influence the general level of economic activity?

14 Regulates monopolies and merger activity?

15 Provides financial assistance to new and existing firms in areas of high unemployment?

16 A Suggest and explain four reasons why the UK government intervenes in product markets.

B What is fiscal policy? How can the policy be used to help create employment and business opportunities?

C What is monetary policy? How can it be used to boost investment in new plant and machinery by business?

D Using examples, explain how indirect taxes can be used to influence the price and quantity traded of particular goods and services.

17 A Suggest and explain two reasons why entire industries in the UK were taken into public ownership in the past.

B What is privatization? List two industries that have been privatized in the UK.

C What are the arguments for and against the privatization of rail services in the UK?

18 A What is difference between a merger and a takeover?

B Explain two reasons for merger and takeovers in business.

C What is the aim of competition policy in the UK?

D Explain the role of the Monopolies and Mergers Commission in UK competition policy.

E Give three examples of other regulations on business activity.

Assessment assignment

Range: Reasons for government intervention
Ways
Evaluate
Government policies

Skills: Communication
Produce written materials
Use illustrations and images
Read and respond to written materials
Application of number
Collect and record data
Interpret and present data
Information technology
Prepare information
Process information
Present information

Business Monthly magazine has asked you to produce an article for their next issue discussing the impact on business of UK and EU government intervention in markets. The article should be produced using a word processor with an ability to capture relevant graphs produced with other software packages or an integrated desktop publishing application.

The magazine editor has asked that the article should include case study material on two chosen local or national markets for particular goods or services. One should be a market served by a newly or soon-to-be-privatized organization.

You have agreed the following format and content list for your article with the editor:

1. A general discussion of the reasons for government intervention in various markets, with examples of markets and measures.
2. A focus on a particular product market to consider the effects of various interventionist measures taken by the UK and EU government. For example, consider the impact on business location of regional policy and planning guidance issued by the UK government to local authorities. Also, what impact will measures undertaken in the last budget have on employment and business opportunities and decisions?
3. A focus on a newly privatized industry or local activity. What were the reasons for privatization? What method of privatization was used? What impact has it had on employees and business? What regulations exist to control the privatized organization and why?

Useful sources of information will include:

- Local and national newspapers (including archive material on CD-ROM)
- Interviews with business owners or managers affected by intervention
- Department of Trade and Industry
- Office of Fair Trading
- Local Authorities

Business Organizations and Systems

Unit Two

unit 2

chapter 4	Business Organizations (Element 2.1)
chapter 5	Administration Systems (Elements 2.2)
chapter 6	Communications Systems (Elements 2.3)
chapter 7	Information Processing (Elements 2.4)

Advanced Business

chapter 4 Business ORGANIZATIONS

This chapter investigates the types of business organization that exist, their purposes and how management and authority is structured and organized within them.

Key ideas

Different types of private-sector business organizations can be distinguished by the way in which they are financed and managed, and the liability of business owners to repay business debts.

Some business owners have **unlimited liability**. If their business fails, they are personally responsible for all business debts. Others may have **limited liability**: if their business fails, they only stand to lose the money they invested in it.

Most private-sector business organizations produce goods and services to make a profit. A business organization may have a number of objectives in addition to seeking profit. These can include **expanding market share, providing a public service**, as well as social, environmental, and **charitable** concerns.

Sole traders are business organizations owned and controlled by one person. **Partnerships** are owned and controlled by more than two people. **Joint stock companies** are owned by their shareholders, who will elect directors to run them.

Public limited companies (plcs) may advertise and sell shares to the general public. Shares in **private limited companies** can only be sold privately to people known to existing shareholders.

Some business organizations have operations in more than one country. These are known as **multinationals**.

Public-sector organizations are owned and controlled by central and local government. They include **government departments, public corporations, enterprise agencies**, and **QUANGO'S**.

The **internal structure** of business organizations will determine the relationships between managers and their subordinates which are necessary to achieve business objectives.

The most common method of establishing formal relationships between individuals is by organizing departments. The human resources in each **department** specialize in a particular task within the organization.

Some departments perform the main **line functions** in a business, namely, **production, sales,** and **marketing**. Others perform a **staff function**, such as **personnel, finance** and **accounting**, and **maintenance**, to provide support for line departments.

The **hierarchy** in a business refers to the layers of management from the most senior managers down to managers or supervisors of the lowest rank. The hierarchy shows the **chain of command**.

A hierarchical organization may be **flat** or **tall** depending on the **span of control** of managers over their subordinates. Flat organizations are those which have relatively few or even just one level of management.

In a **centralized organization**, authority, responsibility, and decision-making are concentrated at the top of the hierarchy. In a **decentralized organization**, authority and responsibility are delegated to lower levels of management.

The structure of an organization may be affected by the **size, location, management style**, and **type of product** of the business, and by external pressures such as **competition, new markets, technology,** and **changes in ownership**.

Section 4.1 Types of business organization

There are three main types of business organization in the UK;

- **Private firms** are owned and controlled by private individuals and can range from small one-person businesses to large multinational corporations.
- **Cooperatives** are owned either by consumers who buy from them or by the employees who work in them.
- **Public-sector enterprises** are owned and controlled by government

▼ Figure 4.1: Types of business organization

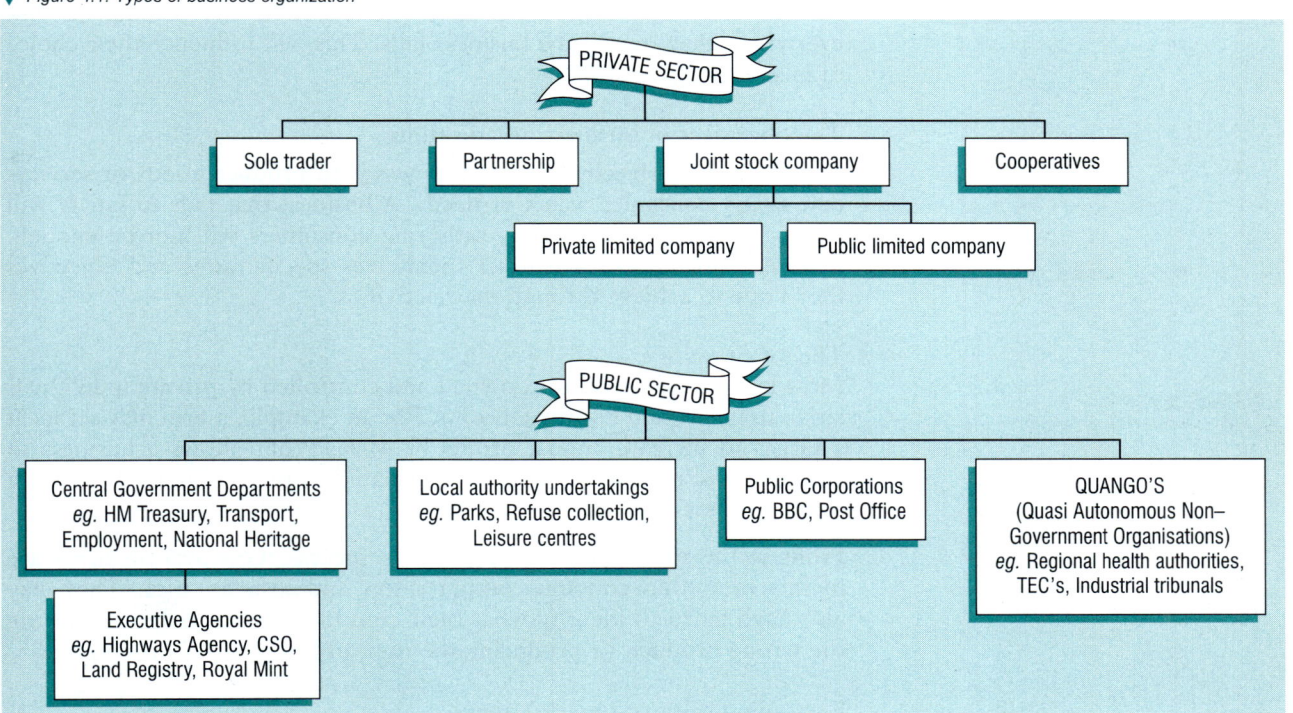

PRIVATE SECTOR
- Sole trader
- Partnership
- Joint stock company
  - Private limited company
  - Public limited company
- Cooperatives

PUBLIC SECTOR
- Central Government Departments
  eg. HM Treasury, Transport, Employment, National Heritage
  - Executive Agencies
    eg. Highways Agency, CSO, Land Registry, Royal Mint
- Local authority undertakings
  eg. Parks, Refuse collection, Leisure centres
- Public Corporations
  eg. BBC, Post Office
- QUANGO'S
  (Quasi Autonomous Non–Government Organisations)
  eg. Regional health authorities, TEC's, Industrial tribunals

A private individual who wishes to start his or her own business will need to consider three main questions.

- **Will I have enough money?** To start a business, an entrepreneur will need capital. This is the money used to buy premises, machinery, equipment, and materials (see 22.1). Some businesses will need more capital than others. If a person cannot raise enough money on their own, they may need to find other people, or partners, who will help finance the business and share in its ownership.

- **Can I manage the business alone?** Running a business on your own will often require working long hours and being a 'jack of all trades'. For example, a self-employed carpenter must not only be a skilled carpenter, but will also need to manage the business, do the accounts, advertise, employ staff if necessary, pay the bills, and much more. Setting up in business with other people can help to spread the load.

Unlimited liability

- **Will I risk everything I own?** The owner of any business is entitled to a share of any profits made. However, if the business fails, they may also be responsible for paying any debts.

Some business owners have **unlimited liability**. This means that they are liable to pay all business debts and may have to sell their personal possessions–house, car, furniture, jewellery - to do so. Business owners can be taken to Court and declared bankrupt if debts are not repaid.

However, some business owners enjoy **limited liability**. This means that if their business fails, they only stand to lose the money they invested in it. They will not have to sell personal possessions to raise money to clear business debts. This reduces their risk. An entrepreneur must therefore decide when financing a business whether they are willing to risk everything they own if the business fails. This will influence their choice of business organization.

The objectives of business organizations

The overriding objective of any business is to produce goods or services that satisfy consumer wants or needs. A business that fails to satisfy will not survive. However, simply satisfying consumers will not be enough. Different organizations will set themselves specific aims and objectives they hope to achieve through their activities.

The profit motive

Most business organizations owned and controlled by private individuals strive to make, and improve, profits. For an example, a firm may set itself a target to increase annual profits by 10%. Profit allows a business to continue and to expand. Profit is calculated as the difference between a firm's revenues and its costs.

Profit is the main measure of business success. Loss-making firms are inefficient and uneconomic: output is low and costs are high. They may also have failed to identify what their consumers want, either producing the wrong product, or producing the right product at the wrong price.

Expanding sales and market share

Not all firms will seek to maximize their profits in the short run. They may have other objectives, such as expanding sales and market share - that is, trying to sell more than rival firms (see 2.1). This may be especially important if the firm is promoting a new product or entering a new market, perhaps overseas. In the short run, they may have to make price cuts and spend heavily on advertising and promotion, both of which can reduce potential profits.

Providing a public service

Organizations owned and controlled by the government have an objective to provide a service that is in the public interest. Some services may be provided free at the point of use, such as the National Health Service, the Police, and street lighting. Other services may be charged for, but may still operate at a loss, such as rail and postal services to rural areas. Losses made by these services are subsidized by profits made by other services provided by the organization, and from general tax revenues.

▼ The NHS provides a public service

Charity

A number of private business organizations belong to what is called the **voluntary sector** of the economy. This consists of charities and other non-profit-making organizations such as:

- Registered charities, for example Save the Children and the RSPCA
- Charitable trusts, which are set up to run schools, homes for the elderly, etc.

Charitable organizations rely heavily on donations of money and endowments to provide help and care for people and animals in need - those without the ability to pay for food, healthcare, and protection from cruelty and exploitation. Organizations such as Liberty, Oxfam, and the British Heart Foundation, do not aim to make a profit from their activities. All monies received by these and other charities are used to cover the cost of their operations.

Some non-profit making organizations, however, are not charities. For example, building societies do not make profits from their activities in the true sense of the word, but do generate revenues in excess of their costs. This surplus revenue is distributed as extra interest on savers accounts or ploughed back into new premises and equipment to expand the organizations. Similarly, local clubs may be run as non profit making enterprises.

Portfolio Activity 4.1

Range: Objectives
Skills: Read and respond to written material

1. Identify the products and objectives of the organizations in the articles and photograph below.

Marlboro price cut made permanent

PHILIP MORRIS, which shocked the tobacco industry in April by cutting the price of its best-selling Marlboro cigarettes, said it will make the cut permanent and extend it to other brands, despite the damage it has caused the company's profits.

The temporary price cut, equal to 40 cents a pack in the US, has reversed the decline in Marlboro's sales, increasing its market share by two to four points, chief executive Michael Miles said yesterday.

The Independent 21.7.93

The League Against Cruel Sports was established in 1924 to oppose cruelty to animals inflicted in the course of human recreation and 'sport'. The League's priority is to campaign for the abolition of 'sports' which cause suffering and death to wildlife – in particular the hunting with dogs of foxes, hares and deer.

In order to expose the cruelties of legal bloodsports and to bring to justice those involved in illegal bloodsports, the League utilises undercover operators and, if necessary, initiates private prosecutions through the courts. The League also offers free legal advice to farmers and landowners whose property is invaded by unwelcome hunts and often provides full legal facilities to enable members to seek redress in the civil courts.

The League also owns 38 wildlife sanctuaries where all bloodsports are prohibited.

LACS Annual Report 1993

Advanced Business

Yesterday's merger between Akzo of the Netherlands and Nobel of Sweden is the largest transaction in the European chemicals industry for a decade.

The industrial and financial logic of the complex deal, effectively a takeover of Nobel by Akzo, is impeccable. Akzo assumes Nobel's crippling debts of SKr10.7bn (£880m) and refinances them at far lower cost. At the same time the Dutch group acquires Nobel's chemicals and coatings operations, creating the largest paints group in the world.

Financial Times 9.11.93

MARGARET FREARSON, of Derbyshire, built up her business supplying agricultural products to local farmers.

This meant convincing a traditionally conservative community that as a woman she should be taken seriously in this sort of business. She had to combine her business with nursing her husband through a long and fatal illness.

Today, Margaret employs seven people and has just taken on a new rep, who is being trained in the business.

Turnover, which is more than £1 million, is already up by £80,000 over the previous year.

Daily Mail 24.1.94

Wychwood gets £500,000 to expand Hobgoblinns

SPIRITS will have been higher than normal at Wychwood Brewery's celebration of Halloween this weekend.

The company has just secured £500,000 to expand its chain of Hobgoblinns – pubs themed on ghouls and ghosties.

The first Hobgoblinn opened a year ago in Staines, Surrey, and has been joined by others in Bristol, Bath, Brighton and High Wycombe. It is planned to open a further four by next spring.

The Independent 1.11.93

2. What are the objectives of your school/college? Find out by interviewing your head teacher or principal. Contrast their business objectives with those of a local business with which you are familiar.

Key words

Capital - money used to finance the purchase of business assets, such as plant and machinery

Unlimited liability - when business owners are liable for all business debts

Limited liability - when business owners can only lose the amount of money they invested in a business and are not liable to repay all business debts

Profit - an excess of revenues over costs

Section **4.2** Private sector business organizations

We can distinguish between the different types of private sector business organizations by asking the following questions:

- Who owns the business?
- Who controls the business?
- What is the main source of finance?

▼ Sole traders

The sole trader

Ownership and control
The oldest and most popular type of business is the sole trader - a business that is owned and controlled by one person. Many small businesses such as local shopkeepers, market stall traders, plumbers, and hairdressers, operate as sole traders. There are more sole traders in the UK than any other type of business. In fact, many of the very large and successful businesses today started life as sole traders many years ago.

Finance
A sole trader is someone who is self-employed. To start their business, they will usually dip into their own savings or borrow from family and friends. Sole traders will also tend to rely on an overdraft facility at the bank in order to make payments, obtain credit from their suppliers, hire purchase for the purchase of equipment, and credit card companies (see 22.2).

Sole traders may grow to employ several people or have a number of branches, but so long as there is only one owner the business will remain a sole trader.

▼ Advantages and disadvantages of being a sole trader

Advantages	Disadvantages
Easy to set up - there are no legal formalities or fees	The owner may have limited funds and may find it difficult to borrow money from banks
The owner is his/her own boss and can make all the decisions	The owner may have to work long hours and cannot afford to be off sick
The owner keeps all the profits	The owner has unlimited liability
Can be set up with relatively little capital	The owner must be a 'jack of all trades'
Personal contact with customers can encourage consumer loyalty	Small businesses are often unable to benefit from bulk purchase discounts

Partnerships

Ownership and control

Under the Partnership Act 1890, a partnership is defined as an agreement between 2 to 20 people providing capital and working together in a business with the objective of making a profit. Partnerships are common in professions such as doctors, insurance brokers, and vets, although they can also be found in other occupations such as builders, garages, and in small factories. Firms of accountants, solicitors, and members of the Stock Exchange are allowed to have more than 20 partners.

Although it is not required in law, most partnerships operate according to terms drawn up in a **Deed of Partnership**. This is a document that sets out matters such as how much capital each partner has invested in the business and therefore how much they own; how profits (and losses) are shared among the partners, and procedures for accepting new partners. If no agreement is drawn up, the rights and obligations of partners are determined by the 1890 Partnership Act.

Finance

A sole trader may find it difficult to manage a business alone or raise enough finance to expand. A partnership can help overcome this problem. To become a partner in a firm, it is necessary for the prospective partner to buy his or her way into the partnership, thus providing existing partners with additional capital.

Banks may be more willing to lend money to a partnership because the security offered by a group of partners is likely to be more than that of sole trader.

▼ *Advantages and disadvantages of a partnership*

Advantages	Disadvantages
Easy to set up. There are few legal formalities	Partners may disagree
More capital can be injected into the business	Partners have unlimited liability
Partners can have a variety of useful skills, bring new ideas and help decision-making	Partnerships may still lack capital
Partners can cover for each other during periods of sickness and holidays	Profits have to be shared
	A partnership will automatically end, or is dissolved, if one partner resigns, dies, or is made bankrupt

Under the 1907 Partnership Act, **ordinary partnerships** can be turned into **limited partnerships** where at least one partner, known as a **sleeping partner**, has limited liability. Sleeping partners provide capital for the business and take a share of the profits but take no active part in the day to day running of it.

Joint stock companies

Joint stock companies are also known as **limited companies**. They differ significantly from sole traders and partnerships in the way in which they are financed, owned, and controlled.

> **Portfolio Activity 4.3**
>
> **Range:** Types of ownership, Differences
> **Skills:** Collect and record data
>
> Look around your local area and identify businesses that are:
> - Sole traders
> - Partnerships
>
> For each business, try to explain why you think the organization, and what it produces, is suited to that particular business type.
>
> Useful sources of information might include:
> - Local business phone directories
> - Local newspaper articles
> - The local council
> - The Chamber of Commerce
> - Training and Enterprise Councils

Finance

Limited companies raise most of their capital through the sale of shares. Money raised from the sales of shares is known as **permanent capital**. That is, shareholders' money never has to be repaid. If a shareholder wishes to get back the money they invested, they must sell their shares to someone else.

Ownership

Limited companies are owned by their shareholders. Each shareholder has limited liability. The liability to pay company debts should the business fail is limited to the amount each shareholder invested in the company. This gives people the confidence to buy shares in the knowledge that their personal possessions are not at risk.

Control

The day-to-day running of a limited company is undertaken by a board of directors. These are elected by shareholders to run and control the company on their behalf (see 13.2). In a small company, shareholders may be directors. However, in very large companies there may be many thousands of shareholders. In these companies there is a 'separation of ownership from control'.

In addition, limited companies will have:

- **A separate legal identity** - that is, the business exists in law separately from its owners (the shareholders). Unlike sole traders and partnerships, the owners of a limited company cannot be sued for damages, recovery of debt, etc.

- **Strict legal requirements**. The 1985 Companies Act requires all companies to publish financial accounts each year and make these available to all shareholders at an annual general meeting (AGM). In addition, all limited companies must be registered with the Registrar of Companies at Companies House, to whom copies of the financial accounts should be sent. Companies are also required to make their accounts available to any member of the public.

There are two main types of limited company. Each must have a minimum of two shareholders. The **private limited company (Ltd)** and the **public limited company (plc)**. Most of the smaller joint stock companies are private limited companies - there are around half a million in existence in the UK. Plcs tend to be much larger in size but fewer in number.

Private limited companies

The founder members of a private limited company are able to sell shares to raise capital but can only do so to family, friends, and associates. This may limit the amount of money they are able to raise.

Selling shares also means that founder members can lose control of their company unless they retain over 50% of the shares they issue. Because there is one vote per share, the shareholder with over 50% of shares is said to have a **controlling interest**. They are able to outvote all other shareholders on matters such as company policy and the election of directors.

Forming a limited company

The promoters of a company are required by law to provide a number of legal documents to the Registrar of Companies:

The **Memorandum of Association** governs the company's relationship with the outside world. It contains important information about the company including:

- The company name (followed by either Ltd or plc)
- The main business address
- The objects of the business, i.e. what it will produce
- A statement of limited liability of the members
- The amount of capital to be raised by issuing shares, for example: £500,000 from the issue of 250,000 ordinary shares with a face value of £2 each
- The agreement of the founder members to form a limited company

The **Articles of Association** control the internal running of the company. These give details such as:

- Procedures for calling a general meeting of shareholders
- The number, rights, and obligations of directors
- Shareholder voting rights

When satisfied that all legal requirements have been met, the Registrar will issue a **Certificate of Incorporation** which permits the new company to start trading.

▼ Table 4.1: The 5 largest private companies, 1993

Company	Sales £bn
John Swire	3.6
Isosceles	3.0
Littlewoods	2.3
John Lewis	2.1
Western United	1.5

Director, November 1993

A shareholder who wants his or her money back must sell their shares to another person with the prior agreement of all the other business owners.

Single member companies

In 1992, new regulations were introduced under the Twelfth Company Law Directive of the European Union, to allow the formation of private limited companies with just one shareholder.

▼ *Advantages and disadvantages of a private limited company*

Advantages	Disadvantages
The sale of shares can raise capital	Founder members may lose control
Owners have limited liability	Shares cannot be advertised or sold on the stock exchange
The company has a separate legal identity from its owners	Setting up can be expansive because of the legal requirements
Owners can appoint directors on their record of achievement and business knowledge	Financial information must be published
Capital raised from the sale of shares never has to be repaid	An annual general meeting of shareholders must be held each year

Public limited companies (plcs)

Plcs are among the largest and most successful organizations in the UK. Examples include British Gas plc, Unilever plc and Tesco plc.

Unlike a private limited company, a plc is able to advertise the sale of shares and sell them to members of the general public through the Stock Exchange (see 22.3).

In addition to the advantages and disadvantages of a private limited company, the plc also has a number of others. These are:

▼ *Two well known public limited companies*

▼ *Advantages and disadvantages of a public limited company*

Advantages	Disadvantages
Owners have limited liability	'Going public' can be expensive
Shares can be advertised	Some plcs can grow so large that they may become difficult to manage effectively
Shares can be sold through the Stock Exchange	Risk of takeover by rival companies who have bought shares in the company
Large plcs may find it easier to borrow from banks	

Cooperatives

A **cooperative** is an organization formed by people joining together for mutual interest to organize production, make decisions, and share profits. All members have an equal say in running the business and share equally in the profits. There are many different types of cooperative but two main types can be distinguished:

Producer (or worker) cooperatives

These are groups of people who have organized themselves collectively to produce goods or services, as in a farming cooperative. They are able to pool their resources to buy expensive equipment and share equally in decision-making and any business profits.

The number of worker cooperatives grew rapidly during the 1970s when unemployment was rising. The government set up the **Cooperative Development Agency (CDA)** to provide advice and financial assistance to help employees buy shares in the ownership of firms which were faced with closure.

Retail cooperatives

The first retail cooperative society was formed in 1844 when a group of workers who were dissatisfied with low pay and high food prices joined together to buy food from wholesalers and take advantage of bulk discounts. The principles of modern retail cooperatives are much the same:

- The cooperative is owned by its members
- Any person can become a member by buying a share for as little as £1
- Members elect a board of directors to run the cooperative
- Each member is allowed one vote regardless of the number of shares they hold
- Profits are shared between members and customers

Today many of the smaller retail cooperative shops have been forced out of business by large supermarkets. In order to compete, a number of cooperatives have formed into larger superstores selling a wide variety of goods and services, normally located on large out-of-town sites. The cooperative movement has also successfully expanded into other activities such as banking, insurance, travel agents, funeral direction, and bakeries. The largest single retailing cooperative is the Cooperative Retail Society based in Manchester.

Cooperative societies are governed by the terms and conditions of the Industrial and Provident Societies Acts 1965 - 1975. Around 11,300 societies are registered in Great Britain. They are responsible to the Registrar of Friendly Societies, to whom they must submit annual accounts.

Franchises

This form of business ownership was first introduced in the USA but is now fast growing in popularity in the UK. A franchise is an agreement between two parties:

- The **franchiser** - an existing, usually well known company with an established market for its product
- The **franchisee** - a person, or group of people, who buy the right to use the trading name of the franchiser and either manufacture, service, or sell its product in a particular location.

Well known examples of franchise operations include McDonalds, Sock Shop, Wimpy, Prontoprint, and BSM. It is also increasingly common for smaller organizations to franchise parts of their operations. For example, milkmen sometimes franchise their round from the local dairy. Department stores will also franchise space within their stores to other retailers.

To buy a franchise, a business can pay around £15,000 - £20,000, plus a percentage of their turnover. In return, the established company will often provide training, equipment, materials, marketing, and help finding premises. The advantage to the franchiser is an increase in the market for their product without the need to expand the firm.

▼ Advantages and disadvantages of buying a franchise

Advantages	Disadvantages
Product name and market likely to be well established	Cost of buying franchise could be high
Franchiser will often market and promote the product	A proportion of business profits are paid to the franchiser
Banks may be more willing to lend money to a well known franchise	Franchise agreement can be withdrawn
Risk of business failure is low	Role of business owners reduced to 'branch manager' Most aspects of business will be dictated by franchiser

Portfolio Activity 4.4

Range: Types of ownership, Objectives
Skills: Read and respond to written material, Collect and record data

1. What business motives has Uniglobe for selling franchises in its travel agency business?
2. What motives had Richard Soule for buying a franchise in Uniglobe?
3. Your local milkman has asked for your advice. The dairy is offering him the chance to franchise his round. He needs advice on the following concerns:
- what is a franchise?
- how does a franchise operate?
- What are the advantages and disadvantages of buying a franchise?
- How will he raise finance?
- What are the sales prospects for doorstep deliveries of milk and dairy products?

You have agreed to produce a short report for him. You can find out more about this fast-growing business sector from the British Franchise Association and from Business Franchise magazine.

Turn over to travel...

THE collapse of High Street agents Exchange Travel three and a half years ago temporarily halted what should have been one of franchising's more profitable operations – business and retail travel agency franchises.

But now the travel agency franchise is back in the frame, with at least four operators offering franchise opportunities, using modern aids like the international airline booking database to gain access to the 11 per cent of consumer spending that travel represents.

The biggest operator is Canadian-based Uniglobe, which has more than 1,000 offices in the UK, North America, Holland, Belgium and Japan.

This year it is targeting Yorkshire, the East and West Midlands, and the North West, and eight London locations within the M25, for further expansion. Total investment is £120,000 depending on location, including £70,000 working capital and a £15,000 initial franchise fee.

The period of contract is ten years renewable, and turnover is projected at £1 million in year one, rising to £2.5 million in year two, yielding a £640,000 net profit.

Richard Soule, 48, bought into Uniglobe Grosvenor Travel for £150,000 two years ago, using savings from his eight tax-free banking years in the Gulf.

'We service oil companies, Government agencies and local businesses from our Grosvenor Gardens, London, office and are now trading at a turnover of £4.5 million for this year,' he says.

Daily Mail 21.1.94

Multinational corporations

A **multinational** is an organization that owns and controls productive activities in more than one country. These companies are some of the largest firms in the world, producing many billions of pounds' worth of goods and services and often employing many thousands of workers.

Imperial Chemical Industries (ICI) is one of the world's largest chemicals groups. The parent company is UK-owned and has manufacturing interests in over 40 countries and sales organizations in more than 60.

Advanced Business

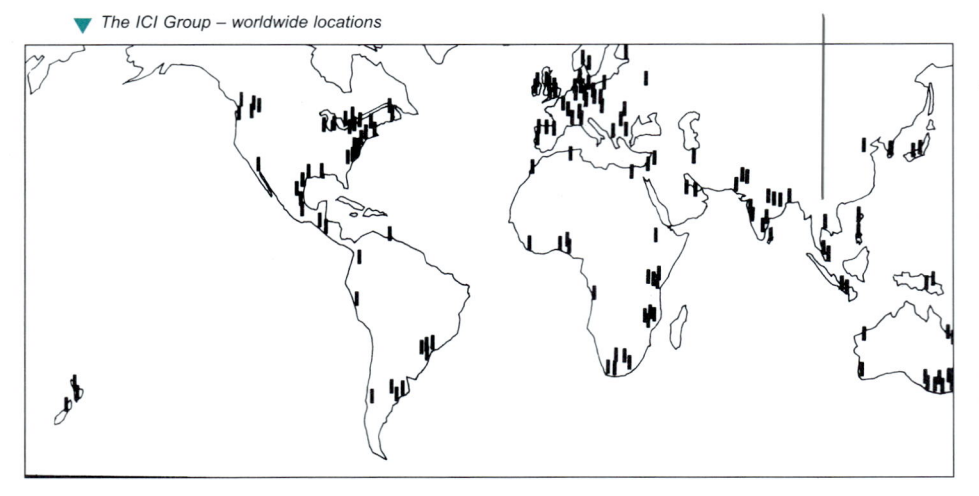

▼ The ICI Group – worldwide locations

However, even the largest UK-owned multinationals are small in comparison to US giants such as Exxon, General Motors, and Ford, and Japanese organizations such as Sony and Mitsubishi. These organizations are able to generate turnovers in excess of the national incomes of all but the very wealthiest nations in the world. Foreign-owned enterprises in the UK account for around 17% of all manufacturing jobs.

▼ Table 4.2: The World's Top 10 Industrial Companies 1992

Company	Country of Origin	Business sector	Sales turnover £bn
Itoh[C.] & Co. Ltd	Japan	Sogo Sosha1	86.6
Mitsui & Co.Ltd	Japan	Sogo Sosha	84.7
Sumitomo Corp.	Japan	Sogo Sosha	81.4
Mitsubishi Corp	Japan	Sogo Sosha	80.2
Marubeni Corp.	Japan	Sogo Sosha	79.5
General Motors	USA	Automobiles	65.9
Exxon Corp.	USA	Oil and gas	61.6
Royal Dutch/Shell	Netherlands/UK	Oil and gas	58.1
Nissho Iwai Corp.	Japan	Sogo Sosha	55.6
Ford Motor Co.	USA	Automobiles	47.3

1 Sogo Sosha companies in Japan are those involved in trading in many different industrial sectors

The Times 1000, 1992-1993

Portfolio Activity 4.4

Range: Business organizations, Organizational structures
Skills: Collect and record data

Below is a list of names of multinational organizations. Try to find out their country of origin, the number of countries they operate in, their main products, and any recent indicators of their business performance. Tabulate the information in an appropriate format.

IBM Toyota	BP	Sears Roebuck
Ciba Geigy	Siemens	GEC
Du Pont	Peugeot	Nestlé
Fiat	AT&T	K Mart
Texaco	Mobil	Nissan
McDonalds	Phillip Morris	Procter & Gamble

> **Key words**
>
> **Sole trader** - a business enterprise owned and controlled by one person
>
> **Partnership** - a business owned and controlled by more than two people
>
> **Sleeping partner** - a person who invests money in a partnership but takes no active role in running the business
>
> **Joint stock (limited) companies** - companies which are owned by their shareholders
>
> **Private limited companies** - companies which cannot advertise share sales and can sell shares only to family, friends, and business associates
>
> **Public limited companies (plcs)** - organizations able to trade their shares with the general public on the Stock Exchange
>
> **Cooperative** - an enterprise run and owned jointly by its members, who have equal voting rights
>
> **Multinational** - a firm that has operations in more than one country

Section 4.3 Public sector organizations

The public sector in the UK is made up of organizations which are funded by, and accountable to, central and local government.

Central government

This is an elected body that operates at national level. Central government departments employ civil servants to administer the economic, social, environmental, and foreign policies of government. There are around 20 central government departments including the Department of Transport, the Treasury, and the Ministry of Defence.

Local government

Some services in the UK are supplied by elected local authorities such as district councils, county councils, and London boroughs. Local authorities provide public services to local businesses and communities, including education, leisure facilities, refuse collection, housing, maintenance of local roads, and parking enforcement.

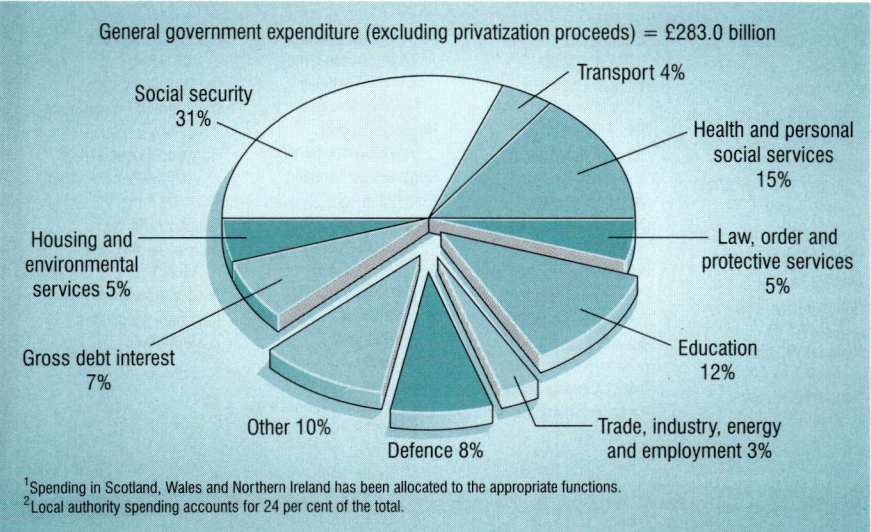

▼ Figure 4.2: General government expenditure (excluding privatization proceeds) by function in 1993-94 [1,2]

General government expenditure (excluding privatization proceeds) = £283.0 billion

- Social security 31%
- Transport 4%
- Health and personal social services 15%
- Law, order and protective services 5%
- Education 12%
- Trade, industry, energy and employment 3%
- Defence 8%
- Other 10%
- Gross debt interest 7%
- Housing and environmental services 5%

[1] Spending in Scotland, Wales and Northern Ireland has been allocated to the appropriate functions.
[2] Local authority spending accounts for 24 per cent of the total.

▼ Figure 4.3: Main central government departments 1995

Defence	Environment
Foreign Office	Home Office
Overseas Development	Education
Agriculture, Fisheries and Food	Health
	Central Statistical Office
Trade and Industry	Social Security
Export Credit Guarantee	Scotland
Employment	Wales
Transport	Northern Ireland
National Heritage	Cabinet Office

Advanced Business

▼ The Bank of England is run by a public corporation.

Public corporations

These are responsible for the day-to-day running of industries and activities owned and controlled by central government. Public corporations have a separate legal identity from the government. This is to protect the government from any legal action against a public corporation.

Public corporations range from those involved in direct trade with consumers, such as the Post Office and British Coal to bodies such as The Bank of England and the Civil Aviation Authority. Each corporation is controlled by a government minister who elects a board of directors. For example, the BBC is accountable to the Home Office minister, Railtrack to the Secretary of State for Transport, and The Bank of England to the Chancellor of the Exchequer.

Executive agencies

The 1988 government report *Next Steps* recommended that a number of public services, such as the Royal Mint, prisons, the provision of statistics, passports, and benefit payments, should be separated from their main

Would you like to run any of these agencies?

Historic Royal Palaces Agency
- Responsibility for Tower of London, Hampton Court, Kensington and Kew palaces, and Banqueting House, Whitehall
- 400 staff
- 1993-94 budget £31.6m
- 11% increase in visitors 1992-93

Royal Mint
- Produces coins and medals for home market and export
- 1,000 staff
- Sales in 1992-93 £104m, including £54.4m (52%) overseas
- Operating profit £11.8m, 7.3% more than 1991-92

Ordnance Survey
- Makes definitive topographic maps of Britain
- 2,327 staff
- Revenue in 1992-93 £49m, against cost of £74.9m
- 34,700 more basic scale maps produced in 1992-93

Meteorological Office
- Provides service to armed forces, shipping, civil aviation, public sector, industry, and general public
- 2,526 staff at home and overseas
- 1992-93 voted expenditure was £129m against voted receipts of £56m
- Contracts out £8m of services per year

Employment Service
- Helps unemployed find work and pays benefits and allowances
- 1,300 local offices where four in five of its 48,000 staff work
- 1992-93 budget £1.18bn
- Efficiency savings of £17.7m achieved in 1992-93

Agencies under review

Accounts Services Agency
ADAS
Building Research Establishment
Cadw: Welsh Historic Monuments
Central Office of Information
Central Statistical office
Central Veterinary Laboratory
Chemical and Bio Defence Est
Civil Service College
Companies House
Compensation Agency
Defence Accounts Agency
Defence Analytical Services Agency
Defence Operational Analysis Centre
Defence Postal and Courier Services
Driver and Vehicle Licensing Agency
Driver and Vehicle Testing Agency
Driving Standards Agency
Duke of York's Royal Military School
Employment Service
Fire Service College
Forensic Science Service
Historic Royal Palaces Agency
Historic Scotland
HMSO
Hydrographic Office
Insolvency Service
Intervention Board (agric.)
Laboratory of the Government Chemist
Land Registry
Medicines Control Agency
Meteorological Office
Military Survey
National Physical Laboratory
National Weights and Measures Lab
Natural Resources Institute
Naval Aircraft Repair Organization
National Engineering Laboratory
NHS Estates
Occupational Health Service
Ordnance Survey
Ordnance Survey of Northern Ireland
Patent Office
Planning Inspectorate
Public Record Office
Queen Elizabeth II Conference Centre
Queen Victoria School
Radiocommunications Agency
RAF Support Command's Maintenance Group Defence Agency
Rate Collection Agency
Recruitment and Assessment Services
Registers of Scotland
Royal Mint
Scottish Agricultural Science Agency
Scottish Fisheries Protection Agency
Service Children's Schools
Social Security Contributions Agency
Social Security Information Technology Services Agency
Teachers' Pensions Agency
The Buying Agency
Training and Employment Agency
Transport Research Laboratory
Passport Agency
Valuation Office
Vehicle Certification Agency
Vehicle Inspectorate
Veterinary Medicines Directorate

Financial Times 10.12.93

policy-making bodies in central government departments. This would allow executive agencies to be run in a more business-like manner with control over their own budgets.

Individual agencies are subject to periodic review to examine the case for allowing private sector firms to carry out their activities.

Quangos (Quasi-autonomous non-government organizations)

These are unelected government bodies run by boards of directors who are responsible for managing particular government initiatives. Examples include regional health authorities, research councils, industrial tribunals, and Training and Enterprise Councils (TECs). In recent years the role of Quangos and the amount of resources they control have increased.

Portfolio Activity 4.5

Range: Business organizations, Types of ownership, Differences

Skills: Collect and record data

1. Complete the following table of features of different types of business organization:

Type of organization	Who owns the business?	Who manages the business?	Who is responsible for business debts?	Does it publish annual accounts?	Main sources of capital
Sole trader	One person	The owner	The owner has unlimited liability	No	Personal and family savings, bank overdraft
Partnership	2 - 20 partners				
Private limited company					
Public limited company					Sale of shares to the general public
Cooperative					
Franchise					
Public corporation		Board of directors appointed by government			

2. For each of the above types of business organization, identify one or two examples, either from your own experience or from other sources, such as a business phone directory or newspaper articles. For each organization, try to find out:

- Its objectives
- The types of goods and services it produces
- How it is financed
- How it is managed

115

> **Key words**
>
> **Central government** - an elected body that operates at national level to control the economy and the overall provision of public services
>
> **Local government** - elected bodies such as district councils, county councils and London borough councils, responsible for running local public services
>
> **Public corporations** - organizations responsible for the day-to-day running of nationalised industries owned and controlled by central government
>
> **Quangos** - unelected, independent bodies running publicly owned enterprises

Section 4.4 Organizational structures

Relationships within an organization

Any business organization, whatever its size, whether in the public or private sector, will need to establish an **internal structure**. The internal structure of a business will show:

- Who is in charge
- Who makes the decisions
- Who carries out decisions
- How decisions and information are communicated

That is, the **organizational structure** will establish the relationships between managers and their subordinates necessary to achieve business objectives (see 4.1).

Organization charts

The **formal structure** within an organization can be represented by means of an **organization chart**. Traditionally, an organization chart is constructed with those individuals near or at the top having more authority and responsibility than those at the bottom.

Figure 4.4 shows the organization chart for Nutmeg UK, a manufacturer of American sports fashion clothing based in Richmond, Surrey. The relative positions of individuals within the boxes show formal relationships, and lines between boxes show formal lines of communication between the individuals.

Departmentalization

The most common method of establishing formal relationships between individuals is by establishing **departments**. A department is defined as a unique group of human resources established by management to perform a particular task within the organization.

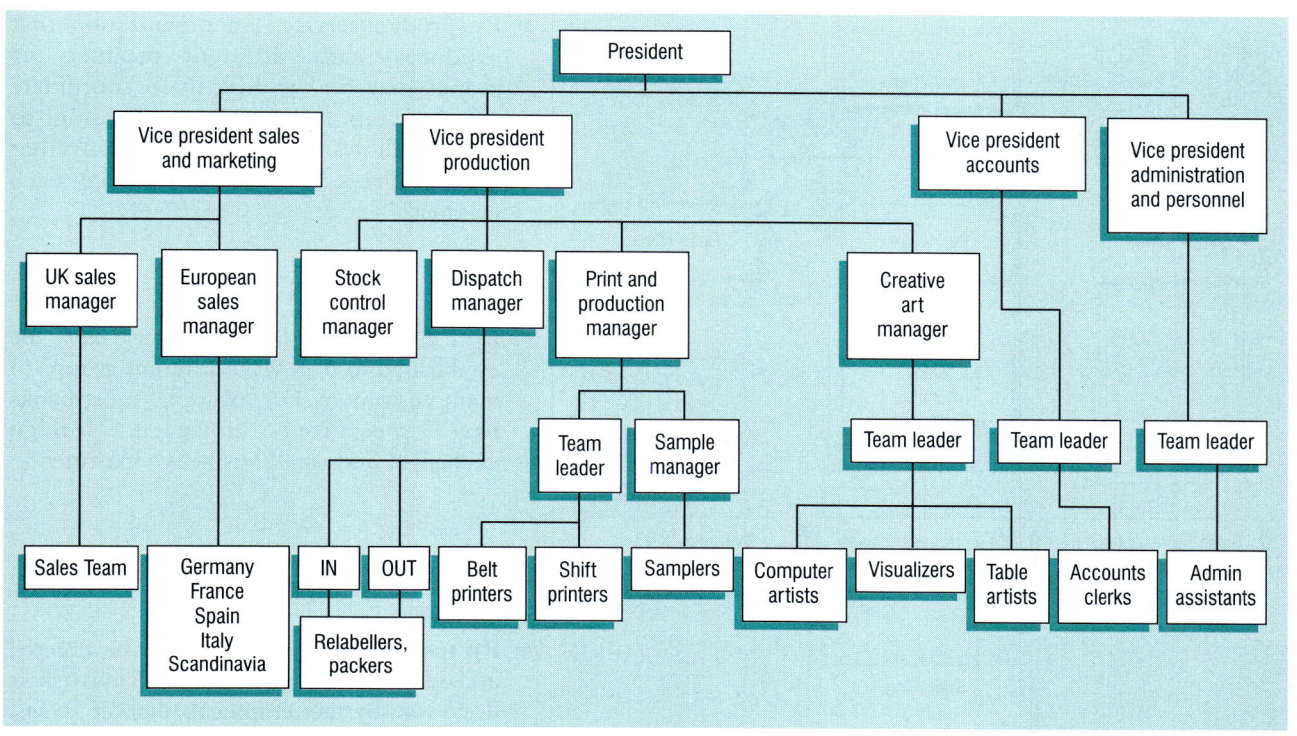

▲ *Figure 4.4: Organization Chart for Nutmeg UK*

▼ **Departmentalization**

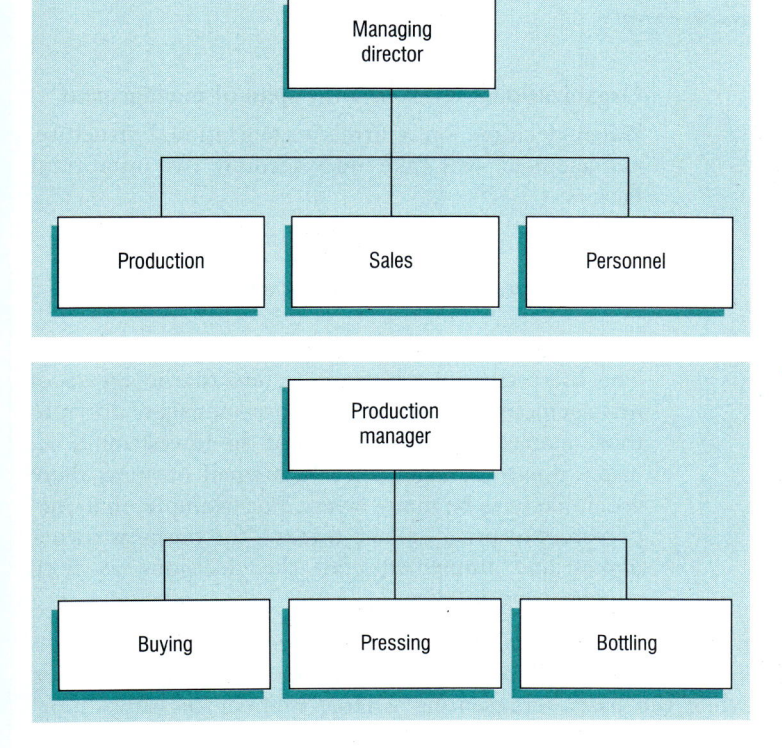

Department groupings can be established in a number of ways. Consider the ways in which a wine producer might be split into departments;

- **By function.** By far the most common method among medium-to-large organizations. Departments are established to perform specific tasks, for example, marketing, finance, production, sales, personnel.

- **By process.** Divisions are based on operations, with each department specializing in a particular task.

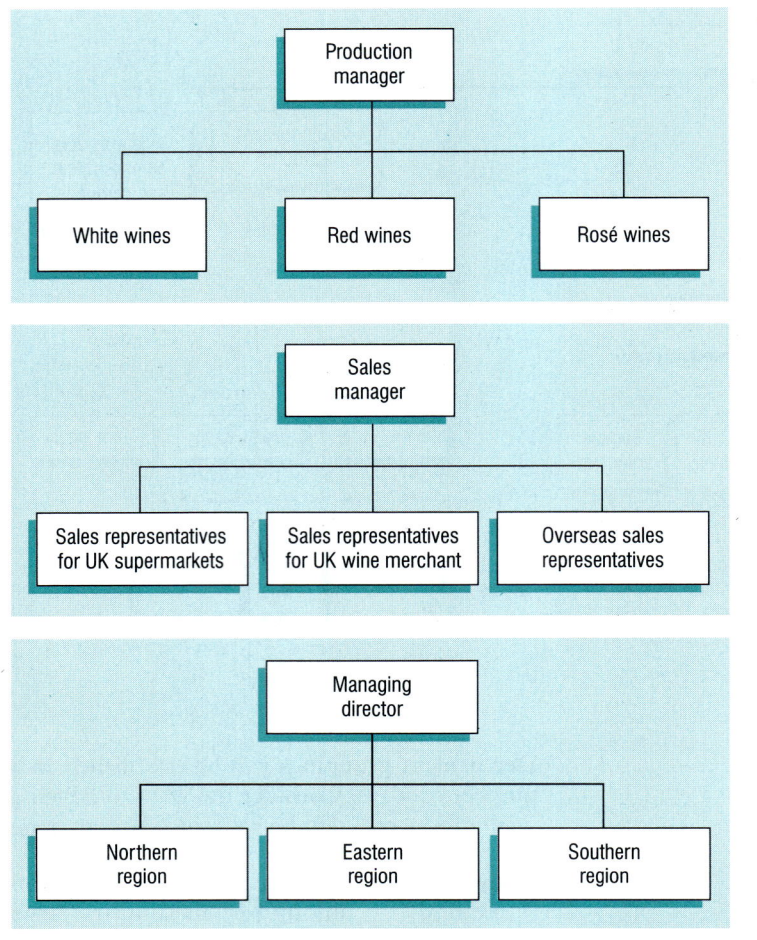

[Diagram: Production manager → White wines, Red wines, Rosé wines]

[Diagram: Sales manager → Sales representatives for UK supermarkets, Sales representatives for UK wine merchant, Overseas sales representatives]

[Diagram: Managing director → Northern region, Eastern region, Southern region]

- **By product/service.** An organization that produces many different products or brands may find it difficult to coordinate across them. Organizing according to product allows managers to group together the resources needed to produce each product.

- **By customer.** Departments can be established to deal with different groups of main customers. For example, most banks have specialized mortgage, foreign exchange, and small business departments

- **By territory.** Departments can be created according to the place in which work is done or by geographical market areas. Most large organizations operate on a regional basis. Multinational organizations will have offices, factories, and often shops in different countries.

Portfolio Activity 4.6

Range: Business organizations, Organizational structures
Skills: Produce written material

Look at the various diagrams above showing how departments may be organized within a business.

Describe the suitability of the different forms of departmentalization for different types of business organization, i.e. sole trader, partnership, limited companies, cooperatives, multinationals, public sector organizations (see 4.1).

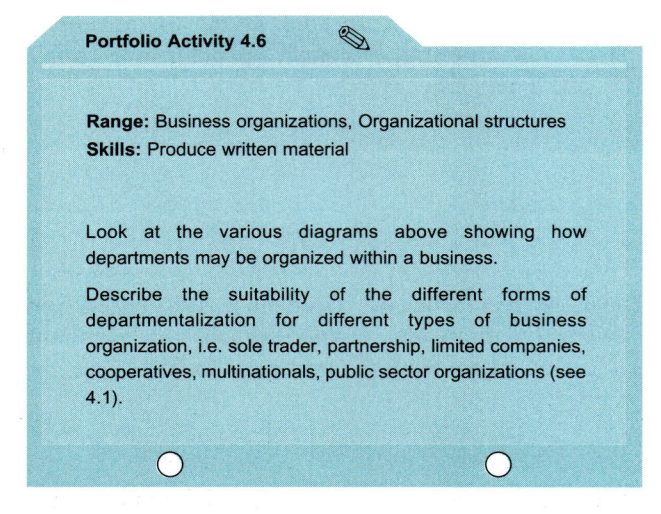

Organizational levels and the span of management

When deciding on a firm's organizational structure, management will take into account two important factors:

- The chain of command
- The span of management (or span of control)

The hierarchical organization

The **hierarchy** in a business refers to the layers of management from the most senior managers down to those managers or supervisors of the lowest rank, i.e. 'top - down management'. In a small business there are unlikely to be many layers. For example, in a one-person enterprise - a sole trader - the business owner makes and implements all the decisions as both manager and worker.

The structure of the **hierarchical organization** is presented as a pyramid (see figure 4.5 on page 120). It is narrow at the top indicating few senior managers, while the base, representing a large number of 'shop-floor' operatives or low-grade workers, is broad.

Line and staff functions

There are three main line functions a business organization will have to perform if it is to achieve its objectives. These are:

- Production
- Sales
- Marketing

Individual departments concerned with performing these functions are called **line departments**. Each line department is supervised by a **line manager** who has **line authority** - the ability to give orders concerning productive activities - over his or her subordinates. For example, the production manager has line authority over the production supervisor, who in turn has line authority over machine operatives.

Staff functions are those which support the main line functions of an organization (see 5.2). These are:

- Research and development
- Purchasing (materials and equipment)
- Distribution
- Finance and accounting
- Human resources (personnel)
- Customer services
- Quality control
- Maintenance (sites, buildings and equipment)
- Communications (see 6.1)
- Information processing (see 7.1)

Employees in these areas work across the organization to provide help and advice to all other departments, but have no authority to make decisions in any other department but their own. For example, personnel managers have responsibility for staff matters and welfare in the whole organization, but have no power to hire or fire staff in the production department without the authority of the production manager. **Staff authority** is the right to advise and assist those who possess line authority and other staff personnel.

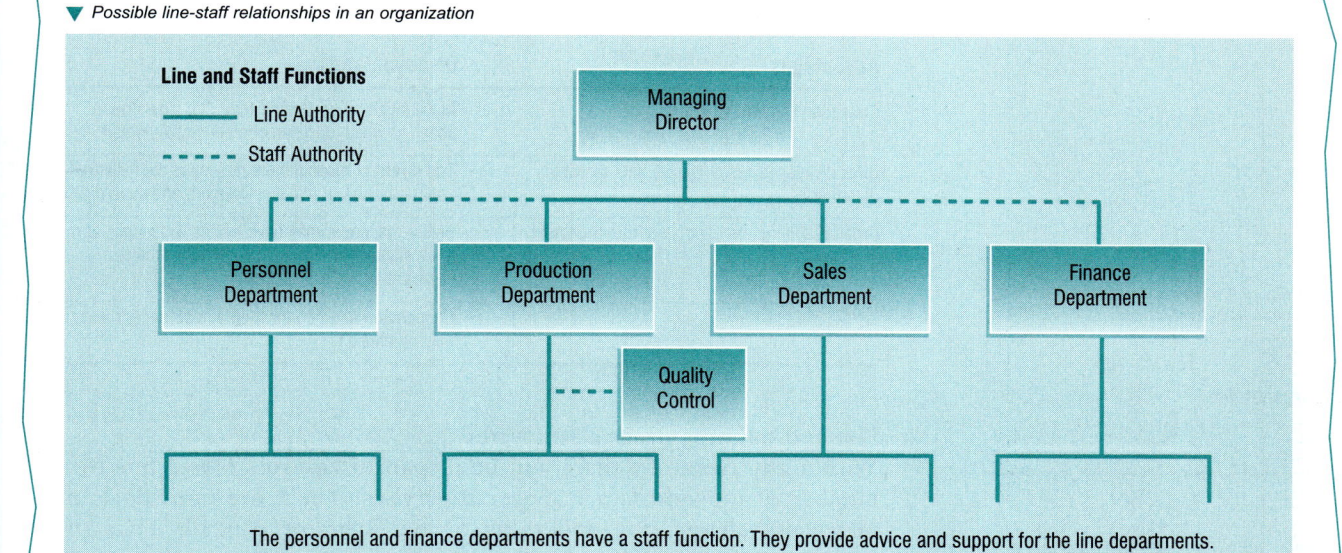

▼ *Possible line-staff relationships in an organization*

Line and Staff Functions

— Line Authority
---- Staff Authority

Managing Director
- Personnel Department
- Production Department
- Sales Department
- Finance Department
- Quality Control

The personnel and finance departments have a staff function. They provide advice and support for the line departments.

The top layers of management - directors or chief executives - are usually concerned with strategic, long-term plans and policies and with checking that subordinates carry these out. A distinct **chain of command** runs in a line from the top layers of management down through each department in the organization to the 'shop floor'. Orders are passed down this chain of command while information on which further decisions are taken - sales, revenues, output, staff turnover, etc. - are passed up the organization.

Figure 4.5: The hierarchical organization structure

CHAIN OF COMMAND

INFORMATION

Directors
Departmental managers
Managers — Middle managers
Supervisors
Shop floor — Operatives/Clerical staff

The main advantages and disadvantages of the hierarchical structure include:

Advantages	Disadvantages
Clear management structure	Many layers of communication can slow down speed at which decisions can be implemented
Clear division of responsibility and allocation of authority	Top layers of management may stifle the initiative and motivation of middle managers and subordinates
Organization can be controlled from the top	Senior managers may have limited experience and understanding of functions within the whole organization
	Cooperation and coordination across departments may be difficult

Figure 4.6: The span of control within organization structures

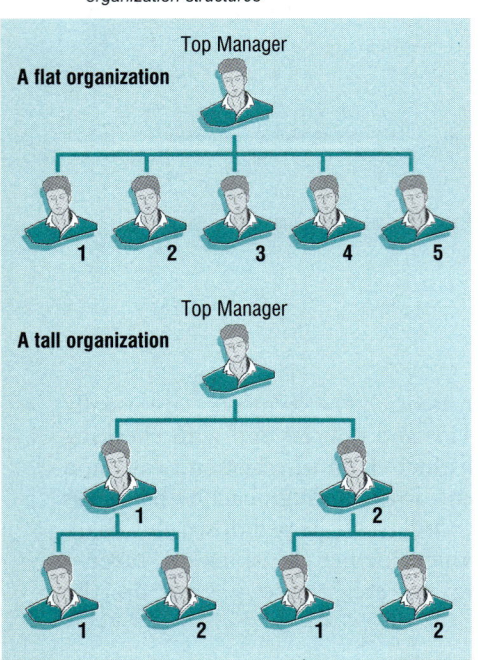

A flat organization
Top Manager
1 2 3 4 5

A tall organization
Top Manager
1   2
1 2   1 2

Flat and tall organization structures

Within any hierarchy there will be a **span of control**. This refers to the number of individuals a manager supervises. The more individuals in a manager's charge, the wider his or her span of control. Thus, if 5 employees are directly under the control of the production manager, his or her span of control is 5.

In general, the greater the height of the organization chart, the smaller the span of control. It follows that the lower the height of the chart, the greater the span of control tends to be.

Organization charts with little height are usually referred to as **flat organizations**, while those with height are referred to as **tall** (Figure 4.6).

Flat organizations are those which have relatively few or even just one level of management. Many UK enterprises have adopted flatter structures in order to reduce levels of management and bureaucracy, and to give their workforce greater decision-making responsibilities.

WIDE SPAN OF CONTROL

Advantages	Disadvantages
Fewer levels of management and decision making	Direct supervision of subordinates can become difficult and management can lose control
Lower supervision costs	Subordinates may have more than one boss
Greater decision-making authority for subordinates can increase job satisfaction	Motivation and output may be impaired if orders become confused
	Flat structure may become unworkable as business expands

NARROW SPAN OF CONTROL

Advantages	Disadvantages
Allows for tight control and close supervision	Subordinates may feel left out of decision-making process and lack motivation
Communication with subordinates is easier	Management and administration costs are high
	Coordinating decisions of numerous managers can be difficult
	Too much supervision may stifle initiative and motivation

Authority, responsibility, and delegation

Employees in a hierarchy will have varying degrees of responsibility and authority. The higher up the hierarchy, the more responsibility and authority an employee will have. Managers need to have **authority** over their subordinates in order for decisions and policies to be implemented. They have to tell their staff what to do and what is expected of them. Although a task may be delegated, or passed down the chain of command, from a manager to a subordinate, the manager will still have the **responsibility** for making sure his or her instructions are carried out.

Delegation is the process of assigning job activities and corresponding authority to specific individuals within the organization. It is essential because it is impossible for one manager to have direct control over all activities. However, for delegation to be effective, a number of conditions must be satisfied:

- The manager must be sure that the subordinate has a clear understanding of what the assigned task entails and its purpose
- The subordinate must be given the right and power of authority within the organization to accomplish the assigned task
- If necessary, training and guidance should be provided to enable employees to complete delegated tasks effectively

"I hate to fire people, so I'm ordering you two to fire each other."

Wall Street Journal 11.9.87

- Whenever possible, tasks should be delegated on the basis of employee interest
- The manager should establish mutually agreed performance criteria for delegated tasks

Centralized and decentralized organizations

If a business is **centralized**, authority, responsibility, and decision-making is concentrated at the top of the hierarchy with a few senior managers. 'Subordinates' have little, if any, authority or power to make decisions. The main advantage of centralization is the ability of senior managers to make quick decisions, especially when the business environment is changing rapidly.

A **decentralized organization** is one in which authority and responsibility have been delegated to lower levels of management. Complete decentralization would mean that subordinates would make all the decisions.

▼ *The advantages and disadvantages of centralized and decentralized organizations*

CENTRALIZED STRUCTURE	DECENTRALIZED STRUCTURE
Advantages	**Advantages**
Senior management maintain control of the business and can make decisions quickly from the point of view of the whole organization	Reduces stress and burden on senior managers. Senior managers can concentrate on strategic decisions
Systems and procedures such as personnel, purchasing, advertising, can be standardized and may gain economies of scale (see 21.2)	Subordinates enjoy more decision-making and improved motivation
Reduces risk of duplication of activities and efforts	Subordinates can make decisions based on local conditions affecting their area of work
Senior managers may be more experienced decision-makers	Delegation allows greater flexibility and a quicker response to changing market conditions
	Middle managers can be groomed for senior positions
Disadvantages	**Disadvantages**
Subordinates may lack motivation	More bureaucracy and consultation is involved
Few opportunities for decisions to be made based on local conditions	Slows down decision-making
Senior managers may have little experience or understanding of activities and constraints in individual departments	Decisions taken by different departments may conflict
	Senior managers lose control

In general, the larger the organization, the more decentralized it is likely to be because it would be impossible for senior management to maintain direct control over all business activities. For example, large retail organizations like Tesco's and B&Q which have a number of branches at different locations operate a decentralized structure. Each store will have a manager able to take decisions on staff requirements, store layout, stock control, etc., but who is ultimately responsible to a regional manager and company directors.

Certain functions within a business will always remain controlled from the centre. For example, decisions about budget allocation between departments, advertising, and growth, are likely to be centralized because they affect the whole organization.

The matrix organization

A **matrix organization** is an organization that has been modified primarily for the purpose of completing a special project. The project - for example, the development of a new product - may either be short-term or long-term, with employees with different skills to complete the project borrowed from various departments within the organization to form project teams.

Figure 4.7 shows one way of changing an organizational structure into a matrix organization. A manager would be appointed for each of the two projects and allocated staff with appropriate skills to complete each one. After the projects were completed, the organization could change back to its original structure.

▼ Figure 4.7: An example of a matrix organization structure

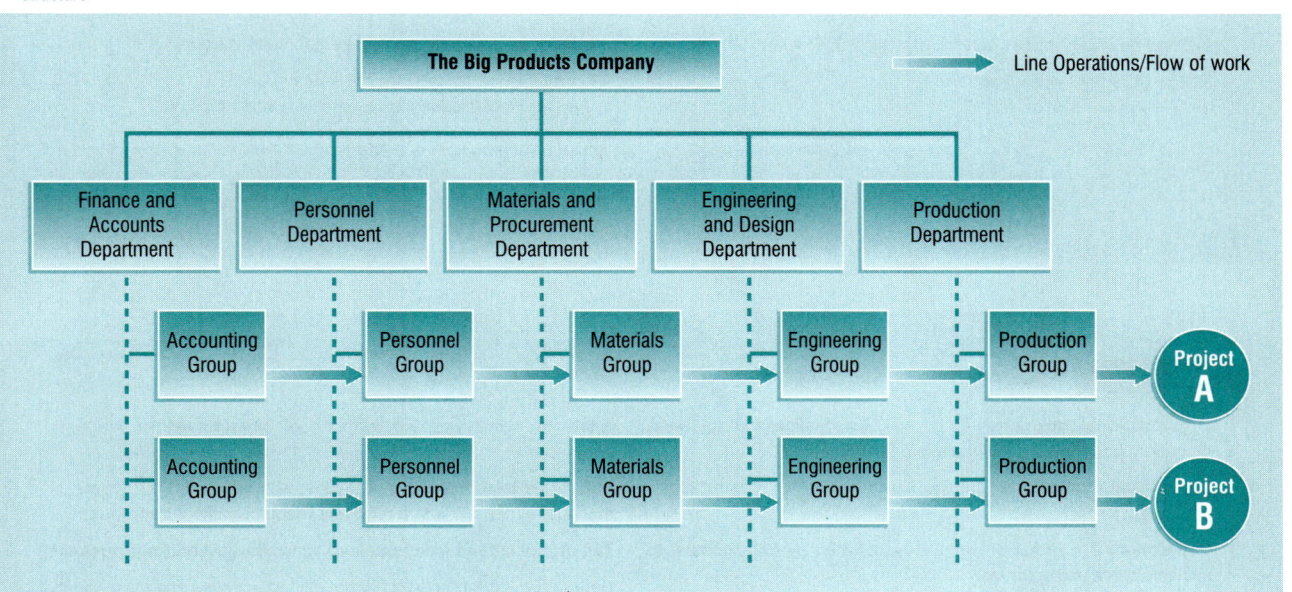

```
                        The Big Products Company                     → Line Operations/Flow of work

    Finance and    Personnel    Materials and   Engineering   Production
    Accounts       Department   Procurement     and Design    Department
    Department                  Department      Department

    Accounting     Personnel    Materials       Engineering   Production     Project
    Group          Group        Group           Group         Group          A

    Accounting     Personnel    Materials       Engineering   Production     Project
    Group          Group        Group           Group         Group          B
```

▼ Advantages and disadvantages of a matrix structure

Advantages	Disadvantages
Communication within the project team is easier	Employees may have more than one boss
Specialist staff can contribute ideas and help to solve problems	Staff loyalties may be divided between their old department and the project team
Team spirit helps to motivate staff	New lines of authority and communication may be difficult to understand

Portfolio Activity 4.7

Range: Organizational structures
Skills: Read and respond to written material

1. How has Barclays Bank plc been reorganized?
2. Why do you think Barclays has been reorganized in this way?
3. Find out how your local Barclays branch is organized. Draw an organization chart for the branch headed by the bank manager/ess.

Taylor reforms Barclays

Mr Martin Taylor, Barclays' new chief executive, yesterday stamped his presence on the UK's largest bank by breaking up its divisional structure and replacing it with a set of management groups reporting directly to him.

His reforms, including the creation of a group offering services to large companies, reduce the influence of Mr Alastair Robinson, head of the former banking division, who was a leading internal contender to be chief executive.

He said Mr Robinson was "a very valuable colleague" but pointed out that he would retire in three years' time. Mr Robinson's remit will include private banking and retail banking in Africa and the Caribbean.

The reforms, which Mr Taylor described as a first step, created groups covering big companies and European retail banking. The new group for UK retail banking will report to Mr Taylor for the first time.

Mr Graham Pimlott, chief executive of merchant banking at the BZW investment banking arm, is to head the group serving large companies.

The bank's former service businesses division – one of three with banking and BZW – will be divided. Mr Joseph De Feo, its chief executive, will retain charge of technology while custody switches to Mr Pimlott's control.

Financial Times 21.4.94

Portfolio Activity 4.8

Range: Organizational structures
Skills: Produce written material, Collect and record data

1. Draw an organization chart for your school/ college.
2. What functions does it perform?
3. Describe the type of structure and span of control.
4. From your own experience, what are the advantages/disadvantages of this type of structure?

Key words

Organizational structure – the various relationships between managers and their subordinates in a business

Organization chart – a graphic illustration of an organization's structure

Department – a group of workers established by management to specialize in a particular task

Line authority – the ability to give orders concerning productive activities, namely the line functions of production, sales, and marketing

Staff functions – those which support the main line functions of an organization, for example, personnel and finance

Staff authority – the right to advise and assist those who possess line authority

Hierarchy – layers of management in an organization

Chain of command – the passage of orders down an organization from top management to the shop floor

Unity of command – the principle whereby any individual within an organization should have only one line manager

Span of control – the number of subordinates a manager supervises

Flat organizations – organizations with relatively few layers of management, each with a relatively wide span of control

Tall organizations – organizations with many layers of management

Delegation – the process of assigning job activities and the authority to carry them out to individuals

Centralized organization – organizations in which authority, responsibility, and decision–making are concentrated at the top of the management hierarchy

Decentralized organization – organizations in which authority and decision–making responsibility are delegated to lower levels of management

Matrix organization – when an organization's structure is modified for the purpose of completing a special project

Section 4.5 Factors that influence the choice of organizational structure

What is structural change?

Many organization structures are **dynamic** - that is, they change or evolve through time. Change will often occur simply as a result of a growth in the size of an organization. But whatever the reason, structural change will be aimed at improving the effectiveness and efficiency of the organization.

There are a number of factors which can influence the choice of organizational structure and prompt change. We can separate these into internal and external pressures:

Internal factors

- **Size:** The larger the organization, the less able top managers will be to control every aspect of the business. Large firms, therefore, tend to have more decentralized and flatter structures than smaller ones. Company directors and/or senior mangers will tend to confine themselves to setting overall objectives and steering the firm, while managers lower down the hierarchy will be responsible for day-to-day activities and the achievement of targets in production, sales, finance, and administration.

- **Location:** Some firms have factories, offices, or shops in more than one location. For example, multinational enterprises operate in several countries. Authority will be delegated to managers in these different locations, since they will be better informed about local conditions, such as labour supply, suppliers, consumer tastes, even languages, currency, and laws.

- **Nature of product:** Management structures tend to be more decentralized in firms supplying goods or services to satisfy specific customer requirements. For example, consider the fitting of double-glazed windows. Responsibility for the measurement and fitting of these windows must rest with those employees who undertake the work. In organizations that mass-produce products for national or even international markets, top-level managers will be able to monitor and control production and marketing efforts more closely.

- **Management style:** The structure of an organization will be a reflection of the particular personalities and management style of top managers. If they enjoy having the power and authority to command all aspects of business activity, then the structure will be tall and centralized, whereas those managers who are more democratic and seek to include employees in decision-making will prefer a flatter, decentralized structure.

- **Changes in working arrangements:** Growing competition has meant that firms are increasingly changing their working methods in an attempt to boost productivity. Work groups are being created in which authority over the organization of tasks and the working environment is delegated to team leaders and supervisors. The idea is that working and problem-solving in groups will provide employees with the incentive and commitment to work harder. Similarly, new production techniques, such as 'Just In Time' production, whereby stocks are ordered and delivered just in time to be processed, require personnel lower down the organizational hierarchy to be able to make quick decisions on the timing and need for further supplies (see 15.2). Such changes in working arrangements have tended to 'flatten' organizational structures and decentralize authority and decision-making.

External factors

- **Increasing competition:** This is perhaps the most important influence on private sector organizational structures. Markets are becoming increasingly competitive at home and abroad. A firm that is slow to react to changing market conditions - for example, new technologies and changing consumer demands - will fail. Passing information up and down a tall chain of command can take precious time and a market opportunity may be missed while top managers decide what to do. Thus, in order to keep pace with changing consumer demands and rivals' marketing strategies, decisions on production, sales, and marketing activities are increasingly being taken by employees 'at ground level'.

- **Entering new markets:** A firm that intends to market a new product may devolve authority and control over the product to an individual department or project group (as in a matrix organization). A firm that enters new markets, especially overseas where there are cultural, language, and legal barriers to overcome, will often need to employ sales and marketing staff with specialized, local knowledge and the authority to take decisions.

- **Technological change:** Businesses have become increasingly aware that communications can be improved by restructuring from hierarchical to flatter structures. This allows information to be transmitted more quickly and easily, and means that managers are given more authority to make decisions. Information Technology is also enabling many office workers to tele-work from home and control their own work tasks and working environment (see 6.1).

- **Change in ownership:** A company that is taken over or merges with another company may often undergo structural change. A takeover occurs when one company buys control of another through the acquisition of shares in the ownership of that company. A firm that is taken over will often lose its original identity and become part of the purchasing or acquiring company.

A merger occurs when two or more firms agree to join together to form a new enterprise with a new legal identity. This is usually done by shareholders of the merging companies exchanging their existing shares for shares in the new organization. The name of the newly created enterprise will normally reflect the names of the merging companies (see 3.4).

Many public sector enterprises have undergone changes in ownership since 1981. Privatization involves the sale of public sector assets by the UK government to the private sector (see 3.5). British Telecom was the first major state-owned, or nationalized, industry in which shares were sold to the private sector in 1984. Since then, many other publicly owned industries have been sold back to the private sector, including British Gas, the electricity supply industry, and regional water supplies. All these industries are now run as public limited companies with boards of directors and business managers, instead of government ministers and public corporations controlling their strategic and day-to-day operations. In the case of electricity the government separated the industry into 12 regional supply companies, a national grid authority owned and controlled by the regional companies, and National Power and Powergen, who own and run power stations.

Reorganizing the railways

In 1994 the government separated British Rail into a number of separate organizations:

- Railtrack, a national track authority responsible for time-tabling, operating signalling systems, and track investment and maintenance
- Regional railway companies, including Scotrail, North East services, Central services, South Wales and West services
- Separate profit centres within some regional companies, such as the separation of Network South East into a number of divisions, for example, the Thames and Chiltern lines, Northern lines, Thameslink services, and the separation of Inter City into East Coast lines, Midland Main line, Gatwick Express, etc.

From 1995, private companies have been able to compete for franchises to run a number of the different regional companies and divisions. A Rail Regulator has been established by the government to oversee the franchise arrangements, issue licences to service operators, protect the interests of rail users, and generally promote competition and the efficient use of the railway

Portfolio Activity 4.9

Range: Organizational structures, Compare

Skills: Read and respond to written material, Collect and record data

1. How is JCB reorganizing its structure? Describe briefly the structure of JCB before and after the reorganization.
2. What motives did the company have for the reorganization?
3. How are working arrangements likely to change in the firm after reorganization?
4. Suggest other factors which might have influenced JCB's decision to reorganize.
5. Investigate the reorganization of railways in the UK:

- How has British Rail been reorganized?
- Why has reorganization taken place?
- What is a franchise? How are these being used to run rail services?
- What is the impact of the reorganization on your local railway line/station? For example, are there physical signs of reorganization/change in ownership, such as logos, uniforms? Have there been any changes in ticket types and/or prices? If possible, interview your local station manager.

The Department of Transport and Railtrack are useful organizations to contact.

Selectors' Choice

There is an office wall at J C Bamford Excavators' headquarters at Rocester, Staffordshire which three of the company's senior executives are unlikely to forget.

At the turn of the year the wall held the names of 300 JCB employees whose individual weaknesses and strengths were discussed and analysed by Henry Shirman, Mike Butler and John Appleby.

The process was a vital prelude to the reorganization into separate product businesses (and profit centres) of the main divisions of the UK's largest construction equipment manufacturing company.

Appointed to the top posts in the new businesses by chief executive Martin Coyne, who conceived the new organization with chairman Sir Anthony Bamford, the three had the unenviable tasks of selecting their teams.

JCB has had a decentralized structure before. In 1984 it broke up a previously tall, centralized organization into product divisions, but four years later went back to the original structure for its main products which helped to tighten management of product design and development. The smaller divisions such as JCB Landpower for agricultural products were kept separate.

The new approach creates divisions which have exclusive responsibility for the future of the main product lines - everything from design and product development to marketing. Basic manufacturing, such as welding, will still be done centrally, but the new divisions will each be responsible for painting and assembly.

The aim is to create multi-disciplinary teams which will sit together and concentrate solely on one product line each, The hope is that by identifying more closely with a particular product employees will understand the need for increased profitability and be encouraged to participate in achieving it.

Financial Times 11.8.93

Further reading

Moynihan, D, and Titley, B: Economics - A Complete Course (Oxford University Press 1993) Chapters 5 and 6

Scott, C, and Jaffe, DT: Managing Organizational Change (Kogan Page 1994)

Advanced Business

Test questions

The following underpinning knowledge will be tested:
1. The objectives of business organizations
2. Differences between types of business ownership
3. Compare organizational structures

1 A US-owned supermarket discount store has recently opened in the UK. In the first year of operation its main business objective is likely to be:

A Gain market share
B Reduce operational costs
C Maximize growth potential
D Restructure the organization

2 Four ex-employees of a large paper mill have started their own business together to manufacture greetings cards. The type of business organization they have formed is a:

A Cooperative
B Sole trader
C Partnership
D Private limited company

3 Which of the following is not a private sector business organization?

A Public limited company
B Worker cooperative
C Public corporation
D Partnership

4 If a business owner has unlimited liability it means:

A The business cannot be declared bankrupt
B The owner must meet all debts
C The business has sold shares
D The organization is non-profit making

5 A public limited company is an organization which:

A Is owned by the government
B Is owned by its workers
C Is listed on the Stock Exchange
D Holds shares in other companies

6 Which of the following is a staff function which supports the main line functions within an organization?

A Marketing
B Finance
C Sales
D Production

Questions 7 - 9 share the following answers:

The aims of business organizations are many and will include:

A Providing a public service
B Profit maximization
C Expanding sales and market share
D Providing a charitable service

Which of the above could explain the following business activities?

7 Two people selling cold cans of drink for £1 each on a beach during a hot summer

8 An electronics company producing video recorders that can play 8mm video tapes from camcorders and full-size VHS tapes

9 Collecting unsold sandwiches from retailers to distribute to homeless people

10 Departments in the organization structure shown below have been organized by:

A Process
B Territory
C Product
D Function

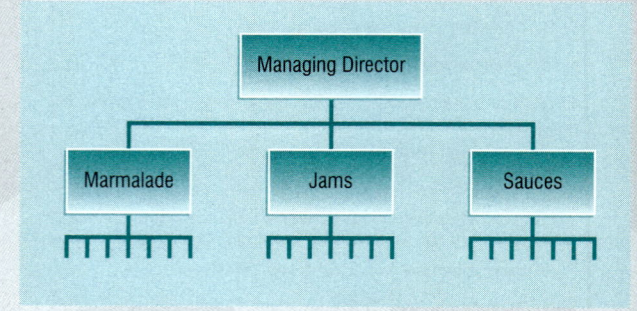

```
              Managing Director
           ┌────────┼────────┐
       Marmalade   Jams    Sauces
       ┌┬┬┬┐     ┌┬┬┬┐    ┌┬┬┬┐
```

11 Which of the following features do you associate with organizational structures which have a wide span of management, or control?

A Management and supervision costs are lower
B Management can lose control
C Subordinates may have more than one boss
D It allows for tight control and close supervision

128

12 Which of the following best describes the organizational structure in the chart below?

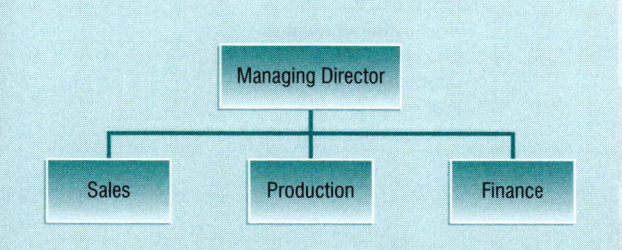

```
        Managing Director
       /        |        \
   Sales    Production   Finance
```

A A centralized, hierarchical structure

B A tall, decentralized structure

C A flat, centralized structure

D A matrix structure

13 (a) Compare the likely objectives of the following organizations:

- ICI (Imperial Chemical Industries PLC)
- Royal Society for the Prevention of Cruelty to Animals (a charity)
- A library run by the local council

(b) ICI is a public limited company (plc). Describe the form of ownership and main method of finance in a plc.

(c) ICI is also a multinational. Explain what is meant by this.

(d) Suggest an appropriate organizational structure for ICI.

14 Explain differences between the following types of business organization in terms of ownership, control, and main method of finance:

- Sole trader
- Partnership
- Private limited company
- Public limited company
- Public corporation

15 (a) What is a sole trader?

(b) Give two advantages and two disadvantages of being a sole trader

(c) Jane Bland owns five electrical stores in the Midlands. Explain why her organization will need a structure.

(d) Suggest an appropriate form of structure for her organization. Give reasons for your answer.

16 (a) What are the span of management and chain of command in an organization?

(b) What are the span of management and chain of command likely to be like in a tall, centralized organization?

(c) Suggest one advantage and one disadvantage of a decentralized organization.

(d) Suggest two factors which might cause a supermarket chain to develop a flat, decentralized structure.

assessment assignment

Advanced Business

Assessment Assignment

Range: Business organizations
Objectives
Differences
Types of ownership
Organizational structures
Compare

Skills: **Communication**
Take part in discussions
Produce written material
Application of number
Collect and record data
Information Technology
Prepare information
Process information

Tasks

1. Examine, and gather information on, the structure of a medium-to-large-sized business organization in the private sector with which you are familiar, and identify the various job roles within the structure.

2. You have been asked by your personnel manager to produce induction material for new employees. The material should be in the form of an attractively designed brochure, produced with the aid of appropriate computer software. The brochure should contain the following information:

- A brief history of the organization and its objectives
- Some data on output and sales over time
- The sector of the economy in which it operates
- The type of organization, for example, partnership, private limited company or plc
- The objectives of the business
- The structure of the organization, for example, hierarchical, flat, tall, matrix, centralized or decentralized
- An organization chart
- Why the organization has chosen this type of structure
- The various departments and their functions
- Line and staff relationships in the organization
- The advantages and disadvantages of the organization structure
- If relevant, how and why the organization has changed its internal structure over time
- Why the internal structure may be reorganized in the future

3. Insert graphs and tables developed from computer spreadsheets in your brochure as appropriate.

4. Complete tasks 1–3 for another organization, preferably in the public sector.

5. Compare the two organizations you have chosen for this assignment in terms of;

- their type of ownership and control
- how they raise finance
- objectives
- organizational structure

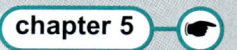

chapter 5

UNIT TWO

CHAPTER 5

chapter 5
Administrative Systems

This chapter investigates the purposes and effectiveness of administrative systems in supporting the functions of business organizations.

Key ideas

An **administrative system** may be defined as a sequence of activities needed by an organization in order to reach an objective.

Businesses need administrative systems to organize their human, financial, and physical resources to perform **routine** and **non-routine functions**.

Administrative systems are used to perform major functions in a firm, including accounts, sales, production, finance, distribution, personnel management, and in the provision of support services such as maintenance and catering.

The introduction of new technology has automated a great deal of day-to-day administration and has reduced the need to employ large numbers of people to carry out the most routine tasks.

The **suitability** of administration systems may be evaluated by the efficiency with which they enable firms to undertake tasks, and their effectiveness in providing information with which to manage and control the business. Administrative systems may also be evaluated through the opinions of users, including employees, customers, suppliers, statutory bodies, etc.

Administration can be improved through **staff training**, **installing new equipment**, and by firms working towards the achievement of recognized **quality standards** such as BS 5750/IS 9000.

Re-engineering, or looking afresh at the administrative systems used in a firm, provides one way in which administration may be improved.

Information technology **hardware** and **software** has revolutionized administration systems. Computer networks have improved productivity and the efficiency of administrative tasks.

Section 5.1 The purposes of administrative systems

What is administration?

> **Portfolio Activity 5.1**
>
> **Range:** Administration systems
> **Skills:** Produce written material
>
> Imagine that you are the owner of a successful small restaurant. You employ five full-time staff, and are kept very busy by regular evening and weekend diners.
>
> Make a list of the typical kinds of routine tasks that would need to be done each week, both by you and your staff.
>
> Can you think of any ways in which the firm could speed up the more repetitive tasks or make the work easier?

Organizing and controlling a business

In a typical business, like the restaurant in Activity 5.1, there are a large number of important jobs which need to be done, and in most cases these will be the same each week or month. A restaurant will need to place regular orders for stocks of food and drink; it will need to check and pay invoices for stock, bank takings, maintain accounts, pay bills and wages, hire and/or train new staff, chase up payments from expense account customers, arrange advertising in the local press, etc. These are the routine tasks which must be carried out repeatedly, but unless they are managed properly, the business will fail. Dealing with these tasks is known as **administration**. Administration is all about the organization and control of business.

The need for good administration

Any business needs to ensure that its administration system is both efficient and effective:

- **Efficiency** refers to how the organization uses its resources.

The aim will be to combine them in the best possible way to maximize output and minimize costs.

- **Effectiveness** refers to how well an organization achieves its objectives, such as increasing sales and/or profits. Good administration lies at the heart of all successful firms.

In the case of the restaurant, if administration is poor, the business may be slow in paying for supplies. This will mean that suppliers may refuse to trade with them and electricity and telephone services may be cut off because bills remain unpaid. Wages, salaries and overtime of staff may not be calculated correctly and the wrong amounts could be paid at the wrong times, leading to unhappy and poorly motivated employees. The restaurant may not keep proper records of its credit customers and so be unable to chase late payers. In the worst case, it may not be able to organize the ordering and delivery of its stocks of food and drink.

The functions of an administrative system

The way in which a business organizes itself in order to cope with day-to-day tasks is known as its **administrative system**.

An administration system may be defined as a sequence of activities necessary to achieve an objective – for example, to order new stock or to pay for goods received. Administration requires that decisions and procedures follow a set of laid-down guidelines based on past good practice. People who carry out these procedures are called administrators.

An example of an administration System

An example of a simple administrative system for processing an order is given below:

1 Order received by the sales department of the firm

2 Warehousing department is informed of the order and checks to ensure that the firm has the right materials to meet it

3 Production department is notified of the requirements of the order

4 Customers informed of delivery date by distribution department

5 Distribution delivers the goods and obtains a **Goods Received Note** (**GRN**) from the customer as evidence of receipt

6 Accounts department sends out an invoice

7 Credit control department chases up late payment of invoice; if necessary

(see also 19.1)

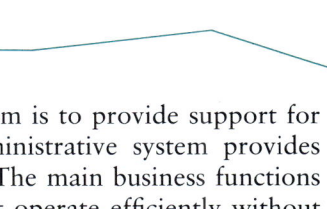

The main function of an administration system is to provide support for **routine and non-routine functions**. An administrative system provides support services for the entire organization. The main business functions of production, sales and marketing could not operate efficiently without this support.

Administrative functions can be classed as either **routine** or **non-routine**

▼ *Paying wages – a routine function*

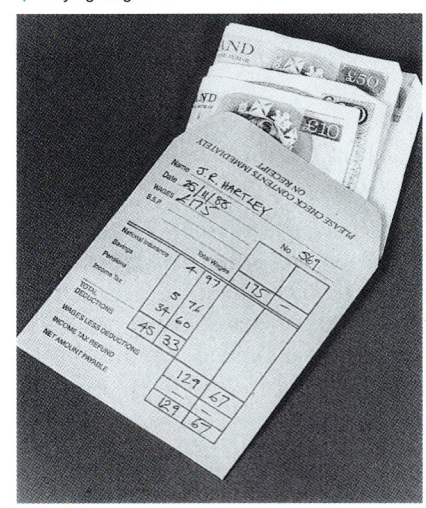

▼ *Dealing with emergencies – a non-routine function*

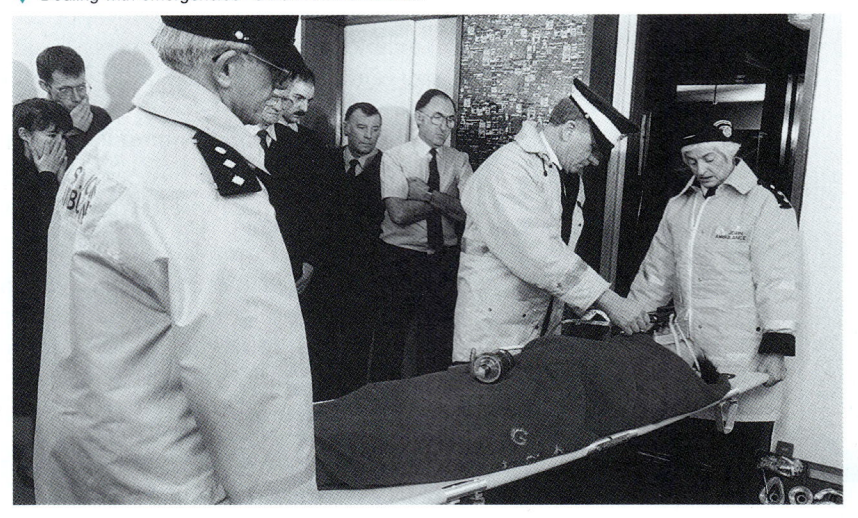

- **Routine functions** are those carried out on a regular basis, such as:

    Organizing financial, physical, and human resources
    Assisting with the smooth production of goods and services
    Assisting with marketing, advertising, and promotions
    Providing accurate and timely information on which to base decisions
    Maintaining sites, buildings, and equipment
    Recording and monitoring business performance
    Meeting external demands for information and legal requirements
    Provide customer service support and dealing with enquiries
    Providing support for quality assurance

    Many of these support functions may be organized into separate departments, for example, finance and accounting, human resources, customer services.

- **Non-routine functions** are those tasks which need to be carried out only at irregular intervals, for example, restructuring the organization, organizing staff cover for absentee workers, dealing with accidents or emergencies, machine breakdowns, legal actions, etc.

The vast majority of business transactions – for example, placing orders for stock, paying wages, loan repayments – occur on a regular basis. Where tasks are routine and predictable, rules and procedures can be established so that the minimum of staff time and thought needs to go into completing the task.

Administrative systems are designed primarily to cope with routine work. However, there will always be some non-routine tasks. For example, a supplier with whom a firm has previously had no contact may require cash payment for their first order. In this case, instead of passing the order through the administrative system, it may need to be passed on to a manager in order that a check can be made on the firm before any money is paid.

A good administrative system will highlight these exceptional or non-routine cases and will have a procedure ready to deal with them.

UNIT **TWO**

CHAPTER 5

Portfolio Activity 5.2

Range: Administration systems, Suitability
Skills: Read and respond to written materials

1. Mail and postal delivery seems to be a straightforward process, which many people would suggest does not need an administrative procedure. Having read the article, to what extent would you agree with this view?

2. What problems are created for firms by not having an agreed administrative system for processing 'urgent' mail?

3. Make some suggestions as to what kind of administrative procedure might help.

Mail Systems to play a larger role

Mailing is a major part of practically any business activity and includes sending sales letters and promotional material as direct mail as well as issuing invoices and statements vital to business cash flow.

The way in which this is achieved, however, through the use of letter post, parcel post and private courier services is often uncontrolled. For this and other reasons the Royal Mail, rated as one of the most efficient services of its kind in Europe, say that British business has been wasting time and money on this exercise through not having a formal distribution policy.

The key issue, says Colin Bok of the Royal Mail is that while nearly five million packages are sent 'urgently' every day, few businesses agree exactly what is meant by urgent. Only a handful of companies have a clear delivery strategy and know the true cost of distribution, especially that of couriers or fax.

Asked what they thought was meant by 'urgent', 75% of secretaries thought something urgent required immediate attention while only just over half of the managers said 'urgent' meant something had to arrive at a specified time, compared with under 20% of secretaries.

The result is unnecessary cost and confusion as secretaries and other staff double guess what their bosses mean by 'urgent' leading to the 'urgency syndrome' which puts too much emphasis on getting the job done quickly rather than getting it done right.

The policy of most companies in not accounting for post to departments or working groups means that many business managers do not know the true cost of distribution because they have become accustomed to it being a 'cost free area'.

Keith Ward, Professor of Financial Strategy at Cranfield School of Management who contributed to the report, says "by introducing a distribution policy it will help companies control costs and cut out wasted time and money in 'urgently' distributing non-urgent items."

Adapted from Business Equipment Digest October 1993

Key words

Administration – the organization of resources to deal with routine and non-routine tasks arising from business activities

Administrative system – the way in which a business organizes it's human, financial, and physical resources

Section 5.2 Administration functions in business

Functional dependency in business

Any business can be viewed as a system of interdependent parts functioning together as a whole to achieve objectives such as improving profit or expanding market share (see 4.1).

Administration involves staff following a set of procedures or rules which set out how things should be done in the firm. Each department or section of a business will operate its own administrative procedures, but all of the systems working within the firm depend on every other system for their own smooth operation. The purpose of administration, therefore, is to bring together all the mutually dependent parts of a business system to make sure they work together in the most efficient way towards the same goals.

Business departments

The most popular way of organizing and administering human, financial, and physical resources in a business system is to divide them into separate departments (see 4.4). Departments allow people to specialize in particular job areas and to improve their skills and performance.

▼ Figure 5.1: Departmental functions

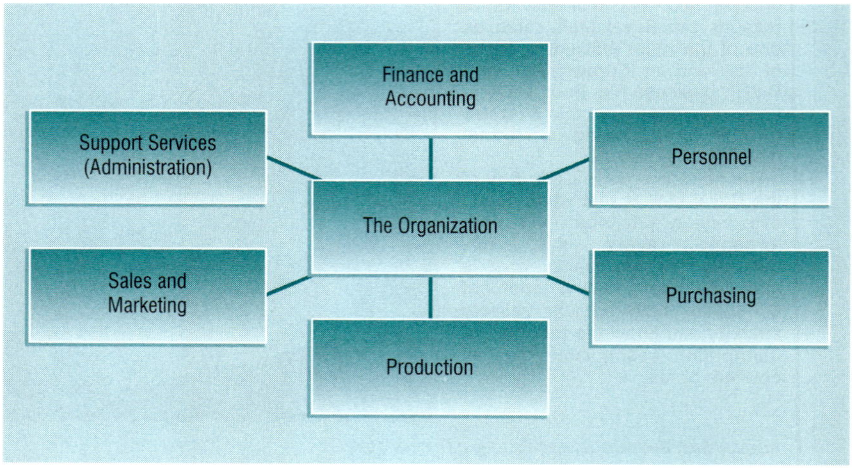

[Diagram: The Organization in the centre, connected to six departments: Finance and Accounting, Personnel, Purchasing, Production, Sales and Marketing, and Support Services (Administration).]

The functions of the various departments one might find in a large organization are detailed below. However, it is important to realize that even in a small organization the same broad functions will need to be performed by staff or owners.

Finance and accounting

The accounting department must operate administrative systems capable of making and recording payments, keeping track of costs, maintaining up-to-date accounts, paying wages, and auditing. These administrative systems must ensure that accounts are kept in an organized and easily accessible form, so that:

- Year-end final accounts can be produced in accordance with the Companies Acts (see 24.1)

- Records can be kept of petty cash and other expenses, and invoices and statements sent to customers
- Careful control can be maintained over debtors and creditors accounts (see 18.2)
- Legal requirements and tax liabilities are met

Information must be available so that the management accountant is able to plan, make decisions, and control the financial operation of the business.

Many organizations today use a computerized accounting system which links the various parts of the accounting records, called an **integrated accounting package** and makes the recording of financial transactions much easier and faster.

Human resources (personnel)

The functions of the personnel department in a firm are many, and will include:

- Recruitment and selection
- Advertising vacant posts
- Education and training
- Health and safety
- Working conditions
- Employee welfare
- Dealing with employee grievances
- Discipline
- Promotions and transfers

The main purpose of an administrative system in personnel, therefore, is to develop routines to carry out these functions and maintain accurate records on each employee, including:

- Name, address, date of birth, telephone number
- Sex, number of dependents, marital status, next of kin
- Nationality and place of birth
- National Insurance number
- Education history and qualifications
- Past and present employment details
- Present job, title, responsibilities
- Salary or wage rate
- Outcome of appraisal interviews
- Any disciplinary actions
- Training and development undertaken

Today, most personnel records are stored on computer. Because much of the information is personal to individual employees, the personnel department must be fully aware of the requirements of the Data Protection Act 1984 (see 7.3).

Purchasing

The main role of the purchasing department is to acquire materials, components, equipment, and other goods and services necessary for production (see 18.2). It involves:

- Finding and negotiating with suppliers
- Ordering
- Dealing with the requirements of other departments
- Taking delivery
- Checking goods and services received against orders
- Arranging the payment of invoices through the finance department
- Keeping records

Production

The role of production is to provide the product at the right quality, quantity, and cost when customers want it. Administration in production can be judged by how successfully the system ensures that production meets these targets. The administrative system must be capable of:

- Ordering materials in advance
- Arranging for storage
- Scheduling routine maintenance of plant and equipment
- Liaison with personnel to ensure that there are sufficient staff with the right qualifications and background
- Providing cost information to the finance department

Sales and marketing

The role of the sales administration system is to ensure that once the customer has agreed to the sale, the transaction is completed quickly and smoothly. For example, the sales system would need to ensure that:

- All sales information is processed quickly
- Customer enquiries are recorded and dealt with promptly
- Sales budgets are prepared and monitored
- Sales representatives' expense claims are checked and then passed to accounts for payment
- Credit is arranged for customers where appropriate
- Customer orders are processed and sent out promptly
- Customer care, such as after-sales service, is provided
- Goods and services are advertised and promoted effectively

- Market research information is collected (see 9.1)

Sales departments in most medium-sized and large organizations keep their customer records on a database along with product details and prices etc. Some businesses, like McDonalds, are able to monitor sales of particular products day by day at their UK headquarters by receiving reports from high street stores via electronic mail. This kind of administrative system allows the firm to adjust its promotions, advertising, and prices in response to local conditions.

An important area of marketing is **customer service** (see 11.1). Good customer service can help to improve an organization's image among consumers, resulting in increased sales. Many organizations have customer service departments to look after customers once a sale has been made and to deal with complaints, repairs, providing replacements, etc. A good administrative system will make sure that customer enquiries, repairs, or complaints are dealt with quickly.

Distribution

The role of distribution is to ensure that goods and services are available to customers when they want them (see 11.2). The function of the administrative system in distribution is to ensure that the right goods are delivered in the right quantities by the time agreed with the customer at the minimum cost. Achieving this may involve the following tasks:

- Delivering supplies to other organizations
- Choosing delivery methods, e.g. by road, rail, air
- Distribution of finished products to wholesalers, retail outlets, or direct to consumers
- Checking in goods received
- Storage
- Checking goods out
- Monitoring the movement of goods and work in progress within a factory
- Monitoring the movement of goods within a retail outlet (i.e. from the stockroom)
- Stock control to ensure goods are available when they are required

Information Technology forms the backbone of most administrative systems in distribution. The use of bar-code readers means that stock can automatically be re-ordered when a central computer notes that remaining stocks are down to a pre-set level. Many large transport firms use 'routemaster' computer programmes which produce a route map for the driver, taking into account the time of day and likely road conditions in order to give the quickest route to the destination.

Support services

The support service department (sometimes known simply as administration) in a firm provides a variety of services to all of the other

Advanced Business

Security – a support service that benefits the whole organization

departments. These services might include cleaning, maintenance of equipment, security systems, central filing, and catering. Often support services may contract out tasks to other organizations, for example offering a cleaning contract for tender. The support services administrative system must be capable of managing contracts and carefully monitoring the quality of services offered by sub-contractors. A good system will also carefully monitor the views of consumers using the services and channel feedback through to service providers.

Catering functions

- Identify catering needs in a firm
- Purchase supplies
- Store food
- Maintain standards of hygiene
- Waste management
- Prepare menus
- Record transactions
- Handle cash

Maintenance functions

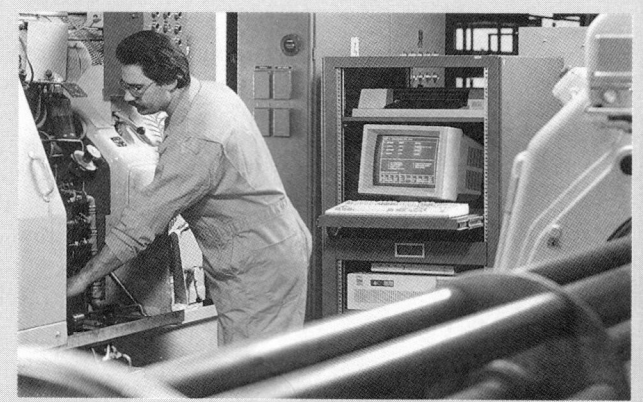

- Create an inventory of all equipment and machinery
- Make regular inspections of all equipment and premises
- Record any faults and repairs undertaken
- Instruct maintenance staff to undertake repairs
- Arrange regular servicing of plant and machinery
- Keep records of maintenance costs

Portfolio Activity 5.3

Range: Administration systems, Information technology
Skills: Take part in discussions, Produce written material

1. Investigate the provision of catering and cleaning services in a business organization you are familiar with. In particular:

   - How are they arranged?
   - Who takes responsibility for arranging these services?
   - Why are these services provided?
   - What are the main functions of these services?
   - What other departments/functions in the organization are required to help provide an efficient catering and cleaning service? (*Hint*: Who keeps details of transactions? Who helps recruit staff?)
   - How are service levels monitored?
   - How is Information Technology used, or how could it be used in future?
   - How might the administration of these support services be improved?

2. Write up your findings in a short report.

3. Prepare a short presentation of overhead slides of your findings to give to your study group.

Section 5.3 **Evaluating administrative systems**

Meeting the requirements of the business

Businesses vary so much in terms of size, structure, location, expertise of staff, and levels of technology used, that no one system of administration will be best for all. Instead, each firm is likely to be better served by creating a tailor-made system to suit its individual circumstances. Bigger firms usually have a greater quantity of decisions to make about purchases, sales, production, finance, distribution, etc., and so will need a more structured and formal system of doing things.

Large firms are able to employ specialist staff to carry out administrative tasks, often aided by the use of computers and other telecommunications equipment such as faxes and modems to link computers through the telephone network. In contrast, in a small sole trader enterprise, most tasks can be undertaken reasonably successfully by just one person doing jobs as and when s/he feels they need to be done.

Sole Trader – Off License

Ordering	Orders placed by telephone daily and given to sales representatives
Stock	Sole trader keeps an informal eye on stock each day and may undertake a formal stock count once a year or month
Distribution	Sole trader employs a delivery boy who makes deliveries in evenings and on Saturdays
Personnel	Sole trader interviews and employs staff her/himself
Accounts	Keeps simple accounts of receipts and payments and hires an accountant to produce annual accounts
Mail	Opens mail her/himself.
Written Communications	Hand writes orders and letters to suppliers. No internal written communications; the sole trader speaks with staff directly.

Public Limited Company – Head office of a large national off-licence chain

Ordering	Central on-line computer receives individual orders from shops and generates bulk orders to wines and spirits suppliers. System managed by a specialist staff of purchasing executives
Stock	Computerized warehouse using bar code readers keeps a minute-by-minute record of all stock held and alerts central computer when stocks of some products are running low.
Distribution	Company operates its own fleet of delivery vehicles based at regional distribution depots.
Personnel	A specialized personnel department places recruitment adverts in the national press and operates a national recruitment and training programme from head office
Accounts	Computerized accounts section employing credit control and budgeting executives
Mail	Mail room employing 10 staff equipped with 5 fax machines receiving 2,000 letters per day
Written Communications	Word-processed internal communications and electronic mail

▲ *How administrative procedures can differ between a sole trader and large PLC*

> **Portfolio Activity 5.4**
>
> **Range:** Administrations systems, Suitability
> **Skills:** Take part in discussions
>
> Select three of the tasks identified in the table above and investigate the administrative systems used to deal with them in an organization with which you are familiar.
>
> Compare these with the systems identified by another student in your study group. Report on some of the differences in administrative systems which you have identified and suggest reasons for these differences. To what extent does the design of each system depend on the size and nature of each firm?

In choosing an administration system a firm will also consider the following:

Do staff have the necessary skills to operate the system?

For example, are staff aware of the rules and procedures which govern the sending and receiving of invoices, arranging maintenance contracts, hiring staff; etc.? Do they know how to use computerized systems? Staff training in administration and the use of Information Technology can help to improve the operation of an administration system.

What are advantages and disadvantages to individuals?

Does the system reduce or increase the workload of individuals? For example, has the creation of standardized documentation helped to improve the efficiency with which documents are processed, allowing staff to use the time saved to concentrate on other tasks?

Computer software packages are now available which can undertake a number of administrative tasks in a fraction of the time it would have taken manually. But does the firm now expect staff to undertake more tasks as a result? Have the procedures for accounting, organizing human resources, or providing support services become so complex that employees are finding it difficult to remember and cope with them all?

Has the administration system implemented health and safety procedures to reduce the number of accidents in the workplace, such as organizing health and safety training, providing protective clothing, or simply producing staff notices?

What are advantages and disadvantages to the firm?

For example, does the system offer value for money? Do the benefits of using the system in terms of increased productivity and reduced overheads exceed the costs of the system in terms of labour, equipment, materials, training, and running costs? Are some tasks more cost effective if undertaken manually rather than with the help of expensive new computer equipment? Is the system secure? What happens if a computer which contains important documents and records is stolen or breaks down?

Monitoring the effectiveness of an administration system

User surveys
One useful way to evaluate the effectiveness and efficiency of administrative systems is to survey the opinions of users. The main users are the staff operating the systems and the customers who purchase the goods or services sold.

There are a range of other business clients who are in contact with firms' administrative systems, including suppliers, government agencies (including the Inland Revenue and Customs and Excise departments), and shareholders. These clients could also provide an insight into administrative efficiency.

The attainment of agreed standards
Administration can be evaluated in each department as well as in the organization as a whole. Administration in a particular department may be judged by identifying the role and purpose of that department and then seeing to what extent its work meets the standards required. For example, a production and distribution department responsible for stock control could have as its aim never to be without any kind of stock for more than one working day and to deliver finished products to customers within three working days.

Portfolio Activity 5.5

Range: Suitability, Improvements

Skills: Take part in discussions, Collect and record data

For any organization that you know (you could choose your own school or college, for example), identify the various departments and their main purposes.

For each department, decide upon a way of measuring the effectiveness of its administrative systems.

Using your chosen method, evaluate the departmental administrative systems and suggest how the overall efficiency of the business may be gauged. Report on your results.

Choose one department and research in detail the views of the users and customers of the system. Recommend improvements to the system.

Ways of improving administrative systems
A firm may seek to improve the operation of their administration system in a number of ways.

Staff training and re-training
A workforce that does not understand the correct procedures to follow, or cannot use equipment properly, will not operate a cost effective administration system. Organizations are using training to create multi-skilled workforces (see 17.2). This refers to training to equip people with a wide variety of skills which they can use to good effect in their organization. For example, skills in using computers, word processing, writing and presentation, negotiating, letting contracts, information processing and managing resources, as well as improving any special skills they may have as economists, production engineers, or accountants.

Introducing quality standards
In a competitive marketplace, successful firms are those which continuously attempt to improve the quality of their goods and services and production methods.

Advanced Business

▲ The BSI kitemark of quality

In order to assist firms to improve the quality of their operations, the **British Standards Institute (BSI)** has introduced quality standards for firms to work towards. The **British Standard 5750** provides a 'kitemark of quality' similar to the British Standards for Safety, which when demonstrated by firms allow them to display the safety kitemark on their products.

For a firm to demonstrate its achievement of BS5750, it must introduce a series of management systems and procedures covering areas such as training, design control, production, purchasing, inspections, and quality audits. These must be clearly documented and well maintained. External inspectors regularly check that the firm is continuing to follow these documented procedures.

The status of BS5750 is recognized internationally and equates with the International Standards Organization ISO 9000 quality standards, which operate in a similar way to BS5750. BS5750 and ISO 9000 standards are interchangeable.

Re-engineering

Business **re-engineering** or **process redesign** provides a way of building new administrative systems into a firm and taking advantage of new technology in order to improve on previous practice. Behind the concept of re-engineering are two key ideas:

- That it is better to re-design all administrative systems in one go rather than to make continual small modifications to an existing system

- That most companies today operate with many thousands of administrative specialists who are judged and rewarded on how well they perform their own specialized tasks, with no concept or interest in how these contribute to the success of the firm as a whole.

By re-engineering and looking at administrative systems from scratch, it is possible to take full advantage of rapid advances in computer technology and falling computer prices in order to build new and better systems.

Re-engineering at Ford

The Ford Motor Car Company re-engineered its administrative procedures to deal with payments to its thousands of suppliers. These payments previously involved 500 staff shuffling purchase orders and invoices among themselves. Ford questioned whether this paperwork was necessary and it now employs 125 staff to do the same job, but much faster. Clerks working at receiving bays use computers to compare deliveries received with the orders placed. If they agree, the goods are accepted and the clerk instructs the computer to pay the supplier. No paperwork is involved.

Key words

Re-engineering – designing new, more effective and efficient administrative systems to replace old systems

British Standards Institute – an organization that inspects firms and products, and awards recognized quality 'kitemarks'.

Section 5.4 — Using Information Technology to improve administration

The power of computing

The operation of administration systems has been greatly assisted by the development and widespread availability of personal computers (PCs). The introduction of new technology can affect the following:

- **Workload:** Information Technology can increase the quantity and quality of work that can be carried out by employees in a firm. This is because computer systems can speed work up and do not make mistakes other than those caused by human error. However, a great deal of effort is required immediately following the introduction of new technology to transfer existing files onto computers and to set up computerized procedures. Initially, therefore, the introduction of new technology can increase the workload of employees before long-term reductions are realized.

- **Stress:** Because change involves new methods of working and procedures, it can be a very stressful time for staff. The introduction of new technology may not only change working methods, but may also lead to redundancies and therefore even greater stress. Stress can be reduced through training in the use of the new equipment and by good communications between management and staff to discuss the new methods and keep people informed.

- **Productivity:** If less inputs are required to produce the same or more output in a firm, then productivity has improved (see 15.1). Information Technology can improve productivity by increasing the speed at which administrative tasks are undertaken, thereby releasing labour to work on other tasks.

- **Efficiency:** A computerized system rarely breaks down and makes mistakes. Information Technology can, therefore, help to increase the speed, accuracy, and efficiency with which administrative tasks are carried out.

Computer hardware

Computer hardware is the physical equipment used by the system. Typically, hardware consists of one or more computers, each possessing a **visual display unit** (VDU), or monitor, and a keyboard with which to enter information and control the software and information output. Use of a mouse, joystick, light pen, and/or touch-sensitive VDU screens, are both alternatives and complements to the keyboard. A printer will be required if information displayed by the VDU is to be output to paper or overhead slide transparencies.

The hardware is driven by one or more **central processing units** (CPUs). The CPU interprets and processes information and commands. The speed and power of CPUs is growing all the time, with 486 and Pentium processors, produced by the American Intel Corporation, being the most common kinds of processor in use today.

Advanced Business

Software

Computer software refers to predesigned packages or programs which give instructions to the computer to process information. A great number of packages are available for business use, including word processing, spreadsheets, databases, graphics, and accounting software (see 7.2).

The tasks software can perform are continually expanding with new developments in processing power, which has also increased the speed at which tasks are completed. For example, desktop video conferencing, whereby staff in different locations can see and talk to each other on their computer screens and work on the same computer files, is now possible using software developed for the Pentium processor.

What is multi-tasking?

The majority of computers used in business today are IBM compatible and will usually run a program called Microsoft *Windows*. *Windows* allows different software packages to be used simultaneously and for information from different applications to be combined. For example, information from a database can be imported into a word processor or into a spreadsheet and turned into a graph, which can then be imported into a word processor to support a report on trends in sales figures. This is known as **multi-tasking**.

Computer hardware systems

MEET OUR FOUNTAIN P75 EXC

Awesome Pentium™ Processor Power from Fountain starts with our Fountain P75 models. The P75 comes in CD-ROM, Multi-Media, On-Line, Video Conferencing and Workstation configurations, all feature the very latest PCI Plug-and-Play technology. All our systems with Pentium™ processors will enable you to blaze through the most demanding of graphic intensive and computational heavy applications and run more conventional applications at speeds hitherto unheard of.

Pentium™ *75MHz Processor with 8Mb RAM*
(Single chip upgradeable CPU, RAM expandable to 128Mb, 16k Internal Cache, 256k Ext Cache)

Toshiba Quad Speed IDE CD-ROM Drive
(MPCII standard, Sub 150ms Access Time, 684Kb per sec data transfer rate, 8.33Mb per sec Burst rate)

850Mb Enhanced IDE HDD

3.5" 1.44Mb Floppy Disk Drive

PCI Bus 32-Bit Expansion Slots
(2 Free 32-Bit PCI Bus and 3 Free 16-Bit ISA Slots)

2Mb PCI Bus Accelerator Graphics Card

SuperScreen 14" .28 Dot Pitch, Energy Saver, Non-Interlaced Super VGA Colour Monitor
(Non-Interlaced, Flicker-Free display, 1024 x 768 resolution, up to 90Hz refresh rate)

Desktop or Midi Tower
(Available for the same price)

12 Months On-Site Warranty Included in the Price
(See Fountain Aftercare Options for additional Options)

FOUNTAIN P75 EXC (EXECUTIVE CD-ROM)

£1299.95 (ex. VAT)

intel inside pentium PROCESSOR

Portfolio Activity 5.6

Range: Information Technology
Skills: Prroduce written material

1. Study the article. What criteria are used to judge the performance of the software? Produce a list of criteria against which you might evaluate another business software application you have access to, for example an accounting package or spreadsheet.

2. Use your list to evaluate the performance of a business software package you have access to. How does the product rate? What are its good points and bad points? What improvements would you recommend, if any?

3. Use your evaluation to write a similar article on your chosen software for the next publication of the computing magazine.

Accounting QuickBooks: Intuit Does Inventory

There's good news for operators of small businesses who are trying to make do with spreadsheets or pencils and ledger paper to maintain their financial records. Get rid of your green eyeshades: The current version of Intuit's QuickBooks now handles inventory management as well as a host of new features, including audit trail and customizable invoices.

Unique among other accounting programs, QuickBooks offers a variety of ways to enter purchased items.

The most useful addition we found was the ability to record the arrival of several elements of a single invoice as they are received, rather than waiting for the complete order to update inventory records.

QuickBooks maintains its forms-based metaphor for entering transactions in this version. Cheques, purchase orders, invoices, and bills are all entered onto screens that mimic the program's forms. There are also more ways to customize forms in this version.

Your accountant will be glad that the program can maintain an audit trail for any data entry errors that occur, though we found that adding audit tracking slowed down transaction processing.

To process payroll, you still need Intuit's QuickPay add-on program. And though Version 3.0 of QuickBooks includes many enhancements, we found several missing elements. The inventory section does not include back-order processing and only maintains a single price for each item (though you can override it during invoice entry). You can customize invoices, but you can only have one invoice layout in use at a time; therefore, you can't create unique invoices for each customer or group.

QuickBooks 3.0 for Windows is a solid performer. If you've got simple inventory management needs and don't want the complexity of a higher-end system, this program is a good choice.

PC Magazine 10.1.95

Computer networks

To allow different parts of an organization to share software and exchange information, computers must be linked in some way. Within an organization this is usually done by creating a **local area network (LAN)**. Networks are either 'wired' together or connected via 'wireless', using radio waves to transmit information between PCs. Increasingly businesses are networking their computers to speed the transfer of information and assist communications. Access to the LAN can be protected by using a password which users must enter before they can log-on.

At the centre of a LAN will normally be a powerful computer which acts as the file server to all the computers—or workstations – linked in the network. A LAN file server will provide:

- Storage space for software programs
- Software applications to workstations on request
- Storage space for files created on workstations
- Temporary storage for files held in a print queue

Advanced Business

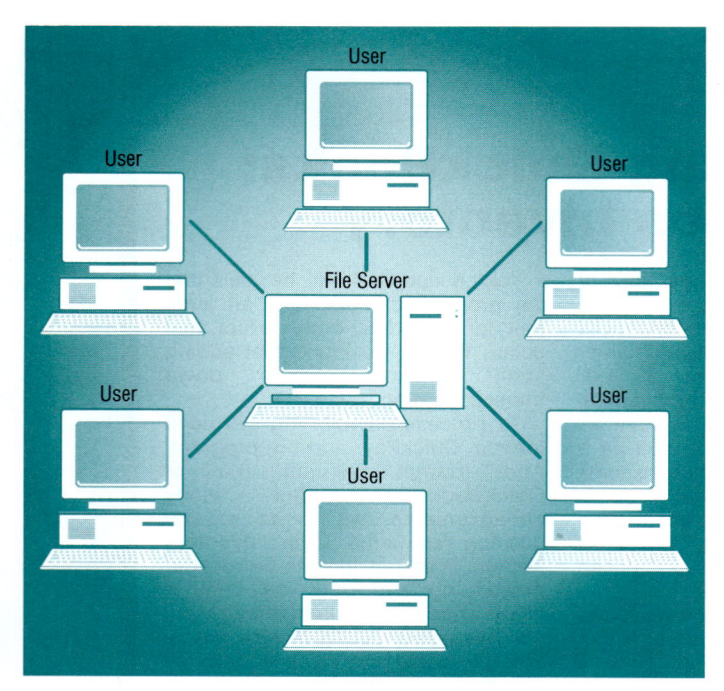

▲ *A Local Area (computer) Network*

Some LANs do not have a file server. Instead, individual workstations use their own hard disks to store software applications and work files which can be made available to the other workstations in the network. These are called **public files**. Microsoft's *Windows for Workgroups* is a software package which can be used to operate this type of network with up to 10 users.

Computers linked through telephone lines form **wide area networks** (WANs). Computers are able to talk to each other using the telephone system. WANS can be used to link different parts of the same organization, or even different organizations, at different sites, including those overseas.

To create a WAN, both the sender and the receiver of information must possess the following facilities and equipment:

- A computer (either a mainframe or PC)
- A telephone socket
- A telephone line
- A **modem** (MOdulator/DEModulator)
- Communications software to operate the modem

Central to the creation of a WAN is the **modem**. This is a device which can change digital signals to analogue signals and back again. Telephone lines were designed for transmitting audible sounds which are transformed for transmission into electrical 'analog' waves. Computers, however, send and receive digital signals made up binary code–a series of 0s and 1s. The combinations of 0s and 1s is infinite and can represent an infinite array of different words, numbers, and pictures when converted.

▼ *Figure 5.2: Creating a Wide Area Network (WAN)*

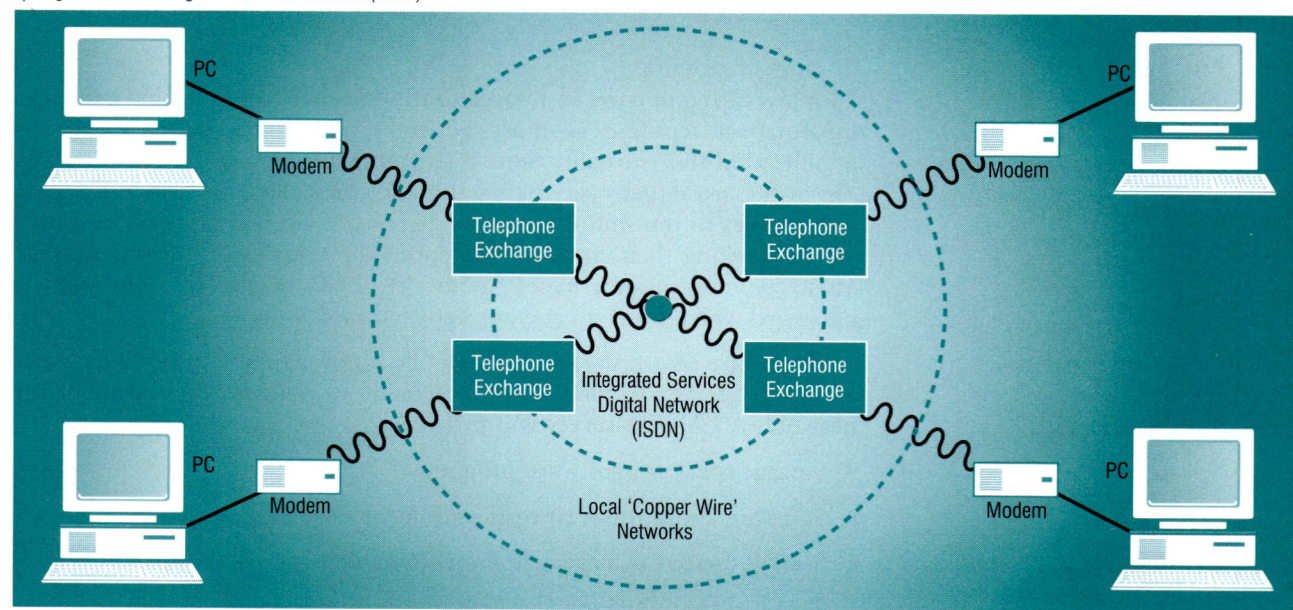

148

Telephone lines between UK exchanges are able to carry digital signals, but most lines from exchanges to homes and organizations remain analogue. Modems are, therefore, needed for computers to communicate with each other until the network in the UK and abroad becomes digital.

Portfolio Activity 5.7

Range: Information Technology, Suitability, Improvements

Skills: Read and respond to written material

1. The Ministry of Agriculture Fisheries and Food (MAFF) has installed a wide area network (WAN) to connect a number of local area networks (LANs). What is the difference between a WAN and a LAN?

2. Explain why modems are vital to the creation of computer networks.

3. How will the networks be used in MAFF?

4. What measures is MAFF taking to ensure that effective and secure use is made of the network?

It's all change at the Ministry

The Ministry of Agriculture Fisheries and Food (MAFF) is equipping 3,000 staff with office automation over the next three years.

The Maiden Project (Ministry of Agriculture Integrated Desktop Environment for the Nineties) is a big challenge for the computing department, which is running the project with support from Siemens Nixdorf Information systems.

The end-users are divided into more than 20 workgroups in half a dozen towns and cities; some are split between sites. The workgroups are largely autonomous and to an extent control their own computing. Most of these staff, who have not used personal computers (PCs) in their work before, are now being given powerful PCs based on Intel's 486 processors. They are also getting Microsoft *Windows* software as needed; *Word* for word processing; the Excel spreadsheet package; *Powerpoint* for graphics and *MS Project* for project management.

The whole lot is being tied together in an electronic mail and data network, providing text communication and access to mainframe computer systems for those who use them.

'We've introduced a management of change process,' says Mr John Kennedy, one of the project's managers. 'We start talking to work groups six months before installation. This is an opportunity for us to start the groups thinking about change management, what needs to be done and the benefits'.

MAFF has analysed the skills of individual users and Siemens Nixdorf has developed training at different levels. PC appreciation courses are available to those new to PCs. There are also courses on using software and advanced courses on the applications, local networking, and system administration.

Everyone gets half a day on electronic mail. Mr Kennedy says all the workgroups see big benefits in this facility, especially those across split sites.

Standard templates have been set up for documents of different types, with specific typefaces and character sizes. As Mr Kennedy says: "A package such as *Word* offers a large number of fonts and if you give people free rein you risk getting some horrendous looking documents."

MAFF is also very serious about illegal software copying (it has recently joined the Federation Against Software Theft) and about viruses - programs which can destroy files.

Financial Times Review, 'Software at Work', Winter 1993

Key words

Hardware – computer equipment

Visual display unit (VDU) – a computer monitor

Computer processing unit (CPU) – the control unit of a computer

Software – computer program, usually supplied on floppy disk or CD-ROM

Multi-tasking – the ability of some computers when using Windows to handle different kinds of information simultaneously

Further reading:

Collins, S: *The Way Computers and MS DOS Work* (Microsoft Press 1994)

Plus any good computer magazines, such as *PC Magazine*, *PC User* or *Personal Computer World*, available from most large newsagents.

Test questions

The following underpinning knowledge will be tested:
1. Administrative systems and support functions
2. How Information Technology can change administration systems
3. The suitability of administration systems
4. Ways to improve administrative systems

1 Which of the following functions can NOT be performed by an administration system?
   A Supporting routine business functions
   B Recording and monitoring business performance
   C Supporting customer service
   D Persuading customers to buy at the point of sale

2 The administrative system used by a business to check its finances for mistakes is known as:
   A Total Quality Management
   B Internal audit
   C Budgetary control
   D Quality control

3 Which of the following criteria could NOT be used for evaluation of the efficiency of an administrative system operated by a firm maintaining photocopiers?
   A Reduced call-out time for copier engineers
   B Increased sales revenues
   C Faster despatch of spare parts to engineers
   D Quicker despatch of reminders to customers who are late payers

4 Which of the following is a non-routine task in a manufacturing firm?
   A Monitoring production costs
   B Recording weekly sales volumes
   C Recording credit sales
   D Dealing with a power failure

5 A primary administrative function of the support services department is:
   A To ensure that accurate records and processing of sales occur
   B To maintain stock levels and to re-order on time
   C To ensure that routine maintenance is undertaken
   D To ensure that materials are purchased on time

6 How best could an organization measure how well it is functioning?
   A Compare actual performance with targets
   B Ask competitors
   C Ask staff and customers' opinions
   D Market research

Questions 7–9 share the following answer options:
   A Finance
   B Personnel
   C Sales
   D Purchasing

Which of the above administrative functions would be used for the following?

7 Recording and dealing with customer enquiries

8 Handling cash and making payments

9 Preparing a job advertisement

10 The main British Standard to measure quality is known as:
   A Total Quality Management
   B ISO 9000
   C The BSI
   D BS 5750

11 a. What is an administration system?

   b. Suggest two examples of a routine function and a non-routine function that an administration system would support in a business.

   c. Explain two ways in which Information Technology can improve the operation of these support functions.

   d. Suggest and explain one other way the operation of the administration system might be improved.

12 a. What is a computer network?

   b. What is the difference between a WAN and a LAN?

   c. Explain how a computer network could help the purchasing department improve its administration in a large firm.

   d. Suggest two software applications a business could use, and how they can be used, to improve the operation of its administration system.

assessment assignment

Assessment assignment

Range: Administration systems
Information Technology
Suitability
Improvements

Skills: Communication
Produce written material
Use images
Information Technology
Process information

You work for a small but rapidly growing firm called Satellite Supplies producing and distributing Satellite TV equipment. The firm started as a sole trader business, with the owner undertaking all of the various tasks needed to run the firm. The tasks varied from banking cash, to ordering supplies, sending out invoices, chasing late payers, taking new orders, and marketing and delivering the goods.

Now the firm has a turnover of £300,000 per annum and employs 5 people. However, it is still being run without any proper business systems, and all decision-making and paperwork still depend for action on the original owner. Recently, because of the heavy workload, it has been decided to look at the kinds of systems that other, more established firms use and then adopt the best of these for Satellite Supplies.

Tasks

You have been asked to prepare a report explaining the administration system used in a firm (or firms) that you have chosen for investigation (this could be a work experience firm, your school/college administration system, or any firm known to you).

Your report should include the following discussion elements:

- Why firms need administration systems
- The kinds of tasks requiring administrative systems at Satellite Supplies and the business functions that would undertake them
- The kinds of international quality standards which could be used by the firm to improve the quality of its administration
- How the suitability of any administrative systems introduced could be evaluated
- The use of a questionnaire to find out the opinions of users, employees, and customers, to help guide the design of an administrative system that could be employed by Satellite Supplies
- How the introduction of computers could help the operation of the administration system, in terms of work load, productivity and other improvements
- What software applications you would recommend to the firm to use in administration

Use word processing or desktop publishing computer software to prepare your report, to cover Information Technology core skills.

Present the main conclusions and recommendations of your report in an oral presentation to your class group, using slides and handouts if appropriate.

Advanced Business

chapter 6 Communications Systems

This chapter examines why businesses need communications systems, the kinds of systems that can be used, and the possible effects of changes to communications.

BUT I DON'T WANT YOU – LET ME TALK DIRECTLY TO THE COMPUTER

Key ideas

Communication is a two-way process which allows information to be passed between people and organizations.

Communication systems are required by businesses in order to assist **internal communication** within the organization and **external communication** with other organizations.

Communication channels are the routes along which information is passed. Channels can be **one-way**, **two-way** or **multi-track**, **open** to all, or **restricted** to certain people and organizations.

The **objectives** of communication include **providing information**, **giving instructions** and **confirming arrangements**. Internally, better cxommunication can **improve team work**.

A variety of communications systems exist for internal and external communications, including **face-to-face** (videoconferencing, round table), **ear-to-ear** (telephone and mobile phone), **written correspondence, sign language, computer-generated speech** and **interactive computer programs**.

Electronic technology is used to assist communications, including **computer networks, electronic mail, enhanced telephone systems** (fax, modem, Internet), **voice recognition** and generation, as well as **touch screens**.

To ensure that full and effective use is made of new communications equipment and systems, a business needs to make sure that users are adequately trained.

Communication systems may be evaluated in terms of their design, **cost and value for money, ease of use, speed and ease of access, accuracy, security,** and how they **improve interaction** between people and organizations.

New communication systems can help to improve the speed of, and ease of access to, communications, and help to create the potential for communication to a wider audience. However, these positive effects must be weighed against the cost of new equipment, the fact that some organizations might be excluded from communication if they do not own the right equipment, and the threat to security from those who can intercept communications.

Section 6.1 Why do businesses need communications systems?

Portfolio Activity 6.1

Range: Communication, Objectives of communication
Skills: Read and respond to written material

Identify two possible means of communication for each of the cases given below:

1. A large high street electrical goods chain has 200 stores. Each store needs to regularly update head office about its daily sales, both to provide central information and also to enable head office to order more stock.

2. A multinational company wishes to consult its national managers on plans for new products. It would like the managers to be able to see and hear each other.

3. A solicitor wants immediate written confirmation that a buyer in Spain has written a cheque to purchase her client's villa.

4. The personnel officer of a large UK insurance company wants to send information detailing a new company training scheme to all of its employees.

What is communication?

Communication is a process which enables information to be passed from one person or organization to another. To be effective, communication will require:

- A **transmitter**: a source or sender of information
- A **transmission**: a message or content
- A **channel**: a route through which information is passed, e.g. different employees and organizations
- A **medium**: a method through which information is passed, e.g. a telephone
- A **receptor**: a person or audience to whom the information is sent
- **Feedback**: to indicate whether not the receptor has understood the message

Thus, for communication to be effective, information passed between two parties must be understood and acceptable to those sending it and to those receiving it. If both the person transmitting information and the person receiving it are within the same organization, communication is said to be **internal**. If information is passed between one organization and another, it involves **external communication**.

Success in business depends on being able to respond to changes in the market and to the actions of competitors quicker than other firms. One very important means of gaining a competitive advantage over rival firms is through fast and efficient communications. Fast and accurate communication means that a firm can find out quickly what is going on in the market and can communicate its response - whether in terms of price changes or the introduction of new or revised products - to its own staff and to customers as quickly as possible.

Advanced Business

▼ *Channels of communication*

Channels of communication

We can define a **communication channel** as either a **formal** or **informal** route between people or organizations along which information passes. For example, informal channels of communication can be 'opened' between people at lunchtime and on social occasions. The people involved may discuss business procedures and policy, but sometimes information communicated through this 'grapevine' method may become distorted. On the other hand, formal communication involves information that is entirely necessary to ensure the effective operation and execution of a business activity.

Most channels of communication involve a two-way process, passing information between two or more parties. However, communication can also be a one-way or multi-track process.

One-way channels

These exist to provide people and organizations with information which requires no direct feedback. Here there is only one transmitter and one receptor. Examples might include the announcement of train departure times at a station, or managers passing simple instructions or other information via a 'vertical channel' to workers on the shop floor.

Two-way channels

Here, the communicators must be both transmitters and receptors of information - for example, a group of managers asking employees for their opinions on the introduction of new technology or proposed changes in working methods, and listening to feedback.

Multi-track channels

These exist when information is passed on by one receptor to a number of receptors who are also able to feedback. For example, manufacturers may provide wholesalers with product information which is then passed onto retailers, who in turn give this information to consumers. Wholesalers, retailers, and consumers may then pass their opinions on the product back to the manufacturer.

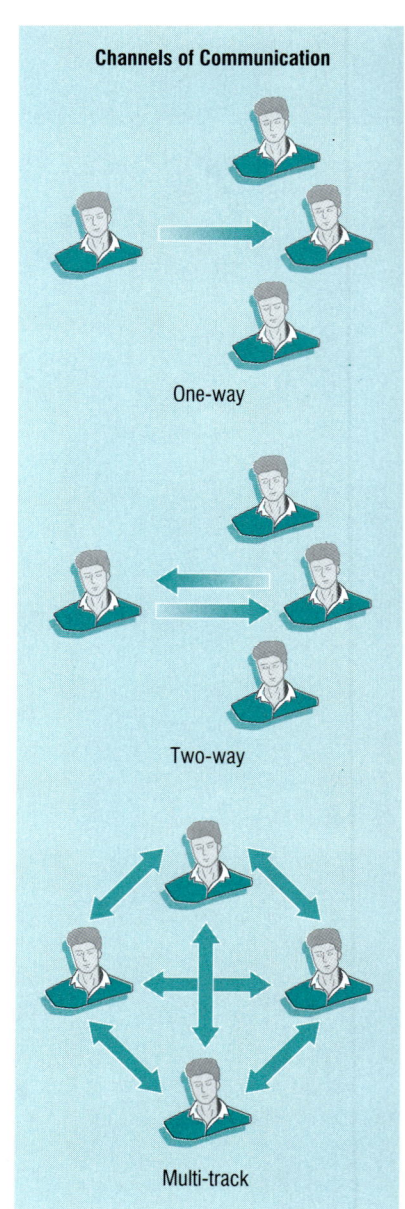

Channels of Communication

One-way

Two-way

Multi-track

Open and restricted channels

If a channel of communication is **open**, it means that anyone can share in the information being transmitted. For example, a noticeboard at work is used to transmit information to anyone who reads it.

However, some information will be confidential, and access to it will be **restricted**. For example, if managers are planning to introduce new machinery which is likely to lead to redundancies, they will need information on which to base this decision, but will not wish their workforce to know until their plans are finalized. An organization will also wish to keep new product developments secret, so that rival firms are unable to copy their ideas.

The objectives of communication

Internal communications in a business between owners and managers, managers and other staff, and between office and shop floor workers, will have the following objectives;

- to provide information on a whole range of matters from organisational goals, costs and performance to simple routine matters such as canteen opening times
- to give instructions on a host of tasks that will help the organisation function effectively and achieve objectives, such as how to organise production, how to design an advertising campaign, how to fill out order forms etc
- to improve team work. Better communication between managers and workers can improve worker morale if they feel their opinions are being considered. Working in teams relies on effective communication between members to get work done.
- to communicate how well individual workers have performed in their jobs either informally or formally via annual job appraisal reviews and to recommend appropriate training and career moves (see 12.2).

The objectives of external communications with other people and organisations will include:

- providing information, such as information on end of year profits to the Inland Revenue or accident statistics to the Health and Safety executive and so on
- giving instructions, such as orders to suppliers, worker selection criteria to employment agencies, credit arrangements to banks and many more
- confirming arrangements, for example, the date, time and venue for a meeting, or travel times and arrangements with transport operators
- receiving feedback, both internally, for example from workers regarding new working methods, or externally, such as consumers opinions of new products.

Advanced Business

> **Portfolio Activity 6.2**
>
> **Range:** Communication, Objectives of communication
> **Skills:** Take part in discussions, Collect and record data
>
> Investigate the Management Information System in an organization of your choice.
>
> - First establish whether an MIS exists. (If organization members say that they do not have an MIS, then ask how managers obtain information with which to make decisions. All managers need information, and the process by which they receive it will be their MIS, although in some organizations the system may be poorly structured.)
> - Find out the information needs of the various managers. (If possible, identify the requirements of the three tiers of management: company directors, middle managers at department level, and supervisors.)
> - Identify relevant sources of information within to the organization and from external sources such as government statistics.

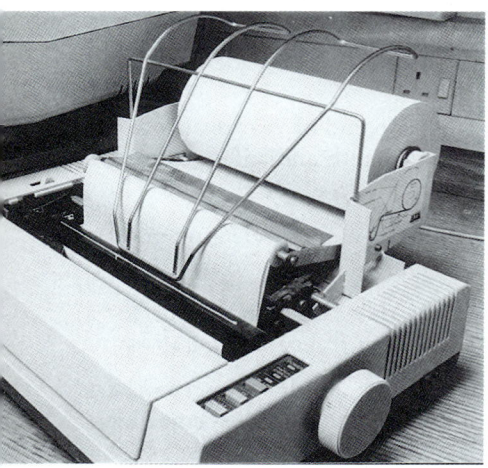

Verbal and non-verbal communication

In general, communication can take two forms:

- **Verbal communication** involves people talking either face-to-face or over a telephone or satellite link. It requires oral and listening skills.
- **Non-verbal communication** refers to all other forms of communication which do not require speech. Information is written and transmitted either by hand or on a computer, and will usually be **paper-based**.

Communications technology

The way in which business organizations communicate has changed significantly in recent times. Information Technology has revolutionized our ability to store, retrieve, and send information to different users. For example, computers and satellites have improved the speed at which information can be passed over long distances. Both sound and vision can be transmitted around the world in just a few seconds. The large number of people who have such equipment as telephones, TVs, videos and computers means that business can communicate with a large audience. This is especially important to firms advertising their products to national and international markets.

However, information technology can be expensive to buy and staff may need a lot of training if they are to use the new equipment effectively. People and firms unable to afford new equipment might be excluded from some communications. The security of information is also threatened by telephone bugging and computer hacking (unlawful access to other peoples and organisations computer files).

Portfolio Activity 6.3

Range: Communication, Analyse, Positive and negative effects
Skills: Produce written material, Collect and record data

Most organizations today, even some of the smallest, will have a vast array of equipment to aid the process of communication. Below is a list of equipment you are likely to find in a busy office:

- Computer terminal
- Modem
- Fax
- Answer machine
- Telex
- Videophone
- Telephone
- Switchboard
- Pager
- Photocopier
- Tannoy
- Television
- Radio
- Intercom

1. Choose an organization with which you are familiar, and find out how many of the above devices they have, how they communicate, and the main types of information they are able to transmit or receive. State whether each piece of equipment is used for one-way, two-way, or multi-track communication.

2. Are there any items of communications equipment that your organization does NOT use or have access to? If so, find out why.

3. Which item, if any, would you recommend your firm to buy or hire to improve communications? Give reasons for your choice.

4. Suggest possible staff training that might be needed to ensure that the new equipment is used effectively and safely.

Key words

Communication - the process of passing information between people and organizations

Communication channel - a link between people and organizations along which information is passed

Open channels - when information is not confidential and can be shared by anyone

Restricted channels - when information is confidential and is directed to those who need, or have paid, to know

Verbal communication - communicating through speech

Non-verbal communication - paper-based and electronic communication

---

Section 6.2

Verbal communication

The easiest way to communicate is simply to talk to people. Today people can talk to each other all over the world using a telephone. However, verbal communication is often complemented by facial expressions - for example, frowning at another person's suggestion - and by body language such as a shrug of the shoulders to suggest indifference. Non-verbal forms of communication such as pictures, graphs, and letters may also form the topic of verbal discussion. Therefore, to be truly effective, verbal communication requires both sound and vision.

Face-to-face communication

The most common method of verbal communication is a face-to-face meeting where people can see who they are talking to. Face to face communications include **interviews**, such as those held to appoint job applicants (see 14.4), and business meetings.

Where people tend not to meet face-to-face this can lead to a 'memo mountain' as managers put off talking through difficult issues with people and instead communicate with staff on paper. This lack of direct contact can quickly lead to misunderstanding and also allows the informal 'grapevine' or 'rumour mongers' to take over the channels of communication. In an effective organization there is no substitute for regular face-to-face contact with staff.

Business meetings

Meetings are the most common means of attempting to resolve difficulties and find solutions to problems. Staff at all levels in an organization will be involved at some time in a meeting. However, meetings among managers tend to be the most frequent. Typically, managers will use meetings to:

- Set business objectives
- Monitor progress and business performance
- Discuss new ideas
- Plan for the future
- Discuss and make decisions

Well-run meetings usually require the following key ingredients:

- A strong **chairperson** who is able to keep people to the point and encourage everybody to have their say, yet at the same time prevent certain individuals from dominating
- An **agenda** issued in advance of the meeting, with a clear list of topics for discussion
- A group of people who are capable of keeping to the point and who are willing to listen to each other, make compromises, and reach a solution.
- Someone who is able to take notes of points and matters arising from the meeting for future reference. These notes can be used to produce the **minutes** of the meeting (see 6.3).

Cascading will often follow senior management meetings at which decisions have been made. This involves setting up a series of meetings between lower-level managers, supervisors, and operatives to pass on and discuss the senior managers' business decisions and ideas, and how they will be put into effect.

▼ *Figure 6.1: An example of an agenda for a business meeting*

KRB FOODS PLC

Notice of Meeting: **Regional Sales Divisions**

Date: 26 March 1995
Time: 2.30 pm
Venue: Head Office, London

Agenda

1. Apologies for absence
2. Minutes of last meeting
3. Action points - budget allocation for IT
   – new promotion campaign update
4. 'Paris' project: tender proposals for research
5. AOB
6. Date of next meeting

▼ Figure 6.2: Cascading

Senior managers meet

Middle managers meet with their supervisors and first line managers

Supervisors meet with operatives

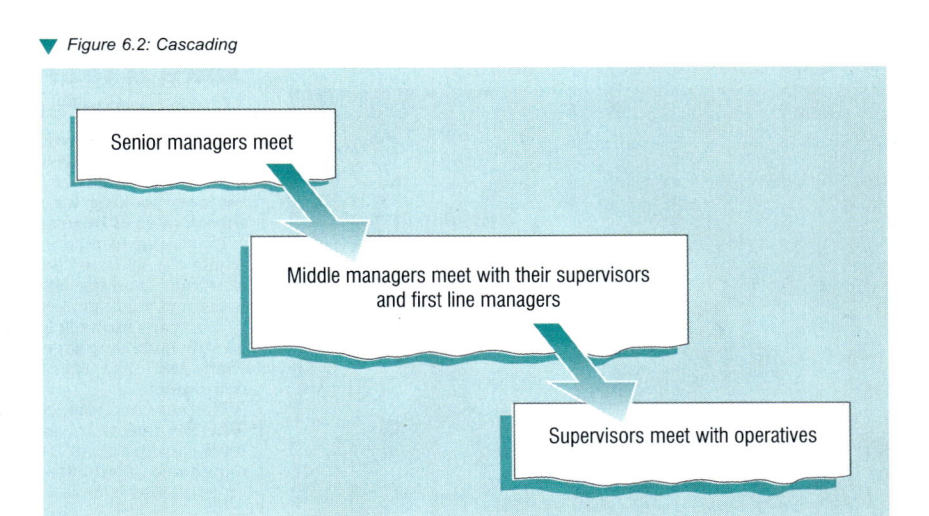

Other types of business meeting

Team meetings - between department managers and their staff teams

Mass meetings - for example, with all the employees, or all the shareholders in a large organization

Presentations - in which one person or group of people present information or demonstrate a product or process to an audience, often using audio and visual methods such as films and slides. Handouts of useful information or speaking notes will also tend to be given to audience members.

▼ Financial Times 28.2.92

Videophone: the next step in communications

European market for videoconferencing
  1990 **$65.44m** estimate
  1995 **$296.00m*** forecast

US market for videoconferencing
  1990 **$894m**
  1995 **$8.3bn** forecast

Number of installed videoconferencing units in US
  1990 **4,660**
  1995 **161,199** forecast

Videophones

These allow users to see and hear each other by means of a built-in camera and small monitor in their telephone sets. Videophones are more expensive to buy than ordinary phones, but they use the same network, and call charges are the same. Business users are likely to find videophones useful because they allow users to make eye contact and to gauge body language, which is an important part of communications.

Videoconferencing

This is a service operated by British Telecom which allows groups of people in different places to be linked using sound and vision. Videoconferencing may be a quicker and cheaper way of achieving a face-to-face meeting than having people travel over long distances. Satellite links can be used to link people in different offices all over the world.

Advanced Business

Videoconferencing can be used for face-to-face communication between people separated by long distances

Take a look at the problem - Videoconferencing helps decisions

Keith Platt, who runs a £3 million turnover insurance business, has been using British Telecom desktop videoconferencing for just over a year to link six sites around the country. "We did it because we were looking for a competitive advantage in a market where direct sales of insurance are cleaning up the business."

Travelling to meetings in London effectively meant writing off a whole day. Now, by linking up on the videophone, he can save hours at a time - and the cost of travelling. He uses the facilities for board meetings, management meetings, presentations, and training.

"You can resolve a lot more things by talking face-to-face. You can see the body language, negotiate, and come to quick decisions," says Platt, who has spent around £40,000 on video communications equipment.

The cost of video communications is coming down all the time. Whereas five years ago it was strictly for the multinationals, who have hundreds of thousands to invest in large systems with expensive, dedicated transmission lines, the entry cost of videophones is now just a few thousand pounds.

Daily Telegraph 8.11.94

Other methods of verbal communication

Telephones

Many firms, even quite small ones, operate an internal telephone system allowing staff all around the building to be in contact with each other. This kind of telecommunications system can speed up decision-making and so increase business efficiency.

British Telecom (BT) and Mercury are the two major suppliers of external telecommunications facilities in the UK. These facilities are much broader than simply telephones: a wide range of electronic and other means of communications are also available for businesses, such as pagers, faxes, and electronic mail.

Mobile phones

Many firms now issue **mobile phones** to staff who need to travel away from their offices. Cellular phones are portable handheld telephones which can communicate with the BT system and with other cellphones using special communications networks such as Cellnet (which is jointly owned by BT and Securicor). These networks relay signals from a series of base stations located around the country.

Mercury also operates a mobile phone network. However, at present it is limited to the area within the M25 around London.

Key words

Face-to-face communication - talking in person to other people

Agenda - notification to those attending a business meeting of the topics to be discussed and the order in which each will be tackled

Cascading - passing information vertically down the chain of command in an organization through a series of meetings between staff at different grades

Videoconferencing - a BT service which allows groups of people to see and hear each other over long distances

Cellular phone - a mobile telephone which can link to the BT system using a nationwide series of relay stations

Section 6.3 Non-verbal communication

A large amount of communication is undertaken using non-verbal methods. These can include **memos, minutes, reports, letters, bulletins,** etc. These are used because it is simply not possible to tell everybody everything they need to know using verbal communication methods. Even if there were time to do this, staff are unlikely to remember everything and will need information written on paper to refer to later.

Paper-based communications have an important role in organizations. However, too much paperwork can result in heavy information flows and very poor communication if staff 'switch off' and do not bother to read it.

Internal communications

People in different parts of an organization will often communicate with each other using a variety of non-verbal paper-based methods. Transmitting information in a written paper-based format has the advantage of providing a record of the message, the person(s) sending and receiving the message, and the date of the communication. The key forms of internal communication are as follows:

- **Memorandums**, or memos, are usually sent through the internal mail and are short communications, focusing on a small number of points.

- **Minutes** provide a summary of decisions made and action resulting from business meetings. They are kept for future reference and may be used at a later date to assess the work and action taken by those at the meeting. For example, minutes produced following the meeting to discuss the agenda in Figure 6.1 might be as shown in Figure 6.4.

▼ *Figure 6.3: An example of a memo*

MEMO
To: All senior managers
Date: 15.8.95
From: JP Smith MD
Subject: Meeting on 25.8.95
Meeting cancelled. Rescheduled to 4.9.95 at 2 pm.
Venue unchanged.
Agenda will be sent prior to meeting.
Please phone Kate Morris (x6783) to confirm attendance.
Apologies for inconvenience. JPS

▼ *Figure 6.4: An example of minutes*

KRB FOODS PLC

Minutes of Regional Sales Divisions Meeting, 26. March 1995

In attendance:
Mr Wood	Sales Director
Mrs James	Scotland & NW
Mr Douglas	NE
Ms Shah	Wales & Midlands
Mr Fawcett	E
Mr Dickens	SW
Mrs Staunton	SE
Mr Hollby	NW Europe

Minutes and Matters Arising:
1. Mr Hallam sent his apologies. Ms Shah to deputize.
2. i. Mr Douglas stated that sales figures from North West division had been misquoted in minutes of previous meeting. Correct figure for Q4 1994 was £1.2m.
   ii. Mr Wood explained that purchasing had now received all requests for new IT equipment. Total bid was £2.7m. Largest element was for networking 160 users in the regional offices at £1.4 million. HQ budget allocation for 1995/96 has now been agreed at £2.4 million. It is envisaged that the current downward trend in prices should mean that all bids can be funded. **No further action required.**
3. Mr Fawcett introduced paper on test-marketing of new 'Champions' chocolate bar in Eastern division territories. Consumer response favourable and sales healthy - 45,000 in first four weeks. A full report was tabled and comments invited before presentation to board of directors on 26.3.95. **Action: All**
4. Mr Hollby explained that 5 tenders had been received from market research organizations invited to bid for the 'Paris' project to examine consumer preferences for confectionery in France. Tenders ranged in price from £150K - £240K. Before the contract for work is let (end of April 1995) the opinions of divisional heads are invited. Copies of the tender documents were tabled. **Action: All - comments, including nil response, by 14.4.95.**
5. Mrs Staunton was currently working up a proposal for in-store customer purchase incentives. Her report will be ready for consideration by 3.4.95 whereupon division heads will be asked for their ideas on how to implement incentives on a regional basis. **Action: Mrs Staunton to report by 3.4.95.**
6. Next meeting fixed for 27 June 1995 at 2 pm. Venue to arranged.

> **Portfolio Activity 6.4**
>
> **Range:** Communication
> **Skills:** Produce written material
>
> 1. Write a memo to your tutor to inform him or her of progress on your assessment assignment(s) in Unit 2 and your expected completion date.
>
> 2. Meet with your class group to plan and discuss assignments and research. Prepare an agenda to follow and produce minutes after the meeting.

- **Reports** tend to be written for specific reasons, for example, to review the effectiveness of a recent sales promotion, or monitor health and safety at work. Reports summarize large quantities of information and draw readers' attention to key issues which need decisions.

- Some firms produce their own regular newsletters or **bulletins**. These usually highlight important new developments in the firm and provide a chance for management to praise their staff. Other organizations may use a daily or weekly bulletin highlighting key points for staff. This might be pinned to a noticeboard, for example, outside the canteen area where everyone will be able to see it.

> **Portfolio Activity 6.5**
>
> **Range:** Communication, Analyse
> **Skills:** Produce written materials
>
> 1. Research into the kinds of non-verbal communication methods used in your college/school or any other organization that you know of. Identify the kinds of methods used and survey the opinions of staff on their effectiveness.
>
> 2. Produce a brief report on the effectiveness of non-verbal communications in the organization and recommend improvements.

External communications

Postal services

These are mainly provided by the Post Office. A wide variety of services are available, including those aimed directly at business users. These include box numbers, recorded delivery, registered post, freepost, and business reply services. There are also a growing number of private postal firms, such DHL, who are willing to guarantee a delivery time for deliveries anywhere in the world.

▼ Postal delivery services

Electronic communications

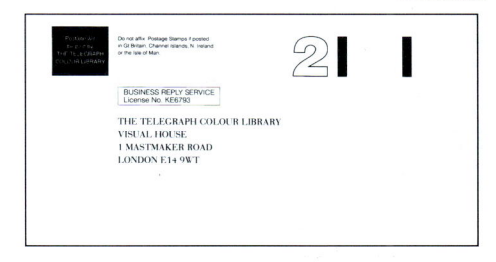

Communications have been revolutionized by affordable personal computers. Using computer networks, business organizations can send, receive, store, and analyse information to and from any part of their organization and other organizations, anywhere in the world, in a matter of seconds (see 5.4). Most paper-based communications are now written, printed, and stored using a wordprocessing package on a computer.

To send and receive information via a computer, it must be connected to other computers in a local area network (LAN) or wide area network (WAN). Once connected to a WAN via a modem, a computer can be used to send and receive information by a variety of means collectively known as **Electronic Data Interchange (EDI)**.

Electronic mail (E-mail)

This is an increasingly popular means of transmitting data between staff within a firm at the same location and also between firms in geographically dispersed locations. Using E-mail, staff may communicate with each other using a computer network.

The advantage of E-mail is that a large number of people can be sent the same message in one transmission. Once sent, the message will wait in electronic mailboxes for the user(s) to access it. The sender is then able to check to see if the messages have been looked at.

Why E-mail?

- Saves stationary and paper costs
- Allows workers to tele-work from home
- Transmission is rapid
- Saves on telephone bills
- Can be integrated with other systems, for example, Internet
- Messages can be stored and prioritized as important or routine
- Messages are automatically dated
- Addresses can be stored and recalled
- It has a multiple addressing facility

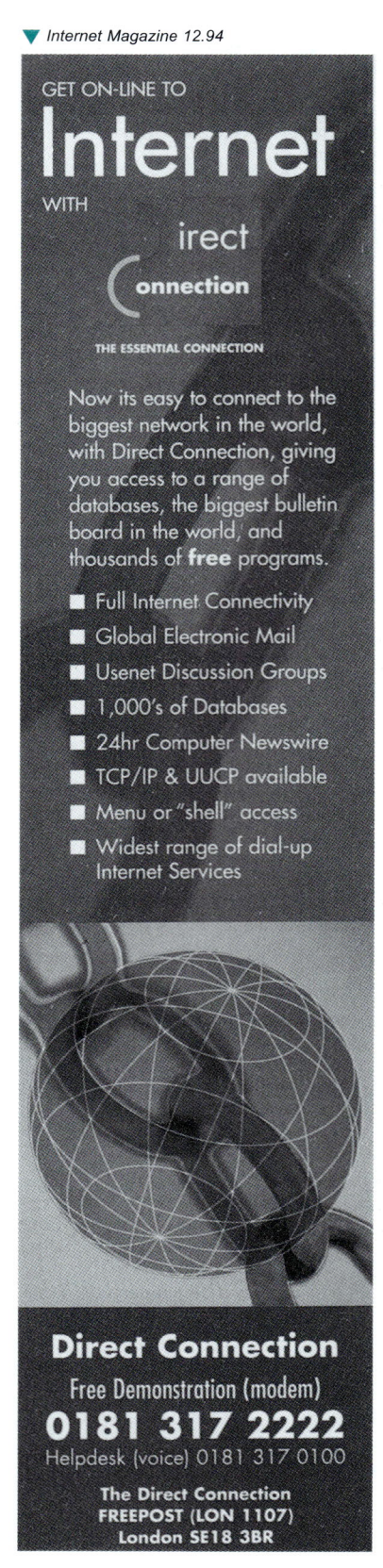

Internet

The Internet is a global computer network made up of links between many smaller networks. In 1995, around 30 million people regularly used the Internet to communicate electronically via computer modem.

The Internet is expected in future to provide not only a fast worldwide communications network, but also a worldwide system for making payments, and a means of receiving banking services, as well as electronic shopping and a wide range of other services.

Computer-generated speech

Voice-recognition and **voice-generation software** is likely to revolutionize communications with computers in the next few years.

Computers with varying degrees of speech recognition are already emerging, and some are beginning to transform the traditional dictation process. Proper dictation systems such as IBM's *Personal Dictation System* provide a highly accurate speech recognition system that analyses spoken words and turns them into text on the screen. These systems allow a user to dictate into software applications at speeds of between 50 and 100 words a minute, using a large vocabulary. The advantages are that the user's hands and eyes are left free, allowing them to get on with the job in hand, or to read from source material at the same time.

Other telecommunications

Pagers

These are small hand-held machines which alert users to the fact that someone is trying to contact them. Message pagers can display a message of up to 15 words.

Facsimile transmissions (fax)

Fax machines are small desktop machines which may be connected to a telephone line. To operate the fax, the user types in the fax number of the recipient of the message. The sender's fax then rings the receiver's fax and establishes contact (this may be heard as a series of screeching tones). Once contact is made, documents placed in the sender's fax machine are read through, one page at a time, and the details sent via the phonelines to appear as an exact copy at the other end.

Fax machines are a useful way of sending pictures, drawings, signatures, and many other very urgent documents.

Telex

This is a service using teleprinter machines (like those seen printing out the football results on television). Telex machines can be left on 24 hours a day and will continue to print out messages received.

Voice messaging

Voice messaging allows telephone users to record a message and have it delivered to an electronic 'mailbox'. The user dials the mailbox and uses a personal identification number (PIN) to listen to the messages. Voice messaging systems (like BT's *Voicebank* and *Voicecom*) are used by

Telex machine

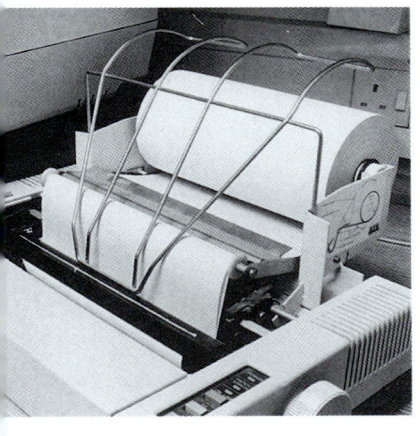

Pager

Fax machine

business people who travel or who are often away from their offices. The advantage of voicemail is that it is useful for communicating out of office hours and across time zones.

Teletext

Teletext refers to the pages of computerized information provided by the BBC (called **Ceefax**) and ITV channels, which can be displayed on TV screens fitted with a teletext decoder. Thousands of pages of information are available, covering a wide variety of subject, including arrival and departure times of planes and trains, as well as share prices and world news.

Viewdata

Viewdata is similar to teletext except that it involves the transmission of information to a specially adapted TV or computer screen by telephone line and allows two-way interaction with the user. For example, the system can be used to book and confirm a holiday, order goods from a supermarket, and for home banking. British Telecom provide an interactive computerized database called Prestel.

Enhanced telephone networks

Fax, E-mail, voice messaging, pagers, videoconferencing, and the Internet are all communications systems offered through an enhanced, and digitized, telephone network. The growing use and power of these telecommunications emphasizes the degree to which much of modern communication depends upon a good telecommunications network.

Surprisingly, a *Financial Times* survey of 300 large firms identified the single most important factor considered by multinationals when deciding where to locate as the quality and reliability of telecommunications in the host country. Thus, the quality of our telephone and telecommunications systems is a key factor in the international competitiveness of our industry.

In 1990 British Telecom introduced the **Integrated Services Digital Network (ISDN)** which is able to transmit digital signals via the existing public telephone lines into homes and organizations without the need for a modem. BT has plans to use the ISDN to transmit video film, games, banking, and shopping services 'on demand' into homes with the appropriate 'smart card interface'. They will then be billed for these services along with their telephone calls each month or quarter. To do this, BT announced a massive investment programme in 1994 aimed at creating 'information superhighways' by replacing much of BT's local 'copper wire' networks with fibre optics. Because of the capacity of the enhanced telephone network to transmit large amounts of audio and visual information at speed, it is also useful for business applications.

Portfolio Activity 6.6

Range: Communication, Positive and negative effects, Analyse
Skills: Take part in discussions

Identify a small or medium-sized firm. Assuming that the firm will grow in future, investigate and report on how the business could use modern technology in order to improve communications. Identify potential suppliers of equipment and costs, and also report on the advantages and any disadvantages associated with your suggestions.

Key words

Memorandum - a set paper-based format for sending information which is urgent or too brief to be sent as a letter

Minutes - a record of who has attended meetings, what was discussed, and what decisions were made.

Reports - documents summarizing large quantities of information and drawing readers' attention to key points

Bulletins - internal newsletters and magazines

Modem - a device, central to the creation of a WAN, which allows computers to communicate with each other over telephone lines

Electronic mail (E-mail) - sending messages between computers over a local or wide area network

Internet - a worldwide computer network linked by modem comprising a vast number of smaller, linked networks.

Facsimile (fax) - a means of transmitting documents by telephone line

Telex - a way of sending information quickly over a worldwide telex network.

Teletext - an information service provided via TV sets with a teletext decoder

Pager - a small portable machine which alerts the user that someone is trying to make contact with them

Voice messaging - a means by which users can send and receive delayed messages using the telephone system.

Section 6.4 Evaluating communication systems in business

Communication breakdowns

Although communications systems are often both costly and sophisticated, they can still fail to work efficiently for a variety of reasons:

- **Poor management** can give rise to unprofessional behaviour and personality clashes which can disrupt communications within an organization. A lack of understanding of the need to motivate employees and involve them in the decision-making process can also lead to poor communications, with staff failing to understand the reasoning behind management decisions.

- **Poor design:** communications systems may be badly designed or out of date. For example, a business with offices on more than one site may find it very difficult to maintain good communications and good staff morale if it relies only on the postal service for communication. Alternatively, a business might outgrow its existing communications network and find, for example, that its existing computer network regularly breaks down because of work overload.

- **Differences in language or culture or large geographical distances between staff in a firm** can also cause problems as firms grow to multinational or global size.
- **Poorly explained or presented messages** can cause confusion and misunderstanding. The sender of the message must have some understanding of the receiver and his/her previous knowledge in order to produce an effective and easily-understood message.
- **Prejudices:** sometimes people interpret a message according to their prejudices - that is, they see what they want to see and not what is actually being communicated.
- **Internal politics:** staff struggling to score points or win political games often attempt to distort communications by spreading rumour and gossip in order to further their own aims, rather than those of the organization.
- **Physiological barriers** such as hearing and sight impairment can hamper communication. However, communications can also be adapted for people with special needs. For example, sign language is commonly used to communicate with deaf or hard-of-hearing workers. This is a quick and surprisingly powerful language in terms of the kinds of information and contexts it can communicate. Braille can be used to communicate written text and numbers to blind people, with words and numbers being represented by a series of raised dots on paper or other surfaces - for example, on lift buttons. Computer programs are also available to convert text directly into braille, and special keyboards with braille keys have been developed for visually handicapped people.
- **Over-use of jargon:** technical terms or 'buzzwords', such as 're-engineering', or obscure acronyms and abbreviations can be a barrier to good communications.

Monitoring effectiveness

Because of the rapid pace of technological change and the pressure to remain competitive, firms nowadays need to continually review the effectiveness of their communications system. The most important question to ask is:

- **How well does it meet business objectives?** For example, if a business finds that its products are always out of date and that it is usually beaten to the market by competitors, this may indicate that its communication system is inefficient. Alternatively, a survey of staff morale and motivation can reveal a great deal about the operation and workings of internal communications within an organization.

Other questions include:

- **Does it offer cost advantages?** Information exchange is now faster than ever before and accuracy has improved, requiring less labour and power input. For example, a table of data can be sent in a matter of seconds via a telephone link between computers, compared to a fax machine, which takes longer and where quality of reproduction can be poor.

- **Does it offer value for money?** Compared to its cost, how well does the system do its job? Are there cheaper ways of doing things which would work just as well? For example, there is little point in a small firm investing thousands of pounds in building a wide area network if it is not going to be used to send and receive messages and share software applications. New communications equipment can be very expensive.

- **Does it provide accurate information?** It is essential that information sent and received by a business is error-free. For example, fax machines, although extremely useful, are not the best method for reproducing small characters. For example, if a faxed order is illegible this could mean that a supplier may deliver the wrong quantity of materials.

- **How easy is it to use and access information?** What do the users of the system both inside the firm and outside, including customers and suppliers, think of it? Communication will be ineffective if users have difficulty operating the equipment or if those organizations you wish to contact, via fax or Email for example, do not possess the necessary equipment. However, new systems may pose a threat to security if communications can be intercepted by unauthorised personnel. Access might need to be restricted in some cases to protect the confidentiality of important business information.

- **What is the speed of access?** Paper-based communication - for example, sending a letter or data by internal mail or external post - can be slow. Technological advance has allowed us to send and receive information from anywhere in the world in just a matter of minutes - for example, via electronic mail.

- **What is its impact on information exchange?** Because of improvements in the speed and cost of data exchange, interaction between individuals and business organizations has increased. Firms are now able to learn of conditions in world markets, such as strikes or wars in countries supplying raw materials, and be able to react immediately to minimize the impact on their business. Much information is freely available on the internet.

- **What is its impact on users?** Prolonged use of computer screens and keyboards can impair eyesight and result in repetitive strain injury (RSI) in users' fingers and wrists (see 7.3). Increasing demands on users for up-to-date information and skills to operate a variety of equipment can also cause stress.

- **Is training adequate?** To ensure that full and effective use is made of new communications equipment and systems, a business also needs to make sure that users are adequately trained. No matter how user-friendly computers and other equipment are today, some basic training will be necessary if employees are to use them to send and receive information. However, training can be expensive.

Further reading

Any good computer magazines, such as *PC User*, *Windows User*, *Personal Computer World* and *Internet*, available from WH Smith and other large newsagents.

Test questions

The following underpinning knowledge will be tested:

1. Communication used in and between business organizations
2. The objectives of internal and external communication
3. Analyse the effectiveness of communications systems
4. Positive and negative effects of changes to communication systems.
5. Suggest changes to improve communications in a business organization

1 What is the correct term for records kept of a business meeting?

A Agenda
B Minutes
C Articles
D Memorandum

2 A head office needs to maintain contact with its sales representatives who travel around the UK. What is the best way to do this?

A Fax
B Mobile phone
C E-mail
D Telex

3 Videoconferencing is a means of:

A Sending text electronically
B Linking staff at different locations using sound and vision
C Communicating using a mobile telephones
D Sending photocopies of documents

4 All of the following are non-verbal methods of communication EXCEPT:

A Memorandum
B Minutes
C Reports
D Meetings

5 If a business installs a new computer into its central services department, what improvements is this likely to lead to?

A Better quality production
B Better motivation amongst workers
C More employment
D Better communications

Questions 6-8 share the following answer options:

Go Ahead is a UK marketing company that devises advertising campaigns for various organizations. The company uses a number of methods to transmit information to its clients. These include:

A Fax
B Telephone
C E-mail
D Paging

Which method is most appropriate to:

6 An informal chat about new campaign ideas with the managing director of a client organization?

7 Sending details of advertising options and costs to the client HQ in New York when a quick decision is needed?

8 Sending weekly sales data for the last five years from the client firm to Go Ahead, so that they can analyse the data and make statistical forecasts?

Questions 9-11 share the following answer options:

A Minutes
B Business letter
C Memo
D Bulletin

Which of the above paper-based communication methods is best used for the following tasks?

9 Informing a senior manager that a meeting has been re-scheduled to another time, date, and venue

10 Recording action points raised at a meeting

11 Informing staff of a change in senior management

12 What type of communication channel would a shop use to pass the following information to all its customers: 'All prices cut by 20%'.

A A one-way channel
B A two-way channel
C A restricted channel
D A multi-track channel

13 a. What is 'communication' and why is it important to business?

b. List three methods of (i) verbal communication, and (ii) non-verbal communication.

c. List three pieces of equipment that might be used to produce non-verbal communication.

d. Explain the difference between external and internal business communications.

e. List three pieces of equipment that can be used for external communications.

14 a. Suggest two advantages and one disadvantage of installing new telecommunications equipment in a firm.

b. What is the difference between a WAN and a LAN?

c. What kinds of communications equipment would you recommend for a firm employing a large number of travelling salespeople who need to communicate complex orders back to head office? Explain your answers.

15 a. What kinds of communications equipment would you recommend for a new electrical chain store needing to despatch customer orders placed in stores from a central depot? Explain your answers.

b. Explain briefly some of the main barriers the organization may encounter preventing the effective use of the new equipment?

Assessment Assignment

Range: Communication
Objectives of communication
Analyse
Positive effects
Negative effects

Skills: **Communications**
Produce written material
Use images
Information Technology
Prepare information
Process information

Can you communicate?

You have been employed as a consultant to report on the effectiveness of communications in an organization and on the kinds of measures, including the introduction of new technology, which can be taken to improve communication in the organization.

Tasks

1. Undertake a study of a communications system used in any organization that you know (this could be in your school/college or a local firm). You should consider the operation of both the formal and the informal ('grapevine') system.

2. Identify communications channels between different employees and departments within the organization and with external organizations. What information is passed along these channels, and why? In each case identify whether channels are formal or informal, open or restricted, one-way, two-way, or multi-track.

3. Describe the communications system and evaluate its effectiveness in supporting the functions of the business - production, sales and marketing, finance and accounts, personnel, etc. Compare this to the kinds of purposes which you think a good communications system should fulfil. In making a judgement about effectiveness, survey the views of the users of the system (e.g. employees, customers, and suppliers).

4. Identify various equipment used by the organization for the purpose of communications. What exactly is the equipment used for?

5. Report on how Information Technology has changed communications within the organization and on how it might do so in future.

6. Recommend possible improvements to equipment and its use, staff training, and channels of communication, and how these might have a positive or negative impact on individuals and/or the organization.

You should prepare a written report in a business-style format, preferably using a computer wordprocessing package, and also present your findings and recommendations to the rest of your group using handouts and a variety of visual aids.

UNIT TWO

CHAPTER 7

chapter 7
Information Processing

This chapter investigates types of business information processing systems, their purposes, and changes brought about by the introduction of new information processing technology.

THE PAPERLESS OFFICE

Key ideas

The purposes of **information processing systems** are to **receive**, **store**, **distribute**, **use**, and **communicate** information.

Information processing systems may be manual or, increasingly in business, electronic. Electronic systems involve a wide range of computer software and hardware.

Computer-based systems typically run a number of **software applications**, including **wordprocessing**, **spreadsheets**, **databases**, **graphics**, **computer-aided design packages**, and **integrated packages**.

The effectiveness of Information Technology hardware and software for information processing may be evaluated by its **fitness for purpose, value for money, security, efficiency, ease of use** and improving the capacity to retain information.

The **Data Protection Act** exists to protect the rights of individuals who have information held about them on computer. Organizations holding information must agree levels of accuracy and security of information with the Data Protection Registrar.

The introduction of new technology usually involves changes within business organizations involving **staff training, improvement of equipment, measures to safeguard information,** and issues relating to the general design of systems to manage computerized information processing.

The introduction of new information processing systems can have **positive** and **negative effects** on businesses and individuals. Businesses may be able to improve the speed, accuracy, reliability and cost of information processing. However, equipment may be expensive and incompatible with existing models.

Individuals may acquire new skills using new equipment and those with disabilities may gain access to information they were previously unable to retrieve or use. However, new technology can replace worker effort and may cause stress.

Advanced Business

Section 7.1 The purposes of information processing

Information processing systems can be manual or electronic.

Handling business information

Businesses transmit and receive vast quantities of information each day. Information about incoming orders, sales, outstanding debts, payments, receipts, purchases, production costs, outputs, personnel, and many other items all have to be handled, interpreted, and distributed to those who need to use the information. Finally, the information must be recorded and stored for future reference.

In order to handle this information as efficiently as possible, businesses set up **information processing systems**. An information processing system is a set of rules or procedures designed to handle information and turn it into a manageable and understandable format which can be referred to in future. The primary purpose of an information processing system is to convert large quantities of data into manageable information.

Manual and electronic systems

Information processing systems can be **manual** - for example, a paper-based filing system - or **electronic**, involving the use of powerful computers to sift, store, and make sense of large volumes of information. Improvements in technology have expanded the capacity of organizations to retain and process ever-increasing amounts of information, from personnel records and market research observations, to financial data. Most firms combine both manual and electronic systems. Paper-based files provide an important extra back-up in case of computer failure or theft.

Information handling: an example

A large business such as a department store may sell many hundreds or even thousands of different types of products each day. The managers of the store will need to know how well products of different kinds are selling in order to adjust advertising and promotions strategies, and also the amount of space given to selling competing products in the shop. A mass of sales data in the form of printed paper receipts or jumbled till rolls will be of little use to them unless it can be converted into useable information.

This conversion is usually done by a computerized information processing system. The process will involve:

- Summarizing total sales figures across all products to make a grand total
- Breaking down sales figures into totals for particular products and categories of products, to give an idea of relative performance
- Communicating the results in an easily understood format to those who need to use the information as the basis for decisions
- Finally, the information will need to be stored for future reference

Clearly a computerized system will be able to handle these information processing tasks more speedily and efficiently than a manual or purely paper-based one.

The main purposes of an information processing system are shown below:

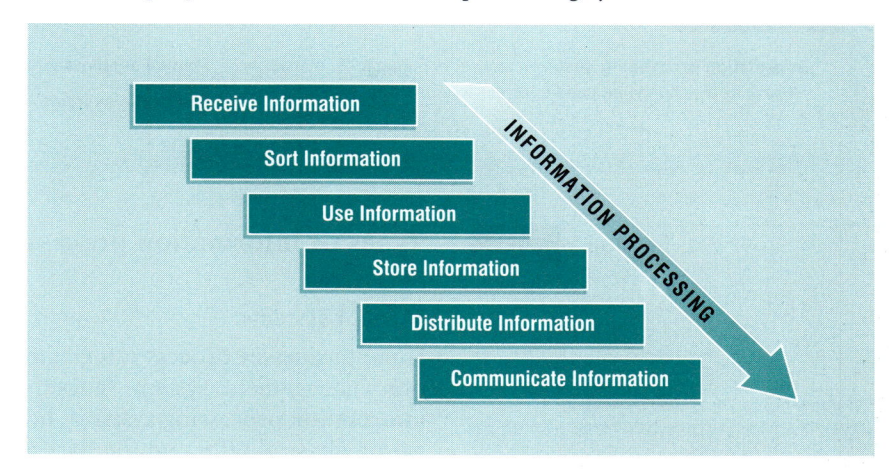

INFORMATION PROCESSING
- Receive Information
- Sort Information
- Use Information
- Store Information
- Distribute Information
- Communicate Information

Information processing will, therefore, involve some or all of the following tasks:

- Retrieving
- Sorting
- Copying
- Researching
- Checking
- Storing
- Classifying
- Filing
- Summarizing
- Analysing
- Calculating
- Comparing
- Presenting
- Communicating
- Distributing
- Collating

Portfolio Activity 7.1

Range: Purposes, Information processing
Skills: Collect and record data

Investigate the types of information processing systems used in an organization of your choice.

- Find out and list the types of information the organization holds on file.
- Why is this information required by the organization?
- Draw up and complete a table like the one started below. For each purpose, give an example of the information used, and the paper-based or electronic method used to process the information.
- If manual or electronic processing methods are NOT used, in each case state why.
- Can you suggest any alternative methods that could be used in each case? For example, instead of always using the post, would you recommend using E-mail? Give your reasons.

Purpose of Information Processing	Example of Information Processed	Manual Processing	Electronic Processing
Receiving	Customer orders	By post, taking telephone messages	E-mail, fax
Sorting		By hand	
Using			
Storing			Computer database
Distributing		By post	
Communicating			

Advanced Business

> **Key words**
>
> **Information processing system** - any set of procedures, manual or electronic, which may be used to organize and process information
>
> **Manual systems** - paper-based information processing
>
> **Electronic systems** - computerized information processing

Section 7.2 — Types of information processing systems

Manual systems

Some businesses process information flows using a paper-based information management system. These systems are sometimes called **manual information processing systems**, because they require a great deal of manual or physical effort on the part of staff to organize, file, store, retrieve, and communicate information to those who need it.

Manual systems rely on internal and external paper-based mail as well as upon the telephone system for the receipt and distribution of information.

Problems with manual systems

Once new information such as details of sales to different customers has been received, it must be organized and sorted, usually by filing clerks working with filing cabinets or card index boxes. This method is both expensive and slow.

When past information has to be retrieved, it needs to be found by someone working with a paper-based filing system. Usually only one person at a time can work at a filing cabinet, so retrieval can be very slow. Because of the bulkiness of paper-based manual systems, they also tend to take up a large amount of space.

If the required information was originally mis-filed, it could take a long time to find. When the information is eventually located and removed, no other member of staff can gain access to it while it is being worked on.

If further calculations need to be performed on the data - for example to calculate sales trends, or percentage changes over time - and the data then needs to be converted into graph form, this will require further effort by staff.

If the information subsequently needs to be communicated to a number of people, for example, department heads, this could require laborious work by secretaries to type, copy, and distribute the data.

For all of these reasons, manual information processing systems have been disappearing very quickly in businesses of all sizes, to be replaced with computerized information processing systems.

Electronic systems

Electronic or computerized systems comprise both hardware and software. Information can be stored on a computer, while the processing of information is carried out by a program held within computer software.

▼ *Paper-based information processing*

Computers provide a powerful and economical way of storing, sorting, analysing, and distributing information. For example, a firm may be able to cut its floorspace requirements and costs by doing away with filing cabinets and storing material on computer disks instead.

Improvements in technology has expanded the capacity of businesses to retain and process ever increasing amounts of information.

Storing information on computers

While the computer is in use, information can be entered and stored temporarily in its 'working' memory or RAM (Random Access Memory). The more memory the computer has, the more it can store in temporary files. Most entry-level personal computers now have eight megabytes of memory (8Mb RAM), while top business machines can have up to 64 megabytes or more. Disks, tapes, and rewritable CD-ROMs provide a permanent storage medium.

- **Floppy disks** are portable and available in two sizes: 3.5" and the now obsolete 5.25".

- **Hard disks** are fixed within the CPU of a computer. Entry-level computers usually provide around 500Mb of disk storage capacity. Some desktop business machines, especially those at the centre of a network, may have up to 3.5 gigabytes of capacity.

  It is sensible to save information on both hard and floppy disks. Hard disks can be corrupted by viruses, or through mistakes made by inexperienced users. They can also be damaged by fire or stolen. Floppy disks can be stored at other locations in fireproof boxes.

- **CD-ROMs** are similar to audio compact discs, except that they can carry much more information than just music. As a result, many newspaper archives, encyclopedias, and atlases are now available on CD-ROM. Data is read by a laser optical drive. Technological advance has greatly reduced the costs of CD-ROM drives and also CDRs (rewritable discs) which allow the user to copy information, including music, onto CD-ROM.

Software applications

There are now thousands of different software packages available from different manufacturers. However, many perform the same or very similar functions, and can be grouped under common headings. The main types of software packages in use in business include:

- Wordprocessing
- Desktop publishing
- Spreadsheets
- Databases
- Graphics packages
- Accounts packages
- Sales and invoicing packages
- Computer-aided design (CAD)

Wordprocessing (WP)

WP software applications are used for letter writing and basic report writing and have replaced typewriters in most businesses. The latest versions of many wordprocessors, like *Word for Windows* and *WordPerfect*, are very like desktop publishing packages (DTP).

Advanced Business

What wordprocessing can do for you

▼ *WordPerfect for Windows*

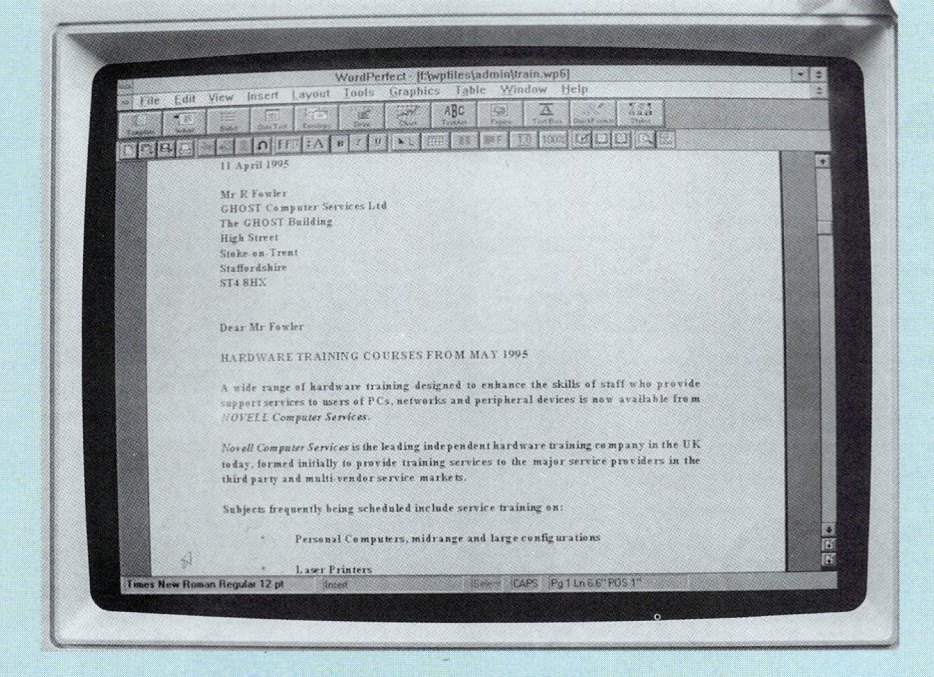

- Provide different fonts and font sizes
- Provide mathematical notation and symbols
- Count the number of words
- Automatically line up (justify) text at each margin
- Cut and copy text
- Correct spellings
- Suggest alternative words in a thesaurus
- Number pages automatically
- Create tables
- Import graphs and tables from other packages
- Make multiple copies
- Print on paper and slide transparencies
- Save and retrieve files

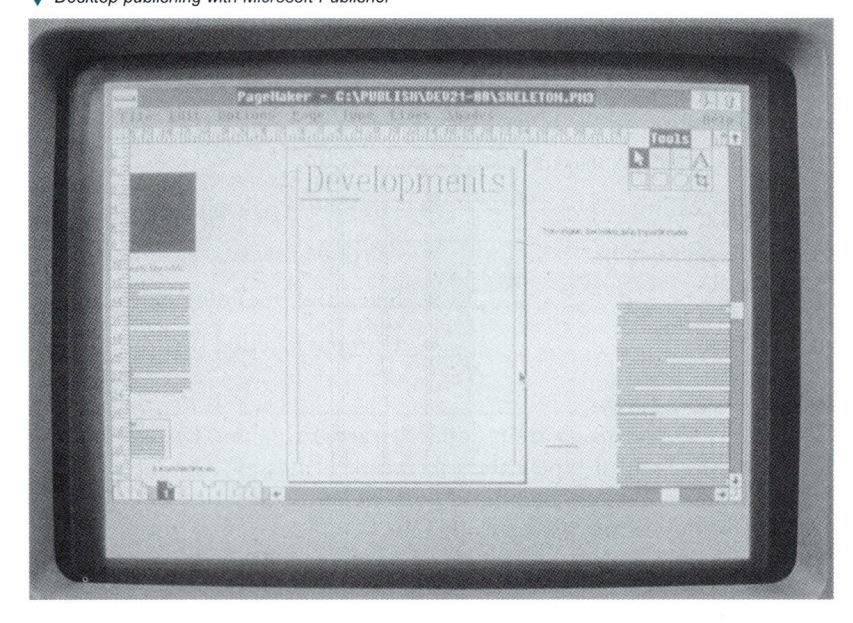

▼ *Desktop publishing with Microsoft Publisher*

Desktop publishing (DTP)

DTP allows users to design a variety of complex page layouts using columns, boxes, diagrams and pictures, in the same way as a newspaper or magazine. DTP programs usually contain a wide variety of fonts (typefaces) and also a picture library to be used in documents. DTP now means that even the smallest firms can produce high-quality publicity and marketing materials using programs such as Aldus *Pagemaker*, *AmiPro*, and Microsoft *Publisher*.

▼ A database of customer addresses

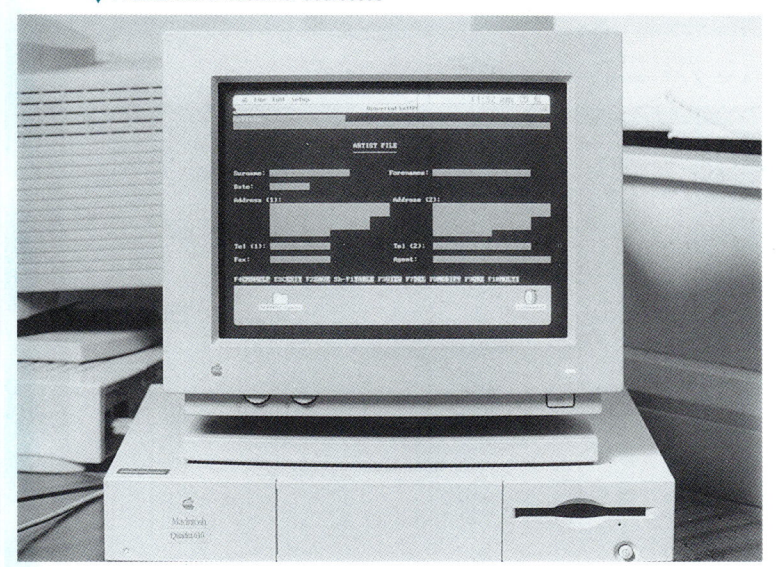

Databases

Databases are programs used to organize and store information. Their special feature is that they allow the user to ask quite complicated questions or queries of the information. Databases are often used to hold customer details such as names, addresses, and information about previous purchases, which is often sold on to other organizations. Databases can be linked with wordprocessing programs to allow the mailmerge of information. A **mailmerge** is a mailshot to a large number of people. The same letter is sent to all, but with a personalized name and address taken from database lists. Mailmerge provides a powerful and cheap means of marketing, and is made possible by the use of powerful computer databases.

Portfolio Activity 7.2

Range: Purposes, Information processing, Analyse
Skills: Read and respond to written material

1. Why do you think BT uses the MERIT system instead of a manual personnel system?
2. What can the MERIT system do that a manual system cannot do?
3. What additional security concerns are needed when operating a computerized information processing system like MERIT? How well do you think BT handles these?

BT on its own MERIT

Merit is BT's new personnel system, introduced in 1993. All MERIT's data is stored in a single computer. Merit holds one complete set of information on each employee, which saves time because information does not have to be duplicated in several departments. It is also more accurate because all the departments are using exactly the same data. The diagram shows how three sets of information are linked in MERIT:

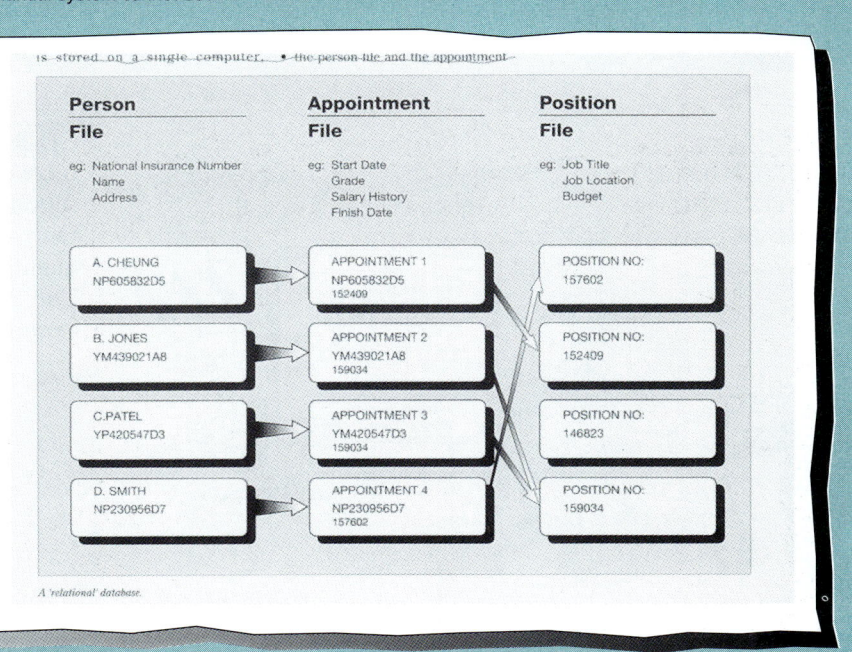

is stored on a single computer. • the person-file and the appointment-

Person File	Appointment File	Position File
eg: National Insurance Number, Name, Address	eg: Start Date, Grade, Salary History, Finish Date	eg: Job Title, Job Location, Budget
A. CHEUNG NP605832D5	APPOINTMENT 1 NP605832D5 152409	POSITION NO: 157602
B. JONES YM439021A8	APPOINTMENT 2 YM439021A8 159034	POSITION NO: 152409
C. PATEL YP420547D3	APPOINTMENT 3 YM420547D3 159034	POSITION NO: 146823
D. SMITH NP230956D7	APPOINTMENT 4 NP230956D7 157602	POSITION NO: 159034

A 'relational' database.

Advanced Business

- The person file holds details of an individual BT employee
- The appointment file holds details of the different jobs an individual employee does within BT from time to time
- The position file holds details of each individual BT job

The diagram shows that each file is linked to others in different categories by using unique numbers.

MERIT operates using a 'graphical interface' - that is, the user sees a screen and makes enquiries by clicking a mouse pointer on parts of the diagram.

MERIT is used by around 1,400 BT staff around the country at any one time. Each operator uses a computer terminal connected by datalink to the MERIT computer.

MERIT is used to find information about individual employees, and statistics about groups of employees. Reports from MERIT can be printed out or copied into a spreadsheet and displayed as charts. A feature called dynamic data exchange means that when figures in MERIT change, reports can be updated with the new figures automatically.

Every effort is made to keep MERIT's data safe, using three different back-up systems:

▼ *BT Factfile No. 8, BT Educational Services*

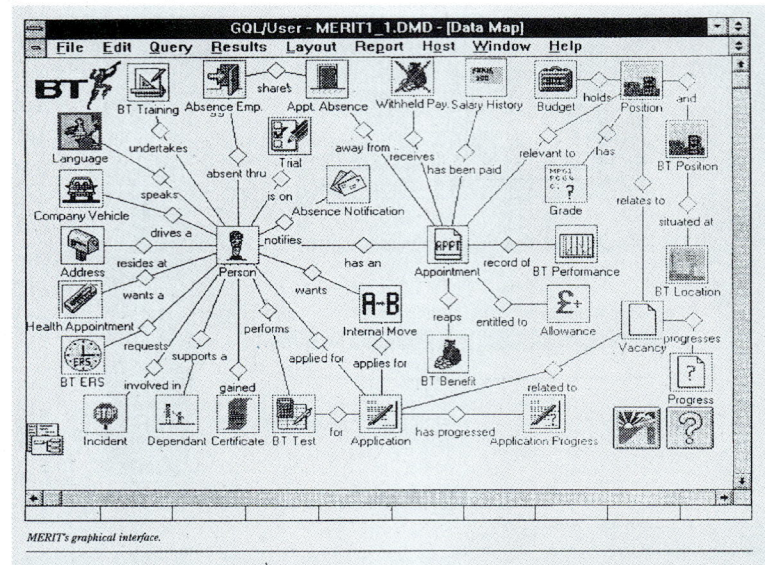

MERIT's graphical interface.

- The whole MERIT database has automatic, real-time micro backup - as every entry is typed into the MERIT system, it is recorded at the same time in a second identical system.
- If this fails, there is a standby system which can be used by up to 250 operators at one time.
- A complete backup of MERIT data is made once a day on tape, and this is kept on a different site for safety.

CD-ROM databases

Increasingly computer software is being supplied on CD-ROM (Compact Disc Read Only Memory). CD-ROMs can store vast quantities of information on a single disk. The Microsoft *Encarta* encyclopedia, for example, holds the equivalent of 28

▼ *Multi-media*

volumes on one CD. CD-ROMs are particularly useful for storing databases, such as telephone directories and reference books. On computers equipped with soundcards and speakers, they also enable information to be more attractively presented, using sound, animated graphics, and video. This format is known as multimedia.

A 'Model Range'

At its 'Face of 1994' competition last week, Storm Management became the first UK model agency to put its portfolio of models onto CD-ROM.

The CD-ROMs, which showed 250 models (six images of each) together with some video clips, were given "a tremendous response" by the photographers and casting directors present.

Storm's clients are now able to search the database looking for models that meet particular criteria such as height or hair colour. Moreover, the CD-ROM is cheaper to mail than Storm's glossy brochure, allowing the agency to send out quarterly updates.

The model catalogue is one example of the way in which CD-ROM technology is making inroads into business. Many large companies now have CD-ROM libraries which stock annual reports, newspapers, legal information, market research, and reference works, as well as producing their own disks for marketing and reference purposes.

▼ *LOTUS 123 for Windows - a powerful spreadsheet package with mathematical and graphics functions*

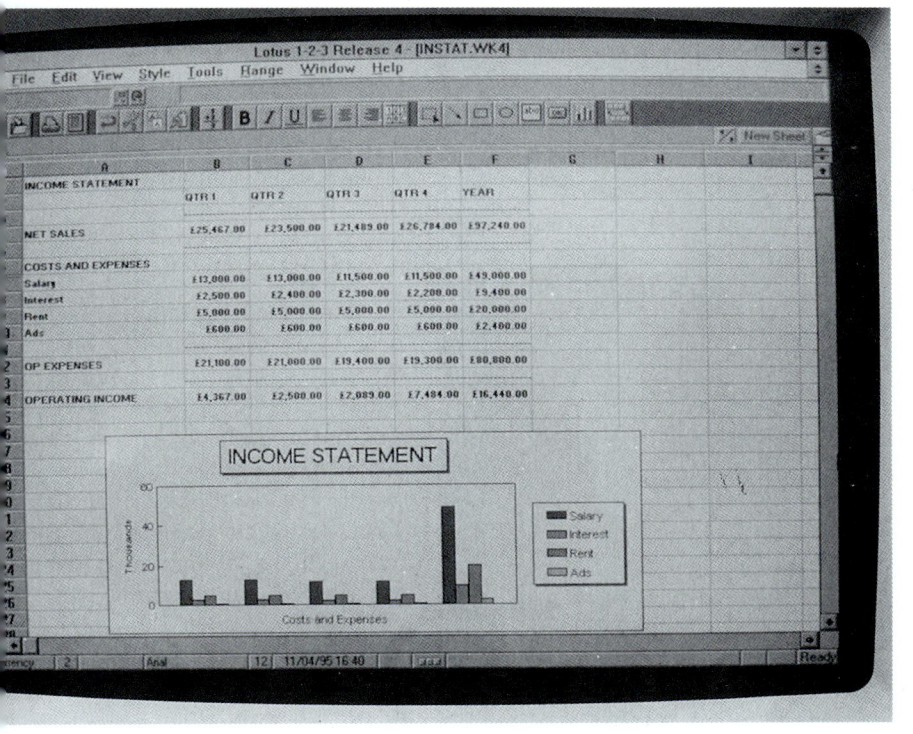

Spreadsheets

A spreadsheet is like a large piece of squared graph paper on a computer screen. Each square is called a **cell**. Cells can be filled with numbers, words, or formulæ. Spreadsheets can be created so that the sheet will automatically sort data and make calculations with the numbers entered. This ability makes them very useful for asking 'What if' questions, or questions designed to show the impact of – say – employing more staff, or spending more on advertising on final figures such as profit or cashflow.

Spreadsheets are often used for budgeting and statistical analysis. Many spreadsheets, such as *LOTUS 123* and *Excel*, can also convert numbers into graphs and charts, making them a very powerful means of processing numerical information.

Graphics packages

Graphics packages are designed to allow users to draw and make new designs quickly. Combined with a new generation of high-quality deskjet and laserjet colour printers, graphics packages such as Harvard *Graphics* and *Freelance Graphics* provide even the smallest of firms with the means to produce high-quality reports, logos, and publicity materials.

What graphics packages can do for you:

- Plot data on graphs and pie charts
- Automatically scale graph axes to data requirements
- Fill areas with patterns or colours
- Copy designs
- Move, shrink, and enlarge designs
- Save and retrieve designs
- Provide pre-designed pictures, maps, and graphs (**clip-art**)
- Provide 'paintbox' facilities for freehand drawing with a mouse or light pen
- Label and title designs

▼ *Computer graphics can be used to produce 3D graphs*

▼ *Computers are now used to design new cars*

Computer-aided design (CAD)

CAD packages allow the user to produce high-quality, detailed design drawings on computer. The best CAD packages allow 3D designs to be rotated and viewed from a variety of angles. Today many new products are designed using CAD packages.

In some high-technology factories, CAD packages are linked directly to Computer Numerically Controlled (CNC) machines, such as robots and automated production lines, which automatically produce what has been designed in the factory. This is known as **computer-aided manufacture** (CAM).

Multi-purpose and single-purpose systems

In the early days of computing, some computers could only be used for a single purpose, for example, wordprocessing or running a computerized payroll. These single-purpose machines were called **dedicated computers**.

Today, because of technological adances in hardware and software production, computers can be used for a variety of purposes. Most office information processing systems are used during the course of the week to write memos and letters, run the payroll, to produce budgets, design publicity material, and many other tasks.

This multi-purpose nature of computing has been assisted by the development of modular software packages. These comprise separate computer programs for different functions such as sales, purchases, cashbook, payroll, stock control, and VAT. Each program does its own job, but each also shares its information with the others and keeps them all updated. This enables all departments to share the same information. Popular modular accounts packages in use include Sage and Pegasus.

▼ Electronic mail

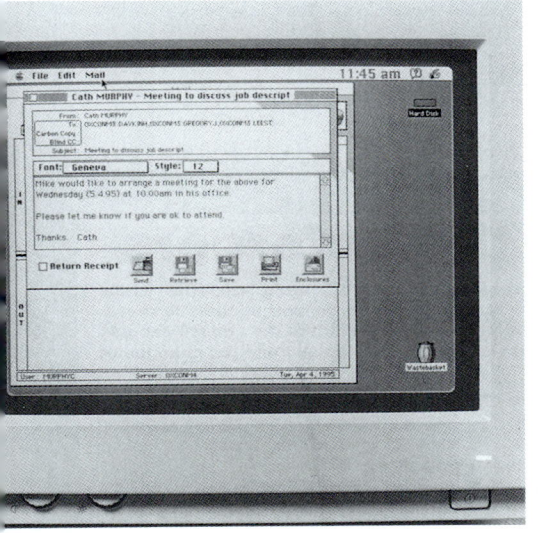

Electronic Data Interchange

Computer software can also be purchased to enable fast communication between computer users. This kind of software is called **electronic mail** or **E-mail** (see 6.3). Using E-mail, a memo or letter can be created and be simultaneously sent to any number of other staff on a computer network (see 5.4). It is possible to 'clip' a file produced using a wordprocessing package or any other software package to an E-mail message and then send it on.

The electronic transfer of information, known as **Electronic Data Interchange (EDI)** is a fast-growing computer application. EDI can replace all human involvement and transfer documents in seconds. Tesco has automated its business chain to such an extent that orders, invoices, and payments are all triggered off by shoppers passing through supermarket checkouts. No other human intervention is required. There are clear benefits of this in terms of speed and in reducing the time needed to get orders placed and delivered.

Portfolio Activity 7.3

Range: Purposes, Information processing
Skills: Collect and record data

1. Investigate the use of computers in your school or college.
   - List the applications for which computers are used.
   - What software is available to users to help them in the applications you have listed?
2. Investigate and suggest:
   (a) the kinds of information dealt with, and
   (b) the uses to which computers are put in the following organizations:

- A central government department
- A large supermarket
- A library
- A bank
- A computer chip manufacturing plant
- A film production company

Key words

Wordprocessor - a computer program used to handle and process text

Spreadsheet - a computer program used to handle and process numbers. Spreadsheets are useful for asking 'What if' questions and for graphical presentation of data.

Database - a computer program used for organizing and classifying information in a way which enables further information processing through the asking of questions or queries

Graphics package - a computer program used for creating presentation graphics in the form of tables, charts, and graphs.

Desktop publishing - a program used to combine text, graphics, and pictures using a variety of presentational styles.

Mailmerge - a way of combining records held in a database with a wordprocessor in order to mass-produce personalized direct mail

Multimedia - the use of sound, video, pictures, and text to present and explain information. Multimedia software is provided on CD-ROM.

Computer-aided design - using computers to design products using complex calculations to specify and plot 3D objects

Computer-aided manufacture - using computers to control automated production

Electronic mail (E-Mail) - an electronic means of sending and receiving information between computer users linked via modems

Section 7.3 The impact of new technology

Portfolio Activity 7.3

Range: Analyse
Skills: Read and respond to written material

1. What kinds of problems do you think existed with the previous manual information processing system?
2. How has the computerized system been of assistance to the department in this case?
3. What problems should management be aware of when introducing computerized information-handling?

Empowering the enforcers

The London Borough of Redbridge has discovered untold benefits since computerizing its busy council planning permissions enforcement section. A seven-person specialist team within the development control section of the council handles around 1,350 cases per year. These break down into new developments, changes of use, untidy land, and advertisements.

A recent review of work focused on the immense amount of documentation generated during planning investigations. The process seemed confused and bureaucratic.

Officers used standard letters but still had to go through the labour intensive tasks of adding typed details of names, addresses, the complaint, references, case officer details, and so on. Because handwritten additions to letters were unacceptable to the authority, over 200 types of standard letter were required. But in 1992 all that changed when the authority introduced a computerized information processing system. Information about planning investigations is stored on a database and can be retrieved selectively and added to reports. The initial improvements have been:

- **Speed;** no need for typists to work on the same old letters, memos, reports, or to add details to standard letters. The database copies the information the officer needs onto the selected standard letter.
- **Priority;** the database has a diary facility which helps to prioritize the work by the date of the last action. A case cannot be lost in the system, it will always appear in the diary until 'no further action' is authorized.
- **Access;** authorized users can access the database and convey the current position of the case in the event of an officer's absence.
- **Monitoring;** the database can print an up-to-the-minute status report on all outstanding work by officers and by case type.
- **Tried and tested;** all documentation set up on the database has been tried and tested for clarity, accuracy, and content. This allows officers to give a consistent approach to complaints when accessing information from the system. The database can do everything for the planning enforcement agency except site visits, investigations, and making judgements. The new system eliminates the repetitive nature of the job and underlines the core activity of investigating and making judgements on enforcement cases.

Planning Week 10.11.94

Information Technology: positive and negative effects

The introduction of new technology to assist in the processing of information has had the following impacts on business:

- **Increased speed (and productivity).** Information technology can perform mundane repetitive tasks, such as ordering and filing information in a fraction of the time it would take under a manual system. In theory this can free up staff to undertake more creative work. In practice, it may lead to job losses.

- **Wider access to information.** In the past, staff wishing to share information stored in different departments would have to request a copy of the information on paper. This could take time if another person was already using it. With a computerized system, authorized staff can access useful information from other departments across the firm, or even information from other organizations, simply by calling it up on a networked computer. Furthermore, the information can be imported into a variety of computer applications and be subjected to further processing if need be.

Open systems

At present, many of the products made by manufacturers of computer equipment and software are incompatible. Many business and accounting packages do not integrate with the wordprocessing, spreadsheet, and database applications used in other offices. Indeed, they often run on completely different computer systems. However, this is rapidly changing.

Growing international markets, and moves towards standardization in the European Union, have put pressure on manufacturers to develop **open systems** - i.e. computer systems that can exchange information from a wide variety of other networks across international boundaries. Open software is also being developed which will provide a standard software solution across Europe, regardless of the country in which it is operated.

Open systems will have a number of important benefits for business:

- Wider choice of suppliers and products
- Lower prices resulting from greater competition in supply
- Improvements in data handling, access, and exchange

- **Improved communications.** Computerized information processing systems mean that firms can be immediately and constantly in touch with their markets and branches worldwide. The use of Information Technology means that information can be shared more easily among those who need it and decisions can be made more quickly.

- **Cost reductions and improved accuracy.** The cost of computer hardware and software has fallen rapidly over time as technology has improved and sales increased, making mass-production possible.

However, purchasing the hardware and software needed to set up even a small network still involves a significant cost, and business managers need to weigh the costs against the expected benefits. The rapid growth in the use of computerized information processing suggests that, for most firms, the long-term benefits of quick access to accurate information which is capable of further processing more than outweigh the short-term costs of purchase.

▼ *Avoid the dangerous angle... and the Cobra... and the Spider*

Avoid the dangerous angle

...and the Cobra

...and the Spider

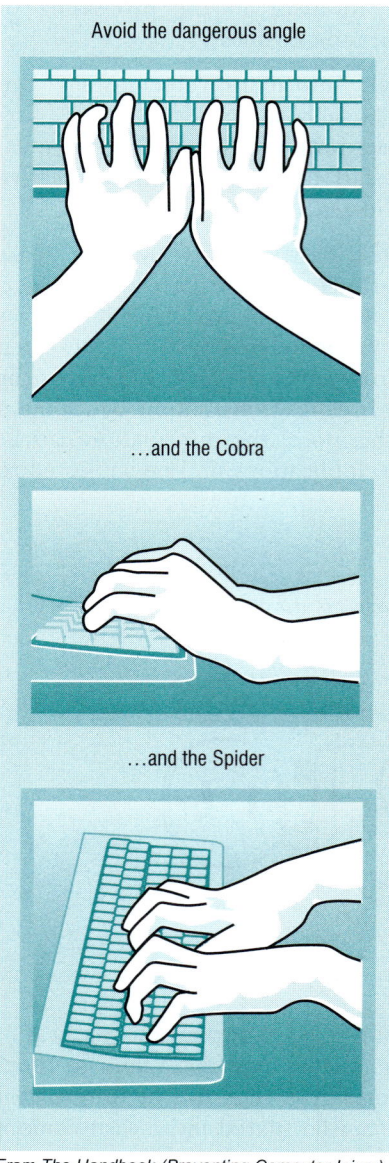

From The Handbook (Preventing Computer Injury) (Ergone International 1994)

▼ *Old and new styles of keyboard*

Computerized information processing systems will also allow employees greater flexibility in their work, and provide them with the information needed to innovate and develop better products and services for customers. Technological improvements such as voice recognition and generation software, braille printers and a host of other software has also enabled blind people and others with disabilities to gain access to more information.

Accuracy is also likely to be improved because networked computers allow managers to monitor very closely the quantity and quality of work produced by employees in a way which has never been possible before.

- **Training and health & safety implications.** Information processing systems based on new technology require staff to be trained with the skills to operate the technology efficiently. A firm that fails to provide employees with sufficient training will find that their new computer system may be less efficient than their old manual systems, simply because staff cannot use it efficiently.

New technology can bring significant benefits. However, if not introduced properly, it can lead to increased stress among employees, ill health, and lower productivity. Any large-scale change in working practices is stressful, and some staff will cope better than others. Careful management of the process can assist the introduction of new technology.

An increasing number of computer users are complaining of repetitive strain injury (RSI) - disorders in the joints and muscles in the fingers, hands and arms, caused by repeated actions in using the keyboard, or by sitting in a particular way. To overcome this, many firms now issue guidelines on how long staff should work at a computer screen without a break, and provide anti-glare screens to fit over monitors to protect users' eyesight.

Some manufacturers are also re-designing keyboards which have for a long time been based on the so-called QWERTY layout of old typewriters. For example, Apple Macintosh and a number of other companies have produced alternative keyboards with keys arranged in a broad circle around the outstretched hand of the user.

> **Key words**
>
> **Open systems** - standardized computer systems that can exchange information from a wide variety of other networks

Section 7.4 Evaluating information processing systems

Evaluation criteria

The advance of Information Technology means that a business must continually review the systems it uses to receive, use, store, distribute, and communicate information. The effectiveness of an information processing system in meeting the needs of a firm can be judged by asking the following questions:

- **Is it fit for its purpose?** A good information system should do the job for which it is intended. If a business regularly needs to analyse large amounts of data, then a manual system would appear to be too slow and cumbersome, especially if the size of the firm has grown over time and its information processing requirements have expanded accordingly. A powerful computer can store millions of data observations and perform quick calculations using statistical techniques to analyse trends and arithmetic means, which can then be interpreted and used in decision-making by business managers.

    An organization that needs a computer simply for writing business letters would not need a machine with a Pentium Processor and expensive CAD software. On the other hand, to run heavyweight graphics-type applications, a more powerful machine would be essential.

- **Is it good value for money?** Before implementing change, a business must weigh up the cost and benefits of an information processing system. Costs will include:

    - Computer hardware and software
    - Installation costs
    - Maintenance
    - Staff training
    - Labour costs
    - Power costs
    - Insurance
    - Cost of providing safe and healthy working environment

    Although manual processing may now appear less attractive than electronic systems, a business must still ask whether the efficiency gains in terms of speed and improved accuracy are enough to justify the expense.

A small shop with minimal information needs would be ill-advised to spend thousands of pounds on the very latest Pentium machines and business software applications. An entry-level machine and simple, bundled business software costing little more than £1,000 at 1995 prices would be more than adequate.

- **Is it secure?** A lot of information held by businesses, such as production costs, product developments, and personnel records, is sensitive and confidential. A good information processing system should ensure that information remains free of error or corruption and safe from unauthorized use. If necessary, filing cabinets should be locked; office staff should put away papers and computer disks at night, and computers should be protected by the use of passwords.

  A business could be open to fraud if unauthorized personnel were able to gain access to the records. It could also encounter trading difficulties if valuable information were lost due to fire, flood, theft, or malicious damage. Many businesses keep copies of important files, either paper-based or on computer disk, at different locations to minimize the risk of loss or damage. Others have been forced to devote more resources to security, in order to prevent systems being accessed by computer hackers.

  Firms also need to consider how well their information processing system meets the requirements of the 1984 Data Protection Act. For businesses using computer networks, this might mean that hardware and software require password protection, or that computers are only available for access in secure rooms. Access to computers by hackers using modems is another risk that big firms must consider.

- **Is it easy to use?** An information processing system will be ineffective if staff cannot understand how to access and use it. For example, lists of files and where to find them need to be produced and regularly updated. Filing cabinets should be labelled. Security procedures need to be understood and adhered to. Users will also need to be aware of which documents to use in order to file and distribute information.

  If a business uses electronic processing, will staff be able to use the new hardware and software? What forms of training are required? Or will so much training be needed that it will be cheaper in the long run to keep the old systems? In recent years, computer software, particularly Windows applications, have become much easier to use, because applications are based on 'user-friendly' pictures or icons and point-and-click operation using a mouse. This has made training easier for most firms. However, like any other equipment, Information Technology can be poorly chosen for the job and be badly used. Mismanagement of Information Technology can mean that the efficiency gains in using new technology are lost. Information Technology on its own does not guarantee that a business will be well run and managed; sound management and an understanding of how to introduce new technology and use it to best effect are also required.

Portfolio Activity 7.4

Range: Analyse
Skills: Read and respond to written material, take part in discussions, Collect and record data

1. What does the article suggest are the costs and benefits of new computer technology?

2. The article suggest that some 40% of companies have not made a business case for network purchases. What are the potential dangers of simply assuming automation can increase productivity without examining the scope for improvements?

3. Computer viruses and security are clearly important issues to business organizations. Investigate and suggest simple measures they could take to reduce these risks.

4. Following the approach outlined in the article, conduct and record a similar survey of business managers in organizations with which you are familiar. Ask them:

   - What are the costs and benefits of computer technology in their organizations?
   - What are the most frustrating aspects of dealing with PCs?

5. If an organization you survey does not currently use computers, try to find out why.

   - Do they intend to in the future? If so, why?
   - Suggest to them how computers might improve their operations, how they might evaluate the new system, and gauge their reaction

The fun starts when users switch on

There is a lot more to office automation than giving everyone a personal computer (PC) and a wordprocessing package. There is the worry of how not to end up in prison for two years - the maximum penalty for copying software. Or losing all the document files. These are management issues which, according to companies interviewed for Software at Work, need at least as much attention as technical matters such as building the office network.

The benefits of basic office automation systems, built around a wordprocessing package and spreadsheet system, appear widely assumed. A recent survey showed that 9 out of 10 managers believe office networks contribute significantly to productivity - but only 1 in 10 measures these gains!

Organizations expect an average increase of 65% in the number of office network users in 1994. But 40% of companies and 80% of public sector bodies do not make any business case for network purchases.

Dr Heather Stark, author of the Ovum study report, sees rapid growth in networked office PCs, especially for electronic mail - "Personal computers will become interpersonal computers" she says. "Most people will use their computers to communicate with each other."

However, management issues arise from the fact that giving office staff PCs gives them the opportunity of bringing in games software and other business packages. This raises the problems of viruses - unwelcome programs which can destroy files and slow down processing speed - and illegal copying.

What also emerges from the interviews is that proper training is vital. When asked to name the most frustrating or irritating aspect of dealing with company office networks, almost 30% of computing managers mentioned 'the users'. Respondents' comments underlined the need for training: "User-ignorance causes many problems"; "Users pull plugs out by mistake and then complain their PCS are not working"; "Users interfere with the networks without authority, for example, by disconnecting their PCs."

Financial Times Review: 'Software at Work,' Winter 1993

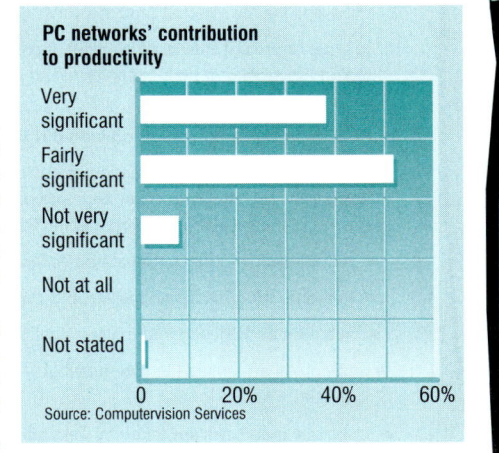

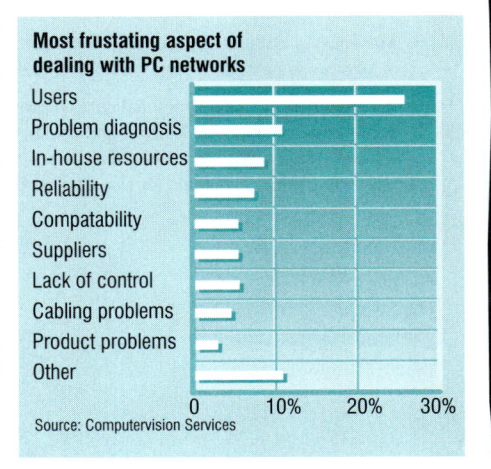

PC networks' contribution to productivity

Very significant	
Fairly significant	
Not very significant	
Not at all	
Not stated	

0   20%   40%   60%
Source: Computervision Services

Most frustrating aspect of dealing with PC networks

- Users
- Problem diagnosis
- In-house resources
- Reliability
- Compatability
- Suppliers
- Lack of control
- Cabling problems
- Product problems
- Other

0   10%   20%   30%
Source: Computervision Services

The Data Protection Act 1984

Why protect data?

More and more information nowadays is being held on computer. Doctors hold detailed medical records on computer, together with addresses and details of next of kin, etc. Government organizations, including the DHSS and police, may hold confidential and personal information. Businesses also keep detailed records on all their employees.

It is possible to learn a great deal about an individual by accessing even a small amount of computer data. For example, by looking at bank and building society records, it is possible to see how much someone earns, what their shopping and spending habits are, and what - and even who - they have spent money on. Computer records may also show potential lenders whether a person is creditworthy or has a history of indebtedness. Many organizations sell information about customers - names, addresses, etc. - to other agencies for marketing purposes.

The risk of misuse of personal information held on computer has never been greater - especially in the light of the growth of global computer communications and the ease with which networks across the world can now be accessed via the Internet (and the consequent increased risk of computer hacking).

In order to protect individual freedom, the European Union has laid down codes of practice for organizations governing the storing of personal information on computers. In the UK, these codes of practice are embodied in the Data Protection Act 1984.

How does the Act protect individual rights?

Organizations holding information about people on computer must register this fact with the **Data Protection Registrar**. The Registrar must be informed about the type of information held, how it is used, who is allowed to see it, and how it was obtained. It is the Registrar's job to ensure that:

- All personal information has been collected legally and is to be used for legal purposes only
- Personal information is accurate and current
- Outdated and unused information must be destroyed when no longer required
- Individuals are entitled to find out what is held on computer about them and, if it is inaccurate, to have it changed
- Security measures are taken by data users to prevent unlawful access, alteration, disclosure, destruction, or loss of personal data

Managing a database to comply with these requirements increases business costs. Large organizations may employ a specialist data protection officer to oversee data management.

Any organization holding personal data on computer that fails to register with the Data protection Registrar can be fined. Organizations that fail to comply with the Data Protection regulations may be required to compensate individuals who suffer because of this. The Act does not apply to information held by the security services and police, nor to information held for statistical purposes only, from which it is not possible to identify individuals.

Test Questions

The following underpinning knowledge will be examined:
1. The purposes of information processing
2. Information processing systems in business
3. The effects of the Data Protection Act
4. Analyse the effectiveness of information processing systems

1 Lewis Locksmiths Ltd has just bought a new computer. Mr Lewis would like to set up his accounts and financial information on computer. What type of software would be best for this?

A A database
B A wordprocessor
C A graphics package
D A spreadsheet

2 The main purpose of the Data Protection Act is to:

A Protect firms by ensuring that they have password protection on all computers.
B Protect the government by ensuring that people cannot have access to secret defence or police information
C Protect individuals by ensuring that organizations holding information about them on computer are required to register this fact and to comply with certain regulations.
D Safeguard information sent on computer disk through the post.

3 A dedicated computer system is one which:

A Rarely breaks down
B Can only run one type of software application
C Can run a variety of different software applications to suit the needs of the user.
D Meets the requirements of the Data Protection Act.

4 The introduction of a new computerized information processing system could be judged to be effective on all of the following criteria EXCEPT:

A Increased speed of information processing
B Lower administrative costs
C Increased paperwork
D Improved information flows for decision-making

5 The main difference between a spreadsheet and a database is:

A A database is not used for handling data
B A database is used for making calculations
C A spreadsheet is used for asking 'What if' questions
D A spreadsheet is mainly used for organizing and categorizing data.

6 All of the following are major purposes of information processing systems EXCEPT:

A Receiving information
B Storing information
C Distributing and communicating information
D Making decisions based on information

Questions 7 - 9 share the following answer options:

A Receiving information
B Storing information
C Using information
D Communicating information

Which of the above purposes of an information processing system do the following situations describe?

7 A telephone call from a angry customer

8 Sending out product details via electronic mail

9 Calculating monthly average sales figures to identify the trend

10 a. Explain the key difference between information processing and Information Technology.

b. What are the differences between computer hardware and software?

c. Suggest five kinds of software application typically used in business to process information.

d. What is an 'open computer system' and why would it be welcomed by business?

Advanced Business

11 The Department of the Environment (DoE) is to move to new offices. The existing library within the Department holds many reference books, newspapers, magazines, and maps. Some information is stored on microfiche slides. Every day the library receives information on new publications, requests from DoE personnel searching for particular items of information or books, and sends out photocopies, items on loan, and loan expiry reminders. Much of the processing of this information is undertaken by hand, and people who request information from the library often complain it is too slow.

The library is currently researching its information processing requirements and has suggested introducing an electronic environment in which as much information as possible is stored on disk which can be accessed by users over a wide area network.

a. What are the main purposes of an information processing system like that in the DOE library?

b. Explain the possible advantages to the DoE library of using an electronic information processing system over their present manual system.

c. Suggest a number of criteria the DoE library could use to evaluate the proposed system against their existing system.

12 Explain the following terms and how each one might help a business:

- Computer-aided design
- Database
- Spreadsheet
- Multimedia
- Electronic Data Interchange
- Computer hardware

13 What are the main implications of the Data Protection Act for a new business?

Assessment Assignment

Range: Purposes
Information processing
Analyse
Effects of the Data Protection Act

Skills: Communications
Take part in discussions
Produce written materials
Use images
Information Technology
Prepare information
Present information

Tasks

Undertake an investigation into the kinds of information processing systems used in a business organization that you know. (This could be your school or college, work placement, or any other organization). Alternatively choose a type of business (e.g. a small factory) and suggest the kinds of information processing systems that would be required for its efficient operation.

1. Describe the information processing systems in use in the business (both computerized and manual) and the purpose of these systems.

2. Evaluate the scope (if any) for further computerization of information processing systems in the organization.

3. Suggest how the effectiveness of the information processing systems in use may be measured, and attempt to evaluate the effectiveness of the systems for your organization. (This section of your report should lead to an identification of strengths and weaknesses in the systems.)

4. Report on the positive and negative effects brought about in the organization because of the introduction of new technology. You should indicate what further changes are likely to occur in future and also include an evaluation of how well the organization has handled some of the major changes so far.

5. What is the purpose of the Data Protection Act, and how does the organization ensure it complies with it? (if possible, include a record of a recent breach of the act).

6. Make a verbal presentation of your report to the rest of your group. This presentation should emphasize the lessons to be learned for organizations in general from your investigation. You should also prepare a detailed written report to hand in, covering the above points.

Marketing

Unit Three

unit 3

chapter 8	The Principles and Functions of Marketing (Element 3.1)
chapter 9	Market Research (Elements 3.2)
chapter 10	Marketing Communications (Elements 3.3)
chapter 11	Customer Service and Sales Methods (Elements 3.4)

Advanced Business

chapter 8
The Principles and Functions of Marketing

This chapter considers the main functions and underpinning principles of marketing, and the different marketing activities used by businesses

> SO, IF YOU WANT TO MAKE A TASTY PROFIT JUST ADD YOUR PRODUCT, PRICE AND PLACE, AND THEN SPRINKLE LIBERALLY WITH PROMOTION

PRODUCT
PRICE
PLACE
PROMOTION

Key ideas

Marketing involves the anticipation, identification, satisfaction and creation of consumer wants for the purpose of generating income or profit.

Marketing involves a variety of **activities** designed to **raise consumer awareness, develop new products, increase market share and profit,** and to **manage the effects of change and competition.**

Effective marketing means that firms must **focus** on every aspect of the business from the perspective of customers.

Firms may adapt a **product-** or **market-orientated** approach to marketing. Product-orientated firms aim to sell what they make, while market-orientated firms focus on their customers by aiming to make what they can sell.

The **growth** of organizations is linked to their ability to develop and sell new products and expand their market shares.

The **marketing mix** consists of all those activities including research, product development, pricing, packaging, advertising, promotion, distribution, selling, and after-sales service that a firm needs to undertake in order to sell its goods or services.

Firms adopt **pricing strategies** based on **production cost, market demand,** and **consumer perception**, or the amount of **competition** in a market.

Promotion involves providing information about products through a variety of media in an attempt to influence consumer buying decisions.

Branding seeks to create a distinctive name or image for a product.

Some goods are consumed relatively quickly and often by consumers. Competition among producers to supply and promote these **fast moving consumer goods** is fierce.

UNIT THREE

Section 8.1 What is marketing?

The need for marketing

Most private-sector business organizations aim to make a profit from the sale of goods and services to satisfy consumer wants. However, there are a number of organizations that do not aim to make a profit - for example, some organizations in the public sector and charities. However, almost all organizations will need to market their goods and services. Marketing can promote sales and higher revenues, while in the case of charities it can generate a stream of donations and increase the take-up of the services they provide.

Marketing principles

Markets are dynamic. They are in a constant state of change due to fluctuations in the economy, changes in the behaviour of competitors, the introduction of new technology, and alterations in government policy. Because of these changes, it is necessary for firms to continually alter and develop their product ranges and promotional strategies to match ever-changing consumer wants.

After sales service

Distribution

In-store promotions

Advertisements

Prices

> **Some definitions of marketing**
>
> *'The identification, satisfaction and regeneration of customers wants at a profit.'*
>
> Marketing is not just about advertising or selling. Marketing involves finding out what kinds of design, packaging, pricing, distribution, advertising, promotion, and after-sales service different kinds of customers want, and satisfying their wants in a way that will encourage them to buy a product over and over again. Marketing affects every department in an organization and the prosperity of the whole organization depends upon successful marketing.
>
> *'Marketing involves identifying and providing what the customer wants both now and in the future.'*
>
> Successful firms are those which can identify and produce what the market wants next and keep ahead of the competition.
>
> *'Marketing is War!'*
>
> Marketing is about competition between rival firms for a limited amount of consumer spending. Winners in the marketing battle will prosper by increasing their market share and earning more profits. Losers will be eliminated and driven out of business. For example, in the UK fast food market, firms like Wimpy lost their dominant market position when they failed to respond to the threat posed by the US firms McDonalds and Burger King, who, by the late 1980s, had successfully taken over the market.

Marketing involves the application of the following principles:

- **Anticipating market opportunities.** Businesses need to identify gaps in markets for new products, or new uses for established products, and be aware of markets in which sales are expanding. For example, in the mid-1990s the market for multi-media personal computers was expanding rapidly.

- **Satisfying consumer expectations.** Consumers will expect the right product to be in the right place at the right time and with the right price and promotion. For example, if the price of a product is above expectations, consumers will not buy it. Similarly, if a high-quality product is priced too low, consumers may be suspicious.

- **Generating revenues (and profits).** The purpose of marketing is to maximize sales through advertising, promotion, and pricing strategies. Expanding sales will increase revenues and the potential for profit. Charities can also generate donations through careful marketing.

- **Utilizing technological developments.** Technological developments can increase the speed at which a firm reacts to the identification of a market opportunity. New machine and production processes can speed up production and reduce costs. Consumers will also expect the latest technological developments in goods and services, such as computer games, home shopping and banking, mobile phones, etc.

- **Maximizing the benefit to the organization.** Marketing will only be cost-effective if the additional income it generates exceeds the costs involved and ensures the long term survival of the business.

Portfolio Activity 8.1

Range: Marketing principles, Marketing functions
Skills: Read and respond to written material, Collect and record data

SMART CARD TO WIPE OUT CASH

The National Westminster Bank, Midland Bank and BT today announced plans to introduce a new plastic 'smart card' which puts Britain ahead in the race to create a cashless society.

The Mondex card, which will be offered to more than 11 million customers of the two banks, could eliminate the use of money for many everyday transactions within a few years.

"We are talking about a cash substitute. This is one step further towards a cashless society," said B Morris, deputy group executive at National Westminster. Instead of carrying hard cash, customers will be able to use the card to pay for anything from a newspaper to a drink. The cards are charged with cash electronically either down a domestic phone line, from a pay phone or through the bank's existing hole-in-the wall cash machine network.

The cards will be far more advanced than existing swipe cards like Switch where transactions depend upon a customer's signature and electronic approval from a bank.

At the moment 90% of all the world's transactions are made with cash. It is hoped that when Mondex is fully implemented, it could account for 40% of all transactions.

Adapted from The London Evening Standard 8.12.93

The Economist 29.1.94

1. To what extent do you think that the launch of the Mondex card by the banks and BT shows evidence of the application of marketing principles?

2. How does the launch of Mondex match the definitions of marketing given above?

3. Research the main marketing objectives for any organizations that you are in contact with. Compare your findings with those of other students. Are they similar? If not, why do they differ?

4. Study the range of marketing activities for any organization that you know. Compare your findings with other students. Do organizations differ in the way they market themselves? If there are differences, do they depend upon the size of the firm, line of business, business sector, etc?

▼ Marketing a family event

▼ Nice product! Pity about the demand

Effective marketing

Customer focus

Effective marketing means that firms must consider every aspect of the business from the perspective of their customers. For example, IKEA, the Swedish furniture company provides basic low, flat-packed furniture. The product range in itself is simple, but the marketing includes cartoon films and playrooms for children, Swedish food, and heavy marketing through home delivery of free catalogues. Through marketing, IKEA is in effect selling not just flat-packed furniture, but a family event. In this way, marketing is said to add value or increase the attractiveness of the product to the final consumer.

Product- versus market-orientated firms

Some firms are **product-orientated**. They introduce new products to a market because they have discovered how to make them, and not because a marketing activity has revealed a consumer want for the product.

Product-orientated firms concentrate on products and production processes. For example, Sinclair Electronics developed and launched the C5 - the first low-cost, mass-produced electric car. This was a technical breakthrough, but the product was a failure because Sinclair had not researched the market. There was little consumer enthusiasm for the product.

A **market-orientated** firm will continually review and analyse consumer wants and modify their product and marketing strategies accordingly. Market-orientated firms tend to be more successful than firms that concentrate on products and processes, because they produce what the market wants. For example, the Japanese Sony Corporation continually adapts its products and product ranges to meet consumer requirements. Because the investment needed to develop and launch products such as the Walkman, 'Easycam', and Mini-disc onto international markets is so huge, Sony must be sure that their marketing is very effective.

Product or market orientation?

What causes a firm to concentrate on product or on the market?

The type of product

Firms producing industrial goods are more likely to concentrate on product. Products like brain scanners and weapon systems are developed for highly specialized markets.

Business objectives

If a firm aims to maximize profits or sales, it will need to be fully aware of consumer wants and adapt its product and approach to marketing accordingly.

Market structure

A firm that faces fierce competition is more likely to be market-orientated. It must know exactly what consumers want or it will lose them to rival products.

The size and nature of the market

In markets that are small and specialized, firms will tend to be product-orientated - for example, antique dealers, craft industries, scientific and specialist magazines.

Mass marketing involves a business aiming its products at large national and international markets. This contrasts with **niche marketing** where a business aims a product at a particular, often very small, segment of a market. However, successful niche markets, for example, connoisseur hi-fi produced by small specialist firms like QUAD and Naim Audio, can attract larger firms like Pioneer and Sony, who are able to offer 'high-end' products at a lower price.

Profitability and accountability

Marketing, such as advertising and other promotions, can be expensive. For marketing to be effective, a firm must weigh up these additional costs, against the benefits it may yield in terms of improved corporate image, higher sales, and increased profits. For example, in 1994 British Telecom spent over £44 million on advertising. At the same time, profits increased by nearly £1 billion, although this may have been due to a great many other reasons than advertising. However, when developing marketing strategies, it is important that firms remain accountable to legal and moral considerations. For example, a firm should not mislead consumers or provide false information about products.

Portfolio Activity 8.2

Range: Marketing functions, Customer focus, Analyse marketing activities, Growth of organizations
Skills: Read and respond to written material

1. What evidence is there from the article to suggest that Coca-Cola is not putting the main principles of marketing into practice?
2. Is Coca-Cola a market- or product-oriented organization? Use evidence from the article to support your view.
3. How is Coca-Cola attempting to change the perception of their own product and those of rival firms by consumers? How effective has their attempt been?
4. Suggest other marketing strategies Coca-Cola or its rivals might use to ensure that consumers make repeat purchases of their products.

Coca-Cola's share of the £670m UK cola market has fallen below 50% for the first time, say figures from Taylor Nelson AGB, the market research group.

The figures - derived from AGB's panel of 1,500 consumers whose grocery purchases are monitored electronically - show that Coca-Cola's market share fell from 54.6% in October to 42.2% in the last week of November.

That was shortly after the arrival of new cola's from Richard Branson's Virgin group and supermarket chain Safeway, and six months after Classic Cola was launched by J Sainsbury.

AGB's figures highlight the threat posed to Coca-Cola which has dominated the market since its UK launch in 1921. AGB's figures show Sainsbury's Classic Cola achieved a share of 12.2% at the end of November, Virgin cola 8.7%, and Safeway's Select Cola together with several other brands held 14.8% of the market. Pepsi-Cola retained the second biggest share with 20.1%.

Coca-Cola is fighting back with a £4m advertising campaign which is a clear attack on own-label copycat brands. Under the slogan 'All colas are not the same', it shows a family attempting to buy Coca-Cola in a ghostly supermarket manned by robot-like assistants selling own-label products only.

Financial Times 19.12.94

Key words

Marketing - the anticipation, identification, satisfaction, and regeneration of consumer wants by business

Product orientation - a business approach which places emphasis on production processes and product

Market orientation - a business approach which places emphasis on consumer wants

Mass marketing - marketing aimed at selling products in huge quantities in large national and international markets

Niche marketing - marketing aimed at small, often specialized, market segments

Section 8.2

Satellite TV, mobile phones, personal computers - expanding markets in the mid 1990s

The objectives of marketing

Marketing objectives and functions

The goals of marketing will reflect the overall objectives of business such as profit maximization, growth, or the provision of a charitable service. Marketing objectives will therefore differ from company to company but are likely to include some or all of the following:

- **Analysing market needs.** Market research can be used to gather information about consumers' buying habits and spending patterns (see 9.1). Firms will use this information to identify market opportunities for new products and marketing strategies.

- **Growth - developing new products.** A firm may set the goal of developing the new product or modifying its existing product range to satisfy consumer requirements. Product development can involve the modification of existing product lines, the creation of new products, and technological breakthroughs (see 9.1). For example, the development of laser and fibre optic technology has brought us products such as compact discs and cable television, as well as applications in the healthcare and defence industries.

- **Growth - entering a new market.** A business must choose wisely which markets to enter to sell its products. It may target overseas markets or particular groups of people within a market - for example, luxury cars aimed at high-income groups.

- **Growth - increasing sales or market share** (see 4.1). In a contracting market, i.e. one where where consumer demand is falling, a firm may aim to keep its total sales the same, while sales in the industry as a whole shrink. This can only be achieved at the expense of competitors' sales and with the help of a very aggressive marketing policy. In expanding markets, for example, in satellite and cable TV systems, it is possible that all firms in the industry will benefit from rising sales, and so the marketing strategy required need not be so aggressive.

- **Increasing profitability or cashflow.** A marketing campaign may be designed to meet profit, cashflow, or in the case of a charity, fundraising targets. A marketing strategy may involve increasing the price of a product, coupled with heavy advertising designed to re-position the product in the consumer's mind as being of higher quality or possessing characteristics which somehow justify the new, higher price. Placing the product in the right retail outlets will also help to promote sales and profits.

- **Optimizing customer perception of organization and/or product range.** Marketing to increase consumer awareness and improve the image of an organization and product is an important objective in competitive and quickly changing markets. A firm may wish to improve the image of its product range, either by changing and 'improving' the products, or by simply re-marketing them as being improved or different in some way - for example by re-launching the product with a new trademark or logo. Similarly, a firm can enhance its image by sponsoring sports events, making public donations to charities, or simply by improving customer services and after-sale care.

▼ *Improving products and product image*

OLD → NEW

- **Managing the effects of change and competition.** Market conditions of demand and supply are in a constant state of change due to fluctuations in the economy, changes in the behaviour of competitors, the introduction of new technology, and alterations in government policy (see 1.4). Firms therefore need to continually alter and develop their product ranges to match ever-changing consumer wants and keep pace with the product and marketing developments of rival firms.

Portfolio Activity 8.3

Range: Marketing functions, Analyse marketing activities
Skills: Gather and process data

1. Some products have such well-known trademarks or symbols that it is often possible to advertise them without using words or pictures. How many of the symbols above can you recognize? Where would you expect to find them? What products do they advertise?

2. Choosing the right name for a product is often as important as what is said about them in an advert. What type of products are these brand names for?

   Bic   Wispa   Blue Stratos   Tipp-ex   Cornetto
   Radox Heineken   Imperial leather   Mars

3. (a) Choose any product - for example, a chocolate bar, a can of fizzy drink, or perfume. Think of 10 names to call your product and design a series of logos (using a computer graphics package if possible) that are both informative and create the image you want for the product.

   (b) Conduct a survey of at least 20 people in your college. First, ask them what product they think each name and logo is for, and record their answers. Then reveal the identity of the product and its intended characteristics - e.g. taste, smell, design, etc. Conduct the survey again, asking which name and logo best describe the product.

   (c) Describe your product, list names and logos, and present the survey results as tables and graphs in a brief report. Which name and logo would you recommend, if any, and what modifications would you advise?

Portfolio Activity 8.4

Range: Growth of organizations, Analyse marketing activities
Skills: Produce written materials, Collect and record data

1. 'The UK toy market is expanding.' Explain the meaning of this statement using information from the article for support.
2. What is meant by the statement 'Video games have a market share of 40%'? How much is this share worth in terms of sales revenues?
3. If video games are to stay ahead in the toy market, what changes to products would you recommend, and why?
4. Identify the main factors behind the rise in the supply of toy bears.
5. Describe the approach to product and image creation being used by manufacturers of toy bears.

Toy industry reports 15% market growth

The UK toy market grew last year by at least 15 per cent to £1.87bn, according to industry estimates released yesterday at the Harrogate International Toy Fair.

Video games are now put at 40 per cent of the total, with sales growth more than trebled in two years and contributing the main driving force in the total toy market's 78 per cent expansion since 1991.

However, industry leaders now believe sales of video games are slowing as the market for the hardware they are played on matures - and as parents turn against the solitary or two-players-only nature of the games.

'Activity' toys such as snooker or darts are second in popularity, with likely sales of £244m last year, or 13 per cent of the market. Games and puzzles came third at £174m, or 9.3 per cent.

"Board games have come back very rapidly in 1993," Mr Graham Scott who organizes the Harrogate Fair said yesterday. "They lost out for a while, but video games cannot be played by whole families. Board games can, and appear to have done well this Christmas."

A rapidly developing segment, however, is 'plush', a cheap synthetic fur which is enabling the market for teddy bears and other cuddly toys to expand rapidly. Plush product sales are growing thanks to cheap labour in China, where high-quality mass-produced plush from Taiwan or South Korea is being turned into teddies by the million. Retail prices of plush bears range from £1.99 to £60.

"It means you can now have a range of bears, with limited editions and a wide choice of options on size to make them more collectible," said Mr Les Vargerson, managing director of Agenta Marketing of Market Harborough in Leicestershire.

He is the UK agent for Althans, which although based near Coburg, Germany, has more than 500 people employed in Hong Kong and China. It is now one of Europe's leading specialists in Asian-made Plüschtierfabrik bears.

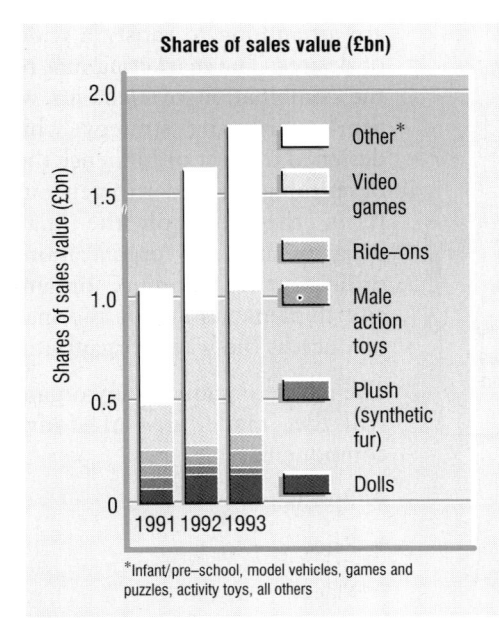

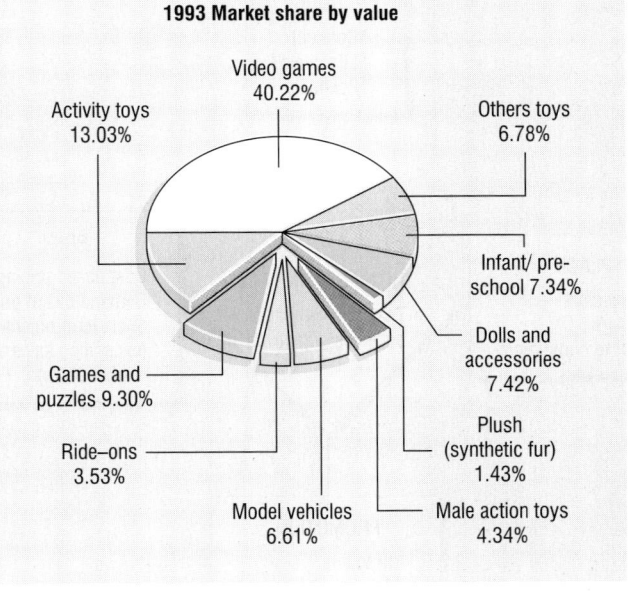

Shares of sales value (£bn)

Categories: Other*, Video games, Ride-ons, Male action toys, Plush (synthetic fur), Dolls

Years: 1991, 1992, 1993

*Infant/pre-school, model vehicles, games and puzzles, activity toys, all others

1993 Market share by value

- Video games 40.22%
- Activity toys 13.03%
- Games and puzzles 9.30%
- Ride-ons 3.53%
- Model vehicles 6.61%
- Male action toys 4.34%
- Plush (synthetic fur) 1.43%
- Dolls and accessories 7.42%
- Infant/pre-school 7.34%
- Others toys 6.78%

FT 10/1/94

6. International animal welfare groups have evidence to suggest that countries such as China and Taiwan trade illegally in parts from endangered species, e.g. bear paws and rhino horn. Campaigners have also gained access to bear farms in China and North Korea where thousands of bears spend their lives locked in cramped cages and are 'milked' of bile from their gall bladders. The bile is a prized remedy in the Far East for colds and other ailments.

If you ran a charity concerned with the protection of wild animals, how might you use knowledge of a growing market for toy bears to bring pressure for change in these countries?

7. Write to an animal charity, such as the WSPA, WWF, or IFAW (see list of useful addresses), to find out more about how they market their 'product' to generate charitable donations. Produce a short report on their marketing activities and suggest ways in which they might be extended.

Key words

Marketing objectives - marketing goals that a business will seek to achieve

Section 8.3 Implementing the marketing mix

Figure 8.1: Elements in the marketing mix

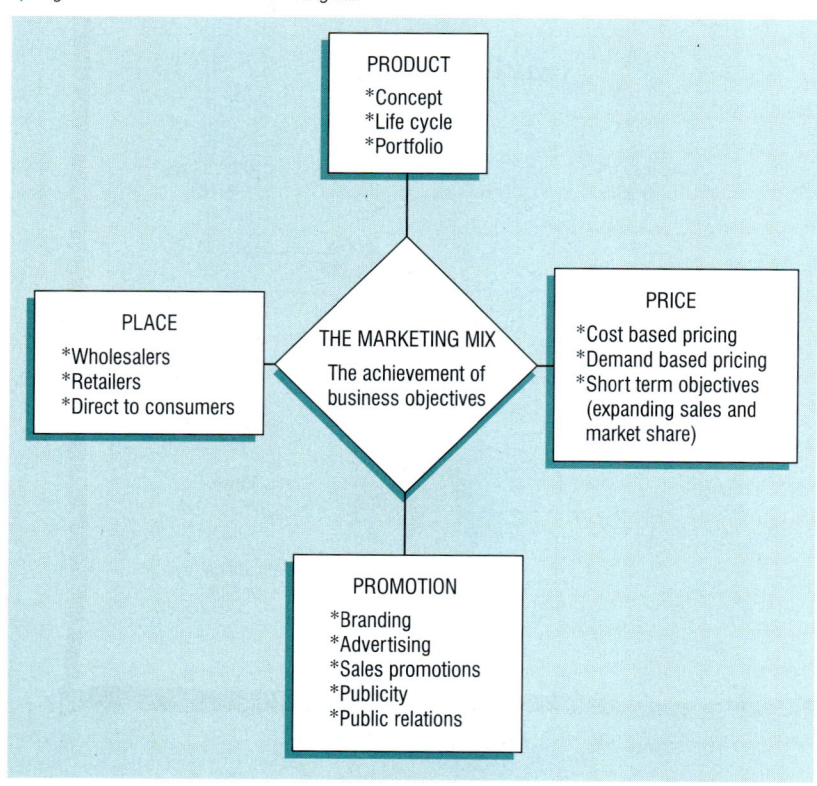

```
                    PRODUCT
                    *Concept
                    *Life cycle
                    *Portfolio

     PLACE                              PRICE
     *Wholesalers    THE MARKETING MIX  *Cost based pricing
     *Retailers      The achievement of *Demand based pricing
     *Direct to      business objectives *Short term objectives
      consumers                          (expanding sales and
                                          market share)

                    PROMOTION
                    *Branding
                    *Advertising
                    *Sales promotions
                    *Publicity
                    *Public relations
```

What is the marketing mix?

When consumers buy a product, they are attempting to satisfy a wide range of desires. The **marketing mix** refers to the combination of elements within a firm's marketing strategy which are designed to meet or influence the wants of customers in order to generate sales. It is the role of the marketing department in any organization to co-ordinate the planning, organization, and implementation of the marketing mix across the whole organization.

The marketing mix of any organization will be made up of four main components:

- Product
- Price
- Place
- Promotion

If a firm is to be successful it must get all four elements right.

A good marketing mix will encourage customers to build up loyalty to a particular product or product range. Additionally, many firms producing items such as hi-fi and video equipment ensure repeat purchases for their products through **built-in obsolescence**. This means that products either last for a limited timespan and then wear out, or have to be frequently updated.

▼ *Built-in obsolescence: the Ford Fiesta in 1978 and 1994.*

Differentiated and undifferentiated marketing

In considering the marketing strategies of different organizations, we can distinguish between **differentiated** and **undifferentiated** marketing.

Differentiated marketing

Not all consumers will want the same things from a product. For example, when buying a hi-fi system, some people may want very high-quality sound, others will look for features and gadgets, while others may desire maximum volume and the latest technology. In such markets, firms will need to adopt a **differentiated** marketing strategy. This involves marketing a product in different ways to different groups of people or market segments, so as to emphasize different aspects of the same product.

In an extreme form, a firm may use concentrated marketing aimed at only one market segment. This can often be a successful and cost-effective method of marketing for small firms serving niche markets. Examples might include polo equipment aimed at high-income groups, student rail passes aimed at people under 26 years of age, or magazines such as *Kerrang* aimed at young people who like heavy metal music.

Undifferentiated marketing

The strategy of broadcasting a single message about a product to the whole market is known as **undifferentiated marketing**. This tends to be used where the product is **homogenous** - that is, where the product cannot be differentiated by producers to suit the needs of different market segments. For example, potatoes are advertised by the Potato Marketing board on behalf of all potato producers, because the product satisfies a basic need for food which is common to all consumers.

▲ *The government-subsidized Potato Marketing Board will end in 1997*

Product

The product is central to the marketing mix. Consumers buy goods and services to satisfy a variety of desires. A firm must be aware of these desires if it is to operate successfully in the market. A firm is not just selling a product, but a whole concept to the consumer (see figure 8.2).

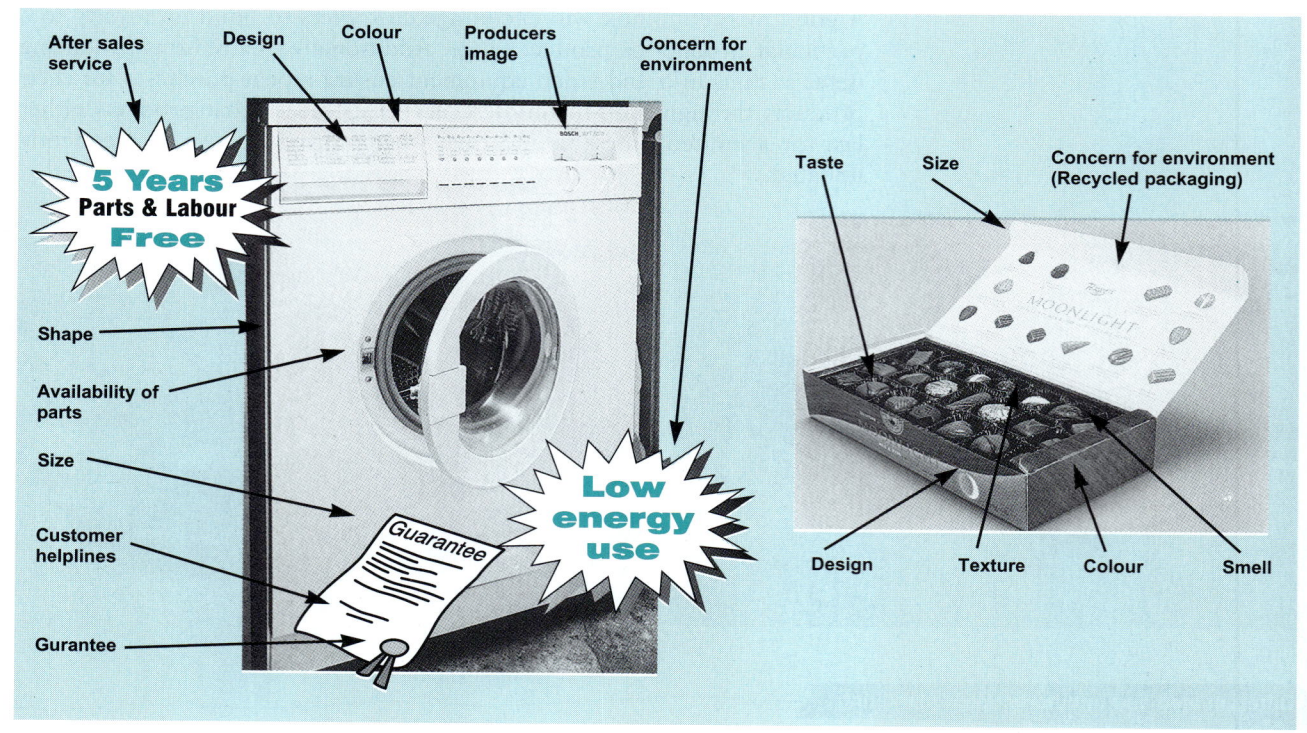

Figure 8.2: The product concept

Price

The prices of all goods and services are likely to vary over time as market conditions alter and marketing objectives change from - say - launching a new product to maximizing profit from it.

Three major factors influence the pricing policies of firms:

- Costs of production
- The level and strength of consumer demand.
- Degree of competition in supply

Short-term objectives, such as responding to the threat of new competitors, or the need to extend the life of the product, may also affect pricing strategies (see 21.1).

Cost-based strategies

Cost-based pricing strategies involve setting price with reference to the costs of production (see 20.1).

Firms will normally calculate the average cost of producing each item before adding a mark-up over cost for profit. However, in the short run, a firm may price below costs, thereby sustaining a loss, in order to promote a new product or fend off competition from rival firms. The aim will be to expand sales and market share.

As sales expand, the firm will be able to increase output and reduce the cost per unit. Cost savings associated with an increase in the size of a firm - for example, the ability to buy in bulk and receive discounts - are known as **economies of scale** (see 21.2).

Demand-based pricing

Instead of basing price on what the product costs to produce, **demand-based pricing** asks the question: 'At what price will the product sell?' To answer this, the firm will need to look carefully at consumers' perceptions of the worth of a product - i.e. their willingness to pay - and at the pricing policies of competitors. Only then will they be able to produce a good or service with the right design and quality to fit the market, and at the right cost to yield a profit.

Place

For the consumer to want to make a purchase, the right product must be transported to the right place at the right time - otherwise the customer will not buy. It will also be necessary for a producer to hold stocks of their product to respond quickly to consumer demand.

▼ Distribution

Distribution refers to the methods by which consumers obtain products from producers. It is a significant element in a firm's costs, and so requires careful management. The firm will need to consider physical distribution, the storage and transportation of goods and services, and the various methods and outlets through which the good or service can be sold to the consumer. These methods will include selling direct to the consumer or selling through **intermediaries** such as wholesalers, retail outlets, or specialist sales agents (see 11.2).

Choosing the distribution channel

A business will need to choose the most efficient channel of distribution for its products: one that will allow them to make their products available to consumers quickly, when they want them, and at minimum cost. Factors to consider will include the following:

- **How big is the market?** Large markets spread over a wide area will usually require intermediaries. International sales may require agents with knowledge of overseas markets and trade regulations.

- **How large is the producer?** Large firms may have the finance and personnel necessary to run their own distribution network of vehicle fleets, warehouses, and even retail outlets.

- **Who are the consumers?** Consumers of low-value, mass-produced goods normally expect to obtain them quickly and easily at retail outlets. Industrial consumers will often require technical details and will deal directly with a manufacturer or agent. They may be willing to wait some time for their order to be fulfilled.

- **What is the product?** Highly specialized or personalized goods and services will require direct contact between producer and consumer. Perishable goods will need to be sold quickly, so speed will be a key factor. Low-value goods sold in bulk are likely to be distributed through intermediaries, thus relieving the producer of the need for, and cost of, storage. New products may meet with some resistance from retailers and may require alternative means of distribution.

- **What is the product image?** Sometimes a firm may wish to restrict the sale of its products to certain shops and stores in order to preserve an exclusive product image.

Promotion

Promotion involves providing information to consumers about products through a variety of media, and attempting to influence buying decisions by stressing certain features. 'Influence' may become 'persuasion' when firms attempt to stress product features which may be more imaginary than real (see 10.2)

Above- and below-the-line promotion

Above-the-line promotion aims at mass markets through independent media such as TV, radio, and press advertising (see 10.2).

Below-the-line promotion refers to the use of media over which the producing firms have more control, allowing them to target their products more closely at particular consumers. Examples include exhibitions, packaging, and in-store sales promotions (see 11.3).

Branding:

- Creates consumer loyalty
- Distinguishes the product from its rivals
- Can help firms justify charging higher prices to their consumers.

Branding

Most forms of promotion seek to create an image to go with the product. **Brand imaging** is an important part of a firm's marketing strategy. Underlying all successful branding is the principle that people not only buy products, they also buy images. For example, Volkswagen advertised the typical VW driver as an affluent, care-free, attractive, professional type of person. The advertizing slogan spoke of 'VW people'. The campaign was successful as a large market segment identified with or wanted to be like the kind of people portrayed as 'VW people'. Sales of the cars rose accordingly.

▲ 'Beanz meanz Heinz'

▲ 'My mate marmite'

▲ 'Have a break, have a Kit Kat'

▼ Table 8.1: Durable brand names in USA

Product category	Market leader 1923	Current market position
cameras	Kodak	1
canned fruit	Del Monte	1
chewing gum	Wrigleys	1
crackers	Nabisco	1
razors	Gillette	1
soft drinks	Coca-cola	1
soap	Ivory	1
soup	Campbells	1
toothpaste	Colgate	2

Boston Consulting Group in Business Week 7.91/Financial Times 22.10.92

'Don't book it, Thomas cook it!'

If branding can make consumers believe that the branded product is better than others, they will be willing to pay a higher price for it. As many rival products are virtually identical, the only way in which a particular one can be made to stand out is often through aggressive branding. This is usually achieved through the use of a brand name, catchphrase, distinctive packaging, and, in the case of soap powders, a scented or coloured powder.

A firm can choose a separate brand name for each of its products or use one name for the whole range. For example, brand names like McDonalds, Sainsbury, and St Michael cover a range of products. Marketing using these brand names means that promoting one product helps the others in the range. However, if one product in the range is not up to standard, this can badly affect the image of the others.

Portfolio Activity 8.5

Range: Marketing functions, Customer focus
Skills: Collect and record data, Produce written material

Consider the following product ranges:
- Washing powders
- Biscuits
- Canned soft drinks
- Toilet rolls and tissues
- Tea and coffee

For each product range investigate:
- The brand names of products (including supermarket own-label brands)
- The images that are created for each brand
- How they are promoted (including advertising, sales promotions, publicity material, etc.)
- The different groups of consumers (or market segments) aimed at by different brands

Fast-moving consumer goods (FMCGs)

Consumer goods such as washing powders, biscuits, canned drinks, and crisps are used up relatively quickly by consumers who may need to make frequent repeat purchases. To meet the high demand for these and other so-called **fast-moving consumer goods**, both retail outlets and manufacturers must frequently re-stock.

Competition among producers to supply FMCGs is fierce. In order to capture market share, producers tend to produce a range of similar products aimed at particular market segments consisting of different groups of consumers with shared characteristics and buying habits (see 10.1). Although there is very little difference between products, distinctive images and brand names can be created for each product in a range by heavy advertising and by the use of different packaging. For example, biscuits such as 'Jammy Dodgers' may be aimed at the youth market segment, while the image created for Bendicks chocolate biscuits is one of luxury and decadence to capture demand from affluent middle-aged and middle-income consumers. Images created for washing powders can emphasize smell, 'whiteness', softness, colour stability, and environmental concern, with each particular image being aimed at a different market segment.

Producers will often spend large amounts of money advertising brands to create customer loyalty and to ensure repeat purchases for their products. This enables them to price their products at a premium, because consumers have been made to believe they are getting something which is worth a higher price. However, in recent years, increasing competition from supermarket own brands and changing consumer attitudes have reduced the demand for well-known brands such as Heinz baked beans and Coca-cola. Supermarkets have also used the power of advertising and price discounts to create an image of 'value for money' for their own-label brands.

Advanced Business

Portfolio Activity 8.6

Range: Marketing functions, Analyse marketing activities
Skills: Read and respond to written material

1. Why were brands so profitable in the past?
2. Explain the meaning of the sentence 'Brands are being bargained, belittled, bartered and battered'.
3. Discuss possible strategies firms could take to save brands.
4. In your view, are there still advantages to business in creating branded products? Support your answer with research into the range of branded products and the competition (price and non-price) between them in your local supermarket.

Shoot out at the check out!

From Marlboro to Kelloggs's, big brands are under siege from supermarkets' own labels. Many brands will perish or never be so profitable again.

What's in a name? In 1988 Phillip Morris bought Kraft for $13 billion and Nestlé spent $4.5 billion on Rowntree. Many people said 1988 was the 'year of the brand.'

It was the spectacular performance of brands and their owners throughout the 1980s that lay behind the large sums paid in these takeovers. By exploiting consumers' loyalty to famous names with price rises well above inflation, firms such as Kellogg and Heinz increased profits by 15% a year. Firms believed that brands would continue to earn a premium well into the future.

Yet that was wrong. Faced with a staggering array of products in every size, shape and shade, many European and American shoppers have correctly concluded that there is little difference between them. Brand loyalty is waning.

The cause is largely to do with firms having encouraged consumers to buy on price by bombarding them with special offers to purchase branded products. Also responsible are retailers' own-label products, which are eating into many brands' market shares. Brands are being 'bargained, belittled, bartered and battered.' According to BBDO, a market research agency, nearly two-thirds of consumers believe there are no relevant or discernible differences between rival brands across a range of products.

Technological advances have raised the quality of most goods and made it easier for competitors to copy one another innovations. Own-label products are increasing and account for more than 20% of sales in some European supermarkets.

Adapted from The Economist 5.6.93

▼ Examples of contracting markets in the mid 1990s include;

Contacting markets	Expanding markets
Typewriters	Multi-media personal computers and software
'Doorstep' milk deliveries	Garden centres
Animal furs	Mineral waters
Tobacco and cigarettes	Herbal drinks
TV repairs	Compact discs
Vinyl LPs	DIY
Coal and solid fuels	Mobil phones
Duplication equipment	Fax machines
Veal	Aromatherapy

The marketing mix and the growth of organisations

Business organisations aiming for growth in their size and scale of production can do so in a number of ways;

- through developing new products to sell
- by expanding their share of a market
- by entering new markets at home or abroad

Product development

Consumer wants are always changing because of various factors - fashion, social and cultural change, growing incomes, new legal requirements, and many more (see 1.2). It is important that firms keep pace with changing wants and develop existing or new products that people will continue to buy. The development of products and their performance in markets are considered in sections 9.1 and 10.3.

Contracting and expanding markets

If consumer demand for a particular good or service is falling over time the market for that product is said to be shrinking or **contracting**. Firms making that good or service will suffer declining sales and profits.

Competition for remaining customers will be fierce among firms and some may close down.

If, on the other hand, consumer demand for a particular good or service is rising over time the market for that product is said to be **expanding**. Those firms already producing the good or service will attract new customers and experience rising sales and profits. They may have to expand production to meet demand and it is likely that other firms will be attracted to the market.

Building market share

Entering a new market will often require a firm initially to charge a relatively low price for its products to attract customers away from established rivals (see 21.3). Heavy advertising and in-store promotions to raise customer awareness about the product will also be necessary (see 10.2). For example, advertising for a new drink called Red Bull was prolific in the summer of 1995 with a number of humorous cartoons being shown on prime time television and posters with the catchy slogan 'It's amazing what a Red Bull can do!'. In this way marketing was being used to gain a foothold in the large canned soft drinks market and to build sales and market share.

Key words

Marketing mix - the elements of a firm's marketing strategy designed to meet consumer wants and generate sales. The four main elements are product, price, place, and promotion.

Differentiated marketing - marketing a product in different ways to different market segments

Concentrated marketing - marketing aimed at one particular market segment

Undifferentiated marketing - marketing a product in the same way to the whole market

Homogeneous products - products which cannot be differentiated

Built-in obsolescence - commodities which are frequently updated or produced in such a way that they wear out relatively quickly

Cost-based pricing - pricing products according to their cost of production

Demand-based pricing - pricing policies based on market conditions and consumer willingness to pay

Economies of scale - cost savings resulting from an increase in the size of a firm

Distribution - the process of getting products from producers to final consumers

Promotion - attempts to influence the buying decisions of consumers.

Above-the-line promotion - promotion aimed at mass markets through independent advertising media such as TV, radio, cinema, and newspapers

Below-the-line promotion - promotional methods such as packaging, trade fairs, in-store merchandising, targeted more closely at the customers of a particular firm

Branding - creating a distinctive name and image for a product to differentiate it from rival products

Fast moving consumer goods (FMCGs) - frequently bought, branded products which are heavily advertised and aimed at different groups of consumers.

Further reading

The following magazines are published weekly and are available from larger branches of WH Smith or on order from local newsagents:

- *Campaign*, Haymarket Business Publications Ltd., 30 Lancaster Gate, London W2 3LP
- *Marketing*, Haymarket Business Publications Ltd., 30 Lancaster Gate, London W2 3LP.
- *Marketing Week*, Centaur Communications Ltd., St. Giles House, 50 Poland Street, London W1V 4AX

Advanced Business

Test questions

The following underpinning knowledge will be tested:

1. Marketing principles and functions
2. How marketing principles underpin marketing functions
3. The need for customer focus and meeting the needs of the organization
4. Marketing activities in business organizations
5. Growth in organizations through product development and expanding sales

1 Which of the following is NOT an objective of marketing?

   A Reducing production costs
   B Market penetration
   C Maintaining market share
   D Influencing consumers' buying choices

Questions 2 - 4 share the following answer options:

   A Offering differentiated products and marketing activities to different groups of consumers
   B Using the same marketing mix on the total population
   C Concentrating on product development only
   D Concentrating the marketing mix on a small niche market

Which of the above approaches to the marketing mix is most likely to be used by each of the following business organizations?

2 A producer of medical equipment

3 A small company producing designer clothing

4 A large manufacturer of cheese and butter products

5 A firm that is product-orientated is most likely to:

   A Aim to maximize sales
   B Undertake extensive market research
   C Produce highly innovative products
   D Practice mass marketing

Questions 6 - 8 share the following answer options:

   A New packaging
   B A new advertising campaign
   C A new consumer phoneline and help desk
   D A new company logo

Which of the above marketing activities could help achieve the following objectives?

6 Satisfying customer requirements

7 Increasing market share

8 Improving corporate image

9 Which of the following is NOT an element of the marketing mix?

   A Product
   B Price
   C Personnel
   D Promotion

Questions 10 - 12 share the following answer options:

   A Distributing video films and compact discs through supermarkets
   B Cutting price below costs to compete with new firms
   C Investigating trends in consumer spending from published data
   D Developing multimedia software for computers

Which of the above would satisfy the following marketing principles?

10 Utilizing technological developments

11 Using data from published sources on trends in consumer spending

12 Generating revenues

13 a. What is marketing?

    b. Give two key principles which underpin marketing.

    c. What is the marketing mix?

    d. Suggest two ways the marketing mix could be used to apply the marketing principles you have suggested above.

14 **a.** Explain why profit-making and not-for-profit organizations need to use marketing.

b. Suggest two ways in which marketing can help an organization achieve growth.

c. Suggest two major factors which can influence the pricing decisions of a firm selling microchip processors for computers.

d. Suggest a possible short-term pricing strategy for a firm faced with a new rival entering the market.

15 **a.** What is branding?

b. Suggest two ways a firm might create a strong brand image for a new chocolate bar.

c. What pricing policy would you advise the firm to pursue in launching the new chocolate bar? Give reasons for your recommendation.

16 'Effective marketing means that firms must consider every aspect of the business from the perspective of the customer.' Explain the meaning of this statement and use examples of how the marketing mix (product, place, promotion, and price) can be used effectively.

Assessment Assignment

Range: Marketing principles
Marketing functions
Customer focus/organization's own needs
Analyse marketing activities
Growth of organizations

Skills: **Communication**
Produce written material
Use illustrations and images
Read and respond to written material
Application of Number
Tackle problems
Information Technology
Process information

RSPCA posters show a pile of dead dogs

By Patrick O'Hanlon

A National poster campaign showing a pile of dead dogs, which calls for government funding for a compulsory dog registration scheme, was launched yesterday "without apologies" by the Royal Society for the Prevention of Cruelty to Animals.

The society, which destroys 350,000 unwanted dogs each year, said it was "sick of doing the Government's dirty work" since dog licences were abolished a year ago.

The £250,000 press and poster campaign was launched after the society said it was advised that the Independent Broadcasting Authority would refuse television time because of the campaign's overtly political nature. One poster shows a photograph of dogs which were destroyed at the society's Birmingham home.

Mr David Wilkins, RSPCA chief veterinary officer, said: "We make no apoligies for the aggression of this campaign."

He said stray dogs cost more than £76 million a year through road accidents, hospital treatment for bites and dog-bourne diseases, livestock attacks, boarding fees and the cost of destroying 1,000 animals a day at £8 each.

Tasks

1. Study the information on the 1989 RSPCA campaign to introduce a compulsory dog registration scheme. Explain how it shows the application of marketing principles.

2. Find out about the aims, services, and campaigns of the RSPCA or any other charity. Explain how these campaigns further demonstrate marketing principles.

3. Identify elements of the marketing mix used by your chosen charity in their efforts to raise income and consumer awareness.

4. Select one private-sector profit-making organization. Compare and contrast the application of marketing principles and the marketing strategies by the organization with your chosen charity.

5. Investigate how the profit-making organization has achieved growth through the development of new products or modification and re-launch of old products.

6. Identify and investigate those factors which have affected, or can affect, the product pricing decisions of your chosen organization.

7. Assemble your research into a carefully produced report using a wordprocessor or desktop publishing package.

Advanced Business

chapter 9 Market Research

This chapter examines sources of marketing information and data collection methods appropriate to a firm researching their market and developing new and improved products to satisfy consumer wants.

Key ideas

A gap in the market for a good or service may be established using **market research** based on original or **primary research**, and/or on **secondary research** using existing sources of information.

Businesses will base their marketing decisions, such as **product development** and pricing, sales and promotional strategies, on information gathered by market research.

Market research information can be used to identify **consumer preferences**, **behaviour** and **spending patterns**, **rising and falling sales**, and the market share and **marketing activities of rival firms**.

A **target market** consists of a group of consumers at which a particular product or marketing activity is aimed.

Because the **target population** of potential consumers of a particular good or service will often be large, a firm will usually select a small sample from which to gather market research information.

It is important that the chosen sample of consumers is representative of all consumers in the target market, otherwise there is high risk that the research information will be **biased**.

A variety of methods can be used to gather **primary market data**, including **questionnaires, interviews, consumer panels, electronic monitoring, test marketing**, or **simple observation**.

Questionnaires will normally contain a mix of **open questions**, which allow a wide variety of answers, or **closed questions**, which restrict the respondent to a limited number of replies

Secondary sources of market research data can either be **internal** to a firm - for example, previous research reports or sales figures - or **external**. External sources can include publications by UK and EU governments, specialist business organizations at home and overseas, and by the media.

The most suitable method of market research for a firm to use will be selected using criteria such as **fitness for the purpose, reliability, cost, speed, accuracy, and accessibility**. A firm will need to determine which criteria are the most important in terms of their particular circumstances.

Section 9.1

What is market research?

Face-to-face interviews with potential consumers

The identification of consumer wants

A business will only be successful if consumers want and can buy what it produces both now and in the future. **Market research** can reduce the risk of producing products that do not appeal to consumers by helping a firm to discover information about their consumers.

Market research involves the gathering, collation, and analysis of data relating to the consumption and marketing of goods and services. The purpose of such research is to identify whether there is want for a particular product - a **gap in the market** - or whether a want can created among consumers by persuasive advertising (see 10.2).

Market research information

In order to identify consumer wants for consumer goods and services and capital goods, firms need to gather information on the following:

- **Consumer behaviour.** For example, how do consumers react to TV advertising or advertising on the radio? Do they like free gifts? How do they react to price changes and new products?

- **Buying patterns and sales trends.** How do buying habits differ between different regions, income groups, age groups, sexes, races? How do buying patterns change over time? Which markets are expanding - i.e. show rising consumer demand and sales? Which markets are contracting - i.e. show falling consumer demand and sales?

- **Consumer preferences.** How do consumers react to different products, styles, colours, tastes, retail outlets, method of payment, promotional devices, etc?

- **Activities of rival firms.** How do competitors adapt their products, ranges, and prices to meet consumers' wants? How well do their products sell? What is their market share? What marketing strategies and what new products are they developing?

Once a firm has identified the kind of market research information it needs, decisions can be taken on how to get the information, how much to spend on collecting it, and how often to undertake research.

A firm also has to consider what it will do with the information it collects. For example, if research shows sales of CD players are falling while sales of mini-discs are rising, will the firm increase advertising expenditure on CD players or will it shift production towards mini-disc machines? Collecting market research information alone will not make an unsuccessful firm successful. Good decisions have to be taken on the basis of the information collected.

Market research and business decision-making

Market research will provide information to a firm on whether the customer will buy the product, and on the design features, colours, packaging, prices, and kinds of retail outlets that consumers prefer.

Advanced Business

▼ Figure 9.1: The stages of market research

STAGE 1
Decide on the purpose of market research. What information do you need? What action will be taken as a result of research findings?

STAGE 2
Decide the most appropriate methods of research given information requirements, time and budget constraints.

STAGE 3
To obtain the information required, how many people should you ask and what type of consumers should they be?

STAGE 4
Undertake the research

STAGE 5
Analyse the results, draw conclusions and make marketing decisions based on the findings.

Portfolio Activity 9.1

Range: Marketing research information
Skills: Read and respond to written material

1. Using the article above, identify as many reasons as you can to explain why market research is an important business activity.
2. Why might it sometimes be very difficult for a firm to act on the results of its market research?

Let The Customer Be Your Guide

When Julian Rankin and Michael Osborn set up their lighting business in London in 1985 they had definite plans for the future. They had set their sights on establishing their company, Ora Lighting, as a manufacturer of well-designed high-quality light fittings.

But instead of being able to sell their range of lighting products they found that seventy percent of their work was special one-off product development. "We tried to steer away from that and impose our own standard ranges of products on the market, but as a small company we didn't have the marketing muscle."

The partners sought advice under the government's Enterprise Initiative. The advice they got from a consultant was to go with the market rather than try to fight it. Now at a time when many competitors have gone out of business, Ora has a turnover of £500,000 and record order books.

Ora's initial approach is not unusual. "A lot of companies think they know who their customers are but never talk to them to find out what they really want. There is a lot of pride involved for someone who has built up his business, he doesn't want somebody telling him he has got it wrong."

Creating a more professional approach to marketing is hampered by widespread ignorance of what marketing actually is. Marketing is not just about selling, instead marketing goes to the heart of a business, determining its field of activity and choice of products. It starts with market research in order to build up a knowledge of customers and competitors. It moves on to designing products or services to suit the market-place and pricing them at the highest level the market will bear.

Businesses which take market research seriously often face painful choices. They may have to give up a cherished product to move into a more promising era. But the alternative to making what your customers want, could be making, and selling, nothing at all.

Adapted from Financial Times 5.10.93

Additionally, research will help to identify the kind of consumer who is likely to purchase the product. For example, market research can reveal information on consumers' likely age range, sex, geographical region, favourite leisure pursuits, and lifestyle. This information will assist in the creation of an appropriate marketing mix to attract customers (see 8.3).

Product development

Take a look around your house. The chances are that you will have a television, a video recorder, a telephone, a compact disc player, a microwave, and a number of other household appliances. Few of these products would have been found in a house 50 years ago. Go back 150 years, and there would have been no cars, aircraft, or plastics, and few of the medicines that we take for granted today. All of the products we are able to enjoy today are the result of innovations and technological breakthroughs.

▼ Figure 9.2: The scope of market research

The need for market research

The marketing mix:

- Product?
- Price?
- Distribution?
- Promotion?

How can market research help?

Identify consumer wants
Test alternative products
Consumer reactions to new products

Consumer willingness to pay
Price elasticity of demand
What forms of payment do people prefer

Where do consumers shop for the type of produce
Wholesalers and retailers reactions to products

Choosing advertising media
Testing new promotional ideas
Effectiveness of promotional campaigns

The market?

Competition?

Market size and conditions
Market segments
Consumer characteristics

Identify competitors, their strengths and weaknesses
Market shares
Information on rivals pricing and strategy

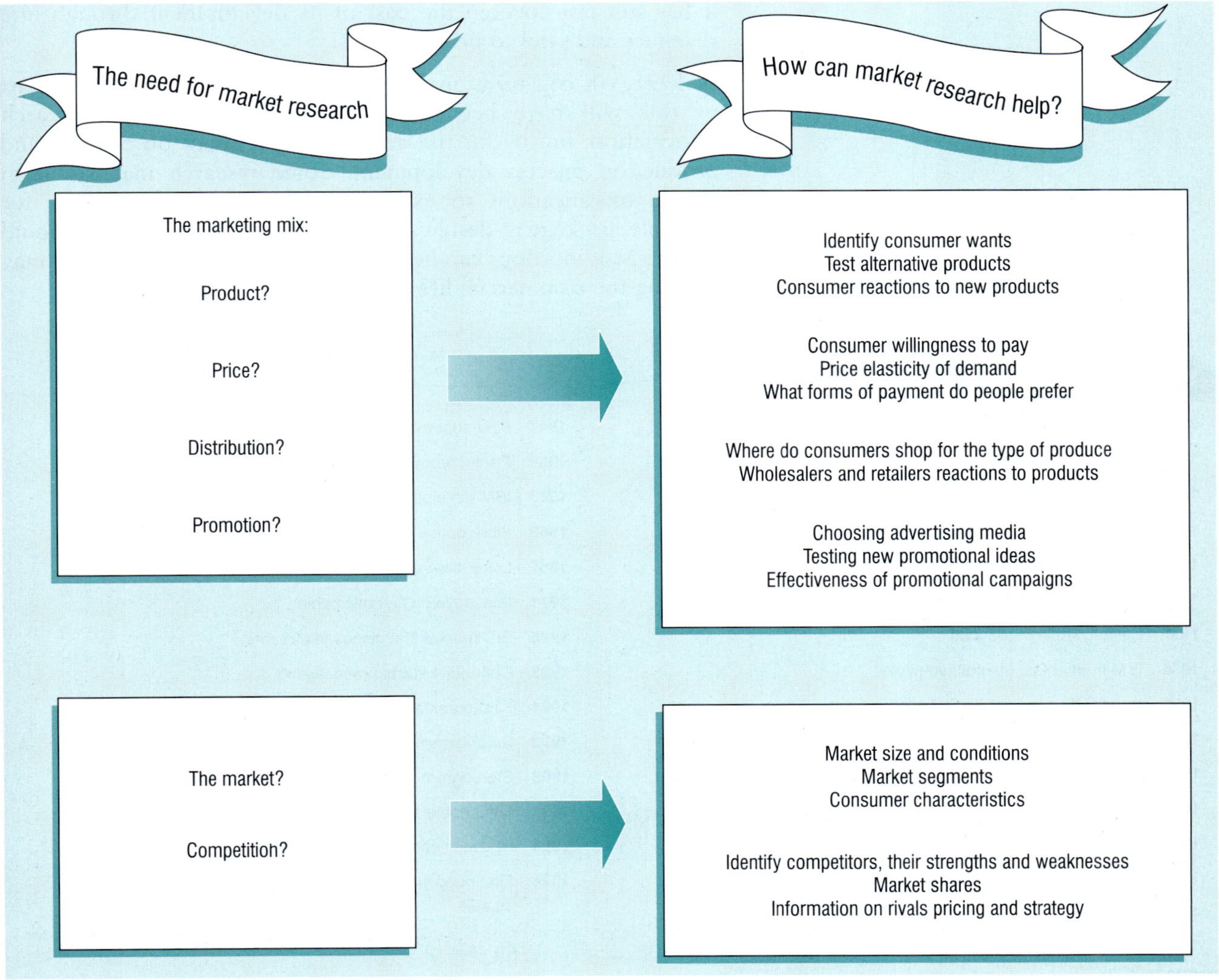

Because fashion, tastes, technology, levels of competition, and the economy are always changing, the market for goods and services is also in a state of continuous change. Change means that firms are increasingly keen to find new products to out-sell their rivals, and new processes to reduce their production costs. This process is called **research and development (R&D)**.

- **Research** is the investigation and discovery of new ideas
- **Development** involves putting ideas into practice

R&D is financed and carried out mainly by businesses, government, and higher education institutions. It is defined as *'creative work undertaken on a systematic basis in order to increase the stock of knowledge, including knowledge of man, culture and society, and the use of this stock of knowledge to devise new applications'*. Sometimes the process can take many years to complete, and success is not always guaranteed. For example, the Concorde supersonic aircraft took around 30 years to develop, yet it has still not covered the cost of its development through fare revenues and sales to other nations.

In 1991, UK organizations spent nearly £12 billion on R&D. Part of this will have been spent on collecting market research information, but by far the most money is spent on product and production process development. Some research may result in simple modifications to existing products and processes - for example, package re-design such as the ringpull can or paper liquid carton. Modifications can help to reduce production costs and may prolong the commercial life of an existing product (see 10.3).

Some important product developments since 1900

Year	Development	Year	Development
1900	Kodak manufacture the first mass-produced camera	1947	First supermarket opens in UK
1903	*Daily Mirror* newspaper is published	1960	Pentel produce felt-tip pen
1908	Henry Ford promotes the sale of the first Model T car	1963	IBM develop wordprocessing for computers
1919	First flight across the atlantic by Alcock and Brown	1966	Fibre optics developed
1927	Warner Bros release first 'talking picture' in USA	1967	Laser beams developed in USA
1928	Limited TV transmissions in USA and UK	1971	Intel develop first microchip
1930	Electric kettle introduced	1975	BIC market first disposable razors
1935	IBM market first electric typewriter	1982	Channel 4 starts broadcasting
1938	Dupont develop non-stick Teflon	1984	First breakfast TV shows launched in UK
1939	ICI develop polythene	1992	Sega launches CD megadrive
1943	Lazlo Biro invents ball-point pen	1993	Stereogram 3D pictures become popular
1955	ITV brodacasts begin in the UK	1994	QVC home shopping channel is launched in UK
1947	British Rail formed	1994	National lottery launched in UK
1948	National Health Service created	1994	First quad speed CD-ROM and rewritable CD-ROM drives on sale
1946	Bikinis introduced		

Some new products and processes are invented by private individuals and inventors purely by chance. For example, 'cats eyes' in roads were the result of the inventor seeing light reflected in broken glass in a road. Inventors can sell their innovations to firms who are willing to produce them for sale. New inventions and ideas can be protected by **patents** which prevent them being copied by other people and firms.

Occasionally, private inventors and organized R&D can result in **technological breakthroughs** leading to the discovery of entirely new products or processes. For example, microchip technology has allowed the development of desktop computers capable of doing work once carried out by computers that filled entire rooms. The invention of lasers has opened the way to the development of micro-surgery in medicine, advanced military weapons, and compact disc players.

Portfolio Activity 9.2

Range: Marketing decisions, Product development
Skills: Read and respond to written materials

Caviar with currents

SAPPORO

There are times when Japan's celebrated long-term approach to business runs wild. Hokkaido Electric Power's interest in caviar farming is one of those times. The firm has a monopoly on the supply of electricity in Hokkaido, Japan's northernmost island. The absence of competitors hands it steady returns: in the year to March Hokkaido Electric clocked up ¥16.3 billion ($131m) in net profits, on revenues of ¥521 billion. Yet the firm's managers fret that their fate is tied to that of Hokkaido's precarious economy. Hence the fish.

Regulation prevents Hokkaido Electric from selling anything except electricity. Undaunted, the firm's researchers have since 1990 been probing the mysteries of the sturgeon's reproductive organs. This year they succeeded in inducing one of 200 captive sturgeon to spawn the eggs that gastronomes call caviar. This was a triumph, but the researchers say it will take a few more years before the technique (which involves hormone injections) is reliable enough to be applied commercially.

What then? Because it is not allowed to sell caviar itself, Hokkaido Electric plans to donate its work to a lucky local company. It the latter prospers, it will need electricity; better still, its newly affluent employees will spend their wages on electricity-consuming gadgets. This is the only return Hokkaido Electric expects from its investment.

The Economist 13.11.93

Advanced Business

1. Explain how each organization has developed products and processes in response to consumer wants. Which organization made the technological breakthrough?

2. What is so unusual about the marketing approach that will be adopted by Hokkaido Electric for the use of their technique to increase the production of caviar? Explain how this marketing approach is designed to create a consumer want that will benefit the company.

Less is more

In the early 1980s, when Proctor & Gamble first test-marketed a highly concentrated laundry product, few people would buy it. Shoppers were put off by what they perceived to be less fabric softener or washing liquid at a premium price. Few of them seemed to care very much that so-called "ultra" products could slash the amount of packaging finding its way into landfills.

But it was hard to keep a good idea down. P&G and other big consumer products manufacturers are now profiting from a shift in consumer sentiment. By 1993, "ultra" – or concentrated – products were capturing about 70 per cent of the laundry market, according to Green MarketAlert, a trade newsletter.

"Consumers once believed more is more, now they think otherwise," says Jacqueline Ottman, a New York environmental consultant.

"Source reduction" is the buzz-word phrase used in the field to describe a movement that embraces package redesign, "light-weighting", and greater use of refillable containers and concentrates. It overlaps with efforts to promote recycling, which slows down demand for virgin materials.

FT 7.12.94

Key words

Market research - the gathering, collation, and analysis of data relating to the consumption and marketing of goods and services

Consumer goods and services - any commodities that directly satisfy a human need or want

Durable goods - products consumed over a long period of time

Non-durable goods - products which are used up quickly

Capital goods - products which are used as an input to further productive activity and which do not satisfy an immediate consumer want

Fast-moving consumer goods (FMCGs) - frequently bought, branded products which are heavily advertised and aimed at different target markets

Product development - the production of new products or the modification of existing ones

Research and development (R&D) - investigating new ideas for products and processes with a view to commercial exploitation

Patents - a licence to protect ideas from being copied

Target market - a group of consumers at which a particular product or marketing activity is aimed

Section 9.2

Sources of marketing information

Information requirements

Information collected by market research can be either **qualitative** or **quantitative**:

- **Quantitative data** refers to numbers - for example, the value and volume of sales per period of time or numbers of shoppers per week - which can be presented in a numerical or graphical format.

- **Qualitative data** refers to information concerning the motives and attitudes of consumers. It focuses, not on how consumers behave, but *why* they behave in certain ways. Qualitative data is a useful supplement to quantitative data. It is sometimes the only source of information when numerical data is scarce.

There are two main sources of market research information: **primary research**, where researchers gather information about the market themselves; and **secondary research**, where researchers use information that has already been collected by other people and organizations.

▼ *Figure 9.3: Sources of information*

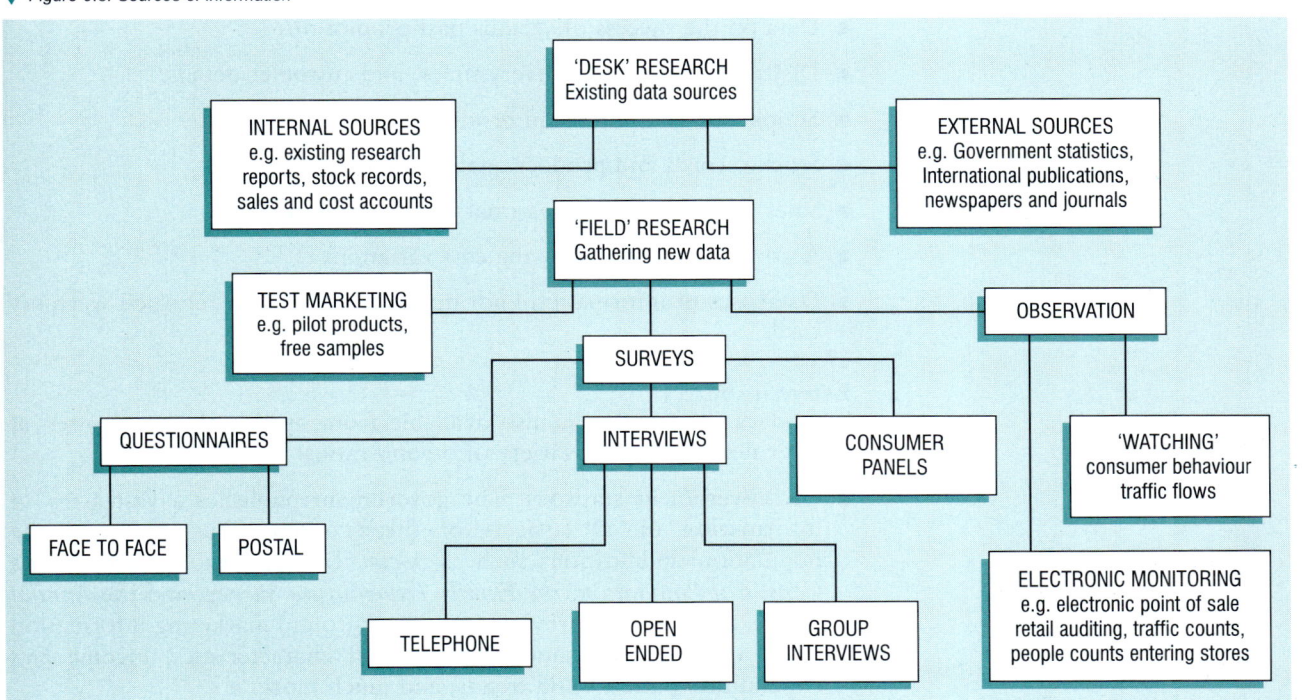

Portfolio Activity 9.3

Range: Marketing research information, Sources
Skills: Collect and record data

A medium-sized high street confectionery chain is considering expanding its product range and also its number of retail outlets.

1. What kind of market research is likely to be available to the firm internally, and how might it use the information?
2. Investigate the kinds of market research information the firm could gather from externally published secondary sources. What can these sources reveal about the environment in which the firm operates?

Secondary data

So-called **desk-based research** makes use of **secondary data**, or data which has already been collected for another purpose. Sources of secondary data may be found both within a business and from outside the firm.

Internal sources

Most firms will find that the experience of their staff and internal business records provide valuable information about the past performance of products. Sources of internal information may include:

- Existing market research reports
- Data on the success of various past promotions
- Distribution data on delivery times, and customer details
- Shopkeepers' opinions on products
- Stock records and product quality audits
- Sales records showing seasonal variations in sales
- Accounting records showing cost variations
- Databases of information built up on customers via returned warranty cards

External sources

Secondary information is also available from outside the firm, often at little or no cost, from a variety of organizations:

- **UK government statistics.** The government publishes a vast array of information on all aspects of the economy, business, and the population. Publications such as *Social Trends, Regional Trends, the Census of Population, the Family Expenditure Survey*, and the *Annual Abstract of Statistics* provide useful background marketing information about regional and national population characteristics, income and expenditure patterns and trends, and much more.

- **Specialist business organizations.** A number of organizations specialize in market research and produce regular reports which can be bought by the public. Examples include Neilsons Retail Audit, Mintel, and Dun and Bradstreet.

Additionally, many sources of secondary market research exist on computer databases and are available to firms with computer links at a charge. These include surveys by The Economist Intelligence Unit, The Financial Times Business Information Service, and economic reports by the OECD (the Organization of Economic Cooperation and Development).

- **International publications.** Organizations such as the World Bank, United Nations, and European Community publish a wide variety of papers and journals containing economic and social data on different countries which are useful to market researchers.

- **Competing firms.** Public limited companies (plcs) are required to produce annual reports on their activities. A rival firm will be able to obtain information about company profits and sales from these reports.
- **The media, TV, and newspapers** will often carry features on economic, business, and social patterns and trends.

Portfolio Activity 9.4

Range: Marketing research information, Marketing decisions, Product development
Skills: Interpret and present data, Present information

You are one of a group of entrepreneurs who have recognized the rapid growth in the market for leisure services. You wish to build and operate a leisure centre as a private company. You hope that the centre will return a healthy profit on your investment.

You must first identify your target market(s). In addition you must find out what types of sports and other facilities your target market(s) are likely to use. Providing the wrong facilities will not attract customers and will not generate revenue for your centre.

▼ Participation in the most popular sports, games and physical activities: by age, 1990

GREAT BRITAIN — **PERCENTAGES AND NUMBERS**

	16-19	20-24	25-29	30-44	45-59	60-69	70 and over	All aged 16 and over	Median age of participants
Percentage in each group participating in each activity in the 12 months before interview									
Walking	72	70	73	73	69	61	37	65	41
Swimming	70	65	63	58	35	20	6	42	34
Snooker, pool, billiards	56	46	37	25	13	7	3	22	29
Keep fit, Yoga	31	35	31	23	14	9	5	19	33
Cycling	41	23	22	22	13	8	4	17	35
Darts	29	26	21	15	10	4	2	13	31
Golf	21	19	18	15	11	7	2	12	35
Tenpin bowls, skittles	26	26	19	15	7	2	1	11	30
Running, jogging	30	20	18	13	3	1	-	9	28
Soccer	33	23	18	9	2	-	-	9	25
Weightlifting, training	27	24	20	10	3	-	-	9	27
Badminton	32	18	13	10	4	1	-	9	27
Tennis	29	16	11	9	3	1	-	7	27
Squash	15	15	15	8	2	-	-	6	27
Fishing	11	7	8	8	6	3	1	6	36

General Household Survey/Social Trends 1994

Advanced Business

▼ Trends in participation in sports, games and physical activities: participation rates in the 4 weeks before interview by sex: 1987 and 1990

PERSONS AGED 16 OR OVER — GREAT BRITAIN

Active sports, games and physical activities*	Men		Women	
	1987	1990	1987	1990
	Percentage participating in the 4 weeks before interview†			
Walking	41	44	35	38
Swimming: indoor	10	11	11	13
Swimming: outdoor	4	4	3	4
Snooker/pool/billiards	27	24	5	5
Keep fit/yoga	5	6	12	16
Cycling	10	12	7	7
Darts	14	11	4	4
Golf	7	9	1	2
Running (jogging, etc.)	8	8	3	2
Weightlifting/training	7	8	2	2
Soccer	10	10	0	0
Tenpin bowls/skittles	2	5	1	3
Badminton	4	4	3	3
Squash	4	4	1	1
Lawn/carpet bowls	2	3	1	1
Tennis	2	2	1	2
Fishing	4	4	0	0
Table tennis	4	3	1	1
Water sports (exc. sailing)	2	2	1	1
Cricket	2	2	0	0
Horse riding	0	1	1	1
Sailing	1	1	0	1
Self defence	1	1	0	0
Ice skating	1	1	1	1
Basketball	1	1	0	0
Athletics - track & field	1	1	0	0
Hockey	0	1	0	1
Climbing	0	1	0	0
Rugby	1	1	0	0
Motor sports	1	1	0	0
Skiing	1	1	0	0
Netball	0	0	1	1
At least one activity (excl. walking)**	57	58	34	39
At least one activity**	70	73	52	57
Base = 100%	9086	8119	10443	9455

* Includes only activities in which more than 0.5% of men or women participated in 4 weeks before interview in 1987 or 1990.
† Interviews were carried out throughout the year so these figures represent average participation in 4 week periods over the year.
** Total includes those activities not separately listed.

General Household Survey 1990

Using the secondary data presented here, try and answer the following questions:

- What are the characteristics of your target population?
- What sports facilities will you provide at your centre?
- What extra facilities could you provide to attract custom from people other than those participating in sporting activities?
- What other information would it be useful to collect to help plan your business?

Produce a report of your research and conclusions. Where appropriate, include graphs and tables you have developed yourself from the secondary data presented. Use a computer to help you if possible.

▼ Rank order of the 'top ten' activities in 12 months before interview

Men	Women	Total
Walking	Walking	Walking
Swimming	Swimming	Swimming
Snooker/pool	Keep fit/yoga	Snooker/pool
Cycling	Cycling	Keep fit/yoga
Darts	Tenpin bowls/skittles	Cycling
Golf	Snooker/pool	Darts
Soccer	Badminton	Golf
Running (excl. track)	Darts	Tenpin bowls/skittles
Weightlifting	Tennis	Running (excl. track)
Tenpin bowls/skittles	Running (excl. track)	Soccer

General Household Survey 1990

▼ Free time in a typical week: by sex and employment status, 1992-93

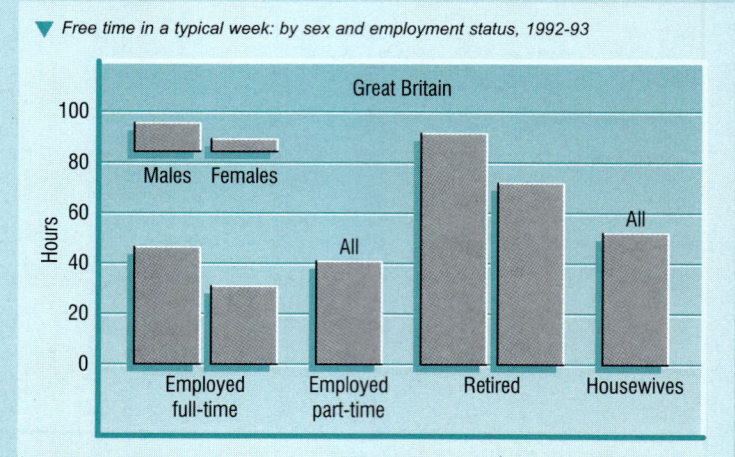

The Henley Centre for Forecasting/Social Trends 1994

220

UNIT THREE

CHAPTER 9

> **Key words**
>
> **Quantitative data** - numerical information
>
> **Qualitative data** - expressing values in words; for example, the weather is very hot, hot, cold, or very cold.
>
> **Primary research** - new market research data gathered by a researcher
>
> **Secondary research** - desk-based research using existing data from a variety of sources
>
> **Secondary data** - data already gathered for another purpose
>
> **Internal data sources** - sources of market research data available from within a firm
>
> **External data sources** - sources of market research data available from other organizations outside the firm.

Section 9.3

Primary research

Primary market research data

Primary data is information which is newly created by field research. Because primary information is newly created, it tends to be more expensive to gather than **secondary data** which is already in existence.

The major advantage of primary data is that, because it is fresh data gathered for a particular purpose, it is likely to match the firm's requirements more closely. It will also be up-to-date and exclusive to the collector.

In the past, most market research was undertaken by specialist research firms like Gallop, Mori, and the Market Research Bureau (MRB). However, new technology increasingly means that firms can carry out their own research. Large superstores can obtain primary marketing information using bar-code readers which immediately register patterns of sales with a central computer. **Electronic Point-of-Sale (EPOS)** systems are now used in nearly all large supermarkets and many other stores. For example, the head office of the McDonalds fast-food restaurant chain can monitor sales in every store daily and can measure the sales response of different products to particular kinds of promotional activities. This gives McDonalds an edge in being able to react very quickly to the market.

▼ *Electronic point-of-sale systems provide valuable consumer data*

Sampling

All of the possible consumers in a market for a particular product taken together are called the **target population**. A survey based on primary research information from the whole population in a market is called a **census**. Because all possible buyers are surveyed, data gathered from a census is likely to be very accurate - and exceptionally expensive in all but the smallest markets.

Because of the expense involved in gathering data from the whole population, researchers usually survey a small part of the whole market. Selecting some of the market for research is called **sampling**.

221

Methods of sampling

The main methods of sampling are:

Random sampling
In a random sample, every member of the population has an equal chance of being surveyed. Random sampling reduces the chance of bias, but may generate some surplus information because people other than those in the target market may be selected.

Systematic random sampling requires that every *n*th member of the population is surveyed, e.g every 20th after the first has been selected at random. One drawback is that the sample may not be a random representation of the whole market.

Stratified sampling
This method involves dividing the sample into market segments made up of particular kinds of consumers, based on existing knowledge of their representation in the entire market population. For example, the market for a certain type of computer game may be 75% male, aged between 13 and 17.

Quota sampling
Truly random sampling requires that particular members of the target market are surveyed. This is time-consuming and expensive because it requires very large sample sizes to ensure that the sample is unbiased. A way of avoiding having to ask particular people questions is for market researchers to focus on a quota of people with certain characteristics. For example, a researcher may be instructed to survey 250 males between the ages of 45 and 65 and 100 males over 65. The danger is that those sampled either may not possess these characteristics, or may not be representative of the whole market.

Due to its low cost, quota sampling is the most popular method and is often used by survey organizations like National Opinion Polls, Mori, and Gallup.

Methods of collecting primary data

Face-to-face survey
A popular method of obtaining primary data is face-to-face questioning based on a pre-designed **questionnaire**. This method is cheap and has the advantage of allowing the interviewer to target particular kinds of people.

Open-ended interview
The advantage of an open-ended interview is that it is flexible. Using this method, the interviewer works from a list of subjects of interest, rather than specific questions. The interviewer can therefore ask questions as s/he wishes and can guide each interview as s/he feels best. This method is useful when the subject is of a confidential or embarrassing nature, or when a very complicated and specialized topic is being researched.

Telephone survey
Telephone surveys allow researchers to target particular respondents by geographical area. However, this method clearly rules out people not listed in the directory and those without telephones, which can cause bias.

Postal surveys
It is possible to select a market research sample through postal sampling. The biggest drawback is that people receiving postal questionnaires may view them as 'junk mail' and throw them away. Postal surveys work best when the customer is given an incentive to reply, perhaps entry into a prize draw or a promise of a free gift.

Consumer panels
A firm can test consumer opinion by inviting a group of potential customers to give their views on products and asking them to allow their spending decisions to be monitored over a period of time. Using a panel,

researchers might ask people to keep records of their purchases over time in order to measure the impact of advertising or of trends in fashion. This method gives a picture over time, rather than just a snapshot of current buying habits, as with the questionnaire.

Observation

Simply observing consumer behaviour - for example, monitoring TV and radio audiences for particular programmes and regions, or counting traffic on roads and at carparks - can generate a great deal of useful market research information. Some firms will use **focus groups** of consumers to monitor spending patterns and behaviour over periods of time.

Experimentation

Sometimes a new product or advertising campaign will be tested on a sample of the target population, perhaps in a particular region of the country. Because of the high cost of launching a product on a national or international market, **test marketing (or field trials)** reduces the risk of making expensive mistakes. If consumers in the test dislike certain aspects of the product or campaign, the firm can make modifications prior to launch.

Wispa bars were launched initially, with great success, in the Tyne Tees TV region in late 1981 prior to national release.

Portfolio Activity 9.5

Range: Marketing research methods
Skills: Read and respond to written material

Below is an example of a badly designed questionnaire. Look at the questions and see if you can identify what is wrong.

1. Do you ever take a bath?   YES?NO

2. When did you last take a bath? _____

3. What is the chemical composition of your present bubble bath?
   _____

4. How much water do you use in your bath?
   50 litres
   100 litres
   150 litres
   More than 150 litres

5. You do use bubble bath, don't you? _____

6. Where do you buy it? _____

7. How much would you pay for bubble bath?
   Less than £1
   £1
   £1.50
   £2
   More than £5

8. Do you think the price and scent of bubble bath is important?   YES/NO

Rules for designing questionnaires

Questionnaires are the most useful method of gaining primary data from consumers. They may be used in face-to-face surveys, telephone surveys, and postal surveys. Administration of questionnaires is much easier today thanks to the use of handheld electronic data processing machines.

However, a badly designed questionnaire can yield poor or inaccurate information. A number of rules must guide the design of a questionnaire. These are:

1. Questions should not be offensive or embarrassing for people to answer. If they are, people will either not answer, or not tell the truth. For example, how often people take a bath may be seen as a personal question by many respondents.

2. Questions should be easy for people to understand and not require specialist knowledge which most people do not possess. For example, most people would not know the chemical composition of their present bubble bath.

3. Questions should not require people to make calculations in their heads. Most people will not be able to calculate the volume of water in their bath tubs. If they give an answer, it is likely to be wrong.

4. Questions should not be loaded or encourage consumers to reply in a particular way. Leading questions like 'You do use bubble bath, don't you?' will encourage people to say 'Yes', even if this is not true.

5. Questions should be designed to limit the number of possible responses that can be made. For example, the question:

    'What price would you be willing to pay for one litre of bubble bath:

    (a) less than £1?

    (b) £1 to £5?

    (c) more than £5?'

    is more likely to give a useful answer than an open-ended question asking how much someone would pay for bubble bath. It is hard for people to give an exact price, but much easier to indicate an ideal range.

6. Questionnaires may be open or closed in design. **Open questions** allow a wide variety of responses and do not pin the respondent down to particular answers. Such questions are likely to lead to fuller, and more varied answers than closed questions.

    Closed questions ask respondents to respond either 'Yes' or 'No', or to pick an answer from a limited range of options, known as **multiple choice questions**. Closed questions lead to a narrower range of responses and make analysis of data much easier. However, they prevent respondents giving opinions or introducing new and unexpected thoughts on the product.

The questions in figure 9.4 were part of a questionnaire containing 73 questions concerning drivers attitudes towards aspects of motorway provision in England, from lighting to roadworks. The questionnaire was completed by drivers as part of a survey commissioned by the Department of Transport in 1992. This first part of the questionnaire aims to establish driver characteristics:

Figure 9.4: An example of a questionnaire

Motorway Drivers' Recruitment Questionnaire — Project 325

Interview name: .... Questionnaire number: [   ]

Respondent name: .... Date: ...../..../.....

Location [   ]
1. Ipswich   5. North London
2. Newcastle   6. Bristol
3. Birmingham   7. Plymouth
4. West London

We are interviewing people at .... between 9.30 am and 4.30 pm. Could you possibly come and contribute to a very important survey? It concerns the Citizen's Charter and the use of motorways. First of all I would like to ask you a few questions to see if you are within the scope of the survey. (There is an incentive of £5.00. The interview lasts from 45 minutes to an hour).

Q1	Do you hold a full valid driving licence? 1. Yes	2. No (THANK & CLOSE)	1	2
Q2	What type of driving licence do you hold? 1. Private car (motorcycles not relevant) 2. Private car and PSV 3. Private car and HGV (Heavy Goods Vehicle) 4. HGV only (military) (THANK & CLOSE)	5. Motorcycle only (THANK & CLOSE) 6. Only Provisional licence for car (THANK & CLOSE) 7. Other .... (PLEASE WRITE IN, CHECK IF IN SCOPE)	1 2 3 4	5 6 7
Q3	Have you driven on the motorway in England in the last 12 months? (EXCLUDE MOTORCYCLES) 1. Yes	2. No (THANK & CLOSE)	1	2
Q4	How often do you drive to and from work on the motorway? (SHOWCARD) 1. Never (go to Q5) 2. Less than once a month (go to Q5) 3. Once a month but less than once a week (go to Q5)	4. Once a week but less than five days a week (go to Q5) 5. Five days a week or more (RECRUIT FOR INTERVIEW AS A COMMUTER CHECK QUOTA)	1 2 3	4 5
Q5	How often do you drive on the motorway for a business journey? (SHOWCARD) 1. Never (go to Q5) 2. Less than once a month (go to Q6)	3. Once a month but less than once a week 4. Once a week but less than five days a week 5. Five days a week or more (3/4/5 RECRUIT FOR BUSINESS JOURNEY CHECK QUOTA)	1 2	3 4 5
Q6	How often do you drive on a motorway for social/leisure purposes (SHOWCARD) 1. Never (THANK & CLOSE) 2. Less than once a month 3. Once a month but less than once a week 4. Once a week but less than five days a week 5. Five days a week or more (2/3/4/5 RECRUIT FOR SOCIAL/LEISURE CHECK QUOTA)	1 2 3 4 5		
Q7	Record appropriate driver/journey type 1. Commuter (CODE 5 IN Q4) 2. Business (CODE 3 FOR INFREQUENT IN Q5) 3. Business (CODES 4 & 5 FOR FREQUENT IN Q5)	4 Social/leisure (CODE 2 FOR INFREQUENT IN Q6) 5 Social/leisure (CODES 3, 4 & 5 FOR FREQUENT IN Q6)	1 2 3	4 5
Q8	How old are you? (CHECK QUOTA) 1. 17-24 2. 25-34 3. 35-44	4 45-54 5 55-64 6 65+	1 2 3	4 5 6
Q9	Record gender (CHECK QUOTA) 1. Male	2 Female	1	2
Q10	What is your occupation? (PLEASE WRITE IN AND CODE) (CHECK QUOTA) .... 1. A/B 2. C1/C2	3 D/E 2	1	3
Q11	Do you have any children under the age of 16 years living at home with you? (CHECK QUOTA) 1. Yes	2 No	1	2

Advanced Business

Portfolio Activity 9.6

Range: Marketing research methods, Suitability
Skills: Read and respond to written material

1. What sampling method and research method do you think the Guardian survey used, and why?
2. What types of business organization are likely to be interested in the findings of the survey?

Students Reject Couch Potato Lifestyle

Students are likely to spend roughly half the national average hours watching television and listening to radio, according to a new survey by the *Guardian*.

Graduate Facts, a survey of more than 2,000 students, found that they watch around 12 hours of TV and listen to about 11 hours of radio a week, compared with the national average of 27.16 hours and 20.8 hours respectively.

The survey found that students are more likely to read broadsheet newspapers. Of those surveyed, 23 per cent read the *Guardian* most often, compared with 16 per cent for the *Independent* and nine per cent for the *Times* and *Daily Telegraph*.

The *Guardian* plans to re-interview the students several times as part of a tracking study.

Media Week 18.2.94.

Choosing the best method of gathering research information

Once the sampling method has been chosen, the next step is to decide exactly how the information will be gathered from the sample. Firms can use a variety of methods of collecting information, including face-to-face interview, postal questionnaire, consumer panel, or electronic data gathering using the latest retail auditing technology.

There is no one 'best' method of gathering information. Whichever method a firm chooses, it will need to weigh up the advantages and disadvantages, using a variety of criteria. These can be identified in the form of questions:

- **Fitness for the purpose** - will the survey collect the data required?
- **Cost** - how much will it cost to collect the data?
- **Speed** - how long will it take to collect data?
- **Accessibility** - how easy will it be to collect data?
- **Accuracy** - how accurate will the data be?

The first step in any research process is to define what information is required, and which consumers need to be surveyed. For example, consider a firm manufacturing baby foods who want to find out if parents and babies like their new recipes, and what price to charge for them. The firm would be ill-advised to gather information by taking a random sample of people leaving a supermarket. A better approach would be to arrange a consumer panel of parents and babies. Panel members might be chosen from details of new births from the register of births, deaths, and marriages.

Each survey method will perform differently on selection criteria, and firms need to determine which features are most important to them before going ahead. For example, if a business is in a highly competitive market like consumer electronics, it will want to bring new products to market very quickly to keep ahead of its competitors. In this case, speed is likely to be more important than cost. Alternatively, a small firm, inexperienced in market research, may choose whichever method is easiest to use.

A large drugs company investing many millions of pounds in the research and development of new products may consider that accuracy is the most important criterion. The greater the amount of information gathered, the more accurate marketing predictions and policies are likely to be.

Limitations of market research

In spite of very large expenditures on market research, around 90% of all new products fail after they have been launched. Market research may sometimes fail because buyers' wants may change more quickly than firms can gather information. When this occurs, researchers say that the data is **biased**.

Bias can arise in primary data in a number of ways:

Sampling bias

If market research is to be of use to a firm, the sample of people chosen for interview must reflect the views and behaviour common to the whole population. If not, the sample will be biased.

Questionnaire bias

Questionnaires must be carefully designed. Leading questions may encourage or force people being interviewed to give particular responses, which may not represent their actual behaviour or views.

Interview bias

People conducting a survey may not always pick people at random. For example, a young male interviewer may be drawn towards asking more young females then he would have done if the selection was purely random.

Response bias

Some people may give misleading or unrepresentative answers to questions simply because they cannot remember how many times they have used a particular good or service, or how they felt about it. Some people may even lie!

Key words

Target population - all possible consumers of a product

Random sample - a representative group of consumers taken from the total population at random

Sampling - selecting a sample of consumers from the target population

Stratified sample - a sample of consumers selected to have characteristics in the same proportions found in the population as a whole

Quota sample - a sample achieved by selecting respondents until predetermined numbers of individuals with specified characteristics have been interviewed

Systematic sample - a non-random sample formed of every nth person

Face-to-face surveys - interviews with potential buyers usually conducted at random in the street

Telephone survey - research conducted by telephone interview

Postal survey - a questionnaire sent and/or returned through the post

Open-ended interview - interview based around a series of topics for discussion rather than set questions

Consumer panel - a group of consumers who allow their buying behaviour to be monitored over time

Electronic monitoring - observation of sales or consumer behaviour using computer technology

Test marketing - testing a product or advertising campaign on a sample of consumers prior to national or international launch

Section 9.4 Market changes

Information on sales

The aim of market research is to identify market opportunities. An important aspect of research is to track sales in order to try to identify those products which are likely to experience rising sales and those which for which sales are declining. Falling sales indicate falling profitability and declining market opportunities. Rising sales indicate an opportunity to expand market share and profits in the long run.

Advanced Business

Consumer spending patterns

Of particular interest to market researchers is how consumer spending patterns change over time. Figure 9.5 shows that between 1957 and 1992, expenditure on food as a percentage of total household expenditure fell from around 34% to 17.5%. However, households are now devoting more of their total expenditure to housing, which has risen from 8.7% of household expenditure to 17.4% in 1992. This is a reflection of the trend towards 'owner occupation' resulting from rising incomes and the aspiration of people to own their own home. The average weekly household income in 1957 was just £18, compared to around £343 in 1992.

However, changes in consumer spending patterns cannot be explained only by the increase in household incomes over time. New products such as videos, camcorders, and compact discs have become available for consumers to want and buy.

There have also been significant cultural and social changes. For example, mainland Europeans, such as the French and Italians, are often characterized as lovers of good food and wine. It is suggested that the increase in foreign travel by UK residents has allowed them to sample and enjoy these aspects of European culture, and this has resulted in the increase in the consumption of wine and meals at restaurants in the UK.

Increasingly consumer spending decisions are linked to the moral views of consumers. Nowhere is this more evident than in the market for 'green' or environmentally friendly products.

Market research suggests that the 1990s could be the decade of the green consumer. When the Consumers' Association surveyed readers of *Which?* magazine, 90% said they were concerned about environmental pollution. Surveys by the market research group Taylor Nelson Applied Futures suggest that 36% of British people subscribe to attitudes which make them green consumers. Research suggests that they are the fastest-growing group in the population.

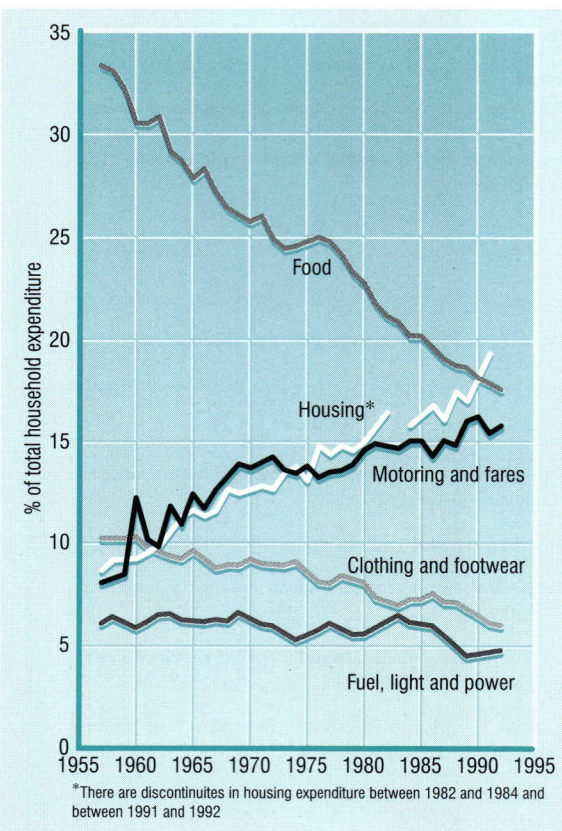

▼ *Figure 9.5: Trends of expenditure for all households, 1957 to 1992*

*There are discontinuites in housing expenditure between 1982 and 1984 and between 1991 and 1992

Family Expenditure Survey

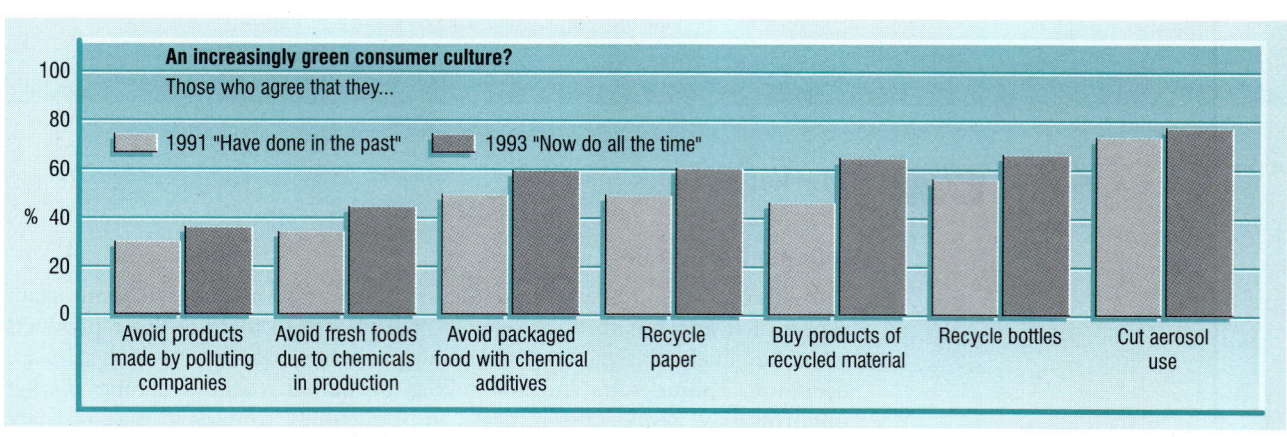

An increasingly green consumer culture?
Those who agree that they...
- 1991 "Have done in the past"
- 1993 "Now do all the time"

Categories: Avoid products made by polluting companies; Avoid fresh foods due to chemicals in production; Avoid packaged food with chemical additives; Recycle paper; Buy products of recycled material; Recycle bottles; Cut aerosol use

▲ *Financial Times 3.3.94*

UNIT THREE

CHAPTER 9

Portfolio Activity 9.7

Range: Marketing decisions, Marketing research information
Skills: Collect and record data, Produce written material

▼ *Changing patterns in the consumption of food at home, Great Britain*

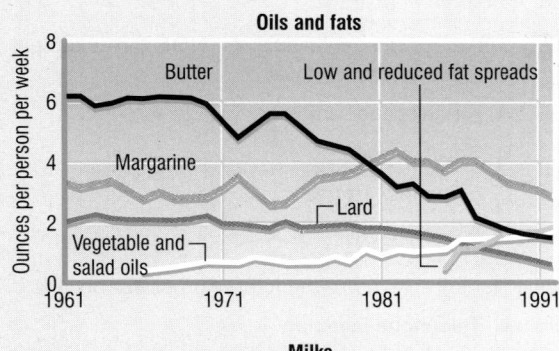

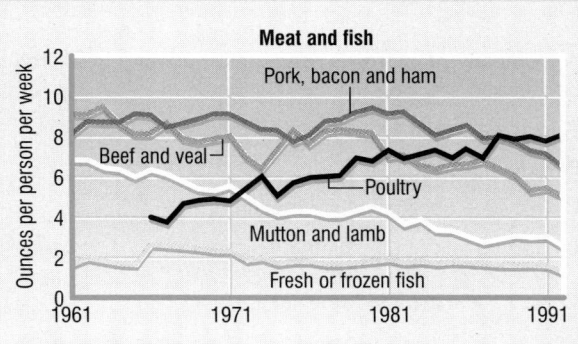

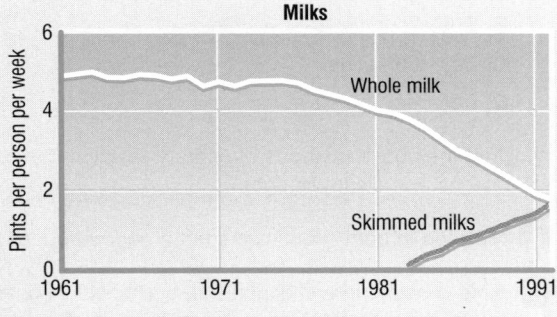

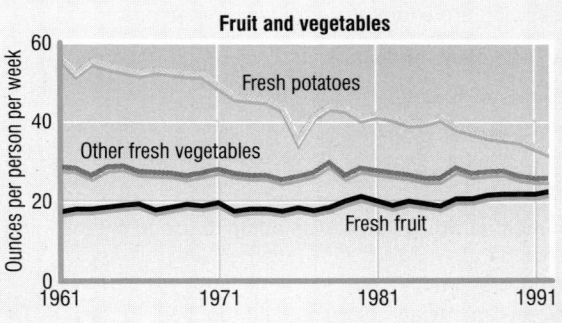

Oils and fats (Ounces per person per week, 1961–1991): Butter, Low and reduced fat spreads, Margarine, Lard, Vegetable and salad oils

Meat and fish (Ounces per person per week, 1961–1991): Pork, bacon and ham, Beef and veal, Poultry, Mutton and lamb, Fresh or frozen fish

Milks (Pints per person per week, 1961–1991): Whole milk, Skimmed milks

Fruit and vegetables (Ounces per person per week, 1961–1991): Fresh potatoes, Other fresh vegetables, Fresh fruit

You are a market analyst for Supreme Supermarkets plc, an organization that owns and operates 100 food stores across the UK. Use the information above to prepare a report for the manager of the purchasing department suggesting how the supermarket should alter their product range over the next five years.

Justify your recommendations using secondary data on forecasts of economic and demographic variables (for example, growth in GDP, lifestyle changes, etc.). Present your ideas formally to the purchasing department (your class), using graphs and overhead slides. Expect them to challenge your ideas and prepare appropriate responses.

Diet-conscious add years to life expectancy

Better diets, medical care and social habits are helping to make Britain a healthier place to live. A baby born today can expect to live until he is 74 and a girl should reach 79; 50 years ago, the figures were 62 and 67 years.

The number of cot deaths was halved between 1991 and 1992, with the rate down to 0.7 per thousand live births.

Infant mortality generally has fallen to 6.6 per thousand, a quarter below the level of five years ago. Changes in diet have been a key factor in improving adult health.

Britain now eats nearly twice as much margarine as butter, red meat consumption has fallen from 9oz to 5oz a week since 1961 and half as many potatoes are eaten today as were consumed 30 years ago.

During the past two decades, cigarette smoking among men has fallen from 52 per cent to 31 per cent and from 41 per cent to 29 per cent among women.

Nearly a quarter of all males drink more than the recommended 21 units a week, while a tenth of women exceed the sale 15-unit limit.

The Times 27.1.94

Further reading
Central Statistical Office: *Social Trends* (published annually by HMSO)

Advanced Business

Test questions

The following underpinning knowledge will be tested:

1. Marketing research methods and their suitability for selected products
2. Marketing research information from different sources and its contribution to marketing decisions
3. Product development with reference to marketing research information

1 A company decides to undertake primary research because it:

   A Is simple to collect
   B Is low cost
   C Provides qualitative information
   D Can be tailored to suit the research

Questions 2 - 4 share the following answer options:

The following are examples of research methods:

   A Telephone interviews
   B Postal surveys
   C Electronic monitoring
   D Face-to-face interviews

Which method would you advise a firm to use in the following situations?

2 When an instant response is required to test a TV advertising campaign

3 When the background to the research needs to be explained in full and requires detailed understanding

4 When respondents wish to remain totally anonymous

Questions 5 - 7 concern the following information:

A DIY superstore intends to carry out some market research. It has identified the following possible methods:

   A Desk-based research
   B Interviews
   C Observation
   D Electronic monitoring

Which method should the store choose if:

5 They want to calculate their share of the total DIY market?

6 They want to find out what people buy, and why?

7 They want to find out patterns of movement around aisles in the store?

8 Which of the following is NOT an example of a secondary source of data?

   A A newspaper article
   B *Social Trends*
   C *Economic Trends*
   D A questionnaire

Questions 9 - 11 share the following answer options:

   A Telephone interview
   B Postal survey
   C Test marketing
   D Personal interview

Which of the above methods of primary research have these advantages and disadvantages?

9 No need to train interviewers but a poor response rate

10 Time consuming and expensive, but individual questions can be probing and answers detailed

11 Reduces risk of expensive national product launch being ill-designed but consumer preferences may differ by area

12 a. Give an example of a consumer durable, and a capital good for industrial use.

   b. What is a fast-moving consumer good? Give an example.

   c. Suggest and explain two ways a firm might gather market research information for each of the examples you have given above.

   d. Suggest two criteria a firm might use in deciding which method of research to use.

13 a. Why do firms research their markets?

   b. What is the difference between primary and secondary market research data?

   c. What is product development? Explain how it is often based on market research information.

   d. Suggest two sources of secondary market research data a firm might use to develop a new washing powder.

assessment assignment

UNIT THREE

CHAPTER 9

Assessment Assignment

Range: Marketing research methods
Suitability
Marketing research information
Marketing decisions
Sources
Product development

Skills: **Communication**
Take part in discussions
Read and respond to written material
Produce written material
Use images
Application of Number
Collect and record data
Information Technology
Process information
Present information

You work in the head office of a medium-sized high street travel agent. Prompted by reports in the press similar to the article below, your line manager has asked you to consider the market for foreign holidays in some detail.

REVIVA ESPANA!

Lunn Poly holiday bookings in 1993 (No. of bookings '000s): Majorca ~360, Ibiza ~120, Minorca ~120, Tenerife ~105, Florida ~105, Costa Blanca ~70, Cyprus ~70, Gran Canaria ~70, Corfu ~55, Algarve ~55.

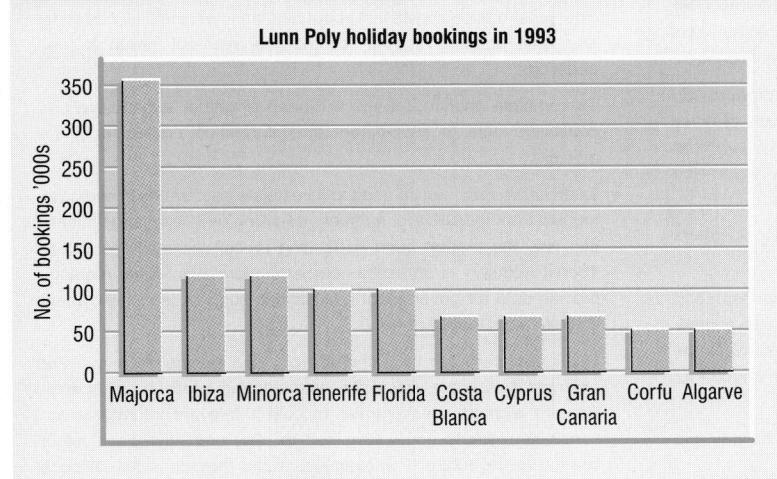

Holidaymakers visiting Spain (No. of visitors millions): 1987 ~3.8, 1988 ~3.6, 1989 ~3.4, 1990 ~2.4 (Gulf war year), 1991 ~2.3, 1992 ~2.5, 1993 ~3.3, 1994 ~4.0.

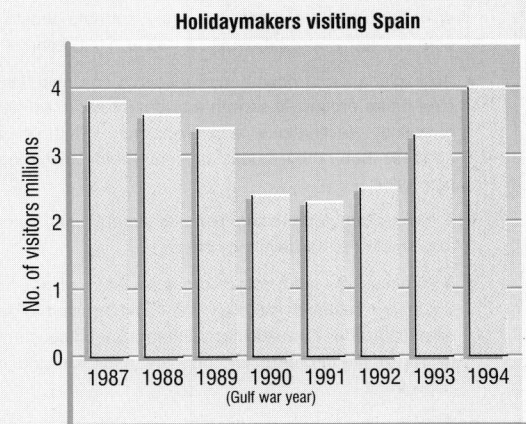

Number of cruise passengers (No. of passengers '000s): 1986 ~90, 1987 ~130, 1988 ~155, 1989 ~170, 1990 ~190, 1991 ~195, 1992 ~220, 1993 ~245.

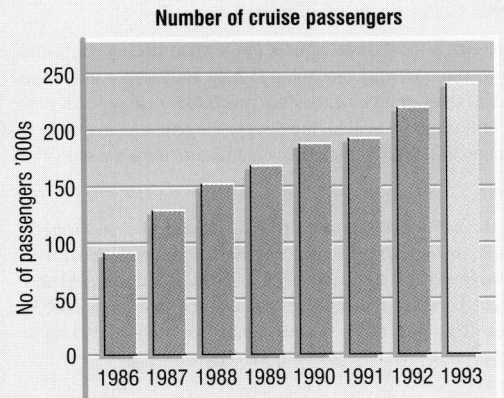

Current country cost comparisons of holiday spending in £ sterling

	Australia	Cyprus	Florida	Hong Kong	Portugal	Spain	St. Lucia	UK
Half pint/ of beer	0.73	0.53	0.40	1.57	0.33	0.85	1.20	0.80
10 min. taxi ride	3.05	2.63	4.68	2.61	3.09	2.33	5.00	5.00
Film 24 exposure	2.73	3.29	1.69	1.74	1.93	3.48	4.51	3.00
Meal for two	29.00	18.42	26.00	40.00	19.34	22.04	31.23	30.00
Bottle of local wine	5.00	1.18	4.73	–	1.55	0.70	–	6.00
Imported wine	10.00	–	6.76	6.97	2.71	–	7.50	4.00

Advanced Business

4m Brits shrug off gloom in sun rush

BRITONS are shaking off the dark clouds of recession – and flocking to sunny Spain again.
You'll probably be bumping into your neighbour on the beach next year as an amazing FOUR MILLION people head for the Costas and the Spanish holiday islands.

That's almost double the number who managed to scrape together enough for a paella and sangria package trip at the height of the slump in 1991.

The figures are revealed today in a major travel survey.

They show that a total of nine million people will take their holidays abroad in 1994 – one in six of every man, woman and child in Britain.

Spain and its islands, including Majorca, Ibiza and Tenerife, are the top destination. More pesetas to the pound and improvements at key resorts are two reasons for the boom.

Holidaymakers will be tucking into bargain-priced meals and local wine at just 70p a bottle.

Greece and its islands such as Rhodes and Corfu come second, while the US is third, despite recent fears about tourist safety.

More people than ever are taking their holidays on floating hotels, says the survey.

Six years ago, fewer than 100,000 people went on a cruise. But this year's bookings have risen to 240,000.

Spain also tops the winter resorts, the survey reveals. Tenerife is the most popular, followed by Benidorm and Malta.

But fewer people will be on the slopes this year. Skiing holidays have slumped to just 12 per cent of the market – mainly due to poor exchange rates at French and Austrian resorts.

Two other top travel agents, Pickfords and Hogg Robinson, also reported a massive surge in trade yesterday. So far, they have taken 1.2 million bookings for 1994 – with increased interest in the Caribbean.

Meanwhile, cross-Channel ferry firms say the number of day-trippers to France has doubled this year as bargain-hunters stock up on cheap booze and duty-free goods.

Daily Mirror 11.11.93

Tasks

1. Write a report on the foreign holiday market, using wordprocessing or desktop publishing software. Relevant data should be tabulated or presented graphically where possible. Your report should contain:

- An explanation of how market research can help the organization plan future product lines with tour operators. (Give details of types of holiday, destinations, accommodation, length of stay, etc., and suggest how they could be marketed, including price and promotion.)

- A description of marketing methods already used by tour operators to promote the holidays they offer

- A summary of useful data sources for information on tourism, and the market research methods that could be used to gather primary data. (Consider what additional information on consumers would be useful to the organization, and the most suitable method(s) of obtaining it.)

- A discussion of how the demand for different types of holiday and destination may change over the next 3-5 years

- Recommendations for product developments and marketing strategies, based on your view of future consumer trends in the holiday market. This should include;
    * changes to the range of holidays offered
    * features of holiday packages
    * holiday sales outlets
    * holiday promotions
    * prices
    * the timing of your marketing communications (see 10.2)

- References to sources of data and other information

2. Prepare and give an oral and visual presentation of your report findings and main recommendations for the management team. Your presentation should last about 5-10 minutes and be followed by an equal amount of time for the management group to ask questions.

To complete your report you will need to gather quantitative and qualitative data to supplement the information presented in the article.

- Quantitative data can be used to investigate past trends in overseas tourism from the UK, e.g. numbers travelling overseas, expenditure, etc. Has the market been expanding or contracting? The British Tourist Authority is an useful source of information. They regularly provide data for government publications such as the Employment Gazette and Social Trends.

Qualitative data can be gathered from your original research. For example, survey the views of people entering a local travel agents. Prepare a short questionnaire to collect relevant information on consumers' wants and willingness to pay, and how these might change in the future. For example, would they consider taking a cruise? What factors would influence their choice?

In addition, visit a local travel agents (on a quiet trading day!) and look through some holiday brochures to help you identify the range of holidays available and how they are marketed. Discuss with staff the types of holidays available, the people they appeal to, and how they are marketed. What is their opinion on future trends in tourism?

Alternatively…

3. Complete the same exercise for a product of your choice. Produce a report and presentation to show how market research could help improve marketing and product design. Investigate and suggest how consumer demand for the product may change over time and, in light of these changes, make recommendations for modifications to the current product and its marketing strategy.

chapter 10

UNIT THREE

CHAPTER 10

chapter 10 Marketing Communications

This chapter evaluates the methods used to communicate information about business products to identified groups of consumers

Key ideas

Any market for a good or service is made up of **market segments**, each consisting of a group of consumers with certain common characteristics, for example, sex, age, or lifestyle. Producers can use their knowledge of market segments to target their products and messages at these different groups of consumers.

Marketing communications involve providing information, through a variety of media, about a product to **target audiences** of consumers in an attempt to influence their buying decisions.

Marketing communications methods include **advertising, publicity, public relations, sales promotions,** and **direct marketing**.

Popular **advertising media** include television, newspaper and magazines, cinema, radio, and posters. Sales leaflets, vehicle livery, letterheads, and signs can provide additional **publicity** for an organization and its products.

Public Relations, such as the issue of press releases, sponsorship of sporting and other events, lobbying Parliament, and community relations, helps to raise the profile of an organization and promote awareness of its aims and products.

Sales promotion methods, such as in-store merchandising, competitions, money-off coupons, special offers, and loyalty incentives help to increase the chance of product purchase and repeat sales.

The effectiveness of marketing communications can be judged in terms of **product performance**, additional sales volumes and revenues generated, the creation of repeat sales and brand loyalty, the extension of a product life-cycle, and increased awareness among consumers.

The **product life-cycle** exhibits five stages: development, launch, growth, maturity, and decline. A sixth stage known as **extension through marketing** is also possible.

The **Advertising Standards Association** monitors non-broadcast advertising in the UK to ensure the **British Code of Advertising Practice** is upheld.

Advanced Business

Section **10.1** Targeting an audience

Market segmentation

Although people talk about a market as if it were one large group of similar consumers, any market is in fact made up of a number of smaller groups of buyers called **market segments**.

A market segment consists of a group of consumers with certain common characteristics, for example, sex, age, or lifestyle. Knowledge of these characteristics can be used by firms to predict consumer response to marketing activities, namely new or improved products, changed pricing strategies, distribution or promotion methods (see 8.3).

Portfolio Activity 10.1

Range: Target audience
Skills: Read and respond to written material

1. What evidence is there in the article to suggest that firms in the past have not seriously considered the results of market research when designing adverts aimed at women?

2. Can women be divided up into target markets? Give reasons for your answer.

3. Pick two products currently advertised on TV which you think could benefit from the type of analysis undertaken by O&M. Suggest how the advertising could be redesigned to take account of the categories suggested by O&M.

Sex, Humour and the 'Me Within'

Women like sex and have a sense of humour; they no longer think of themselves as the 'typical housewife.' A few hours watching UK television commercials, however, might encourage viewers to conclude otherwise. The glum succession of women obsessed with the spotlessness of their floors and weekly wash, and who crave the advice of male scientists contrasts sharply with the humour and inventiveness of, for example, some of the beer advertising aimed principally at men.

Given that most TV commercials are for brands aimed at women, surprisingly little is known about what kind of advertising appeals to them and why, according to advertising agency Ogilvy and Mather.

The agency says commercials aimed at women are often boring and badly made. In an attempt to improve standards the O&M planning department in London, which provides the research that underpins the agency's creative work, has conducted a study among women of a variety of ages and social backgrounds.

The suggestion that women like more sex and humour than advertisers have previously believed and are unlikely these days to think of themselves as housewives are among the study's main conclusions. The survey suggests that 'as a woman progresses through lifestages, she accumulates knowledge, responses, behaviour, like the layers of an onion.' Moving to a new lifestage doesn't mean discarding the experiences and memories of previous lifestages. A woman's sense of identity - the 'me within' as the study refers to it - may be largely submerged or more evident at different stages, but is always there and ready to be accessed or released by advertising.

The 'me' within found by O&M is very strong among single women and those who have partners, but no children. By the time motherhood sets in, women are most likely to describe themselves in terms of roles, such as mum or housekeeper and the 'me' becomes submerged. A return to work is, for many women, a re-emergence of 'me,' as is divorce in some cases.

A detailed study found that women see themselves in a variety of ways which can be tapped by target market advertising.

These are
The wild woman - outrageous, rebellions and sexy
The wicked woman - manipulative, teasing
The free woman - independent, happy in control
The woman on top - one upmanship, subverting expectations
The funny woman - witty and amusing
The return to childhood - fun, naughty
The strong woman - coping, juggling, smiling
The intelligent, creative woman - imaginative, talented
The pampered woman - romantic, indulging, relaxed
The voyeur - enjoying men's bodies
Predictably, advertisements for household cleaning products were among the most irritating to women: the Daz washing-powder commercials featuring doorstep interviews were seen as patronizing, dull and too ready to categorize women as 'housewives'.

The kind of information on target market segments produced by O & M can be used to create attractive advertising aimed at particular target markets.

Financial Times 30.2.94

▼ Markets can be divided up into age and sex groups

Increasing competition between firms in some industrial sectors and between products, especially from a growing number of overseas firms, has made mass marketing more difficult. As a result, firms are increasingly aiming their products and advertising at smaller market segments.

There are a number of ways of dividing up a market into segments:

- Demographic: by age, sex, socio-economic group, income
- Geographic: by country, region, urban, rural
- Lifestyle: by purchasing habits, ethical values, religion, political views

Having identified different market segments, producers can use their knowledge to aim their products and marketing activities at these different groups, known as **target audiences**.

Demographic segmentation

Demography is the study of population. There are various features of the population which can be used to group consumers into different market segments. These may be age, sex, income, socio-economic status, and geographical location.

Age

Markets can be divided into groups of consumers by age. For example, the package holiday industry has designed special holidays and promotional strategies aimed at the 18-30 age group, parents with young children, and the over-50s.

▼ Holidays are targeted at different age groups

Advanced Business

The U.K. age/sex structure

Figure 10.1 shows an **age-sex pyramid** made up of the various age groups in the UK in 1961 and 1991. The number of males and females in the population are shown on the horizontal axis, while the vertical axis shows the ages of each group in the population. The pyramid shows that the average age of the UK population has risen over time. In 1991 there were fewer people in the UK under 20 years of age compared to 1961, but more people between the ages of 20 and 50 and over 65 years of age. An ageing population has important implications for the pattern of consumer spending and therefore for the allocation of resources to different productive activities.

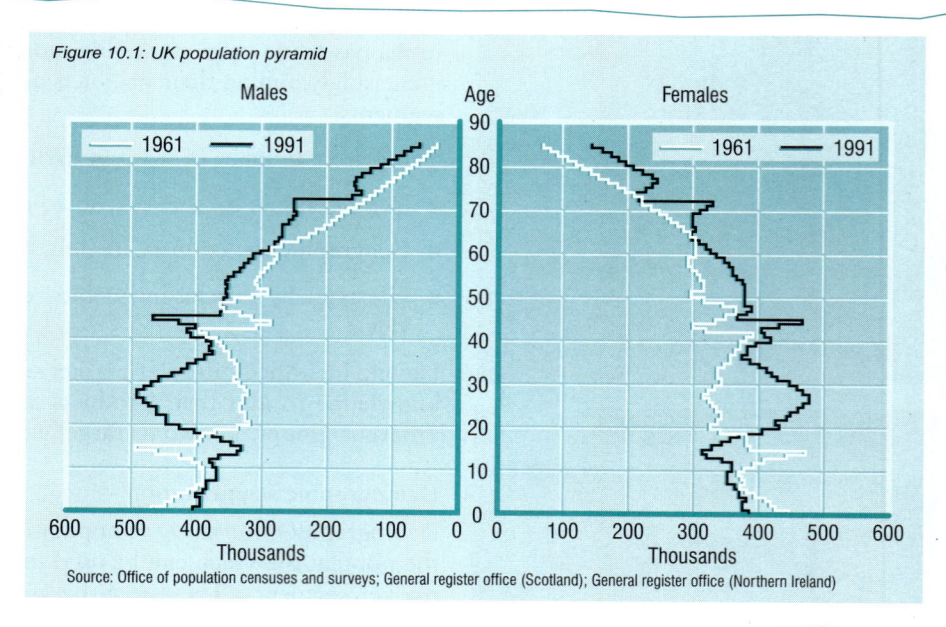

Figure 10.1: UK population pyramid

Source: Office of population censuses and surveys; General register office (Scotland); General register office (Northern Ireland)

Portfolio Activity 10.2

Range: Target audience
Skills: Read and respond to written material

1. Which market segments can be identified from the article?

2. How might a firm make use of the information given in the article? (For example, consider the type of products that are likely to rise in demand, and the promotional strategies that might appeal to the older generation.)

Ageing UK population

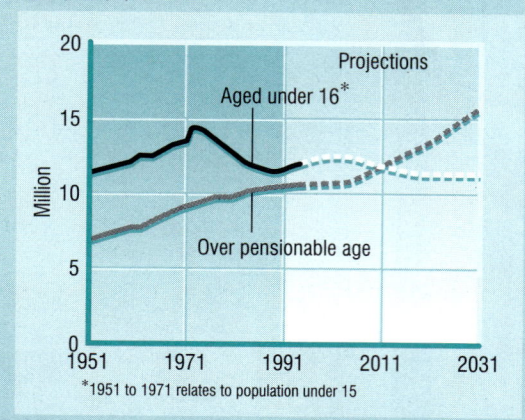

*1951 to 1971 relates to population under 15

Financial Times 27.1.94

Third Age Population to Rise 9%

Consumers aged over 50 exhibit different tastes, social values, shopping habits, and leisure pursuits from younger people, according to a study by Mintel, the market research company.

The number of people in Britain in the over-50 age group will increase by 9% per cent in the 1990s, suggests the study, and those in their early 50s will rise almost a third as the baby boom generation grows older. As a result, a new group of 'third age' consumers is emerging, which embraces people born during the baby boom.

Older consumers eat out and go out drinking more than younger ones, rate quality above fashion in clothing, are more cautious about buying on credit, and value retailers' efficiency above their friendliness, the study says.

The trend is likely to have important economic effects because many 'third age' consumers are affluent. Those aged between 50 and 64 had the highest weekly expenditure in the country of £124 last year. They also spend more of their income than younger people on food, household goods, and motoring, and less on housing, fares, and clothing.

Adapted from The Financial Times 9.11.93 and originally based on 'Third Age Lifestyles 1993' by Mintel

Gender

Men and women have different buying habits and tend to be attracted by different kinds of promotions and marketing activities. For example, a recent study found that, when shopping, men were more likely to pick up and consider products coloured either blue or green, while women were more likely to look at products packaged in lighter shades, particularly pink.

Income

Personal disposable income refers to the amount of income a person has to spend or save after income tax and National Insurance have been deducted.

Different lifestyles and products are enjoyed by people with different levels of disposable income. For example, a Jaguar car, a holiday in the West Indies, and a luxury house are items that are more likely to be bought by people on high incomes. Even within a particular brand there may be differences in the characteristics of consumers who may buy. For example, a top-of-the-range Ford Mondeo car will be more expensive than the basic model and will tend to be bought by a different market segment.

Table 10.1: Distribution of total disposable income, UK 1991 Quintile Groups of individuals

Bottom fifth	Next fifth	Middle fifth	Next fifth	Top fifth	Total
7%	12%	17%	23%	43%	100%

Socio-economic group

Socio-economic status tends to be an indicator of both education and income, and is often used instead of these criteria to segment the market. Research has shown that consumer habits do vary by social class. For example, different classes have quite different media preferences. Upper-class people show preferences for magazines and newspapers, while lower social classes show a preference for television. Even in their TV viewing habits, classes show different preferences, with upper classes favouring news and drama programmes and lower classes preferring soap operas and quiz shows.

There is also some research evidence to suggest that people with more education are more likely to buy cheaper own-label products rather than expensive brand labels. The suggestion is that more educated people are more willing to risk such products because they are less influenced by the heavy advertising that goes with the popular brand names.

Researchers typically use six main categories of social class or **socio-economic groups (SEGs)** to segment the population as in Table 10.2.

Table 10.2: Socio-economic groups, UK 1993

SEG	Description	% of UK population
A - Upper middle class	Higher managerial, administrative or professional	3%
B - Middle class	Intermediate managerial, administrative or professional	13%
C1 - Lower middle class	Supervisory or clerical and junior managerial, administrative or professional	23%
C2 - Skilled working class	Skilled manual labourers	32%
D - Working class	Semi-skilled and unskilled manual workers	19%
E - Very low income earners	Unemployed, pensioners, casual workers	10%

Joint Industry Committee for National Readership Surveys, JICNARS

Portfolio Activity 10.3

Range: Target audience, Advertising
Skills: Collect and record data

Obtain a copy of a popular tabloid newspaper and a more expensive magazine or broadsheet, for example the *Daily Telegraph*.

1. Which social classes are likely to read each paper?
2. Compare advertisements in each publication. How do they compare in terms of the kinds of images, lifestyles, and desires they depict? Do the images and lifestyles match the social classes you identified in question 1?
3. Using figures 10.2 and 10.3, suggest the regions where your chosen publications are likely to sell the most copies. Explain your answers.

The Guardian
The Sun
Daily Mirror
The Daily Telegraph
THE TIMES

Geographical segmentation

Incomes, buying habits, and consumption patterns vary across regions of the country, and segmentation by region is a useful means of identifying target audiences. Consumers within different regions can have very different levels of purchasing power, depending on regional levels of unemployment and the kinds of jobs available (see Figure 10.3). Using this knowledge of broad geographical patterns, market analysts can identify market segments in particular regions and create tailor-made marketing and advertising promotions to stimulate sales.

Figure 10.2: Who's in the money

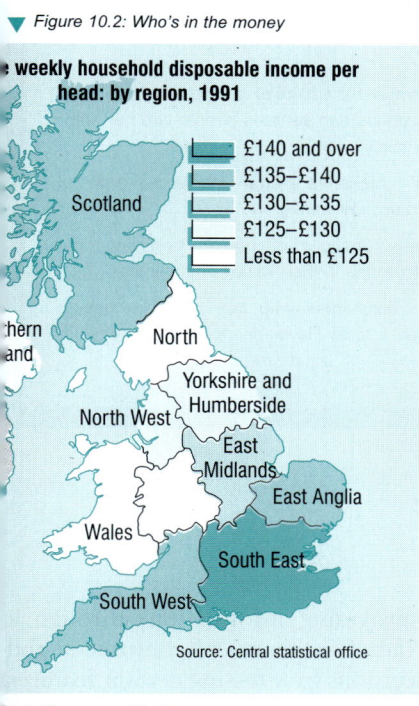

weekly household disposable income per head: by region, 1991

- £140 and over
- £135–£140
- £130–£135
- £125–£130
- Less than £125

Source: Central statistical office

Daily Telegraph 29.1.94

Figure 10.3: Average weekly household expenditure by region, 1992

Source: Family spending 1992

This advertisement for the RAV4 is aimed at young, affluent males - and projects an appealing image and lifestyle to these consumers.

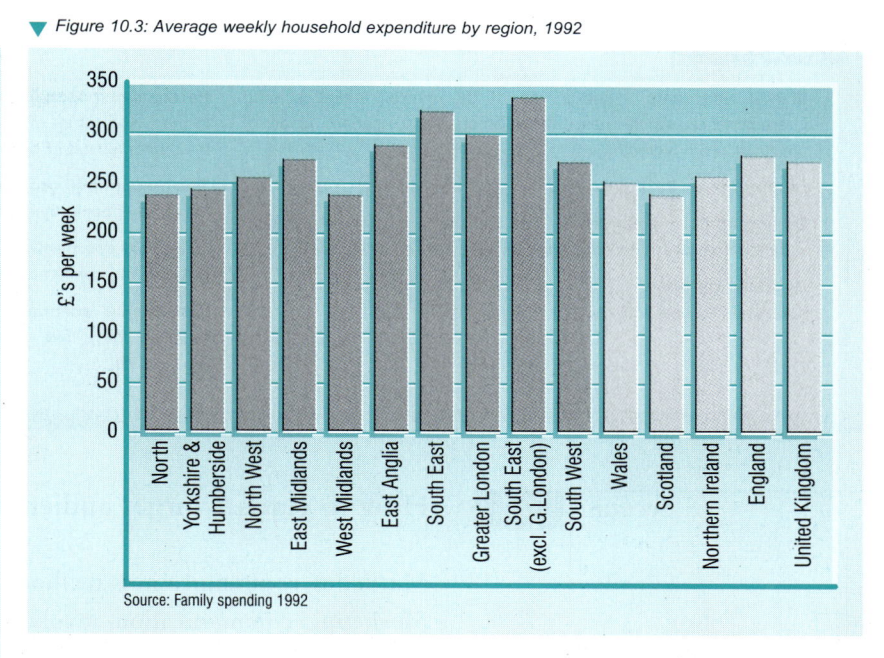

TV regions are often used as a way of identifying regional boundaries and of creating regional segments. Television advertisements can then be designed to appeal to particular regional markets.

Lifestyle segmentation

In recent years researchers have found that there is a less reliable link between social-economic status and buying habits. For example, a builder may drive an expensive sports car while a barrister may drive a Mini.

Lifestyle segmentation involves identifying how groups of people choose to express their personality. Using market research into consumer lifestyles, firms build up profiles which provide information about potential customers. These profiles provide information on day-to-day habits, age, religion, aspirations, leisure pursuits, politics, and many other features of customers. Firms can use this information to develop promotional strategies aimed at different target audiences.

Conscience spending

Increasingly consumer spending decisions are linked to the moral views of consumers. Nowhere is this more evident than in the market for 'green' or environmentally friendly products. For example, sales of roll-on and pump-action deodorant have increased in recent years, while sales of spray cans have fallen due to wider awareness of the effects of chemicals released into the atmosphere.

This growing 'conscience' market segment has been carefully targeted by firms, and appropriate marketing and advertising campaigns have been designed to encourage people to purchase. For example, The Body Shop has built a large chain of stores around Britain by providing a range of cosmetic products which are advertised as untested on animals.

Advanced Business

> **Key words**
>
> **Market segments** - sub-groups of the whole market sharing characteristics which make them amenable to certain kinds of products and advertising.
>
> **Demography** - the study of population characteristics
>
> **Demographic segmentation** - dividing the population into groups with common characteristics such as age, sex, social class, etc.
>
> **Age-sex pyramid** - diagram showing the distribution of the population by age and sex
>
> **Personal disposable income** - a measure of total purchasing power in the UK in terms of the goods and services people can buy with their incomes net of direct taxes
>
> **Socio-economic groups** - categories used by market researchers to classify people by broad occupational group
>
> **Lifestyle segmentation** - analysis of buying behaviour by categorizing consumers according to their values and attitudes
>
> **Conscience spenders** - consumers who buy particular goods because they hold certain ethical views on pollution, cruelty to animals, etc.

Section 10.2 How to reach a target audience

Marketing communications methods

Marketing communication involves providing information, through a variety of media, about a product to target audiences of consumers, and attempting to influence their buying decisions by stressing certain features of the product. 'Influence' may become 'persuasion' when firms attempt to stress product features which may be more imaginary than real. The key methods of marketing communication are:

- Advertising
- Public Relations
- Publicity
- Sales promotions
- Direct marketing

▼ Figure 10.4: UK advertising expenditure by media, 1992

Total expenditure 1992 = £8,769 million

- Cinema (1%) £45m
- Radio (2%) £154m
- Outdoor and Transport (3%) £284m
- Direct mail (11%) £945m
- National newspapers (13%) £1,155m
- Regional newspapers (19%) £1,640m
- Consumer magazines (5%) £432m
- Business and professional (8%) £688m
- Directories (6%) £523m
- Press production costs (5%) £427m
- Television (28%) £2,478m

Advertising Association

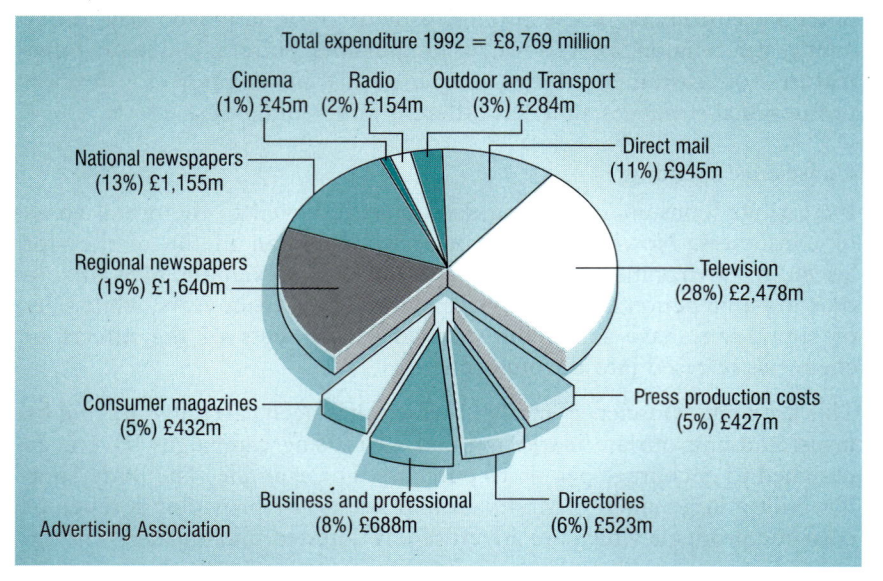

Advertising

Advertising is the main method of promotion used by business. Spending on advertising has grown over time as the real disposable income of households has increased. In 1992, a total of £8.77 billion was spent on advertising in the UK. However, advertising alone will not sell a product; it must be supplemented with other aspects of the marketing mix, including promotion by the sales force, in order to be successful.

Informative and persuasive advertising

The purpose of **informative** advertising is to provide the consumer with information about the product. Examples of purely informative advertising include bus and train timetables and classified advertisements in the local press or phone directories.

Informative or persuasive?

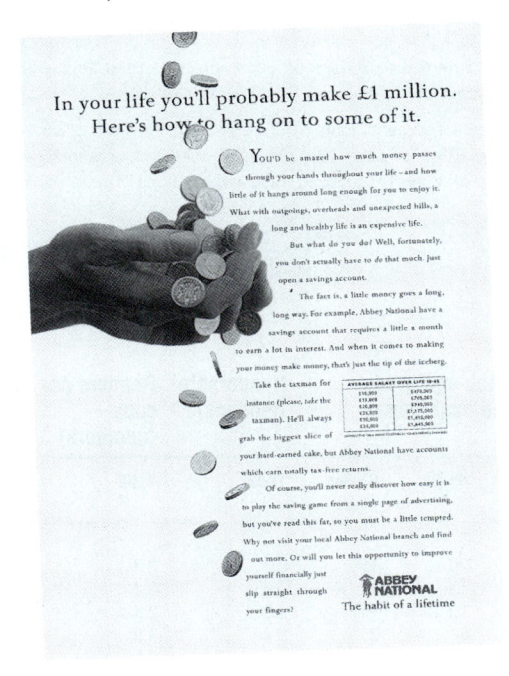

Persuasive advertising is designed to encourage consumers to buy a certain product rather than competitor products. Such advertising will focus on differences with rival products which may be true, or may simply be created by clever advertising. One manufacturer ran a very successful soap-powder advertising campaign for many years claiming that their product washed 'whiter than white' - a meaningless phrase which nevertheless influenced the buying habits of many consumers.

Advertising media

Newspapers and magazines

There are over 11,000 different newspapers and magazines available in the UK, ranging from national daily newspapers to free local newspapers and specialist magazines of limited circulation. Advertising is an important source of revenue for these publications.

In 1992, 60% of all adults read a daily newspaper. Forty-three per cent of all males read either *The Sun* or the *Daily Mirror*.

The Press

- National daily newspapers
- National Sunday newspapers
- Regional daily newspapers
- Local weekly papers
- Local free newspapers
- Consumer magazines
- Specialist interest magazines
- Trade and professional magazines

Advanced Business

Portfolio Activity 10.4

Range: Advertising, Target audience
Skills: Produce written material, Present information

1. You run an advertising agency. You have been approached by firms wishing to advertise the following products:

- Holidays for the under-30s
- Lingerie
- A new video action and adventure film
- Instant coffee powder

What use could you make of the information below to help plan a campaign for each product?

2. Conduct a survey of the advertising used for two different products of your choice. Identify the target markets for the products, and analyse the way they are marketed and advertised in the main media (e.g. TV, radio, particular newspapers), looking carefully at where adverts are placed. How do your findings of how and where your chosen products are advertised tie in with figures from Social Trends and other publications?

3. Chart some figures in table 10.3 below with the help of an IT package, using at least two different means of presentation. Combine your charts with wordprocessed sections of your report.

Table 10.3: Reading of national newspapers and the most popular magazines: by sex and age, 1992

GREAT BRITAIN

	Percentage of adults reading each paper in 1992			Percentage of each age group (millions) reading each paper in 1992				Readership[1] (millions)	Readers per copy (numbers)
	Males	Females	All adults	15-24	25-44	45-64	65 and over	1992	1992
Daily newspapers									
The Sun	24	19	21	28	23	20	15	9.7	2.7
Daily Mirror	19	15	17	18	16	18	17	7.8	2.8
Daily Express	9	8	8	7	6	10	11	3.8	2.5
Daily Star	7	4	5	8	6	5	2	2.4	3.0
The Guardian	3	2	3	3	4	3	1	1.3	3.1
The Times	3	2	2	2	2	3	1	1.0	2.7
Financial Times	2	1	1	1	2	1	-	0.6	3.6
Any national daily newspaper	65	56	60	59	57	64	62	27.3	-
Sunday newspapers									
News of the World	29	26	28	35	31	26	19	12.5	2.7
Sunday Mirror	20	18	19	22	20	20	16	8.8	3.2
The Mail on Sunday	13	13	13	14	14	14	9	5.8	2.9
Sunday Express	11	11	11	10	8	13	14	4.9	2.8
The Sunday Times	9	7	8	9	9	8	4	3.5	3.0
Sunday Telegraph	4	4	4	3	4	5	5	1.8	3.2
Sunday Sport	5	1	3	7	3	1	-	1.3	4.1
Any Sunday newspaper	71	67	69	71	68	72	66	31.3	-
General magazines									
Reader's Digest	14	12	13	9	12	17	14	5.9	3.9
Radio Times	13	12	12	14	12	13	12	5.7	3.6
TV Times	11	11	11	15	10	11	9	5.0	4.5
Viz	14	5	10	29	11	2	-	4.3	1.0
Women's magazines									
Bella	3	14	9	10	11	8	7	3.3	-
Woman's Own	3	14	9	10	10	8	7	3.4	4.9
Woman	2	11	6	6	7	6	5	2.6	3.8
Woman's Weekly	2	10	6	3	4	7	11	2.4	3.2

1 Defined as the average issue readership and represents the number of people who claim to have read or looked at one or more copies of a given publication during a period equal to the interval at which the publication appears.

Social Trends 1994 (National Readership Surveys Ltd)

Television

Television is an ideal means of advertising to reach mass markets, offering the benefits of movement and sound to promote products and services. Commercial television covers the whole of the UK, and advertisements can be broadcast to reach the whole population, or targeted at particular ITV regions.

▼ Figure 10.5: ITV advertising market shares

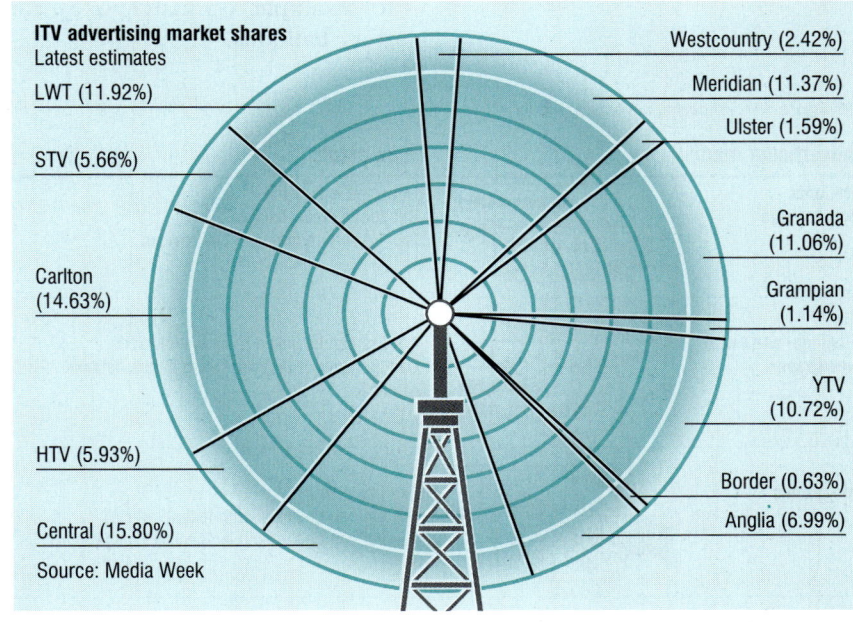

ITV advertising market shares
Latest estimates

- LWT (11.92%)
- STV (5.66%)
- Carlton (14.63%)
- HTV (5.93%)
- Central (15.80%)
- Westcountry (2.42%)
- Meridian (11.37%)
- Ulster (1.59%)
- Granada (11.06%)
- Grampian (1.14%)
- YTV (10.72%)
- Border (0.63%)
- Anglia (6.99%)

Source: Media Week

Financial Times 19.11.93

Due to increasing sales of satellite and cable systems, there are now an increasing number of commercial TV stations in the UK. Because their market is still relatively small, the cost of advertising on these channels tends to be much lower than on ITV and Channel 4, where a 60-second peak-time advert, shown just once, could cost as much as £90,000 in 1994.

Cinema

In 1992, 10.1 million people went to the cinema in the UK. Because of recently growing audiences, advertisers have begun to increase their use of cinema advertising and are now designing adverts specially for cinema release. For example, in 1994, the National Council for Vocational Qualifications promoted the new Advanced GNVQ courses in a series of cinema adverts targeted at 16-18-year-olds attending the films *Wayne's World* (2) and *The Pelican Brief*.

Radio

Radio listening has also increased in recent years. There has been a significant growth in the number of local commercial radio stations, whose main source of funding is revenue from adverts. Local radio provides a relatively cheap and effective means of advertising for many medium-sized and even smaller firms.

Advanced Business

Other advertising media

Large **posters** placed in highly visible sites can be a relatively cheap and effective means of grabbing peoples' attention. Smaller posters placed on the side of buses and taxis, on railway stations, and in airports can be seen by large numbers of people. Sports venues are also popular sites to place posters on hoardings.

Adverts for products can also be placed on the packages of other products - for example, on matchboxes, carrier bags, and T-shirts - and even on hot-air balloons.

▼ Figure 10.6: Choosing advertising media

Advertising media	Plus points	Minus points
National newspapers	 Coverage is national Reader can refer back to advert Product information can be provided	Use of colour limited Smaller adverts tend to get 'lost' among others Readers often ignore adverts
Regional and Local newspaper	 Adverts can be linked to local conditions Can be used for test-marketing before national launch	Reproduction and layout can be poor Average cost per reader relatively high due to more limited circulation
Magazines	 Can use colour Adverts can be linked with feature articles Adverts can be targeted in specialist magazines	Adverts must be submitted a long time before publication Competitors' products often advertised alongside
Radio	 Can use sound and music Relatively cheap to produce Growing number of stations Audiences can be targeted	Non-visual Message usually short-lived Listeners may switch off or ignore adverts
Television	 Creative use of moving images, colour, and sound Can use visual endorsements by well-known personalities Repeats reinforce message Growing number of channels Adverts can be regional	High production costs Peak time can be expensive Message short-lived Viewers may ignore or switch over during adverts
Cinema	 Creative use of images, colour and sound Adverts can be localized Adverts can be targeted at age groups at different films After decline during 1980s audiences increasing again	Limited audiences compared to other media Audience restricted to mainly younger age groups Message may only be seen once due to infrequent visits to cinema
Posters	 Good cheap visual stimulus Can be placed near to points of sale National campaigns possible	Only limited information possible Susceptible to vandalism and adverse weather

UNIT THREE

CHAPTER 10

Publicity

There are a variety of ways a firm can publicize its organization and products:

- **Sales literature** - handouts, leaflet drops, promotional booklets
- **Signs** - on buildings or in windows; for example, pub signs
- **Vehicle livery** - vans and lorries painted in colours and logos associated with a business organization
- **Stationery** - letterheads and logos on paper and documents
- **Point-of-sale** - promotional stands, posters, leaflets at checkouts and shop counters
- **Product placement** - display of products on the sets of major TV and film productions, free gifts, and **product endorsements** from well-known TV and sports personalities who are paid to wear or use particular products.

▼ Leaflets and signs provide useful and relatively inexpensive publicity

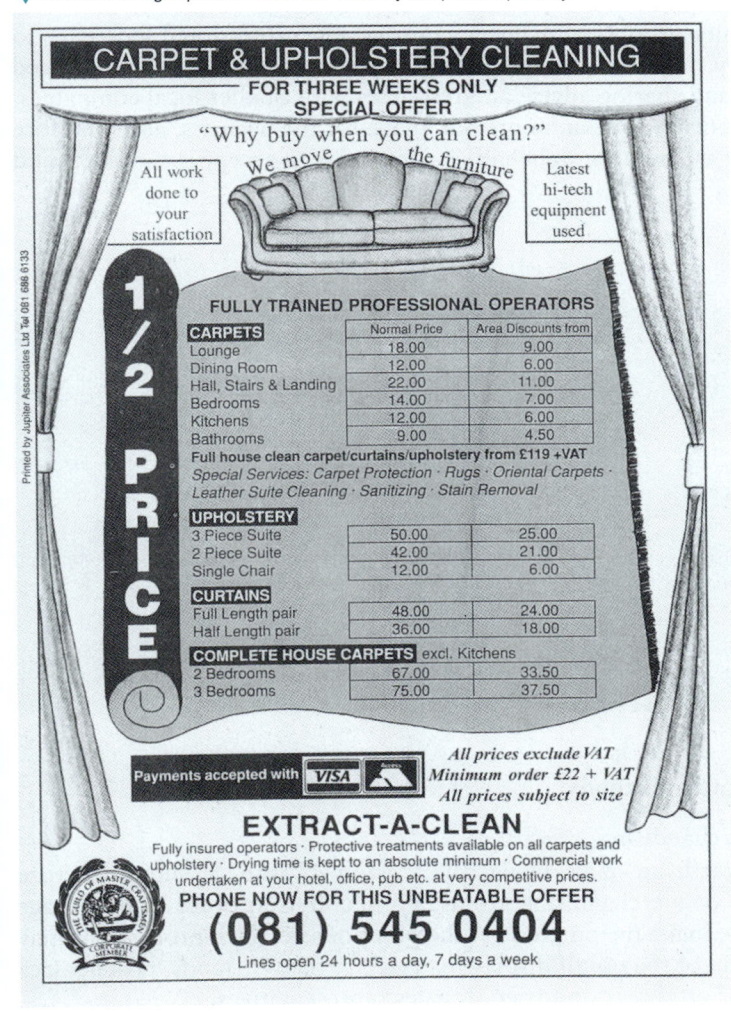

245

Sponsoring a major sporting event is an effective method of improving public relations

Public Relations (PR)

Public Relations involves actions undertaken by a business in the hope of obtaining favourable, and often free, publicity. This is especially important to a firm trying to develop a corporate image or fending off bad publicity. Types of Public Relations activity can include:

- **Press releases:** published statements issued to the media, often offering stories and facts that can be treated as news items

- **Sponsorship:** funding of sporting, cultural, or social events in return for the display of the sponsor company's name and logo. Sponsors may also have an exclusive right to sell their products at the event.

- **Lobbying:** attempts by business or non-profitmaking organizations to influence or persuade decision-makers or those in positions of power. For example, pressure groups like Greenpeace and Friends of the Earth will often lobby Members of Parliament and businesses in an attempt to force changes in the laws governing the treatment of animals and the natural environment.

- **Community relations:** creation of links between businesses and local community groups, with firms contributing professional expertise to voluntary organizations, providing jobs and training to disadvantaged groups, and sharing advice and resources with smaller local companies. The benefits include an improved image for the business, and therefore a greater willingness on behalf of consumers to accept its products and brands.

Portfolio Activity 10.5

Range: Publicity
Skills: Produce written material, Collect and record data

1. Collect sales literature produced by various organizations to promote their products and raise awareness.
2. Study how images and messages are used in the leaflets. Prepare a short report of your findings.
3. From your investigations, design and produce a sales leaflet on a product of your choice, using a desktop publishing package.
4. Find out how business organizations locally and nationally are helping your community. What are their motives?

Sales promotion methods

In-store merchandising

Whilst advertising may bring the customer into a shop, in-store promotions or merchandising are usually required in order to encourage customers to make the purchase at the point of sale. Such promotions may take the form of the use of display material, attractive stands, posters, free samples, and attractive and friendly sales representatives.

In shops, careful thought is also given to design and layout. Sometimes exits are intentionally hard to find, to encourage customers to browse a little longer. Sweets are strategically placed at checkouts to encourage children to pressurize their parents into buying them whilst queuing.

We have ways of making you buy!

Imagine this: a visit to the supermarket in the not-so-distant future. Park your car, grab a trolley, and set off down the first aisle. You plan to buy a jar of your favourite coffee - but even before you reach its shelf, a video ad on the small screen attached to your trolley alerts you to a new coffee which is on offer.

Even before you've scanned your shopping list, your attention is grabbed again. The air is scented with coconut oil. Best buy that suntan cream now, you think, before the Summer holidays.

And so it goes on. The experience of shopping is about to change forever. During the next couple of years, the arrival of sophisticated electronics will change the habits of a generation. Shelves will talk to the customer as s/he walks by, shoppers will add up their own bills with handheld scan guns, and shoplifters may be banished, as electronic tags are embedded in the packaging of every supermarket product.

Interactive couponing machines will be installed so that, using barcodes, the machine can monitor purchases and issue personalized on-the-spot discount coupons to persuade shoppers to buy a rival product next time. For example, Pepsi could negotiate with the supermarket the right to have discount coupons issued for its six-packs of cola each time a similar sized pack of Coke is scanned at the checkout.

The main attraction of developing electronic wizardry is simply to sell more goods by targeting the consumer more directly.

Adapted from The Sunday Times 26.12.93

Other sales promotion methods

- **Competitions:** firms will often run competitions, details of which are displayed on product packaging. To ensure repeat sales, the competition entrant will often be required to collect coupons as proof of purchase.

- **Free mail-ins:** firms may provide free gifts to consumers who collect coupons from product packaging.

- **Money-off coupons:** in magazines, on product packaging, or delivered by direct mail, to encourage sales of a particular product

- **Loyalty incentives:** consumers may be encouraged to remain loyal to a particular product if they are provided with an incentive. This may involve accumulating points which can be used to gain money off future purchases or exchanged for a specific product. For example, petrol station chains such as Shell and Esso give coupons to their customers which can be exchanged for 'gifts'.

- **Sales staff incentives:** firms may offer performance-related pay and gifts to encourage staff to make more sales. For example, staff can earn commission based on a percentage of the sales revenues they generate.

▼ *Competitions, money-off coupons and free gifts are often effective sales promotion methods*

Direct marketing

Direct marketing allows manufacturers to deal directly with consumers without the need for retail outlets or wholesalers (see 11.2). Direct marketing is the fastest-growing method of selling products in the UK.

Mailshots

These are increasingly popular with some manufacturers and can be sent to the homes of thousands of potential consumers. The mailshot contains product details and an order form. Mailshots are usually personalized using modern computer technology, with each letter showing the individual customer's name and address. However, much mailshot marketing is viewed by consumers as 'junk mail' and ends up in the bin.

Portfolio Activity 10.6

Range: Sales promotion methods
Skills: Produce written material

1. Visit a large supermarket. What promotional methods are used in the store to encourage people to buy products? As well as the obvious ones, consider the layout of the store, and any sounds and smells you can detect. Make a list and write short notes on each of the methods you have identified. Compare your list with other students in your group.

2. Gather evidence on other sales promotion methods used by organizations. What is their design and purpose? How do they demonstrate the effective application of marketing principles?

Mail order advertisements

Many firms specialize in selling direct to the consumer through advertisements placed in newspapers, specialist magazines, and other publications. Customers may order products such as computers, cameras, and much more by simply telephoning the firm and quoting a credit card number.

Telesales

Some businesses employ sales staff to telephone potential customers in order to sell them goods and services. This method gives the advantage of allowing the firm to tailor their selling effort to suit the customer. However, many customers do not like being telephoned at home by sales people, and the success rate for such calls is not high.

Home shopping

The development of communications technology such as satellite and cable television has enabled producers to get closer to their target audiences. The QVC home shopping channel began broadcasting on UK screens in 1994, providing 24-hour advertising and product reports enticing viewers to buy direct from the screen. Adverts for sporting events, holidays, and other products can also be found on the BBC Ceefax and ITV Teletext services.

Portfolio Activity 10.7

Range: Direct marketing methods
Skills: Read and respond to written material

1. Compare the form of distribution offered by the QVC home shopping channel with that of mail order catalogues. Suggest at least one advantage to the consumer for each of the two approaches.

2. Suggest and explain how a manufacturer could use the new interactive TV media to develop 'a direct relationship between brands and the consumer'.

A high street in every home

Interactive media will fundamentally change the role of media in marketing, and advertisers should start addressing this now.

Direct response television commercials and the home-shopping channel QVC are already established, but the launch of a whole tier of new interactive services enabling viewers to select exactly what they want to watch and when, is imminent.

In the UK, British Telecom is working with London Weekend Television, Pearson and Kingfisher to develop BT's Video On Demand service, which is due to be tested in Suffolk this spring. If companies are going to exploit the opportunities fully, then they will need the combined strengths of traditional media planning, promotions and direct marketing.

Interactive media will offer the supplier instant feedback on consumer tastes and needs, enabling tighter targeting.

JWT media director David Byles dismisses suggestions that the traditional commercial is doomed.

'There will be high reach advertising-funded channels alongside hundreds of interactive services," he believes. JWT is already running tests overseas on behalf of a number of clients.

Byles adds: "The vision of a direct relationship with a consumer through TV is of immense importance."

"More interesting is the way manufacturers with brands will use interactive TV to develop a direct relationship between brands and the consumer."

Marketing Week 18.2.94

> **Key words**
>
> **Informative advertising** - seeks to provide consumers with product information
>
> **Persuasive advertising** - seeks to influence and persuade consumers to buy a product
>
> **Advertising media** - different means of advertising to consumers, such as TV, cinema, and radio
>
> **Public Relations (PR)** - activities such as sponsorship and lobbying, aimed at raising organizational and product profile
>
> **Sales promotions** - methods used to generate sales and repeat purchases, such as money-off coupons, competitions, and customer loyalty incentives
>
> **Direct marketing** - methods of promoting products direct to consumers, for example, by mailshots, mail order, and telesales

Section 10.3 Product performance

Evaluating marketing communications

The effectiveness of marketing communications in targeting their audience and delivering the right message can be judged by a number of factors:

- **Sales (volumes, values, and growth).** Businesses will often set annual targets for sales levels in both absolute terms and in terms of growth. For example, a company may set an objective to sell 10% more units than last year and attain a total of £3 million in revenues. Failure to achieve these targets may indicate a failure of marketing communications.

- **Repeat sales.** Firms which sell fast-moving consumer goods rely on repeat purchase of their products by consumers. For example, a firm that sells biscuits will try to use marketing communications to ensure that once the consumer has finished the packet, they will immediately want to purchase another one.

- **Brand loyalty.** Through advertising and promotion, a firm will try to make very similar products, like washing powders, appear different and better than their competitors (see 8.3). Creating a strong brand image with which consumers can identify will encourage repeat sales.

- **Extending product life-cycles.** Changes in consumer wants and spending patterns over time will mean that most products have a limited commercial lifespan. However, through appropriate marketing, demand for a product can be maintained and the lifetime of a product extended.

- **Consumer awareness.** Marketing can be judged as effective if it heightens awareness of the product among consumers. If consumers are able to remember a catchy name, logo, or advertising jingle for a product, then there is greater chance they will buy it.

Product life-cycles

Like people, products are born and will eventually die as consumer demand and technology move on. Goods and services change and develop during their lifetimes, and marketing objectives will need to change to match changes in the product. A major marketing tool to help a business plan for the future is **product life-cycle analysis**.

The commercial stages through which a product may pass are known as the product life-cycle. For example, when a new product is launched, it is likely to be relatively unknown, and marketing will need to persuade potential customers, distributors, and retailers to purchase it. The marketing objective will be to get the product established, with sales rising as quickly as possible. On the other hand, a firm with an established product and a large market share may wish to concentrate on making as much profit as possible by creating a strong brand image with higher prices.

▼ *Figure 10.7: The product life-cycle*

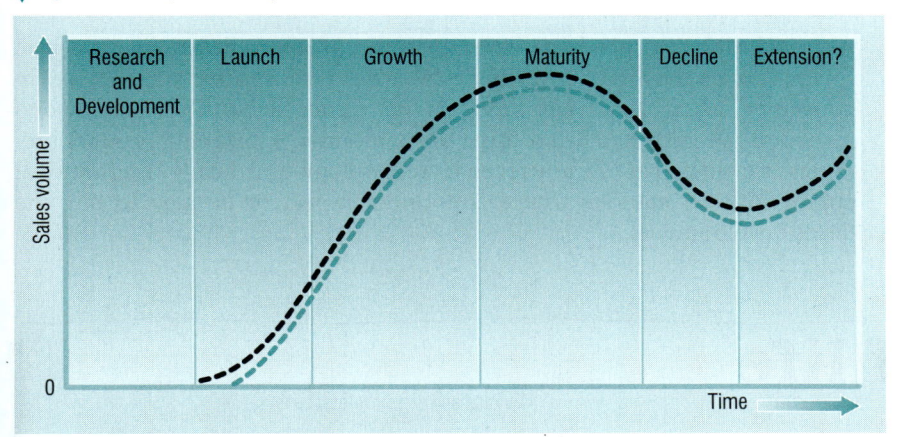

There are five main product life-cycle stages:

1. Research and Development
2. Launch
3. Growth
4. Maturity
5. Decline

A sixth stage, known as **Extension** is possible where a firm may wish to re-launch an old product as 'new' or 'improved'.

Stages in the product life-cycle

Stage 1: Research and Development (R&D)

At this early stage, a business will research the market to find out what the consumer wants and whether it is possible to make and sell the product at a profit. R&D involves research into all aspects of the product, including technical aspects of production, packaging, pricing, and possible market segments.

Stage 2: Launch

This is a very expensive stage in the life-cycle because the product is new and the firm may have to charge consumers a low price and invest heavily in informative advertising to ensure that the market becomes familiar with it. A good example is the launch of Digital Audio Cassettes on the home audio market in 1993.

Stage 3: Growth

During the growth stage, sales will start to rise and advertising will shift from being primarily informative to persuasive advertising to ensure continued demand for the product. Many products falter at the growth stage, when sales fail to take off in spite of heavy marketing. This tends to indicate insufficient care in Research and Development, and/or a poor advertising strategy.

Stage 4: Maturity

At maturity, the product should be well-known and established, and reaching its maximum level of sales and profitability. However, by this time, new firms may be entering the market, and advertising will be needed to maintain market share. Mature products include Kellogs Cornflakes and Oxo cubes, while mature industries include soap powders and newspapers.

Stage 5: Decline

Eventually sales for all products will start to decline. This can be caused by changes in fashion, or, more likely, by new technology which either replaces the product or allows competitors to offer a new or improved version at a lower price. In the 1990s, for example, vinyl records are in decline due to the growth of the CD, while the arrival of powerful 486- and 586-based computers has pushed the 286- and 386-based machines out of the computer market.

Stage 6: Extension

It is possible to extend the life-cycle of a product by convincing customers that the product is somehow different or better than before. Most successful extension strategies start well before the product goes into decline. For example, Oxo cubes were used during the war to give the flavour of meat to other foods when there was very little meat available. After the war, when the supply of meat increased, the life of Oxo was extended by relaunching it as a means of enhancing the flavour of real meat.

Figure 10.8: Different product life-cycles

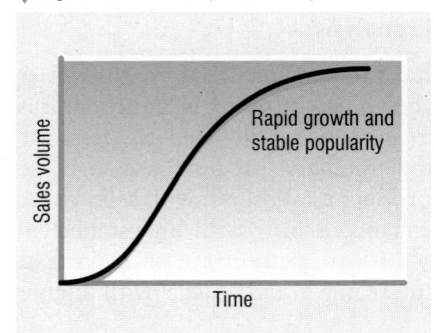

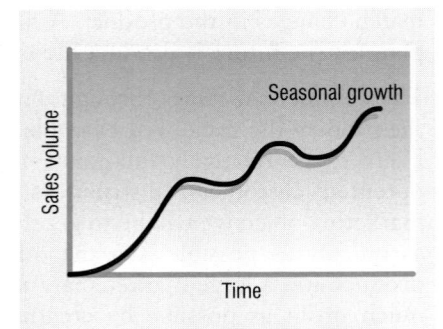

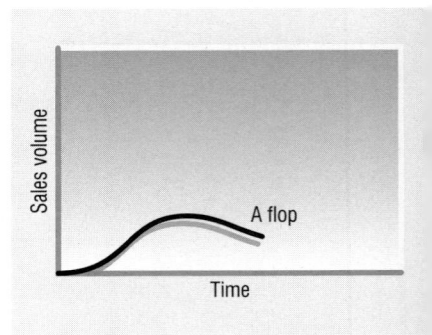

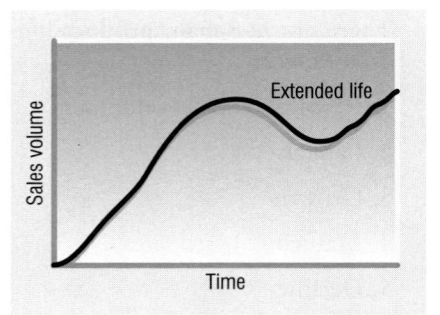

The product portfolio

Although different products have life-cycles of different lengths, it is true to say that on average, most life-cycles are getting shorter and shorter. In consumer electronics, new models of camcorders, TVs, and video recorders are launched every three to six months. Shortening product life-cycles are due to rapid advances in technology and heavy international competition in markets where consumers expect to be able to buy the latest developments.

A matter of life and death

Think of music reproduction. The wind-up gramophone of my grandparents' generation is extinct. In three human generations, five sorts of listening hardware - Edison's cylinders, brittle 78rpm records, vinyl LPs and singles, cassettes, CDs - have arived and become pre-eminent; yet already two have gone. This list does not even include total failures. Eight-track tape and quadraphonic sound died out because they were ill-adapted to capture consumers' money. The heyday of cylinders was ended by discs, which were better adapted for feeding off the world of the consumer.

New Scientist 6.2.93

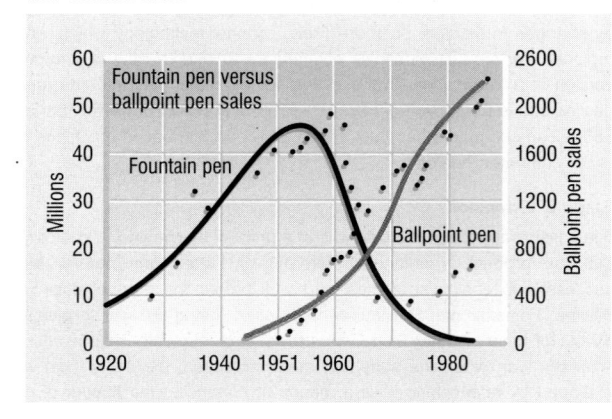

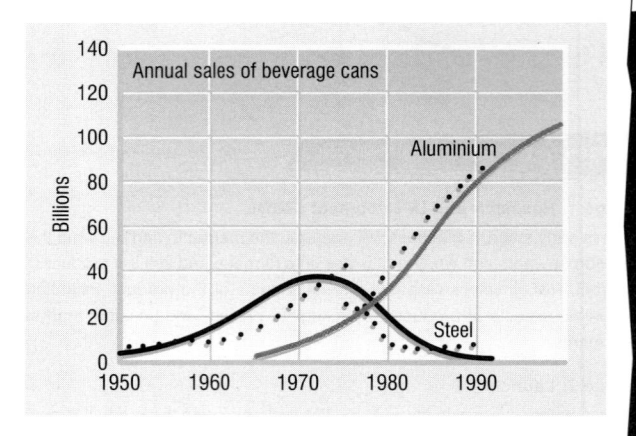

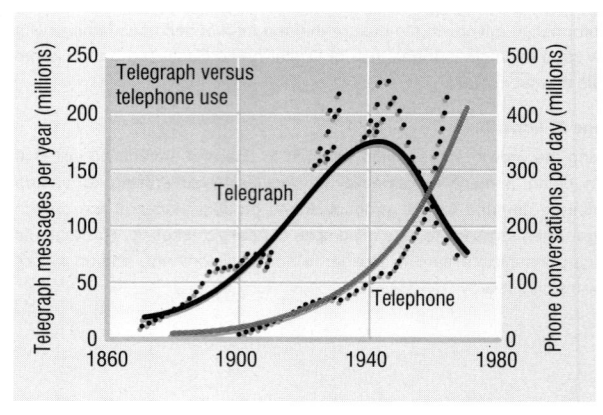

M&S to market pension schemes through its stores

Marks & Spencer, the UK's most profitable retailer, is to offer life and pensions products from next year in addition to its existing financial services.

Financial Times 2.2.94

Because of shortening product life-cycles, many modern organizations produce more than one product and operate in a number of different markets. **Diversification** into other products enables a company to spread the risk of falling consumer demand for one or more of its products. The **product portfolio** (or **mix**) of a firm will include the whole range of products they offer, including all the brands, line extensions, sizes, and types of packaging available.

▼ Figure 10.9: Managing the product portfolio

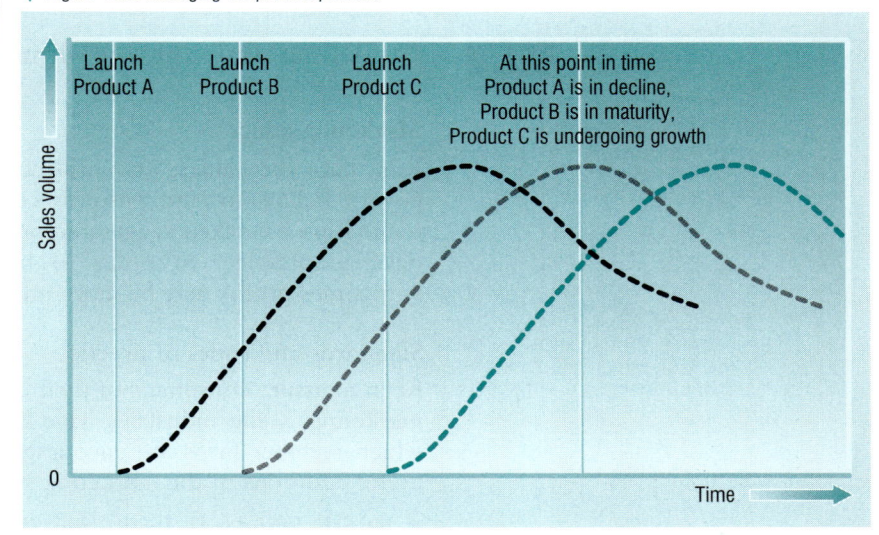

[Graph showing Sales volume vs Time with three overlapping product life-cycle curves: Launch Product A, Launch Product B, Launch Product C. At this point in time Product A is in decline, Product B is in maturity, Product C is undergoing growth.]

Portfolio Activity 10.8

Range: Product performance
Skills: Read and respond to written material

1. Explain why short product life-cycles make up for falling prices during the lifetime of a microchip.
2. What does the text suggest is happening at the Research and Development stage of each new microchip?
3. Explain, with diagrams, how portfolio planning might be of use to chip-makers in this quickly changing market.
4. Suggest marketing communications methods that could be used to promote microchips.

Computer Games on Wall Street

After a miserable 1992, which saw prices fall by 30%, the computer industry had hoped for a breather. The typical personal computer is now almost 20% cheaper than it was in January. However, the microcomputer chip firms such as Intel, Motorola and Advanced Micro Devices (AMD) have thrived by making the microprocessors that are at the heart of PCs. Profit margins on microprocessors are enormous: the Intel 486DX/33, used in many PCs, sells for $283 but costs less than $20 to make. And while profit margins fall quickly during the lifetime of each chip, product life-cycles are short enough for this not to pose much of a problem.

The only snag is that each new generation tends to be far costlier to develop and produce. The biggest chip maker, Intel, will this year spend $900 million on R&D. The biggest headache is growing competition. Rivals to Intel are flooding the market with cheaper chips.

Microchip prices might fall but the industry could still be saved by the creation of new markets for chips including pocket-sized 'personal digital assistants' such as Apple's Newton and microchips for a new generation of digital cellphones and interactive television.

Adapted from The Economist 6.11.93

> **Key words**
>
> **Product life-cycle** - an analysis of the different stages which a product will pass through, and associated sales at each point
>
> **Extension strategies** - methods used to extend the marketable life and sales of a product
>
> **Diversification** - producing a range of commodities for different markets
>
> **Product portfolio** - the mix of products marketed by a firm at a given point in time

Section 10.4 Guidelines and controls on marketing communications

Marketing ethics

Ethics are the values, or moral code, of individuals and society, which govern behaviour and business conduct. In marketing there can be a temptation to make exaggerated or misleading claims about products and business practices in order to boost sales and make larger profits. Sometimes profits may be more important to a firm than ethics.

Standards and codes of practice

Keen to assure consumers of their concern for product quality and ethical marketing, some industries have drawn up voluntary codes of practice which member firms are encouraged to follow. In many ways these are useful additions to the marketing strategies of firms.

▼ *Trademarks which give the consumer quality assurance*

- **British Standards Institution (BSI):** the BSI sets quality and safety standards for a wide range of products. Products meeting the BSI standards are awarded the **kitemark** to indicate that they have reached the necessary standards. Products awarded the kitemark will have a competitive advantage over rival products which fail to display the symbol to the consumer.

- **Professional and trade associations:** Members of trades often set up professional associations in order to protect their interests and improve their reputation with consumers. Examples include the Federation of Master Builders and Association of British Travel Agents (ABTA). These organizations usually specify a code of practice governing the behaviour of members, and consumers can appeal to the associations if they feel that a particular code of practice has been breached.

- **Independent Television Commission (ITC):** the ITC regulates advertisements appearing on television and cable and has its own Code of Advertising Standards and Practice. Certain products and services, including cigarettes, spirits, private investigation agencies, and gambling, may not be advertised on TV. There are also strict rules about advertising aimed at children and about the use of child actors or models in adverts.

- **Advertising Standards Authority (ASA):** the ASA was set up in 1962 to monitor the standard of advertisements in the UK. It covers all advertisements in newspapers, magazines, posters, direct marketing, sales promotions, cinema, video cassettes, and Teletext.

The ASA safeguards the consumer by ensuring that the rules contained in the **British Code of Advertising Practice** are followed by any organization that prepares and publishes advertisements.

> **The essence of good advertising**
>
> The British Code of Advertising Practice states that all advertisements should be:
>
> - Legal, decent, honest and truthful
> - Prepared with a sense of responsibility to the consumer and to society
> - In line with the principles of fair competition generally accepted in business

As well as receiving and investigating complaints from consumers, the ASA advises advertisers, agencies, and publishers how to avoid misleading advertising. If an advertisement is found to be misleading or offensive, the ASA will act to have it changed or withdrawn. Failure to comply with its rulings may lead to adverse publicity in the ASA's monthly report of judgements.

The work of the ASA is financed by a levy of 0.1% on UK advertising expenditures. One criticism, therefore, of the ASA is that it is funded by the very people it is attempting to police, namely the advertising industry.

Advertising on radio is regulated by the **Radio Authority**.

Portfolio Activity 10.9

Range: Guidelines and controls
Skills: Read and respond to written material

Here is an example of a consumer complaint received by the Advertising Standards Authority:

1. Suggest why the marketing activity might be described as 'unethical'. Do you agree? Give your reasons.
2. Investigate and describe how the Advertising Standards Authority might be able to help the consumer in the above case.

Complaint: Objection to a colour supplement mail order advertisement for children's bedding which featured an illustration of a fully-fitted bed, including two pillowcases, and claimed "The bedding consists of a single-size duvet cover and pillowcase set." The complainant found upon receiving her order that only one pillowcase was included.
ASA report 12.93

Key words

Advertising Standards Authority - an independent body that monitors the standard of advertisements in the UK and attempts to enforce the British Code of Advertising Practice

Advanced Business

Test questions

The following underpinning knowledge will be tested:

1. The suitability of advertising and publicity to promote goods, services and organizational image
2. Public Relations to promote products and organizations
3. The use of sales promotion methods to reach target audiences
4. The growth of direct marketing communications
5. The impact of guidelines and controls on marketing communications
6. The effect of marketing communications on product performance

1 The product life-cycle is an essential part of:
  A After-sales service
  B Planning future marketing activities
  C Knowing when the firm will have to shut down
  D Planning how long the product will last before it wears out

2 Which of the following can be used as a means of extending a product life-cycle?
  A Marketing to existing market segments
  B Retaining the existing packaging and advertising
  C Altering packaging and advertising
  D Maintaining present pricing policies

3 The Advertising Standards Authority:
  A Regulates advertising on commercial television
  B Is run by government
  C Ensures adverts are honest and truthful
  D Does not deal directly with consumer complaints

4 Maturity in a product life-cycle is characterized by:
  A Steadily growing sales
  B Steadily falling sales
  C Fierce advertising with competitors
  D High and stable sales

5 Direct marketing methods used by a producer will include:
  A Selling direct to retailers
  B Placing mail order adverts in magazines
  C Using persuasive TV advertising
  D Employing agents to sell products direct to consumers

6 Which advertising media will best suit producers aiming their products at niche markets?
  A Specialist magazines
  B Sky Movie Channel
  C The Daily Mirror newspaper
  D Posters near to point of sale

Questions 7 - 9 share the following answer options:

To help in sales forecasting, consumers can be segmented using the following methods:
  A Age
  B Lifestyle
  C Social class
  D Geographical region

Which method would be most useful in the following situations?

7 When it is considered necessary to group customers according to their values and attitudes

8 When the types of occupations people have is important

9 When a product is to be targeted at young people

10 Which of the following methods would you use to promote the launch of a new product to a mass audience?
  A Sales leaflets
  B Placing an advert in a popular daily newspaper
  C A TV advert
  D Direct mail

Questions 11 - 13 share the following answer options:

A Lobbying members of parliament

B Adverts in local newspapers

C Competitions requiring collection of 5 proofs of product purchase

D Sponsoring a school fête

Which of the above methods would you recommend to the following organizations?

11 A firm wishing to improve community relations

12 Animal rights campaigners wanting an end to blood sports

13 A firm wanting to create product loyalty

14 A new disco is about to open in your local town centre.

a. What is the likely target audience of the disco?

b. Recommend three ways the owners could promote their disco to their target audience. An existing disco nearby has been open for 10 years and is now experiencing a fall in entrance numbers.

c. What does this suggest about the stage in the product life-cycle of the existing disco?

d. Recommend two promotional methods the existing disco might use to extend their product life-cycle.

15 a. Suggest two ways in which a car manufacturer might segment their market into different target audiences.

b. Recommend two advertising media that could be used effectively to promote the product range of the car maker. Give reasons for your choice.

c. Suggest three ways in which the car maker could judge whether these methods have been successful.

d. What is the Advertising Standards Association? Explain how the ASA can influence the marketing communications used by the car maker.

16 A local pressure group wants to mount a campaign against the building of a local by-pass through nearby open land. Advise them on cost-effective promotional methods they might use in their campaign.

Assessment Assignment

Range: Advertising
Publicity
Public Relations
Sales promotion methods
Target audience
Product performance
Direct marketing communications
Guidelines and controls

Skills: Communication
Produce written material
Use images
Read and respond to written material
Application of Number
Tackle problems
Information Technology
Process information

Tasks

Prepare a report, and an oral and visual presentation to your group, on the marketing communications used by two contrasting organizations - for example, a small, local firm serving a niche market, and a large organization selling mass-produced goods to a national market:

1. Gather information on the marketing communications the organizations use to promote themselves and their products. For example, watch TV advertisements, survey national and local newspapers and magazines, examine products for money-off coupons and competitions, etc.

2. Group the methods used by each organization under the following general headings:

- Advertising media
- Publicity
- Public relations
- Sales promotions
- Direct marketing

4. Identify the target audiences at which the products and promotional methods of each organization are aimed.

5. Examine the effectiveness of the promotional methods used in terms of product performance. For example, are consumers more aware of the availability of the product? What is the impact on sales?

6. Suggest other promotional methods the organizations could use to good effect. For example, could they make better use of Information Technology? Give reasons for your recommendations.

7. Discuss how guidelines and controls on marketing communications can affect the way in which your chosen organizations are able to promote information about their products.

Advanced Business

chapter 11
Customer Service and Sales Methods

This chapter investigates how business organizations combine sales methods with the provision of customer services to generate sales revenues and ensure repeat purchases

Key ideas

Customers demand that organizations do more than simply provide goods or services. They require **information**, the ability to make **exchanges, refunds and complaints**, and to have any **special needs**, such as disabilities, catered for.

An organization that fails to respond to customer needs will not achieve its aims of expanding market share and increasing profits.

The ability of an organization to satisfy customer needs can be measured in terms of the **image** of the business, the **impression** left with the customer, and **sales volumes** and **profits**.

Distribution aims to get the right product to the right place at the right time to secure customer purchases.

The **distribution channel**, or route, from producer to consumer can be **direct**, or **indirect** through an **intermediary**, such as a **wholesaler, retailer,** or **agent**.

Direct sales methods include **mail order, TV and radio sales, factory sales, telesales, door-to-door** and **pyramid selling**.

Selling is the final link in the distribution chain and is vital for the success of a business. It will greatly depend on the quality and motivation of sales staff.

Sales communications methods, such as **sales campaigns, meetings, conferences,** and **memos** can be used to inform and motivate sales staff.

In meeting the needs of customers, sales staff have a number of **duties** and **responsibilities.** As well as receiving payments and giving refunds, they must have a knowledge of products and consumer protection laws, and be able to provide adequate customer and after-sales care.

Carrying out these duties will involve **sales administration**, including **processing orders, credit clearance and control, preparing customer accounts, drawing up delivery schedules, maintaining security**, and **prospecting for custom.**

UNIT THREE

Section 11.1 'The customer is always right'

Portfolio Activity 11.1

Range: Needs of organizations, Needs of customers, Customer service

Skills: Read and respond to written material, Collect and record data

1. What, apart from the meal itself, do customers in fast food retail outlets expect the organization to provide? Support your answer by reference to the article and by observing customers in queues and at tables in a fast food outlet.

2. From the article, and your observations, are fast food retailers meeting the needs of their customers?

3. Suggest two likely business objectives of fast food organizations. In the light of your answer to Question 2, do you think the achievement of these objectives is being helped or hindered by the quality of customer services provided?

Secret test criticises fast-food service

By Diane Summers, Marketing Correspondent

Fast-food restaurants, popularly viewed as providing the ultimate in well-drilled friendliness and service, in reality rate worse than banks or, in some respects, British Rail, according to customers who secretly tested them.

A large-scale "mystery shopping" exercise, involving visits to 2,500 retail outlets by researchers posing as consumers, found that fast-food staff scored below the average for all retailers on friendliness, politeness and helpfulness.

Almost 20 per cent of staff forgot part of the order and 15 per cent delivered something that had not been asked for. Twenty five per cent of staff failed to repeat the order as a check that it had been taken correctly. Shoppers also found that almost 20 per cent of restaurants had a litter problem.

The company which conducted the research, the Grass Roots Group, based in Tring, Hertfordshire, sent researchers to a total of 154 branches of McDonald's and Burger King for the study.

Financial Times 17.1.95

The aims of organizations

Production refers to any activity that satisfies a consumer want. It follows that the process of production is not complete until the good or service reaches the consumer. Even then, it may not be complete if after-sales care is required.

Consumers will have many desires to satisfy when making a purchase:

- They will want information about the good or service before they buy
- They will want to receive the good or service they have bought as quickly as possible

Attractively designed catalogues can be provided to customers seeking information about products

- They will want to know that, if anything goes wrong, they can replace the product or get a refund with the minimum of fuss.

An organization that is unable to satisfy these desires will not achieve its aims of expanding market share and increasing profits (see 4.1). There will be no repeat sales or customer loyalty from a dissatisfied customer.

Meeting the needs of customers

If a shop or business is to secure a purchase by a customer, and make them happy enough to want to come back and purchase the same product again, they will need to provide the following functions:

- **Providing information:** product information must be accurate and available on demand. If, for example, a customer phones a supplier of computers, s/he will want to know their latest prices, technical details about product performance, and earliest delivery dates. The person who answers the phone should be able to supply these details verbally or be ready to fax or post them promptly. If they are not quick to respond, the customer may go elsewhere.

Many organizations have a 'no quibble' policy on exchanging goods up to 14 days after the sale.

- **Exchanging goods.** There is nothing more annoying than having the wrong items delivered, or, worse still, finding that a product you have bought does not work properly when you take it home. Making an exchange should be a simple matter of returning the goods to the shop or supplier from which they were purchased. If it is not a simple matter, either because alternatives are unavailable, or because the sales staff are suspicious or uncooperative, then the chances are that the customer will want their money back instead, and the sale will be lost.

- **Giving refunds.** This again should be a simple matter involving no more than some quick paperwork and a signature to verify that money has been refunded. If the honest customer is refused a refund, or has to wait for a long time for a refund, then the organization is unlikely to obtain repeat trade from the customer and may even face a legal action to claim the money back.

- **Dealing with complaints.** Customers who believe they have received poor service should be able to complain on the phone or in writing to someone with enough authority to investigate the complaint and rectify it. Complaints can range from faulty products and inefficient service, to misleading or inaccurate information - for example, the holiday brochure that fails to mention the building site nextdoor to the hotel. Problems will arise, and organizations need to deal with them tactfully and quickly or repeat business will be lost and corporate image may suffer.

- **Catering for special needs.** Although many large firms mass-produce a limited range of products, there are many ways in which products and customer services can be personalized. For example, customers buying new cars may be able to choose different combinations of hi-fi units, upholstery fabrics, exterior paintwork, and colours from a wide range on offer. Cars with chosen features can often be made available within a relatively short period of time. Similarly, following a personal visit from sales staff to take measurements, double-glazing windows can be produced and fitted to meet customer requirements.

  An organization should also not forget that some customers may be disabled. The provision of wheelchair ramps, Braille lettering on lift buttons in shops and offices, and home visits for physically handicapped or housebound customers, are just some ways that these groups can be catered for to secure their purchases and improve the image of the business.

Evaluating customer service

There are a number of ways to judge the success of a business organization in meeting the needs of consumers:

- **The improved image of the business.** Good customer relations will improve the image of an organization and will generate repeat trade and customer loyalty.

- **The impression left with customer.** If refunds are dealt with quickly and without fuss; if complaints are followed up immediately; if information is accurate and freely available, and products and customer services reliable, then the customer will form a favourable impression of the organization and is more likely to deal with them again in future.

  Market research and monitoring customer complaints are two ways an organization might observe changes in customer perceptions of products and image.

- **Business performance.** Improved image and customer relations can be measured in terms of increased cashflow from sales. This ultimately will feed into higher profits.

Section 11.2 Placing the product - distribution

What is distribution?

An organization can spend millions of pounds on developing and advertising products, but if the right product is not in the right place at the right time for a consumer to buy, then all this money and effort will have been wasted. The objective of distribution is to make sure this does not happen.

Distribution is a significant element in a firm's costs and so will require careful management. Firms will need to consider physical distribution, storage and transportation of goods and services, and the various methods and outlets through which a good or service can be sold to a consumer.

Unless the distribution method, location, image, and quality of sales advice offered at the place of sale are right, the customer will not buy. Place of sale is a key ingredient in the marketing mix (see 8.3).

Channels of distribution

A **channel of distribution** refers to the route a producer uses to reach the final consumer of the product. The four main routes are illustrated in Figure 11.1.

▼ *Figure 11.1: Channels of distribution*

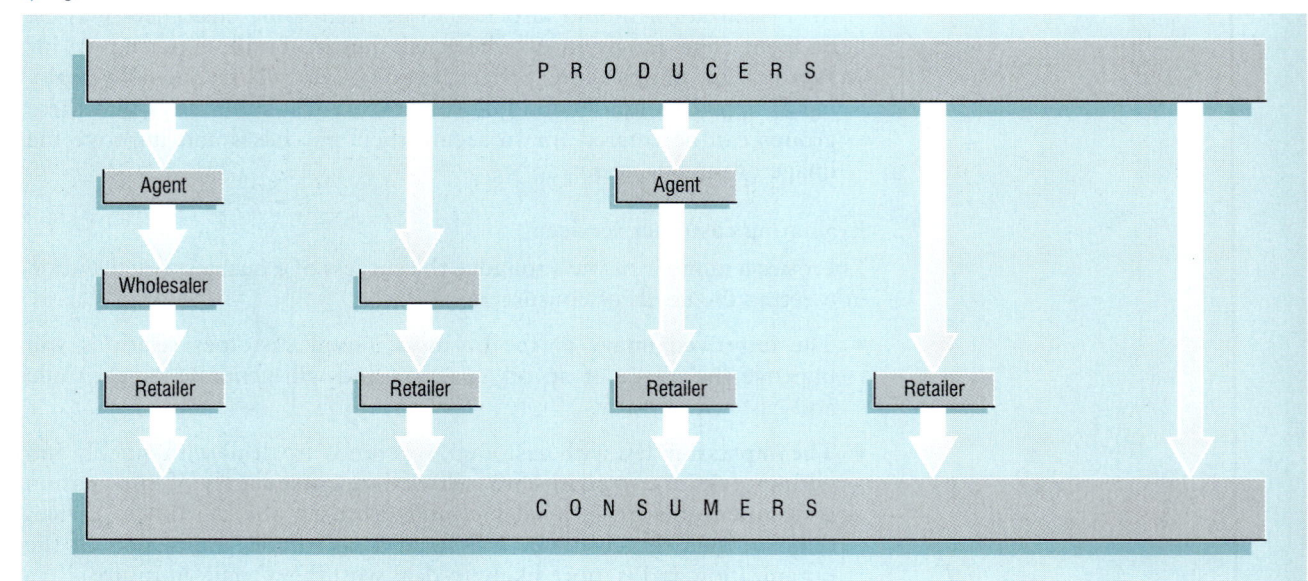

```
PRODUCERS
  │           │           │           │           │
  ▼           │           ▼           │           │
Agent         │         Agent         │           │
  │           │           │           │           │
  ▼           │           │           │           │
Wholesaler    │        [    ]         │           │
  │           │           │           │           │
  ▼           ▼           ▼           ▼           │
Retailer   Retailer   Retailer    Retailer        │
  │           │           │           │           ▼
CONSUMERS
```

There are two main types of distribution channel:

- **Direct** from the product producer or service provider to the consumer. **Direct sale methods** include **factory sales, telesales, personal selling, TV and radio sales, pyramid selling** and **mail/phone/fax order**.
- **Indirect** through an external organization, such as a wholesaler, retail outlet, distributor, or agent. These organizations are known as **intermediaries**.

Distribution channels can be either national or international, involving sales to consumers and other organizations overseas. In some cases, a distribution channel can be made **exclusive** by restricting the number of outlets at which a product can be sold. For example, Dixons has an exclusive deal with Sanyo to sell one of their popular camcorder models.

Some producers distribute directly to the consumer from their factories or to their own retail outlets. For example, a bakery will need to get its products into the shops very quickly before they pass their sell-by date. To guarantee that shops stock their goods, some manufacturers will often own their own chains of retail outlets, and deliver direct. For example, many breweries own public houses. This gives them the advantage of a guaranteed outlet for their beers. It also allows the manufacturer to take all of the profit.

Other manufacturers may prefer to concentrate on making the product, and leave storage, selling, and distribution to outside specialist firms.

Indirect distribution via intermediaries

Wholesalers buy in bulk from manufacturers and are prepared to sell in smaller quantities to local retailers. This can be to the advantage of both the manufacturer and the retailer.

▼ Figure 11.2: The function of the wholesaler

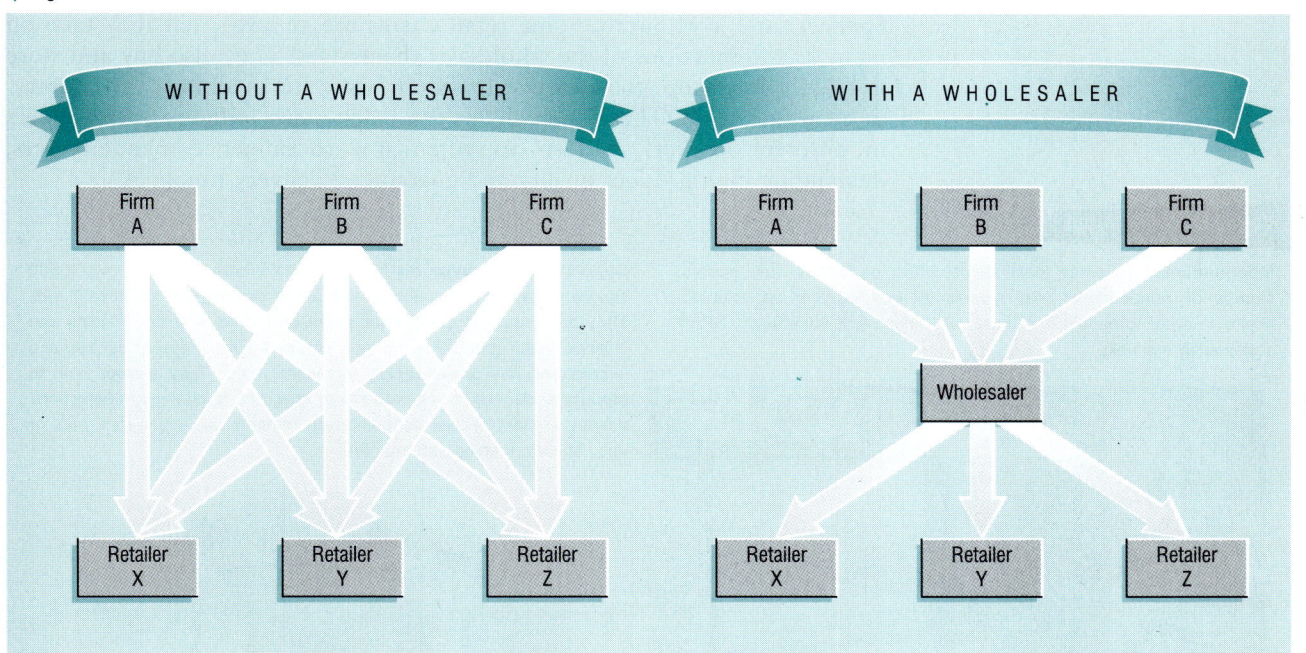

The advantages of using a wholesaler are as follows

Advantages to the manufacturer:	Advantages to the retailer:
The wholesaler will:	The wholesaler will:
• Buy in bulk and pay for storage	• Allow the retailer access to a wide range of products from different manufacturers
• Bear cost of transport to customers/retailers	• Provide a delivery service
• Relieve manufacturers of the cost of administering orders to many customers over a wide geographical area	• Provide information on new product lines
• Provide a source of market research information from contact with retailers	• Sometimes help with storage and give credit

The disadvantages of using a wholesaler

Use of a wholesaler adds to the cost of the final product and so raises the price charged to the consumer. This also reduces the share of profit for the manufacturer and retailer. Because of this, wholesaling has gone into decline in recent years as manufacturers have tried to keep the wholesalers' share of the profit for themselves by selling direct to retailers or straight to the final consumer.

Retailers

The **retail sector** consists of shops and stores who often provide the final link in a chain of distribution from the manufacturer to the final consumer. Retail outlets may either buy products direct from the producer or from a wholesaler, before adding their own mark-up on prices to charge the final consumer in order to cover their overheads and for profit.

A growing number of manufacturers now prefer to use their own distribution networks to sell directly to large retail outlets such as Sainsbury's, Marks & Spencer, and WH Smith. Some retail chains are so large that they take on many of the functions of the wholesaler themselves. They also buy and store in bulk, splitting up stock for distribution to their stores all over the country, or even the world. These large chains can reach many millions of consumers in different markets, and so are often able to influence manufacturers, demanding high product quality and guaranteed delivery times.

Types of retail outlet

Independents are small local shops, often owned by sole traders. Groups of independents may sometimes join together as voluntary chains in order to benefit from joint bulk-buying and advertising. SPAR stores is an example.

Multiple shops tend to be large-scale organizations with more than ten outlets. Multiples tend to specialize in a narrow range of products, for example Boots (primarily cosmetics and medicines), WH Smith (books and stationery), and Our Price (records).

Superstores and hypermarkets are giant stores occupying over 2,500 square metres of floorspace, selling foods, clothes, and electrical items. They are usually found in retail parks on the edge of large towns and close to major roads. The number of out-of-town shopping centres and superstores has grown rapidly in recent years. They answer both to producers' desires to sell products in bulk, and to changing consumers' desires to meet all their shopping requirements under one roof, and for easy access, loading and car parking.

Department stores are a focal point in many town centres, selling a variety of goods and services under one roof. Well-known examples include Selfridges and Harrods in London. There are also department store chains, such as Debenhams.

UNIT THREE

CHAPTER 11

Types of retail outlet

Supermarkets sell mainly food items from floorspace exceeding 400 square metres. This market has grown considerably in recent years with the addition of a number of competitors to established UK supermarket chains such as Tesco and Asda. Aldi, Netto, and Costco, are respectively German, Danish, and US-owned discount stores offering competitive prices to British shoppers.

▼ Mail order adverts

Agents and brokers

Agents are used by producers to obtain sales on their behalf. For example, travel agents sell holidays for tour operators and earn a **commission**, or share of the profits, for doing so. When entering a new foreign market, a firm will often seek the help of a business or individual with local knowledge to act as an agent to help with sales, distribution, and advertising in the overseas market.

Brokers are often used by producers to buy and sell commodities in bulk, such as tea, sugar, gold, and other metals on international markets. The bulk is then usually broken up to be sold on to processing industries.

Distribution direct to the final consumer

Direct selling cuts out the intermediary and allows the manufacturer to deal directly with consumers. This is the fastest-growing method of distribution in the UK. Direct selling methods include:

- **Mail-order advertisement:** many firms specialize in selling direct to the consumer through advertisements placed in newspapers, specialist magazines, and other publications, or by sending mailshots direct to potential customers. Products such as computers, cameras and camcorders, even garages, can be ordered simply by telephoning the firm and quoting a credit card number, or by filling in a printed form and sending it off with a cheque.

- **'Factory' sales:** these are organized by the manufacturer direct to final consumers, either by allowing customers into factories every now and again to sell off surplus or old stock at 'knock-down prices'; by opening up a shop on site, or by mail order. For example, many farms have opened farm shops to sell their produce. Similarly, customers can buy cars 'straight off the production line' at the showrooms at Ford Motors in Dagenham, Essex.

Retailing through the 'Worldwide Web'

Business is making increasing use of the 'web' of connections to the worldwide Internet. In 1994, sales generated in the USA by the Internet was around $100m. By the year 2005, analysts expect it to account for around 30% of the huge US retail market.

At present anyone with a personal computer and a modem link to a telephone line can receive information downloaded through the Internet. At present, most users are business or academics exchanging financial, economic, and business news. However, this is about to change as business organizations begin to sell video films, computer games, music, multimedia books and magazines, and provide dating agencies, home shopping, and banking facilities over the Internet.

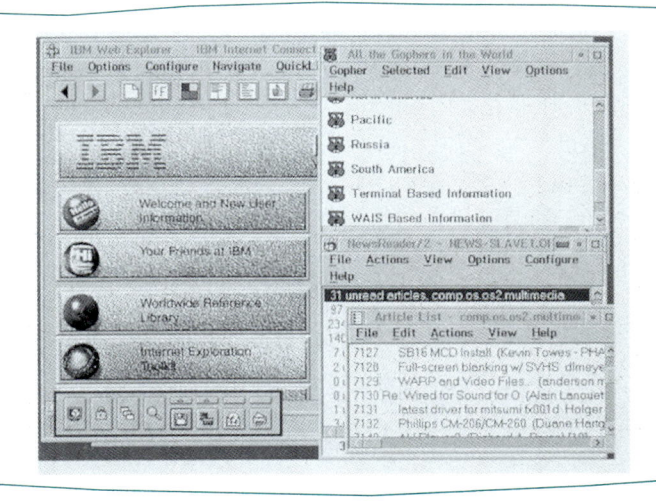

265

Mail order catalogues

- **TV and radio sales:** an increasing number of mail-order adverts are appearing on TV and radio with the benefit of sound and vision. With a growing number of commercial radio stations and cable or satellite TV channels, the cost of advertising via these media has fallen.

- **Mail-order catalogues:** companies such as Littlewoods and Kays which operate mail-order catalogues are simply large wholesalers who deal direct with the general public, splitting bulk into individual items, and allowing the consumer to pay in instalments. The cost of credit and home delivery, which can often take up to 4 weeks, tends to be reflected in higher prices. As a result, the importance of mail-order catalogues in total sales has declined in recent years.

- **Personal selling:** this involves personal contact with the consumer by company sales representatives, either over the phone (telesales), or face-to-face at meetings and 'on the doorstep'. Experienced sales teams can explain how the product works, give demonstrations, and tailor their marketing approach to suit the individual requirements of each consumer. However, personal contact can be expensive, and often consumers react adversely to 'doorstep' sales or being bothered on the phone.

Personal selling is not always welcomed by consumers

- **Pyramid selling:** this system is used successfully by a number of companies, notably the American company Amway, who produce a wide range of products including soap, jewellery, and perfumes from their factories in the USA. These products are sold directly to consumers in many countries, including the UK.

The principle of pyramid selling is that individuals agree to make regular purchases of a company's products to sell on to other consumers - often their family and friends - in their spare time. At the same time, each new salesperson aims to recruit others who are willing to buy products in bulk from them, in order to sell on to other consumers. The incentive to recruit new salespeople is that the person recruiting will earn a percentage of the sales they make. Clearly, the salesperson at the top of the pyramid stands to make the most money by earning a percentage of the sales of each person below him or her.

Salespeople at the bottom of the pyramid often make little money, as people are not always willing to buy products such as cleaning liquids and soaps in bulk for their own use, and on a regular basis - especially from companies they do not know. Selling to friends and family can also be awkward. The result is that the goods bought by sales recruits to sell on to other consumers often remain their own!

▼ *Figure 11.3: How pyramid selling works*

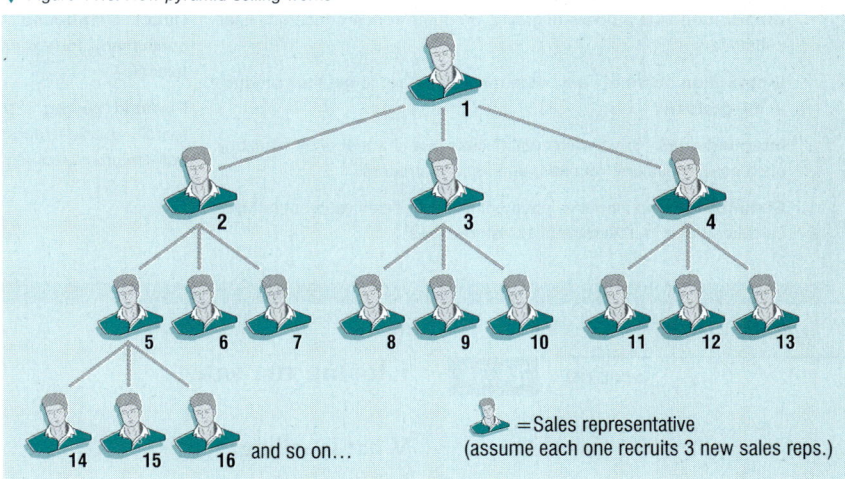

= Sales representative (assume each one recruits 3 new sales reps.)

Portfolio Activity 11.2

Range: Direct and indirect sales methods
Skills: Collect and record data

1. What channels of distribution and sales methods would you use for the following products? Explain your reasons:

   a) Life insurance
   b) Crude oil
   c) Ice cream
   d) Computers
   e) Hamburgers
   f) Furniture
   g) Real ale
   h) Farm tools

2. Undertake research to find out how these commodities are distributed and sold by real-life organizations.

3. Investigate the distribution channel(s) used by an organization of your choice. For example, if you choose a retail outlet, follow the channel back to the manufacturers of the various products sold. If the organization manufactures goods, follow the distribution channel forwards to the final consumer.

Physical distribution

Whatever the channel used to sell a product to the final consumer, most will require movement of goods from one place to another using various modes of transport. Firms will need to consider the relative costs of transport by road, rail, sea, or air, against the speed and possibility of damage, or deterioration of goods. For example, transport by air is very expensive for bulky items, but is a fast method of transporting smaller items over long distances, especially overseas.

Risk of damage to fragile products can be reduced by using packaging materials, while refrigeration units can be used to transport perishable products such as meats and vegetables.

Some large organizations have their own vehicle fleets to transport goods by road within the UK. Distribution facilities are also provided by a large number of private operators such as DHL and TNT, who are willing to guarantee delivery times to their customers.

> **Key words**
>
> **Distribution** - the process of getting products from producers to final consumers
>
> **Distribution channel** - any route taken by a firm to get their product to the customer
>
> **Intermediaries** - firms which act as links in a channel of distribution, such as wholesalers, retailers, agents, and brokers
>
> **Commission** - an incentive payment made to sales representatives, calculated as a percentage of sales revenues
>
> **Direct distribution** - methods of distributing products direct to consumers, for example, by mail order, TV and radio adverts, or telesales
>
> **Pyramid selling** - a method of selling direct to consumers by recruiting sales representatives who are willing to buy products in bulk before personally selling them on to the final consumer

Section 11.3 Closing the sale

What is selling?

Selling can be defined as a personal communication to a customer to make a sale. This contrasts with marketing communications, such advertising, which are not personalized (see 10.2).

Selling is the final link in the distribution chain and is vital for the success of a business. Market research, product development, pricing, and promotion strategies will all have been wasted if an organization cannot 'close the sale'.

Sales communications methods

Producers of goods or services who distribute them directly to the final consumer rely heavily on the skills and efforts of their sales teams to generate sales revenues. If distribution is through an intermediary, then each organization must rely on the sales efforts of every organization in the channel to work towards expanding sales.

Poor sales from one organization will feedback through a distribution channel. For example, if a retail outlet is unable to sell its stock of chocolate bars, it will reduce its order for them from the wholesaler. As stocks build up, the wholesaler will reduce its order from the manufacturer of the chocolate bar. Eventually the manufacturer may take the decision to reduce production and either switch resources to another item, or axe the product altogether.

If sales teams in each organization involved in a channel of distribution are to be effective in making and expanding sales, they will need to be fully informed of product details, new lines, discounts offered, and the various selling techniques they can use to make a sale. The objective of various sales communications methods is to do just that: to inform and motivate sales teams to generate sales.

Sales communication methods include:

- **Sales campaigns:** these can be used to promote an individual product or the product range of a particular manufacturer. A campaign may be agreed between the manufacturer, wholesalers, retailers, and agents in a distribution chain. The sales forces within these organizations will promote the product vigorously, offering price discounts for bulk orders, and distributing promotional materials such as posters, leaflets, or even free gifts and samples to give away. The campaign will also usually be supported by heavy advertising on TV and through other media, such as newspapers and magazines.

- **Sales conferences:** these can either be internal to an organization or, more likely, will involve sales staff from different organizations sharing a common interest in the promotion of a particular product. New product developments and sales techniques can be discussed in lectures and seminars.

- **Sales meetings:** these are internal meetings of sales teams, often from different regions, used to discuss sales performance and set targets for improvement. Meetings may be confined to regional managers of sales teams who will then 'cascade' with their sales teams (see 6.2). Pyramid selling relies heavily on sales meetings, with outsiders often being invited in an attempt to recruit them into the sales teams.

- **Sales letters and memos:** these can be sent out to sales teams on a regular basis to update staff on sales performance, provide product information, news of price discounts and new product lines, sales campaigns, future conferences, and meetings.

- **Trade fairs and exhibitions:** often combined with sales conferences, these are used primarily to promote products directly to consumers - especially to industrial buyers. They are also a useful forum for sales teams from different organizations to investigate rival products and discuss selling techniques. Technical staff will be on hand to demonstrate products and gauge consumer reaction. Well-known examples include the Stitching and Knitting Show, the Motor Show, the Ideal Home Exhibition, and Confex, a trade fair to advertise the services of firms who specialize in the organization and design of exhibitions, stands and advertising.

▼ *Delegates attending sales conferences are keen to learn about new products, promotional strategies, and selling techniques.*

Portfolio Activity 11.3

Range: Sales campaign methods
Skills: Collect and record data

Investigate trade fairs - both national and international - for the following products:
- Computer games
- Military hardware
- Motor cars
- Boats
- Musical instruments
- Two products of your choice

Useful sources of information on trade fairs and exhibitions can be found in specialist magazines and the *Financial Times*.

Advanced Business

The role and responsibilities of sales staff

The quality of sales staff is of vital importance in the marketing mix (see 8.3). Despite heavy investment of time and money in product development, pricing strategies, advertising, and other promotional methods, no organization will succeed in the marketplace if sales staff fail to carry out their duties adequately.

Sales staff in retail outlets or those involved in telesales or door-to-door selling are no longer expected simply to operate tills, telephones, or give product demonstrations. The duties and responsibilities of sales staff are expanding, and training is essential if they are to perform these well. However, training is often overlooked or poorly designed.

Customer care is top priority

London Transport's new chairman Peter Ford is putting customer care at the head of his agenda.

"People can talk about infrastructure. They can talk about equipment. Certainly these things are important, but I think that the single thing that has the biggest impact on the public is their perceived attitude of the staff."

London Direct No.11, October 1994

Portfolio Activity 11.4

Range: Responsibilities of sales persons
Skills: Collect and record data

1. Visit a retail outlet of your choice and observe various sales staff in operation. Make a note of the tasks they are required to perform and how customers benefit from them.

2. Now examine the duties and responsibilities of sales staff who sell products or services directly to consumers over the telephone. Arrange to phone the sales department in an organization of your choice. Ask the sales assistant if they would mind answering a few quick and simple questions about their duties and responsibilities to help you with your project. Have your questions prepared and make a note of their answers.

3. From your notes compiled in Questions 1 and 2, draw up a list, with explanations, of the main duties and responsibilities of sales staff in general.

The main duties and responsibilities of sales staff are to provide:

- **Customer care.** Looking after a customer while they make up their mind is important if they are not to feel rushed into a decision. This could involve helping them try on garments in a shop, giving them a cup of tea and somewhere to sit while they wait at the hairdresser's, or just giving them time to browse without interrupting. Looking after the customer in a helpful, friendly, and caring way increases the chance they will purchase from the organization and remain loyal to it in the future.

- **Point-of-sale service.** This can be as simple as placing shopping in carrier bags for customers, providing product information, or checking that electrical goods work properly before they leave the shop.

- **Product knowledge.** Few consumers have the ability or time to investigate the full range of products available. For example, products such as computers and camcorders are technically very complex, and many are imported from overseas where product standards may differ. Customers will often rely on sales staff, either in a shop or on the telephone direct to the manufacturer, to provide them with technical details of product performance, and to recommend best buys. They will be disappointed if staff are unable to give these details and may go to another organization to make their purchase.

- **Sales information and help.** This can involve providing information on product lines, how to order goods or services, and credit facilities available, or simply pointing out where customers can find the product they are looking for in a shop.

- **Taking payments and giving refunds.** Consumers can now make payment for their purchases in an increasing number of ways. These include cash, cheque, credit card, store cards, direct debit cards such as SWITCH or CONNECT, by credit note issued by the organization against a returned product, and money-off vouchers (see 19.4). Sales staff must know the procedure for accepting different methods of payments and processing - for example, what documentation is required, what information from a credit, debit, or store card is needed, and how the payment method is to be authorized.

▼ *Figure 11.4: Accepting payment by credit card.*

1. Sales assistant checks card number against published list of stolen or missing cards.

2. Card is 'wiped' through electronic till point or manual device to transfer impression of raised numbers on the card onto an issued document. Different cards may require different documents.

3. If manual method is used, the assistant must fill in purchase details on the document and phone the credit card company to obtain clearance for the amount of the purchase.

4. Sales assistant notes clearance code number issued by the credit card company on the document.

5. Customer signs till receipt or card purchase document.

6. Sales assistant checks signature on card with signature on receipt.

- **After-sales service.** A useful way to promote customer loyalty and repeat purchases is to follow up the purchase with after-sales care. This is especially important when the customer has received a service or personalized product, such as carpet cleaning, or double-glazing. A follow-up telephone call or personal visit can establish if the customer is satisfied, or what can be done to overcome any dissatisfaction they may have.

    After-sales service also extends to providing replacement items, spare parts, technical advice, or arranging repairs. Customers need to have confidence that they can find help if anything goes wrong. Organizations that fail to provide this kind of help will soon lose out to rival firms that do offer after-sales care.

▼ *Sales staff must know the requirements of the Sale of Goods Act*

- **Knowledge of Consumer Protection laws.** A number of laws and regulations have been passed by the UK government to protect the consumer from misleading claims and practices by producers. Failure to comply with these laws may involve a company in expensive legal actions. Sales staff must be aware of the requirements of two laws in particular, the **Sale of Goods Act** and the **Trade Descriptions Act** (*see below*).

Consumer Protection Laws

Weights and Measures Act 1963

Pre-packaged products must display the weight or volume of the contents. This Act makes it an offence not to disclose this information and to sell short measures. Certain products must be sold in fixed amounts - for example, milk can only be sold in pints or litres.

Trade Descriptions Act 1968

This Act makes it an offence to mislead consumers in advertising. Descriptions of goods and services must be accurate and must not make false claims. The Act makes it illegal to claim that a good is in a 'sale' unless it has been sold at the higher price for 28 consecutive days in the last 6 months.

Consumer Credit Act 1974

This protects consumers when they buy goods or services on credit, such as hire purchase. For example, credit brokers must obtain a license, provide a copy of any credit agreement to the consumer, always be truthful, and not charge exorbitant interest rates. Advertisements for credit must state the annual percentage rate of interest (APR).

Sale of Goods Act 1979

This has three main parts:

i   Goods must be of merchantable quality - that is, not be damaged, broken, or flawed in any way.

ii Goods must be fit for the purpose they were made for, and this must be made known by the seller. For example, if you ask for trousers that can be machine-washed, a shop cannot sell you trousers that can only be dry-cleaned under the pretence they are machine-washable.

iii Goods must fit the description given of them. For example, if a box of matches is said to contain 250 matches, then it should not contain any less.

If any of these conditions are broken, the shopkeeper must either provide a satisfactory replacement, or refund the consumer's money.

Consumer Protection Act 1987

Under this Act it is a criminal offence for producers to supply goods which are unsafe. The Act also lays down rules governing the use of such terms as 'sales price', 'reduced price' and 'bargain offer'. Prices advertised in this way must be genuine reductions.

Food Safety Act 1990

The main purpose of this Act is to ensure that all food and drugs on sale are pure and wholesome. The Act states that all food must be prepared and sold in hygienic conditions. Prepacked foods must display a list of ingredients, and advertising must not mislead consumers about the nature of the food and drugs.

- **Feedback.** Sales staff are often the 'eyes and ears' in the market for goods and services. They can provide valuable market information on changing customer wants, willingness to pay, and perceptions of products and corporate image.

Sales administration

One of the main responsibilities of sales staff is to ensure that the **administration** and **processing** of sales is quick and cost-effective (see 18.3). Customers will soon become dissatisfied if staff are slow to process their orders or arrange credit, and poor sales administration can lead to higher costs and lower sales.

With the increasing use of computerized administrative procedures, processing nowadays can be considerably easier and quicker, but sales staff need to have the right training. Sales procedures include:

- **Processing orders.** This involves receiving orders for goods or services over the counter, by phone or fax; checking the order against stock; advising the customer of availability, prices, acceptable methods of payment, and delivery dates, and entering this information on computer or paper records.

- **Credit clearance and control.** Increasingly, both organizations and private individuals are making payments on credit extended to them either by the organization from which they are making a purchase, or from a credit card or loan company (see 22.2).

  Sales staff will be expected to administer and control the giving of credit. This will involve the following tasks:

  - Completing credit agreement documents
  - Checking the creditworthiness of a customer with the accounts department in the organization, credit card company, or bank
  - Establishing a credit limit for each customer based on feedback from the accounts department, credit card company, or bank
  - Sending out reminders for late payment
  - Chasing bad debts (see 18.2).

- **Processing customer accounts.** This will involve itemizing purchases on credit made by individual customers, adding up their total bills, sending out accounts, and receiving payments. As many of these tasks are now computerized, sales staff must make sure that the correct details of purchases are entered into the right accounts.

- **Working out delivery schedules based on priorities and routes.** Staff must ensure that deliveries are prompt, and that the right goods reach the right customers in good condition. Routes should be planned to minimize transport costs and travel time betwen different delivery addresses.

- **Maintaining security.** This concerns keeping records of customer names, addresses, payments and accounts confidential, as well as handling money securely.

- **Prospecting.** In many organizations, prospecting and investigating sales leads is done by telephone. Sales staff pick telephone numbers and phone potential customers to see if they are interested in purchasing a particular good or service. This is a popular method used by organizations selling advertising space in newspapers or magazines, and by double-glazing and home security firms.

However, prospecting can also be undertaken by sales staff in shops. Many customers enter shops to browse, not knowing exactly what they want. A sales assistant can offer help and advice, and in so doing, promote various products to customers in the hope of making a sale. A good salesperson will learn to recognize a **buying signal** that suggests a customer is happy with the hard or soft 'sell'.

Improving customer relations at BT

Customer relations

Before the computerised Customer Services System (CSS) was introduced, each department in BT held its own customer records. Dealing with so many departments was frustrating for the customer, and it was time-consuming and expensive for BT to gather nearly thirty pieces of information from separate sources in order to make up each customer's bill.

CSS saves time, money, and customers' temper by bringing together all the separate customer services 'under one roof'. The customer now deals with one department instead of several, and all BT's billing information is held in a single computer system.

What CSS does

Using CSS, it is possible to:
- give an account number to a new customer, and check with a credit agency that the customer has no bad debts;
- place an order for telephone equipment (the CSS database automatically checks that this equipment is in stock, and re-orders when the stock falls below an agreed level);
- arrange for a phone line to be installed at a date and time to suit the customer (this information is automatically displayed at the engineer's workplace);
- answer customers' enquiries about their bills — for example, giving a comparison of this quarter's bill with the same quarter last year;
- run tests to diagnose obvious faults on a customer's line.

CSS holds information about 25 million BT telephone lines.

Key words

Selling - a personal communication to a customer to make a sale.

Sales communications - methods used to inform and motivate sales staff, including sales meetings, conferences, and memos

Further reading
Johnson, N: *How to Sell More* (Kogan Page 1994)

Test questions

The following underpinning knowledge will be tested:

1. Direct and indirect sales methods and how they meet the needs of customers and organizations
2. Sales campaign methods
3. Responsibilities of sales persons
4. The importance of effective sales administration
5. Evaluate customer service in terms of the needs of customers and organizations

1 A direct sales method that can be used by a producer is:
- A Selling direct to retailers
- B Placing mail order adverts in magazines
- C Using persuasive TV advertising
- D Employing agents to sell products direct to consumers

2 Duties and responsibilities of sales staff in an organization are likely to include all of the following EXCEPT:
- A Providing product information
- B After-sales care
- C Making repairs
- D Giving refunds

3 Which of the following is an indirect sales method?
- A Factory sales
- B Using wholesalers
- C Door-to-door selling
- D Pyramid selling

Questions 4-6 share the following answer options:
- A Information
- B Refund
- C Product demonstration
- D Spare parts

Which of the above customer needs could be satisfied by the following customer services?

4 A technical telephone 'hotline'

5 An after-sales service department

6 Point-of-sale services

7 Which of the following Acts protects the consumer from false claims made about products?
- A Sale of Goods Act
- B Weights and Measures Act
- C Trademark Act
- D Trade Descriptions Act

8 Sales staff may be expected to undertake the following administrative tasks EXCEPT:
- A Analysing the results of market research
- B Processing orders and organizing deliveries
- C Credit clearance and credit control
- D Prospecting

9 Which of the following is an indirect method of distribution?
- A Pyramid selling
- B Mail order
- C Agent sales
- D Telesales

10 a. What is distribution, and why is it important?

b. What is a wholesaler?

c. Give two advantages to a manufacturer and a retail chain of using a wholesaler.

d. Suggest two reasons why wholesalers are declining in importance.

11 a. Suggest three needs customers have in making a purchase other than for the products they intend to buy.

b. Suggest and explain three services that sales staff in an organization will be expected to provide in order to meet the customer requirements you have listed in (a).

c. How would you evaluate the performance of an organization and its sales staff in meeting the needs of customers?

d. Outline two sales communications methods an organization could use to inform and motivate their sales staff.

12 a. What is an indirect distribution channel?

b. Explain the role of a wholesaler, retailer, and agent in an indirect distribution channel.

c. Suggest and describe three sales methods a manufacturer could use to distribute products direct to the final consumer.

d. What distribution channel and sales method would you advise the following organizations to use for their products. Give reasons for your recommendations.

 i A large firm selling industrial lasers to a worldwide market

 ii A small carpet cleaning firm serving a localized market

 iii A manufacturer of frozen foods

assessment assignment

Advanced Business

Assessment Assignment

Range: Needs of customers
Needs of organizations
Responsibilities of sales persons
Sales campaign methods
Sales administration
Direct and indirect sales methods
Customer service

Skills: **Communication**
Take part in discussions
Produce written material
Information Technology
Process information
Present information

Preparing a sales staff information and training manual

You work in the human resource department of a large and prestigious department store. The organization is placing increasing importance on the need for skilled and high-quality sales staff to promote sales and customer satisfaction.

Tasks

You have been asked to produce an information pack for new sales staff to explain their duties and responsibilities. The pack should be a well-presented document, produced using computer software. Photographs, video, and audio resources could also be included.

The structure of the information pack should be as follows:

1. A description of the nature and objectives of distribution and the various channels of distribution that exist. It is important to point out what direct and indirect sales methods the organization might use to support and complement the work of its sales staff. For example, the store may also operate a mail-order or phone-order service.

2. An explanation of the importance to the organization of meeting the requirements of customers, and what these requirements include.

3. An explanation of the main duties and responsibilities of the sales staff, and why it is important to perform them well.

4. A description of various sales communications methods the organization may use from time to time to help sales staff in their tasks.

5. A summary of the main administrative tasks staff will be expected to perform, and how new technology can help them.

6. An example to demonstrate the response of consumers to the sales efforts of an organization of your choice. For example, you can measure the success of sales efforts in terms of the image of the organization, sales volumes and values, and profits.

Once you have completed the information manual, you will be required to present its main messages at the next induction course for new sales staff (i.e. your class or group). Your presentation should last no longer than 10-20 minutes and can include video recordings and overhead slides.

This assignment requires you to investigate actual sales methods used in Department stores and other retail outlets before you produce your information pack. Alternatively complete the same tasks for any business organization of your choice

chapter 12

Human Resources

Unit Four

unit 4

chapter 12   Managing Human Resources (Element 4.1)
chapter 13   Job Roles and Change at Work (Elements 4.2)
chapter 14   Job Application and Interviews (Elements 4.3)

Advanced Business

chapter 12
Human Resource Management

This chapter investigates human resourcing and the rights and responsibilities of employees and employers in organizations.

> I TOLD YOU NOT TO BE LATE FOR WORK AGAIN!

Key ideas

The role of the **human resources function** is to secure the best performance possible from an organization's workforce, through **recruitment, training**, and **management of change**. In achieving this performance, human resource managers have a number of **legal and ethical responsibilities** towards their employees.

It is the role of the human resources department to monitor the **training** needs of the organization and the individual employee, and provide this training as and when required to develop employees to their full potential.

Training, **job security**, **regular consulation** with management, **performance related pay**, **job design** and **team working** approaches are important employee motivators.

Employees' rights and responsibilities include the right to **remuneration, good levels of health and safety at work**, and **employers' compliance with the terms and conditions of employment** as laid down in **contracts of employment**.

Employers' rights and responsibilities include the right to expect employees to comply with the terms and conditions of employment as set out in the contract of employment, and with **health and safety regulations**.

Employers are obliged by law to deduct **National Insurance contributions** and **income tax** under the PAYE system, to pay **pension contributions** for contracted workers, and to uphold a wide variety of laws relating to employment.

Trade Unions play an important part in protecting employees' rights. The human resources department often has to negotiate with union staff over pay and conditions of employment.

In the event of a **dispute** between employers and employees, both parties may refer for assistance to the **Advisory and Conciliation Service (ACAS)**, to **industrial tribunals**, the **High Court** or **European Court of Justice**, or to **Trade Unions** and **employers' associations**.

Section 12.1 Managing human resources

What is human resourcing?

The most valuable resource in any business organization is its people, or human resources. There is a direct relationship between the quality of the workforce and business success.

The purpose of **Human Resource Management (HRM)** is to ensure that the employees of an organization are used and developed in such a way that the employer obtains the greatest possible benefit from their abilities. In order to do this, human resource managers must give careful thought to the needs of their employees and the financial and psychological rewards that they receive from their work. The human resource manager must, therefore, work closely with other managers in other departments, including production, marketing, sales, finance, etc.

Human resources are much more difficult to manage than natural or man-made resources, partly because conflict can occur between the aims of the organization and those of their employees, and partly because there is increasingly a desire among employees to share in decision-making about their working environment.

The role and responsibilities of a human resources department

Within a small business, responsibility for Human Resource Management will rest with the owners. Most medium-to-large organizations, however, will have a whole specialist division of employees devoted to staff matters and welfare. It is the role of the **human resources department** (or **personnel** department) to manage human resources within an organization.

The functions of a human resources department are many, including:

- Forecasting future manpower and skill needs in the business.
- Recruitment and selection of staff with the right skills and experience for the job (see 14.1)
- Providing employment advice and information
- Notifying terms and conditions of employment to new employees
- Managing changes in the terms and conditions of existing workers, for example, due to the introduction of new technology, relocation, or internal reorganization (see 4.5)
- Developing and promoting induction courses and training for employees
- Handling staff promotions and transfers
- Developing and administering staff appraisal procedures
- Developing and administering grievance procedures to handle employee complaints
- Handling employee discipline and dismissal
- Implementing non-discriminatory legislation
- Implementing health and safety procedures

- Administering pay, non-financial rewards, and conditions of service, such as holiday entitlements and maternity pay
- Developing good industrial relations and employee consultation
- Taking part in negotiations with employees on pay and conditions and other aspects of their employment

▼ Recruitment

▼ Training

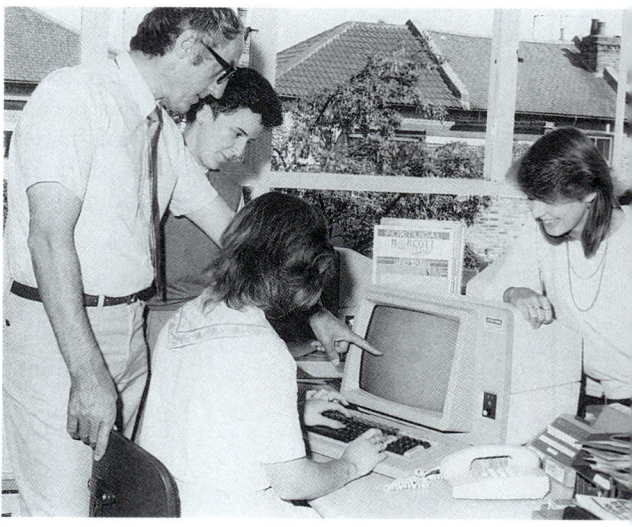

▼ Consultation

In general, the functions of a human resources department are concerned with:

- Using people to achieve the goals of the firm
- Protecting people
- Motivating people

All of these functions tend to be reinforcing: employees who lack motivation, are poorly trained or rarely consulted, and/or who perceive health risks due to poor environmental management at work, are unlikely to work as effectively as they could towards the achievement of organizational goals.

If employers are to get the best from their employees, they must consider their responsibilities to their staff. Some of these responsibilities are required legally, such as good health and safety procedures (see 12.3). Others are ethical and are part of being a good employer, such as giving employment advice and information, handling discipline and grievances in a fair and sympathetic manner, and consulting on a regular basis with employees or their representatives on matters of mutual concern.

UNIT FOUR

CHAPTER 12

Portfolio Activity 12.1

Range: Employer responsibilities, Methods for gaining employee co-operation
Skills: Read and respond to written material, Collect and record data, Take part in discussions

1. What key role might be suggested for a human resources department from the article?

2. Is the primary role of the human resource manager to manage workers' attitudes or to manage the attitudes and develop the skills of other managers? Explain your answer.

3. Investigate the role and responsibilities of the human resource function in an organization of your choice.

4. Arrange for a human resource manager in a medium-to-large organization in your local area to give a talk to your group on the tasks they are required to perform and their general role and responsibilities. Prepare a list of questions you would like him or her to answer after the talk

Silence isn't golden - Firms lose millions by not talking to staff

British business is losing millions of pounds every year because managers lack the basic skills to communicate with their staff.

Instead they push important issues into the shadows leaving problems to fester and making the workforce disillusioned and under-motivated.

Management expert David Hall has dubbed this the 'shadow side' of business.

"Basically it is all the things that don't get talked about in a formal setting," says Hall.

This could be the chairman giving himself an enormous pay rise, while freezing wages on the shop floor, or attempting to change the culture of the company by improving service and not training the staff properly to carry it out.

"It has an enormous impact on business. You are not going to win the hearts and minds of the workforce that way." says Hall.

Daily Mirror 21.9.94

Key words

Human Resource Management (HRM) - the use and development of employees in an organization in the most productive way in order to meet the goals of the organization.

Section **12.2** Investing in human resources

Training, motivating, and developing employees

An important function of the human resources department is to ensure that members of the workforce have the necessary skills to achieve the organization's objectives. It is important that the human resource function not only recruits the right staff, but that it also develops employees to their full potential through training, motivation, and job design.

281

Going back to school

When it comes to job loyalty, it might be a surprise to learn that money is not the number one issue. Instead recent surveys have shown that a happy working environment and good training are top of the list. Money only comes third.

One of the most effective ways of holding onto valued staff is not to give bigger and bigger bonuses but to train them. People want to be rewarded and developed, according to John Miskelly, managing director at JM Management Services.

While most new skills are learnt 'on the job', training reinforces what has been learnt and gives the individual concrete recognition of the skills he or she has gained.

Training increases the skills available within the company and can help it to achieve higher standards.

London Evening Standard 11.1.95

The need for training

Technological progress, changes in consumer wants, and competitive pressures in product markets mean that businesses must continually evaluate how they are organized and their needs for different skills. Training, therefore - whether for machine operatives, office or shop assistants, or managers - should be an ongoing process throughout an employee's career. It is the role of the human resources department to monitor the training needs of the organization and the individual employee, and to provide this training as and when required.

In general, the following training needs will arise within an organization over time:

- Organization of induction courses to introduce new employees to the goals and workings of the organization, and their particular jobs
- Improvement of the skills of existing workers to achieve higher levels of productivity and to reduce production costs
- Facilitation of the successful introduction of new equipment, products, and processes
- Reorganization of job roles and tasks within the organization
- Preparation of individual employees for promotion
- Raising employees' awareness of health and safety to reduce accidents
- Promotion of new skills among existing workers
- Creation of a flexible workforce with a wide variety of skills to adapt to change. This is known as **multi-skilling**.

For employees, training will lead to improved motivation simply because it allows staff to do their jobs better and because it raises confidence and improves promotion prospects.

From the employers' perspective, training may improve employee productivity and bring new ideas and working methods to a firm. Training can also improve health and safety procedures and so reduce accidents. It may also lead to a more positive attitude among workers and so reduce employee turnover (see also 17.2).

People as an asset

Increasingly, successful firms are recognizing that their staff are an asset to be invested in, rather than a cost to be minimized. Investment in this human capital through good induction, training, and career development are of as much benefit to particular businesses as they are to individual employees. This culture is best seen in the Investors In People Award, increasingly sought-after by firms as proof of their commitment to their staff.

Investors In People is a new national standard designed to help British business get the most from employees. Firms may apply to their local Training and Enterprise Council (TEC) to gain IAP status. In order to gain this status a firm must:

- Make a public commitment from the top to develop all employees to achieve its business objectives.
- Regularly review the training and development needs of all of its employees
- Take action to train and develop staff on recruitment and throughout their employment
- Regularly evaluate investment in training and development to assess achievement and improve future effectiveness.

Investors In People is designed to be more than a training initiative: it aims to install permanent systems for continuous improvement and sustained quality within the human resources management of an organization, so as to provide the basis for future business success.

INVESTORS IN PEOPLE

On-the-job training

Types of training

Training to develop work skills is often divided into **on-the-job** and **off-the-job** training. In both cases, instruction in matters of health and safety at work can be an important part of job-related training.

On-the-job training

When training is on-the-job, employees are trained while they are carrying out their normal duties at their place of work. This can take a number of forms:

- **Shadowing.** This is when a new worker is shown what to do by an experienced worker. It can vary from simply sitting next to a machine operator, to attending meetings with another office employee.

- **Coaching.** In the same way as athletes are coached, a trainee employee can be coached by an experienced worker

- **Job rotation.** This involves training employees to do different jobs over short periods of time, either in order for them to become multi-skilled, or simply to give them knowledge of the way in which the whole company functions. This is often an important element in the training of management trainees.

- **Apprenticeships.** Here, the training provided is normally sufficiently thorough to ensure that very little extra training would ever be necessary, apart from some occasional updating of worker skills and knowledge.

Off-the-job training

Off-the-job training involves employees attending courses and training programmes away from their normal jobs, such as:

- **In-house courses.** Some businesses run their own courses for employees. This will often be the case where skills to be taught are **business-specific**, for example, induction programmes for new employees, or when new production methods are introduced. Some large organizations, like banks and building societies, even have their own residential training centres or colleges offering a variety of courses run by specialist training officers.

- **External courses.** These may be with another employer or at a specialist training centre, or with a supplier of new equipment who is willing to train workers how to use it.

- **Vocational and professional courses.** Colleges, universities, and increasingly schools provide courses leading to vocational and professional qualifications which support what is learnt in the workplace. Vocational courses, such as **NVQs**, provide training in competencies or job-related skills. Professional courses, for example, in accountancy, engineering, or law are normally completed by university graduates entering these professions in order to develop their careers.

Was it worth it?

Training can be expensive. A good employer will evaluate the effectiveness of training courses for their workers to see if they have offered value for money. Key questions employers should ask are:

- What skills have workers acquired? For example, can they operate new machinery, implement health and safety procedures, build a brick wall?
- How has job performance or productivity improved?
- What do employees think about their training? Questionnaires at the end of courses can ask workers what they feel the training course has achieved, and how it could be improved.
- What are the benefits to the firm? Have business goals, such as increased profitability, improved customer relations, been achieved?

Evaluation is simple when the result of the training is clear - for example, if workers are now able to operate new machinery. But it is much more difficult when the benefits of training may only be revealed over a longer period of time, as in the case of improved management techniques or communication skills.

Portfolio Activity 12.2

Range: Employer responsibilities, Methods for gaining employee co-operation
Skills: Produce written material, Collect and record data

1. Investigate on-the-job and off-the-job training in the organization.

- What skills/qualifications do the employees need in the organization?
- What methods are used/courses available to train employees?
- What are the organization's immediate and potential future training needs?
- How is the organization responding to these needs?
- Does the organization keep a record of employee training and attendance on courses? What do these records show?
- What further opportunities for training could the organization make use of?

Draw up a short report on methods of training, benefits of training, and training needs in your chosen organization.

2. What other methods are used by the organization to motivate employees and gain their co-operation?

Motivating employees

Employees will need to gain the co-operation of their employees and motivate them towards the achievement of the goals of their organization. Workers who lack motivation will return lower levels of productivity and quality, and higher levels of costs. An important function for the human resources department, therefore, is to recognize the factors that can motivate workers to greater effort. Regular consultation with workers by management on business decisions that may affect them and development through training have already been discussed. However, workers can also be motivated by the sense of satisfaction they feel in their jobs, by working in teams and by financial rewards for their efforts.

Job design

Workers need interesting and varied job tasks, and a sense of responsibility and achievement in their work. These satisfying aspects of employees' work can be achieved through careful job design (see 15.5).

Designing jobs with workers' needs in mind can increase job satisfaction and improve productivity. Jobs can be enriched or expanded so that workers can be given more responsibility, undertake a wider variety of tasks, be more involved in decision-making, and have a greater sense of achievement. Innovations such as **Flexitime** may also improve job satisfaction. Flexitime allows workers to choose when to start and finish work, as long as they complete an agreed number of hours at work per week (see 13.3).

Team working

Research into successful firms indicates that they tend to adopt a team approach, with staff sharing common goals and a shared understanding of what needs to be done. Effective teamwork motivates workers by giving them the feeling that they are shaping their own jobs. Teams can also increase efficiency by eliminating layers of middle management whose job is simply to organize groups of individuals, when in fact teams of people working together can organize themselves (see 15.5).

One approach to team working is the formation of **quality circles**. These are simply groups of employees, usually between 6 and 12, who work for the same supervisor or line manager. Workers in each circle have the responsibility for organising and developing their own jobs. Circle members are usually trained in problem solving techniques. Each quality circle meets regularly to identify and discuss their work related problems and will pass on their findings and any solution to senior management.

Team-based production

Proctor and Gamble report that productivity is up to 40% higher in plants that use team-based production. The company argues that teams eliminate waste by reducing the number of managers. They also encourage innovation by involving the whole workforce in upgrading products and processes, and reduce errors by keeping people interested in their work.

Performance Related Pay (PRP)

PRP is a term used to describe systems that link the pay of workers to some measure of individual, group or organisation effort (see 15.4). For example, individual workers or teams may be rewarded with a pay bonus if they have increased the output or quality of their work. Workers may also participate in profit-sharing and share option schemes, whereby individual employees receive a reward in terms of cash or company shares, the size of which will normally depend on company profits. Because their shares will be worth more, the more profit their company makes, share options are an incentive to employees to work harder.

Key words

Multi-skilling - training employees in a wide variety of skills to increase labour force flexibility

Investors In People - a national standard in training and development designed to help British business get the most from staff

Quality circles - small groups of workers given the responsibility to organize and develop their own jobs

On-the-job training - training employees while they are carrying out their normal duties. It can involve coaching by experienced staff and apprenticeships.

Off-the-job training - training conducted away from the workplace through courses and internal or external training programmes. These can include vocational and professional training courses leading to recognized qualifications.

Performance related pay (PRP) – systems which link pay and other financial rewards to individual, group, or organizational efforts

Advanced Business

Section 12.3 The rights and responsibilities of employees and employers

Human resources managers need to be familiar with legislation regulating employment practices in business, and to make sure that these requirements are upheld. Failure to do so can be costly, both in terms of money, and also in terms of damaged reputation.

Employees' rights nowadays are enshrined in law, and good employers will want to treat their employees properly, not only because of the law, but also because this is ethical behaviour and leads to good labour relations. In return, employers will expect their employees to comply with employment laws, work towards the achievement of organizational goals, meet the needs of customers, and attain agreed standards of quality in their work.

Portfolio Activity 12.3

Range: Analyse, Employer and employee responsibilities
Skills: Understand and respond to written material

1. Using the article above and your own experience, explain why employment legislation is important and who is protected by it.
2. Investigate types of employment protection legislation and how their legal requirements are implemented in a medium-sized organization you are familiar with.

Sunday Working Rights for Shop Staff

New rights for shop workers to protect them from being compelled to work on Sundays are contained in the Sunday Trading Act. The Act, which applies in England and Wales, came into force in August 1994. It puts an end to existing anomalies and confusion surrounding Sunday trading and establishes clear enforceable laws with increased penalties for those who flout them.

The Act allows shops to trade in all goods on Sundays but restricts most larger shops to six hours trading. The conditions of the Act will be enforceable through industrial tribunals. It gives shop workers the right not to be dismissed, made redundant, or subjected to any other detriment for refusing to work on Sundays. Detriment could include, for example, non-payment of normal seniority bonuses, or discrimination in promotion or training opportunities.

With the exception of Sunday-only workers, these provisions apply to all employees required to work in a shop which is open for the serving of customers on a Sunday. They apply irrespective of age, length of service, or hours of work, and even if workers have previously agreed to a contract requiring Sunday trading.

Employment Gazette September 1994

Employee rights

The main statutory rights that the law gives to employees are outlined below:

- The right not to be discriminated against in recruitment or in employment on the grounds of race, sex, or marital status
- The right not to suffer unlawful deductions from pay
- The right to work in a safe and healthy environment
- The right to a written statement of the main terms and conditions of employment
- The right to itemized pay statements
- The right to return to work after illness or maternity leave

- The right not to be discriminated against on grounds of Trade Union membership
- The right of women to receive equal pay with men for work of equal value
- The right of women to a minimum 14 weeks maternity leave, reasonable time off for ante-natal care, and to receive statutory maternity pay (SMP)
- The right to receive statutory sick pay (SSP) during illness
- The right not to be unfairly dismissed
- The right to a written statement of dismissal
- The right to time off work for public duties - for example, jury service
- The right to redundancy payments after two years of continuous service
- The right to time off to look for work or arrange training in a redundancy situation

Both full-time and part-time employees in the UK today have the same statutory rights. This has not always been the case. Prior to 1995 part-time employees working between 8 and 16 hours per week only qualified for the rights in the first half of the list above. They had to complete five years continuous service before they qualified for all the same employment rights as full-time workers, who qualified after two years. Part-time employees working less than 8 hours never qualified. With effect from the 6th February 1995, all hours-of-work thresholds were removed from employment protection legislation.

The legal obligations of employers

Legislation relating to employment provides rights for both employees and their employers. Broadly, the laws governing employment provide protection at each stage of a person's working life, including:

- Recruitment and selection
- The contract of employment
- Sickness, injury, and maternity or paternity leave
- The payment of wages and salaries
- Health and safety in the workplace
- Discipline and dismissal
- Redundancy and retirement

Recruitment and selection
The purpose of recruitment and selection in an organization is to match suitable job applicants with identified job vacancies (see 14.1). The role of the human resources department is to oversee the various stages involved in the process of staff recruitment and selection, and to ensure that all legal requirements are fulfilled.

The main legislation covering recruitment and selection is as follows:

- **The Disabled Persons (Employment) Acts 1944/1958** require employers with 20 or more full-time employees to employ sufficient registered disabled people to make up 3% of their total workforce. In addition, certain jobs, such as car park attendants, should be reserved for disabled people.

- **The Race Relations Act 1976** states that it is illegal for an employer to discriminate on grounds of colour, race, or ethnic origin in employment, education, training, and the provision of housing and other services.

- **The Sex Discrimination Acts 1975/1986** make it illegal to discriminate against a person on grounds of sex or marital status, whether in job adverts, interviews, selection, training, promotion, dismissal, or terms of employment. The 1986 Act also removed restrictions on the hours women could work each week.

If employees feel that they have been discriminated against, they can take their case to an **industrial tribunal** (see 12.4). They can also ask for the help of the **Equal Opportunities Commission (EOC)**, a government body set up in 1975 with the following aims:

- To promote equal opportunities through codes of good practice
- To investigate complaints of discrimination
- To provide legal advice and financial help when a case goes to court or industrial tribunal
- To monitor the pay gap between men and women
- To review the Equal Pay Act
- To issue notices preventing an organization from discriminating

Although not required to do so in law, many firms have devised and operate their own equal opportunities policies which actively seek to remove discrimination in the selection, pay, training, and career opportunities of their workers. Leading public- and private-sector organizations, such as Rank Xerox, Shell UK, British Airways, the BBC, and government departments, have all adopted these type of policies.

Equal Opportunities at the BBC

'Women should be given the opportunity to prove themselves. Since joining the BBC five years ago I've had training in all aspects of technical production, camerawork, cameras, vision operation, sound recording and graphics.'

Nichola Wood,
BBC television operator.

The BBC is committed to equal opportunites for all, irrespective of race, colour, creed, ethnic or national origins, gender, marital status, sexuality, disability or age.

We are committed to taking positive action to promote such equality of opportunity and our recruitment, training and promotion procedures are based on the requirements of a job.

In this policy the BBC include staff whether full time, part time or temporary, and any person who acts as an agent on behalf of the BBC in employment

Taken from 1992-1993 Annual Report of the BBC Television Equal Opportunities Department

Potential costs of equal opportunities	Potential benefits of equal opportunities
• Equal pay can mean higher wage costs	• If everyone has an equal chance of selection, employers are more likely to choose the best person for the job
• Higher wage bills may force firms to cut the number of jobs	• Workers may become more highly motivated if their chances of promotion and/or financial rewards are more equal
• Additional facilities may be required at additional expense, for example, childcare centres, ramps for wheelchairs, etc.	• Improved image may attract higher-quality employees
• Recruitment policies need to be redesigned	• Increased labour flexibility. Evidence suggests that women tend to prefer part-time work, etc. This enables firms to match staffing levels more easily to fluctuations in the pattern of consumer demand

Portfolio Activity 12.4

Range: Employer responsibilities, Analyse
Skills: Read and respond to written material, Collect and record data

Read the article below.

ENGINEERING CHANGE

"WE RECOGNISE that women are a vital part of the workforce. The perspective and style they bring to managerial work contributes significantly to improved performance. Therefore, it makes good business sense to attract and retain our share of all available talent and remove barriers which prevent women realising their full potential."

So says Sir Anthony Gill, chairman of multinational engineering firm Lucas Industries, explaining why he initiated the 'Woman in Lucas Project'.

Of Lucas' 25,000 workforce in the UK, just under a third are women. The majority work in light assembly work, with a much smaller number in professional and managerial positions – a situation which is typical of the engineering industry as a whole.

But far from neglecting its female staff, Lucas has recognised the need to adapt to changing patterns in the labour force.

In 1990 the company launched the 'Women in Lucas Project' based on the findings of a thorough investigation of the situation inside and outside the company.

This produced interesting insights into women's experience of working for Lucas. For example, only half of the sample expected to stay long-term within Lucas – giving a lack of prospects as the main reason for leaving.

Gathering all the information together, Lucas then drew up proposals for action. These are now being developed through the 'Women in Lucas Project', which includes moves to:

- introduce career development programmes for women;
- examine recruitment and selection criteria;
- develop flexible working, maternity and childcare support;
- liaise with schools to promote engineering as a career for girls.

'When I joined Lucas, I felt I had to prove myself as a woman in a predominately male world, but the intensive training and the opportunity to assume responsibility soon helped my build up my confidence.'

Swati Shah, manufacturing systems.

Employment Gazette Feb 93

1. Suggest four ways in which women may have been discriminated against in the engineering industry.
2. Why do you think some firms might discriminate against women and other groups of workers?
3. Lucas Industries has suggested that 'women are a vital part of their workforce'. Explain why they hold this view.
4. Explain how Lucas developed its own equal opportunities policy.
5. What methods are being used by Lucas to promote greater equality in employment? Suggest possible costs and benefits.
6. Obtain a copy of the equal opportunities policy statement for an organization with which you are familiar. Identify ways in which the organization has implemented their policy. Consider the advantages and disadvantages of the policy, and how it might be improved if necessary.

Alternatively...

If your chosen organization does not have an equal opportunities policy, find out if they have plans to introduce one, and why. Prepare a draft policy statement for the organization to discuss with personnel staff, and suggest ways in which they might implement the policy in terms of staff recruitment, pay, training, career development, etc.

The contract of employment

Employers are required to provide both full-time and part-time workers with a 'written statement of their terms and conditions of employment' within 13 weeks of their starting a job.

A **contract of employment** is drawn up by the employer and signed by the employee. It is a legally binding agreement between them and can be enforced by law. A contract can contain any details, but as a minimum it must contain the following:

- The name of employer and employee
- The date on which employment started
- Their job title
- Rates of pay, payment intervals, and method of payment
- Normal hours of work and related conditions, such as meal breaks
- Holiday entitlement, holiday pay, and public holidays
- Conditions relating to sickness, injury, and maternity pay
- Pension arrangements
- Length of notice to quit to and from employee
- Disciplinary rules and procedures
- Arrangements for handling employee grievances
- Other conditions including those relating to Trade Union membership, the need for confidentiality, and working at different locations, etc.

All of the above are called the **expressed terms** of the contract, that is, terms which are openly agreed between employer and employee. Because the range of expressed terms can be enormous, some organizations will not provide full written details in a contract, but will instead direct employees to company handbooks and other documents setting out company rules and policies.

In addition, there will be unwritten **implied terms** which are assumed to be part of a contract. For example, employees will be expected to work towards the achievement of organizational goals, and to produce work to a minimum quality standard. Both employer and employee are expected to be trustworthy, to act in good faith, and to exercise due care to ensure health and safety in the workplace.

The contract of employment is a legally binding agreement on both the employer and the employee, and both parties may reasonably expect the other to work to the terms and conditions agreed in the contract.

The payment of wages and salaries

Wage protection is provided by the **Wages Act 1986**. This sets out conditions for payments to workers, excluding redundancy payments, expenses or loans, and deductions.

Deductions made from wages by employers covered by the Act include:

- Deductions of income tax under the pay-as-you-earn (PAYE) system and National Insurance contributions

- Those displayed in the employment contract, such as contributions to a company pension scheme

- Those agreed by the worker in writing, such as Trade Union membership payments and season ticket loan repayments

Wage protection is also covered by the **Equal Pay Acts of 1970/1983**. These state that an employee doing the same or broadly similar work to a member of the opposite sex in the same organization is entitled to the same rates of pay and conditions - for example, in relation to duties, holidays, overtime, and hours. The 1983 amendment allowed female employees to claim equal pay for work of 'equal value' to that done by a man, in terms of the efforts, skills, and decisions demanded of the employee.

Health and safety

There are a number of specific laws relating to health and safety in factories, offices and shops, and railway stations. However, the main requirements are embodied in the **Health and Safety at Work Act 1974**, which requires employers to 'ensure as far as is reasonably practicable, the health, safety, and welfare at work of all staff' (see also 15.6).

The Act requires that:

- Firms provide all necessary safety equipment and clothing free of charge and ensure a safe working environment

- Union-appointed representatives should have the right to inspect the workplace and investigate the causes of any accidents.

It further requires employees to take reasonable care to avoid injury to themselves or to others by their work activities, and to cooperate with employers and others in meeting statutory requirements. It also states that employees should not interfere with or avoid anything provided to protect their health, safety, or welfare.

The Act is enforced by the **Health and Safety Executive (HSE)** set up by the government. Inspectors appointed by the HSE have the power to enter and inspect workplaces. Legally binding improvement orders can be issued, and in some cases prohibition orders which require the immediate cessation of an unsafe practice or process. The HSE also issues codes of good practice to employers.

> **The Health and Safety 'Six Pack'**
>
> Sweeping new health and safety regulations came into force in the UK in January 1993 to fulfil European Union directives. The regulations cover:
>
> - **Management** - the assessment of risks, the planning, organization, control, and monitoring of health and safety at work, and setting up of emergency procedures
> - **Provision and use of work equipment** - suitability of equipment, employee training, and regular maintenance
> - **Manual handling operations** - assessment of hazardous operations, correct procedures especially for heavy loads, training if necessary
> - **Workplace conditions** - ventilation, temperature, lighting, toilets, washing facilities, canteens, rest areas, clear passageways, ability to open/close windows, etc
> - **Personal protective equipment** - must be provided, maintained and stored correctly, employees to be instructed/trained in use
> - **Display screen equipment** - workstations must be assessed for risks, comply with minimum standards; employees to receive free eye-tests, rest periods and training
>
> Most of the above regulations simply tidied up and clarified existing legal requirements.

Disciplinary and dismissal procedures

An important function of any human resource department is to outline and operate the **disciplinary procedure**. This is the process whereby employees may be disciplined for failing to meet the terms of their contract.

A disciplinary procedure usually involves a series of steps: a verbal warning; a written warning, if the offence persists; a final written warning

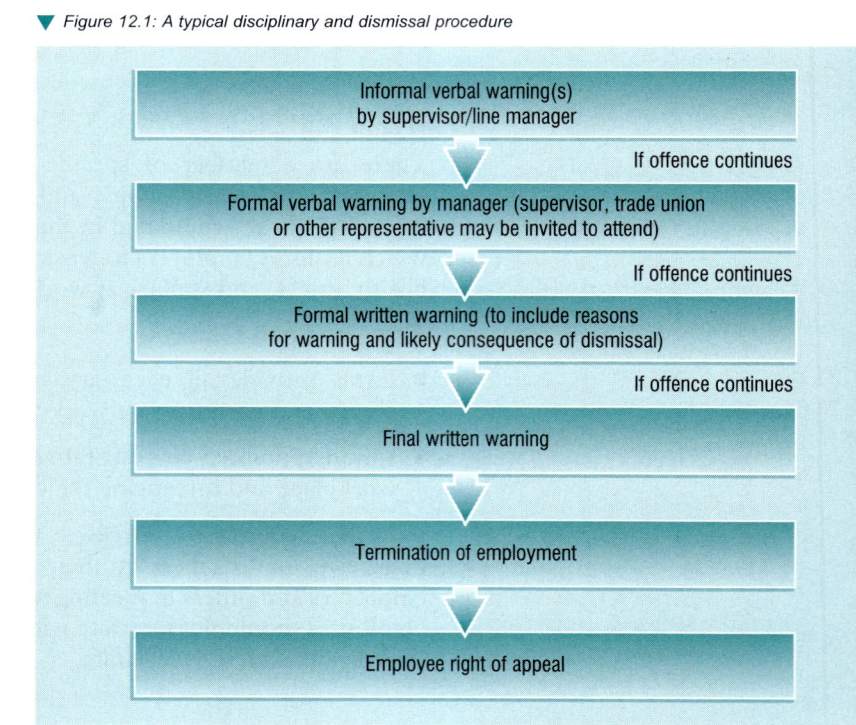

▼ *Figure 12.1: A typical disciplinary and dismissal procedure*

Informal verbal warning(s) by supervisor/line manager
↓ *If offence continues*
Formal verbal warning by manager (supervisor, trade union or other representative may be invited to attend)
↓ *If offence continues*
Formal written warning (to include reasons for warning and likely consequence of dismissal)
↓ *If offence continues*
Final written warning
↓
Termination of employment
↓
Employee right of appeal

and dismissal (if the final written warning is made within twelve months of the first). Alternatively, in the event of a serious breach of company rules (such as theft, or deliberate and dangerous contravention of health and safety rules), an employee may be suspended or dismissed immediately. The employee should be given the right to appeal and independent assessment at any stage in the disciplinary procedure.

Terminating employment

A contract of employment will end when an employee leaves for another job after an agreed period of notice has been given, or if s/he retires, dies, or is dismissed.

Under the **Employment Act 1980**, there are five reasons for dismissal which are considered 'fair' and legal:

- **Redundancy** - when employees are surplus to requirements, possibly due to a decline in business, the introduction of new technology, or structural reorganization. Employees have the right to receive compensation for redundancy, based on their length of service and level of wages.

- **Gross misconduct** - i.e. theft, fraud, wilful disobedience, or negligence which involves a breach of contract

- **Incompetence** - when the worker is clearly not able to do their job and has produced sub-standard work

- **If continued employment contravenes laws** - for example, if a heavy goods vehicle driver has been banned for drink driving

- **Substantive other reasons** - e.g. refusal to accept changes in working practices

---

Key words

Contract of employment - a legal agreement which sets out the terms and conditions of a particular job, and both employers' and employees' responsibilities.

Equal Opportunities Commission - a government body set up to promote equal opportunities through codes of good practice and enforce laws designed to protect employees and potential employees from discrimination on grounds of race, sex, colour, religion, or disability

Health and Safety Executive - government body which enforces health and safety legislation in the workplace

Disciplinary procedure - a set of formal rules and methods governing the disciplining of employees who breach their contract, involving verbal and written warnings and a right of appeal

Redundancy - legal termination of employment, following consultation, when employees are surplus to requirements

---

Section **12.4**

What happens when legislation is not upheld?

Grievance procedures

In any organization, it is the role of human resources management to set out a **grievance procedure** for resolving disputes between employees and management. This a formal means whereby an employee, or his or her representatives, can raise a complaint about his or her treatment or conditions of work.

In some cases complaints can be relatively minor - for example, a lack of clean towels in the toilets, or an absence of vegetarian meals in the canteen. More serious are complaints over possible breaches of the law - for example, employers failing to supply a written contract of employment; refusing to promote an employee on racial grounds; neglecting to provide adequate training to use new machinery, or failing to install proper ventilation on a factory shop floor.

Grievances should be discussed freely with senior managers, and either a compromise position reached, or, in the case of clear breaches of law, necessary changes made. However, if legislation concerning discrimination, contracts of employment, health and safety, unfair dismissal, and redundancy has been broken, then aggrieved parties can seek redress through external organizations.

Portfolio Activity 12.5

Range: Employer responsibilities, Procedures for employees
Skills: Collect and record data, Produce written material

Investigate the grievance, disciplinary, and appeals procedures of a medium-sized organization (over 25 employees) of your choice. Draw a flowchart to illustrate the various stages in these procedures. How effective are the procedures?

What further action can the employee take if they fail to produce a satisfactory outcome through existing channels?

Unfair dismissal

The most common grievance against employers is unfair dismissal. This is defined in law as follows:

- Where employers have failed to give the required period of notice as set out in the contract of employment in the case of redundancy
- Where employees have been dismissed for going on strike, while others who have done the same have not been dismissed
- Where employees have been dismissed for joining or refusing to leave a Trade Union
- Where employees have been dismissed on grounds of sex, race, or religion
- Where employees have been 'wrongfully' selected for redundancy
- Where employees have been dismissed due to illness or pregnancy

Industrial tribunals

In the event of a breach of contract by either an employer or an employee, the aggrieved party can take their case before an **industrial tribunal**. This is a type of court with the legal authority to settle cases brought under a range of employment laws, including wrongful or unfair dismissal, or discrimination. Each tribunal is made up of three people: a legally trained chairperson, an employer, and an employee representative.

A complaint by an employee must be filed within three months of the end of a contract. A notice of application is sent to the employer asking if they wish to contest the case. Details of the case are then sent to the **Advisory, Conciliation and Arbitration service (ACAS)** who will attempt to resolve the dispute before it reaches the tribunal.

If the complaint has to go to tribunal, the employee is entitled to legal advice. After the hearing, the tribunal can either reject the claim, or make one of three decisions in favour of the employee, which the employer is legally obliged to accept. These are:

- The employee to be reinstated in the same job
- The employee to be re-engaged in another job
- The employee to be compensated

Both employer and employee have the right to appeal if the decision of the tribunal goes against them.

In 1993-94 there were over 70 thousand registered applications to industrial tribunals in the UK. Around 57% of these were concerned with unfair dismissal, 15% with contraventions of the Wages Act, and 8% with equal pay and discrimination (see Figure 12.3).

▼ Figure 12.2: The industrial tribunals process

- Employee complains to Industrial Tribunal
- Details passed to ACAS → Settlement reached – case ends
- Pre-hearing assessment Should case go ahead? → No – case ends
- Public hearing → Parties accept decision
- Either party may appeal against decision
- Employment Appeal Tribunal hearing on points of law → Parties accept decision
- Further appeals to: Court of Appeal, EU Court of Justice

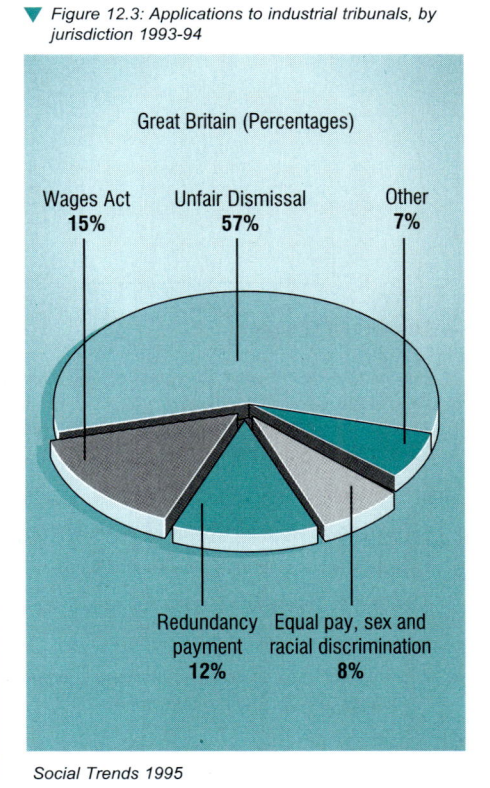

▼ Figure 12.3: Applications to industrial tribunals, by jurisdiction 1993-94

Great Britain (Percentages)

- Wages Act 15%
- Unfair Dismissal 57%
- Other 7%
- Redundancy payment 12%
- Equal pay, sex and racial discrimination 8%

Social Trends 1995

Car firm for 'women only' guilty of bias

A firm which sacked its salesmen to create an all-woman team was found guilty yesterday of 'blatant' discrimination.

Car dealers Swithland motors said it had tried to eradicate the 'Arthur Daley' image by employing all female staff. It felt that women were most sincere and could relate better to customers. But Michael Smith won his claim that he had been discriminated against on the grounds of sex. Mr Smith lost his job when it was taken over by Swithland Motors in 1991. The jobs, he claimed were filled by women.

Swithland denied discrimination, admitting that the majority of the sales staff at its 19 sites were women, but that they were selected purely on merit.

Birmingham industrial tribunal chairman John Macmillan said "The discrimination could scarcely have been more blatant." He awarded Mr Smith £15,000.

Daily Mail 21.6.94

The Arbitration and Conciliation Advisory Service (ACAS)

The **Advisory, Conciliation and Arbitration Service (ACAS)** is an independent organization set up by the government in 1975 to help settle disputes. The aim of ACAS is to improve industrial relations through mediation and by bringing opposing parties together. (ACAS in Northern Ireland is known as the Labour Relations Agency.)

When employers and employees are unable to agree, they may consult an independent organization such as ACAS to help them. In its conciliation role, ACAS will listen to both sides in a dispute and seek to establish common ground. When asked to arbitrate, ACAS will hear both sides and decide on a solution for both parties. Sometimes both sides may agree in advance to abide by whatever ACAS decides.

According to its annual report, ACAS received a total of 75,181 cases in 1993, of which 62% concerned unfair dismissal. Disputes about wages cases accounted for 22%, with the organization handling 1,852 cases of racial discrimination and 1,601 cases involving issues of equal pay. During 1993, 67% of cases handled by ACAS resulted in the parties settling their differences, or agreeing sufficiently to withdraw an application to an industrial tribunal.

Civil legal action

Rather than going to an industrial tribunal, an employee may decide to seek compensation for unfair dismissal by taking their employer to court. This can be expensive because it involves employing a solicitor and sometimes a barrister as well. If the employer wins the case, the employee may have to pay not only their own legal costs but those of the employer as well.

Because court cases can involve bad publicity, employers may sometimes wish to make an out-of-court settlement with a former employee, or suggest that both parties go to arbitration with an independent body deciding the outcome of the case.

The Social Chapter

The aim of the **Social Chapter of the European Union** is to standardize working conditions throughout EU member countries so that all workers within the community are guaranteed the same basic rights. These rights include:

- A maximum working week of 48 hours
- Freedom to join unions and take strike action
- Equal treatment for part-time and full-time workers
- Access to appropriate training and re-training opportunities
- Equal treatment for men and women
- The right to be consulted on changes in organization, new working methods, mergers, and redundancies
- Protection of rights of pregnant women. Working hours and conditions to be adapted if job endangers health
- Freedom to move between EU member states for work, and to enjoy same terms and conditions of employment, such as pay and holidays, as native workers, and have equal recognition of qualifications

The Social Chapter was formally adopted by all EU member states except the UK on 8th December 1989. The UK objected to full implementation of all its directives on the grounds that the restrictions on hours and introduction of a minimum wage would raise business costs and stifle employment opportunities. The UK government had previously abolished wage councils, which had set minimum wage levels in a number of traditionally low-paid industries, such as textiles, retailing, and catering. The Social Chapter may become law in the UK if a future Labour government is elected.

The European Court of Justice

The European Court of Justice is run by judges from the member states of the European Union (see 17.3). The role of the court is to settle cases brought under European Community laws. An employee or employer can appeal to the European Court if they believe that British courts have failed to interpret European law correctly. In practice, rulings of the European Court override UK laws, and decisions relating to employment made by British courts can, in certain circumstances, be overturned on appeal to the European Court of Justice.

Portfolio Activity 12.7

Range: Procedures for employees
Skills: Produce written material, Collect and record data

Using a desktop publishing package, prepare a fact sheet for employees outlining what they can do if they feel they have been unfairly treated. You will need to investigate:

- The grounds on which employees can claim unfair treatment in terms of, for example, discrimination, dismissal, redundancy, and wage payments
- The role of industrial tribunals, ACAS, Civil Courts, and the EU Court of Social Justice, and relevant application procedures.

Key words

Industrial tribunal - a courtroom which is less formal than the law courts, where industrial disputes over unfair treatment can be settled

ACAS - an independent organization providing unbiased advice, arbitration, or conciliation as required, in order to help settle industrial disputes

Civil action - the seeking of redress or settlement of disputes in the courts

European Court of Justice - legal body with the power to pass judgements on European laws, when these are in dispute

Social Chapter - European Union directives aimed at standardizing working conditions and employment rights throughout EU member countries

---

Section 12.5 Trade Unions and employer organizations

Trade unions

A **Trade Union** is defined as *'an organization of workers whose principal purpose is the regulation of relations between workers and employers or employer associations'*. Many Trade Unions for professional and managerial workers prefer to call themselves **staff associations**.

By organizing into groups, unions can attempt to exert influence over the setting of wages, salaries, and terms and conditions of employment by firms.

Total union membership in 1993 was around 10 million. Most unions are quite small, with memberships of less than 1,000. Around 80% of the current membership is accounted for by the 20 largest unions. However,

Advanced Business

▼ Figure 12.4: Trade Unions 1900-1992

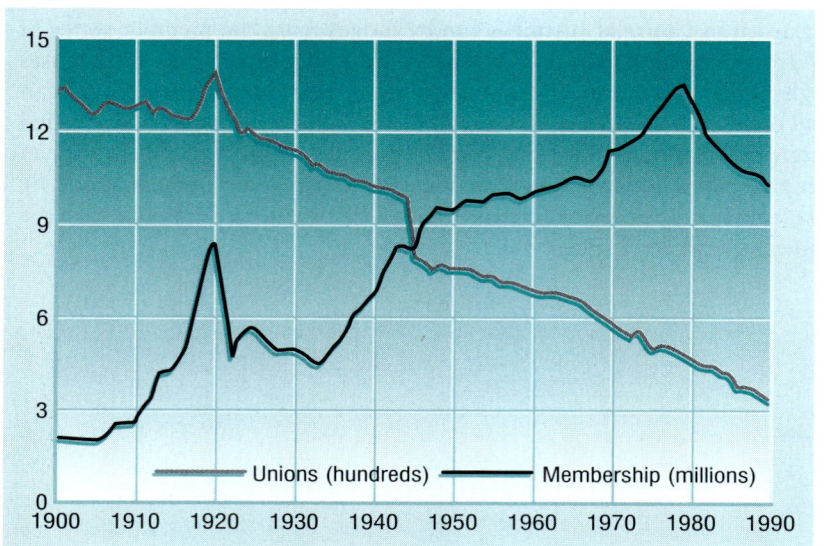

1992 top ten unions	Membership (000s)
Transport and General Workers Union	1,037
Amalgamated Engineering & Electrical Union	884
GMB	799
National and Local Governments Officers' Association	764
Manufacturing Science and Finance Union	552
National Union of Public Employees	527
Union of Shop Distributive and Allied Workers	316
Royal College of Nursing of the UK	299
Graphical Paper and Media Union	270
National Union of Teachers	214

Employment Gazette June 94

union membership has been in decline since the early 1980s. Rising unemployment, the increased participation of women in the labour force, and the growth of part-time employment have all tended to weaken Trade Union membership.

Trade Union aims

The functions of Trade Unions and staff associations are very similar. These are:

- **To defend employee rights.** This will involve campaigning against redundancies, pay cuts, and unreasonable changes in working practices. Unions will help employees with grievance procedures, defend employees who have been unfairly dismissed, disciplined, or discriminated against, and provide information on employee rights, strike pay, and legal aid for their members.

- **To improve working conditions** - for example, health and safety improvements, reduced hours of work, and increased holiday entitlements.

- **To secure adequate pay for their members.** Unions will also try to negotiate improvements in sick pay, pensions, and industrial injury benefits.

- **To provide educational, recreational, and social amenities for members.** Particular emphasis is placed on developing and providing training for new members, and apprenticeships.

- **To increase worker participation in business decision-making.**

- **To ensure their members' interests are represented and considered in all aspects of national life.** To this end, unions play a significant role in politics. For example, the Labour Party developed from the early union movement in the UK and is partly financed from union funds.

Portfolio Activity 12.8

Range: Role of trade unions and staff associations, Analyse
Skills: Read and respond to written material, Take part in discussions

Banning Solvent-Based Eggshell Paints in Local Schools and Premises

Barry Hillyard is a shop steward and spokesperson for UCATT - the Union of Construction Allied Trades and Technicians. He describes a problem some painters were having using eggshell paint.

"Painting schools often involves working in passages, toilets, and other confined areas. Many painters complained to UCATT shop stewards about the fumes. Some suffered badly from nausea and runny eyes and had to take time off sick.

"We contacted the London Hazards Centre who provided our safety representatives with information on the hazards of using solvent-based eggshell paints. We discovered that Trade Unions in Scandinavia were also campaigning on the solvents issue.

"To get a ban we realized we would have to press for an alternative which was water-based but had the same hard-wearing properties and covering as eggshell. Following a meeting with the Chief Architect, we agreed to test two water-based paints and compare these with our existing eggshell variety. We found that a paint called Crown Acrylic Eggshell met the same requirements as the solvent based paint.

"This water-based acrylic paint is now used, and no harmful effects have been reported from our painters."

In groups, discuss the following:

1. What role did UCATT play in ensuring that the painters stopped using solvent-based paints?
2. Why was it necessary for the union to take the lead on this issue?
3. How might the situation have been different in a non-unionized organization?
4. What are the costs and benefits to the employer and the employee of maintaining a high standard of health and safety at work?
5. Ask a local Trade Union official to give a talk to your class group on the objectives of their union, how it is organized, their role and responsibilities. Prepare a list of questions to ask the official at the end of their talk.

Types of Trade Union

Craft unions

These were the earliest form of union and are made up of workers skilled in particular crafts. Craft unions usually include workers with the same skill across several industries - for example, the Electrical, Electronic, Telecommunications and Plumbing Union (EETPU).

General unions

These unions are for semi-skilled and unskilled workers not covered by craft unions. General unions do not restrict membership to workers with specific skills. The Transport and General Workers Union (TGWU) and National Union of Public Employees (NUPE) are general unions.

Industrial unions

These unions cover all workers, regardless of status in a particular industry. The National Union of Mineworkers (NUM) is an example.

White collar unions or staff associations

These unions restrict membership to professional, administrative, and clerical employees. These unions have expanded since 1950, due to the growth of services in the UK economy. This category of union includes the National and Local Government Officers Association (NALGO) and the Association of Scientific, Technical, and Managerial Staffs (ASTMS).

The typical structure of a Trade Union

General Secretary — head of the union

⬇

National Executive — policy-making group. An important role of the executive is to negotiate pay and conditions with employers

⬇

Full-time officials — union members at headquarters who assist local branches

⬇

Union branches — to coordinate the affairs of union members at local level

⬇

Shop Stewards — union officials who conduct the day-to-day business of the union in their places of work, as well as carrying out the job they are employed to do

Trade Union structure

Every union in the UK is entirely independent and self-governing, but most are affiliated to the Trade Union Congress (TUC), which provides coordination and national representation for the entire union movement.

The TUC is headed by the **general council**, which is the TUC's executive decision-making body. It meets every year to discuss and establish policy. Each union can send delegates to the meeting to debate and vote on policy.

The internal structure of Trade Unions varies widely, but there is a typical pattern extending from full-time union officials in the union headquarters, to union members in factories, shops, and offices.

Portfolio Activity 12.9

Range: Role of Trade Unions and staff associations
Skills: Collect and record data

Investigate the types of Trade Unions that are likely to be found at each of the organizations below.

A local college

Hospital

Supermarket

Mainline railway station

Employers' associations

Just as workers have organized into groups, employers in the same industries have joined together to form mutual help associations - for example, the National Farmers' Union, The Builders Merchants' Federation, and the Cement Makers' Federation.

These associations help their members in national wage negotiations with Trade Unions, with the introduction of new pay schemes, and with the provision of legal advice at industrial tribunals. At a national level, associations may try to influence government policy. Many of the employers' associations belong to the **Confederation of British Industry (CBI)**, which is the employers' equivalent to the TUC.

Industrial relations

The term **industrial relations** covers every aspect of the relationship between an employer, or group of employers, and their employees. Good relations will help to prevent conflict over pay and conditions of service, and will motivate employees to higher levels of productivity.

Good relations can be fostered through regular meetings and consultation between employers and unions, and by providing a forum for discussing grievances, proposals for pay increases, changes in working practices, and possible redundancies. Proposals are much more likely to be accepted and successful if workers are consulted and involved in decision-making.

Collective bargaining

The process by which unions and employers settle upon wages and conditions of employment is called **collective bargaining**. While the firm will seek to minimize the cost of its labour, the workforce will aim to maximize the value of its rewards. Somehow an agreement between both sides must be reached. Collective bargaining may be organized so that a negotiated settlement determines pay and conditions for all firms in a particular industry, or by means of local agreements between particular companies and their own workers.

The pay and conditions of some 60-70% of the British labour force is determined either directly or indirectly by collective bargaining. In addition to bargaining on wages and conditions of work, there will also be negotiations about redundancies, demarcation (i.e. who does what job), and the introduction of new technology.

Industrial action

When negotiations fail, **industrial disputes** can occur, and Trade Unions may then resort to the following types of action in an attempt to raise business costs and put pressure on their employers to accept their terms:

- **Overtime ban** - when workers refuse to work more than their normal hours. Many firms rely on overtime to meet production targets and deadlines.

- **Work-to-rule** - when workers comply with every rule and regulation at work in order to slow down production

- **Go-slow** - working deliberately slowly

▼ *Issues over which employees were consulted by their employers*

Health and Safety	54%
Working methods/practices	52%
Training provision	37%
Pay	33%
Quality control	33%
New technology	32%
Physical working conditions	29%
Staffing levels	25%
Environmental policies	13%
None of these	21%
Employees surveyed	1,657

National Opinion Poll Survey of Employee Involvement, April 1993

- **Sit-in** - when workers refuse to leave their place of work, often in an attempt to stop their firm from being closed down
- **Boycott** - sympathy action by one union in support of another that may be on strike. It involves refusing to handle certain goods or work with certain other employees. For example, during the 1984 miners' strike, the rail unions refused to handle coal at their depots.
- **Strike** - when negotiations between unions and employers fail a Trade Union may recommend that their members withdraw their labour altogether and refuse to work. A strike is **official** if it has the backing of the union, or **unofficial** if it is called by workers without the support of their union.

Workers on strike may **picket** their firms by standing outside the organization's premises and trying to persuade others not to enter.

Portfolio Activity 12.10

Range: The role of Trade Unions and staff associations
Skills: Interpret and present data

Labour disputes: working days lost per 1,000 employees in all industries and services 1984–93

	1984	1985	1986	1987	1988	1989	1990	1991	1992	1993
United Kingdom	1,280	300	90	170	180	80	30	20	30	
Belgium	..	40	..	..	70	40	30	20	40	
Denmark	60	1060	40	60	40	20	40	30	30	50
Francec	80	50	60	50	70	50	40	30	30	30
Germany (FR)	250	–	–	–	–	–	10	10	60	20
Greece	320	620	710	9,940	3,550	4,950	12,040	3,020	1,480	840
Ireland	470	520	380	320	180	60	270	100	220	..
Italy	610	270	390	320	230	300	340	200	180	..
Netherlands	10	20	10	10	–	–	40	20	10	10
Portugal	100	100	140	40	70	130	40	40	60	20
Spain	870	440	320	640	1,420	420	280	490	700	250
United States	90	70	120	40	40	150	50	40	40	40
Canada	400	310	690	360	440	330	450	320	190	150

Employment Gazette Dec 1994

1. What trend(s) can you identify in the number of working days lost in the UK between 1984 and 1993? Can you suggest any reasons for these trends? How does the UK compare to other countries?
2. What impact do you think these stoppages would have on the workers and firms involved, and on the competitiveness of UK firms, compared to others?
3. Gather information on recent industrial disputes to compile into a short folder. In each case, try to identify:
   - What unions and employers were involved
   - Why the disputes occurred
   - What action was taken, and how the dispute was eventually settled

Striking will mean a loss of wages for workers and can ultimately lead to loss of employment if the firm is forced to reduce production as a result of lost markets and profits.

In extreme cases an employer may retaliate by locking workers out of the firm with no pay.

When bargaining fails

If collective bargaining fails to resolve a dispute, arbitration may be requested from a third party such as ACAS (see 12.4). If requested, ACAS officials will bring together the two parties in the dispute (**conciliate**) and try to help them reach a compromise position (**arbitrate**).

Portfolio Activity 12.11

Range: Procedures for employers and employees
Skills: Take part in discussions, Produce written material, Present information

1. You are an ACAS negotiator. Produce a short report setting out how you propose to bring together the two sides in the dispute. (*Hint*: what common ground can be established?)

2. Roleplay the dispute in groups of three. One member of the group should play the union leader, the other the employer's representative, and the third, the ACAS conciliator. Set a time limit of two periods of ten minutes for negotiations, separated by a five-minute break.

3. Present the results of your negotiations in the form of a newspaper report, using desktop publishing software. Each group member should write the article from the perspective of their particular role.

ACAS offers peace talks as second rail strike looms

The conciliatory service ACAS will today try to get the two sides in the rail dispute back round the negotiating table. ACAS negotiators, however, face an uphill struggle and with neither side prepared to give way, next Wednesday's 24-hour national rail strike seemed certain to go ahead.

Moves today by ACAS follow individual and 'exploratory' meetings ACAS staff had with employers Railtrack, and Jimmy Knapp's Rail, Maritime, and Transport Union yesterday. Union negotiators are insisting on an 11% pay increase for 4,600 signal staff at the centre of the strike action, in recognition for past productivity and changes in working practices.

Railtrack insists that signal staff have already been compensated for what has gone before, and that any new money must therefore be for future productivity. The Railtrack negotiator said that a pay increase could only be considered in return for productivity improvements and staffing cutbacks.

It is this basic problem that ACAS must overcome if it is to enable the two sides to talk positively and get next Wednesday's scheduled strike called off.

Evening Standard 17.6.94

Single bargaining and non-union organizations

Some companies are non-unionized, either because management discourage unionization, or because staff are offered non-union contracts which provide a package of benefits which may make up for lack of union representation, as in companies such as Marks & Spencer and IBM.

Despite the time and cost savings to industrial firms offered by collective bargaining at national level, there has recently been an increase in single bargaining agreements at company or plant level.

Single bargaining offers the advantages of increased flexibility over pay, especially when related to performance, and job demarcation. In such cases, labour is represented by a single union, and different Trade Unions will compete with one another to represent all the workers in the company - the result being a sort of 'closed shop by competition'. For example, the Japanese car manufacturer Nissan in the North East only allows the EETPU to represent its entire workforce.

Trade Union reforms

Since 1980, successive UK governments have passed laws aimed at curbing the restrictive practices of unions and limiting industrial action.

In the past, the main way in which unions were able to restrict the supply of non-unionized labour to an occupation was through a **closed shop agreement**. This was an agreement between an employer and a union to restrict employment to workers who agreed to join the Trade Union. This increased union bargaining strength enabled agreements with the employer to be enforced without giving benefits to non-union members. Some employers welcomed closed shops because they reduced the need for negotiations with individual workers.

Under the terms of the Trade Union Reform and Employment Rights Act 1993, closed shop agreements can no longer be enforced. Other effects of the legislation include:

- Income Support and other welfare benefits to families of striking workers withdrawn
- Individual workers or employers given the right to challenge closed shops agreed by ballot
- All sympathy actions outlawed
- National unions made liable for damages/losses suffered as a result of any industrial action, even if unofficial
- Employers entitled to dismiss individual employees involved in unofficial action
- Individuals entitled to join any union, regardless of closed shop agreements
- All workers entitled to a full postal ballot, independently scrutinized, prior to any strike action
- Single bargaining encouraged. Employers entitled to offer employees pay inducements to accept individual work contracts

The effect of these reforms has been to diminish the bargaining strength of unions in the workplace.

Key words

Trade Union - an organization representing the interests of its members, usually workers in a particular trade or industry

Trade Union Congress (TUC) - national coordinating and policy-making body for entire union movement in UK

Employers' association - an organization representing the views of companies within an industry

Industrial relations - the relationship between employers and their employees and/or employee representatives

Strikes - withdrawal of labour as a result of an industrial dispute

Collective bargaining - the process of negotiation between workers and employer representatives

Single bargaining - negotiations between employers and individual employees or union representatives conducted at local or plant level

Further reading

Fletcher, C, and Williams, R: *Performance Appraisal and Career Development* (Stanley Thornes 1991)

Collins, H: *Human Resources Management* (Hodder & Stoughton 1993)

Chapman, E: *Improving Relations at Work* (Kogan Page 1989)

UNIT FOUR

CHAPTER 12

Test questions

The following underpinning knowledge will be tested:

1. Analyse the rights of employers and employees
2. Employer and employee responsibilities
3. Procedures available to employers and employees when rights are not upheld
4. The role of trade unions and staff associations
5. Methods for gaining employee co-operation

1 A new member of staff is concerned about the transfer of pension rights from an old employer. Who should s/he talk to first?

A Shop steward
B Human resources manager
C Welfare officer
D Training officer

2 The managing director of a small engineering company holds a series of meetings with staff to discuss company plans to relocate to larger premises. What is the reason for doing this?

A To be popular with employees
B Because it is a legal requirement
C So that staff will feel informed and involved in the decision
D To find out where employees would like to move to

3 Production managers in a firm are concerned about unusually low productivity. What would you advise as their best course of action initially?

A Punish staff for their poor record
B Employ new staff with appropriate skills
C Devise a performance-related pay system
D Form team groups to discuss production problems

Questions 4-7 share the following answer options:

A Equal Pay Act 1970
B Health and Safety at Work Act 1974
C Trade Union Reform and Employment Rights Act 1993
D Sex Discrimination Act 1986

Which of the above laws would an organization be breaking if it:

4 Failed to provide breathing masks for workers who regularly handled asbestos?

5 Terminated the employment of a woman because she was pregnant?

6 Refused to employ a person who would not join a Trade Union?

7 Advertised a job for 'Female drivers only'?

8 Which one of the following statements is false?

A Equal opportunities policies can increase production costs
B The use of equal opportunities policies in firms can improve the allocation of scarce labour resources
C Companies in the UK are required by law to operate equal opportunities policies
D The EU Social Chapter prohibits discrimination in job recruitment, selection, promotion, and pay, on the grounds of sex, race, or religion

9 One of the main responsibilities of the Equal Opportunities Commission is to:

A Monitor race discrimination
B Advise on the employment of older workers
C Monitor discrimination on grounds of sex
D Encourage equal opportunities for disabled people

Questions 10-12 share the following answer options:

A Health and safety
B Wages
C Equal opportunities
D Training

Which of the following information could a company use to monitor its policies on the above?

10 Factory inspection reports

11 Staff attendance records on external vocational courses

12 Staff recruitment and turnover records

305

13 The role of ACAS is to

A Support employers in settling disputes with Trade Unions

B Support Trade Unions in settling disputes with employers

C Make decisions which are legally binding on employers and employees

D Arbitrate and conciliate industrial relations between employees and employers in an independent manner

14 All of the following are responsibilities of human resources management EXCEPT:

A To set up and operate a staff appraisal system

B To ensure that staff wear protective clothing in order to comply with health and safety regulations

C To design a working environment which will motivate staff

D To take part in negotiations with staff and unions

15 Professional unions represent:

A Workers in skilled crafts or trades

B Industrial workers such as mineworkers

C Groups of unskilled workers

D White collar workers

16 Which of the following reasons for dismissal would be unfair?

A For joining a Trade Union

B For redundancy due to a fall in consumer demand

C For consistently poor timekeeping

D For sexual harrassment

17 a. Describe the main functions of a human resources department in a medium-to-large organization.

b. Explain how you might proceed to discipline a new employee who did not attend a week-long external training course that had been arranged.

c. You decide to dismiss the worker for dishonesty. The employee says s/he was ill during the course and claims unfair dismissal. Suggest possible courses of action the employee could take to contest their dismissal.

18 a. What is a Trade Union? Give an example of a union.

b. Suggest four main aims of a Trade Union.

c. Suggest three types of industrial action a union could take during a dispute with an employer. What will be the likely impact on the employees and employer of these actions?

d. Give three reasons why a dispute may occur between a union and an employer.

e. What is ACAS? Explain how ACAS can help to solve industrial disputes.

assessment assignment

UNIT FOUR
CHAPTER 12

Assessment Assignment

Range: Analyse
- The role of Trade Unions and staff associations
- Employer and employee responsibilities
- Procedures for employers and employees
- Methods of gaining employee co-operation

Skills: Communications
- Produce written materials
- Take part in discussions

Information Technology
- Process information
- Present information

Tasks

1. Produce two pamphlets using desk top publishing. One is for employees the other for employers. Both should explain their rights and responsibilities to each other.

   The pamphlets should contain:

   - information about contracts of employment
   - health and safety at work
   - discrimination at work
   - procedures for disciplinary action, the termination of employment contracts and handling grievances
   - examples of two working environments (of your choice) to illustrate how health and safety and anti-discrimination legislation has been introduced (or ignored and the problems of doing so)
   - the role of trade unions and staff associations in negotiating pay and conditions, providing advice, information and legal representation for aggrieved employees, using examples from your own observations of trade union functions in workplaces of your choice.

2. Write a short report which explains how responsibilities for the following functions of human resources management are met by employers:

   - negotiating pay and conditions
   - handling disciplinary or grievance procedures

   Use real examples from your own research wherever possible to illustrate.

   The report should also explain how organisations motivate their employees and gain their co-operation to work towards organisational goals, and how they might improve the level of employees' co-operation.

3. Make a live or video recorded documentary style presentation to your group to summarise the main findings of your report.

chapter 13

Advanced Business

chapter 13
Job Roles and Change at Work

This chapter examines the various job roles and responsibilities in an organization and how working practices and conditions are changing

Key ideas

A number of **job roles** with specific duties and responsibilities can be identified within a company. These are **directors**, **managers**, **supervisors** and **operatives**.

The term **management** not only describes those individuals within an organization who are managers, but also the skills and knowledge they must possess.

Advisers and **consultants** may be employed by an organization on fixed-term contracts to provide specialist skills and knowledge.

All job roles within an organization will have a number of **responsibilities** in common. These include **meeting work objectives, meeting job targets, improving performance, meeting legal requirements, giving advice, handling discipline and grievances**, and **implementing changes in working conditions**.

The **working conditions** of employees include their hours of work, rates of pay, entitlement to sickness leave, holiday, maternity leave and payments, compensation for redundancy, as well as entitlement to healthy and safe working environments.

Business organizations are changing working conditions to create workforces that are **flexible** in terms of skills and hours of work. This is due to **increasing competitive pressures**, and the need to **improve productivity, reduce costs, improve quality**, and **adapt to new technology**.

To increase labour flexibility, improve output and lower costs, many firms have divided their workforces into **core, periphery**, and **external** groups. Core workers are skilled full-time employees performing varied tasks. Peripheral workers are part-timers and temporary staff. External workers are those contracted from other organizations to perform non-core functions, such as cleaning and catering.

Flexibility can also be achieved by the introduction of **new contractual arrangements, teleworking, annualized hours, Flexitime**, and **job sharing**.

A firm can measure the impact of measures to increase workforce flexibility in terms of **improved efficiency, productivity, and quality**.

However, changes in working conditions can also affect the stress and job satisfaction of individual workers.

Section 13.1   **The responsibilities of employees**

The organizational hierarchy

Within any organizational hierarchy a number of key roles can be identified. The structure of the organization will determine the working relationships, and lines of authority and responsibility between them (see 4.4).

▼ Figure 13.1: Job roles in an organization

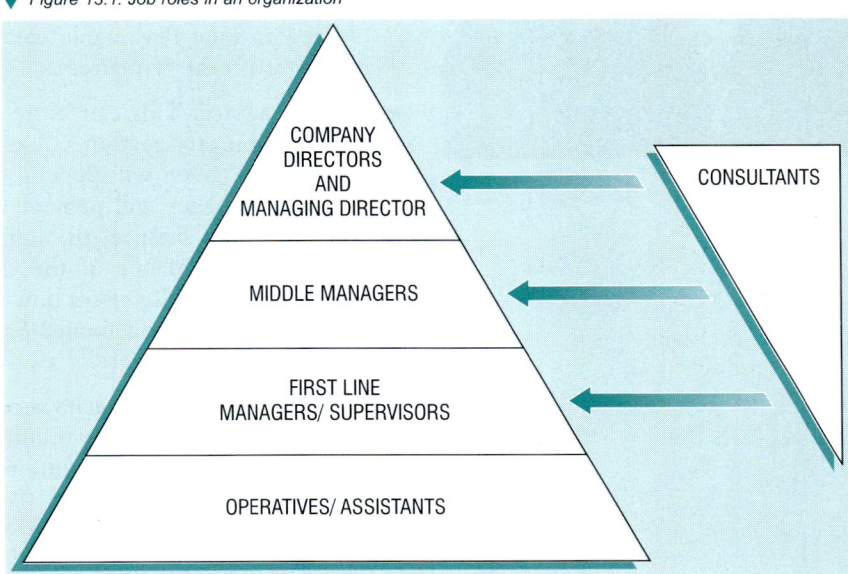

[Pyramid diagram: COMPANY DIRECTORS AND MANAGING DIRECTOR / MIDDLE MANAGERS / FIRST LINE MANAGERS/ SUPERVISORS / OPERATIVES/ ASSISTANTS, with arrows from CONSULTANTS pointing to the top three levels]

General responsibilities

All employees, whether managers or shop-floor workers, will have some general responsibilities in common. Jobs tasks may vary between employees of different grades, but all will be required to:

- **To identify business objectives.** All employees will be expected to work towards the fulfilment of agreed business objectives, for example, to increase output by 10% over the next 12 months, or to improve market share and profits (see 4.1). Senior managers will be responsible for setting these objectives and making decisions on the resource inputs, technology, and working practices necessary to achieve them. Sales teams and workers on the shop floor will be responsible for putting the plans into practice.

- **Meet personal job targets.** Details of personal job targets will usually be contained within individual job descriptions, along with the general duties and responsibilities of the post (see 14.2). A personal target for a department manager, for example, could be to reduce costs by 5% over 12 months. This may be reflected in targets set for his or her staff. Similarly, shop-floor workers may be set production targets.

  Targets may also be set for specific projects - for example, to produce a report on market opportunities in North East England, or implement a new piece of IT equipment.

- **Improve performance.** All employees will be expected by their organization to improve their skills and the amount and quality of their output and decisions over time, and to monitor their performance.

- **Meet legal requirements.** Different jobs will be affected by different laws. For example, personnel staff will have to be aware of laws covering discrimination in recruitment and selection, and pay and promotions (see 12.3). The Data Protection Act will also affect the way records are kept on employees and customers.

  Under the terms of the Health and Safety Act 1974, all employees are obliged to take reasonable care at all times and cooperate with their employer on safety matters.

- **Provide advice.** This can be to other employees inside or outside the organization, to customers, and/or to members of the public. The information given will depend on the employee's job. For example, a financial manager will provide advice to senior managers on methods and sources of finance, the impact of changing interest rates, and the financial performance of the organization. A machine operator may advise a new employee on how to use the machine, or even on matters such as lunch arrangements. Sales assistants will advise customers on product lines and prices.

- **Handle discipline and grievances.** Employees in positions of authority may from time to time be required to discipline other members of staff, for example, for mismanaging resources, for poor work effort, or poor timekeeping. This can take the form of an 'informal chat', or may follow a set of formal procedures including verbal and written warnings (see 12.4).

  Conversely, some employees may complain of being unfairly treated by their fellow workers or by their managers. Grievances such as sexual or racial harassment will need to be handled sensitively, and complaints investigated in full.

  Managers may also have to deal with grievances of suppliers or consultants who feel they have been unfairly treated, or that the organization has strayed from contractually agreed terms and conditions. Sales staff may also have to deal with customer complaints concerning products and customer services (see 11.1)

- **To implement change in working conditions.** The working conditions of employees refer to the time and effort expected of them, their rates of pay, entitlement to sickness, holiday and maternity leave and pay, compensation for redundancy, as well as the physical conditions of their workplace environment in terms of health and safety. Employers may wish to change these conditions over time, for reasons of cost, changes in consumer demands or technology, for example, and employees will be expected to accept them (see 13.4).

The more specific responsibilities of the various job roles within an organization will be examined in Section 13.2 on page 314.

Working conditions

In return for carrying out their responsibilities, all employees in a firm are entitled to some basic rights concerning the terms and conditions of their employment (see 12.3). These are:

- **Knowledge of the terms and conditions of their employment.** When an employer makes an offer of a job and the employee accepts it in return for payment, then a legal agreement or contract exists between them.

  The Trade Union and Employment Rights Act 1993 states that an employee must be given a written statement of the terms and conditions of their service within two months of starting their job. Any changes must be notified in writing within one month.

  A job contract will contain details of job title, rates of pay, hours of work, shift work, place of work, holiday entitlement, sickness benefits, grievance procedures, disciplinary rules, and period of notice required to leave.

  A **contract of employment** can be either **long-term**, binding until either the employer or employee wishes to terminate it, or **short-term** for an agreed period - for example, one year.

- **Sick pay.** Employers are required to pay a minimum amount of sick pay to most employees who are aged over 16, if they have been off work for more than four consecutive days. Statutory sick pay (SSP) is only payable for the first 28 weeks of a long-term illness. However, some employers may continue to pay wages to valued employees who are off work for longer than this.

- **Compensation for redundancy.** Any employee who has worked continuously for two years or more for the same employer is legally entitled to redundancy payment in the event of their contract of employment being terminated because they are no longer required.

  Legal minimum entitlements for each complete year of service, up to a maximum of 20, are given in table 13.1:

▼ Table 13.1: Redundancy entitlement as a percentage of weekly wage

Age range	Entitlement as a percentage of one week's pay
18 - 22	50%
22 - 41	100%
41 - 65	150%

  So for example, a person earning £100 per week on being made redundant at the age of 25, and having worked for the same employer since s/he was 18, would be entitled to £700 in severance pay for redundancy.

- **A healthy and safe working environment.** All employees have a legal right to work in an environment that is free from hazard and pollution, including air and noise. Health and safety measures in the workplace can include:

  - Protection from hazardous substances
  - Training staff in health and safety matters

- Providing ear protectors against noise
- Maintaining safety equipment and clothing
- Breaks for lunch and tea so that workers do not become tired
- Provision of First Aid kits and medical officers
- Controlling workplace temperature

- **Holiday pay.** There is no legislation in the UK to say how much holiday workers should be entitled to or be paid for. However, most full-time workers on long-term contracts get between 20 and 25 days normal paid leave each year.
- **Hours of work.**

The 'basic' working week

All employees will have agreed hours which they are expected to work during the course of a day, week, month, or year, depending on the precise form of their contract of employment.

Actual hours and days worked will vary between jobs. Some employees - for example, retail staff - may have to arrive and leave work at the same time every day to coincide with shop opening and closing times. Many shop workers are also obliged to work some Saturdays and Sundays in return for days off during the week. However, most office staff work what is considered the 'normal' working week, i.e. from 9 am to 5.30 pm, Monday to Friday, each week.

There will also be differences in hours and times due to shift work, annualized hours, and Flexitime arrangements agreed with employers (see 13.4).

The basic working week in the UK is 37.5 - 40 hours a week for manual workers, and 35 - 38 hours for non-manual workers. However, due to overtime, many workers work longer than the basic week, especially in manual occupations (see 16.1).

▼ Table 13.2: Average hours of full-time manual and non-manual employees by industry, UK 1993

	Manual employees	Non-manual employees
Agriculture, forestry and fishing	46.8	41.1
Energy and water supply	43.0	38.7
Extraction of mineral/ores; manufacture of metals & chemicals	44.2	39.0
Metal goods, electronic, and vehicle industries	43.3	39.6
Other manufacturing products industries	44.2	39.4
Construction	44.7	40.0
Distribution, hotels, and catering; repairs	43.4	40.5
Transport and communications	46.8	40.2
Banking, finance, insurance, business services/leasing	46.6	37.3
Other services	42.6	37.3
All industries and services	44.3	38.6

Employment Gazette 8.94

EU Working time directive

The UK has few legal restrictions on hours of work, except where jobs involve driving goods and public service vehicles, which are time-limited for reasons of public safety. However, the UK has been resisting a 1993 European Union (EU) Directive which caps the maximum working week at 48 hours, including overtime, across member countries. The EU directive also sets a minimum entitlement for all workers to four weeks paid holiday and minimum rest periods in each working day.

The UK has argued that restrictions on hours would introduce unnecessary bureaucracy and impose significant costs on UK industry.

Portfolio Activity 13.1

Range: Working conditions, Evaluate
Skills: Read and respond to written material

1. Why should the imposition of a maximum working week of 48 hours impose costs on employers as suggested by the government?
2. Which industries are most likely to be affected by the directive?
3. As an employer, how might you adapt labour recruitment and the deployment of existing labour in your firm to minimize the potential impact of the directive?
4. Explain why it may not be in the interests of the UK to accept the Working Time Directive.

Decision delayed on 48-hour working week limit

Britain has won a delay in a decision to limit the length of the working week across the EU to a maximum of 48 hours.

The UK government has said the Working Time Directive, which also lays down minimum holidays and rest periods, would impose 'crippling costs' on employers and hit the pay packets of millions of workers.

Employment Department officials put the initial cost to Britain's employers of introducing the directive at some £5 billion. This includes the cost of hiring extra staff to cover the 'lost' hours, and assumes that the wages of staff whose hours are cut to 48 hours will not necessarily be reduced 'pro rata'.

Some 3.2 million employees, many construction and postal workers, security guards, hotel and catering staff, agricultural workers and maintenance staff, regularly work overtime which takes them beyond the proposed 48-hour limit.

Employment Gazette 6.92 and 12.92

Number of employees whose total usual weekly hours are over 48 hours by industry (Great Britain, Spring 1992)

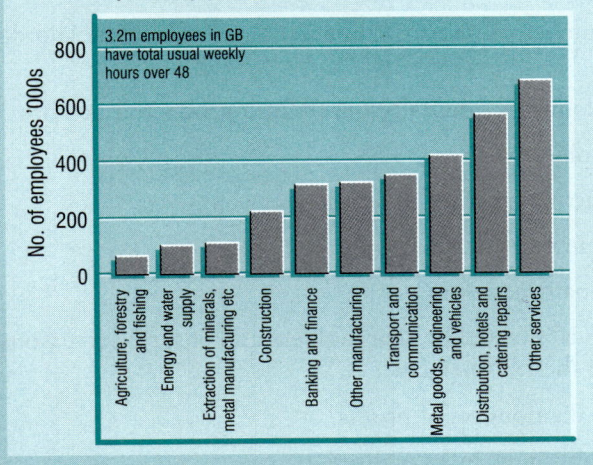

Number of employees whose total usual weekly hours are over 48 hours by occupation (Great Britain, Spring 1992)

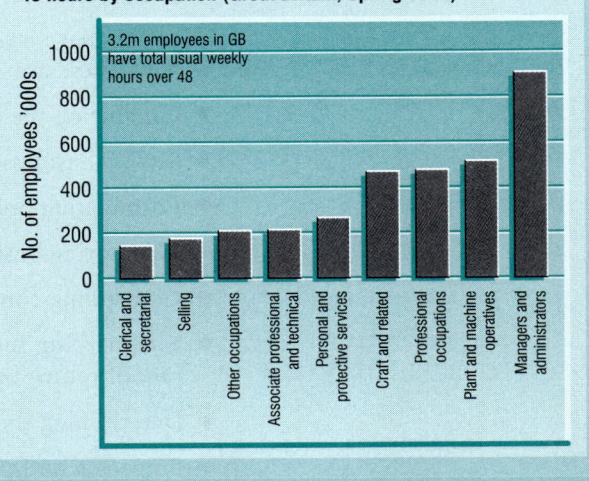

Place of work

A 'usual' place of work is often specified in the employment contract of individual employers. This will be a defined office, shop, or factory location. However, some staff are required to be **mobile** and carry out some, or even all, of their duties at different sites. For some, travel may be infrequent - for example, the occasional business meeting - while other staff such as regional sales teams may be required to be truly mobile. Travel away from a 'usual' place, or work that involves overnight stays, will often require subsistence allowances for travel, hotels, and meals.

A growing number of employees, with the agreement of their employers, are taking advantage of new communications technology that enables them to work from home. This is known as **teleworking** (see 13.3).

Key words

Contract of employment - a legal agreement between employer and employee, setting out terms and conditions of service. Contracts can be permanent, long-term, or short-term for a fixed period, usually around 12 weeks to 5 years

Working conditions - conditions to which employees agree to work, including hours, wages, entitlements to sick leave, holiday, and maternity leave and pay, redundancy, and health and safe working environments.

Section 13.2 Job roles

Directors

The highest level of management in a limited company is the **board of directors**. Directors are elected each year, usually on the basis of their experience and past business performance, and are appointed to run the company on behalf of its shareholders. Some directors may be shareholders in the company themselves.

Directors have a number of responsibilities, some of which are laid down in law. These are:

- Organizing the company and its resources into productive activity
- Setting business objectives
- Formulating policies and plans to achieve set objectives
- Monitoring business performance
- Controlling company activities
- Safeguarding funds invested by shareholders and ensuring a reasonable rate of return on their investment
- Determining the distribution of profits
- Preparing and publishing an annual report
- Protecting the company against fraud and inefficiency

Executive directors have full-time responsibilities and are actively engaged in the running of the company. **Non-executive directors** act only in a part-time capacity. These are people employed for their business knowledge and expertise to attend board meetings and provide an independent and fresh view of decision-making. They may also provide useful links with other organizations because of directorships they hold in other companies.

A firm may also invite an employee representative to sit on the board as a non-executive member. Breaking down divisions between management and employees and encouraging worker participation in the decision-making process is increasing in popularity in the UK (see 13.3).

Managing directors

The **managing director**, or **chief executive**, is a director elected, not by shareholders, but by the board of directors to head the organization. The managing director is responsible to the board, and will usually be appointed on the basis of a proven track record in business management.

Specific duties and responsibilities of the managing director include:

- Appointing senior managers
- Implementing company policies designed to achieve business goals
- Supervising and coordinating day-to-day activities within the company
- Developing an organizational culture
- Meeting important Trade Union and government officials, key suppliers, and customers, and taking part in negotiations with them on major issues

▼ *Figure 13.2: Who's who in the boardroom*

Other board roles

The **company secretary** is not a director, but an executive officer appointed by the board to carry out administrative duties on their behalf. The company secretary has two main obligations:

- The administration of board and shareholders' meetings, including arranging venues and dates, preparing agendas, recording minutes, etc.

- Ensuring that the company meets all its legal requirements, including compliance with the Memorandum and Articles of Association, reporting changes in company directors, preparing and publishing annual company accounts, etc.

The **chairperson** is elected by the board to chair board meetings. S/he may be either an executive or non-executive member of the board.

Portfolio Activity 13.2

Range: Job roles, Responsibilities
Skills: Collect and record data

1. Collect at least five company reports from large public limited companies. These should available to the public on request from the company headquarters.

2. From the reports, identify and compare the various functions of the directors.

▼ Types of managerial positions available

Finance Manager
Broad Commercial Role

Up to £35,000 + Car + Benefits — West Midlands

Outstanding opportunity for commercially focused young finance professional. Wide ranging responsibilities within continuous improvement culture. Director designate position.

THE COMPANY
- Highly successful subsidiary of £500 million plc. Turnover £7 million. Fast growing, 40% compound growth year on year.
- Regarded for product innovation and outstanding customer service.
- Quality focused. Goal to achieve world class manufacturing status.

THE POSITION
- Lead team of 15 in accounts, quality, systems, personnel, warehouse and purchasing functions. Report to Managing Director.
- Ensure the timely and accurate production of financial results. Liaise with divisional and Group Head Offices.
- Develop information systems to support business operations and decisions.
- Significant input into tactical and strategic development of business. Key member of senior management team.

QUALIFICATIONS
- Highly talented qualified Accountant, probably aged between 28 and 35.
- Previous financial management experience within a quality driven company. Ability to combine hands-on/task orientated work with a strategic outlook.
- Bright, resourceful and flexible. Must possess excellent communication and people management skills.

Please send full cv by June 24th, stating salary and ref. GSM2248, to Barkers Response & Assessment, Berwick House, 35 Livery Street, Birmingham B3 2PB

What is management?

Managers influence all aspects of modern organizations. Production managers run manufacturing operations that produce goods to satisfy our wants and needs. Sales managers organize sales teams to market goods and services. Personnel managers provide the organization with skilled and productive human resources.

The term **management** is used in two different ways. It can refer simply to those individuals within an organization who are managers. Or it may describe the skills and knowledge used by managers to achieve organizational goals.

DDD
BUSINESS DEVELOPMENT MANAGER BASED HERTS

Dendron Limited is an independent company achieving enviable growth with a portfolio of well established and successful brands including Ibuleve, Blisteze, Oz and Stain Devils.

The Business Development Manager will play a central role in leading Dendron's future growth by:-

★ Planning and pursuing sales and profit objectives for a group of Brands.
★ Defining category development potential through new product opportunities and existing Brand Activities.
★ Working with the Dendron Sales Team and major customer accounts to address ongoing and future consumer and category sales requirements.
★ Using Strategic and Budget planning procedures to gain management approval for plans.

We require an experienced Brand Manager who is looking for increased responsibility and personal development.

The rewards include a competitive salary, company car, contributory pension scheme, life assurance and the chance to develop a career with a progressive company.

Write with full details or for an application form contact The Personnel Department, DDD Limited, 94 Rickmansworth Road, Watford, Herts WD1 7JJ. Telephone: (0923) 229251.

No Agencies Please

Korean Store Manager and Sales Manager - London

Top Korean tour group luxury goods store requires a store manager and a sales manager. The store manager will have full profit centre, human resource, procurement and merchandising responsibilities; the sales manager will be responsible for outside sales. Candidates should have at least four years experience in merchandising or sales, speak fluent Korean and English, have a higher education qualification and be prepared to work at weekends.

Please apply with full resume and a covering letter in English & Korean to Box GAR88 The Guardian, 164 Deansgate, Manchester, M60

Research Manager

London-based business magazine publisher seeks Research Manager. Responsibilities will include editing two yearbooks/directories; organising market research projects; market data origination, compilation and formatting; and contributing statistical material to company's title. Successful applicant will have research and directory-compiling experience, and be able to produce reports on Mac/Quark XPress or similar electronic systems. Good salary and prospects.

Send CV with samples of work to:
Box GAR58 The Guardian, 164 Deansgate, Manchester, M60 2RR.

BROCKHILL PARK SCHOOL
Business Manager (New Post)
Salary circa £25,000

Brockhill Park School is an 11-18 mixed school of 1100 students set in extensive grounds including a fully operational farm unit. The Governing Body wish to appoint a suitable person to join the school's Senior Management Team with effect from 1st January 1995 under the leadership of the Headteacher Tony Lyng. The school is going through a challenging and exciting phase of development.

The successful applicant must demonstrate that s/he

* is committed to education in the state sector.
* has the business acumen to effectively manage and develop all aspects of school finances, premises and grounds maintenance.
* the ability to communicate effectively and confidently.
* the personnel management skills to manage a wide range of full-time, part-time and temporary support staff.

For further details please apply to:
Mrs A Amos,
Clerk to the Governors, at the school.
Brockhill Park School, Sandling Road, Hythe, Kent CT21 4HL

Closing Date: Monday 5th September 1994.

UNIT FOUR

CHAPTER 13

Some definitions of management

Management...

'...entails activities undertaken by one or more persons in order to coordinate the activities of others in the pursuit of ends that cannot be achieved by any one person'

(Donelly, J, Gibson, J, and Ivancevich, J)

'...is the process of designing and maintaining an environment in which individuals, working together in groups, accomplish efficiently selected aims'

(Koontz, H, and Weinrich, H)

'...is the process of working with and through others to effectively achieve organizational objectives by efficiently using limited resources in a changing environment'

(Kreitner, R)

'...is the coordination of all resources through the processes of planning, organizing, directing and controlling in order to attain stated objectives'

(Sisk, H)

Managers have the responsibility for combining and using productive resources - human, physical, financial - to ensure that organizations achieve their goals. All organizations, business, government, charity, even sports teams, need good management to achieve their objectives. Whether or not an organization achieves its aims depends greatly on the quality of its management.

Portfolio Activity 13.3

Range: Job roles, Responsibilities
Skills: Produce written material, Collect and record data

Use the job adverts for managers on page 316 and your personal knowledge and observations of managers either in your school/college, place of work experience, etc, to identify and list the general functions managers must perform and the qualities you think they need to carry them out.

As part of this exercise, you might ask to spend half a day observing a manager at work. After you have made your observations, discuss them with the manager in question. Find out whether or not the tasks and behaviour you observed were typical.

▼ Figure 13.3: Fayol's activities in business operations

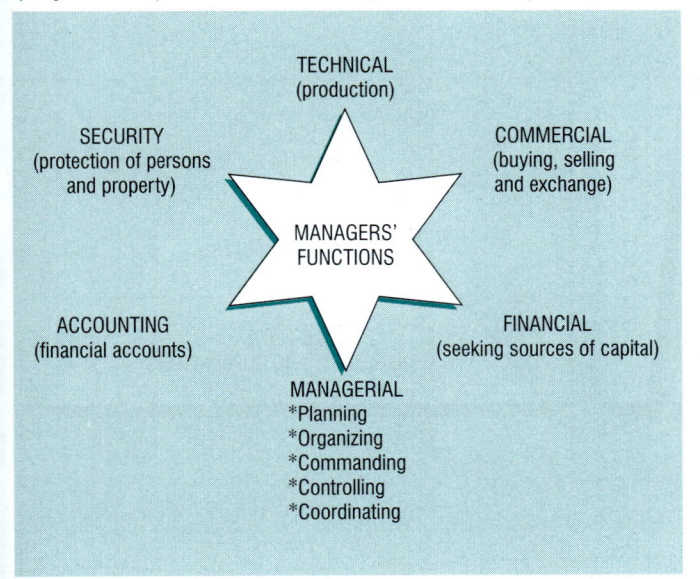

TECHNICAL (production)
COMMERCIAL (buying, selling and exchange)
FINANCIAL (seeking sources of capital)
MANAGERIAL
 *Planning
 *Organizing
 *Commanding
 *Controlling
 *Coordinating
ACCOUNTING (financial accounts)
SECURITY (protection of persons and property)

MANAGERS' FUNCTIONS

The management process

Management science is devoted to understanding and explaining the role and behaviour of management. Henri Fayol, a French industrialist writing in 1916, has become known as the 'father' of modern management theory, and was one of the first to recognize the need to teach good management skills.

Fayol argued that the activities of any business organization could be divided into six groups as shown in Figure 13.3. His analysis concentrates on managerial activities.

Fayol describes five basic managerial functions. These are:

- **Planning:** setting objectives and choosing strategies, policies, and tasks to achieve them. This will include identifying, and meeting, the training needs of their staff.

317

- **Organizing:** establishing an intentional structure of job roles for people to play within an organization. The concept of a 'role' implies that people have a definite purpose or objective to fulfil.

- **Commanding:** giving instructions to subordinates to carry out assigned tasks. Managers have the authority to make decisions and the responsibility to see that they are carried out. This function requires managers to be good leaders - motivating, directing, and mobilizing subordinates toward goal attainment.

- **Controlling:** measuring and correcting the activities of subordinates. Managers must make sure that the performance of individuals and departments within the organization meets pre-established standards. If not, they must put in motion actions to correct poor performance and help ensure that plans are accomplished.

- **Coordinating:** harmonizing individual efforts towards the accomplishment of organizational goals. Not all individuals will identify with, or hold, the same objectives as the organization they work for. It therefore becomes a central task of the manager to reconcile differences in the approach, timing, and efforts of individuals to contribute to the goals of the organization. Some have called this function 'the essence of managership'. Each of the managerial functions is an exercise contributing to coordination.

Levels of management

Within most organizations there will be more than one level of management. All managers will carry out managerial functions, but the time spent on each function may differ between the different levels. Top-level or senior managers will spend much of their time on strategic decision-making and planning. Supervisors and lower-level managers, on the other hand, will spend a great deal of time commanding.

The diagram below shows how much time different managers can be expected to spend on each function within the typical organization, and the various objectives they hope to achieve.

▼ *Figure 13.4: Time spent carrying out managerial functions*

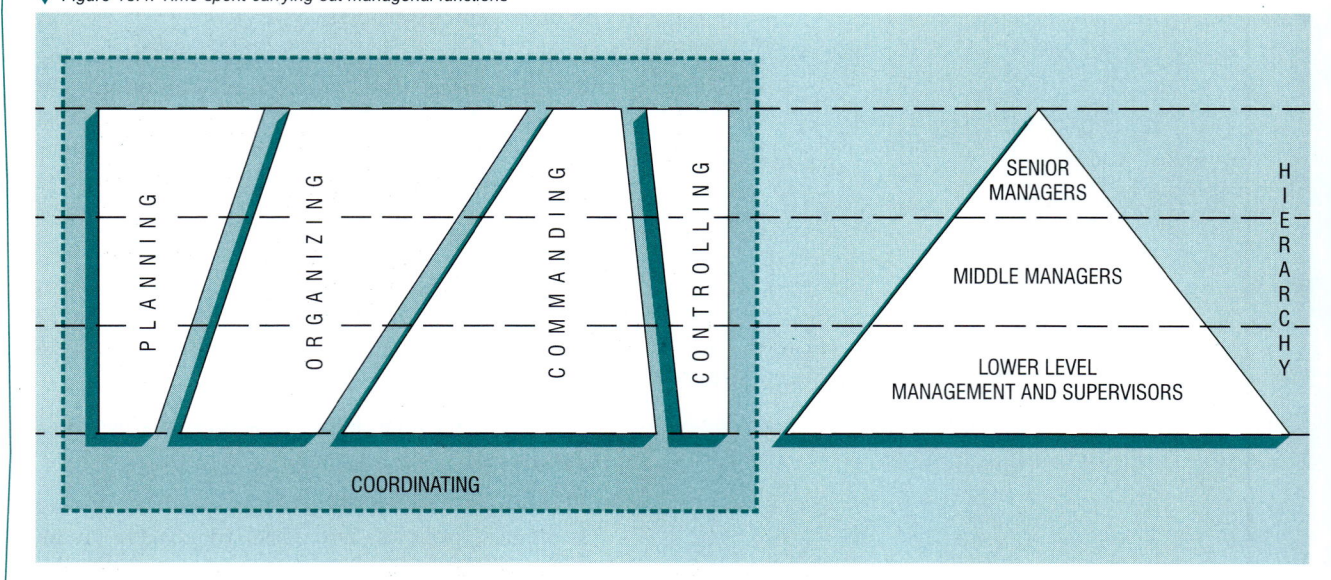

Consultants and advisers

Organizations known as consultancies are able to provide specialist advice to business organizations, who will often contract their services for special one-off projects. For example, firms of consultants may be brought in to advise on new communication systems, office and factory layouts, marketing campaigns, or new constructions, recruitment procedures, and production processes.

Some consultancies, however, may be offered call-off contracts which means that they are paid to provide regular advice as and when necessary - for example, collecting and providing up-to-date economic data from around the world, or giving advice on UK business taxation.

Supervisors

The **supervisor** is usually regarded as the first managerial grade in an organization hierarchy. Supervisors will often be workers promoted off the 'shop-floor' because of their hard work, initiative, and leadership qualities.

The job of the supervisor will vary between organizations but, in general, s/he or she will be a manager who has had extensive contact with 'shop floor' workers and knows how things should be done 'on the ground'. Supervisors are the first in line to deal with day-to-day operations and problems as they occur - for example, a breakdown in a piece of machinery, staff absenteeism, a hold-up in supplies, etc.

▼ *Specialist advice at a price*

Allan C Weller
F.M.S. M.I. Mgt. EURO I.E.

Productivity Improvement Consultant

UK's Leading Authority on M.P.I.P. (Management Performance Improvement Programme)

COMBINING -
- Organisational Analysis
- Operator Involvement
- Problem Solving
- Personnel Development & Training
- Productivity Improvement
- Operational Control

Listed under the D.T.I. Support for Manufacturing Scheme

3 Woodlands Drive, Malpas
Newport, Gwent NP9 6QD
Tel: (0633) 854042

INTERNATIONAL ENQUIRIES WELCOME

Portfolio Activity 13.4

Range: Job roles, Responsibilities
Skills: Read and respond to written material

The two job adverts above are for supervisors in different organizations. Use them to make a list of the general functions a supervisor could be expected to perform, and the personal qualities you think they might need for the job. Draw on any personal experience you have of supervisors in organizations that you know.

SCAFFOLDING SUPERVISOR/ESTIMATOR

MG Scaffolding is a well established scaffolding contractor, and we wish to continue our expansion in the Cambridge area by appointing an experienced Scaffolding/Estimator to join our management team.

To be considered for this position you must be able to demonstrate the following attributes:-
★ Minimum of 5 years experience in the Scaffolding Industry.
★ Proven skills in the planning, motivation and control of labour, and materials planning.
★ The ability to achieve demanding operational and financial targets.
★ Flexible and enthusiastic approach to work.

We offer an attractive remuneration package, including competitive salary, performance related bonus scheme, and Company car.

Please apply in writing enclosing a C.V. to:
The Operations Director
MG Scaffold Limited, Industrial Estate
Stanton Harcourt, Oxford OX8 1SL

Croner Publications Ltd, the country's leading publisher in business information is seeking a

SUPERVISOR

to join our Electronic Product Help Desk to promote quality customer care in the developing field of electronic publishing.

As Supervisor, you will be responsible for providing front-line support to subscribers over the telephone, supporting a team of executives and producing a variety of management information and statistics.

A sound educational background to GCSE level (or equivalent) is necessary, together with a working knowledge of PCs, ideally Wordperfect and Lotus spreadsheet packages.

Previous supervisory experience, preferably with a telephone/customer service environment, is essential, together with a mature and flexible approach to work.

As a progressive company, Croner Publications Ltd offers a competitive salary and an attractive benefits package including life assurance, a pension scheme (subject to qualifying conditions), 28 days' holiday and medical cover. Hours of work are normally 35 per week as appropriate, within an 8am - 6pm framework.

Applicants should write, with a CV and details of current salary, to Moira Jevons at:-
Croner Publications Ltd
Croner House, London Road,
Kingston-Upon-Thames, Surrey KT2 6SR
Tel: 081-547 3333
Fax: 081-541 1733

Closing date: Friday 7 October 1994

NON-SMOKERS PREFERRED

The operative (or shop-floor worker)

The **operative** is a skilled, semi-skilled, or unskilled worker, whether a machine operator in a manufacturing plant, a bank clerk, a sales assistant in a shop, a trainee accountant, or a truck driver. Operatives, or shop-floor workers, undertake essential tasks directly related to the production of goods and services. In an office environment these workers are known as **assistants**.

Operatives are at the bottom of the organizational hierarchy. They are responsible to a manager, usually a supervisor. Some may have a high degree of autonomy and responsibility in their jobs - for example, for quality control, ordering stocks, and problem-solving. Others - for example, an administrative assistant - may carry out a narrow range of repetitive tasks, such as filing and photocopying.

Key words

Board of directors - body elected by shareholders to run a company

Executive directors - directors with full-time responsibilities who are are actively engaged in running a company

Non-executive directors - individuals employed for their expertise or business contacts, who act only in a part-time advisory capacity

Managing director - appointed by the board of directors to implement company policies and supervise and coordinate day-to-day activities

Company secretary - executive officer appointed by a board of directors to carry out administrative duties

Chairperson - elected by a board of directors to chair their meetings

Management - can refer either to people who are managers, or to the various managerial skills and knowledge they must possess in order to achieve organizational goals

Consultant - person, or organization, providing specialist advice, usually under a fixed-term contract

Supervisor - first-line manager with responsibility for day-to-day production issues

Operative - shop-floor worker or office assistant

Section 13.3 Change at work

Towards a flexible workforce

Since the early 1980s, the composition of the UK labour force has changed significantly. By 1994, the UK had witnessed a rise in the number of workers who were either self-employed, working part-time, or in temporary jobs, relative to the number of full-time workers (see 16.3). There was also an increase in the number of workers engaged on short-term contracts.

These changes at work were prompted by the need to create workforces that are flexible to the changing needs of organizations and can be adapted more easily to new products and methods of working.

Many organizations have achieved flexibility by dividing their workforces into 'core', 'periphery', and 'external' groups.

- **Core workers**. These are full-time employees who are multi-skilled in performing varied and mainly key tasks. They will tend to be offered good pay and conditions, and a high degree of job security. This is achieved at the cost of employing 'peripheral' groups of workers, who can be hired and fired as necessary to match changes in consumer demand for a firm's products.

Figure 13.5: Inside a flexible firm

Agency temps, contracted out services, self-employed

Part-time workers, temporary staff

Full-time multi-skilled workers

CORE
PERIPHERAL WORKERS
EXTERNAL WORKERS

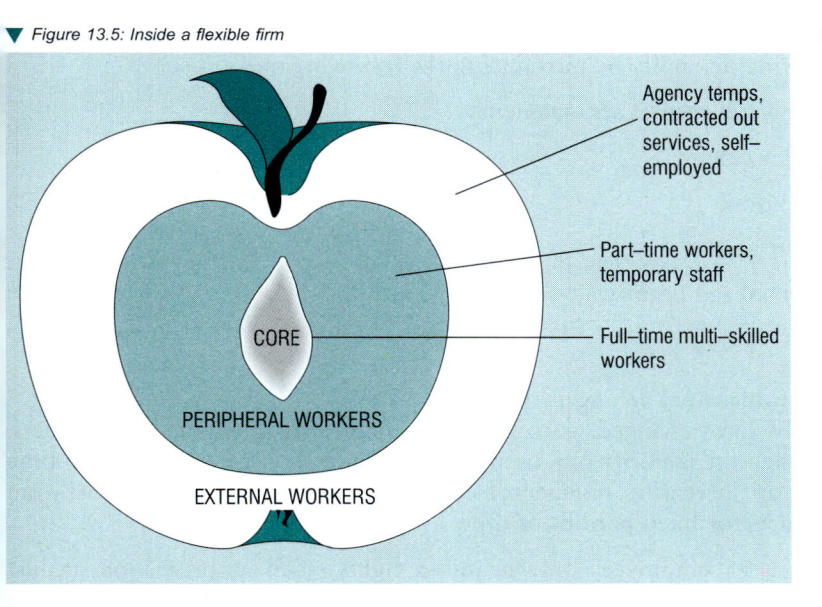

- **Peripheral workers.** These are temporary and part-time workers who receive less favourable pay, conditions, and benefits.
- **External workers.** These are workers who are not directly employed by the firm, such as agency temps, self-employed workers, and sub-contracted workers from other firms. External workers will tend to carry out non-core functions, such as catering, cleaning, computer maintenance, Public Relations, etc. Consultants may also be employed for special one-off projects such as designing and installing new office equipment or advising on a new factory location.

Re-engineering

The term **re-engineering** refers to the way businesses overhaul themselves as part of a process of continuous change. Re-engineering is associated with reducing the size of the business organization, or **downsizing**. As the name suggests, this leads to fewer, but more highly skilled, workers in the 'core', doing more complex and varied work. Downsizing in UK organizations was especially apparent during the economic recession of the early 1980s and again at the beginning of the 1990s, when profits were squeezed by falling consumer demand and there was a need for businesses to trim costs.

Portfolio Activity 13.5

Range: Working conditions, Reasons for change
Skills: Collect and record data, Produce written material

1. Investigate whether it is possible to divide employees in your school/college into core and peripheral workers. Identify the occupations of core and peripheral workers. Are any tasks undertaken by external workers?

2. Contrast the information you have collected from your school/college with another organization with which you are familiar.

3. What do you think are the advantages to both organizations of structuring their workforce into core, periphery and external workers? If possible, try to confirm your views by interviewing head teachers and personnel managers in both organizations.

Other ways to achieve labour flexibility

Increasingly, business organizations are creating workforces that are flexible in terms of skills and the hours they work, so that staffing levels can be adjusted easily to match the fluctuations in consumer demand that occur each week, season, or with cyclical variations in the level of economic activity.

Apart from increasing the use of **non-standard labour**, firms are also achieving flexibility by introducing the following measures:

- New contractual arrangements
- Teleworking
- Flexitime
- Shift work
- Annualized hours
- Job sharing

New contractual arrangements

As jobs have changed, so too has the nature of employment contracts. Although the majority of jobs are still contracted on a permanent full-time basis, an increasing number of employees are being offered short-term contracts for fixed periods of time.

Until 1995 employees only acquired rights, such as protection against unfair dismissal and compensation for redundancy, if they had been in employment for two years or more (see 12.3). By offering contracts for periods of less than two years, firms could avoid the costs associated with these employment rights, and be more flexible in their ability to 'hire and fire' staff to match changing needs.

However, organizations can also negotiate changes to existing long-term employment contracts, for example by:

- Changing hours of work
- Reducing the wage rate
- Introducing performance-related pay
- Altering holiday entitlements
- Introducing new working practices, e.g. Sunday working or night-time shifts
- Re-location
- Introducing additional duties and responsibilities
- Introducing new technology

Of course, workers may resist these changes in negotiations with employees which, if appropiate, will be conducted by via Trade Union representatives (see 12.5).

Introducing changes to existing contracts without the agreement of staff can result in a breach of contract and worker dissatisfaction. This is liable to be reflected in lower productivity and work quality. However, workers may simply be given an ultimatum by their employer either to accept new contracts or face redundancy. To avoid this, many long-term contracts now contain clauses which specifically require the employee to accept change and adapt to the changing needs of the organization.

Teleworking

Home working is a growing feature of the UK labour market. It can be observed in most industries, with particular concentrations in the South East and in the financial and business services sector. So-called teleworking has become feasible because of technological advance. Home workers are now able to keep in touch with their main office via modem links on personal computers, by fax machines, and even with new videophones (see 6.2). However, the number of teleworkers in the U.K. is still relatively small - around 650,000 in 1993.

Portfolio Activity 13.6

Range: Working conditions, Reasons for change, Evaluate
Skills: Read and respond to written material

1. Explain the factors which have led to the introduction of flexible working practices for employees in American Express.

2. What are the advantages of flexible working practices (a) for American Express, and (b) their employees?

3. Consider the introduction of flexible working practices similar to those used by American Express for staff in (a) your school/college, and (b) another medium-sized organization with which you are familiar. Produce a short article, similar to one you might find in *Employment Gazette*, discussing how practical flexible practices might be in each case.

The family-friendly firm   American Express

PRACTICAL EFFORTS to make itself 'the best place to work' and a helpful attitude to working parents recently won American Express the *1991 Employer of the Year Award* from the Working Mothers Association. This award demonstrates how flexible working arrangements benefit both employer and employees.

The UK headquarters of American Express are in Brighton, where it employs 2,500 staff, nearly two-thirds of whom are female. Over the past two years the company has set about adapting its working environment in order to become a 'family-friendly firm'.

Spurred on by predicted demographic changes, a steady loss of female staff leaving work to have children, and a highly competitive local labour market, the management decided to look seriously into how best to retain its skilled employees for the future.

In July 1990 it conducted a 'work and homelife' survey. Staff were asked how they thought the company could help parents combine work and domestic responsibilities. Top of the list came a workplace nursery.

So, American Express joined forces with a local, well-established childcare company, Early Years Childcare plc, to open a nursery for its employees' children.

Both current staff (and new recruits) have been actively encouraged to make use of this facility. It is clear that the nursery is meeting requirements – parents' comments have ranged from "Without the nursery I would probably not have been able to return to work" to "It's the reason I came back to work."

As well as these initiatives in childcare, American Express has introduced comprehensive flexible working policies for its employees. These include flexitime, home working and teleworking, job sharing, school-term contracts, part-time and shift working and extended leave.

Employment Gazette February 1992

▼ Figure 13.6: Occupations of teleworkers

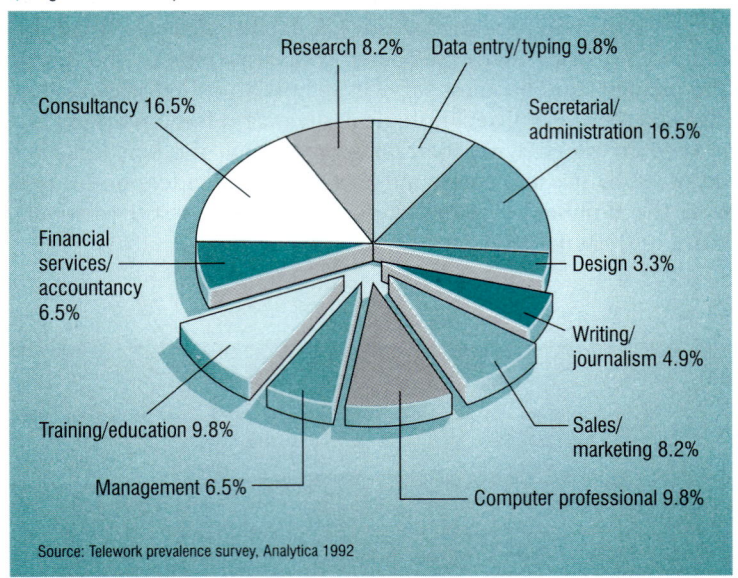

- Research 8.2%
- Data entry/typing 9.8%
- Consultancy 16.5%
- Secretarial/administration 16.5%
- Financial services/accountancy 6.5%
- Design 3.3%
- Writing/journalism 4.9%
- Training/education 9.8%
- Sales/marketing 8.2%
- Management 6.5%
- Computer professional 9.8%

Source: Telework prevalence survey, Analytica 1992

Employment Gazette 2.94

▼ A typical home office

▼ Advantages and disadvantages of teleworking

Advantages to the firm	Disadvantages to the firm
• With more staff working at home, a firm will be able to reduce overall floorspace requirements and associated costs	• Possible loss of management control over home working staff
• Avoidance of commuting can be a significant incentive for employees, while employers may benefit from reduced wage claims to cover rising public transport fares, petrol prices, and parking charges.	• Cost of equipment
	• Communication problems/unavailability of staff for meetings called at short notice
• Home working can motivate staff, reduce stress associated with travel and the office environment, and increase productivity.	• Difficulty of on-job training

Annualized hours systems

Under this system, instead of working a specified number of hours each week, workers are contracted to work a given number of hours over a 12-month period. This means a business can vary the number of hours from week to week or seasonally to meet its requirements - for example, to match fluctuations in consumer demand.

Flexitime

Unlike the annual hours system, **Flexitime** gives the employee the ability to choose, within limits, when to start to start work and when to finish during the working day, as long as a specified number of hours are completed each week. Work in excess of agreed hours can normally count towards extra leave. Because some people like to start early and others will want to start later each morning, a business organization will benefit from an extended period of staff cover in its offices. However, there may be some additional costs to a business. For example, firms will need to pay extra for lighting and heating because workers on Flexitime may be starting earlier and others leaving later at night.

Flexitime tends to be a feature of office-based jobs: it is not very practical for retail outlets or manufacturing plants to allow workers to turn up for work when they want to.

Shift work

Firms that wish to remain operative for more than 8 or 9 hours each day will require their employees to work in **shifts.** Shift work involves using different groups of workers in rotation. For example, a manufacturer who wants to keep running 24 hours a day may employ workers on three shifts: 10pm - 6 am, 6am - 2pm, and 2 pm - 10 pm. Similarly, shops which open from 8am to 9pm may use two or three overlapping shifts, complemented by part-time workers. Workers on night shifts will often be paid an additional shift allowance.

Job sharing

As the name suggests, **job sharing** involves dividing up a full-time job between two or more part-time workers. The main problem is a possible lack of continuity in the job. Those sharing the job need to keep each other informed of the tasks undertaken and their decisions.

▼ Table 13.3 People usually engaged in weekend working, shift work and night work[2], Spring 1994

United Kingdom

	Total (thousands)	As a percentage of all in employment
Saturday working	6,289	24.6
Shift work[3]	4.138	16.2
Sunday working	3,110	12.2
Night work	1,577	6.2

[1] Respondents were asked if they worked unsocial hours: usually, sometimes or never.

[2] It is possible for respondents to appear in more than one category.

[3] Includes both weekend and night shifts.

Social Trends 1995

▼ Table 13.4 Employees with flexible working patterns[1] ... by gender, Spring 1994

United Kingdom   **Percentages**

	Male	Female	All persons
Full-time			
Flexible working hours	9.7	15.4	11.7
Annualized working hours	5.6	6.4	5.8
Term-time working	1.1	4.7	2.4
Job sharing	–	0.2	0.1
Nine day fortnight	0.7	0.4	0.6
Four and a half day week	3.2	3.1	3.1
All full-time employees (= 100%)(thousands)	10,573	5,681	16,254
Part-time			
Flexible working hours	7.3	9.1	8.8
Annualized working hours	3.1	5.3	5.0
Term-time working	4.9	10.3	9.6
Job sharing	1.8	2.5	2.4
Nine day fortnight	–	–	–
Four and a half day week	–	0.3	0.3
All part-time employees (= 100%)(thousands)	745	4,760	5,506

[1] It is possible for respondents to appear in more than one category.

Social Trends 1995

Reasons for change

There are a number of reasons why firms are introducing more flexible working practices and arrangements. These include:

- **Competitive market pressures.** Increasing competition for consumers has meant that firms must reduce their costs if they are to be in a position to cut prices. They also need to be able to react quickly to changes in consumer wants.

  By creating flexible workforces, organizations can match staffing levels more closely to peaks and troughs in consumer demand. If all employees were on long-term contracts for full-time employment, cutting labour requirements during periods of low or falling consumer demand would result in high redundancy payments.

- **To improve productivity.** If a firm is able to produce more output with the same, or fewer, resources, then productivity will increase, and the cost per unit of output produced will fall. If a firm is to be competitive, it must match the productivity gains of rival firms (see 15.1).

- **To reduce costs/improve quality.** An increasing number of larger organizations have downsized and sub-contracted non-core functions such as catering and cleaning to smaller external organizations. Larger firms can insist on quality at competitive rates from small organizations or individuals willing to undertake these functions. For example, many local and central government department functions were 'market tested' in the early 1990s as part of the government's policy of privatization (see 3.5).

- **Diversification.** Rather than producing just one product or service, most medium-to-large organizations produce many different ones, sold in different markets all over the world. Producing a range of products spreads the risk of falling demand or a hold-up in supplies for any one product. However, employees both at the managerial level and on the shop floor must have the necessary skills and be flexible enough to adapt them as required.

- **To motivate employees.** Core workers can be motivated by performance-related pay and job security (see 15.4). However, even peripheral workers may be motivated by the flexibility offered by part-time or temporary work.

- **To adapt to technological changes.** New technology requires new skills and methods of working. In many cases, new technology has also enabled firms to reduce the size of their workforces without reducing output.

- **The need for new skills.** Sometimes firms will not have all the skills they need within their existing workforce. Advancing technology and changing consumer demands create a need for new skills. These skills may be bought into a firm on a temporary basis - for example, a consultancy advising on the introduction of computerized production lines - or may be acquired on a semi-permanent basis, through the employment of self-employed people on renewable short-term contracts.

Implementing and monitoring change

There are three fundamental elements that will make changes to working methods and conditions successful in a business. These are:

- Planning
- Training
- Monitoring

Planning

Changes need to be planned carefully. A business will need a clear idea of how they will effect production, costs and revenues, and how manpower and equipment requirements might change. Explaining the need for change to employees and working out how best to minimise any negative impacts on them is important if workers are to accept changes and continue to work towards the goals of the organisation.

Training

Where new production processes, technology and/or methods of working are introduced, training will be very important if employees are to be able to adopt these changes and use equipment effectively. Business managers will need to identify and meet the training needs of employees.

Portfolio Activity 13.7

Range: Working conditions, Reasons for change, Evaluate
Skills: Read and respond to written material, Take part in discussions

1. What costs does the article suggest are being imposed on workers as a result of changes in employment practices and the nature of contracts in firms, and why?
2. What new skills does Professor Cooper say workers will need to learn?
3. Explain firms' motives for introducing the changes described in the article.
4. What additional costs might be imposed on a firm as a result of increasing the stress on its employees?
5. Conduct a small survey of employees in an organization(s) with you are familiar. Design an appropriate questionnaire to find out their views on changes in their working conditions and pay arrangements, such as performance-related pay. For example:
   - What do they think these changes are designed to achieve, and why?
   - What are their views on these changes and their long-term pay and job prospects?
   - Do they think pressure on them to perform well in their jobs has increased?
   - Do they believe their health has suffered as a result?

Need to tackle stress urged

An age of uncertainty in the workplace is increasing stress among professional and office employees, in spite of the UK's emergence from recession, a stress management expert said yesterday.

Professor Cary Cooper, of Manchester School of Management, said the lack of a 'feelgood factor' was less about short-term job security than about a belief that people would never have the sort of permanent jobs they used to have.

Big companies were continuing to slim down their workforces and using contractors for many activities. While the rate of unemployment was coming down, many new jobs were casual, contract or part-time and project work, he said. This was creating demands for large numbers of freelance employees who often felt they had to work longer hours and miss out on holidays. Domestic pressures had also increased since the family employment pattern had changed, he said. About 65 per cent of women aged between 16 and 59 were now in work.

By the end of the millennium, "people will need training on how to cope with such things as VAT, organizing their work, negotiating contracts and handling computer systems."

Employers need to tackle workplace stress seriously, Prof. Cooper said. Factors forcing them to do so included litigation, increases in corporate health insurance, the estimated £2.2 billion-a-year cost to industry of alcoholism and the estimated £11 billion-a-year cost of sickness absence.

Financial Times 12.1.95

Monitoring

The success of measures designed to make working conditions and labour forces more flexible can be measured in the following ways:

- **Impact on productivity.** Output per employee should be higher than before. A firm will hope to produce more with less labour input.

- **Impact on efficiency.** Costs should be lower and profit margins higher.

- **Impact on quality.** Product quality and/or customer services should have improved, and waste reduced as a result.

However, the effects of increasing flexibility are not felt by firms alone. Individuals can also feel the impact of changes in working practices - both positive and negative:

- **Stress.** The separation of workforces into core, periphery, and external groups of workers will result in unemployment for those unfortunate enough not to be retained as 'core' workers. Full-time workers who lose their jobs may find that they have to take part-time or temporary jobs instead to earn a living. Short-term contracts and contracting out can also lead to increased job uncertainty.

- **Job satisfaction.** On the positive side, those lucky enough to retain their jobs may benefit from the increased flexibility that Flexitime and annualized hours systems give them. Teleworking also relieves people of the need to commute to and from work every day, while job sharing and part-time work may suit many people who have other commitments during the day, for example, meeting children from school, doing voluntary work, or running a small business as a sideline.

Key words

Non-standard labour - Non-full-time workers who are employed either on fixed or short-term contracts or on a more permanent part-time basis

Flexible firm - a firm that divides its workforce into core, peripheral, and external groups

Core workers - full-time employees performing mainly key functions within an organization

Peripheral workers - temporary and part-time workers who tend to be employed to match fluctuations in demand

External workers - sub-contracted labour performing non-core activities such as catering

Downsizing - reducing the size of a business organization by focusing production and the workforce on core functions

Teleworking - employees working from home

Annualized hours - a system of contracting employees to work a specified number of hours each year, rather than a specified number of hours each week

Flexitime - a system which allows workers to choose the time they start and finish work each day within specified hours

Job sharing - when two or more part-time workers share the same full-time job

Re-engineering - looking at, and redesigning from first principles, the structure, job roles, and tasks within an organisation

---

Further reading

Dixon, R: *The Management Task* (Butterworth/Heinemann 1993)

Drucker, P: *The Practice of Management* (Harper & Bros. 1954)

Test Questions

The following underpinning knowledge will be examined:

1. Job roles and responsibilities within organizations
2. Reasons for change to working conditions
3. Evaluate changes to working conditions
4. Plan to implement changes in working conditions

Questions 1 - 3 share the following answer options:

- A Marketing manager
- B Managing director
- C Company secretary
- D Personnel manager

Which of the above will take the responsibility for:

1 Overall control of the company?

2 The legal affairs of the company?

3 Administration within the company?

4 Company directors are elected by shareholders to fulfil all of the following functions EXCEPT:

- A Formulating policies and plans to achieve set objectives
- B Publishing annual accounts
- C Determining the distribution of profits
- D Supervising and coordinating day-to-day company activities

Questions 5 - 7 share the following answer options:

- A Company director
- B Managing director
- C Consultant
- D Supervisor

Which of the above personnel is likely to have the following responsibilities?

5 Providing specialist advice within an agreed contract period

6 Implementing company policies designed to achieve business goals

7 Organizing production on a day-to-day basis

Questions 8 - 10 share the following answer options:

Working practices are becoming more flexible due to:

- A Flexitime
- B Job sharing
- C Teleworking
- D Annualized hours

Which of the above practices do the following describe?

8 Working from home

9 Dividing a full-time job between two or more part-time employees

10 Agreeing to work a set number of hours each year

11 a. Many firms seeking to increase labour flexibility have divided work tasks into core, peripheral, and external activities, and are employing workers on different terms and conditions. Explain what these terms and conditions are in each case.

b. Suggest and explain two other ways a firm might introduce labour force flexibility.

c. Suggest and explain two reasons why firms are introducing more flexible staffing arrangements and working conditions.

d. What impact could the changes in working conditions you have discussed have on employees? Explain your answer.

12 a. Contrast the roles of a managing director and a supervisor in a large office or factory.

b. Suggest two general responsibilities the two job roles will have in common.

c. Why might a business organization introduce shift work for their operatives?

d. Discuss the possible advantages and disadvantages to a firm of allowing middle- and low-grade managers to carry out some administrative work from home on at least one day each week.

assessment assignment

Advanced Business

Assessment Assignment

Range: Job roles
Responsibilities
Reasons for change
Working conditions
Evaluate
Plan to implement change

Skills: **Communication**
Take part in discussions
Produce written material
Application of Number
Collect and record data
Information Technology
Process information
Present information

A day in the life of...

You are a lecturer in Business and Management Science at a local college. You are to develop case study materials for your classes on job roles and responsibilities in two business organizations of your choice.

chapter 14

Tasks

1. Each case study will contain observations on the general and specific duties and responsibilities of people carrying out job roles at different levels in the organizational hierarchy. Where appropriate, these roles will include:

- Director
- Manager
- Supervisor
- Operatives (or assistants in office environments)

Where appropriate, you should distinguish between daily routine tasks associated with each job role, and their long-term strategic responsibilities.

2. Your case studies should also summarize the working conditions and practices of four job roles from senior to junior grades. Each case study should explore:

- How these may have changed over time with the introduction of more flexible working practices, such as teleworking, Flexitime, job sharing, and contracting out.
- Changing contractual arrangements
- The advantages and disadvantages for both employers and employees of changes to working conditions and practices that have taken place, or are about to be introduced.
- those jobs which have responsibility for implementing changes and how changes are planned and reviewed.

Use a word processor to write your case studies.

UNIT FOUR

chapter 14
Job Applications and Interviews

This chapter identifies and evaluates recruitment and selection procedures used by business to fill job vacancies

SO, WHAT MAKES YOU THINK YOU CAN DO THIS JOB THEN?

Key ideas

Recruitment refers to those activities that will generate a pool of suitable job applicants.

Selection involves the assessment of applicants for job vacancies

The purpose of recruitment and selection is to identify human resource needs in a business, match business objectives to jobs, and to match suitable applicants with job vacancies.

Recruitment and selection procedures involve advertising job vacancies, **shortlisting** candidates for interview, assessing candidates, confirming employment with a successful applicant, dealing with unsuccessful candidates, and planning induction programmes.

An organization must ensure that recruitment and selection procedures do not contravene legislation concerning discrimination.

Job analysis is the study of what a job entails in terms of the tasks, skills, and training required.

A **job description** provides information on what a job entails in terms of job title, position in organizational structure, duties and responsibilities, and hours and conditions of work.

A **person specification** describes in broad terms the skills, qualifications, abilities, competencies, and personal qualities a person will need in order to perform a particular job as described in a job description.

Job and person specifications provide information for use in preparing job advertisements and briefing interviewers.

Job vacancies can be filled by **external recruitment**, through adverts placed in local or national newspapers or Jobcentres, or by **internal recruitment**, usually by promoting existing staff

Job applicants can be asked to provide information about their suitability for a job via an **application form, Curriculum Vitae (CV)** or by writing a **letter of application**

Information provided by job applicants should be treated confidentially by the business organization.

The final stage of the selection process is the **interview** of shortlisted candidates. Interviews involve a face-to-face meeting between a candidate and his or her prospective employer.

The recruitment and selection process relies on both the job applicant and the employer being fair, honest, and providing accurate information.

Advanced Business

Section **14.1**

Recruitment and selection

The terms **recruitment** and **selection** are often confused. It is useful to make the following distinction:

- **Recruitment** is the first part of the process to fill a job vacancy. It refers to those activities that will generate a pool of suitable job applicants.

- **Selection** is the next stage, i.e. assessing job applicants by various methods, choosing between them, and making an offer of employment to the right candidate.

Since the 1980s, the UK labour market has undergone significant change. Rising unemployment has produced an over-supply of labour. The number of young people in the population is falling. Many more women are seeking employment. Heavy manufacturing industry has been in decline, to be replaced by high technology and service industries, such as retailing and finance. Consequently, there is growing pressure to get selection right.

▼ Recruitment

The activity of recruitment and selection has therefore had to adapt to overcome the following problems:

- Fewer jobs but larger numbers of applicants
- A need to comply with laws on sex and race discrimination
- Shortages of certain types of skilled labour

Increasing competition among employers for young workers and those with valuable skills is likely to force up wages. Alternatively, employers will need introduce more flexible working practices, such as multi-skilling or job sharing, or adapt their recruitment policies to tap alternative sources of labour - for example, older workers, women, and the disabled. There is already evidence that this is happening.

The need for effective recruitment and selection

It is the role of the human resources manager to identify the need for human resources, to attract the best candidates for new posts, and then to choose, or recruit, the most suitable candidate to fill the vacancy. If a candidate selected is unsuitable, or fails to be motivated by the work, then the business will fail to achieve the best from its human resources.

Selecting an unsuitable candidate to fill a job vacancy can also raise business costs. Output will be lower than it could otherwise be, and more training may be needed. The cost of employing an unsuitable air-traffic controller, for example, could be catastrophic. The process of recruitment and selection, therefore, needs careful planning and handling.

▼ *Figure 14.1: The recruitment and selection process*

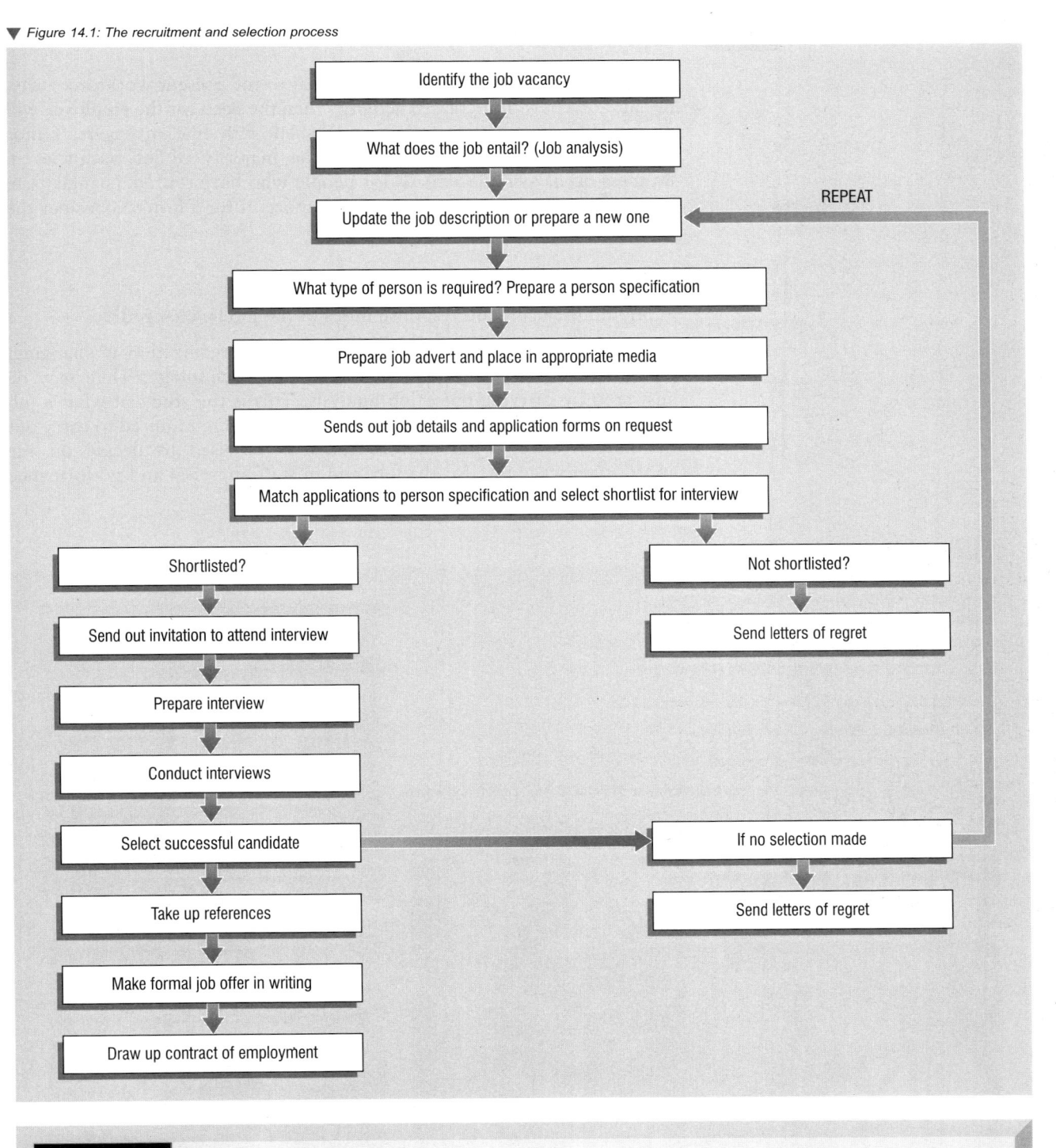

```
                    Identify the job vacancy
                              ↓
            What does the job entail? (Job analysis)
                              ↓
        Update the job description or prepare a new one  ← REPEAT
                              ↓
      What type of person is required? Prepare a person specification
                              ↓
          Prepare job advert and place in appropriate media
                              ↓
         Sends out job details and application forms on request
                              ↓
   Match applications to person specification and select shortlist for interview
                    ↓                              ↓
              Shortlisted?                   Not shortlisted?
                    ↓                              ↓
      Send out invitation to attend interview   Send letters of regret
                    ↓
             Prepare interview
                    ↓
             Conduct interviews
                    ↓
         Select successful candidate  →  If no selection made
                    ↓                              ↓
            Take up references              Send letters of regret
                    ↓
       Make formal job offer in writing
                    ↓
        Draw up contract of employment
```

Key words

Recruitment - the process of generating job applicants, for example from a job advertisement

Selection - assessing the suitability of applicants for a job

Advanced Business

Section **14.2**

The recruitment process

If a job vacancy in a business is additional to the present workforce - say, because of a new or increased activity - then the need for the employee will most likely already have been established with line managers, senior managers, and personnel. However, the majority of job vacancies in business occur as replacements for people who have retired, changed job, or been dismissed. In these cases, it is important for a firm to consider the following questions:

- Is the post still needed?
- Should the tasks and responsibilities of the job be changed?

Questions like these will also arise when the organization is changing, perhaps because of the introduction of new technology. They may be answered by carrying out a **job analysis**. This is the study of what a job entails, namely, the tasks, skills, and training that are required to carry out the job effectively. Job analysis can also be used to decide on the appropriate wage rate for the job, and in staff appraisal and performance monitoring once the post has been filled.

Portfolio Activity 14.1

Range: Job descriptions
Skills: Produce written material

Look at the jobs pictured. For each one, discuss and list:

1. The various tasks and activities involved
2. The skills the job holder must possess
3. Criteria that could be used to assess the appropriate rate of pay for the job and worker performance.

The job description

Once a business has analysed what a job involves, the next step is to prepare a **job description**.

Every job within an organization will have a written job description, usually drawn up immediately prior to the appointment of an employee. Job descriptions can be modified over time to reflect changes in the organization, its business objectives, technology used, products, working conditions, etc. A job description allows a firm to tell applicants what is expected of them, and helps the personnel department to select suitable candidates. Once in post, the performance of the employee can be judged on how well they carry out the tasks identified in their job description.

It is rarely possible to define every feature of a job in a written description, but in general, a job description will contain at least some of the following elements:

The job description

General information
- Job title
- Position in the organizational structure, for example, director, manager, supervisor, etc.
- Department/division
- Name and location of employing firm
- Working conditions, salary details, and other benefits

Job content information
- Main tasks and responsibilities (can be in order of priority)
- General tasks, e.g. post holder should become familiar with administrative arrangements in the office
- Specific tasks, e.g. produce a report
- Purpose of tasks, e.g. to design a new sportswear range
- Methods involved, e.g. use of *LOTUS 123* computer spreadsheet, etc.
- Supervisory/management duties

Performance criteria
- For example, dates for the completion of certain tasks, quality standards, etc.

Special competencies
- Qualifications and skills considered vital to the post, for example, a degree in chemistry, a clean driving licence, fluency in a foreign language, etc.

Advanced Business

Sample job descriptions

Job title: Business Assistant
Responsible to: Group Financial Director
A. Summary of main responsibilities and activities
Help to collate financial reporting information
Maintenance of financial information
Collection, collation, and distribution of marketing materials from and to regional offices
Maintenance of customer lists, customer profiles
Assist in development of marketing materials
Setting up and implementing administrative procedures relating to the above

B. Specific Responsibilities
1. Staff
   (No staff currently reporting to Business Assistant)
2. Planning
   Plan and manage own time to achieve mutually agreed delivery schedules
   Provide advice and input into product planning process
3. Confidential information
   Privy to client data, reference groups, and customer information database
   Privy to group financial information of a confidential nature
4. Contacts
   Liaison with product managers
   Liaison with personnel at regional offices
   External marketing consultants and Public Relations organizations

C. Working conditions
Based at group head office in Warrington
Maybe occasional foreign travel
Salary approx. £20,000+ p.a.
37.5 hours per week (Flexible: core hours 10.00 - 16.00 Mon-Fri)
Additional benefits (subject to medical qualification)
- PPP Private Health Insurance
- Permanent Health Insurance to 75% of salary
- Life Insurance 4 times salary

Job title: Secretary
Reporting to: Financial controller
Hours of work: 09.00 - 17.30 Mon - Fri
Significant working relationships:
All managers and secretaries
All Staff Divisions
Corporate Payroll

Overall purpose:
To provide an administrative and secretarial function to the financial controller and his department

Principal responsibilities:
1. Copy typing department correspondence and reports
2. Filing
3. Making meeting and buffet arrangements
4. Receiving visitors and providing hospitality required
5. Making travel arrangements as necessary
6. Send outgoing faxes
7. Mail distribution to department
8. Order and control stationery for department
9. Provide secretarial support for other staff when required
10. Maintain an internal document logging system for department
11. Any other tasks necessary to ensure the smooth running of the department and division

Training:
Wordprocessing package
Graphics package

Qualifications and personal skills:
Typing
Wordprocessing
Secretarial
Must be able to deal with people

Job title: Sales assistant

Reports to: Store manager

Overall purpose:
To carry out a range of duties specified by store manager

Specific duties:
Greeting and helping customers
Selling
Operating till
Stocktaking
Stock retrieval
Shelf-filling

The right person for the job?

The person specification

A **person specification** describes in broad terms the skills, qualifications, abilities, and personal qualities needed to perform a particular job as described in a job description. The specification forms the basis for the selection of the most suitable job applicant.

A person specification is likely to include many of the following elements:

The person specification

Previous experience and qualifications

- Is experience required or will training be given?
- Evidence of previous experience and qualifications, if necessary, e.g. HGV licence, references from former employers
- Formal education and training qualifications required, e.g. GCSEs, A levels, BTEC, NVQs and GNVQs, university degrees, postgraduate studies, etc.

Special aptitudes

- For example, is the person able to work under pressure? Flexible and adaptable? Good memory?
- Personal qualities and motivation
- For example, is the person willing to take on responsibility? Ambitious? Able to work independently? A 'self-starter'? Reliable and personable?

Special circumstances

- For example, will the person need to travel? Work unsociable hours?

(Note: For some jobs, physical attributes will also be specified for example, there used to be a minimum height requirement for people wishing to join the police. This no longer applies.)

Advanced Business

Sample person specifications

Job title: Business Assistant

A. Physical attributes

Minimum

Good health record. Few absences from work. Tidy appearance.

Desirable

Smart appearance, creates good impression on others

B. Mental attributes

Above average intelligence, good communication skills

C. Qualifications

Minimum

Higher education in a business discipline, e.g. business administration

Desirable

Further education in Public Relations and Marketing

D. Experience, training, and skill

Minimum

Experience of positions involving similar duties

Experience in using PCs as part of daily work, e.g. wordprocessing, spreadsheets, and presentations Desirable

In addition to the above:

Conversational ability in German and French

Job title: Financial Accounts Clerk

Appearance: Needs to be well-groomed and smartly dressed - suits preferred

Desirable Personal Qualities:
- Self-starter
- Able to work independently
- Abundance of common sense
- Sense of humour
- Mature
- Outgoing and lucid communicator
- Open personality, willing to accept change/challenge
- Willing to accept responsibility

Qualifications and Skills:
- Excellent writing skills
- Experience of business and marketing environment
- Numerate
- Not phased by technical activities
- GCSE pass in English and Maths required as minimum

Training:
- Bookkeeping skills

Job title: Sales assistant

Qualities/Skills:
Neat and tidy appearance

Personable, able to get on with people

Reliable and trustworthy

Numerate

Physically fit

Aged 16 - 18 years

Training given:
Operation of till

Stock taking and ordering procedures

> **Portfolio Activity 14.2**
>
> **Range:** Job description, Person specification
> **Skills:** Take part in discussions, Produce written material
>
> 1. Select two employees in an organization you are familiar with. One should be of managerial grade, the other a shop-floor worker. From observations of both employees at work, and from interviews, make a list of the tasks they must perform and the skills and qualities they need.
>
> 2. From your observations, develop a job description and person specification for the jobs performed by your chosen employees.
>
> 3. If possible, discuss the accuracy of your job and person specifications with a personnel manager.

Attracting suitable job applicants

If vacancies exist, then it is up to the personnel department to find suitable staff to fill them. However, in the short term, if a firm is short of funds for additional workers, it may be possible to reorganize the workload so as to fill gaps created by vacant posts. Alternatively, existing workers may be offered overtime as an interim measure before new workers can be hired.

Vacancies will often be filled by **external recruitment**, through adverts placed in local or national newspapers, or Jobcentres. However, some vacancies may be filled by **internal recruitment**, usually by staff on promotion, although this is likely to create vacancies elsewhere in the organization.

Internal recruitment

The advantages of filling a vacancy from the existing workforce in a company rather than from outside are:

- Promotion opportunities can motivate existing workers
- It is more reliable, because existing workers and their abilities will be well-known to the company, while external candidates are not
- An existing worker may feel more committed to the company and the achievement of its goals
- Internal recruitment is relatively cheap and quick

However, there can also be disadvantages:

- Advertising a job internally limits the number of applicants
- External candidates may be more suitable
- It creates vacancies elsewhere in the organization
- External recruitment will still be necessary if no suitable internal candidate can be found

External recruitment

Many vacancies are filled from external sources. This can be time-consuming, expensive, and uncertain, but with careful planning it is possible to minimize these costs.

Choosing the most appropriate method of attracting external candidates will often depend on the type of job and type of employee a business wants. Even during a period of high unemployment, certain types of employee who possess scarce skills may be difficult to find, and employers may have to resort to specialized, and possibly expensive, means of recruitment.

- **Unsolicited applications.** A business will sometimes receive applications from candidates who either call personally looking for work, or write letters of enquiry. Their applications can be placed on file until a suitable vacancy arises.

- **Links with educational establishments.** Many employers maintain links with schools, colleges, and universities. For example, the 'milk round' involves companies visiting universities around the country each year, with the aim of generating interest in posts among final-year students.

- **Trade Unions.** Some employers recruit certain types of workers through appropriate Trade Unions, who are able to endorse candidates as having the necessary skills to undertake a job (see 12.5).

- **Government agencies.** As well as providing careers guidance, the **Careers Service** provides a free or inexpensive means of recruitment for firms. The service collects information about local job vacancies and distributes them to local schools/colleges, training establishments, etc. Some employers may fill a number of vacancies with young people on **Youth Training Schemes (YTS)**. These are guaranteed two-year training courses for under-18-year-olds not in full-time education, involving training and work experience placement with an employer. The cost of employing YTS trainees is heavily subsidized by the government, and firms are also able to have a 'free trial' of prospective employees.

    Job centres are government-run organizations which advertise posts on behalf of employers, and select suitable candidates for interview. The service is free and most useful for advertising skilled, semi-skilled, and unskilled manual and clerical jobs.

- **Professional associations.** Many professional bodies, such as the Institute of Chartered Surveyors or British Medical Association, have an employment service for their members. Employers who use this service can be sure of the professional qualifications of candidates.

- **Private employment agencies.** These are commercial organizations which specialize in recruitment and selection, for example, Alfred Marks, Reed Employment, and Kelly Temporary Services.

    An employer informs the agency of a vacancy, and the agency will then submit a suitable candidate from its register. When a candidate is appointed, the employer pays a fee to the agency. The main advantage of this is time and administration saved by the employer.

    Some agencies specialize in the recruitment and selection of managerial and professional staff, and will complete the entire recruitment process for an employer, including job analysis, job and person specification, sending out application forms, and interviewing suitable candidates. The employer is then presented with a shortlist of candidates for further interview.

▼ *Job centre*

▼ *Employment agency*

Very senior managers or executives are sometimes recruited through a process called **headhunting**, whereby suitable candidates with known specialisms are approached discreetly to discuss a possible appointment with another employer.

The main disadvantages of using an agency, apart from cost, is that the employer loses some control over the recruitment and selection process. Staff recruited through agencies also tend to stay in jobs only a short time.

- **Advertising.** The most popular method of recruitment is to advertise the vacancy and invite candidates to apply to the company.

Job advertisements should aim to produce a small number of well-qualified candidates quickly and cheaply. It is important to make sure that the right advertisement is placed in the right media at the right time. For example, it would be inappropriate to advertise a post for specialist chemical engineers in a mass circulation newspaper like *The Sun*, or to broadcast the vacancy on Radio 1. Adverts for jobs, just like adverts for goods and services, should be aimed as closely as possible at their target audience (see 10.1).

Advertising to get the job done!

If advertising is be cost-effective and attract suitable candidates, the following principles need to be observed:

1. The adverts should contain enough clearly stated and relevant information for people to be able to tell what the job involves and whether they would be suitable candidates. The key elements should be:

- A job title
- Brief details of the job
- Experience, skills, and qualifications required
- Training given
- Pay and working conditions
- A brief description of the organization, including location, whether it has an equal opportunities policy, etc.
- How to apply - for example, by phoning for further details and an application form, or submitting a letter of application and Curriculum Vitae (CV)

In all cases, the information provided must be accurate and honest.

2. The medium chosen for the advertisement should be appropriate. This will depend on factors such as the type of job, the number of vacancies, and the budget available. Where a large number of vacancies exist, mass advertising in national newspapers or on TV may be appropriate, although expensive. For example, the police and armed services sometimes advertise for new recruits on TV.

Some newspapers print specialized job supplements devoted to different types of job on particular days of the week. For example, *The Guardian* advertises jobs in computing every Thursday.

3. The response to the advert must be carefully analysed. For example:

- How many candidates applied?
- Were the applicants suitable for the job?
- Did the advert reach its target audience?

This will help a company to plan and design future job advertisements.

Portfolio Activity 14.3

Range: Recruitment procedures
Skills: Produce written material, Process information

Look at the two job adverts below. One is a good example of how to advertise a job vacancy. The other is not.

1. Use the advertson p.342 to produce a checklist of things a good job advert should have in terms of job details and design.

2. Use your checklist to redraft and redesign the poor advert, using a wordprocessing or desktop publishing package. (Rather than make up details, try to find out the tasks entailed in the advertised job, and the skills, qualifications, and abilities the post holder should have.)

3. In which newspapers would you place the advert? Contact the newspaper(s) to find out how much it would cost.

QUALIFIED MECHANIC REQUIRED
for MOT Kingston
0181-547 1003
(part of the Tradex group)

RAILTRACK

Marketing Assistant

A commercially driven self motivated individual is required to assist the Head of the Leeds Independent Station in maximising the revenue opportunities of the facilities within a terminal used by 50,000 passengers a day.

You will have received some formal training in either marketing or retail and be looking for a challenging opportunity to build your career through practical endeavour.

If you can work on your own initiative, have an ability to develop concepts to practical proposition, are an effective organiser; familiar with market research techniques, and can demonstrate excellent inter-personal skills we would like to hear from you.

The post will require a certain amount of weekend working leading to a salary package of around £15,000.

Please submit a comprehensive CV setting out why you should be appointed to:

**Head of Leeds Independent Station,
Room M59, Headquarters, Station Rise, York YO1 1HT**
to arrive no later than 24 February 1994. Please mark your envelope with reference number ISO/001A.

Railtrack is an equal opportunity employer.

Key words

Job analysis - a study of the tasks, skills, and training that are required to carry out a job

Job description - a summary of what a job entails

Person specification - a profile of the type of person required to do a job

Internal recruitment - filling a job vacancy in an organization from its existing workforce

External recruitment - generating job applicants from outside the organization, for example, by using private employment agencies or advertising in newspapers

---

Section **14.3** Applying for a job

There are a number of ways of inviting people to reply to a job advertisement. For example, they can be asked to:

- Apply for and complete an application form
- Prepare a Curriculum Vitae (CV)
- Write a letter of application

Information provided by job applicants should always be treated confidentially by the business organization receiving it.

The application form

This is sent to applicants on request, usually with further job details. Application forms are often used by business organizations to ensure that important details are not missed out, and that information about candidates is supplied in a logical and uniform manner. This enables information to be processed easily and conveniently, often within a computer database. Standardization also makes for easier comparison of candidates.

Portfolio Activity 14.4

Range: Recruitment procedures
Skills: Read and respond to written material, Collect and record data

1. Select 5-10 different job advertisements for posts at different levels within organizations in different industrial sectors. Check that each advertisement requests the applicant to apply for an application form.
2. Apply for the application forms by writing to the advertised addresses, or by telephoning.
3. Compare and contrast the application forms you receive. Make a list of the main features you think a good application should have. Which of the application forms do you think is (a) the most effective and (b) the least effective? Give reasons.

The layout and design of an application form will depend on the type of job and level of information required. However, in general, an application form will request the following details:

- **Personal details:** name, address (permanent and temporary if applicable), telephone number, date of birth, marital status

- The **name of the post** applied for

- **Education history:** schools, colleges, universities attended, with dates

- **Details of educational and professional qualifications:** exam grades, and dates taken. (*Note*: There are many different types of qualification. The form should allow for these. For example, students in Scotland are not able to list GCSEs and A levels among their educational attainments.)

- **Employment history/previous experience:** names and addresses of former employers, posts held, dates, reasons for leaving. (*Note*: The word **experience** can refer to both **work experience**, and the **skills** the applicant thinks s/he has. The application form should make it clear which meaning is intended.)

- **Medical history:** serious illnesses, disabilities. (These can only be requested if knowledge of them is vital to the execution of the job.)

- **Ethnic origin:** the Commission for Racial Equality code of practice recommends that employers include questions about applicants' ethnic origin on job application forms in order to allow monitoring.

Advanced Business

▼ *Figure 14.2: Example of an application form*

JOB APPLICATION FORM

Please complete this side of the form in BLOCK CAPITALS

Surname (Mr/Mrs/Miss/Ms) _____ Forenames _____

Address (including postcode) _____ Previous name (if applicable) _____

Telephone number _____ Date of birth _____

Names and addresses of schools/colleges since age 11 | Dates attended
From _____ to _____
From _____ to _____
From _____ to _____

Examinations taken or about to be taken

GCSE	Date	Grade	GCSE	Date	Grade	A & A/S levels	Date	Grade

Please list any other courses and qualifications taken or about to be taken

Course/examination	Date	Grade	If you have shorthand/typing qualifications please indicate speeds
			Shorthand _____ wpm
			Audio _____ wpm
			Typing _____ wpm

Please give details of any work experience you have had, including Saturday and holiday jobs

Employer's name and address	Dates of employment	Duties

Please complete this side of the form in your own handwriting unless unable to do so because of physical disability

Indicate your interests and activities – include involvement in voluntary work, clubs and societies, hobbies and sport

Inside school _____ Duties _____

Outside school _____ Duties _____

Provide examples of where you have worked as part of a team. What was your role/contribution?

Please give details of special achievements and/or positions of responsibility (e.g. prefect, Duke of Edinburgh's Award)

Outline any activities you have planned and organised, and how you achieved your results

Please indicate why you are interested in this post, the reasons why you consider yourself suitable and how you see your future with this company

Signed _____ Date _____

- **Interests:** leisure- and work-related; positions of responsibility held at school - for example 'Prefect' - or in organizations related to applicants' leisure pursuits - for example, 'Treasurer of local Ramblers Association'
- **Other information:** for example, why is the applicant interested in the job? What qualities do they have that make them suited to the job?
- **References:** usually, names and addresses of two referees who are able to confirm the applicant's character and suitability for the job.

Most application forms, especially those for higher-level jobs, will contain a mixture of **closed questions** (e.g. 'Please give details of your educational qualifications') and **open-ended questions** (e.g. 'Give reasons why you feel suited to this type of work'). It is important that questions are neither offensive nor illegal (for example, 'Have you got AIDS?' would not be allowed). It is also important for forms to provide enough space for applicants to write their answers.

An application form should make clear where and to whom the completed form should be sent, and the closing date for applications. The completed application provides the basis for selection and is a vital document in an employee's personnel record.

1. Take a photocopy of the form and practise answering the questions in rough.
2. Read all the instructions carefully.
3. Always write clearly in black or blue ink (and use block capitals if asked to do so).
4. Answer questions in full. Do not leave any large gaps. If something does not apply to you, write N/A ('not applicable').
5. Remember to sign and date your completed form.
6. Take a photocopy of your completed form for future reference, should you be called for interview.
7. Ensure that the form is returned promptly to the employer.

The Curriculum Vitae (CV)

Much of the information an application form is designed to extract from a candidate can be provided from a **Curriculum Vitae** or **CV**. Although potentially less structured than an application form, a CV provides a broad summary of the applicant's life and education, and career achievements to date. A job applicant will frequently send a CV along with a letter of application, or application form.

A carefully prepared CV, preferably typed or wordprocessed, is the means by which an applicant will promote themselves to an employer. It is often the first contact between applicant and prospective employer. If it fails to make an impact, then any other efforts the applicant may make will be wasted.

A CV should be no longer than 3-4 sides of A4 paper, and in general should include the following headings:

- Personal details
- Educational history and qualifications
- Training and professional qualifications

Advanced Business

- Employment history and posts held/work experience
- Positions of responsibility held
- Interests
- Other information
- References

Tips on preparing a CV

1. Assemble all the facts about yourself.
2. Prepare a first draft. Use a wordprocessor if possible, as this will make it easier to correct and edit your CV to suit the requirements of different jobs.
3. Use plain white A4 paper and leave enough white space between your details to make presentation attractive and uncluttered.
4. Layout, for example, headings and sub-headings, font size and type, should be consistent.
5. Sentences should be short, to the point, and display a good grasp of English grammar and vocabulary. Try not to be either boring or too fancy.
6. Technical details should be presented in a way that can be understood by a non-specialist reader.
7. Edit and correct mistakes.
8. Print, read through, and redraft if necessary.

Curriculum Vitae

Personal details
Name: Dawn MARTIN
Date of Birth: 6 September 1977
Address: 69 Westbank Road, Tolworth, Surrey, KT5 9GR
Telephone: 0181-330-12345

Education history
1988 - 1993: Tolworth Girls School, Fullers Way North, Tolworth, Surrey
1993 - 1995: Kingston College of Further Education, Kingston-upon-Thames, Surrey

Qualifications
GCSE Subjects:
   Art A
   Biology C
   English Language B
   French A
   History B
   Mathematics C
   Statistics C

GNVQ Subjects:
   Advanced Business Distinction
   Advanced Art and Design Merit

Work experience
Vacation and temporary posts:
June - Sept 1993: Sales Assistant, Bentalls Department Store, Kingston-upon-Thames
June - Sept 1994: Receptionist, Hotel Antoinette, Kingston-upon-Thames
November 1994: Work Placement at Nutmeg UK, assisting manager in design studio

Positions of responsibility
1992: Captain of hockey team 1986
1993: Fifth form prefect
1994: Editor of student magazine

Interests
Watercolour painting, tennis, swimming, rock music, reading

Other information
Special Skills:
Typing (90 wpm) using WordPerfect
User experience of Microsoft *Excel*
Full driving licence for 7 months
Good oral and written French

References
Academic: Mrs B Sure, Department of Art and Design, Kingston College of Further Education, Kingston-upon-Thames KT1 2AQ, Tel: 081-546- 4661
Work Experience: Mr D Jones, Nutmeg UK, Ham Trading Estate, Richmond, Surrey, Tel: 081- 947-6666
Personal: Mrs G Peterson, 45 Park Avenue, Surbiton, Surrey KT6 7NT, Tel: 081-303-0567

Portfolio Activity 14.5

Range: Curriculum Vitae, Appraise
Skills: Produce written material, Prepare information

1. Produce an up-to-date CV for yourself using a wordprocessor.
2. If possible, ask a personnel officer to evaluate your CV. Failing this, present your CV to a careers adviser in your school/college, or to a colleague, and ask them to evaluate your CV against the following checklist:

- Is the content and coverage right?
- Do major achievements stand out?
- Is it concise and to the point?
- Is spelling and grammar correct?
- Is the layout pleasing?
- Is it easily understood?
- Does it create an overall good impression?

The letter of application

Sometimes job applicants may simply be invited to write a letter of application. However, more usually an applicant will use this as a covering letter for a completed application form or CV.

Many employers prefer letters of application to be handwritten. Good handwriting is a requirement in many jobs, particularly in clerical and administrative occupations, and firms may need to see evidence of an applicant's handwriting skills, rather than just a wordprocessed or typewritten application. Handwriting may also be analysed in some cases. The science of **graphology** - the assessment of a person's character from their handwriting - is popular in the USA and some European countries, and is now being used by a number of recruitment agencies in the UK.

Writing a letter of application probably requires more skill than simply filling in an application form or preparing a CV. A letter of application should have a clear structure and give the following information:

- The applicant's reasons for applying for the job
- Skills and knowledge the applicant has acquired that are particularly relevant to the job
- Details of relevant experience and qualifications (if not already provided in a supporting CV)

Tips on writing a letter of application

1. Prepare a first draft.
2. Use plain white A4 paper and try not to write more than one side.
3. Write your permanent address in the top right-hand corner.
4. Write the name and address of the person you are sending your letter to on the left-hand side immediately below your own address.
5. Date the letter below the application address.
6. Use the correct conventions for addressing letters. A letter beginning 'Dear Sir/Madam' should end 'Yours faithfully'. If 'Dear Mr X' is used, the letter should be signed 'Yours sincerely'.
7. Start your letter with a reference to the post you are applying for, and where and when it was advertised.
8. Use good English and try to keep your paragraphs short and to the point.
9. Do not repeat details that are contained in an accompanying CV, but make reference to your attached CV in your letter.
10. Redraft your letter until you are satisfied with it.

Advanced Business

Portfolio Activity 14.6

Range: Recruitment procedures, Appraise
Skills: Read and respond to written material

The letter of application below has been received in response to the advertisement for a data processing assistant. It has been rejected by the employer.

1. List what you think is wrong with the letter, and why.
2. How would you improve the letter? Prepare a new draft.

Data Processing Assistant
Circa £11,000 pa salary depending on experience

A small established busy firm seeks a full time data processing assistant who will probably be aged 18–25. The main role would involve complex database selections being processed and output to numerous media in various formats. The ability to communicate with non-technically minded people is essential since client liaison would be required. Should the successful candidate show the right aptitude, training would be provided to progress into network management and programming. Education to A-level standard or equivalent with some computing experience necessary.

---

57 Letsby Avenue
Trumpington
Cambridge
CR2 1BZ

Ms M Lyes
Personnel Department

Dear Ms Lyes

I would like to apply for the job you advertised recently. I am very interested in computing and think it would be very interesting and rewarding job that I am well suited to carry out.

I am 18 years old and have been studying at college for the last two years. I have just competed GNVQs in Business and Leisure and Tourism. At school I took exams in Maths, English, History, Art, and Computing. I have my own computer at home and am familiar with a number of wordprocessing and spreedsheet programs. Many of my assignments in the two GNVQ courses were completed using a computer. Computer studies was my best subject at school and I got a grade B in the GCSE. I have just enrolled at my college for part-time evening study in A level Computer studies.

I was a fifth form prefect at school and captain of the football team. I am curently working part-time at a local library. this allows me time to ~~pride~~ pursue my hobbies of photography and looking after my aquarium. At the library I have to check incoming and outgoing books, collect fines, order and shelve books and advise customers on library collections.

I am currently preparing my CV and will send this to you within the next few days. Should you require a reference you should contact:

Mr A Young
Head of Computer Studies
Milton High School
Cambridge

My thanks in advance of your consideration.

Yours faithfully
D J Moore
D J Moore (Mr)

References

A **reference** is a confidential statement about a person's character and abilities by a third party, known as a **referee**.

An employer will often request a job applicant to supply two or three referees. One will normally be a personal referee, such as a family friend; the other will be a former or present employer, or, if the applicant is still at school or college, a teacher or tutor. A clear, unbiased description of a candidate's abilities by a former employer can be extremely valuable in selection.

References are normally only taken up by an employer if a candidate is being seriously considered for appointment or has been **shortlisted** (see 14.4). A reference can take many forms:

- **Reference letter** - a formal and confidential written testimonial
- **Reference form** - a structured form of open and closed questions supplied by the prospective employer for the referee to complete

- **Telephone reference** - some organizations may phone referees. Answers to questions, and the tone of voice of the referee may reveal if they are being totally honest about the applicant.
- **Medical references** - these may be required if an employee wishes to join a company pension scheme, or if a job requires specific health standards.

Prospective employers need to treat references with caution. An applicant will naturally choose referees who they think will write complimentary things about them. An applicant who does *not* choose his or her present employer as a referee should therefore be viewed with some suspicion (although this may of course be because the applicant does not want them to know they are thinking of leaving). The present employer of an applicant may also be less than truthful on occasion. For example, they may provide a glowing reference because they secretly hope to get rid of an unsuitable employee.

For these reasons, employers do not usually take up references. Many will already be confident of their chosen candidate's character and abilities from their application and interviews.

Key words

Application form - a standardized set of questions prepared by an organization for job applicants to complete

Curriculum Vitae (CV) - a written summary of a job applicant's life, education, and career achievements

Letter of application - a written letter by a job applicant summarizing information otherwise provided in a CV or an application form

References - a confidential statement about a person's character and abilities by a third party

Section 14.4 Selection

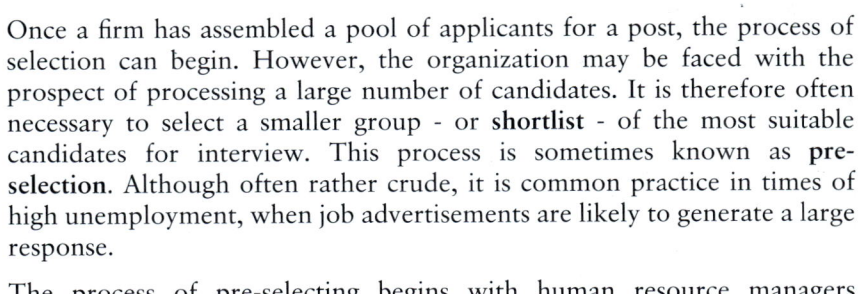

Once a firm has assembled a pool of applicants for a post, the process of selection can begin. However, the organization may be faced with the prospect of processing a large number of candidates. It is therefore often necessary to select a smaller group - or **shortlist** - of the most suitable candidates for interview. This process is sometimes known as **pre-selection**. Although often rather crude, it is common practice in times of high unemployment, when job advertisements are likely to generate a large response.

The process of pre-selecting begins with human resource managers comparing individual applications with the person specification. The aim at this stage is to identify attributes which show candidates to be suitable for the job, and also pinpoint any shortcomings, such as poor presentation, which will either rule them out, or necessitate special training if they are appointed. From this comparison, managers will decide who to invite for interview, and who will be rejected and sent a **letter of regret**. In all cases, selection should be objective and impartial. All applicants should be judged on their own merits - even those who may be internal candidates and known to the pre-selection panel.

Where there are many applicants, pre-selection can be very time consuming. Carefully designed application forms can help by making comparison easier. Some pre-selection procedures will award points to applicants for information which matches the requirements in the person specification - for example, the number of exams passed at grade C and above, previous work experience, etc. Those with the most points will be shortlisted.

Testing

Pre-selection methods used by some organizations include the setting of **tests** for candidates to complete. For example:

- **Tests of numeracy and written communication.** The ability to write good, clear English is an important requirement in many clerical and administrative occupations. Similarly, shop assistants may be set simple arithmetic tests.

- **Practical tests.** These are designed to test whether the candidate can do what they claim to be able to do. For example, a secretary may be set a test to verify a claim to type 100 words per minute.

- **Intelligence tests.** These test applicants' powers of deduction, analysis, and reasoning. The Civil Service often uses these to test candidates for specialist posts. For example, a candidate may be asked to complete a number series, identify the pattern in a line of dominoes, sort jumbled sentences into their correct order, etc.

- **Psychometric and personality tests.** The current trend in job analysis is to concentrate on key behavioural requirements of a job, for example, stamina and mental agility, initiative, working with others, etc. These type of tests may reveal aspects of a candidate's behaviour and attitude to work, and different working practices.

- **Medical tests.** These are used to check specific health standards which are required for a job - for example, a train driver's hearing or colour vision. Medical tests can also be used to protect a firm against claims. For example, an employee may claim that their respiratory problems have been caused by the materials and chemicals they work with. Checking the results of a medical test taken prior to their appointment may reveal that the employee had always suffered from this problem.

Tests require careful design, and the process of compiling and validating tests can be a lengthy and expensive undertaking.

Final selection

The final stage of the selection process is usually the **interview** of shortlisted candidates. Interviews involve a face-to-face meeting between a candidate and his or her prospective employer. An interview is designed to include questions to test achievement and aptitude, and is at present the most commonly used method of personality assessment.

There are three main types of selection interview:

1. A **one-to-one interview** between interviewee (the candidate) and interviewer (a representative of the employer)

2. A **panel interview** involving several interviewers, for example, a senior manager, departmental manager, and personnel manager. Panel interviews have certain advantages:

- Each interviewer can specialize in asking different questions.

- All the interviewers can take part in a joint assessment of the candidate reducing the risk of personal bias.

However, there can also be disadvantages:

- Questioning may be disorganized and repetitive unless questions are planned and agreed before an interview.

- The candidate may feel less at ease.

One-to-one interview

Panel interview

Bored interview!

3. A **board interview** with many more representatives of the employer. For example, boards of over 20 interviewers are not uncommon in the selection of senior civil servants. In addition to the advantages of panel interviews, the board interview is useful to reveal the behaviour of the candidate under stress. However, large numbers of interviewers can make the final assessment of the candidate very difficult.

Sometimes sequential interviews are used in the pre-selection process. A further shortlist of candidates can be drawn up on the basis of their performance during a first interview. Successful candidates may then be invited back for a second interview before final selection is made. Sequential interviews are often used in the selection of senior managers.

Planning an interview

Poorly planned and structured interviews can give an organization a bad image and may result in the selection of an unsuitable candidate. It is therefore important for an employer to plan for an interview. The following steps can be followed:

1. Decide (a) Is a test required? (b) Is interview to be one-to-one or panel?

2. If panel interview, select and invite members

3. Organize a room and facilities for the interview. Make sure the room is quiet and private. If necessary, check access arrangements for any disabled candidates.

4. Send clear instructions on time, date, and venue of interview to candidates and panel members. (Be sure to allow ample time for the interview to be conducted: 30-40 minutes is usual.)

5. Be familiar with the job description and person specification for the post. (Send copies to panel members.)

6. Compare the written application of each candidate with the job description, so that the interviewers can decide where clarification or further information is needed.

7. Make a note of questions to ask each candidate. Some 'control' questions should be common to all candidates in order to aid comparison between them. These might include problem-solving questions, or more open questions, such as 'What qualities do you think a good manager should have?', 'Why do you want to work here?', 'What were your favourite subjects at school?'

8. Agree list of questions between panel members.

Conducting the interview

A well-conducted selection interview should fulfil four main aims:

- To discover information about the candidate's motives and behaviour in order to assess personality
- To check factual information already supplied by the candidate
- To inform the candidate about the job applied for, and the company
- To be fair, so that each candidate feels they have an equal chance and leaves with a favourable impression of the organization

Whether or not an interview fulfils these aims will depend much on the skill and judgement of the interviewers and the questions they ask.

How to conduct an interview

1. Immediately prior to the start of interviews, check the arrangements and facilities are satisfactory. For example, check the seating plan, lighting, refreshments. If interviews are to be conducted across a desk, clear it of any unnecessary equipment. Make sure the room will not be disturbed.

2. Begin the interview with a few remarks and questions designed to welcome the candidate and put them at their ease. For example, 'Did you manage to find your way here OK?'

3. Explain the purpose of the interview to the candidate. For example, will selection be made for the job on the basis of this interview, or is it part of a sequence of interviews used in the process of pre-selection?

4. Ask probing questions. Do not accept candidates' replies to questions at face value. If a candidate says s/he was responsible for a particular activity, or has operated a piece of machinery before, further questions should be asked to find out whether this was in fact the case.

5. As a rule of thumb, in an interview lasting 30 minutes the candidate should be expected to talk for around 20. During this time, interviewers should look interested in what the candidate says, and if necessary make occasional comment to encourage him or her to say more.

6. Observe each candidate during interview. Body language can provide vital clues about the candidate's honesty, personality, and level of stress. For example, observe how they are they sitting, eye movements, and eye contact, arm and hand movements.

7. At the end of the interview, ask the candidate if they would like to ask any questions.

8. Find out whether, if offered the job, the candidate would still want it, and when they could start.

9. Finally, indicate when the interview is over, thank the candidate for attending, and tell them what the next step will be - for example, whether they will be contacted by letter or telephone, and how long they can expect to wait for a reply.

10. Write down any notes on the candidate for your future reference after the interview. Making notes during interview itself may unsettle the candidate.

After the interview

Once all the interviews have been conducted, the interviewer or panel must make their decision on which candidate to appoint. They will compare notes and make a thorough analysis of all the information they have collected on each candidate. Having made their choice, they will then:

- **Send a letter of confirmation.** The successful candidate should be informed promptly, usually by telephone and/or in writing. A letter should confirm essential details such as start date, wage rate/salary, hours of work, and holidays. Offers of employment may be made subject to satisfactory references, and may be conditional on passing a medical exam, university degree, etc.

- **Draw up the contract of employment.** Under the 1978 Employment Protection Act, a new employee is entitled to a written statement of the main terms and conditions of their employment within 13 weeks of appointment (see 12.3).

- **Validate the selection process.** The selection decision can be validated by observing the successful candidate's progress and behaviour once s/he has been working in the job for some time.

What if no appointment is made?

If no suitable candidate can be found to match the organization's specifications, no appointment will be made, and the post will be re-advertised. Internal candidates who fail interviews should be given the chance to discuss their failure with managers at a follow-up meeting, otherwise their motivation can suffer.

What about the candidate?

So far we have focused on how a business organization can prepare and conduct an interview. However, most people reading this book are likely to be more concerned with what they can do as candidates to improve their chance of being successful in interview and getting an offer of a job.

Advanced Business

Portfolio Activity 14.7

Range: Interviewee techniques
Skills: Read and respond to written material

The article contains some good advice on how a candidate should prepare for, and conduct themselves during a job interview. Discuss this advice in groups and draw up a list of 'Do's and Don'ts' for a candidate attending an interview. Use your own experience of any interviews you have had.

Relax – and confidence will do the trick

Getting a job is not just about having ability. It's also about looking the part.

You may have all the qualifications under the sun, but if you don't exude self-confidence you probably won't get a chance to shine.

Rhiannon Chapman, director of The Industrial Society, has spent years sizing up interviewees. The principal quality employers look for in first-time job applicants, she says, is maturity.

Demonstrating that quality is helped by finding out as much as possible about the prospective job and working out how you can demonstrate you could do it. Mrs Chapman says interviewees should be prepared to talk about interests they follow as well as the job they are chasing. This provides clues to their independence and likely performance at work.

High among other factors employers note is appearance.

"People who are clean and tidy and conservatively dressed are looked on most favourably," says Mrs Chapman.

"Jewellery should be kept to a minimum, and if boys have an earring it's probably best to take it out. Hair, too, should be clean and neat.'

And there are a few tips to help you impart that vital air of self-confidence.

"They like people who aren't afraid to ask questions and initiate discussions rather than sit meekly and wait. "They find it enormously endearing if candidates admit they are nervous rather than sit there sweating and pretending everything's OK.

"These days it is difficult to have a hard-and-fast career plan, so it's a good idea to say you are flexible and prepared to try whatever may come up as long as you are learning something.

"That old cliche about telling the boss you want his job is best avoided."

The most important thing of all is probably also the hardest – RELAX.

Daily Mirror 5.7.93

Helpful hints for interviewees

- Acknowledge an invitation for interview promptly, preferably by letter.
- Make any necessary travel and overnight accommodation arrangements well before the interview.
- Find out about the organization, so that you can appear resourceful and knowledgeable during the interview.
- Prepare some questions to ask your interviewers about the job and the organization. For example, 'How has your company been affected by the single European market?', 'What training can I expect to be given?', 'What are the prospects for promotion?'. Questions about pay and holidays are not recommended. You can find out these details from personnel before or after the interview.
- Wear appropriate clothes. For most jobs, this will mean a suit for a man, and skirt and blouse for a woman.
- Hair should be neat and tidy. Jewellery and make-up should be kept to a minimum.
- Arrive no more than 10 minutes before your interview. Do not be late!

- Do not discuss your interview with other candidates who may be waiting. Only make polite conversation.
- Wait to be asked to sit down. Sit upright during interview and appear alert, but more importantly - relax!
- Do not be afraid to ask your interviewers to repeat or clarify questions.
- Take your time. Pause for thought before answering questions.
- Be positive. Speak clearly and with confidence, but always be polite.
- Be truthful. Probing questions will catch you out.
- Look at your interviewers when listening to their questions, and when speaking.
- Be aware of your body language. Do not slouch or keep looking away, and try not to be nervous or use exaggerated hand movements.
- Thank your interviewers and shake hands at the end of the interview.

▼ DO!

▼ DON'T!

Ethical and legal obligations

Matching the right candidate to the right job is essential if an organization is to accomplish set objectives. However, despite careful planning and conduct of the recruitment and selection process, the wrong person may still be chosen. This may be for a variety of reasons. For example, the most suitable candidate may have suffered from nerves during the interview, or may simply have had an off day. Studies have shown that most interviewers form their impression of the candidate within the first few minutes, and spend the rest of the time asking questions that simply reinforce their view. We are all influenced by subjective factors when judging people, for example, how they speak, their school and social background, physical attractiveness, etc. It is important for interviewers not to let these factors cloud their judgement.

The recruitment and selection process relies on both the job applicant and the employer being fair, honest, and truthful. A job advertisement must provide an accurate description of both the job and person required. For example, if the job involves weekend work, it must say so. Similarly, information supplied by a candidate on application forms, CVs, or during interview should be truthful. Failing to disclose information, or giving false information, will invalidate a contract of employment and could lead to dismissal if discovered.

Care must also be taken by an organization to ensure that recruitment and selection procedures do not infringe current employment legislation concerning discrimination. Equal opportunity laws make it an offence for recruiting firms to discriminate on grounds of sex, race, religion, disability, age, Trade Union membership, or against ex-offenders (see 12.3). Job advertisements, application forms, and interviews should be carefully worded to avoid potentially discriminatory statements or questions.

However, it *is* legal to advertise for a person of a particular sex or race if it is a genuine requirement of the job - for example, an attendant for male toilets will need to be male, and an Asian actor portraying an Asian character in a TV programme will need to be Asian.

Many large organizations have developed their own equal opportunities policies which include specific procedures to be followed when hiring employees.

Don't ask!

The following are examples of questions and statements that should be avoided. All are potentially discriminatory and offensive. They have little or no relevance to whether the candidate is capable of doing the job.

'Are you married, Mrs Smith?'

'Male technician required in small engineering company'

'How many children do you have?'

'Have you made arrangements for your children to be looked after during the school holidays?'

'Young girl required for secretarial duties'

'Do you think you are capable of doing this job, Miss Jones?'

'People over 50 need not apply'

'How would you react if a work colleague told a racist joke in your presence?'

'Disabled person needed for simple office duties'

Key words

Shortlisting - selecting a handful of the most promising candidates for interview from the entire set of job applications

Interview - the most common method of personality assessment, involving a face-to-face meeting between a candidate and employers' representatives

Further reading
Lewis, C: *Employee Selection* (Stanley Thornes 1992)

Test Questions

The following underpinning knowledge will be tested:

1. Recruitment procedures
2. How job descriptions and person specifications match applicants with vacancies
3. The content and presentation of letters of application and Curriculum Vitae
4. Practise and appraise interviewer and interviewee techniques
5. Legal obligations and ethical responsibilities in recruitment procedures

1 Which of the following external sources of recruitment is a business seeking an experienced finance manager most likely to choose?

A Local Jobcentre
B University 'milk round'
C Professional recruitment agency
D Trade Union

2 Employers often like job applicants to submit a letter of application for an advertised job because:

A It reveals information not included in an application form
B It is more personal
C It makes shortlisting easier
D It reveals handwriting ability

3 A person specification is designed to:

A Analyse the authority and responsibility involved in a job
B Identify the qualities a worker needs to do a specific job
C Set performance criteria for a job
D Identify the various tasks involved in a job

4 A job selection interview should fulfil all of the following functions except:

A Inform candidates about the job and the organization
B Allow the assessment of the candidate's personality
C Check factual information provided by each candidate
D Agree terms and conditions of employment

5 A company has expanded into new premises and is seeking additional employees. Which of the following represents the usual order of recruitment and selection procedures?

A advertise; applications; shortlist; interviews; appoint
B advertise; shortlist; interviews; applications; appoint
C applications; interviews; shortlist; advertise; appoint
D advertise; applications; interviews; shortlist; appoint

6 A Curriculum Vitae (CV):

A Provides a summary of career details and ambitions
B Provides a summary of personal details and achievements
C Provides a summary of education and professional qualifications
D Provides a summary of personal details and career ambitions

7 A job description should include the following information except:

A Job title and position
B Job tasks and responsibilities
C Personal qualities and attributes
D Job performance criteria

Questions 8 - 10 share the answer options below:

A Keeping eye contact with your interviewers
B Asking questions about the organization
C Asking questions about training and promotion prospects
D Appearing relaxed and confident

If you were being interviewed for a job, which of the above would you use to demonstrate the following?

8 Showing that you are interested in developing your career

9 Showing long-term interest in the job and the company

10 Showing you are telling the truth and can be trusted

11 Shortlisting is:

A Drawing up a list of questions to ask during interview
B Making a list of questions to print on an application form
C Setting criteria by which to judge candidates
D Selecting candidates for interview from applications

Questions 12 - 14 share the answer options below:

- **A** Apply by telephone
- **B** Request and complete an application form
- **C** Write a letter of application
- **D** Provide a Curriculum Vitae and covering letter

Which of the above is likely to be the most appropriate method of applying for the following jobs?

12 A full-time job in a local newsagent's

13 A senior marketing manager in a large multinational

14 Part-time casual work delivering leaflets

15 a. What is the main purpose of recruitment and selection in a business organization?

b. What is the difference between a job description and a person specification? Why are they required?

c. List three items of information a job description and a person specification each will contain.

d. Suggest two ways a person could apply to fill a job vacancy.

e. List five items of information a job applicant should provide to a future potential employer.

16 a. Suggest three ways in which a firm may recruit job applicants externally.

b. List four headings you would expect to find in a CV.

c. What is the purpose of shortlisting?

d. Suggest at least three criteria on which job applicants might be judged for shortlisting.

e. What is the difference between a panel interview and a board interview?

f. How and why should a candidate prepare for a job interview?

g. How and why should an interviewer prepare to interview job candidates?

assessment assignment

Assessment Assignment

Range: Recruitment procedures
Job descriptions
Person specifications
Appraise
Curriculum Vitae
Interviewer techniques
Interviewee techniques
Legal obligations
Ethical responsibilities

Skills: **Communication**
Take part in discussions
Read and respond to written material
Produce written material
Information Technology
Prepare information
Present information

Tasks

Select some job advertisements from your local newspapers. Then in small groups:

1. Prepare a job description and person specification for TWO of the job vacancies.

2. Now select one of the jobs you chose in task 1. Using the job and person specification, devise a series of questions you would ask shortlisted candidates in an interview. Remember the legal obligations of recruitment and selection procedures!

3. Draw up an interview preparation list covering all the other tasks you will need to complete prior to, and after, future interviews. Also include a list of 'do's and don'ts' for interviewers.

4. Now ask another group to reply to your chosen job advert. Working individually, they are to prepare letters of application and Curriculum Vitae for each job. Set a realistic deadline for completion.

5. In your group, read through the letters and CVs and judge them individually in terms of content, clarity, and quality of presentation. Make a note of good and bad points for each one.

6. Now shortlist two applicants to invite for interview by comparing individual applications with the person specification. Look for attributes which show the candidate to be suitable for the job and any shortcomings, such as poor presentation, which may either rule them out or necessitate special training if they are appointed. Give reasons for your choice.

7. Arrange a time and venue for a mock interview, and prepare letters of invitation to the shortlisted candidates, and letters to send out to all other applicants who have not been shortlisted.

   (Job applicants who are invited to interview should prepare by drawing up a plan of action and list of 'do's and don't's' for before and during the interview. This should include a list of questions they could ask their interviewers.)

8. Your group will conduct a panel interview of each shortlisted candidate as arranged. Make some notes during the interview on the performance of each candidate.

9. After the interview, group members should compare notes and reach an unbiased decision on who should be offered the job. The reasons for your choice should be documented.

10. After making your choice, write a letter of confirmation to the successful candidate and a letter of regret to the unsuccessful candidate.

Follow-up evaluation

11. Discuss with each candidate and your tutor how well you think they performed during interview and how they might improve their performance.

12. Discuss with the candidates how well they think you performed as an interviewer. Were the questions fair and relevant? Did it meet its intended purpose? Did it meet legal and ethical obligations? How could the interview have been improved?

Unit Five

unit 5

Production and Employment in the Economy

chapter 15 Production (Element 5.1)
chapter 16 Investigating Employment (Elements 5.2)
chapter 17 The Competitiveness of UK Industry (Elements 5.3)

Advanced Business

chapter 15 Production

This chapter considers how business organizations can improve production.

Key ideas

Production is any activity that seeks to satisfy consumer needs and wants.

Production creates wealth by employing **resources**, in return for payment, to make goods and services people are willing and able to buy.

A firm **adds value** to resources by using them to produce goods and services consumers want.

A business will aim to add value to **meet domestic and international competition**, **survive and grow** and **improve their profits** by being able to **meet customers** requirements better than rival firms.

A business can add value by **improving productivity** (the relationship between inputs and outputs), by reducing costs including **minimising stocks**, **quality assurance** and through greater **marketing effort**.

The level and quality of production in a firm will be affected by the **market price** of their product, **technological change**, the **availability of resources** from suppliers, the **flexibility** of their **labour force** to adapt to change, **competition** and **legislation**, such as controls on pollution.

Productivity is the amount of a good or service produced per unit of resources used. Productivity in a firm will increase if more output can be produced with the same input of resources.

Changes in production can require **changes in relationships with suppliers**, **changes in the demand for labour** and skills, the need for further **research and development**, often to overcome **problems** caused by the changes.

A firm may try to improve production by **improving productivity**, through **total quality** management, **investing in research and development**, **reducing dangers to employees**, and **reducing pollution**.

Productivity can be improved by using advanced technology and processes, and improving worker motivation through a combination of financial rewards and job design.

Research and development (R&D) can result in new products and processes which require less resource input and reduce waste.

If the cost of labour rises relative to the cost of new capital equipment, a firm may decide to **substitute capital for labour**. Technological advance has reduced the cost of capital relative to labour in many industries.

In an attempt to **improve production**, many UK firms are introducing production and management techniques used successfully in Japan and the USA, for example, **Total Quality Management (TQM)**, **Just In Time** inventory control **(JIT)**, and **worker empowerment**.

Performance-related pay describes systems that link wage increases to some measure of individual, group, or organizational effort.

Jobs can be **enlarged** or **enriched** by giving workers more varied tasks, involving them in decision-making, and giving them more regular feedback on their performance. Organizing labour into groups can bring together a variety of skills in **problem-solving teams**.

Work related accidents raise business costs. Dangers to employees can be reduced through **improved health and safety measures**.

Growing concern for the environment amongst consumers has forced many firms to reconsider their production processes and materials to **reduce harmful pollution** and make more environmentally friendly products.

Section 15.1 Production

What is production?

Businesses create wealth by producing goods and services to satisfy consumer demand. **Production**, therefore, can be defined as any activity which is designed to satisfy consumer needs and wants.

Productive activity adds value to resources.

Production involves organizing resources - human, physical, and natural - to produce goods and services. The owners of these productive resources - employees, suppliers - will require payment. They will then be able to use this income to enjoy the benefit of goods and services bought from other business organizations.

By turning resource inputs into outputs which consumers want and are willing and able to buy, productive activity adds value to resources (see 18.1). For example, a firm that produces 1 million chocolate bars which are sold for 50p each but which cost only £200,000 to make, has added £300,000 to the value of the resources used - labour, cocoa powder, milk, paper, plant and machinery, vehicles, power, etc.

Firms can attempt to maximise the added value to the resources they use, measured as the difference between the cost of those resources and the revenues they generate, by;

- **ensuring the best relationship between the costs of imputs and value of final products.** Most firms will attempt to produce as much as they can from the least amount of labour, materials, machinery etc they can. A firm that is able to reduce the amount of inputs they use but still produce the same amount of ouput without employing more inputs, has increased **productivity**.

- **reducing the costs of resource inputs.** This can involve employing workers who are willing to work for lower wages or are more productive than existing workers, buying or hiring more efficient machinery, securing supplies of materials from cheaper suppliers, keeping stocks to a minimum to save storage space, reducing waste and accidents at work.

- **quality assurance.** Poorly produced goods and services do not sell but still cost money to make. Making sure that quality is maintained throughout the production process will result in more revenues from given inputs. The management of 'total quality' in firms is becoming increasingly important.

- **marketing.** The marketing of goods and services is an important part of the whole production process (see 8.3). A firm that is unable to supply the right products in the right amounts at the right price, and in the right place, will be unable to sell their products. Marketing helps a firm increase the value added to resources through the production of goods and services, by informing consumers of the existence of the product and persuading them that the price of the product is worth paying.

The ways in which firms add value and improve added value in production are considered in detail in this chapter.

▼ *Adding value in production From these... (inputs)*

PRODUCTION COSTS OF 100,000 UNITS
LABOUR   £100,000
MATERIALS   60,000
OVERHEADS   40,000
           £200,000

▼ *to these*

REVENUES FROM THE SALE OF 100,000 UNITS
£500,000

Factors that cause changes in production

The decision by a firm to produce a given level of output of a particular good or service, or range of products, will be influenced by the following factors:

- **Market price.** If the price at which a product is sold does not yield an acceptable profit, then firms will be discouraged from producing that product. Firms that are already engaged in the supply of the product may move their resources into the production of other goods or services, or will attempt to reduce costs to increase profit margins (see 1.4).

- **Availability and quality of resources.** Once a firm has decided what to produce, it must engage the necessary resources to achieve its production targets. Some resources - for example, labour with appropriate skills, or natural materials - may be in short supply, and this will force up the supply price, thereby reducing potential profit margins. Labour must also have skills that are flexible and can be adapted to changes in products, production processes and methods of working. The cost and availability of resources will, therefore, affect the production decisions of firms.

  Increasingly, firms are contracting out non-core activities, such as cleaning and maintenance, and specialist services, to external organizations, rather than employing labour to undertake these tasks on a permanent basis (see 13.4). External organizations will often compete to win contracts with firms, and firms who employ them can therefore insist on quality at competitive prices.

- **Technology.** Technological advance has resulted in new materials, products, and processes, and has changed the character, working practices, and production methods of many industries. For example, the manufacture of cars is now almost entirely automated. Automation, robotics, computer aided design and manufacturing, management information systems, are all examples of new technology in production. A firm must not only be aware of change, but must also consider the extent to which it can use new technology to keep ahead of the competition.

- **Legislation.** A number of laws exist which restrict or prohibit the supply of certain products and set strict guidelines on how production should proceed in the workplace. For example, it is illegal to produce hard drugs, or supply cigarettes and alcohol to minors.

  Growing concern for the environment is being reflected in a number of UK and European Union legislative measures concerning protection, preservation, and pollution (see 3.4). These measures are intended to shape and control production decisions that are potentially damaging to the environment. For example, coal-fired power stations have been forced to fit expensive de-sulphurization equipment to reduce the release of harmful pollutants into the atmosphere. Coal-fired stations are also now being phased out, in favour of cleaner, lean-burn gas-powered electricity-generating plants. Similarly, alternative methods of producing veal meat from young calves had to found when the notorious 'veal crate' method was outlawed in the UK.

Firms are also required to invest in health and safety measures, such as training, protective clothing, and rest periods for machine operators (see 12.3). Thus, controls on pollution and health and safety at work may raise the production costs of firms, and in some cases limit resource use and production time.

Portfolio Activity 15.1

Range: Factors, Analyse
Skills: Read and respond to written material

A Black Day for Coal

Amid the deluge of figures on the pit closure controversy, two matter above all others. The world price of coal is £30 a tonne. The stuff British Coal now produces is priced at £43 a tonne.

Given this price gap, almost any economic argument for keeping open loss-making coal mines collapses.

The Economist 24.10.92

Green Powders

Environmentalists began to demand phosphate-free detergents in the mid-1980s as evidence mounted that phosphorous was causing problems in Europe's lakes and rivers. Phosphate is a plant nutrient and too much of it encourages algal blooms.

As demand for green detergents grew, some producers switched to an aluminium-based material called zeolite A. Zeolites soften water, but cannot maintain pH or prevent dirt from resettling on clothes, so an additional ingredient called polycarboxylic acid (PCA) had to be added.

New Scientist 5.2.94

New Plant Puts GM In The Fast Lane

IN EISENACH, where once 10,000 East Germans laboured to build 100,000 rattle-trap Wartburg cars a year, Adam Opel is just three months away from its target of producing 125,000 vehicles with less than 20% of the old workforce.

Patrolling the walkway above the newly robotized welding line in the bodyshop, where human beings do just 2% of the work, he tots up the advantages of Opel's showpiece works. According to the measuring standards set by the Massachusetts Institute of Technology, it takes just 18.3 hours to build a car in Eisenach, compared to around 25 at GM's British subsidiary, Vauxhall. 'But the quality is not as good… We make the best Astra in Europe,' he boasts, claiming that cars come off the Eisenach lines with only half a dozen defects each, compared to 14 in Britain.

Financial Times 9.8.93

'Just in Time' Production Disrupted By Earthquake

Toyota, Japan's largest car maker, yesterday extended assistance to its suppliers hit by the earthquake in Kobe and halted production at all plants for today.

The difficulty in securing supplies from Sumitomo, which makes brake components for Toyota, and Fujitsu Ten, which supplies car audio equipment, was a big factor affecting production at Toyota after the earthquake. The car maker admitted that its Just In Time manufacturing method, which calls for keeping stocks of components at very low levels, meant production was more vulnerable to supply shortages triggered by such disasters.

However, Toyota procures supplies from a number of companies, and the disadvantages of having a low inventory level in an emergency is only one aspect of the Just In Time system which does not affect its overall merits, Toyota said.

Financial Times 20.1.95

Study the articles above. What factors have affected production in each case? What problems have been, or may have been, caused by these changes?

What is productivity?

Production is the total amount of a good or service produced. **Productivity** refers to the amount of output that can be produced from a given input of resources. That is, productivity can be measured as a **ratio of outputs to resource inputs**. Put very simply, a firm that uses 10 units of resources to produce 40 units of output is twice as productive as a firm that uses 10 units of resources to produce 20 units of output.

The aim of any business is to combine its resources in the most efficient way. That is, it will attempt to maximize the productivity of its resources in order to produce as much as it can with as little resource input as possible, and at the lowest cost possible. For example, a construction firm that employs 10 carpenters and yet supplies only 1 hammer, drill, and chisel between them has clearly not combined labour and equipment in the most efficient way. By increasing the input of equipment - i.e. providing more hammers, drills, etc. - the firm is likely to achieve a higher level of productivity.

In general, productivity in a firm will increase if more output can be produced with the same input of resources, or if less resources can be used to produce the same amount of output. Thus, raising productivity adds greater value to resources employed.

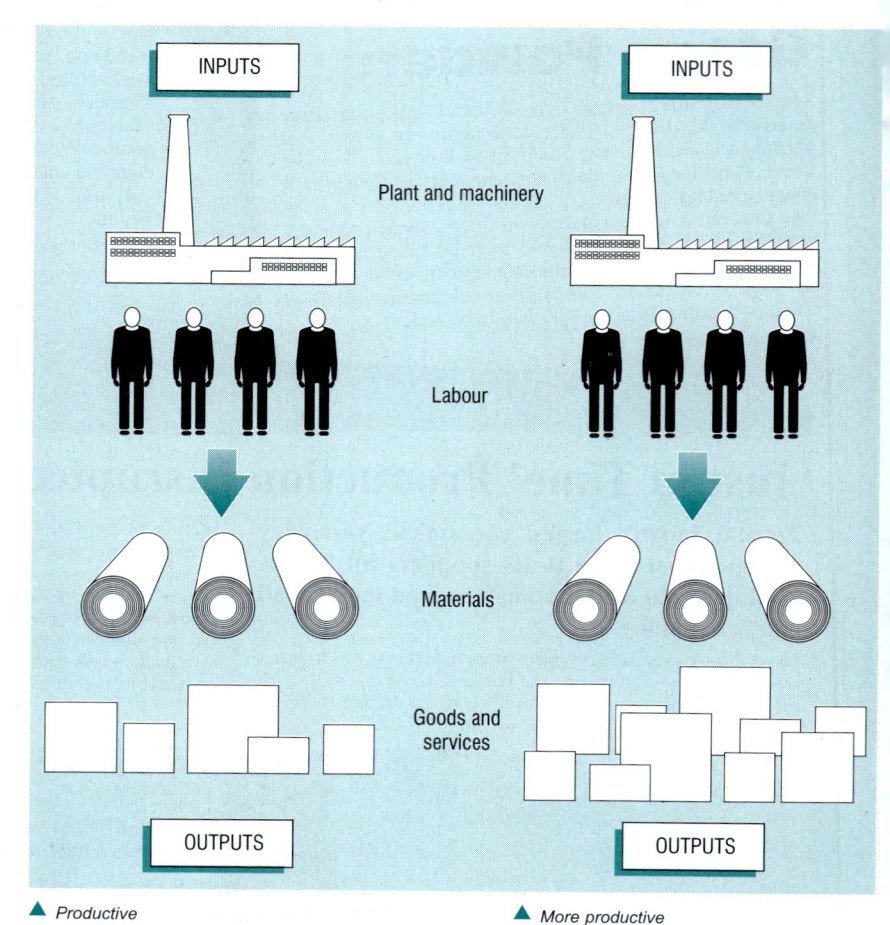

▲ Productive   ▲ More productive

Combining factors of production

In combining resources for productive activity, a firm can decide to use **labour-intensive techniques** involving a larger proportion of labour than capital (i.e. plant and machinery), or **capital-intensive techniques,** using more machinery relative to labour.

▼ *Capital-intensive*

The decision how to combine resources will depend on a number of factors:

- **The nature of the product.** Products in great demand in national and international markets will tend to be mass-produced using a large input of automated machinery.

- **The relative price of labour and capital.** If wages are rising, a firm may decide to employee more capital instead.

- **The size of the firm**. As a firm grows in size, it tends to employ more capital relative to labour.

▼ *Labour-intensive*

Measuring the productivity of labour

Although businesses will aim to improve the productivity of all resources, it is usually the productivity of labour that receives the most attention. Workforce productivity is usually measured by assessing changes in the volume or value of output produced in a company.

Labour productivity in a firm can be calculated by dividing output over a given period of time - for example, each day, week, or month - by the number of workers employed. This will give a measure of the average productivity per worker per period:

$$\text{Average product of labour per period} = \frac{\text{Total output per period}}{\text{No. of employees per period}}$$

The **average product** of labour is a useful measure of the efficiency of the workforce. For example, if a company employs 10 workers to produce 200 terracotta plant pots each day, the average product per employee per day is 20 pots. If daily output is able to rise to 220 pots per day without employing additional workers, then productivity will have increased to 22 pots per worker per day.

How easy is it to measure productivity?

A number of problems arise when using measures of the average product of labour. For example:

- Should all employees be included in the calculation of productivity, including cleaners, management, and admin staff? Or should productivity measures concentrate solely on shop-floor workers?

- How can the measure accommodate 'multi-product' plants, where the efforts of employees might contribute to the production of more than one product?

- How can productivity be measured in organizations that produce services, for example, banks or hairdressers?

In a hair salon we might employ a measure of the number of haircuts per hour, but in many ways the salon will be like a multi-product plant, with some people washing hair, others cutting, applying perms, or cleaning. In this case, a better measure of productivity might be achieved by calculating the **value added** per worker per period (see 18.1). This simply means dividing total sales revenues net of costs by the number of employees, to find the average net revenue per worker.

$$\text{Value added per worker per period} = \frac{\text{Total net revenue per period}}{\text{Number of employees per period}}$$

Similarly, measuring productivity in organizations where there is no physical output or sales revenue - for example, the NHS, the Civil Service, or a state school - also poses problems. Here, clearly, other measures, such as time spent waiting for operations, or meeting deadlines, or numbers of students obtaining qualifications, have to be used.

Why do firms seek to raise productivity?

The performance of a business organisation, in terms of the achievement of certain objectives such as

- business survival

- meeting domestic and international competition

- improving profit

- expanding market share

will depend critically on the level of added value achieved within a firm.

If the same amount of resources can produce more output at the same total cost, then the cost of each unit of output will have fallen. Increasing productivity can therefore lower production costs and increase value added. As costs fall, profit margins rise. A business may also pass on lower costs to consumers in the form of lower prices in an attempt to build and ensure repeat sales at the expense of its rivals.

A firm that fails to increase productivity at the same rate as, or faster than, its competitors will face higher costs and lower profits. Prices cannot be reduced without either sacrificing profits or sustaining a loss. If a firm is unable to offer quality products at competitive prices, then demand for its products will fall. In the long run the firm will face closure, and workers will be made redundant. Adding value is essential to the survival of a firm.

Business organizations in the UK and other developed countries are facing increasing competition from firms in developing economies, such as China, Malaysia, and Taiwan in South East Asia. Wages in these countries are still very low compared to those received by workers in developed countries.

It is therefore vital that firms in the UK increase productivity, reduce unit production costs, and improve product quality in order to compete with overseas organizations and thereby ensure their survival.

Strategies to improve production and productivity

In an increasingly competitive business environment, firms are constantly fighting to raise the productivity of, and add greater value to, their resources. Strategies that aim to improve production and productivity can be grouped into eight main categories. These are:

- secure a reliable source of supplies, and reduce business costs and the need for storage by keeping stocks to a minimum (see 15.2)
- introduce total quality control over the whole production process (see 15.2)
- research, develop and introduce new products and/or production processes and working practices designed to reduce waste, improve quality and increase the output from existing input levels of natural materials, equipment and labour (see 15.3)
- replace old plant and machinery with new, more efficient capital
- increase the amount of new, more productive, capital equipment employed relative to labour (see 15.3)
- increase labour productivity through a combination of training for new and improved skills, financial rewards, changes in working methods and management techniques (see 15.4)
- improve safety and reduce accident costs (see 15.5)
- employ more environmentally friendly materials and processes to limit the amount of pollution (see 15.6)

R&D, new production methods, financial incentives to motivate workers, training, investment in new technology, health, safety and environmental measures - all these imply higher costs and lower profits in the short run. However, if a firm is able to raise productivity and more than offset these higher costs, the long-term reward will be higher profits, and the ability to compete more vigorously on price and market share with rival firms.

Key words

Production - economic activity that satisfies a consumer want

Labour-intensive production - the input of more labour relative to capital

Capital-intensive production - employing more machinery relative to labour

Productivity - the ratio of outputs to inputs in a production process, such as the amount of labour input per period of time

Labour productivity - the amount of output produced per unit of labour input

Average product (of labour) - total output divided by the total workforce

Section 15.2   Just in time production and total quality management

Securing supplies

If production is to run efficiently, resources must be available when they are needed. Production will be slowed or held up if a firm suffers shortages of labour, machine breakdowns, and power failures, or if supplies of natural materials and semi-finished components run out. Keeping a sufficient stock of materials or component parts is, therefore, vital to the production process in any firm. Imagine what would happen if Kwik Fit ran out of car-exhausts and tyres to meet consumer demand one weekend!

However, keeping excessive stocks of materials and work-in-progress is costly in terms of storage space, and because it ties up working capital (see 22.1). Because of this, UK firms are increasingly using techniques such as **Just In Time (JIT)** and **Total Quality Management (TQM)**, developed by Japanese industry and used by Japanese firms with operations in the UK.

Just In Time production

One reason for the high levels of productivity in Japanese industry is the cost reductions achieved by employing **Just In Time inventory control**. This means that suppliers deliver components or materials to production lines 'just in time' for them to be processed. JIT is also known as 'stockless production'.

JIT production is based on the principle that products should be produced when customers need them and in quantities customers want, in order to keep stocks of materials, components, and finished products as low as possible.

For JIT to work, a number of requirements must be met:

- The quality of materials and parts must be high. Poor materials and defective parts can hold up assembly-line production.

- The supplier must be dependable and deliver on time. JIT requires **lead times** between ordering supplies and delivery to be as short as possible. This will be helped if the company and the supplier have a good business relationship.

- It also helps if suppliers are located near the company - but quality and reliability matter more.

Quality assurance

Product quality is an important determinant in the buying decisions of consumers. An organization that fails to assure consumers of quality will lose sales and will eventually be forced to cut back production.

In the past, 'quality control' in many organizations meant inspecting employees' work and products after production had taken place. However, producing poor-quality products and then hunting down the causes in production processes uses up valuable time and resources. Errors are costly.

Total Quality Management (TQM)

To prevent errors happening, Japanese companies have for many years employed methods collectively known as **Total Quality Management (TQM)**. These practices have now been adopted by many UK organizations.

The main aim of TQM is to focus companies on the wants of their customers, and on the relationship between suppliers and customers. It involves building-in quality checks at each and every stage in a production process. In this way, problems can be spotted and solved before products complete the production process. Employees are given the responsibility to control the quality of their output, and make changes if and when they detect a problem.

Features of TQM

Empowerment

This means allowing every employee in an organization to use and realize their full potential and abilities. TQM encourages people at all levels in a company to work in teams to analyse production processes and remove waste and inefficiencies. Teamworking improves communication and cooperation in business.

Continuous monitoring and improvement

Kaizen in Japanese means 'continuous improvement'. A business will use TQM to improve productivity, reduce costs, and satisfy consumer wants more effectively than its competitors. However, if a business is to find scope for improvement, production processes need to be continually monitored. **Statistical process control (SPC)** involves collecting data on business performance. Variations in performance, output, delivery times, product quality, materials, employee efforts, absenteeism, can all be analysed to find out what may have caused changes to occur.

Quality circles

These are simply groups of employees, usually between 6 and 12 in number, who work for the same supervisor or line manager. Workers in each circle are responsible for the organization and development of their own jobs. Circle members are trained in problem-solving techniques, in statistical process control, and working in teams.

Each quality circle meets regularly to identify and discuss their work-related problems. They will pass on their findings and any solutions to problems to senior management.

Quality chains

In any business there will be a whole series of suppliers and customers. For example, a secretary supplies a service to a manager. Canteen staff supply a service to a hungry workforce. These **supply chains** will also include customers and suppliers outside the firm. For example, a company may contract the services of another firm to supply and maintain computer equipment. Suppliers must carry out their services to the satisfaction of their customers. Failure to do so may hold up production or result in poor-quality output. TQM places great emphasis on the effective operation of such quality chains and good relationships between suppliers and the firm.

Benchmarking

This involves observing the products and processes of rival companies and then improving on them to satisfy consumers' ever-changing wants. (see 27.2).

A firm that is able to demonstrate quality in production and products may be able to display trademarks awarded by independent bodies. For example:

- **The British Standards Institution (BSI)** sets quality and safety standards for a wide range of products. Products meeting the BSI standards are awarded the BSI kitemark to indicate that they have reached the necessary standards. Products awarded the kitemark will have a competitive advantage over those which fail to display the symbol to the consumer.

- The **Wool Marketing Board** trademark can be used by manufacturers who have produced garments of quality from pure new wool.

- Organizations can register with professional and trade associations if they follow their codes of practice. Examples include the **Federation of Master Builders, Association of British Travel Agents (ABTA),** and the **Advertising Association.**

Advanced Business

▼ Trademarks of quality

British Wool... naturally

ABTA

Portfolio Activity 15.2

Range: Factors, Improvements in production, Ways to achieve added value, Analyse
Skills: Take part in discussions, Read and respond to written material

Back to basics on the factory floor

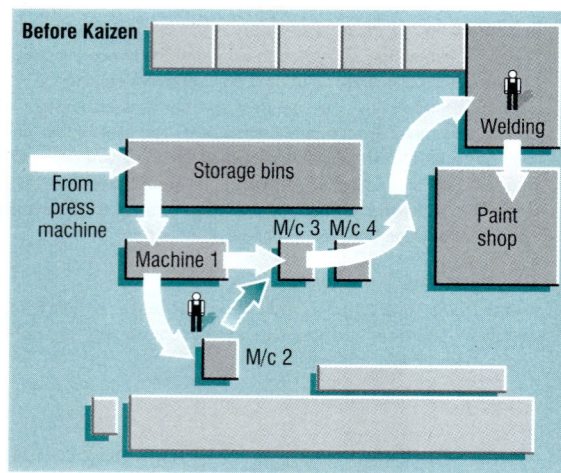

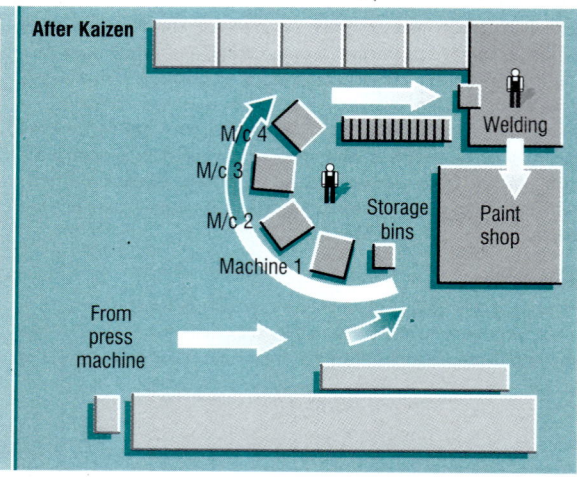

Before Kaizen / **After Kaizen**

It takes a brave man to allow consultants to tear up his factory and re-arrange it overnight.

At the Paddy Hopkirk car accessory factory in Bedfordshire just before Christmas, consultants inspired by the Japanese concept of continuous improvement – or Kaizen – did just that.

One morning the factory was an untidy sprawl of production lines surrounded by piles of crates holding semi-finished components. Two days later, when the 180-strong workforce came to work, the machines had been brought together in tightly grouped "cells". The piles of components had disappeared, and the newly-cleared floor space was neatly marked with colour-coded lines mapping out the flow of materials.

Overnight, there were dramatic differences. In the first full day, productivity on some lines increased by up to 30 per cent, the space needed for some processes had been halved, and work in progress had been cut considerably. The improved lay-out had allowed some jobs to be combined, freeing up operators for deployment elsewhere in the factory.

One of many Japanese management practices which have been adopted in the west, Kaizen is most frequently applied in larger companies. But it is equally valid in smaller factories. Paddy Hopkirk has sales of £6m a year, but with the help of continuous improvement thinks this can reach £9m.

A central tenet of Kaizen is the elimination of waste. It not only exists in obvious piles of excess inventory. It is also wasteful when an operator makes more movements than is necessary to complete a task because his or her machine is badly positioned.

To reduce one of the biggest sources of waste, Kaizen favours one-piece production, involving as many processes as possible being carried out on a single part consecutively rather than one process being done in a big batch. Parts are only delivered to the next stage of the production or assembly process when they are needed.

Another central theme is the drive to reduce the time wasted in processes that do not add value, like carrying parts or moving from one machine to another.

Financial Times 4.1.94

1. What is *Kaizen*?
2. Explain how *Kaizen* has been used successfully in the Paddy Hopkirk Car Accessory factory.
3. **(a)** Gather information on a small local firm, and prepare a short report for management/owners on how they might make use of *Kaizen* to improve productivity. For example, in what ways could their office or factory layout be changed to reduce waste and unnecessary movement? Include 'before and after' layout plans to show the effect of your recommendations.

(b) What other features of Total Quality Management would you recommend your firm to use? Explain the potential advantages and any disadvantages of your recommendations.

(c) Make a short presentation of your recommendations to the management/owners of your firm (or members of your group). Discuss your recommendations with them and evaluate your proposals in the light of their comments. For example, what costs and benefits do they think your recommendations, and TQM in general, may have?

Key words

Job production - producing one product at a time, usually using labour-intensive techniques

Batch production - producing products in batches, for example, of different colours and sizes

Flow production - automated and continuous mass production

Just In Time inventory control (JIT) - keeping stocks and work-in-progress to a minimum by ordering new supplies only when they are needed for production

Lead time - the elapsed time between placing an order for supplies and taking delivery of them

Total Quality Management (TQM) - the continuous improvement of products and processes by focusing on quality at each stage of production

Empowerment - allowing employees to use and realize their full potential and abilities in the workplace

Statistical process control - collecting and analyzing data on business performance

Quality circles - small groups of workers each given the responsibility for the organization and development of their own jobs

Quality chains - groups of interdependent suppliers, each one placing an emphasis on reliability and quality

Best practice benchmarking - observing the products and processes of rival companies in order to learn new and better ways of producing

Section 15.3 The impact of technology

Technological advance

One of the most important factors affecting production this century has been the impact of new technology. For example, advancing technology has brought about the following changes:

- **New products and services**, such as video recorders, compact discs, satellite communications, automated banking

- **New materials**, such as polythene, nylon, and silicon chips for computer motherboards

- **New and more efficient methods of production**, such as computer-aided manufacture (CAM), robotic assembly and welding, genetic engineering to produce hardy vegetable crops, recycling and waste management, laser precision measurements and cutting, 'keyhole' surgery in hospitals

Technological advance in medicine, communications, and robotics

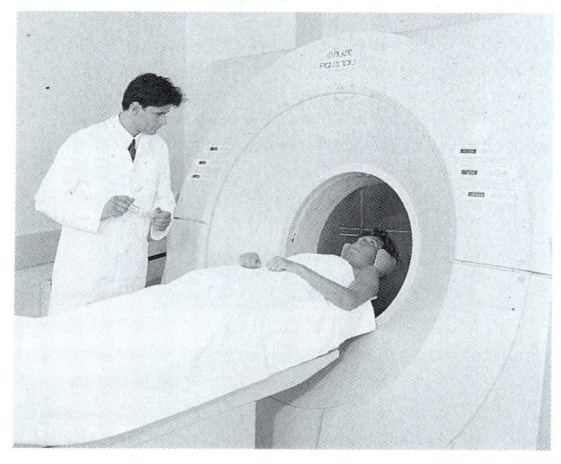

- **New skills,** such as computer technicians, communications engineers, management consultants

- **Changes in business activities,** such as videoconferencing, direct mailing, wordprocessing, computer-aided design (CAD) and management information systems (MIS). A **management information system (MIS)** is a restricted network established within an organisation to provide managers with information and analysis that will help them in their decision making. In a competitive world the faster this information and analysis is received the better and improvements in computer and communications technology has facilitated this.

Each year, industry spends many billions of pounds on the research and development of new products and production processes. In 1992 some £12 billion was spent on R&D in the UK alone (see 9.1).

Technological advance has greatly increased the speed, accuracy, reliability, and cost of new capital equipment to business, resulting in a fall in demand for labour in some occupations and industries. For example, the work of once-skilled typesetters and compositors in the printing industry can now be performed by writers and journalists using desktop publishing software. Intelligent robots controlled by computer are increasingly taking over human tasks in manufacturing processes such as car-assembly and food packaging. This is known as **computer-aided manufacture (CAM).**

What is CAD?

Computer-aided design (CAD) refers to interactive computer software capable of generating, storing, and using geometric graphics. CAD is used by design engineers in many industries for tasks ranging from the development of product packaging to the design of office blocks. The benefits of using CAD are:

- A reduction in lead times between product design and production
- The ability to examine and evaluate a wide range of designs without the need for building 3D prototypes
- The ability to modify designs quickly and easily

Portfolio Activity 15.3

Range: Factors, Improvements in production, Ways to achieve added value

Skills: Read and respond to written material

1. What are the advantages to the French Army of using industrial robots to pack rations?
2. How could the employment of robot technology benefit the food, drink, and confectionery industry?
3. Explain why the robots could be described as 'labour-saving technology'?
4. Describe the main obstacles, past and present, to the employment of robots in UK industry.
5. Investigate the potential for the introduction of labour-saving technology in other industries. What are the implications of this on business, labour, consumers, and the government?

Untouched by human hands

A PLATOON of raw recruits drafted in to the French army to pack combat rations are having to look lively. Up to 10 different menus are needed each month. In order to keep the fighting troops fed, the new recruits have to pack rations at the rate of 24 a minute.

The luckless legionnaires are 13 industrial robots, part of a FFr25m automated packaging and palletising line built for the army by ABB Robotics. Three robots unload boxes of goodies from pallets on to a conveyor which delivers them to the ration packing station.

Here another nine machines, using videos cameras to recognise the right items, pack them into ration boxes in just 2.5 seconds.

David Marshall, responsible for customer training at ABB Robotics in Milton Keynes, fervently hopes that the food, drinks and confectionery industry – including even army rations – will become the next big market for robots.

The reasons for his optimism is that industrial robots have become faster, reliable, more accurate, and easier to incorporate into a production line. Better motor control software has allowed ABB, for example, to squeeze 25 per cent more performance out of the same robot.

Robots are also simpler to program, operate and maintain. And they can lift bigger loads. They can also be washed down with a hosepipe. And prices are coming down to a level where paybacks are acceptable to the food industry.

But what is good for the food and drinks makers is good for manufacturing industry. Mike Wilson, marketing manager at Fanuc Robotics in Coventry, says of the improvements in robot performance: "Our new ARC Mate Welding robot, for example, is 30 per cent cheaper in real terms than a similar model three years ago. And it is 20 per cent faster."

Yet despite the advances in robot technology, Britain has one of the smallest robot populations of all the industrialised nations, around 7,600, compared with Germany's 39,000 and Japan's staggering 350,000.

Even the former USSR has more robots per employee in manufacturing industry than Britain. The problem is the 18 month to two year paybacks demanded in Britain, says Wilson, compared with as long as five years in Japan. "It is very difficult to justify any capital expenditure on an 18 month payback."

Financial Times 25.3.94

Advanced Business

JUST REMEMBER, NO-ONE IS IRREPLACEABLE, No 259 B

The costs of new technology

Despite its undoubted advantages, the increasing use of new technologies in business has not been without cost. Some of the disadvantages include:

- **High 'front-end' costs:** the research and development of new technologies, and their installation and maintenance, are often very expensive. Short-term production costs may also rise if workers need to be retrained, or if labour is laid off and redundancy payments have to be made.

- **Damage to labour relations:** workers may view the introduction of new machinery and production methods with suspicion. Bitter labour disputes between Trade Unions and employers have occurred in the past because of the fear of job losses. New technology has tended to replace manual jobs, but has also created a demand for new, more technical, skills, requiring workforces to undergo retraining.

The substitution of capital for labour in a firm will depend on the type of product and the production process used. In some cases, substitution will not be possible. For example, as yet machines cannot undertake the work of a hairdresser, window-cleaner, economist, or nurse, although clearly many in these occupations will use capital equipment, from hairdriers to computers, to help them in their tasks. In some cases, however, technological advance has increased the demand for labour. For example, the 1980s saw a significant increase in the demand for computer technicians and programmers, following growth in the market for personal computers.

Portfolio Activity 15.4

Range: Ways to achieve added value, Factors, Improvements in Production

Skills: Read and respond to written material, Collect and record data

Investigate the introduction of new equipment in a business organization with which you are familiar. Try to find out:

- The reasons for its introduction
- The cost of the equipment
- The method of finance
- Whether employees were, or will be, given training
- Whether the equipment has replaced labour
- The impact (or expected impact) of the equipment on productivity and quality

---

Key words

Technology - the 'science of the industrial arts', that is, the creative processes which help solve problems and improve efficiency

Computer-aided manufacture (CAM) - automated manufacture controlled by computers

Computer-aided design (CAD) - use of interactive computer software to assist design

Substitution of capital for labour - replacing human with mechanical effort

Section 15.4 Improving the productivity of labour

Why do people work?

If a business organization is to motivate workers to achieve higher levels of productivity and quality, it must first understand why people go to work. The obvious explanation is 'because they need the money'. However, money is not the only need that is satisfied by working. A combination of factors, financial and non-financial, give an employee **job satisfaction**, including:

- Adequate wages and fringe benefits, e.g. pension, company car
- Holiday entitlement
- Pleasant working environment
- Challenging and interesting job tasks
- Variety in the working day
- Opportunities to learn and try new ideas
- Availability of training
- Working as part of a team
- Being consulted on management decisions
- Responsibility
- Regular feedback on performance
- Recognition for good work through pay bonuses or promotion
- Social relationships inside and outside of work with colleagues and managers

A satisfied worker is likely to be more productive, and more committed to the organization and the attainment of its business goals.

Motivation strategies

A variety of strategies can be used by firms to increase job satisfaction and motivate employees to work harder:

- **Performance-related pay (PRP).** Linking pay to the performance of individuals or groups of workers can provide an incentive to greater effort. PRP can be in the form of one-off bonuses, piece rates, profit-sharing, and employee share options.

- **Group working.** Encouraging group working can develop team spirit, which can be beneficial to the organization. Competition between groups may also help to raise output.

- **New methods of working.** Jobs can be enriched or expanded so that workers can be given more responsibility, undertake a wider variety of tasks, be more involved in decision-making, and have a greater sense of achievement.

- Innovations such as **Flexitime** may also improve job satisfaction. Flexitime allows workers to choose when to start and finish work, as long as they complete an agreed number of hours per week (see 13.4).

JOB SATISFACTION LEADS TO:-
- LOWER ABSENTEEISM
- HIGHER MORALE
- BETTER CO-OPERATION
- LOWER STAFF TURNOVER
- INCREASED MOTIVATION
- HIGHER PRODUCTIVITY
- MORE PROFIT
- GOOD CORPORATE IMAGE

- **Managerial communication.** Perhaps the most basic motivational requirement for managers is simply to communicate well with their employees. Communication can satisfy such basic human needs as recognition, security, and a sense of belonging. Managers can praise staff for their efforts, ask their opinions on organizational issues, and involve them in decision-making. In this way managers can change the attitudes of workers so that they are more positive about their work and employers.

- **Rewards and punishments.** If managers want to modify workers' behaviour, they must ensure that appropriate consequences occur as a result of that behaviour. For example, if a worker who arrives on time for work is rewarded in some way, the probability of their arriving on time more often is increased. Conversely, a worker who is reprimanded or punished in some way if late - for example, by loss of earnings - is less likely to repeat the behaviour. An appropriately designed system of rewards and punishments can reinforce good behaviour and help eliminate bad behaviour and poor performance.

Portfolio Activity 15.5

Range: Improvements in production, Analyse
Skills: Read and respond to written material

1. What is a 'quality circle'?
2. What have been the advantages of quality circles to (a) the employees, and (b) the Telco organization?
3. Investigate quality circles in an organization with which you are familiar. Do they exist, and if so, why? If quality circles are not used, why not? Would you recommend them to management? Give reasons.

When Quality is a Way of Life

India may not be the first place to conjure up images of industrial efficiency or Total Quality Management. But if that is now all changing - not least thanks to the economic reforms of finance minister Manmohan Singh - one company stands out as a benchmark for others to follow.

The truck and excavator company Telco (Tata Engineering and Locomotive Company) has developed a peculiarly Indian approach to quality and worker participation.

"Quality and productivity are essential in helping us to compete worldwide," says Sarosh Ghandy, resident director in Jamshedpur. "We are investing in our 'software': building on the skills, commitment and involvement of our workers."

The company launched its own in-house 'human relations at work' (HRW) training programme in 1982. The focus is a three-day course, attended so far by 18,000 of Telco's 20,000 employees. The aim is to empower the workforce to take responsibility.

The visible manifestation has been the birth of shop-floor quality circles. Now nearly 1,300 voluntary groups of 10 to 12 people, involving the bulk of the workforce, meet for an hour each week to iron out problems - and discuss how to tackle alcoholism, family debt, and communal tension in their townships.

One group bailed out a colleague who became heavily in debt after personal problems. Another group repaired a fault on a metal press which had baffled German engineers.

Each year, employees make 100,000 suggestions for improvements, saving Telco nearly £2m, says Ghandy. The company is now making 16,000 more trucks with 6,000 fewer workers, and has enjoyed a strike-free industrial record over the last 21 years.

Financial Times 25.9.93

UNIT FIVE

CHAPTER 15

Motivation and financial rewards

Time rates
Most workers receive wages or salaries based on the number of hours they work each week or year. Time rates are, therefore, used to reward workers for the amount of productive time they spend in work.

Performance-related pay (PRP)
PRP is a term used to describe systems that link the pay of workers to some measure of individual, group or organizational effort. In recent years, PRP schemes have been extended from manual workers to non-manual/white collar occupations. These incentive payment schemes can take many forms:

- **Individual payment by results or piecework** - where an individual's earnings are totally or partially based on their performance, usually in terms of the quantity or value of output they produce. The more they produce the more they are paid.

- **Group payment by results** - where the output or sales-related performance pay is divided between a group of workers according to some pre-determined formula.

- **Plant- or enterprise-wide bonuses** - in which all employees receive a bonus

- **Merit pay** - where the employee receives a level of bonus or basic pay linked to an assessment and appraisal of their performance by their superiors. This system is popular in white-collar occupations.

- **Financial participation** - for example, profit-sharing and share option schemes, whereby individual employees receive a reward in terms of cash or company shares, the size of which will normally depend on company profits over a given period.

Since 1979, a number of Finance Acts have granted tax relief to employers who introduce share and profit-related schemes for their employees. Data from the Inland Revenue shows that by 1993, the number of employees participating in profit-related pay schemes had grown to around 1.2 million.

Other forms of financial incentive include:

- **Commission** - this will often be paid to workers involved in sales, such as insurance and double-glazing salespeople, financial advisers, and travel agents, based on a percentage of the value of sales they achieve.

- **Non-monetary rewards** - these are 'payments' to labour in a form other than money, for example, free medical insurance, subsidized meals, and company cars.

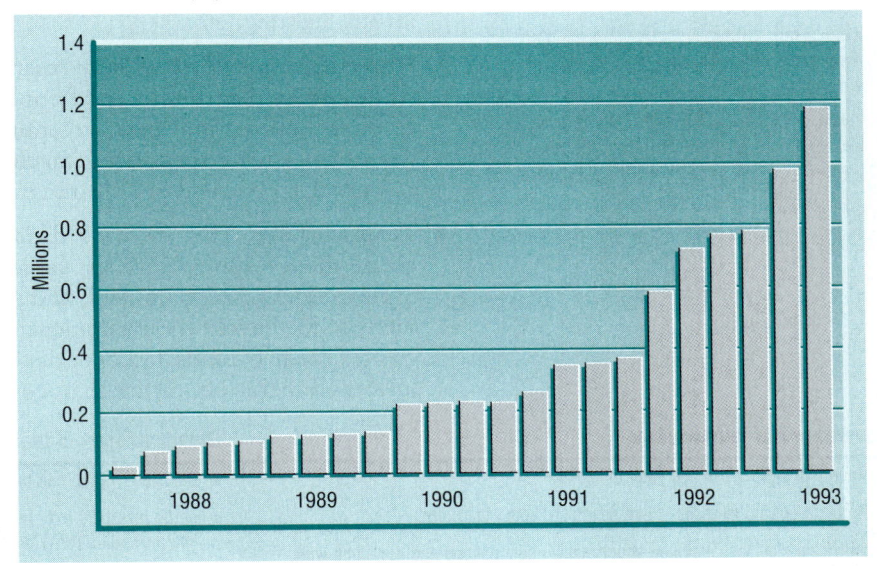

▼ *Figure 15.1: Employees covered by Inland Revenue approved profit-related pay schemes*
Inland Revenue/Employment Gazette September 1993

Working methods and job design

As organizations become more aware of the importance of motivation, a growing number are introducing new methods of working to take into account the needs of employees to enjoy their work, display their creativity, and feel a sense of achievement and responsibility. It is argued that designing jobs with workers' needs in mind will increase quality, productivity and added value, and reduce production costs, absenteeism, and staff turnover.

Various methods have been devised to incorporate workers' needs into jobs. These include:

- **Job enlargement.** This attempts to make a job more varied by removing the boredom associated with repetitive operations. It involves extending the scope of a job by adding similar tasks, but without increasing worker responsibility. For example, instead of an employee bolting the bumpers onto a new car, s/he may also be allowed to fix doors and bonnets. Job enlargement is often criticized because it simply adds to the amount of dull tasks a worker has to perform.

Advanced Business

> **Five steps to job satisfaction**
>
> 1. A job should include all those tasks necessary to complete a finished product or process so that workers can feel a sense of achievement
> 2. Workers, or teams of workers, should take responsibility for the quality of the work and their output
> 3. Workers should be able to carry out a variety of tasks
> 4. Employees should be able to prioritize their work and regulate the speed at which they work
> 5. Employees should have the opportunity to work in groups and socialize with other workers

- **Job rotation.** Instead of enlarging jobs, workers can be organized into small groups and trained to carry out all the jobs in the group. Workers can then swap or rotate their jobs on a regular basis to provide variety. Job rotation is often important in the training of work supervisors or managers. However, if each of the jobs performed is equally boring, motivation is hardly likely to improve as a result.

- **Job enrichment.** This attempts to increase the sense of challenge and achievement in a job. A job may be enriched by giving workers:

   - a greater variety of tasks
   - more freedom in deciding how to plan tasks, order materials, etc.
   - regular feedback on job performance
   - more involvement in analysing and changing physical aspects of their working environment, such as temperature control, office or plant layout, lighting, etc.

   However, some workers may resent an increase in their responsibility, while others may find it hard cope with the added pressure. In other cases, technology may be a constraint. For example, jobs associated with the operation of specialized machinery and assembly-line techniques can never be particularly meaningful.

- **Teamworking.** This involves dividing the workforce into teams and giving them responsibility for areas such as the planning and execution of their work, quality control, and physical aspects of their environment such as the layout of equipment and furniture. Teamwork allows a greater range of skills and experience to be used in problem-solving and fosters cooperation, rather than competition, among team members.

Advantages of teamworking

- Variety of skills leads to greater efficiency
- Problem-solving is easier – 'two heads are better than one'
- Individuals feel less inhibited about making suggestions and decisions with the backing of others – 'strength in numbers'
- Groups may develop a team spirit
- Workers are motivated by team membership and committed to the achievement of group and organizational goals

Disadvantages of teamworking

- Decision-making can be slow, especially in large groups
- Some members may be inhibited by dominant personalities within the team and prevented from making what could have been good suggestions
- Some teams may develop norms and attitudes at odds with the organization, for example, 'Don't work too hard - they won't thank you for it!'
- Team discussions may involve 'too much talk and not enough action'

Teamwork at Volvo

At the Uddevalla Volvo truck plant in Sweden, work teams of between 15-25 employees had a great deal of autonomy. For example, teams chose their own supervisor, assigned tasks among themselves, set their own outputs, and assumed responsibility for quality control. Employees also received immediate feedback on hourly production rates, which were displayed on screens. However, despite the success of this system in the past, the plant was eventually forced to close in 1993 due to high costs.

Portfolio Activity 15.6

Range: Improvements in production, Ways to achieve added value, Analyse
Skills: Take part in discussions, Produce written material

Sue works as a cashier in her local supermarket. Her main tasks are to scan customers' purchases with a bar-code reader, weigh loose fruit and vegetables, and receive payments. Sue also stocks shelves during quieter moments in the store when fewer cashiers are required.

Sue is bored with her job and lacks motivation. Technology has reduced the skills and knowledge needed to do her job. Her cash register is computerized. The bar-code scanner identifies the price of individual items and keeps a running total of the customer's expenditure. Before the new cash registers arrived and the store was reorganized, Sue was required to advise customers on products, input prices manually, subtract any money-off coupons from total bills and calculate the correct change.

1. Suggest how you might redesign Sue's job in line with the 'five steps to job satisfaction' listed on p.000.
2. What are the potential benefits to the supermarket of redesigning the jobs of their cashiers?
3. Investigate the tasks involved in two other jobs carried out by people you know, or are able to contact. (Ideally, one job should be a manual occupation and the other non-manual). Discuss their jobs with them, and their satisfaction or dissatisfaction with their work.

Evaluate the tasks involved in the two jobs and suggest how they might be redesigned to improve worker satisfaction, motivation, and productivity.

Key words

Job enlargement - extending the scope of a job by adding similar tasks without increasing the worker's responsibility

Job enrichment - adding a greater variety of tasks, responsibility, and sense of achievement to a job

Job rotation - workers swapping or rotate their jobs on a regular basis

Job satisfaction - the sense of fulfilment and contentment a worker gains from working in a particular job

Motivation - the incentive to greater effort which can be provided by a variety of financial and non-financial rewards in a job

Performance-related pay - systems which link increases in wage payments to individual, group, or organizational efforts

Teamworking - dividing the workforce into teams and giving them responsibility for the organization of their job tasks and work environment

Section 15.5 Health and safety at work

In a typical week in Britain, 9 workers are killed; a child, an adult, and an elderly person are killed, and 400 people suffer major injuries - all as a result of work-related accidents.

The statistics on work-related accidents in Britain are grim. It is not surprising, therefore, that firms are required by law to provide a healthy and safe environment for their workers and customers (see 12.3). Implementing health and safety measures adds to business costs in the short run. However, a firm that does not consider the interests of its employees is unlikely to achieve its business goals. A healthier workforce, and one that has fewer accidents, is more productive, and will reduce costs in the long run.

Advanced Business

▼ Health and safety at work

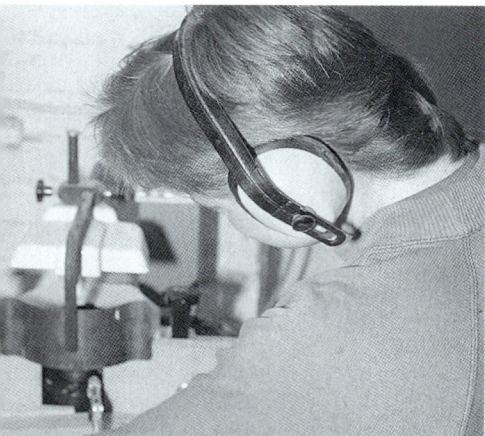

Health and safety measures in the workplace include the following:
- Promoting hygienic conditions
- Protecting workers from hazardous substances
- Training staff in health and safety matters
- Providing ear protectors against noise
- Maintaining safety equipment and clothing
- Allowing breaks for lunch and tea so that workers do not become tired
- Providing First Aid kits and training for medical officers
- Controlling workplace temperature
- Reducing workplace air and noise pollution

Clearly, the need for many of these measures will vary depending on the workplace. For example, office workers will primarily need to be aware of fire drills and precautions relating to the prolonged use of computer screens, the movement of office furniture, etc. By contrast, many industrial workers regularly come into contact with potentially dangerous machinery and substances, and will need much greater levels of protection.

The graphs above show data collected by the Labour Force Survey on the number of employees absent from

▼ Figure 15.2: Percentage of employees absent from work for at least one day in the survey week due to sickness or injury; by industry and occupation, Great Britain, Summer 1994

Percentage of employees absent from work for at least one day in the reference week due to sickness or injury by occupation (Great Britain, Summer 1994, not seasonally adjusted)

GB rate 4.0 per cent (summer 1994)
4.0 per cent (summer 1993)

Occupation	%	(thousands)
Managers and administrators	~3	(82)
Professional	~3	(69)
Craft and related	~4	(89)
Selling	~3.5	(74)
Associate professional and technical	~3.5	(81)
Other occupations	~3.5	(81)
Clerical and secretarial	~4	(160)
Personal and protective services	~5	(119)
Plant and machine operatives	~5	(111)

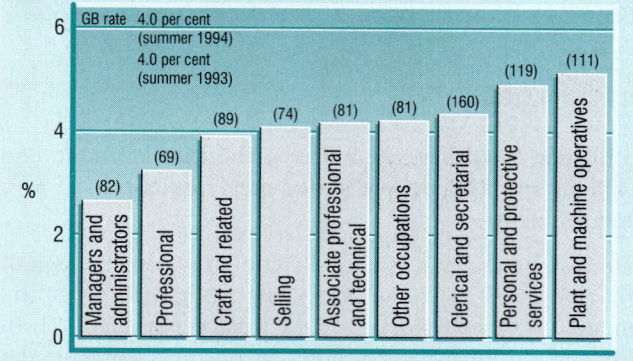

Occupations are coded according to the Standard Occupational Classification
( ) The figures shown in brackets are the number (in thousands) of employees absent from work for at least one day in the reference week

Percentage of employees absent from work for at least one day in the reference week due to sickness or injury by industry (Great Britain, Summer 1994, not seasonally adjusted)

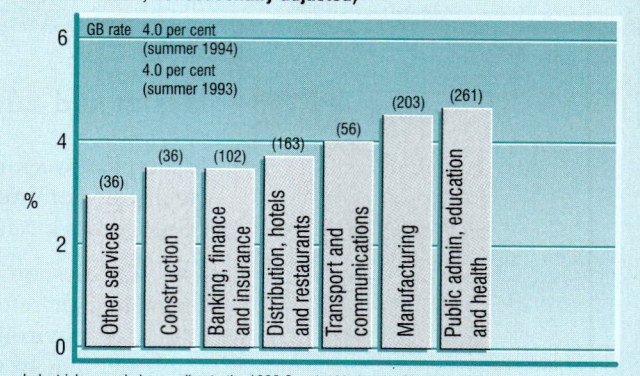

GB rate 4.0 per cent (summer 1994)
4.0 per cent (summer 1993)

Industry	%	(thousands)
Other services	~3	(36)
Construction	~3.5	(36)
Banking, finance and insurance	~3.5	(102)
Distribution, hotels and restaurants	~4	(163)
Transport and communications	~4	(56)
Manufacturing	~4.5	(203)
Public admin, education and health	~5	(261)

Industrial are coded according to the 1992 Standard Industrial Classification
Agriculture, forestry and fishing and energy and water supply industries are not included as estimate less than 10 000 ( ) The figures shown in brackets are the number (in thousands) of employees absent from work for at least one day in the reference week

Employment Gazette 12.94

work due to illness or injury during Summer 1994. Employee absence tends to be higher in primary and secondary industries, namely mineral extraction, manufacturing, and construction, and among plant or machine operatives. However, the data does not distinguish between minor or major injuries, nor does it indicate whether the 'sickness' in question is a common ailment, like a cold, or is related to the working environment.

Portfolio Activity 15.7

Range: Ways to achieve added value, Improvements in production, Analyse
Skills: Read written material, Collect and record data

1. From the articles, explain why it is so important for firms to develop and promote health and safety measures in the workplace.

2. Investigate the health and safety measures employed in your school/college. What improvements would you recommend, if any? To help develop your ideas, it might be useful to collect statistics on past accidents and their causes, to see where improvement might be made. Check with your main school/college office if this information is available.

   Produce a brief report of your findings and ideas to present to senior teachers, following the five-step plan recommended in the article above.

3. Contrast the health and safety measures in your school/college with those employed in another business organization with which you are familiar. Do they differ? If so, why?

Five steps to safety

ADVICE ON how to assess and control risks to health and safety in the workplace is contained in a new free HSE leaflet.

The five steps described in the leaflet are:
- look for the hazards (anything that could cause harm);
- decide who might be harmed and how;
- evaluate the risks arising from the hazards, and decide whether existing precautions are adequate or more needs to be done;
- record the findings; and
- review the assessment from time to time and revise it as necessary.

Employment Gazette March 1994

Accident costs – revealed

EMPLOYERS ARE losing between £4 billion and £9 billion a year through workplace accidents and work-related ill health, says a Health and Safety Executive report.

The losses equate to 5–10 per cent of all UK industrial companies' gross profits in 1990, or between £170 and £360 per year for every employee.

The cost to employers include:
- the damage to materials or finished goods resulting from accidents (accounting for around half of total costs);
- lost output (e.g. through staff absence and disruption to production);
- paying sick pay or compensation to affected workers; and
- extra administration costs.

Advanced Business

Health and safety - the record of achievement

There is little doubt that the introduction of health and safety legislation has been a success. Workplace accidents have fallen, and costs and disruption to production in many firms have been reduced as a result. However, statistics need to be viewed with some caution. Some injuries may not be reported. The overall improvement in workplace injuries is also, in part, a reflection of the shift in employment towards service industries which tend to involve less risk of injury than production in manufacturing industries.

Record low for workplace deaths

THE NUMBER of deaths from accidents at work has been reduced to the lowest on record, says the latest Health and Safety Commission (HSC) annual report.

For the third successive year, the rate of fatal accidents fell in 1992–93 to 1.3 per 100,000 emloyees, generally less than a quarter of the rate 30 years ago. The rate of major injuries fell to 81 per 100,000 employees.

These trends, says HSC, are partly attributable to changes in the structure of industry away from high-risk heavy industry, but also represent genuine improvements in safety particularly in areas such as mining and construction.

Other statistics include:
- 140,365 injuries caused absence from work of more than three days;
- an estimated 3,000 deaths were due to asbestos;
- Some 9,400 accident/incident investigations and 15,090 complaint investigations were made by HSE inspectors;
- 1,843 convictions were made for breaches of health and safety laws, attracting an average fine of £1,384;

Employment Gazette January 1994

Section 15.6 Reducing pollution from production

▼ *Noise pollution*

In the working environment

Some manufacturing processes result in potentially harmful pollutants being released into the air and some can be very noisy. If employees health and stress levels are not to suffer employers must make sure that appropriate measures are taken to reduce air and noise pollution. This can be done by issuing employees with protective clothing and equipment. However, wearing masks and ear mufflers may impede worker efforts and so production processes must be investigated for possible solutions. For example, extractor fans, new less noisy equipment and sound proofing could be deployed.

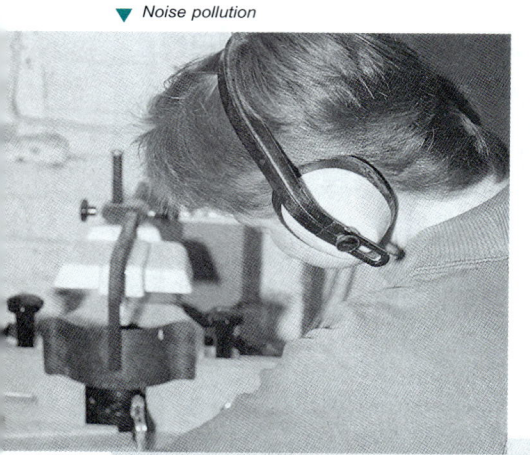

▼ *Chemical pollution*

In the natural environment

However, it is not just workers who may suffer from pollution (see 2.3). Harmful pollutants can be released into the air and water supplies as the result of production in many factories.

Farms may use chemical sprays to protect crops that harm fish and animals. Office work can also result in piles of waste paper. Oil spills can occur at drilling platforms and from tankers. Radiation may leak from nuclear power plants.

Increasing concern for the environment has resulted not only in legislation to control pollution but also firms taking the initiative to make sure they produce goods and services which meet the changing desires of consumers. For example, the *Clean Air Act* and *Environmental Protection Act* set limits on the type and amount of pollutants firms can discharge into the atmosphere, rivers and seas. The new Environment Agency for England and Wales and the Scottish Environment Protection Agency will be largely responsible for the control of industrial pollution and waste, and for the regulation of the water environment (see 3.4).

Changing consumer demands for more environmentally products and less damaging methods of production have also resulted in an increasing number of firms adopting many other environmental measures that has changed the way they produce their goods and services. For example;

- wood merchants and furniture makers making sure their supplies are from renewable forests and not tropical rainforests
- fitting catalytic converters on motor vehicles to reduce exhaust emissions
- using new chemicals in fridges and aerosol cans that no longer destroy the ozone layer
- halting the testing of products and ingredients on animals
- using more recycled materials and biodegradable packaging

Portfolio Activity 15.8

Range: Improvements in production, Factors
Skills: Read and respond to written materials, Collect and record data, Produce written material

Life ever after

To discover how green a product is, companies increasingly look at its environmental effects before, during and after production

One study describes how, after Denmark required refillable containers for drinks, Tetra Pak analysed the environmental effects of its non-refillable paper cartons. It showed they could be packed closer together than glass bottles, thus reducing the number of polluting lorry-loads needed to transport them.

The cartons need less energy to refrigerate and cause less water pollution than glass, which must be cleaned. When bottles are discarded, they take up more space in landfills than lightweight cartons. Confronted with such evidence, the Danish government lifted its ban on non-refillable containers, and in 1993 even lifted its tax on milk cartons.

Adapted from The Economist 9.10.93

Advanced Business

1. Why did the Danish government ban non-refillable cartons? Why was this ban eventually lifted? What likely effect did these changes have on producers of containers?

2. Why did McDonalds initially choose to supply their products in polystyrene containers? What factors caused them to rethink this choice? What were the likely effects of these changes on production and supply chains?

3. Visit a manufacturing plant. Discuss with workers and managers measures that have been used by the firm to reduce pollution (air and noise) in their working environment and in the natural environment. Why has the firm wanted to reduce pollution? What costs have been involved? If the firm has not employed measures to reduce pollution make appropriate recommendations. Write up your findings in a word processed report.

4. Assemble examples from newspapers, magazines and TV, that illustrate how firms are changing their production processes to be more environmentally friendly, or in some cases even less friendly, in your opinion. Analyse how these changes are likely to affect business costs and revenues, labour requirements and relationships with suppliers.

Food for thought

In 1988 McDonald's, America's biggest fast food chain, found itself the target of a vociferous campaign by environmental groups against the enormous amounts of rubbish it produced.

The polystyrene 'clamshells' in which McDonald's hamburgers were sold became a vivid symbol of the throw-away society. The company had chosen polystyrene, a light-weight plastic foam with good insulating properties, because it seemed ideal for packaging fast food. But its use meant that a product which took seconds to consume was carried out of the shop in a package that would take centuries to rot. Customers began posting them back to McDonald's in protest. Schoolchildren demonstrated outside its restaurants.

The company saw such protests as a threat to it future survival. Young people, its most devoted customers, were also those who embraced greenery with the greatest zeal.

At first McDonald's expanded recycling at its restaurants. However, the Environmental Defence Fund (EDF)- one of Americas more innovative environmental research and lobbying groups - urged them to reconsider. In a matter of days McDonalds announced it would replace the clamshell, where possible, with a quilted paper wrap made from a layer of tissue between a sheet of paper and polyethylene.

McDonalds continues to work with the EDF. The company now has a number of goals; reduce, reuse and recycle, for example, by reducing the amount of chlorine bleached paper it uses, and using more recycled materials.

Adapted from The Economist 29.8.92

Further reading

Employment Gazette, official journal of the Employment Department (monthly publication)

Test Questions

The following underpinning knowledge will be tested:

1. Why businesses aim to add value in production
2. Ways to achieve added value
3. Factors that can cause change in production
4. Analyse improvements in production

1 Linking pay to productivity means that workers will only receive a pay rise if:

  A Product demand rises
  B Output rises
  C Production costs fall
  D Product price rises

Questions 2-4 share the following answer options:

The productivity of a workforce may be improved in a firm that offers:

  A Job enrichment
  B Increased job specialization
  C Greater job security
  D Empowerment

Which of the above could be achieved by:

2 Increasing the variety of tasks performed by an employee

3 Offering permanent contracts to temporary employees

4 Improving training opportunities

5 Labour productivity in a firm is most likely to suffer if there is:

  A An increase in overtime working
  B An increase in performance-related gifts
  C An increase in staff turnover
  D An increase in worker participation in decision-making

Questions 6-7 concern the following methods of payment:

  A Time rates
  B Profit sharing
  C Performance-related pay
  D Commission

Which of the above methods describes wage payments which are calculated on the basis of:

6 Systems that link pay to an worker's individual or group productivity

7 The number of hours worked multiplied by the wage rate per hour

8 The payment of non-monetary rewards or 'fringe benefits' to workers by their employers has increased over time. Which one of the following statements could not explain this trend?

  A Firms are increasingly concerned about worker motivation
  B The giving of non-monetary rewards can be cheaper than paying higher wages
  C Increasing competition for skilled labour has made it more difficult to retain staff
  D Unemployment has risen

Questions 9 - 11 share the following answer options:

  A Changing the ratio of capital to labour inputs
  B Total Quality Management
  C Worker empowerment
  D Quality circles

Which of the above describe the following strategies to improve productivity in a firm:

9 Organizing labour into small teams

10 Encouraging greater participation in business decision-making and problem-solving

11 Investment in new plant and machinery

12 The main reason a firm will wish to increase productivity is:

  A To reduce labour input
  B To reduce costs
  C To increase prices
  D To improve quality

13 a. What is production?

  b. What is productivity?

  c. What objectives do firms hope to achieve by increasing productivity?

  d. Explain two ways in which a construction firm might attempt to increase productivity.

  e. What strategies could an office employ to improve productivity?

Advanced Business

    f. Suggest two short-term costs to a firm of introducing methods to increase productivity.

    g. Suggest two long-term benefits of improved productivity to a firm.

14 a. What is 'added value' in production?

    b. Why do firms aim to add value in production?

    c. Suggest and explain three ways a firm might seek to increase added value in production.

    d. Suggest and explain three factors that could affect the production of motor cars.

    e. Suggest and explain three ways the motor car manufacturer could improve production.

15 a. Explain the following terms and suggest how they might help a firm to increase productivity.
- Job redesign
- Performance-related pay
- Just In Time production
- Single sourcing
- Total Quality Management
- Quality circles

    b. Suggest why these measures may not always have the desired impact on added value in production.

Assessment Assignment

Range: Ways to achieve added value
Why businesses aim to add value
Factors
Analyse
Improvements in production

Skills: Communication
Take part in discussions
Produce written material
Use illustrations and images
Application of Number
Collect and record data
Interpret and present data
Information Technology
Prepare information
Present information

Tasks

1. Imagine you are a management consultant and have just been contracted by two organizations to investigate production and productivity in the workplace.

   Based on your findings from site visits, staff interviews, annual reports, and other information sources, produce a report for each organization on the following:

   - How and why each organization adds value
   - How production has been affected by market conditions, resource cost and availability, technological change, labour flexibility, and legislation
   - How levels of labour and capital employment have changed over time
   - How changes in production have affected, and been affected by, investment in research and development and new technology
   - Productivity, and how it has changed over time (consider output levels, input to output ratios, and unit costs)
   - Why each organization wishes to improve productivity
   - A critical evaluation of the success or failure of any measures undertaken in the past to improve production
   - Discussion of how these measures may have altered relationships with suppliers and customers
   - The scope for further improvements in production. Make recommendations for possible strategies. What are the potential costs and benefits of these strategies to the firms and their workers?

2. Discuss the draft report with the owners or managers of each organization and make changes to the text of your report if necessary.

3. Make a presentation (10-15 minutes) of your report findings to the owners or directors. Use overhead projector slides summarizing the main findings, and a selection of tables or graphs to illustrate the main points raised.

chapter 16

UNIT FIVE

chapter 16
Investigating Employment

This chapter examines types, features, and trends in employment in the UK

Key ideas

The **working population** of the UK consists of all those people willing and able to work: employees in employment, the self-employed, claimant unemployed, HM forces personnel, and trainees on work-related government training schemes.

Regional patterns of employment differ. The South East of England has a higher proportion of workers in services than northern England, Wales and Scotland where more workers tend to work in manufacturing industries.

Different **types of employment** exist. People can be employed on a **full-time** or **part-time** basis, on either a **permanent** or **temporary** contract, or be **self-employed**.

The numbers of part-time, temporary and self-employed workers has increased over time to replace a number of full-time permanent jobs. These changes reflect the **needs of business** to **keep down costs**, and **maintain profits** and **levels of productivity** in the face of increasing competition and changing consumer demands to **maintain customer satisfaction**.

Part-time and temporary jobs have implications for the **needs of employees**. They tend to offer lower rates of pay and other benefits, fewer career opportunities and are less secure.

Wage differentials between different people in different occupations and industries occur due to differences in the level and strength of labour demand and supply. The gap between earnings in **manual** and **non-manual occupations** has widened while the gap between male and female earnings has narrowed.

The importance of manufacturing industry in terms of employment and output has declined in many western countries. In contrast, growth in the service sector has been significant; it now employs over 70% of UK employees. This has become known as **deindustrialization**.

The **participation rate** measures the number of people in the UK resident population who are economically active. Increasing numbers of females are participating in the UK labour force. Male participation rates have been falling for many years.

Occupations can be classified according to whether they are **manual** or **non-manual, skilled, semi-skilled** or **unskilled**. There has been a relative growth in the number of non-manual jobs. The demand for skilled labour has increased.

Skill shortages exist when there are not enough workers available with the skills needed to do jobs offered by business organizations.

Changes in the type and nature of employment in the UK have implications for workers. There is pressure on workers to retrain in new skills and to achieve higher levels of productivity. Some jobs are now less secure, and many workers may also face long periods of **unemployment**.

Rising unemployment also has implications for government revenues and expenditure.

Section 16.1 Employment trends

The changing labour market

Labour is an important business resource. It provides the mental and manual skills necessary to organize and undertake the production, marketing, and distribution of goods and services.

In recent years a number of features and trends have emerged in the UK labour market. These are:

- The decline of manufacturing in terms of employment and its contribution to national output
- The growing importance of the service sector as a major employer
- A fall in the number of full-time permanent jobs in favour of increasing part-time and temporary jobs.
- Increasing participation in the labour force by females
- Increasing demand for skilled labour
- Rising national and regional unemployment
- Growth in the number of long-term unemployed
- Growth in 'unofficial' employment and the black economy.

Most of these features are not peculiar to the UK, but can be observed in most developed countries in the world. Many of the changes are market-driven. That is, business organizations want their workforces to be more flexible and able to adapt their skills to changing market conditions, particularly in the face of increasing competition from the developing low-wage economies of South East Asia.

Evaluating changes in the labour market

We can evaluate changes in the UK labour market and employment trends in terms of how they meet the needs of business. **Business needs** will include;

- to control the costs of labour
- to maintain profits
- to maintain levels of productivity
- to meet changing customer demands

The cost of wages is usually the single largest element in the production costs of most firms. Making sure workers do not push for wages ahead of any improvements in output and revenues will be an important consideration for business. Workers may price themselves out of jobs if employers cannot afford to meet their wage demands. Technological advance has often meant replacing workers efforts with machinery and other equipment. For example, many assembly lines are now fully automated and use computer aided robots (see 15.4).

Workers may also need to acquire news skills and be deployed to meet changing consumer demands for products. For example, the demand for late night and sunday shopping has meant many firms have introduced shift working and employed part-timers and temporary workers on new contracts.

However, these employment trends have also affected people in work and looking for work. **Employee needs** in work will include;

- good levels of pay and other benefits such as sickness and holiday leave and pay entitlements
- career progression opportunities
- job security
- agreeable working conditions (see 13.1)

Employers desires for more flexibility in pay arrangements, their ability to hire and fire workers, and in workers skills, may conflict with employees needs. The fall in full-time employment has in part been offset by a rise in part-time employment. Part-time working may suit some people but is unlikely to give them the pay and benefits full-time colleagues would enjoy. The increasing employment of workers on short term contracts means they have less job security and fewer opportunities to progress their career.

▼ Table 16.1: Working population, UK 1981 and 1994

(thousands)	1981	1994
Male	16,288	15,696
Female	10,409	12,179
Total	26,697	27,875
of which:		
Employees in employment	21,870	21,397
Self-employed	2,119	3,266
Unemployed	2,176	2,643
HM forces	334	250
WRGTP	-	319

Annual Abstract of Statistics 1995

The working population

The working population of the UK can be defined as all those people willing and able to work - the total supply of labour. The combination of low birth rates and low death rates in the UK has increased the number of people between the ages of 16 and 65. The increase in the birth rate during the early 1960s fed through to the working population in the 1980s. In 1981 the UK workforce was 26.7 million. This peaked at 28.5. million in 1990 and, in 1994, stood at 27.9 million people.

The working population of the UK includes:

- Employees in employment
- The self-employed
- Claimant unemployed
- HM forces personnel
- Trainees in work-related government training programmes (WRGTP)

Employment in the UK

The numbers of employees in employment in the UK has grown only slowly over time. During the 1950s around 20 million people in the UK were employees. This peaked at just over 23 million in the late 1970s before falling back to around 22 million in the early 1980s. Table 16.1 shows that the number of employees in 1994 stood at 21.4 million.

However, the growth in the number of jobs has not been sufficient to give every person who has joined the working population a job with an employer. The number of **self-employed** has increased significantly from under 2 million in the 1960s to over 3 million in 1994 (see 28.1). However, perhaps the most dramatic change has occurred in national **unemployment**.

Unemployment

During the 1950s and 1960s, no more than 300,000 workers were considered officially unemployed in the UK in any one year. By 1979, this figure had reached 1.2 million, and in 1986 unemployment peaked at 3.1 million - 11.1% of the total working population. That is, approximately 11 out of every 100 workers in the UK were unemployed (see Figure 16.1).

Official unemployment is measured as the number of people out of work who are claiming the Job Seeker's allowance, Income Support, or National Insurance credits. Those unable to claim benefit, such as married women, young people on youth training schemes, part-time workers, or men over 60, are not considered to be officially unemployed, despite the fact that they might be actively seeking full-time employment.

The number of people registered unemployed expressed as a percentage of the total working population is the unemployment rate.

▼ Figure 16.1: Claimant unemployment and Job centre vacancies, UK 1971-1993

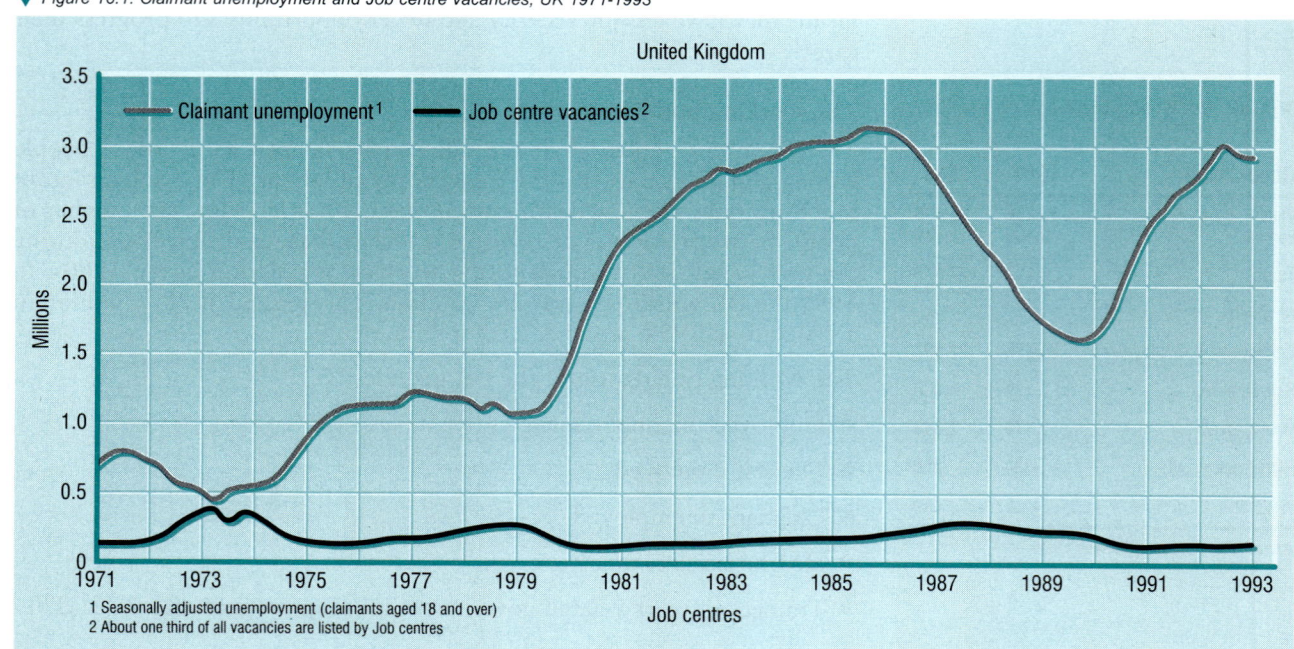

1 Seasonally adjusted unemployment (claimants aged 18 and over)
2 About one third of all vacancies are listed by Job centres

▼ Unemployment rates (%): an international comparison

Country	1981	1992
UK	9.8	9.9
Belgium	10.8	7.9
France	7.4	10.3
Germany	4.4	4.6
Italy	7.8	10.5
Spain	13.9	18.1
Finland	4.8	13.0
Canada	7.5	11.2
Japan	2.2	2.2
USA	7.5	7.3

The amount of time any one person spends unemployed has also increased over time. In 1971, about 15% of the unemployed workforce had been out of work for more than one year. By 1993, this figure had risen to 43% (1.23 million workers), with around 12% of the unemployed having been out of work for over three years (see Table 16.2).

Many young people fared particularly badly in the early 1990s recession. A lack of work experience and a tendency by firms to pursue 'last in, first out' policies in order to minimize redundancy payments resulted in some 1.3 million people between the ages of 16 and 29 being unemployed in Spring 1993.

UNIT FIVE

CHAPTER 16

▼ Table 16.2: UK unemployment[1], by age, sex, and duration, Spring 1994

UNITED KINGDOM — **PERCENTAGES AND THOUSANDS**

Duration of Unemployment (percentages)

	Up to 13 weeks	Over 13 up to 26 weeks	Over 26 weeks up to one year	Over one year up to two years	Over two years up to three years	Over three years	Total[2] (=100%) (thousands)
Males							
16–19	26.8	19.9	26.6	20.2	5.6	–	192
20–29	18.5	17.0	20.0	22.3	11.6	10.3	666
30–39	15.2	14.9	18.5	22.7	11.8	16.8	404
40–49	17.3	14.5	15.5	23.1	11.3	18.1	317
50–64	13.5	14.1	18.9	20.4	10.0	23.1	377
All aged 16 and over[3]	17.6	15.8	19.4	21.9	10.7	14.5	1,967
Females							
16–19	32.9	19.4	24.6	18.4	–	–	126
20–29	29.9	18.1	23.5	16.1	6.5	5.9	321
30–39	24.9	20.0	22.4	17.2	7.7	7.7	207
40–49	27.0	13.7	21.3	19.2	8.4	10.5	142
50–59	20.3	10.8	21.6	20.6	10.5	16.1	106
All aged 16 and over[3]	27.6	17.0	22.7	17.8	7.5	7.4	924
Total persons (thousands)	600	468	591	595	280	354	2,891

1 Unemployment is based on the ILO definition.
2 Includes those who did not state their duration.
3 Includes men aged 65 and over and women aged 60 and over who were unemployed.

Social Trends 1994

Portfolio Activity 16.1

Range: Employment trends, Implications, Evaluate in terms of effects on individuals
Skills: Collect and record data

1. Obtain a copy of the latest *Social Trends* and turn to the chapter on 'Employment'.

2. Compile data on the characteristics of the unemployed, including:
   - Age
   - Sex
   - Race
   - Duration of unemployment
   - Regional patterns

3. Examine the characteristics of the unemployed from the data and write a short paper describing the main patterns you are able to observe.

4. Suggest and explain possible reasons why some groups of people appear to find it more difficult to find work than others.

5. Compare national unemployment characteristics with those of your local economy.

6. Investigate measures taken nationally and locally to reduce unemployment, both in general and for specific groups of people. For example, consider employment law relating to equal opportunities, training schemes, government regional and economic policy, etc.

   Useful data sources include newspapers, local borough councils, Training and Enterprise Councils, and Jobcentres.

What causes unemployment?

There are a number of reasons why unemployment can occur and may persist even when jobs are available:

- A fall in demand for a particular good or service may cause producers to reduce labour input to cut wage costs. This may be more general during an economic recession. As demand for goods and services falls, stocks will rise, and firms will cut back production.

- Technological advance has reduced the cost of capital equipment relative to labour.

- Workers may be occupationally and geographically immobile. This means they have the wrong skills to take up other occupations after being made unemployed, and may be unable to move to areas where jobs are available, due to family ties and the high cost of moving home.

What causes unemployment?...continued

- Workers may 'price themselves out of jobs' by seeking wages that are too high.
- Unemployment benefits may reduce the incentive to work.
- Employers' National Insurance Contributions (NICs) are an additional cost of employing labour and hence reduce the demand for labour by firms. Employers' NICs are related to the wages of an employee and ranged from 0% to 10.2% in 1994.
- Some employers may discriminate against people on grounds of sex, race, religion, and disability in filling job vacancies

Types of unemployment

- **Frictional unemployment** occurs as people move from one job to another and may be out of work for a short period of time. Rising frictional unemployment can be a sign of a booming economy when many attractive jobs are on offer.
- **Structural unemployment** arises from long-term changes in the structure of the economy, for example, the general decline of old 'heavy' manufacturing industries such as shipbuilding, coal mining, textiles, iron and steel. Workers made redundant from these industries have old unwanted skills and are occupationally immobile. Retraining may improve their mobility.
- Many of the old declining industries were located in specific regions of the UK, such as Northern Ireland, Scotland, South Wales, and the North East of England. This has given rise to **regional unemployment**. However, during the economic recession of the early 1990s, London and the South East suffered high regional unemployment as many service-sector organizations cut back their workforces (see Figure 16.2 on page 396).
- **Seasonal unemployment** can arise because the demand for labour by firms, especially those engaged in tourism, leisure, and construction, tends to vary with the weather. Workers on temporary contracts during the summer will boost the numbers unemployed during the winter months.
- **Cyclical or demand-deficient unemployment** occurs when there is a general fall in the demand for goods and services. Falling consumer, business, and/or government expenditure at home or from overseas can increase unemployment as firms experience falling sales. A country which is particularly hard-hit by cyclical unemployment is said to be suffering from a **slump** or **recession**.

Regional levels of employment

Levels of employment differ markedly between different regions of the UK. This will reflect differences in the location of different industries and regional variations in consumer demand. As such regional unemployment rates will also vary because the products of industries in some areas have suffered falling demand while the markets for others have been expanding.

Table 16.3 shows regional variations in employment in different industries. In general, it shows that employment in areas in the north of England, Scotland and Wales is concentrated more in manufacturing industries than in services. Conversely, services tend to employ a higher proportion of workers in the south of England than in most other areas, especially in banking and financial services and public administration. This reflects the concentration of government departments and international banking in London. The table also shows that female employment is concentrated in services.

Old heavy industrial areas in the north of England have suffered high and rising levels of unemployment due to falling demand for their products and overseas competition (see 16.2). However, the economic downturn in the early 1990s affected the south of England badly and many workers in finance, banking and other services lost their jobs. In the early 1990s Greater London had one of the highest unemployment rates in England (see figure 16.2)

Table 16.3: Employees (%) in employment; by industry and sex 1993

	Agriculture, forestry, fishing	Energy and water supply	Metals, minerals and chemicals	Metal goods, engineering and vehicles	Other manu-facturing	Construction	Distribution, hotels and catering, repairs	Transport and commun-ications	Banking, finance, insurance services	Public Administra-tion and other services	All industries and services (=100%) (thousands)
MALES											
United Kingdom	1.9	2.5	4.2	13.5	10.2	6.4	19.1	8.8	12.1	21.3	10,929
North	1.6	3.8	7.2	14.4	10.7	8.9	15.7	7.7	8.2	21.8	550
Yorkshire & Humberside	1.8	3.2	6.8	12.9	13.5	7.0	18.9	7.9	9.0	19.0	923
East Midlands	2.4	3.0	5.1	16.6	16.0	5.6	18.6	7.2	7.6	17.8	759
East Anglia	4.4	2.6	3.1	12.6	12.6	5.7	18.8	10.5	10.0	19.8	406
South East	0.9	1.9	2.3	10.2	7.4	5.3	20.7	10.6	18.0	22.7	3,525
South West	3.3	2.0	2.9	16.3	9.8	5.3	21.4	7.7	11.3	22.0	843
West Midlands	1.7	1.8	6.0	23.9	9.7	6.1	18.2	6.8	9.1	16.7	1,022
North West	1.0	2.1	5.4	15.0	12.1	6.4	18.7	8.4	10.4	20.5	1,153
England	1.6	2.3	4.2	13.9	10.2	6.0	19.5	8.9	12.7	20.7	9,181
Wales	3.1	3.2	7.2	12.9	9.6	7.0	16.9	7.4	8.8	23.0	481
Scotland	2.2	4.5	2.6	12.1	9.9	9.5	17.7	8.6	9.7	23.1	993
N Ireland	6.1	2.1	3.0	8.5	12.2	7.2	17.0	6.0	7.0	30.9	274
FEMALES											
United Kingdom	0.7	0.7	1.4	3.8	7.2	1.3	23.7	2.9	13.0	45.3	10,622
North	0.4	0.9	1.6	3.3	8.0	1.2	25.4	2.0	8.1	49.0	528
Yorkshire & Humberside	0.6	0.7	1.7	2.7	9.8	1.5	24.8	2.3	11.0	44.8	908
East Midlands	1.0	0.5	2.0	3.8	14.8	1.3	22.9	2.3	8.8	42.5	741
East Anglia	2.2	0.7	0.8	3.7	8.0	1.2	25.0	3.1	12.6	42.6	381
South East	0.5	0.7	1.3	3.4	4.7	1.4	22.1	3.8	17.9	44.2	3,375
South West	1.1	0.7	0.8	3.3	5.3	1.2	27.5	2.1	12.5	45.4	841
West Midlands	0.8	0.7	2.2	7.4	6.6	1.4	23.0	2.6	11.6	43.8	952
North West	0.4	0.8	1.8	3.6	7.9	1.1	25.1	2.8	11.2	45.4	1,159
England	0.7	0.7	1.5	3.8	7.1	1.3	24.6	3.0	13.6	44.5	8,885
Wales	0.7	0.8	1.3	4.5	7.4	1.1	24.0	1.9	8.7	49.1	476
Scotland	0.5	0.8	1.0	3.4	7.7	1.4	24.0	2.5	10.9	47.8	991
N Ireland	0.9	0.4	0.6	2.2	9.9	0.8	20.7	1.6	7.6	55.5	270

Regional trends 1994

The costs of unemployment

The cost to individuals

In many countries the unemployed receive benefits from their government. Benefits are financed primarily from tax revenues. However, as unemployment rises, fewer people pay income tax, and reduced spending means less is collected from taxes such as VAT. People in work may, therefore, have to pay higher taxes to pay for unemployment benefits.

In addition, those remaining in work may feel threatened by rising unemployment. People out of work may be willing to accept lower wages in order to get a job. To protect their jobs, those in work may have to accept lower pay rises, or even pay cuts. Because of the uncertainty created by rising unemployment, people in work may become demotivated, and productivity may suffer.

Having suffered a fall in their incomes and purchasing power, unemployed workers may also need to retrain before they have a chance of securing new employment, otherwise they may become **de-skilled** and unattractive to future employers. This is especially true in areas where old industrial factories have closed and the only new jobs on offer are in the service sector.

Advanced Business

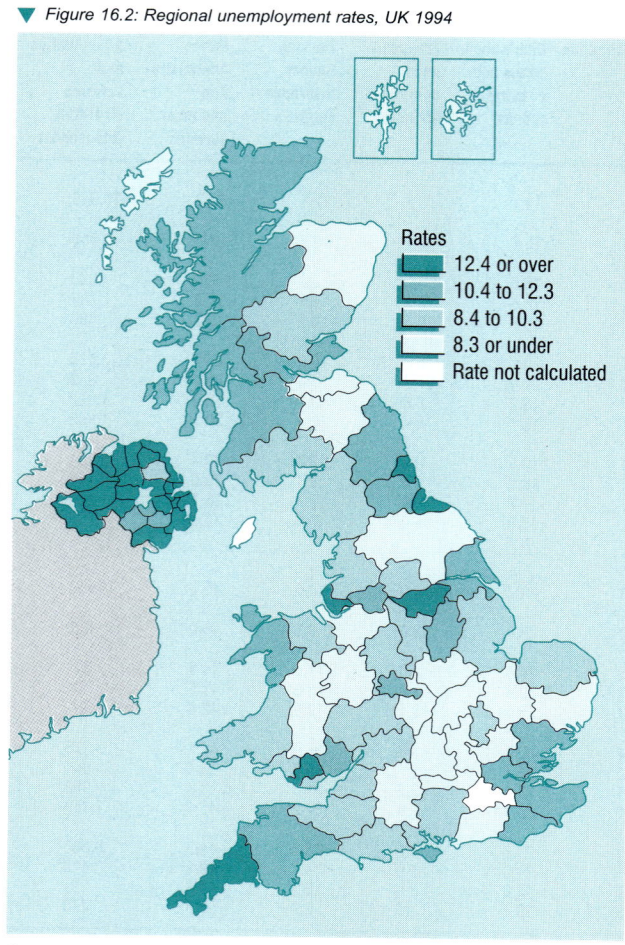

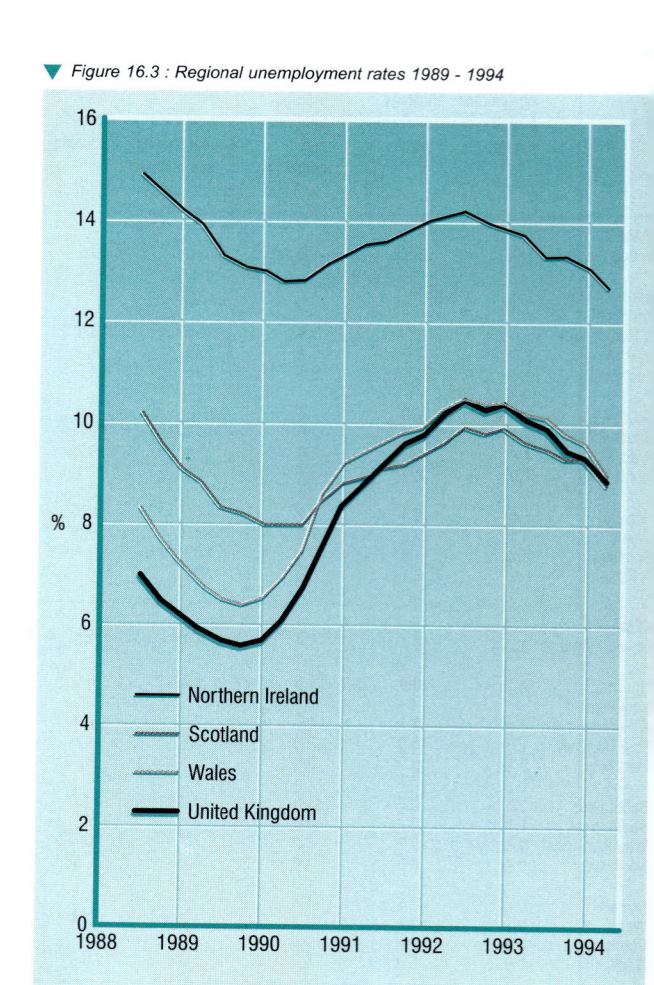

▼ Figure 16.2: Regional unemployment rates, UK 1994

Rates
- 12.4 or over
- 10.4 to 12.3
- 8.4 to 10.3
- 8.3 or under
- Rate not calculated

Regional Trends 1995

▼ Figure 16.3 : Regional unemployment rates 1989 - 1994

— Northern Ireland
— Scotland
— Wales
— United Kingdom

Economic Trends December 1994

The cost to the economy

As unemployment rises in an economy total output falls and people have fewer goods and services to share. That is, the *opportunity cost* of unemployment is the goods and services gone without (see 1.1). In addition, there is an opportunity cost to taxpayers. The tax revenue used to pay for benefits to those out of work could have been used by the government to fund other projects in the economy, for example, new roads, hospitals, or even tax cuts.

The government may also face increased demands to raise spending on their *regional policy* to assist industry in old declining areas of high unemployment and to promote export growth. The UK government offers a considerable amount of free advice and financial assistance in the form of grants, subsidies and training to new and existing firms, to promote employment and regeneration in the so called *Assisted Areas* (see 22.4).

> **Portfolio Activity 16.2**
>
> **Range:** Employment trends
> **Skills:** Collect and record data, Process information, Interpret and present data
>
> 1. Look at table 16.3 on page 395. Describe how the distribution of employees between different industries in your region compares to that of the UK as a whole. Plot this information for your region and the UK on two bar charts for ease of comparison.
>
> 2. Collect up to date information on changes in the level of employment and unemployement in your region and in the UK as a whole over the last five years. Useful sources of information will include the publications Regional Trends and the Employment Gazette.
>
> 3. Use a computer spreadsheet to produce two line graphs to show changes in the level of employment and unemployment in your region and the UK.
>
> 4. Write a commentary below your graphs to explain what has caused the changes they illustrate.

> **Key words**
>
> **Official unemployment** - the number of people out of work who are claiming unemployment benefits
>
> **Unemployment rate** - the number of claimant unemployed expressed as a percentage of the total working population
>
> **Working population** - The total number of people willing and able to work, namely, employees in employment, the self-employed, claimant unemployed, HM forces personnel, and those on work-related government training schemes.
>
> **De-skilling** - a loss of skills by workers due to replacement with new technology or long periods of unemployment.

Section 16.2 Deindustrialization

The three-sector economy

When considering trends in employment it is useful to distinguish between the three major industrial groupings. These are:

- **The primary sector** - normally defined to include agriculture and extractive industries, such as the mining of coal and oil. Primary industries are producers of natural resources.

- **The secondary sector** - in which raw materials are used to make other goods. **Finished** manufactured goods are ready for sale to the consumer, while **semi-manufactured** goods, for example, sheets of metal, or chemicals from crude oil, provide an input to the production of other goods. The secondary sector of the economy includes all manufacturing and construction industries.

- **The tertiary sector** - all those industries involved in the production of a service, including the retail outlets that sell finished goods.

The decline of manufacturing

Between 1973 and 1980, manufacturing output in the UK shrunk by 14%, and the output of the construction industry by 23%. In the decade 1971-1981, nearly 2 million full-time jobs were lost from manufacturing and

▼ Primary industry

construction industries. Over the same period, services such as banking and insurance added a total of 403,000 new jobs, with total employment in service industries rising by 1.8 million. By 1981, some 61% of the UK labour force was employed in the service sector.

▼ Secondary industry

▼ Tertiary industry

▼ Declining

This structural change in the UK economy continued throughout the 1980s and into the 1990s. Employment in manufacturing and construction shrunk by a further 1.8 million between 1981 and 1993, whilst the service sector created an additional 2.1 million jobs. Employment in service industries peaked in 1990 at 15.6 million, before losing around 500,000 jobs during the economic recession of the early 1990s.

Between 1981 and 1994, the working population in the UK expanded by around 1.2 million people (see 16.1). The rise in the number of jobs in the service sector was insufficient to absorb both the increased total supply of labour and displaced manufacturing workers. The net result was rising unemployment.

▼ Growing

▼ Table 16.4: Employees in employment; by sex and industry

Employees in employment: by sex and industry[1]
United Kingdom
Thousands

	1971	1979	1981	1983	1986	1990	1993
All industries	22,139	23,173	21,892	21,067	21,387	22,918	21,341
of which							
Males	13,726	13,487	12,562	11,940	11,7644	12,053	10,852
Females	8,413	9,686	9,331	9,127	9,644	10,865	10,475
Manufacturing	8,065	7,253	6,222	5,525	5,227	5,110	4,289
Services	11,627	13,580	13,468	13,501	14,297	15,986	15,596
Other	2,447	2,340	2,203	2,042	1,863	1,822	1,456
Employees in employment							
Agriculture, forestry and fishing	450	380	363	350	329	297	274
Energy and water supply	798	722	710	648	545	448	357
Other minerals and ore extraction etc	1,282	1147	939	817	729	721	598
Metal goods, engineering and vehicles	3,709	3,374	2,923	2,548	2,372	2,294	1,890
Other manufacturing industries	3,074	2,732	2,360	2,159	2,126	2,085	1,802
Construction	1,198	1,239	1,130	1,044	989	1,087	826
Distribution, catering, and repairs	3,686	4,257	4,172	4,118	4,298	4,853	4,562
Transport and communication	1,556	1,479	1,425	1,345	1,298	1,382	1,269
Banking, finance, insurance, etc	1,336	1,647	1,739	1,875	2,166	2,738	2,617
Other services	5,049	6,197	6,132	6,163	6,536	7,014	7,148

[1] As at June each year

Annual Abstract of Statistics 1994

Portfolio Activity 16.3

Range: Employment trends, Implications
Skills: Interpret and present data

Study the data on employees in employment in Table 16.4.

1. Describe the trends in (a) male and female employment, and (b) employment in the manufacturing and service sectors.

2. Draw line graphs, if possible using a computer spreadsheet, to illustrate the trends you have described in Question 1.

3. (a) Identify from the table an industry in each of the following industrial sectors:

- The primary sector
- The secondary sector
- The service sector

(b) Calculate the change in the numbers employed in each industry between 1971 and 1993.

(c) Investigate the reasons for the change in the numbers employed in each industry.

(d) How is the distribution of employment between the three main industrial sectors likely to change in the future? Give reasons to support your forecast.

4. Identify an industry that is a major employer in your area. What changes have taken place in the numbers employed locally in this industry? How does this change compare with patterns of employment in the industry nationally? (Consult *Regional Trends*, your local TEC and Jobcentres for information.)

▼ Figure 16.4: The growth of the service sector in Europe, USA, and Japan

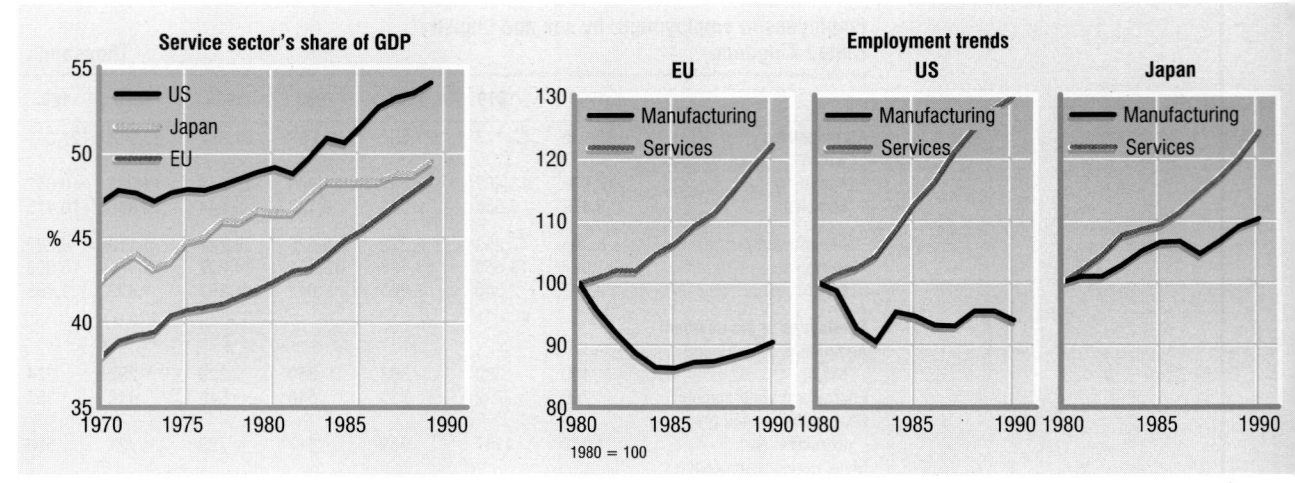

Financial Times 1.3.94

▼ Figure 16.5: Deindustrialization in the UK

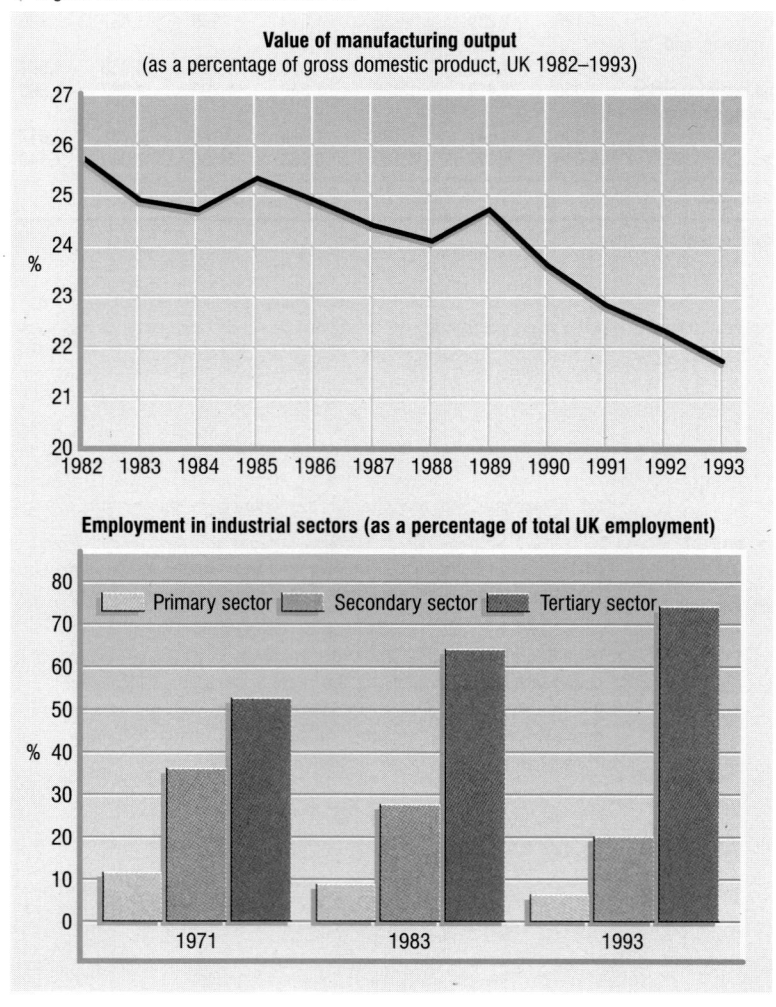

What is deindustrialization?

The structural shift experienced in many developed countries, away from manufacturing and towards the service sector for jobs and output, has been termed deindustrialization. This has been particularly significant in the UK, as Figure 16.5 illustrates.

Primary	Secondary	Tertiary
Declining:	Declining:	Growing:
Agriculture	Iron and steel	Financial and business services
Coal mining	Shipbuilding	Education
Fishing	Motor vehicles	Medical services
Water supply	Machine tools	Communications
	Textiles	Catering
	Construction	

Broadly defined, deindustrialization in the UK refers to:

- Falling employment in manufacturing industry
- Declining importance of manufacturing output in total UK output
- Falling share in the world output of manufactured goods
- Spending on imported manufactured goods exceeding revenues from the sale of UK-manufactured goods overseas

What has caused deindustrialization in the UK?

There is much disagreement among economists, business analysts, and politicians in the UK about the causes of manufacturing decline, but a number of number of factors are thought to be significant:

- The greatest decline in manufacturing has been in traditional industries such as textiles, shipbuilding, and motor vehicles. Rising national income has allowed consumers to devote an increasing proportion of their disposable incomes to leisure and other services. This has resulted in entrepreneurs moving resources away from secondary industries and into these growing markets.

- Traditional industries have suffered increased competition from newly industrialized countries overseas, such as Japan, and now China, Malaysia, and Taiwan.

- The main engines of growth in employment and output in the UK, and in many other developed countries, have been the financial and business services. As people have become wealthier, the demand for personal banking services, property and car insurance, investment services, legal advice, and improved communications has grown.

Portfolio Activity 16.4

Range: Employment trends, Implications, Evaluate in terms of effects on individuals and communities
Skills: Produce written material, Collect and record data

Produce a short report on deindustrialization, covering the following questions:

1. What is meant by 'deindustrialization'?
2. Why do you think deindustrialization gives cause for concern in countries like the UK?
3. What does deindustrialization imply about (a) the level of unemployment in the UK, and (b) the supply of labour with skills required by employers?
4. What evidence is there of deindustrialization in your local area? For example, how many manufacturing and service organizations are there now, compared to, say, 10 or 20+ years ago? Use archive material at your local library to help your investigation. Local Jobcentres may also be able to contribute evidence on the type of job vacancies that have been available over time. Your local Chamber of Commerce may be able to provide additional information.
5. Contrast the experience of your local economy with deindustrialization in the national economy.

Key words

Deindustrialization - a shift observed in many developed economies, away from manufacturing industries and towards the service sector

Primary sector - those activities within an economy that produce natural resources

Secondary sector - those activities within an economy that transform natural resources into goods

Manufacturing - the production of finished and semi-finished goods from natural resources

Tertiary sector - those activities within an economy that produce services

Section 16.3 Types of employment

Working solution to part-time future

If you are one of the lucky ones driving to a full-time job this morning with its promise of security, retirement and a pension, here's something that might make you a little less complacent.

Full-time employment is on the way out. Already employers, both private and Government, are contracting out the services they need to outside firms.

Permanent staff are being replaced by part-timers, by people on short term contracts which may or may not be renewed, or by calling workers in only when they are needed.

In ten years time far fewer of us will have actual jobs, according to US business consultant William Bridges in his book 'Jobshift'.

Instead you may find yourself with a patchwork of part-time jobs and selling your particular skill to several employers for so many days or weeks a month.

Daily Mirror 21.2.95

The nature of employment is changing. Full-time jobs are slowly disappearing and being replaced by part-time and temporary jobs. Increasing numbers of people unable to find work or fed up with working for somebody else are becoming self-employed. In this section we will examine these different types of employment.

Self-employment

People who start and run their own businesses are self employed. But many self employed people may still work for someone else. They will often be employed on short term contracts to complete special projects and can be either full-time or part-time.

The growth in self-employment was one of the most significant changes in the labour market in the UK during the 1980s. In 1994 almost 3.3 million people were self-employed - around 12% of the UK working population.

Self-employment is examined in detail in chapter 28.

Employees in Employment

Most people in work are not self employed. By far the largest group in the UK workforce remains those people who work for someone else. **Employees in employment** totalled 21.4 million in 1994, some 77% of the workforce. They include;

- full-time permanent workers
- part-time permanent workers
- full-time temporary workers
- part-time temporary workers

▼ Table 16.5: Distribution of UK employees (1993)

	Men (000s)	Per cent	Women (000s)	Per cent	All (000s)	Per cent
All in employment	13,934	100	11,446	100	25,381	100
Traditional workforce						
Full-time permanent employees	10,204	61.8	5,480	47.9	15,685	61.8
Flexible workforce						
Full-time temporary employees	393	2.8	266	2.3	659	2.6
Part-time permanent employees	513	3.7	4,204	36.7	4,718	18.6
Part-time temporary employees	174	1.2	451	3.9	624	2.5
Full-time self-employed	2,171	15.6	19	3.7	2,590	10.2
Part-time self-employed	199	1.4	390	3.4	589	2.3
Government training schemes	236	1.7	123	1.1	359	1.4
Unpaid family workers	43	0.3	111	1.0	154	0.6

Employment Gazette July 1994

The traditional workforce vs the flexible workforce

Table 16.5 shows that most full-time and part-time workers are employed on a permanent basis. **Permanent employment** means that employers can only end a contract of employment with an employee if the worker chooses to leave, or if s/he has to be fired for good reason, for example, for stealing, or if s/he has to be made redundant because their job is no longer needed.

People in full-time permanent jobs are often called the **traditional workforce**. It is these jobs which are slowly being replaced by part-time and temporary jobs. Part-timers and temporary workers are being called the **flexible workforce** because employers can hire and fire them more easily than their full-time workers. Many will have only short term contracts of employment which can be renewed if the employer still needs these workers.

Short-term contracts with employees give an employer more flexibility in managing their human resources, but offer their employees less job security and opportunities for career progression. Most short term contracts are for less than two years work. This is because workers who do not complete two years or more continuous service for the same employer are not entitled to employment rights such as appeal against unfair dismissal or redundancy payments (see 12.4).

Full-time employment

Most employees are employed on a **full-time** basis but an increasing number of jobs are either part-time or temporary. There has also been an increase in the numbers of workers employed on short-term contracts for short periods of time after which contracts may or may not be renewed.

Part-time employment

A **part-time employee** is officially defined as a person who normally works less than 30 hours a week excluding lunch breaks and overtime work. Some part-time employment may be the result of **job sharing** whereby two or more workers are employed to carry out one full-time job between them (see 13.4).

In 1971 around 3.4 million people were part-timers. By 1994 almost 6 million people worked part-time compared to around 19 million full-time jobs (see 16.4).

Temporary employment

Temporary workers are used by firms to provide extra help during busy times or to cover for absent employees. Unlike many other employees a temporary worker will not have a permanent contract of employment with his or her employer. They are usually only employed for short periods of time either on a full-time or part-time basis.

Opportunities for career progression and training tend to be limited for temporary workers compared to workers employed on a permanent basis. Their jobs are also less secure.

Examples of temporary workers include;

- many temporary workers are employed as **seasonal workers**. Many jobs in the tourist and construction industries are seasonal jobs involving work only during the summer.
- some temporary workers may be required to 'fill gaps' at short notice, for example, when a full-time employee has gone sick or is on leave. Temporary workers needed at short notice are often recruited from employment agencies and nicknamed **'Temps'**.
- some workers may be employed for one off projects on short term contracts because they have specialist skills required by a business (see below). Workers may also be hired on short-term contracts to provide support services to an organisation such as cleaning, equipment maintenance and catering.
- **causal workers** may be employed on a day to day basis, usually with no formal contract of employment. They may be required to help out in a shop, office or on a building site for example, and will usually receive 'cash in hand' for their efforts. Because casual workers are paid in cash only when they are needed this type of work is often called 'unofficial employment'. As such, casual workers do not qualify for any of benefits that officially employed people do, such as holidays, sick pay, pensions or redundancy payments.

In the summer of 1994 1.45 million employees worked in temporary jobs: 676,000 men and 776,000 women - around 7% of the total UK workforce (see 16.4).

- **Non-contract employment:** this is *unofficial* employment. An employer is required by law to provide a contract of employment to any employee within two weeks of their appointment (see 12.3). However, in doing so, they are also legally obliged to give a worker certain rights, such as sick pay, holidays, etc. The employer may also be liable for additional National Insurance contributions. Because of these additional costs of employment, some employers may employ workers on a casual basis without an employment contract and pay them 'cash in hand'. The employee also benefits by not having to declare this income for income tax purposes. 'Unofficial' employment and cash-in-hand payments are part of the so-called **black economy**.
- **Manual occupations** are those generally thought to require a significant amount of physical effort, usually aided by machinery - for example, jobs such as construction worker, bus driver, or shop assistant. **Non-manual** employees are employed for their mental skills of analysis and thought, usually in office-based work (see 16.4). The growth in the number of non-manual employees reflects the growing importance of the service sector as the major employer.

- **Skilled, semi-skilled and unskilled employment**. We can further distinguish between workers by the level of skills they have. Workers are commonly categorized as either skilled, semi-skilled, or unskilled (see 16.4). The demand for skilled labour by business has increased.

Wage differentials

Just because some people may work more hours than others does not explain why there are large differences in the earnings of people in different jobs (see figure 16.6). **Wage differentials**, differences in the earnings of different people, can be explained by differences in the demand for and supply of labour. For example;

- Workers with skills which are in high demand by firms will tend to receive higher wages than those with old redundant skills, especially if the skilled workers are in short supply.

- Some jobs are dangerous or involve working unsociable hours. If individuals were not compensated, in the form of higher wages, for factors such as risk of injury or unsociable hours then the supply of labour to those occupations will be deficient and firms will find it difficult to recruit workers. For example, miners wages have often been much higher than workers in other manual occupations.

- Some jobs require long periods of education and training. This might discourage people from studying to become doctors, lawyers or other professionals. Wages in these jobs therefore tend to be high because the supply of labour to these occupations is relatively low.

- If consumer demand for a particular good or service is high, firms making those products are likely to have a high demand for labour. This will tend to push up the wages of those workers in demand.

- In some areas of the UK an abundant supply of unemployed labour has tended to depress wage levels. This has resulted in **regional wage differentials** (see table 16.6).

- Wage rates can also reflect regional differences in the cost of living. For example, many firms offer 'London Weighting Allowances' to attract workers to jobs in London and the South East where the prices of goods and services tend to be higher than elsewhere in the country.

▼ Table 16.6 : Average gross weekly earnings for full-time employees, October 1994

Region	Manual (£)	Non-manual (£)
South East	284.0	412.1
East Anglia	259.7	335.4
South West	256.5	339.8
West Midlands	257.7	336.3
East Midlands	254.3	328.0
Yorkshire & Humberside	262.4	327.9
North West	263.4	337.8
North	264.6	325.3
England	267.0	367.8
Scotland	252.7	336.0
Wales	255.8	321.8
Great Britain	264.9	363.2

Employment Gazette 2.95

Portfolio Activity 16.5

Range : Employment trends
Skills : Collect and record data

Choose at least five different job adverts with different levels of pay from your local papers.

1. Using the information presented in each advertisement write down the reasons why you think the wage rates may differ between each job.

2. What methods of payment and any other benefits are being offered in each case?

3. If employers are faced with a shortage or surplus of workers to fill the posts they advertise how might the payments advertised in each case change.

▼ *Figure 16.6 : Average gross weekly earnings by main occupational group, April 1993*

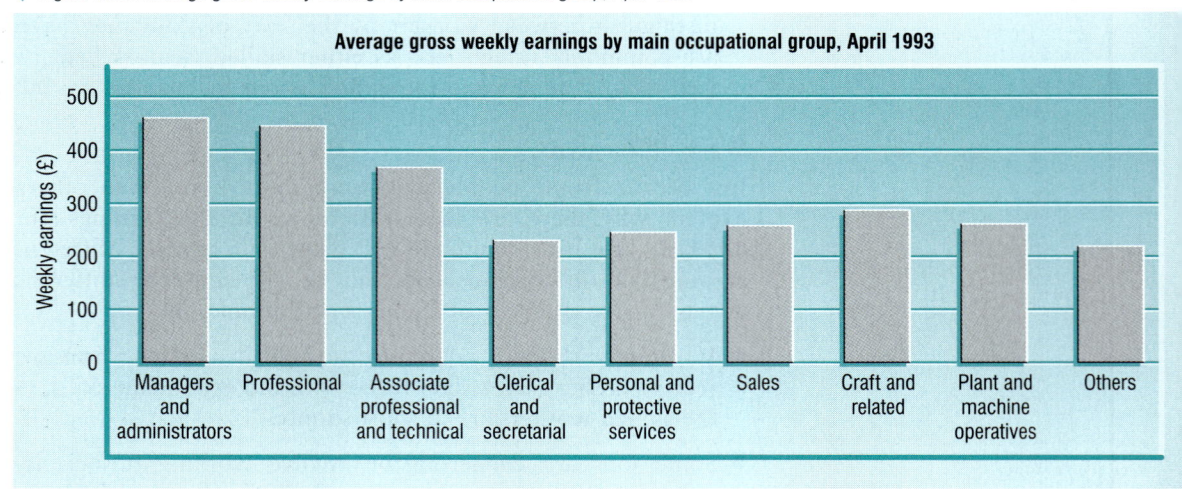

Average gross weekly earnings by main occupational group, April 1993

[Bar chart showing weekly earnings (£) from 0 to 500 for the following occupational groups:
- Managers and administrators: ~460
- Professional: ~450
- Associate professional and technical: ~370
- Clerical and secretarial: ~230
- Personal and protective services: ~245
- Sales: ~260
- Craft and related: ~285
- Plant and machine operatives: ~260
- Others: ~220]

▼ *Average gross weekly earnings, April 1994*

Non-manual workers £360

Manual workers £263

▲ *Male workers £362*

▲ *Female workers £262*

However, some wage differentials can arise for reasons other than those connected with demand and supply conditions in labour markets. This is because;

- workers often lack information about the availability of jobs and the wage rate they attract, and how these compare to other occupations. Finding out this information can be costly. Job search involves much time and effort. As a result some workers work for less pay than they could simply because they are unaware of better paid vacancies elsewhere.

- some employers may discriminate against groups of people. The most common forms of discrimination are refusing to employ women or ethnic minorities in jobs for which they are qualified, employing them only at lower wages, or insisting on higher qualifications than necessary where they are employed at the same wage rate as others.

- some groups of workers may be powerful enough to force their employers to pay them high wages. Some employers also have immense power and may be able to force their workers to accept low wages. The government, for example, is the main employer in the UK of teachers, civil servants and nurses and is therefore virtually the only source of demand for these type of workers.

Average earnings and hours of work

Table 16.7 shows that average gross weekly earnings (including overtime and any performance related pay – see 15.3) of all full-time employees on adult rates working a full week in April 1994 were £326. The gap between earnings in non-manual and manual occupations has widened over time, so that average manual earnings at £263 per week were around 75% of non-manual earnings of £360 per week.

The average working week of full-time employees was 40.1 hours, of which 2.4 hours were for paid overtime. The average working week for manual workers stretched to 43.9 hours, while non-manual employees worked less than 38 hours. Because of these differences in hours worked each week, the gap between average manual and non-manual weekly earnings does not appear as wide as the divergence between their average hourly earnings. Non-manual employees averaged £9.31 per hour in April 1994, manual workers £5.85.

Male and female wage differentials have been closing over time in part due to legislation concerning equal pay opportunities (see 12.3).

▼ Table 16.7: Levels of average pay and hours in April 1994

	Men			Women			Men and Women		
	Manual	Non-Manual	All	Manual	Non-Manual	All	Manual	Non-Manual	All
Average gross weekly earnings (£)	281	428	362	182	278	262	263	360	326
Average gross hourly earnings including overtime (£)	6.31	10.90	8.61	4.53	7.44	6.89	6.02	9.32	8.03
Average total weekly hours	44.7	38.9	41.6	40.1	37.0	37.6	43.9	38.0	40.1
Average weekly overtime hours	5.6	1.4	3.3	2.1	0.6	0.9	4.9	1.0	2.4

Employment Gazette December 1994

Portfolio Activity 16.6

Range: Types of employment, Evaluate in terms of employee needs
Skills: Produce written material, Collect and record data

The following features vary between different types of employment:

- Pay and other benefits
- Hours of work
- Holiday entitlement
- Pension arrangements
- Redundancy entitlements
- Career progression opportunities
- Job security

Produce a short report to discuss how, and why these features differ between the different types of employment.

Included in this chapter to help you compile your report are other tables, charts, and sections of text on employment features by type. You will also find it useful to look at Chapters 13 and 28. However, you should also undertake research and supplement these with data from other sources, including *Social Trends* and the *Employment Gazette*, and from interviews with employees in different types of employment.

Include in your report any relevant tables and charts you have produced yourself from data included in this book and from other sources.

Advanced Business

The average gross weekly earnings of women in April 1994 were £262, representing 72% of average male earnings of £362 per week. This difference in pay is often used as an indication of sex discrimination in the UK labour market. However, the average earnings of women will be lower than those of men for many reasons not necessarily related to discrimination: women tend to work in traditionally lower-paid occupations and industries, and many work part-time. Women employees also worked on average 3 hours less than men per week in April 1994.

Section 16.4 Part-time and temporary employment

Since the early 1980s, the composition of the UK labour force has changed significantly, with a rise in demand for **non-standard labour** - that is, workers who are either self-employed, or willing to work part-time, or in temporary jobs.

Trends in part-time employment

Between 1984 and 1994, the number of women in part-time employment increased by 27% and the number of men working part-time increased by 75%. However, despite this increase, males made up only 16% of part-time employees in 1994. This meant that roughly 1 in every 10 male employees worked part-time. This compared to around 1 in every 2 females in part-time employment. Because part-time jobs tend to be filled by married women and students, the increase in the number of part-time jobs available has had little or no impact on the level of unemployment in the UK.

▼ Table 16.8: Distribution of hours worked by part-time employees

Hours per week	(000's)	Per cent
1 – 5	377	7.0
6 – 10	923	17.2
11 – 15	926	17.3
16 – 20	1,303	24.3
21 – 25	906	16.9
26 – 30	613	11.4
31 – 35	226	4.2
>35	85	1.6

Employment Gazette 12.94

▼ Table 16.9: Full and part-time employment: by sex

United Kingdom **Thousands**

| | Males | | Females | |
	Full-time	Part-time	Full-time	Part-time
1984	13,240	570	5,422	4,343
1985	13,336	575	5,503	4,457
1986	13,430	647	5,662	4,566
1987	13,472	750	5,795	4,696
1988	13,881	801	6,069	4,808
1989	14,071	734	6,336	4,907
1990	14,109	789	6,479	4,928
1991	13,686	799	6,350	4,933
1992	13,141	885	6,244	5,081
1993	12,769	886	6,165	5,045
1994	12,875	998	6,131	5,257

1 Full/part-time is based on respondents self-assessment. Excludes those who did not state whether they were full or part-time.
2 At Spring each year. Includes employees, self-employed, those on government training schemes and unpaid family workers.

Social Trends 1995

UNIT FIVE

CHAPTER 16

Portfolio Activity 16.7

Range: Employment trends, Evaluate in terms of employees' needs
Skills: Read and respond to written material

Read the article below.

1. What motives did Sock Shop have for making its staff change from full-time to part-time contracts of employment?
2. How might their decision affect worker morale and motivation? Why should this be important?
3. Why do you think growth in the employment of part-time workers rather than full-time workers is especially significant in the retail sector?

Sock Shop curbs staff hours

By David Goodhart and Lisa Wood

Sock Shop, the sock and fashion retailer, is to move its 400 staff from full-time to part-time contracts, adopting a growing trend in the retail sector.

Managers of Sock Shop's outlets, of which there are nearly 100, were banned yesterday from giving details of the change, but it is understood that most full-time staff will be switched to 20 hours a week over three days.

One manager, who contacted the Financial Times by telephone, said the company had made quite clear that the switch was mainly to save on employment costs.

Ms Jenny Trotter, personnel manager, would not elaborate on a prepared statement that read: "Sock Shop Holdings Ltd is introducing a number of changes to retail staff contracts. The main modification is in the area of hours worked, so that we have a greater percentage of part-time workers in the company. The changes are being introduced to secure a more flexible and cost-effective workforce."

The changes at Sock Shop are expected to affect about 400 people in nearly 100 shops. The company, built up by Ms Sophie Mirman in the 1980s, was sold for £3.25m after it collapsed in 1990. It was bought by former jeweller Mr Juan Olaso and venture capitalist Mr Barclay Douglas.

Staff at Sock Shop outlets in the City were yesterday unwilling to discuss their employment prospects.

Financial Times 26.1.94

▼ Table 16.10: Reported reasons for employing part-time employees

Reported reason for employment	Per cent of employers citing as reason	Per cent of employers citing as main reason
Tasks requiring a limited time	76	59
To match staffing levels to demand patterns	30	17
To extend opening/production hours	10	3
To reduce wage costs	9	2
Part-timers are less likely to be in unions	1	0
To reduce non-wage costs	4	1
Part-timers have fewer rights under employment protection legislation	1	0
Part-timers are more productive than full-time staff	3	0
Part-timers are easier to recruit	9	1
Applicants want part-time work	33	7
The higher turnover of part-timers gives greater flexibility in staffing levels	4	1
To retain valued staff who can no longer work full-time	21	7
Other reasons	3	2
Number of establishments	**578**	**576**

Employment Gazette May 1992

Why has part-time employment risen?

In 1987, the Department of Employment conducted the Employers' Labour Use Survey (ELUS) to determine the reasons for their employment of non-standard labour. The main reasons given by employers in the ELUS for recruiting part-time workers are set out in Table 16.10.

- **More jobs require only a limited labour input.** Over 75% of employers reported that they employed part-timers to undertake tasks which required only a limited number of hours to complete. Classic examples are cleaners, typically employed for a few hours before or after normal working hours, and catering employees, who commonly work mid-morning to mid-afternoon.

- **More people want to work part-time.** Employment on a part-time basis allows a worker increased flexibility. This might be especially important to women with dependent children.

- **To retain valuable staff who can no longer work full-time.** Employing workers on a part-time basis means firms can still make use of their skills and use them to train possible future replacements.

- **To match employment levels to fluctuations in consumer demand.** Most part-time work is concentrated in the distribution sector. This is partly a reflection of the increased flexibility in trading hours as a result of late-night opening and Sunday trading. Supermarkets and department stores tend to employ part-timers to work lunchtimes and late nights, especially at weekends, to match predictable variations in customer demand. Part-timers are particularly attractive to employers in these situations, because they rarely qualify for overtime rates of pay beyond the standard working day. For example, the Burton retailing group now employs only part-time staff.

- **Staffing levels can be adjusted easily.** One advantage claimed for part-time employment is that higher levels of turnover among staff allow firms to cut their workforces on a voluntary basis when the need arises, without the need for redundancies.

- **To reduce labour costs.** In Table 16.10, the desire to reduce overall labour costs was not given as a particularly important reason by organizations for the replacement of full-time employees with part-time workers. However, there is undoubtedly a financial incentive for firms to offer part-time jobs instead of full-time ones.

In 1993/94 an employer only paid National Insurance contributions (NICs) for an employee if he or she earned over £56 per week. This provided an incentive to employers to keep total earnings below the NIC limit by restructuring hours worked and/or hourly wage rates.

Until 1994, part-time workers were also relatively cheaper to employ because they did not qualify for the same terms and conditions as full-time staff, namely sick pay, holidays, periods of notice, and redundancy payments. Only those employees who worked 16 hours a week or more held the same legal rights as full-time workers (see **Portfolio Activity 16.4**).

Portfolio Activity 16.8

Range: Types of employment, Evaluate in terms of business needs
Skills: Collect and record data, Interpret and present data

1. How many part-time staff are employed in your school/college (a) in total, and (b) as a proportion of all employees? Interview the head of the school/college and ask him/her why part-time workers are employed, their occupations, and how levels of part-time employment have changed over the last 2- 5 years.

2. Repeat Question 1 for another business organization - for example, a large retail outlet - and compare your findings with those from your school/college.

3. Look at Table 16.9 on p.408. Plot the figures for part-time employees as a line graph and update it as necessary. Make a statistical forecast of part-time employment in the UK over the next 3-5 years.

4. Read the article on page 411. What are the possible implications of the government's decision to accept the European directive on business costs and their demand for labour?

5. In the light of the article, would you alter the forecast you developed in Question 3? Explain your decision, and any revised forecasts of future growth in part-time employment you might make.

UNIT FIVE

CHAPTER 16

Sting in tail of work 'win for women'

THE Government bowed to pressure to accept a European directive on part-time workers yesterday.

Hundreds of thousands, most of them women, will now be given the same rights on redundancy payments and unfair dismissal as full-time staff. It was hailed as a victory by women's groups and trade unions.

But there were immediate fears that celebrations could be short-lived.

Employment Secretary Michael Portillo, clearly angry at having to cave in to Europe, predicted that thousands of part-timers could be sacked because the cost of employing them would be too high.

Mr Portillo was backed by employers' groups and small business bosses. They said firms would have to adjust their prices and charges to reflect the increased liability for redundancy and dismissal payouts.

Adapted from the Daily Mail 21.12.94

▶ *The employment of temporary staff is popular in the tourist industry.*

Temporary workers

Why do firms employ temporary labour? The main reasons given by business organizations for employing temporary workers and agency 'temps' are given in Tables 16.11 and 16.12 below. In each case, the majority of employers cited the need for short-term cover to match staffing levels with peaks in demand.

▼ *Table 16.11: Reported reasons for employing temporary employees*

Reported reason for employment	Per cent of employers citing as reason	Per cent of employers citing as main reason
To give short-time cover for absent staff	55	40
To match staffing levels to peaks in demand	35	19
To deal with one-off tasks	29	7
To provide specialist skills	22	11
To screen for permanent jobs	4	0
Temps are not in a union	0	0
To reduce wage costs	1	0
To reduce non-wage costs	1	0
Temps have fewer rights under employment protection legislation	0	0
Temps make it easier to adjust staffing levels	26	12
To provide cover while staffing levels are changed	19	7
Temps are easier to recruit than permanent workers	4	1
Applicants want temporary work	8	0
Other reasons	6	3
Number of establishments	**305**	**283**

▼ *Table 16.12: Reported reasons for employing agency temporaries*

Reported reason for employment	Per cent of employers citing as reason	Per cent of employers citing as main reason
To provide short-term cover	71	62
To match staffing levels to peaks in demand	35	16
To deal with one-off tasks	35	5
To provide specialist skills	16	6
To screen for permanent jobs	11	0
Agency temps are not in unions	0	0
To reduce wage costs	1	0
To reduce non-wage costs	1	0
Agency temps have fewer rights under employment protection legislation	0	0
Agency temps are easier to recruit than permanent workers	15	6
Agency temps make it easier to adjust staffing levels	18	2
Agency temps are cheaper to use than temporary employees	0	0
Other reasons	3	3
Number of establishments	**141**	**138**

Employment Gazette May 1992

Advanced Business

Industries which experience seasonal fluctuations in the demand for their products or services will often employ workers on a temporary basis when demand is high. This is especially the case in tourism and construction. Figure 16.8 shows the seasonal variation in the employment of temporary labour for different industries.

▼ Figure 16.8: Percentage of men and women employees working in temporary jobs; by industry, UK Spring and Summer 1993

Percentage of employees who are in a temporary job

Men (summer 1993): Extraction of minerals, metal manufacturing (14); Other manufacturing (41); Metal goods, engineering and vehicles (67); Transport and communication (44); Banking finance and insurance (61); Distribution, hotels and catering (117); Energy and water supply (25); Construction (66); Other services (217); Agriculture, forestry and fishing (20)

Men (spring 1993): Extraction of minerals, metal manufacturing (12); Other manufacturing (29); Metal goods, engineering and vehicles (56); Transport and communication (36); Banking finance and insurance (53); Distribution, hotels and catering (84); Energy and water supply (23); Construction (51); Other services (190); Agriculture, forestry and fishing (10)

Women (summer 1993): Extraction of minerals, metal manufacturing (*); Construction (*); Energy and water supply (*); Other manufacturing (39); Banking, finance and insurance (74); Metal goods, engineering and vehicles (28); Distribution, hotels and catering (162); Transport and communications (25); Other services (406); Agriculture, forestry and fishing (11)

Women (spring 1993): Extraction of minerals, metal manufacturing (*); Construction (*); Energy and water supply (*); Other manufacturing (20); Banking, finance and insurance (71); Metal goods, engineering and vehicles (29); Distribution, hotels and catering (126); Transport and communications (20); Other services (396); Agriculture, forestry and fishing (*)

( ) Figures in brackets are the numbers (in thousands) of employees in temporary jobs
*Estimate less than 10 000

Employment Gazette March 1994

Temporary workers will often be employed by firms as full-time workers on fixed-term contracts to provide cover for permanent staff on extended leave due to illness or pregnancy, or for those on study leave or secondment to another organization. When the permanent member of staff returns from leave, the contract of employment for the temporary worker will usually be terminated. A temporary worker might also be employed to fill a job vacancy until the person selected for the job is able to take up the post.

Key words

Non-standard labour - workers who do not work full-time on long-term employment contracts, namely self-employed, part-time, temporary, and fixed-contract labour

Wage differentials - differences in earnings between different people in different occupations, industries, and regions

Part-time employee - a person who normally works less than 30 hours a week excluding lunch breaks and overtime work

Short term contract - an employment contract that is time limited normally between 6 month and 2 years

Section 16.5

The economic activity rate

The **economic activity rate**, also known as the **participation rate**, expresses the working population as a percentage of the total resident population. In 1993, the participation rate in the UK was 48%. That is, 48 out of every 100 people could be considered to be participating in the total labour supply.

Activity rates among UK male and females over 16 years of age are among the highest in Europe. In 1992, they were second only to the Danish population, which displayed an economic activity rate of 68.5%.

There has been a tendency for the participation rate of males to fall over the last 3 to 4 decades. Between 1950 and 1993, the activity rate among males fell from 61% of the total male population in the UK, to 56%. In contrast, the participation rate of females has risen substantially. For example, between 1950 and 1992, the participation rate for married women more than trebled, from 22% of the married female population to around 70%.

▼ Table 16.13: Economic activity rates; by sex, EC comparison, 1992

	Percentages		
	Males	Females	All persons
Denmark	74.5	62.7	68.5
United Kingdom	74.0	52.8	63.0
Portugal	71.9	50.2	60.3
Germany[2]	71.5	48.4	59.4
Netherlands	71.1	46.5	58.6
France	65.7	48.0	56.4
Irish Republic	70.6	37.7	53.9
Luxembourg	69.7	39.5	54.2
Italy	65.4	34.9	49.5
Belgium	62.1	39.5	50.4
Spain	65.6	34.1	49.2
Greece	65.5	34.8	49.4
EC average	68.9	44.6	56.2

1 The civilian labour force aged 16 years and over as a percentage of the population aged 16 and over.

2 As constituted since 3 October 1990.

Social Trends 1995

▼ Figure 16.9: Economic activity by sex in the UK, 1981-1992

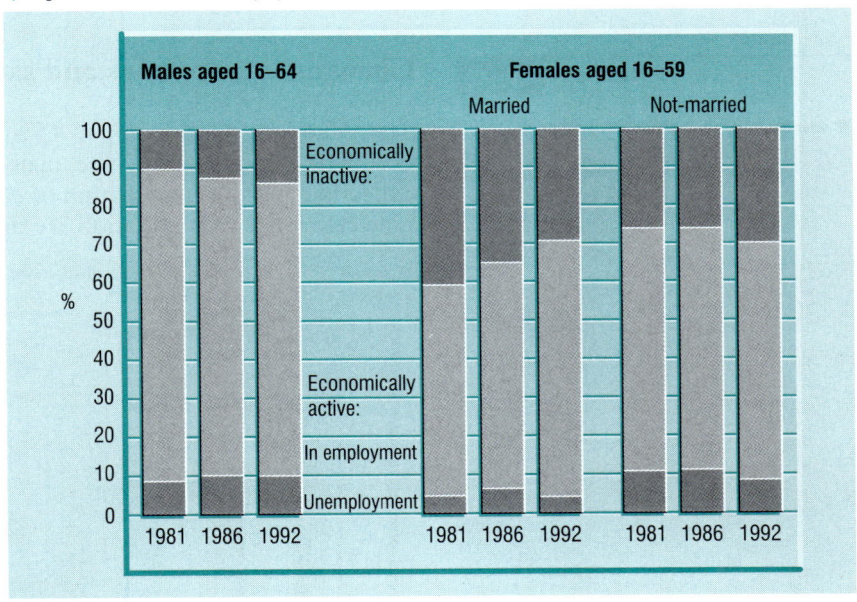

Social Trends 1993

▼ Attitudes towards women going to work have changed significantly.

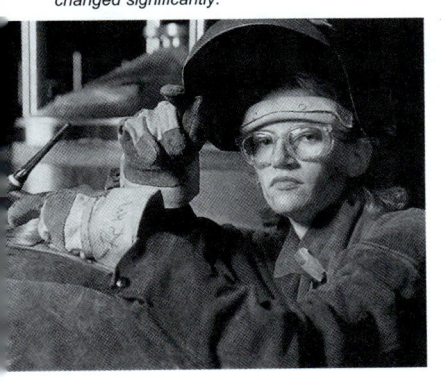

Why have female participation rates increased?

The reasons for the dramatic rise in participation rates among females are complex, but a number of key factors can be identified:

- **Changes in social attitudes** - for example, the trend towards later marriage, falling birth rates, and the increasing emancipation of women from a traditional domestic role. The aspirations of many households to increase their income and wealth have also, in part, been realized by wives going out to work.

Advanced Business

> **Key words**
>
> **Participation rate** - a measure of economic activity, based on the working population in a country as a percentage of the total population

- **Changes in the availability of jobs.** The increase in female activity rates between 1986 and 1993 appears partly due to an increase in the availability of part-time jobs, which has encouraged more women to join the labour force.
- **Legislation concerning equal opportunities** has helped to improve the pay and conditions of women at work (see 12.3).

The overall impact of rising female participation in the UK labour force and falling male participation rates on the sex distribution of the working population has been significant. In 1950, women made up less than a third of the working population. In 1993, they accounted for over 43% of the total labour supply.

According to official figures, occupations in which most women work are also those containing the most part-time workers: clerical and secretarial, childcare and catering, personal services, and sales. This would appear to support the view that women are attracted to occupations which can offer them flexibility to meet domestic commitments. There are also occupations in which more women work than men. These include health associate professionals (nurses, midwives, etc), and teachers.

Section 16.6

▼ *Manual and non-manual occupations*

Changing occupations and skills

The Standard Occupational Classification (SOC) classifies some 374 occupation groups into nine major categories for the purpose of data collection and the examination of employment trends by government. The nine categories of occupation are displayed in Figure 16.10 below.

▼ *Figure 16.10: UK employment by occupation and sex, Summer 1994*

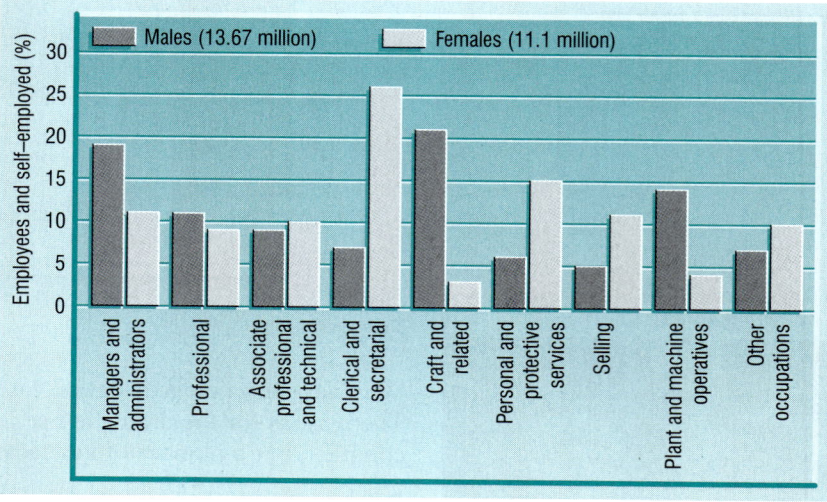

Employment Gazette January 1995

Manual and non-manual labour

Within the SOC we can distinguish between manual and non-manual labour. We normally think of manual labour as undertaking physical work 'by hand', or with the aid of machinery, rather than work 'with the mind', but in fact this distinction is an imperfect one. A more appropriate division

Skilled, semi-skilled, or unskilled labour?

is between 'white-collar workers' who are largely office-based, and manual workers on the shop or factory floor, or out in the open on a building site or farm. However, most manual jobs will require the fulfilment of some administrative or 'white-collar' functions, for example, filling out delivery sheets, invoices, etc.

In the SOC, manual jobs are found in the following groups:

- Craft and related occupations
- Plant and machine operatives
- Other occupations, eg. construction workers

Since the mid-1980s, there has been a marked increase in the number of non-manual employees in the UK. This is a reflection of the growth of the services, particularly in the financial and business services sector of the economy (see 16.2).

Skilled and unskilled labour

Manual work can require either **skilled**, **semi-skilled**, or **unskilled** labour, depending on the precise nature of the work. For example, we might consider an electronic engineer to be skilled, a bricklayer to be semi-skilled, and an agricultural labourer who undertakes a variety of tasks on a farm to be unskilled.

Similarly, non-manual work can be either skilled - for example, a computer programmer - or unskilled - for example, an office messenger. However, in many cases the distinction between what is skilled and unskilled is hard to draw. For example, a photocopy machine operative might be regarded as largely unskilled, but s/he will require some skills in order to respond to peoples' requests, operate the machine effectively, and if necessary undertake some routine maintenance. Similarly, the agricultural labourer referred to above might need skills necessary to operate farm machinery and drive tractors.

Portfolio Activity 16.10

Range: Types of employment
Skills: Collect and record data

Consider the following occupations:

HGV driver	Doctor	Book editor
Computer programmer	Hotel porter	Film cameraman
	Office cleaner	Interior designer
Window cleaner	Secretary	Bricklayer
Marine biologist	Filing clerk	Economist
Army cadet	Holiday rep	Immigration officer
Road sweeper	Science teacher	Hairdresser
Stand-up comedian	Shop assistant	

Make a brief investigation of each occupation and try to decide:

- To which group in the Standard Occupational Classification each occupation belongs
- Whether the occupation is manual or non-manual
- Whether the occupation can be considered skilled, semi-skilled, or unskilled

Using the information above, draw and complete a table like the one started below.

Occupation	SOC	Manual/Non-manual	Skilled/Un-skilled
Bus driver		manual	semi-skilled
Accountant			

▼ Table 16.14: Current hard-to-fill vacancies

Industry sector	Per cent Employers
Mining and quarrying	15
Manufacturing	22
Electricity, gas and water supply	1
Construction	13
Wholesale and retail	18
Hotels and restaurants	41
Transport storage and communication	13
Finance	21
Real estate and business services	18
Public administration, and social security	12
Education	18
Health and social work	29
Other community, social, and personal services	13

Employment Gazette December 1994

In general, workers are considered skilled if they need to undergo intensive education and/or training in order to carry out their job.

Skill shortages

Skill shortages exist when there are not enough workers with the right skills to do the jobs that need doing. A shortage of appropriate skills can be a constraint on the growth of UK industry and its ability to compete with foreign rivals.

Employers' indications of recent or expected recruitment difficulties or hard-to-fill job vacancies are commonly used to measure skill shortages.

Recent trends in skill shortages

Skill Needs in Britain is an annual report by the Employment Department based on a survey of organizations employing 25 or more employees. The 1994 report suggested that recruitment problems among employers had increased, with 21% of employers surveyed experiencing recruitment problems, compared to 16% in 1992 and 1993. More detailed findings of the report were as follows:

- **Skill shortages in industries:** an analysis of hard-to-fill vacancies by industrial sector revealed the highest incidence in the hotels and restaurants health and social work sectors, with 41% of employers in hotels and restaurants experiencing recruitment problems.

- **Skill shortages in occupations:** hard-to-fill vacancies were most often reported for personal and protective services, craft and related occupations, plant and machine operatives, and associate professional and technical occupations.

- **Rising skill needs:** over 60% of employers in the survey reported rising skill needs in each year since 1990. Skill needs have risen due to the introduction of new technology, a shift towards highly-skilled occupations, and new workplace practices. As production processes have become more automated and computerized, the role and skills required of workers have changed. Fewer workers are being asked to specialize in one task among many on mass assembly lines. Instead, more workers are now needed to undertake a number of separate tasks within a firm. This is known as **multi-skilling**.

Job-related training can help to meet skills needed by teaching workers new skills or improving ones they already have.

Key words

Standard Occupational Classification (SOC) - a government classification of occupations into nine major categories for the purpose of data collection and the examination of employment trends

Manual labour - workers in occupations which involve a significant amount of physical effort

Non-manual labour - workers in occupations, often desk-based, which require more written skills and much less physical effort

Skilled labour - workers who have a trained ability and are considered expert in their particular occupation

Skill shortage - when the demand for labour with particular skills outstrips the supply of labour with those skills

Multi-skilling - training workers to carry out several tasks

Skills gap - the difference between the skills possessed by existing employees and the skills their employers would like them to have

Portfolio Activity 16.11

Range: Employment trends, Implications, Evaluate in terms of effects on individuals
Skills: Read and respond to written material

1 Read the article and discuss it in your group. Do you agree with the predictions made about the types of jobs that will be available, say, 20 years from now? What do the predictions suggest about the skills people will need to undertake these jobs? What are the implications for the type of training workers should be receiving and the types of courses and skills you should be taught in school or college?

2 Try to obtain information on skill shortages in your local area from your nearest TEC. How do they compare to the core skills you need to demonstrate in your GNVQ Advanced Business course?

Trading places: is your job safe?

CHANGES in the way we work will make some trades more valuable – and others redundant. The following trades were prominent among those listed in the London Post Office directory of 1900: ash collectors, starchers, blood driers, mourning hatband makers, lamp black makers, lamplighters, ice merchants, soot merchants, spermaceti (whale oil) refiners, saddlers and harness makers, livery stable keepers, soap makers.

None survives in today's (telephone) equivalent, the *London Yellow Pages*. Instead there are computer dealers, advertising agencies, audio-visual services, aircraft component makers ...

But what about a future (electronic) *Yellow Pages* in, say, 20 years' time? What trades will grow, shrink, change – or even be created? Here, *New Scientist* makes its predictions – with a brief explanation.

Shrinking or disappearing trades:

Air couriers (replaced by high-speed data networks); **Answering machines** (computers); **Insurance claims assessors** (neural networks); **Bailiffs** (electronic credit freezes); **Checkout staff** (image recognition software); **Cash register suppliers** (computers); **Coal & solid fuel merchants** (electricity); **Company registration agents** (networks); **Dictation & secretarial services** (voice recognition software); **Layout artists** (computer templates); **Duplicating equipment** (computers); **Factory cleaning** (intelligent robots); **Film processors** (digital, chemical-free film); **Hotel booking agents** (software); **Industrial relations arbitrators** (employment deregulation); **Notaries and commissioners of oaths** (video recordings); **Draughting equipment makers** (computer-aided design); **Typewriter manufacturers** (computers); **Window cleaners** (intelligent robots); **Airlines** (rising fuel prices); **Middle managers** (networks)

Growth areas:

Advertising (fuelled by opportunities in new media); **Alarms & security equipment** (rising crime due to unemployment); **Corporate entertainment** (to keep staff and customers happy); **Sports equipment** (more leisure time); **Hi-fi & computer dealers** (convergence of technologies); **Cellular radio dealers** (more networks); **Cable manufacturers** (more networks); **Environmental systems** (tighter laws); **Recycling** (tighter laws, higher material costs); **Computer programmers** (need for better interfaces); **Designers** (producing and choosing computer templates); **Telemarketing** (chance for wider access to public); **Career consultants** (increased redundancies); **Trauma consultants** (rise in random criminal acts); **Personal matchmakers** (less time for workers to socialise); **Escort services** (importance of appearing sociable in public); **Cruise companies** (for leisurely business trips)

New Scientist 16.4.94

Further reading

Employment Gazette, official journal of the Employment Department (published monthly)

Central Statistical Office: *Social Trends* (published annually by HMSO)

Advanced Business

Test questions

The following underpinning knowledge will be tested:

1. Types of employment
2. Evaluate the effects of changes in types of employment
3. Implications of employment trends
4. Evaluate the implications of employment trends in the local and national economy.

1 Which sector of the economy employs the largest number of workers in the UK?

- A Manufacturing industries
- B Extraction industries
- C Service industries
- D Craft industries

Question 2-4 relate to the answers given below:

Aspects of employment in the UK which have displayed significant growth since the early 1980s include:

- A Part-time employment
- B Temporary employment
- C Self-employment
- D Teleworking

Which of the above are likely to be associated with the following demand- and supply-side factors in labour markets?

2 Seasonal work

3 Increasing economic activity among women with dependent children

4 Improved communications technology

5 Which of the following are NOT included in the measure of the labour force or working population in the UK?

- A Claimant unemployed
- B Self-employed
- C Students
- D HM forces personnel

Questions 6-8 relate to the following identified employment trends:

- A An increase in the number of women at work
- B An increase in the number of people self-employed
- C An increase in the demand for skilled labour
- D A fall in the number employed in manual occupations

Which of the above trends could be explained by the following?

6 The introduction of robotic technology

7 Deindustrialization

8 Changes in social attitudes

9 The most likely outcome from a shortage of skilled labour in the UK is:

- A More government re-training programmes
- B Skilled workers demanding higher wages
- C The increased use of labour with lower skills
- D Falling production costs

10 The most up-to-date and in-depth statistics on employment in the UK are available in:

- A Annual Abstract of Statistics
- B Social Trends
- C Employment Gazette
- D Monthly Digest of Statistics

11 A major cause of the shift of resources from manufacturing towards the service sector in the UK is:

- A Contraction in the youth labour market
- B Rising raw material prices
- C Changing patterns of consumer demand
- D Government competition policy

12 a. Give one example of an industry in each of the following industrial sectors in the UK economy:
  i The primary sector
  ii The secondary sector
  iii The tertiary sector

b. What is 'deindustrialization' and how has it affected the balance of employment between the three industrial sectors?

c. Describe two ways in which the government provides assistance to areas suffering from industrial decline in the UK.

13 In 1993, some 4.7 million workers in the UK were part-time permanent employees, and 630,000 were part-timers on temporary contracts.

a. Explain two reasons for the growth in the number of part-time workers employed in UK firms over time.

b. Suggest how levels of pay and other benefits, hours of work, holiday entitlement, and career progression may differ between part-time and full-time employees.

c. Give one example of:
  i A skilled manual occupation
  ii A non-manual occupation

d. What has happened to the demand for skilled labour in the UK? What effect is this likely to have had on the wages of skilled workers?

assessment assignment

FIVE

Assessment Assignment

Range: Types of employment
Implications
Evaluate in terms of employee needs and business needs
Employment trends
Evaluate in terms of effect on individuals in employment and not in employment, on businesses and communities and government finances

Skills: **Communication**
Produce written material
Use images
Application of Number
Interpret and present data
Information Technology
Process information
Present information

Labour market intelligence report

You work as a business analyst in the UK office of the Nokatomi Corporation. Nokatomi is a Japanese conglomerate which owns companies in all of the main industrial sectors in Japan and the USA. Nokatomi wish to make company acquisitions in the UK and have asked you to investigate the employment trends in the UK. Read the memo from Nokatomi head office below and complete the tasks set.

MEMO

From: Nokatomi Corporation

Japan

1. In our telephone conversation earlier today you agreed to produce a report on UK employment trends ahead of the forthcoming visit to the UK by company chairman Mr Osaka. We agreed that your report should take the following structure;

    (a) Your first task is to identify the main types of employment in the UK and how numbers employed in each type have changed over time. Mr Osaka is particularly keen to know about the growth in part-time, temporary and self-employment at the apparent expense of full-time permanent employment. It would be useful to give examples of the types of occupations and industries which these changes have affected the most.

    (b) You should evaluate the changes in the types of employment you have identified in terms of how well they meet the needs of business and of employees.

    (c) You next major task is to provide an up-to-date picture of national and regional trends in

    * employment in different industrial sectors
    * full-time and part-time employment
    * male and female employment
    * differences in pay

    (d) At this point you should provide some thoughts and evidence on what these employment trends imply for people in work and the unemployed, regional prosperity and UK government finances.

    (e) Mr Osaka is particular keen that you present data in easy to read tabulated and graphical formats in your report. He is aware that the following publications will be extremely useful to you;

    * Social Trends
    * Employment Gazette

2. Mr Osaka will be flying in to Heathrow at 11.45am next Tuesday. I would like you to meet him there and present him with the report. A meeting room has been booked at the airport. Mr Osaka has asked that the findings of your report be explained to him in a short presentation (no longer than 10 minutes).

    I suggest you prepare a one-page summary noting the main findings from your report. This can be handed out to Mr Osaka and his advisers at the start of your presentation.

    Overhead slides of 3 or 4 graphs illustrating the main trends identified should also be presented. I have asked that an overhead projector be provided in the meeting room but should this not be the case, you should have in reserve a set of posters of the same graphs.

3. The report and presentation should be presented to Mr Osaka's aides in both hard copy and disk form. Mr Osaka has made it known he wishes to consult both text and any diagrams on his portable PC as he travels between meetings. Please let me know the wordprocessing, spreadsheet and/or graphics, desktop publishing package(s) you intend to use in good time, so that I can check Mr Osaka's portable for compatible software.

    Remember to check all your work before final completion and quote any data sources you use in your report as Mr Osaka may wish to follow up some of the issues you raise independently.

4. In the event of Mr Osaka being delayed, you may wish to provide an audio-visual copy of your presentation he can watch in his limousine while travelling to his first appointment.

chapter 17

Advanced Business

chapter 17: The Competitiveness of UK Industry

This chapter examines the performance of the UK economy in terms of growth in total output and share of world trade, and efforts by the UK government to improve performance

Key ideas

The performance of the economy and the standard of living in the UK will depend ultimately on the ability of UK firms to compete in domestic and overseas markets.

Gross Domestic Product (GDP) is a measure of the total value of all goods and services produced in a country per period. Growth in the real GDP of the UK has averaged 2.3% per year since 1970. GDP growth tends to rise above this long-term trend during booms, and may even turn negative during economic recessions.

Some of the most significant GDP growth rates since 1980 have been observed in the **emerging markets** of Latin America and South East Asia.

Overseas trade involves the sale of **imports** and **exports** and the movement of capital investments between countries. **Visible trade** involves trade in goods, while **invisible trade** involves the exchange of services.

The difference between flows of money into and out of the UK is known as the **balance of payments**. If payments overseas exceed payments received from abroad, the balance of payments will be in deficit and there will be pressure on the UK sterling **exchange rate** to fall.

The UK share of world export sales fell from 5.7% in 1983 to 4.9% in 1993. Over 50% of UK export sales are to European Union member countries.

The **value of output per person employed** in the UK doubled between 1960 and 1985. However, **unit labour costs** have also grown rapidly in the UK.

The UK government's overall economic objective is to promote sustained economic growth in the total output by establishing a stable economic environment for business, based on low and stable **price inflation**.

The UK government aims to **reduce the burden of taxation** and the **size of government** in order to stimulate demand, reduce interest rates to stimulate investment, and create exchange rate stability to promote exports and curb imported inflation.

Supply-side policies are those which attempt to promote jobs, low inflation, and economic growth by removing barriers which restrict competition and supply in domestic and international markets. Policies include **privatization, deregulation, competition policy, encouraging investment in new technology**, and **expanding education and training**.

UK trade policy operates as part of the **European Union (EU) Common Competition Policy**, while the EU operates within the **General Agreement on Tariffs and Trade (GATT)**, now being taken further in the new **World Trade Organization (WTO)**.

The establishment of a **Single European Market** seeks to remove **tariffs** and administrative barriers to trade between EU member countries.

GATT was established to negotiate mutual reductions in tariffs and restrictions to free trade between participating countries.

Businesses can employ a number of strategies to improve their ability to compete including investing in **new technology**, improving **marketing** efforts, changes in **human resourcing**, expanding the **scale of production**, changing the **organization structure** and **cost control**.

The effectiveness of business strategies can be measured in terms of improved **sales volumes** and **revenues**, **market shares**, productivity, product and service quality.

Section 17.1

The performance of UK industry

What is competitiveness?

Like many countries, the UK faces a world of increasing change as a result of growing foreign competition, increasing consumer power, and new technologies. To meet these challenges, the UK must be able to compete to win business in home and overseas markets. The performance of the economy and the standard of living in the UK will ultimately depend on the ability of UK firms to compete.

For a firm, **competitiveness** means meeting consumers' needs more efficiently and more effectively than its rivals. For an economy as a whole, the Organization for Economic Cooperation and Development (OECD) defines competitiveness as *'the degree to which it can, under free and fair market conditions, produce goods and services which meet the test of international markets, while simultaneously maintaining and expanding the real incomes of its people over the long term'*.

The ability of the UK to compete in international markets and to promote growth in total output and incomes, therefore, requires sustained improvements in productivity and product quality, and reductions in production costs at a rate which exceeds those of countries overseas.

How competitive is the UK?

There are a number of indicators of the changing competitiveness of UK industry as whole over time. Four of the most important and revealing indicators are changes in:

- Real Gross Domestic Product (GDP)
- UK share of world trade
- Output per employee
- Unit labour costs

Gross Domestic Product

If all the firms in an economy manage to produce more goods and services in one year compared to the previous year, the result will be **economic growth**.

Gross Domestic Product (GDP) is a measure of the total value of all goods and services produced in a country per period. Because the production and sale of goods and services generates incomes for the owners of resources - i.e. labour and suppliers of materials and machinery - GDP is, therefore, a measure of the total or national income of a country. Also, because by definition the national income will be spent on goods and services, GDP is a measure of the total expenditure on UK goods.

Revenues from the sale of goods and services will tend to rise each year, simply because prices rise. Economists say this represents a rise in nominal GDP. However, in order for there to be economic growth, the total output of goods and services must also rise. That is, there must be an increase in real output, or real GDP. An increase in real GDP refers to an increase in the quantity and/or quality of goods and services available for an economy to enjoy, and therefore, an increase in real national income.

Gross Domestic product (GDP) =

Total Output =

Total Income =

Total Expenditure

▼ *Figure 17.1: UK Gross Domestic Product 1970-1993*

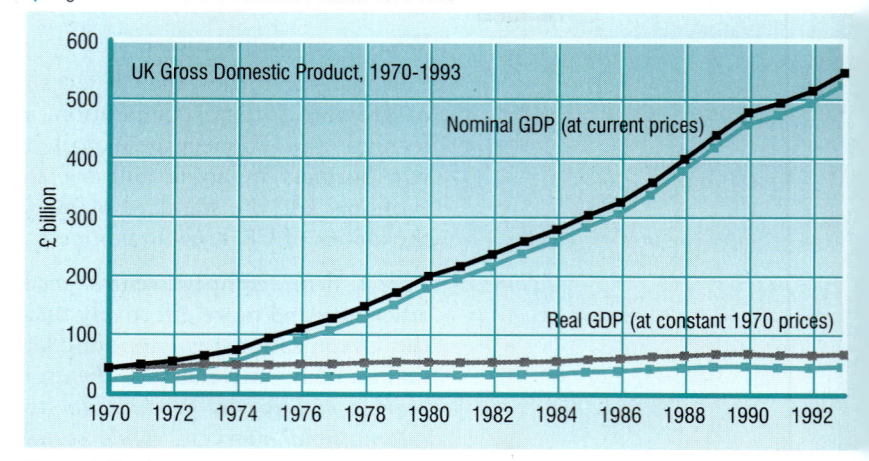

Economic Trends

Figure 17.1 shows the rise in both nominal and real GDP between 1970 and 1993. Over this period, GDP, measured at current market prices increased from £44 billion to £547 billion - an increase of 1,234%. However, after deducting the effect of price inflation on the value of goods and services, real GDP, measured in constant prices, expanded by only 55% over this period - an average increase of 2.3% each year. We might expect this long-term trend rate of growth to continue in the UK. However, in the short term, real GDP can fall during an economic recession, or rise even faster than the trend during a boom. For example, during the economic recession in the early 1990s, UK real GDP fell by 2%.

The business cycle

The continuous fluctuations in real GDP around a long-term trend rate of growth are called the **business cycle** or **trade cycle**. Four stages can be identified in one complete cycle:

1. During an **economic recession** or **slump**, as in the UK in the early 1980s, real GDP tends to fall below trend (see Figure 17.2). There is negative growth. Recessions are characterized by falling output and rising unemployment as a response to falling consumer demand and business investment. Price inflation tends to fall as firms cut prices in a bid to boost sales and maintain shares in shrinking markets. Business profits tend to fall, and an increasing number of firms will close as the slump deepens. However, falling consumer demand for imported goods may improve the balance of international trade.

2. A **trough** occurs when the economy has reached the bottom of the business cycle. Consumer demand and business investment will be low, but will have stopped falling. Unemployment will be high.

3. During an **economic recovery**, incomes and demand start to rise. Stocks of goods will fall, and businesses will respond by increasing output and their recruitment of staff. Unemployment will begin to fall. Growing business optimism may boost investment spending. However, growing demand will tend to suck in more imported goods, and the balance of trade may deteriorate.

4. During a **boom,** real GDP will be rising above trend, as in the mid-to-late 1980s in the UK (see Figure 17.2). Consumer demand, output, sales, and profits will all be buoyant. Unemployment will be low. However, if the supply of goods and services is unable to expand fast enough to meet demand, there will be price inflation.

Economists suggest that the UK completes a full cycle in economic activity every 8 to 12 years.

▼ *Figure 17.2: The UK business cycle*

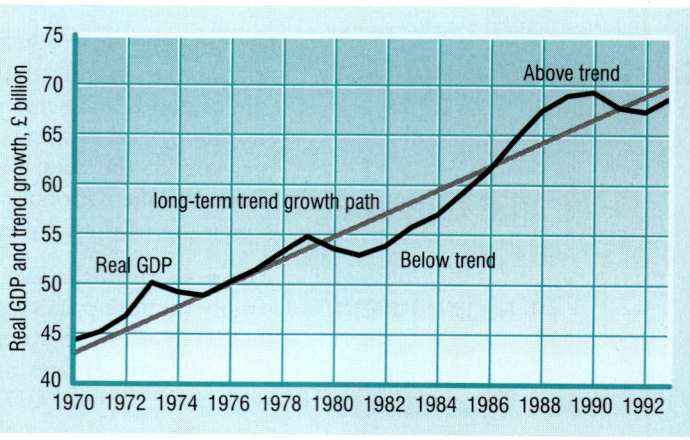

▼ Figure 17.3: Growth in real GDP, selected countries 1976 - 1993

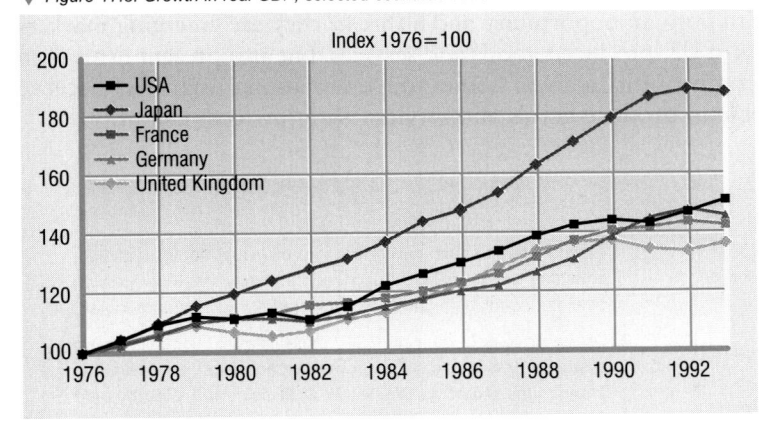

Index 1976=100
- USA
- Japan
- France
- Germany
- United Kingdom

OECD Economic Outlook

▼ Figure 17.4: Growth of real GDP, developing economies 1993

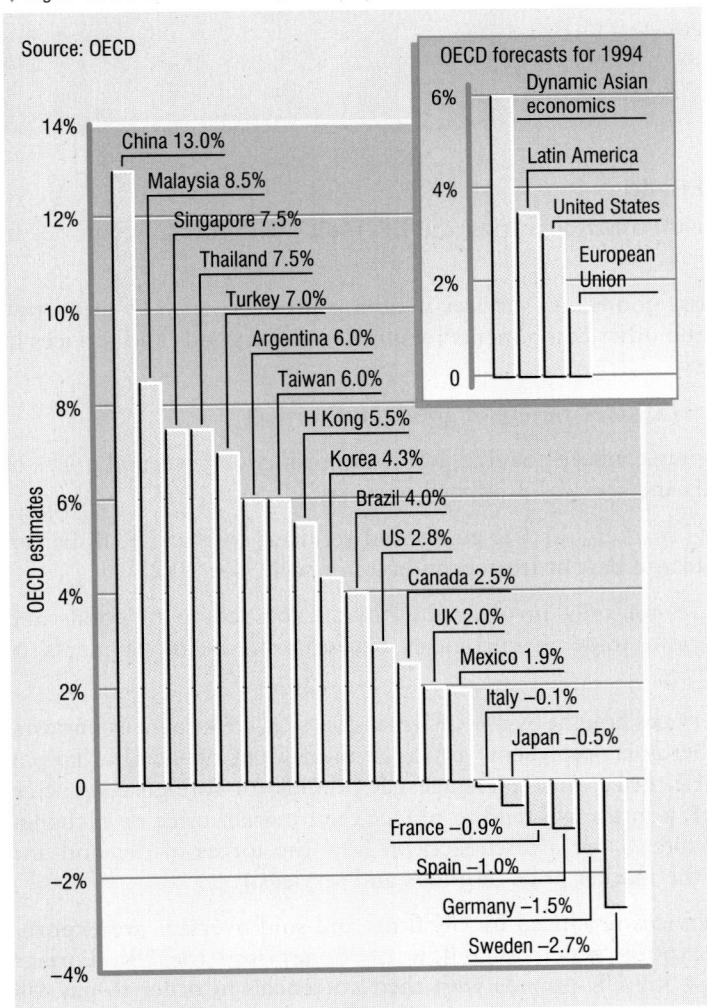

Source: OECD

OECD estimates:
- China 13.0%
- Malaysia 8.5%
- Singapore 7.5%
- Thailand 7.5%
- Turkey 7.0%
- Argentina 6.0%
- Taiwan 6.0%
- H Kong 5.5%
- Korea 4.3%
- Brazil 4.0%
- US 2.8%
- Canada 2.5%
- UK 2.0%
- Mexico 1.9%
- Italy −0.1%
- Japan −0.5%
- France −0.9%
- Spain −1.0%
- Germany −1.5%
- Sweden −2.7%

OECD forecasts for 1994:
- Dynamic Asian economics
- Latin America
- United States
- European Union

Financial Times 7.2.94

Despite the increase in real GDP enjoyed by the UK, some other countries have done much better (see Figure 17.3). Growth rates in real GDP of 4-5% per year were achieved in many of the developed economies of Western Europe, North America, and Japan. Japan especially proved to be an 'economic powerhouse', with an annual average growth rate in real GDP in excess of 6.5%.

However, more recently, growth in many developed western countries has slowed down. In some cases, real GDP growth has even turned negative during the world economic recession in the early 1990s as firms cut back their production. Some of the most significant growth rates since 1980 have been observed in the **emerging markets** of Latin America and South East Asia. For example, in 1993, real GDP in China expanded by 13% (see Figure 17.4). This compared to a fall in the real GDP of Japan by -0.5% and in Germany by -1.5%.

Despite substantial growth in the GDP of **newly industrialized economies** such as China, Malaysia, Mexico, and Brazil, these countries remain relatively poor. In some cases the annual average annual income per head of their populations in 1993 was no

▼ Figure 17.5: Gross Domestic Product per head of population, international comparison 1993

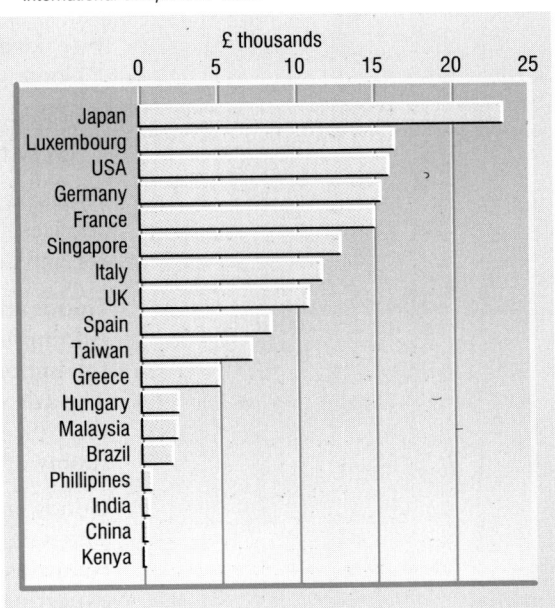

£ thousands (0, 5, 10, 15, 20, 25)
- Japan
- Luxembourg
- USA
- Germany
- France
- Singapore
- Italy
- UK
- Spain
- Taiwan
- Greece
- Hungary
- Malaysia
- Brazil
- Phillipines
- India
- China
- Kenya

more than £200 (see Figure 17.5). They present developed countries like the UK with both an opportunity and a threat: they are **emerging markets** for exports of UK-produced goods and services, but also present firms with growing competition in their home and international markets, because they are able to produce goods and services with low-cost labour.

Portfolio Activity 17.1

Range: Compare performance
Skills: Read and respond to written material, Collect and record data, Interpret and present data

1. Compile an economics and business diary, by collecting newspaper and economics/business magazine articles about the current economic climate in the UK over the next 12-24 months. Include data on changes in GDP, retail sales, investment, industrial output, price inflation, unemployment, overseas trade, and government economic policy, etc.

   From your findings, what stage would you say the UK has reached in the business cycle? Does the information you have collected give conflicting views of recovery or recession in the UK?

   Write a brief commentary at the end of every month to explain emerging trends in the UK economy, and how these compare to other countries, as highlighted by the articles you have collected.

2. Obtain up-to-date data on GDP, price inflation, unemployment, overseas trade, etc., from publications such as *Economic Trends*, the *Monthly Digest of Statistics*, and *Employment Gazette*. Plot graphs of the historical series for these economic variables to include in your diary to illustrate the emerging trends you have discussed.

International trade

In common with other countries, the UK trades with foreign countries in order to:

- Obtain those goods and services it cannot produce, such as many raw materials and other components required to make goods and services in UK industry
- Benefit from a wider variety of goods and services
- Take advantage, where possible, of lower production costs and prices of some goods and services produced overseas
- Expand the markets for UK goods and services, so that UK firms can grow in size and benefit from economies of scale (see 20.2)

Overseas trade not only involves the buying and selling of goods and services, but also trade in currencies necessary to make payments to foreign countries.

Goods and services bought by the UK from overseas are known as **imports**. An import, therefore, represents a flow of money out of the UK. To pay for imports, UK firms must exchange UK pounds for foreign currencies. The sale of UK pounds will tend to reduce their market price or exchange rate. (See Chapter 1 for a discussion on how the forces of demand and supply affect the market price of goods and services.)

Goods and services produced by UK firms and sold overseas are **exports**. The sale of exports generates a flow of money into the UK. Foreign countries must buy UK pounds with their currencies in order to pay UK exporting firms. The demand for the UK currency sterling tends to push up the UK exchange rate.

The balance of payments

The difference between flows of money into and out of the UK is known as the **balance of payments**. If payments overseas exceed payments received from abroad, the balance of payments will be in deficit. The net outflow of money from the UK will tend to reduce the sterling exchange rate on the world currency markets.

▼ Table 17.1: The UK balance of payments (£ million), 1973-1993

	1973	1980	1983	1986	1990	1993
(A) Visible exports	+11,881	+47,149	+60,700	+72,627	+101,718	+121,414
(B) Visible imports	-14,449	-45,792	-62,237	-82,186	-120,527	-134,623
(C) Visible balance (A+B)	-2,568	+1,357	-1,537	-9,559	-18,809	-13,209
(D) Invisible exports	+10,449	+41,041	+65,392	+76,469	+114,504	+116,000
(E) Invisible imports	-8,929	-39,555	-60,326	-67,781	-114,730	-113,102
(F) Invisible balance (D+E)	+1,570	+1,487	+5,066	+8,688	-226	+2,898
(G) Current balance (C+F)	-998	+2,843	+3,529	-871	-19,035	-10,311
(H) Net financial transactions	+924	-3,940	-4,562	-3,115	+18,193	+8,313
Balancing item -(H+G)	+74	+1,097	+1,033	+3,986	+842	+1,998

CSO UK Balance of Payments ('The Pink Book') 1994

There are three main categories of trade and international payments for trade:

- **Visible trade.** This involves trade in physical commodities, such as oil, machinery, foods, chemicals, cars, video recorders, etc. If payments for visible imports exceed payments made for visible exports, the balance of visible trade will be in deficit (see table 17.1).

- **Invisible trade.** This involves international trade in services such as tourism, insurance, and banking. For example, if a UK resident visits a foreign country on holiday, the money s/he spends there represents a flow of money out of the UK and so is classed as an **invisible import**. Conversely, if a foreign shipping firm insures its fleet at Lloyds of London, the premiums paid into the UK are an **invisible export**.

  Invisible exports also include inflows of interest payments on loans made overseas, profits from UK-owned companies overseas, and dividends on shareholdings in foreign companies. Invisible imports include flows of interest, profits, and dividends paid overseas.

  The balance of payments **current account** is a measure of international trading performance. If the total payment made for all imported goods and services in any one period exceeds the total payments received for visible and invisible exports, then the current account will be in deficit as in 1993.

- **Financial transactions.** These are outflows of capital including loans and investments made overseas by UK residents, firms, and government. Inflows are loans and investments in the UK by other countries. If inflows exceed outflows, then the balance of net financial transactions will be in surplus.

Table 17.1 (above) shows the UK balance of payments over a 20-year period to 1993. The balance of payments must, by definition, always balance. Thus, if the current account is in surplus, then net financial transactions must be deficit, and vice versa. For accounting purposes, a **balancing item** is included to account for any errors and omissions made during the collection and compilation of data on the many millions of overseas transactions of UK exporting and importing organizations each year.

The UK share of world trade

The UK is usually a net importer of visibles, but the current account balance has tended to hold up, because it has traditionally performed well on invisibles. This is chiefly due to London being a recognized international centre for banking, insurance, and finance. Figure 17.6, however, shows that since 1986, a worsening deficit in visible trade has overshadowed the surplus on invisible trade, such that the current account balance became negative. Competition from other financial centres such as New York and Tokyo has also tended to reduce the balance on invisible trade.

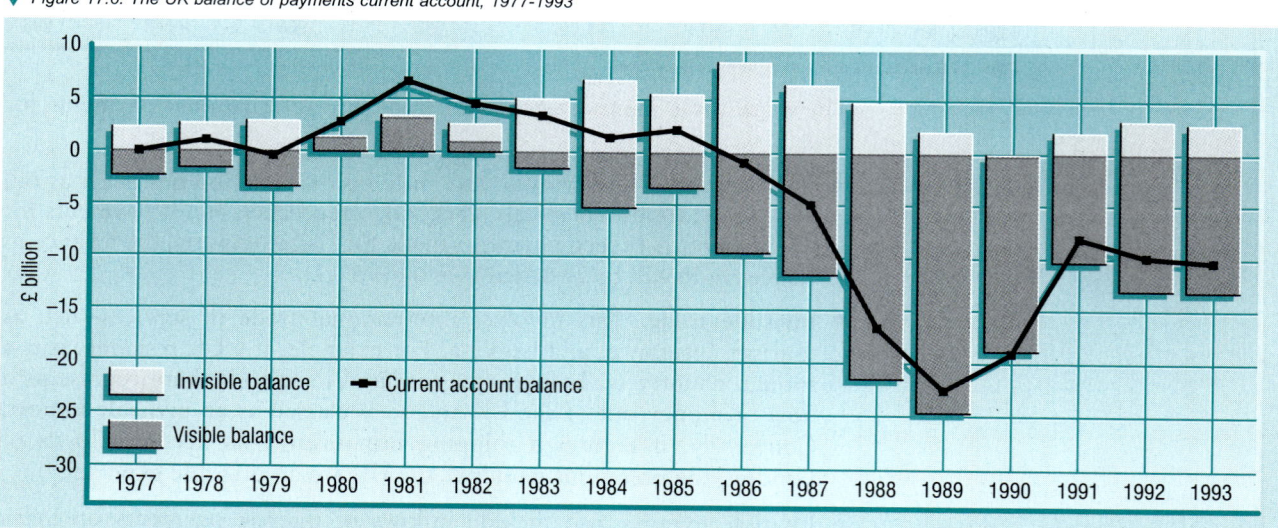

▼ *Figure 17.6: The UK balance of payments current account, 1977-1993*

CSO UK Balance of Payments 1994

The UK has always been a major exporter of manufactured goods, notably machinery. Until 1983, the value of UK exports of manufactures had always exceeded imports. For example, in 1975, UK revenues from the export of manufactures were 25% higher than the value of UK imports. However, in 1983, the balance of trade in manufactures turned negative for the first time in recorded history, and has remained in deficit ever since (see Figure 17.7).

Finished and semi-finished manufactures still account for around 80% of total UK visible exports, but their share of total world export sales has declined significantly over time. In 1950, the UK accounted for 25% of world export sales of manufactures. By 1970, this share had fallen to 11% and is now around 6%.

Figure 17.7: UK trade in manufactured goods, 1974-1993

CSO UK Balance of Payments 1994

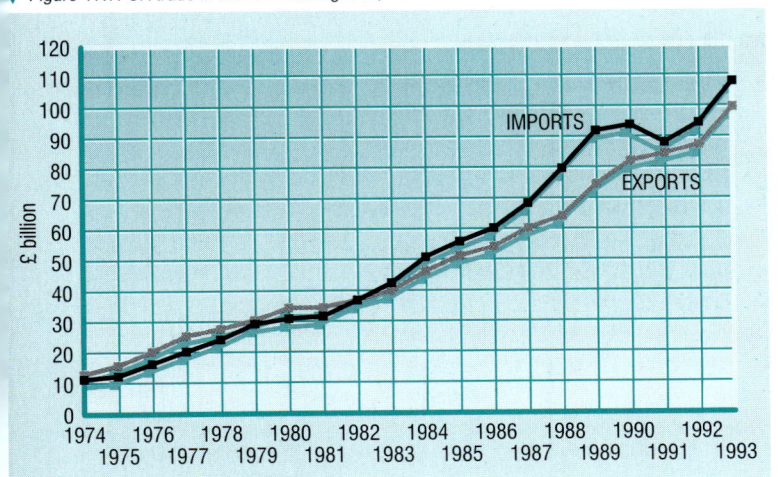

Figure 17.8 shows that in 1980, the UK share of total world export trade in goods and services was 5.7%. Since then it has fallen to around 4.9% of a market worth in excess of £2,400 billion in 1993. At the same time, countries such as Japan, the USA, and a number in South East Asia, were able to increase their share of total export sales.

However, the amount of imports entering the UK has increased over time. The UK accounts for around 5-6% of the world trade in imports. The emerging markets of South East Asia are taking an increasing proportion of world imports as their economies expand and industrialize.

Organization for Economic Cooperation and Development (OECD)		
United States*	Belgium	Norway
Japan*	Luxembourg	Portugal
Germany*	Denmark	Spain
France*	Finland	Sweden
Italy*	Greece	Switzerland
United Kingdom*	Iceland	Turkey
Canada*	Ireland	Australia
Austria	Netherlands	New Zealand

*'Major 7 countries'

Since joining the European Union (EU) in 1972, the UK has enjoyed a growth in her share of intra-EU export trade. In 1958, the UK sold just 22% of her total visible exports to all the other countries who made up the EU in 1994 (see 17.3). By 1983, this share had risen to 46%. In 1993, the EU imported around £63.5 billion of visible exports from the UK, some 53% of total UK visible export sales worth £120.7 billion (see Figure 17.9).

The UK has also enjoyed a growth in her exports to the emerging markets in Asia, while the share going to North America, the largest market for UK goods, has fallen from 16% to around 14% over the 10-year period to 1993.

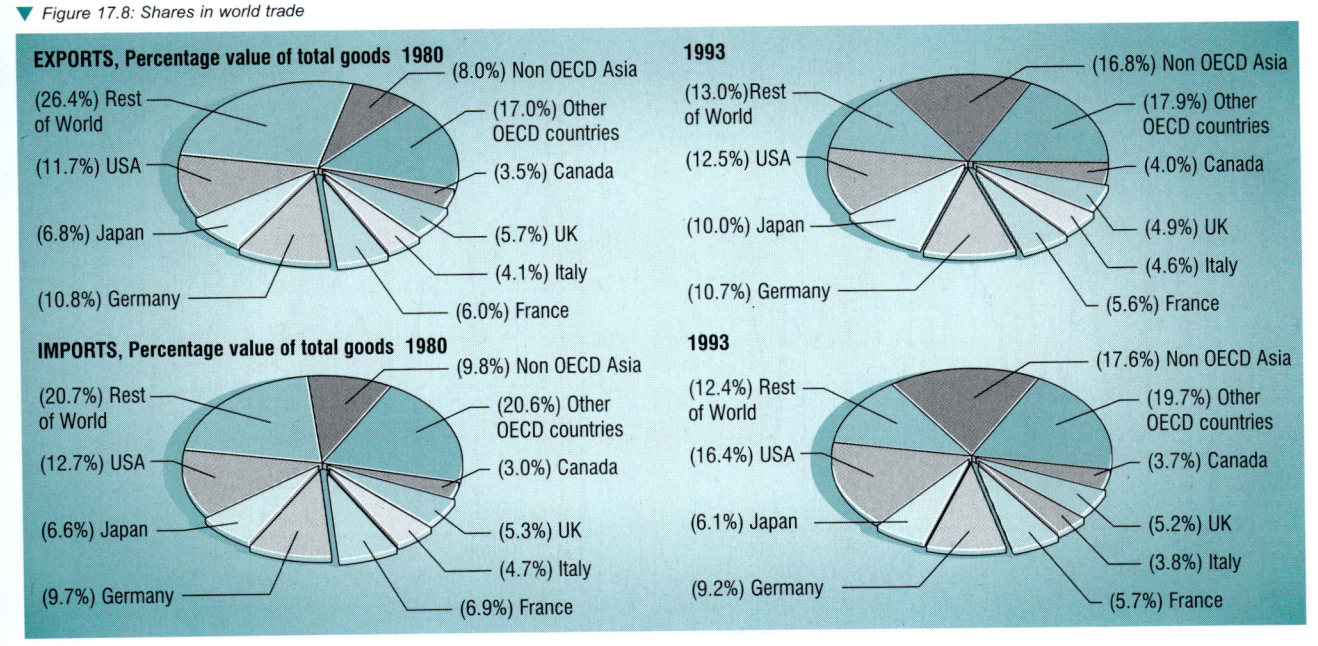

Figure 17.8: Shares in world trade

EXPORTS, Percentage value of total goods 1980
- (26.4%) Rest of World
- (11.7%) USA
- (6.8%) Japan
- (10.8%) Germany
- (8.0%) Non OECD Asia
- (17.0%) Other OECD countries
- (3.5%) Canada
- (5.7%) UK
- (4.1%) Italy
- (6.0%) France

1993
- (13.0%) Rest of World
- (12.5%) USA
- (10.0%) Japan
- (10.7%) Germany
- (16.8%) Non OECD Asia
- (17.9%) Other OECD countries
- (4.0%) Canada
- (4.9%) UK
- (4.6%) Italy
- (5.6%) France

IMPORTS, Percentage value of total goods 1980
- (20.7%) Rest of World
- (12.7%) USA
- (6.6%) Japan
- (9.7%) Germany
- (9.8%) Non OECD Asia
- (20.6%) Other OECD countries
- (3.0%) Canada
- (5.3%) UK
- (4.7%) Italy
- (6.9%) France

1993
- (12.4%) Rest of World
- (16.4%) USA
- (6.1%) Japan
- (9.2%) Germany
- (17.6%) Non OECD Asia
- (19.7%) Other OECD countries
- (3.7%) Canada
- (5.2%) UK
- (3.8%) Italy
- (5.7%) France

OECD Economic Outlook December 1994

Advanced Business

▼ Figure 17.9: UK exports by region

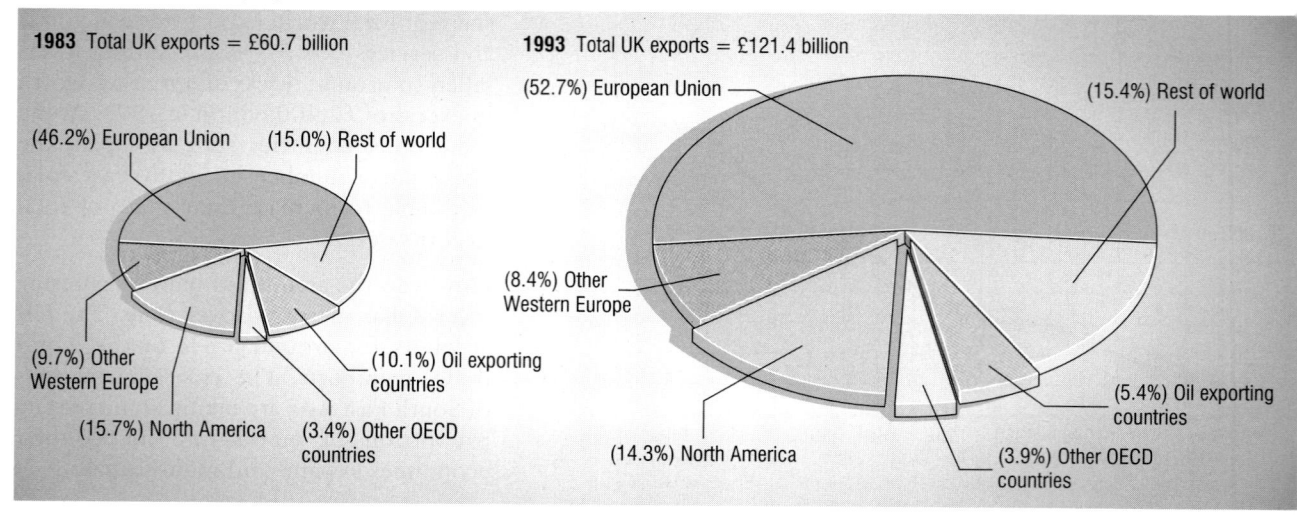

1983 Total UK exports = £60.7 billion
- (46.2%) European Union
- (15.0%) Rest of world
- (9.7%) Other Western Europe
- (10.1%) Oil exporting countries
- (15.7%) North America
- (3.4%) Other OECD countries

1993 Total UK exports = £121.4 billion
- (52.7%) European Union
- (15.4%) Rest of world
- (8.4%) Other Western Europe
- (5.4%) Oil exporting countries
- (14.3%) North America
- (3.9%) Other OECD countries

CSO Monthly Digest of Statistics

Competitiveness and currencies

Competitiveness in world trade is often measured by reference to the relative prices of imports and exports, and the **Sterling Effective Exchange Rate Index**.

The *Index of Relative Export Prices* published in CSO *Economic Trends* is a measure of the average value of UK exports of manufactures, divided by a weighted average of the value of exports of manufactured goods from all other countries expressed in the same currency value. A fall in the relative price index suggests increasing price competitiveness for UK exports.

The **Sterling Exchange Rate Index** measures the average value of the pound against the currencies of all her trading partners. A fall in the index indicates that the average value of the pound has depreciated. This will reduce UK export prices, but raise the price of imports to the UK. An appreciation in the value of the pound against other currencies will raise export prices, but lower import prices.

▼ UK Relative Export Prices Index 1983-1993

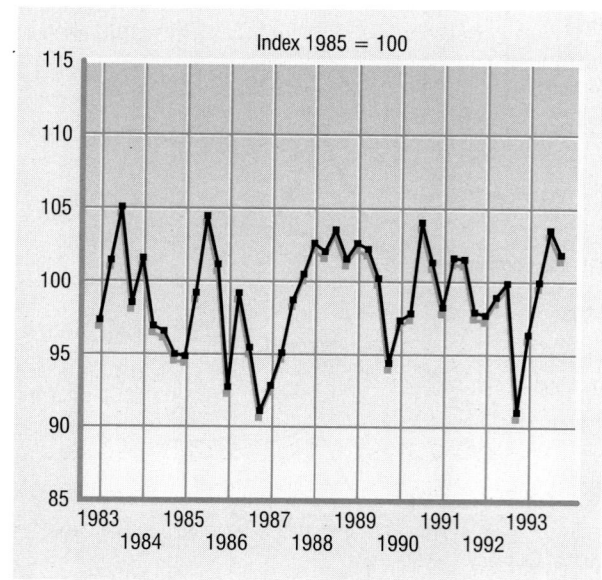

▼ UK Sterling Exchange Rate Index 1983-1992

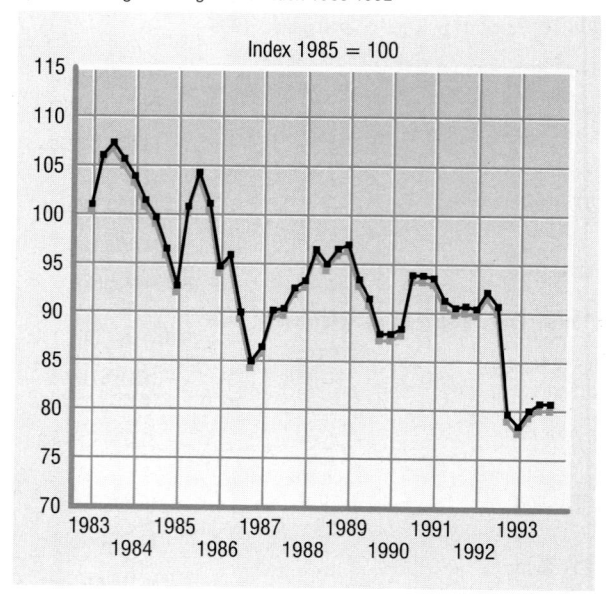

UNIT FIVE

CHAPTER 17

Portfolio Activity 17.2

Range: Compare performance, Major competitors
Skills: Read and respond to written material, Collect and record data, Interpret and present data, Present information

1. What is meant by the 'competitiveness gap' referred to in the article?
2. Obtain data on UK trade performance in exports overseas. Plot data on export volumes and values over the last 5 years.
3. Investigate how the Department of Trade and Industry (DTi) provides help and support to UK firms involved in exporting.
4. Obtain data on measures of UK competitiveness in overseas trade from CSO *Economic Trends*. Produce a short paper discussing what each data series shows, and how UK competitiveness according to these measures has changed over the last five years. Use a computer spreadsheet to plot these data series on a number of line graphs to include in your paper.

First steps on long march to competitiveness

Exports break all records' proclaims a delighted DTi as it watches the swelling tide of overseas sales lift Britain's trading performance.

From coal-powered boilers for China to revolutionary earthquake protection material for Japan, Britain is notching up sales round the world.

But could this buoyant picture merely represent another false dawn for the economy? Although exports last year provided one of the main motors of recovery, the UK is still running a sizeable trade gap.

The Trade and Industry Secretary is predictably optimistic about export growth, but is also the first to sound a note of caution: "The competitiveness gap between the UK and other major economies opened up over a century ago. Despite some recent improvement, it still exists and there is no short cut to eliminating it. We still have a long tail of underperforming companies."

To put the challenge in perspective, Britain will have to make an extra £890 billion of overseas sales by 2000 if it is to raise its 1993 share of world trade from 4.8% to 5.8%. To achieve such a target, UK export performance will have to exceed that of Japan over the last 14 years!

Some analysts have argued that much of the recent growth is explained by the depreciation of sterling, which has left exporters enjoying a short-term competitive advantage. Others point to the recent recession in forcing companies to seek markets overseas in the face of weak domestic demand for their products.

Financial Times 21.2.95

Output per employee and unit labour costs

The value of output per employee is an average measure of the productivity of labour. It is calculated in official statistics as follows:

$$\text{Value of output per person employed} = \frac{\text{Real Gross Domestic Product}}{\text{Total number of employees}}$$

▼ Figure 17.10: Real output per person employed,* UK 1960-1993

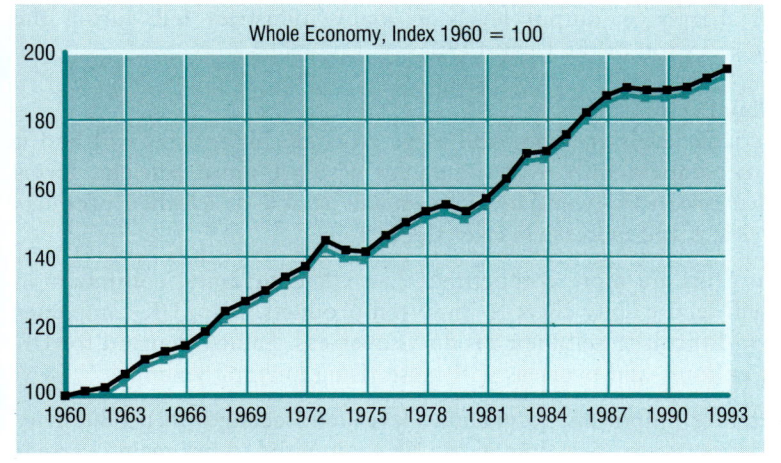

[Graph: Whole Economy, Index 1960 = 100, showing line rising from 100 in 1960 to approximately 195 in 1993]

Whole Economy, Index 1960 = 100
* Output per person employed includes employees in employment, self-employed, and HM forces
CSO Economic Trends

Figure 17.10 shows that significant improvements have been made in the productivity of the employed UK labour force in recent years. The value of output per person employed almost doubled between 1960 and 1993. However, this is unlikely to have been solely due to the increased efforts of the workforce. Increases in productivity will also occur due to:

- Technological advance in equipment and production processes
- The closure of inefficient plants and organizations
- Changes in working practices

429

Output per manshift in coal mining doubled between 1980 and 1990 due to improvements in mining technology and the closure of inefficient mines.

Unit labour costs

Increases in productivity reveal nothing about the cost of production. If, for example, real wage costs (wage increases over and above inflation) have risen faster than productivity, firms will be less competitive.

Unit labour costs for the whole economy can be calculated by dividing the total wage bill for all employees by the total volume of output in the economy. In cash terms, labour costs per unit of UK output increased by 1,180% over the period 1960-1993. However, Figure 17.11 shows that, after deducting the impact of price inflation on wages, real labour costs per unit were only around 1% higher in 1993 than they were in 1960.

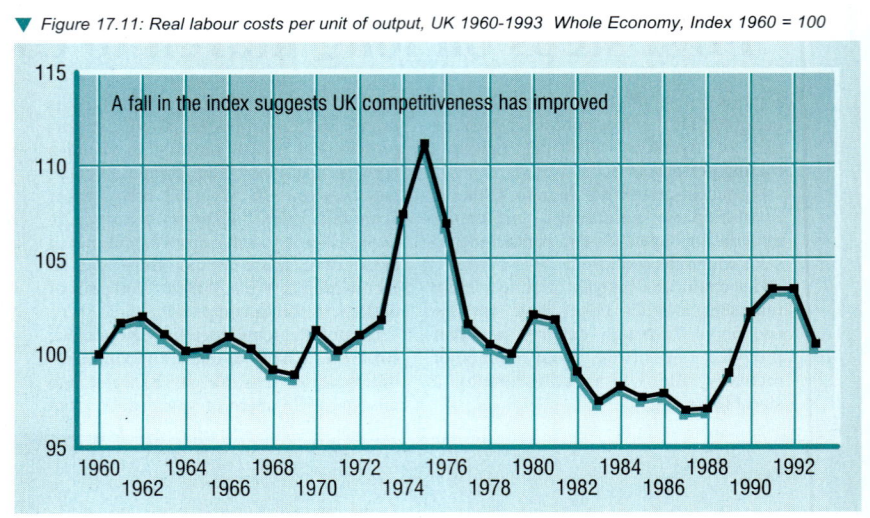

▼ *Figure 17.11: Real labour costs per unit of output, UK 1960-1993 Whole Economy, Index 1960 = 100*

A fall in the index suggests UK competitiveness has improved

European Economy Annual Report 1993

However, Figure 17.11 also reveals notable changes in the competitiveness of UK industry during the early 1970s. Between 1972 and 1975, unit labour costs increased significantly as workers managed to secure wage increases without corresponding productivity gains. In fact, output per employee fell at the same time (Figure 17.10). Real unit labour costs also increased sharply as output levels in many industries fell during the economic recession of the early 1990s.

International comparisons

If productivity levels are poor and wage costs are high, firms will find it difficult to compete with rival companies who are more efficient. Firms with higher productivity and lower costs will be able to sell their products at lower prices and increase market share.

If foreign firms are more competitive than UK companies, consumers in the UK will tend to buy cheaper imported products. Also, UK companies will find it difficult to sell their products overseas. Falling demand for UK products at home and overseas will cause rising unemployment.

It is, therefore, important to examine levels and changes in productivity and unit labour costs over time in the UK, compared to her main overseas competitors.

Table 17.2 suggests that the competitiveness of UK industry is improving, with growth rates in productivity, especially in manufacturing, well above the European Union average, but still below those of Japan. Annual average increases in real labour costs per unit of output have been small, but still above many UK competitors, a number of whom have expanded output faster than real wages, such that unit labour costs have fallen.

▼ Table 17.2: Growth in real output per employee and real unit labour costs, selected countries 1971-1990 (annual average growth rates %)

	1971-1990			1980-1990		
	Productivity in Services	Productivity in Manufacturing	Whole economy Unit Labour costs	Productivity in Services	Productivity in Manufacturing	Whole economy Unit Labour Costs
United Kingdom	1.6	3.1	0.1	1.8	4.6	0.01
Germany	2.3	2.2	0.5	1.4	1.3	0.58
France	2.2	3.0	-0.14	1.8	2.8	-1.04
EU12 Average*	1.5	2.8	-0.22	1.2	2.9	-0.7
USA	0.6	3.2	0.01	0.4	4.2	-0.11
Japan	2.9	6.1	-0.01	2.2	5.8	-0.73

* EU12 = average of 12 European Union members prior to 1.1.95 (see 17.3)
European Economy 1993

However, although the UK may appear to have caught up with the competitiveness of major trading partners, she still has some way to go. Figures 17.12 and 17.13 show the level of average wage costs and value of output per employee in manufacturing in a number of countries.

Despite wage levels being relatively low in the UK, the value of output per employee was also low at around US$45,000 (£79,493) in 1992. The difference between the value of output and the wage cost per worker provides an approximate measure of average profit margins - the difference between revenues and costs. Because the value of output per Japanese worker is high and the wage cost per Japanese employee relatively low, this indicates higher profit margins in Japanese manufacturing than its overseas competitors.

Figure 17.12: Wage costs per employee in the manufacturing sector

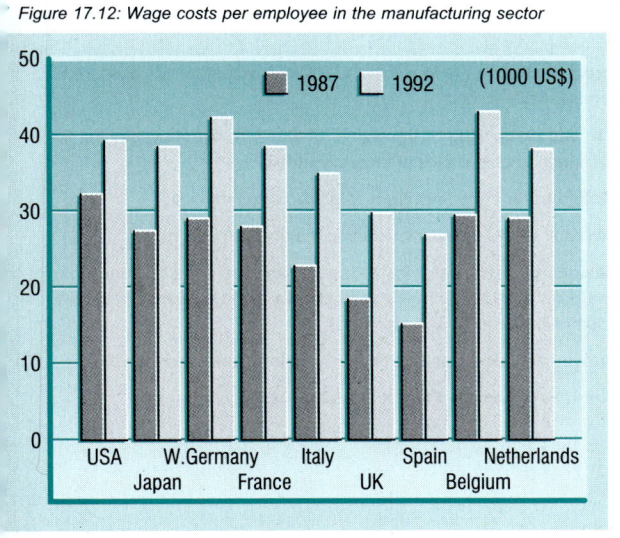

European Economy Annual Report 1993

▼ Figure 17.13: Value of output per employee in the manufacturing sector

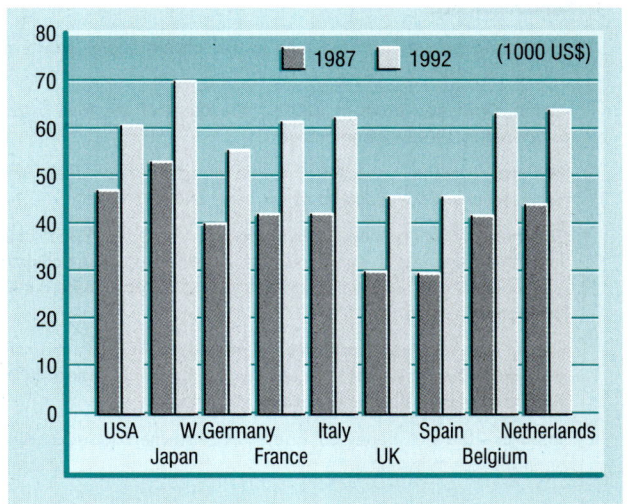

European Economy Annual Report 1993

Advanced Business

Portfolio Activity 17.3

Range: Compare performance, Major competitors
Skills: Interpret and present data

Look at the statistics on changes in output per worker and unit wage costs for the USA, Japan, and EU member countries below. Produce a short report to present to your group covering the following topics:

1. Explain how output per worker and unit labour costs are calculated. Why are they useful measures in business?

2. Suggest which countries have become more competitive and which have become less competitive over time by comparing the changes in output per worker and unit labour costs.

3. What might explain these differences between countries?

4. Plot four graphs each one showing changes in unit labour costs and productivity for the UK, Europe as a whole, the USA, and Japan. When unit labour costs are rising faster than output per worker, profit margins in industry are likely to be falling. If productivity increases faster than unit labour costs, the reverse is probably true. Describe what is happening in each graph.

PERCENTAGE ANNUAL CHANGES IN

	Real output per person employed						Real unit labour costs					
Country	1988	1989	1990	1991	1992	1993	1988	1989	1990	1991	1992	1993
Belgium	3.5	2.2	2.0	1.7	1.1	0.0	-2.7	-3.2	2.4	2.1	0.4	1.7
Denmark	1.8	1.1	2.6	2.2	1.3	1.1	-0.2	-1.5	-1.5	-0.9	-0.1	0.4
Germany	2.9	2.1	2.7	1.9	0.7	-0.2	-1.4	-1.7	-1.1	0.0	0.2	0.1
Greece	2.4	3.0	-1.2	3.5	-0.8	-0.2	0.6	1.7	0.5	-6.9	-1.8	-1.5
Spain	2.3	1.3	0.5	1.8	2.8	3.5	-0.9	-1.8	0.8	-0.8	1.0	-0.2
France	3.6	2.9	1.5	0.7	1.9	0.5	-2.2	3.8	-4.7	0.7	-0.4	-0.1
Ireland	3.2	6.3	5.5	2.7	4.8	1.9	0.0	-3.9	1.5	1.0	0.0	1.0
Italy	3.2	2.9	1.3	0.5	1.8	1.3	-1.2	-0.4	1.8	0.7	-0.9	-2.0
Luxembourg	2.6	2.9	-1.1	-1.2	-0.1	-0.4	-3.3	-2.1	5.0	2.7	0.2	2.9
Netherlands	1.0	2.7	-1.7	0.6	0.6	0.5	-1.3	-3.1	-0.8	0.9	1.5	1.2
Portugal	3.9	4.1	3.5	1.2	1.7	1.5	-2.2	-4.1	0.4	1.5	-0.7	-0.4
UK	1.0	-0.8	-0.2	0.9	2.4	3.3	0.1	2.0	3.2	1.2	-0.2	-2.6
EU 12 (average)	2.6	1.9	1.4	1.3	1.7	1.2	-1.4	-0.1	-0.2	0.3	-0.1	-0.7
USA	1.1	0.2	-0.1	-0.2	2.4	1.2	0.0	-1.2	1.1	0.7	0.4	-1.1
Japan	4.5	2.7	3.0	2.3	0.3	0.2	-1.2	0.0	0.1	0.3	-0.1	-1.3

European Economy November/December 1993

Key words

Economic growth - an increase in the volume and/or quality of output (ie growth in real GDP)

Gross Domestic product (GDP) - the value of the total output produced by UK-owned resources

National income - the total income of all UK individuals and organizations, also measured as the value of GDP

Business cycle - continuous fluctuations in real GDP around some long-term trend rate of growth. Growth below trend is characteristic of economic recession, while growth above trend takes place during an economic boom

Newly industrialized countries - low-wage economies that are developing their industrial base and represent emerging markets for exports from developed economies such as the UK

Imports - flows of money out of the UK in payment for goods and services from overseas

Exports - flows of money into the UK in payment for UK goods and services sold abroad

UK exchange rate - the value of the UK currency sterling in exchange for currencies of other countries

Visible trade - overseas trade in physical commodities

Invisible trade - international trade in services

Balance of payments - the difference between flows of money into and out of the UK for the purpose of inward and outward investment or payment for exports and imports

Current account - the balance of trade in visibles and invisibles

Unit labour costs - the cost of labour per unit of output

Section **17.2** Government action to improve UK competitiveness

Government economic objectives

The UK government's overall economic objective is to promote sustained economic growth in the total output by establishing a stable economic environment for business, based on low and stable price inflation. The government argues that without this, uncertainty will stifle business and employment opportunities, and businesses will be discouraged from investing for the future and developing the products on which UK prosperity depends.

Low and stable price inflation

It is argued that high and volatile price inflation of the kind experienced during the 1970s destroyed jobs, stifled economic growth, and increased the demand for imports from countries with lower price inflation than the UK, thereby causing a balance of payments deficit. At one point, the annual rise in the average level of prices in the economy reached 25%.

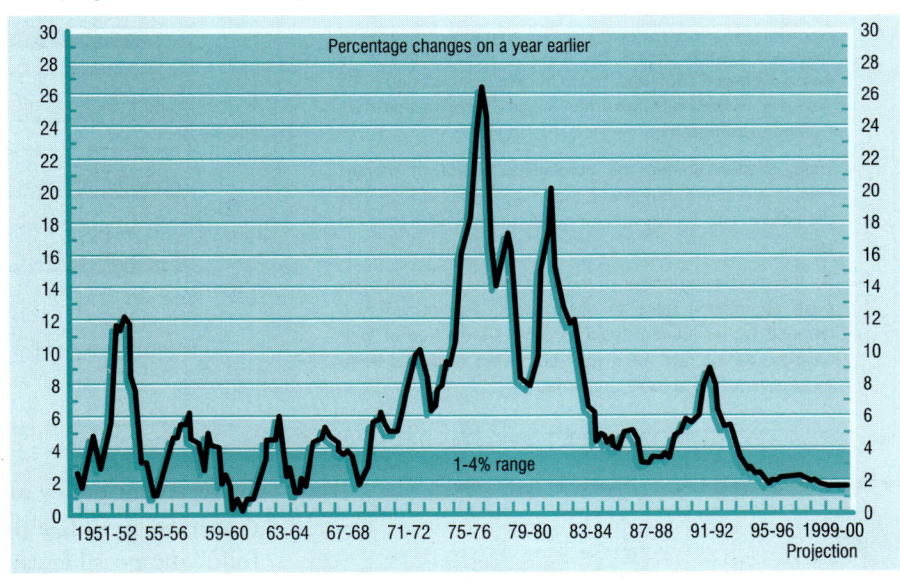

▼ Figure 17.14: Price inflation (percentage annual change in the Retail Prices Index)

Financial Statement and Budget Report (FSBR) 1995-1996 [1994-1995? - please check]

Measuring price inflation

Inflation may be defined as a general and sustained rise in the prices of goods and services. It is measured by calculating the percentage increase in the price level over successive time periods - per month, or per year.

The **Retail Price Index (RPI)** is the main 'headline' measure of price inflation in the UK. It expresses the percentage change in the average level of prices of a 'basket' of some 600 different goods and services, in terms of movement in a single number series. The goods and services in the 'basket' are selected as representative of those purchased by the 'average' UK household, based on a sample of 7,000 households. Approximately 150,000 price quotations are recorded each month by government statisticians from a large number of retail outlets across the UK.

In the **base year**, the average price of the RPI basket is assigned the number 100. If, on average, the price of the basket increased by 10% the following year, the RPI will be calculated as 110. If, over the next year, the average price of the basket rises by 12%, the RPI will be recorded as 123.2 (110 x 1.12).

Taking the year 1974 as a base, the RPI increased from 100 to 550 by 1994. That is, over this period, the prices of goods and services in the basket had, on average, increased by 5.5 times their original 1974 prices.

The **Producer Price Index (PPI)** is calculated from the price movements of approximately 11,000 materials and products purchased and manufactured by UK industry. Increases in material prices paid by producers are likely to feed through to retail prices after a time-lag.

Advanced Business

Since October 1992 the UK government has set an explicit target range for annual inflation of 1-4% that it wishes to achieve.

What is wrong with inflation?

The UK government argues that low inflation - and the confidence that it will be *kept* low - is essential for better economic performance and improved competitiveness. This is because:

- Inflation distorts the price signals in markets on which firms base their decisions about what goods and services to produce (see 1.4). Changes in relative prices become confused by general inflation. Even with general price inflation of only 5% per year, prices double every 14 years.

- High inflation creates uncertainty, which leads to reduced business investment in new plant and machinery - the engine of future economic growth. If firms are unsure about future prices and levels of inflation, they will be less willing to take risks and invest in long-term projects.

- High UK inflation relative to other countries reduces demand for UK exports, but increases the demand for cheaper overseas imports in the UK, thereby destroying jobs at home. Between 1989 and 1993 UK inflation averaged 5.7% per year, somewhat above her major European and non-European competitors.

- High inflation erodes the purchasing power of money. People are able to buy fewer goods and services than they did before, and so demand for goods and services tends to fall.

- As the purchasing power of money falls, lenders of money push up interest rates to compensate. Savers will also demand higher interest rates to protect the value of their savings. As interest rates rise, borrowing becomes more expensive for consumers and firms.

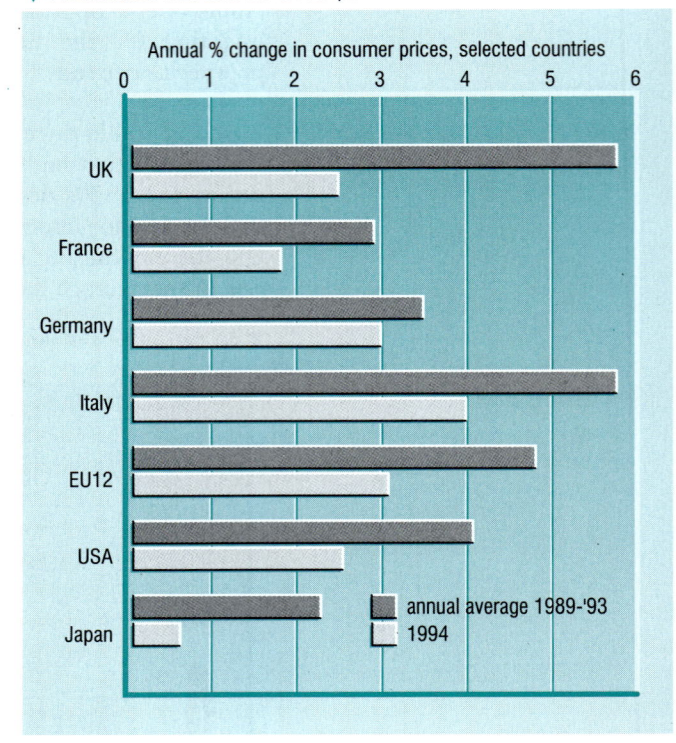

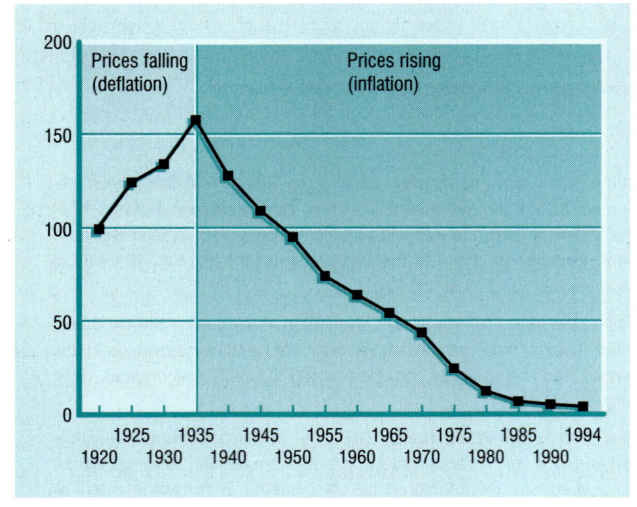

▼ Price inflation: How does the UK compare?

Annual % change in consumer prices, selected countries

(Bar chart showing UK, France, Germany, Italy, EU12, USA, Japan — annual average 1989-'93 and 1994)

▼ Figure 17.15: The purchasing power of £1, 1920-1994

(Line graph showing Prices falling (deflation) and Prices rising (inflation) from 1920 to 1994)

Barclays Bank Economic Review, Q1 1995

Government policy and inflation

Government policy for reducing inflation recognises the following possible causes of rising price inflation:

- **Demand pull inflation** occurs when the total demand for goods and services in the economy exceeds the total output or supply. As a result, prices will be forced up.

- **Cost push inflation** occurs when rising production costs are passed on to consumers in the form of higher prices. Production costs can rise either because workers push for wage increases above increases in productivity, or if the price of materials and components rise. Many economists believe that inflation rates in excess of 20% experienced in the UK in 1974 and 1979 were the result of massive crude oil price increases agreed by the main oil-producing nations.

- **Imported inflation** is said to occur as the result of a fall in value of UK sterling on the foreign exchange market. This will increase the price paid for materials, semi-finished, and finished manufactures, and services purchased from overseas.

Given these possible causes of inflationary pressure in the UK economy, the following government policy measures to control inflation have been developed;

- **Fiscal policy** to control rapid increases in demand for goods and services by raising taxes and/or lowering government spending (see 3.2)

- Using **interest rates** to stabilise the UK exchange rate to encourage exports and to reduce imported inflation (see 3.2)

- **Supply side policies** to improve the ability of UK industry to expand output to meet demand and to reduce business costs and prices. These include;

    – Reducing the size of government in terms of reducing the burden of taxation on consumers and producers and cutting government spending

    – Competition policy to encourage price competition between UK firms (see 3.4)

    – Privatisation: allowing private sector firms to produce goods and services formerly provided by central and local government (see 3.5)

    – Deregulation to remove out of date restrictions on competition and business

    – Promoting skills through investment in education and training

    – Support for innovation and new technology

    – Removing barriers to international trade (see 17.3)

    – Encouraging inward investment (see 17.3)

Fiscal policy

Fiscal policy has been used to control the level of total demand for goods and services in the economy. When demand was rising too fast causing prices to rise governments would raise taxes and lower government spending to reduce the incomes of consumers and business. For example, corporation tax on company profits could be increased to reduce the money they had available to pay to shareholders and to use to invest in new machinery. Incomes taxes could be raised to reduce the amount of income consumers had to spend, and VAT could be increased to increase the price of some goods and services so that consumers could not afford to buy so many of them.

Fiscal policy is still used today to control the level of aggregate demand in the economy. However, the conservative party government in the 1980s and early 1990s disliked trying to use fiscal policy to manage short run changes in the level of demand in the economy and instead placed more emphasis on reducing the size of government over the long term.

▼ Figure 17.16: General government expenditure as a percentage of GDP, UK 1901-1993

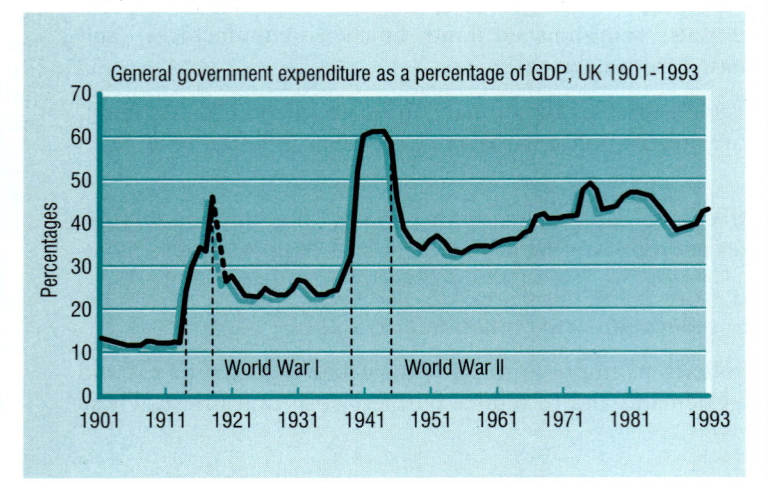

▼ Figure 17.17: Total taxes, as a percentage of GDP, UK 1970-1993

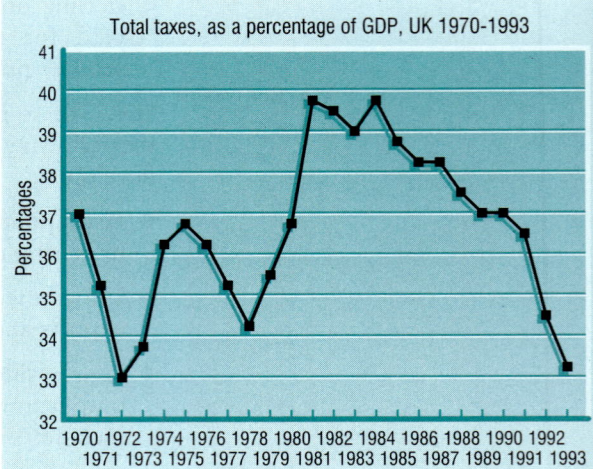

Social Trends 1995

FSBR 1995-96

Reducing the size of government

The present government is committed to reducing the 'size of government' in terms of the amount of total tax it takes from the national income and the proportion of total expenditure accounted for by public spending.

As part of this process, it is encouraging private-sector firms to run activities formerly operated by the government. The **Private Finance Initiative (PFI)** seeks to encourage private firms to build new infrastructure such as road and rail links, prisons, and health centres. Under the PFI, all government departments must consider private funding alternatives to public projects.

Ultimately the commitment to reduce government is linked to an aim to achieve a long-term balance between government spending and revenues and thereby reduce the need for government borrowing. It is argued that too much government borrowing 'crowds out' private-sector borrowing by firms, because the increased demand for borrowed funds by government forces up interest rates. As the cost of borrowing rises, firms tend to cut back their own investment plans.

Government spending as a proportion of GDP has fallen from a peak of over 60% during the Second World War to around 44% in 1994/95 (see Figure 17.16).

Reducing the burden of taxation

The UK government has argued that high income tax rates are a disincentive to greater effort by workers. High corporation tax rates on profits also discourage firms from investing, because any additional profits generated are swallowed up in tax. The government is therefore committed to reducing the burden of direct taxation on the incomes of employees and UK industry.

Since 1979, the burden of taxation has been shifted away from direct taxes on incomes and profits, to taxes on expenditure, such as VAT. However, total taxation as a proportion of national income has tended to rise over time (see Figure 17.17). In 1978, 34.5 pence in the pound was paid in all taxes and National Insurance contributions. By 1984, this had risen to nearly 40 pence in the pound.

Despite the desire to reduce the burden of taxation, the government in fact announced significant tax increases in the 1993 and 1994 budgets. The evidence at the time was that the UK economy had begun to recover from economic recession. The tax increases were therefore designed to control the increase in aggregate demand for goods and services and prevent demand from outstripping supply and leading to higher price inflation, before firms had time to expand their productive capacity.

Interest rates were also on an upward trend, with the government announcing increases in late 1994 and early 1995 in an effort to control rising consumer borrowing and to stabilize the pound.

Stabilizing the exchange rate

Fears of higher price inflation in the UK tends to place downward pressure on the sterling exchange rate. This is because overseas investors, anticipating a fall in the purchasing power of their money held in the UK, will withdraw their investments and sell UK pounds in return for other currencies. As with any other good or service, an increased supply of UK pounds on the world currency market will push down their price. A fall in the value of sterling will raise import prices, and the cost of many raw materials and finished goods will rise also.

UK Sterling Exchange Rates 21.2.95

What the £1 is worth overseas…

Fr	48.043
Fr	8.12
m	2.333
Kr	10.2596
ra	2528
eseta	203.726
	1.583
$	2.226
en	153.505
$	2.511
hekel	4.773
and	6.0769

Portfolio Activity 17.4

Range: Government strategies, Evaluate
Skills: Collect and record data

1. What, according to the article, are the reasons for upward pressure on prices?
2. Explain why 'economists say this adds to the case for an early rise in interest rates'.
3. Suggest the likely impact of an increase in interest rates on the demand for investment and exports.
4. What other measures could the government use to control inflationary pressures? Explain your answers.
5. Investigate the use of fiscal and monetary policy to control the economy. Research your answer from financial and business newspaper articles, and news reports.
6. Using the table of exchange rates above, try to find out which country uses which currency. How have these exchange rates changed over time? Find up-to-date data from newspapers and CSO *Economic Trends*. What do the changes in exchange rates against UK sterling imply about the competitiveness of UK exports?

Borrowers could pay for rising prices at the factory gate

INFLATION fears have risen again after a survey showed another sharp rise in manufacturing industry prices last month. Demand is growing so fast that an increasing number of firms are having trouble keeping up and are raising their prices. Economists say this adds to the case for an early rise in interest rates.

Inflationary pressure is being stoked up by rising costs and shortages of raw materials, according to the Chartered Institute of Purchasing and Supply. Peter Thompson, Director General of the Institute, said: "This strong recovery presents a great opportunity for manufacturers. However, they urgently need to increase capacity and shorten delivery times to consumers if they are to take full advantage of growing demand."

Daily Mail 1.9.94

Interest rates can be used to stabilize the value of the UK currency on world currency markets. Raising interest rates will attract foreign investment to the UK. As foreign currencies are exchanged for UK pounds, the increased demand causes the value of sterling to rise.

Supply-side policies

The aim of government supply-side policies is to free individual markets of imperfections, so as to allow producers to operate and expand more effectively.

Competition policy

This concerns the removal of restrictions to free competition which in turn inhibit market supply, output, and employment. Anti-competitive behaviour in UK markets, such as price-fixing agreements by dominant firms, can be investigated by the Office of Fair Trading, and by the Monopolies and Mergers Commission, who can also recommend corrective measures (see 3.4).

Privatization

This involves the transfer of public-sector activities provided by the government to the private sector. Privatization programmes have involved the sale of state-owned utilities such as British Gas and the regional water boards to private shareholders, and the contracting-out of services such as catering, cleaning, and computer maintenance in hospitals and government departments (see 3.5).

Supporters of privatization argue that such public-sector concerns were often overmanned and inefficient, because they faced no competition and did not have to return a profit. Competition to supply these services for profit therefore improves quality and efficiency. Others argue that privatization has created private monopolies that have increased their profit by exploiting consumers.

Deregulation

The process of removing government restrictions on business and free competition is known as **deregulation**. The Deregulation and Contracting Out Act 1994 aims to remove some 450 statutory regulations on business, ranging from restrictions on opening hours and the sale of methylated spirits, to the licensing of employment agencies (see 3.4). The removal of these restrictions should reduce business costs.

Support for innovation and new technology

The government recognizes the need for research and development (R&D) and implementation of new technologies in UK industry to keep pace with that of our main competitors. New technology can improve the speed, accuracy, and quality of production, and hence release resources that can be used productively elsewhere and reduce costs.

However, the cost of R&D and the implementation of new technology can be high, and the payback in terms of lower costs and increased revenues slow to materialize. In the meantime, uncertainty about the economy, particularly price inflation and exchange-rate and interest-rate stability, can reduce firms incentive to invest in new products, equipment and methods.

Innovation and technology: how does the UK measure up?

Innovation is the successful exploitation of new ideas and technologies. Many innovative UK companies, and some sectors, are world-class:

- UK consumption of medicines accounts for over 3% of the world market, yet the UK produces 5% of the world's needs. Research for 6 out of the top 20 bestselling drugs in 1991/92 was carried out in the UK
- The UK aeronautics industry leads the world in the design and manufacture of advanced systems. The first ever 'fly-by-night' control systems were developed in the UK.
- A medium-sized UK company has won 40% of the world market with an innovative gas-sensing product.

But the need for improvement is shown in a number of ways:

- UK industrial R&D expenditure as a proportion of GDP has fallen behind that of some other leading economies (see Figure 17.18).
- Technical qualifications tend to be less common and less well-rewarded in the UK than in other countries.
- Of a sample of companies surveyed in 1992, one-third had not introduced new technology (automation or flexible manufacturing systems) since 1989, and had no plans to do so.

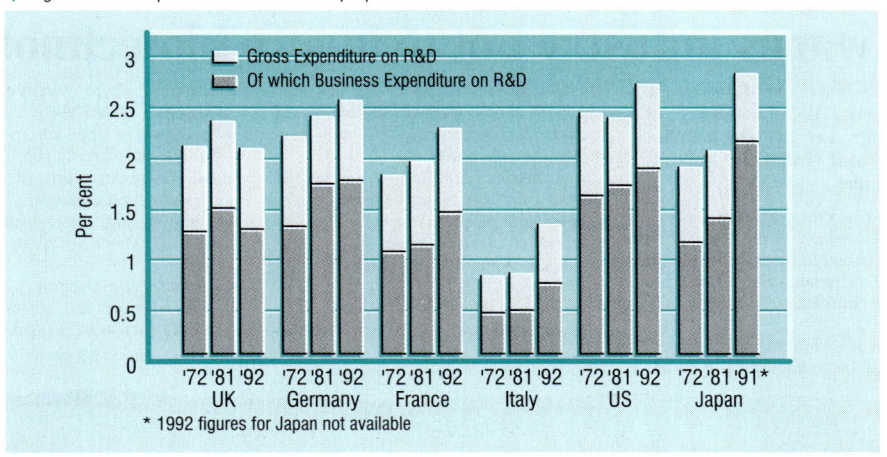

▼ *Figure 17.18: Expenditure on R&D as a proportion of GDP*

Competitiveness - Helping Business to Win (HMSO 1994)

The government is able to encourage firms to invest in R&D and new technologies by providing a stable economic environment, and through a number of other measures:

- Enabling capital expenditure on research and new technology to be offset against corporation tax on company profits.
- Providing funding for skills training in new technologies
- Funding R&D by the science and engineering base (i.e. universities and research establishments), and research commissioned by government departments
- Establishing the **Technology Foresight Programme** to identify opportunities and examine market developments and technological capabilities within the UK
- Providing advice, networking between support organizations at a local and national level, and access to international research programmes, new insights, practices, and technology developed overseas
- Establishing **Business Links** advice centres ('Business Shops' in Scotland) to provide support to UK firms
- Funding specialist Innovation and Technology counsellors in Business Links

Advanced Business

• Encouraging technology transfer partnerships between university departments and industry

Portfolio Activity 17.5

Range: Government strategies, Evaluate
Skills: Read and respond to written material, Produce written material, Collect and record data

1. What are the potential benefits to UK firms and the economy as a whole of the increased application of biotechnology in industry?

2. What reasons might be given by UK firms for not investing as heavily as the DTi would like in biotechnology?

3. Suggest possible government initiatives that could be used to promote increased investment in biotechnology.

4. Investigate sources of support and advice in the UK for firms who may wish to make use of biotechnology. Prepare an information pamphlet to advertise the potential benefits to firms of using such new technologies, and where they can find help.

DTI warns industry not to ignore biotechnology

Much of industry is damagingly ignorant of the benefits of biotechnology, say two Department of Trade and Industry reports published today.

The UK had a strong science base in biotechnology, which is the application of biologically active substances such as bacteria and enzymes, but its use has largely been limited to medicine and agriculture.

The department is "looking at initiatives" to encourage biotechnology's use. Mr Michael Heseltine, trade and industry secretary, quoted forecasts that the world markets for biotechnology could pass £60bn a year by 2000.

The industries identified as having the most to gain from biotechnology were:

• Paper and allied products, where, for example, enzymes could be used to turn low grade raw materials into high grade paper.
• Textiles, in which enzymes could help improve fabric quality and waste disposal.
• Leather, where tanning still uses dangerous chemicals.
• Food, where applications range from the non-mechanical pulping of apples and desegmentation of oranges to contamination detection.
• Metals mining, where bacteria could be used to extract useful materials from rock.
• Oil and gas extraction, where bacteria could change the structure of oil-bearing rock to help expel oil and gas.

Financial Times 16.2.95

What is Investment?

Investment is defined as the act of buying new and often improved plant and machinery by private and public sector business organizations. Investment spending is, therefore, a source of demand and revenue for producers of business premises, machinery and other man-made resources. Investment spending is also known as **gross domestic fixed capital formation**.

Some investment expenditure will be to buy new assets to replace man-made resources - premises, machinery and other equipment - which are old, worn out and no longer productive. Simply replacing old equipment does not add to the ability of firms to increase their output. However, investment in new and additional premises, machinery and other equipment will expand productive capacity.

New investment by business is, therefore, essential if the productive capability of the UK economy is to grow. Investment in new technologies can also mean faster, more efficient production, less wasteful and better quality production. This can lower the cost of producing each unit of a good or service and, therefore, improve the competitiveness of UK industry.

It is often argued that UK firms are reluctant to invest compared to other countries because business owners are often uncertain about the profits they will earn from new investment. For example, in 1993 UK industry invested a total of £111 billion in man made resources, the equivalent of some 15.5% of the total value of UK output of all goods and services. This compared to around 31% of total output in Japan and 22% in Germany (see table 17.3). This suggests that these other countries are devoting a far larger proportion of their total national outputs to investment in new plant and machinery than the UK. However, these figures do not tell us how much of that spending is to replace old and worn out equipment or to increase productive capacity.

▼ Table 17.3 : Gross domestic fixed capital formation, as a % of GDP in selected countries

	1970	1980	1990	1993
United Kingdom	18.9	18.0	19.3	15.5
Germany	25.5	22.6	21.0	21.4
France	24.3	23.0	21.2	19.6
Portugal	23.2	20.2	26.4	25.4
Italy	24.3	24.3	20.2	19.3
EU12*	23.8	22.0	20.9	19.6
USA	18.0	20.2	16.8	15.3
Japan	32.2	31.6	32.2	31.2

* average of the 12 members of the European Union prior to 1.1.95 (see 17.3)

Improving education and training

In order to compete successfully in international markets, it is essential to have a highly trained and skilled workforce. Skill needs in industry are rising as competition and the pace of change in technology increase (see 16.4).

A well-trained workforce can have the following benefits for business:

- **Increased productivity and profitability.** Training can help employees achieve maximum efficiency.

- **A flexible and multi-skilled workforce.** Well-trained personnel will be able to adapt more easily to new products, technology, and production processes.

- **Improved job satisfaction.** Training motivates staff and enables them to derive greater satisfaction from their work. This will help firms retain staff with skills appropriate to their future needs.

- **Reduced accidents and injuries.** Workers who are properly trained in health and safety procedures and able to operate machinery and materials correctly are less likely to be absent from work due to illness or injury.

- **Improved company image** - and therefore, enhanced recruitment potential.

According to the government publication *Training Statistics 1993*, over 3 million employees in Great Britain - around 14.5% of all employees - received some form of job-related training in the four weeks prior to data collection (see Figure 17.19). This compared to some 1.8 million employees, or 9.4% of all employees, reported as receiving training in 1984. This growth in training was particularly evident among young people and women.

According to the report:

- Off-the-job training was the most popular method. Around 70% of people of working age provided with training in the UK did so 'off-the-job' in colleges and other external training organizations.

- Professional and technical occupations tended to receive the most training. Machine operatives and people involved in sales tended to receive the least amount of training.

- Training was more widespread in services, such as banking and insurance, than in manufacturing and construction industries.

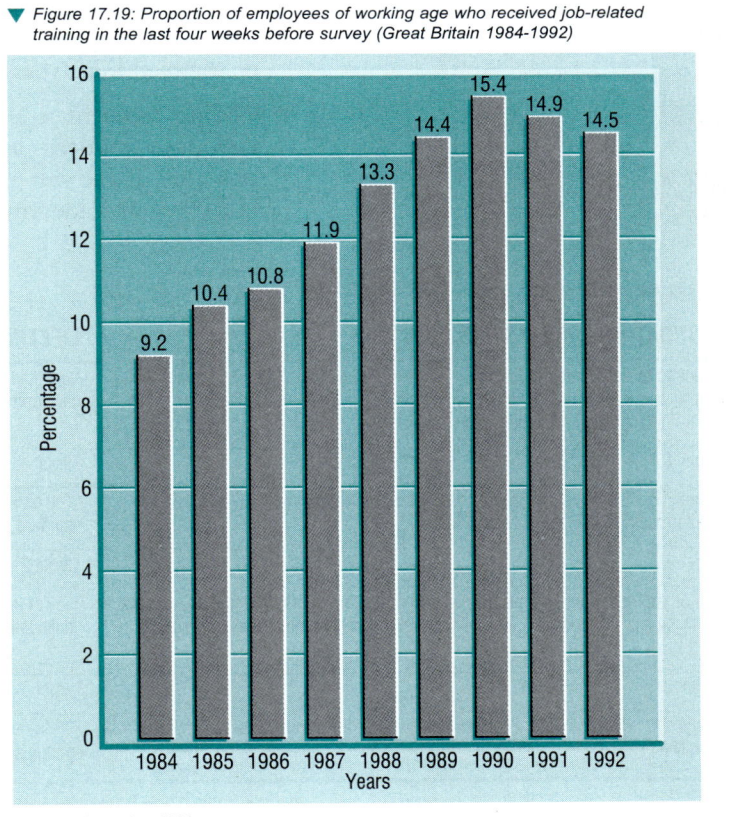

▼ Figure 17.19: Proportion of employees of working age who received job-related training in the last four weeks before survey (Great Britain 1984-1992)

Year	Percentage
1984	9.2
1985	10.4
1986	10.8
1987	11.9
1988	13.3
1989	14.4
1990	15.4
1991	14.9
1992	14.5

Training Statistics 1993

The UK government has taken a number of steps to improve productivity and labour force flexibility through skills training for those in work and the unemployed. Without government intervention, there would be no market for training people without a job, unless they could afford to pay for it.

- Some 82 **Training and Enterprise Councils (TECs)** in England and Wales, and **Local Enterprise Councils (LECs)** in Scotland have been established. The TECs and LECs are managed by employer representatives, and each controls a large training budget funded by central government to pay for work-related further education in its area.

- The government has encouraged the formation of over 120 employer-led **Industry Training Organizations (ITOs),** representing the training interests of around 85% of employees in the UK, ranging from The Biscuit, Cake, Chocolate and Confectionary Alliance to the Security Industry Training Organization Ltd. ITOs cover most industrial sectors. Their objectives are to develop and promote occupational standards, monitor future skill needs, and encourage employers to increase training efforts.

- The government has set ambitious **National Education and Training Targets (NETTS)** for **National Vocational Qualifications (NVQs), General NVQs** and their Scottish equivalents, for the whole workforce.

- **Youth training schemes (YTS)** continue to be the main training route for young people leaving school at 16 or 17. A place on a YTS is guaranteed for 2 years to any young person who is unable to find a job.

- The government is also working with employers, TECs, and ITOs to introduce **modern apprenticeships** for 16-19-year-olds from 1995 onwards. These will offer work-based training to NVQ level 3 or higher in particular trades and skills, such as engineering or carpentry.

▼ *National Education and Training Targets (NETTs)*

FOUNDATION TARGETS FOR 2000	**LIFETIME TARGETS FOR 2000**
Designed to set standards for improving basic attainment levels by young people, and to encourage more young people to continue their education and training through to higher qualifications	Designed to encourage all employees and employers to put training and development at the heart of their strategy for improving performance
Target 1	Target 1
By age 19, 85% of young people to achieve 5 GCSE's at grade C or above, an Intermediate GNVQ or an NVQ level 2	60% of workforce to be qualified to NVQ level 3, Advanced GNVQ or 2 GCE A level standard
Target 2	Target 2
75% of young people to achieve level 2 competence in communication, numeracy and IT by age 19; and 35% to achieve level 3 competence in these core skills by age 21	30% of workforce to have a vocational, professional, management or academic qualification at NVQ level 4 or above
Target 3	Target 3
By age 21, 60% of young people to achieve 2 GCE A levels, and Advanced GNVQ or an NVQ level 3	70% of all organizations employing 200 or more employees, and 35% of those employing 50 or more, to be recognised as Investors in People

- **Training credits** were introduced in 1991, and by 1995/96 will be offered to every 16- and 17-year-old school or college leaver, who can use them to obtain YTS or modern apprenticeships from an employer or other recognized training provider. Similarly, **learning credits** will be provided to 16-19-year-olds to give them the power to buy their own education and training from schools, colleges, employers, and other providers. TECs can tailor the courses on offer to influence occupational choice and help tackle skill shortages.

Portfolio activity 17.6

Range: Government strategies
Skills: Produce written materials, Collect and record data

Produce a series of pamphlets to advertise the types of education and training courses and qualifications available, and their benefits, to the following groups of people:

- 16- to 19-year-old school leavers
- Full-time and part-time employees over 20 years of age
- The long-term unemployed

Details in your pamphlets should be based on your own investigations of courses and qualifications available, and how to gain access to them. Useful sources of information will include:

- Your local TEC/LEC
- ITOs
- Further Education colleges
- Government departments (e.g. Education, Employment, and Trade and Industry)

Key words

Inflation - a sustained increase in the general level of prices, usually measured as a rate of increase

Retail Prices Index (RPI) - a record of the average price level of a representative selection of some 600 household goods and services over time. Changes in the RPI per period provide the headline rate of price inflation in the UK

Producer Prices Index (PPI) - a record of movement in the average price of some 11,000 materials used in manufacturing

Gross fixed capital formation - investment in new and replacement plant and machinery

Private Finance Initiative (PFI) - a government initiative to encourage private-sector organizations to fund activities previously operated by the public sector

Business Links - the DTi business advice shops

Youth Training Scheme (YTS) - on-the-job training provided to all under-19s not in full-time education or a job

Training credits - vouchers that can be exchanged in return for training services provided by colleges and other providers

---

Section 17.3

Government action and international trade

Trade Policy

Markets are becoming increasingly global as real incomes rise in countries all over the world. UK business will be unable to keep pace with international competitors without easy access to overseas markets. Eliminating barriers to free trade and cross-border investment will increase business and consumer choice, and reduce the cost of goods and services.

The UK trade policy operates as part of the **European Union (EU) Common Competition Policy**, while the EU operates within the **General Agreement on Tariffs and Trade (GATT)**, now being taken further in the new **World Trade Organization (WTO)**.

The European Union

The European Community (EC) began in 1958 when six countries - We[st] Germany, Italy, France, Belgium, the Netherlands, and Luxembourg signed the Treaty of Rome, committing themselves to the formation of [a] common market.

By 1993, the UK, Spain, Portugal, Greece, Eire, and Denmark had als[o] joined, making a total of 12 member states (the 'EU12') and forming [a] market of over 350 million people.

On 1 January 1995, the number of EC countries increased to 15, a[s] Austria, Finland, and Sweden became full members. Turkey and Cypru[s] have also applied for membership, with many more considering joining, such as the former communist countries of Poland and Hungary. Since February 1992 the EC has become known as the European Union (EU).

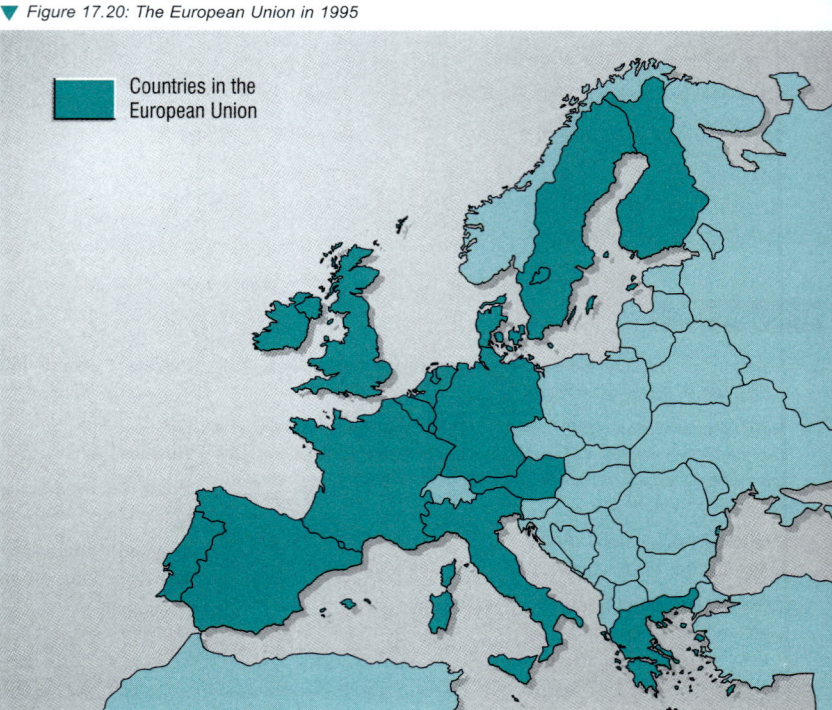

▼ *Figure 17.20: The European Union in 1995*

Decision-making in the EU

There are five main groups which influence decision-making and ensure that decisions are upheld in the EU:

- The **European Commission** is the executive of the EU and makes proposals on policy and legislation.
- The **Council of Ministers** is made up of foreign secretaries from the governments of each member state, who are responsible for all major community decisions on such issues as industry, transport, agriculture, and finance.
- The **European Parliament** consists of elected members from all over the EU. The EU Parliament has powers to approve or recommend changes to the Council's position, but has no powers of veto.
- The **Economic and Social Committee** acts in an advisory capacity to the Council. It is made up of employees, Trade Unions, and independent representatives of the member states.
- The **European Court of Justice** ensures that EU laws are observed in member states and deals with any disputes.

EU objectives

The EU has a number of broad objectives which will dramatically alter the way in which people live and conduct business.

To form a customs union

The EU to be a **customs union** whereby:

- Participating members agree not to place tariffs on goods and services imported from other EU member countries
- EC member countries establish a common external tariff on all goods imported from non-EU countries

The common external tariff is designed to protect business and jobs in the EU from cheap imports from outside the EU. A **tariff** is simply a tax on imports imposed by the importing country to reduce domestic demand for foreign goods. Tariff rates applied to the price of imported goods and services have to be the same in each EU country. If the UK applied a 20% tariff to the price of imports from non-EU countries, while France only applied a 10% tariff, a Japanese firm exporting to the UK could first export their products to France and then ship them to the UK without incurring extra tax.

To encourage freedom of movement

In addition to the removal of tariffs between member countries, the EU aims to remove all barriers to the free movement of goods and services, capital, and people across EU borders. People in the EU should be free to live and work in any member state and be entitled to the same conditions of employment, health care, and social security benefits as anyone else in their chosen member country.

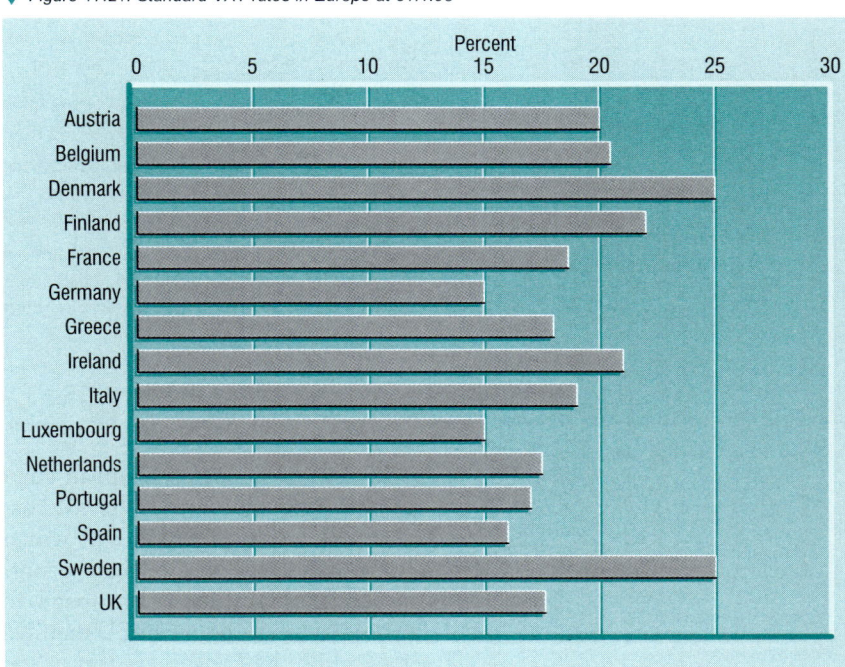

▼ *Figure 17.21: Standard VAT rates in Europe at 31.1.95*

To establish a Single European Market

Although the customs union had been in existence for 30 years, many no[n] tariff barriers to trade remained between EU member countries. The Sing[le] European Market Act 1986 set an agenda and timetable for the removal [of] all other barriers to trade and the free movement of goods, service[s,] capital, and people.

The **Single European Market** (or internal market) came into force [at] midnight 1 January 1993. Member states are now actively workin[g] towards the removal of such barriers to movement and free trade as:

- Frontier checks at custom posts
- Cumbersome importing documentation designed to raise importin[g] costs
- Differential national product and safety standards
- The application of separate - and sometimes unnecessary - health check[s]
- Major differences in indirect taxation, such as rates of value added ta[x,] excise duties and duty-free allowances.

To create economic and monetary union

The European Union (EU) was formally agreed on 7 February 1992, whe[n] individual member governments signed the Maastricht Treaty. The mai[n] focus of the agreement was the creation of a framework for Europea[n] Economic and Monetary Union (EMU), involving the creation of a singl[e] currency and common economic policy by 1 January 1999.

EMU: a three-stage plan

Progress towards European Economic and Monetary Union involves the following three-stage plan:

1. Increased coordination of fiscal and monetary policy between EU members, and completion of the internal market
2. A gradual transfer of economic decision-making power from national central banks, such as the UK Bank of England and the German Bundesbank, to a new single European Central Bank
3. Fixing the value of exchange rates between EU member currencies, a single European monetary policy, and the eventual replacement of national currencies by a single **European Currency Unit (ECU)**.

The Maastricht Treaty states that member states wishing to join EMU Stage 3 must meet the following conditions:

- **Inflation:** annual average price inflation to be within 1.5% of the rate of price inflation of the three EU member states where it is lowest
- **Interest rates:** average long-term interest rates over 1 year to be within 2% of rates in the same three member states
- **Budget deficit:** member states must not have a deficit between public expenditure and tax revenues that is considered 'excessive'
- **Exchange rates:** the national currency of the member country must have been within the narrow band of the European **Exchange Rate Mechanism (ERM)** for at least two years

---

The issue of a single european currency and common economic policy i[n] the EU is controversial. The UK has argued that it will not be bound by th[e] treaty deadline in 1999, and will only fix its exchange rate and adopt [a] single currency if the right economic conditions prevail. The ECU i[s] already used by large European firms and governments to receive an[d] make payments between EU member states, but it will only be available for general use by consumers if it is adopted as the EU currency.

UNIT FIVE

CHAPTER 17

The ultimate aim of 'political union' between EU members is also contentious, involving the eventual harmonization of such non-economic issues as defence, law, education, and health.

The European Exchange Rate Mechanism (ERM)

The ERM is usually regarded as the first step towards economic and monetary union in the EU. It is a system which requires member states to agree, and then 'fix', exchange rates between their currencies. Interest rates could be used to stabilize currency rates. Central banks in EU member countries would also buy up, or sell, a particular EU member currency, in order to raise or lower its value, if necessary, to keep it at the agreed exchange rate.

Exchange rates in the ERM are pegged to the value of the strongest currency in terms of its value against the currencies of non-EU member countries. For many years, the strongest currency in the system was the German Deutschmark, primarily a reflection of the strength of, and confidence in, the German economy. When sterling joined the ERM in October 1990, the value of the UK currency was fixed at £1 = 2.95 Dm. As the value of the Dm appreciates or depreciates against non-EU currencies, so too will all the other currencies tied to it in the ERM. Thus, if £1 = 2.95 Dm = US$1.5, then an appreciation of the Dm would take their values to say 2.95 Dm = US$1.7 = £1.

In practice, currencies in the ERM are allowed to fluctuate within a narrow band (+/-2.5%) around the strongest currency. Recognized as weaker currencies, UK sterling, the Spanish peseta, the Italian lira and Portuguese escudo were allowed to fluctuate within 6% either side of the strongest currency. Sterling, however, left the ERM in September 1993 when interest rates and central bank intervention to buy up pounds failed to stabilize the value of the UK currency, which fell rapidly below the agreed lower band around the Dm.

▼ Figure 17.22: How the ERM works

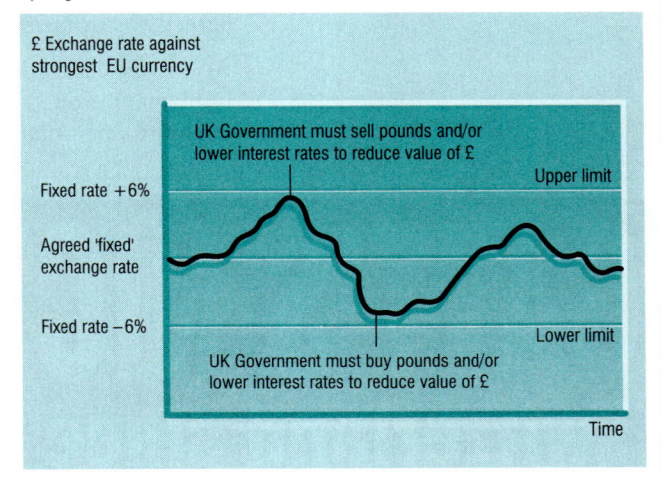

Portfolio Activity 17.7

Range: Government strategies, Evaluate
Skills: Read and respond to written material, Collect and record data

1. What do you think were Bellina's motives in expanding into European markets?

2. How does your understanding of competitiveness help explain how a UK company is able to sell Belgian chocolates to Belgium?

3. With reference to Bellina from the article below, and an organization of your choice, discuss the impact of the Single European Market on their activities.

4. Research and discuss how economic and monetary union, including the introduction of a possible single currency in the EU, may affect government and business in the UK, and trading with Europe.

Belgian Chocolates to Belgium

Mr Ken Ball makes 225,000 Belgian chocolates each week in Ipswich - and now is selling some of them back to Belgium. "We used to send over an empty truck to collect basic ingredients, but now it goes out loaded with chocolates," he says.

Mr Ball, owner-director of Bellina, is modest about his small company's achievements in selling 80 varieties of chocolates - all but the sugar having been imported from Belgium first - to continental markets.

Mr Ball's wife Jennett was responsible for starting the business in 1983 when she opened a shop selling Belgian chocolates in 1983. By 1986, supply problems encouraged the couple to produce their own.

The arrival of the single market at the end of 1992 prompted Bellina to consider other European markets for the first time and the company enlisted the help of the DTi in pursuing contacts. Visits were made to meet importers and to identify the scale and nature of the market.

A decision was taken to give the Continent a try, and now the company is selling to the Netherlands and France as well as Belgium.

Financial Times 21.2.95

Advanced Business

The General Agreement on Tariffs and Trade (GATT)

GATT was established by 23 countries in 1947 with the aim of negotiating mutual reductions in tariffs and restrictions to free trade.

GATT membership has now grown to 117 countries. The latest round of negotiations, which started in 1986 in Uruguay, concluded on 15 December 1993 with the signing of an historic agreement in Switzerland between participating members, including the UK. Its 28 separate accords extended fair trade rules for the first time to agriculture, textiles, services, intellectual property, and foreign investment. Member countries have agreed to cut tariffs on industrial products by a third.

A newly-created **World Trade Organization** will oversee the implementation of the GATT Uruguay round agreements and continue to promote open markets in international trade.

GATT'S NICE
The best thing to come out of Switzerland since the cuckoo clock

| **DOWN** Food prices will be cut | **DOWN** Imported drugs 12% cheaper | **DOWN** £25 annual saving on electrical goods | **DOWN** New jobs will cut dole queues |

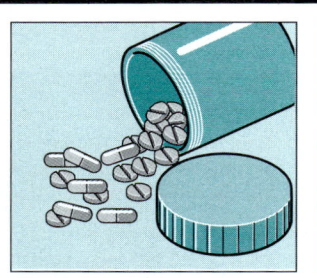

TRADE TRUCE MEANS CHEAPER PRICES AND 400,000 NEW JOBS

CONSUMERS looking for bargains should have their eyes on Geneva today rather than the early winter sales in their high street.

The GATT trade talks in Switzerland may seem like mumbo jumbo from grey men in a boring country but they are vitally important – because they could lead to cheaper prices and thousands of new jobs.

The aim of GATT – the General Agreement on Tariffs and Trade – is to cut the taxes on imports and the subsidies which the 116 negotiating countries currently operate to protect their own industries.

The results would be good news for consumers. Beef prices will fall by 20p a pound, butter by 6p, and the price of a loaf by 3.5p as a direct result of a successful deal.

Experts estimate the average Briton will save £25 a year simply on electronic goods when the deal takes full effect.

Tax on imports into Britain and the rest of the EU will be slashed in exchange for similar moves by the US, Japan and other countries.

Consumers won't be the only people to benefit from the biggest trade deal in history.

Independent experts predict as many as 400,000 jobs in Britain alone will be created within the next six years because of the boost to world trade from the deal – estimated at £142 billion by the end of century.

There will be losers in Britain and all other countries.

Firms who can't sell abroad will find their domestic market under attack from cheaper foreign imports once duty is removed.

It is bound to mean that less competitive firms will close.

But the stakes the negotiators have been playing for in Geneva and around the world since the present negotiations opened back in 1986 are even higher.

Failure to reach a new deal by the December 15 deadline would lead to a vicious trade war with the world's three great trading blocs – the EU, Far East and North America – safeguarding their own industries by keeping out foreign imports.

Daily Mirror 15.12.93

▼ Figure 17.23: Main recipients of US and Japanese investments in the EU

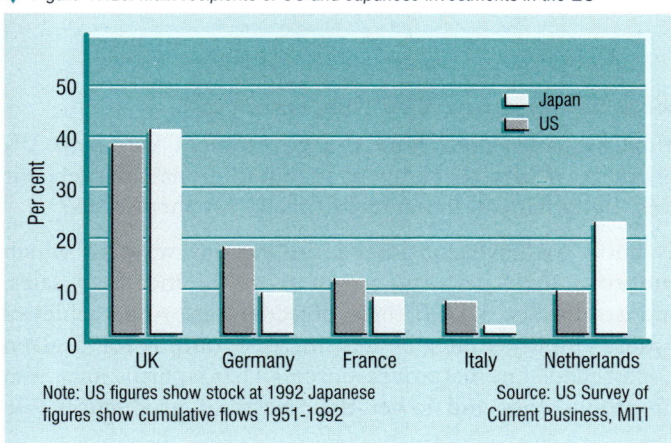

[Bar chart showing per cent of Japanese and US investment by country: UK ~39% Japan, ~42% US; Germany ~18% Japan, ~10% US; France ~12% Japan, ~8% US; Italy ~7% Japan, ~3% US; Netherlands ~10% Japan, ~23% US.]

Note: US figures show stock at 1992 Japanese figures show cumulative flows 1951-1992
Source: US Survey of Current Business, MITI

Competitiveness: Helping Business to Win (HMSO, 1994)

Encouraging inward investment

UK government policy is to encourage both inward and outward investment.

Inward investment refers to the setting up of foreign-owned multinational companies in the UK. By far the biggest foreign investors in the UK are US and Japanese companies. The UK attracts over 40% of all US and Japanese investment in the EU (see Figure 17.23).

Outward investment refers to UK investment overseas. The setting up of UK companies abroad provides access to foreign consumers, allowing UK-owned business to sell more goods overseas and improve the balance of international payments.

The government publication Competitiveness: Helping Business to Win (HMSO, 1994) suggests inward investment has the following benefits:

'Inward investment brings world-class production techniques, technical innovation and managerial skills, which can be transferred to local companies. It has revived the international competitiveness of some sectors of UK industry, such as vehicles.'

Japanese inward investment

Japanese inward investment in the UK vehicle industry has been substantial, with total planned investment of over £2 billion creating over 7,000 direct jobs. Production capacity has increased by around 400,000 cars, predominantly for export. The arrival of world-class Japanese manufacturers, with associated component suppliers, in three areas of England (the North East, Derbyshire, the M4 corridor) and North Wales, has spurred established producers to greater efforts. Continuous improvement has resulted in higher productivity, improved quality, and increased reliability of parts.

▲ Nissan: an example of Japanese investment in the UK

Key words

European Union (EU) - organization of European countries, formerly the European Community, which seeks closer economic and political union between members

Customs union - a group of countries with free trade between them and a common external tariff, like that of the EU

Tariff - a tax placed on an imported good

Single European Market - an agreement by EU member countries to remove all barriers to free trade between them

General Agreement on Tariffs and Trade (GATT) - organization which seeks to promote free trade between member countries

World Trade Organization (WTO) - established to oversee recent GATT agreements and to further promote free trade

Inward investment - the setting up of foreign-owned enterprise in the UK

Outward investment - UK investment overseas

Section 17.4 **Business strategies**

What can businesses do to improve their competitiveness?

In the last section we considered how the government can help UK industry to improve its ability to compete in international markets for goods and services. But what can individual firms do for themselves?

Throughout this book we have considered the various ways in which businesses can improve their performance in terms of increased sales, market shares and profits (see 4.1). If these objectives are to be achieved then businesses must employ strategies that increase output for a given input of human, man-made and natural resources. That is, firms must aim to improve their productivity and lower their costs of production (see 15.1).

Strategies firms have been using to improve their ability to compete for customers and market share include;

- investing in new faster and more efficient machinery and production processes. For example, new technologies such as robotics and computers have revolutionised many manufacturing processes (see 15.3).

- expanding the scale of production to spread fixed costs, such as rent, rates, insurance and other overheads, over a larger output and thereby lowering the average cost per unit of output (see 'economies of scale' 20.2).

- increasing marketing efforts to increase sales, expand market shares and to enter new markets (see 8.1). Marketing will also include using market research to find out about changing consumer wants and the development of new and existing products to satisfy their wants (see 9.1).

- training employees to improve and broaden their skills, and introducing more efficient working methods, for example, team working, quality circles and flexitime (see 13.4 and 15.4).

- Re-designing jobs to improve employee motivation (see 15.4) and increasing the flexibility of human resources by introducing more part-time and temporary employment contracts (see 16.3).

- streamlining administrative procedures and changing the structure of the organization to improve the communication of information on which business decisions are made and the speed at which decisions are implemented by employees (see 4.4).

- cost control by monitoring spending by individual departments, negotiating discounts with suppliers, changing the method of business finance from high cost loans to cheaper sources of funds (see 22.2).

A firm will be able to judge the effectiveness of these strategies on their business performance in terms of;

- increased market shares
- higher sales volumes and revenues
- lower labour costs and improved productivity
- improved products and service quality

For the UK as a whole, the effectiveness of both business and government strategies will be measured in terms of meeting the following objectives;

- economic growth in the national output
- increased levels of employment
- increased export volumes and revenues
- an increased share of the world export market
- low and stable inflation
- an increased standard of living, as measured by the growth in incomes, a wider choice of goods and services, better quality goods and services and less wasteful, more environmentally friendly production

Further reading:

Competitiveness - Helping Business to Win (HMSO 1994)

Competitiveness - Forging Ahead (HMSO 1995)

Bennett, R: Selling in Europe (Kogan Page 1994)

Test Questions

The following underpinning knowledge will be tested:

1. Compare the performance of the UK economy with major competitors
2. Business strategies to improve competitiveness
3. Government strategies to improve competitiveness
4. Evaluate business and government strategies.

1 A common measure used for international comparisons of workforce performance is:

　A The total number or workers employed in the service sector

　B Unit labour costs

　C Basic holiday entitlements and hours of work

　D Average earnings

2 The value of output per worker employed in the UK has more than doubled since the early 1960s. The most likely reason for this is:

　A An increase in the working population

　B Falling prices

　C A shorter working week

　D Technological advance

Questions 3-5 share the following answer options:

　A Imported inflation

　B Cost push inflation

　C Demand pull inflation

　D Deflation

Which of the above types of price inflation will the following changes tend to give rise to?

3 Rising real wages outstripping labour productivity improvements

4 Rising aggregate demand for goods and services outstripping the growth in total supply

5 A fall in the value of UK sterling on the world foreign currency markets

6 Which of the following is an invisible import to the UK?

　A UK machinery sold abroad

　B Japanese investment in the UK

　C A UK resident taking a holiday in Spain

　D A Greek shipping firm insuring their fleet in the UK

Questions 7-9 share the following answer options:

　A Competition policy

　B Monetary policy

　C Trade policy

　D Fiscal policy

Which of the above policies do the following actions concern?

7 Removing tariff and non-tariff barriers

8 Regulating restrictive practices of dominant firms in markets

9 Lowering interest rates to stimulate business investment

10 Which of the following is not an objective of the European Union?

　A Establishing a single European currency

　B Developing common monetary policy

　C Creating a customs union

　D Restricting inward investment

Questions 11-13 share the following answer options:

　A Youth training schemes (YTS)

　B Learning credits

　C Modern apprenticeships

　D National Education and Training Targets

Which of the above government initiatives to improve the skills of the UK workforce do the following describe?

11 Work-based training courses in particular trades for over-19-year-olds

12 Vouchers for 16-19-year-olds to exchange for participation in further education courses provided by schools and colleges

13 Guaranteed 2-year work placements for all under-19-year-olds not in full-time education or work

14

Real Unit Labour Costs 1980-1993
Index 1980 = 100

(Graph showing UK and Japan real unit labour costs from 1980 to 1993, index ranging 90-103)

Using the graph above, which one of the following statements is true?

  A Productivity is lower in Japan
  B UK competitiveness has improved compared to Japan
  C Unit labour costs in Japan have risen
  D The UK competitiveness gap with Japan has increased

15 a. What is meant by international 'competitiveness'?

b. Suggest and explain two measures of UK competitiveness.

c. Suggest and explain three policies the government could use to improve UK competitiveness.

d. Suggest three strategies a firm might devise to help improve its ability to fight international competition.

16 a. What is 'price inflation'?

b. Give three reasons why an important objective of the UK government is to maintain low and stable price inflation.

c. Suggest and explain three major potential causes of price inflation in the UK.

d. List and explain two major policy initiatives the UK government is using in an attempt to improve competitiveness.

17 A headline from the Daily Mirror (15.12.93) read: 'GATT trade truce means cheaper prices and 400,000 new jobs.'

a. Explain how the General Agreement on Tariffs and Trade has the potential to create employment and business opportunities in the UK.

b. Briefly describe what has happened to the UK share of world exports over time, and suggest two possible reasons for these changes.

c. What is the purpose of the Single European Market in the European Union?

d. Give two examples of newly industrialized countries, and suggest why they present both a threat and an opportunity to developed EU member countries, such as the UK and Germany.

assessment assignment

Advanced Business

Assessment assignment

Range: Comparing performance
Major competitors
Business strategies
Government strategies
Evaluate

Skills: **Communication**
Produce written material
Use images
Application of number
Collect and record data
Interpret and present data
Information technology
Process information
Present information

Tasks

The Economist magazine has asked you to write a two page article (the equivalent of around 10 - 12 pages of A4 script) on UK competitiveness and efforts by the UK government to improve it.

Your article should be produced using a word processor with import facilities for graphics generated by spreadsheets, or an integrated desk top publishing package.

The following structure for your article is suggested;

1. A brief introduction explaining what is competitiveness and a summary of recent trends in the UK.

2. A detailed examination of UK economic performance through time in comparison with major European and non-European competitors, for example Japan, USA and newly industrialised countries in SE Asia.

Economic performance indicators may include;

- growth in GDP
- price inflation
- levels of investment
- exchange rates
- shares of world trade
- productivity

You should explain what each of these indicators are and why they are important.

3. A discussion of how the Single European Market and the General Agreement on Tariffs and Trade may affect UK export markets and GDP growth.

4. A discussion of UK government strategies and policy measures aimed at improving competitiveness.

5. A detailed discussion of how government measures to improve competitiveness are affecting one business organization of your choice.

6. A examination of the strategies the same organization has devised itself to improve its ability to fight international competition. How successful have these strategies been for the firm?

7. The article should include relevant computer generated graphs and tables using data from a variety of sources such as;

- Employment Gazette
- CSO Business Monitor (Overseas Trade Statistics)
- CSO Economic Trends
- UK Balance of Payments ('The Pink Book')
- OECD Economic Outlook
- the EU publications European Economy and Eurostat.
- newspapers and magazines

Financial Transactions, Costing and Pricing

unit six

unit 6

chapter 18 *Added Value and the Money Cycle (Element 6.1)*
chapter 19 *Financial Transactions and Supporting Documents (Elements 6.2)*
chapter 20 *Business Costs (Elements 6.3)*
chapter 21 *Pricing Decisions and Strategies (Elements 6.4)*

Advanced Business

chapter 18
Added Value and the Money Cycle

This chapter examines how business creates and distributes wealth, and how the cycle of purchases and sales by a business is controlled and recorded

♪ MONEY MAKES THE WORLD GO AROUND, THE WORLD GO AROUND, THE WORLD GO AROUND... ♪

Key ideas

A business organization that uses resources to produce a good or service is **'adding value'** to their resources by producing something that consumers want.

A business organization will pay the owners of resources for their use. Any surplus of revenues over the cost of buying or hiring resources is the business owner's profit.

Value added (or profit) is the difference between the costs of production and revenues from sales. This added value will be distributed between the tax authorities, business owners, as dividends to shareholders, or retained by the business to pay off loans and to finance business expansion.

The **trading cycle** refers to the continual cycle of ordering materials, receiving supplies, hiring labour and machines, making payments, and turning resources into finished goods and services for sale to consumers in order to make a profit.

The **money cycle** of cash-flows into and out of a business tends to follow the trading cycle. Firms will use their holdings of cash to buy and hire resources to produce goods and services for sale to consumers in return for cash payments.

Goods and services can be sold by **cash sale** on delivery, or by **credit**. It is usual for businesses to allow their customers up to 30, 60, or even 90 days to pay for goods and services.

Most firms employ a **credit control** system to reduce the risk of **bad debts** and cash-flow problems.

The **purchasing** of materials, components, and equipment is an important function in any organization. It involves finding the best suppliers, negotiating prices and delivery dates, placing orders, and taking deliveries.

Efficient **stock control** can improve the performance of a business by keeping storage cost and waste to a minimum.

Section 18.1 Adding value

How productive activity creates wealth

Business organizations turn inputs into outputs. They use natural, man-made and human resources to produce goods and services to satisfy wants (see 1.1). Consider the resources that are inputs to the production of a three-piece suite:

- **Raw materials:** cotton, oil, steel, wood
- **Finished (and semi-finished) goods:** dyes, nails, screws, material
- **Fuel:** oil, gas, electricity
- **Labour:** designers, cutters, carpenter, machine operators, sales teams
- **Capital goods:** machinery, vehicles, factories, offices

If the cost of all these inputs to a furniture manufacturer in one year is £3 million, and the firm produces 10,000 suites which are sold for £800 each, the firm will receive £8 million in revenues. Thus, the **value added** by organizing resources to produce three-piece suites is £5 million.

Any firm that uses resources to produce a good or service is **'adding value'** to their resources by producing something that consumers want.

For example, imagine a dressmaker who has bought material from a mill that spins and dyes raw cotton purchased from a farmer:

- The farmer sells each bale of raw cotton to the mill for £20. This covers his costs of production and yields him a small profit. The mill can use a bale of cotton to make four yards of material. To allow for a small profit over the cost of the raw cotton and the cost of labour, machines, transport, power, rent, and other overheads, the mill sells the material to the dressmaker for £35. The £15 difference between the price paid for the bale of cotton and the price of the material is the value added, or wealth created, by the mill.

- The dressmaker is able to use the material to make a dress to sell to a shop for £50. This money covers the cost of the material, the dressmaker's labour, the machines she hires, and the power she uses. Any money left over from the sale of the dress after these payments have been deducted is her profit. However, in making the dress for sale at £50 she has added another £15 in value to the resources that have produced the dress.

- The final link in this chain of activity is the shop, which, after deducting the cost of employing shop assistants, power, and rent, plus a mark-up for profit, sells the dress for £70. The shop owner has therefore added a further £20 to the value of the resources that have produced the dress, from the raw cotton in the farmer's fields to the final sale of the finished garment to the consumer.

Firms that provide services are also adding value to the resources they use. For example, a bank provides saving schemes and loans. It will use peoples' savings to make loans and invest in the shares of limited companies. A bank will earn revenues from interest payments on loans and dividend payments on shares. Out of this money it will pay interest to savers, wages to its staff, electricity bills, invoices for office supplies, rent and rates. Any money left after these payments have been made is the bank's profit - a measure of the value it has added to the resources it has used.

Figure 18.1: Adding value through a chain of production

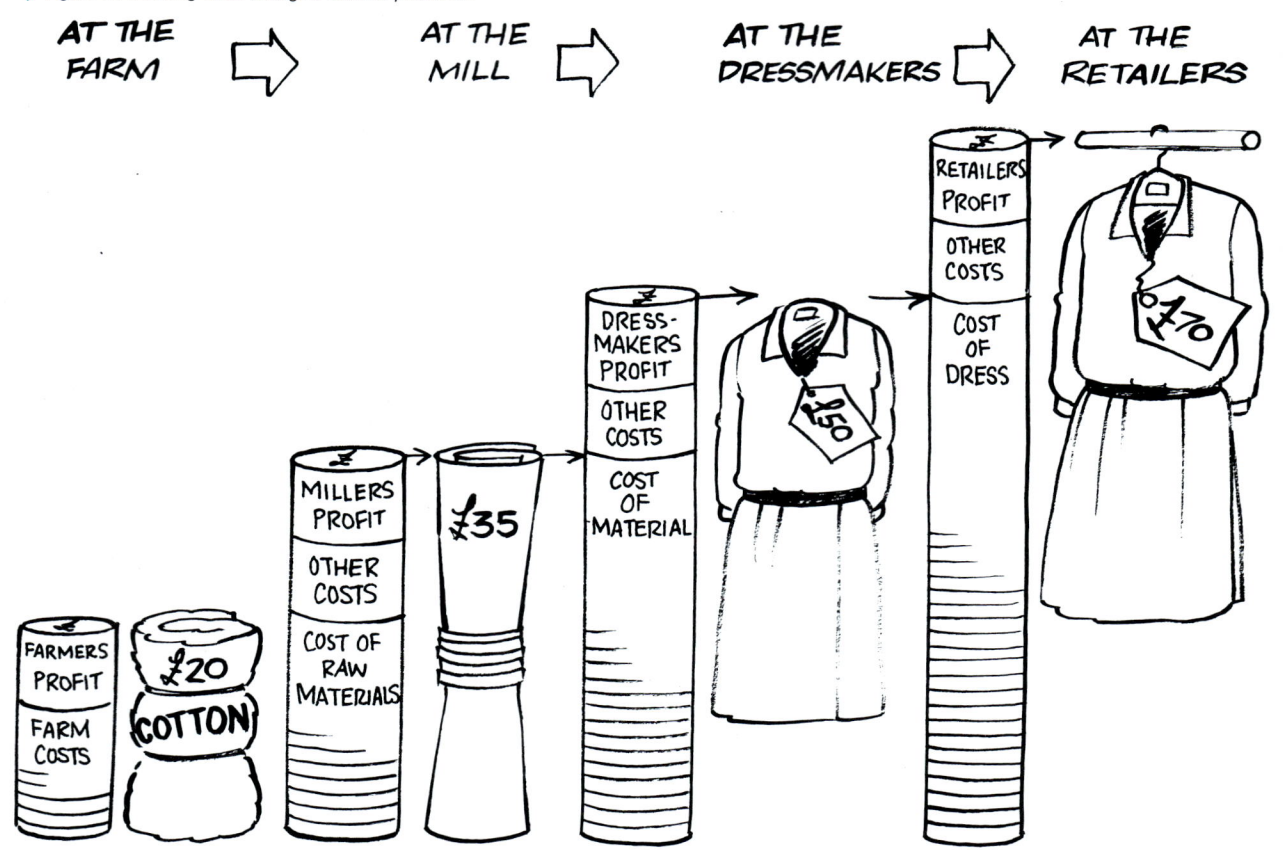

The distribution of added value

Business owners provide their organizations with capital to buy or hire business assets such as machinery, vehicles, premises, raw materials, and labour. If a business needs more money than its owners are able to provide it may borrow additional funds from banks and other financial institutions. Once a business has acquired the assets it needs, it can start production.

When consumers buy goods and services or make donations to charities they provide organizations with revenue. Business organizations can use these revenues to buy or hire the resources they need to make more goods and services to sell.

In hiring or buying resources a firm will face the following costs:

- Employees' wages and salaries
- Raw materials

- Power supplies
- Office supplies
- Equipment and machine purchases
- Hire purchase and/or leasing instalments on machinery and vehicles
- Interest payments on loans
- Office and factory rents to landlords
- Business rates to local authorities

Clearly, what is a cost to one person or business is income to another person or firm. People earn wages by supplying their labour; electricity suppliers earn revenues from the sale of power; banks earn interest from loans. In addition, the government will earn revenue from Value Added Tax on many of the goods and services businesses and consumers buy - and so on.

Profit is a surplus of revenue over and above production costs. It is also the reward to business owners for risking their money in a business venture rather than placing it in a risk-free deposit account with a bank or building society. However, before profit can be distributed to owners, a business organization must pay corporation tax on its profits to the government (see 3.2).

In a sole trader enterprise, any profits after tax belong to the owner. Where there is more than one owner, profits will be divided up according to the amount of capital each owner contributed to the business. In limited companies, profits are distributed as dividends on shareholdings (see 4.2). However, not all profits after tax will be distributed to business owners. Most firms will retain some profits to finance further asset purchases.

To summarize, all revenues received by a firm will be paid out to other people and firms in the following ways:

- Wages and salaries
- Payments for other goods and services
- Interest on loans
- Taxes
- Dividends to business owners
- Retained profits

In turn, people and firms who receive incomes will use these to buy goods and services and add to their stock of wealth. This cycle of activity can be represented as a diagram to show how added value is distributed and wealth created by using resources to produce goods and services.

Table 18.1 shows that wages (and salaries) accounted for nearly two-thirds of all income received in the UK in 1992.

▼ Table 18.1: Shares in domestic income, UK 1992

	% share
Income from employment (wages)	66
Income from self employment	11
Gross trading profits of companies	13
Gross trading profits of public corporations	1
Rent	9
Total domestic income (£516.6 billion)	100

Annual Abstract of Statistics 1994

Advanced Business

▼ *Figure 18.2: The cycle of economic activity*

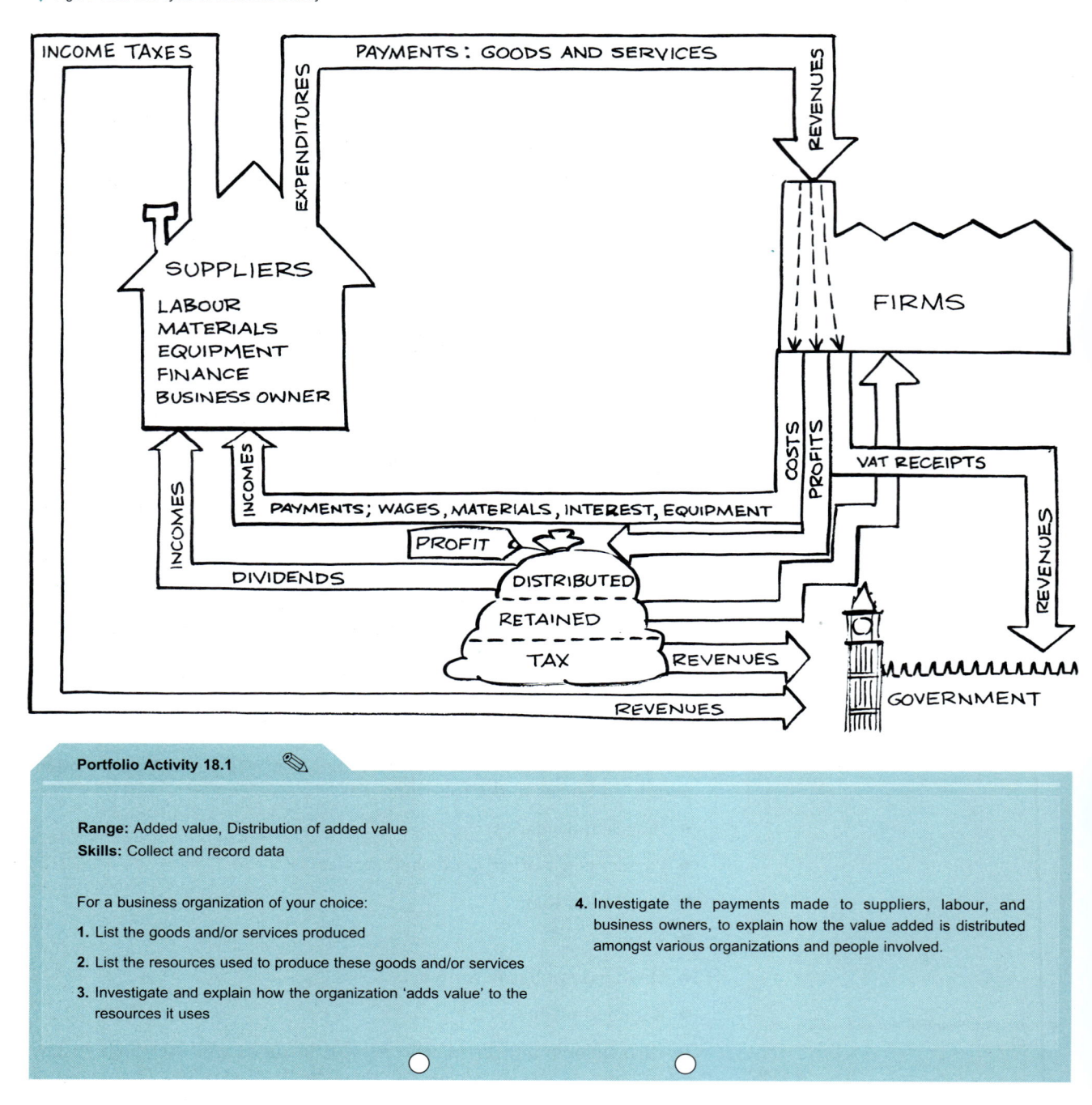

[Diagram: The cycle of economic activity showing flows between Suppliers (labour, materials, equipment, finance, business owner), Firms, and Government. Flows include: Income Taxes, Expenditures, Payments: Goods and Services, Revenues, Costs, Profits, VAT Receipts, Payments: wages, materials, interest, equipment, Incomes, Dividends, Profit (Distributed, Retained, Tax), Revenues.]

Portfolio Activity 18.1

Range: Added value, Distribution of added value
Skills: Collect and record data

For a business organization of your choice:

1. List the goods and/or services produced
2. List the resources used to produce these goods and/or services
3. Investigate and explain how the organization 'adds value' to the resources it uses
4. Investigate the payments made to suppliers, labour, and business owners, to explain how the value added is distributed amongst various organizations and people involved.

Key words

Added value - wealth created by the processing of resources into goods and services to satisfy consumer wants

Section 18.2 Buying and selling

The trading cycle

Production is defined as any activity that satisfies a consumer want or need. The process of production is, therefore, not complete until the final good or service reaches the intended consumers.

The production of any good or service involves a chain of activities, from the extraction or growing of the required raw materials, through a processing stage to turn them into finished products, and finally to distribution either directly, or through a network of wholesalers and retailers, to the final consumer (see 11.2). The motive for production of most business organizations is to earn a profit. Business owners will wish to earn a return on the money they have invested in the assets of their business.

The success of any business organization will depend on its ability to identify a consumer want and deliver the right product to their consumers, in the right amounts, at the right price and at the right time. To do this requires research and careful planning.

If a firm is to produce a good or service in the 'right' amounts, it must ensure it has the necessary natural, man-made, and human resources to do so. It must also try to obtain the best resources it can at the most competitive price, and ensure that the product can be produced at a price which consumers are willing to pay but which will more than cover production costs. If materials are of a poor quality; if machines continually break down, and labour is unskilled, product quality and output will be lower than expected, costs will rise, and the company will make less profit, or even run at a loss.

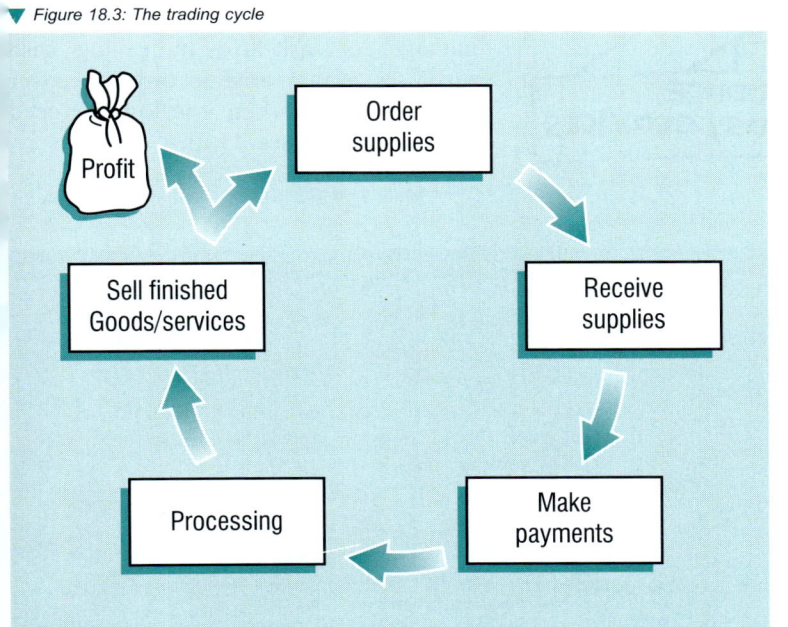

▼ Figure 18.3: The trading cycle

The **trading cycle** refers to this continual cycle of ordering materials, receiving supplies, hiring labour and machines, making payments, turning resources into finished goods and services to meet customer requirements, and selling these products to earn a profit.

The same is true of non-profit-making organizations. Although the objective is not to make as much profit as possible, they too will be concerned with the cost of their operations. For example, a charity will need to order supplies, hire staff and equipment, make payments, and use its resources to help those people or animals it intends to reach. Instead of revenues, a charity relies on donations and gifts of money from which to make payments.

The money cycle

To complete the trading cycle, a firm will need cash. This can be in the form of notes and coins or money in a bank or building society account from which payments can be made, usually in the form of a cheque (see 19.4).

Cash-flows into and out of a business tend to follow the trading cycle. Starting with an initial holding of cash, a firm will buy materials and hire labour and premises. It can then produce goods and services for sale. Most business organizations allow their customers some time after taking delivery of goods or services to pay for them. Payments for goods and services after an agreed credit period are a cash inflow to a business organization from which they can make payments to their suppliers. And so the cycle starts over again, starting with a cash outlay and ending with a cash inflow.

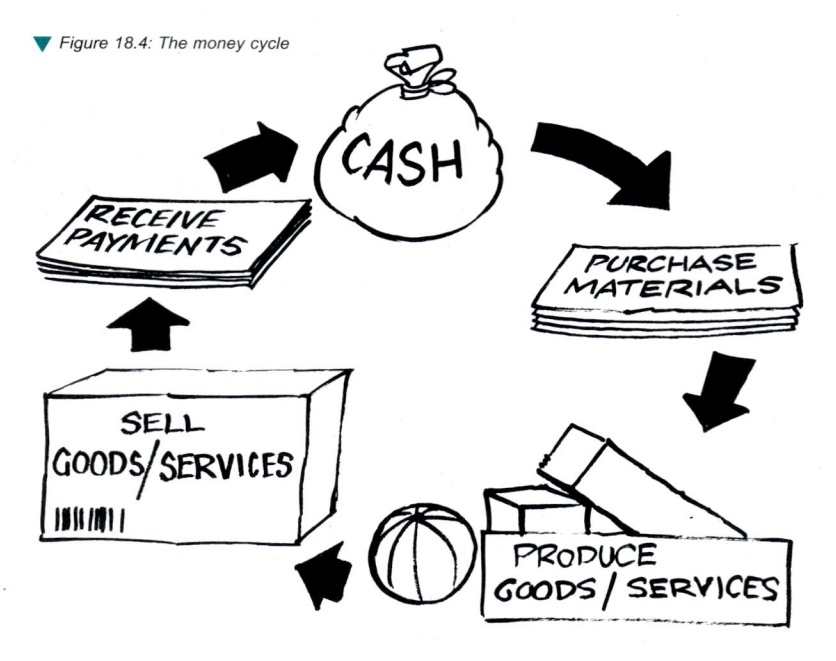

▼ *Figure 18.4: The money cycle*

A firm that is unable to pay its debts is said to be insolvent. This will happen if a firm runs out of cash to make payments and is unable to raise money quickly from other sources, for example, by selling off assets, such as stocks of finished goods, or by obtaining an overdraft facility at a bank (see 22.2). Cash-flow problems may arise in a firm if customers who have purchased goods or services on credit are late in making payment. It is important, therefore, that businesses control the amount of credit they give to their customers. A business should also manage its cash-flow by saving cash surpluses as they arise in order to cover those periods when outflows exceed inflows of cash (see 23.2).

Portfolio Activity 18.2

Range: Trading cycle, Money cycle
Skill: Collect and record data, Produce written material

1. Investigate, and describe and draw in a short report, the trading cycle and how it gives rise to a cycle of cash-flows into and out of a business organization with which you are familiar.

Try to find out:

- Who the suppliers are
- How payments are made
- How payments are received
- Costs and revenues for the business
- The value added (or profit/loss) of the business
- How the profit is distributed (ie to tax authorities, owners or retained by the business to pay debts or buy new equipment).

2. Use the information on cash-in flows and out flows from the business to enter into a suitable spreadsheet to show how the money cycle starts and ends with cash.

3. Discuss what can go wrong in the cycle and how these problems can affect the prosperity of the business; for example, materials not delivered on time, poor quality materials, machine breakdown late payments etc. How does, or could, the business organization attempt to overcome these and other problems?

Selling goods and services

In general, goods and services are sold in one of two ways:

- **Cash sale:** This means that goods and services are paid for immediately they are received. Most shops sell goods and services on this basis. When you buy a bar of chocolate or a CD, you will normally pay for it there and then by cash or by cheque (see 19.4).

Cash is generally thought of as notes and coins. Small purchases tend to be made with cash, but around 90% of the total value of all payments today are made by other means. This is because handling cash can be time-consuming; because cash in large amounts can be bulky, and because it is less secure than other forms of payment. Some small businesses like to receive payment in cash because there is little chance of it being traced if they do not declare it to the Inland Revenue for tax purposes. This is illegal.

- **Credit:** It is usual for businesses to allow other firms up to 30, 60, or even 90 days to pay for goods and services they have received. This is known as **trade credit**.

High street shops also extend credit to their customers. Many people today make purchases using a credit card. The credit card company, for example, Access, Visa, or American Express, will pay the shop on receipt of an invoice and expect the card-holder to make payment after an agreed period, usually between 4-6 weeks (see Figure 18.5). If payment is not made in full, the credit card company will charge interest on the outstanding balance.

▼ Figure 18.5: Payment by credit card

1. Customer pays £50 for goods with credit card
2. Shopkeeper issues credit card invoice for £50
3. Shopkeeper deposits invoice copy in his/her bank account Bank
4. Shopkeeper's bank arranges for invoices to be sent to credit card company
5. Credit card company pays £50 to shopkeeper's bank
6. Credit card company sends account statement of purchases to customer £50
7. Customer settles account balance with credit card company.

People and organizations to whom goods or services have been sold on credit are known as **debtors**. The business organization that has extended credit to its debtors is, therefore, their **creditor** until they pay for the goods and services they have received.

Credit control

Most businesses need to employ some form of **credit control** system. Credit arrangements are clearly of benefit to the person or business that is buying goods and services, but they can cause problems for the suppliers.

Every business will need cash to make payments. It is, therefore, vital that a business is able to collect money owing to it quickly and with ease. If a firm adopts a 'tight credit' policy, it means it may limit the amount of credit it allows, reduce repayment periods, and give credit only to its most valued and reliable customers. This will reduce the risk of bad debts and improve cash-flow.

An 'easy credit' policy of allowing customers longer to pay and larger credit limits, may be used to encourage sales, particularly if the firm is entering a new market, or to clear old stocks of finished goods. It may also be designed to help out valued customers who may be experiencing financial difficulties of their own.

Each system will differ but, in general, good credit control will involve the following:

- **Credit checks:** The bank at which a firm keeps its accounts will often be willing to enquire into the credit status of a potential customer by contacting their bank to see if there have been any problems.

- **Establishing a credit limit for each customer:** This will often be based on the bank's report on the customer's credit worthiness. If the value of orders exceeds this limit, the firm should investigate and, if necessary, either insist that outstanding invoices are paid first, or simply refuse the order.

- **Making sure outstanding invoices are 'aged':** By keeping an **aged debtors list** of customer names, including the date at which they received credit and the amount, a firm can easily identify customers as their debts fall due for payment at the end of an agreed credit period. Conversely, a firm can also keep an **aged creditors list** in which to record the names of their creditors, the amount of credit they were extended, and when payment falls due. This will help ensure they do not overlook paying their suppliers.

- **Sending out reminders:** Each debtor should be sent a copy of their invoice with 'reminder' stamped across it or written in a covering letter around 10 days before their payment falls due.

- **Chasing bad debts:** A **bad debt** is caused by a debtor failing to pay an outstanding invoice for goods or services delivered. Bad debts can cause cash-flow problems, especially in smaller firms who may be forced out of business if they lack the money to pay for resources to continue production. It is usual for a firm to chase up outstanding debts first with a payment reminder. If this does not work, the next step is a strongly worded letter or personal visit to the debtor. As a last resort the firm may threaten and eventually be forced to take legal action to recover monies owed to it.

> **Portfolio Activity 18.3**
>
> **Range:** Factors when selling
> **Skills:** Collect and record data, Produce written material
>
> Continue the investigations you started in **Portfolio Activity 18.2** by examining and reporting on the credit control system employed in your chosen organization. In particular, consider the following questions:
>
> - How is the system designed?
> - How are bad debts chased up?
> - What has been the impact, if any, of bad debts on the business?
> - How could the system be improved?

How to buy goods and services

Purchasing is an important function in any organization. It involves buying materials, components, power supplies, fuel, tools, equipment, stationary, and services such as cleaning.

Manufacturing businesses must purchase raw materials, semi-finished goods, finished goods, and components. A car manufacturer, for example, may buy oil, sheet metal, electrical wiring, microchips, tyres, cloth, nuts, bolts, and car radios from a host of other business organizations. These stocks of materials and goods are used to produce cars to sell to people and other firms.

The importance of purchasing will vary according to the nature and size of the business. Purchasing is especially important in a manufacturing firm where the cost of materials and components can often form a large proportion of total production costs. For a firm to remain competitive, it must be able to obtain the best quality materials it can, at the lowest possible price, where and when it wants. Large firms will therefore tend to employ specialist buyers to seek out sources of supply and examine quality. In a small one-person business or partnership, purchasing will often be just another task to be carried out by the business owner (or owners).

Centralized v. decentralized purchasing

Some business organizations use **centralized purchasing**, whereby the acquisition of materials, components, and other goods and services is carried out by a specialized department. This has the following advantages:

- Staff have, and can build up, specialist knowledge of product qualities and purchasing procedures
- Business is able to take advantage of bulk-buying discounts
- Quality and standards of materials are consistent throughout the whole business
- Storage and distribution can be planned more easily

Decentralized purchasing means that individual parts of a business acquire the goods and services they need themselves. This has the advantage that staff within each area of a business are likely to be more in touch with their needs than a centralized purchasing unit. For example, a store manager in a particular locality will be in a better position than his or her headquarters to judge which products are selling well to local customers.

The main tasks of purchasing can be summarized as follows:

- **Finding the best source of supply.** Materials, components and equipment must be of good quality, 'fit for the purpose', the right size, style, and available at acceptable prices from reliable suppliers
- **Buying in bulk.** Large firms are able to enjoy discounts offered by suppliers to buy materials and equipment in bulk. With firms who place large regular orders under contract, suppliers are willing to negotiate on prices and offer priority delivery.
- **Ordering.** Firms need to ensure that orders are made out correctly and in time to obtain materials and equipment when they are needed
- **Handling requisitions.** This involves dealing with written requests from other departments, offices, factories or shops in the business, for the purchase of goods and services
- **Taking delivery** - and chasing up late deliveries
- **Checking goods received** - to ensure that they meet the requirements of an order
- **Paying invoices** - for goods and services delivered and accepted. Some firms may offer price discounts for prompt payment or even payment in cash.

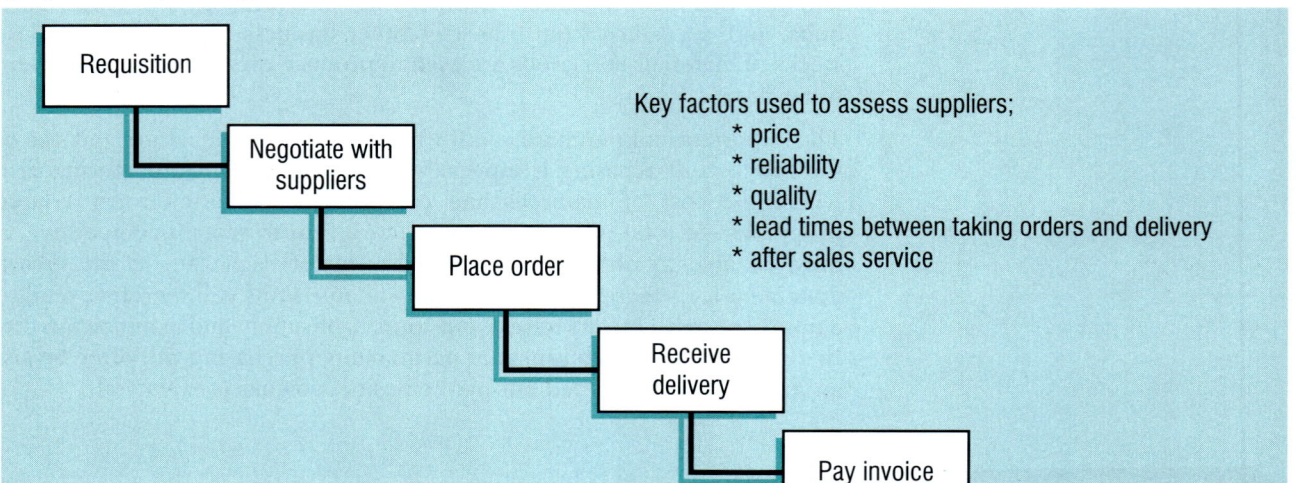

▼ *Figure 18.6: The purchasing process*

Requisition → Negotiate with suppliers → Place order → Receive delivery → Pay invoice

Key factors used to assess suppliers;
* price
* reliability
* quality
* lead times between taking orders and delivery
* after sales service

Stock control

A purchasing department may also be responsible for running a warehouse and managing the flow of stocks into and out of stores. Careful control of stock levels can improve the performance of a business. High levels of stock can be costly for a business:

- Money used to buy stocks of materials and components could have been put to other uses

- Storage costs will be incurred, including rent for premises, heating, lighting, refrigeration, security
- Some stock may perish or deteriorate in quality over time

On the other hand, holding too few stocks could mean that production is held up if stocks run out and the firm has to wait for further deliveries. Lost production also means lost revenues from sales.

'Just In Time' production

One reason for the high levels of productivity and value added in Japanese industry is the cost reductions it manages to achieve by employing Just In Time inventory control (JIT). This means that suppliers deliver components or materials to production lines 'just in time' for them to be processed. JIT has often been called stockless production.

JIT production is based on the principle that products should be produced when customers need them and in quantities customers want, in order to keep stocks of materials, components, and finished products as low as possible. This will reduce the costs normally associated with organizing and storing stocks.

For JIT to work, a number of requirements must be met:

- The quality of materials and parts must be high. Poor materials and defective parts can hold up assembly-line production.
- The supplier must be dependable and deliver on time. JIT requires that lead times between placing orders and delivery be kept as short as possible. It helps if the company and the supplier have a good business relationship.
- It also helps if suppliers are located near the company, but quality and reliability matter more.

Many UK companies are now employing JIT in an attempt to improve productivity and lower their production costs.

Key words

Trading cycle - the continual flow of resources and payments between organizations necessary to acquire materials to process into goods and services to satisfy consumer wants

Money cycle - the cycle of cash payments and receipts into and out of a business

Cash sale - selling goods and services in return for immediate payment

Credit sale - selling goods and services on credit

Trade credit - credit arrangements between business organizations

Debtors - people and firms who owe an organization money

Creditors - people and firms to whom an organization owes money

Credit control - the monitoring and collecting of monies owed to a business

Aged debtors list - a list of debtors' names, the dates at which they each received credit, and the amount owed

Aged creditors list - a list of creditors' names, amounts owed to them, and dates when payments fall due

Bad debts - caused by debtors failing to pay outstanding invoices for goods or services received

Purchasing - securing sources of supply of materials, components, equipment, and services used in a business

Centralized purchasing - purchasing carried out by a specialized department for the whole organization

Decentralized purchasing - acquisition by individual parts of a business of the goods and services they need

Just In Time production - delivery of materials and components immediately before they are due to be processed in order to keep stocks as low as possible

Further reading
Pullen, M: *Business Cash Books Made Easy* (Kogan Page 1994)

Advanced Business

Test questions

The following underpinning knowledge will be tested:
1. The distribution of added value
2. The trading cycle of goods and services and their value added
3. The money cycle
4. Factors to consider when selling
5. Factors to consider when buying

1 The money cycle in a business starts and ends with cash. However, a firm may become insolvent if
- A in-flows of cash exceed outflows
- B creditors pay their invoices late
- C it runs out of money to pay off debts
- D it fails to chase up bad debts

2 Productive activity creates and distributes wealth by adding value to resources used up in making goods and services. The last group of people to whom added value is distributed are:
- A Suppliers of raw materials
- B Workers
- C Business owners
- D The government

3 The trading cycle refers to the flow of resources and payments involved in productive activity. Which of the following options best describes the typical order of events within a trading cycle beginning with the ordering of raw materials and components?
- A Order, payment, supply, processing, selling, profit
- B Order, supply, processing, selling, payment, profit
- C Order, payment, supply, profit, processing, selling
- D Order, supply, payment, processing, selling, profit

4 A firm producing paper has the following annual costs:

Wood and other materials	£140,000
Labour	£160,000
Power	£16,100
Rent and rates	£13,900
Admin. and other expenses	£40,000

It produces 10,000 reams of paper for sale to magazine producers at £50 per ream. What is the value added by the paper manufacturer?
- A £500,000
- B £200,000
- C £130,000
- D £170,000

5 Which of the following is not a function of a purchasing department in a large organization?
- A Negotiating with suppliers
- B Chasing bad debts
- C Paying invoices
- D Ordering

6 A tight credit policy could involve all of the following except:
- A Giving credit only to valued customers
- B Refusing credit to new customers
- C Limiting the total amount of credit given
- D Extending repayment periods

7 Just In Time production is based on the principle that products should be produced only when customers want them and in the quantities they require, in order to keep stocks of materials and work in progress as low as possible. This will involve:
- A Increasing product lead times between orders and deliveries of materials
- B Insisting on high-quality supplies and reliable delivery times
- C Only ordering stocks when they have been fully used up
- D Using only those suppliers who are located near to the company

8 Which of the following factors used by a purchasing department do you think is the least important in assessing the suitability of suppliers?
- A Price
- B Location
- C Lead times
- D Quality

9
- A What is 'added value' in production?
- B Suggest three ways a firm may distribute it's added value.
- C What is the trading cycle?
- D What is the purpose of the money cycle in business?

assessment assignment

UNIT SIX   CHAPTER 18

Assessment Assignment

Range: Trading cycle
Added value
Distribution of added value
Money cycle
Factors when selling
Factors when buying

Skills: Communication
Take part in discussions
Produce written material
Use images
Application of Number
Collect and record data
Tackle problems

You have been asked by a trade magazine for restaurateurs to study and evaluate this article. Produce an article to include in the next issue of the magazine, using the questions below to guide your choice of structure and content.

EXPERTS HIT AT OVER-PRICED, POOR QUALITY WINE

We're plonkers to put up with this

A NIGHT out, a relaxing meal, good conversation. And then a major let down – the wine.

Although we drink twice as much wine as we used to – more than 16 litres a year each in restaurants and bars – it's likely to taste like vinegar and be three times dearer than plonk from the local supermarket.

The Good Food Guide, which surveyed more than 13,000 pubs, bistros and restaurants, has hit out at greedy restaurateurs eager to charge over the odds for plonk.

Editor Jim Ainsworth says: "There is no excuse for a restaurant failing to offer half a dozen good house wines for less than £10 a bottle.

"We know from the wine we can buy in supermarkets that there is a wide range of excellent ones available.

"What we don't understand is why we can't buy it in restaurants. It is outrageous that some restaurants charge an extra 15 per cent service charge on top of the mark up."

Some restaurants assume anything under £20 is inferior, while most of us feel anything more than £20 is too expensive.

"Restaurants seem to be far behind the times in what they serve the customer," says Jim.

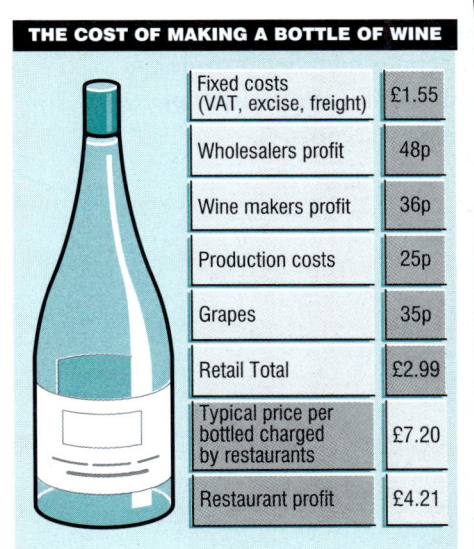

Daily Mirror 7.10.94

THE COST OF MAKING A BOTTLE OF WINE

Fixed costs (VAT, excise, freight)	£1.55
Wholesalers profit	48p
Wine makers profit	36p
Production costs	25p
Grapes	35p
Retail Total	£2.99
Typical price per bottled charged by restaurants	£7.20
Restaurant profit	£4.21

Tasks

1. List the resources that are used to produce wine.

2. Suggest how the diagram in the article helps to illustrate how the production of wine adds value to the resources it uses up.

3. Explain how the diagram can help to illustrate how that added value is distributed

4. Arrange and prepare for an interview with a local restaurant owner or manager to provide information for tasks 5-8.

5. Consider the resources used up in running a restaurant, the costs of running a restaurant, and how it adds value. Now critically examine the following statement: 'Restaurants are unjustified in charging their customers so much more for a bottle of wine'.

6. Investigate and explain the trading cycle of purchases and sales involved in running a local restaurant.

7. Explain the money cycle generated by the restaurant activity and collect data on cash in-flows and out-flows from the restaurant over a period of time to illustrate it.

8. Suggest factors the restaurant should take into account when selling their services to customers, and when buying supplies from other organizations.

chapter 19

Advanced Business

chapter 19
Financial Transactions and Supporting Documents

This chapter examines the various kinds of business documentation that are used to record financial transactions and that provide the foundation for the creation of accounting records.

I'M FOLLOWING THE AUDIT TRAIL!

Key ideas

Documentation is kept in most businesses to record details of transactions relating to **purchases, sales, payments,** and **receipts**. This documentation provides the basic records used to create business accounts which give information about the performance of the business.

Purchases documentation includes **orders placed, purchase invoices**, and **goods received notes**.

Sales documentation includes **orders received, delivery notes, sales invoices, credit** and **debit notes,** and **statements of account**.

Payment documents include **cheques, BACs** (Banking Automatic Credits systems), **EDI** (Electronic Data Interface), **debit cards** and **credit cards**.

Receipts documents include cash and **goods receipts, cheques, paying-in slips,** and **bank statements**.

Business documentation provides an **audit trail** - the means by which past transactions of a business can be traced and checked.

Correct completion of documents is essential. Wrongly completed documents can result in inaccurate accounting records and misleading information about business performance, which can be the basis for bad management decisions.

Businesses can reduce the risk of fraud and financial loss by introducing a range of security measures including **authorization of orders, checking invoices** against orders and goods received notes and **authorized cheque signatures**.

Section **19.1**   ## The need for financial documents

Why document financial transactions?

Financial information is essential to all organizations engaged in productive activities. It is important that all financial transactions are recorded, that records are kept up to date, and that information can be retrieved easily when required, for the following reasons:

- **To monitor business performance:** Business managers need financial records in order to be able to measure how well their organization has performed. This will assist them in future business planning.

- **To record all purchases and sales:** A business will need to keep track of total purchases and sales so that the firm can know how much money they owe to suppliers and how much is owed to them by their debtors.

- **To produce final accounts:** Business owners and managers need to see financial accounts at the end of the financial year in order to judge the total worth of the business and how much profit or loss has been made. Limited companies are required by law to produce annual accounts (see 24.1).

- **To fulfil legal requirements:** Organizations are required by law to produce accounts so that the tax authorities can calculate how much corporation tax and VAT they are liable to pay.

- To confirm mutual understanding between buyer and seller.

Any exchange of goods or services between organizations and individuals is called a **transaction**. A transaction is a two-way process. It will involve one firm making a purchase and another making a sale. It is, therefore, important that both buyers and sellers can confirm arrangements for orders, delivery dates, prices and methods of payments. This can only be done by making sure each has a copy of relevant documents.

For all of these reasons, accurate financial records must be maintained. The recording of financial information is called **bookkeeping**. These records are based upon the many thousands or millions of transactions made by firms each day. In the vast majority of firms, the daily and weekly transactions are far too many to be remembered, so every sale or purchase, or business expense, must be recorded on paper for subsequent entry into the bookkeeping system.

Using documents

Recording information about transactions often requires a lot of paperwork. To speed this process up, businesses have devized special documents to use. Invoices, order forms, purchase documents, bank paying-in slips, and sales invoices are just a few of the kinds of documents used to record transactions. Information from these documents is then transferred to the bookkeeping system in order to record totals for sales, purchases, and other business expenses.

Financial documents are required not only to assist business managers in remembering transactions, but also to provide evidence that the transactions actually took place. For example, it might be tempting for some business managers to attempt to hide sales in order to avoid tax, but a quick check through the invoices raised by the firm by independent auditors (accountants) will usually reveal the true picture.

Advanced Business

Portfolio Activity 19.1

Range: Documents, Purposes
Skills: Take part in discussions

Imagine that you are a sole trader running a small newsagent's shop. List the different kinds of financial transactions that you would regularly need to undertake; suggest how you would record them, and the types of documents you would need.

Undertake research into any small business that you know. Find out about the different kinds of documents that the business uses, and why it uses them. Compare these to your original list.

▼ Figure 19.1: Documents involved in a typical business transaction

Example: The household insurance department in a large insurance company head office purchases new office equipment from a stationary and office supplies company

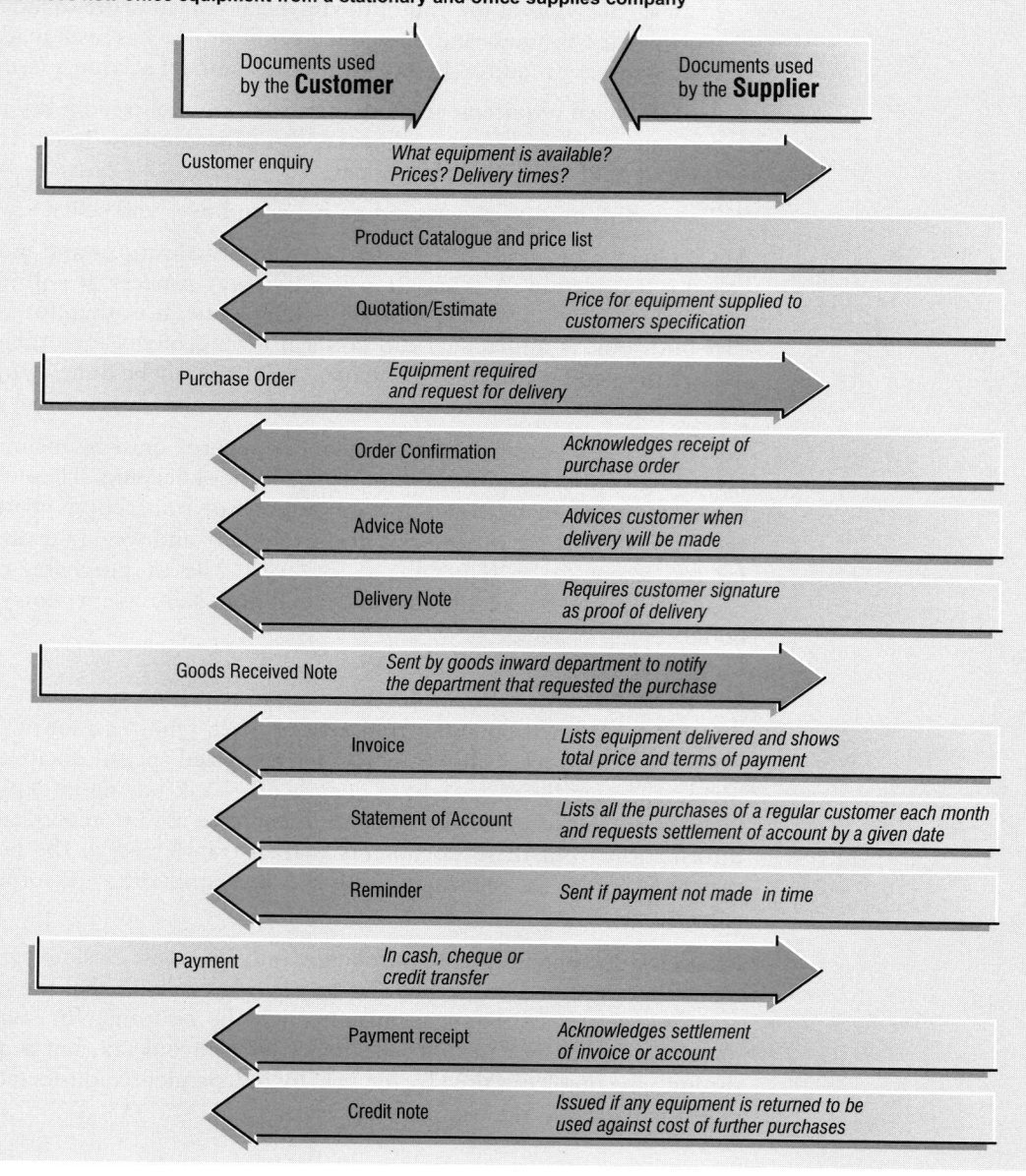

Documents used by the **Customer**		Documents used by the **Supplier**
Customer enquiry	What equipment is available? Prices? Delivery times?	
	Product Catalogue and price list	
	Quotation/Estimate	Price for equipment supplied to customers specification
Purchase Order	Equipment required and request for delivery	
	Order Confirmation	Acknowledges receipt of purchase order
	Advice Note	Advices customer when delivery will be made
	Delivery Note	Requires customer signature as proof of delivery
Goods Received Note	Sent by goods inward department to notify the department that requested the purchase	
	Invoice	Lists equipment delivered and shows total price and terms of payment
	Statement of Account	Lists all the purchases of a regular customer each month and requests settlement of account by a given date
	Reminder	Sent if payment not made in time
Payment	In cash, cheque or credit transfer	
	Payment receipt	Acknowledges settlement of invoice or account
	Credit note	Issued if any equipment is returned to be used against cost of further purchases

Section **19.2**

Purchase documents

Making purchases

The function of the purchasing department in a business is to buy in materials of the right quality, in the right quantities, at the right time, and at the lowest cost (see 18.2). Every pound saved by purchasing is an extra pound made in profits, so it is essential that purchasing works efficiently. The different stages in the purchasing process require different kinds of documentation.

Before any documentation is drawn up, the purchasing department will make enquiries with different suppliers in order to get a range of **estimates** or **quotations** as to the best deal available. Once the best supplier is identified, a purchase order is drawn up. This is a legal offer to the supplier.

The purchase order

Figure 19.2 shows an order for computer equipment made by Iles Textiles Ltd.

▼ *Figure 19.2: An example of a purchase order*

Iles Textiles Ltd
21 Bedford Way
London WC2
Tel: 0171-123-6789
Fax: 0171-123-6780
VAT Reg No. 4333 5432 18

Purchase Order No. 9285

To: Computer Supplies Ltd

1 Megadrive Way

Milton Keynes MK6

DATE	DESCRIPTION	QTY	CAT.No	PRICE	TOTAL
24.8.95	486 DX 66MHz 8 Mb RAM 15" monitor Keyboard and mouse	1	928/C	£1,250	£1,250

Other charges			**Delivery**	£30
Deliver to above address			**Sub-total**	£1,280
			VAT @ 17.5%	£224
			Total	£1,504

Authorized by: *J. Iles* for Iles Textiles Ltd.

An order for goods and/or services to be supplied should specify:

- The purchaser's name and address for delivery of goods and for receipt of payment documentation
- Precise details of the goods or services being purchased, including make, model number, unit price, VAT payable
- The total price
- The delivery date required. If delivery by a certain date is very important, this should be stated clearly on the order.
- The order should be signed by someone with sufficient authority to approve it.

A copy of the **purchase order** will also be forwarded by the purchasing department to the accounts department. When the supplier sends the request for payment, called an **invoice**, the accounts department can compare this bill to the original order to check that the goods in question were actually ordered by the firm and at the price stated on the invoice.

Purchase invoice

A supplier demands payment for goods delivered to a customer by sending an **invoice**. The invoice will detail the name and address of the supplier and customer. Sometimes the address for the invoice is different from the address for delivery of goods. For example, when delivering goods to a chain store, the goods will go to the main warehouse or to individual stores, but the invoice requesting payment will go to the accounts department at the company's head office.

An invoice will normally contain the following information:

- Customer's account number
- Invoice reference number
- A full description of the goods supplied and their reference numbers
- Unit price of the goods
- If the charge for delivery is included in the price, the invoice states 'carriage paid'
- Total price
- Deductions for any cash or trade discounts
- The total net price after including VAT and any deductions
- The date by which the invoice should be paid
- Some businesses may also include a *remittance advice* with their invoices. This may take the form of a tear off slip summarising the main points on an invoice. The buyer simply returns this with the payment so that it is easily matched to the correct transaction.

An invoice is a legal document. Firms must keep all their invoices in order to provide evidence of the amount they have spent on purchases, both for VAT inspectors and for the Inland Revenue. VAT-registered businesses can claim back VAT paid on purchases, and some may be tempted to claim they have purchased more than they really have. Similarly, a firm may be tempted to mislead the tax authorities by claiming more purchases were made than actually occurred in order to reduce the profit declared in the accounts and so reduce corporation tax liability. Both practices are illegal.

To the firm making a purchase, an invoice from a supplier is known as a **purchase invoice** because the payment made by the purchasing firm to settle it will be entered as a debit in their business accounts.

Figure 19.3 shows the invoice sent by Computer Supplies to Iles Textiles Ltd following delivery of the computer they ordered, using the purchase order in Figure 19.2.

▼ Figure 19.3: An example of an invoice

INVOICE

Computer Supplies Ltd

1 Megadrive Way
Milton Keynes MK6
Tel: 01908-6566
Fax: 01908-6560
VAT Reg No. 234 8899 14

To: Iles Textiles Ltd
21 Bedford Way
London WC2

DATE	Order No	Account No.	Invoice No
8.9.95	9285	702316	18967

QTY	Description	Cat No.	Unit Price	Total
1	486DX 66Mhz 8 Mb RAM 15" Monitor Keyboard & mouse	928/C	£1250	£1250
1	Delivery		£30	£30

Sub-total	£1280
Cash discount	−£32
Total (ex. VAT)	£1248
VAT @ 17.5%	+£218.40
Total due	+£1466.40

Terms:
Payment due 30 days from date of invoice.
Cash discount of 2.5% if payment received within 10 working days from date of invoice

E & OE

Cash discounts

In order to speed up the payment of invoices, many suppliers offer a **cash discount**. This discount is a percentage of the goods total (usually around 2.5%) which the buyer can deduct if he or she pays immediately rather than waiting until the end of the period specified on the invoice.

Trade discounts

In addition to a discount for paying cash, some suppliers also give a discount to regular customers, called **a trade discount**. For example, most retailers will receive trade discount from their suppliers. The discount is deducted from the invoice total and will often vary with the quantity purchased. Bigger discounts tend to be given for bigger orders.

Invoice errors and omissions

The abbreviation E & OE on an invoice stands for 'errors and omissions excepted', which means that if the supplier has made any mistakes or left anything off the invoice, the supplier has the right to correct the mistake later and demand full payment.

Goods received note (GRN)

Before paying for the goods, Iles Textiles Ltd accounts department will need signed proof that the goods have actually been received by their firm. This is usually in the form of a **goods received note** signed by a representative of the purchasing firm on delivery of the goods. Once the purchase order, purchase invoice, and goods received note are compared and found to agree, the invoice is paid.

▼ Figure 19.4: An example of a Goods Received Note

Iles Textiles Ltd
GOODS RECEIVED NOTE

Supplier: Computer Supplies Ltd
1 Megadrive Way
Milton Keynes MK6

GRN NO: 2546
Date: 6.9.95
Re; Delivery Note: 10/6789

ORDER NO.	QTY	DESCRIPTION	REF NO:
9285	1 (2 boxes)	486DX 66Mhz 8Mb RAM Keyboard + Mouse 15" monitor	928/C

Received by: *A Bowme*
for Iles Textiles Ltd.

Key words

Purchase order - a request for the delivery of goods or services sent to a supplier

Invoice - a request for payment from a supplier

Goods received note - proof that goods have been delivered completed by a representative of the firm that ordered them and then sent to the accounts department

Cash discount - a deduction from the total price on an invoice in return for immediate payment

Trade discount - a deduction made by a supplier to regular customers, often for making bulk purchases

Remittance advice - form summarising details on an invoice that is returned by the buyer with payment.

Section 19.3 Sales documents

Making a sale

The main objective of the sales department in an organization is to generate sales and to record revenues accurately, so that it can judge how well it is meeting its targets. In making sales, fulfilling customer orders, and obtaining payments, a sales department will issue a variety of documents.

Orders received

When a purchase order is received from a customer, the details are recorded by the sales department. The sales department then has to check that the firm can meet the order and supply the goods in the right quantity at the right price by the date requested in the order. The sales department may then send a **written acknowledgement** to the customer to confirm receipt of their order and giving precise details of the delivery date and time.

If goods are to be in transit for some time, the sales department may also send an **advice note** to tell the customer that the goods are on their way. This will give details of the date the goods were despatched, and how they have been sent - for example, by parcel post or courier.

Delivery note

When goods are delivered by vehicle, either by the supplier or by an outside carrier, the driver is given a **delivery note** (see figure 19.5). This gives a full description of the goods and states the number of packages. On receipt of the goods, the customer is able to check delivered items against the note in order to identify any errors or damage. The delivery note is usually carbonated with two copies. It is signed by the customer, and one copy is kept by the driver as proof that the goods were delivered as required.

Figure 19.5: An example of a delivery note

Computer Supplies Ltd

1 Megadrive Way
Milton Keynes MK6
Tel: 01908-6566
Fax: 01908-6560
VAT Reg No. 234 8899 14

Ref No: 10/6789

Delivery address: Iles Textiles Ltd
21 Bedford Way
London WC2

Delivery date: 6.9.95

DATE	Order No	Account No.	Invoice No
5.9.95	9285	702316	18967

QTY	Catalogue No.	Description
1	928/C	486DX 66MHz 8 Mb RAM 15" Monitor Keyboard & mouse

Delivery by: Parcel Express
No. of items: 2 (CPU and Monitor separate)
Goods received by: _____ (signature)
_____ (please PRINT name)

G Hubble

G Hubble
Sales Manager
Computer Supplies Ltd

Please retain this copy as proof of receipt

▼ *Figure 19.6: An example of a credit note*

Computer Supplies Ltd

1 Megadrive Way
Milton Keynes MK6
Tel: 01908-6566
Fax: 01908-6560
VAT Reg No. 234 8899 14

To: Iles Textiles Ltd
21 Bedford Way
London WC2

CREDIT NOTE NO.
CN3457

DATE	Reference Invoice No.	Customer Account No.
22.9.95	18436	702316

QTY	Description	Cat No.	Unit Price	Total
4	Diskettes (box of 10)	344/D	£10	£40

Reason for credit:
Diskettes returned as faulty

Sub-total	£40
Cash discount	£0
Total (ex. VAT)	£40
VAT @ 17.5%	+£7
Total credit	£47

Sales invoice

After delivering goods or services a supplier will send an invoice to the customer. The invoice requests payment for the goods or services delivered and gives information on any discounts included in the final price and the date by which payment must be made (see 19.2). To the selling organization the invoice is a **sales invoice**. Sales on credit are entered as a credit in the accounts of the business.

Credit and debit notes

A **credit note**, often printed in red, is issued by the sales department to a customer if a deduction needs to be made from an invoice. This may be because:

- The supplier has made a mistake and overcharged
- Goods were not delivered because they were lost or stolen in transit
- The customer has returned unsatisfactory or faulty goods

Figure 19.6 shows a credit note issued by Computer Supplies Ltd to Iles Textiles Ltd after they had returned four boxes of floppy disks which were found to be faulty from an earlier delivery.

A **debit note** will be sent to a customer if the amount on their invoice is insufficient - for example, if payment is late and is subject to a surcharge, or where boxes or crates used to deliver goods were on loan but have not been returned.

Statement of account

When a firm regularly uses the same supplier, it is likely to receive a number of invoices each month. In this case, rather than send out lots of individual invoices, it is more efficient for the supplier to send out a statement of account summarizing all the purchases made by that customer each month. It is also more convenient for a customer to make one payment each month than to have to make numerous payments to settle each separate invoice. The monthly statement shows the amount owed or balance outstanding at the beginning of the month, adding any invoices raised during the month, and deducting any payments received. The balance left at the end of the month is the amount owed. The monthly statement is, therefore, both a summary of transactions made during the month and a request for payment.

Figure 19.7 shows the account of Iles Textiles Ltd with Computer Supplies Ltd for the month of September 1995. Included are references to the purchase order in Figure 19.2 and the credit note in Figure 19.6. A further order for supplies was made by Iles Textiles during the month. This was invoiced by Computer Supplies Ltd on the 25th September.

▼ Figure 19.7: Example of a monthly statement of account

Computer Supplies Ltd

1 Megadrive Way
Milton Keynes MK6
Tel: 01908-6566
Fax: 01908-6560
VAT Reg No. 234 8899 14

Account No: 702316

Iles Textiles Ltd

21 Bedford Way

London WC2

Statement date: 30.9.95

Date	Details	Debit (Dr)	Credit (Cr)	Balance
1.9.95	Balance brought forward	£700.60		£700.60 Dr
8.9.95	Goods Invoice No. 18967	£1466.40		£2167.00 Dr
20.9.95	Payment-thank you		£2500.00	£333.00 Cr
22.9.95	Refund CN.3457		£47.00	£380.00 Cr
25.9.95	Goods Invoice No. 19543	£560.00		£180.00 Dr
		Balance now due		£180.00 Dr

Terms: Payment by 14.10.95 required

Advanced Business

Portfolio Activity 19.2

Range: Purchase documents, Sales documents
Skills: Read and respond to written material

1. Based on the purchase order below from P Lewis Builders Merchants, design and complete a sales invoice from Johnson Office Supplies (preferably using a computer desktop publishing package). The invoice number is 9513. The VAT rate is 17.5%. Goods are subject to a 15% trade discount and a 5% cash discount if paid for within ten days of the invoice date.

2. Include the following information on your sales invoice and explain what is meant by each term:

   Product code or catalogue number, Unit price, Carriage paid, E % OE , Cash Discount 5 days , Deliver to ... , Sub-total, VAT

3. Prepare a flowchart to show each of the firms involved and the departments concerned in processing the documentation generated by the purchase order by P Lewis Builders Merchants.

4. Explain why the accounts department of P Lewis Builders Merchants will need to see a copy of a purchase order, purchase invoice, and goods received note for the same transaction before it pays for goods delivered.

P Lewis Builders Merchants

4 West Hill Way, Bromley BR4 05N

Tel: 0181-466-0001, Fax: 0181-123-0002

VAT Reg No. 2867 0823 9

Purchase Order No. 909867

To: Johnson Office Supplies

98 High Street, Coulsdon

DATE	DESCRIPTION	QTY	CAT.No	PRICE	TOTAL
7.6.94	Photocopy paper	30	P567/2	£5 per ream	£150
	Tippex fluid	20	P345/7	£1.50	£50
	Staplers	2	P23/1	£4.25	£8.50

Other charges		Delivery	£2
Deliver to above address		Sub-total	£210.50
		VAT @ 17.5%	£36.84
		Total	£247.34

Authorised by: *P Lewis*

P Lewis

UNIT SIX

CHAPTER 19

Key words

Advice note - informs the customer that ordered goods have been despatched.

Delivery note - statement issued to the purchaser on taking delivery of goods, listing the items that have been despatched

Sales invoice - request sent out by a supplier for the payment of credit sales

Statement of account - a summary of all the purchases made by a regular customer in a month and the balance of money owed to the supplier

Credit note - notice of a reduction in the amount on an initial invoice, for example, if a customer has been overcharged, goods are lost in transit, or are returned as faulty

Debit note - notice of an increase in the amount owed on an initial invoice, for example, if a customer has been undercharged

Section 19.4

Payment documents

Making payments

Once the goods have been received by a purchasing firm and the accounts department has checked that the purchase order, goods received note, and invoice all match, payment will be made. The most common method of payment used by individuals and business is cash and cheques. However, increasingly transfers between bank and building society accounts are being made electronically, without the need for buyers and sellers to exchange paper and coins. **Credit cards** are also increasing in use (see 18.2).

CONSUMER PAYMENT; BY METHOD

Great Britain	Percentages	
	1981	1992
All payments		
cash	88	76
Non-cash	12	24
Non-cash payments		
cheque	68	46
BACS/CHAPS	20	25
Plastic cards	9	25

Social Trends 1994

Payment by cheque

Most business debts are settled by cheque. Unless a cheque is made payable to 'cash', a cheque is simply a way or arranging a transfer of money between two bank or building society accounts. The person or firm who owns the account from which money will be debited is known as the **drawer**. The person or firm named on the cheque to receive payment is

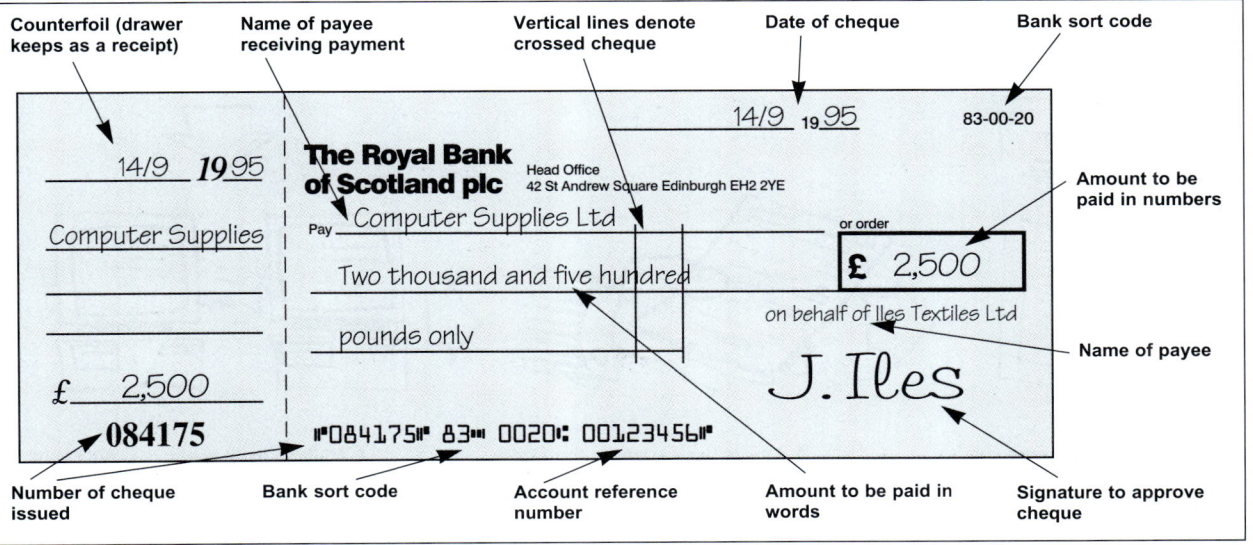

▼ Figure 19.8: An example of a cheque

481

called the **payee**. Each cheque has a serial number, a sort code to identify the bank or building society, and the drawer's account number. It is usual to write out the sum to be paid in figures as well as in words on a cheque so that the precise amount cannot be mistaken. The drawer must also sign each cheque with his or her usual signature.

In all but the smallest firms, cheques can only be signed by authorized staff, usually in the accounts department. For larger sums, signatures of two staff are often required, one at a senior managerial level.

In most business organizations, employees who are in a position to order goods and services by raising purchase orders are not in a position to make payment for them as well by writing cheques. This provides an important safeguard against fraud. Clearing banks also keep specimen signatures of those staff authorized to sign cheques in order to provide further checks.

Cheque validation

A cheque is valid if:

- It is written in ink or printed
- It is signed by the drawer who is paying the money
- The amount in words is the same as the amount in numbers
- The cheque is made payable to someone or to the bearer (the person holding the cheque)
- The cheque is dated and is not more than six months old

▼ *Figure 19.9: Payment by cheque-an example*

1. Customer pays £25 with cheque from the Lloyds bank
2. Shopkeeper 'pays' cheque into his/her account at the Midland bank
3. Midland bank credits shopkeeper's account with £25
4. Midland bank contacts Lloyds bank
5. Lloyds bank arranges transfer to Midland bank
6. Lloyds bank debits customer's account by £25

Cheques can be either **open** or **crossed**.

- A **crossed** cheque has two parallel lines across it. This signifies that it must be paid into the payee's account, regardless of who presents the cheque at a bank for payment. This safeguards the drawer and payee against theft. For additional security, the words 'A/C payee' are often written between the two lines to make sure that the cheque can only be paid into the payee's account.
- An **open** cheque, which does not have the two lines, can be cashed over a bank counter to whoever presents it.

Most businesses will not accept cheques as payment unless they are backed by a cheque card.

Cheque cards are issued by banks and building societies to their reliable account-holders. These are used to guarantee payment of the cheque even if the account upon which it is drawn does not contain enough money to cover it. However, certain conditions apply:

- The maximum sum guaranteed must be as stated on the cheque card (either £50 or £100)
- The cheque card number should be copied onto the back of the cheque
- The name and signature on the cheque should match those on the cheque card

Increasingly, account-holders are able to use their cheque guarantee cards to make payments using systems such as SWITCH (operated primarily by Midland and National Westminster banks) and CONNECT (Lloyds and Barclays). These so-called **debit cards** offer both customer and supplier a much simpler method than payment by cheque, because the card-holder's account is debited immediately by electronic transfer. Retailers who belong to either system have to pay a fixed charge for its use, but they benefit from having their account credited immediately payment by card is made.

Bankers Automated Clearing Services (BACS)

Paying by cheque and taking cheques and other payments to and from banks can be time-consuming. In order to speed up payments to regular suppliers, many firms send the money from their bank account through the banking system to the bank account of the supplier, using computer links. These transfers of funds are made using a system known as **BACS** (Bankers Automated Clearing Service).

A bank customer wishing to make regular payments completes a standing order form telling the bank who to pay, how much to pay them, and how often. The bank will then input these instructions to a computer and the payments will be made automatically.

Where the amounts paid regularly are likely to vary, the customer can change the amount using an 'autopay' version of the BACS system. This is usually achieved by giving the details on each series of payments to the bank on computer disk, or by sending the information via the telephone line using a modem (see 5.4). The banks provide the software programs which create the required format. Today, most workers, especially those in medium-to-large organizations, are paid their wages directly into their bank of building society accounts through BACS. Each worker will receive a monthly statement telling him or her how much money will be credited to their account after deductions for income tax, National Insurance

Advanced Business

contributions, and perhaps a company pension or season ticket loan repayments.

Clearing House Automated Payments System (CHAPS)

CHAPS is used by banks for making urgent payments of £1,000 or more. The payments are transferred via the CHAPS computer system. Once accepted, the payment cannot be stopped and so the funds are considered to be cleared by the banking system. The money can then be used immediately by the person or organization that has received payment.

Electronic Data Interchange (EDI)

Just as it is possible for computer users to communicate with each other via modem, it is also possible for businesses to send large quantities of information to each other via modem links. In fact, all of the purchases, sales, and payments documents considered in this chapter can be transmitted between firms electronically using EDI.

At present EDI is used mainly by larger retailing organizations which need to replenish stocks regularly. Bar-code readers monitor sales at supermarket checkouts and maintain an up-to-date record of stocks. When stock reaches a certain pre-set minimum level, the computer generates an order for more stock electronically via a modem link to the supplier. Payment is also subsequently made electronically via BACS. Using the EDI system, paperwork, and the need for labour to administer the documents, is cut to the minimum.

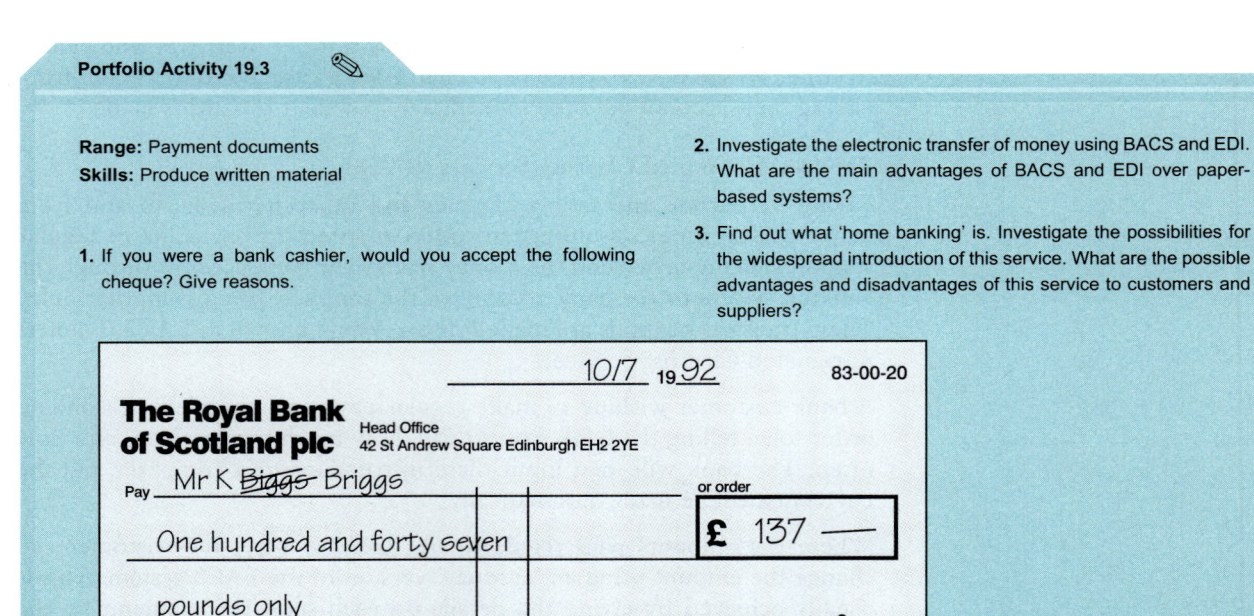

Portfolio Activity 19.3

Range: Payment documents
Skills: Produce written material

1. If you were a bank cashier, would you accept the following cheque? Give reasons.

2. Investigate the electronic transfer of money using BACS and EDI. What are the main advantages of BACS and EDI over paper-based systems?

3. Find out what 'home banking' is. Investigate the possibilities for the widespread introduction of this service. What are the possible advantages and disadvantages of this service to customers and suppliers?

The Royal Bank of Scotland plc
Head Office
42 St Andrew Square Edinburgh EH2 2YE

10/7 19 92   83-00-20

Pay Mr K ~~Biggs~~ Briggs   or order

One hundred and forty seven pounds only

£ 137 —

D Smith

⑈084175⑈ 83⑆ 0020⑆ 00123456⑈

Key words

Cheque - a written instruction to a bank or building society to transfer money from the account of the cheque drawer to a named payee

Cheque card - a guarantee that a cheque will be honoured up to a specified limit, usually £50 or £100

BACS (Banking Automated Clearing Services) - a computerized system which transfers money between accounts without the need for cash or cheques

CHAPS (Clearing House Automated Payment System) - a computer system used by banks to make immediate payments of £1,000 or more.

EDI (Electronic Data Interchange) - the interchange of financial documents and other information between organizations using computers linked by modems

Section 19.5 Receipts documents

The proof of purchase

When you buy a good or service in a shop, you will receive a receipt as **proof of purchase**. Similarly, when an organization makes payment it will require proof that payment has been made for its own records and for the purpose of informing the tax authorities about its expenses.

A number of documents can provide proof that a transaction has taken place.

Sales receipts

A **sales receipt** is usually issued when payment for goods or services received is immediate. It can take many forms, but will include the following information:

- The name and address of the organization that has made the sale
- The date the transaction took place
- A description of the goods or services purchased
- The cost of each item
- The total cost of all items
- The method of payment

Figure 19.10: An example of a sales receipt

```
       WELCOME
          TO
     WH SMITH LTD
                        £
Stationery           15.95
Newspaper             0.50
Book                 22.50

Balance due          38.95

CASH                 50.00
CHANGE               11.05

 4280  07  5  1615   11:03:05
          21SEPT95

 THANK YOU FOR SHOPPING AT
       WH SMITH LTD
    KINGSTON-UPON-THAMES
```

Portfolio Activity 19.4

Range: Receipts documents
Skills: Tackle problems

Assume that you work in the spare components section of Speed Ltd, a large garage. Usually the computer system prints out receipts for customers. However, today the system is not working and you must design your own receipt. N Mansell has just purchased a new set of tyres for £250 and paid in cash. Produce a handwritten receipt for the customer.

Advanced Business

Paying-in slip

When a firm pays in cash and cheques to its bank, it will complete **paying-in slip** or **bank giro credit** slip. The slip, along with cash and cheques, is handed to the cashier. The bank cashier will stamp and initial both the slip and the counterfoil. The counterfoil acts as the customer receipt. The paying-in slip counterfoil allows the business to check that the subsequent entries on its bank statement are correct.

▼ *Figure 19.11: A bank giro credit slip*

Paying-in slips can be used to show the following information:

- The date money was paid into the account
- The bank (or building society) branch at which money was paid in
- The branch sort code
- The account-holder's name
- The number of the account to be credited
- The amount to be credited
- The name and signature of the person paying in the money

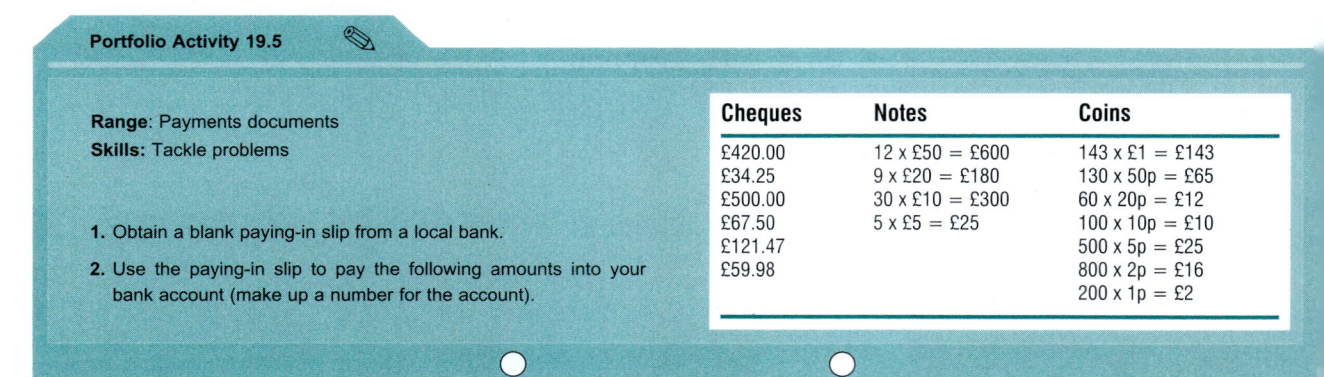

Portfolio Activity 19.5

Range: Payments documents
Skills: Tackle problems

1. Obtain a blank paying-in slip from a local bank.
2. Use the paying-in slip to pay the following amounts into your bank account (make up a number for the account).

Cheques	Notes	Coins
£420.00	12 x £50 = £600	143 x £1 = £143
£34.25	9 x £20 = £180	130 x 50p = £65
£500.00	30 x £10 = £300	60 x 20p = £12
£67.50	5 x £5 = £25	100 x 10p = £10
£121.47		500 x 5p = £25
£59.98		800 x 2p = £16
		200 x 1p = £2

Bank statement

A **bank statement** provides a summary of receipts and payments made to and from a bank account. Building societies also provide their account-holders with regular statements.

▼ Figure 19.12: Example of a bank statement

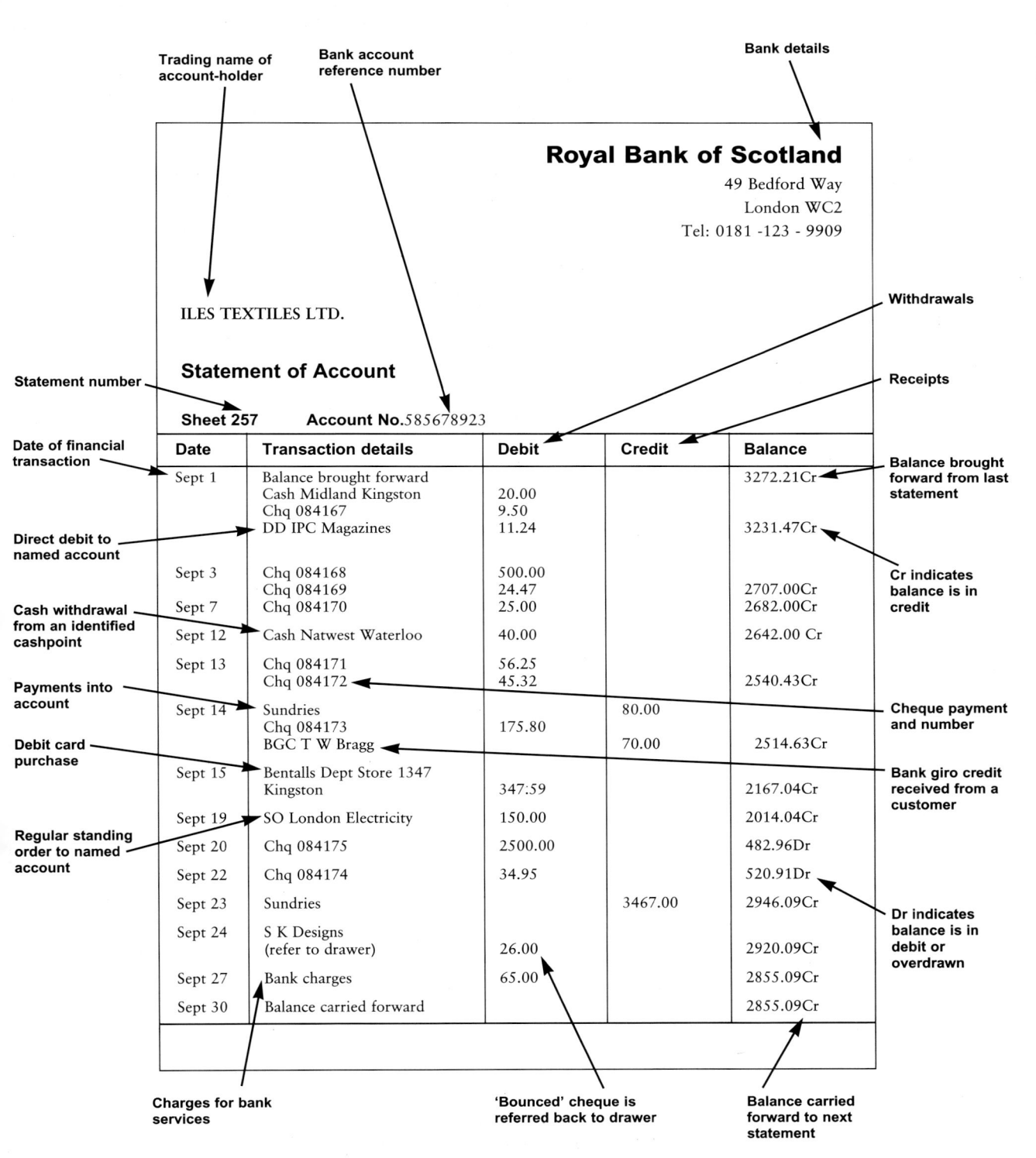

Trading name of account-holder

Bank account reference number

Bank details

Royal Bank of Scotland

49 Bedford Way
London WC2
Tel: 0181 -123 - 9909

ILES TEXTILES LTD.

Withdrawals

Statement of Account

Receipts

Statement number — Sheet 257   Account No. 585678923

Date of financial transaction

Date	Transaction details	Debit	Credit	Balance
Sept 1	Balance brought forward			3272.21Cr
	Cash Midland Kingston	20.00		
	Chq 084167	9.50		
	DD IPC Magazines	11.24		3231.47Cr
Sept 3	Chq 084168	500.00		
	Chq 084169	24.47		2707.00Cr
Sept 7	Chq 084170	25.00		2682.00Cr
Sept 12	Cash Natwest Waterloo	40.00		2642.00 Cr
Sept 13	Chq 084171	56.25		
	Chq 084172	45.32		2540.43Cr
Sept 14	Sundries		80.00	
	Chq 084173	175.80		
	BGC T W Bragg		70.00	2514.63Cr
Sept 15	Bentalls Dept Store 1347 Kingston	347.59		2167.04Cr
Sept 19	SO London Electricity	150.00		2014.04Cr
Sept 20	Chq 084175	2500.00		482.96Dr
Sept 22	Chq 084174	34.95		520.91Dr
Sept 23	Sundries		3467.00	2946.09Cr
Sept 24	S K Designs (refer to drawer)	26.00		2920.09Cr
Sept 27	Bank charges	65.00		2855.09Cr
Sept 30	Balance carried forward			2855.09Cr

Direct debit to named account

Cash withdrawal from an identified cashpoint

Payments into account

Debit card purchase

Regular standing order to named account

Charges for bank services

Balance brought forward from last statement

Cr indicates balance is in credit

Cheque payment and number

Bank giro credit received from a customer

Dr indicates balance is in debit or overdrawn

'Bounced' cheque is referred back to drawer

Balance carried forward to next statement

A bank statement can be checked for any mistakes against documentary proof that the transactions have been made, such as entries on cheque counterfoils, counterfoils issued when SWITCH or CONNECT cards are used, and paying-in counterfoils. This process is known as **bank reconciliation**. Differences between the bank statement and the firm's records may arise due to:

- Clerical errors causing figures to be wrongly entered or missed out
- Payments made into the bank which have not been entered in the firm's records
- Cheques presented to the bank which have not yet been cleared.
- Bank charges representing interest on loans or overdrafts and/or charges for other services (some current accounts also pay interest on credit balances)

Figure 19.12 shows the bank statement of account of Iles Textiles Ltd for September 1995. Note the drawing of the cheque for £2,500 by Computer Supplies Ltd on 20.9.95 as shown in the customer account statement in Figure 19.7.

Portfolio Activity 19.6

Range: Receipts documents
Skills: Tackle problems

1. Create a table in a computer word processing package in which to enter a bank statement.

2. Use the statement to record the following transactions made by a business account-holder during one month. Entries should appear in date order:

3. Remember to calculate and show the 'balance carried forward' to the next statement.

Date	Details	Amount
1	Balance brought forward	−£24
	Drawings:	
4	Cheque No. 15326	£35.25
7	Cheque No. 15327	£157.50
15	Cheque No. 15328	£12.99
12	Cheque No. 15329	£79
25	Cheque No. 15330	£230.70
9	Standing order to British Gas	£50
10	Cash dispenser	£60
18	Cash dispenser	£40
14	Standing order to N&P Building Society	£380
14	SWITCH Tesco Superstore	£49.45
28	SWITCH Houghtons Garage	£16.75
21	Bank Charges	£10.25
	Receipts:	
1	Credit transfer from XYZ Ltd	£1,425.50
8	Cheque No.26893 received	£56.90
18	Cheque No.99901 received	£10.25

> **Key words**
>
> **Sales receipt** - a proof of purchase
>
> **Paying-in slip (or bank giro credit)** - form used to identify the account into which accompanying cash or cheques must be paid
>
> **Bank statement** - a summary of payments to and from a bank account
>
> **Bank reconciliation** - the process of checking bank statement entries against actual payments and receipts documents

Section 19.6 The accuracy and security of financial records

The consequences of incorrect completion of documents

A business uses its documentation on purchases, sales, payments, and receipts to complete its annual accounts (see 23.4). However, errors and omissions are inevitable - for example, recording the wrong price for an item, calculating VAT incorrectly, not adding up prices correctly, or mislaying an order or cheque payment.

Failing to complete documents accurately can cause problems for an organization:

- **Incorrect purchases:** If purchases are incorrect, this could lead to the wrong materials being bought in, which in turn could lead to expensive re-ordering, a slowdown in production and possible waste if the materials cannot be returned.

- **Incorrect sales:** If sales are incorrect, customers may be supplied with the wrong goods, leading to returns and a poor business image.

- **Incorrect payments and receipts:** If receipts and payments records are incorrect, this could lead to over- or undercharging of customers, late payment, disputes, and consequently dissatisfied customers and suppliers.

- **Incorrect accounts:** If there are errors in documentation relating to purchases, sales, or expenses, the final accounts will be incorrect and the business owners may get the wrong impression about the value of their firm and the profit it has made. The tax authorities also use the accounts to calculate the amount of tax a firm is liable to pay. If they discover any mistakes in the accounts, the firm could be fined heavily.

- **Misleading information on past business performance:** As decisions on how to manage the business are based on the accounting records, the business could be badly managed as a consequence of incorrect or sloppy handling of the basic financial documentation. This could lead to future financial difficulties.

The need for security

Whatever the methods used to purchase and pay for goods and services, a business must be aware of the risk of theft and fraud. For example, following the death of newspaper tycoon Robert Maxwell in 1991, it was discovered that he had illegally transferred over £400 million from his employees' pension fund to finance other business ventures. Pensioners are still trying to recover their money. In order to minimize the risk of theft or fraud and to protect both the firm and the reputation of individual employees, it is necessary to have a series of checks and financial controls.

For example:

- **Use an audit trail.** The primary safeguard in maintaining financial records is to provide an audit trail. An **audit trail** is simply a means of checking the passage of a transaction through a business by checking through the records and documentation, from the generation of a purchase order or sale to the stage where the payment appears in the bank statement. If there is no audit trail - that is, if the transaction disappears somewhere in the firm and no further records can be found - the firm is open to fraud, because the transaction will be impossible to check.

By law, each year external independent auditors will sample some transactions in companies and follow the audit trail in the documentation through from beginning to end. Today, much of the audit trail is held on computer.

- **Use only authorized personnel to countersign orders and cheques.**

    Allowing just anybody to authorize payments opens a firm to risk of fraud because some employees may be tempted to issue payments to bogus companies operated by their friends or family. Ensuring that only staff with appropriate levels of seniority always sign purchase orders and cheques provides some control. For large transactions, often two signatures will be required. Clearing banks also maintain sample copies of authorized signatories in order that they can check the transactions of their customers.

    When payment is made by cheque, it is also important to make sure it is crossed. Most cheque slips supplied by banks have two lines and the words 'A/C payee' already printed across them (see 19.4).

- **Always cross-check documents.** Checking of documents against external source documents such as invoices and goods received notes also provides a means of ensuring that the business only pays for what it has received.

- **Give responsibility for receiving goods and paying for goods to different people.** If the same person in an organization takes delivery of goods and makes payment for them they could defraud their employer or be tempted to steal. This is because they could lie about goods being delivered but still make payment. Or pay money to a bogus company operated by a friend or family member without having received any supplies.

- **Install security equipment.** This can include video cameras in delivery bays and at checkouts and the installation of safes in which to deposit money during the day to reduce the risk of theft.

Portfolio Activity 19.7

Range: Security checks for business documents
Skills: Take part in discussions

Your school or college will have its own financial controls to assist with security. Arrange for one member of your group to contact the finance department of your school/college to set up a presentation on these procedures. Follow this up with questions and answers from your group.

Contact another organization if you can, and find out what kinds of controls they use. (Alternatively see if you can get a representative of a local accountancy firm to come in and give a presentation on the kinds of procedures which are typically used in firms - with some examples of bad, as well as good, practice.)

Prepare a short report comparing and contrasting the two presentations and suggest your own ideal system, giving reasons for your choice.

UNIT SIX
CHAPTER 19

Test questions

The following underpinning knowledge will be tested:
1. The purposes of financial documentation
2. The use of purchases and sales documents
3. The use of payments and receipts documents
4. Security checks for business documents
5. Why is it important to complete documents accurately and possible consequences of incorrect completion

1 The primary function of financial documentation in business is to:
- A Provide information for lenders, for example, the bank
- B Provide information for the government
- C Provide information which will assist in monitoring and controlling the business
- D Provide information for the registrar of companies

2 The person who signs a cheque to make payment is:
- A The person who is paying the money
- B The branch bank manager
- C The person to whom the cheque is paid
- D The person who pays the cheque in to the bank account

Questions 3-5 share the following answer options:
- A An audit trail
- B Checking invoices against purchase orders
- C Requiring two authorized personnel to sign orders
- D Checking invoices against goods received notes

Which of the above security measures could reduce the risk of the following situations occurring?

3 Paying invoices for goods not ordered.

4 Authorizing payment for goods not delivered.

5 Authorized personnel making fraudulent payments to their own bank account.

6 Which of the following would a firm send to a supplier requesting delivery of goods?
- A Statement of account
- B Purchase order
- C Goods received note
- D Invoice

Questions 7-9 share the following answer options:
- A A sales invoice
- B A delivery note
- C A statement of account
- D A sales receipt

Which of the above documents would be used to:

7 Provide proof that a purchase has been made?

8 Inform a customer of the value of goods supplied and terms of payment?

9 Request payment for goods delivered?

Questions 10-12 share the following answer options:
- A Delayed payments
- B Delivery of the wrong goods
- C Misleading the tax authorities
- D Unhappy customers cancelling further orders

Which of the above problems could be caused by the following sources of error?

10 Unclear instructions on a purchase order

11 Overcharging vat on an invoice

12 Making an error in the final accounts

13
- A What is a purchase order and what information should it contain?
- B What is the difference between a goods received note and a delivery note. Explain why they are needed.
- C What is the purpose of a sales invoice and what information should it contain?
- D Explain why it is important to check invoices against orders and goods received notes.
- E How is a cheque able to be both a method of payment and a receipt?

assessment assignment

Assessment Assignment

Range: Purposes
Purchase documents
Sales documents
Payments documents
Receipts documents
Consequences of incorrect completion
Security checks

Skills: **Communication**
Produce written material
Use images
Application of Number
Collect and record data
Tackle problems
Information Technology
Prepare information
Present information

Tracey Lane has set up a new restaurant called 'Nibbles' in your local high street. Tracey has no experience of keeping financial records and is worried that she will either get into trouble with the tax authorities, or go out of business through lack of knowledge. Tracey has agreed to pay you to help her with recording financial transactions.

Tasks

1. Produce a brief report for Tracey explaining:

   A Why she needs to keep accurate records of financial transactions

   B The main kinds of documents she should keep.

2. Design, preferably using a DTP package, the main documents she will use on a regular basis. Include copies of these in your report.

3. Tracey has already been trading for a brief period and has made the transactions given below. She would like you to fill in the documents you have designed to show them.

- A local business, Office Solutions, has an account with 'Nibbles'. Office Solutions regularly entertain clients at the restaurant and usually prefer to pay on receipt of a statement each month rather than on invoice. Transactions this month include:

8.11.95	Meals	Invoice no. 765	£250
11.11.95	Take away	Invoice no. 892	£50
21.11.95	Meals	Invoice no. 969	£100
25.11.95	Payment	Invoice no. 223	£50

- B Kennington has also opened a business account and incurred a meals bill for £300, net of VAT, by 25.11.95. Nibbles offers a 2% discount for payment within 5 days.

- Office Solutions would like a receipt for a £150 payment on 25.10.95

- 'Nibbles' delivers food to parties and business functions and requires customers to sign on receipt of the order. Aldhouse Bricks Co. of Leigh in Kent have ordered a buffet for 50 people to be delivered in 10 sealed packs on 1.1.96.

4. Tracey now needs to order more supplies as follows:

   10 chickens at £3 each

   50 lbs of potatoes @ 35 pence per pound

   20 lbs of Salmon at £2 per lb

   20 lbs of steak at £1 per lb

   50 bottles of wine at £5 per bottle

   Supplies are bought from L Thomas of Whitehead Street, London E1.

   Draw up an appropriate purchase order for her, then complete a cheque for full payment to L Thomas.

5. Tracey usually pays her invoices using cheques. Explain in your report to her how, and why, she could make use of electronic banking methods instead.

6. Tracey hopes to be able to expand in future and so would like to take on other staff to assist her, especially with paperwork and administration. You have been asked to write a brief report explaining the kinds of steps she could take in order to reduce the risks of fraud or misunderstandings and so improve security.

UNIT SIX

CHAPTER 20

chapter 20 Business Costs

This chapter investigates how businesses identify and calculate their costs of production

Key ideas

Costs may be classified as **direct costs** or **indirect costs**.

Direct costs are those which can be clearly associated with the production of a particular good or service, e.g. **wages, materials,** and **depreciation.**

Depreciation refers to a fall in the value of **fixed assets**, such as machinery and vehicles, due to wear and tear.

Indirect costs, or **overheads,** are those costs which are incurred by the whole organization and cannot be associated with a particular good or service, e.g. management, administration, marketing, and day-to-day running expenses.

Costs can also be classified according to how they vary with production levels. **Fixed costs** do not vary with the level of output, for example rent and rates. Costs, such materials and labour, which do vary with the level of output are **variable costs**.

The **total cost** of producing a given level of output is equal to the sum of direct and indirect costs, which is equivalent to the sum of fixed and variable costs.

The **average cost** of a unit of output is calculated by dividing total costs by total output. If the firm charges a price above average cost for the sale of that unit the revenue will cover both direct and indirect costs and yield a profit.

The extra cost incurred by increasing output by one unit is known as the **marginal cost** of production. If the extra revenue generated by the sale of that item does not cover its marginal cost it is not worth producing.

Advanced Business

Section 20.1

The costs of production

Identifying business costs

In most cases, running a business is all about making decisions on how best to use scarce resources in order to make a profit, where:

Profit = Sales Revenues − Costs

Every business decision, whether to launch a new product, change advertising methods, or to expand production, has cost implications. Because the primary purpose of most private-sector firms is to make a profit, it is essential that businesses are able to keep a tight control on their costs. Cost control is equally important to public-sector organizations and charities who do not seek to make a profit, but will nonetheless want to minimize the cost of their operations.

In order to control costs, it is first necessary to be able to identify business costs, calculate how much these costs are, and then to set targets for future cost levels.

Classifying costs

There are two main ways in which costs can be classified and calculated in order to assist managers in planning and controlling the operation of a business:

- **Direct and indirect costs** are definitions used for accounting purposes to calculate the level of profit before tax for a particular good or service
- **Fixed and variable costs** are classified according to how they vary as the level of output of a good or service is varied (see also 21.2).

Direct costs

Costs which can be directly identified with a particular product or activity are known as **direct costs** or **prime costs**. These will include:

- **Direct materials:** the raw, or semi-finished materials used to make a product
- **Direct labour:** the wages of employees directly involved in making or assembling a product
- **Direct design costs:** costs incurred at the product planning stage
- **Other direct costs:** including the costs of power used in production, hire charges for machinery specifically employed in the production process, and the costs of any work subcontracted to other businesses
- **Depreciation:** an allowance made to cover a fall in the value of fixed assets, such as machinery, vehicles, computers, etc., due to wear and tear

▼ Direct costs

Indirect costs

In most business organizations there will be costs which are not directly related to the production of a particular good or service, but which result from the operation of the entire organization. For example:

- Rent and business rates

▼ *Indirect costs...*

- Lighting and heating
- Equipment maintenance
- Insurance
- Cleaning
- Sales and distribution costs, such as advertising and transport
- Bank charges on loans
- The wages and salaries of office staff, managers, accountants, etc.
- Depreciation of equipment used for administrative purposes

These are all known as **indirect costs** or **overheads**.

The sum of direct and indirect costs gives the **total cost** of an organization's activities. It is important to know total cost in order to be able to work out **total profit**.

▼ *Indirect costs...*

Portfolio Activity 20.1

Range: Direct and indirect costs
Skills: Collect and record data

Collect information on all the things a business organization of your choice has to pay for. Draw a table like the one started opposite for a local builders and sort out the cost items into direct costs and indirect costs.

Direct Costs	Indirect Costs
Sand	electricity bills
cement	motor vehicle duty
...	...

Depreciation

The **fixed assets** of a business, such as machinery and vehicles, are used over and over again in the production process. Over time, their value will fall due to wear and tear, or perhaps because changing technology makes some of them obsolete. A fall in the value of fixed assets is known as **depreciation** and represents a cost to business.

Each year a business must work out how much depreciation to allow for each fixed asset. That is, it must put aside a certain amount of money each year so that, when the asset wears out, it will have saved up enough to buy a replacement.

▼ *Depreciation*

There are two main methods used by businesses to work out depreciation. These are:

- **The straight line method:** this divides the cost of the asset by the number of years it is expected to remain in service. For example, if a machine cost £1,000 and is expected to last 5 years, then the value of that machine will depreciate by £200 each year.

- **The reducing balance method:** this assumes that the depreciation charge in the earlier stages of the expected life of an asset will be greater than in later years. The value of the asset is therefore depreciated by a constant percentage each year. For example, if the value of the £1,000 machine is depreciated over 5 years at 25% each year then the depreciation charge in the first year will be £250, in the second year £187.50 (i.e. 25% of £750), in the third £140.60 - and so on, until all that remains after 5 years is the expected scrap value of the asset.

Variable costs

To expand production a firm is likely to need more materials or components, and more power to drive machinery, or to heat and light premises for longer periods. They may also need to take on more workers or employ existing workers on overtime to produce more.

Costs that vary with the level of output, such as materials, power, and the wages of production workers, are called **variable costs**. For example, if the variable cost of producing one television set is £100, then the cost of producing 1000 television sets is likely to be £100,000, unless costs savings can be made from workers and machinery working much harder and improving their productivity (see 15.1).

Variable costs are, therefore, just the direct costs of productive activity.

Fixed costs

Costs that do not vary with the level of output but remain fixed how ever many units are produced are known as **fixed costs**. For example, if it costs £5000 each month to rent a factory in which to produce television sets this cost will be unchanged whether 1 or 1000 television sets are produced. Other fixed costs will include, rates, lighting and heating, insurance, cleaning and all other overheads - that is, all indirect costs.

Calculating the total cost of production

The **total cost** of producing a given level of output in an organization is the sum of it's fixed and variable costs. Since the total costs of the same business is also the sum of its direct and indirect costs it follows that the

MABELS MUGS
(costs per month)

Direct costs		Indirect costs	
labour	£700	rent	£120
materials	£300	rates	£40
	£1,000	insurance	£35
		power	£30
		telephone	£25
		loan repayment	£35
		advertising	£15
			£300

total cost of producing a given level of output per period in any business is equal to;

Direct costs + Indirect costs = Fixed costs + Variable costs

Consider the following example. Mabels Mugs is small pottery manufacturing business which makes large, hand painted drinking mugs. Mabel, the owner of the business, has calculated that her direct costs are £1,000 each month, and her indirect costs are £300 each month. Total costs are, therefore, £1,300 per month.

These costs are based on Mabel's usual output of 500 mugs each month. That is, she allocates all her business costs to the production of her mugs. She would like to increase her output to 600 mugs each month. Her indirect costs are unlikely to increase simply because she has produced 100 more mugs. So, to find out how much extra 100 mugs would cost her she calculates that the variable cost of producing each mug in terms of labour and materials (her direct costs) is £2 (ie. £1000 / 500 mugs). Using this information Mabel calculates not only the total cost of producing 600 mugs each month but also other levels of output assuming her indirect costs remain fixed (see table 20.1).

▼ Table 20.1: How Mabels Mugs costs vary with output

Number of mugs per month	Fixed costs (£) per month	Total variable costs (£) for the level of output			Total cost (£) per month for the level of output
0	300	(£2 × 0)	=	0	300
100	300	(£2 × 100)	=	200	500
200	300	(£2 × 200)	=	400	700
300	300	(£2 × 300)	=	600	900
400	300	(£2 × 400)	=	800	1100
500	300	(£2 × 500)	=	1000	1300
600	300	(£2 × 600)	=	1200	1500
700	300	(£2 × 700)	=	1400	1700

So for example, Mabel calculates the total cost of producing 600 mugs is equal to £300 of fixed costs and £1200 of variable costs–a total of £1500 per month. If she increased production by 100 to 700 mugs per month her total variable costs will rise to £1400–an increase of £200. Fixed costs will be unchanged and so the total cost of making 700 mugs per month will be £1700.

Will fixed costs always remain fixed?

As a firm expands output it may come to a point when its existing premises and amount of machinery are simply not enough to carry on producing more and more. That is, its productive capacity will be fully utilised - it has no spare capacity to produce any more output. If the firm is to expand production further it must take on larger premises and more machinery. The firm may also find it needs to take on more administrative staff to deal with orders, deliveries and payments. These fixed costs, may not, therefore, always be fixed as firms expand production. For example, if Mabels Mugs wanted to produce 1000 mugs each month instead of 600 mugs it may need to buy a computer to help with office functions, a larger kiln in which to bake the clay mugs and a power driven potters wheel rather to replace one operated by foot.

Advanced Business

Portfolio Activity 20.1

Range: Direct and indirect costs, Fixed and variable costs
Skills: Produce written material, Tackle problems

The table opposite shows details of costs incurred by a small fast food pizza business over a 6 month period.

1. Which items are direct costs?
2. Which items are indirect costs?
3. Calculate total direct costs and total indirect costs for the business over the 6 month period.
4. Try to find out the actual costs involved in running a real-life small fast food business. How, if at all, are costs apportioned to different products/activities?
5. The pizza business has calculated that its fixed costs are £1,500 each month, while its variable costs per pizza are £2. Use a spreadsheet to calculate the total cost of producing the following number of pizzas each month;
   - 0 pizzas
   - 500 pizzas
   - 1000 pizzas
   - 2000 pizzas

Purchases of pasta, tomatoes, oils, and toppings	£1,500
Drinks	£2,000
Telephone bill	£400
Wages of cook	£10,000
Wages of part-time bookkeeper	£5,000
Electric bill	£850
Sales assistants' wages	£7,000
Wages for take-away delivery boy	£2,500
Business rates	£900
Insurance for employees	£450
Insurance for the public	£500
Hire of pizza oven	£500
Pizza poster advertising	£100
Consumables (paper, pens, cleaning fluid, order books, paper towels, etc.)	£800

Calculating total costs in multi-product organizations

The total profit of an organization is calculated as the difference between total sales revenues and total costs.

If a firm produces only one product then all the costs that arise in the firm will be the result of producing and selling that one product. That is, all costs are incurred, or absorbed, by that product. This is known as **total absorption costing**. However, a firm that produces a number of different products will want to know how much the total costs and revenues are of each product, otherwise it will not be possible to see which products are making a profit.

The direct costs of producing one pair of shoes, a compact disc, a sack of potatoes, one haircut, will be easy to calculate from their costs of materials, labour and other items used in production. However, in a firm producing two or more products it will be difficult to apportion indirect costs. For example, how much rent, rates, marketing or insurance costs is accounted for by each product?

There are a number of different ways firms can choose to apportion their indirect cost to different products. One of the easiest ways is simply to apportion indirect costs in the same proportions as direct costs in total costs.

Imagine that a firm is producing two types of duvet - one for single beds and the other for double beds. The direct costs of producing single and double duvet covers are as follows:

Direct costs of duvet production per year

Single bed duvet	£60,000	(40% of total direct costs)
Double bed duvet	£90,000	(60% of total direct costs)
Total direct costs	£150,000	

The firm also incurs indirect costs of £40,000, representing equipment maintenance, administration, and office costs. It decides to apportion these costs to each product in the same proportions as direct costs.

The single bed duvet is, therefore, apportioned £16,000 (40% of £40,000) and the double duvet cover incurs £24,000 (60% of £40,000) of indirect costs. The total cost of each product can now be calculated as follows:

Total costs of duvet production per year

	Direct costs	Indirect costs	Total costs
Single bed duvet	£60,000	£16,000	£76,000
Double bed duvet	£90,000	£24,000	£114,000
Total costs	£150,000	£40,000	£190,000

Alternatively the duvet firm may choose to apportion indirect costs based on the amount of floorspace used in the factory to produce single and double duvets. It may choose this method because the cost of factory rents, rates and insurance are such a large proportion of total indirect costs. If the production of single duvets takes up 30% of the factory while double duvets take up 70% of the factory then a different total costs per product will be calculated as follows:

Total costs of duvet production per year

	Direct costs	Indirect costs	Total costs
Single bed duvet	£60,000	£12,000 (30%)	£72,000
Double bed duvet	£90,000	£28,000 (70%)	£118,000
Total costs	£150,000	£40,000	£190,000

Clearly, different methods of apportioning indirect costs to different products will give different answers for total costs and profits when costs are compared to revenues.

UNIT SIX

CHAPTER 20

> **Key words**
>
> **Direct costs** - costs which can be directly related to the production of a particular good or service
>
> **Depreciation** - an allowance made by a business for the fall in the value of its fixed assets over time
>
> **Indirect costs** - costs which cannot be directly related to the production of a particular good or service, for example, the costs of business administration
>
> **Overheads** - indirect costs
>
> **Fixed costs** - costs that do not vary with the level of output
>
> **Variable costs** - costs that do vary with the level of output

Section 20.2 Calculating unit costs

Once the total cost of each product has been calculated, it is possible to calculate how much, on average it costs to produce each unit of output (or cost unit). This is particularly useful for a business to know.

A **cost unit** is simply a unit of product, the cost of which can be calculated and compared to revenues earned from its sale. A cost unit can be any good, for example, a car, a compact disc, a box of washing powder, a lawn mower, a chest of drawers and so on. Or the cost unit can be a service, such as one hour of labour form a car mechanic or hairdresser, one passenger mile on an aeroplane, train or bus, or one minute of time using a telephone.

Calculating average costs

The **average cost per unit** of output of a particular good or service produced can be calculated using the following formula;

$$\text{Average cost per unit} = \frac{\text{Total Cost of Output}}{\text{Total Output}}$$

Consider a manufacturer of toy dinosaurs. If the variable cost of producing each toy dinosaur is 50 pence and fixed costs are £150,000 per year, then the total cost of producing 200,000 toy dinosaurs each year will be £250,000, ie.

Total variable costs = 200,000 × 50 pence = £100,000
Total fixed costs per year = £150,000
Total costs of 200,000 units per year = £250,000

Thus, the average cost of each toy dinosaur is £1.25 (ie. £250,000 / 200,000). If the business wanted to sell each toy for £2 it will make a profit of 75 pence per dinosaur, or a total profit of £150,000 if all 200,000 units are sold. That is, the price of £2 absorbs both direct and indirect production costs and leaves a surplus for profit.

In the same way we can calculate the average cost per unit of a service, for example one hour of labour from a car mechanic or one air passenger mile. All we would need to know is the total cost of both direct and indirect costs associated with these activities. So, for example, if a mechanic spends 7 hours working on a car at a total cost of £350 in labour, materials,

Advanced Business

power, administration and other overheads, then the average cost per labour hour is £50 (ie. £350 / 7 hours).

Similarly, if it costs a total of £50,000 to fly 100 passengers 2000 miles - a total of 20,000 passenger miles - then the cost per passenger mile is £2.50 (ie. £50,000 / 20,000 miles).

Calculating marginal cost

Sometimes it is useful for a business not just to know how much it costs on average to produce each unit of output but how much it would cost to produce just one more unit of output. If a firm wants to expand production it would like to know how much it will cost. It can then decide if this cost is worth paying. That is, will the sale of the extra output generate sufficient revenues to cover the cost of producing it?

Consider the firm producing toy dinosaurs. It wants to expand production by 50,000 units. However, this will mean hiring extra machinery and moving to larger premises. The extra annual cost of machine hire, rent and rates is estimated to be £100,000. If the variable cost of producing each toy dinosaur is 50 pence then to produce an extra 50,000 toys each year will cost;

$$\text{Additional total variable costs} = 50,000 \times 0.50 \text{ pence} = £25,000$$
$$\text{Additional fixed costs} = £100,000$$
$$\text{Total additional costs} = £125,000$$

Portfolio Activity 20.2

Range: Direct and indirect costs, Fixed and variable costs
Skills: Produce written material, Tackle problems

Janine Nichols runs her own small craft business making soaps with natural herbal ingredients. She produces two soap products: 'Cool Blue' and 'Summer Meadow', which are sold to shops all over the UK.

Her costs of production each month are as follows:

Indirect costs		Direct costs	
Rent	£100	**Cool Blue:**	
Rates	£65	Labour	£120
Insurance	£35	Materials	£160
Power	£80		
Advertising	£25	**Summer Meadow:**	
Travel	£45	Labour	£150
Telephone	£25	Materials	£250
Loan repayment	£25		

Janine apportions her total indirect costs to the two products as follows;

Cool Blue   40%
Summer Meadow   60%

Output per month is currently 2,000 bars of Cool Blue soap and 4,000 bars of Summer Meadow soap.

Using this information;

1. Calculate the total cost of producing each level of output for each soap.

2. Calculate the average cost of producing one bar of Cool Blue soap and one bar of Summer Meadow.

3. Calculate the prices Janine should charge for each Cool Blue and Summer Meadow soap bar is she wants to earn of total profit of £560 and £960 on each brand respectively.

4. Summer Meadow is selling well and Janine would like to increase production by 1000 bars per month. She has calculated that she will need to work longer and incur additional fixed costs (mainly power) of £50 per month. The variable cost of producing each bar of soap will remain the same.

   a. Calculate the marginal cost of producing each extra bar of Summer Meadow soap.

   b. Advise Janine whether you think it would be worth producing the additional 1000 bars for sale at the same price you advised her to charge in task 3.

This means that it would cost £2.50 to produce each one of the additional 50,000 dinosaurs (ie. £125,000 / 50,000). Because the firm has chosen to price each dinosaur at £2 each it will not make a profit from the additional output unless it raises their price. However, this may price the toys beyond what consumers are willing to pay for them.

The additional cost of raising output is called the **marginal cost** of production. The marginal cost per unit of extra output is, therefore, calculated as follows;

$$\text{Marginal cost of an extra unit of output} = \frac{\text{Change in Total Cost}}{\text{Change in Total Output}}$$

Economies of scale

Economies of scale refer to the reductions in average cost per unit of output brought about by an increase in the scale or size of a firm. In general, as output is increased, the average cost per unit will tend to fall, as fixed costs are spread over more and more units of output.

For example, consider a power station generating electricity. Fixed costs of production are £10,000 per week regardless of how much electricity is produced. If 10,000 watts of electricity are produced each week, the average fixed cost per watt will be £1. Doubling output to 20,000 watts per week will reduce average fixed costs per watt to 50 pence. The variable cost per unit of output may also fall as output is increased. For example, the power station may be able to buy more coal and obtain a discount from suppliers.

Falling average costs are an important benefit to firms. If, however, average cost rises as output is increased, then a firm will experience **diseconomies of scale**, because it will be producing beyond it's optimum level of output.

We can plot the relationship between average cost and output in a typical firm on a graph, as follows:

▼ *Figure 20.1: An average cost curve*

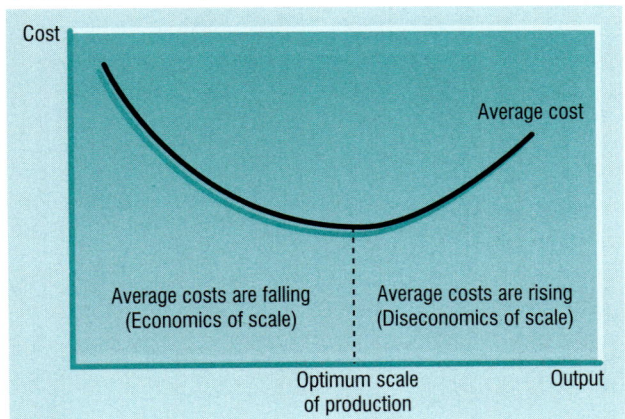

In general, the average cost curve for a given firm is U-shaped. At first, as the scale of production expands, there are cost savings resulting from increases in the scale of output. However, after a certain point, if the firm expands too much, production will become less efficient, and average costs will begin to rise. The firm will then experience diseconomies of scale.

The optimum scale of production, or most efficient size of a firm, is therefore where the average cost of producing each car, toy, pair of shoes, therm of gas, microchip, etc., is at the lowest level possible. At this point, it will be possible to combine and organize resources in the most efficient or cost-effective way. Lowering average production costs will either increase the profit margin on that product, or allow the firm's owners to lower price to attract more sales.

Economies of scale - the advantages of large-scale production

When a firm expands the scale of production, it has a chance to become more efficient and reduce average costs. This is because expansion can give business managers and owners a chance to reorganize the way in which their firm is run and financed. The advantages which result from this are known collectively as **internal economies of scale**, and include the following:

- **Financial economies**. A large firm may be able to obtain finance from a greater variety of financial institutions, for example, by selling shares on the Stock Market (see 22.3).

- **Marketing economies**. Large firms, with the necessary finance and storage space, can often take advantage of discounts for bulk purchases offered by suppliers. They may employ specialist sales teams to market their products, and will also have the financial resources to advertise widely through a variety of media to reach and expand their market.

- **Technical economies**. The research and development of new, faster, and more efficient methods and products is often very expensive. A large firm will be able to spread this cost across a large output, and can therefore afford to use a wider range of production methods. It will also be able to benefit from bulk carriers such as juggernauts, or in the case of oil companies, pipelines, and supertankers, to meet its vast distribution requirements.

- **Risk-bearing economies**. A large firm can attempt to minimize or spread risk in a number of ways not open to a smaller enterprise. It can buy materials in bulk from a number of suppliers to minimize the risk of a hold-up in supplies from one outlet. It may also diversify production lines - i.e. produce a range of different products for sale in case the demand for one falls.

Diseconomies of scale - the disadvantages of large-scale production

However, if a firm becomes too large, production may become inefficient. Average costs will rise. This is caused by diseconomies of scale, for example:

Economies of scale...continued

- **Management diseconomies.** Large firms can often suffer from too many layers of management, leading to communication problems.

- **Labour diseconomies.** Large firms will use specialized mass-production techniques in an attempt to reduce average production costs. However, as production of the final product is divided up into many specialized tasks, workers may become bored with their repetitive and often monotonous jobs, and productivity and product quality may suffer.

Key words

Cost unit - a unit of a good or service to which costs can be charged and compared to revenues.

Marginal cost - the cost of producing an additional unit of output

Under-recovery - if the price per unit recovers a smaller proportion of the indirect costs apportioned per unit than initially anticipated

Average cost - total cost divided by total output to give the cost per unit of output

Further reading
Gittas, JF: *Controlling Costs* (Kogan Page 1992)

Test Questions

The following underpinning knowledge will be tested:
1. Direct and indirect costs
2. The calculation of direct costs of goods or services per period of time
3. The calculation of indirect costs per period of time
4. The total cost of a unit of production or service
5. Variable and fixed costs and their relationship with production
6. The marginal cost of a unit of production or service

1 All of the following business costs will usually be classified as direct costs **except**

A business rates
B raw materials
C production workers wages
D depreciation

2 Depreciation as a business cost is

A a fall in the value of foreign currency holdings
B a fall in the value of current assets
C a fall in the value of stocks held
D a fall in the value of fixed assets

3 Which of the following is **not** an indirect cost to business?

A the purchase of photocopying paper
B allowances for the depreciation of machinery
C office heating bills
D after sales care

Questions 4 - 6 share the following answer options;

A passenger mile
B call unit
C labour hour
D barrel

Which of the above cost units will be used by the producers if the following goods and services to compare unit costs and revenues?

4 oil

5 piano lessons

6 coach travel

7 Which of the following costs is likely to vary with the level of output in a firm?

A rent
B overheads
C component parts
D insurance

8 What annual depreciation charge would you advise a firm to use against a machine that cost £5,000 and lasts 10 years?

A 0
B £1,000
C £500
D £50

9 Which of the following cost items are unlikely to vary with the level of output on a farm?

A seeds
B petrol for a tractor
C business rates
D fertilizer

10 A firm wants to expand production by 10,000 units over current levels of output. To do this it will need to hire additional machinery at a cost of £5,000 per year. If the cost of labour and materials to produce each unit of production is £3, what is the marginal cost of each additional unit?

A 70 pence
B £3.50
C £7
D £3

Questions 11 - 14 are based on the following information;

ABC Ltd has calculated that its fixed costs are £10,000 per month. Variable costs are £2 per unit produced.

11 What are the total cost of producing 5000 units each month?

A £12,000

B £200,000

C £10,000

D £20,000

12 What is the average cost of producing each unit of the total output of 5000 units per month?

A £4

B £2

C £40

D £20

13 If ABC Ltd wanted to earn a profit of £10,000 on the production and sale of 5000 units per month what price per unit should they charge?

A 60 pence

B £60

C £2

D £6

14 a. List three cost items in a computer assembly plant that could be classed as i. direct costs, and ii. indirect costs

b. Why are some cost items referred to as 'fixed'?

c. i. Explain what is meant by the marginal cost of production?

ii. Why is information on the marginal cost of production useful to a firm investigating possibilities for expansion?

d. What is depreciation? Explain using examples.

assessment assignment

CHAPTER 20

Assessment Assignment

Range: Direct costs
Indirect costs (overheads)
Fixed costs
Variable costs
Unit of production
Unit of service
Time period

Skills: **Communication**
Produce written material
Application of number
Collect and record data
Tackle problems
Interpret and present data
Information technology
Process information
Present information

Waterhouse Waffles produces cream filled waffles for sale in supermarket freezer sections.

The accounts department has calculated that the cost of producing 400,000 waffles each quarter are as follows;

Direct costs

Labour	£70,000
Materials	£25,000
Power	£5,000

Indirect costs per Qtr

Rent	£5,100
Rates	£1,000
Power (offices only)	£1,250
Marketing	£1,550
Telephone	£650
Business travel	£550
Office supplies	£850
Insurance	£450
Depreciation	£250
Other overheads	£350

Using this information, Accounts have calculated that the variable cost of producing each waffle is 25 pence. It has also estimated that indirect costs would remain the same for levels of output between 200,000 waffles per quarter and 600,000 waffles per quarter. At 600,000 waffles per quarter the factory is working at full capacity.

To increase output above 600,000 waffles per quarter the firm would need to expand into new premises and install new computer controlled equipment. A nearby factory unit meeting the requirements of such expansion plans has been identified and will cost a total of £9,000 in quarterly rent and rates - £2,900 more than at present. A long term loan to buy the new equipment would cost £3,300 per quarter in repayments. Other indirect costs are assumed to rise by around £800. The variable cost per waffle would stay the same.

Tasks

1. Produce a short report for the Managing director of Waterhouse Waffles, explaining the difference between;

- direct and indirect costs
- fixed and variable costs
- average and marginal costs per waffle

Also include in your report an explanation of the following terms;

- cost units
- depreciation

Now use a computer spreadsheet to undertake tasks 2 - 5 below. Generate computer print outs of your calculations to include in your report.

2. Using the information above calculate the total cost of producing the following amount of waffles each quarter;

- 200,000
- 400,000
- 600,000

3. What is average cost of producing each waffle at the present level of output of 400,000 waffles per quarter?

4. If Waterhouse Waffles wanted to make a profit of £128,000 each quarter from the sale of 400,000 waffles what price should it charge for each waffle?

5. Suppose the firm does to decide to expand production to 800,000 waffles each quarter. Calculate the total cost of this level of output and then use the information on the change in total costs and output to calculate the marginal cost of producing each additional waffle over an output of 600,000.

6. Assuming the firm is able to sell the additional waffles at the same price chosen in task 4 would you advise the firm to go ahead with its expansion plans?

chapter 21

Advanced Business

chapter 21
Pricing Decisions and Strategies

This chapter examines the pricing decisions and strategies used by different business organizations and the factors that influence these decisions

Key ideas

Three major factors will influence the pricing decisions of a business organization: costs of production, level and strength of consumer **demand**, and **competition** with rival suppliers.

Cost-based pricing strategies involve setting the price of a product above its variable and fixed costs of production.

In the short run, a firm must set a price which will generate revenues sufficient to cover its variable costs, such as materials and labour, in order to continue production.

Pricing at **marginal cost** involves setting a price equal to (or just above) the cost of producing one more unit of a good or service. For example, because the cost of carrying one more passenger is small, airlines often sell off unused seats at bargain 'marginal cost' prices.

In the long run, a firm must be able to cover its fixed costs such as rent and rates, if it is to survive.

The **break-even level of output** for an organization occurs where total sales revenue from the sale of a product equals total costs of production, such that profit is zero.

Economies of scale refer to cost savings achieved as firms grow in size.

Demand-based pricing strategies are based on the price that consumers are willing to pay for a product. For example, pricing may be kept low to launch a new product and to expand sales.

A firm may use **competition-based pricing strategies** to expand, or at least preserve, market share in highly competitive markets.

A **price war** may develop between suppliers, involving retaliatory price cuts. Unless total sales increase as a result, the only winner in a price war is the consumer.

Section **21.1**

The pricing decision

What determines prices?

Deciding on the price at which to sell a product is one of the most important decisions an organization can make. If price is set too high, consumers may be unwilling to buy the product. If price is set too low, a firm may not be able to cover its costs of production.

The prices of all goods and services are likely to vary over their product life-cycles as the marketing objectives of different organizations change - for example, from launching a new product, to maximizing profit from the product (see 4.1). At any given time, short-term objectives, such as the need to fight off new competitors or to extend the life of the product, may affect the pricing strategy of a firm. Pricing low to generate sales and fight off competition may cause a firm to lose money in the short term. However, in the long run, if a firm is to stay in business it must be able to cover its costs of production with sales revenues.

Three major factors can, therefore, be identified as influencing the pricing decisions of firms. These are:

- The costs of production (and the desire for profit)
- The level and strength of consumer demand
- The level of competition among producers to supply the market

Factors influencing pricing decisions

Prices set by a firm with reference to its costs of production will be greatly influenced by the particular aims and objectives agreed by the organization.

The need to survive

Underlying all business is the need to survive. To do this, a firm must be able to generate enough revenues to cover its costs of production. This is of particular importance to non-profit-making organizations such as charities. All donations or monies they receive are spent on their particular activities. That is, income should exactly equal costs. However, because flows of income and expenditures do not necessarily occur at the same time, charities must be careful not to overspend and operate at a loss.

The desire for profit

Covering costs may ensure business survival, but most business owners also want to earn a profit from their activities. The level of return on their investment will need to be at least as much as the interest they could have earned by placing the money in a bank account instead. In order to earn this profit, they will need to set a price for their product which will generate revenues to exceed production costs.

Expanding sales

When a firm enters a market for the first time with a new product, its long-term objective may be to maximize profit, but in the short term it will have other aims as well. For example, in order to ensure a successful launch for the product, it may decide to pitch price low and cut its profit margins to the bone. If there are a number of other similar products already on the

Promotional pricing to boost sales

market, it may need to keep price at this low level in order to build market share and maximize potential sales. If sales do not match expectations, it may find itself left with underused capacity, in terms of labour, stocks or materials, machines, and other equipment.

However, in other circumstances, launching an entirely new and unique product may allow a firm to pursue a high-price strategy. Consumers may be willing to pay a premium price for a new product. A high selling price may also be the only way the firm can justify the high cost of product research and development (R&D) and an initial supply. It may be that sales will need to expand before a firm can benefit from cost savings associated with mass production and be able to pass these on to consumers in the form of lower prices (see 20.2).

External factors influencing pricing decisions

Setting price with regard only to the costs of production ignores the constraints imposed by external factors such as:

- The level of consumer demand (see 1.2)
- The amount of competition among producers (see 2.2)
- Government intervention in product markets (see 3.3)

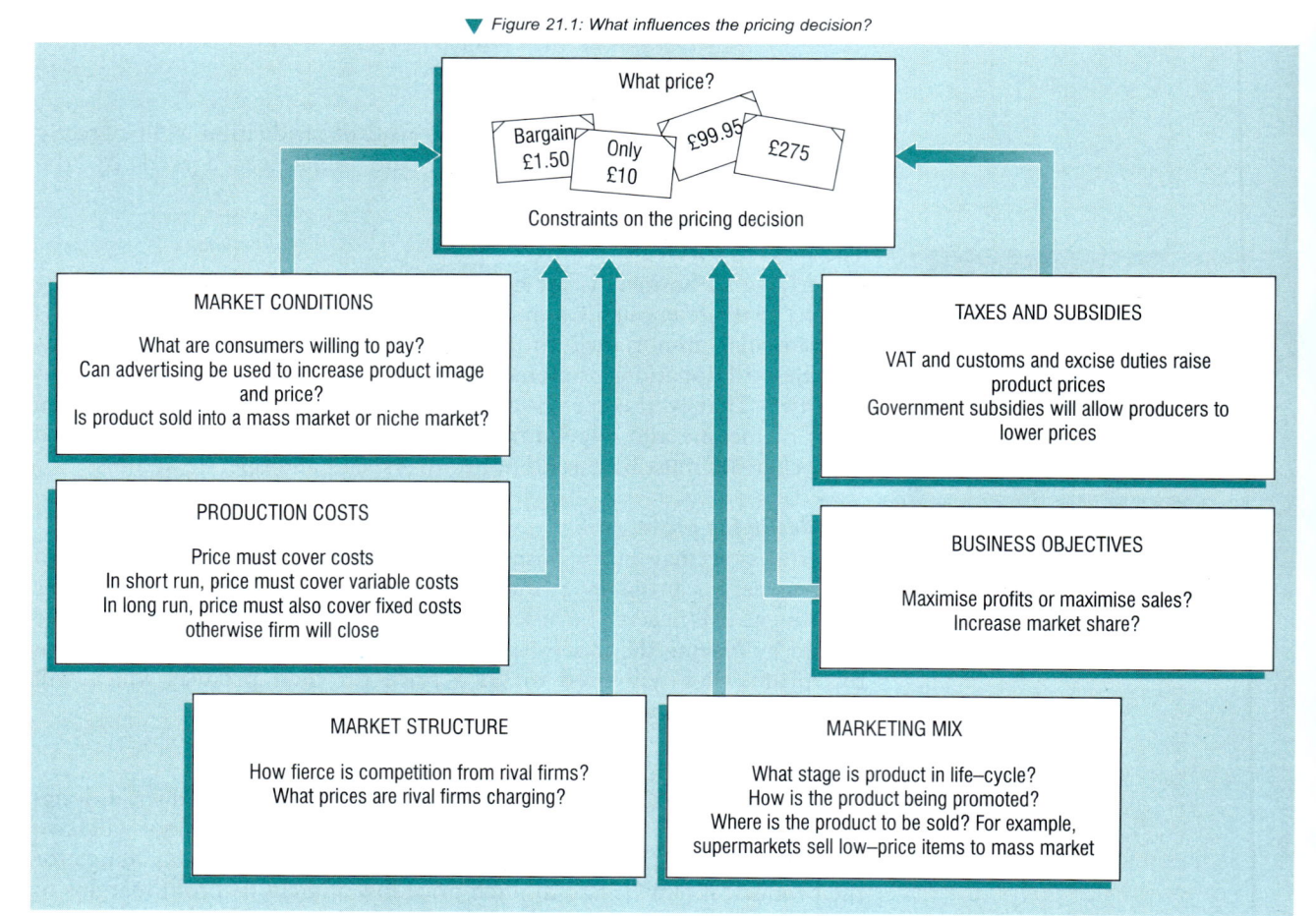

Figure 21.1: What influences the pricing decision?

What price?

Bargain £1.50 | Only £10 | £99.95 | £275

Constraints on the pricing decision

MARKET CONDITIONS

What are consumers willing to pay?
Can advertising be used to increase product image and price?
Is product sold into a mass market or niche market?

PRODUCTION COSTS

Price must cover costs
In short run, price must cover variable costs
In long run, price must also cover fixed costs otherwise firm will close

MARKET STRUCTURE

How fierce is competition from rival firms?
What prices are rival firms charging?

TAXES AND SUBSIDIES

VAT and customs and excise duties raise product prices
Government subsidies will allow producers to lower prices

BUSINESS OBJECTIVES

Maximise profits or maximise sales?
Increase market share?

MARKETING MIX

What stage is product in life-cycle?
How is the product being promoted?
Where is the product to be sold? For example, supermarkets sell low-price items to mass market

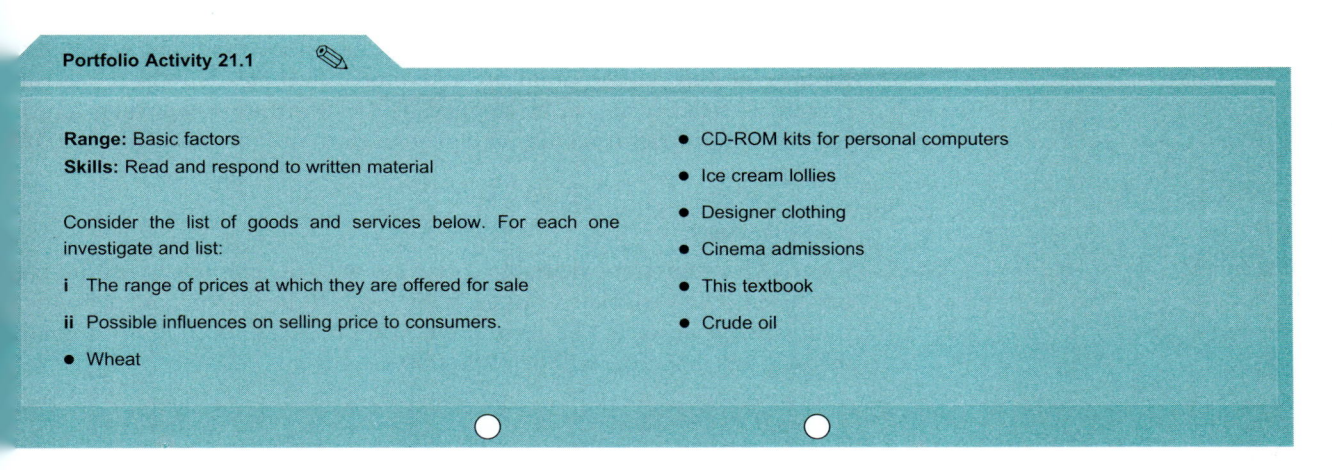

> **Portfolio Activity 21.1**
>
> **Range:** Basic factors
> **Skills:** Read and respond to written material
>
> Consider the list of goods and services below. For each one investigate and list:
>
> i The range of prices at which they are offered for sale
>
> ii Possible influences on selling price to consumers.
>
> - Wheat
> - CD-ROM kits for personal computers
> - Ice cream lollies
> - Designer clothing
> - Cinema admissions
> - This textbook
> - Crude oil

Section 21.2 Cost-based pricing

Cost-based pricing methods involve setting price with reference to costs. For this purpose, it is important for a business to understand how costs may change with the level of output and over time, especially if the business is considering expanding production.

Fixed and variable costs

In chapter 20 we learnt that **fixed costs**, such as rent, rates and other running expenses, do not vary with the level of output. Costs that do vary as a direct result of changes in the level of output, such as purchases of raw materials and wages, are called **variable costs**.

We will now consider how fixed and variable costs can be presented on graphs to help a business plan for future levels of production.

Figure 21.2 depicts the relationship between fixed costs and output in a graph for a business making toy animals. It shows that fixed costs are £50,000 regardless of the amount produced, up to 200,000 units of

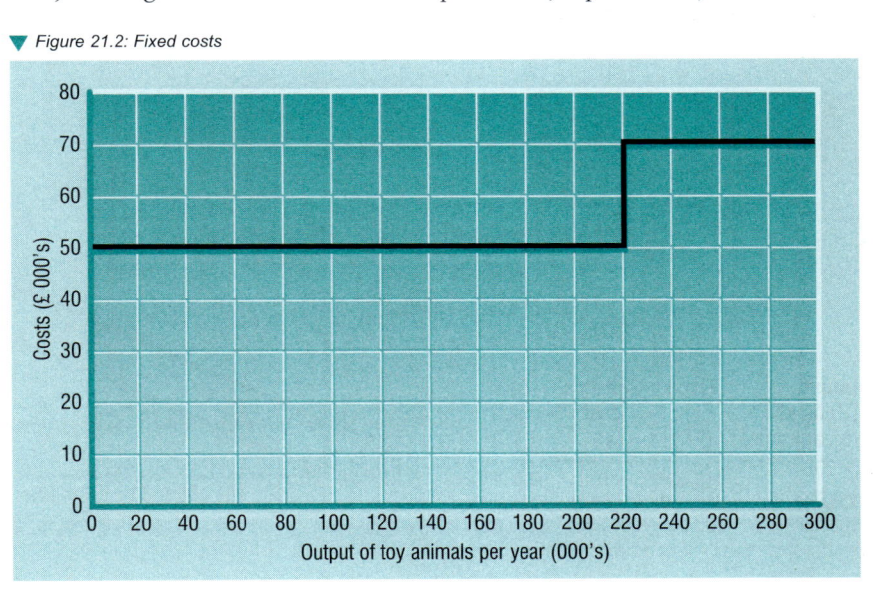

▼ Figure 21.2: Fixed costs

product per year. If the firm wants to produce more than this, it will need to hire or buy larger premises and more machines. In the long run therefore, fixed costs can be stepped up (or down), but will then remain fixed at their higher level of £70,000 at levels of output exceeding 200,000 units per year.

Variable costs

Figure 21.3 shows how variable costs vary with the amount of toy animals produced. The variable cost of each toy is £1. If the firm produces no toys total variable costs will be zero. If the firm produces 200,000 toy animals its total variable costs will be £200,000.

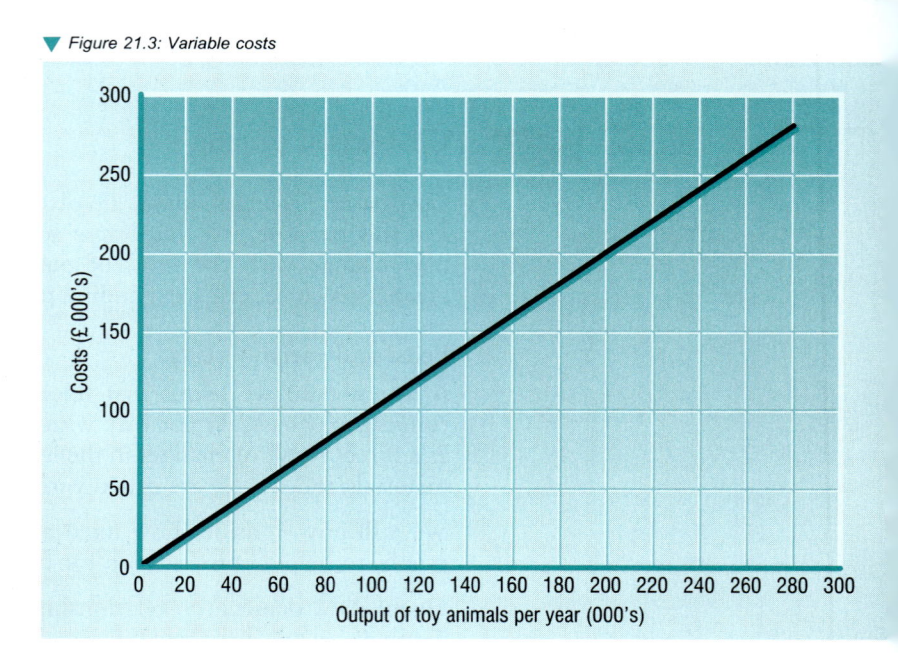

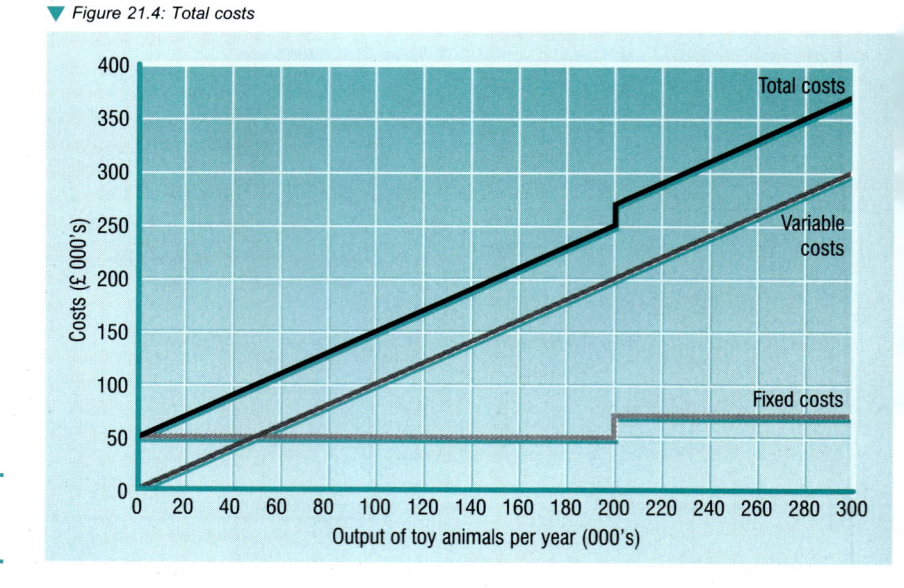

▼ *Figure 21.3: Variable costs*

▼ *Figure 21.4: Total costs*

Output (Units of toy animals)	Fixed cost (FC)	Variable cost (VC)	Total cost (TC)
0	£50,000	0	£50,000
100,000	£50,000	£100,000	£150,000
200,000	£50,000	£200,000	£250,000

Total costs

From chapter 20 we know that adding fixed and variable costs together gives the total cost of production.

$$\text{Total Cost (TC)} = \text{Fixed Cost (FC)} + \text{Variable Cost (VC)}$$

The total cost of production is the cost of producing any given level of output. As output rises, total cost will increase because of variable costs. The relationship between total cost and output for the toy animal manufacturer is shown in Figure 21.4.

> **Semi-variable costs**
>
> Some costs do not fit neatly into the categories of 'fixed' and 'variable'. The cost of hiring labour is a good example. If a business employs ten people on a permanent basis, the total wage bill will be the same each week, regardless of the level of output. However, if the employees are asked to work overtime to produce more output, then the extra cost of their employment will be variable. Such labour costs are said to be **semi-variable**. Only if the employees' wages are linked directly to output, for example, through the payment of piece rates, will the whole wage bill be a variable cost to the business.
>
> Other examples of costs which are often thought of as semi-variable are telephone and electricity charges. These consist of a fixed standing charge which is the same no matter how many calls are made or how much electricity is used, plus a variable charge dependent on the number of units used up.

What is break-even analysis?

A business will often want to know how much they will have to produce and sell of a good or service at a chosen price before they make a profit. Classifying costs as fixed or variable allows managers to undertake this calculation, and to decide on appropriate selling prices for their products.

The **break-even level of output** is where total sales revenue is exactly equal to total costs. At this point, the firm makes neither a profit nor a loss. That is, the break-even point occurs where:

$$\text{Total Revenue (£)} = \text{Fixed Costs} + \text{Variable Costs} = \text{Total Costs}$$

Break-even analysis seeks to predict the level of sales a business will need to achieve in order to break even, and to determine how changes in output, costs, and/or price will affect the break-even point and their possible profits.

Calculating break-even point

A firm can calculate its break-even point if it knows its costs and the price it can charge for each unit of output. Consider the following example.

Geoff's Knitwear Ltd has fixed costs each year of £200,000, and variable costs of £5 per jumper produced. The jumpers are sold for £30 each. The break-even level of output for Geoff's Knitwear can be calculated as follows:

$$\text{Total Cost (TC)} = \text{Fixed Costs} + \text{Variable Costs}$$
$$\text{TC} = £200,000 + (£5 \times Q)$$

and:

$$\text{Total Revenue (TR)} = \text{Price} \times \text{Quantity Sold}$$
$$\text{TR} = £30 \times Q$$

(where Q is the quantity of jumpers produced and sold)

At break-even output, total cost equals total revenue. That is:

$$TC = TR$$
$$£200{,}000 + (£5 \times Q) = £30 \times Q$$

Thus, to solve the equation by finding Q:

$$£200{,}000 = £25 \times Q$$
$$\frac{£200{,}000}{£25} = Q$$
$$8{,}000 = Q$$

That is, Geoff's Knitwear must produce and sell 8,000 jumpers at a price of £30 each to break even. If more than 8,000 jumpers are sold, the firm makes a profit, while if less than 8,000 are made, the firm makes a loss.

We can check this calculation by returning to the formula TC = TR;

$$£200{,}000 + (£5 \times 8000 \text{ jumpers}) = £30 \times 8000 \text{ jumpers}$$
$$£200{,}000 + £40{,}000 = £240{,}000$$
$$£240{,}000 \text{ costs} = £240{,}000 \text{ revenues}$$

We can, therefore, be confident that 8000 jumpers is the break even level of ouptut in Geoff's Knitwear Ltd.

Break-even charts

The break-even point can also be found by plotting total costs and total revenues on a **break-even chart**.

The first step is to calculate total costs and total revenues for a number of different levels of output. (As an absolute minimum, two levels of output should be chosen - zero and one other.) Table 21.1 is a schedule of outputs for Geoff's Knitwear Ltd, ranging from 0 to 12,000 jumpers per year, with corresponding costs and revenues. These figures can be used to plot the two line graphs in the break-even chart in Figure 21.5.

▼ Table 21.1: Schedule of outputs, costs and revenues for Geoff's Knitwear Ltd

Jumpers per year (Q)	Total costs (£200,000 + (£5 x Q))	Total revenue (£30 x Q)
0	£200,000	0
2,000	£210,000	£60,000
4,000	£220,000	£120,000
6,000	£230,000	£180,000
8,000	£240,000	£240,000
10,000	£250,000	£300,000
12,000	£260,000	£360,000

In a break-even chart, output or sales are measured on the horizontal (x) axis, while costs are measured on the vertical (y) axis. Break-even output is found at the point at which the total revenue line crosses the total cost line. The area between the two lines represent a loss when TC is greater than TR, and a profit when TC is less than TR.

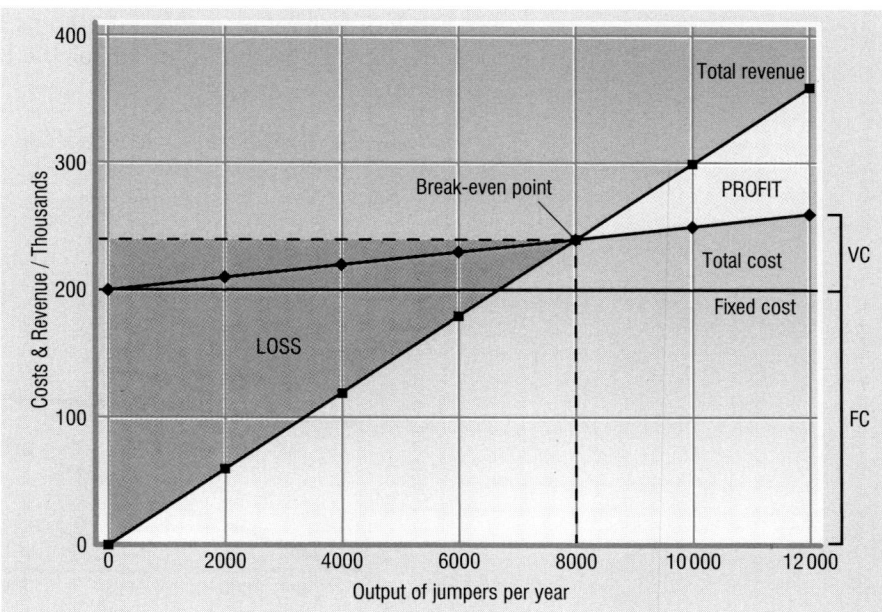

▼ *Figure 21.5: Break-even chart for Geoff's Knitwear Ltd*

Portfolio Activity 21.2

Range: Break-even point, Reasons, Analyse
Skills: Tackle problems

Bear Necessities is a small toy firm producing hand-made teddy bears, owned by Bev Johnson. Bev rents a small factory unit on an industrial estate for £100 per week. She pays out £5 a week on heat and light (subsidized by the council), and £50 a week to repay a bank loan. She hires machinery at a cost of £45 per week, and employs her two brothers to help her make bears. At present, they pay themselves £1 for each bear they complete. Materials to make the bears cost £6, and foam costs £1. Bev initially charges £20.00 for each bear sold.

1. Calculate the total fixed costs of Bear Necessities and the variable cost per bear.

2. For the following levels of output of bears each week, calculate total cost, total revenue, and profit (or loss):

   (a) 0
   (b) 0
   (c) 40

3. What is the average cost per bear when:

   (a) 10 bears are produced each week

   (b) If bear production is 40 per week

   What do you conclude about the relationship between average cost and output? Why is this relationship unlikely to hold if bear production is expanded indefinitely? (see 20.2)

4. Calculate how many bears Bev Johnson needs to produce and sell each week to break even.

5. What will happen to her break-even level of output if:

   (a) She finds a new supplier who offers her a bulk discount, such that material costs per bear fall to £4

   (b) She has to reduce the price of each bear to £15 to encourage sales (costs are as calculated in Question 1)

6. Suggest how break-even analysis can assist Bear Necessities in planning future production and prices.

'What if' analysis

Break-even charts are a useful business planning tool because they allow managers to project what might happen to the break-even output and profits if costs alter, or if the price of the product is changed. For example, if prices are cut, the break-even level of output will rise, since more units will need to be sold to cover production costs.

Figure 21.6 shows the effect of a price-rise to £37 per jumper on the break-even level of output for Geoff's Knitwear Ltd. Only 6,250 jumpers now have to be sold in order for the business to break even, rather than 8,000.

▼ Figure 21.6: The impact of a price-rise on break-even

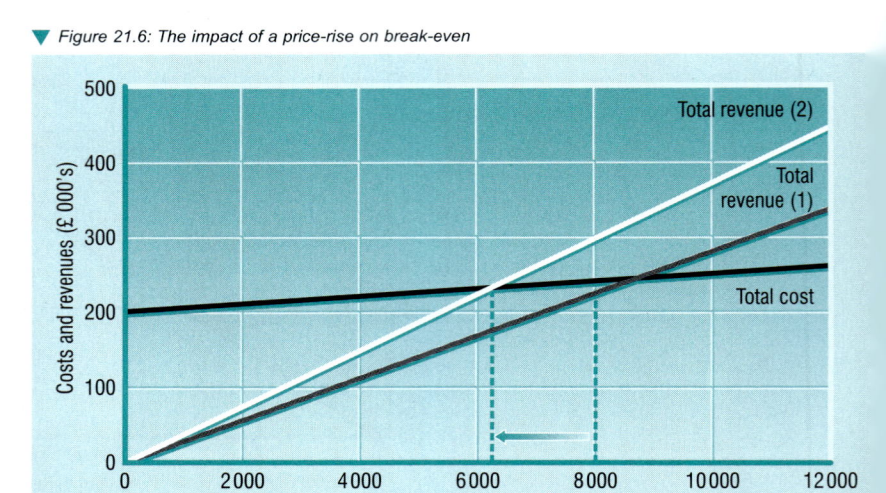

Figure 21.7 shows the impact of a rise in materials costs on the knitwear business. Variable costs per jumper are now £10. In order to break even the company must now sell 10,000 jumpers per year. An increase in fixed costs would have a similar impact.

▼ Figure 21.7: The Impact of an increase in variable costs on break-even

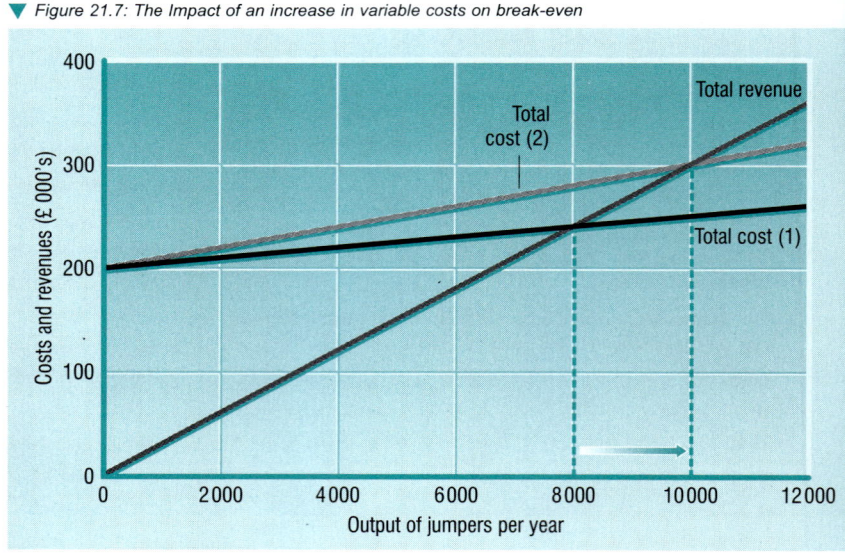

The margin of safety

Once a business has forecast the level of sales it must achieve at a given price in order to break even, it must then attempt to exceed this level in order to make a profit. In the example above, Geoff's Knitwear might plan to sell 10,000 jumpers next year - 2,000 more than required to break even.

The firm would then be operating above break-even output and will therefore be in the area of profit. This difference between forecast sales and break-even output is known as the **margin of safety**. In other words, Geoff's Knitwear has incorporated a margin of safety of 2,000 units into its sales forecast. Sales of jumpers can therefore fall short of the forecast by up to 2,000 (or 20%) before the firm will start to make losses (see Figure 21.8).

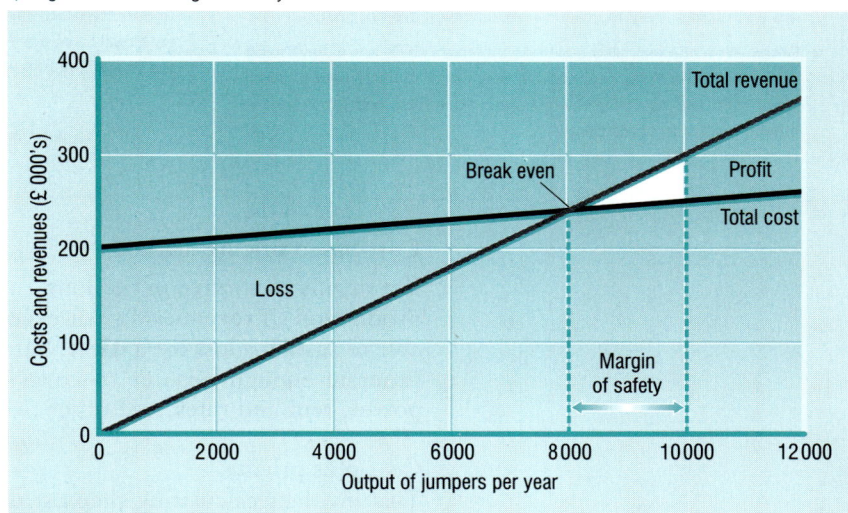

▼ Figure 21.8: the margin of safety for Geoff's Knitwear Ltd

Portfolio Activity 21.3

Range: Break even point, Label, Analyse
Skills: Interpret and present data, Process information

1. Input the following table into a computer spreadsheet:

FINANCIAL INFORMATION FOR SWIZZ MAGS LTD
Teen Dream Magazine (Retail Price £1.50)

Fixed costs per month £10,000
Variable cost per unit £0.25

Magazines per month	Total cost	Total revenue	Profit/Loss
0	?	?	?
4,000			
8,000			
2,000			
16,000			
20,000			
24,000			
28,000			

2. Input commands to automatically compute each cell in the columns for total cost, total revenue, and profit/loss for each level of output.

3. What is the break-even level of output?

4. Use the information to produce a break-even chart from your spreadsheet table. Make sure you use the following labels

- Area of profit/loss
- Total cost and Total revenue
- Costs and level of output
- Break even point
- Fixed costs and variable costs

5. For each of the following events in isolation, recalculate each column in your table, and then replot your break-even chart to show the effect of:

(a) an increase in product price to £1.85

(b) an increase in the variable cost per unit to 50 pence

(c) an increase in fixed costs to £12,000 per month, due to an increase in insurance and business rates

Limitations of break-even analysis

Break-even analysis is a useful aid to business planning, but managers need to be aware of its limitations as a decision-making tool. For example:

- Break-even analysis assumes that the quantity of goods produced is actually sold, and that no stocks are held. In reality, however, firms will often need to build up stocks to cope with seasonal variations or unforeseen changes in demand. This means that they are sometimes likely to produce goods which are not sold.
- Break-even analysis also assumes that fixed costs are always fixed. However, when output expands, it may become necessary to install more plant and equipment, which can cause fixed costs to increase. Inflation will also affect costs.
- The conditions of demand and supply are constantly changing (see 1.4). That is, costs and the prices at which goods or services can be sold will not be static. As conditions change, it becomes harder to predict the break-even level of output.
- Break-even analysis relies on accurate cost and sales data. If data is inaccurate or forecasts poor, then break-even analysis will yield inaccurate advice. For example, if fixed costs have been underestimated, break-even analysis will suggest a lower level of sales will be needed to cover costs than will actually be the case and the firm will risk making a loss.

Cost-based pricing methods

If a firm is to survive in the long run, it must be able to cover its costs of production. If revenues do not exceed costs, it will make a loss. It may be able to sustain a loss for a while, but in order to continue operating, it must generate enough revenue to cover wage bills and pay for materials and power, rent and rates, and other overheads.

Cost-plus pricing

This involves calculating the cost of producing each unit of output, and then adding a mark-up for profit. For example, if a firm produced 10,000 units of a product costing £20,000, the average cost would be £2 (see 20.2). A 10% profit mark-up would mean that units would be priced for sale at £2.20 each.

Contribution pricing

It is relatively easy to calculate the variable costs of producing each unit of output. However, it is often difficult to calculate what proportion of fixed costs such as rent and rates, heating, nighttime security, etc., to apportion to each product. **Contribution pricing**, therefore, involves setting a price for each unit that covers its variable cost and makes a contribution towards total fixed costs, as well as a mark-up for profit.

The contribution per unit of output can be calculated as follows:

$$\text{Contribution per Unit (£)} = \text{Selling Price} - \text{Variable Cost}$$

The selling price of each unit of output will be chosen so that the total contribution covers fixed costs and yields an acceptable profit, where:

$$\text{Profit} = \text{Total Contribution} - \text{Total Fixed Costs}$$

Contribution pricing can also be used to find the level of output at which a firm will break even. For example, returning to the case of Geoff's Knitwear Ltd, we can calculate the contribution each jumper makes towards fixed costs as follows:

$$\text{Contribution per Jumper Sold (£)} = £30 - £5 = £25$$

Figure 21.9: Cost-based pricing

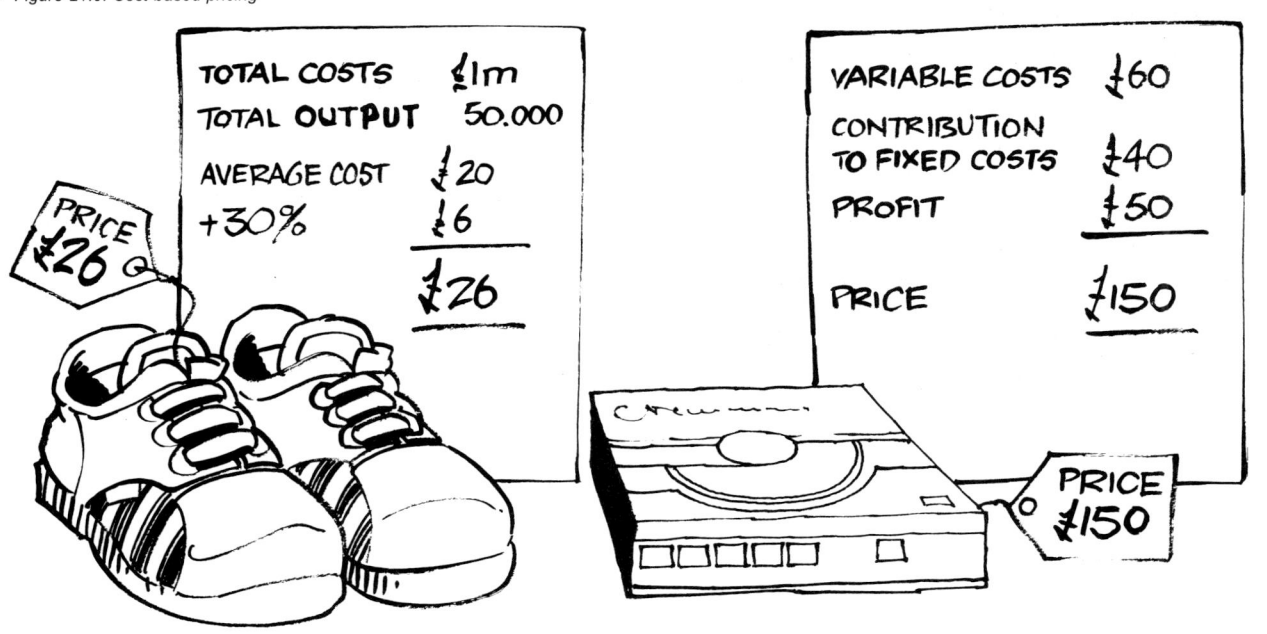

At the break-even output of 8,000 jumpers, the total contribution will be £200,000 (ie. 8000 × £25) - exactly equal to total fixed costs. Profit is zero. However, the 8001st jumper sold will yield a profit of £25 and so on.

The break-even level of output can therefore be calculated using the following formula:

$$\text{Break-even Output} = \frac{\text{Fixed Cost}}{\text{Contribution}} = \frac{£200,000}{£25} = 8,000$$

Contribution pricing methods can be a very useful means of assessing the performance of a business, allowing management to measure and compare the contribution made by all of the various products the firm produces. Some products may make a negative contribution - that is, variable costs may exceed the selling price - in which case, total profit may be increased by halting their production. However, sometimes firms may deliberately produce and sell a product generating a negative contribution as a **loss-leader**, in order to encourage interest in other products in the range. Closing down the production of such a product could damage sales of the other products, and reduce their contribution as well. For example, the Mini car is a popular make which car-dealers like to display in their showrooms to attract people in to browse - and hopefully to buy. However, for many years the production of the Mini resulted in a loss for its manufacturer.

Similarly, a product may make a negative contribution if it is a relatively new, competitively priced item, in the launch or growth stage of its life-cycle (see 10.3).

▼ *Flight bargains offered by 'bucket shops' - an example of marginal cost pricing to use up spare capacity*

Daily Mirror 7/2/95 'Classifieds'

Marginal cost pricing

The addition to total cost resulting from the production of an additional unit of output is known as the **marginal cost** (see 20.2). A decision to expand output by one or more units will be based on an assumption that unit price will be at least sufficient to cover marginal costs, such that the total profit earned on all previous units is not reduced.

Sometimes firms will price just above marginal cost in order to use up spare capacity and ensure that at least a small contribution to fixed costs is made. For example, consider an airline selling flights to New York. Whether the plane flies full or half-empty, it will incur the same fixed costs for fuel, flight crew, and staff. Suppose 80% of seats at the standard fare are sold, yielding a reasonable profit on the flight. In an attempt to fill the plane, the airline can offer remaining seats at bargain prices. The marginal cost of each additional passenger will be small - just the cost of additional administration and on-board refreshments. As long as the fare price more than covers these small additional costs, the airline will be able to add to its profit.

Problems with cost-based pricing

Cost-based pricing strategies make no allowance for the market and what people are already paying for similar products. Once a mark-up for profit has been added on top of allocated costs per unit, the product price may be too expensive compared to rival products, and the firm will find it difficult to make sales. In the short run, therefore, a firm may be forced to cut price and take a loss in order to fight off competition.

Key words

Fixed costs - costs that do not vary with output, for example, rent and overheads

Variable costs - costs which vary with the level of output, such as the cost of materials

Average cost - the average cost per unit of output, calculated by dividing total costs by total output

Break-even level of output - the level of output at which total revenue is equal to total costs, i.e. profit is zero

Margin of safety - the difference between planned output and an associated level of profit, and the break-even point

Cost-plus pricing - setting product price equal to average cost, plus a mark-up for profit

Profit mark-up - the margin added to cost to give the price of a product, as used in cost-plus pricing

Contribution pricing - setting product price to cover variable cost, plus a proportion of fixed costs

Contribution - selling price per unit less variable cost per unit. If a sufficient total contribution is made to cover fixed costs, a business will make a profit

Loss-leader - an unprofitable product which continues to be produced and sold because it has a positive effect on the sales of other products produced by the same organization

Marginal cost pricing - setting price equal to or just above the cost of producing an extra unit of output

Section 21.3 Market-based pricing

Demand based pricing

Market- or **demand-based** pricing strategies tend to involve pricing products at 'what the market will bear'. That is, producers will price high if consumer demand is high. For example, high prices are often charged for unique products, like rock festivals and designer clothes, because demand will normally outstrip supply.

Short-term pricing objectives

The product price charged by a firm will largely depend upon the target market for the product and the objectives of the firm. For example, in some markets, such as supermarket own-brand products, firms will need to adopt a low-price strategy to attract customers away from well-known brand leaders. In other markets, high price can actually be an attraction because it lends exclusivity or 'snob appeal' to the product. Products in Hamleys Toy Shop in London's Regent Street, for example, are sometimes priced 400% above those for the same toys in high street shops, yet the toys will still sell because of the exclusivity and image of the store.

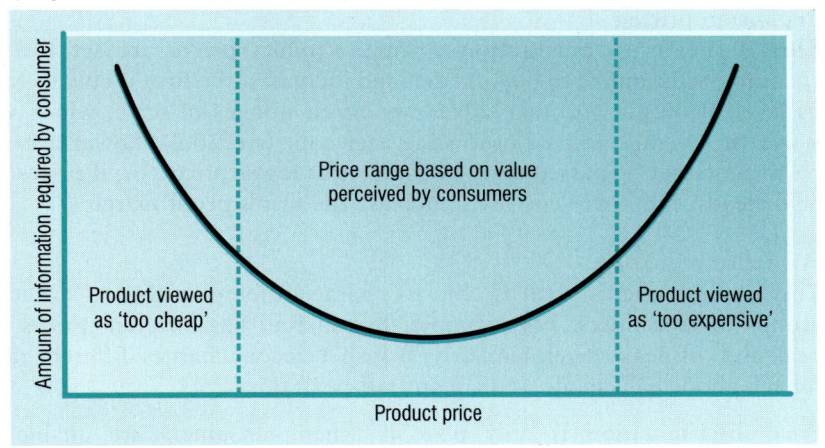

▼ Figure 21.10: The relationship between price and consumer information requirements

[Graph showing U-shaped curve with "Amount of information required by consumer" on y-axis and "Product price" on x-axis. Left side labeled "Product viewed as 'too cheap'", right side labeled "Product viewed as 'too expensive'", middle region labeled "Price range based on value perceived by consumers".]

Adapted from 'Directing the Marketing Effort' by R Willsmer (Pan)

If customer's perception of the product does not match the price, extra marketing effort will required to justify the difference (see Figure 21.10). This is true whether the price is lower or higher than the customer would normally expect to pay. Both 'bargain' prices and excessively high prices are likely to arouse suspicion. The greater the difference between the consumer's expected price and the actual selling price, the greater the marketing effort required to convince the customer that the price charged is justifiable.

Instead of reflecting what the product costs to produce, demand-based pricing asks: 'At what price will this product sell?' In adopting this approach, firms will need to carry out careful market research to find out what consumers are willing to pay, and also study the pricing policies of their competitors (see 9.1). Only then will they be able to produce a good or service with the right design and quality to fit the market, and at the right cost to yield a profit.

Market skimming

This strategy, also known as **price creaming**, is often used when there is little competition in a market. It involves charging a high price for a new product to yield a high initial profit from consumers who are willing to pay extra because the product is new and unique. As competitors enter the market, prices are reduced to encourage the market to expand.

Market skimming is a practice often observed in markets for audio and video products. For example, Sony and Phillips were the first manufacturers to release compact disc players in the UK during the mid-1980s. Initially, the players were priced at £500 or more. By 1995, there existed a bewildering variety of CD players, some priced as low as £50.

Penetration pricing

This strategy is used by firms trying to gain a foothold in a new market. It is a high-risk, high-cost strategy that tends to be confined to large firms who supply mass markets.

Penetration pricing involves setting product price low to encourage consumers to try the product and to build sales. This will also encourage retailers and wholesalers to stock the product and in doing so reduce their demand for competitors' goods and services. In addition, the firm may boost sales by lowering price if demand is price-elastic (see 1.5). Cutting price tends to increase total sales revenue if demand is price-elastic.

However, in markets where the supply side is very competitive, a **price war** may develop among rival firms. Any rise in sales from price cuts may be shortlived, as rival firms slash prices in an attempt to retain their market shares. It is often said that only the consumer wins in a price war.

Expansion pricing

This is similar to penetration pricing. Product prices are set low to encourage consumers to buy. As demand increases, the firm is able to raise its level of output and take advantage of economies of scale, which will lower the average cost of producing each unit (see 20.2). Lower average costs can either be passed on to consumers as lower prices, or, if prices are held steady, the lower costs will increase the firm's profit margins.

Price discrimination

This is used when a firm is able to charge different prices to different groups of consumers. For example, British Rail has different prices for peak and off-peak travel. Similarly, British Telecom charges different rates for telephone calls made at peak and off-peak times.

Price discrimination is only possible when consumers are unable to undercut higher prices by reselling the product from low-price markets to higher-priced ones. Thus, it is often possible to charge different prices for the same product or service in different regions of the country or world, if the cost of sending the product elsewhere more than offsets any saving in price between areas.

Competition-based pricing

Where there is fierce and direct competition between suppliers to a market, firms will often adopt **competition-based** pricing strategies.

Price leadership

This will tend to occur where firms are reluctant to start a price war by cutting their prices. They will therefore tend to price their products in line with those charged by their competitors. In some cases, a dominant firm may take on the role of **price leader**, and rival firms will raise or cut prices as dictated by the dominant firm. **Price leadership** tends to occur in markets dominated by a handful of large and powerful suppliers, such as petrol retailing (see 2.2).

Portfolio Activity 21.4

Range: Related pricing strategies
Skills: Read and respond to written material, Collect and record data

1. What is a 'price war'? What evidence is there from the article that supermarkets chains are engaged in a price war?
2. What motives has Gateway for cutting the prices of a number of its products?
3. What will be the likely impact of the price war on small, local supermarkets and grocery shops?
4. Collect evidence from competing supermarkets to support the view that they are engaged in a price war:
5. (a) Compile a list of items that are likely to appear in a typical household's weekly shopping basket.

   (b) Find out the price of these items from 3-4 different supermarkets in your area every 2 weeks for a 20-week period. How do prices change over time, and how do they compare between your chosen supermarkets?

6. Collect evidence from newspapers on price competition in other markets. Keep a scrapbook, and write a brief evaluation of each article you find. For example, list the main organizations competing on price, their motives, and what their pricing strategies have achieved so far.

Gateway to cut prices of 150 lines

GATEWAY TURNS up the heat on the big three supermarket groups today with steep price cuts on a range of luxury items in the run-up to Christmas. The retail chain has slashed its turkey prices to 42p a lb – almost half the price of the birds at J. Sainsbury and Safeway, and cut some other products by up to a third.

The move is the latest in a fierce price war between supermarket chains that intensified last week when Sainsbury, Britain's biggest supermarket chain, cut the price of 300 of its most popular own-label products.

Other retailers yesterday signalled their determination not to be beaten on price. Asda, the food and consumer goods superstore chain, said yesterday it would do everything to maintain prices which it froze 10 days ago. "We intend to remain the lowest-priced superstore and have not the slightest intention of losing the high ground," an official said.

The share prices of the sector have fallen in response to the price war. Sainsbury fell 34p last week to 366p. Argyll fell 32p to 260p, Asda fell more than 4p to $49\frac{1}{2}$p and Tesco fell $10\frac{1}{2}$p to 195p.

Mr Simmons said that Gateway's effort so far to trim prices, which began in May, had more than paid for itself in additional sales. "The extra customer traffic has more than compensated for any margin cuts." The chain has seen an additional 1m customers a week on top of its usual 6m to 7m weekly shoppers, Mr Simmons added.

A strong challenge is being mounted on margins by the rise of discount chains such as Germany's Aldi and the UK's Kwik Save.

Chains such as Asda have been laying stress on permanently low prices and Mr Simmons said he believed cut-price deals are here to stay. "Once the customer has a taste for value, it's hard to shake that," he said.

Financial Times 8.11.94

Destroyer pricing

A more drastic version of penetration pricing, **destroyer pricing** is used when the objective is to destroy the sales of competitors' products, or to warn off new entrants to the market. Trading losses resulting from destroyer pricing strategies cannot usually be maintained for long. Freddie Laker, owner of Laker Airways in the 1980s, accused large airlines of operating destroyer pricing on transatlantic air routes, causing his business to collapse.

Problems with demand- and competition-based pricing

Cost-based pricing ignores the influence of the market conditions of consumer demand and supply on price. Conversely, the main problem with price-setting with reference to market conditions is that it may ignore the production costs which a firm must at least cover through sales revenues if it is to survive.

Advanced Business

Portfolio Activity 21.5

Range: Related pricing strategies
Skills: Produce written material, Collect and record data

1. Identify the pricing strategy which appears to be in use to launch the Eurotunnel rail services. Comment on how effective this policy might be.
2. Explain some different pricing strategies which could have been adopted by Eurotunnel when launching rail services to Europe.
3. How might ferry operators adapt their pricing strategies when faced with new competition from Eurotunnel?
4. What is a 'price war' and who will be the most likely winners?
5. (a) Explain, using examples, how the ferry operators discriminate between different market segments using price.

   (b) Collect information to prepare a brief report on the use of price discrimination in other markets. (Information on rail fares and phone tariffs will be a good start.) Conclude your report by discussing how practical price discrimination is as a general pricing policy for business. For example, would it be useful to price Mars bars or computer games in this way?

How cross-Channel fares line up

Eurotunnel	P&O	Stena
Standard return (car - unlimited passengers)	Standard return (Car - up to 9 passengers)	Standard return (Car - up to 5 passengers)
£220 Blue (Nov-Dec)	£139 low season	£126 low season (10 Jan-24 Mar)
£260 White (Sep-Oct)	£221 mid-season (May, June)	£188 mid-season (25 Mar-7 Jul & 5 Sep-31 Dec)
£280 Red (May-Jun & Jul-Aug, not Fri-Sat)	£289 peak season (July, Aug)	£220 peak season (8 July-4 Sep)
£310 Gold (May bank holiday & July-Aug, Fri-Sat)	£320 August Bank Holiday weekend	£270-£320 peak weekend
5-day return	5-day return	5-day return
£130 Blue	£77 low season	£76 low season
£160 White	£124 mid-season	£124 mid-season
2-day introductory return	£160 peak season	£126 peak season
£125 Sun 5 Jun-Thur 21 Jul	£175 peak weekend	
(travel to France on Sun to Thur only)		

The eagerly awaited announcement yesterday of Eurotunnel's cross-Channel fare tables suggests that the company is seeking a premium price on its first few months of operation, but Eurotunnel's rivals, the ferry operators, and observers in the travel industry said it could be forced to reduce its tariffs once the novelty had worn off.

In its early months, Eurotunnel will have limited shuttle capacity and may be unable to meet demand from first-time users of its service.

But as deliveries of the special rolling stock to carry cars, coaches, and trucks through the 32-mile tunnel build up, and the frequency of shuttle departures increases from two to four an hour, there is a strong chance that it will be forced to reduce its fares to fill the space available.

P&O Ferries said: "There is nothing in the Eurotunnel tariffs to panic about." And Hoverspeed said: "We are very pleased at what has been revealed and it shows we are very competitive."

Stena Sealink was quick to point out that savings of up to £92 on the Eurotunnel tariffs are possible from its own peak-season schedule.

Mr Christopher Garnett, Eurotunnel commercial director, stressed yesterday that the company did not plan to wage a price war. "We are a unique service comparable with the impact of the opening of the transatlantic airline routes on the ocean liners," he said.

Others are not so sure. Mr Keith Betton, head of corporate affairs at the Association of British Travel Agents, said: "We expect Eurotunnel will need to adjust its fares downwards when it comes to attracting travellers for a second time."

Travel industry observers are also uncertain about whether Eurotunnel will be able to maintain its policy of charging the same rate throughout the day. Stena Sealink last week fell in with this previously announced Eurotunnel policy when it announced its fares for this year.

Financial Times 12.1.94

As long as a firm is able to cover its variable costs of production in the short run, it can continue production and carry on with objectives such as launching a new product or expanding market share. However, a firm cannot go on making a loss indefinitely. Eventually it must be able to pay for its fixed costs of production, namely rent, rates, and overheads. In the long run, therefore, pricing decisions must take into account total costs, including fixed costs, as well as market conditions. If a firm is only able to cover its costs by setting its product price higher than rival products, then to make sales and survive, it will need to examine the scope for cost-cutting and increasing productivity (see 15.1).

Key words

Demand-based pricing - pricing policies based on market conditions and consumer willingness to pay

Market skimming - high-price strategies used to maximize profits from a new product in the short run when there is little competition

Penetration pricing - low-price strategies aimed at boosting total sales and expanding market share

Price discrimination - charging different prices to different market segments for the same product

Competition-based pricing - setting prices with reference to prices charged by rival firms

Price leadership - when rival firms in a market set their prices in accordance with those charged by a dominant firm

Destroyer pricing - low-price strategies adopted by a firm or group of firms to force competitors out of the market

Further reading
Lewis, G: *Pricing for Profit* (Kogan Page, 1993)

Test Questions

The following underpinning knowledge will be tested
1. Factors which determine price
2. Related pricing strategies
3. Break-even level of production and sales
4. Draw, label and analyse break even charts
5. Reasons for using a break even chart

1 The break-even level of output in a firm can be found at the point at which:

A Total Sales Revenue = Business Start-up Costs
B Total Sales Revenue = Total Costs
C Total Sales Revenue = Indirect Costs
D Total Sales Revenue = Direct Costs

2 If a business plans for a 'margin of safety', it has planned to:

A Increase its cash holdings in a bank account
B Produce at the break-even level of output
C Produce an output greater than break-even
D Produce any output where sales revenue covers direct costs

3 A firm which produces wide-screen televisions has fixed costs of £500,000. The variable cost per TV is £500. If each TV is sold for £1,000, how many TVs must the firm produce and sell to break even?

A 5,000
B 100
C 1,000
D 500

Question 4 and 5 are based on the following information:
Costs of producing 'Blaster' CD-ROM game for computers
Fixed costs per year   £30,000
Variable cost per CD-ROM   £15

4 If the firm produces 10,000 CD-ROM games what will be the average cost per unit?

A £15
B £5
C £21
D £18

5 If the firm plans to earn a contribution of £25 per unit sold, the price it must charge for each CD-ROM game will be:

A £40
B £43
C £50
D £46

6 A firm produces and sells 40,000 units annually. Variable costs per unit are £2, while fixed costs total £100,000. If the firm adds a 20% mark-up for profit, each unit will sell for:

A £5.40
B £4.50
C £2.40
D £3.00

7 Which of the following is unlikely to be an important objective of penetration pricing strategies?

A Increasing market share
B Launching a new product in a competitive market
C Maximizing sales revenue
D Maximizing short-term profits

8 You are a business manager in a large, well-established firm. A new firm has entered the market and threatens to reduce your market share. Which of the following pricing strategies would you advise your organization to adopt in the short term?

A Market skimming
B Destroyer pricing
C Price discrimination
D Contribution pricing

9
a. Suggest and explain a pricing strategy a firm could adopt to launch a new product.

b. How might established firms in the same market adapt their pricing strategies in the face of the new competition?

c. Using examples, explain the term 'price discrimination'.

d. Explain why a holiday company may offer foreign holidays at bargain prices within a few days of their departure dates.

10
a. A small firm producing candles has fixed costs of £60,000 per year and variable costs of 50 pence per candle. Each candle is sold for £2.50. How many candles must the firm produce and sell each year to break even?

b. How much profit would the firm earn if it produced and sold 80,000 candles each year?

c. Use the information from (b) and (c) above to draw a break-even graph for levels of output between 0 and 80,000 candles. Mark the area of profit and loss.

d. Explain, using examples, why break even analysis and the use of break even charts is so useful to new and existing businesses.

assessment assignment

Advanced Business

Assessment Assignment

Range: Basic factors
Break even point
Label
Analyse
Reasons
Related pricing strategies

Skills: **Communication**
Produce written material
Use images
Application of Number
Collect and record data
Represent and tackle problems
Interpret and present data
Information Technology
Process information
Present information

What price promotion?

You work for a newly created company which is about to launch a new type of canned cola drink into the soft drinks market. Your managing director has asked you to consider and research possible short- and long-term pricing strategies for the new product.

You are to write up the findings of your research and make recommendations in a full report. The document should be produced using a wordprocessor. A spreadsheet can be used to make calculations and generate graphs to import into your report where appropriate.

You have made the following list of tasks to complete before you begin to write up your report.

Tasks

chapter 22

1. Set up a table in a spreadsheet with 6 columns and 6 rows. Label the columns in the first row in the following order
   - Number of cans
   - Fixed costs
   - Total variable costs
   - Total costs
   - Total revenues (1)
   - Total revenues (2)

2. Calculate the total cost of producing a range of outputs from 0 to 2 million (in steps of 500,000 cans). Annual costs for the new drink are identified as follows:

Fixed costs (incl. rent, rates, and overheads)	£200,000
Variable costs per can (labour and materials)	10 pence

   Complete columns 1-4 in the table accordingly.

3. Plot a total cost line on a graph. Remember to label axes appropriately.

4. Calculate the average cost of producing each can of drink at each level of output. Choose an appropriate price per unit for your product to cover your costs of production, and will earn a reasonable level of profit at a given level of output.

5. Use your chosen price to calculate expected total revenues for sales of between 0 and 2 million cans. Use this information on total revenues to complete column 5 in the table. Also complete the graph started in Task 3 and find the break-even level of output.

6. Confirm the break-even level of output from the graph using the following equation:

   Total Revenue (TR) = Total Cost (TC)

   where:

   TR = Price per Unit × Quantity

   TC = Fixed Costs + (Variable Cost per Unit × Quantity)

7. Investigate the range of prices offered by rival firms in the market. Write up the findings of the investigation and describe a possible pricing strategy to establish the new product in the market. Explain the possible reaction of competitors.

8. How, if at all, does the price per can chosen in Task 7 differ from the chosen price in Task 3? If price differs, recalculate expected total revenues in column 6 of the table.

9. What is the impact of this new price on the break-even level of output? Show this on a new graph of total costs and total revenues for a range of outputs above zero.

10. Consider medium-term pricing objectives for when the product's market position has been established. What pricing strategy could be adopted in the event of its losing market share to new competition? What would be the aim and likely effect of this strategy?

11. Write up your findings and recommendations in a report. This should include an explanation of why break even analysis is useful to new and existing business organizations.

Financial Forecasting and Monitoring

Unit Seven

unit 7

chapter 22 *Business Finance (Element 7.1)*
chapter 23 *Cashflow Forecasting (Elements 7.2)*
chapter 24 *Profit and Loss Statements and Balance Sheets (Elements 7.3)*
chapter 25 *Monitoring Business Performance (Elements 7.4)*

Advanced Business

chapter 22 Business Finance

This chapter identifies the need for, and sources of, finance for various types of business organization

Key ideas

Businesses need **capital** for a wide variety of reasons including business start-up, expansion, introducing new technology, and R&D.

Capital is used to provide **long-term assets**, such as land, buildings, machinery, and equipment. **Working capital** is for the purchase of items to be consumed over a short period of time, such as materials, financing for work in progress and stocks of finished goods, and for paying off loans.

Most business organizations rely on bank **overdrafts** and **trade credit** to fund their working capital requirements.

Some capital may be raised internally within an organization from **owners' savings, retained profits, asset management**, and by improving the management of working capital.

Capital to finance business assets can also be raised externally from the **sale of shares** to investors, or via **loan capital** in the form of **loan stocks, bank loans, hire purchase, leasing, mortgages,** and **venture capital**.

All limited companies may issue **ordinary and preferences shares**, but only **public limited companies (plcs)** may trade their shares through the Stock Exchange.

A wide variety of institutions may assist in the raising of finance for business, including individual and institutional investors, banks, building societies, leasing and factoring companies, government agencies, and venture capital firms.

When choosing the best method of finance, firms' selection criteria may include the amount to be raised, the purpose for which the finance is required, the cost of finance, the firm's status as a borrower, the general economic environment, and the firm's level of **gearing** (ratio of debt finance to total finance).

Section 22.1

Why do businesses need capital?

What is capital?

Capital refers to money introduced into a firm by its owners to purchase **assets**, such as land, buildings, machinery, vehicles, and office equipment. Businesses need capital to finance business start-ups, to expand, to pay for research and product development, and to finance the introduction of new technology. This chapter considers the ways in which firms can 'raise capital'.

Capital can be described in a number of ways, depending on how it is used by an organization:

- **Venture capital** is often used to describe money used to finance new business start-ups, mainly of private limited companies
- **Investment capital** is money used to buy new **fixed assets**, such premises, machinery and other equipment that have relatively long productive lives
- **Working capital** is money used to pay the day-to-day running expenses of a business, such as raw materials, electricity, telephone bills, insurance, loan repayments, etc.

Working capital can be held in the form of the following **current assets**, which are used up by a business over a relatively short period of time;

- Cash 'in hand' and in bank or building society accounts
- Liquid assets, such as stocks and work in progress which can be sold quickly to raise cash
- Debtors – people and firms who owe money to the business. This money can be recalled to raise cash.

Working capital is equal to the value of current assets less any current liabilities, namely any outstanding bills yet to be paid or bank overdrafts which will reduce the amount of cash available to a business.

Portfolio Activity 22.1

Range: Common methods of finance, Assets, Working capital
Skills: Collect and record data, Produce written material

You are a sole trader preparing to set up a newsagent's store. Before you can begin to trade, the shop you intend to buy will need re-fitting with shelves, a counter, a store room, lighting and heating, and a new shopfront.

1. Make a detailed list of all the things that you will need to spend money on. (Pay a visit to a local newsagent to help you.) Divide your list into fixed assets and current assets.
2. Make estimates of how much each list will cost you and justify these estimates.
3. Consider how you might raise the money to finance this expenditure.
4. If you intend to borrow money, consider how you might convince people and other organizations to finance your business.
5. Some sources of finance might be better for financing assets, and others for providing working capital. Investigate and explain.
6. How do you think your answers to Questions 1-5 would differ for a large chain of newsagency and stationery stores owned by a public limited company, for example, WH Smith?

Internal sources of asset finance

A business organization may already have some capital of its own to contribute to asset and working capital finance. The main sources of **internal finance** are:

- **Personal savings:** the use of personal savings remains an important, and often principal, source of finance for many small firms, especially sole traders and partnerships (see 4.2).

- **Retained profits:** ploughed-back or retained profits amount to around 50% of the total finance used by companies. These are a cheap source of finance because the funds are not borrowed and no interest need be paid for their use.

  In small businesses, including sole traders and partnerships, it is unlikely that there will be enough retained profit to use as a source of finance. Limited companies are more likely to make sufficient profits to provide reserves for the future. However, because all profits after tax belong to the business owners, any profits retained by managers must be justified to them.

- **Asset management:** a firm may raise funds by selling off some of its existing assets such as machinery or fixtures and fittings. Because asset sales tend to reduce the ability of a firm to trade, this is a fairly drastic means of raising finance.

- **Management of working capital:** by careful planning, it is possible to manage the flow of cash into and out of a firm so as to avoid the need for short-term finance (see 23.2). A surplus of cash one month can be saved, to cover a deficit later on, when outflows of cash exceed inflows - for example, when a large bill for electricity or deliveries of materials has to be paid.

External sources of finance

Most firms will be unable to finance all their asset and working capital requirements from internal sources. They will therefore raise the money they need from external sources, such as banks and other financial institutions. Charities will rely on gifts, donations and membership fees.

In order to raise **external finance**, it is usually necessary for a business to produce a plan detailing how exactly it intends to use the finance raised. This is called a **business plan** (see 27.1).

It is good financial practice to match the source of finance with the kind of asset required. For example, it would not be a good idea to purchase a large piece of capital equipment which will pay for itself over ten years, with an overdraft requiring repayment in six months!

Because fixed assets, such as buildings and machinery, remain productive for a long time, a company will often be willing to pay for them over many years, and will seek sources of **long-term finance**. In contrast, **short-term finance** is available from a variety of sources to fund working capital requirements and enable firms to meet day-to-day bills and debts. As a rule of thumb, short-term finance is normally repaid within three years while medium- to long-term finance is repaid over many more.

Long- or short-term external finance?

Short term finance	Long-term finance
To cover short term losses and net outflows of cash	To purchase long-term or fixed assets including equipment
To meet working capital requirements	To finance expansion
To finance exports	To cover costs of long-term projects, for example, building a new office or factory
To puchase low-cost fixed assets, eg. a new computer	

Figure 22.1 summarizes the various sources of external short- and long-term finance available to a business organization.

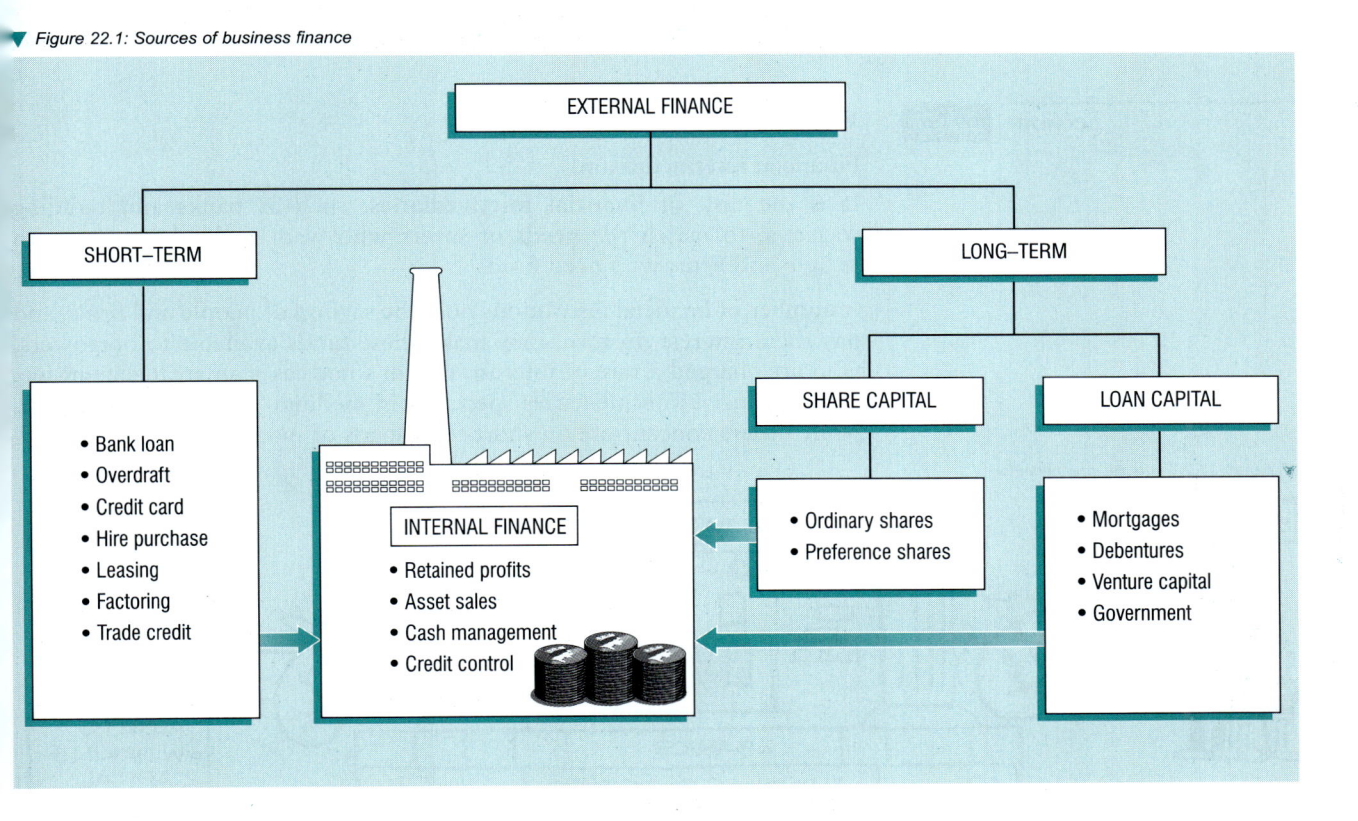

Figure 22.1: Sources of business finance

EXTERNAL FINANCE

SHORT–TERM
- Bank loan
- Overdraft
- Credit card
- Hire purchase
- Leasing
- Factoring
- Trade credit

LONG–TERM

SHARE CAPITAL
- Ordinary shares
- Preference shares

LOAN CAPITAL
- Mortgages
- Debentures
- Venture capital
- Government

INTERNAL FINANCE
- Retained profits
- Asset sales
- Cash management
- Credit control

There are two main sources of long-term external finance. These are:

- **Loan capital:** this is any money borrowed over a period of time which has be repaid by an agreed date, usually with interest, either as a lump sum or in regular instalments (see 22.2).

- **Share capital:** limited companies are able to sell shares to raise finance (see 22.4). The sale of shares can raise very large amounts of money. Unlike a loan, share capital is **permanent** capital because it is not normally redeemed, i.e. a firm never has to repay shareholders' money. To get their money back, a shareholder must sell their shares to someone else.

Advanced Business

> **Key words**
>
> **Capital** - finance or money used in a business to purchase assets
>
> **Assets** - resources owned by a business and used up in production
>
> **Fixed assets** - business assets, such as plant and machinery, used over a long period of time
>
> **Venture capital** - money used to finance a new business start-up
>
> **Investment capital** - money used to buy plant and eqiupment
>
> **Current assets** - assets used up over a short period of time, such as stocks of finished products and raw materials
>
> **Working capital** - funds available for use in the day-to-day operation of the business
>
> **Internal finance** - capital raised from sources inside a business from retained profits, the sale of assets, or by cash management
>
> **External finance** - capital raised from sources outside a business
>
> **Loan capital** - money borrowed by a business for a long period of time
>
> **Share capital** - money raised by the sale of shares in a business
>
> **Permanent capital** - money that never has to be repaid

Section 22.2 Raising loan capital

Financial intermediation

It is the task of **financial intermediaries**, such as banks and building societies, to match the needs of savers who want to lend money, with people and firms who need funds.

A number of financial institutions hold the savings of people and firms, and pay them interest. In turn, they make these funds available to borrowers, who are charged a rate of interest, and in some cases an arrangement fee. Some financial intermediaries specialize in medium- to long-term finance, while others concentrate on short-term loans of money.

▼ *Figure 22.2: Financial intermediation*

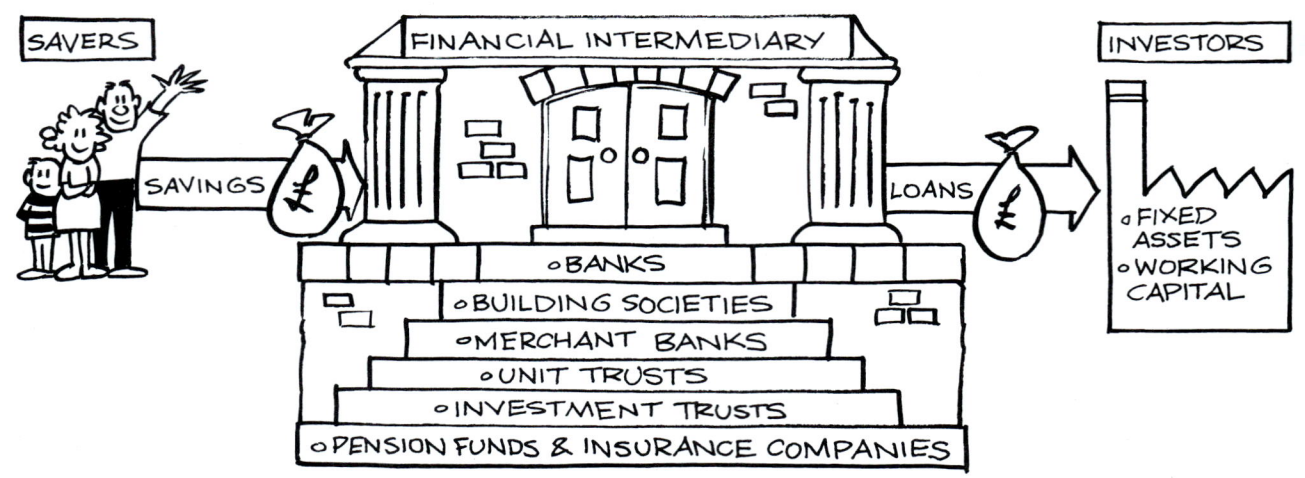

Securing finance

Loans may be **secured** or **unsecured**. Some financial institutions may insist on **security** or **collateral** against a loan, especially when the amount of money involved is large. This refers to an asset, or assets, of value equal to the amount borrowed, which is tied to the loan. In the event of non-payment or default, the lender is legally entitled to take possession of the secured assets, and to sell them to obtain their money.

Credit cards provide a useful method of short term finance

Assets most likely to be accepted as security for a loan include:

- Property
- Money saved in endowment and life insurance policies
- Shareholdings

Assets which lose their value quickly or are difficult to sell - for example, specialized machinery - are unlikely to be accepted by banks and other lenders as suitable forms of security.

The money market

Short-term finance is available on the **money market**. This is made up of people and firms who want to borrow money for relatively short periods of time, and those people and organizations willing and able to provide it.

The supply of short-term finance is dominated by the major commercial banks, also known as **clearing banks**, such as Lloyds, Barclays, Midland, and the Cooperative Bank. These lend money to firms in the same way as they lend money to private individuals. Short-term finance is available in the form of a bank loan or overdraft. The major banks can also arrange, often through specialized companies which they own, other methods of finance, such as leasing and factoring services, and commercial mortgages.

Methods of short-term finance

- **Overdraft:** overdrafts are frequently used to ease cashflow problems associated with working capital requirements in many business organizations. Under an overdraft agreement, a bank allows a business to make payments or withdrawals in excess of the amount held in its account, up to a specified limit. Banks normally insist that overdrafts are paid off relatively quickly. Interest is charged on the amount of the overdraft on a daily basis, and is normally slightly lower than the rate charged on loans.

- **Bank loan:** banks can advance loans to businesses, to be repaid in regular fixed monthly instalments over an agreed period of time. Loan terms can be anything from six months to ten years, but most tend to be relatively short. Interest is charged on the total amount of the loan, and is fixed from the outset. A borrower is locked into that rate, even if interest rates fall during the period of the loan.

  Loans and overdrafts can be an expensive way of borrowing, but they are one of the most popular forms of short-term finance available to sole traders and partnerships (see 4.2).

- **Credit cards:** Visa, Access, American Express, and Diners Club are examples of credit card companies. Depending on the credit card, users can pay bills and make purchases, and defer payment until up to eight weeks later. Each month, users receive a statement of their transactions. They can then decide whether to pay the balance in full or in part. If payment is made in full, no interest is charged. Interest is charged only on the outstanding balance, but can be quite high.

- **Hire purchase:** this is a popular method of finance, often used by smaller firms to buy plant and machinery. A hire purchase agreement will normally require a firm to pay a deposit on equipment purchased, and then to pay off the balance, with interest, in regular instalments over a few months or several years.

  Hire purchase can be arranged through a bank or, more often, through a finance house. Because finance houses tend to be less selective in granting loans, their rates of interest tend to be higher. The finance house will buy the equipment for the buyer, and will be the legal owner of it until the last payment has been made. If the buyer is unable to pay the agreed instalments, the finance house can legally repossess the equipment.

- **Leasing:** Leasing is a way of paying rent for the loan of equipment for a fixed period. At the end of the period, the equipment is returned to its owner. The advantage is that businesses can get expensive equipment such as computer systems without making a large capital outlay. During the period of the lease, maintenance and servicing of equipment are the responsibility of the owner of the equipment rather than the lessee. Once the period of the lease is over, the firm can return the old computer system and lease a more up-to-date version.

  A number of specialist leasing companies will buy plant and machinery to order from a company wanting to rent the equipment. Over a long period of time, leasing can be more expensive than buying equipment outright. Leasing is, however, an increasingly popular means of obtaining equipment.

Leasing

New lease on life

When Ian Dyson wanted to start a Sheffield bus company in 1990, he was faced with a problem. He and his three partners, all former senior depot managers for the nationalised bus company, had little money and less collateral. To achieve critical mass they needed at least 15 double-decker buses.

The solution was to buy 12-year-old vehicles – but who would finance such aged assets? After exploring a number of cul-de-sacs, including bank loans, Dyson found Close Asset Finance, a specialist leasing company.

Whereas banks were not interested in his collateral, Close Asset Finance took a view on the residual value of the assets in the event of default, entered a hire-purchase arrangement and Sheffield Omnibus was born. Four years later, the company has 85 buses, employs 220 people full-time and is still using leasing for its asset financing.

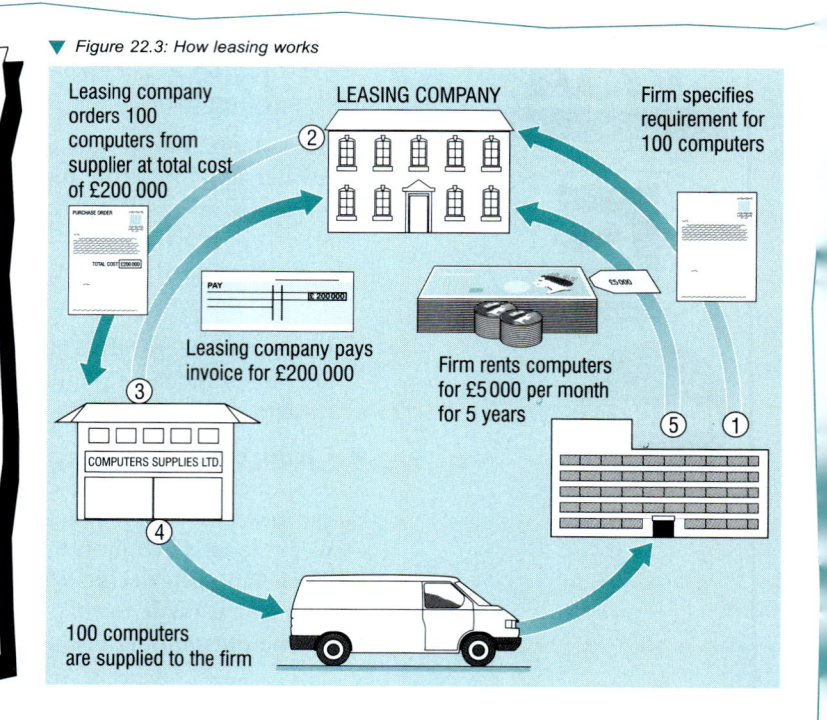

▼ *Figure 22.3: How leasing works*

- Leasing company orders 100 computers from supplier at total cost of £200 000
- Firm specifies requirement for 100 computers
- Leasing company pays invoice for £200 000
- Firm rents computers for £5 000 per month for 5 years
- 100 computers are supplied to the firm

- **Trade credit:** many businesses rely on their creditors as a form of short-term finance. Because most suppliers allow their customers to take somewhere between one and three months to pay for goods supplied, the debtor company can use what is effectively an interest-free loan of up to 90 days to pay other bills. Creditors will often give incentives in the form of cash discounts if payment is made earlier, but by delaying payment, the debtor can use money owed to finance other current assets.

  An estimated £50 billion-plus was owed by late payers in mid-1994. It was claimed that many of the worst offenders were huge corporations which did not fear legal action as they would have no trouble finding other suppliers if one went out of business.

- **Factoring:** late payment of invoices for goods delivered can cause considerable financial hardship for creditors. **Debt factoring** involves a specialist company, known as a **factor**, paying off the unpaid invoices of supplies.

  It is common for a factoring company to agree to pay 80% of the amount of the invoice on issue, paying the remaining 20% when the debtor settles the invoice with the factor. This provides the creditor with early payment of debts and leaves the chasing-up of payments to the factoring company.

  The profit of the factoring company is the difference between what they have paid to the supplier to settle the invoice and the full amount of the invoice eventually paid by the debtor.

Portfolio Activity 22.2

Range: Common methods of finance, Usual sources of finance
Skills: Take part in discussions

Bank loan

This is a role-play exercise based around an interview between a bank manager and a person wishing to borrow money to start a new business. On the basis of the information provided, and the details that emerge from the interview, it is up to the bank manager to decide whether or not to grant a loan. The bank is interested in making loans, but must be convinced that it will receive back at a later date a larger sum plus interest. There will always be the risk that the borrower may not be able to repay. How much of a risk this is must be judged in each case by the bank manager.

The customer's role

You are Beverley Johnson, aged 24. You work as a secretary in a small company. During evenings and at weekends you help out at a friend's gym and fitness studio. She pays you £70 for your help each week, before tax. This is in addition to your salary of £16,000 per year before tax. You pay tax of £334 each month.

You live in a rented house and pay £150 each week for your rent and bills. Other outgoings, such as food, clothes, and entertainment amount to £300 per month. The remainder is saved in a building society account which totals £1,000 so far.

You want to start your own dance and fitness studio above a local supermarket. Rent would be £600 per month, while fittings and decorations have been estimated to be £5,000. You hope a friend will help out in the evenings for £60 per week.

You decide to sell your idea to your bank manager, and arrange an interview for a loan. You will need to prepare an action plan to convince the bank of the potential for profit from your business proposal.

The bank manager's role

Your job is to decide whether or not to loan money to Beverley Johnson who has approached you for a loan to finance her business start-up. In order to make your decision you will need to know:

- How much money is needed and what is it needed for?
- For how long will Beverley need the loan?

- Has she any savings she can put into her business?
- What is her character like? Is she trustworthy?
- What are her personal incomes and expenditures?
- Has she any security to offer against the loan?
- Has she enough experience to run the type of business proposed?

- Will the business succeed?
- What about local competition?
- Will it generate enough revenue and earn profits?

The following form will help you to assess her position in the interview. Assume interest is charged on business loans at 10% per year (see repayment table below).

Loan Approval Form

Part 1: Customer details

Name .... Age .... years ....

Address ....

....

Number of years account held at bank ....

Has customer bank account been satisfctory? YES/NO

If not, give reasons ....

....

INCOME
(Customer income per month after tax,   £ ....
National Insurance)

EXPENDITURE
(Customer outgoings per month)

        Rent/Mortgage   £ ....

        Other loans/HP   £ ....

        Other expenses   £ ....

        Total expenditure   £ ....

DISPOSABLE INCOME   £ ....
(Income - expenditure)

Part 2: Details of loan

Purpose of loan ....

Total cost of customer project   £ ....

Customer contribution to project   £ ....

Amount of loan requested   £ ....

Length of loan requested   £ ....

Annual interest rate   .... %

Total interest payable   £ ....

Total cost of loan (interest + loan)   £ ....

Monthly repayment   £ ....

Can the customer offer any security?
(e.g. house, shares, life insurance)

....

Part 3: Manager's decision

Loan approved ?   YES/NO

Reasons for decision ....

....

Repayment table: Annual interest rate 10%

Amount of loan*	Monthly Repayments (loan + interest)			
	12 months	24 months	36 months	60 months
£1,000	£91.66	£50.00	£36.11	£25.00

*Therefore, for a loan of £10,000 multiply all figures by 10, etc.

What is the capital market?

The **capital market** brings together people and firms who want to borrow a lot of money for long periods of time with those who are willing and able to supply funds on this basis. Borrowers tend to be limited companies seeking to fund large-scale replacement of fixed assets or expansion.

Methods of long-term finance

- **Mortgages:** a commercial mortgage is a long-term loan, typically over 25 years, of up to approximately 80% of the purchase price of a business property. Business owners may also remortgage their existing premises in order to raise finance for use elsewhere in the business. The business premises provide security for the loan, and, in the event of a failure to repay regular instalments, the lender can take possession of the property.

  Mortgages are available from building societies and banks.

▼ *Investors in Industry (3i) is a specialist provider of venture capital*

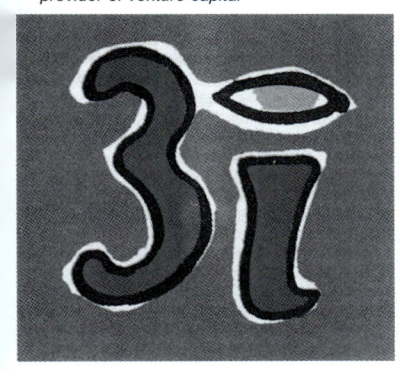

- **Venture capital:** start-up funds for new limited companies are available from specialist venture capital companies. These are commercial organizations specializing in loans to new and risky businesses who might otherwise find it difficult to raise finance. Investors in Industry (3i) plc, Equity Capital for Industry, and the clearing banks are the biggest and best-known venture capital firms. These firms usually lend in return for shares in the ownership of the company (or **equity stakes**), hoping for an eventual capital gain on the value of their shares, rather than for interest or dividends.

  Merchant banks also provide venture capital. These are financial institutions specializing in advice and financial assistance to limited companies, for example, to fund business expansion, takeovers of other companies, or management buyouts.

  The venture capital industry in the UK has grown very quickly, providing a valuable source of finance to small firms and high-risk enterprises. Venture capital lending rose from £66 million in 1981 to £1.4 billion in 1989.

Money going begging: recession worries lead to cash mountain

Sir George Russell, the chairman of 3i, is a puzzled man. Last Tuesday, he reported that the venture-capital giant had £1 billion ready to invest in new and growing companies - but not enough suitable takers for the cash.

At a time when most of the comment about small firms focuses on a perceived gap in available funds, Russell's revelation threatens to stand conventional wisdom about the threat to small-business growth on its head.

It was the second time in a few months that 3i had indicated it had cash to spare for investment "We have been underwhelmed," Russell said last week.

"Companies are not queuing up at the door. And, if there are no new small companies today, there will be no new medium-sized companies in two or three years time."

The reason appears clear. Badly burned by the recession, entrepreneurs are being highly cautious about committing themselves to expansion again. Many are delaying investment decisions until recovery seems more certain.

Adapted from The Sunday Times 12.1.93

- **Loan stocks:** these are certificates issued for sale by limited companies, which acknowledge that the bearer has lent a company money and is to be repaid at a specified future date, known as **maturity**. Government is also able to borrow money by issuing loan stocks for sale to the general public.

Loan stocks are sold to raise finance - around £10 billion in 1993. They offer holders a fixed rate of interest each year until the loan is repaid by the issuing company. If, during the period of the loan, the holder wishes to get their money back, the loan stock can be sold to another person or company. Loan stocks can be in the form of:

- **Debentures** issued by public limited companies (see 4.2)
- **Local government bonds** issued by local authorities
- **Gilt-edged securities** issued by central government, normally lasting 25 years

A **debenture** may be secured or unsecured on specific property owned by the company. When debentures are issued, the company agrees to repay the loan with interest on maturity.

The Stock Exchange

The capital market is dominated by the **Stock Exchange** in London. The main function of the Stock Exchange is to provide a market where the owners of loan stocks and shares can sell them to other people and firms who want to buy them (see 22.3). The total market value of all stocks and shares (collectively known as **securities**) traded on the Stock Exchange is called the **market capitalization**. At the end of March 1993, this value stood at £2,605 billion.

The people and organizations that provide companies with capital by buying shares in them are called **investors**. Most shares traded in the UK are bought by investment trusts, unit trusts, pension funds, and insurance companies. These companies accept people's savings and use the money to invest in shares and government stocks. Dividends, interest on stocks, and capital gains in the value of shares are passed on, in part, to savers.

▼ *Figure 22.4: Total market value of securities quoted on the UK Stock Exchange*

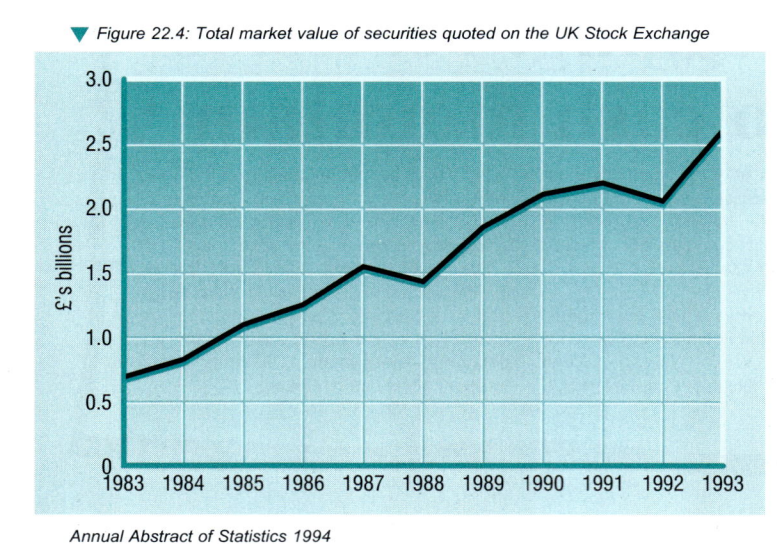

Annual Abstract of Statistics 1994

▼ *Figure 22.5: Shares held in UK companies, by sector*

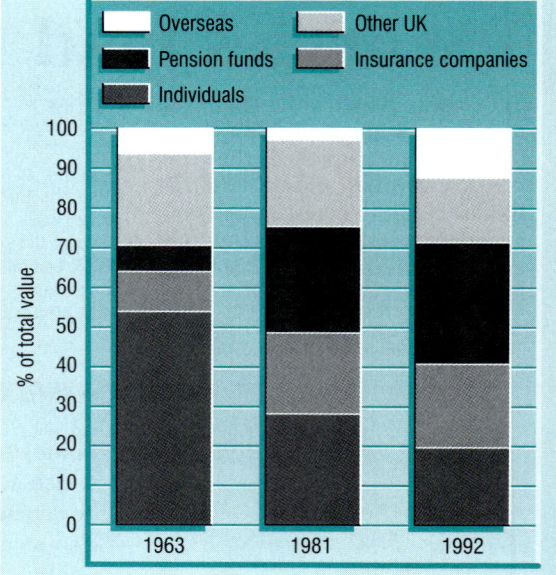

Social Trends 1993

> **Key words**
>
> **Financial intermediary** - an institution, such as a bank or building society, which accepts deposits and uses this money to make loans
>
> **Collateral** - an asset which provides security for a loan
>
> **Money market** - the market for short-term finance, consisting of borrowers and lenders
>
> **Commercial banks** - high street banks that accept deposits from, and make loans to, the general public and business organizations
>
> **Bank loan** - money borrowed for a specified period from a bank that has to be repaid with interest, usually in equal monthly instalments
>
> **Overdraft** - short-term finance provided by overdrawing from a bank account
>
> **Credit cards** - issued by companies providing short-term credit for payments made with them. If full payment is made to the credit card company within a specified period, usually 6-8 weeks, no interest is charged
>
> **Hire purchase** - taking delivery of goods after paying a deposit, and then paying the balance with interest in equal monthly instalments over an agreed period
>
> **Finance house** - specialist providers of finance for hire purchase
>
> **Leasing** - renting equipment for an agreed period, after which it can be bought at a discount or returned to the owner
>
> **Trade credit** - when a supplier gives a customer time to pay for goods or services delivered
>
> **Creditor** - a supplier who has granted trade credit
>
> **Factoring** - borrowing money to cover unpaid invoices
>
> **Capital market** - the market for long-term finance made up of borrowers and lenders
>
> **Commercial mortgage** - a loan secured on the value of property
>
> **Venture capital** - funds lent to high-risk (usually new) companies
>
> **Merchant banks** - specialist banks for limited companies
>
> **Loan stocks** - tradeable certificates sold by companies to raise long-term finance. At maturity, they entitle their holder to the face value at which they were sold, plus interest
>
> **Debentures** - loan stocks issued by companies
>
> **Gilt-edged securities** - loan stocks issued by government, often for up to 25 years
>
> **Stock Exchange** - the UK market for the sale of loan stocks and shares issued by public limited companies and the government
>
> **Market capitalization** - the value of shares quoted on the Stock Exchange
>
> **Investors** - people and organizations who provide share capital

Section 22.3   Raising share capital

Issuing shares

A **share** is simply part of a company offered for sale. The price printed on the front of a share certificate is its **face value**, that is, the price at which it was first sold by the company. Selling shares in the ownership of a company is the usual way of raising money for private and public limited companies (see 4.2).

Private limited companies can only sell shares to people connected with the business in some way, such as family, friends, workers, etc. (see 4.2). This limits their ability to raise finance through the issue of shares. However, a company that 'goes public', i.e. becomes a public limited company (plc), will obtain a listing on the Stock Exchange and be able to advertise and sell a new issue of shares to members of the public from all over the world. The launch of a company's shares on the Stock Exchange is known as a **flotation**.

Before an organization can offer its shares for sale, the Council of the Stock Exchange will investigate it to ensure it is trustworthy and meets certain standards of practice and size. For example, a company must have authorized share capital of at least £50,000, of which it must sell at least a quarter. People will then buy shares in return for a share of any profits made, called a **dividend**. Once a share is sold, the company does not have to return the money to the shareholder. If shareholders want their money

Types of shares

Preference shares

These pay a **fixed dividend**. For example, a preference share worth 100 pence with a fixed return of 10% will pay a 10 pence dividend per year. However, if no profit is made, then no dividend is paid. If the shares are **cumulative preference shares**, profits not paid in one year will be paid in the next year in which profits are made.

Even if a company has a very profitable year, preference shareholders receive no more than the fixed rate of return, unless they hold **participating preference shares**. This type of share allows its holder to receive a sum out of profits in addition to their fixed dividend, after other shareholders have been paid their dividends.

Redeemable preference shares are issued for a specified period of time, after which they will be repaid by the company.

Preference shareholders are not usually allowed to vote for company directors at annual general meetings. Companies can raise capital by selling preference shares without the existing owners losing control.

Ordinary shares

These are the most commonly issued type of share. According to *CSO Financial Statistics*, UK companies raised £16.3 billion from new issues in 1993, compared to just £570 million raised from the sale of new preference shares.

Ordinary shares (or **equities**) pay a dividend based on what is left from profits after interest on loans and dividends to preference shareholders have been paid, and after some profit has been retained for future investment.

Holding ordinary shares can be risky, because the price of the shares can go up and down, depending upon the performance of the company and the opinions of investors as to its future performance. In addition, the dividend payment may also fluctuate depending on the amount of profit made, and how much of this profit company directors decide to pay out to shareholders.

Owners of ordinary shares are allowed to vote. One vote per share is allowed, and voting takes place at the **annual general meeting (AGM)**. At the AGM, directors report on how the company has performed in the previous twelve months, and shareholders vote on whether or not they wish the present directors to continue in post.

Shares can go up as well as down

Weak clothing sales leave Bodycote lower

Shares in Bodycote International fell 13p to 292p yesterday as the metal technology, packaging and textiles group blamed weak clothing sales for a 13 per cent decline in profits.

Mr Roger Green, finance director, said: "Pricing has been cut-throat and we were disappointed with the figures, particularly in Holland."

Earnings per share fell from 15.8p to 14.1p, but Mr Green said confidence about future prospects justified a final dividend of 3.25p, making a total of 5.25p (5p).

Financial Times 20.4.94

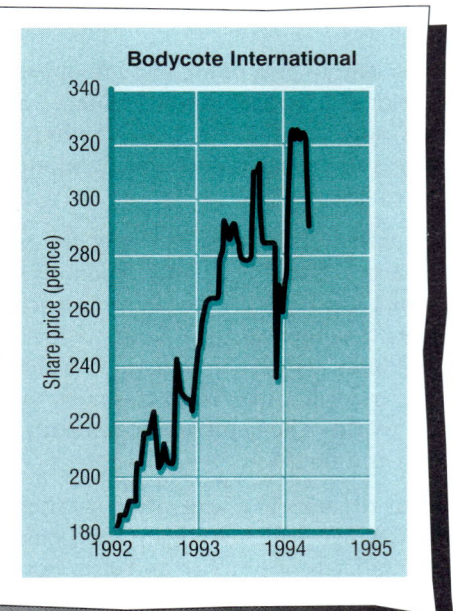

Like the price of any other commodity, share prices reflect market conditions of demand and supply. For example, if a company announces poor profits, shareholders may want to sell their shares because they will not receive a high dividend. The increase in the supply of shares in that company will drive down the price at which they can be sold on the stock market.

The movement in share prices can therefore reveal a great deal about the performance of individual companies. However, share prices may also fluctuate, due to **speculation**, which may or may not be based on the true performance of a company.

The **FT-SE Actuaries All Share Index** provides a daily summary of how share prices are performing relative to a base value of 1,000 points on 1 January 1985. The average value of 860 shares listed on the Stock Exchange is calculated every day to form the index number series. A rise in the index indicates rising share prices on average. By close of trading on 8 September 1994, the index had reached 1606 points.

The **FT-SE 100** index (nicknamed the 'Footsie') is recalculated every minute, to provide a measure of share prices in 100 of the largest UK companies.

Shares can go up as well as down ....continued

FT-SE 100 index reaches a 'real' all-time high

The FT-SE 100 index reached an all-time inflation-adjusted peak of 2,136.91 on Monday. As the chart points out, the previous high point for the index was reached on July 13 1987, writes Steve Thompson.

The stock market crash, which saw the FT-SE 100 plunge 500 points, or around 20 per cent, in two trading days, took place in October 1987.

Market strategists, while pointing out that current markets are looking stretched, yesterday highlighted the contrasting outlook for interest rates and inflation between 1987 and now. Retail investment is focusing on higher returns from the stock market than are available from building societies.

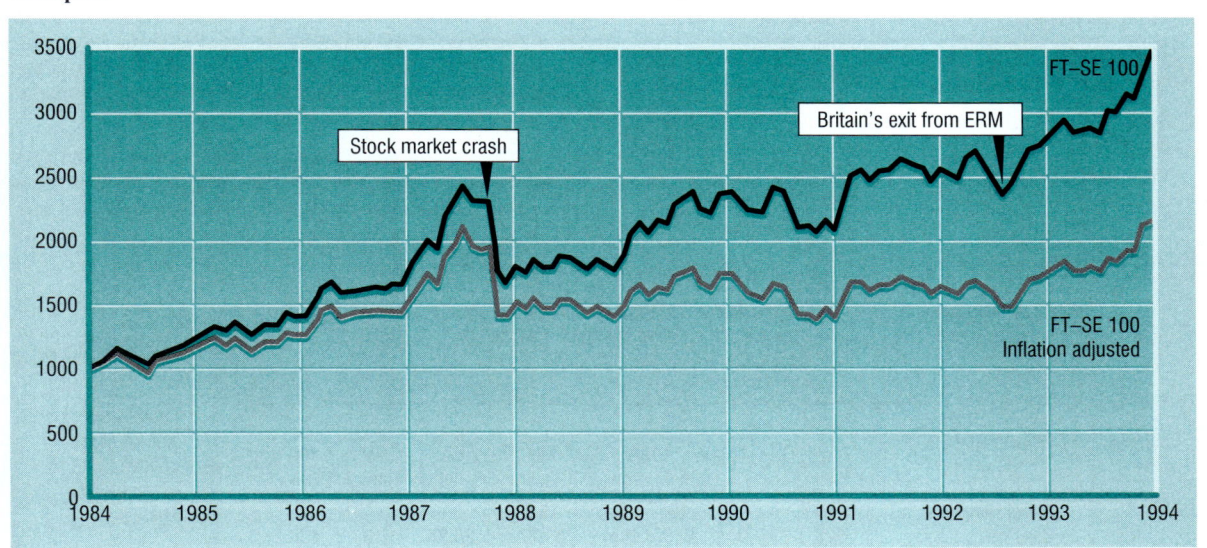

Financial Times 2.2.94

Portfolio Activity 22.3

Range: Usual sources of finance
Skills: Interpret and present data, Process information

Play the Stock Market!

Imagine you have £10,000 to invest in the shares of different companies in different industrial sectors. Your holding of shares will be known as your **portfolio**. Choose your shares from those listed every day at the back of the *Financial Times*.

Assume for the moment that you want to invest all your money in the shares of the Bass brewery. The number of shares you can buy at a price of 576 pence per share would be 1,736. If the price of shares rose to 600 pence each the following week, your portfolio would be worth £10,416 (1,736 x 600 pence).

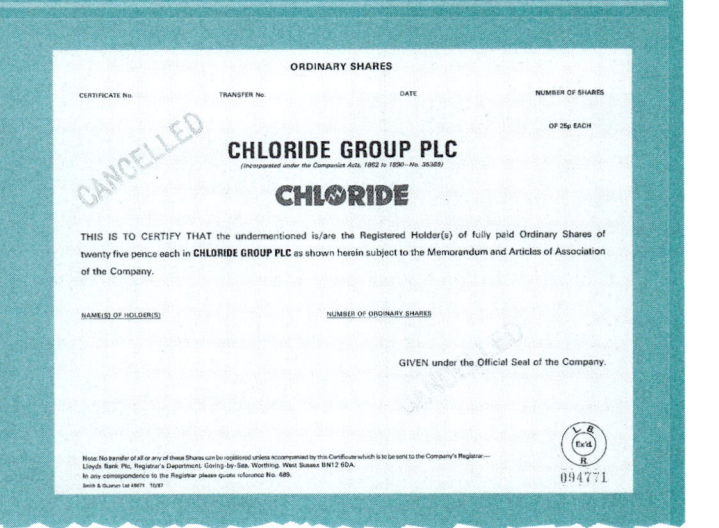

Advanced Business

The aim of this game is to double your money from capital gains. Compete against students in your class. The person with a portfolio worth nearest to £20,000 after six months wins.

To play you must follow these rules:

1. You are only allowed to hold shares in up to 10 different companies at any one time.
2. If you want to revise your portfolio, you may do so only on one day each week to be agreed by all the players in the game.
3. Every time you buy or sell shares, no matter what their value, you will have to pay a stockbroker £50 from your portfolio.

During the game:

- Obtain information on past company performance. Write to those companies you intend to buy shares in and ask for a copy of their annual report.

- Calculate an index number series of the average value of your shareholdings on the same day each week, using a computer spreadsheet. Compare the movement in the value of your share portfolio with changes in the FT All Share index. Is your portfolio performing better or worse than all other shares? If your portfolio is underperforming (i.e. the average value of your portfolio is falling or rising at a slower rate than the FT index) you may wish to reconsider your shareholdings and sell them in order to buy shares which are rising faster.

- Watch the market. Read the financial press and listen to the business news. What companies are about to announce profits? Are profit expectations high or low? How might changes in the economy affect your companies? How will these factors affect your decision to hold shares?

- Keep a detailed record of the shares you buy and sell on your computer spreadsheet, and justify your decisions in writing. You may discuss possible purchases with 'financial advisers' (e.g. your parents, guardians, or teachers).

▼ *How to read the financial pages in newspapers*

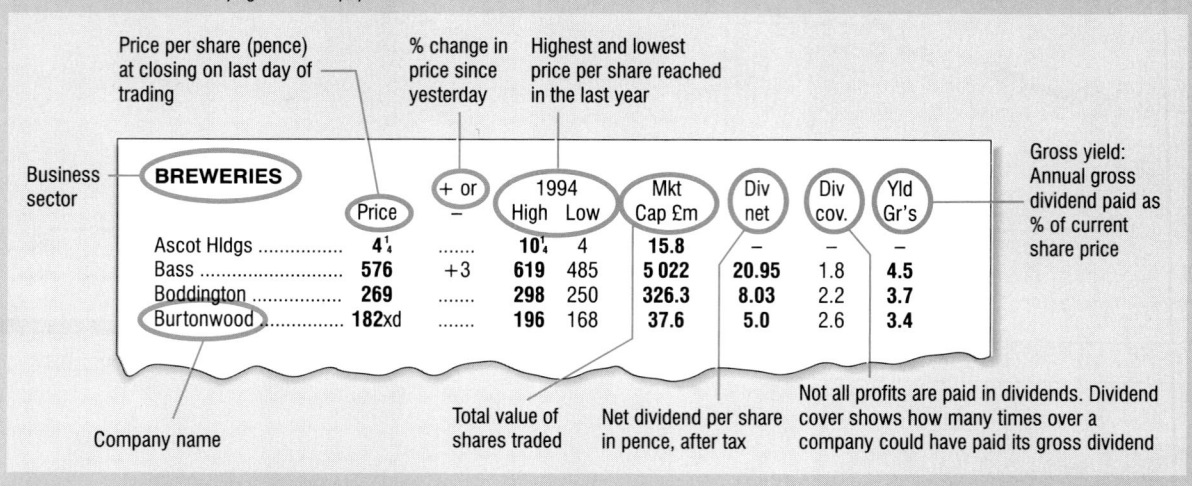

Business sector — **BREWERIES**

Price per share (pence) at closing on last day of trading — **Price**

% change in price since yesterday — **+ or −**

Highest and lowest price per share reached in the last year — **1994 High Low**

Total value of shares traded — **Mkt Cap £m**

Net dividend per share in pence, after tax — **Div net**

Not all profits are paid in dividends. Dividend cover shows how many times over a company could have paid its gross dividend — **Div cov.**

Gross yield: Annual gross dividend paid as % of current share price — **Yld Gr's**

Company	Price	+ or −	1994 High	Low	Mkt Cap £m	Div net	Div cov.	Yld Gr's
Ascot Hldgs	4½	......	10½	4	15.8	–	–	–
Bass	576	+3	619	485	5 022	20.95	1.8	4.5
Boddington	269	......	298	250	326.3	8.03	2.2	3.7
Burtonwood	182xd	......	196	168	37.6	5.0	2.6	3.4

Portfolio Activity 22.4

Range: Usual sources of finance
Skills: Read and respond to written material

1. Compare the two articles. What do they illustrate about the risk of holding ordinary shares in a company?
2. How is NFC raising money? Investigate other methods the company might consider using.
3. Investigate share issues, and the role of the Stock Exchange. Look in the financial press for an advertisement for a sale of company shares to the general public. Apply to the company for a prospectus. Why, and how, are they issuing shares? Also, contact the Stock Exchange for information on how the Stock Market works and how it is regulated. What is the role of a stockbroker?

£265 million shaker for BOC shares

More than £265 million was wiped off the stock market value of industrial gases group BOC today after chairman Pat Rich issued a gloomy trading statement and warned that operating profits will not match last year's. The shares plunged 59p to 654p within minutes.

London Evening Standard 10.8.93

UNIT SEVEN

CHAPTER 22

Road to riches with NFC

It has been a stupendous investment. Every £1 put up by the army of removal men, tea ladies, and warehouse managers who helped buy the National Freight Corporation from the Government in 1982 is now worth £160. Britain's wealthiest employees have already built up hefty nest eggs running well into six figures.

Now the Pickfords to BRS empire is launching its first cash call - to raise £263 million - since its flotation four years ago.

The money will be used to help integrate the BRS and Excel logistics business, and provide them with better Information Technology. It will also be used to fund growth of the firm in the UK, US, and mainland Europe, and to pay for the development of strategic alliances with companies in the US.

London Evening Standard 8.12.93

Key words

Share - a certificate of part ownership in a limited company

Face value - the price at which shares are first issued

Listing - obtaining permission to sell shares through the Stock Exchange

Flotation - when shares are sold in a public limited company for the first time

Dividend - a proportion of company profits paid per share in that company

Capital gain - an increase in the market value of shares

Preference shares - shares which are entitled to a fixed dividend if sufficient profits are made

Ordinary shares - shares in the ownership of a limited company which allow their holders to vote at annual general meetings. Dividends are variable depending on profits.

Equities - ordinary shares

Section **22.4**

Government assistance

The government offers a considerable amount of free advice and financial assistance in the form of grants, subsidies, and training to new and existing firms, to promote employment and economic growth (see 17.1).

Regional policy

The UK government has operated a **regional policy** for many years designed to encourage firms to locate and start up in areas of high unemployment and industrial decline.

Two types of area have been identified by the Department of Trade and Industry (DTi) as eligible for assistance (see Figure 22.6). The **assisted areas** are:

- Development Areas (DAs)
- Intermediate Areas (IAs)

543

Advanced Business

Three forms of financial assistance are available in these areas.

1. **Regional selective assistance:** discretionary grants for companies of any size with investment projects, primarily in manufacturing, that are commercially viable and will create or safeguard employment.

2. **Regional enterprise grants:** for small firms of less than 25 employees with investment projects, to cover 15% of the cost of new plant and machinery, up to a maximum of £15,000. Also available are 'innovation' grants of 50% of the cost of new product and process development, up to a maximum of £25,000.

- **Consultancy initiative:** firms with less than 500 employees can claim two-thirds of the cost of hiring business consultants to provide advice on marketing, planning, finance, design, and other aspects of business. Firms in non-assisted areas can also claim up to half the cost of approved business consultancy.

▼ Figure 22.6: Assisted Areas and Urban Programme Areas

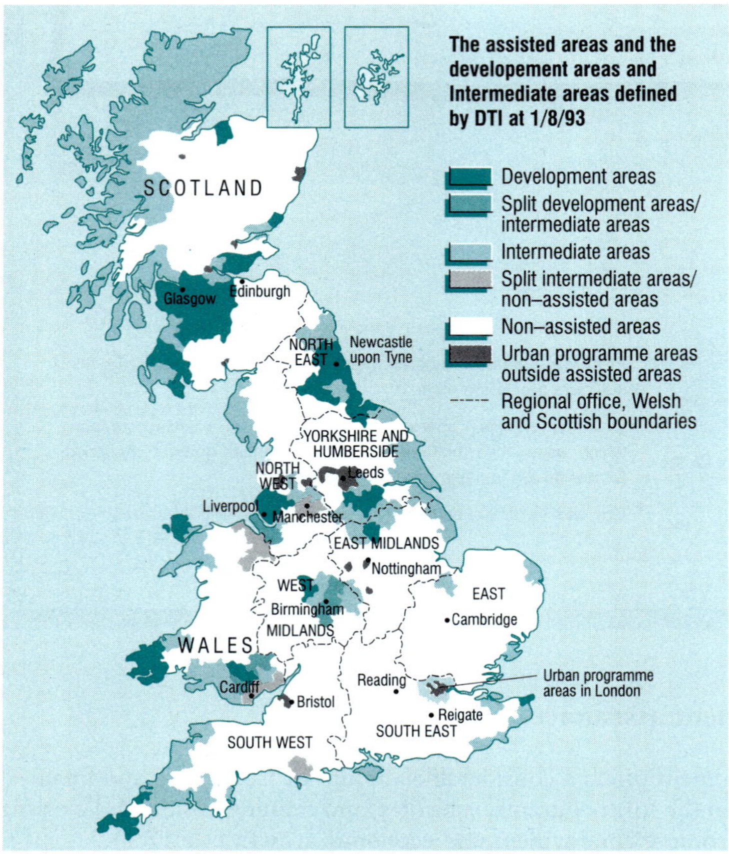

The assisted areas and the developement areas and Intermediate areas defined by DTI at 1/8/93

- Development areas
- Split development areas/ intermediate areas
- Intermediate areas
- Split intermediate areas/ non-assisted areas
- Non-assisted areas
- Urban programme areas outside assisted areas
- Regional office, Welsh and Scottish boundaries

From 'The Enterprise Initiative' DTi, September 1993

Urban policy

Inner City Task Force Areas

Inner City Task Forces operate in around 16 run-down urban areas, outside of the Assisted Areas, in major conurbations such as Edinburgh, Leeds, and London. They are able to provide grants and loans through Task Force Development Funds (TFDFs).

Enterprise Zones

There are around 26 of these zones earmarked for major office, factory, housing and leisure development, for example Docklands to the east of London, Telford and the Swansea Valley. New business location in these zones will be exempt from rates and almost free of planning controls. 100% capital allowances are available on the construction of property within these areas.

Other assistance

- **The Single Regeneration Budget (SRB)** was introduced in England in 1994 to focus support on local needs and priorities. About £100 million was made available in 1995/96, to be allocated on the basis of competitive bids from local authorities, Training and Enterprise Councils (TECs), and firms seeking assistance.

- **The Business Start-Up Scheme** is run by TECs and provides finance and training to selected unemployed people who wish to start their own business. Schemes vary (see 26.4). Although now part of the **Single Regeneration Budget**, start-up schemes are likely to continue.

- **The Loan Guarantee Scheme** seeks to encourage banks to lend money to small firms. The government offers to pay back 85% of loans over 2-7 years, up to a maximum of £250,000, if the business that has borrowed the money fails to repay.

- **Small Firms Training Loans**, to finance training programmes in firms with less than 50 employees, were introduced in 1994 by the government, in conjunction with Barclays, and the Cooperative and Clydesdale banks. Repayment can be deferred for up to 13 months. The government pays the banks interest during this period.

- **Local Authorities** may also be able to provide funds for local business start-ups, job creation and re-location. For example, a local authority may be willing to defer rent and rate payments to businesses occupying premises owned by the council (known as **landlord finance**).

- The **European Commission** also provides funds for regional development. The **European Regional Development Fund (ERDF)** provides help for infrastructure projects such as road building, telecommunications, etc. The UK was allocated £571 million in 1993. The **European Social Fund (ESF)** provides money for training and other schemes to promote employment and worker productivity. The **European Agricultural Guidance and Guarantee Fund (EAGGF)** provides grants to promote employment in rural areas. The **European Investment Bank** is also able to offer some low-interest loans to industry and infrastructure developments in depressed areas.

Key words

Assisted Areas - depressed areas, suffering from high unemployment and a lack of business opportunities, designated by government as in need of financial assistance

---

Section 22.5

Choosing a method of finance

When selecting methods of finance, firms will use the following criteria:

- **Amount:** the larger the amount of capital required, the less likely it is to be raised from internal sources. If large amounts of capital are required for long periods, then it may be worth the expense of raising finance through a share issue.

- **Cost:** any business will want to raise capital in the cheapest way possible, both in terms of administration costs and interest charges. Selling shares can be expensive in terms of administration, advertising, etc., whereas borrowing for a short period of time on credit cards or by trade credit can be interest-free. However, share sales can raise large amounts of permanent capital for a firm.

In general, the longer the period of a loan, and the more risk that the borrower will fail to repay, the higher the rate of interest charged.

- **Purpose:** firms will tend to seek long-term sources of finance in order to spread the cost of fixed asset purchases, such as premises and new machinery, over a number of years. For example, mortgages can spread the cost of buying or building a new factory over 25 years. In contrast, working capital requirements will tend to be funded from short-term sources, such as trade credit and overdrafts.

- **Status and size of the borrower:** small sole traders tend to be limited in their choices of finance, and will often lack assets to offer as security against a large long-term loan (see 22.2). The high failure rate of small businesses also tends to scare off potential lenders, who will only be willing to lend in return for a high rate of interest. In contrast, banks and other lenders regard lending to large, profitable companies such as Unilever and ICI, as being as safe as lending to the government. This means that these firms can raise finance more easily and at lower cost.

- **The economic environment:** economic factors can influence a firm's choice of finance. For example, in times of rising inflation, firms may find it of benefit to borrow at fixed rates of interest. If the general level of prices rises, then the real value of the sum paid back is reduced. During a recession, when sales and profits are likely to be falling, it would be unwise for a firm to take on hefty loan repayments, unless it can be sure of a future economic recovery (see 17.1).

- **Gearing:** the proportion of total finance raised in a firm from borrowing is called the **gearing ratio**, and has an important impact on how a company can raise further finance.

A high gearing ratio means that a firm has, in the past, raised a large proportion of its total capital through borrowing, and so has a large amount of fixed interest payments to make from future profits. This interest must still be paid on debt, even when profits are low or non-existent. This tends to make further borrowing a riskier form of raising finance than selling shares. With equities, no set amount must be paid to shareholders out of profits.

Portfolio Activity 22.5

Range: Usual sources of finance, Common methods of finance, Characteristics, Types of business organization
Skills: Produce written material, Collect and record data

1. In each of the following cases, investigate and select the type of borrowing you think would best suit the circumstances. Justify your choices (more than one answer may be correct). In each case, what will be the approximate duration and cost of repayment? Will security be needed? What security could be offered?

- A large multinational company wishes to borrow £20 million to finance the construction of a new factory.
- A corner shop would like £5,000 to improve the decoration of the premises.
- A furniture company is seeking finance to build up its stock of wood.
- A private hospital would like to raise £50,000 for a new brain-scanning machine.
- A large British plc is considering the location of a new factory in the North East of England. The area has very heavy unemployment and the firm wishes to raise £1.5 million.

2. Identify, with examples, those sources of finance which would be most useful to a business for:

   (a) Long-term borrowing (over 5 years)
   (b) Medium-term borrowing (3-5 years)
   (c) Short-term borrowing (less than 3 years)

Portfolio Activity 22.6

Range: Common methods of finance
Skills: Read and respond to written material

1. The article suggests that many owner-managed businesses are 'constrained by high gearing'. Explain what this means.

2. Give reasons why companies appear to dislike factoring and venture capital as methods of finance.

3. What methods of finance have been used by a business organization that you are familiar with? Arrange an interview with the owners or managers, and ask them which sources of capital are available to them, which they prefer, and why?

Dependent on the overdraft

Owner-managed businesses in the UK are still "depressingly dependent" on the overdraft as a means of financing their long-term development, according to a survey* carried out by the accountancy firm Touche Ross.

This reliance increases with the size of the business, the survey of 264 companies with sales of £5m to £150m shows.

On the whole, owner-managed businesses appear to be reducing their external borrowing but they remain constrained by high gearing. Peter Morgan, Touche Ross partner responsible for owner-managed businesses in London, says he is pessimistic about the chances of many raising money as the economy recovers.

Perhaps the most revealing section of the report is the list of the methods companies least like to choose to raise money. Businesses most want to avoid factoring, followed by venture and development capital. Leasing and hire purchase came next, with the sale of equity and commercial mortgages "least disliked" apart from the bank overdraft.

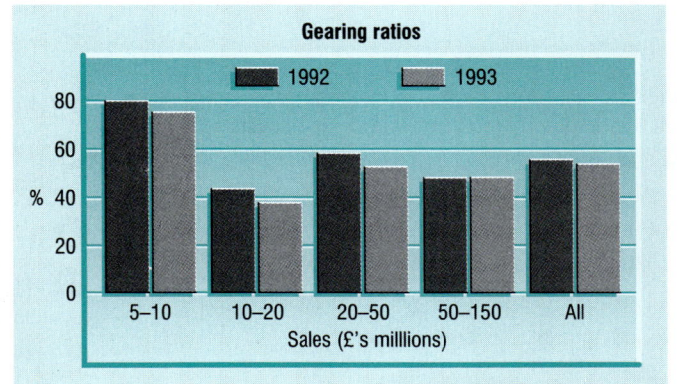

Financial Times 9.11.93

Key words

Gearing ratio - the proportion of total finance raised by a company from borrowing

Further reading

Moynihan, D, and Titley, B: *Economics - A Complete Course* (Oxford University Press 1993), Chapter 6

Useful articles on business finance can be found in *Managing Your Business* (published quarterly by Chase Communications Publishing Ltd., Arena House, 66-68 Pentonville Road, London N1 9HS)

The high street banks also publish various guides to sources of financial help for business. These are available free of charge.

Advanced Business

Test Questions

The following underpinning knowledge will be tested:
1. The financing requirements of a business
2. Assets and working capital.
3. Common methods of finance
4. Usual sources of finance for different types of business organizations.
5. Characteristics of common methods of finance

1 Which of the following is a permanent source of business finance?
- A Bank loan
- B Bank overdraft
- C Leasing
- D Equity capital

2 All of the following are factors to consider when choosing the best method of finance for a firm, except:
- A Gearing ratio
- B Amount required
- C Purpose
- D The amount of competition in the industry

3 Which form of finance is most appropriate for an expanding public limited company?
- A Bank loan
- B Overdraft
- C Share capital
- D Trade credit

4 All of the following provide internal sources of finance for a business except:
- A Retained profits
- B The sale of fixed assets
- C Government loans
- D Personal savings

5 Ordinary shares:
- A Give one vote per share at the AGM
- B Carry a fixed rate of return
- C Are not as risky as preference shares
- D Are paid back by the company when the shareholder wishes to sell

6 All of the following provide methods of external finance for business except:
- A Retained profits
- B Share sales
- C Increasing gearing
- D Trade creditors

7 Long-term finance is likely to be used for:
- A The purchase of fixed assets
- B Meeting working capital requirements
- C Covering short-term losses
- D Financing exports

Questions 8–10 share the following answer options:
- A Overdraft
- B Hire purchase
- C Trade credit
- D Share sales

Which of the above:

8 Is the most appropriate method of financing working capital?

9 Is a source of long-term finance?

10 Is granted by suppliers?

Questions 11-14 share the following answer options:
An expanding business needs to buy the following assets:
- A New premises
- B A computer system
- C A delivery van
- D Stocks of raw materials

Which is most likely to be bought using:

11 A lease contract?

12 A mortgage?

13 A bank loan?

14 Trade credit?

15
- A Make a list of the fixed assets you might expect to find in a large car manufacturers.
- B Suggest three methods of long term finance the car manufacturing company could use to finance the purchase of fixed assets.
- C What is the difference between a secured and unsecured loan?
- D What is working capital? Suggest and justify a suitable method of financing working capital requirements in a small sole trader business.
- E Why does the UK government offer financial help to some business organizations? Explain, using examples of the type of financial assistance available.

assessment assignment

UNIT SEVEN

CHAPTER 22

Assessment Assignment

Range: Financing requirements
Assets
Working capital
Common methods of finance
Usual sources of finance
Characteristics
Types of business organization

Skills: **Communication**
Read and respond to written material
Use images
Produce written material
Application of Number
Collect and record data
Tackle problems
Information Technology
Process information
Present information

Why City Players Tune In For United's Results

Most public companies report at most four times a year. At present Manchester United must feel as if it is reporting four times a week.

In the past month, the shares have risen and fallen on results from places as far afield as Swindon, Blackburn, and Wembley. Every time United or its premiership rival Blackburn Rovers play, the City adjusts the price. The defeat by Aston Villa at Wembley last Sunday sent United's down 30p, but Blackburn's defeat on Tuesday saw it recover much of the loss.

Broker Smith New Court's Roy Owens says, " The sharp swings are slightly artificial. There is not much volume in trading the shares and every game at this stage of the season is crucial."

But United's shares have been closely tracking events on the field for some time. Last year the shares jumped 22p to 474p when it won the Premier League. When it crashed out of the European Cup to Turkish side Galatasary in October, the shares fell 52p to 527p, and when it lost to Chelsea last month, the first home defeat for 17 months, the share slipped 10p to 690p.

Even player behaviour seems to affect the stockmarket. Eric Cantonas' sending off wiped 21p off the shares, while his dismissal in the next game knocked 5p off.

Sharp swings in the shares have been noted by City cynics, who argue that football clubs make poor public companies. They point to a history of boardroom unrest, soaring debts, and financial scandal and claim that profits are often sacrificed for performance on the field.

Adapted from The Daily Telegraph 3.4.94

chapter 23

Tasks

1. Manchester United FC is a business organization which aims to make a profit from organizing resources into a sporting activity. Explain who owns and controls Manchester United FC. How does this compare to the ownership and control of football clubs that have not sold shares to raise finance?

2. Why would a football team need to raise finance? Make a list, and attach cost estimates, of fixed and current assets a football club such as Manchester United might have.

3. Investigate sources, methods, and costs of asset and working capital finance available to a Premier League football club. Match these to their possible capital requirements identified in Task 2. How might these sources of nance differ from those available to a fourth division team?

4. Why would people buy ordinary shares in a football club? What is the role of the Stock Exchange?

5. Why do you think the share price of Manchester United has varied so much? Do you think the reasons you have given really do affect the future prosperity of the club, and should be reflected in sharp price swings?

6. Contrast Manchester United FC with a business organization of your choice. Investigate methods and sources of finance used by, and available to, your chosen organization.

- What are the asset and working capital requirements of the business?
- What methods of finance does it use and why?
- What other methods of finance could the business use? Give reasons for your recommendations.

549

Advanced Business

chapter 23 Cashflow Forecasting

This chapter explains why business organizations hold cash and how they forecast inflows and outflows of cash

Key ideas

Businesses need to hold sufficient **cash** and other **liquid assets** to meet day-to-day running expenses, debts, and unexpected business costs.

Liquid assets are those assets which can be quickly converted into cash.

Without enough liquidity, even a profitable firm can be forced to close down if it cannot meet its debts.

A **cashflow forecast** provides a business with an estimate of future **cash inflows and outflows**. Such a forecast enables managers to plan ahead in order to ensure that the business has enough liquidity to meet its debts and expenses.

Cashflow forecasts are used by business managers to monitor the performance of the firm. The forecast will also be used by people and firms who lend money to a business to gauge whether or not it will be able to make repayments.

Cashflow forecasts will be derived from spending plans in the **capital budget** and projections of running costs and sales in the **trading forecast**. The capital budget will include the costs of purchasing or hiring premises, machinery and other fixed assets.

Cash inflows include start-up capital, loans, sales revenues, and interest earnings on loans made by the business. **Cash outflows** include purchases, wages and salaries, and overheads, including loan repayments.

Cashflow is affected by the timing of payments made by and to a firm. A firm may attempt to manage the timing of these items in order to improve cashflow performance.

If a cashflow forecast is inaccurate, a firm may experience a shortage of cash and have to borrow money at high rates of interest. In the worst case, creditors may force the firm into **liquidation** and closure.

Cashflow difficulties can be caused by a variety of factors, including overtrading, the purchase of too many fixed assets, overstocking, poor credit control, and uncertainty and seasonal variations in sales.

Cashflow problems may be resolved by seeking additional finance, selling stock, delaying payments to creditors, or speeding receipt of payments from debtors, and changing pricing policies.

Section 23.1 Why is cash important?

Portfolio Activity 23.1

Range: Purpose of forecasts
Skills: Read and respond to written material, Collect and record data

1. What kinds of costs are involved in holding cash?
2. How else could consumer purchasing power be stored?
3. Given the costs involved, why do consumers and businesses continue to hold income and wealth in the form of cash?
4. Attempt to find out how much cash a business organization that you are familiar with holds on an average day on the premises, and in bank or building society deposits. Establish the reasons why this quantity of cash is held. For example, why does the organization not hold more or less cash? What are the advantages and disadvantages?

Paying with cash costs UK consumers £800m a year

It costs the British £800 million a year in lost interest income to carry around banknotes and coins in wallets and handbags, according to a study of the costs of circulating cash around the economy.

The first detailed study for 20 years estimates that it costs £4.5 billion to lubricate the £250 billion flow of cash payments made in Britain each year.

Individuals pay £800m, with a further £800m from shops and business, £700m from the Post Office, and £2.2bn from the Bank of England and commercial banks.

The study carried out by the Boston Consulting Group for De La Rue, the banknote printers, estimates that the use of cash costs each of Britain's 22 million households £210 a year in lost interest and handling expenses. It has been estimated that each household holds an average of £460 in cash at any one time. The figure is thought to be high because it is artificially boosted by the 'black economy' of unregistered and criminal enterprises which deal largely in cash.

Financial Times 18.11.93

The importance of cash

Any business will need to pay its bills with cash either in the form of notes and coins held by the firm, or by converting a variety of assets which are of value into cash. Assets which can be turned into cash quickly are known as **liquid assets**. The term **liquidity** refers to the ability to exchange such assets for cash without a loss of value.

Cash is the most liquid asset a firm can hold. It refers to notes and coins held on business premises or in bank or building society current accounts which can be withdrawn at short notice, usually by using a cheque to make payment. Cash is part of, but not the same as, working capital, which is money used to meet the day-to-day running expenses of a business (see 22.1). Working capital includes other current assets, such as money owed by debtors, which will need to be paid before the cash is available to the business to pay bills.

If a firm runs short of cash, it may be able to exchange some of its assets for cash. However, some assets may be **illiquid**, i.e. difficult to convert into cash quickly. For example, it might be difficult to sell partly-finished products or raw materials very quickly in order to pay a bill. Even if these assets could be sold, there is no guarantee that they would be worth as much to others as they are to the firm selling them. For example, stocks of soft lead, enamel paint, and partly-finished toy soldiers will be of limited value to firms other than toy makers, and even then will only be of worth to those firms wishing to make lead toy soldiers.

Other assets might be easier to sell and have a more definite value, for example, a factory building, vehicles, and plant and machinery. But even the sale of these can take time, and if a firm has to sell these kinds of assets in order to meet a bill, it may then find it difficult to continue trading. Because of these problems, wise business managers always ensure that they hold sufficient cash as one of their assets to meet bills.

It is possible to imagine a whole 'spectrum of liquidity', that is, a range of assets that could be converted into cash by a business, given a long enough period of time (see Figure 23.1).

▼ *Figure 23.1: A simple liquidity spectrum*

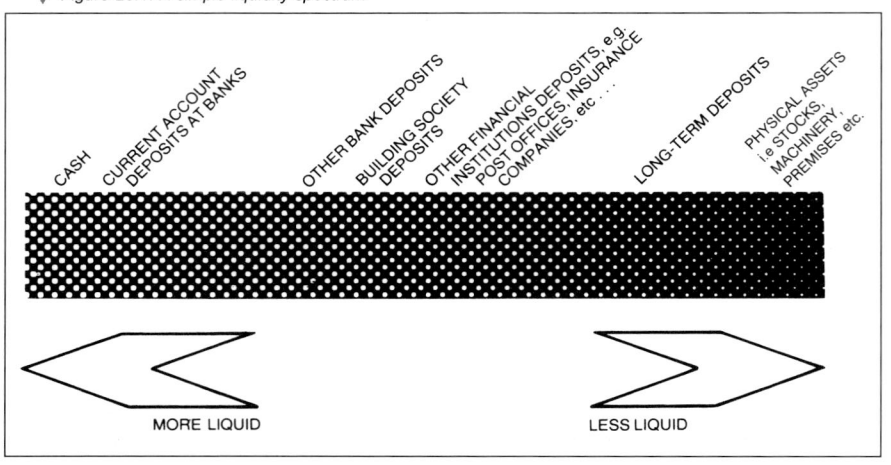

[Figure: A liquidity spectrum showing from left (MORE LIQUID) to right (LESS LIQUID): CASH, CURRENT ACCOUNT DEPOSITS AT BANKS, OTHER BANK DEPOSITS, BUILDING SOCIETY DEPOSITS, OTHER FINANCIAL INSTITUTIONS DEPOSITS, e.g. POST OFFICES, INSURANCE COMPANIES, etc..., LONG-TERM DEPOSITS, PHYSICAL ASSETS, i.e. STOCKS, MACHINERY, PREMISES etc.]

How much cash should a business hold?

Knowing exactly how much cash to hold, and being able to forecast future cash requirements, is one of the most important and difficult jobs facing business managers. A business can be very profitable 'on paper', but if it invests all of its cash into new machinery and plant, it may not have the funds available to meet day-to-day bills. When this happens, a firm is said to be **insolvent**.

If a firm is insolvent, it may be forced to borrow money from banks and other lenders at high rates of interest. If interest rates rise quickly, an otherwise profitable firm may find itself unable to meet its debts. At this point, creditors - the people or other firms to whom the firm owes money - may decide to demand repayment. The firm will then have to stop trading and shut down in order to be able to sell off key assets such as premises and machinery to meet bills. This is known as **liquidation**.

At first, it may seem odd that a profitable business could end up in this situation. However, cashflow problems may occur because of the time difference between receiving revenues from sales and making payments. For example, wages and salaries have to be paid out in cash each month, and raw materials must also be paid for, usually before the finished product can be sold to a customer. Thus, a firm incurs a number of cash costs before the good or service it produces is ready for sale. Even then, it may have to grant up to three months credit to customers, making a lengthy time-lag between paying out cash and receiving cash from sales. A business may, therefore, appear profitable 'on paper' - that is, revenue owed to the firm may be greater than its costs - but it can lack the liquidity needed to survive.

The continuous flows of cash into and out of a firm is often referred to as the **cashflow cycle** (see Figure 23.2).

▼ Figure 23.2: The cashflow cycle

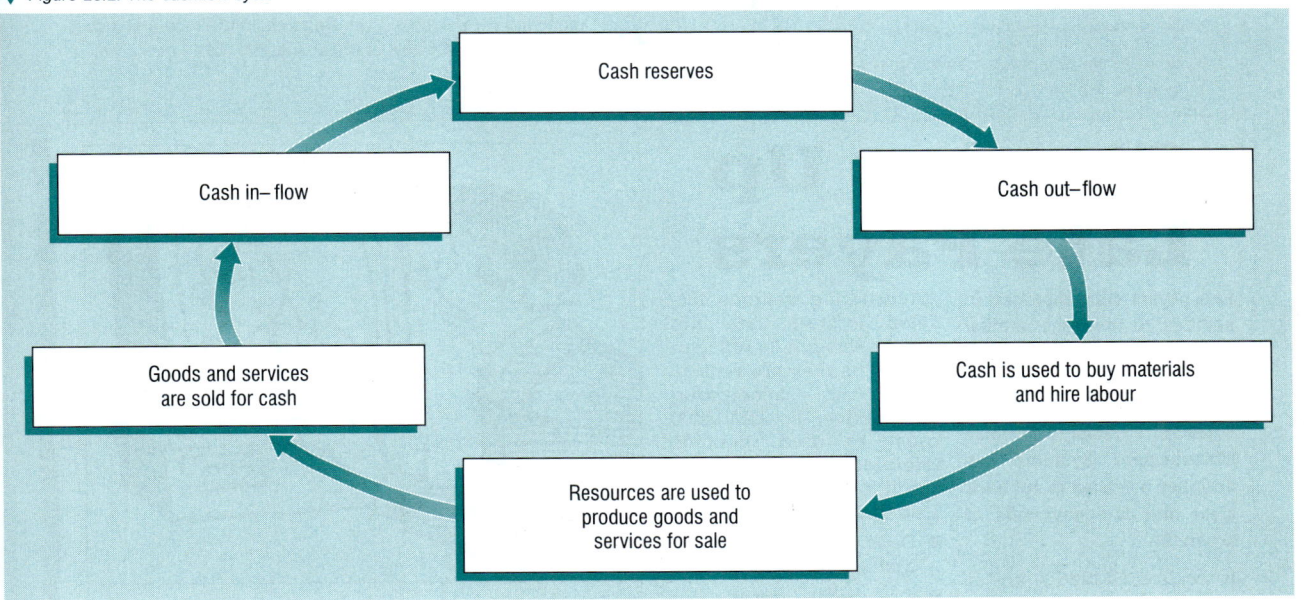

[Diagram showing cyclical flow: Cash reserves → Cash out-flow → Cash is used to buy materials and hire labour → Resources are used to produce goods and services for sale → Goods and services are sold for cash → Cash in-flow → Cash reserves]

The difference between cash and profit - an example

Top Chocs has just started selling high-quality chocolates imported from Belgium. The sole trader firm sells an average of 500 boxes per month. Top Chocs sells the boxes for £10 each, making sales of £5,000 in the first month of trading.

The boxes of chocolates cost £5 each to buy, and the total wage bill for the firm is £1,500 per month. Rent costs are £500 per month, and insurance and energy costs add another £200 per month.

REVENUES

500 boxes x £10	= £5,000

COSTS

Chocolates (500 boxes)	= £2,500
Wages	= £1,500
Rent	= £ 500
Insurance and energy	= £200
	£4,700

PROFIT

Revenues - Costs	= £300

Thus, after subtracting trading costs from sales revenues, Top Chocs has made a trading profit of £300 in its first month of operation. However, the owner, Ms Soft-Centre is worried, because even though she is making a profit on paper, her bank balance has fallen.

When the chocolates are imported, foreign suppliers will only despatch orders for 150 or more boxes to UK customers. Because Top Chocs sells four types of chocolate box, this means she has had to buy a total of 600 boxes at a total cost of £3,000 (600 x £5).

By the end of the first month, Ms Soft-Centre had spent the following cash sums:

Chocolate	£3,000
Rent	£ 500
Wages	£1,500
Insurance	£ 100
Energy	£100
	£ 5,200

In other words, the £300 profit was made on the quantity of chocolate boxes actually sold, but because so much stock had to be purchased initially, the firm is worse off in terms of cash holdings by a sum of £200, being the difference between sales revenue and total costs. The remaining extra stock will no doubt be profitably sold in the future, but in the meantime the Top Chocs cash balance has been reduced by a profitable transaction.

Advanced Business

Portfolio Activity 23.2

Range: Purposes of forecasts, Significance of timing
Skills: Read and respond to written material

1. Why do 'late payers kill companies'?
2. Is late payment something which can be estimated accurately when producing a cashflow forecast?
3. How might the technology described in this article be of use in managing cashflow?
4. Gather data on the extent of the problem of late payment in firms with which you are familiar, and report on what could be done by firms themselves and the government in order to assist business in obtaining timely payment. You may wish to use your local authority Enterprise Unit and other national sources for information - for example, the Department of Trade and Industry (DTi), the Confederation of British Industry (CBI), etc.

Chasing Up Late Payers

Late payers kill companies! In addition to the large number of bankruptcies caused, many companies go through damaging cashflow problems. Software developers Eastside Management Systems has designed a system to cut back slow and late payments of accounts.

It's called CMS2000 and it is able to take information from any computerized order processing or sales ledger system. It then takes over everything from invoicing and credit control to court action against late payers, if this becomes necessary. The package costs about £4,000.

Accounting systems, like sales ledgers, are not flexible enough for efficient control as they are written from the accounting perspective, so CMS2000 tries to find specific information needed for credit management.
This includes:

- Daily list of calls made and letters sent
- On-screen details of each account in debt
- Information of the approach to be taken with each customer

The package allows the credit manager to get any information needed from any part of the system. An analysis of debts by age can be produced and if cash is coming in more slowly than expected a report can be produced to redefine collection tactics.

The system manages cash collection by dictating the action to be taken by the credit controller, who has details of each debt displayed on the screen and details of how the customer should be approached.

The credit controller then has to make notes of each call, and this information is kept for future reference. If payment is not received by the due date, a note of this appears in the next day's diary. If letters are needed the system will produce them.

Daily Mail 24.1.94

Key words

Cash - notes and coins and money held in bank or building society current accounts

Liquid assets - assets which can be converted into cash

Liquidity - the ability to exchange assets for cash without a loss of value

Illiquid assets - assets which cannot easily or quickly be converted into cash

Insolvency - when a firm does not have enough assets to pay its debts

Liquidation - selling off a firm's assets after the collapse of the business

Section 23.2 Cashflow forecasting

Why do firms forecast cashflows?

An important part of business planning and management is the setting of targets, and preparation of plans to achieve them. Organizations will set objectives, such as increasing profits or market share, and then devise plans for the use of materials and labour, the level of production and sales, and the cash requirements to meet their objectives.

Making plans involves making forecasts. Important forecasts for a business are;

- **Capital budget** – this involves forecasting the timing and amount of necessary expenditures on premises, machinery, vehicles and other fixed assets (see 22.1). New fixed assets will be needed to replace old assets or to expand a new or existing business.

- **Trading forecast** – this involves forecasting spending on activities that enable the firm to produce and sell goods and services. These include forecasts of spending on raw materials, wages, telephones, power, rent and rates, and all other day to day running costs. Sales revenues resulting from trading activities will also be forecast.

- **The cashflow forecast** – this is a forecast of expected cash in-flows from sales and any other incomes, for example bank loans, and expected cash out-flows to pay for the bills forecast to arise in the capital budget and trading forecast.

We shall now consider the purposes and format of a cashflow forecast.

Cashflow smoothing

An important aspect of business success is to plan ahead and forecast inflows and outflows of cash, in order to be able to anticipate future difficulties and take appropriate action. If a forecast shows that the business is likely to run short of cash in a particular month, because cash outflows exceed cash inflows, managers can either decide to cut costs now, or attempt to raise revenues in future in order prevent the shortfall from happening. It is much better to be able to take time in deciding what should be cut, than to be forced into a rush decision.

A **cashflow forecast statement** is simply a budget for cash. It lists all expected monthly receipts and payments over a given period of time - usually six or twelve months - so that the firm can identify when cash will be short or in surplus. Using this information, the firm can then arrange a loan to cover a cash shortfall or, if a cash surplus is likely to be earned at another time in the year, save it for use later in the year, when cash reserves are low.

Using cashflow forecasting to even-out cash surpluses and deficits into the future is sometimes known as **cashflow smoothing**. A firm will be able to test the impact on cashflow of different forecasts of spending on fixed assets and trading activities, and different assumptions about the future level of sales. In this way it will be able to have courses of action planned in case the firm runs short of cash.

Monitoring business performance

The cashflow forecast also provides a useful method by which business managers can monitor the performance of the firm. The forecast can be used to compare actual cashflow with plans on a regular basis, so as to help identify any differences which may require attention.

Raising capital

In addition, a cashflow forecast can be used to illustrate the future prospects for a business to a potential lender. For example, a bank manager will want to be assured that the firm will have sufficient cash each month to meet loan repayments. A healthy cashflow forecast can increase the confidence both of new and existing investors in the business.

The cashflow forecast statement

The precise format of a cashflow forecast statement will vary between firms. However, within any forecast there will be three main sections:

- **Receipts:** details of cash inflows from various sources, for example, revenues from cash sales, cash from debtors, and injections of new capital from loans or share sales. Interest payments on any surplus cash invested in a bank deposit account or other interest-bearing accounts can also produce cash for a business.

- **Payments:** details of cash outflows to pay for various items such as wages and salaries, purchases of raw materials and fixed assets, and overheads, such as telephone and electricity bills, office supplies, rent and rates, which tend not to vary with the level of output (see 20.1). Loan repayments, including any interest, will also be included within this section.

- **Summary balance:** this section at the bottom of the forecast statement sums total receipts and payments for each month. The net cashflow is then added to the cash balance available at the beginning of each month to give the closing balance of cash available at the end of each month.

Figure 23.3 shows an example of a cashflow forecast for a firm over a period of eight months. The **cash inflow** in each month represents expected monthly cash. The firm has also just received a bank loan of £2 million in January to replace some old equipment. Sales invoices outstanding since the previous December are also repaid in February, to add £800,000 to cash inflows.

The forecast sales figures for each month could be based on previous experience or, in the case of a new business, on the average cash sales made by similar-sized competitors in the industry, or from market research into consumer demand for the firm's products. Financial advisers and accountants may also be able to help a new business forecast its cashflow. However, it is important to remember that a cashflow forecast only shows cash receipts, and that actual sales may be quite different to the cash figure if some sales are made on credit.

Cash outflows in the form of purchases, wages, and overheads are given each month. Again, these figures represent the expected cash payments made. Spending plans in the capital budget and trading forecast may differ from cash outflows - for example, if the firm is allowed credit by materials suppliers, or if assets are bought on hire purchase.

▼ Figure 23.3: Example of a cashflow forecast

ALL FIGURES £000'S

Month	Jan	Feb	Mar	Apr	May	June	July	Aug
RECEIPTS: (cash inflows)								
Cash sales	3,000	2,500	1,900	1,800	1,800	1,500	1,200	1,000
Cash from debtors		800		500		500		300
Loan capital	2,000							
Interest payments						100		
Total receipts (A)	5,000	3,300	1,900	2,300	1,800	2,100	1,200	1,300
PAYMENTS: (cash outflows)								
Cash purchases (incl. VAT)	3,000	2,000	2,500	2,000	2,000	2,000	1,500	1,500
Credit purchases (incl. VAT)	500							
Wages/salaries	820	800	800	800	800	800	800	800
Overheads:								
Rent/rates	150	150	150	150	150	150	150	150
Transport	30	26	19	17	17	17	12	12
Hire Purchase	5	5	5	5	5	5	5	5
Leasing payments	25	25	25	25	25	25	25	25
Loan repayments		100	100	100	100	100	100	100
Electricity				60	60			
Gas				13	10			
Telephone				25	25			
Post	4	3	2	2	2	2	2	2
Insurance	6	6	6	6	6	6	6	6
VAT			-2,000			1,600		
Other expenses	30	25	25	25	25	25	20	20
Total payments (B)	4,570	3,140	1,730	3,130	3,130	3,225	4,220	2,620
Net Cashflow (A-B)	430	160	170	-830	-1,330	-1,225	-3,020	-1,320
+ Opening Bank Balance	1,000	1430	1590	1760	930	-400	-1525	-4545
= Closing Bank Balance	1,430	1,590	1,760	930	-400	-1,525	-4,545	-5,865

The **net cashflow** for each month is given as total receipts minus total payments. This information can be usefully plotted on a graph (see Figure 23.4).

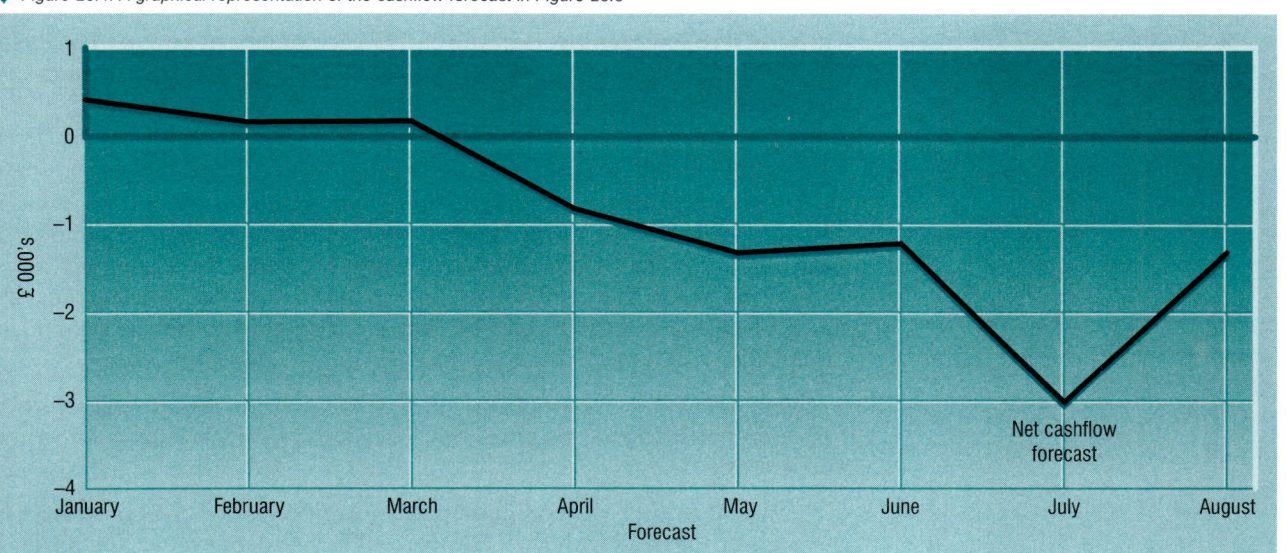

▼ Figure 23.4: A graphical representation of the cashflow forecast in Figure 23.3

Inflows and outflows will affect the balance of cash held by the firm at the bank. In figure 23.3, the business started with a bank balance of £1 million. The last rows of the cashflow forecast show the opening balance at the bank, and the impact on this balance of the net cashflow each month. Opening balance plus cashflow gives the closing balance at the bank each month. The closing balance then becomes the opening bank balance in the next month.

The cashflow forecast in figure 23.3 predicts a cash surplus in the first three months of the trading period, and then a deficit in each of the remaining five months, reflecting the seasonal nature of sales. However due to the strong cashflow performance in the first few months, the forecast shows that the bank balance of the business is able to stay in credit for the first four months, before going into debit. The looming negative balance of nearly £6 million in August, not helped by a large VAT payment made to Customs and Excise in June at a time when sales were falling, will force the firm to plan ahead in an attempt to cover the expected cash deficit. Possible solutions to this cashflow problem are discussed in Section 23.3 below.

The timing of cash inflows and outflows

Credit periods

The example above illustrates the importance of correct timing when calculating cashflow figures. Purchases and sales are not necessarily entered into the cashflow when they happen, but are entered when a cash receipt or payment occurs. Given trade credit periods of up to three months, the time difference between entering transactions into the accounts and cashflow entries can be very significant (see 22.2). For example, a business may make sales on credit today of £10,000. A figure of £10,000 is entered into the accounts immediately, and is used in calculating the profit figure. However, the cashflow will only show the £10,000 cash received when it is paid to the firm in a few months time.

Wages and salaries

It is usual to pay employees at the end of each month in arrears. This helps to delay cash outflows, often until cash receipts for each month are available to pay the wages bill.

Value Added Tax (VAT)

VAT is a percentage tax added to the price of many goods and services. Some goods, known as zero- rated, are exempt from VAT. Examples of zero-rated goods include children's clothes, books, food, and rail fares. Rates and wages and salaries are also exempt from VAT. The current rate of VAT is 17.5%, but this may be changed from time to time in the budget (see 3.2).

Traders are legally required (except if zero-rated) to collect VAT on their sales on behalf of the Customs and Excise department. This is known as **output tax**.

In 1994/95, a firm with an anticipated turnover of £45,000 or more had to register for VAT with the Customs and Excise department. If a business is VAT-registered, then the trader may reclaim any VAT it has paid on its own purchases as a business expense. VAT is likely to be paid by firms on purchases of stock, fixed assets, and overhead expenses. Since 1994 VAT has also been levied on gas and electricity bills but at a lower rate of 8%. Reclaimed VAT is known as **input tax**. This VAT may be claimed against the tax the trader passes on to Customs and Excise. That is:

VAT payable to Customs and Excise = Output Tax - Input Tax

For example, a firm makes sales of £571,428 in a given month, on which £100,000 will be owed to Customs and Excise in VAT (**output tax**). To produce the goods for these sales, the firm purchased £200,000 of stock, and of this sum, 17.5% or £35,000 was paid in VAT (**input tax**). The business can reclaim the input VAT it has paid and so only passes on the difference of £65,000 between output VAT and input VAT, (ie. £100,000 - £35,000), to Customs and Excise.

Since the output tax will nearly always be greater than the input tax, businesses will almost certainly end up paying some cash to the Customs and Excise department for VAT. This is because output tax is based on selling prices, whereas input tax is based on cost prices of materials bought into the business before value is added (see 18.1).

Only zero-rated firms, for example, those in the food industry, are not required to charge VAT on their sales. However, they may have to pay out large sums in input VAT on purchases of raw materials and components. In this case, the Customs and Excise Department will owe the trader money. Zero-rated traders can reclaim this input tax every month, thereby boosting cashflow.

Portfolio Activity 23.3

Range: Cash in-flow headings, Cash out-flow headings, Significance of timing
Skills: Process information

Completing a cashflow forecast can be time-consuming. Incorrect entries may also be overlooked and carried forward from one month to the next. Because of this, many businesses prefer to set up a spreadsheet on a computer. In this way, cashflow and closing balances at the end of each month can be automatically recalculated each time a new figure is entered into an appropriate cell.

1. Load a spreadsheet package, for example EXCEL or LOTUS 123, on to your computer and set up the cashflow forecast statement from Figure 23.3.

- Enter appropriate formulae to sum column totals for receipts and payments each month.

- Also enter formulae to calculate net cashflow each month, by subtracting the cell containing total payments from the cell containing total receipts.

- Enter formulae to calculate the opening balance and closing balance and to carry forward the closing balance each month.

- Check that your spreadsheet works before proceeding.

2. Use your spreadsheet to adjust the cashflow forecast in Figure 23.3 to allow for the following additional flows:

- A VAT bill for £600 is received in March but paid in April. The firm has paid £300 of VAT input tax which can be offset against this bill.

- The firm delivered goods to a customer with an invoice for £400 in April. The sum was paid in June.

- There was an unpaid energy bill for £200 outstanding in August.

- Sales on credit worth £600 were made in February. Payment was received in May.

- Sales on credit worth £400 were made in June. Payment was received in August.

In the case of quickly-growing small firms, there is often a temptation to use VAT as a source of extra finance by delaying payment to Customs and Excise, so that total receipts including VAT can be used to boost net cashflow. However, fines for late payment of VAT are severe, and the cost of these fines would more than outweigh the benefits gained from using VAT money for a short period.

It is essential to make correct estimates as to the timing and size of VAT payments. At 17.5% of sales revenue, VAT can have a major impact on cash inflows and outflows.

Key words

Capital budget - a plan for future purchases of fixed assets such as premises, machinery and other equipment.

Trading forecast - a plan for production (raw material purchases, wage payments), overheads and sales in a business.

Cashflow forecast statement - a prediction of all expected monthly business receipts and payments over a future time period, to show the forecast cash balance at the end of each month

Cashflow smoothing - using a cashflow forecast to plan the management of cash to smooth out surpluses and deficits and minimize the need to borrow capital externally

Net cashflow - total cash inflows less total cash outflows

Output tax - Value Added Tax (VAT) collected by business as a percentage of their sales of certain goods and services which must be paid to the Customs and Excise department

Input tax - VAT on purchases made by a business which can be reclaimed as a business cost from the Customs and Excise department

Section 23.3 Cashflow problems

Causes of cashflow shortages

A business that fails to forecast cashflow accurately will fail to manage and control its working capital. The result can be a shortage of liquidity, which may force the business to sell important assets and therefore lead to a reduction in future profitability. Alternatively, the firm may have to borrow at high rates of interest, which will drain away profits. In the worst case, a lack of liquidity can lead to closure.

Cashflow difficulties may arise because of the following:

- **Overtrading.** A firm that attempts to increase the scale of production too quickly without regard to the impact of growth on cashflow, is said to be **overtrading**. Increased sales create the need for more cash to pay for extra raw materials and work in progress. Without having secured long-term funds in advance, the business is forced into delaying payment to creditors and attempting to obtain early payment from debtors. If a creditor insists on early payment, the firm may have to go into liquidation.

- **Too many fixed assets.** Spending too much money buying fixed assets, such as new plant and machinery, is a significant drain on business cash reserves. It may be better to lease fixed assets or purchase them on HP, rather than pay for them up-front in full.

- **Overstocking.** Another difficulty is caused when too much stock is purchased. The more specialized the stock is, the harder it will be to sell off quickly in a cashflow crisis in order to raise working capital. Large quantities of stock also tie up cash unnecessarily, which could be used to earn interest. Stocks may also become obsolete if fashions or technology change, or if there is fall in demand for the product.

- **Too much credit.** A firm may raise its capital internally from its owners, or externally by borrowing (see 22.2). The larger the proportion of capital raised through borrowing, the larger will be the interest payments which the business has to make. If interest rates rise, the burden of interest payments faced by a heavily indebted firm will also increase. These payments are likely to be a severe drain on cashflow and profit.

- **Poor credit control.** Many small firms find themselves faced with cashflow difficulties either because sales are less than expected, or because credit customers take longer than expected to pay their debts. Often this is due to poor credit control, and the granting of credit to firms who are themselves experiencing cashflow difficulties.

- **Inflation.** Cashflow difficulties may arise because the general level of prices rises by more than was anticipated. If, for example, wages and raw materials costs rise suddenly and unexpectedly, then cash reserves may be used up, leaving too little cash for other eventualities. Firms often underestimate the impact of rising prices on their costs in their cashflow forecasts. Both capital budgets and trading forecasts should allow for an anticipated increase in prices over the forecast period.

- **Seasonal fluctuations.** Some businesses are seasonal, with cash inflows and outflows varying by time of year. For example, firework manufacturers may spend money throughout the year in producing fireworks, but find that their main source of cash inflow is in the weeks leading up to early November. While this may be anticipated, it takes very careful planning and discipline to ensure that the cash inflow is held over, to be spread across the full year.

Solving cashflow problems

The main ways of solving a cashflow crisis are either to foresee the problem and take preventative action (such as cutting cash outflows or raising inflows), or to find additional sources of finance to cover the deficit.

Specific cashflow remedies might include the following:

- **Negotiate short-term finance.** It may be possible to negotiate an overdraft with a bank in order to cover a potential cashflow difficulty. The disadvantage of this is that interest will have to be paid on the money borrowed, and if the firm is already in difficulty, it may be hard to find a lender to borrow from.

- **Convert current assets into cash.** A business may be able to sell some of its stock in order to raise cash. Debtors can also be chased for payment, or offered discounts to pay up more quickly.

- **Sell off fixed assets and lease back.** Fixed assets owned by a business such as plant, vehicles, and machinery can be sold off to raise cash. The amount raised from the sale of fixed assets is known as their **net realisable value**. This may be less than their '**book value**' (ie cost price less an allowance for depreciation – see 20.1).

  However, fixed assets will be needed to produce goods and services for sale. By leasing these assets, a firm agrees to rent them for a fixed period from a leasing company, and is therefore able to carry on production (see 22.2). However, the regular monthly payments made to a leasing company will increase cash outflows over the period of asset hire.

- **Alter pricing policy.** Sometimes cutting product selling prices can result in increased cash sales if the quantity sold rises by a sufficiently large amount. If this happens, demand for the product is said to be **price elastic** (see 1.5).

- **Tie cash outflows to sales.** This means that spending on items other than current wages and production supplies is postponed until after a target level of sales revenue has been reached. For example, a firm may delay replacing equipment and non-essential consumables until sales have picked up.

Portfolio Activity 23.4

Range: Significance of timing
Skills: Take part in discussions, Collect and record data

1. In small groups, investigate how a debt factoring service can assist firms with cashflow problems. (see 22.2)
2. Undertake research into how a real small firm manages its cashflow. Investigate;
- how it produces capital spending plans and trading forecasts
- how the cashflow is produced, how cashflow is reviewed and monitored, and what kinds of action follow as a result.
- Would you advise the firm you have chosen to use a debt factoring service? Explain your answer. (If you use a firm which is new to you, you are more likely to be able to fulfil the range requirements of communications core skills in this task, in dealing with people not in frequent contact with you.)

Sources of information may include the Business Advisory Service of the local authority, or local firms on an industrial estate.

Avoiding cashflow problems

Businesses can adopt some practical strategies right from the start of trading, in order to minimize the risk of future cashflow crises. For example:

- Avoid reliance on a few big customers. If one closes down or switches supplier, it will hit cashflow very badly.
- Send out invoices as quickly as possible. If a contract involves a long period of work before a final invoice can be sent out, agree in advance to invoice at key points as the work progresses.
- Give debtors an incentive to pay up quickly by offering discounts for prompt payment. Be firm with late payers.
- Try to arrange to pay large bills in instalments.
- Once a good relationship has been built up with suppliers, try to re-negotiate credit and discounts with them in order to reduce costs.
- Avoid carrying too high a level of stock. Stock is important, but it represents business capital tied up, and can be costly if financed by a bank loan on which interest is paid.

Portfolio Activity 23.5

Range: Consequences of incorrect forecasting
Skills: Read and respond to written material

1. What is a 'negative cashflow'?

2. Why might a negative cashflow be associated with business expansion and growth, rather than contraction? Give some practical examples to explain.

3. Is cashflow on its own a sufficient indicator of business success? If not, what kinds of indicators would be?

4. Undertake research into two or three firms of different sizes. Establish from these firms how much they rely on cashflow forecasts, and to what extent they supplement cashflow with other forms of performance monitoring. Draw up an action plan and keep a lrecord of how you have tackled this investigation.

5. Prepare a brief report summarizing your views on what potential investors should look for in the performance of a business before investing their money.

The Lessons of Agony and Excess

The last five years have been traumatic for most businesses. The period has seen prominent scandals (Maxwell and Polly Peck), some astonishing collapses (Canary Wharf, Coloroll), and many calamities that have left companies such as Next, Storehouse, Saatchi & Saatchi much smaller than before.

Defining measures of success is not easy, especially at a time when companies were making merry with lax accounting rules to dress up their performance figures. Cashflow is often a useful measure in the absence of clear profit figures, but it can also be misleading.

The list of companies with significant negative cashflows during this period includes expected victims such as British Aerospace, Burton, Forte, Lonhro and Ratner. All of these companies experienced negative cashflows in four of the five years under review.

But so did successful businesses such as Sainsbury, Tesco, Cable & Wireless, and United Biscuits. Their cashflows were associated with expansion, rather than recession and catastrophe.

No single measure is sufficient to capture business performance, but a collection of indicators does separate the winners from the losers. Combining sales, earnings, employment, investment, and net profits, some companies do stand out.

These companies include three supermarket groups (KwikSave, Sainsbury, and Tesco), but also one of their suppliers, Cadbury Schweppes, the services group Rentokil and Glaxo.

Adapted from The Guardian 18.9.93

Key words

Overtrading - when a firm expands too quickly without obtaining the necessary long term finance

Net realisable value - the value at which old fixed assets can be sold off

Book value - the cost price of replacing old fixed assets less an allowance for their depreciation

Further reading
Hopkins, C: *Cashflow and How To Improve It* (Kogan Page, 1993)

Advanced Business

Test Questions

The following underpinning knowledge will be tested:
1. The purposes and components of forecasts
2. Capital budget and Trading forecast headings
3. The purpose of a cash flow as a component of a forecast to a business seeking finance
4. Cash in-flow and out flow headings
5. The consequences of incorrect forecasting
6. Produce forecasts for cash in flows and outflows from a 12 month period

1 The purpose of a cashflow forecast is to:
- A Show the amount of profit made
- B Provide a tool for managing cashflow
- C Show expenses actually incurred
- D Provide information on sales actually made

Questions 2-4 relate to the simple cashflow forecast for a four-month period shown below:

Month	Jan	Feb	Mar	Apr
Receipts £				
Sales	500	800	600	1,300
Payments £				
Wages	600	600	600	600
Energy costs	100	100	100	100
Raw materials	100	200	300	300
Administration costs	50	50	40	20
Total payments	850	950	1,040	1,020

2 In which month does cash inflow exceed cash outflow for the first time?
- A January
- B February
- C March
- D April

3 All of the following are true statements about the forecast except:
- A the firm will need an overdraft in April
- B the amount of overdraft needed in January is £350
- C Cashflow will be negative in March
- D The closing balance at the end of February will have been increased by £150

4 Assume now that the firm borrows £500 in February. If nothing else changes, net cashflow in March will be:
- A + £500
- B 0
- C - £150
- D + £360

5 In a trading forecast, cash outflows may include all of the following except:
- A Wages
- B Energy costs
- C Long-term creditors
- D Rent

Questions 6-9 share the following answer options:
- A An unplanned cash surplus
- B An unplanned bank overdraft
- C An increase in money owed by the firm
- D No impact on cashflow

Which of the above impacts on cashflow would result from:

6 Some debtors unexpectedly going bankrupt?

7 Payment by a customer of a previously written-off debt?

8 Purchases of machinery not accounted for in the capital budget?

9 The firm experiencing an increase in credit sales?

10 A business has produced a cashflow forecast which predicts a closing balance at the bank at the end of the year of £5,000. The following mistakes are then discovered:
- Sales for the year should be £7,000 higher
- An increase in wages in the trading forecast of £4,000 was ignored

What should the new forecast for the closing balance be, taking into account these changes?

- A £8,000 surplus
- B £16,000 surplus
- C £6,000 deficit
- D £2,000 surplus

11 A cashflow forecast will show:

- A Profit or loss
- B Depreciation of assets
- C Cash receipts and payments
- D Balances on customer accounts

12 When a business applies for a loan it is usual to produce a cashflow forecast. The main reason for this is:

- A The cashflow forecast gives the lender unlimited liability
- B It is a legal requirement
- C It shows that borrowing requirements have been accurately estimated
- D It shows that the business has a good accounting system

13 A firm registered for VAT makes payments to the Customs and Excise department every three months. Its cashflow forecast for the next three months has left out VAT. The likely consequence of this is that the firm:

- A Will be charged too much VAT by its suppliers
- B Pays Customs and Excise too much money
- C May not have sufficient funds to make the VAT payment
- D Will be exempt from payment

14 The graph below is a plot of the net cashflow forecast of a small business that is due to start trading one month from now:

What is the most likely explanation for the negative cashflow expected in the first four months of trading?

- A Payment of VAT to Customs and Excise department
- B The receipt of a bank loan
- C Sales on credit
- D The purchase of fixed assets

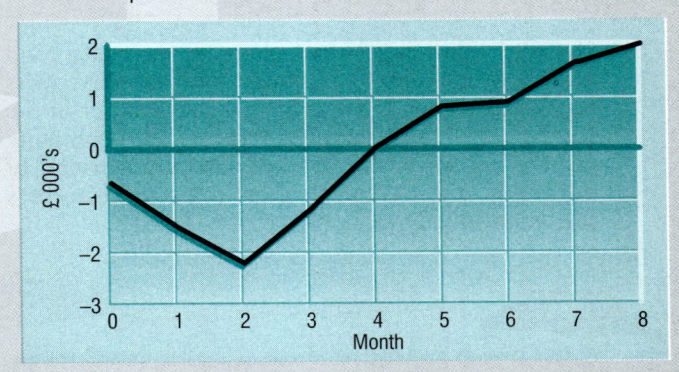

15 A What are the main purposes in business of producing forecasts of capital spending on fixed assets, sales and costs incurred in trading and cashflows? Explain your answer.

B Explain what might happen if a firm gets their forecasts wrong.

C Suggest and explain at least two reasons why a firm may make inaccurate forecasts of cashflow

D Explain the difference between a cash inflow and cash outflow using examples of the various headings you would expect to find in a cashflow forecast.

assessment assignment

Advanced Business

chapter 24

Assessment Assignment

Range: Purposes of forecasts
Components of forecasts
Capital budget headings
Trading forecast headings
Cash inflow headings
Cash outflow headings
Significance of timing
Consequences of incorrect forecasting

Skills: Communication
Produce written material
Application of Number
Tackle problems
Interpret and present data
Information Technology
Process information
Present information

Hot Pizza Ltd is a small chain of two fast food outlets which started business on 1 January. Miss Katrina Sorrento is the principal shareholder in the company. Other shareholders in the company include her sister and brother. You are a friend of the family, and have been asked to provide business and financial advice.

Tasks

1. Miss Sorrento has asked you to produce a cashflow forecast for the new company over the twelve-month period to next December. You decide to set up a spreadsheet model (like that in Figure 23.3) to calculate total expected receipts and payments each month, so that you can examine the effect on cashflow of a variety of assumptions. You base your forecast on the following information provided by Miss Sorrento:

- The Sorrento sisters use £20,000 of their savings to start the business on 1 January

- Miss Sorrento arranges to have stock worth £5,000 delivered every quarter on the first day of the month, starting in January. This must be paid for in cash two months after delivery.

- Her brother uses his savings to buy a van for £5,000 cash, and pays £3,000 cash for fixtures and fittings. He also decides to buy a personalized number plate for the van, registration P1ZA 1 for £1,000 cash.

- Hot Pizza sales in January are expected to be low, at around £1,000 for the month, but thereafter steady sales of £3,000 per month are expected.

- Miss Sorrento has taken on a contract to supply Pizzas to the staff of the local hospital each weekday. This is on a credit basis, and is in addition to the £3,000 expected sales per month. The hospital contract is expected to earn £500 a month, with payment received one month in arrears. The first month of the contract will be in March.

- Hot Pizza Ltd will employ three staff in the two outlets at a total wage cost of £1,500 per month.

- Energy costs are expected to be £500 per quarter.

- Insurance for public liability, employee liability, equipment, and vehicle insurance will come to £400 per month.

- Advertising and other miscellaneous expenses will total to £250 per month

- The Sorrento's hope to be able to draw out a total of £1200 a month to live on.

   Remember to check that your spreadsheet and the formulae you have input are working correctly, by manually calculating the Hot Pizza cashflow forecast. Rectify any faults.

2. Miss Sorrento is unhappy with the notion that transactions only affect the cashflow when money is received or paid, not when a transaction is made. She asks you to explain the importance of cashflow timings and how this works. Write a brief explanatory note to her, using examples taken from her own cashflow situation. Also explain the possible consequences on the pizza business of incorrect forecasting.

3. Is the business viable with the initial capital and forecast expenses that the Sorrento family is putting in? What advice would you give them?

4. From your spreadsheet, produce a graph of cashflow, showing the net cashflow surplus or deficit month by month. Include this in your report to Miss Sorrento.

5. Miss Sorrento has asked you to consider an optimistic scenario in which cash sales are £1,000 more each month than first expected as from April. If this is the case, she thinks additional expenses will be as follows:

- Two part-time workers should be employed at a total cost of £380 per month

- Additional stock each quarter of £1,000

- Increased energy costs of £100 per quarter

- A bank loan of £2,000 in August to purchase two more large ovens

   Recalculate the cashflow forecast using this information. Describe how it compares with the first forecast. What other forms of finance would you advise Miss Sorrento to consider to purchase the ovens?

UNIT SEVEN

chapter 24
Profit and Loss Statements and Balance Sheets.

This chapter investigates how to create the main accounting records kept by business - the profit and loss account and balance sheet.

Key ideas

Accounts summarize records of business transactions and performance over each **accounting period**, usually of 12 months duration.

The final accounts of a business will be used by the tax authorities to assess its tax liability, and by the business owners to monitor its performance, and to secure and maintain appropriate sources of finance.

It is the role of **accountants** to maintain the bookkeeping records upon which company accounts are based. By law, the accounts of all companies must be checked by independent auditors before publication.

Businesses need **assets** in order to trade. Assets can be financed in two ways: through the owners' own money, called **proprietors' capital**, or via money borrowed from other people, called **liabilities**.

A **balance sheet** is an account which records the assets and liabilities of a business. It is typically laid out in a vertical format which clearly shows working capital.

The accounting equation, **Assets = Liabilities + Capital** underpins the construction of the balance sheet.

The **profit and loss account** shows the profit or loss in a business over a period of time. This account is made up of three parts: the **trading account** showing gross profit, the **profit and loss account** showing net profit after tax and interest, and the **appropriation account** showing how the final profit has been distributed.

Any profits retained by a business at the end of a trading period are carried over from the profit and loss account to the total of **accumulated reserves** in the balance sheet.

Business documents, such as invoices and receipts, will be used to keep up to data accounting records. **Ledger accounts** are summaries of the total amounts owed by, and owed to, a business.

A **trial balance** will list all the balances on individual ledger accounts at the end of a trading period. Once the trial balance has been checked and sums to zero, the various entries can be transferred to final balance sheet and profit and loss statement.

Advanced Business

Section 24.1 The purpose of accounts

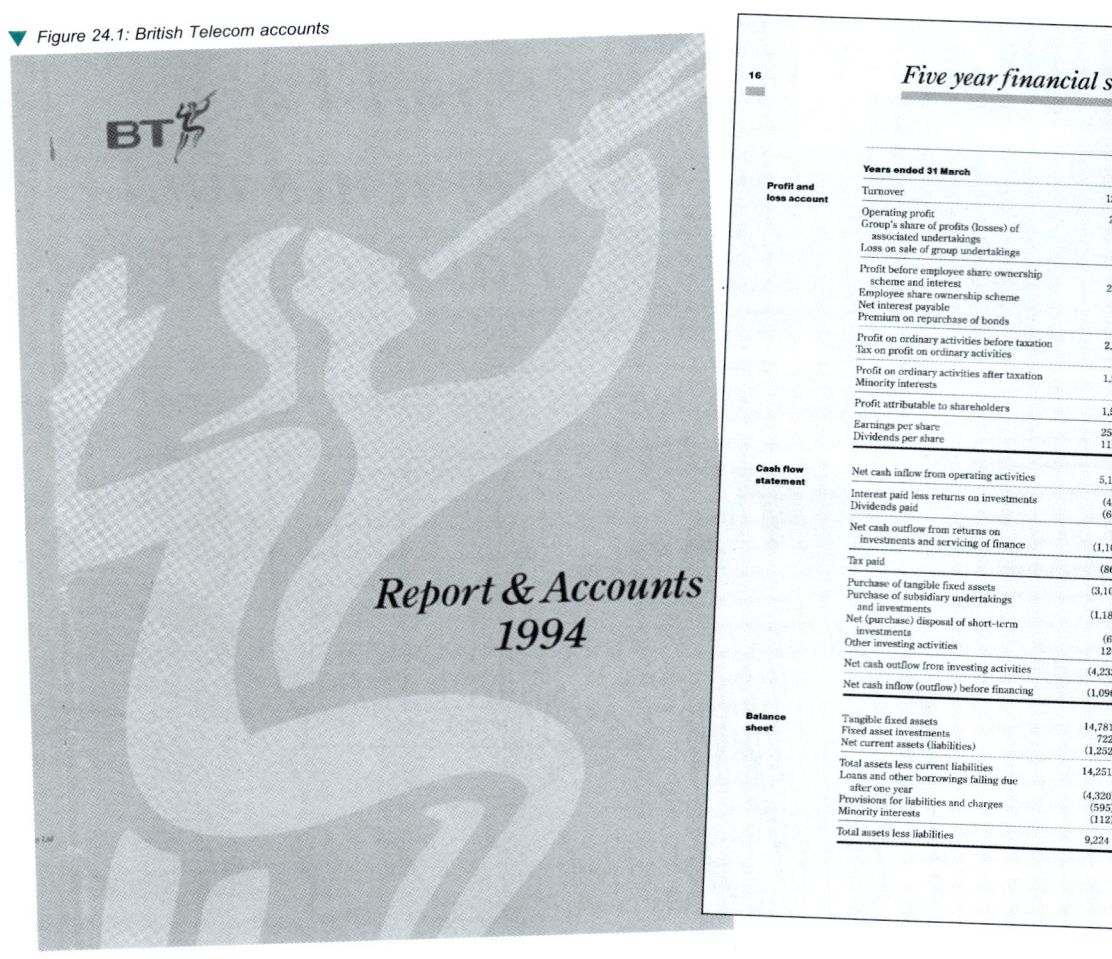

▼ Figure 24.1: British Telecom accounts

Five year financial summary

	Years ended 31 March	1990 £m	1991 £m	1992 £m	1993 £m	1994 £m
Profit and loss account	Turnover	12,315	13,154	13,337	13,242	**13,675**
	Operating profit	2,826	3,537	3,408	2,436	**3,015**
	Group's share of profits (losses) of associated undertakings	(6)	(6)	7	13	**18**
	Loss on sale of group undertakings	–	–	–	(132)	**(14)**
	Profit before employee share ownership scheme and interest	2,820	3,531	3,415	2,317	**3,019**
	Employee share ownership scheme	34	39	38	33	**33**
	Net interest payable	484	417	304	256	**230**
	Premium on repurchase of bonds	–	–	–	56	**–**
	Profit on ordinary activities before taxation	2,302	3,075	3,073	1,972	**2,756**
	Tax on profit on ordinary activities	767	995	999	724	**951**
	Profit on ordinary activities after taxation	1,535	2,080	2,074	1,248	**1,805**
	Minority interests	26	–	30	28	**38**
	Profit attributable to shareholders	1,509	2,080	2,044	1,220	**1,767**
	Earnings per share	25.0p	34.0p	33.2p	19.8p	**28.5p**
	Dividends per share	11.8p	13.3p	14.4p	15.6p	**16.7p**
Cash flow statement	Net cash inflow from operating activities	5,107	5,470	5,710	5,127	**4,914**
	Interest paid less returns on investments	(444)	(411)	(351)	(314)	**(184)**
	Dividends paid	(663)	(769)	(859)	(931)	**(1,014)**
	Net cash outflow from returns on investments and servicing of finance	(1,107)	(1,180)	(1,210)	(1,245)	**(1,198)**
	Tax paid	(863)	(894)	(897)	(975)	**(605)**
	Purchase of tangible fixed assets	(3,103)	(2,875)	(2,565)	(2,148)	**(2,161)**
	Purchase of subsidiary undertakings and investments	(1,189)	(48)	(52)	(27)	**(612)**
	Net (purchase) disposal of short-term investments	(67)	(619)	(416)	327	**(463)**
	Other investing activities	126	138	95	92	**168**
	Net cash outflow from investing activities	(4,233)	(3,404)	(2,938)	(1,756)	**(3,068)**
	Net cash inflow (outflow) before financing	(1,096)	(8)	665	1,151	**43**
Balance sheet	Tangible fixed assets	14,781	15,480	15,785	15,736	**15,584**
	Fixed asset investments	722	639	660	735	**1,312**
	Net current assets (liabilities)	(1,252)	(385)	(150)	322	**125**
	Total assets less current liabilities	14,251	15,734	16,295	16,793	**17,021**
	Loans and other borrowings falling due after one year	(4,320)	(4,468)	(3,768)	(3,386)	**(3,199)**
	Provisions for liabilities and charges	(595)	(602)	(665)	(1,117)	**(701)**
	Minority interests	(112)	(92)	(108)	(72)	**(95)**
	Total assets less liabilities	9,224	10,572	11,754	12,218	**13,026**

Why do firms keep accounts?

All businesses need to keep financial records summarizing how well or how badly they are performing over time. These records will include financial data on costs, the value of assets, debts, sales, and profits. The final accounts of an organization summarize this financial information at the end of each trading period. The main financial summaries of a business are;

- The balance sheet
- The profit and loss statement

Accounting periods

It is normal to publish accounts on an annual 'financial year' basis, over the previous 12-month trading period, the start of which will normally have been determined by the date at which the business started to trade. For example, if a firm started trading on 1 July 1973, it may keep financial records over each 12-month period from 1 July each year to the following 31 June. It is not necessary to produce accounts running from 1 January to 31 December each year. Some large companies may even publish accounts more than once each year, for example, on a quarterly basis.

Business organizations produce accounts for a number of reasons:

- **To monitor business performance.** The final accounts provide a record of how well a business has performed over the last accounting period in terms of sales, cost control, and profits. These figures can be compared to those from earlier periods to see how business performance has improved (see 24.2). If business performance has worsened, managers can take action they think is appropriate to turn the fortunes of their organization around, for example, by cutting product prices, launching a new advertising campaign, streamlining the workforce, or employing new equipment.

- **To secure and maintain finance.** All businesses need capital to buy or hire assets such as premises, machinery, and land (see 22.1). Most business organizations raise capital from external sources such as banks and finance companies. These providers of finance will wish to use the accounts to judge whether or not the business will be in a position to repay loans. Similarly, before private investors are willing to buy shares in the ownership of a limited company, they will wish to know if the company is profitable and is able to pay its shareholders healthy dividends.

- **To meet legal requirements.** All firms must provide financial records to the Inland Revenue so that it can calculate corporation tax or income tax liabilities on their profits. The Customs and Excise department will also need to check VAT liabilities. Limited companies are required by law to provide annual accounts to their shareholders and on request to the general public.

The role of accountants

It is the job of the accountant to keep financial records, and to turn these into a form that can be understood by business managers and other users of accounting information.

Businesses usually employ two kinds of accountant:

- **Financial accountants** are responsible for the production of final accounts in accordance with the various Companies Acts, in order to provide interested parties, such as the owners of the company, with an accurate picture of the firm's progress and financial position.

- **Management accountants** produce and use accounting information for internal management purposes. The management accountant may, for example, produce budgets and various forecasts in order to assist management in planning and controlling the business. Whereas the work of the financial accountant is made public in the annual report and accounts, the work of the management accountant is usually for confidential use only within a business.

By law, company accounts must be checked by independent accountants to ensure that they provide a 'true and fair view' of the position of the company. These independent accountants, called auditors, are hired to audit or check the company accounts before they are published. This is an important safeguard in helping to ensure that accurate information is presented to shareholders and other interested parties in the published accounts.

Financial statements

Limited companies are required by law to publish their accounts once a year, and to file these with the **Registrar of Companies** (see 4.2). These accounts are then made available to any member of the public who wishes to see them. The final accounts of a limited company will usually include the following sections:

Directors' report

This is a report written by the company directors in the annual accounts, which is required by the Companies Act 1985. The report usually:

- Reviews the development of the company during the year
- Informs shareholders of future developments
- Details the firm's health and safety policy
- Lists any political or charitable donations
- Lists directors' shareholdings and share options
- Details any changes in the membership of the board of directors
- States the amount of profit recommended to be paid as dividends to shareholders, and the amount to be retained for re-investment in the firm.

The chairman's statement

Large companies will often include a statement by the chairman in the accounts, although this is not required by law. The statement will normally include a review of the performance of different parts of the company and forecasts for the future.

Balance sheet

The balance sheet of a firm shows how the business has used its money, and where the money came from. The balance sheet contains two sections: the first lists the company assets (**capital**), the second summarizes what it owes (**liabilities**), on a particular date, for example, 31 December. The balance sheet is useful because it shows the value of the owners' investment in the firm at the given date. The balance sheet can also be used to calculate various statistical measures of the financial health and performance of the business (see 25.3).

The profit and loss account

The profit and loss account provides a picture of the firm's trading activities over the course of a trading period. It shows the sales revenues received, the direct and indirect trading costs incurred during the period, and the profit or loss made at the end of the period.

Cashflow statement

Large companies must also provide a cashflow statement which summarizes the sources and uses of cash over the accounting period.

Notes to the accounts

Notes to the accounts provide a detailed explanation of the accounts and how they have been constructed.

Auditor's report

The independent auditors are required by law to give an opinion on the accounts. They must state whether or not they feel that the accounts present a 'true and fair view' of the affairs of the company.

Portfolio Activity 24.1

Range: Purposes, Accounting periods
Skills: Collect and record data

Public limited companies are required by law to provide copies of their annual accounts on request to any member of the public. Write to a selection of plcs that you are aware of in different business sectors, asking for copies of their latest published accounts.

On receipt, study the accounts. What information do they provide? For what reasons have your chosen companies produced accounts? How does the performance of each company compare:

i Over time

ii With the other companies in your selection

What factors might explain any differences?

Key words

Accounts - financial records showing the performance of a business over time, as used by owners, managers, the Inland Revenue, potential investors, and competitors

Financial accountant - a specialist employed by a company to produce financial accounts according to the requirements of the Companies Acts

Management accountant - a specialist employed by a company to produce financial information for internal purposes of planning and control of the business

Auditor - an independent accountant hired to check whether the company accounts provide a 'true and fair view' of the company performance

Section 24.2 Creating a balance sheet

What is a balance sheet?

A **balance sheet** provides the following details about a business at a given point in time:

- **The value of fixed and current assets held** (see 22.1)
- **Liabilities** - money owed by the business to external creditors
- **Capital** - money invested in the business by its owners

By presenting information on the value of fixed and current assets held by a business, a balance sheet will provide an indication of the total worth of that business. However, certain assets, such as customer loyalty to a branded product, or the good reputation of company among staff, suppliers and customers, which may have taken many years to develop, are difficult to value with any precision. These are often known as **intangible assets** because, although they are very important to the continued financial health of a business, they have no physical existence. Other intangible assets may include patents, copyrights, and trademarks.

Business assets

Firms will wish to hold some of their capital as cash in a bank account, to make any immediate or unforeseen payments. However, the purpose of raising finance is not usually to hold cash, but rather to buy the assets needed to operate as a business.

Businesses purchase two main kinds of tangible assets. These are:

- **Fixed assets**: for example, buildings, plant and machinery, and vehicles. These are physical assets which will in general last for a long period of time, usually defined as more than one year.
- **Current assets**: these are assets which are used up relatively quickly during trading. Current assets include:

    - Stocks of raw materials
    - Stocks of semi-finished goods (work in progress)
    - Stocks of finished goods
    - Money owed by debtors
    - Cash held in the business ('cash in hand')
    - Cash held in a bank account ('cash in tills')

Current assets are defined as those items which can be converted into cash within one year. Stocks can be sold to raise cash relatively quickly, and money owed by debtors can be called in for payment. Cash is needed by a business to fund day-to-day trading, for example, to pay wages or settle bills for electricity, gas, telephones, and other overheads. The amount of money available to a firm for this purpose is called **working capital** or **circulating capital**.

Working capital is equal to the value of current assets less any current liabilities, namely any outstanding bills yet to paid, and a bank overdraft (see 22.1).

▼ *Fixed and current assets*

Fixed and current assets are purchased with capital provided by the business owners, usually in the form of **share capital** (see 22.3), or from funds borrowed from external sources such as banks and trade creditors (see 22.2). All of the money used in a business to purchase assets is therefore owed to someone, either to the business owners or to other creditors. That is, all of the money invested in fixed and current assets by a business, is balanced pound for pound by its **liabilities**.

Liabilities

A liability refers to a sum of money owed. The liabilities of a business can be split into two kinds:

- **Liabilities to owners (shareholders' capital).** This represents the money invested by business owners in a firm, such as share capital, plus the accumulated profits made by the firm and not paid out to owners in previous years of trading. Accumulated profits retained by a business and not distributed to owners are known as **reserves**. Thus,

    Shareholders' Funds = Capital + Reserves

- **Liabilities to other creditors.** Businesses will often raise capital by borrowing money form external sources such as banks, or by withholding payment of invoices for goods delivered by a supplier for an agreed period of time.

    Current liabilities are those which normally have to be repaid within twelve months, for example:

    - Trade credits
    - Tax debts
    - Outstanding expenses (accruals)
    - Overdrafts

Other liabilities may only need to repaid in full after a period of more than one year. These are known as **long-term liabilities**. For example:

- Long-term loans
- Loan stocks, i.e. debentures (see 22.3)

'A balance sheet must always balance'

The total value of all current and long-term liabilities of a business, including liabilities to its owners, is used to finance fixed and current assets. This relationship can therefore be represented in the following accounting equation:

Assets = Liabilities + Capital

Assets and liabilities in a balance sheet must always be equal, because the money needed to purchase business assets must have been financed from liabilities of one kind or another - hence the name 'balance sheet'.

An example of a balance sheet

Table 24.1 below shows the types of asset and liability that might appear in the balance sheet of a limited company.

▼ Table 24.1: Assets and liabilities in the balance sheet

LEIGH Ltd
Balance Sheet as at 31.12.95

Liabilities (Sources of capital)		Assets (Uses of capital)	
Capital and Reserves		**Fixed Assets**	
Shareholders' capital	£80,000	Premises	£90,000
Retained profit (Reserves)	£12,000	Computer equipment	£4,000
		Machinery	£30,000
Long-term Liabilities			
Bank loan	£20,000	**Current Assets**	
Current Liabilities		Stock	£10,000
		Debtors	£10,000
Trade creditors	£35,000	Cash at bank	£16,000
Taxation	£13,000		
Total Liabilities	£160,000	**Total Assets**	£160,000

In Table 24.1 Leigh Ltd has liabilities totalling £160,000. Of this amount, £80,000 is money invested in the business by its shareholders. Profits retained by the business and not paid out in dividends to shareholders total £12,000. The firm has also obtained a bank loan of £20,000 and received goods and services on credit from trade suppliers worth £35,000. The firm also owes £13,000 to the Inland Revenue in corporation tax on last year's profits. Total money owed by the company is £160,000.

On the other side of the equation, Leigh Ltd has used £160,000 to purchase various assets - premises valued at £90,000, computer equipment, and machinery costing £34,000, and current assets worth £36,000, which includes £16,000 held as cash to pay bills.

The balance sheet in Table 24.1 demonstrates that total assets must always equal total liabilities, because all of the capital a firm has must be owed to someone, either its owners, or people outside the business. Thus, whenever a transaction is made by the business, it will affect both assets and liabilities. For example, if Leigh Ltd decides to purchase more computer equipment costing £5,000 on credit, this will increase fixed assets by £5,000 and current liabilities **(trade creditors)** by £5,000. The balance sheet totals will also rise by £5,000. Similarly, when Leigh Ltd pays the £13,000 tax it owes to the Inland Revenue, this will reduce its cash holdings by £13,000, and the balance sheet totals will fall by £13,000.

▼ Table 24.2: The Body Shop company balance sheet as at 28.2.93

Notes on page 575

		1993 £000	1992 £000
1 →	**Fixed Assets**		
	Intangible assets	5,256	
2 →	Tangible assets	49,999	47,094
	Investments	9,647	13,952
(A)		64,902	61,046
3 →	**Current Assets**		
	Stocks	20,576	20,158
	Debtors and prepayments	28,845	44,881
	Cash at bank	9,200	37
(B)		58,621	65,076
4 → (C)	**Current Liabilities**		
	Amounts falling due within one year	26,770	35,774
5 → (D)	**Net Current Assets**		
	[Working Capital] (B−C)	31,851	29,302
6 → (E)	**Total assets less current liabilities**		
	[A+D]	96,753	90,348
7 → (F)	**Long-term Liabilities**		
	Amount falling due in more than one year	(3,380)	(2,419)
8 → (G)	**Provision for liabilities and charges**		
	Deferred taxation	(3,527)	(2,091)
9 → (H)	**Net Assets**		
	(E−(F+G))	89,846	85,838
(I)	**Capital and Reserves**		
10 →	Called-up share capital	9,363	9,361
11 →	Share premium account	33,530	33,502
12 →	Revaluations	-	-
13 →	Accumulated Reserves	46,953	42,975
14 →	**Shareholders' funds (I = H)**	**89,846**	**85,838**

Adapted from 'The Body Shop 1993 Annual Report and Accounts'

Conventional balance sheet formats

Balance sheets are usually laid out in a vertical format. The advantage of this is that it clearly shows the **working capital** (current assets - current liabilities) of the firm: that is, the amount of money available to pay the day-to-day bills, which is a vital indicator of the financial health of a business.

An example of a vertical format balance sheet is given in Table 24.2.

Company balance sheet terminology
(to be read in conjunction with table 24.2)

1 Fixed assets - assets which will last for longer than one year, namely physical assets such as buildings, machinery, vehicles, etc. For the purpose of compiling a balance sheet, the estimated value of intangible assets such as customer loyalty, goodwill, patents, and trademarks, are also classed as fixed assets.

2 Investments - these are **financial assets**, usually shares held in other companies. If a company holds more than 50% of the shares of another company, that company is known as a **subsidiary**. If the holding is between 20% and 50%, the company is known as an **associated company**. Holdings of less than 20% are called **trade investments**. For example, the Body Shop Group includes companies such as Body Shop Worldwide Ltd, Eastwick Trading BV, Soapworks Ltd, Body Shop Inc, and Normaland Ltd. Investments may also include holdings of government bonds or deposits of foreign currency. Investments are included at cost in the balance sheet.

3 Current assets - assets which are generally used up in the business in less than one year, e.g. cash, stocks, debtors. Sometimes firms pay certain expenses in advance, for example, insurance premiums. Where these are paid in advance, for part of the next financial year they are **prepayments** and are counted as debtors.

4 Current liabilities - for example, creditors, overdrafts, accruals, or bills outstanding. Current liabilities include those debts which are likely to fall due within one year.

5 Net current assets - the difference between the value of current assets and current liabilities. This calculates the sum available to the business to pay for day-to-day running costs, otherwise known as working capital.

6 Total assets less current liabilities - fixed assets plus working capital

7 Long-term liabilities - debts which do not need be settled within one year, e.g. bank loans, mortgages, debentures.

8 Provisions for liabilities and charges - money put aside to cover certain future liabilities, notably deferred taxation arising from timing differences between corporation tax liabilities on profits and claims for allowances against tax for capital expenditures and pension provisions, etc.

9 Net assets - the worth of the business to its owners, calculated by adding fixed assets to working capital and deducting long-term liabilities. The sum left represents the liability of the firm to its owners.

10 Called-up share capital - also known as **issued capital**. This is the amount of money received from selling shares valued at their face value. For example, selling 10,000 x £1.00 ordinary shares will give a company £10,000 of called-up share capital.

11 Share premium - because of a high level of demand for their shares, a company that issues shares may be able to charge more for them than their face value (see 22.3). For example, a firm may issue 10,000 ordinary shares with a nominal or face value of £1.00, but sell them for a market price of £1.50 each. In this case there is a premium of 50 pence per share over and above the face value. The share premium gives the business additional cash to use and is also a liability owed to the shareholders. Share premium is shown separately in the reserves section of the balance sheet.

12 Revaluations - because of inflation, the current value of some assets can be much higher than their original cost. Because of this, firms may wish to revalue their assets from time to time. Although not shown in the Body Shop balance sheet, this is common within the capital and reserves section of balance sheets. For example, if a firm revalues the property it owns, or if there is an appreciation in the value of its foreign currency holdings, then the value of fixed assets will increase, and liabilities in the form of reserves, shown by the revaluation account, will also rise.

13 Reserves (or retained profits) - some profits are retained each year in order to invest within the business. These retained profits are a liability of the firm to shareholders. Only a small part of the reserves will be held as cash; most of it will be re-invested in assets of different kinds.

14 Shareholders' funds - the total amount of money owed by the business to its owners. This should be exactly equal to net assets, because the total worth of the business belongs to its owner.

Advanced Business

Portfolio Activity 24.2

Range: Balance sheet
Skills: Tackle problems

1. Input the balance sheet in Table 24.1 for Leigh Ltd into a suitable spreadsheet. Use sum commands to automatically calculate column totals for assets and liabilities, as individual number entries to the balance sheet are changed.

2. Check that your spreadsheet balance sheet always balances, after allowing for the following transactions taking place on 31.12.95:

- Leigh Ltd decides to add to its vehicle fleet by purchasing a new van at a cost of £12,000 on Hire Purchase.
- The business decides to expand into new premises. It sells its existing premises and takes out a mortgage to pay for the additional cost of a £150,000 small factory and office unit.
- The Inland Revenue informs Leigh Ltd that it had overestimated its tax liability by £5,000.

The balance sheet and the law

The 1985 Companies Act requires that limited companies include the following information in their balance sheets or accompanying notes:

- Authorized capital - the amount of share capital the company is allowed to issue, as approved by the Registrar of Companies
- Called-up share capital - how much the company has actually raised from a share issue. Not all of the authorized capital may have been issued
- The amount of share premium (over and above the face value of shares)
- Reserves (or retained profits)

- Details of fixed and current assets
- The method used to value fixed assets
- The total amount of depreciation in the value of fixed assets allowed for
- The value of any investments and shares held by the business in subsidiaries
- Any returns due from investments or shareholdings in subsidiaries
- Corresponding figures for the previous year for comparison

Portfolio Activity 24.3

Range: Balance sheet
Skills: Tackle problems

You have been employed as an accountant to draw up a company balance sheet as at today's date, from the following information for XYZ Ltd. You may produce the balance sheet either manually or using a computer spreadsheet or accounting software.

	£000
Issued ordinary shares (400,000 × £2 each)	800
Retained profit	810
Trade creditors	700
Share premium account	270
Bank overdraft	310
Taxation accrual	120
Long-term loan	500
Debentures	360
Dividends payable	50
Buildings	1000
Machinery	1000
Vehicles	250
Cash at bank	750
Debtors	750
Insurance prepayment	200

The balance sheet of a sole trader

A sole trader is a business owned and controlled by one person (see 4.2). The format of the balance sheet of a sole trader firm will differ from that of a limited company for the following reasons:

- Sole traders do not have shareholders, and therefore the sole trader balance sheet will not show shareholders' funds or dividends
- Sole traders are likely to make regular drawings from their business in the form of wages or to pay for living and other personal expenses.
- A sole trader enterprise will have been set up with the personal capital of its owner. This will appear in the balance sheet as 'opening capital', and, as the owner injects more money into their business, as 'capital introduced'.

Table 24.3 provides an example of a sole trader balance sheet.

▼ Table 24.3: Balance sheet of Brennan's General Store as at 31.5.95

		£	£
	Fixed Assets		
	Premises		50,000
	Fixtures and fittings		10,000
	Delivery van		8,000
(A)			68,000
	Current Assets		
	Stocks	10,000	
	Debtors and prepayments	1,500	
	Bank account	2,500	
	Cash in tills	1,000	
(B)		15,000	
(C)	less Current liabilities (C)		
	Trade creditors	10,000	
(D)	Working capital (B – C)		5,000
	NET ASSETS (A + D)		**73,000**
	FINANCED BY:		
	Opening capital		45,000
	Capital introduced		22,000
	add Net profit		17,000
			84,000
	less Drawings		11,000
			73,000

Advanced Business

Portfolio Activity 24.4

Range: Balance sheet
Skills: Tackle problems

Mario decides to start a mobile hairdressing business, using his personal savings. He starts by getting a bank loan for £2,000 to a buy a car so that he can visit his clients.

1. Below is a summary of his business transactions for the first month of trading. Draw up a balance sheet in the sole trader format to show the position of the business at the end of the first month of trading.

- £1,000 savings are put into bank account
- Received a bank loan of £2,000
- Buys car for £2,200
- Bought for cash a hairdryer for £30
- Bought on credit brushes and combs worth £50
- Bought for cash and used up shampoo and dyes costing £10
- Received in cash from customers for services rendered £60, which was immediately banked
- Is owed £50 by Mrs Gerkhin for her perm

2. Mario has discovered that he has left the following transactions out of his balance sheet. Re-write the balance sheet to allow for them

- He uses a £200 overdraft facility to buy more stock
- Debtors worth £150 were forgotten
- He buys some more new equipment for £400 on credit and discovers other creditors, previously forgotten, worth £60
- He has paid car and personal liability insurance of £350, representing £250 for the year to 31.12.95, with the balance being an advance payment for the following year.

Key words

Accounting equation - Assets = Liabilities + Capital

Balance sheet - a statement of a firm's assets and liabilities, the main purpose of which is to show the value of the business

Intangible assets - assets which have no physical existence, but which help to provide benefits for the firm, for example, suppliers' goodwill, customer loyalty to a branded product

Liabilities - money owed by the business to its owners or to external sources. These may either be current liabilities falling due within one year, or long-term liabilities which will need to be repaid some time after one year

Subsidiary - a company in which another company holds more than 50% of issued shares, i.e. has the controlling interest

Working capital - money available to a business to pay for its day-to-day running expenses

Called-up share capital - total funds raised through the issue of equities valued at their nominal or face value

Share premium - those funds raised from the sale of equities over and above their face value

Revaluation - a change in the book value of assets and liabilities due to a periodic revaluation of assets, for example, to allow for the effect of rising inflation on property values

Reserves - the total of retained profits held by a business over many years, shown as a liability to shareholders on a company balance sheet

Section 24.3

The profit and loss statement

What is a profit and loss statement?

With the exception of charities, profit is the prime objective of most private-sector businesses and of organizations in the public sector (see 4.3). A profit is made when sales revenues, or turnover, exceed expenses. A loss, or **negative profit**, occurs when expenses exceed all revenues.

If a profit is made at the end of a trading period, some is likely to be paid out to the business owners, either in the form of drawings, or dividends on their shares. The remainder of the profit after tax will be retained in the business for future investment.

The profit and loss account shows how much profit or loss a firm has made during a trading period, usually over 12 months.

Businesses incur three main types of expense, but not all are used in the calculation of profit or loss in the profit and loss accounts:

Revenue expenses - these are the day-to-day running costs of the business, for example, travel expenses, advertising, electricity, gas, petrol, rent and rates, insurance, repairs, wages, etc. These expenses may be associated either with production on the shop-floor, or with administrative functions. With the exception of the wages of production workers, most of these costs are not directly related to the level of output produced. These indirect costs are also known as **overheads** (see 20.1). Such expenses are included in the calculation of profits in the profit and loss accounts.

Capital expenses - these are the expenses incurred in buying fixed assets such as plant and machinery. Because fixed assets tend to remain productive for a long time, the cost of buying them is not included in the calculation of profit in the profit and loss accounts.

However, fixed assets will tend to wear out, and this will reduce their value over time. **Depreciation** is an allowance for wear and tear, and is included as a cost in the profit and loss accounts (see 20.1). For example, a machine bought for £1,000 may be depreciated at 10% per year over 10 years, when it is eventually replaced. Thus, a depreciation charge of £100 per year will appear in the annual profit and loss accounts.

Private expenses - these are expenses privately incurred by the business owners, and are not charged against the profits of the business. A small-business owner will take money from his or her business in the form of drawings, which appear in the balance sheet, but these are not included in the calculation of profit in the profit and loss account.

The calculation of profit and loss

The profit and loss account of a business will be divided into three parts:

- The **trading** account
- The **profit and loss** account
- The **appropriation** account

An example is given in Table 24.4 overleaf.

The trading account

The trading account shows sales revenues for the year, less the cost of these sales. The **cost of sales** refers to all costs of production associated with those goods and services actually sold.

It will often be necessary to adjust the cost of materials for changes in stocks over the trading period. The cost of sales for Mountain Bikes Ltd in Table 24.4 is £55,000. This will consist mainly of the cost of purchasing bicycles for resale. However, it is likely that some of the bikes sold this trading period were purchased in the last period, while some of this period's stock may remain unsold until next year.

These adjustments can be made by adding purchases of stock made during the trading period to the opening stock (the value of stock held at the start of the year), and then deducting closing stock - that is, the value of stock left at the end of the trading period. This calculation gives the cost of stock actually sold during trading.

Cost of Sales = Opening Stock + Purchases - Closing Stock

The closing stock at the end of one period, therefore, is the opening stock in the next.

Thus:

Gross Profit = Sales revenue - Cost of Sales

The differences between sales revenue and cost of sales is known as **gross profit**. In the example above, Mountain Bikes Retail Ltd made sales during the year of £100,000. It started the year with an opening stock of £10,000 and made purchases of £60,000, finishing the year with a closing stock of £15,000. Using the formula for cost of sales given above, this gives a cost of sales of £55,000 for the stocks of bikes, and a gross profit of £45,000.

The profit and loss account

The trading account gives the amount of profit made on trading activities - that is, on buying in stocks and then selling goods or services. However, gross profit is not the final profit available to the business managers to pay out to shareholders or to re-invest in their firm. Overheads and tax owed

▼ Table 24.4: The profit and loss account of Mountain Bikes Retail Ltd

MOUNTAIN BIKES RETAIL LTD
Profit and Loss Account for the year ended 31.12.95

		£	
TRADING ACCOUNT	**Turnover**		100,000
	Less cost of sales		
	Opening stock (1.1.95)	10,000	
	Add Purchases	60,000	
		70,000	
	less Closing stock (31.12.95)	15,000	
			55,000
PROFIT AND LOSS ACCOUNT	**Gross profit**		45,000
	less		
	Expenses		
	Heat and light	1,000	
	Printing and stationery	1,500	
	Advertising	750	
	Insurance	500	
	Wages & salaries		
	(Admin only)	10,000	
	Business rates	1,500	
	Telephone	300	
	Provision for bad debts	1,300	
	Depreciation	2,000	
		18,850	
	Net profit		26,150
	add Non-operating income	1,850	
	less Interest payable	600	
APPROPRIATION ACCOUNT	**Profit before tax**		27,400
	less Corporation tax	6,825	
	Profit after tax		20,575
	less Proposed dividends	10,000	
	Retained profit for the year		10,575

have to be deducted from profit first. In addition, firms may have extra income to add, known as **non-operating income**, which is not earned from trading, for example, interest on holdings of government bonds, and earnings from shares held in other companies.

The profit and loss account starts by deducting total operating expenses from gross profit. Expenses here are those overheads or indirect costs which are not incurred 'on the shop floor' as a result of the production of goods and services, for example, the wages of administrative staff, office supplies, business rates, etc. Thus,

Net (or Operating) Profit = Gross Profit − Expenses

Any expenses incurred but not yet paid must still be deducted from profit. For example, if a bill for water rates of £3,000 was received in December and not paid until the new financial year in January, the expense must still appear in the previous year's profit and loss account.

Many businesses will earn income from their own investments. This non-operating income must be added to net profit. In the example, Mountain Bikes Retail Ltd has a cash balance at the bank which earned £500 in interest in 1995, and the firm holds shares in a bicycle parts manufacturing company which have earned £750 in dividend payments, making a non-operating income of £1,850.

However, the firm took out a loan in the past and has paid £600 in interest during the year on this loan. This must be deducted from net profit before the tax liability can be calculated. Thus;

Profit before tax = Net profit + non-operating income − interest payable

'Taxation' in company accounts refers only to corporation tax - that is, tax levied on company profits. Other taxes, including local business rates, are included as business expenses in the profit and loss account.

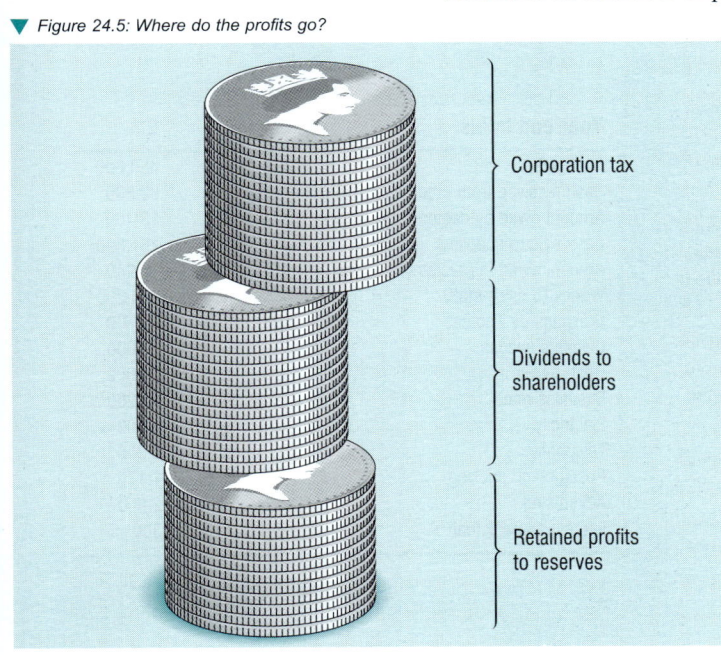

▼ Figure 24.5: Where do the profits go?

Appropriation account

The **appropriation account** shows what happens to the final profit - how much is distributed to shareholders as dividend payments, and how much is retained by the company to add to reserves.

Dividends are not an expense, because they do not affect the amount of profit made by a business. Rather, they are a way of using the profits which have been earned. In the case of Mountain Bike Retails Ltd, dividends of £10,000 have been paid out, leaving £10,575 as the profit retained by the business. This sum is allocated to accumulated reserves in the balance sheet and may, for example, be re-invested in new plant and machinery which increases the amount of fixed assets in the balance sheet.

Advanced Business

Adjustments to the profit and loss accounts

Carriage inwards and outwards

This is a delivery cost. **Carriage inwards** is the cost of delivery paid by a firm's customers for goods received. It is therefore an additional source of revenue that should be added to turnover in the trading account.

On the other hand, when the firm takes delivery of materials or goods, it will have to pay for **carriage outwards**. This is an expense which will need to be deducted from gross profit in the profit and loss account.

Purchase returns

Money paid by the firm for any faulty goods or poor-quality materials subsequently returned to suppliers will have to be refunded. Unless refunds are subtracted from stock purchases in the trading account, gross profit will be understated.

Sales returns

Any finished goods returned by consumers in return for their money back will need to be subtracted from turnover in the trading account, otherwise gross profit will be overstated.

Discounts

Any discounts granted by the business in return for bulk purchases or prompt payment of outstanding sales invoices are counted as an expense, and deducted from gross profit in the profit and loss account.

Value Added Tax (VAT)

When companies charge VAT on goods or services, they are collecting the tax on behalf of the government and must pass this tax revenue on to the Customs and Excise department. It would, therefore, be wrong to include VAT at 17.5% in the value of sales turnover, because this would give the impression that profits were much higher. Thus, turnover excludes VAT in company accounts.

Bad debts

Sometimes customers may not pay for goods delivered or services received as agreed. These customers are known as **bad debtors**. When this happens, some adjustment will need to be made to the accounting figures to correct for bad or outstanding debts. Instead of reducing the sales figure, bad debts are considered to be an expense and are deducted from gross profit in the profit and loss account.

Portfolio Activity 24.5

Range: Profit and loss
Skills: Tackle problems

Thomas Smith opened an art supplies shop ten years ago. Four years ago, he formed a limited company by selling shares in his business to two of his friends. With the money he raised, he opened a large art supplies discount warehouse.

Opposite is a summary of his transactions for a full 12 month accounting period. Produce a profit and loss account for Thomas from these figures, and from the additional information provided below.

- At the start of the 12-month trading period, Thomas had no debtors or creditors, but did own £70,000 of stock left over from the previous period. Closing stock at the end of the trading period was valued at £55,000.
- Thomas owes his accountant £1,000 for work done during the year, and has promised his staff a Christmas bonus of £300 each, and £200 for the cleaners.
- Corporation tax is calculated as 20% of net profit. Dividends worth 40% of net profit after tax are paid to shareholders.

Year end totals	£
Cash sales	450,600
Cash received from credit sales	92,500
Amount owed by debtors	13,400
Cash paid to suppliers	181,800
Amount owed to creditors	16,240
Wages (5 sales staff)	104,200
Drawings by Thomas	18,700
Cleaners' wages	10,000
Rent	26,000
Business rates	11,260
Electricity	4,500
Telephone	2,300
Postage and packing	1,170
Advertising	2,800
Interest on bank loan	300

How are the balance sheet and profit and loss accounts related?

The balance sheet and profit and loss accounts are linked in the following ways:

1. Profit belongs to the business owners, whether it is held in reserve by the business, or paid out to shareholders in dividends. Retained profit in a particular year increases the assets available to the business shown on the balance sheet, and at the same time increases the liabilities on the balance sheet owed by the firm to its owners. Accumulated reserves on the balance sheet represent the sum total of all of the retained profits held back during the life of the business.

   When a loss is made, this may be covered by drawing on reserves built up during previous years, as detailed in the balance sheet. If a business has no reserves, any loss would have to be paid for by borrowing money, or from a further sale of shares.

2. Allowances for depreciation reduce the value of fixed assets on the balance sheet, and are charged to gross profit as an expense.

3. Outstanding tax payments and dividends proposed but not yet paid to shareholders are shown as current liabilities on the balance sheet, and are also charged against profits as an expense.

4. Investments listed in the balance sheet as fixed assets may give rise to dividend or interest payments. This non-operating income is added to net profit in the profit and loss account to obtain profit before tax.

Non-profit-making organizations

Private-sector organizations, such as charities or clubs and societies, which do not aim to make a profit from their activities are not required to produce a profit and loss account. Instead, they will normally draw up a **receipts and payments account** recording all monies received and paid out over a given period, along with an opening and closing cash and bank balance.

At the end of a trading period, these organizations may produce a more formalized **income and expenditure account**, following a very similar format to the profit and loss account. Local authorities must, by law, produce such an account at the end of each financial year.

Key words

Profit and loss statement - (1) an account showing the profit or loss made by a business over a period of time

Trading account - that part of the profit and loss statement which shows gross profit as being the difference between total sales and the cost of those sales

Cost of sales - the costs associated with the production of goods and services actually sold

Opening stock - the value of unsold stock held over from the previous trading period

Closing stock - the value of stock unsold at the end of the current trading period

Overheads - costs that are not linked directly to the production process, for example, rent, heating, and lighting

Non-operating income - income earned by a firm from investments and sources other than its own trading activities

Appropriation account - statement of how the profit after tax has been used by the company, either in payments to shareholders or in retained profits for re-investment

Net profit = gross profit less expenses

Section 24.4 Trial balance and final accounts

In order to create the final accounts at the end of a trading period it is important that a business keeps accurate and up to date records of all business transactions throughout the period (see 19.1). The purpose of business documents for payments and receipts is to provide the information for these financial records.

Every business transaction has two elements. For example, if a firm buys stock for cash, its cash reserves will decrease, whilst its stock will increase. If instead the stock is bought on credit, the firm's liabilities to creditors will increase, and stock will increase. This twin effect is the basis for **double entry bookkeeping**.

Double-entry bookkeeping is the system used by all firms where every transaction affects two different accounts. One account is said to be **credited** (added to) and the other is **debited** (taken from). This means that every transaction affecting a balance sheet or a profit and loss account will always have two effects. For example, if a company buys a new vehicle with cash, this will raise fixed assets and reduce the cash balance on the balance sheet.

Ledger accounts

The effects of business transactions are recorded in **ledger accounts**. Businesses will keep ledger accounts for:

- Sales (and money owed by debtors)
- Purchases (and money owed to creditors)
- Stationery expenses
- Rent and business rates
- Wages
- VAT
- Capital spending to buy fixed assets
- All other headings under which transactions are made

A **general ledger** will summarise all the details of incomes and expenditures entered into all the individual ledger accounts. Because entries in these accounts are often made on the left or right-hand side of a 'T', they are also sometimes known as 'T' **accounts**. Entries on the left are known as **debits**, whilst entries on the right are called **credits**. Most accounts will have entries on both sides (see figure 24.6). At the end of a trading period, an accountant will want to use these accounts to produce the balance sheet and profit and loss account.

Books of Prime Entry

Ledger accounts are summaries of the total amount owed by individual debtors and owed to individual creditors. However, on a day to day basis an organization will tend to record written details of invoices sent out and payments in so called **books of prime entry**. These include;

- **the sales daybook** – this records all the credit sales made by the organization from the invoices it has issued.
- **the purchase daybook** – this records all the credit purchases made by an organization and is prepared from invoices received from suppliers.
- **the returns books** – records credit notes issued or received from suppliers for returns. Goods returned by customers are known as

returns inwards or sales returns. A **credit note** will be issued for each sale return (see 18.2). Issued credit notes will be entered into the **returns inward daybook**. On the other hand, goods that have been purchased by the organization but sent back to their supplier are known as **returns outwards** or purchases returns. Credit notes issued for these goods by their suppliers are entered into the **returns outward daybook**.

- **the cashbook** – records dates and details of payments and receipts. These can either be in the form of actual notes and coins paid out and received, or deposits and withdrawals to and from a bank or building society account.

At the end of each month entries into the daybooks for sales and purchases can be added up to provide totals to enter either as a credit or debit into the ledger accounts.

Figure 24.6: Examples of 'T' accounts

Sales Account

Date	Debit	£	Date	Credit	£
			1 May	Balance b/d	200
2 May	Returns from Cam Ltd	100			
5 May	Returns from A Smith	75	10 May	Sales	250
			14 May	Cam Ltd	150
		425			
		---			---
	Balance c/d	600	31 May		600
		---			---
			31 May	Balance b/d	425

Purchases Account

Date	Debit	£	Date	Credit	£
			1 May	Rerturns	100
8 May	Paper	40			
15 May	Computer disks	50			
			18 May	Returns	50
29 May	Stock	500		Balance c/d	440
		---			---
31 May		590			590
		---			---
31 May	Balance b/d	440			

* c/d = carried down   b/d = brought down

When is a transaction a debit or a credit?

A transaction will be a debit - i.e., recorded on the left of the 'T' account - if it is:

- An increase in assets, for example, the purchase of a car
- An expense to the firm, for example, wage payments
- A reduction in a liability, for example, a cash payment to a creditor

A transaction will be a credit - i.e. recorded on the right-hand side of the 'T' account - if it is:

- An increase in a liability, for example, an increase in creditors
- A reduction in the value of assets held, for example, the sale of a vehicle
- Income received, for example, sales revenue

From trial balance to final accounts

Final accounts are produced by calculating the balance on each individual 'T' account at a particular date. For example, there is a balance of £185 on the sales account in figure 24.6 at the end of May, and this is a credit balance. If May is the end of an accounting year, this is the sales figure that will be used in the trading account in the year-end profit and loss statement. In the same way, the balance on each 'T' account will provide a figure for either the balance sheet or profit and loss statement compiled at the end of an accounting period.

In practice, a business will have by the end of its financial year a wide range of accounts, listing many hundreds, thousands, or even millions of transactions, covering fixed assets, cash, debtors, creditors, expenses, accruals, prepayments, VAT, sales, bad debts, etc.

The trial balance

Before using the figures in 'T' accounts to produce the final accounts, it is useful to check if the figures are correct. This check can be made by creating a **trial balance**.

A trial balance is simply a list of all the balances on the 'T' accounts written as a simple column indicating whether each item is a debit or credit balance. Because each bookkeeping transaction always has two matching effects, the sum of the debits should equal the sum of all the credits.

Thus, in the trial balance, the following equation should always hold:

Credits − Debits = 0

If this is not the case, then a mistake is likely to have been made somewhere in the accounts, and this will need to be corrected. It is much better to test the accounts using a trial balance than to go to the trouble of creating the balance sheet and profit and loss accounts, only to find that the figures do not add up because of an error somewhere in the 'T' accounts.

▼ Table 24.5: Example of a trial balance for a sole trader

TRIAL BALANCE AS AT 31 DECEMBER 1995

'T' Accounts	Credit	Debit	Which final account?
	£	£	
Proprietor's capital	12,000		balance sheet
Plant and machinery		3,000	balance sheet
Depreciation		500	profit/loss
Freehold property		5,000	balance sheet
Opening stock		2,000	profit/loss
Purchases		1,000	profit/loss
Sales	10,650		profit/loss
Business rates		500	profit/loss
Wages		9,750	profit/loss
Sundry expenses		50	profit/loss
Cash account		750	balance sheet
Debtors		700	balance sheet
Creditors	600		balance sheet
Total Credits/Debits	23,250	23,250	

Once the trial balance sums to zero, the various 'T' account balances can be transferred to the balance sheet and profit and loss accounts with more confidence that they are likely to be correct. Each trial balance item appears only once in the balance sheet or profit and loss account. The value of closing stocks at the year end does not appear in the trial balance, but usually as a footnote underneath. Closing stock appears both in the balance sheet, as a current asset, and in the profit and loss account, as part of the cost of sales.

Portfolio Activity 24.6

Range: Trial balance
Skills: Tackle problems

The following are the balances on the accounts for Jane Iles Ltd. Jane is not sure which of the accounts should be credit or debit balances and because of this, she cannot make the trial balance sum to zero. You have been employed as an accountant to identify the credit and debit balances, and to check if these do in fact sum to zero. There are no prepayments on any accounts.

Lay the trial balance out as a single column, and write 'credit' or 'debit' next to each item as appropriate.

	£
Drawings	250
British Telecom (bill unpaid)	52
Sales	9,000
Electricity	40
Cash	15,485
Capital	10,000
Rent	200
Advertising	25
Dawling Ltd (debtor)	1,000
Purchases	4,000
Threads plc (creditor)	2,000
Post Office	52

Key words

Double-entry bookkeeping - method of recording business transactions based on the idea that there are two aspects to all transactions, a source of funds and a use of funds

Ledger accounts - up to date records summarising business transactions during a trading period. These are used to compile a trial balance.

Books of prime entry - daily records of purchases, sales, returns and cashflows

'T' account - means of presenting individual transactions and a final balance in an account, using a simple 'T' layout

Trial balance - a list of credit and debit account balances in a business used to compile the final accounts. It is used as a means to establish whether all business transactions have been properly recorded

Further reading

Starting in Business, Inland Revenue Guide IR28, available free from the Inland Revenue

Bright, G, and Herbert, M: *Mastering Accounting* (Macmillan Master Series 1990)

Test questions

The following underpinning knowledge will be tested:

1. Basic accounting system for a small business
2. Accounting periods
3. Extracting a trial balance for given accounting records
4. Identify each account in a trial balance in relation to profit and loss or balance sheet items
5. Produce and explain profit and loss and balance sheet in vertical form from a trial balance
6. The purpose of balance sheets and profit and loss statements

1 Which of the following is a current liability of a business?
   A Buildings
   B Stock
   C Cash
   D Overdraft

2 Which of the following is a long-term business liability?
   A Vehicles
   B An accrual for wages
   C Creditors
   D Debentures

Questions 3-5 share the following answer options:
   A Business owners
   B Employees
   C Central government
   D Suppliers

Which of the groups of people listed above will be interested in examining the final accounts of a limited company for the following purposes?

3 To negotiate pay and productivity agreements

4 To check business performance

5 To calculate liability for corporation tax

6 For a balance sheet to balance, only one of the following equations is correct and must hold. Which?
   A Assets + Capital = Liabilities
   B Fixed assets − Liabilities = Current Assets
   C Gross Profit = Sales revenue − Cost of sales
   D Assets = Liabilities + Capital

7 The main purpose of a balance sheet is to:
   A Satisfy the Inland Revenue on tax liabilities
   B Provide information for potential investors
   C Show the value of the business
   D Allow creditors to assess the firm's ability to repay debts

8 In which account would overhead expenses appear?
   A Balance sheet
   B Trading account
   C Profit and loss account
   D Appropriation account

9 The balance sheet will include information on
   A Sales
   B Purchases
   C Dividends paid
   D Debtors

10 The amount of money raised by a company in excess of the face value of shares issued is known as
   A Revaluation account
   B Retained profits
   C Share premium account
   D Minority interests

11 A link is provided between the balance sheet and profit and loss accounts through:
   A Retained profit for a trading period
   B Business expenses actually paid
   C Fixed assets
   D Sales

12 The trading account of a business will give details of:
  A The cost of goods sold
  B The liquidity position of the business
  C The current value of the business
  D The loss in value of assets for the period

13 The purpose of a trial balance is to
  A monitor business performance
  B calculate tax liabilities
  C check figures used to compile the final accounts
  D prepare a profit and loss statement

Questions 14 and 15 share the following answer options;
  A £35,000
  B £60,000
  C £27,000
  D £17,000

From the jumbled list of financial information for a small business given below, what is:

14 Net profit?

15 Profit after tax?

	£000
Corporation tax	8
Turnover	100
Non-operating income	5
Cost of sales	40
Expenses	30
Dividends payment proposed	10

16 A Why do firms keep financial accounts?
  B What is the purpose of a trial balance in compiling final accounts?
  C Explain the main differences between a balance sheet and a profit and loss statement.

assessment assignment

Advanced Business

Assessment Assignment

Range: Basic accounting system
Accounting periods
Trial balance
Profit and loss
Balance sheet
Purposes

Skills: **Communication**
Produce written material
Application of Number
Tackle problems
Information Technology
Process information
Evaluate the use of information technology

CRUMBZ!

You live in an area with a large number of office blocks. Although there are quite a few restaurants and eating places, you know that many office workers would rather have food delivered to their office than have to leave their place of work. You decide to set up a sandwich making and delivery service called 'Crumbz'.

chapter 25

Tasks

1. Investigate and produce a financial plan detailing the types of assets (including fixed and working capital) you will need to purchase for your business, how much these are likely to cost, and the amount of finance you will need to raise to start up.

   Your report should weigh up a range of alternative sources of finance and you should recommend your chosen sources of finance with justification (see 22.1 - 22.4).

2. Write a short report explaining the basic accounting system you intend to use for your business i.e what financial documents, ledger accounts, trial balance and final accounts will you need to produce?

3. At the end of your second year of trading you have produced the trial balance opposite. You will now need to produce the year-end balance sheet and profit and loss statement from the trial balance. If possible, use a computer spreadsheet package with which you are familiar to input the information and to derive your final accounts. Remember to check for errors before printing out your final hard copies.

   (Alternatively, you may have access to business accounting software designed to help firms produce final accounts. What advantages does this business software offer your business over manual means of information-handling, or more conventional computer spreadsheets? If you do not have access to accounting software, you may wish to investigate the availability and facilities of such software designed for balance sheet applications. What advantages could this software offer your business and would they justify the cost of purchase?)

TRIAL BALANCE AS AT 31.12.95

	£
Capital introduced at 1 January 1995	2,000
Cash	3,680
Cost of sales	10,300
Sales turnover	29,600
Drawings	12,000
Rent	2,800
Casual wages	3,800
Electricity	700
Office furniture and fittings	760
Debtors	4,300
Creditors	2,340
Other receipts	420
Telephone	320

Closing stock is £3910, opening stock was £6910

4. You have decided to employ a friend from school to run your office, answer the telephone, and take orders for food. You hope that your friend will eventually take over the bookkeeping, and you decide to write him a brief report explaining why businesses need a trial balance, balance sheet, and profit and loss account, and how useful these are to business owners. Use examples taken from your own accounts produced under Task 2 above to illustrate points made in writing.

UNIT SEVEN

CHAPTER 25

chapter 25

Monitoring Business Performance

This chapter explains how and why business organizations monitor the achievement of their financial targets and objectives

PROFIT MARGINS ARE UP AND OVERHEADS ARE STABILISING

Key ideas

All business organizations set aims and objectives to strive towards. Some objectives, such as increasing profits, sales, and/or market share, can be expressed in money terms and are called **quantitative targets**.

Other business targets may be difficult to express in terms of money, for example, building a good reputation among customers. These are known as **qualitative** or **non-financial targets**. They require subjective judgements to be made on success or failure.

Accounting information from the profit and loss statement and balance sheet, can be used to monitor the performance of a business organization. Key data will include profits, assets, liabilities, working capital, overheads, stock, and debtors.

A **budget** is a financial plan agreed in advance by managers which shows how much money the business will need in the future and how it will be financed.

Variance analysis involves investigating the reasons for differences between actual results and budget plans.

Budgetary control is the process of setting targets, preparing budgets, monitoring those budgets, and analysing variances.

The financial performance of a business can be monitored using **ratio analysis** to compare figures taken from final accounts, profit and loss accounts, balance sheets, and cashflow statements.

There are three main types of financial ratio: **liquidity ratios, performance ratios**, and **activity ratios**.

Liquidity ratios are used for measuring the solvency of a business.

Profitability ratios examine how well a business is doing, using information on profits to calculate gross and net profit margins, and the rate of return on capital employed.

Activity ratios consider how efficiently a firm is using its resources. They include the administration expenses to sales ratio, asset and stock turnover, and average debt collection period.

591

Advanced Business

Section 25.1

Accounting for business control

Setting business targets

Financial accounts, such as balance sheets and profit and loss accounts, are used by business managers in order to plan and to control the activities of their organization.

The planning of business activities requires businesses to identify the long-term targets it wants to achieve in the future. These could be to:

- Maximize or increase profit
- Maximize or increase sales revenues
- Increase market share
- Expand into new or overseas markets
- Step up internal growth by increased investment in plant and equipment
- Promote external growth through the acquisition or takeover of other companies

Targets like these, which can be expressed in financial or money terms, are known as **quantitative targets** (see 4.1).

An organization may have other targets which are less easy to measure in money terms - for example, to improve the reputation of the business, or to increase loyalty among the workforce. Non-profit-making organizations, such as charities, may set targets such as increasing donations, saving more animals from exploitation, housing more homeless people, etc. Targets such as these are known as **qualitative**, or **non-financial targets**. How well an organization succeeds in meeting these targets is a matter of subjective judgement.

The objectives of The Body Shop

A qualitative target:

'The Body Shop aims to integrate itself into the communities in which it operates so that it can be sensitive to local needs. Top of our agenda are our community projects. We are also committed to education, not just for staff but for customers. An open exchange of information is something we value because knowledge is a healthy step towards responsibility and self-empowerment.'

'The Body Shop - Annual Report and Accounts 1993'

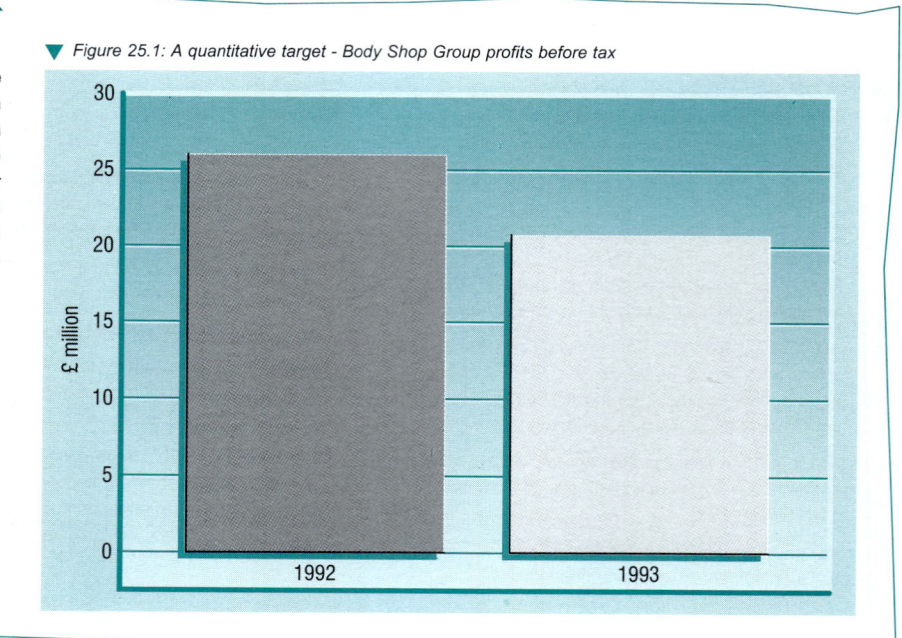

▼ Figure 25.1: A quantitative target - Body Shop Group profits before tax

Business plans and targets can usually be found in the chairman's statement in the annual report and accounts of individual limited companies. The accounts themselves, including the profit and loss statement and balance sheet (see 24.1), represent an organization's progress to date in achieving its quantitative targets. The financial accounts of an organization can, therefore, be used to measure or monitor progress towards business objectives, as well as to set out targets for the future.

Portfolio Activity 25.1

Range: Users, Reasons for monitoring
Skills: Produce written material

1. Using the extract from the Boots The Chemist annual report and accounts, identify the kinds of aims and objectives which the company has set.

2. Which of their aims are (a) quantitative, and (b) qualitative?

3. Investigate the business aims of a firm with which you are familiar. How well have they achieved their aims in the last 3 to 5 years?

Boots The Chemist plc

Group sales at £3.66 billion increased 2.5% and profit at £374.2m increased 7.2%. Our main retail business, Boots The Chemist, turned in an excellent performance, particularly when viewed against the retail sector as a whole. Profit at £246.2m was up 7.6%, on a sales increase of 4.7%.

An extensive store refurbishment programme and investment in information systems have clearly helped. Electronic Point of Sale (EPOS) and Direct Product Profitability (DPP) give management the ability precisely to control their business, and plan future development. We are transferring the skills and lessons learned from Boots The Chemist to our other retail businesses, where we expect to make significant performance advances.

New stock systems are already benefiting the key process of inventory rationalization in Do It All, our joint venture with WH Smith.

Boots Properties continues to be very successful. Our approach to property development has been cautious and we have used the opportunity of a depressed market to improve our property holdings.

Analysis leading to investment and improved systems is also the picture in Boots Opticians, where there has been an excellent result.

Capital is also being invested in manufacturing plants in the US for drugs like Ibuprofen and in the UK for Manoplax.

Generally in assessing current business and investment for the future we are taking a more radical approach. All existing businesses and all new investments must be value-creating, thus generating more than the cost of capital.

The business is managed for its cash-generating potential which will secure the company's future, making funds available for paying dividends and for re-investment, thereby enhancing shareholder value. More importantly we continue to invest in our people. We aim to recruit, train and motivate the best and our results are a consequence of their hard work.

Adapted from 'Boots the Chemist PLC - Annual Report and Accounts 1993'

Advanced Business

Reasons for monitoring business performance

In order to plan and control the running of a business, it is necessary to be able to identify the kinds of information that accounts can give, and how these can be interpreted to show how well a firm is doing.

Accounts can provide a way of monitoring:

- **Solvency:** whether or not a firm has enough assets (both fixed and current) to be able to trade into the future. For example, if a firm is short of cash, it may not be able to meet its debts and be forced to sell off fixed assets, such as machinery and vehicles. Cashflows can be monitored and forecast in order to make provision for periods when cash may be short (see 23.2).

- **Profitability:** profit is one of the most significant measures of business performance. A firm will judge how well it has performed compared to past profit levels and to those of other firms in the industry.

- **Achievement of targets:** for example, has the firm achieved its target of a 10% increase in profits, a 5% growth in its market share, a 20% cut in operating costs, cut bad debts in half, etc.? Financial information can be used to identify areas where an organization can improve its performance. Actual results can be monitored and action taken if the firm appears to be off-target.

- **Tax:** a business can monitor and prepare for the amount of tax due to be paid to the Inland Revenue and Customs and Excise department.

- **Financial requirements:** a business must monitor loan and credit repayments and make sure they do not fall behind, as this may jeopardize any future requests it makes for loans or credit.

- **Performance:** a business can compare its performance over time and with rival firms in the same industry and other industries.

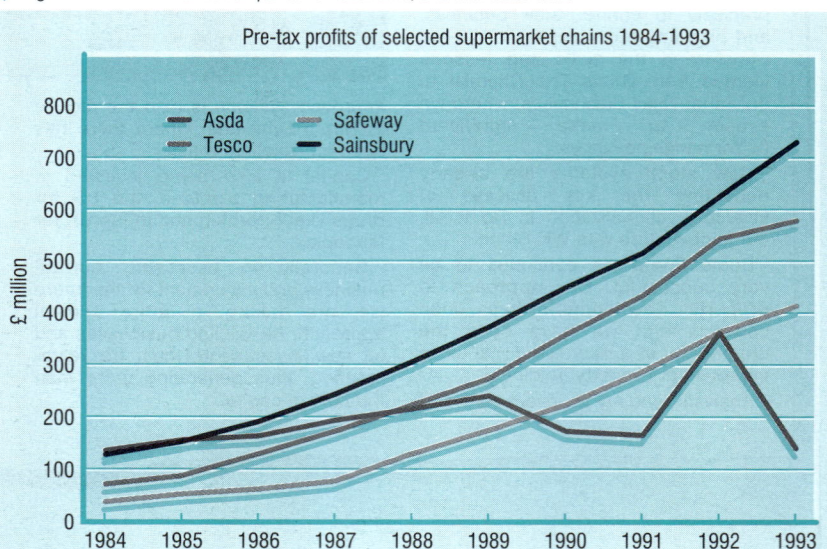

▼ *Figure 25.2: Performance comparisons - over time, and with other firms*

Accounting information can also be used to:

- **Identify trends and forecast future performance:** in order to make an informed guess at the future performance of a business, it is useful to look at its past performance and see if there are any trends which might be expected to continue into the future. For example, if sales have on average risen by 10% each year, one might reasonably forecast sales to rise at this rate in the future. However, the past is not always the best guide to what might happen in the future. Market conditions are constantly changing. New suppliers entering the market, shortages of raw materials, changing consumer demand, new government policy - all these factors and more can affect the performance of a business. Judgement is, therefore, required.

During the course of each trading period, a business will continually monitor whether or not it is 'on target' to achieve its objectives. If the firm is 'off target', or under-performing, managers can make changes to the operation of the business in order to move the firm back towards its goals. For example, a firm selling chocolate bars may aim to capture 25% of the market by the end of the year. To do this, it forecasts it must increase sales by 5% each month. If, midway through the year, sales of its chocolate bars are low and are being outstripped by sales of a competitor's product, the firm may plan a new advertising campaign to raise sales, or may even lower price to boost demand. Plotting actual sales against forecast sales on a graph is a useful way to monitor the achievement of this target (see Figure 25.3).

Similarly, a firm may set a target to increase annual profits by 10% over the previous year. If, at the end of the first quarter, profits are down, it can take action either to boost revenues or cut costs, for example, by buying materials from a cheaper source of supply.

Using accounting information to assist managers in planning, decision-making, and guiding a business is known as **management accounting**.

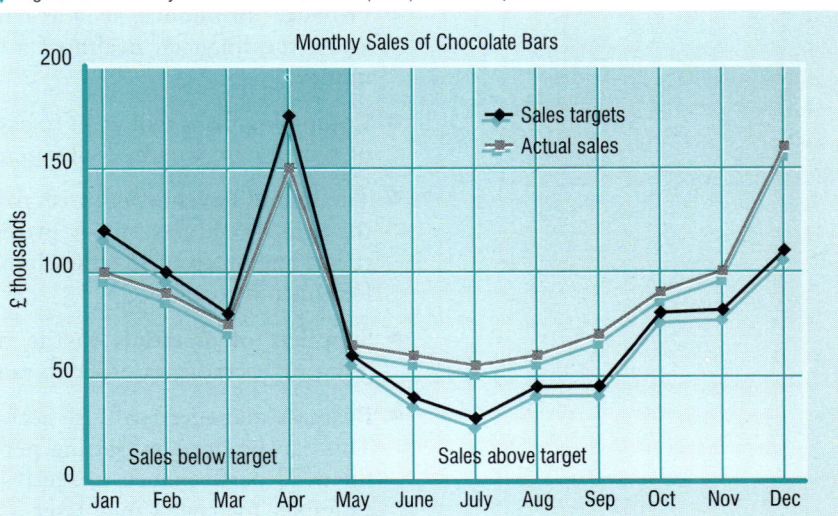

▼ *Figure 25.3: Monthly sales of chocolate bars (£000) – an example*

Key components of accounting information

In an efficient organization, monitoring is continual. To do this, financial information must be recorded accurately and be readily available, so that business managers can make decisions and take steps to ensure that their organization is working towards its targets. Such information will be available to business managers from the following sources:

- **Forecasts:** expectations of future costs, production levels, sales, stocks, input requirements, cash inflows and outflows, and profits

- **Operating budgets:** used to plan the day-to-day use of resources in an organization. The operating budget will show expenditures and receipts agreed by business managers as required to meet set targets. Budgets will be prepared for all key areas of business activity: output, sales, inputs of labour and materials, overhead expenses, cash inflows and outflows (see 25.2).

- **The master budget:** a summary of total expenditure and expected receipts across the entire organization (see 25.2).

- **Aged creditors reports:** lists of suppliers to whom the organization owes money for goods and services delivered, with details of when each debt is due to be repaid

- **Aged debtors reports:** lists of customers who owe the organization money, and how long each debt has been outstanding

- **Balance sheet:** showing the assets and liabilities of a business at the end of each trading period (see 24.2).

- **Profit and loss statement:** a summary of all the financial transactions undertaken by a business within a trading period. It records total revenue and expenditure, and shows profit or loss (see 24.3).

- **Cashflow statement:** a summary of total cash inflows and outflows at the end of each trading period.

- Accounting information from the previous years trading against which changes in performance can be judged.

Who uses information on business performance?

A variety of people and organizations will wish to use data to monitor business performance:

- **Business owners** will want to see the accounts in order to know how well the firm is doing, how much profit is being made, and how much their investment in the firm is worth.

- **Employees** and **Trade Unions** may use published accounts to determine target pay settlements. If the accounts reveal that the company has gained a significant increase in profits, then employees may feel justified in asking for a large increase in their pay.

- **Potential future investors**, including individuals and other organizations, will wish to see accounts in order to judge whether or not to invest in the company. Accounts allow investors to compare the performance of different companies over time.

- **Providers of finance**, such as banks and building societies, will wish to know the financial health of a business organization before lending it money.

- **Competing firms** will want to assess the financial strength and efficiency of a rival company by looking at its published accounts.

- The **Inland Revenue** will wish to see accounts to calculate how much tax the firm should pay on any profits. All businesses are required by law to reveal any profit or loss they have made at the end of each financial year for this purpose.

- **Suppliers of materials** to the firm will wish to see accounts before granting it credit, in order to judge if it will be able to pay invoices.

- **Business managers** will use accounting records to control the business. This can be done by setting performance targets and then monitoring financial performance to see if the outcomes match expectations. For example, managers might set a target for profit before tax to rise by 10% over a 12-month period. The actual percentage change in profit each week or month can then be compared to the 10% target. Accounts will provide a picture of the performance of a firm over time.

Business managers can make use of two important techniques to monitor the performance of their organization using financial information. These are:

- **Variance analysis**: this involves examining reasons for differences between business budget plans or forecasts and actual results.

- **Ratio analysis**: this involves comparing key financial figures from the final accounts.

These techniques are considered in detail in the following sections.

> **Key words**
>
> **Management accounting** - using accounts to monitor the performance of a business and changing the way in which it is managed in order to improve performance
>
> **Quantitative targets** - business targets which can be expressed in money terms
>
> **Qualitative targets** - non-financial targets such as improving product quality
>
> **Solvency** - the ability of a business to meet its debts

Section 25.2 Budgetary control

Preparing a budget

Budgeting allows business managers to improve their control over individual departments or divisions within their organization. **A budget** is a financial plan or statement which is agreed in advance. It is not a forecast, but a planned outcome which a firm hopes to achieve. It shows how much money is needed for spending, and how this expenditure might be financed. Most budgets will cover the next 12-month period, but some budget plans are drawn up for longer periods of time. For example, R&D may involve spending large amounts of money over many years.

The UK government also prepares a budget each December for the economy as a whole (see 3.2). This is a statement of planned public expenditures and expected revenues in the coming financial year.

The preparation of budgets is an important aspect of business planning. Budgets will help an organization to:

- Appraise alternative courses of action - for example, identifying the costs and benefits of employing additional labour to raise output, or investing in new machinery instead

- Present information to potential lenders to raise finance

- Set business targets, as expressed by the amount and cost of resources shown in budget plans

- Monitor business performance by comparing plans with actual results

Drawing up a budget involves a number of steps, as illustrated in Figure 25.4.

Advanced Business

▼ Figure 25.4: Preparing a budget

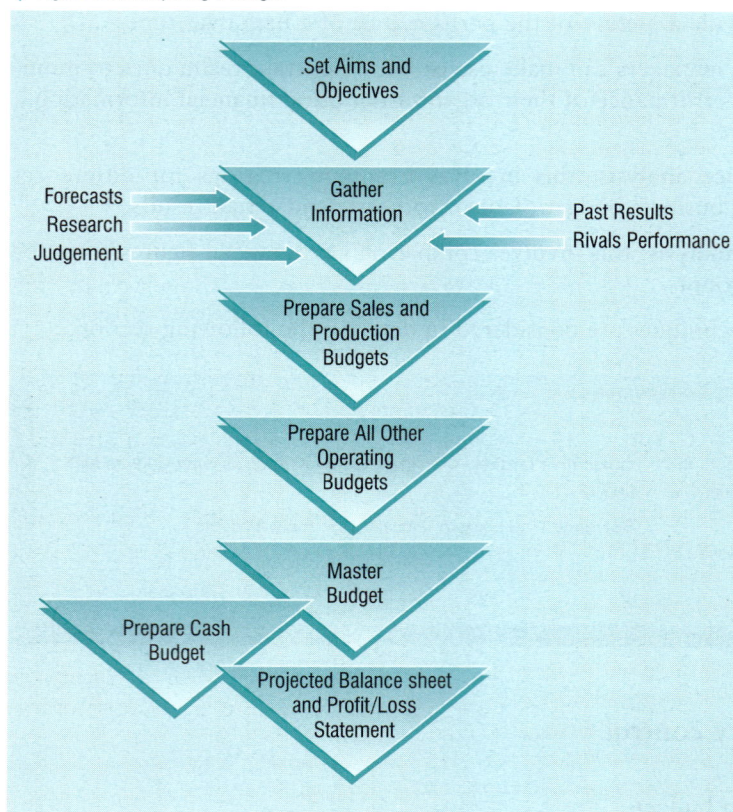

Flowchart (left side):
- Set Aims and Objectives
- Gather Information ← Forecasts, Research, Judgement / Past Results, Rivals Performance
- Prepare Sales and Production Budgets
- Prepare All Other Operating Budgets
- Master Budget
- Prepare Cash Budget
- Projected Balance sheet and Profit/Loss Statement

Stage 1: Decide upon a budget period. Most budgets are produced annually. It is usual for an annual budget to be broken down into quarterly or monthly budgets for easier control.

Stage 2: Agree business objectives and set targets. For example, to expand market share by 5%. In a large organization, individual targets will be agreed for each factory or office, or each department, area, or product to achieve. Targets should be challenging, but at the same time realistic.

Stage 3: Obtain information on which to base budgets. Most budgets are based on past spending levels, adjusted for the impact of price inflation on costs.

Stage 4: Prepare key operating budgets for sales, production, materials, labour, overheads, and cashflow, in line with agreed targets.

Stage 5: Draw up the master budget. This is a summary statement combining all individual budgets. It shows estimated revenues and planned expenditures and also, therefore, the expected profit.

Stage 6: Use the master budget and cash budget to prepare the projected balance sheet, to show the value of business assets and liabilities expected at the end of the budget period.

Types of budget

- **Zero-based budgets** are *not* based on past information. They ignore the past and make a fresh start. Each activity is evaluated against its relevance to the business, and whether or not the expenditure will yield benefits. For example, a firm that decides to install a computer network in its offices for the first time would have no past experience of computer costs. If it thinks computerization will increase output and efficiency by more than the cost of the equipment, then it will go ahead and prepare an IT budget based on cost estimates.

- **Flexible budgets** are adjusted over time in response to unforeseen changes in the level of activity in a firm. For example, the photocopying unit in a firm may need to buy a new machine to cope with an increased demand for photocopying minutes and reports, or an office may need to buy new computer equipment to replace a faulty machine.

- **Fixed budgets** remain the same, even if the level of activity in an organization differs from what has been predicted.

Monitoring budgets

If an organization is to be successful, it is important that it is always fully aware of its current financial situation. Business managers must therefore make sure that certain key areas of the organization are closely monitored:

- The **sales budget** shows planned revenues the firm hopes to achieve each month. This is calculated by multiplying predicted sales by the product prices the firm hopes to achieve.

- The **production budget** shows the amount of materials, labour hours, and machine hours needed to meet sales targets.

All other operating budgets for individual departments or activities will be based on the sales and production budgets. These will include budgets for labour and materials, overheads, and cashflow (see 23.2).

Summary budgets may also be drawn up separately for all capital and current expenditures. Current expenditures include wages, materials purchases, spending on power, and overhead expenses. Capital expenditures include spending on plant and machinery, vehicles, and other equipment that will remain productive for a long time. It will also include plans for loans to finance such expenditure.

It is possible to monitor business performance and the attainment of targets by comparing actual results, or outturn, with what had been planned for each month. The difference between what was planned and what is actual is called the variance. For example, suppose that the personnel department in a firm has been allocated a budget for consumables, such as paper and pens, of £100 per month. If it spends £150 on these items in one month, then the variance is negative. That is, £50 more was spent than had been budgeted for. If the department is unable to cut back its spending on these items in future months, this negative variance will be carried forward to the end of the year.

At the end of each budget period, the projected balance sheet can be compared with the balance sheet drawn up on the basis of actual results.

Variance analysis

This involves investigating the reasons for differences between actual results and budgeted figures, either in terms of money or in terms of volumes - for example, the number of labour hours, or amount of materials used in production.

Variances can be:

- **Negative** or **adverse** - if outturn sales are less than planned, or if outturn costs exceed budget

- **Positive** or **favourable** - if outturn sales revenues are more than planned, or if outturn costs are below budget

There are a number of important variances a firm will seek to monitor and analyse. The profit variance is usually the most important, showing the extent to which actual profit is greater or less than planned profit from the master budget.

Type of variance	Some reasons for variance
Sales variance	Unforeseen price changes
	Higher or lower sales volume than expected
Direct materials	Higher or lower prices than usual
	Increased wastage or inefficiency
Direct labour	Increased overtime working
	Negotiated pay settlement
	Cut in labour force
	Change in labour productivity
Overheads	Equipment breakdown
	Paper wastage
	Power cut
	Rise in price of materials

Budgetary control, therefore, is the process of setting targets, preparing budget plans, monitoring those plans, and then analysing variances.

▼ Figure 25.5: The process of budgetary control

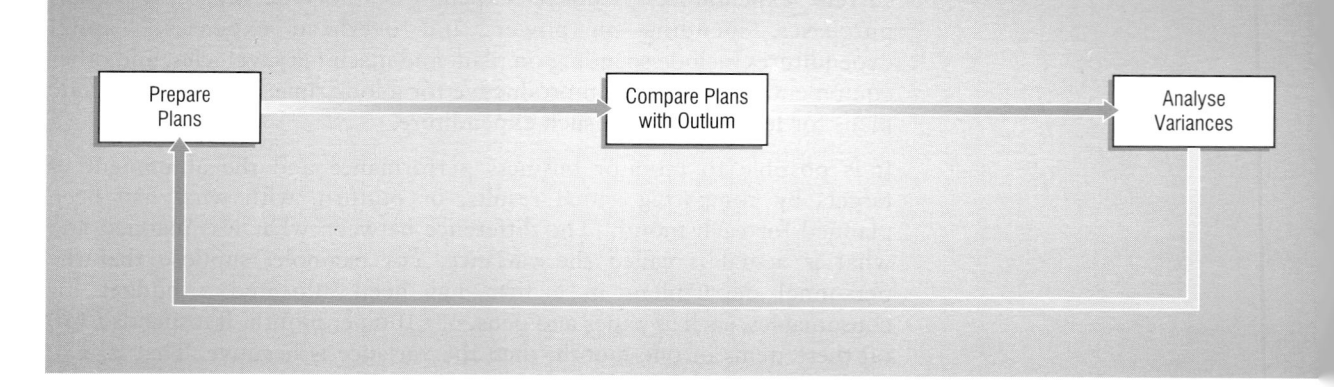

```
Prepare Plans → Compare Plans with Outurn → Analyse Variances → (loops back to Prepare Plans)
```

Portfolio Activity 25.2

Range: Comparisons and variance
Skills: Interpret and present data

Examine the sales budget of the business organization below.

Month	Price	Sales targets (units)	Target revenues £	Actual revenues £	Variance +/−
January	£10	2000	20,000	21,000	
February	£10	1400	14,000	15,400	
March	£10	1200	12,000	12,500	
April	£10	1600	16,000	15,000	
May	£10	2200	22,000	18,200	
June	£12	2500	30,000	22,100	
July	£12	2700	32,400	29,500	

1. Suggest what information the sales budget may have been based on.
2. What is the danger of being too optimistic in the sales budget, and how might this impact on other operating budgets the business is likely to have drawn up?
3. Calculate the sales variances for each month.
4. What might have caused the large variances in sales?
5. How could management use this information?
6. Which variance(s) will the following factors affect? Are the factors adverse or favourable?
   - Discounts to customers who buy in bulk
   - Improved working conditions
   - Rise in staff absenteeism
   - Increasing competition from rival firms
   - Economic downturn
   - Favourable response to advertising campaign
   - Savings from contracting out office cleaning
   - Machine breakdown
   - Incorrect recording of hours worked
7. Investigate how budgets are prepared in a business organization with which you are familiar.

Key words

Budget - a financial plan agreed in advance by managers

Sales budget - details of planned revenues

Production budget - details of factor inputs needed to achieve planned production targets

Current expenditure - spending on resources used up quickly, such as materials, labour, and power

Capital expenditure - spending on capital goods, such as plant and machinery

Master budget - a summary statement detailing the total budget for an organization, expected sales, and anticipated profits

Variance - the difference between an actual figure and a planned figure

Variance analysis - the investigation of reasons for variances

Section 25.3

Ratio analysis

What is a financial ratio?

An accounting ratio or **financial ratio** is simply the comparison of two figures in company accounts produced by dividing one key figure by another, and usually taking a percentage.

Data on profit, sales, or capital employed in a firm alone tells us very little about how well a business is doing. **Ratio analysis** uses financial ratios to make meaningful comparisons of business performance over time and between different firms.

Even simple comparisons of financial data may reveal a great deal. For example, an investor has the choice of either placing money in a safe bank account and earning a guaranteed rate of interest, or risking money by buying shares which might provide a high rate of return - or none at all. Which is the best investment? A simple comparison of two figures could provide the answer. A bank account might pay 8% interest each year - that is, a return of 8 pence in every pound. If a firm received £100,000 in shareholders' funds and earned a profit of £5,000, this is only a return of 5%, which is significantly worse than the 8% which could be earned elsewhere. In this case, the investor would be better off placing savings in the bank. In making such a calculation, the investor is working out a financial ratio or comparing the return on savings to the return on investment in shares.

The key accounting ratios used by business organizations are:

- **Liquidity ratios** - to measure the ability of a firm to meet its debts
- **Profitability ratios** - to measure how well an organization is doing
- **Activity ratios** - to measure how efficiently a firm is using its resources

Figure 25.6 presents the final accounts for Motorcade plc, a small car retail chain dealing in new and second-hand vehicles. Business managers at Motorcade are confident that performance has improved since 1994. We will use these accounts to show how financial ratios can be used to provide valuable information on business performance.

Liquidity ratios

The **liquidity** of a firm is measured by comparing those assets which can be turned into cash quickly, known as **current assets**, and those liabilities which have to be paid out in the short term, known as **current liabilities** (see 23.1).

If a firm has plenty of assets which can easily be converted to cash in order to meet liabilities which are due to be paid out soon, it is said to be **liquid**. If, however, it is **illiquid**, it may have to obtain an expensive bank loan or sell off important fixed assets, such as machinery, to raise cash in order to meet its business debts.

Liquidity ratios, also known as **solvency ratios**, are useful as they can give early warning of financial problems which might occur if there is a sudden demand for cash.

▼ Figure 25.6: Final accounts for Motorcade plc

MOTORCADE PLC
Profit and Loss Account for the year ended 31 December 1995

	1995 £000s	1994 £000s
Turnover	1,455	1,380
Less Cost of sales	935	905
Gross profit	520	475
Less operating expenses	170	150
Net profit	350	325
Less Interest payable	47	39
Profit before tax	303	286
Less Taxation	76	71
Profit after tax	227	215
Less Dividends	180	170
Retained profits	47	45

MOTORCADE PLC
Balance Sheet as at 31 December 1995

	1995 £000s	1994 £000s
Fixed assets	778	743
Current assets		
Stock	218	201
Debtors	130	115
Cash at bank	23	33
	371	349
Current liabilities		
Creditors – amounts falling due within one year	185	180
Net current assets	186	169
Total assets less current liabilities	964	912
Creditors – amounts falling due after one year	260	270
	704	642
Net assets		
Capital and reserves	377	364
Called-up share capital	30	28
Share premium account	297	250
Retained profits	704	642

Current ratio

The ability of a firm to meet its short-term debts is measured by a liquidity ratio known as the current ratio, where:

$$\text{Current Ratio} = \frac{\text{Current Assets } (£)}{\text{Current Liabilities } (£)}$$

A generally accepted rule is that current assets should be about double current liabilities, to give a current ratio of 2:1. Any lower, and a firm could be in danger of running out of cash. A ratio any higher than 2:1 means that too much money is tied up in cash and not enough is being invested, either in interest-earning bank accounts or in capital equipment.

A ratio of less than 1:1 means that current liabilities exceed current assets, and the firm will not be able to pay its immediate debts and may have to sell some of its fixed assets.

Using the balance sheet for Motorcade plc in figure 25.6, the current ratio may be calculated for 1994 and 1995 as follows:

Current ratios for Motorcade plc:

	1994	1995
Current assets (£000) : Current liabilities (£000)	$\frac{349}{180} = 1.94:1$	$\frac{371}{185} = 2:1$

Motorcade PLC has therefore maintained a reasonable level of liquidity in both 1994 and 1995.

Acid test ratio
An alternative ratio for measuring liquidity is known as the **liquidity ratio** or **acid test ratio**.

$$\text{Acid Test Ratio} = \frac{\text{Current Assets (£) - Value of Stock (£)}}{\text{Current Liabilities (£)}}$$

The acid test ratio excludes stocks of finished products and materials from the calculation of current assets. That is, the ratio measures whether or not a business is able to meet its short-term debts without having to sell off stocks. This is because when a firm needs to raise cash quickly, it may be quite difficult to sell its stocks of finished goods.

As a general rule, an acid test ratio of 1:1, where current assets minus stocks equals current liabilities, is considered reasonably safe for a business, because it can meet all its short-term debts without having to sell off stocks. If the ratio falls below 1:1, then the firm could face problems if all its creditors demand to be paid in full at the same time. In this case, it would need to sell stocks to meet these debts and, should this not be possible, either borrow the money or sell fixed assets.

Acid test for Motorcade Ltd:

	1994	1995
Current assets less stock (£000): Current liabilities (£000):	$\frac{349 - 201}{180} = 0.82$	$\frac{371 - 218}{185} = 0.83$

Using the acid test ratio, Motorcade displays a reasonable level of liquidity, although the business managers should be careful not to let this ratio fall any further below 1:1 in future years by reducing their current liabilities.

Profitability ratios
There are a number of ratios which can be used to measure how well a business is doing. These are:

- Gross profit margin
- Net profit margin
- Return On Capital Employed (ROCE)

Gross profit margin
The gross profit margin is a measure of how much total profit is made as a percentage of sales. The ratio is a measure of trading efficiency. The higher the percentage, the better the business trading performance.

$$\text{Gross Profit Margin (\%)} = \frac{\text{Gross Profit (£)} \times 100}{\text{Turnover (£)}}$$

Using the profit and loss statement in figure 25.6 the gross profit margin for Motorcade PLC is calculated as follows;

	1994	1995
Gross Profit (£000): Turnover (£000):	$\frac{475}{1,380} \times 100 = 34.4\%$	$\frac{520}{1,455} \times 100 = 35.7\%$

That is, in 1995 every £1 of sales at Motorcade generated just under 36 pence in profit - a good result.

Advanced Business

Margins rise cheers Tesco

Tesco today lifted a little of the gloom which has for months surrounded the food retailers, with news that margins have risen in the past few weeks and the trading environment appears to have stabilized.

"Our gross margin has improved from the 0.7% decline reported in the second half of last year. I would think we will progress very well in 1994," said chairman Sir Ian MacLaurin.

He admitted that competition on pricing remains fierce but said the introduction of pharmaceuticals, CDs and tapes, as well as technical improvements on the cost side, have helped to boost the group's overall margin.

Evening Standard 12.4.94

Net profit margin

Net profit is arrived at after overhead expenses, such as electricity, telephones, and gas, have been paid out from gross profit. The difference between gross and net profit therefore gives an indication of a firm's ability to control its costs. The higher the net profit margin, the smaller the difference between costs and revenues.

$$\text{Net Profit Margin (\%)} = \frac{\text{Net Profit (£)}}{\text{Turnover (£)}} \times 100$$

The net and gross profit margins provide a useful means of judging business performance when comparing performance across two or more years. If gross margins stay constant but net margins decrease, this means that overheads must have increased during the year. With this information management may wish to investigate cost control and budgeting for overhead costs.

For example, sales staff may spend increasing amounts on entertaining clients with expensive lunches in order to generate sales and earn more commission. Whilst gross profits will stay high due to extra sales, net profits may begin to fall, because of the increased expense involved in earning these extra sales. In this case, the self-interest of sales staff in earning high commission works against the good of the firm, because it leads to lower net profits. By monitoring changes in net profit margins over time, business managers can identify any potential future problems and take corrective action.

Motorcade plc net profit margins:

	1994	1995
Net Profit (£000) : Turnover (£000) :	$\frac{325}{1,380} \times 100 = 23.5\%$	$\frac{350}{1,455} \times 100 = 24\%$

Return On Capital Employed (ROCE)

This ratio expresses the net profit of a business as a percentage of the total value of its capital invested in fixed and current assets.

$$\text{Return on Capital Employed (\%)} = \frac{\text{Net profit (£)}}{\text{Total Assets (£)}} \times 100$$

The return on capital should ideally be higher than the rate of interest a business could earn by placing money in a bank or building society account. If not, then the business might just as well convert its assets to cash and put the money into an interest-earning account.

In limited companies, the business owners are its shareholders and they expect to be paid a dividend from company profits. They will clearly be interested in earning more from their money invested in shares than they would get from an interest-earning account, or from investing their money in another business venture. The ROCE ratio allows them to compare all these alternatives.

The higher the ROCE, the better it is for business owners. Profits are high, and therefore the dividends on their shares will be healthy. Judge for yourself if Motorcade plc is making a good return on capital employed, by comparing its rate of return with the rate that could currently be earned on savings accounts:

Return on capital employed in Motorcade plc:

	1994	1995
Net Profit (£000) :	$\frac{325}{1{,}092} \times 100 = 29.7\%$	$\frac{350}{1{,}149} \times 100 = 30.5\%$
Total Assets (£000) :		

Return on net assets

This is very similar to ROCE, but measures the ratio on long-term capital only. Short-term sources of capital, such as creditors, are excluded. Deducting current liabilities from total assets in the balance sheet gives a figure for net capital employed or net assets.

$$\text{Return on Net Assets (\%)} = \frac{\text{Net Profit (£)}}{\text{Net Assets (£)}} \times 100$$

This ratio should be higher than ROCE, because net assets will be less than total capital employed.

Activity (or performance) ratios

There are a number of ratios which examine whether or not a business is using its resources efficiently. These include:

- Administration to sales
- Asset turnover
- Stock turnover
- Debt collection period

Administration expenses to sales

Another way in which a business can monitor how well it is controlling its costs is by calculating the ratio of administration or overhead expenses to sales revenue or turnover. The larger the percentage of sales revenues used to pay for administration expenses, the worse the cost control performance of the firm.

$$\text{Administration to Sales (\%)} = \frac{\text{Administration Expenses (£)}}{\text{Sales Revenue (£)}} \times 100$$

Administration expenses (or operating expenses) as a percentage of sales for Motorcade plc were as follows:

	1994	1995
Administration Expenses (£000) :	$\frac{150}{1{,}380} \times 100 = 10.9\%$	$\frac{170}{1{,}455} \times 100 = 11.7\%$
Turnover (£000) :		

Motorcade plc has a good record of cost control. However, the slight rise in the proportion of total sales accounted for by overheads in 1995 may cause some concern for business managers, who may want to keep a tight control on these expenses in the following year.

Asset turnover

Since the net assets of a business represent the value of the capital invested in it, it is useful to see how many times a business can generate sales in a year equal to the value of its capital or net assets. **Asset turnover** is a measure of the number of times that net assets are 'turned over' in sales in a year.

This is another means of measuring the productivity of a business.

$$\text{Asset Turnover} = \frac{\text{Turnover } (\pounds)}{\text{Value of Net Assets } (\pounds)}$$

We can calculate the asset turnover ratio for Motorcade plc by taking sales revenues from the profit and loss account and net assets from the balance sheet, as follows:

	1994	1995
Turnover (£000) : 1,380 Net Assets (£000) : 704	$\frac{1{,}380}{704} = 1.96$	$\frac{1{,}455}{642} = 2.26$

That is, in 1995 Motorcade generated sales of 2.26 times the value of its net assets.

Stock turnover

The **stock turnover ratio** measures the number of times in a year that a business sells the value of its stocks. It is a measure of business activity. The faster the rate of sales, the more times stocks will need to be replaced. If sales are poor, stocks will build up, indicated by a low and falling ratio, and production will have to be cut.

$$\text{Stock Turnover} = \frac{\text{Turnover } (\pounds)}{\text{Value of Stocks } (\pounds)}$$

The stock turnover ratio for Motorcade plc can be found by taking the sales figure from the profit and loss account and the value of stocks figure from the balance sheet:

	1994	1995
Turnover (£000) : 1,380 Value of Stocks (£000) : 201	$\frac{1{,}380}{201} = 6.86$	$\frac{1{,}455}{218} = 6.67$

Therefore, Motorcade had to replace its stock of cars roughly 7 times in each year. Generally, the higher the rate of stock turnover, the better the sales performance of the firm. Ratios of around 6-7 are probably acceptable for a car dealer.

What is an acceptable level of stock turnover will vary with the type of business. For example, a high-quality jeweller may only replace his or her stock of expensive rings and necklaces once each year, whilst a bakery would expect to replace its stock of fresh bread every day, giving a ratio of 365.

Debtor collection period

It is possible to measure how well a firm is controlling the giving of credit to its customers by calculating the average amount of time taken by debtors to pay their invoices.

Most firms give credit to their trade customers. The credit period will vary by the type of firm. Typically, firms will give trade customers up to 60 days to pay invoices for goods or services delivered. If debtors are taking longer than this to pay, it indicates that the firm may have given credit unwisely and could be left with bad debts. However, some large firms may give credit for 90 days, while some small firms may struggle if their debts are not repaid within 30 days.

Because it is assumed that debtors will pay their invoices in the near future, sales on credit are treated as a current asset in the balance sheet. However, the larger the proportion of sales accounted for by credit sales, the more serious the consequences for the business if some of the debtors fail to pay.

Businesses can calculate the average number of days it takes for debtors to settle their debts. To do this, it is first necessary to work out the figure for an average day's sales, by dividing total sales revenue by 365 days in a year. The next step is to calculate how many average days' sales is represented by the debtors figure:

$$\text{Debt Collection Period (Days)} = \frac{\text{Debtors (£)}}{\text{Average Daily Sales (£)}}$$

$$= \frac{\text{Debtors (£)}}{\text{Turnover (£)}/365}$$

For example, a firm may have average daily sales of £300 and total credit sales during a year of £6,000. This means that the debtors figure represents on average 20 days of sales revenues (i.e. £6,000/£300). That is, debtors take on average 20 days to settle invoices. Or, to look at it another way, it would take 20 days of sales to cover the credit sales to debtors if they should all fail to pay up within an agreed period.

The average debt collection period in Motorcade plc can be found by taking sales in each year from the profit and loss account and dividing by 365, and then dividing this into the debtors figure found on the balance sheet:

	1994	1995
Debtors :	$\frac{£115,000}{£3,780.80} = 30.4$ days	$\frac{£130,000}{£3,986.30} = 32.6$ days
Turnover/365 :		

In 1994, customers owing money to Motorcade paid up, on average, 30.4 days after receiving an invoice. In 1995, this had increased to an average of just under 33 days. As both figures are within the typical 60-day credit period, this does not indicate that the firm has a credit control problem. If the figure was greater than 60 days, this would indicate that some of the debtors had gone beyond the normal period of credit and so are unlikely to pay. In this case, the firm should review its policy on giving credit.

Long delays in receiving payments from debtors can create cashflow problems for a business (see 23.3). Businesses will, therefore, normally operate a system of credit control, using an aged debtors list (see 18.2). This lists the names and the 'ages' of the debts of all the firm's debtors. The business can then concentrate on collecting the oldest, or longest-outstanding, debts. Those debts that cannot be recovered after written warnings and even legal action are written off as bad debts.

Other performance indicators

To complete the picture of past performance, there are a host of other indicators an organization might use. For example:

- Advertising costs per unit of sales
- Output per employee

- Average time taken to produce a unit of output
- Staff absenteeism
- Man days lost due to illness, machine breakdowns, disputes, etc.
- Number of faulty or sub-standard goods
- Number of customer complaints
- Average response time to customer orders

> **Portfolio Activity 25.3**
>
> **Range:** Performance of a business, Ratios
> **Skills:** Interpret and present data
>
> 1. Write to a well-known public limited company of your choice, and ask them to send you a copy of their most recent annual report and accounts.
> 2. Study the profit and loss account and balance sheet for your chosen company and calculate as many financial ratios as you can.
> 3. Comment briefly on the performance of your chosen company over the two-year period reported in the accounts.
> 4. What other information might be useful to examine the overall performance of the company?

The limitations of financial ratios

Although financial ratios are very helpful in analysing accounts, they have some important limitations.

- Accounting information alone cannot tell us everything about company performance. For example, accounts give no indication of changes in economic conditions, changes in the activities of a business - for example, the release of a new product - or about the quality of a firm's workforce, all of which can affect business performance.

- The balance sheet is simply a snapshot of performance at a particular moment. If the business is a seasonal one, like a seaside hotel, the balance sheet might look particularly healthy during the summer months, but this will not give a true picture of the overall performance of the business throughout the year.

- Different firms may compile their accounts in different ways - for example, in the way they value stocks, or account for the impact of price inflation on the value of assets such as land and buildings. This makes inter-firm comparisons difficult. Additionally, firms may have financial years which end on different dates, which also makes comparison difficult, especially where seasonal factors affect the business.

- Past performance may be a poor guide to future performance. Any analysis of past accounting information to inform future decision-making and business planning must be treated with caution.

Non-financial business objectives

Many firms have non-financial objectives which represent important targets that cannot be measured simply by looking at the financial performance of the company. Increasingly, firms are becoming aware of environmental issues and are setting targets relating to cleaning up their production processes, reducing waste, and repairing environmental damage caused by their past activities. Customer care is also important in an increasingly competitive business environment.

Objectives like these are usually outlined in the annual company report and accounts, together with a review of how well the company has progressed towards achieving them, for example, through buying wood from renewable sources and not from tropical rainforests, abolishing tests of cosmetics on animals, etc. With an increasing number of green consumers, firms are unlikely to be able to continue to make profits without taking an increasingly public environmental stance.

Portfolio Activity 25.4

Range: Performance of a business, Ratios
Skills: Produce written material

On the right are a selection of accounting ratios for a firm, calculated over successive years. Interpret these figures and draw some conclusions about the performance of the business.

	1993	1994	1995
Gross profit as a percentage of sales	33%	35%	42%
Net profit as a percentage of sales	19%	21%	26%
Rate of return on capital employed	8%	9%	12%
Current ratio	1:1	1.4:1	2:1
Debt collection period	95 days	97 days	40 days
Stock turnover	5	5.2	6

Key words

Ratio analysis - a way of interpreting accounting information by comparing two figures from company accounts, usually expressing one as a percentage of another, for example, profits as a percentage of turnover

Liquidity ratios - ratios measuring the extent to which assets, which can be quickly converted into cash, are available to a firm to meet its liabilities as they become due. These include the current ratio and acid test ratio

Profitability ratios - ratios that measure the profitability of a business

Net profit margin - measures a firm's ability to control overhead costs and expresses net profit as a percentage of turnover

Return On Capital Employed (ROCE) - a measure of the productivity of business capital, calculated by expressing the net profit of a business as a percentage of the value of its total assets

Activity ratios - ratios that examine how efficiently a firm is using its resources, including ratios for administration expenses to sales, stock and asset turnover

Asset turnover - the amount of times total sales generate the same value as the net assets of a business in a trading period

Stock turnover - the number of times in a year a firm has to replace its stock of finished or semi-finished goods

Debt collection period - the average number of days taken by debtors to pay their invoices

Aged debtors list - a list of debtors' names and the 'age' of their outstanding invoices

Further reading

Hall D, Jones, R , and Raffo, C: *Business Studies* (Causeway Press 1993) Unit 45

Test Questions

The following underpinning knowledge will be tested;

1. Uses of accounting information
2. Reasons for monitoring a business
3. Key components of accounting information used in monitoring
4. Comparisons and variance analysis
5. How ratios are used to interpret accounting information
6. Implications for the performance of a business from accounting information

1 The acid test ratio is used to identify an organization's:
- A Profitability
- B Use of assets
- C Ability to meet its debts
- D Long-term liabilities

2 During a trading period, the rate of stock turnover is best described as:
- A Total revenue from monthly sales of stocks
- B The average level of stocks held per month
- C The average cost per month of holding stocks
- D The number of times that stocks levels are replaced

3 The ability of a firm to control credit can be measured by:
- A Creditors divided by sales
- B Debtors divided by daily sales
- C Profits divided by debtors
- D Debtors divided by creditors

4 Calculating the return on capital employed by a company provides information on:
- A Profitability
- B How efficiently assets are used
- C Liquidity
- D Capital structure

5 All of the following are financial performance ratios used by business organizations except:
- A Return on net assets
- B Asset turnover
- C Stock turnover
- D Acid test ratio

Questions 6-8 are based on the following jumbled financial information for an organization over a 12-month period.

	£000
Turnover	365
Fixed assets	400
Current assets	200
Current liabilities	50
Gross profit	90
Overheads	30
Debtors	60

6 The gross profit margin is
- A 45%
- B 28.5%
- C 15%
- D 24.7%

7 The return on capital employed is
- A 15%
- B 22.5%
- C 10%
- D 16.4%

8 The average debt collection period is
- A 60 days
- B 6 days
- C 10 days
- D 75 days

9 The most likely reason for an adverse variance between the overheads budget and outturn is:
- A A cut in the price of electricity
- B A machine breakdown on the shop-floor
- B An increase in the standing charge for telephone lines
- D The purchase of a new, more efficient photocopier

10 If the budget for a particular business activity is zero-based, it means that:
- A The business has planned not to spend any more money on it
- B It is based on past information adjusted for inflation
- C It is fixed until the end of the budget period
- D It ignores past information in its preparation

11 A firm will wish to monitor its solvency because:
- A It reveals how much profit it is making
- B It reveals its ability to cover its debts
- C It reveals its tax liabilities
- D It reveals information on non-financial targets

12 Explain how and why business organizations monitor their performance using accounting information. Use examples to illustrate your answer.

UNIT SEVEN
CHAPTER 25

Assessment Assignment

Range: Users
Reasons for monitoring
Comparisons and variance
Key components of accounting information
Performance of business
Solvency ratios
Profitability ratios
Performance ratios

Skills: **Communication**
Read and respond to written material
Produce written material
Application of Number
Collect and record data
Tackle problems
Information Technology
Prepare and process information

Tasks

1. Obtain the final accounts of two large public limited companies of your choice in the same industry.

2. You have been asked to advise a large bank that is keen to invest money in the shares of these companies. You are to produce a report containing the following information:

   - A brief history of each company
   - Objectives of each company
   - Why accounting information is used by business managers
   - Sources and key components of accounting information
   - How accounts can be used to examine financial performance
   - Evaluation of the financial performance of each company in terms of:
     - liquidity
     - sales
     - profits
     - costs
     - stock turnover
   - Whether each organization achieved its targets
   - Reasons for changes in the performance of each company over the two-year period contained in their accounts
   - An inter-firm performance comparison and an evaluation of any differences
   - Your recommendations to the bank - should they buy shares in one or both of these companies? Justify your choice.

3. Use ratio analysis to examine financial performance in your report. Make sure that any calculations are set out clearly and explained.

   To calculate financial ratios from information contained in company accounts, you may use a computer spreadsheet. You will first need to input information in an appropriate format from the profit and loss statement and balance sheets. You may then input formulae referring to the appropriate cells in each case to calculate the various ratios. Always check your calculations.

4. You should also consider any other means of measuring business performance, including performance in meeting non-financial objectives.

5. Also comment on how other factors, including the economic climate, government economic policy, and exchange rates may have affected performance.

chapter 26

Business Planning

Unit Eight

unit 8

chapter 26   *The Business Plan – Preparing and Collecting Data (Element 8.1)*

chapter 27   *How to Prepare and Produce a Business Plan (Elements 8.2)*

chapter 28   *Planning for Employment or Self-employment (Elements 8.3)*

Advanced Business

chapter 26
The Business Plan - Preparing and Collecting Data

This chapter introduces the key issues to be considered when preparing the groundwork for a new business proposal in the form of a business plan.

Key ideas

Businesses will have a range of financial **objectives** including, at the very least, to break even, or to maximize profits. Business managers need to plan in order to achieve objectives.

A standard format for outlining what an organization aims to achieve and how it aims to do this is known as a **business plan**.

Business plans are typically used by firms to present their ideas to potential lenders to raise finance, and as a tool for management to monitor progress towards business objectives.

A good business plan will show an appreciation of competing firms and products, the likely demand and repeat business for a product, and forecasts of sales volumes, values and profits.

Business activities usually have **legal and insurance implications**, and a good business plan will consider how these implications will be managed. The main areas of legislation a business will need to be aware of are employment, health and safety, environmental protection, and consumer protection. A business is required by law to have public, product, and employee liability insurance cover.

The key to good management is to organize the human, physical, and financial **resources** available, in order to achieve the targets or goals of the organization within a given time period. The business plan should detail the kinds of resources required to achieve business goals and how these will be managed.

A business must manage time effectively. Critical activities such as planning, marketing, production and selling should be identified and planned for accordingly.

A wide range of support and advice is available to **entrepreneurs** wishing to start up in business, including small-business advisers, local authority enterprise agencies, accountancy firms, Training and Enterprise Councils, local Chambers of Commerce, and many more. Much of this advice is provided free of charge, or at a low cost.

UNIT EIGHT

CHAPTER 26

Section 26.1   What is a business plan?

Portfolio Activity 26.1

Range: Business objectives, Purposes of a business plan
Skills: Read and respond to written material

1. What objectives might somebody like Ian Beale have had in setting up his new fish and chip shop, for the first month, year, and first five years of trading?

2. The article suggests that Ian spent some time planning his business before he opened, whereas Steve did not. What kinds of things in particular, do you think that Ian might have included in his plans for his new business?

3. Give examples of how a lack of planning could have made things more difficult for someone like Steve in starting up a new business.

Ian Shows Who's the Soap Rival Boss

When it comes to starting up and running a business, Ian Beale, budding entrepreneur from Eastenders, is streets ahead of struggling Steve McDonald of Coronation Street.

Steve's T-shirt printing business filled a gap in the market, but he failed to draw up a long-term plan to manage it effectively. Not surprisingly, he has run into difficulties with Mike Baldwin, who has been quick to exploit Steve's lack of business skills, says Barclays Bank.

By contrast, when Ian Beale decided to open a fish and chip shop, he researched his market, took advice and used past experience to plan his venture. "The fact that Ian spent time planning how his business would run and Steve didn't explains why Ian's fish and chip shop is thriving and Steve's business is struggling," says David Lavarack, Head of Small Business Services at Barclays Bank. David says Steve should follow five key points for starting up a small business:

- Prepare a business plan; your blueprint for success
- Research and understand your market
- Gain a clear idea how to sell and promote your business
- Adopt the right pricing policy
- Watch your cashflow

Daily Mirror 22.11.94

Starting a new business

Business know-how, or the ability to organize and manage production, is known as **enterprise**. The people who have enterprise are known as **entrepreneurs**. They are the people who take the risks and decisions necessary to make a firm run successfully.

What do entrepreneurs do?

Innovate
Entrepreneurs have business ideas. Shami Ahmed started the 'Joe Bloggs' clothing company. Anita Roddick thought of The Body Shop.

Organize
Entrepreneurs hire resources and organize them to produce goods and services. They decide what to produce, where to locate business premises, methods of production, job specifications, how much labour and capital to employ, wage levels, and prices.

Take risks
Running a business is risky. An entrepreneur may borrow money, or use personal savings to invest in a business to pay for materials, premises, and labour. If the business fails, the entrepreneur will lose this money.

'Don't go into business to make money for money's sake. Choose something that fascinates you, like I did with the music industry. Since you're going to spend your life working on it, it is important you enjoy the work.

'Make sure there's an obvious need. If it's not being done well by somebody else, you can fill a gap in the market.'

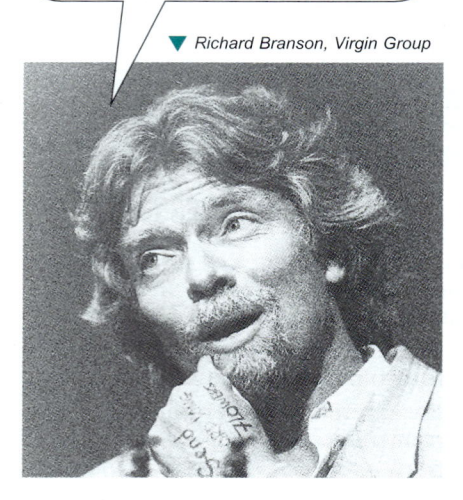

▼ *Richard Branson, Virgin Group*

▼ *Product innovations*

Starting a new business is not easy, because there are so many factors an entrepreneur cannot control, for example, legislation affecting the business, changes in taxes, economic conditions, consumer demand, and competition. About one in four businesses fail in their first few years. Starting a new business, therefore, needs careful planning and research.

Evaluating a business idea

When evaluating a business idea, the key questions to ask are:

- Will you enjoy the work?
- Have you identified a gap in the market?
- Have you assessed the market potential?
- Who are your competitors?

Turning to the business itself, what is that you want to produce? Is it a good or a service? Is the product something people will buy on a regular basis, such as food, or something that they are likely to want only every now and again, for example expensive jewellery or a carpet-cleaning service?

It is not always necessary to be innovative and make an entirely new product. You can provide a good or service that is already available - but do it better than the competition.

Many of the products we take for granted today started as the innovations of private individuals. For example, Percy Shaw became a multi-millionaire after inventing 'cats eyes' for roads as a result of seeing his car headlights reflected in some broken glass. Swedish brothers Gad and Hans Rausing made £5.2 billion from their invention, the Tetra Pak Carton.

A 'gap in the market'

Spotting a gap in the market means identifying a consumer want that is not being satisfied - either because a particular product is not available, or because existing products are unsatisfactory in some way. A business that is able to satisfy these consumer desires stands a good chance of succeeding.

For example, mobile phones have filled a gap in the market for improved communications. Microwave ovens have filled a gap in the market for reduced cooking times, as the number of single working households has increased and more women go out to work. Even if a good or service is generally available, a gap may still exist in the market at a local level. For example, a small village may not be served by a newsagent's shop or hairdressing salon.

Market potential

More opportunities for new business organizations exist in markets which are expanding. This means that sales of a particular good or service are rising. It is important for budding entrepreneurs to assess the future potential demand for their product ideas, by identifying trends in sales for similar products from published sources, such as the *Annual Abstract of*

The herbal drinks market was expanding in the early 1990s

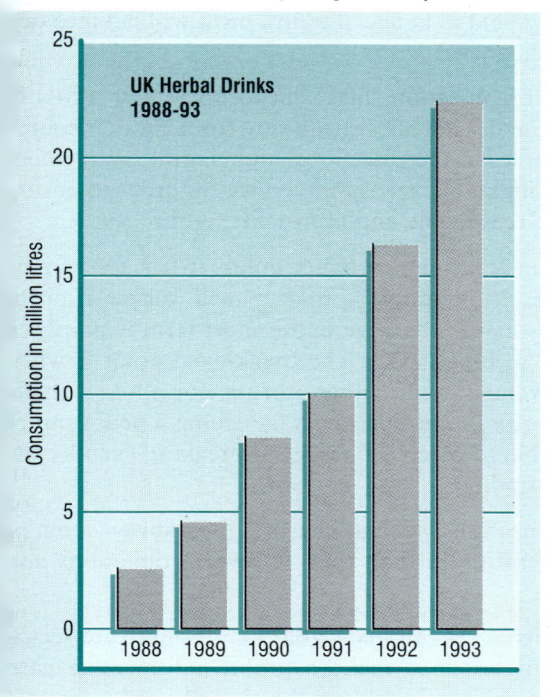

UK Herbal Drinks 1988-93
Consumption in million litres

- 1988: ~2.5
- 1989: ~4.5
- 1990: ~8
- 1991: ~10
- 1992: ~16
- 1993: ~22.5

Daily Mirror, December 94

Statistics, or, in the case of entirely new products, by using primary market research to gauge consumer demand (see 9.2).

Market research can help to identify who is likely to buy your new products, and how much they are willing to pay. The target audience for your product and advertising can be identified by age, sex, income, lifestyle, and geographical location (see 10.1). Expanding markets in the early 1990s included gardening products and DIY, personal computers, mobile phones and fax machines, CD-Roms, camcorders, aromatherapy, and herbal drinks.

Competition

Unless your good or service is unique, you can expect to encounter competition from rival business organizations. You can attempt to minimize competition by offering better quality and service, lower prices, faster delivery, better customer care and after-sales service, advertising, longer opening hours, and so on, and generally differentiating your product or service from that of your rivals.

It will be important to study the strengths and weaknesses of rival organizations in terms of price, promotion, quality, image, and customer care. Size and location will also be important. For example, it would be madness to think you could successfully compete against giant organizations such as Sony in the market for recorded music. Similarly, it would also be risky to open a hairdressing salon in an area already served by many competing salons.

Setting business objectives

One of the very first tasks for a budding entrepreneur is to identify business objectives for the short, medium, and long term. Once identified, these will provide the goals towards which the business works, and by which its success can be

---

Portfolio Activity 26.2

Range: Business objectives, Supporting information
Skills: Collect and record data

1. From your own knowledge and further research, identify markets that are currently expanding or contracting, and gather supporting information.
2. For the goods and services you have identified, list and explain possible reasons for their growth or decline in sales. Useful sources of data will include:

- CSO Social Trends
- CSO Annual Abstract of Statistics
- Newspapers and magazines
- Specialist marketing magazines
- Discussions with shop sales staff

measured. Businesses may have many different objectives. However, all objectives will be reinforcing, and in financial terms, most will fall into one or other of the following categories:

- **To be subsidized:** some organizations may aim to operate at a loss in order to keep prices low, and will receive a subsidy from another source to break even. For example, in the past, local and central government have subsidized loss-making public transport services in order to ensure that the public receives a reasonable and affordable level of service.

- **To break-even:** when a new business sets up, unless it has a very new and innovative product, it is unlikely that it will make a profit immediately. A more reasonable objective in the short term is simply to avoid making a loss, i.e. to break even. The break-even point is where total costs equal total revenues, and neither a profit nor a loss is made (see 21.2). The vast majority of entrepreneurs launching a new venture are quite pleased to be able to reach the target of breaking even by the end of their first year of trading.

  Non-profit-making organizations, such as charities, will always attempt to break even, spending no more than they receive in donations and other incomes.

- **To maximize profits:** this is the ultimate goal of most private-sector business organizations. In order to make a profit, a firm must earn revenues in excess of total costs. To achieve this, it will need to meet a number of other shorter term (or tactical) objectives along the way, such as establishing a product and brand name, gaining market share and customer loyalty, etc. Similarly, large firms may subsidize new subsidiaries or products if they are aiming to enter a new market, in order to help them to get established.

Only the fittest survive

When the going gets tough, the main objective of any business is survival. About half a million new businesses start up every year in the UK. About one in four fail in their first few years of operation. Business survival is especially important in the early stages of trading, when consumers know little about the new company or their product, and when competition from existing firms in the market will be especially fierce. Survival is also important when there is a slump in consumer demand during an economic recession, or when a company is under threat of takeover by a rival firm.

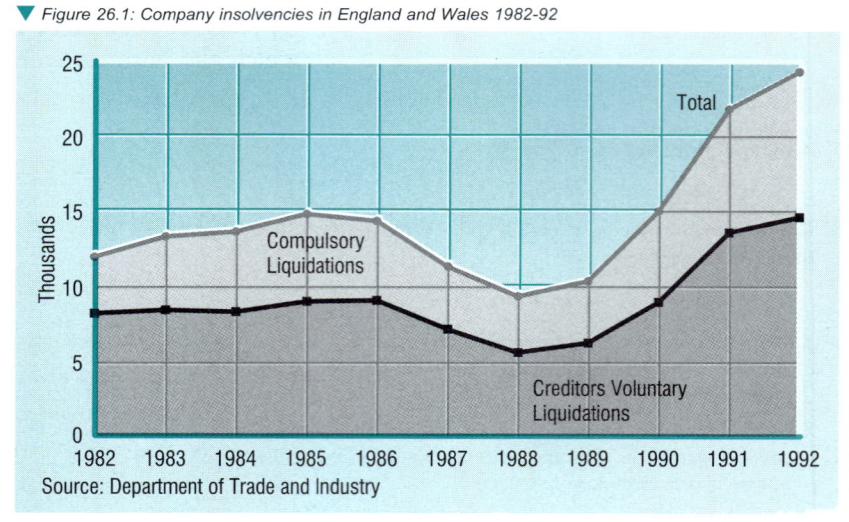

Figure 26.1: Company insolvencies in England and Wales 1982-92

Source: Department of Trade and Industry

CSO Annual Abstract of Statistics 1994

Mission statements

Many organizations summarize their business objectives in a **mission statement**. Such a statement is useful to inform both employees and the public of the goals and purpose of the business. Mission statements usually highlight the key business objectives of the organization, as well as wider social goals, such as care for the environment, and being a responsible employer.

British Telecom's Mission Statement

BT's mission, our central purpose, is to provide world-class telecommunications and information products and services, and to develop and exploit our networks, at home and overseas, so that we can:

- meet the requirements of our customers,
- sustain growth in the earnings of the group on behalf of our shareholders, and
- make a fitting contribution to the community in which we conduct our bussiness.

The purposes of a business plan

Once an entrepreneur has a business idea and an agreed set of objectives, it is usual to set these out in a document known as a **business plan**. The plan will identify the objectives of the business, and detail how it intends to achieve them. It has been suggested that 'a business that fails to plan is one that plans to fail.' There is no set format for a business plan. The structure and content will vary widely from business to business, depending on its size, the nature of the product, and the expertise of the writer. However, it is important for any business plan to consider the following five areas in some detail:

- Objectives
- How the business/product will be marketed
- How production will be organized, and the methods to be used
- Resource requirements (physical, human, and financial)
- Methods of finance

These five sections in a business plan are considered in more detail in Chapter 27.

Producing a well-structured business plan is important for a number of reasons:

- **It is a valuable exercise for the owner(s).** It forces them to evaluate their business idea, market potential, and competition, assess their present financial situation, plan for the future, and set realistic output, sales, and profit targets

- **To identify resource requirements.** For example, the plan will set out the business experience and skills of the owners, how many workers they will need, the skills they require, equipment and vehicle requirements, the size and location of suitable premises, and types and amounts of materials. Business start-up costs will also be identified, and the amount of external finance needed.

- **To support an application for finance.** A bank will insist on seeing a business plan before deciding to lend the owner(s) money. A plan will identify the key factors that will determine the success of the business, and how much of their own money the owners are willing to invest in the venture.

- **To monitor business performance.** The plan allows the business owner(s) to compare actual figures against projections. Forecasts of outputs, sales, cashflows, profit and loss accounts, and balance sheets can be compared against outturn, usually every month or every three months.

Key words

Entrepreneur - a person who starts up, owns, and runs a business

Business plan - a report detailing objectives, marketing strategy, production costings, and financial implications of a new business idea

Break-even - when revenues are equal to costs

Profit - an excess of revenues over costs

Mission statement - a summary statement of the long-term objectives of a business

---

Section 26.2 Legal and insurance implications

Business Law

An entrepreneur setting up a new business must have an understanding of the basics of business law. This is because being in business brings a wide variety of legal and other responsibilities which, if ignored, can be very costly and disruptive to the running of the organization. If a business does break the law, it is not an acceptable defence to plead ignorance. The major categories of law which affect businesses are as follows:

Employment law

The relationship between employers and their employees is regulated by a number of laws in the UK (see 12.3). The main ones are:

- Industrial Relations Act 1971
- Race Relations Act 1976
- Employment Protection (Consolidation) Act 1978
- Employment Act 1980
- Equal Pay Acts 1970, 1983
- Sex Discrimination Acts 1975, 1986
- Wages Act 1986

- Employment Act 1989
- Trade Union Reform and Employment Rights Act 1993

Together, these acts give employees the right to:

- A written statement of terms and conditions of employment
- Guaranteed payment of wages
- An itemized pay slip
- Statutory sick pay
- To return to the same job after illness
- Redundancy payments
- Maternity leave for female employees and the right to return to the same job afterwards
- Non-discrimination on grounds of sex, race, marital status, religion, and Trade Union membership
- Protection against unfair dismissal
- Notice of termination of employment
- Time off for public duties

In December 1994, the UK government accepted an European Union (EU) Directive calling for part-time workers to be given the same redundancy payments and unfair dismissal rights as their full-time colleagues after two years' continuous service. Employers also need to be aware that employees must be at least 16 years old in order to enter into full-time employment. Legislation has also changed recently to lift the retirement age of women to 65 years, the same as men. Employment law is likely to continue to change and develop, due to Britain's membership of the European Union.

Health and safety

A number of laws have been existence for many years to protect employees and members of the public from health and safety hazards at work (see 12.3). These include:

- The Factories Act 1961
- The Offices, Shops and Railway Premises Act 1963
- The Fire Precautions Act 1971
- The Health and Safety at Work Act 1974
- Control of Substances Hazardous to Health Regulations (COSHH) 1988

In January 1993, six new Directives of the European Union came into force concerning health and safety in member countries. The so-called 'six pack' of legislative measures cover:

- Management of health and safety
- Provision and use of work equipment
- Manual handling operations

- Workplace conditions
- Issue of personal protective equipment
- Use of display screen equipment

Health and safety legislation in the UK requires employers 'to ensure as far as is reasonably practicable, the health, safety and welfare at work of all staff'. Positive steps to prevent accidents and to promote health and safety must be taken by all organizations. Employers must:

- Develop and display a written policy on health and safety
- Maintain a safe working environment
- Provide safety equipment and, where appropriate, clothing free of charge
- Keep detailed records of accidents, and make regular assessments of health and safety risks in the workplace

All new businesses need to consider very carefully how they will ensure health and safety at work. The penalties for negligence on the part of employers can be very severe. New entrepreneurs should seek advice on health and safety before setting up in business.

Environmental protection

The Environmental Act 1990 and a growing body of European law on the environment regulate the behaviour of firms in the UK, and this is supported in Britain by the Inspectorate of Pollution (see 3.4). Taken together, these laws control many thousands of different industrial processes, which might, if uncontrolled, cause noise or chemical pollution in the air, land, or water. Local authorities are also required by government to monitor some 30,000 industrial processes for unacceptable levels of pollution.

Firms breaking anti-pollution laws may be subject to heavy fines. Therefore, it is essential for new businesses starting out to establish whether or not any of their production processes are likely to contravene the law, and, if so, what it would cost to put this right. For example, does the business result in hazardous waste by-products? How can waste be kept to a minimum, and how can it be disposed of safely?

Portfolio Activity 26.3

Range: Legal implications
Skills: Take part in discussions

1. In groups, discuss the following questions arising from the article:

    (a) In what ways can environmental and other kinds of legislation affect business costs?

    (b) If business costs in the UK rise, how and why might this affect international competitiveness?

    (c) What are the likely costs and benefits to producers, consumers, and citizens in the UK, of more legislation to protect the environment?

2. Survey any organization with which you are familiar in order to establish the kinds of costs which management feel are imposed by legislation of various kinds. Do they see the legislation as necessary? Would their views conflict with those of the general public? Report on your findings and prepare a short presentation to the rest of your group.

UNIT EIGHT

CHAPTER 26

CBI appeals for reinforcements on the green front

British businesses are starting to chafe under the weight of environmental regulation. They feel the government is creating laws without sufficiently balancing the costs and benefits. They also wish the government would make up its mind about environmental issues. These concerns will be reflected in a report to be published by the Confederation of British Industry (CBI). "At present too many businesses are falling foul of the pitfalls, rather than seizing the opportunities of environmental regulation," the CBI says.

A further problem is the effect of regulation on international competitiveness. A quarter of respondents to a CBI poll said they were experiencing difficulties gaining access to foreign markets, mainly because of eco-labelling schemes in other countries. 30% said they suffered specific disadvantages because of standards imposed domestically, and the stricter enforcement of EU legislation in the UK than in other countries. According to the CBI, environmental regulators are not sufficiently sensitive to the costs that they impose. "This is not a report which says 'We can't afford all this environmental regulation'. But it does reflect frustration over a lot of wasted effort," says Howard Davies, CBI Director General.

Financial Times 4.11.94

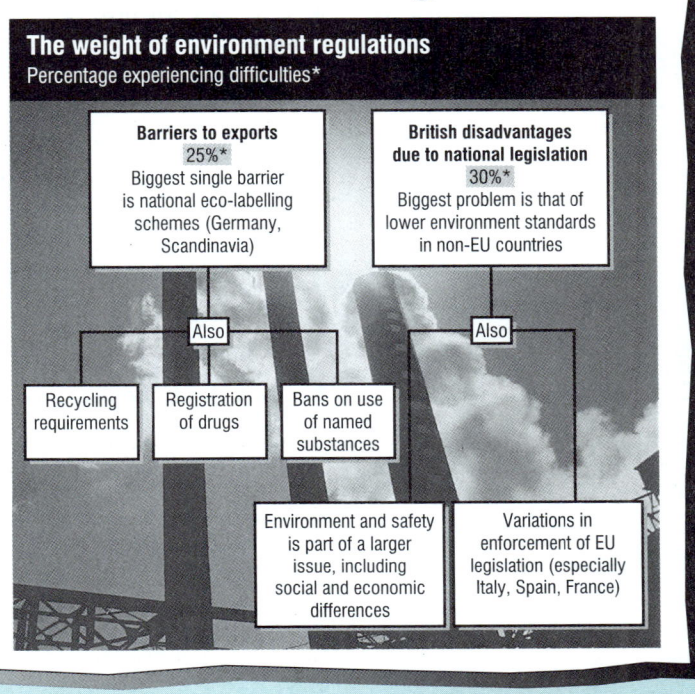

The weight of environment regulations
Percentage experiencing difficulties*

- **Barriers to exports 25%***
  Biggest single barrier is national eco-labelling schemes (Germany, Scandinavia)
- **British disadvantages due to national legislation 30%***
  Biggest problem is that of lower environment standards in non-EU countries

Also:
- Recycling requirements
- Registration of drugs
- Bans on use of named substances

- Environment and safety is part of a larger issue, including social and economic differences
- Variations in enforcement of EU legislation (especially Italy, Spain, France)

Consumer protection law

A body of laws exist to protect consumers from misleading claims by producers and from the sale of goods of poor quality (see 11.3). These include:

- Food and Drugs Act 1955
- Weights and Measures Act 1963
- Trade Descriptions Act 1968
- Unsolicited Goods Act 1971
- Consumer Credit Act 1974
- Consumer Safety Act 1978
- The Sale of Goods Act 1979
- Foods Act 1984
- Consumer Protection Act 1987
- Food Safety Act 1990
- Trademark Act 1994

Together these acts make it illegal to:

- Prepare or sell food in unhygienic conditions

- Use false or misleading weighing equipment
- Give short measure
- Give false or misleading descriptions of goods and services
- Send goods to customers who have not ordered them and then demand payment
- Not provide consumers with copies of credit agreements
- Not provide correct and full details of credit arrangements
- Sell goods which might be harmful to consumers
- Sell goods that are not of merchantable quality
- Sell defective goods that may cause damage or harm to consumers or their property
- Copy the trademark, logo, or name of another business or product

In addition a number of laws exist to control anti-competitive behaviour by firms, such as colluding to fix prices (see 3.4). These are:

- Monopolies and Trade Practices Act 1948
- Restrictive Trade Practices Act 1956
- Fair Trading Act 1973
- Restrictive Practices Act 1976
- Competition Act 1980
- Monopolies and Mergers Act 1965

Most of these laws will apply to large well-established firms who are able to dominate markets, known as **monopolies** and **oligopolies** (see 2.2). However, even small firms may be able to dominate the supply of a good or service to a local market and use this power to fix high prices and deter new competition.

Additional laws regulate opening times for shops and public houses, and forbid the sale of cigarettes, alcohol, and fireworks to children.

Portfolio Activity 26.4

Range: Legal implications
Skills: Collect and record data

There are many other laws in the UK which can affect business, and which must be taken into consideration when starting up and running your business, and when planning business expansion. These include:

- Data Protection Act
- Insolvency Act
- Copyright Act
- Patents Act
- Business Names Act
- Partnership Act
- Companies Act
- Sunday Trading Act

Try to find out the various requirements of these laws. How might they affect a new or existing business?

UNIT EIGHT

CHAPTER 26

Portfolio Activity 26.5

Range: Legal and insurance implications
Skills: Read and respond to written material, Collect and record data

1. From the articles and picture, suggest why businesses need insurance.
2. Make a list of risks a business will need to insure against.
3. Try to confirm your list in Question 2 by talking to managers of an organization with which you are familiar, and/or by gathering information on cover provided by major insurance companies, such as the Prudential or Legal & General.

Unions win £335m damages total

Britain's trade unions in 1994 won £335m in legal damages for members who suffered injury or ill-health as a result of their work, the TUC says in a survey published today.

Unions provided at least 125,000 members with free legal advice and representation against their employers, insurance companies and government compensation schemes.

Financial Times 28.12.94

QE2 passengers start moves to sue Cunard

A group of passengers who travelled on the Queen Elizabeth 2's ill-fated Christmas cruise from Southampton to the US have taken the first step in their intended legal action against Cunard, the ship's owner.

A claim letter has been sent to Cunard's offices in New York and Southampton by New York lawyers Kreindler & Kreindler ahead of the filing of a class action suit, probably this week.

"Each passenger has suffered damages of from $50,000 to $100,000," the letter states. Passengers are demanding a full fare refund plus damages for mental stress, physical injuries and impaired health.

The list of grievances includes:
- Exposure to asbestos dust and other noxious fumes.
- Fear from unsafe practices, including "blocked passageways to the deck areas in case of a need to evacuate the vessel, or to reach deck areas in an emergency".
- Lack of proper water, heat and air conditioning as well as lack of agreed accommodation.

Financial Times 30.1.95

Insurance

Asset insurance

A large proportion of capital in a business will be invested in physical assets, such as buildings and machinery (see 22.1). **Asset insurance** aims to protect firms, through financial compensation, in the event of loss or damage to these assets. Because types of insurance and premiums vary, it is often worthwhile to seek the advice of a specialist **insurance broker**. Organizations will usually insure their assets against the following risks:

- **Fire:** damage to assets resulting from fire, flood, lightning, storms, riots, and vandalism

- **Theft:** loss of assets through theft. Many businesses pay an extra insurance premium to cover assets both when they are on the firm's

625

premises, and when they are authorized to be removed for use elsewhere (known as **all risks cover**). In such cases, it is essential to make sure that a sufficiently high insurance premium is paid to cover the full replacement value of the assets.

- **Disruption of trading:** this covers the firm against loss of earnings from sales, usually as a result of claims under fire insurance cover. Fire and disruption of trading insurance, taken together, will pay for damage to assets, and compensate the firm for any loss of earnings due to damaged assets.

Firms are not required by law to take out asset insurance. However, it would be very foolish for a firm not to insure against this kind of loss or damage, given the high proportion of business capital that assets consume, and the difficulty of replacing them without financial compensation. Although premiums can be high, the consequences of a fire or theft on a business can be devastating.

Public, product, and employers' liability

Firms are, however, required by law to insure for public, product, and employers' liability. Again, the costs are justified, because a successful claim for damages by a member of the public or employee could bankrupt a firm.

- **Public liability insurance:** firms must insure themselves against causing injury to a member of the public as a result of their business activities - for example, if a highly polished floor in a shop caused a customer to slip over and hurt themselves. Such insurance also covers loss or damage to customers' property. This is an important safeguard for the public and for firms, because without it, a claim from a member of the public for damages could easily bankrupt a business. The insurance is important for the public, because it guarantees them compensation if the firm is at fault.

- **Product liability insurance:** firms must also insure themselves against claims by members of the public for damages due to loss or injury caused by the use of their goods or services - for example, if an electrical product catches fire and causes damage, due to an internal fault. This insurance also covers a business for the legal costs which might be incurred in defending itself against claims made against it by a member of the public.

- **Employers' liability:** this provides protection against claims for compensation from employees involved in accidents at work.

Other types of business insurance

- **Bad debts** - caused by customers not paying sales invoices
- **Fidelity guarantee** - to protect against theft and dishonesty by staff
- **Legal insurance** - to protect the organization from prosecutions for breaches of the law such as restrictive trading practices, river pollution, or unfair dismissal
- **Motor** - third-party insurance is a minimum legal requirement to protect passengers and pedestrians from injuries sustained through motor vehicle accidents.

> **Key words**
>
> **Employment law** - legislation which defines the relationship between employers and their employees
>
> **Health and safety law** - designed to protect workers and members of the public from hazards at work
>
> **Environmental protection laws** - legislation to prevent harm or damage to the natural environment
>
> **Consumer protection law** - designed to protect consumers from misleading claims and anti-competitive behaviour by business organizations
>
> **Asset insurance** - insurance against damage to, or theft of, fixed assets such as machines and equipment, and disruption of trading
>
> **Insurance broker** - specialist adviser on insurance and insurance cover
>
> **Public liability insurance** - compulsory insurance designed to protect members of the public and their property against loss or injury directly or indirectly caused by a business
>
> **Product liability insurance** - compulsory insurance cover designed to protect consumers against loss or injury caused by the use of a firm's goods or services

Section 26.3 Business resources

Planning, organizing and managing resources

In order to create a successful business, it is necessary to obtain and manage human, physical, and financial **resources** in order to achieve business goals within specific timescales. The hardest tasks in setting up a new business are to:

- Correctly identify the quantity and quality of resources required
- Obtain the resources needed at a reasonable cost
- Manage the resources efficiently and effectively over a period of time, in order to achieve desired goals

This section considers some of the resource issues and questions which must be asked by entrepreneurs starting a new firm.

Portfolio Activity 26.6

Range: Resource requirements
Skills: Read and respond to written material

1. What kind of business costs are demonstrated in the article?
2. What has this entrepreneur done in order to minimize his costs?
3. Make a list of all other resources Charles Webb will require to run his business.

Charles Webb, proprietor of the Camden Bus estate agency in north London, is doing well selling flats to first-time buyers, Webb, 34, who set up the company seven years ago, was feeling flush and decided a company car was required. When your head office is a 1984 Route Traveller, what could be better for ferrying potential customers about than a black cab? The 'office' cost him £5,000 and his rent is £12,000 a year - about £15,000 less than conventional premises would cost in the same area. Rates too are less than half the going business rate for the area, at £1,500 a year - the initial calculation of £3,500 provoked complaints even from Webb's competitors in the area, demonstrating a rare streak of decency among estate agents. "We don't make heaps of money," admits Webb. "But we make a steady profit".

Daily Telegraph 13.8.94

Human resources

Labour, or human resources, provides the physical and mental effort necessary to run a business. To be successful, a business needs the right management and workforce. The first step an entrepreneur should take when setting up a new business is to ask: 'Do I have the necessary experience and expertise to run this business? If not, how will I be able to run it, and who else can help me?'

Sometimes the answer may prompt the entrepreneur to become an employee first in a similar kind of business, in order to 'learn the ropes'. It is clearly also very important to consider the kind of skills that would-be employees might need, and how staff with the right skills might be recruited. This might involve undertaking a survey of the employment market, in order to see what terms and conditions of employment staff are offered elsewhere.

Once the entrepreneur has identified whether or not the right management and staff can be found, it is necessary to look at the kinds of systems that will be needed to manage the human resources of the organization. As a business begins to grow and take on more staff, the owners will have to ensure that they can meet the requirements of employment legislation and can manage the deduction of income tax under the **PAYE** (pay-as-you-earn) system and the payment of National Insurance contributions (see 28.3). The costs of advertising, recruiting, and training staff must all be carefully estimated, because these will make up a significant proportion of the total costs of setting up a new business.

Physical resources

Physical resources include the premises that the business will operate from, the machinery and equipment it will use, and the stocks of materials and other consumables, such as paper, it will need to purchase. Choosing the right premises in the right location and at the right price is a key factor in the success of any new business, particularly a retail outlet.

Types of business premises can include:

- Shop
- Office
- Factory unit/Factory
- Home

An increasing number of people are running small businesses from home, because it is often the cheapest and most convenient option. Many home businesses will either manufacture products that do not require a large amount of machinery and other equipment, such as stuffed toys or dried flower arrangements, or will provide services such as child-minding, cleaning, photography, or painting and decorating.

Because working from home changes the use of the property, it may be necessary to obtain planning permission from the local authority before the business can be established. Certain mortgages or leases also contain conditions which limit the use of the property.

However, operating from home is not usually an option for people who start up new retail outlets or factories. Shops will need to be accessible by car and public transport, and near to other shops to pick up passing trade. A factory will need to house machinery and receive deliveries. The best location will, therefore, vary with the kind of business in question.

Choosing premises

When considering premises, traders should consider the following issues:

- Are there any plans which might change the character of the area in future, for example, new roads, office blocks, or changes to parking regulations?
- Are there any financial gains to be had by locating in the area? For example, is it a development area which qualifies for government financial assistance? (see 22.4).
- What local authority grants are available for new start-ups in the area?
- What is the availability of labour in the area?

Traders should also consider:

- The location of suppliers who will make regular deliveries to the business
- Ease of access, both for customers and for suppliers (e.g. locating in a restricted parking area may cause problems)
- Security of the premises, and how much it would cost to make them secure (wire grills, locks, alarms, etc.)
- Availability of facilities such as washbasins and toilets, and whether they meet health and safety requirements
- Storage facilities
- Floor area in relation to anticipated sales turnover and number of employees
- Fire exits, stairways, and lifts
- Space for expansion, car parking, etc.
- Costs of legal fees, rent, rates, refurbishment, and insurance
- Costs and other terms and conditions of the letting
- Local competition. For example, it would be unwise to set up yet another shoe shop in a small town already served by ten others.

Once suitable premises have been found, it is necessary to consider carefully the basis on which the property will be occupied. If the land and and property are **freehold,** the owner can buy them outright and use them as they wish (subject to planning and local authority regulations). However, freehold ownership is not the norm for new businesses, because of the heavy financial commitment involved in taking out a commercial mortgage, and also because commercial properties tend to be available only on a **leasehold** basis.

Leasehold land or property is rented from its owner for a set number of years. This is the cheaper option, and the basis on which most firms operate.

If premises have been used for different purposes in the past, the entrepreneur will need to ask the local authority if formal planning permission is required for a 'change of use'. For example, a scheme to establish a wine bar in premises previously used as a furniture store will certainly need formal permission from the council. Obtaining planning permission will involve the local council investigating the views of other traders and local residents and considering any objections they may have. Some businesses may also require a special licence from the local authority to operate. For example, restaurants, bars, tobacconists, and nurseries all require a local authority licence. The licence may be removed at any time, if the local authority has evidence that the trader is not operating to the required standards.

Advanced Business

Financial resources

When setting up a business, the owners need to consider:

- How much start-up capital they can raise from their own savings, or from family and friends
- The balance which needs to be raised from external sources (see 22.1).

Calculating a realistic figure for the amount of external finance to be raised when starting a business is one of the most difficult tasks in business planning. Entrepreneurs are often unrealistic and underestimate the amount of money they will need. However, lenders, such as banks, are unlikely to be sympathetic if the business later starts to struggle because of a lack of finance.

Portfolio Activity 26.7

Range: Resource requirements
Skills: Read and respond to written material

1. Why do you think the bank manager asked Frank to prepare a business plan before considering his application for a loan?
2. Make a list of the type of questions the bank manager might have wanted the business plan to answer.
3. Make a list of the fixed assets, such as machinery, that Frank might have needed to start up and run his small bakery.
4. What 'hidden costs' was Frank unprepared for?
5. How does an overdraft differ from a loan? What do overdrafts tend to be used for in a business?
6. Why do you think the bank withdrew its support for Frank?
7. What 'cautionary tales' does the article tell about the pitfalls of starting a new business and arranging external finance? Make a list of useful tips for would-be entrepreneurs.

Crumbling fortune

When Frank Evans needed a loan to set up a business, Barclays Bank couldn't wait to lend him the cash.

The 53-year-old former truck driver had been made redundant and saw the bakers shop in Bacup, Lancashire, as an ideal little earner. His confidence was even boosted by the bank's own enthusiasm. But when the business hit a rocky patch, all that changed, and Frank is now in danger of losing his home.

The nightmare started in 1990. Frank visited his local Barclays Bank manager who asked him for a business plan. Frank saw an accountant, a business plan was prepared, and the bank manager visited the shop. He then suggested that Frank re-mortgage his house - on which he owed £6,500 - for £28,000. This would provide the £10,000 Frank would need to refurbish the bakery.

He also insisted Frank take out a mortgage care insurance. For £20.12 per month, the policy would provide £449 monthly income in case of sickness or accident.

Frank then set to work renovating the shop. Three months later Frank opened for business. He was soon earning £600 per week.

But refurbishing the run-down shop to Health and Safety standards cost more than he bargained for. He took out a loan for £5,000 and his overdraft went up to £6,000. As the expenditure was essential, he had no reason to doubt that Barclays would support him.

He was wrong. Seven months after opening, the bank manager told him here would be no more money. Frank managed to carry on for two more years until disaster struck and he had to go into hospital for three operations. The bakery was put up for sale and he was offered £20,000.

This amount fell far short of the £30,000 Frank had spent on improvements - and his years of hard work. The buyer, who also banked with Barclays, soon learned that Frank had financial problems. 'After that he kept knocking the price down,' says Frank. 'In the end I got only £7,000!'

Daily Mirror 26.4.94

A new business will require finance for:

- The purchase of fixed assets such as buildings and machinery
- Working capital, or the day-to-day financing requirements of the firm

In considering which sources of finance to use, business owners will need to carefully consider:

- The **total amount** of money required
- **How long** they need to borrow money for
- The **relative costs** of different sources of finance

A variety of external organizations will consider providing finance to businesses on different terms over different periods of time. These include banks, building societies, finance companies, and venture capitalists (see 22.2). Hire purchase and leasing should also be considered as methods of financing equipment.

Time management

Good management requires that resources are used to achieve particular goals within specified periods of time. For example, capital borrowed from a bank must be converted into goods and services for sale, and back into cash for repayment of the loan, within a period acceptable to the bank. One of the key issues in time management is the prioritizing of tasks, so that the most urgent ones are identified and carried out first. For example, when converting business premises, planning permission needs to be obtained *before* builders are contracted to make the alterations. Although this may seem obvious, when many hundreds of tasks need to be completed, the planning and organizing of tasks in this way is essential.

Businesses use two key techniques to help them plan and manage tasks:

- **Critical path analysis (CPA)** is a technique used to break down a project into its component activities, place them in the right sequence, and then decide when to carry them out. The aim is to identify the minimum amount of time required to complete the entire project.

    For example, in marketing there are a series of stages, including market research, research and development (R&D), test marketing, pricing, distribution, promotion, selling and after-sales service, which can be further broken down into key steps and prioritized (see Unit 3). Some of these activities are **critical**, such that if they are delayed, the whole project will take longer than expected. For example, the lead time between ordering and taking delivery of materials is critical in production.

    The objective of CPA is to schedule tasks in a way that minimizes time and costs. A series of lines, each one representing an activity, can be drawn in the form of a network diagram, or **PERT** chart **(Program Evaluation and Review Technique)**. Adding the time each activity is expected to take allows a business to identify the **critical path** of the project - that is, the minimum time needed to complete it.

    Figure 26.2 shows a PERT chart for a project to install new computer equipment in an office. It shows that no activity in the network can be started until all preceding activities have been completed. To complete all the individual tasks would take 31 days. But because some tasks can be carried out at the same time, the whole project could be completed in 20 days. A delay in any one of the activities on the critical path will delay the whole project.

▼ *Figure 26.2: A PERT chart for installing new computer equipment*

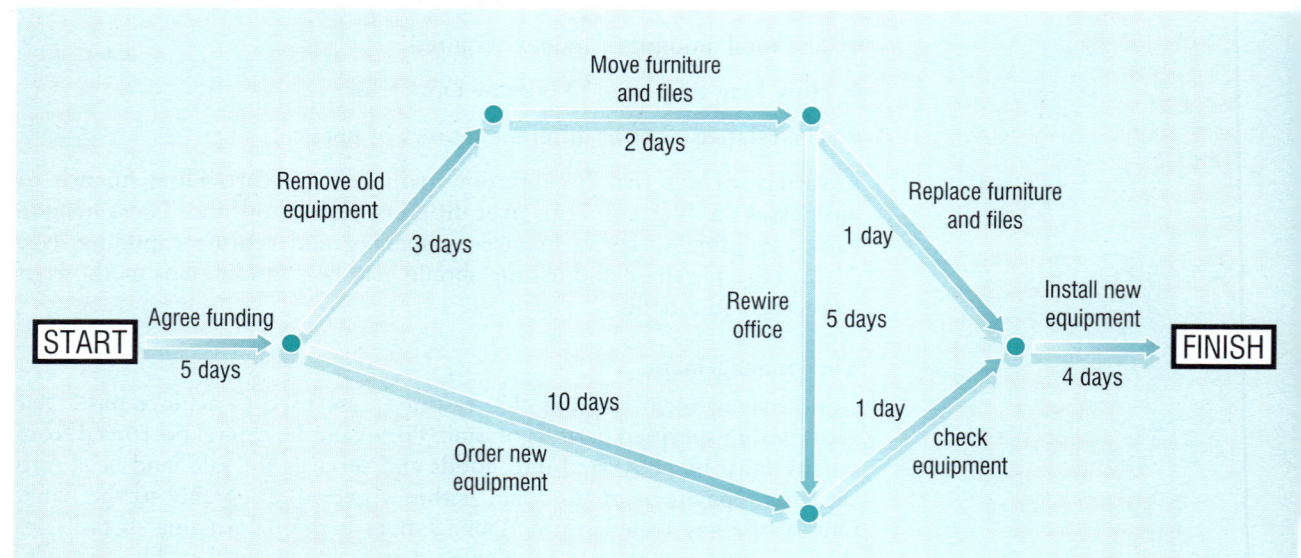

- A **GANNT chart** is simply a horizontal bar chart, each bar representing a different activity. The vertical axis records the different activities which need to be undertaken, and the horizontal axis records time. The length of each bar is determined by the amount of time needed to complete an activity. Bars can also be shaded to show how much work has been completed under each task (see Figure 26.3).

▼ *Figure 26.3: A GANNT chart for installing new computer equipment*

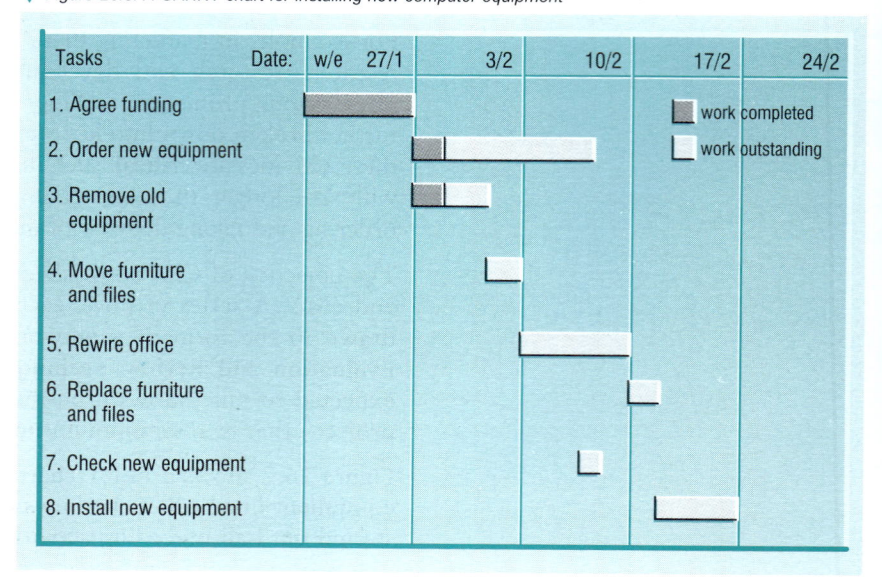

To prepare a GANNT chart, a manager will list all the activities necessary to complete a project, and then estimate the time required for each one. Progress is then checked against the chart. If the project is ahead of schedule, the manager may decide to move some employees to another project. If the project is behind schedule, extra labour may be required to finish it on time.

Portfolio Activity 26.8

Range: Timescales
Skills: Tackle problems

A friend of yours knits jumpers with personalized designs. Business is good, but her knitting machine is slow and out of date. She has decided to replace it with new computerized equipment. At the same time, she wants to relocate her equipment and stores from her spare bedroom to a purpose-built extension at the back of her house. She has listed the following tasks she will need to complete, together with estimates of how long they will take to complete, as follows:

- Plan equipment needed (1 day)
- Place order for equipment (10 days to deliver)
- Remove old equipment (1 day)
- Remove furniture and storage cupboards from bedroom (1 day)
- Wire and fit new plug points in extension (3 days)
- Decorate extension (5 days)
- Order new stock of wools and cotton (1 day)
- Delivery of materials ordered (5 days)
- Install furniture and storage cupboards in extension (2 days)
- Set up new equipment in extension (1 day)

Your friend has asked you to:

1. Calculate the critical path for her project
2. Produce a PERT chart and a GANNT chart to illustrate the timing and sequencing of the tasks she needs to complete.

Key words

Freehold property - property owned outright by the business

Leasehold property - property rented for a specified period from its owner

Critical Path Analysis (CPA) - diagrammatic technique used to plan and analyse the scheduling of activities in business projects

GANNT chart - type of bar chart used to assist in the planning of timings and sequencing of activities in business projects

Section 26.4 Potential support for a business plan

Why do businesses need support?

The main aims of a business plan are to raise finance from sources external to the business, such as banks, and to provide a means of monitoring and evaluating the progress of the business over time by comparing outturn to plans. Although a wide range of people may expect to see a business plan, would-be entrepreneurs are not expected to produce the business plan single-handed. A wide range of help and advice is available.

When writing a business plan for a new venture, the following kinds of expertise will be needed:

- **Financial:** to help construct a cashflow forecast, open a balance sheet and profit and loss statement (see 24.2–24.3), and advise on VAT, National Insurance, and income tax (see 28.3)

- **Legal:** to assist in registering a company and drawing up contracts with suppliers, customers, and staff
- **Human resources:** to advise on employment law, advertising, recruitment, selection, and training (see 12.1)
- **Production:** to help set up, run and manage production facilities, develop products, select suppliers, machinery, and premises, and negotiate contracts
- **Sales and marketing:** to organize market research, create and implement a sales and marketing plan, determine product promotion, distribution, and selling strategies, sales targets and after-sales service (see 8.3)
- **Management:** to assist in setting realistic and achievable deadlines and targets for parts of the business plan. This kind of experience is also needed in order to advise on establishing monitoring and review systems for the business.
- **IT:** increasingly firms are making use of new technology to help with administration, communications, and information processing (see 7.3). Buying and installing IT will require some technical knowledge.

For an existing business considering expansion into a new venture, advice on the above areas is likely to be available from staff already working in the accounts, administration, human resources, production, and sales and marketing departments. But for those businesses newly starting up, advice and support from a variety of external sources will be required. Existing organizations can also take advantage of this support.

External sources of business support

A wide range of organizations and individuals can provide advice to business start-ups:

- **Accountants** will be able to assist with the creation of cashflow forecasts and initial accounts, as well as with setting up accounting systems in the new firm.
- **Banks** now all have special business start-up advisers at their local branches, who will offer help, particularly on finance, or suggest other sources of advice.
- **Independent financial advisers** can investigate and advise on the best sources of business finance and the costs involved, but will charge for this service.
- **Solicitors** can advise on all legal matters relating to the purchase of leases or freeholds, registration of companies or partnerships, and contracts.
- **'Business Angels'** are individuals and organizations willing to invest money in small businesses in return for a share of the profits. The Natwest Bank has set up a national register to bring together 'angels' and small businesses to discuss investment opportunities.
- **Local authorities** can offer advice and information to businesses in their area to help with marketing, locating premises, training, and raising finance.

▲ *Business angels?*

The Kent TEC Business Start-Up scheme is called 'Selfstart'

- **Local Enterprise Agencies** offer a 'one-stop shop', providing advice and counselling on all aspects of business start-up, often at little or no charge. There is a network of around 400 LEAs in the UK.

- **Training and Enterprise Councils (TECs)** and **Local Enterprise Companies (LECs)** can assist local business by providing information, advice, counselling, and training services. Through the **Business Start-Up Scheme**, they are also able to provide financial assistance to unemployed people who want to start up new businesses. In 1993, payments ranged from £20 to £90 per week, spread over periods between 26 and 66 weeks. Around 80 TECs operate in England and Wales, and 22 LECs in Scotland.

- **Chambers of Commerce** are run by local employers, and can be a good source of advice on practical matters. They will also be able to point out all of the available sources of advice to business start-ups.

- The **Confederation of British Industry (CBI)** can provide support and advice to local businesses through a number of regional offices. The CBI aims to represent a united voice for its membership, which is drawn from private-sector enterprises, major public-sector employers, some employer and trade associations, and Chambers of Commerce.

- **Business in the Community (BITC)** works with some 450 of its member companies to help raise business awareness of community issues and encourage partnerships between the public, private, and voluntary sectors. This includes sharing resources, including expertise and training, with small local businesses.

- **ACAS (Advisory, Conciliation and Arbitration Service)** offers free advice on employment issues (see 12.4)

- The **Prince's Youth Business Trust** helps 18- to 29-year-olds who are out of work or finding it hard to get started, by backing them with cash. The Trust gives grants of up to £1,500 to individuals, or £3,000 for groups setting up in business, and up to £5,000 for expanding businesses.

- **Other self-employed people and local firms** may often be willing to share their experiences and advice on sources of help which they found useful.

- The **Department for Trade and Industry (DTi)** can provide practical help and guidance through its Enterprise Initiative. This includes:

  - financial assistance to help small firms obtain specialist advice on marketing, design, business planning, management information systems, and other topics

  - practical guidance on topics such as new product development through their 'Managing in the 90s' programme

- regional selective assistance to firms in development areas (see 22.4)
- assistance for innovation, including grants towards collaborative research projects, and access to existing technology through case studies and information
- access to relevant overseas information and advice to exporters

- The **Department of the Environment (DoE)** can provide advice on planning issues and reducing energy costs
- A host of specialist organizations and consultants exist to provide advice on every aspect of running a business from research and development to production and marketing, communications systems and management structure. However, this advice may be expensive.

Portfolio Activity 26.9

Range: Potential support
Skills: Collect and record data, Present information

1. Choose three organizations from the above list of organizations offering support to new businesses. Compare in detail the assistance each organization is able and willing to give, and investigate whether there are any costs involved.

2. Use this and any other information you can collect to produce a leaflet advising on sources of help available to new businesses. Prepare your leaflet on a computer word processor or desk top publishing package.

Further reading

Foster, T: *101 Great Mission Statements* (Kogan Page 1994)

Ingham, C: *101 Ways to Start Your Own Business* (Kogan Page 1994)

Singleton, S: *You and the Law* (Kogan Page 1994)

Some Review Questions

1. What is a business plan? Give three reasons why a person wishing to start up a new business will need to complete one.

2. Outline three types of insurance a new business is likely to need.

3. Suggest the likely resource requirements of a new small business producing picture frames.

4. What is a 'mission statement'?

5. Suggest how an entrepreneur could evaluate a new business idea.

6. What is meant by 'an expanding market'? Suggest two markets that are currently expanding.

7. a. Explain why a business must have an understanding of current legislation concerning employment and health and safety.

b. What other laws are likely to affect the running of a small business?

8. A small retail business has just moved into new premises to sell computer games. It intends to decorate and refurbish the shop to install new counters, shelving, carpets, and TV monitors, so that customers can try out the games at different games consoles. Advise the owners on how they can plan and schedule the work required, using Critical Path Analysis and GANNT charts.

9. List the likely overheads involved in running a small hairdressers.

10. Why do small businesses need external support? Suggest three sources of support for small businesses.

(assessment assignment)

Advanced Business

Assessment Assignment

Range: Purposes of a business plan
Business objectives
Supporting information
Legal and insurance implications
Resource requirements
Timescales
Potential support

Skills: **Communications**
Take part in discussions
Produce written materials
Use images
Application of Number
Collect and record data
Information Technology
Process information

Unit 8 requires you to prepare and produce a business plan for a business idea of your own, whether you intend to start up the business or not.

The Assignment details are given at the end of Chapter 28. However, in preparation, you are now required to undertake the following tasks, either on your own or as part of a group:

chapter 27

Tasks

1. Think up a business idea (and possible alternatives). You can produce a good or service. Develop ideas for your product (or shop) design, including features, if appropriate, such as size, shape, colours, quality, incorporated technology, taste, smell, packaging, labelling, logos, level of service, and business trading name.

2. Evaluate your business idea(s) in terms of:
- Market potential for the good or service
- Level and strength of demand for the product
- Number of potential customers
- Likelihood of repeat trade
- Competition

The following sources of information may be useful:
- Face-to-face interviews with consumers, using questionnaires
- Government statistical publications
- Newspapers and magazines
- Surveys of local businesses

3. Investigate the materials you will need to make your product, and possible methods of production. For example, what ingredients would you need to produce chocolate cakes? Should you produce them individually or in large batches? Materials will also be important for many services, but methods of production will tend to be 'customized'.

4. Identify potential sources of support for your business idea.

5. Gather information on:
- Your resource requirements, including availability of suitable premises, suppliers of materials, suitable labour
- Legal and insurance requirements
- Start-up costs
- Realistic timescales in which to acquire resources and start your business idea
- Potential sources of external finance

Useful additional information sources to those you identified in Task 3 will include commercial property agencies, other business organizations, and Jobcentres.

6. Investigate suitable methods and costs of promoting your new business and product to customers, including advertising and publicity.

7. Draw up an action plan identifying the actions you need to take in order to finalize your business plan, within an appropriate timescale.

UNIT EIGHT

CHAPTER 27

chapter 27
How to Prepare and Produce a Business Plan

This chapter examines how to prepare and complete a business plan for a single product or service.

Key ideas

A **business plan** should contain the following five sections:

(1) A section outlining the **business objectives** and the timescale for achieving them. Objectives will include supplying a good or service that consumers want, achieving sales volume or sales value, building market share, breaking even, and eventually making a profit.

(2) A **marketing plan** which sets out how an organization intends to market its goods or services, focusing on pricing, promotion, distribution, selling, after sales care and the timing of the marketing plan.

(3) For an organization selling a manufactured product, the business plan should contain a **production plan**. This should set out details of design, product development, premises, machinery, materials to be used, labour requirements, quality assurance and timescales.

(4) The **resource requirements** of the business, in terms of the human, financial, physical and time resources required.

(5) A **financial plan** with a cashflow forecast, start-up balance sheet, and profit and loss statement, as well plans for regular monitoring and review of the major accounts.

The business plan can be used to monitor the performance of the business once in operation, to see how well it meets its objectives.

639

Section 27.1 Planning business objectives and timescales

The business plan

A new business that has considered in some detail its business idea and market potential, and has worked out plans that will help it achieve set objectives, will stand a better chance of survival than a business that has not. One in four new businesses fail in their first few years of operation. Drawing up a business plan can significantly improve the chances of survival.

In Chapter 26 we learned that the function of a business plan is to:

- Set business objectives and targets
- Identify resource requirements of the new business venture
- Support applications for finance
- Monitor business performance

The following table outlines the typical contents of a business plan, as suggested by a large firm of accountants.

Business plan checklist

Business	Description of the business
	Business objectives
	Ownership
	Key personnel
Management	Managers
	Missing skills, and how these will be provided
Products	Description of products
	Why products are better or different
Marketing	Major customers
	Size of market
	Predicted market share
	Major competitors
	Market strategy
	Pricing
	Methods of sale
	Average size of orders
	Advertising methods and costs
Production plan	Details of product design and development
	Raw materials needed and availability
	Suppliers
	Number of employees
	Skills required
	Training needed
	Premises location
	Equipment required and prices
	Lead times in delivery
Financial Plan	Cashflow forecast
	Projected balance sheet
	Projected profit and loss statement
	Mechanisms for monitoring and review of accounting records

Ernst & Whinney: 'Starting Your Own Business'

Portfolio Activity 27.1

Range: Business objectives
Skills: Take part in discussions, Produce written materials

Survey any business managers that you know, either in your own school or college, or in firms that you have attended for work experience. Identify their current business objectives, and find out how and why these have changed over time. Produce a brief report on the kinds of objectives that different kinds of firms have, and why these may change and develop over time.

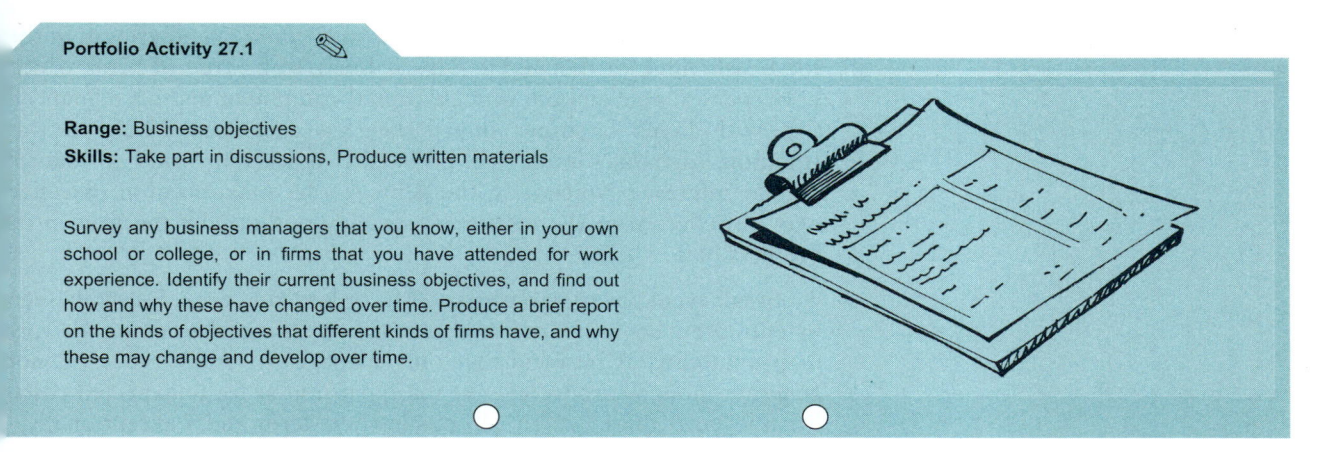

Business objectives

Producing a business plan is an important means of clarifying businesses objectives. The plan should outline a range of objectives to be achieved over a period of time. A firm cannot hope to make a profit immediately, but is likely to set it as a long-term objective. In the short run, establishing the product and building sales are by far the most important objectives.

Objectives

Short term	Medium term	Long term
Achieve sales volume →		
	Achieve sales value →	
	Break even →	
		Build market share →
		Make a profit →

- **To supply a good or service:** the first aim of any business that wants to be a success must be to produce a good or service that people either need or want. A business that aims to make a profit will stand no chance of doing so if people are not willing to buy their product.

- **To achieve sales volume:** if a business can supply the right product in the right place at the right time and at the right price, it has a good chance of making a sale. Setting price low initially and advertising will help to generate sales for a new product. However, selling at a low price at first is unlikely to make the business very profitable. When a business is new and output is low, the cost per unit of production is high, because fixed costs, such as rents, rates, and insurance, are spread over a small output. This usually leads to high prices in order to cover costs, and so makes the firm uncompetitive.

A business may aim to achieve a higher level of output in order to expand production, and so achieve **economies of scale** (see 20.2). As output and sales rise, fixed costs are spread more evenly over a larger number of units, and so cost per unit falls. Therefore, a certain target sales volume may be a vital objective, enabling a firm to achieve a low enough level of costs to be competitive in the marketplace.

- **To achieve sales value:** some businesses may aim for high growth in the total cash value of their sales. This is likely to be true of firms which have spent a large amount on new capital equipment and have financed this with loans or other interest-bearing debt (see 22.2). In this situation, high sales value will be needed quickly in order to finance regular interest payments on the debt. A sales maximization objective may be reflected in the marketing strategy outlined by the firm in its business plan.

- **To break even:** covering business costs, or breaking even, is usually seen by entrepreneurs as an intermediate target to be reached along the way to profitability. A business that only manages to break even will not generate enough surplus revenue for expansion or for unexpected costs. Break-even is therefore an acceptable short-term and - exceptionally - medium-term goal, but is not a sufficient target for a profit-seeking business in the long term. Non-profit-making organizations, such as charities, will always plan to break even and not to spend more than they generate in donations and other incomes.

- **To achieve market share:** once a product is established, a firm's medium-term objective may be to expand market share at the expense of rival organizations. In order to achieve a reasonable share of total sales in a market, a business must adopt a marketing mix geared for growth, including product, pricing, distribution, and promotion strategies (see 8.3). A business plan identifying this objective will need to indicate clearly how the firm would cope with competitors' responses.

- **Making a profit:** profit is the main motive for production in most private-sector firms. However, the importance of making a profit depends upon the stage an organization has reached in its development. Other objectives, including becoming established in the market, or removing competitors, may be more important in the short term. Profit is likely to be a long-term objective.

Portfolio Activity 27.2

Range: Business objectives, Marketing plan
Skills: Read and respond to written material

Read the article on page 643

1. What motives do you think Penguin had in discounting its books in response to the entry of Wordsworth into the discounted book market?

2. What advantages might Wordsworth have in the sales battle with Penguin, even though it is smaller than Penguin?

3. If Wordsworth had anticipated that Penguin and other large competitors might react in this way, what plans could they have made to counteract their competitors' actions?

The Classic Rivals - Penguin to Move in on £1 Novels

One of Britain's biggest publishers is launching a sales war with novels at £1 each.

The books will be paperbacks of literary classics. The move by Penguin follows soaring sales of Wordsworth Classics, launched 18 months ago by Michael Trayler. Wordsworth are also charging £1 a book and will make a £1.5 million profit this year after selling 18 million copies worldwide.

Their list of 120 favourites includes the works of Dickens, Jane Austen, and the Brontë sisters. Now Penguin has decided to hit back by bringing out 12 classics each month, including Jane Austen's Emma, Conrad's Lord Jim, Great Expectations by Dickens and Defoe's Robinson Crusoe.

A spokesman said: "Wordsworth has done a marvellous job, establishing that there is a market for cut-price classics. We want to be in that market too."

The £1-a-time titles are out of copyright and therefore incur no royalties. Mr Trayler said "We identified people who enjoy reading classics but who could not find them at affordable prices. Imitation is the sincerest form of flattery. We are a young company and Penguin are huge, but we are not frightened. We have made a good start and we are small and adaptable."

Daily Mail 10.2.94

Section 27.2

The marketing plan

Choosing the right mix

The marketing section of a business plan should aim to outline how the business intends to price, promote, distribute, and sell the product - the **marketing mix** (see 8.3).

Having a good product, with clever design, is not enough in itself to sell a product. In order to make sales, the product must be carefully targeted at those consumers who are likely to buy. This targeting requires that the product is designed to appeal, not just in its physical design, but also in its price, promotion, packaging, and distribution.

All aspects of a business are concerned with marketing, because everything a business does has some impact on sales, and ultimately profits. Marketing is a total approach to business which focuses on the needs of customers, from something as simple as the trading name of the business, the design of stationery, the helpfulness and knowledge of sales staff, to the price and quality of the product itself.

The marketing section of the business plan is very important, not just in encouraging business managers to organize their thoughts about how to achieve sales, but also in persuading potential lenders that the business will work. It should contain a realistic sales target (in terms of both volume and value) and details of how the marketing mix will be used to achieve it.

Advanced Business

Your business market

This section provides an overview of some of the important marketing questions you will need to address in your business plan.

1. Is the market declining/static/increasing, and why?

   _____
   _____
   _____

2. Who are your major competitors?

   _____
   _____
   _____

3. What features of their products/services enable them to compete successfully with you?

   _____
   _____
   _____

4. What are your major strengths and those of your products/services that make you competitive in your business market?

   _____
   _____
   _____

5. What level of sales do you anticipate achieving?

   In the next 6 months £

   In the following 6 months £

6. What makes you certain of achieving these levels of sales?

   _____
   _____
   _____

7. What methods do you intend using to market and sell your products/services (e.g. advertising, direct mailing, trade fairs)?

	Cost (estimates)
_____	£ _____
_____	£ _____
_____	£ _____
_____	£ _____
_____	£ _____

   Midland Bank, Credo - Planning The Business Plan

What's in a name?

You may choose to name your business after your own name. However, from a promotional point of view, it may be better to choose a trading name that reflects the product you are selling, or one that suggests a particular feature of the business, such as quality, speed of service, or value for money. For example, consider the following business names: General Motors; Richer Sounds; Prontaprint; Kwik Save. What do they tell you about these businesses?

Portfolio Activity 27.3

Range: Marketing plan
Skills: Collect and record data

Survey the trading names of businesses in your local area, by visiting your town centre and/or looking in your local business phone directory.

Pick some business names, including those not well known to you.

What do they tell you about the business, the product they sell, or the type of customer services they provide?

Now choose a business name for your own business idea. Conduct some market research to see if the name you have chosen is effective and will create the right image for your business.

Product

Choosing the right product is vitally important. Unless your product is unique and you can create a want for it through advertising, it is important to produce a product for which the market is expanding. This will require research (see 9.1).

The appearance of a product, in terms of size, shape, colour, texture, taste, smell, labelling, brand image, and incorporated technology, will all influence the buying decision of the consumer.

Because consumers' desires are forever changing, it is important for a business to keep researching the market and adapting products accordingly. Product development - strategies, costs, and resources involved - is normally considered within a **production plan** (see 27.3).

▼ *Product features: consumers who buy watches are not just buying something from which to tell the time.*

Organizations will often use **best practice benchmarking** in product development. This involves observing the products and processes of rival companies, and then improving on them (see 15.2).

Methods of benchmarking can include taking apart rival products to see how they were made, analysing published data (for example, in company reports), or simply talking to suppliers, distributors, and customers.

Advanced Business

> **Value analysis**
>
> This is an attempt by business to ensure that the customer receives value for money from a good or service. All elements of the marketing mix are examined to eliminate unnecessary or wasteful effort, and expenditures checked in order to keep costs as low as possible without compromising product quality and reliability.

▼ *Getting the price right*

Pricing

The price at which a product will sell will ultimately be determined by the forces of consumer demand and producer supply (see 1.4). If price is set too high, the product will not sell. If set too low, there will be an excess of demand which will force the firm to raise price, at least until they can expand output to meet the demand.

Choosing the right price is, therefore, a key part of the marketing mix (see 21.1). But this does not mean that the good or service has to be cheap in order to attract customers. Consumers may be suspicious of a low price because it may suggest poor quality. Whatever price is charged should be consistent with all of the other marketing messages given by the marketing mix. For example, if the promotion, advertising, packaging, and retail outlets through which the product is distributed all suggest high quality, then the price should be correspondingly high.

Costs will also need to be taken into account in the pricing decision. If price fails to cover the cost of production, the firm will make a loss (see 21.2).

In the long term, the best price for a product is one that will maximize profits by creating the best combination of sales volume, price, and costs. However, in the short term, the goals for pricing might be different. For example, price may be set low initially in order to build the business by gaining sales.

In practice, many small businesses take a lead from other businesses, by charging a similar price to that of their rivals.

Promotion

A good product will not sell, even if the price is right, if customers do not know it exists. Ensuring that the market knows about the firm's products is known as **product promotion** (see 10.3).

The key steps in efficient product promotion are as follows:

- Tell potential customers of the existence of the firm and/or its products
- Get customers to visit the firm and/or to see the products
- Encourage customers to buy
- Persuade customers to make a repeat purchase in future.

Effective promotion is about turning the target market into loyal and satisfied customers. A business outlining its promotional strategy for its business plan will therefore need to ask the following kinds of questions:

- **What is the promotion seeking to achieve?** The objectives of a promotion could be simply to ensure that customers know of the existence of a new business, or to persuade them to ask for further information, or to visit the business, or to place an order, and to continue to make repeat orders.

UNIT EIGHT

CHAPTER 27

Some promotional messages

HER SOUNDS VIRGINS!
Ever been to a Richer Sounds before? - No, then you're a Richer Sounds Virgin!". If it's your 1st visit to one of our stores simply announce it's your first time and you'll get your free gift!

Guinness Book of Records
THE WORLD'S BUSIEST RETAILER 1991, 92, 93 & 94 EDITIONS
Ambition of Mr Richer's fulfilled. Sandwiched between General Motors, biggest company in the world with sales of $123.8 billion for 1991 and the most profitable corporation in history is your favourite hi-fi store:

Sales per unit area The record for the greatest sales based on square footage of selling space is held by Richer Sounds plc, the hi-fi retail chain, with sales at their busiest outlet at London Bridge Walk reaching £17 553 per square foot.

Without your support we'd never have done it. Thanks
Copyright © Guinness Publishing Ltd 1993.

You'll be singing in the rain!
All customers purchasing hi-fi when it's raining, if you need an umbrella, just ask and you'll receive an attractive automatic one completely free!

- **What kind of promotional message will achieve the objectives?** To create a persuasive message, a business needs to identify what is different or special about the product or business - that is, its **unique selling point**. If there is little about the product which is different, the owners need to ask what can be portrayed through advertising and promotions as being different - for example, quality, after-sales care, free gifts, helpful sales staff, etc. In this way, promotion creates a brand image in the mind of the consumer.

SALE! SALE! SALE! SALE!
HALF PRICE NAKAMICHI CD SCOOP
SALE PRICE **£249**
BRAND NEW BOXED
NAKAMICHI MB3 Bringing together 7 disc convenience and Nakamichi's reputation for outstanding build and sound quality - and at half price!! We must be mad!! WERE £499.95 Stocks Ltd.

- **What media will be used?** A wide variety of media can be used to communicate the firm's promotional message. These may vary from promotions on free carrier bags, to primetime television advertising. The choice of promotional medium is as important as the promotional message, because if the right message is sent out using the wrong media, the target market will not hear it, and the promotion will fail.

Clearly, the right media is not just the one which reaches the target market: the media also has to be affordable. Many small businesses use *Yellow Pages*, local newspaper advertising, specialist magazines and leaflets, as low-cost ways of reaching their target market.

Promotional media
Television (including satellite and cable)
National and local press
Radio
Cinema and video films
Posters and leaflets
Direct mailshots
Exhibitions
(see 10.3)

A Meat-eoric Success:
Salami Man Sells An Extra 95 Tonnes

HE'S a walking, talking sausage who eats his own arms and has a wicked sense of humour - and he's proving that if you make the customers laugh, they are more likely to buy your product.

This unlikely character has increased sales of Pepperami, the savoury sausage snack, by 33% in six months, which converts into an extra 95 tonnes of Pepperami sold.

Daily Mirror 26.10.94

Distribution

Distribution is about where and how the product is sold (see 11.2).

In buying a product, consumers consider its place and method of sale along with the features of the product itself. For example, people buying bread and milk late on a Sunday evening or Bank holiday from a local 'corner shop' will often pay up to double the price they would pay at a supermarket on a weekday. This is simply because of the convenience of being able to shop late at night, when other stores are closed. In other words, the benefits of timing and ease of access to the local store are being sold along with the bread and milk.

A plan for distribution may be created by asking the following questions:

- **Who will buy the product or service?** The aim here is to identify a target market segment. This will help identify the kinds of outlet where the product should be distributed in order to reach the target market.

- **Why will customers buy?** The answer to this will reveal the package of features and benefits that customers will look for. If, for example, it includes 'good after-sales service,' the product might need to be distributed through established department stores and high street shops. If not, then mail order or distribution through discount chains might be appropriate.

Distribution will also involve a consideration of the cost, speed, and security of physically transporting products by road, rail, sea, or air. Transport costs can often be a significant element in the total costs of a business.

Selling methods

The organization of sales and sales staff requires careful planning. Sales staff need to be carefully trained in order to acquaint them with the features of the product and how it can be favourably compared to competitors' products. The selling section of the marketing plan may aim to target particular types of customer, by choosing retail outlets in particular localities or by targeting mailshots at certain customer groups. The sales section of the plan should make it clear how the business will:

- Influence customers' attitudes towards the product
- Make people desire the product
- Convince customers that buying the good is the right decision

Selling methods might include:

- Visiting customers
- 'Cold calling' by telephone or doorstep calls
- Mailshots
- Telesales
- Trade magazines and trade fairs
- Contacting wholesalers
- Advertising in business directories and *Yellow Pages*

- Posters and leaflet distribution
- Local and national radio advertising
- Free gifts and samples
- Cards in shop windows
- Catalogues and mail order
- Home demonstrations and sales parties in homes

Preparing a marketing budget

A good marketing plan will estimate the costs of the proposed marketing strategy, and express this in a **budget**.

A budget will enable the entrepreneur to evaluate whether or not the marketing plans are realistic. Once costed, the marketing plans could prove to be too expensive and so have to be scaled down; alternatively, the cost could be very modest and so allow some extra marketing effort. The budget will also provide a means by which the entrepreneur can monitor and control the operation of the marketing plan in practice, by carefully comparing actual marketing expenditure to planned expenditure.

The budget should estimate the amount likely to be spent on each aspect of the marketing plan. This will include market research, all types of advertising, promotions, distribution, and selling. The costs of many of these items can be estimated accurately. For example, press and leaflet advertising can be costed simply by contacting local newspapers and printers. Other items, such as the amount to be spent on selling expenses (e.g. expense accounts and training for sales staff), cannot be costed by contacting outside agencies, but will have to be estimated by business managers.

A number of different methods are used by firms in order to allocate funds to these kind of subjective budget headings. Methods can be based on:

- A fixed percentage of the next year's estimated sales value
- A fixed percentage of this year's sales value
- Estimates of what competitors spend
- Estimates of how much extra revenue an activity will generate

The marketing budget should also indicate how the planned expenditure will be phased across the year, usually using a monthly breakdown. The budget should be presented in a similar format to other kinds of operating budgets (see 25.2).

Timing and scheduling the marketing plan

In order to ensure that the marketing plan is successful, it is necessary to carefully work out priorities, and then schedule the timing of activities, so that the key marketing activities are carried out in the correct sequence. For example, the product must be designed, packaged, and priced *before* sales staff can be trained. Shop-counter promotions created to encourage consumers to sample the product can only take place once the product has been distributed - and so on.

Advanced Business

Techniques such as the GANNT chart and Critical Path Analysis (CPA) ca assist with the timing and scheduling of marketing activities (See 26.3).

How customers' needs have changed

1992
1. Convenience of location
2. Wide choice
3. Good quality
4. Good value
5. Easy parking

1994
1. Convenience of location
2. Good value
3. Wide choice
4. Good quality
5. Easy parking

British Shopping Trend Surveys/Dr Robert East, Kingston University

Key words

Marketing mix - the elements of a firm's marketing strategy designed to meet consumer wants and generate sales. The four main elements are: product, price, place, and promotion.

Marketing plan - sets out how an organization will use the marketing mix to achieve its business objectives

Marketing budget - a forward plan of costed marketing activities

Unique selling points - features of a product or business that differentiate it from its rivals

Best practice benchmarking - observing the products and processes of rival companies in order to learn new and better ways of producing

Section 27.3 The production plan

What is a production plan?

The aim of the production plan is to organize premises, machinery, labour, and raw materials efficiently, so that the firm can produce the goods required by customers in the right quantities and at the right time. The production plan will outline the action to be taken both immediately and in the medium-to-long term.

Portfolio Activity 27.4

Range: Production plan
Skills: Read and respond to written material

Using the article on page 651:

1. What evidence is there to suggest that many British manufactured goods are poorly designed? Why is product quality important?

2. Why does the article suggest that planning for the introduction of new products is needed now, more than ever?

3. What kinds of strategies might be adopted by a new business in order to help get its product launch right?

UNIT EIGHT

CHAPTER 27

Time for an Action Plan

The successful introduction of new products is one of the keys to profitable manufacturing, but, for many UK manufacturers, improving the process is still in its infancy.

This is one of the findings of an updated edition of *Manufacturing into the Late 1990s*, which has been prepared by the Department of Trade and Industry by Tony Roberts and Mark Smalley at PA Consulting group.

"Product design often takes years for many engineering-type products," he says. The complexity of new product introduction for many engineering products means it is less well understood than other industrial processes. It involves highly skilled people who are accustomed to working at their own pace.

The study gives advice to managers on how to improve their manufacturing responses to the challenges in the 1990s. It identifies four themes:

- Higher customer expectations. "Customer power continues to grow and to compete effectively you must satisfy existing and new customers profitably."
- Greater business complexity. Multi-technologies in the product and the manufacturing process, a wider product range, customization, and market niches.
- More uncertainty, stemming from a wider range of customers, shorter product lifecycles and more competition. This means greater uncertainty about the life of products and the investment decisions associated with them.
- Growing competitive and legislative pressure, such as that concerned with health and safety and product liability.

Because of these pressures successful new product introduction is seen as so important. The key ways to achieve this include getting designers close to customers, using multi-discipline teams with clear objectives about delivering their product on time, and having the design effort managed by a product director with clear authority to deliver.

Planning should also include the design of better factories, including flexible manufacturing processes with focused units which can handle variations in type of production for production runs of short lifecycle.

Roberts is encouraged by what has been happening in manufacturing. "There is a much greater awareness of the need for a strategy - something that makes sense of all of the elements of design and manufacture to produce a competitive and profitable business," he says.

Financial Times 3.9.93

A business may plan to vary the priorities for its product and production processes over time. The table below illustrates how this might be achieved.

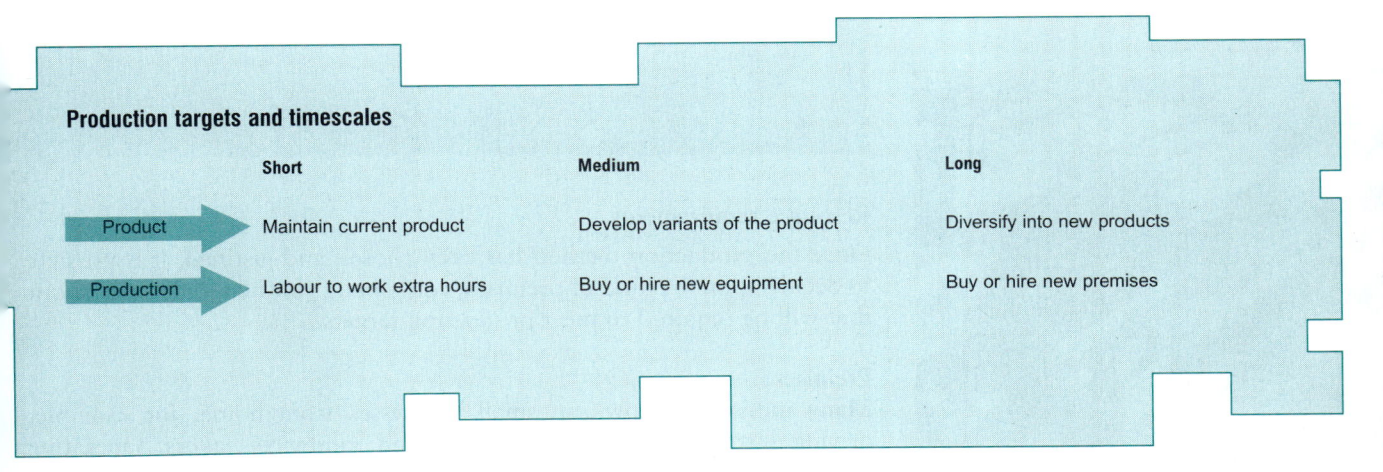

Production targets and timescales

	Short	Medium	Long
Product	Maintain current product	Develop variants of the product	Diversify into new products
Production	Labour to work extra hours	Buy or hire new equipment	Buy or hire new premises

Types of production

The way in which production is organized will depend upon the method of production adopted by the business. Three possible methods are:

- **Job production:** this method is used for producing single or one-off orders, where each order is custom built. For example, personal services, such as hairdressing, painting and decorating, arranging flowers for weddings, are all examples of job production.

▼ Job production

▼ Flow production

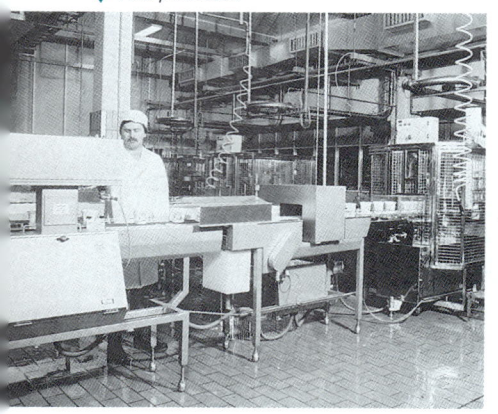

▼ Batch production

- **Flow production**: this method involves the manufacture of a product in a continuously moving process. Flow production is used to mass-produce identical products for huge national or international markets.
- **Batch production**: this method is used for producing a limited number of identical products to meet a specific order, for example, 1,000 calling cards, 50,000 pre-recorded video cassettes of a particular film, or runs of daily newspapers.

The precise method of production chosen will clearly depend on the answers to a number of questions:

- **What is the nature of the product?** For example, is it a personalized good or service? Do materials need careful handling?
- **What is the size of the market?** This will determine the volume of output required.
- **What is the nature of demand?** Will consumers purchase the product on a regular basis (e.g. washing powder), or infrequently (e.g. furniture and electrical goods)?
- **What is the capacity of the business?** If necessary, does the business have enough resources to produce on a large scale?

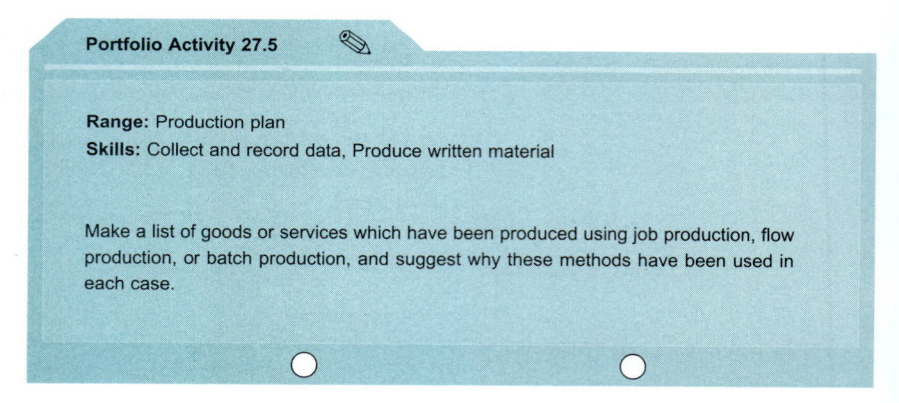

Portfolio Activity 27.5

Range: Production plan
Skills: Collect and record data, Produce written material

Make a list of goods or services which have been produced using job production, flow production, or batch production, and suggest why these methods have been used in each case.

Resource requirements

Once the production method has been chosen and justified, it is possible to decide upon the kind of premises, equipment, raw materials, and labour that will be required to meet production targets.

Premises

Many individuals now run small businesses from home, for example, driving instructors, window-cleaners, and sandwich-makers. Operating from home can save money, but care needs to be taken to ensure that running a home business does not infringe local authority planning regulations or the conditions of the householder's mortgage. Most businesses are operated from leased premises (see 26.3).

It is useful in a production plan to draw a diagram of the premises and the layout of benches, counters, tables, machinery, and other equipment you intend to use.

Machinery

The production plan should identify the machinery and other equipment required, for example, tools and computers, and name some potential suppliers. This section should indicate whether or not the business intends to hire, lease, or buy equipment, and should also outline the estimated total cost of what it intends to do. The plan should detail the support available for servicing and maintaining the machinery, where this support will come from, and how much it will cost.

The impact of any plans to buy additional equipment in the future should also be outlined in the plan.

Labour

Will production be labour-intensive or capital-intensive? The production plan should outline the firm's labour requirements - that is, numbers of employees, their skill levels, and previous experience required. The plan should indicate where these employees are to be found, how they will be recruited, methods of payment, and future training needs.

The cost of labour varies enormously across different regions in the UK. Labour costs in the South East are the highest in the country, while costs in parts of the North of England and Northern Ireland are among the lowest. The entrepreneur will need to consider the impact of the geographical location of the firm on its labour costs. A business requiring a large amount of unskilled labour might locate in a region with high unemployment and find that it can recruit cheaply. However, a business needing highly specialized labour, for example, those with computer system design skills, may need to locate near similar organizations, for example in 'Silicon Valley' in Cambridge, and may be forced to pay very high wages to attract staff from rival firms.

Raw materials

If the business needs raw materials, it is important that the entrepreneur identifies suppliers in advance who are able to supply materials of the right quality in the right amounts at the right time, and who are prepared to trade on terms acceptable to the firm. Many suppliers will be cautious of giving credit to new and unknown businesses. Therefore, it is essential that the terms and conditions of supply of materials are established before the business starts up.

This section should also outline the stock levels that the firm intends to carry.

Just In Time production (JIT)

Just In Time production is a system designed to reduce the costs of holding stocks of raw materials, work in progress, and finished goods, through careful scheduling of the production process. JIT is sometimes known as supply chain management, because it involves a great deal of work with suppliers to achieve high levels of quality and reliability in supplies.

JIT means that finished goods are produced to order and 'just in time' to be sold, thereby reducing storage times. Similarly, raw materials and components arrive at the factory 'just in time' to be used, thereby reducing storage costs (see 15.2).

Quality assurance

The production plan should also detail how product quality will be assured.

The production of poor-quality products, and the resulting search for weaknesses in production processes, use up valuable time and resources in a business. Errors are costly. Furthermore, should any poor quality products reach consumers, company image and reputation can be damaged.

To prevent errors happening, organizations are increasingly turning to the techniques of **Total Quality Management (TQM)**. This involves building-in quality checks at each and every stage in a production process, the aim being to identify problems and solve them *before*, rather than after, products have completed the production process (see 15.2).

Quality control objectives

Quality control aims to produce goods that:

- Satisfy consumer wants
- Work properly
- Can be repaired
- Conform to safety standards
- Are produced cost-effectively

A company that fails in quality control is unlikely to realize revenue, profit, or growth objectives.

Key words

Production plan - this sets out details of design, product development, premises, machinery, materials to be used, and labour requirements.

Job production - completing one job before moving on to another

Flow production - continuous mass-production

Batch production - producing a limited number of identical products to meet a specific order. Work is completed for a whole batch before the next batch is begun

Just In Time production (JIT) - keeping stocks and work in progress to a minimum by ordering new supplies only when they are needed for production

Total Quality Management (TQM) - the continuous improvement of products and processes by focusing on quality at each stage of production

---

Section 27.4 The financial plan

Making financial projections

Setting clear business objectives involves more than just producing words in a business plan. Business managers must translate their objectives into figures or targets expressed in money terms. **Financial plans** are needed to focus a firm on its targets and to help provide the entrepreneur with the answers to key questions once the business is trading. For example:

- What is the cash position of the business?
- What profit is being made?
- What are the business overheads?
- What are the variable costs?
- How much does the firm owe?
- How much is owed to the firm?
- How much working capital does the business have?

The financial plan in Figure 27.1 gives examples of the kind of questions that an entrepreneur would be asked by a bank when starting up a new business venture.

The purpose of these questions is to establish how much money the firm will need to spend on its major cost items, including freehold or leasehold premises and rates, as well as plant, machinery, and equipment. Set against this are any assets which the entrepreneur can make available to the lender as security, and any capital to be provided by the entrepreneur. At the bottom of the plan is the amount to be raised externally.

In order to answer these questions, firms typically produce **cashflow forecasts, balance sheets,** and **profit and loss accounts** on a regular, sometimes monthly, basis.

The cashflow forecast

Cashflow refers to the money which flows into and out of a business over a period of time, usually one year (see 23.2). A **cashflow forecast** should be constructed for the first year of trading (some lenders ask to see forecasts for the first three years).

A cashflow forecast gives the estimated sum of cash inflows into a business, minus the sum of cash outflows. **Inflows** of cash can arise from cash sales, debtors paying cash, interest received, and sales of any assets. Cash **outflows** may be caused by cash purchases of stock, purchases of materials or of assets, or by settling debts owed to creditors. The cashflow forecast shows the net effect of cash inflows and outflows each month, and the impact of these on the firm's bank balance.

The advantage of cashflow forecasting is that it allows the business to spot in advance any shortfalls in cash during particular months, and to take appropriate action. If a deficit is anticipated, the firm can attempt either to reduce cash outflows in advance, or to raise cash inflows. Failing this, it can attempt to arrange an overdraft to cover the deficit. The cashflow forecast also allows the firm to identify where cash surpluses are likely to be made, and to plan to use these efficiently, for example, by investing the surplus or holding it over to meet a future deficit.

An example of a blank cashflow forecast statement is given in Figure 27.2. The forecast contains columns for both predicted and actual cashflow. By comparing the two, it is possible to identify differences or **variances** from the plan, and to investigate these as they happen (see 25.2).

Advanced Business

▼ Figure 27.1: A financial plan questionnaire

Name of business _____ Type of Business _____

Business Address _____

_____ Principal activities of business _____

_____ Date business commenced _____

KEY PERSONNEL

Name   Position Held   Salary

_____

_____

Please also attach details on separate (sheet(s) of any additions to management team necessary for the growth of the business.

COST OF PREMISES

Freehold
Value (give basis and date) £ _____
Mortgate outstanding £ _____
Monthly repayment figure £ _____

Leasehold
Term of Lease _____
Period outstanding _____
Option to renew YES/NO
Present Rent per annum £ _____
Frequency of Payment _____
Next rent review _____

Rates
Amount (half-yearly) £ _____
Date due (half-yearly) _____

PLANT AND MACHINERY, EQUIPMENT AND VEHICLES (EXISTING)

Description   Life Expectancy   Value £

_____

_____

What capital expenditure do you anticipate during the next 12 months? Please attach details on separate sheet.

PRODUCT OR SERVICE AND THE MARKET PLACE

Please give brief details of your product or service _____

Market size and potential (quote sources of information) _____

Major competitors and their existing market share _____

Has your product or service been market tested? _____
Please attach details on separate sheet together with firm orders, letters of intent etc.
Marketing and sales methods including costs involved _____

ASSETS AVAILABLE AS SECURITY

Business (description)   Value (to include basis and date)

_____

Personal (description)   Value (to include basis and date)

_____

FINANCIAL REQUIREMENTS

Total cost of project
Own recources   £ _____
Grants   £ _____
Other sources (please specify)   £ _____
    £ _____

Bank requirements:
Overdraft (as per cashflow)   £ _____
Loans and terms (years)   £ _____
Other (please specify)   £ _____
Total bank requirements _____
Total   £ _____

This Financial Plan to be used in conjunction with Cash Flow Forecast and trading Forecast in order to provide a comprehensive Business Plan.

Adapted from Banking Information Service Financial plan

▼ Figure 27.2: A cashflow forecast proforma

PERIOD (EG 4 WEEKS/MONTHS/QUARTER)	Budget	Actual	Budget	Actual	Budget	Actual	Budget	Actual
Orders: Net of VAT								
Sales								
Receipts								
Cash Sales								
From Debtors								
Other Revenue Sources								
Total Receipts A								
Purchases								
Payments								
Cash Purchases								
To Creditors								
Wages/Salaries/PAYE								
Rent/Rates/Insurance								
Light/Heat/Power								
Transport/Packing								
Repairs/Renewals								
VAT – Net								
HP Payments/Leasing Charges								
Bank/Finance charge/Interest								
Sundry Expenses								
Tax								
Dividends								
Drawings/Fees								
Loan Repayments								
Capital Expenditure/Inflow								
Total Payments B								
A-B (net inflow) or C Cr								
B-A (net outflow) Dr								
Bank balance at end of Cr								
previous period brought fwd... D Dr								
Bank balance at end of period Cr								
carried fwd to aggregate (C&D) Dr								
Agreed overdraft facility								

Banking Information Service

A projected balance sheet

A potential lender will also require information about:

- The total capital (money) needed by a business
- What the business intends to do with its capital
- How much of the owner's money is being put into the firm
- Where the rest of the capital is to be raised from

This information is usually shown in the form of an **opening balance sheet**. A balance sheet is a statement of an organization's assets and liabilities at a particular point in time (see 23.2). Assets will include premises, machinery, and equipment owned by the firm, and holdings of cash, bank, or building society deposits, or sales on credit. **Liabilities** refers to money owed by the business to other people and organizations, for example, bank loans, hire purchase, leasing agreements, or purchases made on credit.

In the case of a new business, the balance sheet statement is likely to be drawn up for the first day of trading. It is common practice to include in a business plan both an opening balance sheet, and a projected balance sheet for the end of the first year of trading.

Figure 27.3 shows an opening balance sheet for a new business – Splash Decorating Services – and the balance sheet for the same business one year later.

▼ Figure 27.3: Opening and projected balance sheet for Splash Decorating Services

	OPENING BALANCE Sheet 1.6.96 £	PROJECTED BALANCE Sheet 31.5.97 £
Fixed assets		
Machinery	2,000	1,600 (less 20% depreciation)
Vehicles	2,500	2,000 (less 20% depreciation)
(A)	4,500	3,600
Current assets		
Stocks	2,000	2,500
Debtors	–	500
Cash	1,500	2,000
(B)	3,500	5,000
Less Current liabilities (C)		
Bank overdraft	2,000	1,600
Trade creditors	500	250
(C)	2,500	1,850
Working capital (D=B−C)	1,000	3,150
Net assets (A+D)	5,500	6,750
Financed by		
Bank loan	4,500	4,500
Overdraft facility	–	1,000
Owners' savings	1,000	–
Net profit	–	1,250
	5,500	6,75

The opening balance sheet shows the capital requirements of the firm, and what it intends to do with this capital in terms of distributing it between fixed and current assets (see 22.1). The balance sheet also shows, in the 'Financed by' section, how the business intends to raise its finance - in this case, by taking out a bank loan, and from the owners' savings. In this way, a start-up balance sheet can provide a great deal of useful information to a potential lender.

The projected balance sheet for the end of the first year shows the assets and liabilities the business expects to hold by 31 May 1997. By the end of the year, fixed assets such as machines and vehicles will have reduced in value because of depreciation (see 20.1). At the same time, the values for current assets and liabilities will change from their opening position, due to business trading.

In order to produce the end-of-year balance sheet forecast, the values of some of the balance sheet figures, such as stocks and cash, can be estimated from the cashflow forecast for the year. The firm will have some money owed from sales to debtors by the end of the year, and in this example, will have recorded its first retained profit, a predicted sum of £1,250.

The projected year-end balance sheet allows potential lenders to see the likely value of the business one year from starting trading, and so gives them an idea of the likelihood of the business being able to repay its loan.

The projected profit and loss statement

The profit and loss statement shows the profit made by a business during a particular trading period. It is calculated as total sales revenue minus total costs (see 23.3). Unlike a balance sheet, which gives a picture at a particular moment in time, the profit and loss statement shows profit made over a period of time.

Figure 27.4 provides an example of a projected profit and loss statement for Splash Decorating Services:

▼ *Figure 27.4: Trading and profit and loss statement for Splash Decorating Services as at 31.5.97*

	£	£
Turnover		45,000
Opening stock (1.6.96)	4,500	
Add Purchases	12,000	
	16,500	
Less Closing stock (31.5.97)	2,500	
		14,000
Gross profit		**31,000**
Less Rent	4,000	
Rates	500	
Light/heat	450	
Telephone/Post	150	
Insurance	250	
Hire Purchase	400	
Advertising	400	
Loan repayments	500	
Provisions for bad debts	300	
Depreciation	400	
Drawings	4,000	
Other expenses	750	
Total expenses	12,100	
Net profit		**18,900**

If a profit is projected after tax and other expenses, the business owners can then decide how much to retain in the business and how much to pay out to themselves. If a loss is projected, the owners can plan in advance how to raise the finance necessary to pay for the loss.

▼ Figure 27.5: Proforma for monthly profit and loss statement forecast

Month TOTAL £	1	2	3	4	5	6	7	8	9	10	11	12	
Sales Less opening stock Add purchases													
Gross profit (A)													
Expenses:													
Rent													
Rates													
Electricity													
Gas													
Advertising													
Insurance													
Stationery, postage													
Telephone													
Bank charges													
Loan repayments													
Hire Purchase													
Depreciation: equipment vehicles													
Provision for bad debts													
Owners' drawings													
Other expenses:													
_____													
_____													
_____													
_____													
Total expenses (B)													
Net profit/loss (A-B)													

Notes:
1. *Opening stock should appear in Month 1 cost of sales. (Add purchases)*
2. *Allowance for depreciation of equipment and vehicles is usually entered in last month.*
3. *Drawings can be thought of as a monthly wage paid to the small business owner.*

New firms are usually required to produce a projected profit and loss statement for their first year of trading in order to give potential lenders an estimate of how well the firm is likely to do. Once the business has started, managers are likely to produce a profit and loss statement every one to three months in order to monitor business performance (see Figure 27.5).

Monitoring and reviewing business performance

Once a new business is up and running, managers will want to monitor its financial performance very closely in order to be in a position to take immediate corrective action when required. Potential lenders will look for evidence that the business is going to be run according to principles of sound financial management, and will expect to see details of how this is going to happen in the business plan.

The main means of monitoring used by small firms are as follows:

1. Regular monitoring of cash inflows and outflows against the cashflow forecast.

2. Comparing actual sales and purchases against operating budget plans. A comparison of plans with outturn can be made using **variance analysis** (see 25.2). It is important for an organization to keep its costs as low as possible, and within budget.

3. Producing monthly or three-monthly profit and loss statements and balance sheets. These accounts can reveal a great deal about business performance. Financial performance can be monitored using **ratio analysis**, for example, measuring profit margins, return on capital employed, and liquidity ratios (see 25.3)

4. Monitoring **aged creditors lists** and **aged debtors lists** (see 25.3). This will tell a business how much is owed to suppliers and when payments have to be made, and how much is owed to the business for sales made on credit. Chasing up late payers may be required to keep cashflow projections on target and to provide funds, so that creditors can be paid on time.

Business planning

To be workable a business plan must be realistic; it must take account of the shortcomings of the firm and of the people involved. This will help to ensure that the plan is achievable within the resources available. For an average business, a three-year projection will be adequate, with the first year shown in detail, and the next two in outline. In quickly changing industries, such as computers or consumer electronics, the planning horizon may need to be shorter - perhaps 18 months to 2 years.

A business plan should not be seen as a rigid, inflexible answer to a firm's problems. Business conditions are continually changing, and a good business will adapt its plans to suit changes in the market or other circumstances. Business plans are only useful if they are realistic. A plan serves no purpose unless it can be delivered.

Research into small business growth and success both in the UK and USA suggests that there is a clear correlation between the amount of time invested in business planning and the ability of firms to sustain stable growth over time.

Further reading

Daily Telegraph Enterprise Guides: *How to Start Up Your Own Business* (Kogan Page 1994)

National Westminster Bank: *The NatWest Business Start-Up Guide* (NatWest Small Business Services)

Advanced Business

Some review questions

1. Suggest and explain some business objectives a newly-created small business might set in the short, medium, and long term.
2. What are the five main parts of a business plan?
3. What is the 'marketing mix'? Outline its importance in a business plan.
4. What is the difference between job production, batch production, and flow production?
5. What type of production process would you recommend organizations producing (a) ice lollies and (b) dried flower arrangements to use, and why?
6. Why is cashflow so important to a business?
7. Suggest two ways in which a new firm can use its business plan to monitor performance.
8. Explain the possible resource requirements of a new business selling hand-printed silk ties.
9. What promotional methods would you recommend a newly self-employed plumber to use to publicize his service? Give reasons.
10. A friend of yours is investigating premises for her new hairdressing salon. What factors would you advise her to consider when choosing premises, and what potential costs should she be aware of?
11. You have been operating a mobile car repair service for six months. You decide to buy a bigger van using a loan from your bank. How will these transactions affect both your balance sheet and profit and loss account?
12. What factors should you consider in designing a product to sell?

chapter 28

Assessment Assignment

Range: Business objectives
Marketing plan
Production plan
Resource requirements
Financial data and forecasts

Skills: Communication
Take part in discussions
Produce written materials
Use images
Application of Number
Collect and record data
Tackle problems
Interpret and present data
Information Technology
Prepare, process and present information

Tasks

1. Prepare a business plan in five parts for a good or service of your choice. The purpose of the plan is to secure finance from a lender, and the plan should be produced with this in mind.

   The plan should contain a section on each of the following:

   - Your business objectives for the short, medium, and long term
   - An outline marketing plan covering your product idea, its market potential, pricing and promotion strategies, distribution, methods of selling, and a marketing budget. The marketing plan should suggest a schedule of timings for each of these items.
   - An outline production plan, covering product design, development, and production methods
   - The resource requirements of the business, covering human, physical, financial, and time resources
   - Financial data and forecasts, including a cashflow forecast, opening and projected balance sheet and profit and loss statement, and an outline of your proposed means of monitoring and reviewing business performance and your financial systems

   In each section, you must justify the choices you have made - for example, your choice of product, size and location of premises, production method.

   Where appropriate, graphs and tables should be included in the text of your plan. Useful illustrations will include:

   - A table of your business start-up costs
   - A bar chart of your expected monthly sales revenues
   - A line chart of your projected net cashflow
   - A break-even graph to show expected revenues and costs at different levels of output (see 21.2)
   - GANNT and PERT charts of your planned marketing and production activities (see 26.3)

   You should look closely at the Application of Number and Information Technology core skills when preparing your plan, in order to ensure that you produce the required evidence towards them.

2. Prepare and make a short presentation of the main points of your plan to your lender. Use a range of visual aids, including charts and graphs, and prepare a brief summary of the plan to hand out to the lender.

Using pre-prepared plans and proforma

Most high street banks can supply business plan forms on request from their small business service. Cashflow forecast and monthly profit and loss statement proforma are also available from them. The Banking Information Service is also able to supply these documents for you to complete.

Alternatively, use the proformas in Figures 27.2 and 27.5. However, in all cases it is suggested that you use printed plans and proforma only as a guide. Ideally, you should adapt them to meet your own requirements, using a wordprocessing and/or spreadsheet package.

UNIT **EIGHT**

CHAPTER 28

chapter 28
Planning for Employment or Self-employment

This chapter examines the personal skills needed for employment and self-employment, the statutory requirements for employees and employers, and the sources of information available to assist people in starting up their own businesses.

Key ideas

A person can become **self-employed** by setting up their own business or buying an existing business. Business start-ups can take a variety of forms, including a sole trader enterprise, partnership, shareholder in a limited company, or franchise.

Paid employment may be either in the **private** or **public sector**. People engaged in **voluntary work** provide their labour for free.

Becoming self-employed involves meeting statutory requirements, including registration with the Inland Revenue and the Department of Social Security, and making arrangements to pay taxes and National Insurance Contributions at agreed intervals. The self-employed must also keep detailed records for VAT purposes.

Employers must organize income tax and National Insurance contributions for their employees.

Opportunities for employment and self-employment may present themselves both locally, in other parts of the UK, in the European Union, or elsewhere in the world.

To take advantage of opportunities for self-employment, would-be entrepreneurs need to have certain skills: **personal skills** to evaluate their own strengths and weaknesses, an ability to work with others, and the drive and determination to work alone; **organizational skills**, including planning and managing resources, decision-making, and problem-solving; and skills in **communication**, **numeracy**, and the use of **Information Technology**. Success in paid or voluntary employment, and progression to better jobs, will also require these skills.

Information and advice about opportunities for employment or self-employment are available from a wide range of sources, including local Training and Enterprise Councils (TECs), the Department of Trade and Industry (DTi), Voluntary Service Overseas, Citizens' Advice Bureaux, and many others.

It is a good idea to prepare a personal plan for employment or self-employment, outlining the things you will need to do to prepare for work, the dates by which these will be done, and to identify your information requirements and sources.

Section 28.1 Types of employment and self-employment

Going to work

An enormous variety of employment opportunities are open to workers in the UK. These include a vast range of jobs and careers working for others, as well as opportunities for self-employment.

One of the main disadvantages of self-employment is the risk the entrepreneur takes that the venture may not succeed, and that he or she may lose the money they invested in the business. By working for someone else, this worry is removed. Working for someone else is, in many ways, less risky and more secure than being self-employed.

Unlike the self-employed, employees can expect to receive a regular income each week or month for the duration of their paid employment. Employees will also benefit from paid holidays, sick pay, and maternity leave. Self-employed people must find others whom they can trust to run their businesses while they are ill or on holiday, and they do not benefit from paid maternity leave.

However, being an employee has the disadvantage that you have to do what others tell you - and, of course, there are very few really wealthy employees.

Employment in the public and private sectors

The **private sector** in the UK consists of private individuals, the business organizations they own and control, and the **voluntary sector** (see 4.2). Private-sector business organizations consist of:

- Sole traders
- Partnerships
- Limited companies
- Cooperatives

The **public sector** in the UK consists of organizations funded by, and accountable to, central and local government (see 4.3). These are:

- Central government departments, e.g. Transport, Environment, Health
- Local government departments
- Public corporations that run state-owned industries, e.g. the Post Office
- Executive agencies, for example, the National Physical Laboratory and the Royal Mint
- Quangos (Quasi-autonomous non-government organizations), for example, the Regional Health Authorities

In 1994 there were 6 million and 15.2 million employees in the public and private sectors respectively.

Figure 28.1 shows the relative proportions of employees in each broad occupational category in UK public and private-sector organizations. The public sector employs a large number of people in professional, clerical, and secretarial occupations, compared to the private sector. This reflects the large number of civil service employees in central government departments and agencies. Employees in selling, craft, and related occupations, and plant and machine operatives are concentrated in the private sector.

Figure 28.1: Public and private-sector employees, UK 1993-94

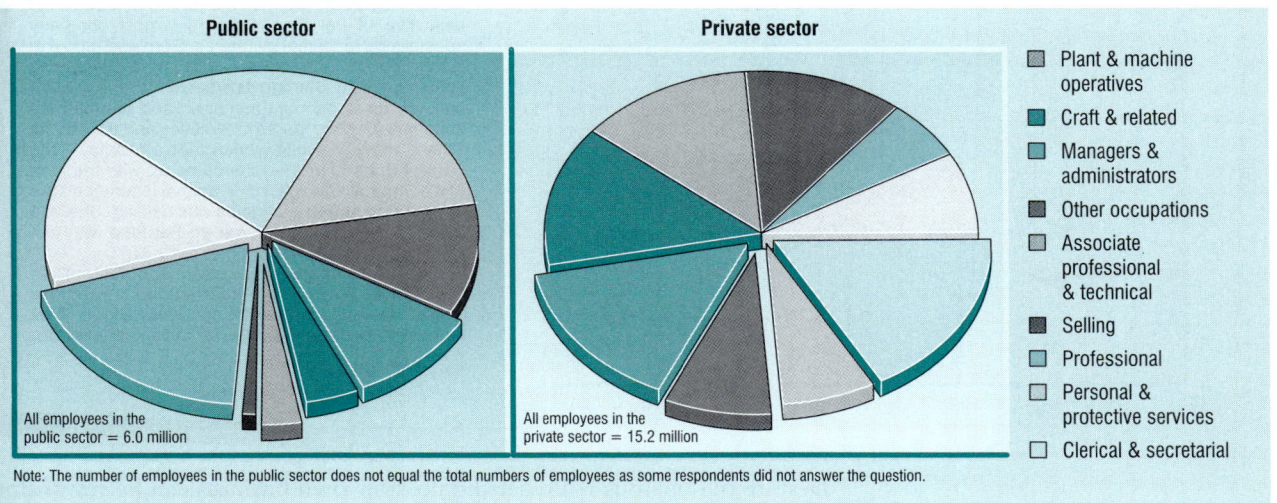

Public sector

Private sector

- Plant & machine operatives
- Craft & related
- Managers & administrators
- Other occupations
- Associate professional & technical
- Selling
- Professional
- Personal & protective services
- Clerical & secretarial

All employees in the public sector = 6.0 million

All employees in the private sector = 15.2 million

Note: The number of employees in the public sector does not equal the total numbers of employees as some respondents did not answer the question.

Employment Gazette, Labour Force Survey, August 1994

Opportunities in the private and public sector

Employment in the public sector has always been considered secure compared to working in the private sector, with little risk of redundancy. Whereas private-sector firms are continually striving to reduce costs, of which labour is a significant proportion, and can go bankrupt, most public-sector organizations are not engaged in trading activities. Those that were in the past, such as British Steel and British Rail, were not usually required to make a profit and were often subsidized by taxpayers' money.

However, in recent years, public-sector employment has become much less secure. This is due to the privatization of many once state-owned industries, which are now run for profit (see 3.5). The Civil Service is also being reduced in size to reduce costs, with departments being replaced by independent agencies working within tight budgets. Many areas of work once undertaken by civil servants and other public-sector workers are now being 'market tested' to see if the private sector can deliver an improved and cheaper service - for example, private refuse collection.

The nature of private-sector employment has also changed, due to restructuring of the UK economy and increased competition from overseas organizations. The increase in employment in service-sector industries has not been sufficient to 'mop up' the job losses from manufacturing. Both service-sector and manufacturing jobs are also under threat from the emerging markets in South East Asia, where labour and materials are much cheaper (see 16.2).

Being your own boss

More and more people in the UK are choosing to become self-employed. In 1981, around 2 million people were self-employed. By 1993, this had risen to just under 3 million - 11% of the total UK working population.

▼ Figure 28.2: Total self-employment, UK 1951-93

ED Quarterly series

I DIDN'T GET WHERE I AM TODAY WITHOUT ...

PATSY BLOOM, 53, is the founder and chief executive of Pet Plan, Britain's largest company specialising in animal insurance. Born and raised in North London, she took her first job in advertising at the age of 16. Starting as a secretary, she worked her way up to account manager, and handled the accounts for Mary Quant Cosmetics and the charity Oxfam. In 1977, while working for a charity — the Central British Fund — she came up with the idea of a company specialising in animal insurance after her pet dog suffered a series of illnesses. She and a friend, David Simpson, set up Pet Plan with just £500 capital.

Today, the company has a turnover of £32 million and runs successful international franchise operations in Canada and Italy. Patsy Bloom lives alone with her Yorkshire Terrier in Central London.

Daily Mail 10.2.94

Despite the obvious risks, setting up your own business can be rewarding, both financially and in terms of personal satisfaction. Many people become self-employed after being made redundant, as an alternative to unemployment. But self-employment is also appealing to people who feel trapped in a boring job, perhaps working for someone they dislike, in return for a relatively low level of pay. However, unless you have a sound business proposal, leaving paid employment for these reasons to set up in business is not a good idea. There is no guarantee of success in business. It may also involve long hours of work, more worry, and a big financial risk.

But not all self-employed people run a small business. Some do a job for someone else just like many other employees. However, self-employed people will usually only be employed on a short term contract, often to provide specialist skills and expertise needed for a particular project. They will also not qualify for many of the benefits of ordinary employees such as sick pay and redundancy compensation.

Small firms are the business!

Britain's 5-million-strong army of small businessmen and women is clocking up long hours to help lift the country out of recession. A survey by Lloyds Bank today reveals that more than half - 55% - put in more than 50 hours a week.

It shows that 39% of their time is spent on producing goods and services, 21% on paperwork, 15% on the phone, 11% at meetings, 8% travelling, and 6% dealing with the taxman.

Almost all - 95% - work more than the national employee average of 38 hours a week. Seven percent work more than 70 hours, while over a third work every weekend and only one in ten never work Saturdays. The findings come from the Lloyds Bank/Small Business Research trust quarterly Small Business Management Report.

Daily Mirror 9.6.93

Why has the demand for self-employed labour increased?

In 1987, the Employment Department commissioned the **Employers' Labour Use Survey (ELUS)** to investigate - amongst other questions - why employers use the services of self-employed workers. The reasons given were as follows:

▼ Table 28.1: Reported reasons for using the self-employed

Reported reason for employment	Per cent of employers citing as reason	Per cent of employers citing as main reason
To provide specialist skills	60	53
To match staffing levels to peaks in demand	29	17
Self-employed workers are not in unions	1	0
Self-employed are more productive	8	6
Self-employed are more committed	1	0
Self-employed have fewer rights under employment protection laws	2	0
To avoid administering PAYE and NI	3	0
To reduce wage costs	9	7
To reduce non-wage costs	6	0
To reduce overheads	4	1
Workers prefer to be self-employed	28	14
To reduce training costs	0	0
Other reasons	4	4
Number of establishments	183	168

Employment Gazette, May 1992

- **The need for specialist skills:** by far the most important reason given by employers for the use of self-employed labour was the provision of their specialist skills (Table 28.1).

- **To match skills and staffing levels to changes in demand:** of the sample of employers, 29% suggested that matching staffing levels more accurately with peaks in demand was an important reason for recruiting the self-employed.

- **More workers prefer to be self-employed:** as a result, self-employed workers tend to be more motivated. Absenteeism among the self-employed may therefore be lower, and productivity higher.

- **To reduce costs:** an increasing number of larger organizations have 'downsized' and subcontracted non-core functions such as catering and cleaning to smaller external organizations (see 13.3). Larger firms can insist on quality at competitive rates from small organizations or individuals willing to perform the work. For example, many local and central government department functions were 'market tested' in the early 1990s, as part of the government's policy of privatization (see 3.5).

Why has the supply of self-employed labour increased?

- **Changes in the structure of consumer demand:** there has been an increase in consumer demand for more specialized and personalized products, which can best be met by small firms and self-employed individuals.

- **Technological advance:** technological change has improved the productivity of many items of equipment and reduced their cost, so that small firms and people working at home are now able to afford them.

- **Worker attitudes and demographic effects:** workers' dissatisfaction with their employment, pay, and promotion prospects may have grown. Self-employment allows people to be their own boss, choose their own hours of work, and to specialize in those activities they either enjoy the most, and/or are best able to do.

- **The business cycle:** opportunities for individuals to set up in business successfully on their own will tend to rise during economic booms, when demand for goods and services is buoyant. However, during economic recessions, rising unemployment and a general lack of job vacancies may force individuals into self-employment. This is likely to have been a significant explanatory factor underlying the growth in the number of self-employed during the early-to-mid-1980s.

- **Government policy:** the government has actively encouraged people to become self-employed by providing advice and financial help. A network of **Training and Enterprise Councils (TECs)** provide business information, advice, training, and counselling. The **Business Start-Up Scheme (BSUS)** is run by TECs to help unemployed people start their own business (see 26.4). It involves the payment of an allowance to help bridge the gap between loss of unemployment benefit and the time when the self-employed person begins to make a profit. Clearly, it is a legal requirement that a previously unemployed person claiming benefit must inform their local Benefits Agency office that they have become self-employed.

Portfolio Activity 28.1

Range: Types, (plus employment trends from Element 5.2)
Skills: Produce written material, Interpret and present data

Look at the tables and charts set out below. Use them to write a brief report entitled 'Features of the Self-employed Workforce'. Set out your report in point form, identifying the most significant features of the self-employed. Support these where appropriate with precise figures.

Gather any other information you feel is necessary to produce your 'profile of the self-employed' from government publications and other sources of data.

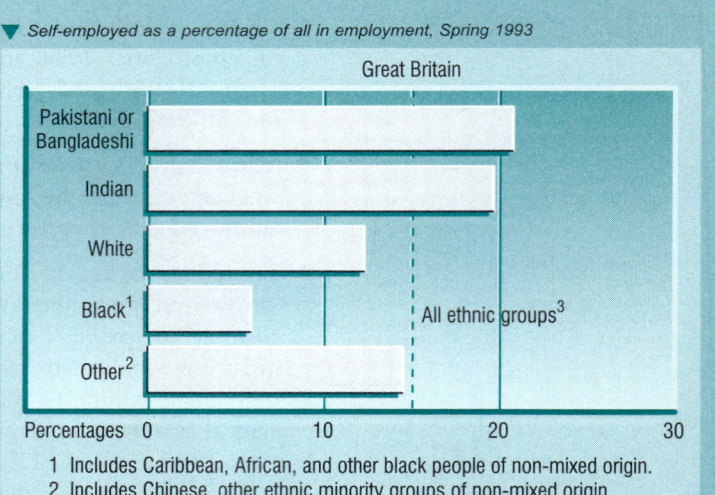

▼ *Self-employed as a percentage of all in employment, Spring 1993*

Great Britain

Ethnic group	Percentage
Pakistani or Bangladeshi	~23
Indian	~20
White	~13
Black[1]	~6
Other[2]	~13

All ethnic groups[3] ~ 15

Percentages 0 10 20 30

1 Includes Caribbean, African, and other black people of non-mixed origin.
2 Includes Chinese, other ethnic minority groups of non-mixed origin, and people of mixed origin.
3 Includes ethnic group not stated.

Social Trends 1994

UNIT EIGHT

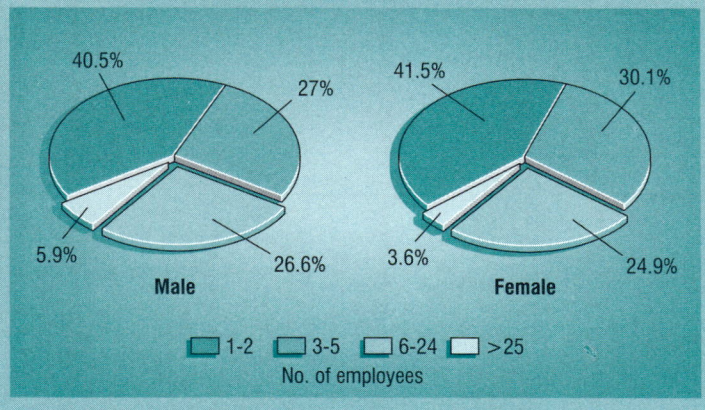

CHAPTER 28

▼ Self-employed with employees, by number employed

Male
- 40.5%
- 27%
- 5.9%
- 26.6%

Female
- 41.5%
- 30.1%
- 3.6%
- 24.9%

□ 1-2 □ 3-5 □ 6-24 □ >25
No. of employees

Employment Gazette, June 1992

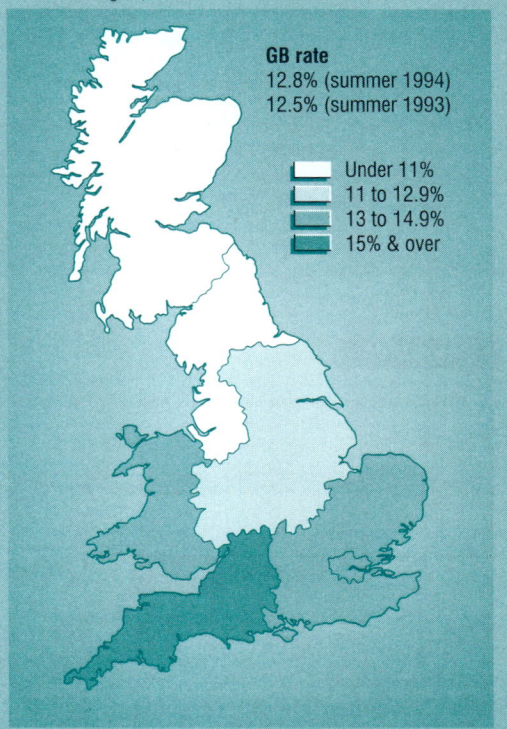

▼ Self-employed as a percentage of the total in employment in each region, UK 1994

GB rate
12.8% (summer 1994)
12.5% (summer 1993)

- Under 11%
- 11 to 12.9%
- 13 to 14.9%
- 15% & over

Employment Gazette, January 1995

▼ Self-employed: by sex and industry, UK 1986 and 1992[1]

SELF-EMPLOYED: BY SEX AND INDUSTRY, 1986 AND 1992[1]

United Kingdom	Thousands	
	1986	1992
All industries[3]	2,799	3,212
of which		
Males	2,109	2,422
Females	690	791
Manufacturing	257	348
Services	1,694	1,871
Other	844	981
Self employed by industry		
Agriculture, forestry and fishing	265	294
Energy and water supply	3	11
Other minerals and ore extraction, etc	20	27
Metal goods, engineering and vehicles	83	107
Other manufacturing industries	154	214
Construction	575	676
Distribution, catering and repairs	823	746
Transport and communication	120	173
Banking, finance, insurance, etc	299	447
Other services	452	506

1 At Spring each year.
2 Standard Industrial Classification.
3 Includes workplace outside the UK and industry group not stated.

▼ Number of days usually worked each week

NUMBER OF DAYS USUALLY WORKED PER WEEK (UK)

	Self-employed		
	All	Full-time	Part-time
Total (000s)	3,212	2,662	550
			Per cent
Nine-day fortnight	*	*	*
Four-and-half day week	0.8	0.9	*
1 Day per week	2.0	*	11.3
2 Days per week	2.5	*	13.6
3 " " "	3.7	0.6	18.5
4 " " "	3.4	1.5	12.1
5 " " "	37.8	40.2	26.1
6 " " "	25.0	28.9	6.2
7 " " "	24.7	27.5	11.6
Total	100	100	100

Source: spring 1992 LFS estimates
Employment Gazette. Sept 93

669

Advanced Business

Portfolio Activity 28.2

Range: Skills

Skills: Take part in discussions, Read and respond to written material

Do you know anyone who is self-employed? If so, interview them to find out the type of work they do, and why they chose to become self-employed. What skills do they need? What are the advantages and disadvantages of 'being your own boss'?

Key words

Private sector - private individuals and business organizations

Public sector - organizations funded by, and accountable to, central and local government

---

Section 28.2 Going into business

Some businesses have been in families for generations. Many of today's large companies, like Marks & Spencer and John Lewis Partnership, started life many years ago as small sole traders - organizations owned and controlled by one person. In many cases, members of the founder's family still own part of the company and take an active interest in its running.

Small family businesses may also be passed on from one generation to the next, like Pete Beale's stall in BBC TV's *Eastenders*. Perhaps you know someone who intends to work in their parent's shop or small business? Consider how many small local firms have '... & Son' in their name.

▼ Keeping it in the family

In 1994, almost two-thirds of some 370,000 business start-ups in the UK had no full-time employees apart from their immediate family.

Starting your own business

If stepping into a family business is not an option, it is still possible to become self-employed by starting up your own small business. Often, finding the money to finance a business start-up is the main hurdle. Money from savings, family, and friends may have to be topped up from banks and other lenders.

There are a number of legal forms of business enterprise a person can start up, or buy into (see 4.2). These are:

- **Sole trader:** the simplest way to become self-employed is to set up as a sole trader. Start-up involves little expense and formality, and allows the entrepreneur to be his or her own boss.

  A sole trader can trade under his or her own name, or under a suitable trading name. The name of the business does not have to be registered, but care must be taken not to use the name of another business, or one that would imply a connection with royalty or government. For example, if you were to set up a small record shop, you could not call it 'Tower Records' or 'Royal Records'.

- **Partnership:** it is also possible to start up in business with others as partners, either by buying into an existing partnership or by creating a new one.

  Being in a partnership means that there are others to share in decision-making, and the partnership allows the firm to employ people with a range of skills and abilities.

  To create a partnership, it is advisable to have a solicitor draw up a Deed of Partnership agreement between the partners. This is a document that sets out matters such as how much capital each partner is to invest in the business, how profits (and losses) are to be shared among the partners, and procedures for accepting new partners. If no agreement is drawn up, the rights and obligations of partners are determined by the 1890 Partnership Act.

- **Limited company:** the owners of a limited company are its shareholders. Shares are sold to raise money for the business venture. A **single-member company** has one shareholder, but most private limited companies have several, often family and friends.

  A **private limited company** may grow large enough to be listed on the Stock Exchange. It can then sell shares to members of the general public (see 22.3).

  A limited company has the attraction that its owners are not liable for the debts of the business. This is known as **limited liability**.

  To form a limited company, you will need to draw up legal documents with the help of a solicitor, and send copies of these to the Registrar of Companies. The **Articles of Association** define the internal rules of the company and give details such as the number of directors, the voting rights of shareholders, and how profits are to be shared out. The

Memorandum of Association gives details of the business name, objectives, and capital.

- **Buying an existing business:** it is possible to buy an established business, either by buying out an existing sole-trader business, buying into a partnership, or becoming a shareholder in a limited company, or by buying a franchise.

- **Buying a franchise:** in taking out a franchise, an entrepreneur can buy into an established product and brand name, and potentially benefit from the support and advice of an already successful company (see 4.2). Body Shop, British School of Motoring, Pizza Hut, Benetton, and Kentucky Fried Chicken are examples of popular and successful franchise organizations in the UK. Buying into a franchise can be expensive, and will usually involve paying a share of the profits to the parent company, but the risk of business failure is greatly reduced, due to the track record and market position of the parent company.

Sometimes, less successful firms franchise their operations as a way of making their owners wealthy. When considering buying a franchise, it is therefore vital to obtain professional and financial advice before proceeding.

Portfolio Activity 28.3

Range: Identify opportunities for employment and self-employment

Skills: Read and respond to written material

1. What is the popular view of the job-creating powers of small firms?
2. Why does the article suggest that this may not be so?
3. Undertake some research on employment and business size in your region. Which types and sizes of firms seem mainly responsible for new job creation? Which types and sizes of business appear to be actively 'downsizing' - cutting jobs? How do your findings compare with your answers to Questions 1 and 2 of this exercise? (Useful sources of information will include local newspapers, Jobcentres and TECs/LECs.)

From tiny acorns ...

Net change in employment as % of total employment, annual rates
no of employees

		Total	1–19	20–99	100–499	500+
Britain	1987–1991	2.7	1.6	0.4	0.3	0.4
Canada	1983–1991	2.6	2.2	0.6	0.1	–0.3
Denmark	1983–1989	2.2	2.3	0.3	–0.4*	
Finland	1986–1991	–1.6	0.9	–0.7	–1.1	–0.7
France	1987–1992	0.9	0.4	0.4	0.3	–0.2
New Zealand	1987–1992	–4.1	0.4	–1.9	–1.5	–1.1
Sweden	1985–1991	1.3	2.6	–0.2	–0.5	–0.6

*100 and over
Economist 23.7.94

Belittled: small firms

Are small firms really the engine of job creation in modern economies? In the past decade or so, many economists and politicians have claimed exactly that, elevating the notion that 'small is beautiful' from a cliché to a creed. But according to the OECD's annual Employment Outlook they have oversold their case.

How so? The evidence in favour of small firms looks compelling. The late 1980s and early 1990s saw big companies suffer. Some went bust; others broke themselves up; most slashed their workforces. Most net new jobs were created by small companies.

Yet, says the OECD, this picture is less clear-cut than it seems at first. For a start, it is no surprise that most new jobs are created by small firms, since companies with under 100 workers employ between 40% and 70% of workers in OECD countries anyway. The 1980s saw a rapid growth in subcontracting by big firms, especially of services: many new small firms are in effect subsidiaries of larger ones. Rapid structural change can magnify the role of small firms in employment: firms in declining industries shrink from now-unsupportable sizes, while those in newer industries grow from small beginnings.

Transitory factors may have an impact. When times are tough, a firm will be below its average size and may be misclassified as 'small'. When things pick up and the firm returns to its natural size, it will look as if it is a small firm, growing.

The truth seems to be that small firms both take on and sack a disproportionate number of employees. In all the countries in the table below, firms with fewer than 100 employees accounted for over half of all hirings and firings. The debate continues.

The voluntary sector

A growing number of people are using their knowledge and skills to help those who are less fortunate than themselves. Voluntary work is unpaid and can be full-time, part-time, or very occasional. A great many voluntary organizations exist which rely on the unpaid skills and help of different people. Charities, for example, require the help of a wide range of people, from those who can simply hand out leaflets and collect donations, to specialists able to advise on anything from accounting procedures to construction projects.

Voluntary Service Overseas (VSO) arranges work overseas for UK residents who apply, and who it considers to have the necessary skills to undertake fixed-term contracts. VSO organizes contracts which pay living expenses, or a small income to cover essentials only.

Why they queue up for a new life as a volunteer

Claims that we are living in a less caring society get short shrift from the workers of Voluntary Service Overseas. More people than ever want to make a contribution to the lives and prosperity of developing countries and the rebuilding of Eastern Europe, according to VSO, the largest agency of its kind in the world.

It handled 67,000 inquiries last year, received 7,500 firm applications, and at any time has around 1,700 workers in 55 countries.

"There has been a steady increase in people applying to do VSO in the past five years, and statistics show that numbers have kept rising since we launched in 1958," said Frances Tuke of VSO.

Volunteers want to go abroad for various reasons - following redundancy, as a career break, a change of direction in lifestyle, or simply to make a contribution to another society. At least 1 in 10 applicants is aged over 50. VSO is frequently asked for accountants, craft business advisers, legal specialists, and managers. Teachers and mid-wives are always in short supply.

Daily Mail 10.2.94

Advanced Business

Key words

Sole trader - a business enterprise owned and controlled by one person

Partnership - a business owned and controlled by more than two people

Limited company - a business organization owned by its shareholders

Franchise - an agreement whereby an existing business (the franchiser) sells rights to another business or individual (the franchisee) to produce and/or sell their products using the same business name

Section 28.3 Statutory requirements for employment and self-employment

Portfolio Activity 28.4

Range: Statutory requirements
Skills: Read and respond to written material

1. What taxes will affect a business?
2. Why would being reclassified as an employee rather than as self-employed lead to some people paying more tax?
3. Why is a self-employed person financially better off than an employed one, even if both earn the same amount?
4. Survey some self-employed people and find out what they think are the financial benefits of self-employment.
5. Find out more about business taxation. Useful sources of information will include the Inland Revenue and Customs & Excise department, Citizens' Advice Bureaux, and other business advice centres (see 28.6).

Self-employed under taxman's microscope

The Inland Revenue is scrutinizing the distinction between thousands of self-employed people and employees, to see if more tax could be raised. This could mean reclassifying some people who say they work for themselves as employees.

Being self-employed offers various advantages. Maurice Parry-Wingfield, tax partner at accountants Touche Ross, said: "Employees pay tax on schedule E on a monthly basis, but the self-employed pay tax twice a year in January and July - giving them a cashflow advantage."

In addition, self-employed people can offset more expenses against tax. Mike Warburton, head of tax at accountants Grant Thornton, said: "If you are an employee, you can set any expenses that are wholly and exclusively necessary for your employment against your tax. But if you are self-employed, expenses do not need to be 'necessary,' so more can be allowed. For example, if you are self-employed you could claim relief on your wife's wages as your secretary.

National Insurance is another area where the self-employed are better off. Sue Sinagola, tax partner at Ernst & Young, said: "Clearly you will pay less National Insurance as a self-employed person than as an employee. Although your basic pension entitlements will be no different, you will not be entitled to statutory sick pay or unemployment benefit."

All in all Mr Warburton estimates that a self-employed person earning £22,360 in the next tax year would pay about £1,452 in National Insurance contributions. An employee earning the same would pay about £2,236, and his employer would also have to pay 10.2% of his wages in National Insurance Contributions.

The main disadvantage of being self-employed is having to register for VAT if you make above a certain threshold income per year. In this case, recipients of your services must pay VAT as well.

But you cannot simply decide to be treated as self-employed. Mr Parry-Wingfield said: "If you provide services regularly for one person or organization, then you are likely to be taxed as an employee whatever you may describe yourself as."

Daily Telegraph 18.12.93

Any person starting in self-employment, or paid employment, will need to know about various legal, or statutory requirements that may affect them. The main areas affected are;

- Business start-up
- Company registration
- Pension arrangements
- Taxation
- Business rates
- Licences

Business start-up
Anybody that has been unemployed and claiming the job seekers allowance must notify their local Benefits Agency office if they find paid work or become self-employed. It is illegal to continue to claim benefits to cushion against the loss of income suffered while unemployed.

In some cases certain benefits may still be paid to people in work or starting their own business. For example, income support may be available to people on low wages. Financial assistance may also be available to new business owners during the first few months of trading from their local Training and Enterprise Councils (see 28.1).

Company registration
If the business a person starts up is a private limited company they will need to inform the governments Registrar of Companies based in Cardiff at Companies House (see 4.2).

The Registrar keeps details of all limited companies and requires them to send to Companies House a copy of their annual accounts each year (see 24.1). The company must also send in details each year of the company directors, their shareholdings, share capital issued and any company property that has been mortgaged.

Pension arrangements
A **pension** is a form of lifetime saving to provide an income for retirement from work. There are a number of different types of pension available to people in work.

- A **state pension** is payable on retirement to men over 65 years of age and women over 60 (The statutory retirement age for women is to be raised gradually to 65 years by the year 2010). The state pension is a relatively low flat rate decided each year by the government. In 1995 the state pension was just under £59 per week for a single person.

The state pension can usually be topped up by SERPS (State Earnings Related Pension Scheme) under which an additional amount is paid based on the employees former earnings and how much National Insurance he or she paid. Self-employed people are not eligible for SERPS. Since 1988, employees in SERPS have been able to 'contract out' by taking out a personal pension scheme instead.

- If you want to have a bigger pension when you retire than the state pension then it is likely you will need to pay regular amounts from your earnings into a **contributory pension** scheme. These savings build up over time with interest and pay out on retirement usually in the form of a lump sum plus regular payments. The more you contribute the more your pension is likely to be.

Some contributory pensions are also paid into by employers for their employees. Some may even operate their own company pension scheme run by the employer. Payments into the scheme by employees receive tax relief and are deducted from their wages.

Self-employed people must make their own arrangements for a pension with a bank or specialist pension fund provider. Payments can be offset against tax liabilities.

- In some cases workers may not have to pay into a pension scheme because their employer makes regular fixed contributions on their behalf, usually related to the amount they earn each month. These are called **non-contributory pensions**.

Taxation

Both employed and self-employed workers are required by law to pay income tax and National Insurance contributions (NICs). Self-employed people who employ staff of their own may also have to collect income tax and NICs on their behalf.

In addition, some self-employed workers must also register as eligible to pay Value Added Tax (VAT). When entering employment or self-employment, it is important to understand how these statutory requirements work.

Income tax

Self-employed and employed workers are taxed differently. An employee is taxed under the **Pay-As-You-Earn (PAYE)** system, whereby tax is deducted from their wage or salary 'at source' by their employer each week or month. Income tax is therefore automatic for employees, and all of the work in calculating the amount of tax due and when it should be paid is the responsibility of the employer. The employer must, therefore, organize the operation of the PAYE system for their employees.

A self-employed person must arrange to pay tax on their own earnings direct to the Inland Revenue. In order to do this, they must first tell their local tax office the date on which they propose to start being self-employed. Self-employed people normally pay tax in two instalments, in January and July of each year.

The general rule is that tax liability on self-employed earnings is based on profits made in the previous twelve months. This means that self-employed people pay tax one year in arrears. For example, a tax assessment for 1997 will be based upon earnings, net of expenses, in 1996. (A tax year runs from 1 April to 31 March the following year). Because tax is paid in two lump sums, it is necessary to hold over enough earnings in order to meet the tax bill. This requires an element of self-discipline - another possible burden not placed on employees.

UNIT EIGHT

CHAPTER 28

Allowable business expenses

As a self-employed person, you are able to deduct from your earnings any expenses which are wholly and exclusively incurred in carrying out your business. However, the tax authorities will require proof of the expenditure to be detailed in your business accounts.

Allowable business expenses can include:

- Cost of materials - for example, a self-employed decorator can deduct the cost of paints.
- Goods bought for resale - for example, to sell in a shop
- VAT on purchases
- Wages and salaries of employees (including members of your family)
- Business travel
- Interest charges on loans and overdrafts
- Business insurance
- Professional fees - for example, payments to accountants, financial advisers, or solicitors
- Business gifts and entertaining staff and clients
- Subscriptions to professional and trade magazines
- Bad debts (i.e. non-payment of invoices by debtors)
- Running costs (overheads such as rent, rates, electricity and gas, telephone, cleaning, advertising, etc).

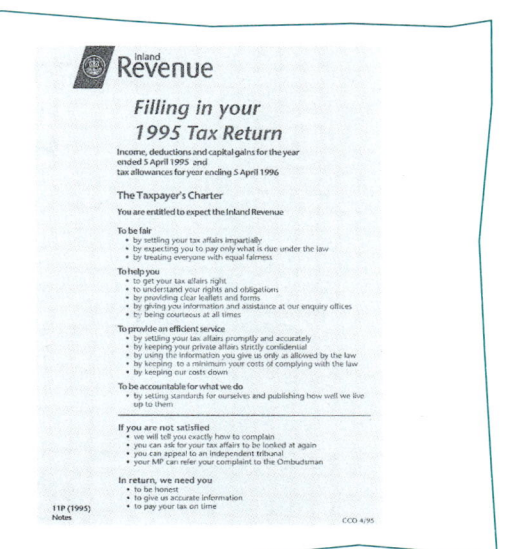

Corporation tax

Profits made by a limited company are liable for **corporation tax**. The tax is usually paid after the end of the company's trading year, and is based on a percentage of the company's profits.

In 1995, a business earning more than £300,000 profit per year was taxed at a marginal rate of 33%. Small businesses, with profits less than £300,000 per year, paid corporation tax at 25%.

National Insurance

Self-employed workers pay National Insurance at a different rate to employees. In order to arrange this, self-employed workers must inform the Department of Social Security.

Self-employed business owners who employ staff will also need to deduct employees' National Insurance Contributions (NICs) from their wages, and pay the additional contributions for each person they employ earning over £59 per week in 1995. National Insurance is calculated as a rising percentage of employees' earnings (see Table 28.2).

▼ Table 28.2: Structure of National Insurance Contributions, 1995-96

Weekly earnings	Employees	Employers
	PERCENTAGE NIC RATE	
Below £59	0	0.0
£59 - £104.99		3.0
£105 - £149.99	2% of £59 plus 10%	5.0
£150 - £204.99	of earnings between	7.0
£205 - £440	£59 and £400	10.2
Over £440		10.2

Value Added Tax (VAT)

In the 1995/96 tax year, a business that expected sales to exceed £46,000 that year had to register for VAT with the Customs & Excise department. VAT charged on goods or services sold to customers must be paid to the

Customs & Excise department every month or quarter, less any VAT paid on goods and services supplied to the business (see 23.2).

If an eligible business fails to register and subsequently claims not to have known about VAT, ignorance will not be accepted as a defence in law. Even if the business failed to charge VAT to its customers, Customs & Excise will still require that any VAT that should have been charged is passed on to them.

Business rates
Unless you run your small business from home, your business will have to pay a lump-sum tax to your local authority, based on the value of the business property.

Licences
Many kinds of business require licences in order to run. These include child-minding, money-lending, and gambling. In addition, taxis, food, and catering are covered by legislation governing business conduct.

When starting a new firm, it is sensible to consult with the local authority planning department, environmental health department, and trading standards office, in order to see how the business might be affected by existing regulations.

Key words

Income tax - tax levied on personal income

National Insurance contributions - payments made by employees and employers to the government in the form of an insurance premium to help cover the cost of unemployment, sickness, bereavement, pensions, and other benefits

Corporation tax - tax levied on business profits

Value Added Tax - tax levied on the price of most goods and services

Pension - a saving scheme to provide income after retirement

Section 28.4 Opportunities for employment and self-employment

Opportunities for employment worldwide
Opportunities for employment and self-employment may present themselves locally, or in other parts of the UK, or even abroad. The more mobile workers are, the more likely they are to find employment. British workers have in the past been notoriously reluctant to move region in order to find employment. This phenomenon, known as **geographical immobility**, has been largely due to a preference for staying in their own home area, but also due to a relative shortage of private rented accommodation in the UK, compared to other countries.

The Single European Market
On 1 January 1993 the **Single European Market** came into being. The creation of a single 'internal' market was intended to remove barriers to trade and allow the free movement of goods, services, and people across European Union member countries (see 17.3).

Britain out in front as jobs centre of Europe

By DAVID NORRIS, Industrial Correspondent

JOB prospects in Britain are brighter than anywhere else in the EU, a report says.

Bosses here are the most optimistic about taking on more workers and helping to cut the dole queue, according to the European Chambers of Commerce, which surveyed 120,000 firms in 11 member states.

Second in the jobs confidence league was Ireland, followed by Greece, Italy and Luxembourg. Significantly, the most pessimistic country was Germany, once hailed as the 'post-war economic miracle'.

Employers there blame statutory worker benefits and the stranglehold of union collective agreements for the country's failure to create more jobs.

Daily Mail 2.2.95

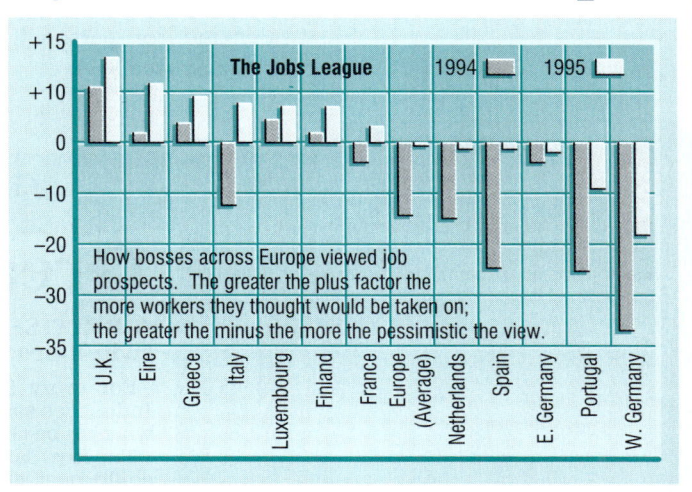

The Jobs League — 1994, 1995

How bosses across Europe viewed job prospects. The greater the plus factor the more workers they thought would be taken on; the greater the minus the more the pessimistic the view.

Countries: U.K., Eire, Greece, Italy, Luxembourg, Finland, France, Europe (Average), Netherlands, Spain, E. Germany, Portugal, W. Germany

---

With the opening of European markets, more and more opportunities for employment and self-employment will present themselves, as workers are allowed to travel freely to live and work in other EU countries.

The European Social Chapter

The European Social Chapter is designed to create similar conditions of employment across Europe, in order to improve labour mobility. This process is being further assisted by the increasing trend towards European-wide recognition of qualifications, as part of the move to the single market. However, barriers to employment mobility still exist between countries, including different languages, different cultures, and, in the case of non-European nations, very different legal systems and product standards. Many overseas governments also require foreign workers to obtain strictly limited permits or visas which will allow them to work in their countries.

Unemployment in Europe

In spite of measures to increase worker mobility across Europe, European unemployment remains high, with an average rate of unemployment of around 11.5% throughout 1993 and 1994. Since large numbers of Europeans are unable to find work in their own countries, it is unlikely that there will be many opportunities there for workers from other parts of Europe. Those opportunities that do exist are for highly qualified, usually professional people, with some command of a foreign language.

Opportunities for self-employment

Opportunities for self-employment in the UK are increasing in the 1990s, due to the tendency of larger firms to shed staff and then re-employ them on a self-employed basis, paid to undertake particular tasks. This reduces costs for employers, who only have to pay staff for the actual work that they do, and gives them the flexibility to employ people as and when they are needed (see 13.3). Also, there will be opportunities for business start-up in new and expanding markets. For example, in 1995 consumer demand for personal computers, DIY and health foods was growing strongly (see 8.3).

Portfolio Activity 28.5

Range: Identify opportunities for employment and self-employment

Skills: Read and respond to written material, Collect and record data

1. What reasons are given for the relocation of BPI to China?

2. What does this suggest about future opportunities for people seeking work in the UK?

3. Collect evidence of further relocations of business activities overseas from local and national newspapers and other sources. How many UK jobs are affected in each case? What are the reasons for relocation?

4. Investigate getting a job overseas in a European Union or non EU country. Produce a short report on:
    - What types of job opportunities exist that interest you?
    - How to apply?
    - What cultural differences should you be aware of?
    - What legal restrictions apply (eg visas)?
    - How will you be taxed on your earnings?

Great call of China

A BRITISH firm is to axe one of its factories and switch production to China to cut costs.

For every £10 of its UK payroll bill, British Polythene Industries says it will spend just £1 in China. Raw materials will also be cheaper.

The firm said yesterday that the move was the only way it could beat cheap imports from the Far East. Around 150 jobs will be lost when it closes its factory at Telford, Shropshire, which makes thin carrier bags for supermarkets.

The move will be seen by unions as another example of an alarming trend. Far Eastern countries rapidly industrialising, are intent not only on undercutting products made in Europe and America with cheap labour and cut-price raw materials, but also on 'importing' jobs from the well-paid West.

In 1992, the London International Group, makers of Durex condoms, shed 650 UK jobs when it switched surgical and kitchen-glove manufacture to Malaysia in a cost-cutting move.

Daily Mail 7.2.95

Section 28.5 Skills for self-employment

Not everybody is suited to self-employment. Being self-employed means being able to manage yourself and others; to prioritize and organize your own time, and decide what to do, without anyone telling you. Some people enjoy managing themselves, while others prefer to work for someone else and have their work organized for them. Not everyone wants to be in a position of being entirely responsible for their own hours of work, their own earnings, and their own success or failure.

To be successful in self-employment requires a variety of different skills. A small business may not be able to afford to buy in these skills from other people or organizations, and so many self-employed people must be 'jacks of all trades'.

UNIT EIGHT

CHAPTER 28

Portfolio Activity 28.6

Range: Skills
Skills: Read and respond to written material

What skills do you think Keith needed to start up his own business and run it successfully?

Cheers, lads!

Like most students, Keith Matthewman would spend ages discussing the problems of the world over a pint of beer. And one of those problems was... the beer. Keith and his counterparts at Blackburn Polytechnic felt that mass-produced British beer couldn't hold a candle to lovingly brewed and matured continental brews.

So he set up his own off-licence - and now he's pulling in £1,000 a week.

Keith says: "I had been in Belgium as a student and realized how superior Belgian beers were to anything produced in England. So when I finished my business studies course, I thought I'd see if there was an opening to sell them here in England."

But as an ex-student Keith had no money to start up in business. So he turned to his friends for capital, borrowed £8,000 and opened an off-licence specializing in stocking the best beers in the world - especially those Belgian beers.

They include 'devil' beer brewed to 8.5 per cent proof, and Bush Beer, brewed to 12 per cent. He also decided to stock the best beers from Lapland, Germany, Italy, and Czechoslovakia.

Daily Mirror 13.9.94

Have you a head for business?

"My best advice is to believe that your position in life will depend to a large extent on the amount of effort you are prepared to put into it. Everybody can't reach the top. But if you have the will, you can find a way to get the most from talents that you are blessed with. Take a step at a time, and you will usually find there is another one ahead if you wish to take it."

Margaret Thatcher, ex-Prime Minister

"To succeed you need determination, single-mindedness, and the ability to grasp opportunities when they arise."

Jennifer D'Abo, Chairman of Ryman Limited

"You need:
- A burning wish to succeed
- A pride in being different
- A desire to be a boss
- A realization that success is 90% hard work and tenacity, and only 10% talent!"

Dr Leah Hertz, authoress and businesswoman

"Never take no for an answer. Even if the group outcome looks bleak, never lie down and die until you're dead."

Richard Branson, Chairman of the Virgin group

681

Useful skills in employment and self-employment

Personal skills	Organizational skills	Communication skills	Numerical skills	Information technology
Working independently	Planning	Oral and written skills	Gathering and handling data	Hands on experience of hardware and software
Working with others	Setting targets	Negotiating	Analysis	
Evaluating your own strengths and weaknesses	Managing time and people	Presentation	Mathematical/statistical	
Reliability under pressure	Monitoring and reviewing performance		Graphical	
Judgement and foresight	Problem-solving		Accounting and book-keeping	
Drive and determination	Information-seeking and handling			

So you think you can run your own business?

Entrepreneurs need to have certain qualities. The following questions will help you find out if you are the right type of person to start up and run your own successful business. For each question, tick the answer you think describes yourself the best. Try to be honest!

1. Are you a self-starter?

   (a) I do things on my own initiative. I don't need anyone to tell me what to do.

   (b) Once someone's explained what to do, I get on with it.

   (c) I bide my time. I won't put myself out unless I have to.

2. How do you get on with people?

   (a) I like people. I get on with just about anybody.

   (b) I have my close circle of friends - I don't really need anyone else.

   (c) I'm never at ease with company. Most people irritate me.

   (d) I'm never comfortable with strangers.

3. Can you lead and motivate others?

   (a) I can get most people to go along with me when I start something.

   (b) I'm very good at giving orders once I know what to do.

   (c) Once something is moving, I'll probably join in.

4. Can you take responsibility?

   (a) I like to take charge and see things through.

   (b) I'll take over if I have to, but I'd prefer someone else to be responsible.

   (c) There's always an eager beaver around waiting to show off. I leave it to them.

   (d) 'Never volunteer' That's my motto.

5. Are you a good organizer?

   (a) I like to have a plan to work to. Most of my friends leave it to me to get things organized.

   (b) As long as I can keep to a plan, it's plain sailing. When unexpected problems arise, I get confused.

   (c) You can get everything carefully prepared, then something comes along to upset the apple cart. So I just take things as they come.

6. How good a worker are you?

   (a) I know what it means to work long hours. I'm quite willing to work hard for something I want.

   (b) I'll work hard for a while, but when I've had enough - that's it.

   (c) I can't see that working hard is that important. Look at all the people who take it easy and still have a good life.

7. Can you make decisions?

   (a) I often make snap decisions. They usually work out well.

   (b) Yes, if I have time to think about them. If I don't have much time, I often regret them later.

   (c) I prefer to leave it to others.

8. Can people trust what you say?

   (a) I'm as straight as a die. I don't say things I don't mean.

   (b) I won't actually lie - but I will sometimes change my mind about things.

   (c) I find it hard to say things which I know will upset people or lead to conflict.

9. Can you stay the course?

   (a) If I decide to do something, nothing will stop me.

   (b) I usually finish what I start - if it goes well.

   (c) If it doesn't go right the first time, I lose interest.

10. How good is your health?

    (a) I can keep going from dawn to dusk, no problem.

    (b) I have enough energy to do most of the things I want to do.

    (c) I seem to run out of energy before most of my friends

Self-employed people need to be able to communicate orally and in writing with a wide range of people, from customers and suppliers, to the Inland Revenue and Customs & Excise department. As they often have to communicate figures to these organizations, skills in numeracy, such as accounting and bookkeeping, are also valuable.

Increasingly, self-employment also requires skills in Information Technology. Even the smallest of businesses now use wordprocessing, mailmerge, spreadsheet and desktop publishing packages to advertise and to communicate with customers and suppliers.

As well as these core skills, it is necessary to be able to plan ahead, to manage others, to take decisions, and to solve problems. With an open mind, all of these skills can be learned.

In self-employment, good organizational skills are absolutely essential because there is no one else to tell you what to do and when to do it. Self-employed business people stand or fall on their own abilities.

Portfolio Activity 28.7

Range: Skills
Skills: Collect and record data

Using the questions given above, and your knowledge of yourself and how you perform in different situations, produce an analysis of your own strengths and weaknesses for employment and self-employment. You might wish to use the careers software of your school or college to assist you, such as Job Information-Generating Computer-Assisted Learning (JIG-CAL).

How can you build on your strengths and correct your weaknesses?

Section 28.6 Sources of information for employment and self-employment

A wide variety of private- and public-sector organizations exist to support people wishing to become employed or self-employed in the UK. These organizations can provide information on employment and business opportunities, as well as advice, guidance, training, and in some cases, capital and grants.

Some of the major sources of information include:

- **Jobcentres:** these can provide information on jobs available in your area. One-to-one interviews and 'Workwise' courses can be arranged, providing intensive help in how to look for work.

- **Training and Enterprise Councils/Local Enterprise Councils:** these are government agencies with offices across the UK, providing a range of training and enterprise support measures. TECs are locally based and are able to identify local business skill shortages and training needs. TECs also operate a range of enterprise and business start-up schemes to help unemployed people to start their own businesses.

- **Chambers of Commerce:** locally based, these provide a range of services for members, including information, conferences and exhibitions, registers, publications, and legal advice.

- **Libraries:** local libraries provide a range of facilities of use to new businesses, including a free enquiry service to callers, database searching, and, in larger libraries, market research and trade directories.

NatWest Small Business Start-up Index

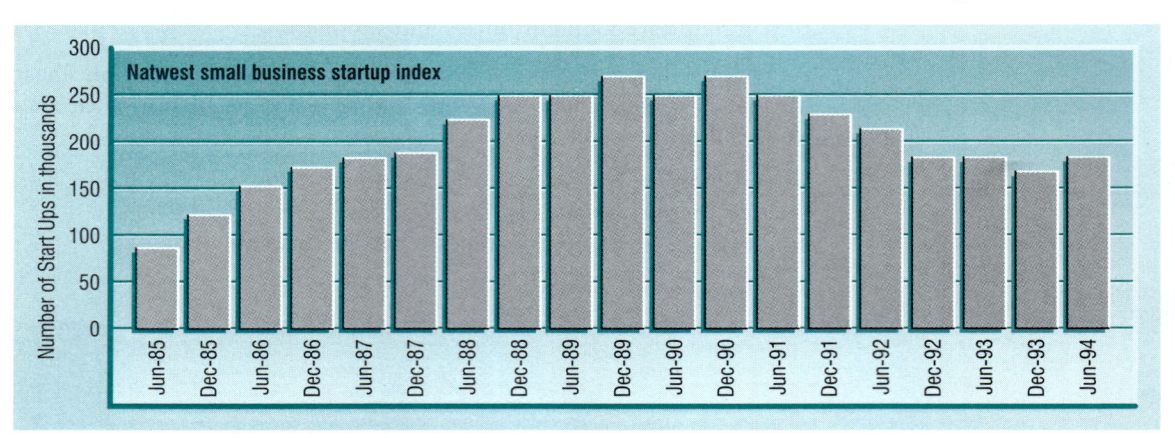

Small businesses could be missing out, due to a lack of awareness of low-cost government and European Union loan schemes. Barclays research has shown that of 400 small business owners, 74% would consider a Government or European institution loan if they needed funds to expand. And 53% would consider changing banks if their own could not offer these loan schemes.

The research showed that awareness of subsidized loan schemes varies. Highest awareness was for the loan guarantee scheme, which was known by 43% of small businesses.

Daily Mirror 22.11.94

- **Commercially produced publications:** commercially available market overview reports give an overall picture of who buys what and why, future trends, and the main operators in a market. These include publications by The Economist Intelligence Unit, *The Financial Times*, and the Mintel market research organization, among many others. Newspapers and magazines also advertise a wealth of jobs.

- **Commercial banks:** the main high street banks produce industry-sector reports, as well as reports on particular countries. They can also give help in preparing business plans and financial advice.

- **Citizens' Advice Bureaux:** these provide a range of advice to individuals on legal matters, and are a good starting point for anyone seeking advice on starting up in business.

- **The Department of Trade and Industry (DTi):** the DTi offers direct support to industry and commerce through its sponsorship of a variety of enterprise initiatives (see 26.4). It can provide an overview of government policies affecting small firms, as well as regional policy, competition policy, and policy on overseas trade (see 3.4).

- **Business directories:** these can be particularly useful as a source of information about competitors. Examples include *Kelly's Business Directory* and *Kompass*, which provides company information on manufacturers and products and services. Specialist directories also provide lists of solicitors, accountants, and business consultants.

- **Employment Department (ED):** the Employment Department is a government department with specific responsibility for employment policy. It publishes a number of free information leaflets and booklets which are generally available from Jobcentres, employment offices, benefit offices, and regional offices of the Employment Department. These can provide a valuable source of information on employment rights for employees.

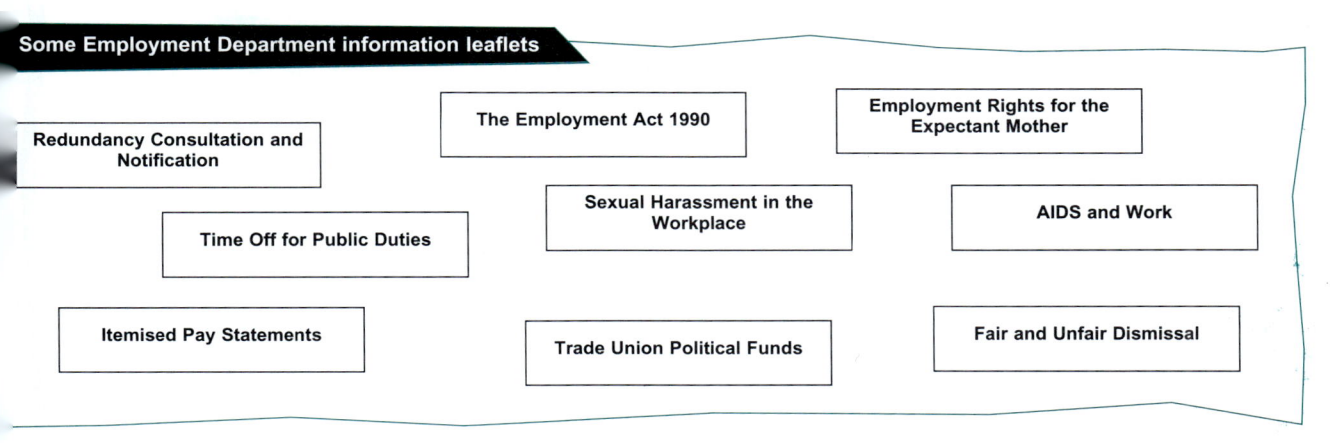

Some Employment Department information leaflets

- Redundancy Consultation and Notification
- The Employment Act 1990
- Employment Rights for the Expectant Mother
- Time Off for Public Duties
- Sexual Harassment in the Workplace
- AIDS and Work
- Itemised Pay Statements
- Trade Union Political Funds
- Fair and Unfair Dismissal

- **Voluntary Service Overseas (VSO):** VSO is an agency for volunteers who wish to make a contribution to charitable work overseas (see 28.2). VSO takes people with a wide range of skills and practical abilities, and attempts to match them with placements abroad.

Section 28.7 Preparing a personal plan for employment or self-employment

In order to achieve success in finding rewarding employment or self-employment, you need to plan in advance. This will help you to prioritize your objectives and avoid wasting time on unimportant issues.

When considering becoming employed or self-employed, there are a wide variety of things to be investigated, considered, and decided upon. The best way to organize them is to create an **action plan**. The plan should list the key things that need to be done, in order, and also give timescales for completion, and sources of information, advice, and support to be used along the way. This can provide a very useful framework for actions to achieve your objectives.

A personal plan

An example of a plan for self-employment is given below. Because each business is different, this plan will not be appropriate in every case, but it does list some of the important issues to be considered when setting up a new firm. Use this plan to help you devise and complete a personal plan for the Assessment Assignment at the end of this chapter. In the 'Achieved' column, if your answer to a question is 'Yes', then you should say how; if your answer is 'No', give reasons.

Advanced Business

▶ *A personal plan for self-employment*

	Achieved	To do	By when?	Support from?
The business Have you chosen a business idea that will suit your personal aptitudes and strengths? Have you identified and taken into account your strengths and weaknesses in relation to running the business on a day-to-day basis? Have you thought about contingency plans for running the business if you should become ill or have an accident? Have you considered your immediate, short-term (1-12 months) and long-term (1-5 years) objectives?				
Sales and marketing Have you identified your main selling points? Have you identified your target market segments and identified their characteristics, including their needs and purchasing behaviour? Have you estimated likely market share and growth of sales? Have you produced projected sales figures for your first year of trading? Have you analysed your strengths, weaknesses, market opportunities, and threats from competition? Have you decided how you will distribute your product? Have you a promotional strategy?				
Costs Have you estimated your costs? Do you know when you will have to pay the costs? Have you worked out break-even levels of output and price?				
Accounting and finance How much working capital will your business require? Have you created a cashflow forecast? Have you anticipated any cashflow problems and worked out a strategy to cope with them? Have you worked out how much you will need, and for what? Have you produced a business plan? Do you need an overdraft in the first year, and have you spoken to the bank about this? Have you identified grants and other sources of external finance which can be used?				
Fixed assets Do you know what fixed assets you will need? Have you worked out where to get them, and on what terms? Have you decided between leasing and buying?				
Location Have you identified a location for the business?				

A plan for **paid employment** (or **voluntary work**) might include:

- An investigation of types of occupation available
- Consideration of the advantages and disadvantages of different jobs
- Consideration of the experience and skills required for particular jobs
- How and when you will acquire these skills
- Methods of job search
- Preparation of a Curriculum Vitae
- Preparation for any job interviews you are invited to (see 14.4).
- Consideration of skills you want to have in 12 months'/5 years' time
- Consideration of the position you want to reach in 12 months' /5 years' time

Plans for both employment and self-employment should also consider the effect of statutory regulations. For example, a potential employee might wish to find out about law relating to equal opportunities, and how this might affect the interview process and employment in general. The action plan should also outline sources of useful advice and information (see 28.5).

Key words

Action plan for employment or self-employment – plan outlining the timescales, legal considerations, and sources of support to be used when seeking employment or self-employment

---

Further reading

Tolley's Tax Guide (usually updated annually)

Armstrong, K: *Taxes on Business* (Kogan Page 1994)

Golzen, G: *Working for Yourself* (Kogan Page 1992)

Some Review Questions

1 What are the main differences between paid employment, voluntary work, and self-employment?

2 Suggest three reasons why self-employment in the UK has risen.

3 What forms of taxation will a self-employed person have to deal with (a) as a self-employed person, and (b) if appropriate, as an employer?

4 What are business rates and how are they calculated?

5 What is the Single European Market? Suggest what impact its creation might have on opportunities for employment for UK citizens. Give reasons for your answer.

6 Suggest two sources of information for an unemployed person looking for paid employment.

7 Suggest three sources of information for a person investigating opportunities for self-employment.

8 List ten skills a person will need to run a business and perform well in paid employment.

Assessment Assignment

Range: Types
Statutory requirements
Skills
Sources of information
Personal plan

Skills: **Communication**
Take part in discussions
Produce written material
Application of Number
Collect and record data
Information Technology
Prepare information
Process information
Present information

Produce a personal plan for employment or self-employment

You are required to investigate alternative ways of becoming employed or self-employed, either as a sole trader, partner, franchise-holder, or any other method that appeals to you, including voluntary work. You should identify the area of business which you would like to enter.

Tasks

1. Choose a route to employment or self-employment (or voluntary work), and justify why this is best for you by referring in detail to an assessment of your own strengths and weaknesses. Suggest possible strategies to overcome any weaknesses that you have identified and build on your strengths.

2. For your chosen kind of employment, draw up a personal plan showing how you might achieve your short-term and long-term goals. The plan should indicate:

- The steps which you would need to take to become employed or self-employed
- The timescales by which you would hope to achieve your goals
- The information sources and sources of support or help that you would wish to call on
- Statutory requirements for your selected employment or self-employment opportunity

Appendix

Appendix: Sources of further information

Useful contact addresses

Advertising Association
Abford House
15 Wilton Road
London SW1V 1NJ

Advertising Standards Authority
Brook House
2-16 Torrington Place
London WC1E 7HN

Arbitration, Conciliation and Advisory Service (ACAS)
Clifton House
83 Euston road
London NW1

Association of British Insurers
51 Gresham Street
London EC2V 7HQ

Association of British Travel Agents (ABTA)
55 Newman Street
London W1

Banking Information Service
10 Lombard Street
London EC3V 9AT

Bank of England Information Division
Threadneedle Street
London EC2R 8AH

Barclays Bank plc
54 Lombard Street
London EC3P 3AH

The Body Shop International plc
Watersmead
Littlehampton
West Sussex BN17 6LS

Boots Company plc
1 Thane Road West
Nottingham

BBC Education and Training
BBC Enterprises
Woodlands
Wood Lane
London W12 0TT

British Cement Association
Wexham Springs
Slough
Berkshire SL3 6PL

British Computer Society
Station Road
Swindon
Wiltshire SN1 1TG

British Gas plc
326 High Holborn
London WC1B 7PT

British Institute of Management
Management House
Cuttingham Road
Corby
Northants NN17 1TT

British Petroleum plc (Educational Service)
Brittanic House
Moor Lane
London EC2Y 9BU

British Standards Institution
Linford Wood
Milton Keynes
Buckinghamshire MK14 6LE

British Telecom Education Service
2-10 Gresham Street
London EC2V 7AG

British Textile Confederation
British Textile and Apparel Centre
7 Swallow Place
London W1R 7AA

British Tourist Authority
Thames Tower
Blacks Road
London W6 9EL

Cadbury World
Linden Road
Bournville
Birmingham B30 2LD

Careers and Occupational Information Centre
Moorfoot
Sheffield S1 4PQ

Careers Research and Advisory Centre
Hobsons Press (Cambridge)
Bateman Street
Cambridge CB2 1LZ

Central Statistical Office
Government Buildings
Cardiff Road
Newport
Gwent NP9 1XG
(Enquiries 01633 812973)

Centre for Alternative Technology
Llwyngwern Quarry
Machynlleth
Powys
Wales SY20 9AZ

Chemicals Industries Association Ltd
Kings Buildings
Smith Square
London SW1P 3JJ

Coca Cola GB
Pemberton House
Wrights Lane
London W8 5SN

Commission of the European Communities
8 Storeys Gate
London SW1P 3AT

Confederation of British Industry (CBI)
Centre Point
103 New Oxford Street
London WC1A 3AT

Conservation Trust
Basingstoke Road
Reading
Berkshire RG2 0EN

Conservative Research Department
33 Smith Square
Westminster
London SW1P 3HH

Construction Industry Training Board
Bircham Newton
Kings Lynn
Norfolk PE31 6RH

Consumers' Association
14 Buckingham Street
London WC2N 6DS

Cooperative Bank plc
1 Bloom Street
Manchester M60 4EP

Cooperative Retail Services Ltd
54 Maryland Street
Stratford
London E15 1JE

Cooperative Union Ltd
Stamford Hall
Loughborough
Leics. LE5 5QR

Corporation of City of London
Guildhall
London EC2P 2EJ

Council for Environmental Education
University of Reading
London Road
Reading
Berkshire RG1 5AQ

Customs and Excise Department
New Kings Beam House
22 Upper Ground
London SE1 9PJ

Daily Express
121 Fleet Street
London EC4P 4JT

Daily Mail
Carmelite House
Carmelite Street
London EC4Y 0JA

Daily Mirror
33 Holborn
London EC1

Department of Employment
Public Enquiry Office
Caxton House
Tothill Street
London SW1H 9NA

Department of the Environment
2 Marsham Street
London SW1P 3EB

Department of Trade and Industry (DTi)
Ashdown House
123 Victoria Street
London SW1E 6RB

Department of Social Security
Adelphi
1-11 John Adams Street
London WC2N 6HT

Economist Newspaper Ltd
25 St James Street
London SW1A 1HG

The Employment Service
Rockingham House
123 West Street
Sheffield S1 4ER

Engineering Training Authority
41 Clarendon Road
Watford
Hertfordshire WD1 1HS

Esso UK plc Public Affairs Dept.
Esso House
Victoria Street
London SW16 5JW

European Parliament UK Office
2 Queen Anne's Gate
London SW1

Exports Credit Guarantee Department
2 Exchange Tower
Harbour Exchange
London E14 9GS

Federation of Recruitment and
Employment Services
26-38 Mortimer Street
London W1N 7RB

Federation of Small Businesses
140 Lower Marsh
London SE1 7AE

Financial Times Ltd
1 Southwark Bridge
London SE1 9HL

APPENDIX

Food and Farming Information Service
European Business Centre
462 Fulham Road
London SW6 1BY

Friends of The Earth
377 City Road
London EC1V 1NA

GALLUP
307 Finchley Road
London NW3

General Agreement on Tariffs and Trade (GATT)
Center William Rappard
Rue de Lausanne 154
CH-1211 Geneva
Switzerland

Greenpeace
Canonbury Villas
London N1 2PN

Health and Safety Executive
Baynards House
1 Chepstow Place
London W2 4TF

HMSO Publications Centre
PO Box 276
London SW8 5DT
(Enquiries 0171 873 0011)

Investors in Industry (3i)
91 Waterloo Road
London SE1 8XP

Imperial Chemicals Industries plc (ICI) School Liaison Section
Group Personnel Department
Bessemer Road
Welwyn Garden City
Herts AL7 1HD

Independent Broadcasting Authority
70 Brompton Road
London SW3 1EY

Industrial Society
Peter Runge House
3 Carlton House Terrace
London SW1 5DG

Board of Inland Revenue
Somerset House
London WC2R 1LB

Institute of Marketing
Moor Hall
Cookham
Buckinghamshire

Institute of Materials
1 Carlton House Terrace
London SW1Y 5DB

Institute of Personnel Management
Camp Road
Wimbledon
London SW19 4UX

International Labour Office
96-98 Marsham Street
London SW1P 4LY

John Lewis Partnership
4 Old Cavendish Street
London W1A 1EX

Labour Party
150 Walworth Road
London SE17 1JT

Labour Research
78 Blackfriars Road
London SE1 8HF

Liberal Party
1 Whitehall Place
London SW1A 2HE

Lloyds of London
Publicity and Information Dept.
Lime Street
London EC3M 7HA

Lloyds Bank plc
Black Horse House
78 Cannon Street
London EC4P 4LN

London Chamber of Commerce and Industry
Marlowe House
Station Road
Sidcup
Kent DA15 7BJ

Marks & Spencer plc Public Relations Dept.
Michael House
47 Baker Street
London W1A 1DN

Midland Bank plc Schools Liaison Office
3 Kings Arms Yard
London EC2R 7BA

Ministry of Agriculture, Fisheries and Food (MAFF)
Whitehall Place
London SW1A 2HH

Monopolies and Mergers Commission (MMC)
New Court
48 Carey Street
London WC2A 2JT

MORI
26 Bloomsbury Square
London WC1

Motor Industry Education Service
Society of Motor Manufacturers and Traders
Forbes House
Halkin Street
London SW1X 7DS

Advanced Business

National Farmers' Union
Agriculture House
25-31 Knightsbridge
London SW1X 7NJ

National Girobank plc
Bootle
Merseyside GIR 0AA

National Opinion Poll (NOP)
1 Berners Street
London W1

National Westminster Bank plc
41 Lothbury
London EC2P 2BP

Nestle UK Ltd Consumer Services
St George's House
Croydon
Surrey CR9 1NR

Northern Ireland Department
Dundonald House
Belfast BT4 3SB

Nuclear Electric plc
Barnett Way
Barnwood
Gloucestershire GL4 7RS

Office of Electricity Regulation
Hagley House
Hagley Road
Edgbaston
Birmingham
B16 8QG

Office of Fair Trading (OFT)
Field House
15-25 Breams Buildings
London EC4A 1PR

Office of Gas Supply (Ofgas)
Stockley House
130 Wilton Road
London SW1V 1LG

Office of Population Censuses and Surveys
Census Information Unit
54 St Catherine's House
10 Kingsway
London WC2B 6JP

Office of Telecommunications (OfTel)
50 Ludgate Hill
London EC4M 7JJ

Office of Water Services (OfWat)
Centre City Tower
7 Hill Street
Birmingham B5 4UA

Organization for Economic Cooperation and Development (OECD)
2, Rue Andre-Pascal
75775 Paris CEDEX 16
France

Overseas Development Administration (ODA)
94 Victoria Street
London SW1E 5JL

Procter and Gamble Ltd
City Road
Newcastle upon Tyne NE99 1EL

Royal Bank of Scotland plc
Public Relations Office
42 St Andrew Square
Edinburgh EH2 2YE

Royal Society for the Prevention of Cruelty to Animals (RSPCA)
Causeway
Horsham
W. Sussex
RH12 1HG

Scottish Office
Pentland House
47 Robbs Loan
Edinburgh EM14 1TG

Shell UK
Shell Mex House
Strand
London WC2R 0DX

The Stock Exchange
Information Dept.
London EC2N 1HP

Tesco Stores Ltd
Customer Services Dept.
Tesco House
Delamare Road
Cheshunt
Waltham Cross
Hertfordshire EN8 9SL

Trade Union Congress (TUC)
Congress House
Great Russell Street
London 3LS

HM Treasury
Treasury Chambers
Parliament Street
London SW1P 3AG

Unilever
Unilever House
Blackfriars
London EC4P 4BQ

Welsh Office
Cathays Park
Cardiff CF1 3NQ

World Bank
New Zealand House
London SW1

World Society for the Protection of Animals (WSPA)
2 Langley Lane
London SW8 1BR

APPENDIX

Useful statistical references

CSO Annual Abstract of Statistics (HMSO)

A comprehensive document of annual economic, vital and industrial statistics over the preceding 10-year period. Detailed information on the outputs and performance of individual industrial sectors is given, along with macro-economic information on prices, employment, overseas trade, public expenditure, and national income.

Bank reviews

All the main high street banks produce quarterly economic reviews and bulletins, usually free of charge. These will contain articles and data on UK economic and business performance.

CSO Blue Book - UK National Accounts (HMSO)

This annual publication provides detailed information on total output, income, and expenditure in the UK. Output is disaggregated by industrial sector and expenditure by category.

CSO Business Monitors (HMSO)

Up-to-date monthly publication of statistics on a variety of topics, including overseas trade, product and retail price indices, overseas travel and tourism, and production in a number of industrial sectors: coal, oil and gas, car and commercial vehicles, retail sales, aerospace, and electronics.

OECD Economic Outlook (OECD)

Twice a year the OECD surveys the latest economic developments in OECD countries and assesses policies and future prospects, making use of an internationally consistent set of quantitative forecasts. The surveys provide analysis and projection of real growth in total output and incomes; the evolution of domestic demand, costs, and product; unemployment and productivity; foreign trade; developments in major non-OECD countries; international financial developments, and more. OECD Economic Outlook is also available on disk.

CSO Economic Trends (HMSO)

A highly recommended publication which brings together all the main economic and business indicators. The largest section gives time series over the last five years or so, preceded by several pages of the latest information, and followed by an analysis of indicators in relation to the business cycle over the last 20 years. Other articles comment on and analyse economic statistics. Economic Trends is the primary publication for details of quarterly national accounts and the balance of payments. It is published monthly with four quarterly supplements and an annual supplement.

Employment Gazette (Department of Employment)

A highly recommended monthly publication by the Department of Employment, containing a wealth of data on the UK labour market - employment, average earnings and hours, productivity, unemployment, training - and international comparisons. Particular features and surveys of the labour market are reported in depth, with supporting graphs, tables, and charts, many in colour. New employment and training initiatives, policies, and parliamentary questions feature as news items in the magazine.

European Economy (Office for Official Publications of the European Communities)

Published four times a year in March, May, July, and November, this journal contains important reports and communications from the European Commission and Council of Ministers on the economic situation and developments in European Union (EU) member countries. It also presents reports and studies on problems concerning economic policy. Two supplements accompany the main journal. These are:

• European Economy Supplement Series A: Economic Trends: published 11 times a year, this describes with the aid of graphs and tables the most recent trends of industrial production, consumer prices, unemployment, the balance of payments, exchange rates, and other indicators. It also presents the Commission's forecasts of these variables.

• European Economy Supplement Series B - Business and Consumer Survey Results: also published 11 times a year, this gives the main results of opinion surveys of industrial executives (e.g. on orders, stock levels, production outlook, etc.) and consumers (e.g. on the general economic and financial situation, outlook, etc.) in EU member countries, and other business cycle indicators.

Eurostat (Office for Official Publications of the European Communities)

A very useful handbook published every year, containing a wealth of data on all the countries in the European Union. Information is provided on economic variables such as GDP, prices, the balance of payments, and government finance; plus statistics on population, employment, wages, primary and industrial production, foreign trade, transport and communications, and the environment. Eurostat can be obtained from HMSO.

Financial Statement and Budget Report (HMSO)

This is published once a year following the UK government's budget. The report contains background discussions of economic trends in the UK economy, and details of the changes to taxes and public spending announced in the budget.

CSO Financial Statistics (HMSO)

This provides data on a wide variety of financial topics, including the financial accounts of the economy, government income and spending, public-sector borrowing, banking statistics, investment by financial institutions, company finance and liquidity, share prices and exchanges, and interest rates. It is published monthly with an annual supplement.

CSO Monthly Digest of Statistics (HMSO)

This monthly publication provides basic information on 20 subjects, including population, output, employment and prices, energy, social services, construction, manufacturing, transport, catering, national and overseas finance. It contains mostly runs of monthly data and quarterly estimates for at least two years, and annual figures for several more.

New Earnings Survey (HMSO)

This is an annual six-part comprehensive report on earnings and hours of work in the UK, published by the Department of Employment. It contains analyses giving results for employees in particular wage negotiation groups, industries, age/sex groups, occupations, regions, and sub-regions.

CSO Pink Book - UK Balance of Payments (HMSO)

This contains the most comprehensive annual data on UK international payments accounts over the last decade. It details export and imports by value and volume, type, origin, and destination, and flows of investments into and out of the UK. It is published annually.

CSO Regional Trends (HMSO)

This annual publication provides a unique description of the regions of the UK, covering a wide range of social, vital, demographic, industrial, and economic statistics

CSO Social Trends (HMSO)

This annual publication draws together statistics from a wide range of government departments and other organizations to provide a broad picture of British society today, in terms of population and household characteristics, education, employment, income and wealth, expenditure patterns, health, leisure pursuits, crime and justice, housing, transport, and the environment. Social Trends is a must for students of business. It is also available on CD-Rom.

The Times 1,000 (Times Books)

This is an annual review of the world's leading industrial and financial companies, in terms of their turnover, capital employed, stock market values, number of employees, and profits. Top performing organizations are ranked for their position in the world, Europe, the UK, and a host of other countries, including the USA and Japan.

National newspapers

Newspapers such as the Financial Times, The Times, the Independent and the Guardian contain up-to-date news items and special features on almost all aspects of daily business activities and trends in the UK and world economies. The Daily Mirror and Daily Mail also carry useful business articles.

The European also sometimes carries useful articles on developments in the European Union.

Specialist magazines

There are a wealth of business magazines available on all aspects of business, from management to marketing, and from franchising to finance. Many are available 'off the shelf' in large newsagents and book stores. Further reading lists in each chapter will indicate which are the most appropriate.

Index

A

About Advanced GNVQ 2-7
Above and below the line promotion 204
Absorption costing 498
Accountability 196
Accountants 569
Accounting
 final accounts 585
 balance sheet 571–78
 profit and loss 568, 579, 580–1, 578–83, 596
 ratios 601–7
 trial balance and final accounts 583–7
Accounting periods 568
Accounting to control business 592–3
Acid test ratio 603
Activity ratios 601, 605–7
Adding value 457–60
Administration 132
Administration expenses to sales ratio 605
Administrative functions 136–140
Administrative systems 131–51
Advertising 55, 240–4, 341
Advertising Standards Authority 254
Advice note 477
After sales service 271
Age market segmentation 235
Age-sex pyramid 236
Aged creditors 464, 596
Aged debtors 464, 596
Agenda 158
Agents 265
Aggregate demand 75
Aims of business 259–61
Amplification and guidance for GNVQ specifications 3
Analysing data 15–19
Annualized hours systems 324
Application form 342–5
Apprenticeships 283
Appropriation account 579, 581
Arbitration and Conciliation Service (ACAS) 296, 635
Arithmetic mean 16
Articles of Association 108, 671
Asset insurance 625
Asset management 530
Asset stripping 86
Asset turnover ratio 605–6
Assets 529
 current 529, 571, 575
 fixed 571, 575
Assisted areas 543
Audit trail 490
Auditors 569
Average costs 499

B

Average earnings 405
Average product of labour 367

Bad debts 464, 582
Balance of payments 74, 425
Balance sheet 568, 571–8, 596
 formats 575–7
 projected for a new business 658–9
Balancing item 426
Bank Giro Credit 486
Bank loan 533
Bank reconciliation 488
Bank statement 486–8
Bankers Automated Clearing Service (BACS) 483
Bar charts 9, 10
Barter 21
Batch production 373, 652
Below the line promotion 204
Benchmarking 371, 645
Board of directors 314
Book value 562
Books of prime entry 584
Boom 422
Boycott 301
Brand loyalty 250
Branding 204
Break even analysis 511–16, 618
British Standards Institute (BSI) 144, 254, 372
BS5750 144
Budget deficit 77
Budgets 596, 597–9
Built-in obsolescence 201
Business cycle 422, 668
Business Directories 684
Business Links Advice Centres 439
Business meetings 158
Business objectives 102, 617–19, 641–2
Business optimism 37
Business organizations 101
Business Plan 531
Business Plan purposes of 619–20
Business planning 615–619, 640–61
Business planning Support for 633–6
Business planning, law relating to 620–4
Business planning, managing resources 627–33
Business rates 677
Business start up 675
Business Start up Scheme 544, 668
Business targets 592–3
Buying and selling 461–3

C

Called up share capital 575
Capital 23, 101, 529, 571
Capital budget 555
Capital gain 540
Capital goods market 28
Capital intensive production 367
Capital market 536–8
Carriage inwards and outwards 582
Cascading information 160
Cash 551, 553
Cash discounts 475
Cash inflows 556
Cash outflows 556–7
Cash sale 463
Cashbook 585
Cashflow 655–7
Cashflow cycle 553
Cashflow forecasting 555–9
Cashflow problems 560–2
Cashflow smoothing 555
Cashflow statement 596
Casual workers 403
CD-ROMS 175, 178–9
Cellular phones 160
Central government departments 101
Central Processing Unit (CPU) 146
Certificate of incorporation 108
Chairperson 158, 315
Chambers of Commerce 635, 684
Changes in demand 30,31
Changes in production 364–5
Changes in supply 35–8
Channels of communication 154
Charities 103, 507
Cheque cards 483
Cheques 481–3
Chief Executive 315
Citizens Advice Bureaux 684
Clean Air Act 385
Clearing banks 533
Clearing House Automated Payments System (CHAPS) 484
Closed questions in market research 224
Coaching 283
Collateral 532
Collective Bargaining 301
Commission 265, 379
Commodities market 28
Common Agricultural Policy (CAP) 82
Communication breakdowns 166–8
Communication objectives 155
Communication Systems 153–70
Communications technology 156
Companies (see limited companies)
Companies Acts 107
Company registration 675
Company secretary 315

695

Competition 51–5
Competition based pricing 520–1
Competition policy 85, 438
Competitiveness 421
Complementary goods 32
Computer Aided Design (CAD) 180, 374–5
Computer Aided Manufacture (CAM) 180, 374
Computer networks 148
Conscience spending 239
Consultancy initative 544
Consultants 319
Consumer Credit Act 272
Consumer goods market 27
Consumer panels 222
Consumer protection 88, 272, 623
Consumer Protection Act 272
Consumer spending patttens 228
Consumers 24
Contract of employment 290–311
Contracting out 89, 93
Contribution pricing 516–7
Controlling interest 108
Cooperatives 101
Core skills 3
Core workers 320
Corporation tax 676
Cost based pricing 202, 509–11, 516–8
Cost of sales 579
Cost plus pricing 516
Cost push inflation 434
Costs of production 37, 497
Council of Ministers 444
Craft unions 299
Credit 584
Credit cards 533
  clearance and control 273, 464
  note 478, 585
  periods 558
  sale 463
Critical path analysis 631–2
Crossed cheque 483
Cumulative frequency curves 11
Cumulative preference shares 540
Current account (balance of payments) 425
Current assets 529, 571, 575
Current liabilities 572, 575
Current ratio 602
Curriculum Vitae 345
Customer care 270
Customer focus 195
Customs union 445

D

Data Protection Act 186, 188, 310
Databases 177
Debentures 538
Debit 584
Debit note 478

Debtor collection period ratio 606–7
Debtors 464, 529
Deed of partnership 106
Deindustrialisation 397–401
Delivery note 477
Demand
  based pricing 203
  changes in 30–1
  curves 29–30, 40–1, 43–4, 52, 55, 82
  elasticity of demand 43, 44, 52, 94
  excess 40
Demand push inflation 434
Demographic segmentation 235
Department of Trade and Industry 635
Departments 136
Depreciation 496
Deregulation 93, 438
Desktop publishing software 176
Destroyer pricing 521
Destruction pricing 54
Development Areas 84, 543
Differentiated marketing 201
Direct costs 494
Direct marketing 248–9
Direct taxes 76
Disabled Persons Act 287–8
Disciplinary procedures at work 292–3
Discounts 582
Diseconomies of scale 502
Disruption of trading insurance 626
Distribution 139, 203, 261–8, 648
Diversification 253, 326
Dividend 539
Double entry bookkeeping 584
Downsizing 321
DTI 684

E

Economic activity rate 412–14
Economic and Social Committee 444
Economic bads 63
Economic goods 63
Economic growth 63, 74, 421
Economies of scale 95, 202, 501–2
Economy 23
Education and training 441–3
Effectiveness 132
Efficiency 132
Elastic demand 44, 52
Elasticity of demand 43
Elasticity of supply 46
Electronic communications 163
Electronic Data Interchange (EDI) 163, 181, 484
Electronic Information Processing 172, 174–81
Electronic Mail (E-mail) 163, 181
Electronic Point of Sale (EPOS) 221
Emerging markets 423–4

Employee rights 286–7
Employers Associations 301
Employers liability insurance 626
Employment 664–6
Employment Act 293
Employment agencies 340
Employment department 684
Employment law 620–2
Employment trends 390–6
Employment types 402–3
Empowerment 371
Enhanced telephone networks 165
Enterprise Zones 544
Entrepreneurs 615
Environmental protection 85, 90, 385, 622
Equal Opportunities Commission 288
Equal pay Act 291
Equities 540
Estimates 473
European Commission 444, 545
European Court of Justice 297, 444
European Currency Unit 446
European Investment Bank 545
European Parliament 444
European Regional Development Fund (ERDF) 545
European Social Fund (ESF) 545
European Union 444–7
European Union working time directive 313
Evidence indicators 3
Excess demand 40
Excess supply 40
Exchange Rate Mechanism (ERM) 446–7
Exchange rates 79, 428
Executive directors 315
Exchange rate stabilization 437
Expansion pricing 54, 520
Exports 424, 427
External communication 153, 155, 162–5
External recruitment 339–40
External sources of finance 530–1
External workers 321
Externalities 64–5

F

Face to face communication 157
Face to face survey 222
Face value 539
Facsimile 164
Factoring 535
Factory sales 265
Fair Trading Act 86
Franchise 672
Fast moving consumer goods (FMCG) 206
Finance and accounting department 136–7
Final Accounts 585

INDEX

Financial
  accountants 569
  documents 471–6
  economies 502
  intermediation 532
  planning 654
  records, accuracy and security of 489–90
  policy 76–7, 435,
  statements 570
  transactions 425
Fixed assets 571, 575
Fixed budget 598
Fixed costs 494, 496–7, 509
Flexible budget 598
Flexible worforce 320, 441
Flexitime 324, 377
Floppy disks 175
Flotation 539
Flow production 652
Focus groups 223
Food Safety Act 272
Forecasts 596
Foreign Currencies 428
Foreign exchange market 28
Formal communication 154
Franchising 93
Freehold 629
FT-SE 100 540
FT-SE Actuaries All Share Index 540
Full time employment 402

G

GANNT Chart 632
Gap in the market 616
Gearing ratio 546
Gender market segmentation 237
General Agreement on Tariffs and Trade (GATT) 448
General ledger 584
General National Vocational Qualifications 442
General unions 299
Geographical market segmentation 238
Gilt-edged securities 538
Go-slow 301
Goods Received Note (GRN) 476
Government
  assistance 543–5
  economic objectives 433
  intervention in markets 70
  spending 436
  statistics 218
Grading, GNVQ 5
Graphics packages 180
Grievance procedures 293, 310
Gross Domestic Product (GDP) 421
Gross misconduct 293
Gross profit 580
Gross profit margin 603

H

Hard disks 175
Hardware 146
Headhunting 341
Health and Safety 184, 291–2, 310, 381–3
Health and Safety Executive 292
Health and Safety law 621–2
Henry Fayol 317
Hire purchase 534
Histograms 11
Home shopping 249
Homogeneous product 201
Hours of work 405
Human resources 23, 27, 137, 279, 628

I

Impact of new technology 182–4
Imported inflation 435
Imports 424, 427
In-house training courses 283
Income 32, 237
Income and expenditure accounts 583
Income elasticity 46
Income tax 675
Incomes policy 80
Incompetence in employment 293
Independent Television Commission 254
Index numbers 13
Indirect costs 494–5
Indirect taxes 76, 82
Industrial
  action 301
  relations 301
  tribunal 288, 294–5
  unions 299
Industry training organizations 442
Inelastic demand 44, 94
Infant industries 84
Inflation 74, 433–4
Informal communication 154
Information processing systems 171–90
Informative advertising 241
Inner City Task Force Areas 544
Innovation 439
Input tax 559
Insolvency 552
Insurance 625–6
Intangible assets 571
Intemediaries in distribution 263
Interest rates 435
Intermediate Areas 543
Internal communication 153, 155, 161
Internal finance 530
Internal recruitment 339
International trade 424
Internet 164
Interview bias 227

Interviews 350–5
Investment 440, 575
Investment capital 529
Investors 539
Investors in People Award 282
Invisible
  export 425
  import 425
Invisible trade 425
Invoice 474–5
  errors and omissions 476
ISDN 149, 165
IT in administration 145–9

J

Job
  analysis 334
  centres 340, 684
  description 335–6
  design 284, 379
  enlargement 379
  enrichment 380
  production 373, 651
  roles 314
  rotation 283, 380
  satisfaction 327, 441
  sharing 325
  targets 309
Joint stock companies 106
Joint ventures 93
Just in time production 370–1, 467, 653

K

Kaizen 371

L

Labour 23
Labour intensive production 367
Labour market 28
Labour market, changes in 390–1
Law relating to business 620–4
Learning credits 443
Leasehold 629
Leasing 534
Ledger accounts 584
Legal obligations of employers 267
Legislation 73, 85–90
Letter of application 347
Liabilities 571–2
Licences 677
Lifestyle market segmentation 239
Lifetime targets 442
Limited companies 108–9, 671
Limited liability 102, 671
Limited partnerships 106
Line graphs 12
Liquid assets 529, 551
Liquidation 552
Liquidity 551
Liquidity ratios 601
Loan capital 531

697

Loan Guarantee Scheme 545
Loan stocks 537–8
Local area network 148, 163
Local authorities 101, 545
Local Enterprise Agencies 635
Local Enterprise Councils (LECs) 442
Local government bonds 538
Long term finance 531

M
Macro-economic policy 74–80
Mail order 24, 265–6
Mailmerge 177
Mailshots 248
Management 316–18
Management accountants 569
Management accounting 595
Management diseconomies 502
Management Information System (MIS) 374
Managers 316
Managing director 315
Manual and non–manual labour 414–15
Manual information processing 172, 174
Manual occupations 403
Margin of safety 514–15
Marginal cost 500
Marginal cost pricing 518
Market
   based pricing 519–23
   demand 28
   failure 71
   niche marketing 195
   orientated approach 195
   potential 616–17
   prices 38–40
   research 210–57
   research stages 212
   segments 234–7
   share 52, 102
   skimming 54, 519
   structure 195, 508
   supply 33–8
Marketing
   budget 649
   communication methods 240
   economies 502
   ethics 254
   mass 195
   mix 200–07, 643–50
   objectives 197–9
   operation of 50–69
   place in marketing 203
   plan 643
   principles 193–4
   promotion 203–7, 246–7, 646–8
   test marketing 223
   undifferentiated marketing 201

Markets
   defined 27
   expanding 207
   contracting 207
Mass marketing 195
Master budget 596
Measures of central tendency 16–19
Median 17
Meetings-types of 159
Memorandum of Association 672
Memorandums 161
Merchant banks 537
Mergers 85–6
Micro-economic policy 73, 81–4
Microsoft Windows 147
Middle managers 318
Minutes 161
Mission statements 619
Mobile phones 160
Mode 17
Modem 148
Modern apprenticeships 442
Monetary Policy 78–80
Money 22
Money cycle 462
Money market 533–5
Monitoring business performance 594, 661
Monopolies 94–5, 624
Monopolies and Mergers Commission 87
Monopolies and Trade Practices Act 86
Mortgages 537
Motivating employees 284–5
Motivation strategies 377–80
Multi-purpose computer systems 180
Multi-skilling 416
Multi-tasking 147
Multi-track communication 154
Multimedia 179

N
National Education and Training Targets 442
National insurance 77, 409, 677
National Vocational Qualifications 283, 442
Nationalization 96
Nationalized industries 91, 94
Natural monopolies 91
Natural resources 23, 27
Needs and wants 20
Net assets 575
Net Profit margin 603, 604
Net realizable value 562
NETTS 442
Niche marketing 195
Non-contract employment 403
Non-executive directors 315
Non-operating income 581

Non-price competition 55
Non-profit making organizations 583
Non-standard labour 322
Non-verbal communication 161–5

O
OECD 421, 427
Off the job training 283
OFFER 95
Office of fair trading 86
OFGAS 95
OFTEL 95
OFWAT 95
Oligopolies 624
On the job training 283
One way communication 154
Open cheque 483
Open communication 155
Open ended interview 222
Open questions 224
Open systems 183
Operating busgets 596
Operatives 319–20
Opportunities for employment 665
Opportunity cost 27
Optimum scale of production 502
Ordinary shares 540
Organizational hierarchy 309
ORR 95
Output per employee 429
Output tax 559
Overdraft 533
Overheads 495
Overstocking 561
Overtime ban 301
Overtrading 560

P
Pagers 164
Part time employment 402, 407–9
Participating preference shares 540
Participation rate 412
Partnership 671
Partnerships 106
Patents 214
Pay-As-You-Earn 675
Paying in slip 486
Payments documents 481–4
Penetration pricing 54, 520
Pension 675
Performance criteria 3
Performance related Pay (PRP) 285, 377, 379
Peripheral workers 321
Permanent capital 531
Person specification 337–8
Personal disposable income 237
Personal savings 530
Personal selling 266
Personnel–see Human resources
Persuasive advertising 241

INDEX

Physical distribution 267
Physical resources in business 628
Pie charts 9
Place in marketing 203
Planned economies 23
Plant 24
Point of sale service 270
Policy instruments 75
Pollution 384–6
Population changes 33
Portfolio management 4
Postal services 162–3
Postal survey 222
Preference shares 540
Presenting data 8–14
Price
   creaming 519
   determination 507, 520
   elasticity of demand 43
   elasticity of supply 46
   floors and ceilings 81–2
   leadership 520
   marketing 202
   leadership 520
   mechanism 41
   war 54
Pricing-influences on 507, 508
Primary research 217, 221–7
Primary sector 397
Princes Youth Business Trust 635
Private costs and benefits 64
Private Finance Initative 436
Private firms 101
Private Limited Company 671
Private sector businesses 105, 664
Privatization 74, 92, 438
Processing orders 273
Producer price index 433
Producers 24
Product
   development 213–14
   focus 195
   marketing 201
Product liability insurance 626
Product life cycle 250–1
Product performance 250
Product portfolio 252–3
Product superiority 52
Production 24, 363–88
   budget 598
   department 138
   plan 650–54
   value added in production 457
Productivity 145, 363, 366–9
Professional associations 340
Profit and Loss 568, 596
   account 579, 580–1
   statement 578–83
   projected 659–60

Profit
   before tax 581
   maximization 618
   motive 102
   retained 530
   gross 580
   net profit margin 603, 604
Profitability ratios 601, 603–4
Profitability 594
Promotion 203–7, 646–8
Proof of purchase 485
Property market 28
PSBR 77
Public interest 95
Public Liability insurance 626
Public ownership 91
Public relations 246
Public sector 92, 664
Public sector enterprises 101
Public service 102
Publicity 245
Purchase
   day book 584
   invoice 475
   order 473–4
   returns 582
Purchasing 465–6
Purchasing department 138
Pyramid selling 266

Q

Qualitative data 15, 217
Qualitative targets 592
Quality assurance 363, 371, 654
Quality
   chains 371
   circles 285, 371
   standards 144
Quangos 101
Quantitative
   data 15, 216
   targets 592
Questionnaire
   bias 227
   design 223–5
Quota sampling 222
Quotations 473

R

Race Relations Act 288
Raising share capital 539–41
Random sampling 222
Range 3, 18
Ratio analysis 597, 601–9
   limitations of 608–9
Re-engineering 144, 321
Receipts documents 485–8
Recession 75, 422
Recovery 75, 422
Recruitment and selection 332–56

Redeemable preference shares 540
Reducing balance depreciation 496
Redundancy 293, 311
References 348–9
Regional
   employment 394
   enterprise grants 544
   policy 84, 543–4
   selective assistance 544
Regulation and deregulation 89
Repeat sales 250
Reports 162
Research and Development 438–9
Reserves 575
Resources 23
Response bias 227
Responsibilities of employees 309
Restricted communication 155
Restrictive Practices Act 86
Retail Price Index 433
Retailers 264
Retained profits 530
Return on capital employed 603, 604–5
Returns book 584
Revaluations 575
Routine and non-routine functions 133–4
RPI 433

S

Sales 250
   administration 273–4
   and marketing 138
   budget 598
   campaigns 269
   communication methods 268
   conferences 269
   day book 584
   documents 477–80
   invoice 478
   meetings 269
   promotion methods 246–7
   prospecting 274
   receipt 485
   revenues 44
Sampling 221
   random 222
   quota 222
   stratified 222
   systematic 222
Sampling bias 227
Seasonal fluctuations 561
Seasonal workers 403
Secondary research 217–8
Secondary sector 397
Securing finance 532
Security 532
Self employment 402, 664–8
   opportunities 679
   planning for 685–7

699

Selling 268
Selling methods 648
Semi-skilled employment 403
Sex Discrimination Act 288
Share capital 531
Share Premium 575
Shareholders funds 575
Shares 539–41
Shift work 325
Shop floor workers 319
Short term finance 530
Shortlist 349
Sick pay 311
Single bargaining 303
Single European Market 446–7, 678
Single member companies 108–9
Single member company 671
Single purpose computer systems 180
Single Regeneration Budget 544
Skill shortages 416
Skilled and unskilled labour 415
Skilled employment 403
Sleeping partners 106
Small Firms Training Loans 545
Social Chapter 296, 678
Social costs and benefits 62–6
Socio-economic groups 237
Software 146
Software applications 175
Sole trader 105–6, 671
Solvency 594
Solvency ratios 601
Sources of further information 689–92
Specialization 21
Spreadsheets 179
Stacked bar charts 10
Staff associations 297
Standard Occupational Classification 414
State pension 675
Statement of account 478
Statistical references 693–4
Sterling, effective exchange rate 428
Stock control 466
Stock Exchange 538
Stock turnover 606
Straight line depreciation 496
Stratified sampling 222
Stress 327
Strike 301
Subsidies 84, 618
Subsiduary 575
Substitutes 32, 45
Supervisors 319
Supply
  side policies 435, 438
  changes in 35–38
  curves 34–5, 40–1, 46, 52, 55, 82, 83
  elasticity of 46

Support Services 139
Survey methods 222–5
Systematic sampling 222

T

T accounts 584
Tables 8
Takeovers 85
Targeting the market 234
Tariff 445
Tariffs and quotas 84
Tastes 32
Tax and supply curves 83
Tax Burden 436
Taxes and subsidies 508
Team working 285, 380
Technical economies 502
Technological advance 374–6
Technology Foresight Programme 439
Telephone survey 222
Telephones 160
Telesales 249
Teletext 164
Teleworking 323
Telex 164
Temporary employment 403, 410–11
Terminating employment 293
Tertiary sector 397
Test marketing 223
Time management in business 631
Time rates 379
Total costs 496–7
Total Quality Management (TQM) 370–3, 654
Trade 21
  associations 254
  credit 463, 535
  creditors 574
  cycle 422
Trade Descriptions Act 272
Trade discounts 476
Trade fairs and exhibitions 269
Trade policy 443
Trade Union and Employment Rights Act 311
Trade Union Congress (TUC) 300
Trade Unions 297–300
Trade Unions structure 300
Trading account 579–80
Trading cycle 461
Trading forecast 555
Training 184, 281–3
Training and Enterprise Agencies 635
Training and Enterprise Councils (TECs) 442, 668, 684
Training and re-training 143–4
Training Credits 443
Trends in business performance 595
Trial balance and final accounts 583–87
TV and radio sales 266

Two way communication 154
Types of competition 54–5

U

Undifferentiated marketing 201
Unemployment 74, 392–3, 679
  costs of 395–6
Unfair dismissal 294
Unit elastic demand 44
Unit labour costs 429–30
Unlimited liability 102
Urban policy 544
User surveys 143

V

Value added 457
Value added per worker 368
Value Added Tax (VAT) 82, 558–9, 582, 677
Value added, distribution of 458
Variable costs 494, 496, 509–510
Variance analysis 597, 599–600
VDU 146
Venture capital 529, 537
Verbal and non-verbal communication 155, 157–60
Videoconferencing 158
Videophones 158
Viewdata 165
Visible trade 425
Voice messaging 164
Voice recognition software 164
Voluntary sector 103, 673
Voluntary Service Overseas 673

W

Wage differentials 403–6
Wages and Salaries 291
Wealth creation 22
Weights and Measures Act 272
What-if analysis 513–14
White Collar
  unions 299
  workers 414
Wholesalers 263–4
Wide area network 148, 163
Wordprocessing software 175–6
Work shadowing 283
Work to rule 301
Working capital 529, 571
Working conditions 310–11
Working population 391
Working week 312
World trade 426
World Trade Organisation 448

Y

Youth Training Scheme (YTS) 340, 442

Z

Zero based budget 598